ROMANTIC POETRY AND PROSE

THE OXFORD ANTHOLOGY OF ENGLISH LITERATURE
General Editors: Frank Kermode and John Hollander

Medieval English Literature
J. B. TRAPP, Librarian, Warburg Institute, London

The Literature of Renaissance England
JOHN HOLLANDER, Hunter College;
and FRANK KERMODE, University College London

The Restoration and the Eighteenth Century
MARTIN PRICE, Yale University

Romantic Poetry and Prose
HAROLD BLOOM, Yale University;
and LIONEL TRILLING, Columbia University

Victorian Prose and Poetry
LIONEL TRILLING and HAROLD BLOOM

Modern British Literature
FRANK KERMODE and JOHN HOLLANDER

Romantic Poetry and Prose

HAROLD BLOOM
Yale University

LIONEL TRILLING
Columbia University

New York OXFORD UNIVERSITY PRESS
London Toronto

Selections from works by the following authors were made possible by the kind permission of their respective publishers and representatives:

Thomas Lovell Beddoes: The Works of *Thomas Lovell Beddoes*, edited by H. W. Donner, reprinted by permission of Oxford University Press, London.

William Blake: *The Poetry and Prose of William Blake*, by David V. Erdman with commentary by Harold Bloom, copyright © 1965 by David V. Erdman and Harold Bloom; reprinted by permission of Doubleday and Company, Inc.

John Clare: *The Poems of John Clare*, edited with an introduction by J. W. Tibble, copyright © 1935 by J. M. Dent & Sons Ltd.; reprinted by permission of J. M. Dent and Sons Ltd., and E. P. Dutton, Inc. *Selected Poems and Prose of John Clare*, edited by Eric Robinson and Geoffrey Summerfield, copyright © 1967 by Eric Robinson; reprinted by permission of Curtis Brown Ltd., and Oxford University Press, London.

John Keats: *The Letters of John Keats*, edited by Robert Gittings, reprinted by permission of Oxford University Press, London. *The Letters of John Keats*, edited by Hyder Edward Rollins, reprinted by permission of Harvard University Press.

Percy Bysshe Shelley: *"The Triumph of Life"*: A Critical Study by Donald H. Reiman, reprinted by permission of The University of Illinois Press.

Dorothy Wordsworth: *The Journals of Dorothy Wordsworth*, edited by Mary Moorman, reprinted by permission of the editor and Oxford University Press, London.

William Wordsworth: "The Ruined Cottage" taken from *William Wordsworth* by Jonathan Wordsworth, reprinted by permission of A. D. Peters and Company.

General Editors' Preface

The purpose of the Oxford Anthology is to provide students with a selective canon of the entire range of English Literature from the beginnings to recent times, with introductory matter and authoritative annotation. Its method is historical, in the broadest sense, and its arrangement, commentary, and notes, both analytic and contextual, have benefited not only from the teaching experience of the several editors, but from a study of the virtues and shortcomings of comparable works. A primary aim has been to avoid the insulation of any one section from the influence of others, and more. positively, to allow both student and instructor to come to terms with the manner in which English literature has generated its own history. This aim has been accomplished in several ways.

First, a reorganization of chronological phases has allowed the Tudor and Stuart periods to be unified under the broad heading of the English Renaissance, with two editors collaborating over the whole extended period. Similarly, the nineteenth century has two editors, one for the poetry of the whole period, and one for the prose. This arrangement seemed appropriate in every way, especially since neither of these scholars could be called a narrow specialist in "Romantic" or "Victorian," as these terms are used in semester- or course-labels.

Every contributing editor has worked and taught in at least one period or field outside the one for which he is, in this anthology, principally responsible, and none has ever allowed specialization to reduce his broader commitment to humane studies more largely considered. Thus we were able to plan a work which called for an unusual degree of cross reference and collaboration. During a crucial phase in the preparation of the text, the editors held daily discussions of their work for a period of months. By selection, allusion, comparison, by direction and indirection, we contrived to preserve continuity between epochs, and to illuminate its character. At the same time, the close co-operation of the various editors has precluded the possibility of common surrender to any single dominating literary theory; and the teacher need have no fear that he must prepare to do battle with some critical Hydra showing a head on every page.

The method of selecting text was consistent with these principles. In the eighteenth- and nineteenth-century sections it was our general policy to exclude the novel, for obvious reasons of length; but in the twentieth, where short fiction becomes more prominent and more central, we have included entire works of fiction, or clearly defined parts of them—for example, *Heart of Darkness*, "The Dead," the "Nausicaa" episode of *Ulysses*, and *St. Mawr*. On the other hand we were persuaded, after much reflection, that a different principle must apply in the cases of Spenser and Milton, where we waived the requirement of completeness. To have given the whole of one book—say, the First of *The Faerie Queene*—would have been a solution as easy as it is, no doubt, defensible; but it is asking a great deal of students to see that portion of the poem as an epitome of the rest, which is often so delightfully different; and we decided that we must provide selections from the whole poem, with linking commentary. We did the same for *Paradise Lost* though without abandoning the practice of providing complete texts when this was both possible and desirable; for example, *Comus* is reprinted entire, and so is a lesser-known but still very important masque, Jonson's *Pleasure Reconciled to Virtue*, which is interesting not only in relation to *Comus* but as an illustration of the part poetry can play in political spectacle and—more generally—in the focusing of the moral vision. Minor texts have been chosen for their exemplary force and their beauty, as well as to embody thematic concerns. If the teacher wishes, he or she may work, both within and across periods, with recurrent patterns as large as the conception of the Earthly Paradise, or with sub-genres as small but as fascinating as the Mad Song. It will also be evident from certain patterns of selection—*The Tempest* as the Shakesperean play, the very large amount of Blake, the emphasis given to D. H. Lawrence's poems as well as his fiction—that a genuinely modern taste, rather than an eager modishness, has helped to shape our presentation of the historical canon. It is also hoped that the unusually generous sampling of material in certain sections—notably the Renaissance, eighteenth century, and the Romantics—will allow the teacher to use secondary or minor works, if he so chooses, to highlight these newer concerns or to fill in contextual background.

As for the annotations, the editors have never been afraid to be lively or even speculative. They have consistently tried to avoid usurping the teacher's role, as providing standard or definitive readings might do. On the other hand, the commentary goes beyond merely providing a lowest common denominator of information by suggesting interpretive directions and levels along which the teacher is free to move or not; and of course he always has the freedom to disagree. The editors have been neither prudish nor portentous in their tone, nor have they sought—in the interests of some superficial consistency, but with leaden effect—to efface their personal styles.

Texts have all been based on the best modern editions, which happen quite often to be published by the Oxford University Press. Spelling and punctuation have been modernized throughout, save in three instances: portions of the medieval period, and the texts of Spenser and Blake, two poets whose spelling and punctuation are so far from idiosyncrasies to be silently normalized that they constitute attempts to refashion poetic language. In the medieval section, modern verse translations of *Beowulf* (by C. W. Kennedy) and of *Gawain* (by Brian Stone) have been adopted. Glossaries of literary and historical terms in all periods have been provided, sometimes keyed to the annotations, sometimes supplementing the larger headnotes. These, it will be noticed, seek to illuminate the immediate contexts of the literature of a period rather than to provide a dense précis of its social, political, and economic history. Similarly, the reading lists at the end of each volume are not exhaustive bibliographies; in the happy instance where a teacher finds an extensive bibliography advisable, he or she will want to supply one.

A word about the pictures. They are not to be thought of simply as illustrations, and certainly not as mere decorations, but rather as part of the anthologized material, like the musical examples and the special sections (such as the one on Ovidian mythology in the Renaissance and on the Urban Scene in the eighteenth century). Throughout, the reader is introduced to the relations between poem as speaking picture, and picture as mute poem. Aside from contextual and anecdotal illustration, of which there is indeed a good deal, the pictorial examples allow teachers, or students on their own, to explore some of the interrelations of texts and the visual arts in all periods, whether exemplified in Renaissance emblems or in contemporary illustrations of Victorian poems.

Finally, an inevitable inadequate word of acknowledgment. To the English Department of Dartmouth College the editors are deeply indebted for having so generously and hospitably provided a place in which to work together for a sustained period. The staff of the Dartmouth College Library was extraordinarily helpful and attentive.

All of the editors would like to extend a note of gratitude to the many academics throughout the United States who willingly made suggestions as to what should be included as well as excluded. A special note of thanks to Jim Cox of Dartmouth College and Paul Dolan of the State University of New York at Stony Brook for their challenging and always helpful comments.

And finally to the entire staff of the New York branch of the Oxford University Press who have done more than could be humanly expected in connection with the planning and execution of this book. We would especially like to thank our editor John Wright, as well as Leona Capeless and her staff, Mary Ellen Evans, Patricia Cristol, Joyce Berry, Deborah Zwecher, and Jean Shapiro. An unusual but very deserved note of thanks to the Production people, especially Gerard S. Case and Leslie Phillips and to the designer, Frederick Schneider, whose excellent work speaks for itself.

Frank Kermode
John Hollander

New York
September 1972

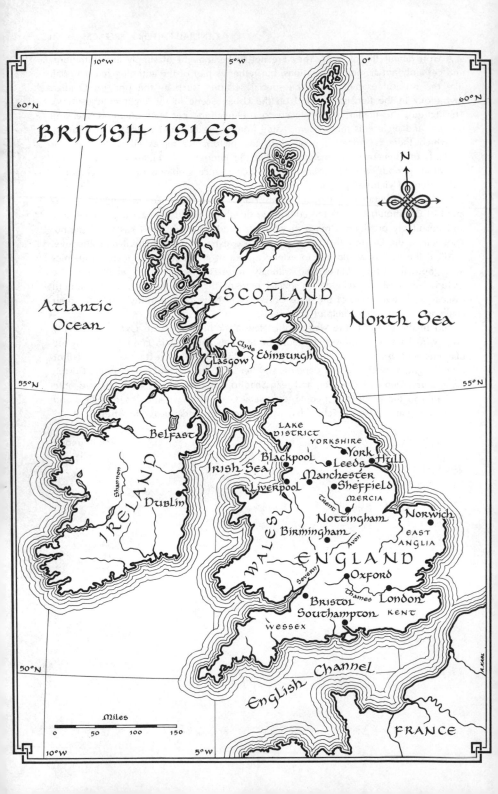

BRITISH ISLES

SCOTLAND

Atlantic Ocean

North Sea

Clyde
Glasgow• •Edinburgh

LAKE DISTRICT

YORKSHIRE

Belfast•

Shannon

IRELAND

Blackpool• York• •Hull
•Leeds

Irish Sea Manchester•

Liverpool• •Sheffield

Dublin• **MERCIA**

Trent

•Norwich

Nottingham•

Birmingham• **EAST ANGLIA**

WALES

ENGLAND

Avon

Severn

•Oxford

Thames

•Bristol •London

Southampton• **KENT**

WESSEX

English Channel

Miles

0 50 100 150

FRANCE

N

Contents

* An asterisk is used to indicate that a work does not appear in its entirety.

ix

Other Romantic Poets, 559

ROMANTIC PROSE, 591

ROMANTIC POETRY AND PROSE

Romantic Poetry

ROMANTICISM

Romanticism resists its definers, who can fix neither its characteristics nor its dates. It is a broad movement in the history of European (and American) consciousness, but whether it represented a genuine change in consciousness we still cannot know. In the later seventeenth century, the European Enlightenment or triumph of rationalism was one such change, and marked the end of the last stage of the Renaissance. Just as Romanticism still prevails today, for all the modernist rebellions against it, so it may be that Romanticism is only a very late phase of the Enlightenment against which it vainly rebelled. The spiritual differences between Pope and Blake, large as they are, quite fade away when we compare either writer with a representative current figure like Norman Mailer or Robert Lowell. Milton and Wordsworth, Tennyson and Yeats, contrasted with any of our contemporaries, are Enlightened rationalists, for all believed—as did Pope and Blake—in the power of the mind over the universe of sense. All believed that the poet's mind could make, or be found by, a coherent order in history or nature or society, or some combination thereof. None of them beheld a vision of chaos without believing also that chaos was irrational, and capable therefore of being organized into an intellectual coherence.

In this anthology, English Romanticism, as a historical phase of literature, is taken as extending from Blake's earliest poems (printed in 1783) up to Tennyson's first public volume (1830). These dates are arbitrary and, to some extent, now traditional. Romantic poetry in English does not end with the young, unhappy poets of the 1820's (Clare, Beddoes, Darley) but continues its complex course through Victorian and modern poetry. Yeats is not less Romantic than Blake, or Hardy than Shelley. Nor can we say just where English Romantic poetry, let alone Romantic poetry, begins. English Romanticism, whether rightly or not, saw itself as a Renaissance of the English Renaissance, a return to Spenser, Shakespeare, and Milton, and a repudiation of the literature of Enlightened England. But this return had begun long before Blake's *Poetical Sketches* of 1783. That volume owes most to the poetry of Sensibility—of anguished feeling—that had attempted a return to a pre-Enlightened age some forty years before. Yet we cannot say now that Collins, Gray, Cowper were closer to Milton than Pope was, nor would we quite know what we were talking about if we debated whether Spenser or Milton was the more Romantic poet. In a very broad sense *The Odyssey* is a Romantic poem, or at least much more Romantic than *The Iliad*. What can we mean when we call a poem or a person (or an idea) Romantic?

Plotinus, the third century neoplatonic philosopher, proposed an allegorical reading of the story of Odysseus, in which the seafarer's journey back home was interpreted as the soul's quest back to the Divine Unity. Though various Romantics seem to echo this interpretation of *The Odyssey*, their actual quests took them back not so much to a Christian or neoplatonic homecoming but rather outwards and downwards to a series of individual and glorious defeats. The major Romantic questers, whether we see these as the poets themselves or as the quasi-autobiographical heroes of their poems, are all engaged in the extraordinary enterprise of seeking to re-beget their own selves, as though through the imagination a man might hope to become his own father, or at least his own heroic precursor.

The temptations that haunted Odysseus—Circe and Calypso in particular—become in Romantic poetry the mysterious forms of Nature herself. Wordsworthian Nature, with all her representatives—Lucy, Margaret, the image of the child—is the most complex and positive of these temptations. The idealized heroines of Byron, Shelley, and Keats yield to purgatorial figures—the Moneta of *The Fall of Hyperion* and the "Shape all light" of *The Triumph of Life* being the most memorable. "I loved but woman fell away," the tragic John Clare proclaims, and this is the darker Romantic pattern, lamented by Coleridge and thoroughly analyzed and attacked by Blake. Because the quester demands more love and beauty than nature can give (or than a merely natural man could sustain on receiving), nature is discovered to be inadequate to the Romantic imagination.

Older scholarly views of Romanticism have tended to emphasize the movement's emotional naturalism, its supposed return to feeling, to folk traditions, to stories of the marvelous and supernatural. Romanticism was a health-restoring revival of the instinctual life, in contradistinction to eighteenth-century restraints that sought to sublimate the instincts in the united names of reason and society. Such views are not wrong except as they are inadequate in not going far enough. Romanticism, even in Wordsworth, depends finally upon a fuller sublimation of the instinctual life than had been thought necessary in all the centuries of European thought and feeling. By demanding more of natural love and of sensuous beauty than these could afford, the High Romantics each in turn attained a crisis in the instinctual life that could be overcome only by a yielding up of the instinctual life to a fully self-conscious creative mind. By a profound irony, the most heroic exalters of human emotion became responsible for an enormous sacrifice of instinct upon the altar of imaginative form. Keats delighted in every sensuous experience; yet he admits at last that he cannot unperplex joy from pain, if he is to write poems. Shelley, the Orphic priest of a healing Eros, ends with a vision of judgment in which Eros is much more of a destroyer than a preserver. Romantic love, the legacy of which still torments us all, could not solve the dilemma of the self and the other, any more than Romantic vision could heal the dumbfoundering abyss between the subject and the object. Though these were spiritual failures, they tended also to be aesthetic triumphs, for Romantic poetry has the sharp poignance of awakening every reader's own nostalgias for the unending quest after the love and beauty that come to us only imperfectly in our post-Romantic lives.

The discrimination between Romanticisms generally ends in a hopeless jumble, and none will be attempted here. We need a meaning for the term comprehensive enough to make coherent such statements as these: that Ezekiel is a more Romantic prophetic poet than Isaiah; that Emerson and his American descendants, from Whitman to Wallace Stevens and Hart Crane, are Romantic poets; that D. H. Lawrence is a central figure in Romantic tradition. Yet the term's usage must be narrow enough to have a period meaning also. This editor suggests that, as a literary period in England, from the American Rebellion through the First Reform Bill (1832), we speak of a High Romantic Age. Romanticism, as an ageless and recurrent phenomenon, cannot be defined, but the High Romantic, manifest at somewhat varied times in England, America, France, Germany, Italy, can sustain a simple historical definition. It is the literary form of the Revolution, which began in America and the West Indies, flowered in France, and spread from France through space and time into the continuing world upheaval of our century.

The virtual identity between High Romanticism and Revolution marks the French visionary, Jean-Jacques Rousseau, as the central man of Romantic tradition: ". . . it was Rousseau who brought the feeling of irreconcilable enmity to rank and privileges, *above humanity*, home to the bosom of every man—identified it with all the pride of intellect, and with the deepest yearnings of the human heart." To this remark of Hazlitt, one can add that it was Rousseau who completed the process of "inventing" adolescence and also of raising the vision of external nature to an ecstasy. Unfortunately, this ecstasy was a reduction, since it was purchased at the price of estrangement, of making nature wholly other than the human viewer. Ruskin, who consolidated so much of Romantic criticism, calculated the price of this estranging ecstasy as what he called "the pathetic fallacy," the imputation of consciousness to an objective world secretly known to be lifeless. Though himself an inheritor from Wordsworth and Coleridge, Ruskin expressed profound uneasiness as to this characteristic mode of Romantic vision.

For even High Romanticism was divided severely against itself, precisely where it quested most urgently to correct the Enlightenment. It was as dualistic as the empiricists in its actual emphasis on the power of creative mind as contrasted to the phenomenal universe, which widened still further the split between subject and object. Against this involuntary dualism, High Romanticism stressed a doctrine or principle (perhaps more nearly, an analogue) of Organicism. Taking the universe primarily as a process, Romanticism tried to believe that a poem resulted from the same process, one that produced simultaneously a tree, a world, and a work of art. Pater, protesting Coleridge's reliance upon this analogue, observed that it negated each artist's hard struggle, the mind's heroic effort to make something of its own. In twentieth-century criticism Pater's dark prophecy of the negative effects of Organicism has been fulfilled, but in Coleridge and his contemporaries the analogue had a pragmatically liberating effect.

This effect was felt most strongly in the idea (or complex of ideas) that High Romanticism called the Imagination. Though Wordsworth refers to the Imagination as a glorious faculty, neither he nor his major contemporaries considered Imagination as one faculty among many making up the human endowment. Though only Blake overtly denied it was a faculty at all, most of the High Romantics came close to Blake's identification of the Imagination with what he called the Real Man, the unfallen human potential. Bewilderingly as all of these poets used the term, what seems central is a common tendency in them (at their most concentrated and intense) to insist that the Imagination or creative power is autonomous. The implications of this autonomy are still being worked out in modern literature, but each major High Romantic poet either argues or sometimes verges on assuming that the Imagination can both perceive and at least half-create reality and truth, far more reliably than any other mode of apprehension.

The center of High Romantic consciousness is found in each poet's difficult realization of the Sublime, a realization that internalizes the quest-pattern of the ancient literary form of the romance, or marvelous tale, suspended in its context halfway between natural and supernatural realms. Quite narrowly, High Romanticism can be called the internalization of quest-romance, with the poet as quester, a principle of Selfhood (manifested as excessive self-consciousness) his antagonist, and a Muse-figure his goal (frequently shadowy). The goal of the quest from Wordsworth's "Solitary" through Yeats's wandering Oisin is sublimity, but this is a sublimity not easy to distinguish from solipsism, that is, from the sense that all other selves and the external world are unreal compared with the quester's own exalted self-consciousness. This sublimity, unlike the eighteenth-century Sublime, is not a Sublime of great conceptions, before which the self feels small, but rather of a hoped-for potential, in which the private self turns upon infinitude, and so is found by its own greatness.

Quest becomes the journey to re-beget the self, to be one's own father, and the pattern of the poetic career assumes the shapes of the life cycle of what we now call Freudian or Psychological Man. The High Romantic mythology of love, still prevalent among us, deliberately confuses yearnings for a more-than-natural, a Sublime apotheosis, with a purely erotic fulfillment. More than any poetry, before or since, High Romanticism offers a vision of desire as being its own value, with necessarily a counter-version of hell as failed or frustrated desire. Romantic love, as a passion, was hardly the creation of High Romanticism, but to see love as "the sanction which connects not only man with man but with everything that exists," as Shelley phrased it, was to burden love with a hope that no relation could sustain.

Love taken up into the Imagination tended to be the High Romantic formula for apocalypse, the final or total form subsuming the Revolution, which was thus reduced to an omen or a promise. No burden could have been greater for poetry, and High Romanticism, risking everything by its astonishing ambitions, necessarily lost nearly as much as it gained by such aspiration. A vision that was meant to become a continuity became instead a discontinuous recording of Good Moments, whose life was menaced by the tendency to memorialize them even before they had passed. A poetry that had insisted "If not now, when?" became a study of the nostalgias, of the lost childhood of each creator. The preference for the Sublime over the Beautiful, for a wild infinity over an orderly bounded vista, dwindled to an ambivalent concern with the terrors of individual Selfhood. The High Romantic, whether as alternative to or extension of the Enlightened mind, became a failed quest for a widened consciousness. Self-consciousness, conceived as the Romantic antagonist, became the central Romantic characteristic.

But "failure" itself is a dialectical term when applied to the High Romantic enterprise. Matthew Arnold, who believed that the Romantics had "failed" for not knowing enough, nevertheless received his psychological education from Romantic poetry, and could not go on as a creator when he became anti-Romantic. He demonstrated, unintentionally, what all poets in English have demonstrated since. We have been, and still are, in a phase where our poets are Romantic even as once poets were Christian, that is, whether they want to be or not. Wordsworth, with his massive turn to the subjective, changed Western poetry as decisively as Homer had, or as Freud, with his Romantic rationalism, was to change Western psychology.

THE ROMANTIC POETS

Of the six major poets now commonly grouped as the English Romantics, two clearly stand in eminence just after Chaucer, Spenser, Shakespeare, and Milton among all English poets. Blake and Wordsworth have little in common beyond this shared greatness, despite their similar desire to awaken us from the sleep of death, which we call life. Wordsworth insists he will do this by words that speak of nothing more than what we already are, while Blake urges us to cast away everything we are, in the name of what we were and might be again. Whether or not Wordsworth was a poet of Nature, he refused to yield up human nature or the external world, and at least attempted to hallow the commonplace. The human heart by which we live is to him a perpetual cause for thanksgiving, and even the most Sublime of his ecstasies are grounded in ordinary experience. No poet before him—not even Homer or Shakespeare—so exalts the common decencies that bind human beings together.

But, to Blake, the human heart was a hopeless labyrinth of "selfish virtues," and Nature the den of Ulro, the ultimate error nurtured by the fallen understanding. The outward creation, he asserted, was hindrance to him, not action, no part of him. His strenuous enterprise seeks to burn away every context—conceptual, societal, natural—that limits the human from becoming the Divine. Nature, to Wordsworth, was a saving process and a benign Presence. To Blake, Nature's final form is a mythological triple Whore, whom he called Rahab, Vala, Tirzah, or secrecy, illusive beauty, necessity. Though he read Wordsworth with uneasy admiration, Blake saw in Wordsworth the Natural Man rising up against the Spiritual Man continually, and for Blake the Natural Man was at enmity with God. Yet Blake and Wordsworth, as poets, shared the same prime precursor, Milton, and both began with the same hope, that the French Revolution would fulfill Milton's vision of England "rousing herself like a strong man after sleep."

The English government under which Blake and Wordsworth lived was engaged either in Continental warfare or in suppressing internal dissent, or both together, for most of their lives. The London of the last decade of the eighteenth century and the first of the nineteenth is the London shown in Blake's poem of that title in *Songs of Experience:* a city in which the traditional English liberties of free press, free speech, and the rights of petition and assembly were frequently denied. A country already shaken by war and anarchic economic cycles was beginning to experience the social unrest that had overthrown the French social order, and the English ruling class responded to this challenge by a vicious and largely effective repression.

Voices raised against this repression included Tom Paine, who had to flee for his life to France, where he then nearly lost it again, and a much more significant figure, the philosophical anarchist William Godwin, who was the major English theorist of social revolution. Godwin subsided into a timid silence during the English counter-terror, but his philosophic materialism was crucial for the early Wordsworth and the young Shelley alike, though both poets were to break from Godwin in their mature works.

Behind the materialist vision of Godwin was a consciousness that older modes of thought were dying with the society that had informed them. When Blake was eight years old, in 1765, the steam engine was perfected, and what were to be the images of prophetic labor in Blake's poetry, the hammer and the forge, had their antagonist images prepared for them in the furnaces and mills of another England. In the year of Wordsworth's birth, 1770, we have the ironical juxtaposition of Goldsmith's poem *The Deserted Village*, a sad celebration of an open, pastoral England vanishing into the isolated farm holdings, and wandering laborers, resulting from enclosure. "Nature," insofar as it had an outward, phenomenal, meaning for Pope, was a relaxed word, betokening the gift of God that lay all about him. Wordsworthian nature, the hard, phenomenal otherness that opposes itself to all we have made and marred, takes part of its complex origin from this vast social dislocation.

The real misery in England brought about through these economic and social developments was on a scale unparalleled since the Black Death in the fourteenth century. The French wars, against which all of Blake's prophetic poetry protests with Biblical passion, were typical of many modern wars fought by industrial nations. Enormous profits for the manufacturing classes were accompanied by inflation and food shortages for the mass of people, and victory over Napoleon brought on an enormous economic depression, unemployment, hunger, and more class unrest.

This unrest, which there was no means of channeling into organization or a protest vote, led to giant public meetings, riots, and what was called frame-breaking, a direct attempt to end technological unemployment by the destruction of machines. The government reacted by decreeing that frame-breaking was punishable by death. The climax of popular agitation and government brutality came in August 1819, in the Peterloo Massacre at Manchester, where mounted troops charged a large, orderly group that was meeting to demand parliamentary reform, killing and maiming many of the unarmed protesters. For a moment, England stood at the verge of revolution, but no popular leaders of sufficient force and initiative came forward to organize the indignation of the mass of people, and the moment passed. A similar movement was to come in 1832, at the start of another age, but then revolution was to be averted by the backing-down of Parliament, and its passage of the First Reform Bill that helped to establish the Victorian compromise. So the political energies of the age were not without issue, even in England; yet to idealists of any sort living in England during the first three decades of the nineteenth century it seemed that a new energy had been born into the world and then had died in its infancy. The great English writers of the period reacted to a stagnant situation by withdrawal, as Milton had withdrawn internally before them. In Blake and Wordsworth this internal movement helped create a new kind of poetry; it created modern poetry as we know it.

Coleridge, less clearly in Milton's shadow and so less concerned with the failures of revolutionary energies, did not emulate the Miltonic disillusion as closely as Blake and Wordsworth did. Coleridge suffered the anxiety of Milton's influence more in the passive manner of the poets of Sensibility like Collins and Cowper, than in the active, struggling way of Blake in his *Milton* or Wordsworth in his *Recluse* fragment. Coleridge had a deeper fear of profaning Nature than even Wordsworth had, and this joined itself, in Coleridge, to an inhibition that prevented him, except in fragments, from following Milton into a daemonic Sublime.

With the second generation of major Romantic poets the reaction to the failures of the Revolution are less personal, but the uneasy dialectic of Nature and Imagination, and the struggle with Milton's influence, became yet more complex because of the shadow of Wordsworth's achievement. Shelley, Byron, and Keats each responded very differently to Wordsworth (as they did also to Milton), but their poetry, even the scoffing Byron's, could not get beyond the dilemmas of Wordsworth's humanized Sublime. Shelley's visionary skepticism, Byron's satiric near-nihilism, and Keats's carefully qualified and finally tragic naturalism, all accept as the given a Wordsworthian account of the relations between Nature and poetic consciousness. Shelley emphasized a division in this heightened consciousness, between distrusting head and loving heart, and exported something like such a division into Nature itself. An unwilling dross, a ruin that is love's shadow, stalks every aspiration in Shelley's poetry, but this was Shelley's own reading of Wordsworth's poetry, as the entire Wordsworth-haunted sequence from *Alastor* through to *The Triumph of Life* makes clear. Byron, who bitterly read the "Solitary" of Wordsworth's *The Excursion* as a moralizing portrait of himself, became an obvious if involuntary Wordsworthian in *Childe Harold's Pilgrimage III* and *Manfred*. Where Byron is most himself, in *Don Juan* (acclaimed by Shelley as the greatest poem of the age), he still uneasily continues an argument with the Wordsworthian analysis of the self-destructiveness of the solitary consciousness. Keats, the natural heir of Wordsworth, read more receptively than his two great contemporaries, and so his poetic argument with Wordsworth is deeper and subtler. Wordsworth, with all his sense of imaginative loss, declined to take a tragic view of natural existence. Though Wordsworth's hidden subject is almost always mortality, his poetry frequently evades its own darkest implications. Keats, whose heroic stance evades no difficulties, engages the themes of mortality more directly than any poet but Shakespeare.

The ambition of all the High Romantic poets was to reach and even surpass Milton in epic. Necessarily, this ambition was frustrated, but the large-scale internalized romance, in one form or another, became one of the two prime Romantic achievements. *Milton, Jerusalem, The Prelude, Prometheus Unbound, Don Juan,* and the two *Hyperions;* for all their limitations, these constitute the last full-scale attainments of the Sublime in English poetry. More influential on Victorian and modern poetry, the Romantic lyric achievement surpassed the expectations and even the designs of its makers. The great invention of Coleridge and Wordsworth was the crisis-lyric, by which the poet saved himself for the next poem, and for at least the possibility of a fuller life. Though the High Romantics intended to continue and to extend Milton, the characteristic art of the therapeutic lyric was born instead. When we think of Romantic poetry (or, if our perspective is larger, of modern poetry), we think first of poems like "Resolution and Independence," "Dejection: An Ode," "Ode to the West Wind," "To Autumn." The major paradox of High Romanticism is that its minor mode became its central (and still unsurpassed) legacy.

It is difficult now, when we have seen so many disasters, human and societal, emerge from Romanticism, whether recurrent or High, to arrive at any last judgment upon its values and its achievements. Recurrent romanticism is apparently endemic in human nature; all men and women are questers to some degree. Those who quest beyond reason, beyond societal and familial constraints, who like Shelley go on until they are stopped and never are stopped, stand beyond aesthetic judgment in any case. High Romanticism is, by now, largely an aesthetic phenomenon and invites an aesthetic judgment. Whatever its human cost, the literature of internalized quest, of Promethean aspiration, is the most vitalizing and formidable achievement in the Western arts since the Renaissance.

WILLIAM BLAKE
1757–1827

Blake was born in London on November 28, 1757, into the family of a hosier. He had no formal education, but was apprenticed to an engraver, James Basire. In 1782 he married Catherine Boucher; the marriage was childless, and went through intense difficulties, particularly in early 1793, when Blake complained bitterly of her sexual jealousy, but eventually the relationship became serene and very close. Blake died on a Sunday evening, August 12, 1827, Catherine by his side, and by all accounts he died majestically, a fulfilled and happy man.

There were almost no outward events in Blake's life. He was not a professional poet or man of letters, but earned his living, sometimes very precariously, as an engraver. Insofar as he had any public reputation during his lifetime, it was as a failed, eccentric painter. But some of his lyrics were known and admired by Coleridge and other literary men, and his paintings were valued by some of the better artists of his time. Almost unknown, however, were what are widely (and rightly) now regarded as his most important achievement, a series of visionary poems culminating in three brief or foreshortened epics, works demonstrating probably the greatest conceptual power ever to appear among poets.

Blake, for all his gifts, is not a poet of the eminence of Chaucer, Shakespeare, or Milton, yet he gives his readers not only what can be expected from a great poet, but a profundity of schematized psychological insight comparable to Freud's, and a disciplined intellectual inventiveness comparable to Hegel's. His difficulty for readers, and his unique value, is that he offers even more than that, for he is, as he insisted, a prophet, in the precise sense that Isaiah and Ezekiel (he would have added Milton) are prophetic poets. His poems, which are always poems, are astonishingly ambitious, even for the Romantic Age, into which he survived. They propose nothing less than to teach us how to live, and to explain to us what has made it so hard to live as fully human rather than merely natural beings.

Blake, a self-taught London radical Protestant, was more than deeply read in the King James Bible, and in Milton. In the Talmudic phrase, he had "eaten those books," and they account for all but an insignificant part of his literary tradition, and indeed of his knowledge. Much scholarship has wasted itself, from Yeats to the present moment, in attempting to trace Blake's ideas and images to a large number of arcane traditions. But Blake was a very impatient reader, except of the Bible and Milton, and though he glanced at anything he encountered, he would have snorted at the suggestion that he give serious effort to the study of alchemy, mysticism, theosophy, esoteric forms of neoplatonism, occult "science," latter-day gnosticisms or any of the crankeries that have elicited respectful concentration from some of his scholarly pursuers.

To comprehend Blake, his reader needs to understand how Blake read the Bible and Milton, or as Blake might have said, how to read poetry. For Blake was primarily an intellectual revisionist, even as Nietzsche, Marx, Freud, in the longest perspective, seem most important as revisionists of the European Enlightenment. Blake, like the major Romantics after him, sought to correct the Enlightenment, and not to abolish it. He had no quarrel with reason itself but only with inadequate accounts of reason, and he refused to distinguish between "the intellectual powers" and what he called "the Real Man the Imagination," whose most complete expression was in the arts of poetry and painting. The Bible, whose degree of historical validity was quite irrelevant to Blake, represented for him the Great Code of Art, the total form of what he called the Divine Vision, which he believed to have been so obscured by the nightmare of history as to be all but totally darkened in his own time.

Most of what currently passes for movements of human liberation would have been condemned by Blake as what he bitterly called Druidism, taking the name from what he judged to have been the native British version of natural religion. All of Blake's work is based on a firm distinction between what is imaginative and what is merely natural in us, with the natural rejected, cast out beyond the balance of what Blake termed "contraries." The revolt of youth-as-youth Blake saw as a cyclic self-defeat, the sad destiny of the eternal rebel he called Orc. The revolt of women-as-women (as exemplified in his acquaintance Mary Wollstonecraft) he judged also as doomed to the perpetual failure of natural cycle, for all natural women, like all natural men, were subject to what he named the Female Will, always rampant in nature. The revolt of the heart against the head (as represented by Rousseau) he pungently characterized as "reasoning from the loins in the unreal forms of Beulah's Night," Beulah being a lower paradise of illusory appearances. D. H. Lawrence, a lesser Blake, inveighed against "sex in the head," following Blake's prophecy, but proceeded, like so many since, to reason from the loins, hardly a more humanizing procedure, in Blake's view.

Blake's view was what he himself always termed Vision or Intellectual Vision, which he took ironic care to distinguish from the literalism of the natural eye, and from the chemistry of the natural mind. He saw with the eye of the imagination, and without the aid of artificial paradises of any kind whatsoever. His visions are what Ezekiel and Milton saw, and what he believed all of us could see, by the hard efforts of poetry and painting, or of learning to apprehend the poets and the painters, and so to re-create their worlds after them. He hoped to rescue English culture from what he interpreted as its decadence, by restoring poetry to what it had been in Milton and the Renaissance writers before Milton, and by raising English painting to what it had never been, the spiritual art of Michelangelo and Raphael.

Yet Blake's own genius was curiously divided. As poet and as painter he excels as a caricaturist, an intellectual satirist, and a master of a new kind of vitalizing but ironic parody, which first triumphs in The Marriage of Heaven and Hell. Where he wished most to excel was in the Sublime of Milton and Michelangelo, and here his achievement was only partial, though larger in poetry than in painting. His painting was anachronistic in a somewhat crippling sense, and his failure to understand Rubens and Rembrandt was more self-defeating than it need have been. In his Sublime poetry, he is least successful where he is most directly Miltonic, and rather closer to the highest kind of accomplishment when he is even more Hebraic than Milton is. But there too, his stature is lessened when he is read in direct juxtaposition with the Bible. His own true Sublime comes in another mode, a Northern one, in the tradition of the Icelandic Eddas, and in the less strenuous but still Miltonic eighteenth-century English tradition of James Thomson, Thomas Gray, William Collins, and William Cowper, the poets of Sensibility, as recent scholarly criticism has begun to call them. After Milton, Blake felt closer to Cowper than to any other English poet, and though he read, admired, and (very complexly) protested Wordsworth's poetry, he always was more comfortable with an ode like Gray's "The Progress of Poesy" than with one like "Intimations of Immortality."

The Miltonizing poets of Sensibility failed, in Blake's opinion, because they were not sane enough to overthrow a world view Blake regarded as totally mad, and which he associated with Bacon, Newton, and Locke in metaphysics and with Dryden, Pope, Dr. Johnson, and Sir Joshua Reynolds in the arts. This world view is so savagely caricatured by Blake that we need to be very wary about accepting his version of it as being in any way adequate to those thinkers and artists. But Blake was no more unjust than the Augustan satirists were, from their almost opposite points of departure. Blake was politically of the permanent Left, like Shelley in the next generation, and to him the Augustan trinity of Reason, Nature, and Society was a three-headed beast or triple whore responsible for the sufferings of the lower classes of England, out of whom he had come and with whom he defiantly remained. The Revolution did not come to England, the repression of Pitt did its work well, and Blake learned the joyless wisdom of public timidity. He secretly raged, in his notebooks and his poems, but he accurately said of his outward obedience: "I am hid." When he did speak his mind, he suffered for it, whether in defying patrons or in angrily throwing a soldier out of his garden. The first brought on Jobean trials of poverty for himself and his loyal, suffering wife, and the second brought on him the ordeal of trial for treason (he was acquitted, but the terror of the experience is intense throughout his greatest poem, *Jerusalem*). Too profound a consciousness to accept any easy explanations for the torments of his fellows and himself, Blake prophetically indicted the English conservative cultural tradition in its totality. In his gathering vision all fit together: the theology of the English state church, the political theory of Burke, the deistic natural religion which he believed the church only pretended to oppose, the poetics of Pope and the aesthetics of Reynolds, the philosophy of Locke, the physics of Newton, the morality of Bacon. The aggregate of all this, quite unfairly but wholly unforgettably, Blake fused together as the Accuser of Sin, the spectral torturer of English man, of Albion. His mature poetry became an attempt to identify, with final clarity, this Accuser, in the belief that to know the clear outline of error, particularly within the self, is to make its destruction inevitable.

To achieve this identification, Blake tried several times to organize his vision, so as to tell a comprehensive story of how mankind fell into its present condition, what that condition was, and how mankind was to be freed from all conditions, particularly from the confining context of nature. We begin to apprehend Blake when we realize that for him "human nature" is a wholly unacceptable phrase, an absolute contradiction, or, as he said, "an impossible absurdity." What was human about us, Blake insisted, was the imagination; what was natural about us had to be redeemed by the imagination, or else it would destroy us. The imagination, to Blake, was not a faculty, however glorious, but was the Real Man, the unfallen unity we had been and must become again.

Blake's story is too complex and long for this introduction, and one major aspect of it is sketched in the Headnote to the selection from the epic *The Four Zoas*. But it is crucial, as we begin to read Blake, that we ask why he made his story so difficult for us. Though several major poets since Blake have invented mythologies, and though there are mythopoeic elements in all major poets, Blake's myths are the most formidable and complete in the language. Northrop Frye, probably Blake's best critic, has insisted that Blake's poetic procedures were as central as any poet's, and this may be so; yet the experience of most common readers seems to tell them otherwise. What can be made explicit to the idiot, Blake said, was not worth his care, and so he addressed a sublime allegory to the intellectual powers. But need his address have been so solitary a one? Could he have been more direct and immediate, as apparently he was in his earlier work, or is there convincing inner necessity in his initially strange procedures? Did a voice crying in the wilderness of 1790–1810, the years of his major works, have to cry aloud in so subtly complex a language that it seems always to need translation for even willing auditors?

There are no certain answers, yet one can be ventured, by comparing Blake's poetry to that of his older contemporary, Cowper, and his younger contemporary, Wordsworth. Cowper is so Milton-haunted that he never fully finds his own voice, and so afflicted by a sense of worthlessness and damnation that he scarcely can find his way past fear and trembling. When we read Cowper, if we read acutely and sympathetically, we are very moved, but what moves us is the pathos of Cowper's predicament, and his helplessness at breaking out of it. Blake's was a fierce spirit, akin to the greatest dissenters that the "inner light" tradition of Protestantism has produced among the English. He would not allow himself to be a victim or a latecomer, like the poets of Sensibility before him, and so he resolved to break through every net, external and internal, that had blocked his precursors from joining themselves to Milton's greatness, even the net of Milton himself.

Wordsworth, born thirteen years after Blake, was also a titanic individuality, a consciousness fierce enough not to accept victimization by history and circumstances, or even by Milton, whom he revered quite as much as Cowper and Blake did. But Wordsworth chose another way, not a personal mythology, but a de-mythologizing so radical that it enabled him to create modern poetry, if any single figure can be said to have done so. He is ultimately a more difficult poet than Blake, if "difficult" means problematic, as it should. Once a reader has mastered Blake's initial complexities, he goes on encountering vast profundities, but his way is clear before him. A little way into Wordsworth, the reader begins to encounter enormous and legitimate obscurities and dark passages, whereas Blake gives almost too continuous and directing a light. For Blake is not only more systematic than Wordsworth; he is also far closer than Wordsworth to English Renaissance poetry, and necessarily far less modern, however you want to interpret "modern." It is one of the disturbing paradoxes about Blake that, lifelong rebel though he was, his mature work increasingly seems conservative in the longest perspectives we can achieve. An enemy of the rationalists, he was a great rationalizer; an exploder of the mythologies, he re-mythologized so extensively as to help preserve the cultural life of many phenomena he wished to bury. Though he has been reclaimed for the latest movements of social, political, and artistic revolt from late nineteenth-century England down to this present moment, he is farther away from any and all of us than he is from the Enlightenment he prophesied against.

Blake could or would not do what Hazlitt rightly said Wordsworth had done: begin anew on a *tabula rasa* ("clean slate") of poetry, almost as though none had been written before him. *Jerusalem,* at first reading, may baffle or repel an unprepared contemporary reader, but so does Ezekiel, and so does John Milton. Poetry meant too much to Blake to abandon the main continuities of what it had been; poetry meant a great deal to Wordsworth, but nature meant more. Yet to Blake, nature was hindrance, not action, and so no part of him. He undertook the immense task of his mythologizing so as to begin the preservation of man by the preservation of poetry, in a form still fundamentally recognizable as a major creation of the English Renaissance. Though, in his own terms, he did not fail, and on any terms he became one of the half-dozen or so poets in the language, he did not succeed as Wordsworth was to succeed. Blake became the last epic poet in the old sense of epic. It was left for Wordsworth to become a new kind of poet, one which, perhaps to our sorrow, is necessarily with us still.

The texts reprinted here are from *The Poetry and Prose of William Blake,* edited by David Erdman. Blake's original spelling and punctuation have been preserved to give the reader the full sense of Blake's extraordinary individuality. Blake himself would have sanctioned this refusal to modernize, for most of his poetry was engraved by him in this form.

From Poetical Sketches°

To Spring°

O thou, with dewy locks, who lookest down
Thro' the clear windows of the morning;° turn
Thine angel eyes upon our western isle,
Which in full choir hails thy approach, O Spring!

The hills tell each other, and the list'ning
Vallies hear; all our longing eyes are turned
Up to thy bright pavillions: issue forth,
And let thy holy feet visit our clime.

Poetical Sketches Blake's early poems, written between the ages of twelve and twenty-one, are collected in this, his only conventionally printed volume (1783); like the poets of Sensibility, Blake explicitly imitates Spenser, Shakespeare, and Milton in his first poems, but already these lyrics foreshadow the crucial element in his mature mythology, the coexistence of "states-of-being," even of contrary states, though this is not yet a psychological doctrine, as it will become by 1788–89.

To Spring The first poem in his first book, this will be significantly echoed in Night IX, "The Last Judgment," of *The Four Zoas,* initially intended to be his definitive epic; here it introduces four poems addressed to the seasons, stanzaic but unrhymed, in imitation of James Thomson's blank verse poem *The Seasons,* itself a Miltonic imitation.
clear . . . morning See *The Four Zoas,* Night IX, 120:50, where this is assimilated to Rahab's "window" of Joshua 2:18.

10 Come o'er the eastern hills,° and let our winds
Kiss thy perfumed garments; let us taste
Thy morn and evening breath; scatter thy pearls
Upon our love-sick land that mourns for thee.

O deck her forth with thy fair fingers; pour
Thy soft kisses on her bosom; and put
Thy golden crown upon her languish'd head,
Whose modest tresses were bound up for thee!
1769–77   1783

To the Evening Star°

Thou fair-hair'd angel of the evening,
Now, while the sun rests on the mountains, light
Thy bright torch of love;° thy radiant crown
Put on, and smile upon our evening bed!
Smile on our loves; and, while thou drawest the
Blue curtains of the sky, scatter thy silver dew
On every flower that shuts its sweet eyes
In timely sleep. Let thy west wind sleep on
The lake; speak silence with thy glimmering eyes,
10 And wash the dusk with silver. Soon, full soon,
Dost thou withdraw; then the wolf rages wide,
And the lion glares thro' the dun forest:
The fleeces of our flocks are cover'd with
Thy sacred dew: protect them with thine influence.
1769–77   1783

Song°

How sweet I roam'd from field to field,
    And tasted all the summer's pride,
'Till I the prince of love° beheld,
    Who in the sunny beams did glide!

He shew'd me lilies for my hair,
    And blushing roses for my brow;
He led me through his gardens fair,
    Where all his golden pleasures grow.

---

eastern hills See the Song of Solomon 2:8 ff.
To the Evening Star See Spenser's *Epithalamion,*
ll. 285–95, for Blake's prime source; this poem
is a precursor of the *Songs of Innocence.*
torch of love the Evening Star, Venus

Song The tradition is that Blake wrote this poem
before he was fourteen; it is a precursor of the
Songs of Experience.
prince of love Eros, or Cupid, who usurps the
role of Phoebus, the sun god, and glides down
in Phoebus' chariot

With sweet May dews my wings were wet,
    And Phoebus fir'd my vocal rage;
He caught me in his silken net,
    And shut me in his golden cage.

He loves to sit and hear me sing,
    Then, laughing, sports and plays with me;
Then stretches out my golden wing,
    And mocks my loss of liberty.
    1769–77   1783

Mad Song°

The wild winds weep,
    And the night is a-cold;
Come hither, Sleep,
    And my griefs infold:
But lo! the morning peeps
    Over the eastern steeps,
And the rustling birds of dawn
The earth do scorn.

Lo! to the vault
    Of paved heaven,°
With sorrow fraught
    My notes are driven:
They strike the ear of night,
    Make weep the eyes of day;
They make mad the roaring winds,
    And with tempests play.

Like a fiend in a cloud
    With howling woe,
After night I do croud,
    And with night will go;°
I turn my back to the east,
From whence comforts° have increas'd;
For light doth seize my brain
With frantic pain.°
1769–77   1783

Mad Song Blake's first intellectual satire, based
on the Elizabethan "mad songs" and their later
imitations; the singer is being satirized, but so
is the mental world he seeks to escape; he can
be regarded as a poet of Sensibility like Cowper,
whose madness (in Blake's judgment) is an eva-
sion of the burden of prophecy.
paved heaven The singer's heaven is the self-
paved "vault" of materialist concepts of space.

After . . . go Crowding after night, the singer
seeks to escape a materialist (and self-imposed)
concept of time.
comforts a grim humor on Blake's part; the singer
cannot bear "comforts"
frantic pain another satiric suggestion that the
singer wishes to be more insane than he has
managed (so far) to make himself

To the Muses°

Whether on Ida's° shady brow,
  Or in the chambers of the East,
The chambers of the sun, that now
  From antient melody have ceas'd;

Whether in Heav'n ye wander fair,
  Or the green corners of the earth,
Or the blue regions of the air,
  Where the melodious winds have birth;

Whether on chrystal rocks ye rove,
10 Beneath the bosom of the sea
Wand'ring in many a coral grove,
  Fair Nine, forsaking Poetry!

How have you left the antient love
  That bards of old enjoy'd in you!°
The languid strings do scarcely move!
  The sound is forc'd, the notes are few!
1769–77   1783

Songs of Innocence and of Experience

There are twenty-one copies of *Songs of Innocence,* and twenty-seven of the combined work, but no separate copies at all of *Songs of Experience.* Blake therefore was willing to have *Songs of Innocence* read separately (he continued to issue it after he had combined the two groups) but not the contrary work. These are works in illuminated printing, engraved after a process of Blake's own invention, in which he applied words and pictures to copper plates, and then etched surrounding surfaces away. The colors of inks and the tints and washes, some translucent, some opaque, vary from copy to copy.

Together with some early tracts, Blake's *Songs of Innocence* and *The Book of Thel* begin his deliberate canon of engraved works. The first drafts of three of the *Songs of Innocence* are to be found in a satirical context in the early prose fragment *An Island in the Moon,* and satire of a very subtle kind is crucial throughout the combined work, in which Innocence and Experience are so juxtaposed as to demonstrate one another's inadequacies.

The *Songs of Innocence* are indeed "of" and not "about" the state of innocence. There is much critical debate about Blake's Innocence, and little that is definitive can be said about it. The reader should know that the root meaning of innocence is "harmlessness," the derived meanings "guiltlessness" and "freedom from sin." But Blake uses the word to mean "inexperience" as well, which is a very different matter.

To the Muses This is a defiant and confident "lament," employing the diction of Augustan minor verse to mock that verse's failure of inspiration. There are overtones of Milton's *Comus,* ll. 98 ff., and Psalms 19:4–5.
Ida's Mountain in Crete; there is also one of the same name near Troy; both are notable in Greek poetry.
How . . . you you loved Spenser and Milton, and the other bards of Britain, but now you have become faithless

As the contrary of Experience, Innocence cannot be reconciled with it within the context of natural existence. Implicit in the contrast between the two states is a distinction Blake made between "unorganized innocence," unable to sustain experience, and an organized kind which could. On the manuscript of *The Four Zoas*, he jotted down: *"Unorganized Innocence: An Impossibility.* Innocence dwells with Wisdom, but never with Ignorance."

Since Innocence and Experience are states of the soul through which we pass, neither is a finality, both are necessary, and neither is wholly preferable to the other. Not only are they satires upon one another, but they exist in a cyclic relation as well. Blake does not intend us to see Innocence as belonging to childhood and Experience to adulthood, which would be not only untrue but also uninteresting.

The relation of the matched pairs of poems, where they exist, does not appear to be schematic, but varies from instance to instance. The matching of "The Divine Image" and "The Human Abstract" seems to be the crucial one, since it shows the widest possibilities of relationship, and demonstrates vividly what readers are too likely to forget, which is that Innocence satirizes Experience just as intensely as it itself is satirized by Experience, and also that any song of either state is also a kind of satire upon itself.

From Songs of Innocence and of Experience

Shewing the Two Contrary States of the Human Soul

Songs of Innocence

1789
The Author & Printer   W Blake

Introduction

Piping down the valleys wild
Piping songs of pleasant glee
On a cloud I saw a child.
And he laughing said to me.

Pipe a song about a Lamb;
So I piped with merry chear,
Piper pipe that song again—
So I piped, he wept to hear.

Drop thy pipe thy happy pipe
10   Sing thy songs of happy chear,
So I sung the same again
While he wept with joy to hear

Piper sit thee down and write
In a book that all may read—
So he vanish'd from my sight.
And I pluck'd a hollow reed.

And I made a rural pen,
And I stain'd° the water clear,
And I wrote my happy songs
20 Every child may joy to hear
1789

The Lamb

Little Lamb who made thee
Dost thou know who made thee
Gave thee life & bid thee feed.
By the stream & o'er the mead;
Gave thee clothing of delight,
Softest clothing wooly bright;
Gave thee such a tender voice,
Making all the vales rejoice!
Little Lamb who made thee
10 Dost thou know who made thee

Little Lamb I'll tell thee,
Little Lamb I'll tell thee!
He is called by thy name,
For he calls himself a Lamb:°
He is meek & he is mild,
He became a little child:
I a child & thou a lamb,
We are called by his name.
Little Lamb God bless thee.
20 Little Lamb God bless thee.
1789

The Little Black Boy°

My mother bore me in the southern wild,
And I am black, but O! my soul is white;°

stain'd as a painter stains, yet the sense including an overtone of "polluted"
Lamb Christ as the Lamb of God
The Little Black Boy The speaker applies his mother's teachings to the dilemma of his own condition. Her wisdom is a summary of the beliefs of the Innocent state of the soul: God is a loving father, nature is a loving mother, and all children share a brotherhood from nature under God. Though the voice singing this song is poignant and admirable, the poem explores the inadequacy of Innocence to sustain that voice's idealizations.
And I . . . white The Black Boy has been taught a pernicious dualism, at once metaphysical and societal.

White as an angel is the English child:
But I am black as if bereav'd° of light.

My mother taught me underneath a tree°
And sitting down before the heat of day,
She took me on her lap and kissed me,
And pointing to the east began to say.

Look on the rising sun: there God does live
10   And gives his light, and gives his heat away.
And flowers and trees and beasts and men receive
Comfort in morning joy in the noon day.

And we are put on earth a little space,
That we may learn to bear the beams of love,
And these black bodies and this sun-burnt face
Is but a cloud, and like a shady grove.

For when our souls have learn'd the heat to bear
The cloud will vanish we shall hear his voice.
Saying: come out from the grove my love & care,
20   And round my golden tent like lambs rejoice.

Thus did my mother say and kissed me,
And thus I say to little English boy.
When I from black and he from white cloud free,°
And round the tent of God like lambs we joy:

Ill shade him from the heat till he can bear,
To lean in joy upon our fathers knee.
And then I'll stand and stroke his silver hair,
And be like him and he will then love me.

                                        1789

The Chimney Sweeper°

When my mother died I was very young,
And my father sold me while yet my tongue,
Could scarcely cry weep weep weep weep.°
So your chimneys I sweep & in soot I sleep.

---

bereav'd Here "dispossessed" or "divested"; the child has been taught a myth of the Fall of Man. **underneath a tree** Any teaching beneath a tree (thus shrouded by nature) is abhorred by Blake, for whom all trees are versions of the Tree of Mystery (see "The Human Abstract"). **When I . . . free** a line implying all the ambiguities of Innocence **The Chimney Sweeper** As in "The Little Black Boy," here an innocent speaker condemns societal and psychic repressiveness without being aware of the full burden of his own song. The Chimney Sweeper is a charity child sold into commercial bondage by his father and the English church. Here too there is no consciously directed irony on the child's part, but an enormous moral urgency is developed against the forces of exploitation, particularly at their success in conditioning the child's mind and even his dreams. **weep** The lisping little children pronounce "sweep" as "weep."

Theres little Tom Dacre, who cried when his head
That curl'd like a lambs back, was shav'd, so I said.
Hush Tom never mind it, for when your head's bare,
You know that the soot cannot spoil your white hair.

10 And so he was quiet, & that very night,
As Tom was a sleeping he had such a sight,
That thousands of sweepers Dick, Joe Ned & Jack
Were all of them lock'd up in coffins of black°

And by came an Angel who had a bright key,
And he open'd the coffins & set them all free.
Then down a green plain leaping laughing they run
And wash in a river and shine in the Sun.

Then naked & white, all their bags left behind,
They rise upon clouds, and sport in the wind.
And the Angel told Tom if he'd be a good boy,
20 He'd have God for his father & never want joy.

And so Tom awoke and we rose in the dark
And got with our bags & our brushes to work.
Tho' the morning was cold, Tom was happy & warm,
So if all do their duty, they need not fear harm.°

                    1789

The Divine Image°

To Mercy Pity Peace and Love,
All pray in their distress:
And to these virtues of delight
Return their thankfulness.

For Mercy Pity Peace and Love,
Is God our father dear:
And Mercy Pity Peace and Love,
Is Man his child and care.

For Mercy has a human heart
10 Pity, a human face:
And Love, the human form divine,
And Peace, the human dress.

Then every man of every clime,
That prays in his distress,

coffins of black the chimneys, and also the blackened bodies of the chimney sweepers
So . . . harm Compare the effect of this with the similar moral tags at the end of "The Little Black Boy" and the "Holy Thursday" of Innocence.
The Divine Image Note the absence of imagery in this lyric of abstractions, and compare it to the contrary of Experience, "The Human Abstract."

Prays to the human form divine
Love Mercy Pity Peace.

And all must love the human form,
In heathen, turk or jew.
Where Mercy, Love & Pity dwell
20   There God is dwelling too.
        1789

Holy Thursday°

Twas on a Holy Thursday their innocent faces clean
The children walking two & two in red & blue & green
Grey headed beadles walkd before with wands as white as snow°
Till into the high dome of Pauls they like Thames waters flow

O what a multitude they seemd these flowers of London town
Seated in companies they sit with radiance all their own
The hum of multitudes was there but multitudes of lambs°
Thousands of little boys & girls raising their innocent hands

Now like a mighty wind they raise to heaven the voice of song
10   Or like harmonious thunderings the seats of heaven among
Beneath them sit the aged men wise guardians of the poor
Then cherish pity, lest you drive an angel from your door°
1784   1789

Songs of Experience

1794
The Author & Printer   W Blake

Introduction°

Hear the voice of the Bard!
Who Present, Past, & Future sees
Whose ears have heard,

Holy Thursday These are the chimney sweepers again, charity wards of the exploiting church, being led into St. Paul's Cathedral on Ascension Day, the fortieth day after Easter Sunday, on which Christ ascended into Heaven. Their march is regimented, and the poem, depending upon perspective, can be read as either the bitterest or most idyllic of Blake's songs.
as white as snow leprously white, in Blake's symbolism. The beadles are church flunkeys whose "wands" are also disciplinary rods, as well as badges of office.
multitudes of lambs See Joel 3:14, where the prophet sees "multitudes, multitudes in the valley of decision."
Then cherish . . . door a bitter contrast to Hebrews 13:2: "Be not forgetful to entertain strangers: for thereby some have entertained angels unawares"
Introduction Blake is no more to be identified with the Bard of Experience than he is with the Piper of Innocence, though the Bard speaks for a larger and more urgent component of his imagination, as the deliberate echoings of Jeremiah and Milton here indicate.

The Holy Word,
That walk'd among the ancient trees.°

Calling the lapsed Soul°
And weeping in the evening dew;
That might controll,
The starry pole;
10 And fallen fallen light renew!

O Earth O Earth return!°
Arise from out the dewy grass;
Night is worn,
And the morn
Rises from the slumberous mass.

Turn away no more:
Why wilt thou turn away
The starry floor
The watry shore
20 Is giv'n thee till the break of day.°

                                    1794

Earth's Answer°

Earth rais'd up her head,
From the darkness dread & drear.
Her light fled:
Stony dread!°
And her locks cover'd with grey despair.

Prison'd on watry shore
Starry Jealousy does keep my den
Cold and hoar
Weeping o'er
10 I hear the Father of the ancient men

Selfish father of men
Cruel jealous selfish fear
Can delight
Chain'd in night
The virgins of youth and morning bear?

---

ancient trees See Genesis 3:8.
lapsed Soul This is not Blake's view, but the Bard's.
return See Jeremiah 22:29 and Milton's allusion to this in his *The Ready and Easy Way to Establish a Free Commonwealth.*
break of day Apocalypse, when the "starry floor" and "watry shore" will be swept away
Earth's Answer Like the Earth, mother of Prometheus, in Shelley's *Prometheus Unbound,* Act

I, this Earth is fearful of "Starry Jealousy" or the "Selfish father of men," Shelley's Jupiter or Blake's Urizen-Jehovah. Yet her bitter point against the Bard (and all men) seems justified. Where the Bard blames nature for turning away, nature replies by blaming men, for not freeing love.

Stony dread There is here a suggestion of Medusa, whose glance turned men to stone.

Does spring hide its joy
When buds and blossoms grow?
Does the sower?
Sow by night?
20   Or the plowman in darkness plow?

Break this heavy chain,
That does freeze my bones around°
Selfish! vain,
Eternal bane!
That free Love with bondage bound.
1793   1794

Holy Thursday

Is this a holy thing to see,
In a rich and fruitful land,
Babes reducd to misery,
Fed with cold and usurous hand?

Is that trembling cry a song?
Can it be a song of joy?
And so many children poor?
It is a land of poverty!

And their sun does never shine.
10   And their fields are bleak & bare.
And their ways are fill'd with thorns.
It is eternal winter there.

For where-e'er the sun does shine,
And where-e'er the rain does fall:
Babe can never hunger there,
Nor poverty the mind appall.
1793   1794

The Chimney Sweeper

A little black thing among the snow:
Crying weep, weep, in notes of woe!
Where are thy father & mother? say?
They are both gone up to the church to pray.

Because I was happy upon the heath,
And smil'd among the winters snow:

Break . . . around The chain of jealousy is
derived from the chain used to bind Loki in
the Northern Prose Edda.

They clothed me in the clothes of death,
And taught me to sing the notes of woe.

And because I am happy, & dance & sing,
10 They think they have done me no injury:
And are gone to praise God & his Priest & King
Who make up a heaven of our misery.
1793   1794

The Sick Rose°

O Rose thou art sick.
The invisible worm,
That flies in the night
In the howling storm:

Has found out thy bed
Of crimson joy:
And his dark secret love
Does thy life destroy.
                    1794

The Tyger°

Tyger Tyger, burning bright,
In the forests of the night;
What immortal hand or eye,
Could frame thy fearful symmetry?

In what distant deeps or skies
Burnt the fire of thine eyes!
On what wings dare he aspire?°
What the hand, dare sieze the fire?°

And what shoulder, & what art,
10 Could twist the sinews of thy heart?

The Sick Rose Note that the Rose's bed is "of crimson joy" *before* the worm finds it out. The bed is concealed, and evidently a place of self-gratification. "Dark secret love" comes and destroys, possibly because a bright open love would have been rejected anyway.
The Tyger This is the most disputed of Blake's lyrics among interpreters. The increasingly rhetorical questions are akin to those asked by God at the end of the Book of Job, and the Tyger is a kind of cousin to the Leviathan and Behemoth with whom God confronts Job. However the poem is interpreted, the reader should be wary of identifying the poem's chanter with Blake, who did not react with awe or fear to any natural phenomenon whatsoever.
   Blake probably had considerable satirical in-
tention in this lyric, as a juxtaposition of his verbal description of the Tyger with his illustration seems to suggest. The poem's speaker, though a man of considerable imagination (quite possibly a poet like William Cowper), is at work terrifying himself with a monster of his own creation. Though Blake may mean us to regard the poem's questions as unanswerable, he himself would have answered by saying that the "immortal hand or eye" belonged only to Man, who makes both Tyger and Lamb. In "the forests of the night," or mental darkness, Man makes the Tyger, but in the open vision of day Man makes the Lamb.
On . . . aspire a suggestion of Icarus
What . . . fire a hint of Prometheus

And when thy heart began to beat,
What dread hand? & what dread feet?°

What the hammer? what the chain,
In what furnace was thy brain?
What the anvil? what dread grasp,
Dare its deadly terrors clasp?

When the stars threw down their spears°
And water'd heaven with their tears:
Did he smile his work to see?
20   Did he who made the Lamb make thee?

Tyger, Tyger burning bright,
In the forests of the night:
What immortal hand or eye,
Dare frame thy fearful symmetry?
1793   1794

Ah! Sun-flower°

Ah Sun-flower! weary of time,
Who countest the steps of the Sun:
Seeking after that sweet golden clime
Where the travellers journey is done.

Where the Youth pined away with desire,
And the pale Virgin shrouded in snow:
Arise from their graves and aspire,
Where my Sun-flower wishes to go.
                              1794

London°

I wander thro' each charter'd° street,
Near where the charter'd Thames does flow.

what dread feet David Erdman notes that "& what dread feet?" was altered in ink to "formed thy dread feet" in a late copy; another late source gives "forged thy dread feet."
When . . . spears The stars, or fallen angels, never throw down their spears and surrender in Milton's *Paradise Lost*; in Night V of Blake's *The Four Zoas*, Blake clearly associates "The Tyger" with the Fall of Urizen, who says: "I call'd the stars around my feet in the night of councils dark; / The stars threw down their spears & fled naked away. / We fell."
Ah! Sun-Flower In Blake's poem *Europe*, heaven is described as "an allegorical abode where existence hath never come." Blake's Sun-Flower is weary of time because it is trapped in heliotropic bondage, in perpetual cycle, and longs vainly for such an allegorical abode. The reader

should ask himself whether the three "where"s of this poem are not the same place.
Blake is giving his own version here of Ovid's story of Clytia, who was first loved but then abandoned by Helius, the sun god. As she still gazed at him, with yearning, she was metamorphosed into a heliotrope or sunflower.
London This greatest of Blake's prophetic lyrics is based on Ezekiel, and associates London under Pitt's counter-revolutionary repression with Jerusalem waiting for its destruction. But only the third stanza centers upon societal repression; the other three describe every person's all-too-natural abandonment of his own liberty.
charter'd A bitter, multiple usage; it refers to "the charter'd rights of Englishmen," curtailed by Pitt, but also to commercial chartering, and finally to "natural" chartering (the Thames is "bound" or chartered between its banks).

And mark in every face I meet
Marks of weakness, marks of woe.°

In every cry of every Man,
In every Infants cry of fear,
In every° voice: in every ban,°
The mind-forg'd manacles I hear

10　How the Chimney-sweepers cry
Every blackning Church appalls,°
And the hapless Soldiers sigh,°
Runs in blood down Palace walls

But most thro' midnight streets I hear
How the youthful Harlots curse
Blasts the new-born Infants tear°
And blights with plagues the Marriage hearse°
1793　　　　　　　　　　　　　1794

The Human Abstract°

Pity would be no more,
If we did not make somebody Poor:
And Mercy no more could be,
If all were as happy as we;

And mutual fear brings peace;
Till the selfish loves increase.
Then Cruelty knits a snare,
And spreads his baits with care.

He sits down with holy fears,
10　And waters the ground with tears:

marks of woe Here, and later in the poem, Blake closely echoes Ezekiel, as he will in the larger structure of his epic *Jerusalem*; see Ezekiel 9:4, where God says: "Go through the midst of the city, through the midst of Jerusalem, and set a mark upon the foreheads of the men that sigh and that cry for all the abominations that be done in the midst thereof."
every The emphasis on "every" should make us wary of a purely societal interpretation; Blake means *natural* fear, which warrants the repetition of "every."
ban the marriage announcement as well as all societal prohibitions
appalls drapes in a pall
sigh Like "cry" in l.9, this derives from Ezekiel 9:4.
new-born Infants tear Newborn infants have no tears until their eyes are moistened by doctor or midwife; Blake attributes a natural fact to the harlot's curse; the other meaning found here by interpreters, that the infant suffers prenatal blindness, caused by the parent's venereal dis-

ease by earlier infection from the harlot, blends into the curse as spell; the curse is a shouted outcry in the street (most of the poem consists of *sounds*) which "blasts" the tear in the sense of scattering it, as if by wind; the harlot ultimately is Nature herself, as we should expect in Blake.
Marriage hearse Blake means that every marriage whatsoever rides in a hearse, rather than in a celebratory coach.
The Human Abstract This contrary poem to "The Divine Image" of Innocence is as much an organic and terrible image as that poem is a deliberately confused tangle of abstractions. All the virtues of "The Divine Image" are revealed here as stemming from the selfishness of the natural heart. "Abstract" is not to be understood in the sense of the Latin *abstractus* ("separated," "drawn apart"), because Blake does not mean that human nature is split in the state of Experience, but probably that we reduce the truly human to a pernicious series of misleading abstractions.

Then Humility takes its root
Underneath his foot.

Soon spreads the dismal shade
Of Mystery over his head;°
And the Catterpiller and Fly,
Feed on the Mystery.

And it bears the fruit of Deceit,
Ruddy and sweet to eat;
And the Raven° his nest has made
20   In its thickest shade.

The Gods of the earth and sea,
Sought thro' Nature to find this Tree°
But their search was all in vain:
There grows one in the Human Brain
1793   1794

To Tirzah°

Whate'er is Born of Mortal Birth,
Must be consumed with the Earth
To rise from Generation° free;
Then what have I to do with thee?°

The Sexes sprung from Shame & Pride
Blow'd in the morn: in evening died
But Mercy changd Death into Sleep;
The Sexes rose to work & weep.°

Thou Mother of my Mortal part°
10   With cruelty didst mould my Heart,

Soon . . . head This is the Tree of Mystery,
the Norse Yggdrasil that the god Odin hanged
himself upon, in order to gain knowledge of the
runes, or riddles of Mystery.
the Raven Odin's emblem, here a scavenger
upon humanity's repressed desires
The Gods . . . Tree After Loki, by trickery,
arranged for Balder to die by a mistletoe branch,
the gods searched through nature to find the
tree, so as to restore Balder; Blake's tree is
natural enough, but grows in our minds, which
have fallen into nature.
To Tirzah This poem, the last of the *Songs of
Experience*, with its illustration showing the
raising of the Spiritual Body from death, was
added late to the song cycle, perhaps as late
as 1805, which makes it one of Blake's final
poems, since he wrote little in the last twenty
years of his life. The most difficult of the songs,
it condenses the entire argument of Blake's work.
"To Tirzah" repudiates both Innocence and
Experience, for Tirzah presides over both states.
Tirzah was the capital of the Northern king-

dom of Israel, and so the contrary city to the
Jerusalem of the Prophets, capital of the Southern kingdom of Judah; the two tribes of the
Southern kingdom were redeemed from the captivity, but the ten lost tribes of Tirzah never returned from Babylon; even as Jerusalem is for
Blake the Emanation or spiritual freedom of
man, so Tirzah is his natural bondage; in Blake's
longer poems she turns the spindle of Necessity,
so that to defy her is to deny natural religion,
but also all natural limitation.
Generation sexual generation, but also Blake's
technical name for the state of Experience
what . . . thee Jesus to Mary his mother in
John 2:4
The Sexes . . . weep Blake says that the sexual
act preceded the Fall, yet sexual division with
its present limitations came from a "Shame
& Pride" not originally human; the "Mercy"
here is Time.
Mortal part Nature is not the mother of Blake's
Imagination, his immortal part.

And with false self-deceiving tears,
Didst bind my Nostrils Eyes & Ears.

Didst close my Tongue in senseless clay°
And me to Mortal Life betray:
The Death of Jesus set me free,°
Then what have I to do with thee?
1805   1805

The Book of Thel

This Blakean version of pastoral is an extended Song of Innocence, written in Blake's
characteristic long line, the fourteener, and in the genre of the Renaissance mythological epyllion, or brief epic. The pathos of Thel's story is a function of her weakness
of will, and her failure to endure the necessary sufferings of the state of Experience
is both a failure of desire, and another exposure of the limitations of Innocence.
Blake shows her as an unborn being discontented with her paradisal abode, yet not
courageous enough to sustain the will to be born. She is an image of Innocence
unwilling to carry herself over into the world of Experience, and so she comes to
represent a failure in desire. The reader is left free to interpret her failure on many
levels, from a thought that does not permit itself to find expression to a love that
does not allow itself to be realized by sexual fulfillment.

The Book of Thel°

The Author & Printer   Willm Blake, 1789

PLATE i

Thel's Motto,°
Does the Eagle know what is in the pit?
Or wilt thou go ask the Mole:
Can Wisdom be put in a silver rod?
Or Love in a golden bowl?

senseless clay The "red clay" (literal meaning
of "Adam") of the fallen human form; notice
that Blake grants nature's power to curtail only
four senses, but not the fifth sense, the sexual
one of touch.
set me free not from the orthodox notion of
original sin, but from the deceits of natural
religion
Thel From the Greek for "will" or "wish"; like
so many of Blake's names, this is a grim irony
as well as a gentle pathos, because Thel fails in
will, in the strength of desire.

Motto The source is Ecclesiastes 12:4–7: "and
all the daughters of musick shall be brought
low; / . . . and fears shall be in the way . . .
and desire shall fail: because man goeth to his
long home . . . / Or ever the silver cord be
loosed, or the golden bowl be broken . . . /
Then shall the dust return to the earth as it was.
. . ." The Mole is in the pit of Experience,
where knowledge of Experience must be sought.
Wisdom and Love must be put into a rod and
bowl of flesh, the organs of fallen human generation.

PLATE 1

Thel

I

The daughters of Mne Seraphim° led round their sunny flocks,
All but the youngest. she in paleness sought the secret air.
To fade away like morning beauty from her mortal day:

Down by the river of Adona° her soft voice is heard:
And thus her gentle lamentation falls like morning dew.

O life of this our spring! why fades the lotus of the water?
Why fade these children of the spring? born but to smile & fall.
Ah! Thel is like a watry bow, and like a parting cloud,
Like a reflection in a glass. like shadows in the water.
10 Like dreams of infants. like a smile upon an infants face,
Like the doves voice, like transient day, like music in the air;
Ah! gentle may I lay me down, and gentle rest my head.
And gentle sleep the sleep of death. and gentle hear the voice
Of him that walketh in the garden in the evening time.°

The Lilly of the valley breathing in the humble grass
Answer'd the lovely maid and said; I am a watry weed,
And I am very small, and love to dwell in lowly vales;
So weak, the gilded butterfly scarce perches on my head
Yet I am visited from heaven and he that smiles on all.
20 Walks in the valley. and each morn over me spreads his hand
Saying, rejoice thou humble grass, thou new-born lilly flower,
Thou gentle maid of silent valleys. and of modest brooks;
For thou shalt be clothed in light, and fed with morning manna:
Till summers heat melts thee beside the fountains and the springs
To flourish in eternal vales: then why should Thel complain,

PLATE 2

Why should the mistress of the vales of Har, utter a sigh.

She ceasd & smild in tears, then sat down in her silver shrine.

Thel answerd. O thou little virgin of the peaceful valley.
Giving to those that cannot crave, the voiceless, the o'ertired.
Thy breath doth nourish the innocent lamb, he smells thy milky garments,
He crops thy flowers. while thou sittest smiling in his face,
Wiping his mild and meekin mouth from all contagious taints.

Mne Seraphim The Seraphim were the highest order of angels, generally pictured as having the heads of children; in *Tiriel*, an earlier experiment at a mythological brief epic, Blake made Mnetha (a compound of Mnemosyne, or memory, and Athena) the goddess of the vales of Har, or world of the ungenerated. Thel and her sisters are thus angelic daughters of Mnetha, pastoral shepherdesses more ornamental than functional in their unborn realm.
river of Adona See *Paradise Lost* I.450–52 and Spenser's Garden of Adonis, *The Faerie Queene* III.vi.29.
the voice . . . time See Genesis 3:8; Thel's prison-paradise is thus identical with the Hebraic Garden of Eden.

Thy wine doth purify the golden honey, thy perfume,
Which thou dost scatter on every little blade of grass that springs
10   Revives the milked cow, & tames the fire-breathing steed.
But Thel is like a faint cloud kindled at the rising sun:
I vanish from my pearly throne, and who shall find my place.

Queen of the vales the Lilly answered, ask the tender cloud,
And it shall tell thee why it glitters in the morning sky,
And why it scatters its bright beauty thro' the humid air.
Descend O little cloud & hover before the eyes of Thel.

The Cloud descended, and the Lilly bowd her modest head:
And went to mind her numerous charge among the verdant grass.

PLATE 3

II

O little Cloud the virgin said, I charge thee tell to me,
Why thou complainest not when in one hour thou fade away:
Then we shall seek thee but not find; ah Thel is like to Thee.
I pass away. yet I complain, and no one hears my voice.

The Cloud then shew'd his golden head & his bright form emerg'd,
Hovering and glittering on the air before the face of Thel.

O virgin know'st thou not. our steeds drink of the golden springs
Where Luvah° doth renew his horses: look'st thou on my youth,
And fearest thou because I vanish and am seen no more.
10   Nothing remains; O maid I tell thee, when I pass away,
It is to tenfold life, to love, to peace, and raptures holy:
Unseen descending, weigh my light wings upon balmy flowers;
And court the fair eyed dew. to take me to her shining tent;
The weeping virgin,° trembling kneels before the risen sun,
Till we arise link'd in a golden band, and never part;
But walk united, bearing food to all our tender flowers
Dost thou O little Cloud? I fear that I am not like thee;
For I walk through the vales of Har.° and smell the sweetest flowers;
But I feed not the little flowers: I hear the warbling birds,
20   But I feed not the warbling birds. they fly and seek their food;
But Thel delights in these no more because I fade away,
And all shall say, without a use this shining woman liv'd,
Or did she only live. to be at death the food of worms.

The Cloud reclind upon his airy throne and answer'd thus.

Then if thou art the food of worms. O virgin of the skies,
How great thy use. how great thy blessing; every thing that lives,

Luvah the first appearance of one of Blake's Zoas, the "Giant Forms" or Titans of his comprehensive mythology. In his fallen form Luvah will be Orc, the fiery rebel of unbridled sexual energy, but here he is unfallen, and presides over a world of only infantile sexuality.
weeping virgin the vaporizing half of the water cycle in nature, from cloud to rain to sea to cloud again
vales of Har Har is Hebrew for "mountain"; the name also suggests the Miltonic alternate placing of the earthly paradise in Abyssinia or Ethiopia.

Lives not alone, nor for itself: fear not and I will call
The weak worm from its lowly bed, and thou shalt hear its voice.
Come forth worm of the silent valley, to thy pensive queen.

30   The helpless worm arose, and sat upon the Lillys leaf,
And the bright Cloud saild on, to find his partner in the vale.

PLATE 4

III

Then Thel astonish'd view'd the Worm upon its dewy bed.

Art thou a Worm? image of weakness. art thou but a Worm?
I see thee like an infant wrapped in the Lillys leaf:
Ah weep not little voice, thou can'st not speak. but thou can'st weep;
Is this a Worm? I see thee lay helpless & naked: weeping,
And none to answer, none to cherish thee with mothers smiles.°

The Clod of Clay heard the Worms voice, & raisd her pitying head;
She bow'd over the weeping infant, and her life exhal'd
In milky fondness, then on Thel she fix'd her humble eyes.

10   O beauty of the vales of Har. we live not for ourselves,
Thou seest me the meanest thing, and so I am indeed;
My bosom of itself is cold. and of itself is dark,

PLATE 5

But he that loves the lowly, pours his oil upon my head.
And kisses me, and binds his nuptial bands around my breast,
And says; Thou mother of my children, I have loved thee.
And I have given thee a crown that none can take away
But how this is sweet maid, I know not, and I cannot know,
I ponder, and I cannot ponder;° yet I live and love.

The daughter of beauty wip'd her pitying tears with her white veil,
And said. Alas! I knew not this, and therefore did I weep:
That God would love a Worm I knew, and punish the evil foot
10   That wilful, bruis'd its helpless form: but that he cherish'd it
With milk and oil. I never knew; and therefore did I weep,
And I complaind in the mild air, because I fade away,
And lay me down in thy cold bed, and leave my shining lot.

Queen of the vales, the matron Clay answerd; I heard thy sighs.
And all thy moans flew o'er my roof. but I have call'd them down:
Wilt thou O Queen enter my house. 'tis given thee to enter,
And to return; fear nothing. enter with thy virgin feet.°

---

mothers smiles An appeal to Thel's repressed
maternal impulses; the worm is emblematic of
sexual generation, but also of death.
cannot ponder The Clod of Clay represents both
the Adamic flesh and the grave, the worm's two
aspects, and so speaks for it; the Clay's puzzle-
ment is a gentle satire upon natural innocence,
which is unorganized and thus ignorant.
virgin feet The feet, for Blake, always represent
visionary stance; here an irony, as only Thel's
feet will cease to be virgin, in her brief encounter with Experience.

PLATE 6

IV

The eternal gates terrific porter lifted the northern bar:°
Thel enter'd in & saw the secrets of the land unknown;
She saw the couches of the dead, & where the fibrous roots
Of every heart on earth infixes deep its restless twists:°
A land of sorrows & of tears where never smile was seen.

She wanderd in the land of clouds thro' valleys dark, listning
Dolours & lamentations: waiting oft beside a dewy grave
She stood in silence. listning to the voices of the ground,
Till to her own grave plot° she came, & there she sat down.
10   And heard this voice of sorrow breathed from the hollow pit.

Why cannot the Ear be closed to its own destruction?
Or the glistning Eye to the poison of a smile!
Why are Eyelids stord with arrows ready drawn,
Where a thousand fighting men in ambush lie?
Or an Eye of gifts & graces, show'ring fruits & coined gold!
Why a Tongue impress'd with honey from every wind?
Why an Ear, a whirlpool fierce to draw creations in?
Why a Nostril wide inhaling terror trembling & affright
Why a tender curb upon the youthful burning boy!
20   Why a little curtain of flesh on the bed of our desire?°

The Virgin started from her seat, & with a shriek.°
Fled back unhinderd° till she came into the vales of Har
        THE END
1789–91   1789–91

The Marriage of Heaven and Hell

This is Blake's manifesto, his declaration of spiritual independence, and his version of what it means to rise in the body at thirty-three, the age at which Christ died. Deliberately, he makes it the entry-way into the canon of his mature work, his highly organized story of how man and the universe got into their present sorry condition,

northern bar See the *Odyssey* XIII. where the Cave of the Naiades or sea nymphs has two entrances, a northern one for men, and a southern one for gods; some scholars see Blake's source here as the neoplatonic philosopher Porphyry's commentary on the Cave of the Nymphs, but Blake is closer to Spenser's double gates and their double-natured porter in the Garden of Adonis (*The Faerie Queene* III.vi.31–32); in his epic *Milton* 26:16–18, Blake identifies his porter as Los the Poetic Genius; Spenser's porter is Old Genius. So the northern gate is the gate for men, not gods, from Innocence to Experience; Thel passes out and then flees back through the northern gate.
every heart . . . twists the naturalized heart,

a labyrinth of jealousy and selfishness
grave plot where Thel would be buried eventually if she accepted natural incarnation; the lament that rises would be her own voice
Why cannot . . . desire The lament's vocabulary is Petrarchan-Elizabethan in its erotic conventions; Thel protests the excessive strength of four senses, but bewails the failure of the fifth, the sexual sense of touch, to be strong enough to have broken through her inhibitions; even in Experience, she would have remained a virgin.
shriek the reverse of a birth shriek, since Thel refuses to be born
unhinderd ironic, since she is choosing "hindrance, not action"

and his prophecy of what should be done by every man who wishes to work free of a merely natural or given condition.

The central element in this prose poem is Blake's presentation of his dialectic, his imaginative but still rational process of arriving at truth through the progression of contraries, opposites which are not negations or denials but partial truths. What makes The Marriage initially a little difficult is that its rhetoric of presentation and its complex and experimental literary form embody a dialectical argument, so that the shock value of the work goes beyond its actually quite restrained wisdom. Commenting on Emanuel Swedenborg (Swedish theologian and mystic, 1688–1772) in 1788, Blake wrote, "Good and Evil are here both Good and the two contraries Married"; Blake's contraries replace Swedenborg's "correspondences," which are mutually absorbing categories, identities between the spiritual and natural worlds. By "marriage" Blake means that the contraries are to be reconciled, but are not to absorb or subsume one another. Blake was never a Swedenborgian, but may have believed him to be a fellow visionary, until by reading more of Swedenborg, he came to know better. In another 1788 comment on Swedenborg, Blake wrote, "Heaven and Hell are born Together," meaning that Swedenborg never knew this, since that onetime rebel against Calvinism had embraced the doctrine of Predestination. Blake begins and largely continues as though he were on the "Devil's" or imaginative rebel's side, and certainly he is more in that camp than among "Angels" or the timidly orthodox, but his final stance transcends any upsurge of energy and desire. Just as the states of Innocence and of Experience satirize one another, so the contraries of Devil and Angel satirically reveal one another's limitations.

The Marriage, then, is an intellectual satire, but it is also a qualified prophecy of an apocalypse that may be imminent. Rabelais (whom Blake never read) provides the closest analogue to Blake's tone, with the difference that Blake sees in his contemporary time of troubles the presages of the promised end. Not so much the French Revolution but the English reaction against the spread of revolution is Blake's starting point. The notes below trace his movement from that point to his overt declaration of election as the prophet his bad time requires.

The Marriage of Heaven and Hell

The Argument°

PLATE 2
Rintrah° roars & shakes his fires in the burdend air;
Hungry clouds swag° on the deep

Once meek, and in a perilous path,
The just man kept his course along
The vale of death.

The Argument This introductory lyric obliquely presents the contraries of Devil and Angel as an endlessly unresolved cycle of just man driven out and villain accepted by society.
Rintrah representative of prophetic wrath in Blake's mythology. He is a forerunner, like Elijah or John the Baptist, and his fury precedes the turning over of a societal and natural cycle, but he himself is only a harbinger, not a redeemer.
swag sway or lurch

Roses are planted where thorns grow.
And on the barren heath
Sing the honey bees.

Then the perilous path was planted:
10   And a river, and a spring
On every cliff and tomb;
And on the bleached bones
Red clay° brought forth.°

Till the villain left the paths of ease,
To walk in perilous paths, and drive
The just man into barren climes.

Now the sneaking serpent walks
In mild humility.
And the just man rages in the wilds
20   Where lions roam.

Rintrah roars & shakes his fires in the burdend air;
Hungry clouds swag on the deep.

PLATE 3
As a new heaven is begun, and it is now thirty-three years since its advent:
the Eternal Hell revives.° And lo! Swedenborg is the Angel sitting at the
tomb; his writings are the linen clothes folded up.° Now is the dominion of
Edom, & the return of Adam into Paradise; see Isaiah xxxiv & XXXV Chap:°
Without Contraries is no progression. Attraction and Repulsion, Reason and
Energy, Love and Hate, are necessary to Human existence.
From these contraries spring what the religious call Good & Evil. Good is
the passive that obeys Reason[.] Evil is the active springing from Energy.
Good is Heaven. Evil is Hell.°

PLATE 4
   The Voice of the Devil°
All Bibles or sacred codes. have been the causes of the following Errors.
   1. That Man has two real existing principles Viz: a Body & a Soul.

Red clay literal meaning of the Hebrew "Adam"
Then forth The general source is Exodus 17:1–8.
As . . . revives In Swedenborg's book *Last Judgment*, Blake had read: "The evil are cast into the
hells, and the good elevated into heaven, and thus
that all things are reduced into order, the spiritual equilibrium between good and evil, or between heaven and hell, being thence restored.
. . . This Last Judgment was commenced in the
beginning of the year 1757. . . ." Blake was
born in 1757; writing in 1790, aged thirty-three,
he ironically sees his birth as the contrary to
Swedenborg's pronouncement of a new heaven
of Angelic restraint.
Swedenborg . . . folded up See Matthew 28:
1–7.
XXXV Chap The red man of Edom was identified with Esau, tricked of the inheritance by

his brother Jacob or Israel in Genesis 28:40,
where their father Isaac then prophesies the
eventual dominion of Esau's descendants. Isaiah
63:1–4 amplifies this prophecy by the vision of a
savior coming out of Edom, taken by Christian
exegetes as a foretelling of Christ. Blake associates both these texts with the earlier prophecy in
Isaiah 34 and 35, where the desolate land of
Israel is restored, once the wicked are cut off.
As Blake displaces the prophecy into the situation of 1790, Edom is France, and the red man
will soon be identified as Orc, the Revolution
threatening to cross the English Channel.
Evil is Hell ironical identifications, as Blake
adopts the vocabulary of the Angels.
the Devil again an irony of stance, "diabolical" only to the Angels

2. That Energy. calld Evil. is alone from the Body. & that Reason. calld Good. is alone from the Soul.

3. That God will torment Man in Eternity for following his Energies. But the following Contraries to these are True

1. Man has no Body distinct from his Soul for that calld Body is a portion of Soul discernd by the five Senses, the chief inlets of Soul in this age°

2. Energy is the only life and is from the Body and Reason is the bound or outward circumference of Energy.

3. Energy is Eternal Delight

PLATE 5

Those who restrain desire, do so because theirs is weak enough to be restrained; and the restrainer or reason usurps its place & governs the unwilling.

And being restrained it by degrees becomes passive till it is only the shadow of desire.

The history of this is written in Paradise Lost.° & the Governor or Reason is call'd Messiah.

And the original Archangel or possessor of the command of the heavenly host, is calld the Devil or Satan and his children are call'd Sin & Death

But in the Book of Job Miltons Messiah is call'd Satan.°

For this history has been adopted by both parties

It indeed appear'd to Reason as if Desire was cast out, but the Devils account is, that the Messi[PL 6]ah fell. & formed a heaven of what he stole from the Abyss

This is shewn in the Gospel, where he prays to the Father to send the comforter or Desire that Reason may have Ideas to build on, the Jehovah of the Bible being no other than he, who dwells in flaming fire.° Know that after Christs death, he became Jehovah.

But in Milton; the Father is Destiny, the Son, a Ratio° of the five senses. & the Holy-ghost, Vacuum!

Note. The reason Milton wrote in fetters when he wrote of Angels & God, and at liberty when of Devils & Hell, is because he was a true Poet and of the Devils party without knowing it°

A Memorable Fancy°

As I was walking among the fires of hell, delighted with the enjoyments of Genius; which to Angels look like torment and insanity. I collected some of their Proverbs: thinking that as the sayings used in a nation, mark its character,

---

in this age Though Blake is rejecting the Pauline dualism of body and soul, he does not equate body and soul, as a pure naturalist would; "this age" is fallen, and so the Body is all of the Soul that our shrunken senses can perceive.

The history . . . Paradise Lost This is an aesthetic reading of the poem's design, and not a reading of Milton's intentions; Blake traces the declining movement of creative energy from the active of the early books to the passive of the poem's conclusion, and particularly has in mind the poem's continual denigrations of fallen man's creative powers.

But . . . Satan In the Book of Job, Satan is a moral accuser who torments Job with physical pain; in *Paradise Lost* Christ is instrumental in carrying the fire of God's wrath down into the abyss, so that Hell is created as a place of moral and physical punishment; so Blake arrives at the equation: Job's Satan is Milton's Messiah.

This . . . fire See John 16:7 for the Comforter or Paraclete, but the reference is probably to John 14:16–17, with "the Spirit of Truth" interpreted by Blake as Desire.

Ratio rationalistic reduction

Note . . . it This means that for a poet *as poet* the energy of human desire cannot be separated from the imagination.

A Memorable Fancy This, and subsequent sections with the same title, are parodies of what Swedenborg called "Memorable Relations," literal-minded reports of his spiritual visions.

so the Proverbs of Hell, shew the nature of Infernal wisdom better than any description of buildings or garments.°

When I came home; on the abyss of the five senses, where a flat sided steep frowns over the present world. I saw a mighty Devil folded in black clouds, hovering on the side of the rock, with cor[PL 7]roding fires he wrote the following sentence now perceived by the minds of men, & read by them on earth.°

> How do you know but ev'ry Bird that cuts the airy way,
> Is an immense world of delight, clos'd by your senses five?°

Proverbs of Hell°

In seed time learn, in harvest teach, in winter enjoy.

Drive your cart and your plow over the bones of the dead.

The road of excess leads to the palace of wisdom.

Prudence is a rich ugly old maid courted by Incapacity.

He who desires but acts not, breeds pestilence.

The cut worm forgives the plow.

Dip him in the river who loves water.

A fool sees not the same tree that a wise man sees.

He whose face gives no light, shall never become a star.

10   Eternity is in love with the productions of time.

The busy bee has no time for sorrow.

The hours of folly are measur'd by the clock, but of wisdom: no clock
    can measure.

All wholsom food is caught without a net or a trap.

Bring out number weight & measure in a year of dearth.

No bird soars too high. if he soars with his own wings.

A dead body. revenges not injuries.

The most sublime act is to set another before you.

If the fool would persist in his folly he would become wise

Folly is the cloke of knavery.

20   Shame is Prides cloke.

PLATE 8

Prisons are built with stones of Law, Brothels with bricks of Religion.

The pride of the peacock is the glory of God.

The lust of the goat is the bounty of God.

---

any description . . . garments a parody of the Devil's activities in *Paradise Lost* II, after Satan goes off on his voyage through Chaos
I saw . . . earth The "mighty Devil" is Blake at work engraving the *Marriage*, the "corroding fires" are of his satiric art, and the "rock" is our fallen human minds, as we read and study his engraved plates.
How . . . five The couplet the Devil Blake etches is a tribute to Thomas Chatterton, closely following a quatrain from his "The Dethe of Syr Charles Bawdin," ll.133–36: "How dydd I knowe thatt ev'ry darte, / That cutte the airie waie, / Myghte nott fynde passage toe my harte, / And close myne eyes for aie?" Blake's parody of this reminds us of our perceptive limitations.
Proverbs of Hell "Diabolic" or antinomian in their rhetoric, these seventy proverbs depend

upon a dialectical definition of an "act," and have been generally misunderstood, particularly in recent years. In his annotations to Johann Kaspar Lavater's (1741–1801) *Aphorisms on Man*, Blake wrote: "As I understand Vice it is a Negative—It does not signify what the laws of Kings and Priests have calld Vice . . . Accident is the omission of act in self and the hindering of act in another, This is Vice but all Act is Virtue. To hinder another is not an act it is the contrary it is a restraint on action both in ourselves and in the person hinderd. for he who hinders another omits his own duty at the time. Murder is Hindering Another. Theft is Hindering Another. Backbiting, Undermining, Circumventing and whatever is Negative is Vice." The reader needs to apply these ideas of act and hindrance to the Proverbs.

The wrath of the lion is the wisdom of God.
The nakedness of woman is the work of God.
Excess of sorrow laughs. Excess of joy weeps.
The roaring of lions, the howling of wolves, the raging of the stormy sea, and
    the destructive sword. are portions of eternity too great for the eye of man.
The fox condemns the trap, not himself.
Joys impregnate. Sorrows bring forth.
³⁰ Let man wear the fell of the lion. woman the fleece of the sheep.
The bird a nest, the spider a web, man friendship.
The selfish smiling fool. & the sullen frowning fool. shall be both
    thought wise. that they may be a rod.
What is now proved was once, only imagin'd.
The rat, the mouse, the fox, the rabbet; watch the roots, the lion, the tyger, the
    horse, the elephant, watch the fruits.
The cistern contains: the fountain overflows
One thought. fills immensity.
Always be ready to speak your mind, and a base man will avoid you.
Every thing possible to be believ'd is an image of truth.
The eagle never lost so much time. as when he submitted to learn of the crow.

PLATE 9
⁴⁰ The fox provides for himself. but God provides for the lion.
Think in the morning, Act in the noon, Eat in the evening, Sleep in the night.
He who has sufferd you to impose on him knows you.
As the plow follows words, so God rewards prayers.
The tygers of wrath are wiser than the horses of instruction
Expect poison from the standing water.
You never know what is enough unless you know what is more than enough.
Listen to the fools reproach! it is a kingly title!
The eyes of fire, the nostrils of air, the mouth of water, the beard of earth.
The weak in courage is strong in cunning.
⁵⁰ The apple tree never asks the beech how he shall grow, nor the lion. the horse,
    how he shall take his prey.
The thankful receiver bears a plentiful harvest.
If others had not been foolish, we should be so.
The soul of sweet delight, can never be defil'd,
When thou seest an Eagle, thou seest a portion of Genius. lift up thy head!
As the catterpiller chooses the fairest leaves to lay her eggs on, so the priest
    lays his curse on the fairest joys.
To create a little flower is the labour of ages.
Damn. braces: Bless relaxes.
The best wine is the oldest. the best water the newest.
Prayers plow not! Praises reap not!
⁶⁰ Joys laugh not! Sorrows weep not!

PLATE 10
The head Sublime, the heart Pathos, the genitals Beauty, the hands & feet
    Proportion.
As the air to a bird or the sea to a fish, so is contempt to the contemptible.

The crow wish'd every thing was black, the owl, that every thing was white.
Exuberance is Beauty.
If the lion was advise'd by the fox. he would be cunning.
Improve[me]nt makes strait roads, but the crooked roads without Improvement,
    are roads of Genius.
Sooner murder an infant in its cradle than nurse unacted desires
Where man is not nature is barren.
Truth can never be told so as to be understood, and not be believ'd.

70   Enough! or Too much

PLATE 11°
    The ancient Poets animated all sensible objects with Gods or Geniuses,
calling them by the names and adorning them with the properties of woods,
rivers, mountains, lakes, cities, nations, and whatever their enlarged & numerous
senses could perceive.
    And particularly they studied the genius of each city & country. placing it
under its mental deity.
    Till a system was formed, which some took advantage of & enslav'd the
vulgar by attempting to realize or abstract the mental deities from their objects;
thus began Priesthood.
    Choosing forms of worship from poetic tales.
    And at length they pronounced that the Gods had orderd such things.
    Thus men forgot that All deities reside in the human breast.

PLATE 12
    A Memorable Fancy
    The Prophets Isaiah and Ezekiel dined with me, and I asked them how they
dared so roundly to assert. that God spake to them; and whether they did not
think at the time, that they would be misunderstood, & so be the cause of
imposition.
    Isaiah answer'd. I saw no God, nor heard any, in a finite organical perception;
but my senses discover'd the infinite in every thing, and as I was then per-
swaded, & remain confirm'd; that the voice of honest indignation is the voice
of God, I cared not for consequences but wrote.
    Then I asked: does a firm perswasion that a thing is so, make it so?
    He replied. All poets believe that it does, & in ages of imagination this firm
perswasion removed mountains; but many are not capable of a firm perswasion
of any thing.
    Then Ezekiel said. The philosophy of the east taught the first principles of
human perception   some nations held one principle for the origin & some another, we of Israel taught that the Poetic Genius (as you now call it) was
the first principle and all the others merely derivative, which was the cause
of our despising the Prisets & Philosophers of other countries, and prophecying
that all Gods [PL 13] would at last be proved to originate in ours & to be the
tributaries of the Poetic Genius, it was this. that our great poet King David
desired so fervently & invokes so patheticly, saying by this he conquers enemies

Plate 11 This section describes the codification
of poetry into scripture, in a little history of
religion.

& governs kingdoms; and we so loved our God. that we cursed in his name all the deities of surrounding nations, and asserted that they had rebelled; from these opinions the vulgar came to think that all nations would at last be subject to the jews.

This said he, like all firm perswasions, is come to pass, for all nations believe the jews code and worship the jews god, and what greater subjection can be

I heard this with some wonder, & must confess my own conviction. After dinner I ask'd Isaiah to favour the world with his lost works, he said none of equal value was lost. Ezekiel said the same of his.

I also asked Isaiah what made him go naked and barefoot three years? he answerd, the same that made our friend Diogenes the Grecian.°

I then asked Ezekiel. why he eat dung, & lay so long on his right & left side? he answerd. the desire of raising other men into a perception of the infinite this the North American tribes practise. & is he honest who resists his genius or conscience. only for the sake of present ease or gratification?°

PLATE 14
The ancient tradition that the world will be consumed in fire at the end of six thousand years is true. as I have heard from Hell.°

For the cherub with his flaming sword is hereby commanded to leave his guard at tree of life, and when he does, the whole creation will be consumed, and appear infinite. and holy whereas it now appears finite & corrupt.°

This will come to pass by an improvement of sensual enjoyment.°

But first the notion that man has a body distinct from his soul, is to be expunged; this I shall do, by printing in the infernal method, by corrosives, which in Hell are salutary and medicinal, melting apparent surfaces away, and displaying the infinite which was hid.°

If the doors of perception were cleansed every thing would appear to man as it is, infinite.

For man has closed himself up, till he sees all things thro' narrow chinks of his cavern.°

PLATE 15
    A Memorable Fancy°
I was in a Printing house in Hell & saw the method in which knowledge is transmitted from generation to generation.

I also . . . Grecian See Isaiah 20:3; Diogenes (412–323 B.C.) was a Cynic philosopher, noted for eccentric behavior.
I then . . . gratification See Ezekiel 4:4–12.
The ancient . . . Hell The tradition was hardly ancient, since Blake relies upon later Christian interpretations of II Peter 3:8.
for the . . . corrupt The cherub is from Genesis 3:24, but assimilated to the Covering Cherub of Ezekiel 28:11–16, with whom Blake identified Satan in his poem *Milton* 9:30–35.
sensual enjoyment the necessary first step for Blake, but only a first step
this I shall do . . . hid Note that Blake refers to his satiric art as poet and visionary art as engraver, and not to mysticism or extraordinary states of consciousness.

cavern our body as it is now
A Memorable Fancy An allegory of artistic creation; it begins with the Dragon or phallic man improving sensual enjoyment, while the Dragons expand our other senses; the Viper of repression seeks to conceal our fallen condition, but the Eagle or portion of Genius defeats the Viper and raises us to infinite potential; the "Eagle like men" are artists; in the fourth chamber appearances are melted down into the stuff of poetry by the Lions who represent archetypes of imagination; in the fifth chamber, which influenced the "golden smithies" of Yeats's "Byzantium," the flood of spirit is broken by forms of art; the metals are then cast into the sixth chamber, where the creative process culminates.

In the first chamber was a Dragon-Man, clearing away the rubbish from a caves mouth; within, a number of Dragons were hollowing the cave,

In the second chamber was a Viper folding round the rock & the cave, and others adorning it with gold silver and precious stones.

In the third chamber was an Eagle with wings and feathers of air, he caused the inside of the cave to be infinite, around were numbers of Eagle like men, who built palaces in the immense cliffs.

In the fourth chamber were Lions of flaming fire raging around & melting the metals into living fluids.

In the fifth chamber were Unnam'd forms, which cast the metals into the expanse.

There they were reciev'd by Men who occupied the sixth chamber, and took the forms of books & were arranged in libraries.

PLATE 16

The Giants who formed this world into its sensual existence and now seem to live in it in chains, are in truth. the causes of its life & the sources of all activity, but the chains are, the cunning of weak and tame minds. which have power to resist energy, according to the proverb, the weak in courage is strong in cunning.

Thus one portion of being, is the Prolific. the other, the Devouring: to the devourer it seems as if the producer was in his chains, but it is not so, he only takes portions of existence and fancies that the whole.

But the Prolific would cease to be Prolific unless the Devourer as a sea received the excess of his delights.°

Some will say, Is not God alone the Prolific? I answer, God only Acts & Is, in existing beings or Men.

These two classes of men are always upon earth, & they should be enemies; whoever tries [PL 17] to reconcile them seeks to destroy existence.

Religion is an endeavour to reconcile the two.

Note. Jesus Christ did not wish to unite but to seperate them, as in the Parable of sheep and goats! & he says I came not to send Peace but a Sword.°

Messiah or Satan or Tempter was formerly thought to be one of the Antediluvians° who are our Energies.

A Memorable Fancy°

An Angel came to me and said   O pitiable foolish young man! O horrible! O dreadful state! consider the hot burning dungeon thou art preparing for thyself to all eternity, to which thou art going in such career.

I said, perhaps you will be willing to shew me my eternal lot & we will contemplate together upon it and see whether your lot or mine is most desirable

Thus one . . . delights The most central passage in *The Marriage*, making clear that Blake goes beyond Devil as well as Angel, and the one passage in *The Marriage* free of all irony; the Devourer is the outer limit of the Prolific, as Freud's ego is of his id, but the Devourer cannot operate independently; the Prolific, unlike Freud's id, is not chaotic, yet needs the Devourer to avoid chaos.
Note . . . Sword For the Parable, see Matthew 25:32–33; Christ's remark is in Matthew 10:34.
Antediluvians the Giant Race before the Flood that only Noah and his family survived
A Memorable Fancy The "stable" is where Jesus was born, the "vault" where he was buried, the "mill" represents rationalistic reduction; the "winding cavern" suits rationalistic metaphysics, and the "void" is nature; Hell, an orthodox illusion, scares away the Angel, allowing Blake the solitude of his own creative vision.

So he took me thro' a stable & thro' a church & down into the church vault at the end of which was a mill: thro' the mill we went, and came to a cave. down the winding cavern we groped our tedious way till a void boundless as a nether sky appeard beneath us. & we held by the roots of trees and hung over this immensity, but I said, if you please we will commit ourselves to this void, and see whether providence is here also, if you will not I will? but he answerd, do not presume O young man but as we here remain behold thy lot which will soon appear when the darkness passes away

So I remaind with him sitting in the twisted [PL 18] root of an oak. he was suspended in a fungus which hung with the head downward into the deep;

By degrees we beheld the infinite Abyss, fiery as the smoke of a burning city; beneath us at an immense distance was the sun, black but shining[;] round it were fiery tracks on which revolv'd vast spiders, crawling after their prey; which flew or rather swum in the finite deep, in the most terrific shapes of animals sprung from corruption. & the air was full of them, & seemd composed of them; these are Devils. and are called Powers of the air, I now asked my companion which was my eternal lot? he said, between the black & white spiders

But now, from between the black & white spiders a cloud and fire burst and rolled thro the deep blackning all beneath, so that the nether deep grew black as a sea & rolled with a terrible noise: beneath us was nothing now to be seen but a black tempest, till looking east between the clouds & the waves, we saw a cataract of blood mixed with fire and not many stones throw from us appeard and sunk again the scaly fold of a monstrous serpent[.] at last to the east, distant about three degrees appeard a fiery crest above the waves[.] slowly it reared like a ridge of golden rocks till we discoverd two globes of crimson fire, from which the sea fled away in clouds of smoke, and now we saw, it was the head of Leviathan, his forehead was divided into streaks of green & purple like those on a tygers forehead: ° soon we saw his mouth & red gills hang just above the raging foam tinging the black deep with beams of blood, advancing toward [PL 19] us with all the fury of a spiritual existence.

My friend the Angel climb'd up from his station into the mill; I remain'd alone, & then this appearance was no more, but I found myself sitting on a pleasant bank beside a river by moon light hearing a harper who sung to the harp, & his theme was, The man who never alters his opinion is like standing water, & breeds reptiles of the mind.

But I arose, and sought for the mill, & there I found my Angel, who surprised asked me, how I escaped?

I answerd. All that we saw was owing to your metaphysics: for when you ran away, I found myself on a bank by moonlight hearing a harper, But now we have seen my eternal lot, shall I shew you yours? he laughd at my proposal; but I by force suddenly caught him in my arms, & flew westerly thro' the night, till we were elevated above the earths shadow: then I flung myself with him directly into the body of the sun, here I clothed myself in white, & taking in my hand Swedenborgs volumes sunk from the glorious clime, and passed all the planets till we came to saturn, here I staid to rest & then leap'd into the void, between saturn & the fixed stars.

tygers forehead This confirms the association in "The Tyger" with the Leviathan of Job.

Here said I! is your lot, in this space, if space it may be calld, Soon we saw the stable and the church, & I took him to the altar and open'd the Bible, and lo! it was a deep pit, into which I descended driving the Angel before me, soon we saw seven houses of brick,° one we enterd; in it were a [PL 20] number of monkeys, baboons, & all of that species chaind by the middle, grinning and snatching at one another, but witheld by the shortness of their chains: however I saw that they sometimes grew numerous, and then the weak were caught by the strong and with a grinning aspect, first coupled with & then devourd, by plucking off first one limb and then another till the body was left a helpless trunk. this after grinning & kissing it with seeming fondness they devourd too; and here & there I saw one savourily picking the flesh off of his own tail; as the stench terribly annoyd us both we went into the mill, & I in my hand brought the skeleton of a body, which in the mill was Aristotles Analytics.°

So the Angel said: thy phantasy has imposed upon me & thou oughtest to be ashamed.

I answerd: we impose on one another, & it is but lost time to converse with you whose works are only Analytics

Opposition is true Friendship.

PLATE 21

I have always found that Angels have the vanity to speak of themselves as the only wise; this they do with a confident insolence sprouting from systematic reasoning;

Thus Swedenborg boasts that what he writes is new; tho' it is only the Contents or Index of already publish'd books

A man carried a monkey about for a shew, & because he was a little wiser than the monkey, grew vain, and conciev'd himself as much wiser than seven men. It is so with Swedenborg; he shews the folly of churches & exposes hypocrites, till he imagines that all are religious. & himself the single [PL 22] one on earth that ever broke a net.

Now hear a plain fact: Swedenborg has not written one new truth: Now hear another: he has written all the old falshoods.

And now hear the reason. He conversed with Angels who are all religious, & conversed not with Devils who all hate religion, for he was incapable thro' his conceited notions.

Thus Swedenborgs writings are a recapitulation of all superficial opinions, and an analysis of the more sublime, but no further.

Have now another plain fact: Any man of mechanical talents may from the writings of Paracelsus or Jacob Behmen, produce ten thousand volumes of equal value with Swedenborg's. and from those of Dante or Shakespear, an infinite number.°

seven houses of brick the seven churches in Asia to whom St. John addressed his Revelation
Aristotles Analytics his writings on logic, which contributed to the theological monkey-quarrels the passage satirizes
Have now . . . number It is vital to get this passage right; Paracelsus (Theophrastus Bombastus von Hohenheim, 1493–1541, the subject and title of a Browning poem) was an alchemist; Jacob Behmen (Böhme, 1573–1624) was a theosophist and mystic; scholars delight in trac-

ing their "influence" on Blake, but such scholars show a more exemplary patience with obscurantism than Blake did. This passage insists that the alchemists and theosophists are more imaginative than poor Swedenborg, but then goes on to say that these spiritual amateurs are only candles in sunshine when compared with Dante and Shakespeare, who in turn meant very little to Blake when compared with Milton and the Bible.

But when he has done this, let him not say that he knows better than his master, for he only holds a candle in sunshine.

A Memorable Fancy

Once I saw a Devil in a flame of fire, who arose before an Angel that sat on a cloud. and the Devil utterd these words.

The worship of God is. Honouring his gifts in other men each according to his genius. and loving the [PL 23] greatest men best, those who envy or calumniate great men hate God, for there is no other God.°

The Angel hearing this became almost blue but mastering himself he grew yellow, & at last white pink & smiling, and then replied,

Thou Idolater, is not God One? & is not he visible in Jesus Christ? and has not Jesus Christ given his sanction to the law of ten commandments and are not all other men fools, sinners, & nothings?

The Devil answer'd; bray a fool in a morter with wheat. yet shall not his folly be beaten out of him: if Jesus Christ is the greatest man, you ought to love him in the greatest degree; now hear how he has given his sanction to the law of ten commandments: did he not mock at the sabbath, and so mock the sabbaths God? murder those who were murderd because of him? turn away the law from the woman taken in adultery? steal the labor of others to support him? bear false witness when he omitted making a defence before Pilate? covet when he pray'd for his disciples, and when he bid them shake off the dust of their feet against such as refused to lodge them? I tell you, no virtue can exist without breaking these ten commandments. . Jesus was all virtue, and acted from im[PL 24]pulse. not from rules.°

When he had so spoken: I beheld the Angel who stretched out his arms embracing the flame of fire & he was consumed and arose as Elijah.°

Note. This Angel, who is now become a Devil, is my particular friend: we often read the Bible together in its infernal or diabolical sense which the world shall have if they behave well

I have also: The Bible of Hell:° which the world shall have whether they will or no.

One Law for the Lion & Ox is Oppression°
1790–93   1793

Visions of the Daughters of Albion

Like Shelley's *Epipsychidion*, this is a rapturous hymn to free love, but where Shelley will see free love fail because of the incurable solitariness of individuals, Blake sees it as doomed because of what the Blake scholar Peter Fisher called "the failure of the fallen understanding to cope with the organization of desire." Oothoon is defeated

those who envy . . . God This ought not to be confused with the egregious Hero Worship of Carlyle, for "greatest men" here means greatest artists, and no one else.
not from rules Blake's Jesus is an antinomian or rebel against the Moral Law.
Elijah biblical model for Blake's Rintrah

The Bible of Hell the canon of Blake's engraved works, evidently anticipated here
One Law . . . Oppression This accompanies the illustration of Nebuchadnezzar eating grass (Daniel 4:33), which is the final plate of *The Marriage*; see Bromion's questioning use of this in *Visions of the Daughters of Albion* 4:22.

because both her lovers are imaginatively inadequate, and so the poem is essentially a vision of the limitations of male jealousy and of male sexual fearfulness.

Bromion's name is from the Greek "bromios," for "roaring," ordinarily a Dionysiac title, but used ironically here, since Bromion is a puritanical deist with nothing Dionysiac about him. He despises his own lust, and is a rather Dickensian satiric villain, as he roars out his conventional and disgusting morality. Theotormon, Oothoon's wretchedly weak betrothed, is tormented by his absurd notions of god, as his name is meant to indicate. Oothoon's mellifluous name is a variant on the *Oithona* of James MacPherson (Ossian), and satirizes the conventional heroine of that tiresome prose poem, since Oithona prefers death to the dishonor of rape, while Oothoon, after being raped, attempts to choose a more abundant life. Blake's insights here into the psychic origins of sexual jealousy have not been surpassed. Oothoon wishes to offer herself sexually to Theotormon, but is taken forcibly by Bromion. After a brief period in which she accepts the conventional morality which would condemn her as a harlot (for having enjoyed the sexual act, though it was a rape) she rises into an imaginative freedom that Theotormon can neither understand nor accept, and that Bromion understands but rejects out of natural fear.

Visions of the Daughters of Albion°

The Eye sees more than the Heart knows.°

Printed by Will:ᵐ Blake: 1793.

PLATE iii

The Argument°
I loved Theotormon
And I was not ashamed
I trembled in my virgin fears
And I hid in Leutha's vale!
I plucked Leutha's flower,
And I rose up from the vale;
But the terrible thunders tore
My virgin mantle in twain.

PLATE I

Visions
Enslav'd, the Daughters of Albion weep: a trembling lamentation
Upon their mountains; in their valleys. sighs toward America.

Visions of the Daughters of Albion The title's reference is to what the Daughters *see*, since their function throughout is to be a lamenting chorus. Blake elsewhere identifies Albion with the Greek Titan Atlas, which identifies the Daughters with the Hesperides, who live in a last remainder of Lost Atlantis, and there guard a golden apple tree, which in Blake's poem becomes a flower, "the bright Marygold."
The Eye . . . knows vision surpasses the limited awareness of the natural heart
The Argument Spoken by Oothoon, and sum-

marizing the first seventeen lines of what follows, but significantly different in tone; the Argument indicates that Oothoon's initial timidity was due only to sexual inexperience; Leutha will appear in Blake's *Europe* as a sexual temptress, and in his *Milton* as Sin to Blake's version of Milton's Satan; to hide in Leutha's vale is to repress sexuality, and to pluck her flower and rise up from her vale is to achieve the first step in sexual liberation, but the rapist Bromion intervenes.

For the soft soul of America, Oothoon wanderd in woe,
Along the vales of Leutha seeking flowers to comfort her;
And thus she spoke to the bright Marygold of Leutha's vale

Art thou a flower! art thou a nymph! I see thee now a flower;
Now nymph! I dare not pluck thee from thy dewy bed?

The Golden nymph replied; pluck thou my flower Oothoon the mild
Another flower shall spring, because the soul of sweet delight
10   Can never pass away. she ceas'd & closd her golden shrine.

Then Oothoon pluck'd the flower saying, I pluck thee from thy bed
Sweet flower. and put thee here to glow between my breasts
And thus I turn my face to where my whole soul seeks.

Over the waves she went in wing'd exulting swift delight;
And over Theotormons reign, took her impetuous course.

Bromion rent her with his thunders. on his stormy bed
Lay the faint maid, and soon her woes appalld his thunders hoarse

Bromion spoke. behold this harlot here on Bromions bed,
And let the jealous dolphins sport around the lovely maid;
20   Thy soft American plains are mine, and mine thy north & south:
Stampt with my signet° are the swarthy children of the sun:
They are obedient, they resist not, they obey the scourge:
Their daughters worship terrors and obey the violent:

PLATE 2
Now thou maist marry Bromions harlot, and protect the child
Of Bromions rage, that Oothoon shall put forth in nine moons time

Then storms rent Theotormons limbs; he rolld his waves around.
And folded his black jealous waters round the adulterate pair
Bound back to back in Bromions caves terror & meekness dwell°

At entrance Theotormon sits wearing the threshold hard
With secret tears; beneath him sound like waves on a desart shore
The voice of slaves beneath the sun, and children bought with money.
That shiver in religious caves beneath the burning fires
10   Of lust, that belch incessant from the summits of the earth

Oothoon weeps not: she cannot weep! her tears are locked up;
But she can howl incessant writhing her soft snowy limbs.
And calling Theotormons Eagles to prey upon her flesh.°

signet Bromion is a slave-owner and the signet
is his seal or mark of ownership.
Then storms . . . dwell This is a fantasy of
what Theotormon would like to see.
Oothoon weeps . . . flesh The subtlest passage
in the poem (ll. 11–19); she *begins* by trying
to accept the morality of Bromion and Theotormon, but the psychic actuality of her reaction to sexual experience belies her conventional
acceptance; though she tries to weep, she can't,
and the writhing of her limbs shows that Theotormon ought to save the situation by fulfilling
her sexual desires, and ignoring the rape; his
failure brings about the sado-masochistic substitute gratification of her submission to a Pro-
metheus-like punishment; when she next speaks
in the poem, she will have surmounted all this.

I call with holy voice! kings of the sounding air,
Rend away this defiled bosom that I may reflect.
The image of Theotormon on my pure transparent breast.

The Eagles at her call descend & rend their bleeding prey;
Theotormon severely smiles. her soul reflects the smile;
As the clear spring mudded with feet of beasts grows pure & smiles.

20   The Daughters of Albion hear her woes. & eccho back her sighs.
Why does my Theotormon sit weeping upon the threshold;
And Oothoon hovers by his side, perswading him in vain:
I cry arise O Theotormon for the village dog
Barks at the breaking day. the nightingale has done lamenting.
The lark does rustle in the ripe corn, and the Eagle returns
From nightly prey, and lifts his golden beak to the pure east;
Shaking the dust from his immortal pinions to awake
The sun that sleeps too long. Arise my Theotormon I am pure.
Because the night is gone that clos'd me in its deadly black.
30   They told me that the night & day were all that I could see;
They told me that I had five senses to inclose me up.
And they inclos'd my infinite brain into a narrow circle.
And sunk my heart into the Abyss, a red round globe hot burning
Till all from life I was obliterated and erased.
Instead of morn arises a bright shadow, like an eye
In the eastern cloud: instead of night a sickly charnel house;
That Theotormon hears me not! to him the night and morn
Are both alike: a night of sighs, a morning of fresh tears;

PLATE 3
And none but Bromion can hear my lamentations.

With what sense is it that the chicken shuns the ravenous hawk?
With what sense does the tame pigeon measure out the expanse?
With what sense does the bee form cells? have not the mouse & frog
Eyes and ears and sense of touch? yet are their habitations.
And their pursuits, as different as their forms and as their joys:
Ask the wild ass why he refuses burdens: and the meek camel
Why he loves man: is it because of eye ear mouth or skin
Or breathing nostrils? No. for these the wolf and tyger have.
10   Ask the blind worm the secrets of the grave, and why her spires
Love to curl round the bones of death; and ask the rav'nous snake
Where she gets poison: & the wing'd eagle why he loves the sun
And then tell me the thoughts of man, that have been hid of old.

Silent I hover all the night, and all day could be silent.
If Theotormon once would turn his loved eyes upon me;
How can I be defild when I reflect thy image pure?
Sweetest the fruit that the worm feeds on. & the soul prey'd on by woe
The new wash'd lamb ting'd with the village smoke & the bright swan

By the red earth of our immortal river: I bathe my wings.
20 And I am white and pure to hover round Theotormons breast.

Then Theotormon broke his silence. and he answered.

Tell me what is the night or day to one o'erflowd with woe?
Tell me what is a thought? & of what substance is it made?
Tell me what is a joy? & in what gardens do joys grow?
And in what rivers swim the sorrows? and upon what mountains

PLATE 4
Wave shadows of discontent? and in what houses dwell the wretched
Drunken with woe forgotten. and shut up from cold despair.

Tell me where dwell the thoughts forgotten till thou call them forth
Tell me where dwell the joys of old! & where the ancient loves?
And when will they renew again & the night of oblivion past?
That I might traverse times & spaces far remote and bring
Comforts into a present sorrow and a night of pain
Where goest thou O thought? to what remote land is thy flight?
If thou returnest to the present moment of affliction
10 Wilt thou bring comforts on thy wings. and dews and honey and balm;
Or poison from the desart wilds, from the eyes of the envier.°

Then Bromion said: and shook the cavern with his lamentation

Thou knowest that the ancient trees seen by thine eyes have fruit;
But knowest thou that trees and fruits flourish upon the earth
To gratify senses unknown? trees beasts and birds unknown:
Unknown, not unpercievd, spread in the infinite microscope,
In places yet unvisited by the voyager. and in worlds
Over another kind of seas, and in atmospheres unknown:
Ah! are there other wars, beside the wars of sword and fire!
20 And are there other sorrows, beside the sorrows of poverty!
And are there other joys, beside the joys of riches and ease?
And is there not one law for both the lion and the ox?
And is there not eternal fire, and eternal chains?
To bind the phantoms of existence from eternal life?°

Then Oothoon waited silent all the day. and all the night,

PLATE 5
But when the morn arose, her lamentation renewd,
The Daughters of Albion hear her woes, & eccho back her sighs.

Tell me . . . envier Theotormon lives only in a "present moment of affliction," bound in by the circumference of his sexual envy; Blake's insight is that jealousy stems from an acceptance of a materialist concept of limited time, from the fear that there can never be enough time, which is a fear of death; sexual jealousy is thus death-in-life.

Thou knowest . . . life Bromion, an insane and debased rationalist, is far more complex in his fears; he dreads the potential chaos of experience, and so insists upon the necessity for uniform laws (which, ironically, he is incapable of obeying himself); but notice how intelligent Bromion is in his sickness, for he does not deny the reality of Oothoon's vision (as Theotormon does) but admits that he fears the vision's implications.

O Urizen!° Creator of men! mistaken Demon of heaven:
Thy joys are tears! thy labour vain, to form men to thine image.
How can one joy absorb another? are not different joys
Holy, eternal, infinite! and each joy is a Love.

Does not the great mouth laugh at a gift? & the narrow eyelids mock
At the labour that is above payment, and wilt thou take the ape
For thy councellor? or the dog, for a schoolmaster to thy children?
10 Does he who contemns° poverty, and he who turns with abhorrence
From usury: feel the same passion or are they moved alike?°
How can the giver of gifts experience the delights of the merchant?
How the industrious citizen the pains of the husbandman.
How different far the fat fed hireling with hollow drum;
Who buys whole corn fields into wastes, and sings upon the heath:
How different their eye and ear! how different the world to them!
With what sense does the parson claim the labour of the farmer?
What are his nets & gins° & traps. & how does he surround him
With cold floods of abstraction, and with forests of solitude,
20 To build him castles and high spires. where kings & priests may dwell.
Till she who burns with youth. and knows no fixed lot; is bound
In spells of law to one she loaths: and must she drag the chain
Of life, in weary lust! must chilling murderous thoughts. obscure
The clear heaven of her eternal spring? to bear the wintry rage
Of a harsh terror driv'n to madness, bound to hold a rod
Over her shrinking shoulders all the day; & all the night
To turn the wheel of false desire: and longings that wake her womb
To the abhorred birth of cherubs in the human form
That live a pestilence & die a meteor & are no more.
30 Till the child dwell with one he hates. and do the deed he loaths
And the impure scourge forces his seed into its unripe birth
E'er yet his eyelids can behold the arrows of the day.

Does the whale worship at thy footsteps as the hungry dog?
Or does he scent the mountain prey, because his nostrils wide
Draw in the ocean? does his eye discern the flying cloud
As the ravens eye? or does he measure the expanse like the vulture?
Does the still spider view the cliffs where eagles hide their young?
Or does the fly rejoice. because the harvest is brought in?
Does not the eagle scorn the earth & despise the treasures beneath?
40 But the mole knoweth what is there, & the worm shall tell it thee.
Does not the worm erect a pillar in the mouldering church yard?

PLATE 6
And a palace of eternity in the jaws of the hungry grave
Over his porch these words are written. Take thy bliss O Man!
And sweet shall be thy taste & sweet thy infant joys renew!

Urizen The first appearance of Urizen by name
in Blake's work; his name comes from the Greek
for "to draw with a compass, to circumscribe,"
and echoes the sound and meaning of "horizon,"
based on the same Greek word.

contemns despises
are they moved alike? a profound question
that Blake wants his reader to answer
gins snares

Infancy, fearless, lustful, happy! nestling for delight
In laps of pleasure; Innocence! honest, open, seeking
The vigorous joys of morning light; open to virgin bliss,
Who taught thee modesty, subtil modesty! child of night & sleep
When thou awakest. wilt thou dissemble all thy secret joys
Or wert thou not, awake when all this mystery was disclos'd!
10   Then com'st thou forth a modest virgin knowing to dissemble
With nets found under thy night pillow, to catch virgin joy,
And brand it with the name of whore; & sell it in the night,
In silence. ev'n without a whisper, and in seeming sleep:
Religious dreams and holy vespers, light thy smoky fires:
Once were thy fires lighted by the eyes of honest morn
And does my Theotormon seek this hypocrite modesty!
This knowing, artful, secret, fearful, cautious, trembling hypocrite.
Then is Oothoon a whore indeed! and all the virgin joys
Of life are harlots: and Theotormon is a sick mans dream
20   And Oothoon is the crafty slave of selfish holiness.
But Oothoon is not so, a virgin fill'd with virgin fancies
Open to joy and to delight where ever beauty appears
If in the morning sun I find it: there my eyes are fix'd

PLATE 7
In happy copulation; if in evening mild. wearied with work;
Sit on a bank and draw the pleasures of this free born joy.

    The moment of desire! the moment of desire! The virgin
That pines for man; shall awaken her womb to enormous joys
In the secret shadows of her chamber; the youth shut up from
The lustful joy. shall forget to generate. & create an amorous image
In the shadows of his curtains and in the folds of his silent pillow.
Are not these the places of religion? the rewards of continence?
The self enjoyings of self denial? Why dost thou seek religion?
10   Is it because acts are not lovely, that thou seekest solitude,
Where the horrible darkness is impressed with reflections of desire.

Father of Jealousy. be thou accursed from the earth!
Why hast thou taught my Theotormon this accursed thing?
Till beauty fades from off my shoulders darken'd and cast out,
A solitary shadow wailing on the margin of non-entity.

I cry, Love! Love! Love! happy happy Love! free as the mountain wind!
Can that be Love, that drinks another as a sponge drinks water?
That clouds with jealousy his nights, with weepings all the day:
To spin a web of age around him. grey and hoary dark!
20   Till his eyes sicken at the fruit that hangs before his sight.
Such is self-love that envies all! a creeping skeleton
With lamplike eyes watching around the frozen marriage bed.

But silken nets and traps of adamant will Oothoon spread,
And catch for thee girls of mild silver, or of furious gold;

I'll lie beside thee on a bank & view their wanton play
In lovely copulation bliss on bliss with Theotormon:
Red as the rosy morning, lustful as the first born beam,
Oothoon shall view his dear delight, nor e'er with jealous cloud
Come in the heaven of generous love; nor selfish blightings bring.

30 Does the sun walk in glorious raiment. on the secret floor

PLATE 8
Where the cold miser spreads his gold? or does the bright cloud drop
On his stone threshold? does his eye behold the beam that brings
Expansion to the eye of pity? or will he bind himself
Beside the ox to thy hard furrow? does not that mild beam blot
The bat, the owl, the glowing tyger, and the king of night.
The sea fowl takes the wintry blast. for a cov'ring to her limbs:
And the wild snake, the pestilence to adorn him with gems & gold.
And trees. & birds. & beasts. & men. behold their eternal joy.
Arise you little glancing wings, and sing your infant joy!
10 Arise and drink your bliss, for every thing that lives is holy!

Thus every morning wails Oothoon. but Theotormon sits
Upon the margind ocean conversing with shadows dire.

The Daughters of Albion hear her woes, & eccho back her sighs.
       THE END
1793   1793

America a Prophecy

This is Blake's first poem fully set in his own mythic universe. Throughout Blake's
life and work, the American Revolution counted for much more than the French, not
only because it came first and so seemed the "voice of the morning," but because
Blake wanted to see it as a more genuinely imaginative change in history, and not
just as the organic, cyclic revolution of repressed energies that took place in Europe.
It does not matter that Blake knew too little about American conditions; for him
America was the Golden World of Atlantean symbolism, and the prophetic force of
his poem's hopefulness still endures.

America *a Prophecy*

Lambeth
Printed by William Blake in the year 1793

PLATE 1

Preludium°
The shadowy daughter of Urthona° stood before red Orc.°
When fourteen suns had faintly journey'd o'er his dark abode;
His food she brought in iron baskets, his drink in cups of iron;°
Crown'd with a helmet & dark hair the nameless female stood;
A quiver with its burning stores, a bow like that of night,
When pestilence is shot from heaven; no other arms she need:
Invulnerable tho' naked, save where clouds roll round her loins,
Their awful folds in the dark air; silent she stood as night;
For never from her iron tongue could voice or sound arise;
10 But dumb till that dread day when Orc assay'd his fierce embrace.

Dark virgin; said the hairy youth, thy father stern abhorr'd;
Rivets my tenfold chains while still on high my spirit soars;
Sometimes an eagle screaming in the sky, sometimes a lion,
Stalking upon the mountains, & sometimes a whale I lash
The raging fathomless abyss, anon a serpent folding
Around the pillars of Urthona, and round thy dark limbs,
On the Canadian wilds I fold, feeble my spirit folds.°
For chaind beneath I rend these caverns; when thou bringest food
I howl my joy! and my red eyes seek to behold thy face
20 In vain! these clouds roll to & fro, & hide thee from my sight.

PLATE 2

Silent as despairing love, and strong as jealousy,
The hairy shoulders rend the links, free are the wrists of fire;
Round the terrific loins he siez'd the panting struggling womb;
It joy'd: she put aside her clouds & smiled her first-born smile;
As when a black cloud shews its light'nings to the silent deep.

Preludium This myth-making fantasia gives the primordial prelude to the poem's visionary politics; behind political revolution lurk these tremendous images of sexual bondage and triumphant sexual release; the world shown has come only recently into life, as its emblems indicate: shadows, clouds, darkness, silence, namelessness, all of which cause imprisoned sexuality to attack the female ministering to it; as in all subsequent poetry by Blake, the male personages symbolize humankind, male and female alike; the female figures all represent different aspects of the confining natural context that limits or confines the human.
shadowy daughter of Urthona Nameless in this poem, but later to be called Vala (from "veil," and pronounced like it), the beauty of the visible world; Urthona's name may be formed from "fourth one," whose form "is like the Son of God," and who appears in the burning fiery furnace of Daniel 3:25. In Blake's story, he is

the most important of the Four Zoas, and appears in our fallen world of time as Los the Poetic Genius. In *America*, Urthona is a recently fallen, primitive smith god, like Thor or Vulcan, and his dens imprison energy under Urizen's promptings.
red Orc The fallen form of the Zoa, Luvah; Orc (from *orcus*, Latin for hell, or a hell-like monster, because he seems that to the Angels) is the force of libido, of organic energy, the youth of nature, the Promethean element of fire, and politically the permanent Left; he can make revolutions, and prefigure the apocalypse, but himself cannot bring apocalypse about.
His food . . . iron Blake's naïve notion of an Iron Age; the general atmosphere and appearances suggest the influence of Norse mythology.
Sometimes . . . folds The various animals are emblems of contemporary revolutions in the Western hemisphere.

Soon as she saw the terrible boy then burst the virgin cry.°
I know thee, I have found thee, & I will not let thee go;
Thou art the image of God who dwells in darkness of Africa;°
And thou art fall'n to give me life in regions of dark death.
On my American plains I feel the struggling afflictions
Endur'd by roots that writhe their arms into the nether deep:
I see a serpent in Canada, who courts me to his love;
In Mexico an Eagle, and a Lion in Peru;
I see a Whale in the South-sea, drinking my soul away.°
O what limb rending pains I feel. thy fire & my frost
Mingle in howling pains, in furrows by thy lightnings rent;
This is eternal death; and this the torment long foretold.°

The stern Bard ceas'd, asham'd of his own song; enrag'd he swung
His harp aloft sounding, then dash'd its shining frame against
A ruin'd pillar in glittring fragments; silent he turn'd away,
And wander'd down the vales of Kent in sick & drear lamentings.°

PLATE 3
       A Prophecy
The Guardian Prince of Albion° burns in his nightly tent,
Sullen fires across the Atlantic glow to America's shore:
Piercing the souls of warlike men, who rise in silent night,
Washington, Franklin, Paine & Warren, Gates, Hancock & Green;°
Meet on the coast glowing with blood from Albions fiery Prince.

Washington spoke; Friends of America look over the Atlantic sea;
A bended bow is lifted in heaven, & a heavy iron chain
Descends link by link from Albions cliffs across the sea to bind
Brothers & sons of America, till our faces pale and yellow;
Heads deprest, voices weak, eyes downcast, hands work-bruis'd,
Feet bleeding on the sultry sands, and the furrows of the whip
Descend to generations that in future times forget.—

The strong voice ceas'd; for a terrible blast swept over the heaving sea;
The eastern cloud rent; on his cliffs stood Albions wrathful Prince
A dragon form clashing his scales° at midnight he arose,
And flam'd red meteors round the land of Albion beneath[.]
His voice, his locks, his awful shoulders, and his glowing eyes,

virgin cry Nature, barren when not possessed by man, now breaks silence for the first time.
Thou art . . . Africa Blake identified the biblical Egypt with all of Africa, and both with primordial natural religion .
I see . . . away Though embraced by Orc, her father's false teachings prevail in her, and she dreads the emblems of revolt.
This . . . foretold "Eternal death" is Blake's irony, and means generative life, a torment from the unfallen point of view in Eternity; see the opening of "The Mental Traveller."
The stern . . . lamentings The Bard is not Blake, and is ashamed because the shadowy female is unconverted.
Prince of Albion King George III, also called Albion's Angel; a dragon form even as Pharaoh was called a dragon by Ezekiel
Washington . . . Green all leaders and agitators of the American Revolution
A dragon . . . scales Both Albion's Angel and Orc are dragon forms of death, from one another's perspective; Blake's insight is that there is an Orc-Urizen cycle, in which revolution always transforms itself into the repression it seeks to destroy.

PLATE 4
Appear to the Americans upon the cloudy night.

Solemn heave the Atlantic waves between the gloomy nations,
Swelling, belching from its deeps red clouds & raging Fires!
Albion is sick! America faints! enrag'd the Zenith grew.
As human blood shooting its veins all round the orbed heaven
Red rose the clouds from the Atlantic in vast wheels of blood
And in the red clouds rose a Wonder o'er the Atlantic sea;
Intense! naked! a Human fire fierce glowing, as the wedge
Of iron heated in the furnace; his terrible limbs were fire
10 With myriads of cloudy terrors banners dark & towers
Surrounded; heat but not light° went thro' the murky atmosphere

The King of England looking westward trembles at the vision

PLATE 5
Albions Angel stood beside the Stone of night,° and saw
The terror like a comet, or more like the planet red°
That once inclos'd the terrible wandering comets in its sphere.
Then Mars thou wast our center, & the planets three flew round
Thy crimson disk; so e'er the Sun was rent from thy red sphere;
The Spectre° glowd his horrid length staining the temple long
With beams of blood; & thus a voice came forth, and shook the temple

PLATE 6
The morning comes, the night decays, the watchmen leave their stations;
The grave is burst, the spices shed, the linen wrapped up;°
The bones of death, the cov'ring clay, the sinews shrunk & dry'd.
Reviving shake, inspiring move, breathing! awakening!
Spring like redeemed captives when their bonds & bars are burst;
Let the slave grinding at the mill, run out into the field:
Let him look up into the heavens & laugh in the bright air;
Let the inchained soul shut up in darkness and in sighing,
Whose face has never seen a smile in thirty weary years;
10 Rise and look out, his chains are loose, his dungeon doors are open.
And let his wife and children return from the opressors scourge;
They look behind at every step & believe it is a dream.
Singing. The Sun has left his blackness, & has found a fresher morning
And the fair Moon rejoices in the clear & cloudless night;°
For Empire is no more, and now the Lion & Wolf shall cease.

heat but not light See *Paradise Lost* I.62–63.
Stone of Night See the pillows of Jacob in Genesis 28:11; the stone tablets of the Law of Sinai hover in the background.
planet red Mars. There is no precedent for Blake's fantastic astronomy here, nor does he develop it elsewhere.
Spectre Albion's Angel; the word means a phantom; in Blake, the shadow of desire, or withered form of repression.
The morning . . . wrapped up This image of Christ's Resurrection echoes *The Marriage;* the entire speech echoes Oothoon's great chants.
The Sun . . . cloudless night Orc's final lines will be repeated in Blake's depiction of the Last Judgment, *The Four Zoas* Night IX, 138:20–21.

PLATE 7

In thunders ends the voice. Then Albions Angel wrathful burnt
Beside the Stone of Night; and like the Eternal Lions howl
In famine & war, reply'd. Art thou not Orc; who serpent-form'd
Stands at the gate of Enitharmon° to devour her children;
Blasphemous Demon, Antichrist, hater of Dignities;
Lover of wild rebellion, and transgresser of Gods Law;
Why dost thou come to Angels eyes in this terrific form?

PLATE 8

The terror answerd: I am Orc, wreath'd round the accursed tree:°
The times are ended; shadows pass the morning gins° to break;
The fiery joy, that Urizen perverted to ten commands,
What night he led the starry hosts thro' the wide wilderness:°
That stony law I stamp to dust: and scatter religion abroad
To the four winds as a torn book, & none shall gather the leaves;
But they shall rot on desart sands, & consume in bottomless deeps;
To make the desarts blossom, & the deeps shrink to their fountains,
And to renew the fiery joy, and burst the stony roof.
10   That pale religious letchery, seeking Virginity,
May find it in a harlot, and in coarse-clad honesty
The undefil'd tho' ravish'd in her cradle night and morn:
For every thing that lives is holy, life delights in life;
Because the soul of sweet delight can never be defil'd.
Fires inwrap the earthly globe, yet man is not consumd;°
Amidst the lustful fires he walks: his feet become like brass,
His knees and thighs like silver, & his breast and head like gold.°

PLATE 9

Sound! sound! my loud war-trumpets & alarm my Thirteen Angels!°
Loud howls the eternal Wolf! the eternal Lion lashes his tail!
America is darkned; and my punishing Demons terrified
Crouch howling before their caverns deep like skins dry'd in the wind.
They cannot smite the wheat, nor quench the fatness of the earth.
They cannot smite with sorrows, nor subdue the plow and spade.
They cannot wall the city, nor moat round the castle of princes.
They cannot bring the stubbed oak to overgrow the hills.
For terrible men stand on the shores, & in their robes I see
10   Children take shelter from the lightnings, there stands Washington
And Paine and Warren with their foreheads reard toward the east

Enitharmon Queen of Heaven, her name is derived from the Greek for "numberless," as she is also Blake's Eve, mother of numberless mankind.
accursed tree The Tree of Mystery, which Orc will climb, in order that he be crucified like Christ and Odin, so as to become Jehovah or a repressive god.
gins begins
What night . . . wilderness Orc identifies Urizen with the Jehovah of Exodus.
fire . . . consumd Redeemed man is identi-

fied with the walkers in the furnace; see Daniel 3:25.
Amidst . . . gold Renovated man is the image seen in King Nebuchadnezzar's dream, Daniel 2:31–35, but there is a subtle, crucial difference, for Orc's man is one level nearer to ultimate salvation, since the feet of iron and clay are now feet of brass, the thighs of brass are now silver, and the silver breast is now golden, like the head.
Thirteen Angels the colonies in America

But clouds obscure my aged sight. A vision from afar!
Sound! sound! my loud war-trumpets & alarm my thirteen Angels:
Ah vision from afar! Ah rebel form that rent the ancient
Heavens; Eternal Viper self-renew'd, rolling in clouds
I see thee in thick clouds and darkness on America's shore.
Writhing in pangs of abhorred birth; red flames the crest rebellious
And eyes of death; the harlot womb oft opened in vain
Heaves in enormous circles, now the times are return'd upon thee,
20   Devourer of thy parent, now thy unutterable torment renews.
Sound! sound! my loud war trumpets & alarm my thirteen Angels!
Ah terrible birth! a young one bursting! where is the weeping mouth?
And where the mothers milk? instead those ever-hissing jaws
And parched lips drop with fresh gore; now roll thou in the clouds
Thy mother lays her length outstretch'd upon the shore beneath.
Sound! sound! my loud war-trumpets & alarm my thirteen Angels!
Loud howls the eternal Wolf: the eternal Lion lashes his tail!

PLATE 10
Thus wept the Angel voice & as he wept the terrible blasts
Of trumpets, blew a loud alarm across the Atlantic deep.
No trumpets answer; no reply of clarions or of fifes,
Silent the Colonies remain and refuse the loud alarm.

On those vast shady hills between America & Albions shore;
Now barr'd out by the Atlantic sea: call'd Atlantean hills:°
Because from their bright summits you may pass to the Golden world
An ancient palace, archetype of mighty Emperies,
Rears its immortal pinnacles, built in the forest of God
10   By Ariston° the king of beauty for his stolen bride,

Here on their magic seats the thirteen Angels sat perturb'd
For clouds from the Atlantic hover o'er the solemn roof.

PLATE 11
Fiery the Angels rose, & as they rose deep thunder roll'd
Around their shores: indignant burning with the fires of Orc
And Bostons Angel cried aloud as they flew thro' the dark night.

He cried: Why trembles honesty and like a murderer,
Why seeks he refuge from the frowns of his immortal station!
Must the generous tremble & leave his joy, to the idle: to the pestilence!
That mock him? who commanded this? what God? what Angel!
To keep the gen'rous from experience till the ungenerous
Are unrestraind performers of the energies of nature;
10   Till pity is become a trade, and generosity a science,
That men get rich by, & the sandy desert is giv'n to the strong

Atlantean hills The American Revolution promises to restore Atlantis, the lost, unfallen world.
Ariston Greek name meaning "the best"; Blake's
source is Herodotus VII.61–66; that the bride

is "stolen" is Blake's characteristic hint that the
Greek archetype of Atlantis was stolen from a
Hebrew original; cf. the Preface to Blake's *Jeru-
salem*.

What God is he, writes laws of peace, & clothes him in a tempest
What pitying Angel lusts for tears, and fans himself with sighs
What crawling villain preaches abstinence & wraps himself
In fat of lambs? no more I follow, no more obedience pay.

PLATE 12
So cried he, rending off his robe° & throwing down his scepter.
In sight of Albions Guardian, and all the thirteen Angels
Rent off their robes to the hungry wind, & threw their golden scepters
Down on the land of America. indignant they descended
Headlong from out their heav'nly heights, descending swift as fires
Over the land; naked & flaming are their lineaments seen
In the deep gloom, by Washington & Paine & Warren they stood
And the flame folded roaring fierce within the pitchy night
Before the Demon red, who burnt towards America,
10   In black smoke thunders and loud winds rejoicing in its terror
Breaking in smoky wreaths from the wild deep, & gath'ring thick
In flames as of a furnace on the land from North to South

PLATE 13
What time the thirteen Governors that England sent convene
In Bernards house;° the flames coverd the land, they rouze they cry
Shaking their mental chains they rush in fury to the sea
To quench their anguish; at the feet of Washington down fall'n
They grovel on the sand and writhing lie, while all
The British soldiers thro' the thirteen states sent up a howl
Of anguish: threw their swords & muskets to the earth & ran
From their encampments and dark castles seeking where to hide
From the grim flames; and from the visions of Orc: in sight
10   Of Albions Angel; who enrag'd his secret clouds open'd
From north to south, and burnt outstretchd on wings of wrath cov'ring
The eastern sky, spreading his awful wings across the heavens;
Beneath him roll'd his num'rous hosts, all Albions Angels camp'd
Darkend the Atlantic mountains & their trumpets shook the valleys
Arm'd with diseases of the earth to cast upon the Abyss,
Their numbers forty millions, must'ring in the eastern sky.

PLATE 14
In the flames stood & view'd the armies drawn out in the sky
Washington Franklin Paine & Warren Allen Gates & Lee:
And heard the voice of Albions Angel give the thunderous command:
His plagues obedient to his voice flew forth out of their clouds
Falling upon America, as a storm to cut them off
As a blight cuts the tender corn when it begins to appear.

rending off his robe Taking off the garment of
the Law; the great instance of this in Blake is
in Milton's declaration of descent in the poem
Milton (the declaration is included in this anthology).

Bernards house The Angels become Devils and
follow Boston in rebellion; the colonial governor
Bernard was recalled from Massachusetts in
1769, but he represents British rule in general.

58   WILLIAM BLAKE

Dark is the heaven above, & cold & hard the earth beneath;
And as a plague wind fill'd with insects cuts off man & beast;
And as a sea o'erwhelms a land in the day of an earthquake:

10   Fury! rage! madness! in a wind swept through America
And the red flames of Orc that folded roaring fierce around
The angry shores, and the fierce rushing of th'inhabitants together:
The citizens of New-York close their books & lock their chests;
The mariners of Boston drop their anchors and unlade;
The scribe of Pensylvania casts his pen upon the earth;
The builder of Virginia throws his hammer down in fear.

Then had America been lost, o'erwhelm'd by the Atlantic,
And Earth had lost another portion of the infinite,
But all rush together in the night in wrath and raging fire
20   The red fires rag'd! the plagues recoil'd! then rolld they back with fury°

PLATE 15
On Albions Angels; then the Pestilence began in streaks of red
Across the limbs of Albions Guardian, the spotted plague smote Bristols
And the Leprosy Londons Spirits, sickening all their bands:
The millions sent up a howl of anguish and threw off their hammerd mail,°
And cast their swords & spears to earth, & stood a naked multitude.
Albions Guardian writhed in torment on the eastern sky
Pale quivring toward the brain his glimmering eyes, teeth chattering
Howling & shuddering his legs quivering; convuls'd each muscle & sinew
Sick'ning lay Londons Guardian, and the ancient miter'd York°
10   Their heads on snowy hills, their ensigns sick'ning in the sky
The plagues creep on the burning winds driven by flames of Orc,
And by the fierce Americans rushing together in the night
Driven o'er the Guardians of Ireland and Scotland and Wales
They spotted with plagues forsook the frontiers & their banners seard
With fires of hell, deform their ancient heavens with shame & woe.
Hid in his caves the Bard of Albion° felt the enormous plagues.
And a cowl of flesh grew o'er his head & scales on his back & ribs;°
And rough with black scales all his Angels fright their ancient heavens
The doors of marriage are open,° and the Priests in rustling scales
20   Rush into reptile coverts, hiding from the fires of Orc,
That play around the golden roofs in wreaths of fierce desire,
Leaving the females naked and glowing with the lusts of youth

For the female spirits of the dead pining in bonds of religion;
Run from their fetters reddening, & in long drawn arches sitting:

The red . . . fury David Erdman relates this reversal of the plagues onto England's shores to the Great Pestilence of 1348, which followed English aggression upon France; Blake's symbolic point is clear enough in contemporary America.
The millions . . . mail the troops desert

miter'd York the Archbishop, who like the King sickens almost to madness
Bard of Albion the (as usual) undistinguished Poet Laureate, William Whitehead (1715–85)
And a cowl . . . ribs See Paradise Lost X.511 ff., where Satan and his host become reptilian.
The doors . . . open the societal restrictions upon sexuality fall away

They feel the nerves of youth renew, and desires of ancient times,
Over their pale limbs as a vine when the tender grape appears

PLATE 16
Over the hills, the vales, the cities, rage the red flames fierce;
The Heavens melted from north to south; and Urizen who sat
Above all heavens in thunders wrap'd, emerg'd his leprous head
From out his holy shrine, his tears in deluge piteous
Falling into the deep sublime! flag'd with grey-brow'd snows
And thunderous visages, his jealous wings wav'd over the deep;
Weeping in dismal howling woe he dark descended howling
Around the smitten bands, clothed in tears & trembling shudd'ring cold.
His stored snows he poured forth, and his icy magazines
10 He open'd on the deep, and on the Atlantic sea white shiv'ring.
Leprous his limbs, all over white, and hoary was his visage.°
Weeping in dismal howlings before the stern Americans
Hiding the Demon red with clouds & cold mists from the earth;
Till Angels & weak men twelve years° should govern o'er the strong:
And then their end should come, when France reciev'd the Demons light.°

Stiff shudderings shook the heav'nly thrones! France Spain & Italy,
In terror view'd the bands of Albion, and the ancient Guardians
Fainting upon the elements, smitten with their own plagues
20 They slow advance to shut the five gates of their law-built heaven°
Filled with blasting fancies and with mildews of despair
With fierce disease and lust, unable to stem the fires of Orc;
But the five gates were consum'd, & their bolts and hinges melted
And the fierce flames burnt round the heavens & round the abodes of men°
    FINIS
1793   1794

From Blake's Notebook

Never Pain To Tell Thy Love

Never pain to tell thy love
Love that never told can be
For the gentle wind does move
Silently invisibly

I told my love I told my love
I told her all my heart

Leprous . . . visage Urizen is exposed as being leprous and impotent.
twelve years the time span between the American and French Revolutions
Demons light appearance of Orc's revolutionary fire in France
They slow . . . heaven The tyranny of society is founded upon natural law, founded in turn upon the barred gates of the five fallen senses.
And . . . men Flames of desire burn *round* but not yet *through* the five fallen senses; natural tyranny is threatened, but not yet overthrown.

Trembling cold in ghastly fears
Ah she doth depart

Soon as she was gone from me
10 A traveller came by
Silently invisibly
O was no deny
1793?   1863

To Nobodaddy°

Why art thou silent & invisible
Father of Jealousy
Why dost thou hide thyself in clouds
From every searching Eye

Why darkness & obscurity
In all thy words & laws
That none dare eat the fruit but from
The wily serpents jaws
Or is it because Secrecy
10 gains females loud applause
1800–1803   1863

What Is It Men in Women Do Require?

What is it men in women do require?
The lineaments° of Gratified Desire
What is it women do in men require?
The lineaments of Gratified Desire
1800–1803   1863

My Spectre Around Me Night & Day

The Spectre is Blake's term for the isolate Selfhood, the spirit of solipsism that Shelley
(on Peacock's advice) called the *alastor* or self-avenging *daemon*. Each human is
isolated from his bride, which means that everyone is in his Spectre's power. The
bride Blake calls an Emanation, the total form of what any human being creates and
loves. In this frightening lyric from the Notebook, the Spectre "guards" only as a
menace keeping all others from the Self. The Emanation at first has failed to
emanate, and keeps far within the psyche, weeping for a sin which is the Self's
failure to create and love. Throughout the lyric, the speaker is trapped in what Blake
calls the state of Ulro (ultimate error), or single vision, the world of egomania. To

Nobodaddy God the Father is actually no-   **lineaments** features
body's daddy.

break the cycle of frustrated flight and pursuit, in which the elusive Emanation, after venturing out, cannot be embraced, the speaker at last vows to "turn from Female Love." This does not mean that the speaker intends to be ascetic or homosexual, but that he will give up love as what the Female Will understands it to be. The reader needs to remember that Female Will means natural will, and that the poem's speaker can be either a man or a woman, who heroically breaks out of isolation into the prophetic mode of Oothoon, who urged a love that does not seek to drink the beloved up, or absorb the other.

My Spectre Around Me Night & Day

My Spectre around me night & day
Like a Wild beast guards my way
My Emanation far within
Weeps incessantly for my Sin

A Fathomless & boundless deep
There we wander there we weep
On the hungry craving wind
My Spectre follows thee behind

10   He scents thy footsteps in the snow
Wheresoever thou dost go
Thro the wintry hail & rain
When wilt thou return again

Dost thou not in Pride & Scorn
Fill with tempests all my morn
And with jealousies & fears
Fill my pleasant nights with tears

Seven of my sweet loves thy knife
Has bereaved of their life
Their marble tombs I built with tears
20   And with cold & shuddering fears

Seven more loves weep night & day
Round the tombs where my loves lay
And seven more loves attend each night
Around my couch with torches bright

And seven more Loves in my bed
Crown with wine my mournful head
Pitying & forgiving all
Thy transgressions great & small

When wilt thou return & view
30   My loves & them to life renew

When wilt thou return & live
When wilt thou pity as I forgive

Never Never I return
Still for Victory I burn
Living thee alone Ill have
And when dead Ill be thy Grave

Thro the Heaven & Earth & Hell
Thou shalt never never quell
I will fly & thou pursue
40   Night & Morn the flight renew

Till I turn from Female Love
And root up the Infernal Grove
I shall never worthy be
To Step into Eternity

And to end thy cruel mocks
Annihilate thee on the rocks
And another form create
To be subservient to my Fate

Let us agree to give up Love
50   And root up the infernal grove
Then shall we return & see
The worlds of happy Eternity

& Throughout all Eternity
I forgive you you forgive me
As our Dear Redeemer said
This the Wine & this the Bread
1800–1803   1863

Mock on Mock on Voltaire Rousseau

Mock on Mock on Voltaire Rousseau°
Mock on Mock on tis all in vain
You throw the sand against the wind
And the wind blows it back again

And every sand becomes a Gem
Reflected in the beams divine
Blown back they blind the mocking Eye
But still in Israels paths they shine

The Atoms of Democritus°
10   And Newtons Particles of light°

Voltaire Rousseau deists and so (in Blake's view) enemies of imaginative religion
Democritus (460–362 B.C.), Greek philosopher who taught a version of atomic theory
Particles of light corpuscular theory of light, which Blake doubted (with good reason)

Are sands upon the Red sea shore
Where Israels tents do shine so bright
1800–1803   1863

Morning

To find the Western path
Right thro the Gates of Wrath°
I urge my way
Sweet Mercy leads me on
With soft repentant moan
I see the break of day

The war of swords & spears
Melted by dewy tears
Exhales on high
10 The Sun is freed from fears
And with soft grateful tears
Ascends the sky
1803?   1863

When Klopstock England Defied°

When Klopstock England defied
Uprose terrible Blake in his pride
For old Nobodaddy aloft
Farted & Belchd & coughd
Then swore a great oath that made heavn quake
And called aloud to English Blake
Blake was giving his body ease
At Lambeth beneath the poplar trees
From his seat then started he
10 And turnd himself round three times three
The Moon at that sight blushd scarlet red
The stars threw down their cups & fled
And all the devils that were in hell
Answered with a ninefold yell
Klopstock felt the intripled turn
And all his bowels began to churn
And his bowels turned round three times three

To find . . . Wrath This opening couplet is
the epigraph to the American poet Hart Crane's
"The Tunnel," the descent into a subway hell
in his brief epic *The Bridge* (1930).
When Klopstock England Defied Friedrich Gott-
lieb Klopstock (1724–1803), German poet, whose
religious epic *Messias* was influenced by *Paradise
Lost*. Someone told Blake that Klopstock was
Germany's answer to Milton. This poetic im-
promptu is Blake's answer to Klopstock, and is
rather more active than anything in *Messias*, a
work renowned for the continuous piety of its
sentiments, and its author's studious genius for
avoiding mere incidents, or anything else that
might have made his poem readable.

And lockd in his soul with a ninefold key
That from his body it neer could be parted
20 Till to the last trumpet it was farted
Then again old Nobodaddy swore
He neer had seen such a thing before
Since Noah was shut in the ark
Since Eve first chose her hell fire spark
Since twas the fashion to go naked
Since the old anything was created
And so feeling he begd him to turn again
And ease poor Klopstocks nine fold pain
From pity then he redend round
30 And the Spell removed unwound
If Blake could do this when he rose up from shite
What might he not do if he sat down to write
1797–99   1965 (in this form)

[Epigrams]

Some people admire the work of a Fool
For its sure to keep your judgment cool
It does not reproach you with want of wit
It is not like a lawyer serving a writ

Her whole Life is an Epigram smack smooth & neatly pend
Plated quite neat to catch applause with a sliding noose at the end

When a Man has Married a Wife
he finds out whether
Her knees & elbows are only
glued together

Grown old in Love from Seven till Seven times Seven
I oft have wished for Hell for Ease from Heaven

The Hebrew Nation did not write it
Avarice & Chastity did shite it

To God

If you have formed a Circle to go into
Go into it yourself & see how you would do

Since all the Riches of this World
May be gifts from the Devil & Earthly Kings
I should suspect that I worshiped the Devil
If I thanked my God for Worldly things

The Mental Traveller

Like "The Crystal Cabinet," this poem exists in a fair copy manuscript that Blake may have intended for engraving. Both poems are highly finished, economical, complex ballads, and seem to be deliberate experiments at telling versions of Blake's myths without using a technical vocabulary or private personages. "The Mental Traveller" foreshadows the entire Orc-Urizen cycle, and is perhaps the bleakest of Blake's comprehensive accounts of fallen existence. Yeats acknowledged its influence upon his mythological book *A Vision*. Few poems in the language do so much so grandly and so grimly in just over a hundred lines.

The poem may be described, briefly, as a report upon a grotesque planet given by a being alien to it, who cannot quite understand the horrors he sees. He describes two cycles moving in opposite directions, and out of phase with one another. The natural cycle (symbolized by the female) is moving backward, the human (symbolized by the male) forward. There are only two personages in the poem, but they move through several phases, and phantoms of earlier phases sometimes linger. The human cycle moves between an infant Orc and an aged, beggared Urizen, and then back again. The natural sequence is Tirzah (Nature-as-Necessity), Vala (Nature-as-Temptress), and Rahab (Nature-as-Destroyer), and then back again.

The Mental Traveller°

I traveld thro' a Land of Men
A Land of Men & Women too°
And heard & saw such dreadful things
As cold Earth wanderers never knew°

For there the Babe is born in joy
That was begotten in dire woe
Just as we Reap in joy the fruit
Which we in bitter tears did sow°

And if the Babe is born a Boy
10   He's given to a Woman Old
Who nails him down upon a rock
Catches his shrieks in cups of gold°

She binds iron thorns around his head
She pierces both his hands & feet°
She cuts his heart out at his side
To make it feel both cold & heat°

The Mental Traveller The speaker is one of Blake's Unfallen Eternals, who descends from a world where "Mental Things alone are Real."
Women too Before the Fall the Zoas were not separate from their Emanations, and each human was both man and woman.
And heard . . . never knew Human beings hear and see the horrors of existence, but cannot convert sounds and sights into knowledge; the Mental Traveller can.

for there . . . sow The Traveller sees fallen sexual intercourse as "dire woe" and the pain of fallen birth as "joy"; he compares this to the strife of Eternity, which ensues in reconciliations; Blake's Eternity is a realm of "mental fight," and not a static heaven.
Who nails . . . gold the fate of Loki in the Norse Edda
She binds . . . feet the crucified Christ
She cuts . . . heat the torment of Prometheus

65

Her fingers number every Nerve
Just as a Miser counts his gold
She lives upon his shrieks & cries
20   And she grows young as he grows old

Till he becomes a bleeding youth
And she becomes a Virgin bright
Then he rends up his Manacles
And binds her down for his delight

He plants himself in all her Nerves
Just as a Husbandman his mould
And she becomes his dwelling place
And Garden fruitful seventy fold

An aged Shadow soon he fades
30   Wandring round an Earthly Cot
Full filled all with gems & gold
Which he by industry had got

And these are the gems of the Human Soul
The rubies & pearls of a lovesick eye
The countless gold of the akeing heart
The martyrs groan & the lovers sigh

They are his meat they are his drink
He feeds the Beggar & the Poor
And the wayfaring Traveller
40   For ever open is his door

His grief is their eternal joy
They make the roofs & walls to ring
Till from the fire on the hearth
A little Female Babe° does spring

And she is all of solid fire
And gems & gold that none his hand
Dares stretch to touch her Baby form
Or wrap her in his swaddling-band

But She comes to the Man she loves
50   If young or old or rich or poor
They soon drive out the aged Host°
A Beggar at anothers door

He wanders weeping far away
Untill some other take him in
Oft blind & age-bent sore distrest
Untill he can a Maiden win

Female Babe an infant Rahab or baby whore,
Blake would have commented

aged Host the earlier self, now abandoned by
nature

And to allay his freezing Age
The Poor Man takes her in his arms
The Cottage fades before his sight
60   The Garden & its lovely Charms

The Guests are scatterd thro' the land
For the Eye altering alters all
The Senses roll themselves in fear
And the flat Earth becomes a Ball°

The Stars Sun Moon all shrink away
A desert vast without a bound
And nothing left to eat or drink
And a dark desert all around

The honey of her Infant lips
70   The bread & wine of her sweet smile
The wild game of her roving Eye
Does him to Infancy beguile

For as he eats & drinks he grows
Younger & younger every day
And on the desert wild they both
Wander in terror & dismay

Like the wild Stag she flees away
Her fear plants many a thicket wild
While he pursues her night & day
80   By various arts of Love beguild

By various arts of Love & Hate
Till the wide desert planted oer
With Labyrinths of wayward Love
Where roams the Lion Wolf & Boar

Till he becomes a wayward Babe
And she a weeping Woman Old
Then many a Lover wanders here
The Sun & Stars are nearer rolld°

The trees bring forth sweet Extacy°
90   To all who in the desert roam°
Till many a City there is Built°
And many a pleasant Shepherds home°

But when they find the frowning Babe
Terror strikes thro the region wide

The Senses . . . Ball Blake insisted that to an imaginative eye, the Earth was flat; to see it as a Ball rolling through space was to yield to a dehumanization of our context.
nearer rolld meaning that this is the one opportunity of breaking the cycle, through a humanizing love, but it is not broken

Extacy Generation or Experience
To all . . . roam the Ulro
City there is Built the state of Eden, a city not a garden
Shepherds home the state of Beulah, a pastoral garden

They cry the Babe the Babe is Born
And flee away on Every side

For who dare touch the frowning form
His arm is witherd to its root
Lions Boars Wolves all howling flee
100 And every Tree does shed its fruit

And none can touch° that frowning form
Except it be a Woman Old
She nails him down upon the Rock
And all is done as I have told
1803?   1863

The Crystal Cabinet

The Maiden caught me in the Wild
Where I was dancing merrily
She put me into her Cabinet°
And Lockd me up with a golden Key

This Cabinet is formd of Gold
And Pearl & Crystal shining bright
And within it opens into a World
And a little lovely Moony Night°

Another England there I saw
10   Another London with its Tower
Another Thames & other Hills
And another pleasant Surrey Bower

Another Maiden like herself
Translucent lovely shining clear
Threefold each in the other closd°
O what a pleasant trembling fear

O what a smile a threefold Smile
Filld me that like a flame I burnd
I bent to Kiss the lovely Maid
20   And found a Threefold Kiss returnd°

I strove to sieze the inmost Form°
With ardor fierce & hands of flame
But burst the Crystal Cabinet
And like a Weeping Babe became

An none can touch The cycle grows harsher, as history grinds on; the Babe of the third stanza could be given to the terrible foster-mother but now he is more fearsome, and only she can touch him.
Cabinet quite possibly the vagina
Moony Night the state of Beulah

Threefold . . . closd three mirror-outlines enclosed one within the other
Threefold Kiss returnd cf. *Jerusalem* 70:20–27, where the Maiden is Rahab the Whore
inmost Form which cannot be grasped in the phenomenal shimmer-of-appearances that is Beulah

A weeping Babe upon the wild
And Weeping Woman pale reclind
And in the outward air again
I filld with woes the passing Wind°
1803?   1863

Auguries of Innocence°

To see a World in a Grain of Sand
And a Heaven in a Wild Flower
Hold Infinity in the palm of your hand
And Eternity in an hour

A Robin Red breast in a Cage
Puts all Heaven in a Rage
A dove house filld with doves & Pigeons
Shudders Hell thro all its regions
A dog starvd at his Masters Gate
10   Predicts the ruin of the State
A Horse misusd upon the Road
Calls to Heaven for Human blood
Each outcry of the hunted Hare
A fibre from the Brain does tear
A Skylark wounded in the wing
A Cherubim does cease to sing
The Game Cock clipd & armd for fight°
Does the Rising Sun affright
Every Wolfs & Lions howl
20   Raises from Hell a Human Soul
The wild deer wandring here & there
Keeps the Human Soul from Care
The Lamb misusd breeds Public strife
And yet forgives the Butchers Knife
The Bat that flits at close of Eve
Has left the Brain that wont Believe
The Owl that calls upon the Night
Speaks the Unbelievers fright
He who shall hurt the little Wren
30   Shall never be belovd by Men
He who the Ox to wrath has movd
Shall never be by Woman lovd
The wanton Boy that kills the Fly
Shall feel the Spiders enmity

A weeping . . . Wind compared to the opening stanza, the speaker has suffered only loss, through seeking in sexual experience a finality it cannot afford anyone
Auguries of Innocence The title, which probably refers only to the opening quatrain, means omens or divinations, that is, tokens of the state of Innocence; this is not so much a single poem as a collection of aphorisms and epigrams.
armd for fight in cockfighting sport

He who torments the Chafers° sprite
Weaves a Bower in endless Night
The Catterpiller on the Leaf
Repeats to thee thy Mothers grief
Kill not the Moth nor Butterfly
40 For the Last Judgment draweth nigh
He who shall train the Horse to War
Shall never pass the Polar Bar
The Beggers Dog & Widows Cat
Feed them & thou wilt grow fat
The Gnat that sings his Summers song
Poison gets from Slanders tongue
The poison of the Snake & Newt
Is the sweat of Envys Foot
The Poison of the Honey Bee
50 Is the Artists Jealousy
The Princes Robes & Beggars Rags
Are Toadstools on the Misers Bags
A truth thats told with bad intent
Beats all the Lies you can invent
It is right it should be so
Man was made for Joy & Woe
And when this we rightly know
Thro the World we safely go
Joy & Woe are woven fine
60 A Clothing for the Soul divine
Under every grief & pine
Runs a joy with silken twine
The Babe is more than swadling Bands
Throughout all these Human Lands
Tools were made & Born were hands
Every Farmer Understands
Every Tear from Every Eye
Becomes a Babe in Eternity
This is caught by Females bright
70 And returnd to its own delight
The Bleat the Bark Bellow & Roar
Are Waves that Beat on Heavens Shore
The Babe that weeps the Rod beneath
Writes Revenge in realms of death
The Beggars Rags fluttering in Air
Does to Rags the Heavens tear
The Soldier armd with Sword & Gun
Palsied strikes the Summers Sun
The poor Mans Farthing is worth more
80 Than all the Gold on Africs Shore

Chafers beetle's

One Mite wrung from the Labrers hands
Shall buy & sell the Misers Lands
Or if protected from on high
Does that whole Nation sell & buy
He who mocks the Infants Faith
Shall be mock'd in Age & Death
He who shall teach the Child to Doubt
The rotting Grave shall neer get out
He who respects the Infants faith
90   Triumphs over Hell & Death
The Childs Toys & the Old Mans Reasons
Are the Fruits of the Two seasons
The Questioner who sits so sly
Shall never know how to Reply
He who replies to words of Doubt
Doth put the Light of Knowledge out
The Strongest Poison ever known
Came from Caesars Laurel Crown
Nought can deform the Human Race
100   Like to the Armours iron brace
When Gold & Gems adorn the Plow
To peaceful Arts shall Envy Bow
A Riddle or the Crickets Cry
Is to Doubt a fit Reply
The Emmets° Inch & Eagles Mile
Make Lame Philosophy to smile
He who Doubts from what he sees
Will never Believe do what you Please
If the Sun & Moon should doubt
110   Theyd immediately Go out
To be in a Passion you Good may do
But no Good if a Passion is in you
The Whore & Gambler by the State
Licencd build that Nations Fate
The Harlots cry from Street to Street
Shall weave Old Englands winding Sheet
The Winners Shout the Losers Curse
Dance before dead Englands Hearse
Every Night & every Morn
120   Some to Misery are Born
Every Morn & every Night
Some are Born to sweet delight
Some are Born to sweet delight
Some are Born to Endless Night
We are led to Believe a Lie
When we see not Thro the Eye

Emmets ant's

Which was Born in a Night to perish in a Night°
When the Soul Slept in Beams of Light
God Appears & God is Light
130   To those poor Souls who dwell in Night
But does a Human Form Display
To those who Dwell in Realms of day
1803?   1863

The Four Zoas

The subtitle of Blake's first epic describes the poem with great precision: *The Torments of Love and Jealousy in the Death and Judgment of Albion the Ancient Man.* Albion is mentioned by Spenser and Milton as the father of the British people, after whom the island is named. Blake's Albion is his version of Milton's Adam, with the enormous difference that unfallen Albion is both Man and God, a vision of all that was. In the pre-existent unity which Blake posits, Albion contained, in a harmony of creative tensions, his own female principle or Emanation, Jerusalem, who represented his freedom from strife or, as Milton would have said, his Christian Liberty. He contained also four sons (or principles, faculties, elements), named Urthona, Urizen, Luvah, and Tharmas.

Blake's source is essential knowledge here, and makes clear how central and traditional a mythic structure is being elaborated. The Bible forbids the Jews to make images of God, but allows one complex image anyway, the vision of the Divine Chariot (*Merkabah* in Hebrew) that opens the book of the prophet Ezekiel. Ezekiel sees what he calls "the wheels and their work," a crystalline fire of swift movement. In the midst of the fire are "four living creatures" that "had the likeness of a man," each with four faces and four wings. These "living creatures" themselves constitute what Blake calls "the Vehicular form of Divinity," the Chariot in which an enthroned Man rides, "and this was the appearance of the likeness of the glory of the Lord." In Revelation 4:6 (based upon Ezekiel), "four beasts full of eyes before and behind" surround God's throne. The New Testament Greek word for these beasts is adapted by Blake for his Zoas or Giant Forms, as he also called them.

Blake's Zoas, in their fallen form, together with their emanations, are in every human being, man and woman alike (Blake's symbolism does *not* suggest that each male among us is possessed by the Four Zoas, and each female by their four emanations). It is a mistake to translate the Giant Forms into allegorical equivalents, though this is by now a very traditional error in the criticism devoted to Blake. Urizen is not intellect, Luvah is not the passions, Tharmas is not the instincts, and Urthona is not the imagination. The Zoas and their emanations are *what they do* in the poetry. But since any reader must begin by translating, and since Freud's psychic cartography is the common mythology we now share, it can be useful to translate (warily) Blake's beings into their very rough Freudian equivalents. In their fallen forms, Los (Urthona) is the ego, the Spectral or Satanic Urizen the superego, the inchoate Tharmas the id, and Orc (Luvah) the libido rising out of the id. Of the fallen emanations, the lost delight in his true function of each Zoa, Enitharmon is the spatial consciousness of the time-ridden ego, Los; Ahania is the Urizenic super-ego's dread of futurity; Enion is the lost sense of the id's unity with the object-world; and Vala is the troubling, narcissistic beauty of the object-world that the libido vainly seeks to possess.

Given below are two extraordinary biblical chants that conclude Night II of the poem, and the whole of the dazzling fury of Night IX, the last Night and the Apocalypse or Last Judgment.

From The Four Zoas

[Song of Enitharmon°]
Night passd & Enitharmon eer the dawn returnd in bliss
She sang Oer Los reviving him to Life his groans were terrible.
But thus she sang I sieze the sphery harp I strike the strings

At the first Sound the Golden sun arises from the Deep
And shakes his awful hair
60 The Eccho wakes the moon to unbind her silver locks
The golden sun bears on my song
And nine bright spheres of harmony rise round the fiery King°

The joy of woman is the Death of her most best beloved
Who dies for Love of her
In torments of fierce jealousy & pangs of adoration.
The Lovers night bears on my song
And the nine Spheres rejoice beneath my powerful controll

They sing unceasing to the notes of my immortal hand
The solemn silent moon
70 Reverberates the living harmony upon my limbs
The birds & beasts rejoice & play
And every one seeks for his mate to prove his inmost joy

Furious & terrible they sport & rend the nether deeps
The deep lifts up his rugged head
And lost in infinite hum[m]ing wings vanishes with a cry
The fading cry is ever dying
The living voice is ever living in its inmost joy

Arise you little glancing wings & sing your infant joy
Arise & drink your bliss
80 For every thing that lives is holy for the source of life
Descends to be a weeping babe
For the Earthworm renews the moisture of the sandy plain

Song of Enitharmon a triumph-hymn of the Female Will and particularly admired by Yeats fiery King the fallen sun as Enitharmon's son,

Orc, born of her in fallen nature; nine spheres because in Blake's day only seven planets were known, to which he adds the sun and the moon

Now my left hand I stretch to earth beneath
And strike the terrible string
I wake sweet joy in dens of sorrow & I plant a smile
In forests of affliction
And wake the bubbling springs of life in regions of dark death

O I am weary lay thine hand upon me or I faint
I faint beneath these beams of thine
90   For thou hast touchd my five senses & they answerd thee
Now I am nothing & I sink
And on the bed of silence sleep till thou awakest me

PAGE 35
        [Song of Enion°]
I am made to sow the thistle for wheat; the nettle for a nourishing dainty
I have planted a false oath in the earth,° it has brought forth a poison tree
I have chosen the serpent for a councellor & the dog
For a schoolmaster to my children
I have blotted out from light & living the dove & nightingale
And I have caused the earth worm to beg from door to door
I have taught the thief a secret path into the house of the just
I have taught pale artifice to spread his nets upon the morning
My heavens are brass my earth is iron my moon a clod of clay
10   My sun a pestilence burning at noon & a vapour of death in night

What is the price of Experience do men buy it for a song°
Or wisdom for a dance in the street? No it is bought with the price
Of all that a man hath his house his wife his children
Wisdom is sold in the desolate market where none come to buy
And in the witherd field where the farmer plows for bread in vain°

It is an easy thing to triumph in the summers sun
And in the vintage & to sing on the waggon loaded with corn
It is an easy thing to talk of patience to the afflicted
To speak the laws of prudence to the houseless wanderer

PAGE 36
To listen to the hungry ravens cry in wintry season
When the red blood is filld with wine & with the marrow of lambs
It is an easy thing to laugh at wrathful elements
To hear the dog howl at the wintry door, the ox in the slaughter house moan
To see a god on every wind & a blessing on every blast
To hear sounds of love in the thunder storm that destroys our enemies house
To rejoice in the blight that covers his field, & the sickness that cuts off his
        children

Song of Enion The burden of this terrifying chant is that, in our fallen existence, we can only be happy by ignoring the torments of all other beings; the page numbers are Blake's.

I have . . . earth See Zechariah 8:17.
What is . . . song See Job 28:12–13.
Wisdom . . . vain Blake himself is both seller and farmer.

While our olive & vine sing & laugh round our door & our children bring fruits
   & flowers

Then the groan & the dolor are quite forgotten & the slave grinding at the mill
10 And the captive in chains & the poor in the prison, & the soldier in the field
When the shatterd bone hath laid him groaning among the happier dead

It is an easy thing to rejoice in the tents of prosperity
Thus could I sing & thus rejoice, but it is not so with me!
1796–1807?   1893

Night the Ninth
Being The Last Judgment

This extraordinary final section of *The Four Zoas* is the culmination of the first phase
of Blake's rhetorical art, which becomes considerably more chastened and subdued
in *Milton* and in *Jerusalem*. The continuous exuberance of violent invention in Night
the Ninth is regulated as a series of approaches to Apocalypse, rather than a single
outburst of finality, but the intensity and driving energy of the whole Night is
remorseless and even awesome, perhaps unmatched in the language.

    Blake's starting point in Night IX is not Revelation, though he will weave in a number
of significant allusions to the Apocalypse of St. John the Divine (and to St. John's
principal source, Ezekiel), but Paul Henri Mallet's *Northern Antiquities,* translated by
Bishop Percy from the French. Compare to the opening of Night IX the opening
of Mallet's Fable 32, "Of the Twilight of the Gods":

> Then will happen such things as may well be called prodigies. The Wolf
> FENRIS will devour the Sun. . . . Another monster will carry off the Moon
> . . . the stars shall fly away and vanish from the heavens; the earth and the
> mountains shall be seen violently agitated; the trees torn up from the earth
> by the roots; the tottering hills to tumble headlong from their foundations;
> all the chains and irons of the prisoners to be broken and dashed in pieces.
> Then is the Wolf Fenris let loose; the sea rushes impetuously over the earth,
> because the great Serpent, changed into a Spectre, gains the shore. . . . The
> great Ash Tree of Ydrasil is shaken: nor is any thing in heaven or earth exempt
> from fear and danger.

The unique tone of Night IX stems from its displacement of the Hebrew-Christian
account of the Last Things into this world of a Northern Apocalypse, where even
finality is not quite final. Everything in Blake that belonged emotionally to Orc,
despite Blake's dialectical awareness of organic energy's limitations, is allowed its
absolute expression for once in Night IX. Though Blake evidently judged Night IX to
be a spiritual failure, and rejected its violence and wish-fulfillment by refraining from
engraving *The Four Zoas,* the poem remains his most titanic and strenuous attempt
at the Sublime, and the culmination of what Martin Price has called the Theater of
Mind, the characteristic creation of the eighteenth-century poets of Sensibility.

Night the Ninth
Being The Last Judgment

And Los & Enitharmon builded Jerusalem weeping
Over the Sepulcher & over the Crucified body°
Which to their Phantom Eyes appear'd still in the Sepulcher
But Jesus stood beside them in the Spirit Separating
Their Spirit from their body. Terrified at Non Existence
For such they deemd the death of the body. Los his vegetable hands
Outstretchd his right hand branching out in fibrous Strength
Siezd the Sun. His left hand like dark roots coverd the Moon
And tore them down cracking the heavens across from immense to immense°
10 Then fell the fires of Eternity with loud & shrill
Sound of Loud Trumpet thundering along from heaven to heaven
A mighty sound articulate Awake ye dead & come
To Judgment from the four winds Awake & Come away
Folding like scrolls of the Enormous volume of Heaven & Earth°
With thunderous noise & dreadful shakings rocking to & fro
The heavens are shaken & the Earth removed from its place
The foundations of the Eternal hills discoverd
The thrones of Kings are shaken they have lost their robes & crowns
The poor smite their opressors they awake up to the harvest
20 The naked warriors rush together down to the sea shore
Trembling before the multitudes of slaves now set at liberty
They are become like wintry flocks like forests stripd of leaves
The opressed pursue like the wind there is no room for escape°
The Spectre of Enitharmon let loose on the troubled deep
Waild shrill in the confusion & the Spectre of Urthona

Recievd her in the darkning South their bodies lost they stood
Trembling & weak a faint embrace a fierce desire as when
Two shadows mingle on a wall they wail & shadowy tears
Fell down & shadowy forms of joy mixd with despair & grief

And Los . . . Crucified body At the close of Night VIII, Blake brings his story to his own historical moment, with Rahab the Whore triumphing, in the guise of the English state church sacrificing the sons of England on the altar of Urizen-as-war god. But Satan divides against Satan, Rahab begins to waver, and what Blake saw as the particular spiritual significance of Deism now emerges. In the exhaustions of natural religion, Blake sees the decadence of Babylon begin anew, and at last history is ripe for the Last Judgment. As Night IX begins, Los and Enitharmon are in despair, but they continue their creative labor of building Jerusalem, which means that the crucified body of Jesus is not still in the sepulcher, as they fear, but stands beside them, freeing them from nature. Los, aware that his body is dying (Blake's subtle indication of the contemporary low state of the arts, in his opinion) but not knowing that Jesus actively prepares the resurrection of his body, reaches out in a shudder of revulsion and begins the Apocalypse by a frontal attack upon nature. This, on one level, is the act of Blake in writing Night IX, his own desperate shudder against the darkness of the age.

Los his . . . immense As in the Norse Twilight of the Gods, Apocalypse's first stage attacks sun and moon, the centers of the universe of death, the sun that once was unfallen Urizen and the moon that was unfallen Luvah; though this attack is inadequate, being only a natural impulse ("fibrous Strength," "dark roots"), it begins a more-than-natural movement of release, since it is the natural reaction of Los the imaginative man.

folding . . . Earth See Revelation 6:14, and its source in Isaiah 25:3–4.

The opressed . . . escape See Revelation 6:9–10.

Their bodies buried in the ruins of the Universe
Mingled with the confusion. Who shall call them from the Grave°

Rahab & Tirzah wail aloud in the wild flames they give up themselves to
    Consummation

The books of Urizen unroll with dreadful noise the folding Serpent
Of Orc began to Consume in fierce raving fire his fierce flames
10 Issud on all sides gathring strength in animating volumes
Roaming abroad on all the winds raging intense reddening
Into resistless pillars of fire rolling round & round gathering
Strength from the Earths consumd & heavens & all hidden abysses
Wherever the Eagle has Explord or Lion or Tyger trod
Or where the Comets of the night or stars of asterial day
Have shot their arrows or long beamed spears in wrath & fury

And all the while the trumpet sounds from the clotted gore & from the hollow
    den
Start forth the trembling millions into flames of mental fire
Bathing their limbs in the bright visions of Eternity

20 Then like the doves from pillars of Smoke the trembling families
Of women & children throughout every nation under heaven
Cling round the men in bands of twenties & of fifties pale
As snow that falls around a leafless tree upon the green
Their opressors are falln they have Stricken them they awake to life
Yet pale the just man stands erect & looking up to heavn
Trembling & strucken by the Universal stroke the trees unroot
The rocks groan horrible & run about. The mountains &
Their rivers cry with a dismal cry   the cattle gather together
Lowing they kneel before the heavens. the wild beasts of the forests
30 Tremble the Lion shuddering asks the Leopard. Feelest thou
The dread I feel unknown before My voice refuses to roar
And in weak moans I speak to thee This night
Before the mornings dawn the Eagle calld the Vulture
The Raven calld the hawk I heard them from my forests black
Saying Let us go up far for soon I smell upon the wind
A terror coming from the South. The Eagle & Hawk fled away
At dawn & Eer the sun arose the raven & Vulture followd
Let us flee also to the north. They fled. The Sons of Men
Saw them depart in dismal droves. The trumpet sounded loud
40 And all the Sons of Eternity Descended into Beulah

PAGE 119
In the fierce flames the limbs of Mystery lay consuming with howling
And deep despair. Rattling go up the flames around the Synagogue
Of Satan   Loud the Serpent Orc ragd thro his twenty Seven

Recievd . . . Grave A conceptual allegory revitalized; the spectre of Urthona is clock-time, the spectre of Enitharmon "yardstick-space" (Northrop Frye's phrase); they are overthrown together and go down with the ruined wall of nature.

Folds. The tree of Mystery went up in folding flames
Blood issud out in mighty volumes pouring in whirlpools fierce
From out the flood gates of the Sky The Gates are burst down pour
The torrents black upon the Earth the blood pours down incessant
Kings in their palaces lie drownd Shepherds their flocks their tents
Roll down the mountains in black torrents Cities Villages
10   High spires & Castles drownd in the black deluge Shoal on Shoal
Float the dead carcases of Men & Beasts driven to & fro on waves
Of foaming blood beneath the black incessant Sky till all
Mysterys tyrants are cut off & not one left on Earth

And when all Tyranny was cut off from the face of Earth
Around the Dragon form of Urizen & round his stony form
The flames rolling intense thro the wide Universe
Began to Enter the Holy City° Entring the dismal clouds
In furrowd lightnings break their way the wild flames whirring up
The Bloody Deluge living flames winged with intellect
20   And Reason round the Earth they march in order flame by flame
From the clotted gore & from the hollow den
Start forth the trembling millions into flames of mental fire
Bathing their Limbs in the bright visions of Eternity

Beyond this Universal Confusion beyond the remotest Pole
Where their vortexes begin to operate there stands
A Horrible rock far in the South° it was forsaken when
Urizen gave the horses of Light into the hands of Luvah
On this rock lay the faded head of the Eternal Man
Enwrapped round with weeds of death pale cold in sorrow & woe
30   He lifts the blue lamps of his Eyes & cries with heavenly voice
Bowing his head over the consuming Universe he cried

O weakness & O weariness   O war within my members°
My sons exiled from my breast pass to & fro before me
My birds are silent on my hills flocks die beneath my branches
My tents are fallen my trumpets & the sweet sounds of my harp
Is silent on my clouded hills that belch forth storms & fires
My milk of cows & honey of bees & fruit of golden harvest
Are gatherd in the scorching heat & in the driving rain
My robe is turned to confusion & my bright gold to stones
40   Where once I sat   I weary walk in misery & pain
For from within my witherd breast grown narrow with my woes
The Corn is turnd to thistles & the apples into poison
The birds of song to murderous crows My joys to bitter groans

Holy City Golgonooza, Blake's City of Art, the
name based on the Hebrew for "hidden hub or
center"; compare ll. 16–23 to Yeats's "Byzantium," which they influenced.
rock far in the South Not the Rock of Ages,
but the rock where Orc (like Loki or Prometheus) was tortured by Urizen earlier in the

poem; the South is Urizen's abandoned realm
in Eternity; Urizen's move to the North (like
similar directional moves by Milton's Satan and
Isaiah's Lucifer) began his Fall.
within my members Within the Zoas; the tone
of this is Pauline, but its thrust is against all
dualisms, St. Paul's included.

PAGE 120

The voices of children in my tents to cries of helpless infants
And all exiled from the face of light & shine of morning
In this dark world a narrow house I wander up & down
I hear Mystery howling in these flames of Consummation
When shall the Man of future times become as in days of old
O weary life why sit 1 here & give up all my powers
To indolence to the night of death when indolence & mourning
Sit hovring over my dark threshold. tho I arise look out
And scorn the war within my members yet my heart is weak
And my head faint Yet will I look again unto the morning
Whence is this sound of rage of Men drinking each others blood
Drunk with the smoking gore & red but not with nourishing wine

The Eternal Man sat on the Rocks & cried with awful voice

O Prince of Light where art thou   I behold thee not as once
In those Eternal fields in clouds of morning stepping forth
With harps & songs where bright Ahania sang before thy face
And all thy sons & daughters gatherd round my ample table
See you not all this wracking furious confusion
Come forth from slumbers of thy cold abstraction come forth
Arise to Eternal births shake off thy cold repose
Schoolmaster of souls great opposer of change arise
That the Eternal worlds may see thy face in peace & joy
That thou dread form of Certainty maist sit in town & village
While little children play around thy feet in gentle awe
Fearing thy frown loving thy smile O Urizen Prince of light

He calld the deep buried his voice & answer none returnd

Then wrath burst round the Eternal Man was wrath again he cried
Arise O stony form of death O dragon of the Deeps°
Lie down before my feet O Dragon let Urizen arise
O how couldst thou deform those beautiful proportions
Of life & person for as the Person so is his life proportiond
Let Luvah rage in the dark deep even to Consummation
For if thou feedest not his rage it will subside in peace
But if thou darest obstinate refuse my stern behest
Thy crown & scepter I will sieze & regulate all my members
In stern severity & cast thee out into the indefinite
Where nothing lives, there to wander. & if thou returnst weary
Weeping at the threshold of Existence I will steel my heart
Against thee to Eternity & never recieve thee more
Thy self destroying beast formd Science shall be thy eternal lot
My anger against thee is greater than against this Luvah
For war is energy Enslavd but thy religion
The first author of this war & the distracting of honest minds

dragon of the Deeps See Psalms 148:7.

Into confused perturbation & strife & honour & pride
Is a deceit so detestable that I will cast thee out
If thou repentest not & leave thee as a rotten branch to be burnd
With Mystery the Harlot & with Satan for Ever & Ever
Error can never be redeemd in all Eternity
But Sin Even Rahab is redeemd in blood & fury & jealousy
50   That line of blood that stretchd across the windows of the morning
Redeemd from Errors power.° Wake thou dragon of the Deeps

PAGE 121
Urizen wept in the dark deep anxious his Scaly form
To reassume the human & he wept in the dark deep

Saying O that I had never drank the wine nor eat the bread
Of dark mortality nor cast my view into futurity nor turnd
My back darkning the present clouding with a cloud
And building arches high & cities turrets & towers & domes
Whose smoke destroyd the pleasant garden & whose running Kennels
Chokd the bright rivers burdning with my Ships the angry deep
Thro Chaos seeking for delight & in spaces remote
10   Seeking the Eternal which is always present to the wise
Seeking for pleasure which unsought falls round the infants path
And on the fleeces of mild flocks who neither care nor labour
But I the labourer of ages whose unwearied hands
Are thus deformd with hardness with the sword & with the spear
And with the Chisel & the mallet I whose labours vast
Order the nations separating family by family
Alone enjoy not   I alone in misery supreme
Ungratified give all my joy unto this Luvah & Vala
Then Go O dark futurity I will cast thee forth from these
20   Heavens of my brain nor will I look upon futurity more
I cast futurity away & turn my back upon that void
Which I have made for lo futurity is in this moment
Let Orc consume let Tharmas rage let dark Urthona give
All strength to Los & Enitharmon & let Los self cursd
Rend down this fabric as a wall ruind & family extinct
Rage Orc Rage Tharmas Urizen no longer curbs your rage

So Urizen spoke he shook his snows from off his Shoulders & arose
As on a Pyramid of mist his white robes scattering
The fleecy white renewd he shook his aged mantles off
30   Into the fires Then glorious bright Exulting in his joy

He sounding rose into the heavens in naked majesty
In radiant Youth. when Lo like garlands in the Eastern sky
When vocal may comes dancing from the East Ahania came
Exulting in her flight as when a bubble rises up
On to the surface of a lake. Ahania rose in joy
Excess of Joy is worse than grief—her heart beat high her blood
burst its bright Vessels She fell down dead at the feet of Urizen°
Outstretchd a Smiling corse they buried her in a silent cave
Urizen dropt a tear the Eternal Man Darkend with sorrow

40   The three daughters of Urizen guard Ahanias Death couch
Rising from the confusion in tears & howlings & despair
Calling upon their fathers Name upon their Rivers dark

And the Eternal Man Said Hear my words O Prince of Light

PAGE 122
Behold Jerusalem in whose bosom the Lamb of God
Is seen tho slain before her Gates he self renewd remains
Eternal & I thro him awake from deaths dark vale
The times revolve the time is coming when all these delights
Shall be renewd & all these Elements that now consume
Shall reflourish. Then bright Ahania shall awake from death
A glorious Vision to thine Eyes a Self renewing Vision
The spring. the summer to be thine then sleep the wintry days
In silken garments spun by her own hands against her funeral
10   The winter thou shalt plow & lay thy stores into thy barns
Expecting to receive Ahania in the spring with joy
Immortal thou. Regenerate She & all the lovely Sex°
From her shall learn obedience & prepare for a wintry grave
That spring may see them rise in tenfold joy & sweet delight
Thus shall the male & female live the life of Eternity
Because the Lamb of God Creates himself a bride & wife
That we his Children evermore may live in Jerusalem
Which now descendeth out of heaven a City yet a Woman°
Mother of myriads redeemd & born in her spiritual palaces
20   By a New Spiritual birth Regenerated from Death

Urizen said. I have Erred & my Error remains with me
What Chain encompasses in what Lock is the river of light confind
That issues forth in the morning by measure & the evening by carefulness

Ahania . . . Urizen Ahania, Urizen's emanation, normally represents the intellect's legitimate pleasure in itself, debased in the Fall to the intellect's sado-masochistic self-hatred, or acute self-consciousness. This revival and subsequent apparent "death" of Ahania is a crucial moment in Night IX. Her premature reunion with Urizen represents Blake's warning against self-deception (his own and ours) in an apocalyptic age, when the apparently renovated mind becomes suddenly too joyful at taking pleasure in itself again, a too-easy gratification that cannot precede, but must follow, a terrible struggle toward self-integration.
the lovely Sex Again the reader must remember that this refers to the self-sacrifice of the emanations in the unfallen life of Eden; Blake does not mean it to be a paradigm for human female behavior, since it refers to natural forms (in the fallen world) and human creations (in Eternity) and not to human beings at all, female or male.
a City yet a Woman See Revelation 21:2–10,

Where shall we take our stand to view the infinite & unbounded
Or where are human feet for Lo our eyes are in the heavens

He ceasd for rivn link from link the bursting Universe explodes
All things reversd flew from their centers rattling bones
To bones Join,° shaking convulsd the shivering clay breathes
Each speck of dust to the Earths center nestles round & round
30   In pangs of an Eternal Birth in torment & awe & fear
All spirits deceasd let loose from reptile prisons come in shoals
Wild furies from the tygers brain & from the lions Eyes
And from the ox & ass come moping terrors. from the Eagle
And raven numerous as the leaves of autumn   every species
Flock to the trumpet muttring over the sides of the grave & crying
In the fierce wind round heaving rocks & mountains filld with groans
On rifted rocks suspended in the air by inward fires
Many a woful company & many on clouds & waters
Fathers & friends Mothers & Infants Kings & Warriors
40   Priests & chaind Captives met together in a horrible fear
And every one of the dead appears as he had livd before

PAGE 123
And all the marks remain of the slaves scourge & tyrants Crown
And of the Priests oergorged Abdomen & of the merchants thin
Sinewy deception & of the warriors ou[t]braving & thoughtlessness
In lineaments too extended & in bones too strait & long

They shew their wounds they accuse they sieze the opressor howlings began
On the golden palace Songs & joy on the desart the Cold babe
Stands in the furious air he cries the children of six thousand years
Who died in infancy rage furious a mighty multitude rage furious
Naked & pale standing on the expecting air to be deliverd
10   Rend limb from limb the Warrior & the tyrant reuniting in pain
The furious wind still rends around they flee in sluggish effort

They beg they intreat in vain now they Listend not to intreaty
They view the flames red rolling on thro the wide universe
From the dark jaws of death beneath & desolate shores remote
These covering Vaults of heaven & these trembling globes of Earth
One Planet calls to another & one star enquires of another
What flames are these coming from the South what noise what dreadful rout
As of a battle in the heavens hark heard you not the trumpet
As of fierce battle While they spoke the flames come on intense roaring

20   They see him whom they have piercd they wail because of him°
They magnify themselves no more against Jerusalem Nor
Against her little ones the innocent accused before the Judges
Shines with immortal Glory trembling the Judge springs from his throne
Hiding his face in the dust beneath the prisoners feet & saying

rattling . . . Join See Ezekiel 37:7.   **They see . . . him** See Revelation 1:7.

Brother of Jesus what have I done intreat thy lord for me
Perhaps I may be forgiven While he speaks the flames roll on

And after the flames appears the Cloud of the Son of Man°
Descending from Jerusalem with power and great Glory
All nations look up to the Cloud & behold him who was Crucified

30   The Prisoner answers you scourgd my father to death before my face
While I stood bound with cords & heavy chains. your hipocrisy
Shall now avail you nought. So speaking he dashd him with his foot

The Cloud is Blood dazling upon the heavens & in the cloud
Above upon its volumes is beheld a throne & a pavement
Of precious stones. surrounded by twenty four venerable patriarchs°
And these again surrounded by four Wonders of the Almighty
Incomprehensible. pervading all amidst & round about
Fourfold each in the other reflected they are named Life's in Eternity°
Four Starry Universes going forward from Eternity to Eternity
40   And the Falln Man who was arisen upon the Rock of Ages

PAGE 124
Beheld the Vision of God & he arose up from the Rock°
And Urizen arose up with him walking thro the flames
To meet the Lord coming to Judgment but the flames repelld them
Still to the Rock in vain they strove to Enter the Consummation
Together for the Redeemd Man could not enter the Consummation

Then siezd the Sons of Urizen the Plow they polished it°
From rust of ages all its ornaments of Gold & silver & ivory
Reshone across the field immense where all the nations
Darkend like Mould in the divided fallows where the weed
10   Triumphs in its own destruction they took down the harness
From the blue walls of heaven starry jingling ornamented
With beautiful art the study of angels the workmanship of Demons
When Heaven & Hell in Emulation strove in sports of Glory

The noise of rural work resounded thro the heavens of heavens
The horse[s] neigh from the battle the wild bulls from the sultry waste
The tygers from the forests & the lions from the sandy desarts
They Sing they sieze the instruments of harmony they throw away
The spear the bow the gun the mortar they level the fortifications
They beat the iron engines of destruction into wedges°
20   They give them to Urthonas Sons ringing the hammers sound

the Son of Man See Luke 21:27, and Revelation
1:7.
in the cloud . . . patriarchs See Revelation 4:2–4.
Life's in Eternity The Zoas, in Eternity, define
truly what Life is.
And the . . . Rock a crucial moment, like
Prometheus being unbound from his ravine, but
the passage goes on to apply the lessons learned

from the failure of the French Revolution
Then siezd . . . polished it The work of restora-
tion begins in our minds, where the reclaimed
Urizen now assumes his proper place; the mind
must plow up the hell of the physical universe,
in a truly humanistic Harrowing of Hell; see
Revelation 14:15–20.
They beat . . . wedges See Isaiah 2:4.

In dens of death° to forge the spade the mattock & the ax
The heavy roller to break the clods to pass over the nations

The Sons of Urizen Shout Their father rose The Eternal horses
Harnessd They calld to Urizen the heavens moved at their call
The limbs of Urizen shone with ardor. He laid his ha[n]d on the Plow
Thro dismal darkness drave the Plow of ages over Cities
And all their Villages over Mountains & all their Vallies
Over the graves & caverns of the dead   Over the Planets
And over the void Spaces over Sun & moon & star & constellation

30   Then Urizen commanded & they brought the Seed of Men°
The trembling souls of All the Dead stood before Urizen
Weak wailing in the troubled air East west & north & south

PAGE 125
He turnd the horses loose & laid his Plow in the northern corner
Of the wide Universal field. then Stepd forth into the immense

Then he began to sow the seed he girded round his loins
With a bright girdle & his skirt filld with immortal souls
Howling & Wailing fly the souls from Urizens strong hand

For from the hand of Urizen the myriads fall like stars
Into their own appointed places driven back by the winds
The naked warriors rush together down to the sea shores
They are become like wintry flocks like forests stripd of leaves
10   The Kings & Princes of the Earth cry with a feeble cry
Driven on the unproducing sands & on the hardend rocks
And all the while the flames of Orc follow the ventrous feet
Of Urizen & all the while the Trump of Tharmas sounds
Weeping & wailing fly the souls from Urizens strong hand
The daughters of Urizen stand with Cups & measures of foaming wine
Immense upon the heavens with bread & delicate repasts

Then follows the golden harrow in the midst of Mental fires
To ravishing melody of flutes & harps & softest voice
The seed is harrowd in while flames heat the black mould & cause
20   The human harvest to begin Towards the south first sprang
The myriads & in silent fear they look out from their graves

Then Urizen sits down to rest & all his wearied Sons
Take their repose on beds they drink they sing they view the flames
Of Orc in joy they view the human harvest springing up
A time they give to sweet repose till all the harvest is ripe°

dens of death Dens of Urthona, the Ulro; this underworld or unconscious must be broken through before Luvah's world of Experience or Generation and the Innocence or Beulah of Tharmas can be reclaimed.

Seed of Men after the plowing, the sowing for the human harvest; see Matthew 13:3–8
A time . . . ripe See Revelation 14:15; Urizen's initial labor has been performed, and his momentary rest permits Ahania now to be truly revived.

And Lo like the harvest Moon Ahania cast off her death clothes°
She folded them up in care in silence & her brightning limbs
Bathd in the clear spring of the rock then from her darksom cave
Issud in majesty divine   Urizen rose up from his couch
On wings of tenfold joy clapping his hands his feet his radiant wings
In the immense as when the Sun dances upon the mountains
A shout of jubilee in lovely notes responding from daughter to daughter
From son to Son as if the Stars beaming innumerable
Thro night should sing soft warbling filling Earth & heaven
And bright Ahania took her seat by Urizen in songs & joy

The Eternal Man also sat down upon the Couches of Beulah
Sorrowful that he could not put off his new risen body°
In mental flames the flames refusd they drove him back to Beulah
His body was redeemd to be permanent thro the Mercy Divine

PAGE 126
And now fierce Orc had quite consumd himself in Mental flames°
Expending all his energy against the fuel of fire
The Regenerate Man stoopd his head over the Universe & in
His holy hands recievd the flaming Demon & Demoness of Smoke
And gave them to Urizens hands the Immortal frownd Saying

Luvah & Vala henceforth you are Servants obey & live
You shall forget your former state return O Love in peace
Into your place the place of seed not in the brain or heart
If Gods combine against Man Setting their Dominion above
The Human form Divine. Thrown down from their high Station
In the Eternal heavens of Human Imagination: buried beneath
In dark oblivion with incessant pangs ages on ages
In Enmity & war first weakend then in stern repentance
They must renew their brightness & their disorganizd functions
Again reorganize till they resume the image of the human
Cooperating in the bliss of Man obeying his Will
Servants to the infinite & Eternal of the Human form°

Luvah & Vala descended & enterd the Gates of Dark Urthona
And walkd from the hands of Urizen in the shadows of Valas Garden
Where the impressions of Despair & Hope for ever vegetate
In flowers in fruits in fishes birds & beasts & clouds & waters
The land of doubts & shadows sweet delusions unformd hopes
They saw no more the terrible confusion of the wracking universe
They heard not saw not felt not all the terrible confusion

And Lo . . . clothes Ahania is one with the harvest goddess here.
The Eternal . . . body Albion wishes to enter Eden, the condition of fire, but it is still Millennium, and he must abide in Beulah or redeemed nature for a time.
And now . . . flames The focus moves now from Urizen and Ahania to Luvah and Vala;

Orc, as natural man, is burned up, and his eternal forms of Luvah and Vala reappear, the children of Experience abandoning what D. H. Lawrence called "sex in the head" and returning to their generative "place of seed."
If Gods . . . form Ll. 9–17 summarize the moral of the entire poem.

For in their orbed senses within closd up they wanderd at will
And those upon the Couches viewd them in the dreams of Beulah°
As they reposd from the terrible wide universal harvest
Invisible Luvah in bright clouds hoverd over Valas head
And thus their ancient golden age renewd for Luvah spoke
30   With voice mild from his golden Cloud upon the breath of morning

Come forth O Vala from the grass & from the silent Dew
Rise from the dews of death for the Eternal Man is Risen

She rises among flowers & looks toward the Eastern clearness
She walks yea runs her feet are wingd on the tops of the bending grass
Her garments rejoice in the vocal wind & her hair glistens with dew
She answerd thus Whose voice is this in the voice of the nourishing air
In the spirit of the morning awaking the Soul from its grassy bed

PAGE 127
Where dost thou dwell for it is thee I seek & but for thee
I must have slept Eternally nor have felt the dew of thy morning
Look how the opening dawn advances with vocal harmony
Look how the beams foreshew the rising of some glorious power
The sun is thine he goeth forth in his majestic brightness
O thou creating voice that callest & who shall answer thee

Where dost thou flee O fair one where dost thou seek thy happy place

To yonder brightness there I haste for sure I came from thence
Or I must have slept eternally nor have felt the dew of morning

10   Eternally thou must have slept nor have felt the morning dew
But for yon nourishing sun tis that by which thou art arisen
The birds adore the sun the beasts rise up & play in his beams
And every flower & every leaf rejoices in his light
Then O thou fair one sit thee down for thou art as the grass
Thou risest in the dew of morning & at night art folded up°

Alas am I but as a flower then will I sit me down
Then will I weep then Ill complain & sigh for immortality
And chide my maker thee O Sun that raisedst me to fall

So saying she sat down & wept beneath the apple trees

20   O be thou blotted out thou Sun that raisedst me to trouble
That gavest me a heart to crave & raisedst me thy phantom
To feel thy heat & see thy light & wander here alone
Hopeless if I am like the grass & so shall pass away

Rise sluggish Soul why sitts thou here why dost thou sit & weep
Yon Sun shall wax old & decay but thou shalt ever flourish

Luvah . . . Beulah Ll. 18–26 deliberately echo
The Book of Thel for the renovated Vala is the
contrary to the pathetic Thel, and welcomes
entry into a humanized Generation.
Thou . . . folded up See Psalm 90:6.

The fruit shall ripen & fall down & the flowers consume away
But thou shalt still survive arise O dry thy dewy tears°

Hah! Shall I still survive whence came that sweet & comforting voice
And whence that voice of sorrow O sun thou art nothing now to me
30 Go on thy course rejoicing & let us both rejoice together
I walk among his flocks & hear the bleating of his lambs
O that I could behold his face & follow his pure feet
I walk by the footsteps of his flocks come hither tender flocks
Can you converse with a pure Soul that seeketh for her maker
You answer not then am I set your mistress in this garden
Ill watch you & attend your footsteps you are not like the birds

PAGE 128
That sing & fly in the bright air but you do lick my feet
And let me touch your wooly backs   follow me as I sing
For in my bosom a new song arises to my Lord
Rise up O Sun most glorious minister & light of day
Flow on ye gentle airs & bear the voice of my rejoicing
Wave freshly clear waters flowing around the tender grass
And thou sweet smelling ground put forth thy life in fruits & flowers
Follow me O my flocks & hear me sing my rapturous Song
I will cause my voice to be heard on the clouds that glitter in the sun
10 I will call & who shall answer me   I will sing   who shall reply
For from my pleasant hills behold the living living springs
Running among my green pastures delighting among my trees
I am not here alone my flocks you are my brethren
And you birds that sing & adorn the sky you are my sisters
I sing & you reply to my Song   I rejoice & you are glad
Follow me O my flocks we will now descend into the valley
O how delicious are the grapes flourishing in the Sun
How clear the spring of the rock running among the golden sand
How cool the breezes of the vally & the arms of the branching trees
20 Cover us from the Sun come & let us sit in the Shade
My Luvah here hath placd me in a Sweet & pleasant Land
And given me fruits & pleasant waters & warm hills & cool valleys
Here will I build myself a house & here Ill call on his name
Here Ill return when I am weary & take my pleasant rest

So spoke the Sinless Soul & laid her head on the downy fleece
Of a curld Ram who stretchd himself in sleep beside his mistress
And soft sleep fell upon her eyelids in the silent noon of day

Then Luvah passed by & saw the sinless Soul
And said   Let a pleasant house arise to be the dwelling place
30 Of this immortal Spirit growing in lower Paradise

Where . . . tears Ll. 7–27 echo *The Book of
Thel,* again providing a positive contrary to
Thel's pathos.

He spoke & pillars were builded & walls as white as ivory
The grass she slept upon was pavd with pavement as of pearl
Beneath her rose a downy bed & a cieling coverd all

Vala awoke. When in the pleasant gates of sleep I enterd
I saw my Luvah like a spirit stand in the bright air
Round him stood spirits like me who reard me a bright house
And here I see thee house remain in my most pleasant world

PAGE 129
My Luvah smild I kneeled down he laid his hand on my head
And when he laid his hand upon me from the gates of sleep I came
Into this bodily house to tend my flocks in my pleasant garden

So saying she arose & walked round her beautiful house
And then from her white door she lookd to see her bleating lambs
But her flocks were gone up from beneath the trees into the hills

I see the hand that leadeth me doth also lead my flocks
She went up to her flocks & turned oft to see her shining house
She stopd to drink of the clear spring & eat the grapes & apples
10   She bore the fruits in her lap she gatherd flowers for her bosom
She called to her flocks saying follow me o my flocks

They followd her to the silent vally beneath the spreading trees
And on the rivers margin she ungirded her golden girdle
She stood in the river & viewd herself within the watry glass
And her bright hair was wet with the waters She rose up from the river
And as she rose her Eyes were opend to the world of waters°
She saw Tharmas sitting upon the rocks beside the wavy sea
He strokd the water from his beard & mournd faint thro the summer vales

And Vala stood on the rocks of Tharmas & heard his mournful voice

20   O Enion my weary head is in the bed of death
For weeds of death have wrapd around my limbs in the hoary deeps
I sit in the place of shells & mourn & thou art closd in clouds
When will the time of Clouds be past & the dismal night of Tharmas
Arise O Enion Arise & smile upon my head
As thou dost smile upon the barren mountains and they rejoice
When wilt thou smile on Tharmas O thou bringer of golden day
Arise O Enion arise for Lo I have calmd my seas°

So saying his faint head he laid upon the Oozy rock
And darkness coverd all the deep the light of Enion faded
30   Like a fa[i]nt flame quivering upon the surface of the darkness

My Luvah . . . waters In this beautiful passage
(ll. 1–16), the redeemed Vala surmounts an
Eve-like narcist contemplation of her own
beauty, and by opening her eyes to the world
of waters begins the redemption of Tharmas and
Enion, the mother and father figures of the
world of Innocence; Experience having been
purged, Beulah or Innocence can be recovered.
calmd my seas From having been the harmony
and instinctual unity of the Eternal world,
Tharmas has fallen into the Old Man of the Sea
or voice of Chaos; repenting, he calms his seas,
which means that his emanation, the Earth
Mother, is able to return to him.

Then Vala lifted up her hands to heaven to call on Enion
She calld but none could answer her & the Eccho of her voice returnd

Where is the voice of God that calld me from the silent dew
Where is the Lord of Vala dost thou hide in clefts of the rock°
Why shouldst thou hide thyself from Vala from the soul that wanders desolate

She ceas'd & light beamd round her like the glory of the morning

PAGE 130
And She arose out of the river & girded on her golden girdle

And now her feet step on the grassy bosom of the ground
Among her flocks & she turnd her eyes toward her pleasant house
And saw in the door way beneath the trees two little children playing°
She drew near to her house & her flocks followd her footsteps
The Children clung around her knees she embracd them & wept over them

Thou little Boy art Tharmas & thou bright Girl Enion
How are ye thus renewd & brought into the Gardens of Vala

She embracd them in tears. till the sun descended the western hills
10   And then she enterd her bright house leading her mighty children
And when night came the flocks laid round the house beneath the trees
She laid the Children on the beds which she saw prepard in the house
Then last herself laid down & closd her Eyelids in soft slumbers

And in the morning when the Sun arose in the crystal sky
Vala awoke & calld the children from their gentle slumbers

Awake O Enion awake & let thine innocent Eyes
Enlighten all the Crystal house of Vala awake awake
Awake Tharmas awake awake thou child of dewy tears
Open the orbs of thy blue eyes & smile upon my gardens

20   The Children woke & smild on Vala. she kneeld by the golden couch
She presd them to her bosom & her pearly tears dropd down
O my sweet Children Enion let Tharmas kiss thy Cheek
Why dost thou turn thyself away from his sweet watry eyes
Tharmas henceforth in Valas bosom thou shalt find sweet peace
O bless the lovely eyes of Tharmas & the Eyes of Enion

They rose they went out wandring sometimes together sometimes alone
Why weepest thou Tharmas Child of tears in the bright house of joy
Doth Enion avoid the sight of thy blue heavenly Eyes
And dost thou wander with my lambs & wet their innocent faces
30   With thy bright tears because the steps of Enion are in the gardens
Arise sweet boy & let us follow the path of Enion

clefts of the rock See Song of Solomon 2:14.   the *Songs of Innocence* return as a restored
two little children playing The lost children of   Tharmas and Enion.

So saying they went down into the garden among the fruits
And Enion sang among the flowers that grew among the trees
And Vala said Go Tharmas weep not Go to Enion

PAGE 131
He said O Vala I am sick & all this garden of Pleasure
Swims like a dream before my eyes but the sweet smelling fruit
Revives me to new deaths I fade even like a water lilly
In the suns heat till in the night on the couch of Enion
I drink new life & feel the breath of sleeping Enion
But in the morning she arises to avoid my Eyes
Then my loins fade & in the house I sit me down & weep

Chear up thy Countenance bright boy & go to Enion
Tell her that Vala waits her in the shadows of her garden

10   He went with timid steps & Enion like the ruddy morn
When infant spring appears in swelling buds & opening flowers
Behind her Veil withdraws so Enion turnd her modest head

But Tharmas spoke Vala seeks thee sweet Enion in the shades
Follow the steps of Tharmas, O thou brightness of the gardens
He took her hand reluctant she followd in infant doubts

Thus in Eternal Childhood straying among Valas flocks
In infant sorrow & joy alternate Enion & Tharmas playd
Round Vala in the Gardens of Vala & by her rivers margin

They are the shadows of Tharmas & of Enion in Valas world
20   And the sleepers who rested from their harvest work beheld these visions
Thus were the sleepers entertaind upon the Couches of Beulah

When Luvah & Vala were closd up in their world of shadowy forms
Darkness was all beneath the heavens only a little light
Such as glows out from sleeping spirits appeard in the deeps beneath
As when the wind sweeps over a Corn field the noise of souls
Thro all the immense borne down by Clouds swagging in autumnal heat
Muttering along from heaven to heaven hoarse roll the human forms
Beneath thick clouds dreadful lightnings burst & thunders roll
Down pour the torrent Floods of heaven on all the human harvest
30   Then Urizen sitting at his repose on beds in the bright South
Cried Times are Ended° he Exulted he arose in joy he exulted
He pourd his light & all his Sons & daughters pourd their light
To exhale the spirits of Luvah & Vala thro the atmosphere
And Luvah & Vala saw the Light their spirits were Exhald
In all their ancient innocence the floods depart the clouds
Dissipate or sink into the Seas of Tharmas   Luvah sat
Above on the bright heavens in peace. the Spirits of Men beneath

Times are Ended See Revelation 10:6; Urizen's   16, as he becomes the joyful reaper of the now
role in 131:22–132:1 fulfills Revelation 14:14–   fully prepared harvest.

Cried out to be deliverd & the Spirit of Luvah wept
Over the human harvest & over Vala the sweet wanderer
40   In pain the human harvest wavd in horrible groans of woe°

PAGE 132
The Universal Groan went up the Eternal Man was Darkend

Then Urizen arose & took his Sickle in his hand
There is a brazen sickle & a scythe of iron hid
Deep in the South guarded by a few solitary stars°
This sickle Urizen took the scythe his sons embracd
And went forth & began to reap & all his joyful sons
Reapd the wide Universe & bound in Sheaves a wondrous harvest
They took them into the wide barns with loud rejoicings & triumph
Of flute & harp & drum & trumpet horn & clarion°
10   The feast was spread in the bright South & the Regenerate Man
Sat at the feast rejoicing & the wine of Eternity
Was servd round by the flames of Luvah all Day & all the Night
And when Morning began to dawn upon the distant hills
a whirlwind rose up in the Center & in the Whirlwind a shriek
And in the Shriek a rattling of bones & in the rattling of bones
A dolorous groan & from the dolorous groan in tears
Rose Enion like a gentle light° & Enion spoke saying

O Dreams of Death the human form dissolving companied
By beasts & worms & creeping things & darkness & despair
20   The clouds fall off from my wet brow the dust from my cold limbs
Into the Sea of Tharmas Soon renewd a Golden Moth°
I shall cast off my death clothes & Embrace Tharmas again
For Lo the winter melted away upon the distant hills
And all the black mould sings. She speaks to her infant race her milk
Descends down on the sand. the thirsty sand drinks & rejoices
Wondering to behold the Emmet the Grasshopper the jointed worm
The roots shoot thick thro the solid rocks bursting their way
They cry out in joys of existence. the broad stems
Rear on the mountains stem after stem the scaly newt creeps
30   From the stone & the armed fly springs from the rocky crevice
The spider. The bat burst from the hardend slime crying
To one another What are we & whence is our joy & delight
Lo the little moss begins to spring & the tender weed
Creeps round our secret nest. Flocks brighten the Mountains
Herds throng up the Valley wild beasts fill the forests

groans of woe at not yet being reaped, and so
still enduring nature and history
Then Urizen . . . stars To perform his labors
as reaper, Urizen dismantles his star world,
formerly one of Blake's prime images of tyranny
and repression.
This sickle . . . clarion See Revelation 14:14–16.
Rose . . . light Enion's rising is the particular

joy of the body's resurrection, in *The Marriage's*
sense of the body's being all of the soul that the
five senses can apprehend; Enion's "gentle light"
is the body's joy at finding itself whole again.
Golden Moth A butterfly, for which see "Auguries of Innocence," ll. 39–40; as Tharmas hu-
manizes, all instinctual life acquires a human
awareness.

Joy thrilld thro all the Furious form of Tharmas humanizing
Mild he Embracd her whom he sought he raisd her thro the heavens
Sounding his trumpet to awake the dead on high he soard
Over the ruind worlds the smoking tomb of the Eternal Prophet°

PAGE 133
The Eternal Man arose He welcomd them to the Feast
The feast was spread in the bright South & the Eternal Man°
Sat at the feast rejoicing & the wine of Eternity
Was servd round by the flames of Luvah all day & all the night

And Many Eternal Men sat at the golden feast to see
The female form now separate They shudderd° at the horrible thing
Not born for the sport and amusement of Man but born to drink up all his
     powers
They wept to see their shadows they said to one another this is Sin
This is the Generative world they rememberd the Days of old

10   And One of the Eternals spoke All was silent at the feast

Man is a Worm wearied with joy he seeks the caves of sleep
Among the Flowers of Beulah in his Selfish cold repose
Forsaking Brotherhood & Universal love in selfish clay
Folding the pure wings of his mind seeking the places dark
Abstracted from the roots of Science then inclosd around
In walls of Gold we cast him like a Seed into the Earth
Till times & spaces have passd over him duly every morn
We visit him covering with a Veil the immortal seed
With windows from the inclement sky we cover him & with walls
20   And hearths protect the Selfish terror till divided all
In families we see our shadows born. & thence we know ⎤ Ephesi-
That Man subsists by Brotherhood & Universal Love   ⎬ ans iii c.
We fall on one anothers necks more closely we embrace ⎦ 10 v°

Not for ourselves but for the Eternal family we live
Man liveth not by Self alone but in his brothers face
Each shall behold the Eternal Father & love & joy abound

So spoke the Eternal at the Feast they embracd the New born Man
Calling him Brother image of the Eternal Father. they sat down
At the immortal tables sounding loud their instruments of joy
30   Calling the Morning into Beulah the Eternal Man rejoicd°

tomb . . . Prophet The natural world now transcended is the tomb of Jesus; Jesus is Los, and Los is now again Urthona.
The feast . . . the Eternal Man Unfallen Albion's head was in the South, realm of Urizen, once the zenith, and now the place of celebration in the Apocalypse.
They shudderd because the emanations still retain separate existence, since the feast is in Beulah, and the integration of Eden has not yet been reattained.
Ephesians iii c.10 v An ironical reference, in part, since the text is: "To the intent that now unto the principalities and powers in heavenly places might be known by the church the manifold wisdom of God," to which compare Blake's motto to the whole of The Four Zoas, from Ephesians 6:12: "For we wrestle not against flesh and blood, but against principalities, against powers, against the rulers of the darkness of this world, against spiritual wickedness in high places." The juxtaposition of passages reminds the reader that the English state church is the enemy of Revelation.
Eternal Man rejoicd but he is still in Beulah, the garden of the South, so the joy is not yet final.

When Morning dawnd The Eternals rose to labour at the Vintage°
Beneath they saw their sons & daughters wondering inconceivable
At the dark myriads in Shadows in the worlds beneath

The morning dawnd Urizen rose & in his hand the Flail
Sounds on the Floor heard terrible by all beneath the heavens
Dismal loud redounding the nether floor shakes with the sound

PAGE 134
And all Nations were threshed out & the stars threshd from their husks°

Then Tharmas took the Winnowing fan the winnowing wind furious
Above veerd round by the violent whirlwind driven west & south
Tossed the Nations like Chaff into the seas of Tharmas

O Mystery Fierce Tharmas cries Behold thy end is come
Art thou she that made the nations drunk with the cup of Religion°
Go down ye Kings & Councillors & Giant Warriors
Go down into the depths go down & hide yourselves beneath
Go down with horse & Chariots & Trumpets of hoarse war

10 Lo how the Pomp of Mystery goes down into the Caves
Her great men howl & throw the dust & rend their hoary hair
Her delicate women & children shriek upon the bitter wind
Spoild of their beauty their hair rent & their skin shriveld up
Lo darkness covers the long pomp of banners on the wind
And black horses & armed men & miserable bound captives
Where shall the graves recieve them all & where shall be their place
And who shall mourn for Mystery who never loosd her Captives

Let the slave grinding at the mill run out into the field
Let him look up into the heavens & laugh in the bright air
20 Let the inchaind soul shut up in darkness & in sighing
Whose face has never seen a smile in thirty weary years
Rise & look out his chains are loose his dungeon doors are open
And let his wife & children return from the opressors scourge

They look behind at every step & believe it is a dream°
Are these the Slaves that groand along the streets of Mystery
Where are your bonds & task masters are these the prisoners
Where are your chains where are your tears why do you look around
If you are thirsty there is the river go bathe your parched limbs
The good of all the Land is before you for Mystery is no more

30 Then All the Slaves from every Earth in the wide Universe
Sing a New Song° drowning confusion in its happy notes
While the flail of Urizen sounded loud & the winnowing wind of Tharmas

When . . . Vintage This begins with threshing
and winnowing, for which Blake had no precedent in Revelation, but see Matthew 3:12.
And all . . . husks With some variants this is
used by Yeats as the epigraph to the early group
of lyrics he later called "Crossways."

Mystery the Harlot of Revelation 17
Let the slave . . . dream Ll. 18–24 are repeated from America 6:6–12, but note the enlargement of their power in this more comprehensive context.
New Song See Revelation 5:9.

So loud so clear in the wide heavens & the song that they sung was this
Composed by an African Black from the little Earth of Sotha°

Aha Aha how came I here so soon in my sweet native land
How came I here Methinks I am as I was in my youth

PAGE 135

When in my fathers house I sat & heard his chearing voice
Methinks I see his flocks & herds & feel my limbs renewd
And Lo my Brethren in their tents & their little ones around them

The song arose to the Golden feast the Eternal Man rejoicd
Then thé Eternal Man said Luvah the Vintage is ripe° arise
The sons of Urizen shall gather the vintage with sharp hooks
And all thy sons O Luvah bear away the families of Earth
I hear the flail of Urizen his barns are full no roo[m]
Remains & in the Vineyards stand the abounding sheaves beneath
10 The falling Grapes that odorous burst upon the winds. Arise
My flocks & herds trample the Corn my cattle browze upon
The ripe Clusters The shepherds shout for Luvah prince of Love
Let the Bulls of Luvah tread the Corn & draw the loaded waggon
Into the Barn while children glean the Ears around the door
Then shall they lift their innocent hands & stroke his furious nose
And he shall lick the little girls white neck & on her head
Scatter the perfume of his breath while from his mountains high
The lion of terror shall come down & bending his bright mane
And couching at their side shall eat from the curld boys white lap
20 His golden food and in the evening sleep before the Door

Attempting to be more than Man We become less said Luvah
As he arose from the bright feast drunk with the wine of ages
His crown of thorns fell from his head he hung his living Lyre
Behind the seat of the Eternal Man & took his way
Sounding the Song of Los descending to the Vineyards bright
His sons arising from the feast with golden baskets follow
A fiery train as when the Sun sings in the ripe vineyards
Then Luvah stood before the wine press all his fiery sons
Brought up the loaded Waggons with shoutings ramping tygers play
30 In the jingling traces furious lions sound the song of joy
To the golden wheels circling upon the pavement of heaven & all
The Villages of Luvah ring the golden tiles of the villages
Reply to violins & tabors to the pipe flute lyre & cymbal
Then fell the Legions of Mystery in maddning confusion
Down Down thro the immense with outcry fury & despair
Into the wine presses of Luvah° howling fell the Clusters
Of human families thro the deep. the wine presses were filld

Sotha Associated in Blake's poem "Africa" (part of *The Song of Los*) with a code of war; the African is now set free from the code.
Vintage is ripe See Revelation 14:17–19.

wine presses of Luvah see Revelation 14:17–19 again; Blake's Vintage is at once a festival of rebirth, the terror of the Napoleonic Wars, and the self-sacrifice of the natural man.

The blood of life flowd plentiful Odors of life arose
All round the heavenly arches & the Odors rose singing this song

PAGE 136
O terrible wine presses of Luvah O caverns of the Grave
How lovely the delights of those risen again from death
O trembling joy excess of joy is like Excess of grief

So sang the Human Odors round the wine presses of Luvah

But in the Wine presses is wailing terror & despair
Forsaken of their Elements they vanish & are no more
No more but a desire of Being a distracted ravening desire
Desiring like the hungry worm & like the gaping grave
They plunge into the Elements the Elements cast them forth
Or else consume their shadowy semblance Yet they obstinate
Tho pained to distraction Cry O let us Exist for
This dreadful Non Existence is worse than pains of Eternal Birth
Eternal Death who can Endure. let us consume in fires
In waters stifling or in air corroding or in earth shut up
The Pangs of Eternal birth are better than the Pangs of Eternal Death

How red the sons & daughters of Luvah how they tread the Grapes
Laughing & shouting drunk with odors many fall oerwearied
Drownd in the wine is many a youth & maiden those around
Lay them on skins of tygers or the spotted Leopard or wild Ass
Till they revive or bury them in cool Grots making lamentation

But in the Wine Presses the Human Grapes Sing not nor dance
They howl & writhe in shoals of torment in fierce flames consuming
In chains of iron & in dungeons circled with ceaseless fires
In pits & dens & shades of death in shapes of torment & woe
The Plates the Screws and Racks & Saws & cords & fires & floods
The cruel joy of Luvahs daughters lacerating with knives
And whip[s] their Victims & the deadly sports of Luvahs sons

Timbrels & Violins sport round the Wine Presses The little Seed
The Sportive root the Earthworm the small beetle the wise Emmet
Dance round the Wine Presses of Luvah. the Centipede is there
The ground Spider with many Eyes the Mole clothed in Velvet
The Earwig armd the tender maggot emblem of Immortality
The Slow Slug the grasshopper that sings & laughs & drinks
The winter comes he folds his slender bones without a murmur
There is the Nettle that stings with soft down & there
The indignant Thistle whose bitterness is bred in his milk
And who lives on the contempt of his neighbour there all the idle weeds
That creep about the obscure places shew their various limbs
Naked in all their beauty dancing round the Wine Presses
They Dance around the Dying & they Drink the howl & groan

PAGE 137

They catch the Shrieks in cups of gold they hand them to one another
These are the sports of love & these the sweet delights of amorous play
Tears of the grapes the death sweat of the Cluster the last sigh
Of the mild youth who listens to the luring songs of Luvah

The Eternal Man darkend with Sorrow & a wintry mantle
Coverd the Hills   He said O Tharmas rise & O Urthona

Then Tharmas & Urthona rose from the Golden feast satiated
With Mirth & Joy Urthona limping from his fall on Tharmas leand°
In his right hand his hammer Tharmas held his Shepherds crook
10   Beset with gold gold were the ornaments formd by sons of Urizen

Then Enion & Ahania & Vala & the wife of Dark Urthona
Rose from the feast in joy ascending to their Golden Looms
There the wingd shuttle Sang the spindle & the distaff & the Reel
Rang sweet the praise of industry. Thro all the golden rooms
Heaven rang with winged Exultation   All beneath howld loud
With tenfold rout & desolation roard the Chasms beneath
Where the wide woof flowd down & where the Nations are gatherd together

Tharmas went down to the Wine presses & beheld the sons & daughters
Of Luvah quite exhausted with the Labour & quite filld
20   With new wine, that they began to torment one another and to tread
The weak. Luvah & Vala slept on the floor o'erwearied

Urthona calld his Sons around him Tharmas calld his sons
Numrous. they took the wine they separated the Lees
And Luvah was put for dung on the ground by the Sons of Tharmas & Urthona
They formed heavens of sweetest wo[o]d[s] of gold & silver & ivory
Of glass & precious stones They loaded all the waggons of heaven
And took away the wine of ages with solemn songs & joy

Luvah & Vala woke & all the sons & daughters of Luvah
Awoke they wept to one another & they reascended
30   To the Eternal Man in woe he cast them wailing into
The world of shadows thro the air till winter is over & gone

But the Human Wine stood wondering in all their delightful Expanses
The Elements subside the heavens rolld on with vocal harmony

Then Los who is Urthona rose in all his regenerate power
The Sea that rolld & foamd with darkness & the shadows of death
Vomited out & gave up all° the floods lift up their hands
Singing & shouting to the Man they bow their hoary heads
And murmuring in their channels flow & circle round his feet

on Tharmas leand Blake wisely qualifies his
apocalypse, even in this first and most exuberant of its versions; Urthona, though restored,
is still a crippled smith god, though no longer
a mere Thor or Vulcan, which means the imagination is not yet wholly healed; by leaning on
Tharmas, who is once more the human integral
or instinctual wholeness, he finds support and
can hope.
The Sea . . . gave up all See Revelation 20:13.

PAGE 138
Then Dark Urthona took the Corn out of the Stores of Urizen
He ground it in his rumbling Mills Terrible the distress
Of all the Nations of Earth ground in the Mills of Urthona
In his hand Tharmas takes the Storms. he turns the whirlwind Loose
Upon the wheels the stormy seas howl at his dread command
And Eddying fierce rejoice in the fierce agitation of the wheels
Of Dark Urthona Thunders Earthquakes Fires Water floods
Rejoice to one another loud their voices shake the Abyss
Their dread forms tending the dire mills The grey hoar frost was there
10   And his pale wife the aged Snow they watch over the fires
They build the Ovens of Urthona Nature in darkness groans°
And Men are bound to sullen contemplations in the night
Restless they turn on beds of sorrow. in their inmost brain
Feeling the crushing Wheels they rise they write the bitter words
Of Stern Philosophy & knead the bread of knowledge with tears & groans

Such are the works of Dark Urthona Tharmas sifted the corn
Urthona made the Bread of Ages & he placed it
In golden & in silver baskets in heavens of precious stone
And then took his repose in Winter in the night of Time°

20   The Sun has left his blackness & has found a fresher morning°
And the mild moon rejoices in the clear & cloudless night
And Man walks forth from midst of the fires the evil is all consumd
His eyes behold the Angelic spheres arising night & day
The stars consumd like a lamp blown out & in their stead behold
The Expanding Eyes of Man behold the depths of wondrous worlds

One Earth one sea beneath nor Erring Globes wander but Stars
Of fire rise up nightly from the Ocean & one Sun
Each morning like a New born Man issues with songs & Joy
Calling the Plowman to his Labour & the Shepherd to his rest
30   He walks upon the Eternal Mountains raising his heavenly voice
Conversing with the Animal forms of wisdom night & day
That risen from the Sea of fire renewd walk oer the Earth

For Tharmas brought his flocks upon the hills & in the Vales
Around the Eternal Mans bright tent the little Children play
Among the wooly flocks The hammer of Urthona sounds
In the deep caves beneath his limbs renewd his Lions roar
Around the Furnaces & in Evening sport upon the plains
They raise their faces from the Earth conversing with the Man

How is it we have walkd thro fires & yet are not consumd
40   How is it that all things are changd even as in ancient times

---

Nature in darkness groans For a last time, we
are back in the nightmare of history.
Winter in the night of Time the moment poised
just before breakthrough

The Sun . . . morning Apocalypse proper begins with this line.

PAGE 139
The Sun arises from his dewy bed & the fresh airs
Play in his smiling beams giving the seeds of life to grow
And the fresh Earth beams forth ten thousand thousand springs of life
Urthona is arisen in his strength no longer now
Divided from Enitharmon no longer the Spectre Los
Where is the Spectre of Prophecy° where the delusive Phantom
Departed & Urthona rises from the ruinous walls
In all his ancient strength to form the golden armour of science
For intellectual War The war of swords departed now
10   The dark Religions are departed & sweet Science reigns°
      END OF THE DREAM

1796–1807?   1893

Milton

Though Blake may have worked at revising *The Four Zoas* as late as 1807, he seems to have chosen to write a poem or poems to replace it as early as 1800. Some version of *Milton* existed by 1803, but revision presumably continued until the etching of the plates in 1809–10 (I am following David Erdman's datings). *Milton* is a deliberately foreshortened or "brief" epic, on the model of John Milton's *Paradise Regained*, which itself took the Book of Job as a thematic model.

Both *Paradise Regained* and the Book of Job justify God's ways through dramatic dialogues, but Blake's *Milton* is a more internalized and autobiographical work, though the self-portrayal has little to do with either personality or character. Blake is his own Job, and overcomes a personal Satan by following the example of his great precursor, Milton. The most original element in Blake's poem is that his precursor is the poem's Sublime hero, not just a moral guide like Virgil in Dante's *Comedy*, or a dark parody of such a guide like Rousseau in Shelley's *The Triumph of Life*. Discontented with the extraordinary mythopoeic rival to *Paradise Lost* that he had attempted in *The Four Zoas*, Blake turned to the spiritual form of John Milton to serve him as an epic hero. The audacity of such a procedure is astonishing; try to conceive of *Browning: a Poem in 2 Books* by Ezra Pound, or an *Eliot Agonistes* by Robert Lowell. Blake's success was proportionate to his audacity and, genius aside, can be tracked to his own enormous need of the work, which is as much a crisis poem as Wordsworth's *The Prelude*, but also to Blake's profound and intense relation to John Milton.

Blake's crisis took place at Felpham village in Sussex where he lived from 1800 to 1803 under the patronage of the wealthy William Hayley, minor poet and biographer of William Cowper. The crisis was double, in Blake's own sense of his epic vocation, and in an accusation of treason against him made by a soldier named Schofield. The treason accusation and subsequent trial (Blake was acquitted) play their part in *Jerusalem*; the crisis in poetic self-confidence is the hidden subject of *Milton*, particularly of the first part of Book I of the poem, a "Bard's Song," which appears to be grounded in a quarrel about Blake's work as artist and poet that occurred between Blake and Hayley. Menaced by these outer circumstances, and by

Spectre of Prophecy Los, as opposed to Urthona, the Zoa of Prophecy
sweet Science reigns not the science of the

deists and empiricists but the totally organized
imaginative knowledge attainable only through
the experience of art

inner doubts, Blake turned to a purgatorial theme of temptation and endurance, and to Milton as a kind of savior.

Yet Blake, from *The Marriage of Heaven and Hell* onward, had sought not only to weather Milton's influence upon him, but to swerve away from Milton by creatively "correcting" his Sublime precursor. Blake's Milton is therefore a marvelously complex figure, and the selections that follow have been chosen to reveal this complexity.

From Milton

a Poem in 2 Books

The Author & Printer W Blake 1804

To Justify the Ways of God to Men°

PLATE 1

Preface

The Stolen and Perverted Writings of Homer & Ovid: of Plato & Cicero. which all Men ought to contemn:° are set up by artifice against the Sublime of the Bible. but when the New Age is at leisure to Pronounce: all will be set right: & those Grand Works of the more ancient & consciously & professedly Inspired Men, will hold their proper rank, & the Daughters of Memory shall become the Daughters of Inspiration. Shakspeare & Milton were both curbd by the general malady & infection from the silly Greek & Latin slaves of the Sword.

Rouze up O Young Men of the New Age! set your foreheads against the ignorant Hirelings! For we have Hirelings in the Camp, the Court & the University: who would if they could, for ever depress Mental & prolong Corporeal War. Painters! on you I call! Sculptors! Architects! Suffer not the fash[i]onable Fools to depress your powers by the prices they pretend to give for contemptible works or the expensive advertizing boasts that they make of such works; believe Christ & his Apostles that there is a Class of Men whose whole delight is in Destroying. We do not want either Greek or Roman Models if we are but just & true to our own Imaginations, those Worlds of Eternity in which we shall live for ever; in Jesus our Lord.

> And did those feet in ancient time.
> Walk upon Englands mountains green:
> And was the holy Lamb of God,
> On Englands pleasant pastures seen!
>
> And did the Countenance Divine,
> Shine forth upon our clouded hills?
> And was Jerusalem builded here,
> Among these dark Satanic Mills?°

To Justify . . . Men See *Paradise Lost* I.26.
The Stolen . . . contemn See Milton's *Paradise Regained* IV.331–64, where Jesus sets the Hebrew Scriptures over Greek literature, asserting "that rather Greece from us these Arts derived; / Ill imitated."

dark Satanic Mills These are not industrial mills, but mills of the mind; see *Milton* 4:2–3, "where the Starry Mills of Satan / Are built beneath the Earth and Waters," hardly locations for industry.

Bring me my Bow of burning gold:
10   Bring me my Arrows of desire:
Bring me my Spear: O clouds unfold!
Bring me my Chariot of fire!°

I will not cease from Mental Fight,
Nor shall my Sword sleep in my hand:
Till we have built Jerusalem,
In Englands green & pleasant Land.

Would to God that all the Lords people were Prophets.°
                                        Numbers XI. ch 29 v.

PLATE 14
        [Milton's Descent°]
10 Then Milton rose up from the heavens of Albion ardorous!°
The whole Assembly wept prophetic, seeing in Miltons face
And in his lineaments divine the shades of Death & Ulro°
He took off the robe of the promise, & ungirded himself from the oath of God

And Milton said, I go to Eternal Death!° The Nations still
Follow after the detestable Gods of Priam;° in pomp
Of warlike selfhood, contradicting and blaspheming.
When will the Resurrection come; to deliver the sleeping body
From corruptibility: O when Lord Jesus wilt thou come?
Tarry no longer; for my soul lies at the gates of death.
20 I will arise and look forth for the morning of the grave.°
I will go down to the sepulcher to see if morning breaks!
I will go down to self annihilation and eternal death,
Lest the Last Judgment come & find me unannihilate
And I be siez'd & giv'n into the hands of my own Selfhood.
The Lamb of God is seen thro' mists & shadows, hov'ring
Over the sepulchers in clouds of Jehovah & winds of Elohim°
A disk of blood, distant; & heav'ns & earth's roll dark between
What do I here before the Judgment? without my Emanation?

Chariot of fire a reference to the vision of Milton in Thomas Gray's Pindaric ode "The Progress of Poesy"
Would . . . Prophets a reproof of Moses to Joshua, who urged the Lawgiver to silence "unauthorized" prophets
Milton's Descent These passages are all from Book I of the poem, the plate and line numbers being 14:10–17:20, 18:51–19:14, 20:7–21:14.
Then . . . ardorous Unhappy in his own Heaven, Milton has just heard the Bard's Song, which turns upon the imaginative realization that Pity and Love are part of the Human Abstract, and not of the Divine Vision. His poetic ardor reawakened, he is weary of an unimaginative heaven where he has nothing to do but walk about "pondring the intricate mazes of Providence," in parody of his own Fallen Angels. His rising up means that he has decided to go down from Eternity into time, not as a mere Mental Traveller, but as the prophet armed that he was in his heroic life.
Death and Ulro that is, he will descend into their world, giving up immortality and Eden
Eternal Death our life, from the perspective of Eternity
Gods of Priam Priam was king of Troy, father of Hector; in his "Descriptive Catalogue" Blake said of the "gods of Priam" that they were "destructive to humanity." Blake's Milton's reference here is to the invocation to Book IX of *Paradise Lost*, which attempts to change the theme of epic from warfare to heroic martyrdom. But the nations of Europe, England included, have failed to learn Milton's lesson.
I will . . . grave Milton renews the role of the disciples who watched at the sepulcher.
The Lamb . . . Elohim Neither clouds nor winds are anything but negative, natural emblems for Blake, and both serve here to obscure the Lamb of God.

With the daughters of memory, & not with the daughters of inspiration[?]°
30 I in my Selfhood am that Satan: I am that Evil One!
He is my Spectre! in my obedience to loose him from my Hells
To claim the Hells, my Furnaces,° I go to Eternal Death.
And Milton said. I go to Eternal Death! Eternity shudder'd
For he took the outside course, among the graves of the dead
A mournful shade. Eternity shudderd at the image of eternal death

Then on the verge of Beulah he beheld his own Shadow;
A mournful form double; hermaphroditic: male & female
In one wonderful body. and he enterd into it
In direful pain for the dread shadow, twenty-seven-fold°
40 Reachd to the depths of direst Hell, & thence to Albions land:
Which is this earth of vegetation on which now I write.

The Seven Angels of the Presence° wept over Miltons Shadow!

PLATE 15
As when a man dreams, he reflects not that his body sleeps,
Else he would wake; so seem'd he entering his Shadow: but
With him the Spirits of the Seven Angels of the Presence
Entering; they gave him still perceptions of his Sleeping Body;
Which now arose and walk'd with them in Eden, as an Eighth
Image Divine tho' darken'd; and tho walking as one walks
In sleep; and the Seven comforted and supported him.°

Like as a Polypus° that vegetates beneath the deep!
They saw his Shadow vegetated underneath the Couch
10 Of death: for when he enterd into his Shadow: Himself:
His real and immortal Self: was as appeard to those
Who dwell in immortality, as One sleeping on a couch
Of gold; and those in immortality gave forth their Emanations
Like Females of sweet beauty, to guard round him & to feed
His lips with food of Eden in his cold and dim repose!
But to himself he seemd a wanderer lost in dreary night.

Onwards his Shadow kept its course among the Spectres; call'd
Satan, but swift as lightning passing them, startled the shades

---

With . . . inspiration See this distinction in the Preface to the poem; it was implicit already in the boyish "To the Muses."
the Hells, my Furnaces The furnace is the creative mind, going back to Hebrew prophetic imagery, particularly Daniel 3:19–26; see also the remarkable "the furnace shall come up at last" in Christopher Smart's *Jubilate Agno;* Milton here undoes the "errors" of *Paradise Lost* and goes to reclaim his cast-out energies of desire.
twenty-seven-fold The shadow of the cycles of history; they moved in a lunar twenty-eight-phase sequence, called Churches by Blake, but the twenty-eighth is Apocalypse and so does not belong to the shadow.

The Seven . . . Presence Opposed to the spectral cycle of the Churches are the Seven Angels or Eyes of God, who impose prophetic order upon fallen history; they weep because Milton is re-entering the nightmare of history.
As when . . . supported him Though Milton goes down into illusion, his spiritual body joins the Seven Angels as an Eighth walker in Eden (thus associating Milton's self-sacrifice with that of Jesus) even as his material body sleep-walks first in Beulah and then in Generation.
Polypus Greek name for hydra or water snake; Ovidian emblem of materiality or natural existence

Of Hell beheld him in a trail of light as of a comet
20   That travels into Chaos:° so Milton went guarded within.

The nature of infinity is this: That every thing has its
Own Vortex;° and when once a traveller thro' Eternity
Has passd that Vortex, he percieves it roll backward behind
His path, into a globe itself infolding; like a sun:
Or like a moon, or like a universe of starry majesty,
While he keeps onwards in his wondrous journey on the earth
Or like a human form, a friend with whom he livd benevolent.
As the eye of man views both the east & west encompassing
Its vortex; and the north & south, with all their starry host;
30   Also the rising sun & setting moon he views surrounding
His corn-fields and his valleys of five hundred acres square.
Thus is the earth one infinite plane, and not as apparent
To the weak traveller confin'd beneath the moony shade.
Thus is the heaven a vortex passd already, and the earth
A vortex not yet pass'd by the traveller thro' Eternity.

First Milton saw Albion upon the Rock of Ages,°
Deadly pale outstretchd and snowy cold, storm coverd;
A Giant form of perfect beauty outstretchd on the rock
In solemn death: the Sea of Time & Space thunderd aloud
40   Against the rock, which was inwrapped with the weeds of death
Hovering over the cold bosom, in its vortex Milton bent down
To the bosom of death, what was underneath soon seemd above.°
A cloudy heaven mingled with stormy seas in loudest ruin;
But as a wintry globe descends precipitant thro' Beulah bursting,
With thunders loud, and terrible: so Miltons shadow fell,
Precipitant loud thundring into the Sea of Time & Space.

Then first I saw him in the Zenith as a falling star,
Descending perpendicular, swift as the swallow or swift;°
And on my left foot falling on the tarsus,° enterd there;
50   But from my left foot a black cloud° redounding spread over Europe.

Onwards . . . Chaos Coming down through
the Shadow, Milton seems to be a comet, ironically suggesting the fall of his own Satan.
The nature . . . Vortex A difficult and powerful conceptual image, probably a bitter parody
of the materialist theory of perception of Descartes. The vortex is the whirlpool or eddy of
unfallen consciousness. At its center is any object that unfallen consciousness sees and so creates. Since, in unfallen vision, center and circumference are one, the eternal perceiver is
simultaneously at the apex of his own vision,
and yet able to regard it from a distance. But
Milton, passing into Beulah, forsakes eternity for
time, and so becomes the apex of his own
vision. This objectifies him, and the eternal circumference of his vision rolls up behind him,
solidifying into the globed universe of Newto-
nian and Cartesian perception. But, even in
time, Milton retains his imagination, and can
achieve an approximation of eternal perception
by seeing the object world as human (l. 27)
and so encompass his vortex.

Rock of Ages not in Blake a reference to Matthew 16:18, but the rocky shore that is the
physical universe
Hovering . . . above Milton, emerging into
time and space, sees Man as a fallen giant,
Albion, and enters Albion's heart, again passing
through an apex of vision; he discovers that
fallen Urizen ("cloudy heaven") and fallen
Tharmas ("stormy seas") have usurped that
heart, excluding Orc and Los. The "vortex"
Milton has invaded rolls up behind him, forming a falling globe, again resembling the falling
Satan. Milton will enter Blake by the "left
foot," thus provisionally changing Blake's prophetic stance.
swift a bird outwardly resembling a swallow;
noted for quickness
tarsus The ankle: but there is a pun on Saul of
Tarsus, who became St. Paul.
black cloud Foster Damon identified this as
Puritanism.

Then Milton knew that the Three Heavens of Beulah° were beheld
By him on earth in his bright pilgrimage of sixty years

PLATE 16

PLATE 17
In those three females whom his Wives, & those three whom his Daughters°
Had represented and containd, that they might be resum'd
By giving up of Selfhood: & they distant view'd his journey
In their eternal spheres, now Human, tho' their Bodies remain clos'd
In the dark Ulro till the Judgment: also Milton knew: they and
Himself was Human, tho' now wandering thro Death's Vale
In conflict with those Female forms, which in blood & jealousy
Surrounded him, dividing & uniting without end or number.

He saw the Cruelties of Ulro, and he wrote them down
10 In iron tablets: and his Wives & Daughters names were these
Rahab and Tirzah, & Milcah & Malah & Noah & Hoglah.°
They sat rang'd round him as the rocks of Horeb round the land
Of Canaan:° and they wrote in thunder smoke and fire
His dictate; and his body was the Rock Sinai; that body,
Which was on earth born to corruption: & the six Females
Are Hor & Peor & Bashan & Abarim & Lebanon & Hermon
Seven rocky masses terrible in the Desarts of Midian.°

But Miltons Human Shadow continu'd journeying above
The rocky masses of The Mundane Shell;° in the Lands
20 Of Edom & Aram & Moab & Midian & Amalek.°

. . . .

PLATE 18
Urizen emerged from his Rocky Form & from his Snows,

PLATE 19
And he also darkend his brows: freezing dark rocks between
The footsteps. and infixing deep the feet in marble beds:
That Milton labourd with his journey, & his feet bled sore

Three . . . Beulah threefold or sexual vision, hence limited
In . . . Daughters Milton had three wives and three daughters; Blake accepted the bad tradition that Milton lived unhappily with all of them.
Rahab . . . Hoglah Rahab is chief of Milton's emanations; the other wives and daughters were the daughters of the sonless Zelophehad (Numbers 26:33) for whom Moses (reluctantly) legislated a separate female inheritance; Blake interprets this to mean that Milton yielded to his Female Will, with the destructive Rahab presiding over his five fallen senses.
They sat . . . Canaan This is an extraordinary vision of Milton (who by tradition dictated his major poems to his daughters) serving as the

Rock Sinai and dictating the Law to six lesser masses of rock; though this is austerely sublime, it is also satirical.
Hor . . . Midian These are all biblical mountains or high regions; in a burst of visionary geography, Blake places them in the Midian desert, thus associating Milton's errors with the symbolic desert-wanderings of Moses and of Christ in the Temptation.
Mundane Shell the fallen world, in its most illusory aspect, hence merely mundane and, even more merely, a shell
Edom . . . Amalek These are all lands that opposed the Israelites; Blake associates them with Urizen's Mundane Shell, the twenty-seven natural religions, each with its own absurd Heaven and demonic Hell.

Upon the clay now changd to marble; also Urizen rose,
And met him on the shores of Arnon;° & by the streams of the brooks

Silent they met, and silent strove among the streams, of Arnon
Even to Mahanaim,° when with cold hand Urizen stoop'd down
And took up water from the river Jordan: pouring on
To Miltons brain the icy fluid from his broad cold palm.°
10 But Milton took of the red clay of Succoth,° moulding it with care
Between his palms; and filling up the furrows of many years
Beginning at the feet of Urizen, and on the bones
Creating new flesh on the Demon cold, and building him,
As with new clay a Human form in the Valley of Beth Peor.°

. . .

PLATE 20

. . . Silent Milton stood before
The darkend Urizen; as the sculptor silent stands before
His forming image; he walks round it patient labouring.
10 Thus Milton stood forming bright Urizen, while his Mortal part
Sat frozen in the rock of Horeb: and his Redeemed portion,
Thus form'd the Clay of Urizen; but within that portion
His real Human walkd above in power and majesty
Tho darkend; and the Seven Angels of the Presence attended him.

O how can I with my gross tongue that cleaveth to the dust,
Tell of the Four-fold Man,° in starry numbers fitly orderd
Or how can I with my cold hand of clay! But thou O Lord
Do with me as thou wilt! for I am nothing, and vanity.
If thou chuse to elect a worm, it shall remove the mountains.
20 For that portion namd the Elect:° the Spectrous body of Milton:
Redounding from my left foot into Los's Mundane space,
Brooded over his Body in Horeb against the Resurrection
Preparing it for the Great Consummation;° red the Cherub° on Sinai
Glow'd; but in terrors folded round his clouds of blood.

Now Albions sleeping Humanity began to turn upon his Couch;
Feeling the electric flame of Miltons awful precipitate descent.

Arnon The Arnon river divides the trans-Jordan lands of Israel from Moab; in Numbers 21:14, the Arnon is associated with the Red Sea, and is therefore a River of Error; crossing it, or the Red Sea, is thus a movement from death to life, Moab to Canaan, Urizen to Luvah-Christ. Later in this poem (Plate 38) and in *Jerusalem* 89:25 the Arnon is identified with possessive natural love or the Selfhood's murderous jealousy, the two being the same for Blake. In this passage, Urizen fails to stop Milton by transforming the clay Adamic earth into purgatorial marble, and so Urizen is forced to wrestle Milton, even as Jehovah wrestled Jacob. But Milton is the New Israel, and instead of seeking Urizen's blessing, labors to remake Urizen-Jehovah, and so humanize him.

Mahanaim See Genesis 32:1–2; this is the place where Jacob meets the angels of God.
And took . . . palm a parody of baptism
Succoth See Kings 7:46 and Genesis 33:17.
Beth Peor the burial place of Moses; see Deuteronomy 34:6
Four-fold Man unfallen Albion, both Man and God
Elect Used sardonically; the Elect are the Angels or time-serving orthodox; the Reprobate are the Devils or imaginative rebels; the Redeemed are everyone else, and ironically their name means that they require redemption.
Great Consummation Apocalypse
Cherub the Covering Cherub, in Blake's symbolism the fallen Tharmas; see Genesis 3:24 and, more crucially, Ezekiel 28:14–16

Seest thou the little winged fly, smaller than a grain of sand?
It has a heart like thee; a brain open to heaven & hell,
Withinside wondrous & expansive; its gates are not clos'd,
30 I hope thine are not: hence it clothes itself in rich array;
Hence thou art cloth'd with human beauty O thou mortal man.
Seek not thy heavenly father then beyond the skies:
There Chaos dwells & ancient Night & Og & Anak° old:
For every human heart has gates of brass & bars of adamant,
Which few dare unbar because dread Og & Anak guard the gates
Terrific! and each mortal brain is walld and moated round
Within: and Og & Anak watch here; here is the Seat
Of Satan in its Webs; for in brain and heart and loins
Gates open behind Satans Seat to the City of Colgonooza°
40 Which is the spiritual fourfold London, in the loins of Albion.

Thus Milton fell thro Albions heart, travelling outside of Humanity
Beyond the Stars in Chaos in Caverns of the Mundane Shell.
But many of the Eternals rose up from eternal tables
Drunk with the Spirit, burning round the Couch of death they stood
Looking down into Beulah: wrathful, fill'd with rage!
They rend the heavens round the Watchers in a fiery circle:
And round the Shadowy Eighth: the Eight close up the Couch
Into a tabernacle, and flee with cries down to the Deeps:
Where Los opens his three wide gates, surrounded by raging fires!
50 They soon find their own place & join the Watchers of the Ulro.

Los saw them and a cold pale horror coverd o'er his limbs
Pondering he knew that Rintrah & Palamabron° might depart:
Even as Reuben & as Gad;° gave up himself to tears.
He sat down on his anvil-stock; and leand upon the trough.
Looking into the black water, mingling it with tears.

At last when desperation almost tore his heart in twain
He recollected an old Prophecy in Eden recorded,
And often sung to the loud harp at the immortal feasts
That Milton of the Land of Albion should up ascend
60 Forwards from Ulro from the Vale of Felpham; and set free
Orc from his Chain of Jealousy, he started at the thought

PLATE 21
And down descended into Udan-Adan;° it was night:
And Satan sat sleeping upon his Couch in Udan-Adan:
His Spectre slept, his Shadow woke; when one sleeps th'other wakes.

Og & Anak giants who opposed the Israelites; see Numbers 21:33 and Joshua 11:21
Golgonooza Blake's New Jerusalem of Art or, as he will call it, the "spiritual fourfold London"; very roughly akin to Spenser's Cleopolis, which, however, is an earthly city only
Rintrah & Palamabron sons of Los. Rintrah is the angry "Science of Wrath"; Palamabron the gentle "Science of Pity": both are, or should be, civilizing forces.
Reuben . . . Gad sons of Jacob; see Joshua 22: 9–34. This seems a later attempt by Blake to integrate *Milton* into the denser biblical symbolism of *Jerusalem*.
Udan-Adan world of illusive appearances

But Milton entering my Foot; I saw in the nether
Regions of the Imagination; also all men on Earth,
And all in Heaven, saw in the nether regions of the Imagination
In Ulro beneath Beulah, the vast breach of Miltons descent.
But I knew not that it was Milton, for man cannot know
What passes in his members till periods of Space & Time
10   Reveal the secrets of Eternity: for more extensive
Than any other earthly things, are Mans earthly lineaments.

And all this Vegetable World appeard on my left Foot,
As a bright sandal formd immortal of precious stones & gold:
I stooped down & bound it on to walk forward thro' Eternity.°

. . . .

PLATE 28
        [The World of Los]
But others of the Sons of Los build Moments & Minutes & Hours
And Days & Months & Years & Ages & Periods; wondrous buildings
And every Moment has a Couch of gold for soft repose,
    (A Moment equals a pulsation of the artery)°
And between every two Moments stands a Daughter of Beulah
To feed the Sleepers on their Couches with maternal care.
50   And every Minute has an azure Tent with Silken Veils.
And every Hour has a bright golden Gate carved with skill.
And every Day & Night, has Walls of brass & Gates of adamant,
Shining like precious stones & ornamented with appropriate signs:
And every Month, a silver paved Terrace builded high:
And every Year, invulnerable Barriers with high Towers.
And every Age is Moated deep with Bridges of silver & gold:
And every Seven Ages is Incircled with a Flaming Fire.
Now Seven Ages is amounting to Two Hundred Years
Each has its Guard. each Moment Minute Hour Day Month & Year.
60   All are the work of Fairy hands of the Four Elements
The Guard are Angels of Providence on duty evermore
Every Time less than a pulsation of the artery
Is equal in its period & value to Six Thousand Years.°

PLATE 29
For in this Period the Poets Work is Done: and all the Great
Events of Time start forth & are concievd in such a Period
Within a Moment: a Pulsation of the Artery.

The Sky is an immortal Tent built by the Sons of Los°
And every Space that a Man views around his dwelling-place:

I stooped . . . thro' Eternity a crucial moment,
for in it Blake and Milton become one poet
But others . . . artery Book I of *Milton* ends
with one of Blake's very rare positive (though
qualified) visions of Experience as being in its
best sense the creation of Los and his children;
this passage is a saving vision of time as the
mercy of Eternity *through* the poet's work,
which takes place *in* time, but in its smallest
indivisible unity—the pulsation of an artery.
Six Thousand Years Blake's notion of the historical span between Creation and Apocalypse
The Sky . . . Los The sky is a tent just as
the Israelites moved their tents in their God-
directed wanderings back to their own land.
We move our sky as our divine imagination de-

Standing on his own roof, or in his garden on a mount
Of twenty-five cubits° in height, such space is his Universe;
And on its verge the Sun rises & sets. the Clouds bow
To meet the flat Earth & the Sea in such an orderd Space:
10   The Starry heavens reach no further but here bend and set
On all sides & the two Poles turn on their valves of gold:
And if he move his dwelling-place, his heavens also move.
Wher'eer he goes & all his neighbourhood bewail his loss:
Such are the Spaces called Earth & such its dimension:
As to that false appearance which appears to the reasoner,
As of a Globe rolling thro Voidness, it is a delusion of Ulro
The Microscope knows not of this nor the Telescope. they alter
The ratio of the Spectators Organs but leave Objects untouchd
For every Space larger than a red Globule of Mans blood.
20   Is visionary: and is created by the Hammer of Los
And every Space smaller than a Globule of Mans blood. opens
Into Eternity of which this vegetable Earth is but a shadow:
The red Globule is the unwearied Sun by Los created
To measure Time and Space to mortal Men every morning.

.   .   .

The Vision of Beulah

This opens Book II of *Milton* and is Blake's most extensive single account of what
he called "lower paradise," organized Innocence, the sexual state at its most favorable,
and his culmination of pastoral convention. Blake's prime sources for his Beulah were
Isaiah and John Bunyan. Isaiah 62:4 reads:

> Thou shalt no more be termed Forsaken; neither shall thy land any more
> be termed Desolate; but thou shalt be called Hephzibah, and thy land
> Beulah; for the Lord delighteth in thee, and thy land shall be married.

Bunyan's *The Pilgrim's Progress* reads (with reference to the Song of Solomon 2:10–12,
as well as to Isaiah 62:4–12):

> Now I saw in my Dream, that by this time the Pilgrims were got over the
> Inchanted Ground, and entering into the Country of *Beulah*, whose Air was
> very sweet and pleasant, the way lying directly through it, they solaced them-
> selves there for a season. . . . Here they were within sight of the City they
> were going to. . . . For in this Land the shining Ones commonly walked,
> because it was upon the Borders of Heaven. In this Land also the contract
> between the Bride and the Bridegroom was renewed. . . .

---

sires, and see as we create. Each loss of a
human being literally diminishes the heavens,
for all empirical observation is a delusion or an
ultimate error, since space as well as time is
visionary (*not* subjective). The only irreducibles
are the Minute Particulars, the red globule of
human blood that is true space, and the pulsation's artery that is true time. To go beyond
these, or to reduce them, we would need to open
into Eternity, beyond space and time. Finally,
the Minute Particulars themselves are the creations of Los, invisible suns within us giving out
the pure flame that is life.

cubits A cubit was 18 to 22 inches; 25 cubits
comes to about 40 feet, evidently about as high
a merely natural aggregate as Blake was willing
to tolerate.

Book II of *Milton* centers on the self-purgations of Milton and Ololon, his composite Emanation, and their recovery of Innocence. It begins therefore in Beulah, as that state requires purgation from its own ambiguities. Beulah, for all its attractions, is relatively static, and represents the threefold sexual, and not the fourfold or wholly human. All contraries are equally true in it, and since progression is only by the strife of contraries, *human* existence is not possible in Beulah. In one of Blake's hardest paradoxes, taking us back to the early *Songs*, Beulah is both a higher and a lower state than Generation.

In this passage, Beulah is the loving Mother Nature, but only to its own proper dwellers, its unregenerated Daughters. To the Sons of Eden, like Milton, it can only be a rest.

PLATE 30

[The Vision of Beulah]
There is a place where Contrarieties are equally True
This place is called Beulah, It is a pleasant lovely Shadow
Where no dispute can come. Because of those who Sleep.
Into this place the Sons & Daughters of Ololon° descended
With solemn mourning, into Beulahs moony shades & hills
Weeping for Milton: mute wonder held the Daughters of Beulah
Enrapturd with affection sweet and mild benevolence

Beulah is evermore Created around Eternity; appearing
To the Inhabitants of Eden, around them on all sides.
10 But Beulah to its Inhabitants appears within each district
As the beloved infant in his mothers bosom round incircled
With arms of love & pity & sweet compassion. But to
The Sons of Eden the moony habitations of Beulah,
Are from Great Eternity a mild & pleasant Rest.

And it is thus Created. Lo the Eternal Great Humanity°
To whom be Glory & Dominion Evermore Amen
Walks among all his awful Family seen in every face
As the breath of the Almighty. such are the words of man to man
In the great Wars of Eternity, in fury of Poetic Inspiration,
20 To build the Universe stupendous: Mental forms Creating

But the Emanations trembled exceedingly, nor could they
Live, because the life of Man was too exceeding unbounded
His joy became terrible to them, they trembled & wept
Crying with one voice. Give us a habitation & a place
In which we may be hidden under the shadow of wings°
For if we who are but for a time, & who pass away in winter

Ololon Sometimes an individual, sometimes a host, she is the goal of Milton's quest, and ironically descends to seek him even as he descends after her, as evidently no one gets to meet a bride or husband of the imagination in Heaven (where the orthodox, after all, say there is no giving or taking in marriage); her name stems from a Greek word for the lamenting outcry of women to the gods (see the English "ululate").
the Eternal Great Humanity Blake's God
shadow of wings The reference is to the caduceus or winged staff of Hermes; see the commentary of George Sandys to his translation of Ovid's *Metamorphoses* II.

Behold these wonders of Eternity we shall consume
But you O our Fathers & Brothers, remain in Eternity
But grant us a Temporal Habitation. do you speak
30 To us; we will obey your words as you obey Jesus
The Eternal who is blessed for ever & ever. Amen

So spake the lovely Emanations; & there appeard a pleasant
Mild Shadow above: beneath: & on all sides round,

PLATE 31
Into this pleasant Shadow all the weak & weary
Like Women & Children were taken away as on wings
Of dovelike softness, & shadowy habitations prepared for them
But every Man returnd & went still going forward thro'
The Bosom of the Father in Eternity on Eternity
Neither did any lack or fall into Error without
A Shadow to repose in all the Days of Happy Eternity

Into this pleasant Shadow Beulah, all Ololon descended
And when the Daughters of Beulah heard the lamentation
10 All Beulah wept, for they saw the Lord coming in the Clouds.
And the Shadows of Beulah terminate in rocky Albion.
And all Nations wept in affliction Family by Family
Germany wept towards France & Italy: England wept & trembled
Towards America: India rose up from his golden bed:
As one awakend in the night: they saw the Lord coming
In the Clouds of Ololon with Power & Great Glory!

And all the Living Creatures of the Four Elements, wail'd
With bitter wailing: these in the aggregate are named Satan
And Rahab: they know not of Regeneration, but only of Generation
20 The Fairies, Nymphs, Gnomes & Genii of the Four Elements
Unforgiving & unalterable: these cannot be Regenerated
But must be Created, for they know only of Generation
These are the Gods of the Kingdoms of the Earth: in contrarious
And cruel opposition: Element against Element, opposed in War
Not Mental, as the Wars of Eternity, but a Corporeal Strife
In Los's Halls continual labouring in the Furnaces of Golgonooza
Orc howls on the Atlantic: Enitharmon trembles: All Beulah weeps

Thou hearest the Nightingale begin the Song of Spring;°
The Lark sitting upon his earthy bed: just as the morn
30 Appears; listens silent; then springing from the waving Corn-field! loud

Song of Spring This is an expression of the
glory of Beulah as seen from the standpoint of
Generation, for in Generation any song of Beulah must be a Song of Spring (like Solomon's
Song) just as in Eden the songs of Beulah
would mean Autumn, while a song of Generation would seem like Spring. Since the "Thou"
addressed in this lyric is generative man, ourselves, the poem's subtle beauty depends on the

paradox that a lamentation of Beulah sounds
to us, necessarily, as a Song of Spring. The
Daughters of Beulah (Blake's Muses, insofar
as he would tolerate them, but not very brilliant
girls) lament the descent of Ololon from Eden
through Beulah to Generation. But their tears
are spring rain to us, for to us any song of the
Earthly Paradise seems happy. Blake knew better.

He leads the Choir of Day! trill, trill, trill, trill,
Mounting upon the wings of light into the Great Expanse:
Reecchoing against the lovely blue & shining heavenly Shell:
His little throat labours with inspiration; every feather
On throat & breast & wings vibrates with the effluence Divine
All Nature listens silent to him & the awful Sun
Stands still upon the Mountain looking on this little Bird
With eyes of soft humility, & wonder love & awe.
Then loud from their green covert all the Birds begin their Song
40 The Thrush, the Linnet & the Goldfinch, Robin & the Wren
Awake the Sun from his sweet reverie upon the Mountain:
The Nightingale again assays his song, & thro the day,
And thro the night warbles luxuriant; every Bird of Song
Attending his loud harmony with admiration & love.
This is a Vision of the lamentation of Beulah over Ololon!

Thou percievest the Flowers put forth their precious Odours!
And none can tell how from so small a center comes such sweets
Forgetting that within that Center Eternity expands
Its ever during doors, that Og & Anak fiercely guard[.]
50 First eer the morning breaks joy opens in the flowery bosoms
Joy even to tears, which the Sun rising dries; first the Wild Thyme°
And Meadow-sweet downy & soft waving among the reeds.
Light springing on the air lead the sweet Dance: they wake
The Honeysuckle sleeping on the Oak: the flaunting beauty
Revels along upon the wind; the White-thorn lovely May
Opens her many lovely eyes: listening the Rose still sleeps
None dare to wake her. soon she bursts her crimson curtaind bed
And comes forth in the majestiy of beauty; every Flower:
The Pink, the Jessamine, the Wall-flower, the Carnation
60 The Jonquil, the mild Lilly opes her heavens! every Tree,
And Flower & Herb soon fill the air with an innumerable Dance
Yet all in order sweet & lovely, Men are sick with Love!
Such is a Vision of the lamentation of Beulah over Ololon

PLATE 40
[Milton's Declaration]
But turning toward Ololon in terrible majesty Milton
Replied.° Obey thou the Words of the Inspired Man
30 All that can be annihilated must be annihilated
That the Children of Jerusalem may be saved from slavery
There is a Negation, & there is a Contrary
The Negation must be destroyd to redeem the Contraries°

Wild Thyme one of Blake's transcendent puns
But . . . Replied This is the poem's great climax, and one of Blake's luminous triumphs of
prophetic oratory; Ololon has rejected, as a
true poet's loved creation should, natural religion
and the Female Will, thus compelling Rahab to

a negative epiphany as the Whore of Revelation; Milton approvingly replies, but urges her to
go farther as he now will in self-annihilation.
The Negation . . . Contraries Milton and
Ololon must war as creative Contraries in Eden,
but these will be the "wars of life."

The Negation is the Spectre; the Reasoning Power in Man
This is a false Body: an Incrustation over my Immortal
Spirit; a Selfhood, which must be put off & annihilated alway
To cleanse the Face of my Spirit by Self-examination.

PLATE 41
To bathe in the Waters of Life; to wash off the Not Human
I come in Self-annihilation & the grandeur of Inspiration
To cast off Rational Demonstration by Faith in the Saviour
To cast off the rotten rags of Memory by Inspiration
To cast off Bacon, Locke & Newton from Albions covering°
To take off his filthy garments, & clothe him with Imagination
To cast aside from Poetry, all that is not Inspiration
That it no longer shall dare to mock with the aspersion of Madness
Cast on the Inspired, by the tame high finisher of paltry Blots,
10 Indefinite, or paltry Rhymes; or paltry Harmonies.
Who creeps into State Government like a catterpiller to destroy
To cast off the idiot Questioner° who is always questioning,
But never capable of answering; who sits with a sly grin
Silent plotting when to question, like a thief in a cave;
Who publishes doubt & calls it knowledge; whose Science is Despair,
Whose pretence to knowledge is Envy, whose whole Science is
To destroy the wisdom of ages to gratify ravenous Envy;
That rages round him like a Wolf day & night without rest
He smiles with condescension; he talks of Benevolence & Virtue
20 And those who act with Benevolence & Virtue, they murder time on time
These are the destroyers of Jerusalem, these are the murderers
Of Jesus, who deny the Faith & mock at Eternal Life!
Who pretend to Poetry that they may destroy Imagination;
By imitation of Natures Images drawn from Remembrance
These are the Sexual Garments, the Abomination of Desolation°
Hiding the Human Lineaments as with an Ark & Curtains
Which Jesus rent:° & now shall wholly purge away with Fire
Till Generation is swallowd up in Regeneration.

·   ·   ·

1800–1809?   1809–10

To cast off . . . covering The imagery of removing false garments goes through the whole
poem; see Yeats's use of this in "Supernatural
Songs."
idiot Questioner the spectre within every man,
Blake included
Abomination of Desolation False or pagan god
placed in the Jerusalem Temple, prototype of
the Antichrist; here, the "Sexual Garments"
meaning what Blake called "Female Love,"
that is, merely natural or selfish, possessive love

as opposed to human love, which Ololon and
Milton now accept; again, this does *not* mean
they are to abandon sexual love-making, a common or vulgar error in much interpretation of
Blake.
Which Jesus rent The "Ark" and "Curtains"
refer to the Holy-of-Holies in the Jerusalem
Temple; Blake means that his Jesus came to
destroy all Mystery, all concealment, as his
heroic Milton has now done, and persuaded
Ololon to do also.

Jerusalem
The Emanation of the Giant Albion

Jerusalem is Blake's definitive poem, his most finished and profound work, but also his most difficult, in form and argument. The three brief excerpts that follow cannot represent it, but are given here because of their own unique values, even ripped from context, and to aid in the apprehension of other Blakean poems and extracts in this volume. The passages in Blake's plate and line numbering are 10:23–65, 45:2–42, 90:67–91:57.

Much of *Jerusalem* turns on a harsh internal conflict between Los-in-Blake and the Spectre of Urthona in Blake, defined as the despair of the imaginative man—and on his own terms he *is always right*. He is a reductionist, who insists always on knowing by knowing the worst, particularly concerning the self and its tribulations with others. His ancestry in Blake's work is complex, but fundamentally he began as a satire upon the poets of Sensibility, a satire all the more moving because it was self-satire, since Blake started as a Bard of Sensibility, and developed into the greatest poet of the group while growing well beyond it. Though we tend now (and rightly, I think) to read and study Blake in the company of other High Romantics, from Wordsworth to Yeats, he himself never lost his passion for William Cowper, who meant more to him than any English poet except Milton; and his deep affinities persisted also with Thomson, Collins, Gray, and Chatterton.

The Spectre of Urthona is not a satire on any particular poet (and certainly least of all on the beloved Cowper) but on a sinister tendency in all men, one to which poets at certain historical moments are peculiarly vulnerable. Yet a particular annotation by Blake is helpful in apprehending the Spectre of Urthona. Reading Spurzheim's *Observations on . . . Insanity*, some time after 1817, Blake jotted down a remarkable observation:

> Cowper came to me and said, o that I were insane always I will never rest. Can you not make me truly insane. I will never rest till I am so. O that in the bosom of God I was hid. You retain health and yet are as mad as any of us all—over us all—mad as a refuge from unbelief—from Bacon, Newton and Locke.

This covers a wide range of Blake's work in its reference, from the early "Mad Song" to the Spectre of Urthona in *Jerusalem*. For the Spectre of Urthona is the anxiety of the imagination itself, fearful that its words can never become deeds, and yet desiring only to continue in that fear. Hating his own separate existence, and yet sensing the danger (and excitation) of every threat that might end separation, the Spectre of Urthona is a personified Dread, and a menace to every one's continued imaginative functioning.

From Jerusalem
The Emanation of the Giant Albion

PLATE 10
[The Spectre of Urthona]
Shuddring the Spectre howls. his howlings terrify the night
He stamps around the Anvil, beating blows of stern despair
He curses Heaven & Earth, Day & Night & Sun & Moon
He curses Forest Spring & River, Desart & sandy Waste
Cities & Nations, Families & Peoples, Tongues & Laws
Driven to desperation by Los's terrors & threatning fears

Los cries, Obey my voice & never deviate from my will
30 And I will be merciful to thee: be thou invisible to all
To whom I make thee invisible, but chief to my own Children°
O Spectre of Urthona: Reason not against their dear approach
Nor them obstruct with thy temptations of doubt & despair[.]
O Shame O strong & mighty Shame I break thy brazen fetters
If thou refuse, thy present torments will seem southern breezes
To what thou shalt endure if thou obey not my great will.

The Spectre answer'd. Art thou not ashamd of those thy Sins
That thou callest thy Children? lo the Law of God commands
That they be offered upon his Altar: O cruelty & torment
40 For thine are also mine! I have kept silent hitherto,
Concerning my chief delight: but thou hast broken silence
Now I will speak my mind! Where is my lovely Enitharmon
O thou my enemy, where is my Great Sin? She is also thine
I said: now is my grief at worst: incapable of being
Surpassed: but every moment it accumulates more & more
It continues accumulating to eternity! the joys of God° advance
For he is Righteous: he is not a Being of Pity & Compassion
He cannot feel Distress: he feeds on Sacrifice & Offering:
Delighting in cries & tears & clothed in holiness & solitude
50 But my griefs advance also, for ever & ever without end
O that I could cease to be! Despair! I am Despair
Created to be the great example of horror & agony: also my
Prayer is vain I called for compassion: compassion mockd[,]
Mercy & pity threw the grave stone over me & with lead
And iron, bound it over me for ever: Life lives on my
Consuming: & the Almighty hath made me his Contrary°
To be all evil, all reversed & for ever dead: knowing

my own Children Los's creative acts, but the Spectre is willing to surrender them, as in relation to any making he is merely a passive instrument, a temporal will opposed to creation.
joys of God The Spectre's God is fallen Urizen, as the Spectre is the sickness unto death, in despair at the meaninglessness of his own repetitive existence, yet dreading to see it end; the Spectre attacks Los (and of course Blake) cunningly, where any imagination is most vulnerable, in its creative jealousy of its own emanations, its possessive love for what it has made.
his Contrary See Milton's Satan on Mt. Niphates, *Paradise Lost* IV.32–113; Spenser's Despair in *The Faerie Queene* I.ix is also in the background.

And seeing life, yet living not; how can I then behold
And not tremble; how can I be beheld & not abhorrd

60   So spoke the Spectre shuddring, & dark tears ran down his shadowy face
Which Los wiped off, but comfort none could give! or beam of hope
Yet ceasd he not from labouring at the roarings of his Forge
With iron & brass Building Golgonooza in great contendings
Till his Sons & Daughters came forth from the Furnaces
At the sublime Labours, for Los compelld the invisible Spectre

PLATE 45
            [The Minute Particulars]
Fearing that Albion should turn his back against the Divine Vision
Los took his globe of fire to search the interiors of Albions
Bosom,° in all the terrors of friendship, entering the caves
Of despair & death, to search the tempters out, walking among
Albions rocks & precipices! caves of solitude & dark despair,
And saw every Minute Particular° of Albion degraded & murderd
But saw not by whom; they were hidden within in the minute particulars
Of which they had possessd themselves; and there they take up
10   The articulations of a mans soul, and laughing throw it down
Into the frame, then knock it out upon the plank, & souls are bak'd
In bricks to build the pyramids of Heber & Terah.° But Los
Searchd in vain: closd from the minutia he walkd, difficult.
He came down from Highgate thro Hackney & Holloway towards London
Till he came to old Stratford & thence to Stepney & the Isle
Of Leuthas Dogs, thence thro the narrows of the Rivers side
And saw every minute particular, the jewels of Albion, running down
The kennels of the streets & lanes as if they were abhorrd.
Every Universal Form, was become barren mountains of Moral
20   Virtue:° and every Minute Particular hardend into grains of sand:
And all the tendernesses of the soul cast forth as filth & mire,
Among the winding places of deep contemplation intricate
To where the Tower of London frownd dreadful over Jerusalem:
A building of Luvah builded in Jerusalems eastern gate to be
His secluded Court: thence to Bethlehem where was builded
Dens of despair in the house of bread: enquiring in vain
Of stones and rocks he took his way, for human form was none:
And thus he spoke, looking on Albions City with many tears

Fearing . . . Bosom This introduces a central passage of the poem, as Los goes within Albion, questing for evidences of incorruptibility, in the prophetic faith that he can search out alien invaders within Albion.
Minute Particular The irreducible individualities that make up the human; the phrase occurs in Dr. Johnson's *Life of Waller*, which Blake had read.
Heber & Terah Terah was Abraham's father; Heber was Terah's ancestor, but the name is also that of the husband of Jael who, in the Song of Deborah, Judges 5, slays Sisera in his tent.

Blake's immensely grim point is that there are no alien invaders. The Minute Particulars are murdered by the Satanic Accusers who are intimate parts of every man, and these Accusers are like brickmakers who reduce our individual articulations into the sameness of bricks in the pyramid of bondage. Since Albion is Israel, Heber and Terah are his ancestors also, and Albion, like Sisera, is slain by the Female Will.
Every . . . Virtue a violent protest against the 18th century's proclivity for making moral generalizations

What shall I do! what could I do, if I could find these Criminals
30 I could not dare to take vengeance; for all things are so constructed
And builded by the Divine hand, that the sinner shall always escape,
And he who takes vengeance alone is the criminal of Providence;
If I should dare to lay my finger on a grain of sand
In way of vengeance; I punish the already punishd: O whom
Should I pity if I pity not the sinner who is gone astray!
O Albion, if thou takest vengeance; if thou revengest thy wrongs
Thou art for ever lost! What can I do to hinder the Sons
Of Albion from taking vengeance? or how shall I them perswade.
So spoke Los, travelling thro darkness & horrid solitude:
40 And he beheld Jerusalem in Westminster & Marybone,
Among the ruins of the Temple: and Vala who is her Shadow,
Jerusalems Shadow bent northward over the Island white.

·   ·   ·

PLATE 90
[The Declaration of Los]

67 But still the thunder of Los peals loud & thus the thunder's cry°
These beautiful Witchcrafts of Albion are gratifyd by Cruelty

PLATE 91
It is easier to forgive an Enemy than to forgive a Friend:
The man who permits you to injure him, deserves your vengeance:°
He also will recieve it; go Spectre! obey my most secret desire:
Which thou knowest without my speaking: Go to these Fiends of Righteousness
Tell them to obey their Humanities, & not pretend Holiness;
When they are murderers: as far as my Hammer & Anvil permit
Go, tell them that the Worship of God, is honouring his gifts
In other men: & loving the greatest men best, each according
To his Genius: which is the Holy Ghost in Man; there is no other
10 God, than that God who is the intellectual fountain of Humanity;°
He who envies or calumniates: which is murder & cruelty,
Murders the Holy-one: Go tell them this & overthrow their cup,
Their bread, their altar-table, their incense & their oath:
Their marriage & their baptism, their burial & consecration:°
I have tried to make friends by corporeal gifts but have only
Made enemies: I never made friends but by spiritual gifts;
By severe contentions of friendship & the burning fire of thought.°
He who would see the Divinity must see him in his Children
One first, in friendship & love; then a Divine Family, & in the midst
20 Jesus will appear; so he who wishes to see a Vision; a perfect Whole

But . . . cry This is the triumph of Los, akin
to Milton's great declaration on Plate 41 of that
poem; Milton's speech was addressed to Ololon
and overheard by Blake, but the speech of Los
is made to the Spectre of Urthona, and is the
utterance of a unified being who is also Blake.
It is . . . your vengeance undoubtedly a re-

flection on the relationship between Blake and
Hayley (see Headnote to *Milton*)
go, tell . . . Humanity This echoes the fifth
Memorable Fancy in *The Marriage*.
go tell . . . consecration an echo and expansion from Blake's Milton when he resolved
to descend
fire of thought Blake's vision of Eden

Must see it in its Minute Particulars;° Organized & not as thou
O Fiend of Righteousness pretendest; thine is a Disorganized
And snowy cloud: brooder of tempests & destructive War.
You smile with pomp & rigor: you talk of benevolence & virtue!
I act with benevolence & Virtue & get murderd time after time:
You accumulate Particulars, & murder by analyzing, that you
May take the aggregate; & you call the aggregate Moral Law:
And you call that Swelld & bloated Form; a Minute Particular.
But General Forms have their vitality in Particulars: & every
30   Particular is a Man; a Divine Member of the Divine Jesus.°

So Los cried at his Anvil in the horrible darkness weeping!°

The Spectre builded stupendous Works, taking the Starry Heavens
Like to a curtain & folding them according to his will
Repeating the Smaragdine Table of Hermes° to draw Los down
Into the Indefinite, refusing to believe without demonstration[.]
Los reads the Stars of Albion! the Spectre reads the Voids
Between the Stars; among the arches of Albions Tomb sublime
Rolling the Sea in rocky paths: forming Leviathan
And Behemoth: the War by Sea enormous & the War
40   By Land astounding: erecting pillars in the deepest Hell,
To reach the heavenly arches; Los beheld undaunted furious
His heavd Hammer; he swung it round & at one blow,
In unpitying ruin driving down the pyramids of pride°
Smiting the Spectre on his Anvil & the integuments° of his Eye
And Ear unbinding in dire pain, with many blows,
Of strict severity self-subduing, & with many tears labouring.

Then he sent forth the Spectre all his pyramids were grains
Of sand & his pillars: dust on the flys wing: & his starry
Heavens; a moth of gold & silver mocking his anxious grasp
50   Thus Los alterd his Spectre & every Ratio of his Reason
He alterd time after time, with dire pain & many tears
Till he had completely divided him into a separate space.°

He who . . . Particulars Both a moral and an aesthetic argument; to "organize" the Particulars is to attain vision; in the "aggregate" they disorganize into the Moral Law.
& every . . . Jesus The Minute Particulars, because they stand for human wholeness and integrity, stand also for Blake's Jesus.
So . . . weeping Though this speech is masterly and assured, its situation is terrible, as Los weeps in a darkness just preceding the advent of Apocalypse.
Smaragdine Table of Hermes The central text of occult tradition, clearly repudiated (and all occultism with it) by Blake-Los in this passage. "Smaragdine" means resembling an emerald or emerald-green in color, while Hermes here is the fictive Hermes Trismegistus ("thrice greatest"), supposedly an Ancient Egyptian authority, but the Table is actually a late medieval forgery with Hellenistic antecedents; the crucial part of this Table reads: "That which is above is as that which is below, and that which is below is as that which is above, to accomplish the one thing of all things most wonderful." Yeats cites the Table (or Tablet) approvingly in his "Supernatural Songs," but Blake dislikes it for the same reason Yeats approves it, that it states a correspondence between a suprasensual "above" and the sensual "below," a "below" Blake was determined to see burned up, and upon which he was not willing to build a model for Eternity. Here it is a magical spell of the Spectre to trap Los in nature, the "below," is rejected as another "rational" mode of demonstration, just another variety of natural religion.
the Spectre . . . pride The Spectre emulates the God of the Book of Job by confronting Los with emblems of the sanctified tyranny of nature over man, Leviathan and Behemoth; Los smashes them also with the hammer of his art.
integuments natural coverings
Thus . . . space The Spectre of Urthona is finally subdued by breaking up its desperate continuities, which are mostly temporal; by destroying its repetition-compulsiveness, as we might say.

Terrified Los sat to behold trembling & weeping & howling
I care not whether a Man is Good or Evil; all that I care
Is whether he is a Wise man or a Fool. Go! put off Holiness
And put on Intellect: or my thundrous Hammer shall drive thee
To wrath which thou condemnest: till thou obey my voice

                      ·   ·   ·

1804–15?   1815–20?

From The Gates of Paradise°

[Epilogue]

To The Accuser who is
The God of This World°

Truly My Satan thou art but a Dunce
And dost not know the Garment from the Man
Every Harlot was a Virgin once
Nor canst thou ever change Kate into Nan°

Tho thou art Worshipd by the Names Divine
Of Jesus & Jehovah: thou art still
The Son of Morn in weary Nights decline
The lost Travellers Dream under the Hill
1818?   1818?

From [A Vision of the Last Judgment]°

PAGE 70
     For the Year 1810
     Additions to Blake's Catalogue of Pictures &ᶜ

    The Last Judgment [will be] when all those are Cast away who trouble
Religion with Questions concerning Good & Evil or Eating of the Tree of
those Knowledges or Reasonings which hinder the Vision of God, turning all
into a Consuming Fire. When Imagination, Art & Science & all Intellectual Gifts,
all the Gifts of the Holy Ghost, are look'd upon as of no use & only Contention
remains to Man, then the Last Judgment begins, & its Vision is seen by the
Imaginative Eye of Every one according to the situation he holds.

PAGE 68
    The Last Judgment is not Fable or Allegory, but Vision. Fable or Allegory
are a totally distinct & inferior kind of Poetry. Vision or Imagination is a

---

The Gates of Paradise Blake engraved a little
emblem book with this title in 1793; perhaps as
late as 1818 he reissued it, with new text, including this confident "Epilogue."
To . . . World to Satan, in his role as God's
Accusing Angel of the Book of Job, and in his
power as the principle worshiped by the orthodox of this world under the names of Jesus and
Jehovah

Every . . . Nan Even the spouse of Blake's
Satan, Rahab the Harlot (the English state
church), was once a Virgin and will be so again;
Kate (Blake's wife's name) signifies wholesome-
ness and Nan whorishness.
[A Vision of the Last Judgment] a commentary
in the Notebook by Blake upon one of his
major paintings, now unfortunately lost

Representation of what Eternally Exists, Really & Unchangeably. Fable or Allegory is Form'd by the daughters of Memory. Imagination is surrounded by the daughters of Inspiration, who in the aggregate are call'd Jerusalem. Fable is Allegory, but what Critics call The Fable, is Vision itself. The Hebrew Bible & the Gospel of Jesus are not Allegory, but Eternal Vision or Imagination of All that Exists. Note here that Fable or Allegory is seldom without some Vision. Pilgrim's Progress is full of it, the Greek Poets the same; but Allegory & Vision ought to be known as Two Distinct Things, & so call'd for the Sake of Eternal Life. Plato has made Socrates say that Poets & Prophets do not know or Understand what they write or Utter; this is a most Pernicious Falshood. If they do not, pray is an inferior kind to be call'd Knowing? Plato confutes himself.°

PAGES 68–69

The Last Judgment is one of these Stupendous Visions. I have represented it as I saw it; to different People it appears differently as everything else does; for tho' on Earth things seem Permanent, they are less permanent than a Shadow, as we all know too well.

The Nature of Visionary Fancy, or Imagination, is very little Known, & the Eternal nature & permanence of its ever Existent Images is consider'd as less permanent than the things of Vegetative & Generative Nature; yet the Oak dies as well as the Lettuce, but Its Eternal Image & Individuality never dies, but renews by its seed; just so the Imaginative Image returns by the seed of Contemplative Thought; the Writings of the Prophets illustrate these conceptions of the Visionary Fancy by their various sublime & Divine Images as seen in the Worlds of Vision.

PAGES 71–72

. . . Let it here be Noted that the Greek Fables originated in Spiritual Mystery & Real Visions, which are lost & clouded in Fable & Allegory, while the Hebrew Bible & the Greek Gospel are Genuine, Preserv'd by the Saviour's Mercy. The Nature of my Work is Visionary or Imaginative; it is an Endeavour to Restore what the Ancients call'd the Golden Age.

PAGES 82–84

. . . If the Spectator could Enter into these Images in his Imagination, approaching them on the Fiery Chariot of his Contemplative Thought, if he could Enter into Noah's Rainbow or into his bosom, or could make a Friend & Companion of one of these Images of wonder, which always intreats him to leave mortal things (as he must know), then would he arise from his Grave, then would he meet the Lord in the Air & then he would be happy. General Knowledge is Remote Knowledge; it is in Particulars that Wisdom consists & Happiness too. Both in Art & in Life, General Masses are as Much Art as a Pasteboard Man is Human. Every Man has Eyes, Nose & Mouth; this Every Idiot knows, but he who enters into & discriminates most minutely the Manners & Intentions, the Characters in all their branches, is the alone Wise or Sensible Man, & on this discrimination All Art is founded. I intreat, then, that the Spectator will attend to the Hands & Feet, to the Lineaments of the

Plato confutes himself in the dialogue *Ion*

Countenances; they are all descriptive of Character, & not a line is drawn without intention, & that most discriminate & particular. As Poetry admits not a Letter that is Insignificant, so Painting admits not a Grain of Sand or a Blade of Grass Insignificant—much less an Insignificant Blur or Mark.

. . .

A Last Judgment is Necessary because Fools flourish. Nations Flourish under Wise Rulers & are depress'd under foolish Rulers; it is the same with Individuals as Nations; works of Art can only be produc'd in Perfection where the Man is either in Affluence or is Above the Care of it. Poverty is the Fool's Rod, which at last is turn'd on his own back; this is A Last Judgment—when Men of Real Art Govern & Pretenders Fall. Some People & not a few Artists have asserted that the Painter of this Picture would not have done so well if he had been properly Encourag'd. Let those who think so, reflect on the State of Nations under Poverty & their incapability of Art; tho' Art is Above Either, the Argument is better for Affluence than Poverty; & tho' he would not have been a greater Artist, yet he would have produc'd Greater works of Art in proportion to his means. A Last Judgment is not for the purpose of making Bad Men better, but for the Purpose of hindering them from opressing the Good with Poverty & Pain by means of Such Vile Arguments & Insinuations.

Around the Throne Heaven is open'd & the Nature of Eternal Things Display'd, All Springing from the Divine Humanity. All beams from him. He is the Bread & the Wine; he is the Water of Life; accordingly on Each Side of the opening Heaven appears an Apostle; that on the Right Represents Baptism, that on the Left Represents the Lord's Supper. All Life consists of these Two, Throwing off Error & Knaves from our company continually & Recieving Truth or Wise Men into our Company continually. He who is out of the Church & opposes it is no less an Agent of Religion than he who is in it; to be an Error & to be Cast out is a part of God's design. No man can Embrace True Art till he has Explor'd & cast out False Art (such is the Nature of Mortal Things), or he will be himself Cast out by those who have Already Embraced True Art. Thus My Picture is a History of Art & Science, the Foundation of Society, Which is Humanity itself. What are all the Gifts of the Spirit but Mental Gifts? Whenever any Individual Rejects Error & Embraces Truth, a Last Judgment passes upon that Individual.

PAGES 90–91

Here they are no longer talking of what is Good & Evil, or of what is Right or Wrong, & puzzling themselves in Satan's Labyrinth,° But are Conversing with Eternal Realities as they Exist in the Human Imagination. We are in a World of Generation & death, & this world we must cast off if we would be Painters such as Rafael, Mich. Angelo & the Ancient Sculptors; if we do not cast off his world we shall be only Venetian Painters, who will be cast off & Lost from Art.

PAGES 91–92

Many suppose that before the Creation All was Solitude & Chaos. This is the most pernicious Idea that can enter the Mind, as it takes away all sublimity from the Bible & Limits All Existence to Creation & to Chaos. To the Time &

Satan's Labyrinth See *Paradise Lost* II.561.

Space fixed by the Corporeal Vegetative Eye, & leaves the Man who entertains such an Idea the habitation of Unbelieving demons. Eternity Exists, and All things in Eternity, Independent of Creation which was an act of Mercy. I have represented those who are in Eternity by some in a Cloud within the Rainbow that Surrounds the Throne; they merely appear as in a Cloud when any thing of Creation, Redemption or Judgment are the Subjects of Contemplation, tho' their Whole Contemplation is concerning these things; the Reason they so appear is The Humiliation of the Reason & doubting Self-hood, & the Giving all up to Inspiration. By this it will be seen that I do not consider either the Just or the Wicked to be in a Supreme State, but to be every one of them States of the Sleep which the Soul may fall into in its deadly dreams of Good & Evil when it leaves Paradise following the Serpent.

PAGE 91

The Greeks represent Chronos or Time as a very Aged Man; this is Fable, but the Real Vision of Time is in Eternal Youth. I have, however, somewhat accomodated my Figure of Time to the common opinion, as I myself am also infected with it & my Visions also infected, & I see Time Aged, alas, too much so.

Allegories are things that Relate to Moral Virtues. Moral Virtues do not Exist; they are Allegories & dissimulations. But Time & Space are Real Beings, a Male & a Female. Time is a Man, Space is a Woman, & her Masculine Portion is Death.

PAGES 86, 90

The Combats of Good & Evil & of Truth & Error which are the same thing is Eating of the Tree of Knowledge. The Combats of Truth & Error is Eating of the Tree of Life; these are not only Universal, but Particular. Each are Personified. There is not an Error but it has a Man for its Agent, that is, it is a Man. There is not a Truth but it has also a Man. Good & Evil are Qualities in Every Man, whether a Good or Evil Man. These are Enemies & destroy one another by every Means in their power, both of deceit & of open Violence. The deist & the Christian are but the Results of these Opposing Natures. Many are deists who would in certain Circumstances have been Christians in outward appearance. Voltaire was one of this number; he was as intolerant as an Inquisitor. Manners make the Man, not Habits. It is the same in Art: by their Works ye shall know them; the Knave who is Converted to Deism & the Knave who is Converted to Christianity is still a Knave, but he himself will not know it, tho' Every body else does. Christ comes, as he came at first, to deliver those who were bound under the Knave, not to deliver the Knave. He Comes to deliver Man, the Accused, & not Satan, the Accuser. We do not find any where that Satan is Accused of Sin; he is only accused of Unbelief & thereby drawing Man into Sin that he may accuse him. Such is the Last Judgment—a deliverance from Satan's Accusation. Satan thinks that Sin is displeasing to God; he ought to know that Nothing is displeasing to God but Unbelief & Eating of the Tree of Knowledge of Good & Evil.

PAGE 87

Men are admitted into Heaven not because they have curbed & govern'd their Passions or have No Passions, but because they have Cultivated their Understandings. The Treasures of Heaven are not Negations of Passion, but

Realities of Intellect, from which all the Passions Emanate Uncurbed in their
Eternal Glory. The Fool shall not enter into Heaven let him be ever so Holy.
Holiness is not The Price of Enterance into Heaven. Those who are cast out
are All Those who, having no Passions of their own because No Intellect,
Have spent their lives in Curbing & Governing other People's by the Various
arts of Poverty & Cruelty of all kinds. Wo, Wo, Wo to you Hypocrites. Even
Murder, the Courts of Justice, more merciful than the Church, are compell'd
to allow is not done in Passion, but in Cool Blooded design & Intention.

The Modern Church Crucifies Christ with the Head Downwards.

PAGES 92–95

. . .

Thinking as I do that the Creator of this World is a very Cruel Being, &
being a Worshipper of Christ, I cannot help saying: 'the Son, O how unlike
the Father!' First God Almighty comes with a Thump on the Head. Then
Jesus Christ comes with a balm to heal it.

The Last Judgment is an Overwhelming of Bad Art & Science. Mental
Things are alone Real; what is call'd Corporeal, Nobody Knows of its Dwelling Place: it is in Fallacy, & its Existence an Imposture. Where is the Existence
Out of Mind or Thought? Where is it but in the Mind of a Fool? Some People
flatter themselves that there will be No Last Judgment & that Bad Art will be
adopted & mixed with Good Art, That Error or Experiment will make a Part
of Truth, & they Boast that it is its Foundation; these People flatter themselves: I will not Flatter them. Error is Created. Truth is Eternal. Error, or
Creation, will be Burned up, & then, & not till Then, Truth or Eternity will
appear. It is Burnt up the Moment Men cease to behold it. I assert for My
Self that I do not behold the outward Creation & that to me it is hindrance
& not Action; it is as the Dirt upon my feet, No part of Me. 'What,' it will
be Question'd, 'When the Sun rises, do you not see a round disk of fire somewhat like a Guinea?' O no, no, I see an Innumerable company of the Heavenly
host crying 'Holy, Holy, Holy is the Lord God Almighty.' I question not my
Corporeal or Vegetative Eye any more than I would Question a Window
concerning a Sight. I look thro' it & not with it.

[END OF A VISION OF THE LAST JUDGMENT]

1810   1810

From The Letters

To Dr. Trusler [1] 23 August 1799

Revd Sir,

I really am sorry that you are fall'n out with the Spiritual World, Especially
if I should have to answer for it. I feel very sorry that your Ideas & Mine on
Moral Painting differ so much as to have made you angry with my method
of Study. If I am wrong, I am wrong in good company. I had hoped your plan

---

1. John Trusler (1735–1820), an Enlightened
clergyman, wrote the words "Blake, dimmed with
Superstition," on the margin of this letter.

comprehended All Species of this Art, & Expecially that you would not regret that Species which gives Existence to Every other, namely, Visions of Eternity. You say that I want somebody to Elucidate my Ideas. But you ought to know that What is Grand is necessarily obscure to Weak men. That which can be made Explicit to the Idiot is not worth my care. The wisest of the Ancients consider'd what is not too Explicit as the fittest for Instruction, because it rouzes the faculties to act. I name Moses, Solomon, Esop, Homer, Plato.

But as you have favor'd me with your remarks on my Design, permit me in return to defend it against a mistaken one, which is, That I have supposed Malevolence without a Cause. Is not Merit in one a Cause of Envy in another, & Serenity & Happiness & Beauty a Cause of Malevolence? But Want of Money & the Distress of A Thief can never be alledged as the Cause of his Thieving, for many honest people endure greater hardships with Fortitude. We must therefore seek the Cause elsewhere than in want of Money, for that is the Miser's passion, not the Thief's.

I have therefore proved your Reasonings Ill proportion'd, which you can never prove my figures to be; they are those of Michael Angelo, Rafael & the Antique, & of the best living Models. I percieve that your Eye is perverted by Caricature Prints, which ought not to abound so much as they do. Fun I love, but too much Fun is of all things the most loathsome. Mirth is better than Fun, & Happiness is better than Mirth. I feel that a Man may be happy in This World. And I know that This World Is a World of imagination & Vision. I see Every thing I paint In This World, but Every body does not see alike. To the Eyes of a Miser a Guinea is more beautiful than the Sun, & a bag worn with the use of Money has more beautiful proportions than a Vine filled with Grapes. The tree which moves some to tears of joy is in the Eyes of others only a Green thing that stands in the way. Some See Nature all Ridicule & Deformity, & by these I shall not regulate my proportions; & Some Scarce see Nature at all. But to the Eyes of the Man of Imagination, Nature is Imagination itself. As a man is, So he Sees. As the Eye is formed, such are its Powers. You certainly Mistake, when you say that the Visions of Fancy are not to be found in This World. To Me This World is all One continued Vision of Fancy or Imagination, & I feel Flatter'd when I am told so. What is it sets Homer, Virgil & Milton in so high a rank of Art? Why is the Bible more Entertaining & Instructive than any other book? Is it not because they are addressed to the Imagination, which is Spiritual Sensation, & but mediately to the Understanding or Reason? Such is True Painting, and such was alone valued by the Greeks & the best modern Artists. Consider what Lord Bacon says: 'Sense sends over to Imagination before Reason have judged, & Reason sends over to Imagination before the Decree can be acted.' See Advancem^t of Learning, Part 2, P. 47 of first Edition.

But I am happy to find a Great Majority of Fellow Mortals who can Elucidate My Visions, & Particularly they have been Elucidated by Children, who have taken a greater delight in contemplating my Pictures than I even hoped. Neither Youth nor Childhood is Folly or Incapacity. Some Children are Fools & so are some Old Men. But There is a vast Majority on the side of Imagination or Spiritual Sensation.

To Engrave after another Painter is infinitely more laborious than to Engrave

one's own Inventions. And of the size you require my price has been Thirty
Guineas, & I cannot afford to do it for less. I had Twelve for the Head I sent you
as a Specimen; but after my own designs I could do at least Six times the quantity of labour in the same time, which will account for the difference of price
as also that Chalk Engraving is at least six times as laborious as Aqua tinta. I
have no objection to Engraving after another Artist. Engraving is the profession
I was apprenticed to, & should never have attempted to live by any thing else,
If orders had not come in for my Designs & Paintings, which I have the
pleasure to tell you are Increasing Every Day. Thus If I am a Painter it is not
to be attributed to Seeking after. But I am contented whether I live by Painting
or Engraving.

I am, Rev⁴ Sir, your very obedient servant,

William Blake

13 Hercules Buildings
Lambeth
August 23. 1799

To George Cumberland [1] 12 April 1827

Dear Cumberland,

I have been very near the Gates of Death & have returned very weak & an
Old Man feeble & tottering, but not in Spirit & Life, not in The Real Man The
Imagination which Liveth for Ever. In that I am stronger & stronger as this
Foolish Body decays. I thank you for the Pains you have taken with Poor Job.
I know too well that a great majority of Englishmen are fond of The Indefinite
which they Measure by Newton's Doctrine of the Fluxions of an Atom, A Thing
that does not Exist. These are Politicians & think that Republican Art is Inimical
to their Atom. For a Line or Lineament is not formed by Chance: a Line is a
Line in its Minutest Subdivisions: Strait or Crooked It is Itself & Not Intermeasurable with or by any Thing Else. Such is Job, but since the French Revolution Englishmen are all Intermeasurable One by Another, Certainly a happy
state of Agreement to which I for One do not Agree. God keep me from the
Divinity of Yes & No too, The Yea Nay Creeping Jesus, from supposing Up &
Down to be the same Thing as all Experimentalists must suppose.

You are desirous I know to dispose of some of my Works & to make them
Pleasin[g]. I am obliged to you & to all who do so. But having none remaining
of all that I had Printed I cannot Print more Except at a great loss, for at the
time I printed those things I had a whole House to range in: now I am shut up
in a Corner therefore am forced to ask a Price for them that I scarce expect to
get from a Stranger. I am now Printing a Set of the Songs of Innocence & Experience for a Friend at Ten Guineas which I cannot do under Six Months
consistent with my other Work, so that I have little hope of doing any more of
such things. The Last Work I produced is a Poem Entitled Jerusalem the
Emanation of the Giant Albion, but find that to Print it will Cost my Time the
amount of Twenty Guineas. One I have Finish'd. It contains 100 Plates but it
is not likely that I shall get a Customer for it.[2]

1. Writer on art and one of Blake's patrons.   2. This is the unique colored copy of *Jerusalem.*

As you wish me to send you a list with the Prices of these things they are as follows

	£	s	d
America	6.	6.	0
Europe	6.	6.	0
Visions &c	5.	5.	0
Thel	3.	3.	0
Songs of Inn. & Exp.	10.	10.	0
Urizen	6.	6.	0

The Little Card I will do as soon as Possible but when you Consider that I have been reduced to a Skeleton from which I am slowly recovering you will I hope have Patience with me.

Flaxman[3] is Gone & we must All soon follow, every one to his Own Eternal House, Leaving the Delusive Goddess Nature & her Laws to get into Freedom from all Law of the Members into The Mind, in which every one is King & Priest in his own House. God send it so on Earth as it is in Heaven.

I am, Dear Sir, Yours Affectionately

William Blake

12 April 1827
N 3 Fountain Court Strand

WILLIAM WORDSWORTH
1770–1850

Born near, and raised in, the English Lake District, Wordsworth was left alone with the visible world at an unnaturally early age. Though he had three brothers and a sister, Dorothy, to whom he was closer than ever he would be to anyone else, he still had to sustain the death of his mother when he was just eight, and of his father when he was thirteen. His "family romance" (as Freud would have called it) was primarily with the natural world, surpassingly beautiful in the Lake Country.

From 1787 to 1791 Wordsworth attended St. John's College, Cambridge, where he did nothing particularly remarkable. In the summer of 1790 he went on a walking tour of the Alps and France (see The Prelude VI) and observed France at the height of its revolutionary hopefulness, which he shared. He returned to France and lived there for a turbulent year (November 1791–December 1792), during which time he associated himself with the moderate faction of the Revolution, fell in love with Annette Vallon, and fathered their daughter, Caroline. Abandoning both mother and child, and his political friends, he returned to England, to spend five years troubled by guilt and remorse, not only about these near-betrayals, but concerning also his identity as Englishman and as poet. Though the continued presence of Dorothy (she never married) was an essential element in Wordsworth's recovery from this long crisis, the catalyst for his renovation was his best friend, Coleridge, whom he first met early in 1795. Coleridge gave Wordsworth rather more than he took, intellectually and poetically, but in return Wordsworth gave Coleridge something necessary out of his

3. John Flaxman, eminent sculptor and Blake's friend, had died a few months before.

own massive (though still turbulent) emotional strength. Later in 1795 a friend's legacy enabled Wordsworth to free himself from financial burdens. By 1797 Wordsworth had surmounted his crisis, and in the almost-daily company of Coleridge was able to begin upon his mature and characteristic work, first published (anonymously) in 1798 as *Lyrical Ballads, With a Few Other Poems.* The ballads included Coleridge's "The Ancient Mariner," and the other poems included "Tintern Abbey." Historically considered, this remains the most important volume of verse in English since the Renaissance, for it began modern poetry, the poetry of the growing inner self.

The birth of this self had preceded Wordsworth, and is located variously by different intellectual historians. It seems clear that the inner self was a Protestant creation, and that before Luther it was prefigured in Catholic thinkers as diverse as the furious reformer Savonarola and the meditative Thomas à Kempis, who wrote *The Imitation of Christ.* In Luther, though, the inner self achieves the kind of prominence that made a writer like Rousseau possible. As the inner self grew, landscape paradoxically began to enter European literature, for the inner self made landscape visible precisely through a devaluation of everything else that the self would not contain. The outer world moved more outward as the inner self grew more inward, until the estrangement between the two worlds produced the phenomenon of Rousseau's ecstatic nature worship. Confronting what had ceased to be a world in which he shared, Rousseau was moved by love and longing for what he had lost. The next and all-important step in poetry was taken by Wordsworth, who did for literature what Freud was to do for modern psychology, nearly a century later.

The immense burden of Wordsworth's poetry is the contradiction that he understood better than all his followers down to today: self-consciousness is essential for modern poetry, yet self-consciousness is the antagonist of poetry, the demon that needs to be exorcised. Before Wordsworth, poetry had a subject. After Wordsworth, its prevalent subject was the poet's own subjectivity. Before Wordsworth, any poet, professional or amateur, would in some sense *choose a subject* in order to write a poem. After Wordsworth, this is no longer true, and so a new poetry was born.

Hazlitt, in some ways a more acute critic of Wordsworth than Coleridge (because much more detached), reviewed *The Excursion* in 1814, and said of its poet: "He sees all things in himself," and added that his mind was "conversant only with itself and nature." Lecturing on the "living poets" in 1818, Hazlitt emphasized Wordsworth's astonishing originality, and simply observed that the poet "is his own subject." Rightly associating Wordsworth's poetical revolution with the French Revolution, Hazlitt nevertheless added the stern warning that a poet of Wordsworth's school necessarily manifested an "egotism [that] is in some respects a madness." Yet Wordsworth knew this better than Hazlitt did, as "Resolution and Independence" and *The Prelude* show.

What was Wordsworth's "healing power"? How does his best poetry work so as to save not only the poet himself in his own crises, but so as to have been therapeutic for the imagination of so many poets and readers since? Five generations have passed since Wordsworth experienced his Great Decade (1797–1807), and still the attentive and dedicated reader can learn to find in him the human art he teaches better than any poet before or since, including precursors greater than himself (but no successors as yet, of his eminence). The art is simply what Keats, Shelley, Arnold, Emerson, and others called it: *how to feel.* Wordsworth, by a primordial power uncanny in its depths, educates the affective life of his reader. He teaches precisely what he knew he could teach: how to become, within severe limitations, a renovated spirit, free of crippling self-consciousness yet still enjoying the varied gifts of an awakened consciousness. He proposes to observe nature with an eye steadily on the object, and yet not to lose his freedom to the tyranny of the eye, while also preserving the integrity of nature from our profane tendency to practice analysis upon it.

This is the primary Wordsworth of whom Matthew Arnold was the classical critic, the poet "Of blessed consolations in distress, / Of moral strength and intellectual powers, / Of joy in widest commonalty spread—." Arnold superbly located Wordsworth's healing effect in *power*, "the extraordinary power with which Wordsworth feels the joy offered to us in nature, the joy offered to us in the simple primary affections and duties . . . and renders it so as to make us share it." Like Tolstoy at his finest, like the great sages of Judaic and some aspects of Christian tradition, this Wordsworth hallows the commonplace, celebrates the common, human heart by which we live, and the nature that cares for and refreshes that heart.

But there is another Wordsworth, and he is a great poet also, but more problematic and far less heartening. Arnold turned away from the Miltonic, strong, sublime, non-Coleridgean side of Wordsworth, as the critic A. C. Bradley first demonstrated early in the twentieth century. Recent critics have followed Bradley in exploring Wordsworth's uneasiness with nature, his dark sense that nature was a hidden antagonist to the full, Miltonic development of his own imagination. The hidden story of The *Prelude* and of the great crisis poems of 1802 (e.g. "Resolution and Independence" and the "Intimations" ode) is largely concerned with this struggle, and the inability to resolve this conflict between questing self and adherence to nature may be the clue to Wordsworth's rapid, indeed catastrophic decline after 1807, at the very latest.

Certainly the facts of Wordsworth's own mature biography do little to explain his poetic decay. He settled, with Dorothy, late in 1799 at Grasmere, not far from the beloved scenes of his boyhood. Coleridge settled nearby. Wordsworth married, happily, in 1802, but sorrows began to shadow him. His closest brother, John, drowned in 1805; the friendship with the increasingly unhappy Coleridge began to fade, and largely ended in a dreadful quarrel in 1810. Two of his children died in 1812, and the fear of his own mortality, always strong in him, necessarily augmented. He became outwardly well-off, politically a champion of the established order, and eminently orthodox in the Church of England. He iced over.

But the astonishing poems remained, and cannot die. In them, more than any other in the language before or since, we find ourselves, and this "we" is very nearly universal. The great poems do not champion any cause or urge any vision but one: to know ourselves, sincerely, in our own origins and in what we still are. The hiding places of every person's power, Wordsworth insisted, are in his own past, however painful that past might have been. To live life, and not death-in-life, Wordsworth gently but forcefully advises us to find the natural continuities between what we were and what we are. If he himself never quite became what he might have been, that does not matter. Though he himself could not sustain even the strength he attained, that also does not matter. What matters is that his poetry found a way of showing how much a natural man might do for himself, by the hard discipline of holding himself open both to imagination and to nature.

Lines Written in Early Spring

I heard a thousand blended notes,
While in a grove I sate reclined,
In that sweet mood when pleasant thoughts
Bring sad thoughts to the mind.

To her fair works did Nature link
The human soul that through me ran;
And much it grieved my heart to think
What man has made of man.

Through primrose tufts, in that green bower,
The periwinkle trailed its wreaths;
And 'tis my faith that every flower
Enjoys the air it breathes.

The birds around me hopped and played,
Their thoughts I cannot measure—
But the least motion which they made,
It seemed a thrill of pleasure.

The budding twigs spread out their fan,
To catch the breezy air;
And I must think, do all I can,
That there was pleasure there.

If this belief from heaven be sent,
If such be Nature's holy plan,
Have I not reason to lament
What man has made of man?
1798   1798

Expostulation and Reply

'Why, William, on that old grey stone,
Thus for the length of half a day,
Why, William, sit you thus alone,
And dream your time away?

'Where are your books?—that light bequeathed
To Beings else forlorn and blind!
Up! up! and drink the spirit breathed
From dead men to their kind.

'You look round on your Mother Earth,
As if she for no purpose bore you;
As if you were her first-born birth,
And none had lived before you!'

One morning thus, by Esthwaite lake,
When life was sweet, I knew not why,
To me my good friend Matthew spake,
And thus I made reply:

'The eye—it cannot choose but see;
We cannot bid the ear be still;
Our bodies feel, where'er they be,
20 Against or with our will.

'Nor less I deem that there are Powers
Which of themselves our minds impress;
That we can feed this mind of ours
In a wise passiveness.

'Think you, 'mid all this mighty sum
Of things for ever speaking,
That nothing of itself will come,
But we must still be seeking?

'—Then ask not wherefore, here, alone,
30 Conversing as I may,
I sit upon this old grey stone,
And dream my time away.'
1798   1798

The Tables Turned

An Evening Scene on the Same Subject

Up! up! my Friend, and quit your books;
Or surely you'll grow double:
Up! up! my Friend, and clear your looks;
Why all this toil and trouble?

The sun, above the mountain's head,
A freshening lustre mellow
Through all the long green fields has spread,
His first sweet evening yellow.

Books! 'tis a dull and endless strife:
10 Come, hear the woodland linnet,
How sweet his music! on my life,
There's more of wisdom in it.

And hark! how blithe the throstle sings!
He, too, is no mean preacher:
Come forth into the light of things,
Let Nature be your Teacher.

She has a world of ready wealth,
Our minds and hearts to bless—
Spontaneous wisdom breathed by health,
20   Truth breathed by cheerfulness.

One impulse from a vernal wood
May teach you more of man,
Of moral evil and of good,
Than all the sages can.

Sweet is the lore which Nature brings;
Our meddling intellect
Mis-shapes the beauteous forms of things:—
We murder to dissect.

Enough of Science and of Art;
30   Close up those barren leaves;
Come forth, and bring with you a heart
That watches and receives.
1798   1798

To My Sister

It is the first mild day of March:
Each minute sweeter than before,
The redbreast sings from the tall larch
That stands beside our door.

There is a blessing in the air,
Which seems a sense of joy to yield
To the bare trees, and mountains bare,
And grass in the green field.

My Sister! ('tis a wish of mine)
10   Now that our morning meal is done,
Make haste, your morning task resign;
Come forth and feel the sun.

Edward will come with you—and, pray,
Put on with speed your woodland dress,
And bring no book; for this one day
We'll give to idleness.

No joyless forms shall regulate
Our living calendar;
We from today, my Friend, will date
20   The opening of the year.

Love, now a universal birth,
From heart to heart is stealing;

From earth to man, from man to earth:
—It is the hour of feeling.

One moment now may give us more
Than years of toiling reason;
Our minds shall drink at every pore
The spirit of the season.

Some silent laws our hearts will make,
30   Which they shall long obey;
We for the year to come may take
Our temper from today.

And from the blessed power that rolls
About, below, above,
We'll frame the measure of our souls:
They shall be tuned to love.

Then come, my Sister! come, I pray,
With speed put on your woodland dress;
And bring no book: for this one day
40   We'll give to idleness.
1798   1798

The Ruined Cottage

The Tale of Margaret, first published belatedly as Book I of *The Excursion*, exists in
several different versions. This one, transcribed by Jonathan Wordsworth in his book
The Music of Humanity (1968), is by common scholarly agreement now considered the
most effective.

Though the simplicity of Margaret's story is crucial, it is important to note that she is
destroyed by excess of hope, and not of sorrow. She stands for something dangerous
and poignant in Wordsworth's consciousness, for a preternatural strength of hope that
can destroy what is most necessary for continued existence, our ability to come to
terms with human loss.

The Ruined Cottage

First Part
'Twas Summer and the sun was mounted high.
Along the south the uplands feebly glared
Through a pale steam, and all the northern downs,
In clearer air ascending, showed far off
Their surfaces with shadows dappled o'er
Of deep embattled clouds. Far as the sight
Could reach those many shadows lay in spots
Determined and unmoved, with steady beams

Of clear and pleasant sunshine interposed—
10 Pleasant to him who on the soft cool grass
Extends his careless limbs beside the root
Of some huge oak whose agèd branches make
A twilight of their own, a dewy shade
Where the wren warbles while the dreaming man,
Half conscious of that soothing melody,
With sidelong eye looks out upon the scene,
By those impending branches made more soft,
More soft and distant.

              Other lot was mine.
Across a bare wide Common I had toiled
20 With languid feet which by the slippery ground
Were baffled still, and when I stretched myself
On the brown earth my limbs from very heat
Could find no rest, nor my weak arm disperse
The insect host which gathered round my face
And joined their murmurs to the tedious noise
Of seeds of bursting gorse that crackled round.
I rose and turned towards a group of trees
Which midway in that level stood alone;
And thither come at length, beneath a shade
30 Of clustering elms that sprang from the same root
I found a ruined house, four naked walls
That stared upon each other. I looked round
And near the door I saw an agèd Man,
Alone and stretched upon the cottage bench,
An iron-pointed staff lay at his side.
With instantaneous joy I recognized
That pride of nature and of lowly life,
The venerable *Armytage,* a friend
As dear to me as is the setting sun.

40   Two days before
We had been fellow travellers. I knew
That he was in this neighbourhood, and now
Delighted found him here in the cool shade.
He lay, his pack of rustic merchandise
Pillowing his head. I guess he had no thought
Of his way-wandering life. His eyes were shut,
The shadows of the breezy elms above
Dappled his face. With thirsty heat oppressed
At length I hailed him, glad to see his hat
50 Bedewed with waterdrops, as if the brim
Had newly scooped a running stream. He rose
And pointing to a sunflower, bade me climb
The [   ] wall where that same gaudy flower
Looked out upon the road.

                    It was a plot
Of garden ground now wild, its matted weeds
Marked with the steps of those whom as they passed,
The gooseberry trees that shot in long lank slips,
Or currants hanging from their leafless stems
In scanty strings, had tempted to o'erleap
60   The broken wall. Within that cheerless spot,
Where two tall hedgerows of thick alder boughs
Joined in a damp cold nook, I found a well
Half covered up with willow flowers and grass.
I slaked my thirst and to the shady bench
Returned, and while I stood unbonneted
To catch the motion of the cooler air,
The old Man said, 'I see around me here
Things which you cannot see. We die, my Friend,
Nor we alone, but that which each man loved
70   And prized in his peculiar nook of earth
Dies with him, or is changed, and very soon
Even of the good is no memorial left.
The Poets, in their elegies and songs
Lamenting the departed, call the groves,
They call upon the hills and streams to mourn,
And senseless rocks—nor idly, for they speak
In these their invocations with a voice
Obedient to the strong creative power
Of human passion. Sympathies there are
80   More tranquil, yet perhaps of kindred birth,
That steal upon the meditative mind
And grow with thought. Beside yon spring I stood,
And eyed its waters till we seemed to feel
One sadness, they and I. For them a bond
Of brotherhood is broken; time has been
When every day the touch of human hand
Disturbed their stillness, and they ministered
To human comfort. When I stopped to drink
A spider's web hung to the water's edge,
90   And on the wet and slimy footstone lay
The useless fragment of a wooden bowl.
It moved my very heart.

                    'The day has been
When I could never pass this road but she
Who lived within these walls, when I appeared,
A daughter's welcome gave me, and I loved her
As my own child. Oh Sir, the good die first,
And they whose hearts are dry as summer dust
Burn to the socket. Many a passenger
Has blessed poor Margaret for her gentle looks

100 When she upheld the cool refreshment drawn
From that forsaken spring, and no one came
But he was welcome, no one went away
But that it seemed she loved him. She is dead,
The worm is on her cheek, and this poor hut,
Stripped of its outward garb of household flowers,
Of rose and sweetbriar, offers to the wind
A cold bare wall whose earthy top is tricked
With weeds and the rank spear grass. She is dead,
And nettles rot and adders sun themselves
110 Where we have sate together while she nursed
Her infant at her breast. The unshod colt,
The wandring heifer and the Potter's ass,
Find shelter now within the chimney wall
Where I have seen her evening hearthstone blaze
And through the window spread upon the road
Its cheerful light. You will forgive me, sir,
But often on this cottage do I muse
As on a picture, till my wiser mind
Sinks, yielding to the foolishness of grief.

120 'She had a husband, an industrious man,
Sober and steady. I have heard her say
That he was up and busy at his loom
In summer ere the mower's scythe had swept
The dewy grass, and in the early spring
Ere the last star had vanished. They who passed
At evening, from behind the garden fence
Might hear his busy spade, which he would ply
After his daily work till the daylight
Was gone, and every leaf and flower were lost
130 In the dark hedges. So they passed their days
In peace and comfort, and two pretty babes
Were their best hope next to the God in Heaven.

'You may remember, now some ten years gone,
Two blighting seasons when the fields were left
With half a harvest. It pleased heaven to add
A worse affliction in the plague of war,
A happy land was stricken to the heart,
'Twas a sad time of sorrow and distress.
A wanderer among the cottages,
140 I with my pack of winter raiment saw
The hardships of that season. Many rich
Sunk down as in a dream among the poor,
And of the poor did many cease to be,
And their place knew them not. Meanwhile, abridged
Of daily comforts, gladly reconciled
To numerous self-denials, Margaret

Went struggling on through those calamitous years
With cheerful hope. But ere the second autumn
A fever seized her husband. In disease
150   He lingered long, and when his strength returned
He found the little he had stored to meet
The hour of accident, or crippling age,
Was all consumed. As I have said, 'twas now
A time of trouble: shoals of artisans
Were from their daily labour turned away
To hang for bread on parish charity,
They and their wives and children, happier far
Could they have lived as do the little birds
That peck along the hedges, or the kite
160   That makes her dwelling in the mountain rocks.

'Ill fared it now with Robert, he who dwelt
In this poor cottage. At his door he stood
And whistled many a snatch of merry tunes
That had no mirth in them, or with his knife
Carved uncouth figures on the heads of sticks.
Then idly sought about through every nook
Of house or garden any casual task
Of use or ornament, and with a strange
Amusing but uneasy novelty
170   He blended where he might the various tasks
Of summer, autumn, winter, and of spring.
But this endured not, his good humour soon
Became a weight in which no pleasure was,
And poverty brought on a petted mood
And a sore temper. Day by day he drooped.
And he would leave his home, and to the town
Without an errand would he turn his steps,
Or wander here and there among the fields.
One while he would speak lightly of his babes
180   And with a cruel tongue, at other times
He played with them wild freaks of merriment.
And 'twas a piteous thing to see the looks
Of the poor innocent children. "Every smile,"
Said Margaret to me here beneath these trees,
"Made my heart bleed." '

                    At this the old Man paused
And looking up to those enormous elms
He said, ' 'Tis now the hour of deepest noon.
At this still season of repose and peace,
This hour when all things which are not at rest
190   Are cheerful, while this multitude of flies
Fills all the air with happy melody,

Why should a tear be in an old man's eye?
Why should we thus with an untoward mind,
And in the weakness of humanity,
From natural wisdom turn our hearts away.
To natural comfort shut our eyes and ears.
And, feeding on disquiet, thus disturb
The calm of Nature with our restless thoughts?'
    END OF THE FIRST PART

    Second Part
He spake with somewhat of a solemn tone,
But when he ended there was in his face
Such easy cheerfulness, a look so mild,
That for a little time it stole away
All recollection, and that simple tale
Passed from my mind like a forgotten sound.
A while on trivial things we held discourse
To me soon tasteless. In my own despite
I thought of that poor woman as of one
Whom I had known and loved. He had rehearsed
Her homely tale with such familiar power,
With such an active countenance, an eye
So busy, that the things of which he spake
Seemed present, and, attention now relaxed,
There was a heartfelt chillness in my veins.
I rose, and turning from that breezy shade
Went out into the open air, and stood
To drink the comfort of the warmer sun.
Long time I had not stayed ere, looking round
Upon that tranquil ruin, I returned
And begged of the old man that for my sake
He would resume his story.

                            He replied,
'It were a wantonness, and would demand
Severe reproof, if we were men whose hearts
Could hold vain dalliance with the misery
Even of the dead, contented thence to draw
A momentary pleasure, never marked
By reason, barren of all future good.
But we have known that there is often found
In mournful thoughts, and always might be found,
A power to virtue friendly; were't not so
I am a dreamer among men, indeed
An idle dreamer. 'Tis a common tale
By moving accidents uncharactered,
A tale of silent suffering, hardly clothed
In bodily form, and to the grosser sense

But ill adapted, scarcely palpable
To him who does not think. But at your bidding
I will proceed.

          'While thus it fared with them
To whom this cottage till that hapless year
Had been a blessed home, it was my chance
240   To travel in a country far remote;
And glad I was when, halting by yon gate
That leads from the green lane, again I saw
These lofty elm trees. Long I did not rest:
With many pleasant thoughts I cheered my way
O'er the flat common. At the door arrived,
I knocked, and when I entered, with the hope
Of usual greeting, Margaret looked at me
A little while, then turned her head away
Speechless, and sitting down upon a chair
250   Wept bitterly. I wist not what to do,
Or how to speak to her. Poor wretch, at last
She rose from off her seat, and then, oh Sir,
I cannot tell how she pronounced my name.
With fervent love, and with a face of grief
Unutterably helpless, and a look
That seemed to cling upon me, she enquired
If I had seen her husband. As she spake
A strange surprise and fear came to my heart,
Nor had I power to answer ere she told
260   That he had disappeared—just two months gone.
He left his house: two wretched days had passed,
And on the third by the first break of light,
Within her casement full in view she saw
A purse of gold. "I trembled at the sight,"
Said Margaret, "for I knew it was his hand
That placed it there. And on that very day
By one, a stranger, from my husband sent,
The tidings came that he had joined a troop
Of soldiers going to a distant land.
270   He left me thus. Poor Man, he had not heart
To take farewell of me, and he feared
That I should follow with my babes, and sink
Beneath the misery of a soldier's life."

'This tale did Margaret tell with many tears,
And when she ended I had little power
To give her comfort, and was glad to take
Such words of hope from her own mouth as served
To cheer us both. But long we had not talked
Ere we built up a pile of better thoughts,
280   And with a brighter eye she looked around,

As if she had been shedding tears of joy.
We parted. It was then the early spring:
I left her busy with her garden tools,
And well remember, o'er that fence she looked,
And, while I paced along the footway path,
Called out and sent a blessing after me,
With tender cheerfulness, and with a voice
That seemed the very sound of happy thoughts.

'I roved o'er many a hill and many a dale
290   With this my weary load, in heat and cold,
Through many a wood and many an open ground,
In sunshine or in shade, in wet or fair,
Now blithe, now drooping, as it might befall;
My best companions now the driving winds
And now the "trotting brooks" and whispering trees,
And now the music of my own sad steps,
With many a short-lived thought that passed between
And disappeared.

          'I came this way again
Towards the wane of summer, when the wheat
300   Was yellow, and the soft and bladed grass
Sprang up afresh and o'er the hay field spread
Its tender green. When I had reached the door
I found that she was absent. In the shade,
Where we now sit, I waited her return.
Her cottage in its outward look appeared
As cheerful as before, in any show
Of neatness little changed, but that I thought
The honeysuckle crowded round the door,
And from the wall hung down in heavier tufts,
310   And knots of worthless stonecrop started out
Along the window's edge, and grew like weeds
Against the lower panes. I turned aside
And strolled into her garden. It was changed.
The unprofitable bindweed spread his bells
From side to side, and with unwieldy wreaths
Had dragged the rose from its sustaining wall
And bent it down to earth. The border tufts,
Daisy, and thrift, and lowly camomile,
And thyme, had straggled out into the paths
320   Which they were used to deck.

            'Ere this an hour
Was wasted. Back I turned my restless steps,
And as I walked before the door it chanced
A stranger passed, and guessing whom I sought,
He said that she was used to ramble far.

The sun was sinking in the west, and now
I sate with sad impatience. From within
Her solitary infant cried aloud.
The spot though fair seemed very desolate,
The longer I remained more desolate;
330   And looking round I saw the cornerstones,
Till then unmarked, on either side the door
With dull red stains discoloured, and stuck o'er
With tufts and hairs of wool, as if the sheep
That feed upon the commons thither came
Familiarly, and found a couching place
Even at her threshold.

     'The house clock struck eight:
I turned and saw her distant a few steps.
Her face was pale and thin, her figure too
Was changed. As she unlocked the door she said,
340   "It grieves me you have waited here so long,
But in good truth I've wandered much of late,
And sometimes, to my shame I speak, have need
Of my best prayers to bring me back again."
While on the board she spread our evening meal,
She told me she had lost her elder child,
That he for months had been a serving boy,
Apprenticed by the parish. "I perceive
You look at me, and you have cause. Today
I have been travelling far, and many days
350   About the fields I wander, knowing this
Only, that what I seek I cannot find.
And so I waste my time: for I am changed,
And to myself," she said, "have done much wrong,
And to this helpless infant. I have slept
Weeping, and weeping I have waked. My tears
Have flowed as if my body were not such
As others are, and I could never die.
But I am now in mind and in my heart
More easy, and I hope," she said, "that heaven
360   Will give me patience to endure the things
Which I behold at home."

      'It would have grieved
Your very soul to see her. Sir, I feel
The story linger in my heart. I fear
'Tis long and tedious, but my spirit clings
To that poor woman. So familiarly
Do I perceive her manner and her look
And presence, and so deeply do I feel
Her goodness, that not seldom in my walks
A momentary trance comes over me,

370   And to myself I seem to muse on one
       By sorrow laid asleep or borne away,
       A human being destined to awake
       To human life, or something very near
       To human life, when he shall come again
       For whom she suffered. Sir, it would have grieved
       Your very soul to see her: evermore
       Her eyelids drooped, her eyes were downward cast,
       And when she at her table gave me food
       She did not look at me. Her voice was low,
380   Her body was subdued. In every act
       Pertaining to her house affairs appeared
       The careless stillness which a thinking mind
       Gives to an idle matter. Still she sighed,
       But yet no motion of the breast was seen,
       No heaving of the heart. While by the fire
       We sate together, sighs came on my ear,
       I knew not how, and hardly whence they came.
       I took my staff, and when I kissed her babe
       The tears stood in her eyes. I left her then
390   With the best hope and comfort I could give:
       She thanked me for my will, but for my hope
       It seemed she did not thank me.

                              'I returned
       And took my rounds along this road again
       Ere on its sunny bank the primrose flower
       Had chronicled the earliest day of spring.
       I found her sad and drooping. She had learned
       No tidings of her husband; if he lived,
       She knew not that he lived; if he were dead,
       She knew not he was dead. She seemed the same
400   In person or appearance, but her house
       Bespoke a sleepy hand of negligence.
       The floor was neither dry nor neat, the hearth
       Was comfortless,
       The windows too were dim, and her few books,
       Which one upon the other heretofore
       Had been piled up against the corner panes
       In seemly order, now with straggling leaves
       Lay scattered here and there, open or shut,
       As they had chanced to fall. Her infant babe
410   Had from its mother caught the trick of grief,
       And sighed among its playthings. Once again
       I turned towards the garden gate, and saw
       More plainly still that poverty and grief
       Were now come nearer to her. The earth was hard,
       With weeds defaced and knots of withered grass;

No ridges there appeared of clear black mould,
No winter greenness. Of her herbs and flowers
It seemed the better part were gnawed away
Or trampled on the earth. A chain of straw,
420   Which had been twisted round the tender stem
Of a young apple tree, lay at its root;
The bark was nibbled round by truant sheep.
Margaret stood near, her infant in her arms,
And, seeing that my eye was on the tree,
She said, "I fear it will be dead and gone
Ere Robert come again."

                'Towards the house
Together we returned, and she enquired
If I had any hope. But for her Babe,
And for her little friendless Boy, she said,
430   She had no wish to live—that she must die
Of sorrow. Yet I saw the idle loom
Still in its place. His Sunday garments hung
Upon the selfsame nail, his very staff
Stood undisturbed behind the door. And when
I passed this way beaten by Autumn winds,
She told me that her little babe was dead,
And she was left alone. That very time,
I yet remember, through the miry lane
She walked with me a mile, when the bare trees
440   Trickled with foggy damps, and in such sort
That any heart had ached to hear her, begged
That wheresoe'r I went I still would ask
For him whom she had lost. We parted then,
Our final parting; for from that time forth
Did many seasons pass ere I returned
Into this tract again.

              'Five tedious years
She lingered in unquiet widowhood,
A wife and widow. Needs must it have been
A sore heart-wasting. I have heard, my friend,
450   That in that broken arbour she would sit
The idle length of half a sabbath day;
There, where you see the toadstool's lazy head;
And when a dog passed by she still would quit
The shade and look abroad. On this old Bench
For hours she sate, and evermore her eye
Was busy in the distance, shaping things
Which made her heart beat quick. Seest thou that path?
The green sward now has broken its gray line—
There to and fro she paced through many a day
460   Of the warm summer, from a belt of flax

That girt her waist, spinning the long-drawn thread
With backward steps. Yet ever as there passed
A man whose garments showed the Soldier's red,
Or crippled Mendicant in Sailor's garb,
The little child who sate to turn the wheel
Ceased from his toil, and she, with faltering voice,
Expecting still to hear her husband's fate,
Made many a fond enquiry; and when they
Whose presence gave no comfort, were gone by,
470 Her heart was still more sad. And by yon gate,
Which bars the traveller's road, she often stood,
And when a stranger horseman came, the latch
Would lift, and in his face look wistfully,
Most happy if from aught discovered there
Of tender feeling she might dare repeat
The same sad question.

                    'Meanwhile her poor hut
Sunk to decay; for he was gone, whose hand
At the first nippings of October frost
Closed up each chink, and with fresh bands of straw
480 Chequered the green-grown thatch. And so she lived
Through the long winter, reckless and alone,
Till this reft house, by frost, and thaw, and rain,
Was sapped; and when she slept, the nightly damps
Did chill her breast, and in the stormy day
Her tattered clothes were ruffled by the wind
Even at the side of her own fire. Yet still
She loved this wretched spot, nor would for worlds
Have parted hence; and still that length of road,
And this rude bench, one torturing hope endeared,
490 Fast rooted at her heart. And here, my friend,
In sickness she remained; and here she died,
Last human tenant of these ruined walls.'

The old Man ceased: he saw that I was moved.
From that low bench rising instinctively,
I turned aside in weakness, nor had power
To thank him for the tale which he had told.
I stood, and leaning o'er the garden gate
Reviewed that Woman's sufferings; and it seemed
To comfort me while with a brother's love
500 I blessed her in the impotence of grief.
At length towards the cottage I returned
Fondly, and traced with milder interest,
That secret spirit of humanity
Which, 'mid the calm oblivious tendencies
Of nature, 'mid her plants, her weeds and flowers,
And silent overgrowings, still survived.

The old man seeing this resumed, and said,
'My friend, enough to sorrow have you given,
The purposes of Wisdom ask no more:
510 Be wise and cheerful, and no longer read
The forms of things with an unworthy eye.
She sleeps in the calm earth, and peace is here.
I well remember that those very plumes,
Those weeds, and the high spear grass on that wall,
By mist and silent raindrops silvered o'er,
As once I passed, did to my mind convey
So still an image of tranquillity,
So calm and still, and looked so beautiful
Amid the uneasy thoughts which filled my mind,
520 That what we feel of sorrow and despair
From ruin and from change, and all the grief
The passing shows of being leave behind,
Appeared an idle dream that could not live
Where meditation was. I turned away,
And walked along my road in happiness.'

He ceased. By this the sun declining shot
A slant and mellow radiance, which began
To fall upon us where beneath the trees
We sate on that low bench. And now we felt,
530 Admonished thus, the sweet hour coming on:
A linnet warbled from those lofty elms,
A thrush sang loud, and other melodies
At distance heard, peopled the milder air.
The old man rose and hoisted up his load.
Together casting then a farewell look
Upon those silent walls, we left the shade;
And, ere the stars were visible, attained
A rustic inn, our evening resting place.
        THE END
1797–99   1968

Home at Grasmere

['Prospectus' to *The Excursion*]

These are the final one hundred and seven lines of "Home at Grasmere," Book One of
Part One of the projected epic *The Recluse*, and almost all of that poem ever
written, except for *The Excursion*, which was to be Part Two of three parts. Wordsworth waited sixteen years before publishing these lines, as a "Prospectus" to *The
Excursion* in 1814. *The Prelude* was not part of the design of *The Recluse*, but was
intended as a preparatory poem toward the (hopefully) greater work. Wordsworth, a
little defensively, characterized the relation between the completed but unpublished *Prelude* and the incomplete but partly published *Recluse* as being like the one

that "the ante-chapel has to the body of a gothic church. Continuing this allusion, he may be permitted to add, that his minor Pieces, which have been long before the public, when they shall be properly arranged, will be found by the attentive reader to have such connection with the main work as may give them claim to be likened to the little cells, oratories, and sepulchral recesses, ordinarily included in those edifices."

This fragment, extraordinary in itself as Wordsworth's most defiantly unorthodox manifesto of a naturalistic humanism, is vital also as a central influence upon Keats and Shelley. It provoked Blake to passionate protest, and his comments have been integrated with the notes below.

From Home at Grasmere

['Prospectus' to *The Excursion*]

On Man, on Nature, and on Human Life,
Musing in solitude, I oft perceive
Fair trains of imagery before me rise,
Accompanied by feelings of delight
Pure, or with no unpleasing sadness mixed;
And I am conscious of affecting thoughts
And dear remembrances, whose presence soothes
Or elevates the Mind, intent to weigh
The good and evil of our mortal state.
10   —To these emotions, whencesoe'er they come,
Whether from breath of outward circumstance,
Or from the Soul—an impulse to herself—
I would give utterance in numerous verse.°
Of Truth, of Grandeur, Beauty, Love, and Hope,
And melancholy Fear subdued by Faith;
Of blessed consolations in distress;
Of moral strength, and intellectual Power;
Of joy in widest commonalty spread;
Of the individual Mind that keeps her own
20   Inviolate retirement, subject there
To Conscience only, and the law supreme
Of that Intelligence which governs all,
I sing—'fit audience let me find though few!'°

So prayed, more gaining than he asked, the Bard—
In holiest mood. Urania,° I shall need
Thy guidance, or a greater Muse, if such
Descend to earth or dwell in highest heaven!
For I must tread on shadowy ground, must sink
Deep—and, aloft ascending, breathe in worlds

---

numerous verse See *Paradise Lost* V.150.   **fit . . . few** *Paradise Lost* VII.31
Urania See invocation to Bk. VII, *Paradise Lost*.

30   To which the heaven of heavens is but a veil.
      All strength—all terror, single or in bands,
      That ever was put forth in personal form—
      Jehovah—with his thunder, and the choir
      Of shouting Angels, and the empyreal thrones—
      I pass them unalarmed.° Not Chaos, not
      The darkest pit of lowest Erebus,°
      Nor aught of blinder vacancy, scooped out
      By help of dreams—can breed such fear and awe
      As fall upon us often when we look
40   Into our Minds, into the Mind of Man—
      My haunt, and the main region of my song.
      —Beauty—a living Presence of the earth,
      Surpassing the most fair ideal Forms
      Which craft of delicate Spirits hath composed
      From earth's materials—waits upon my steps;
      Pitches her tents before me as I move,
      An hourly neighbour. Paradise, and groves
      Elysian, Fortunate Fields°—like those of old
      Sought in the Atlantic Main—why should they be
50   A history only of departed things,
      Or a mere fiction of what never was?
      For the discerning intellect of Man,
      When wedded to this goodly universe
      In love and holy passion, shall find these
      A simple produce of the common day.
      —I, long before the blissful hour arrives,
      Would chant, in lonely peace, the spousal verse°
      Of this great consummation—and, by words
      Which speak of nothing more than what we are,
60   Would I arouse the sensual from their sleep
      Of Death, and win the vacant and the vain
      To noble raptures; while my voice proclaims
      How exquisitely the individual Mind
      (And the progressive powers perhaps no less
      Of the whole species) to the external World
      Is fitted—and how exquisitely, too—
      Theme this but little heard of among men—
      The external World is fitted to the Mind;°
      And the creation (by no lower name

All strength . . . unalarmed (ll. 31–35) Blake
commented: "Solomon when he Married Pharaoh's daughter and became a Convert to the
Heathen Mythology Talked exactly in this way
of Jehovah as a Very inferior object of Mans
Contemplations he also passed him by unalarmed and was permitted, Jehovah dropped
a tear and followed him by his Spirit into the
Abstract Void it is called the Divine Mercy
Satan dwells in it but Mercy does not dwell in
him he knows not to Forgive."

Erebus antechamber to Hades
Fortunate Fields the place of the blessed in
the afterlife, islands where Achilles is said to
have gone, beyond Gibraltar, out in the Atlantic, and sometimes associated (as by Wordsworth here) with lost Atlantis
spousal verse a nuptial song, an epithalamion
The external . . . Mind Blake snapped: "You
shall not bring me down to believe such fitting
and fitted I know better and Please your Lord-
ship."

70 Can it be called) which they with blended might
Accomplish—this is our high argument.
—Such grateful haunts foregoing, if I oft
Must turn elsewhere—to travel near the tribes
And fellowships of men, and see ill sights
Of madding passions mutually inflamed;
Must hear Humanity in fields and groves
Pipe solitary anguish; or must hang
Brooding above the fierce confederate storm
Of sorrow, barricadoed evermore
80 Within the walls of cities—may these sounds
Have their authentic comment; that even these
Hearing, I be not downcast or forlorn!°—
Descend, prophetic Spirit! that inspirest
The human Soul of universal earth,
Dreaming on things to come;° and dost possess
A metropolitan temple in the hearts
Of mighty Poets: upon me bestow
A gift of genuine insight; that my Song
With starlike virtue in its place may shine,
90 Shedding benignant influence, and secure,
Itself, from all malevolent effect
Of those mutations that extend their sway
Throughout the nether sphere!—And if with this
I mix more lowly matter; with the thing
Contemplated, describe the Mind and Man
Contemplating; and who, and what he was—
The transitory Being that beheld
The Vision; when and where, and how he lived—
Be not this labour useless. If such theme
100 May sort with highest objects, then—dread Power!
Whose gracious favour is the primal source
Of all illumination—may my Life
Express the image of a better time,
More wise desires, and simpler manners—nurse
My Heart in genuine freedom—all pure thoughts
Be with me—so shall thy unfailing love
Guide, and support, and cheer me to the end!
1798   1814

—Such . . . forlorn (ll. 72–82) Blake un-
derlined "Humanity in fields and groves /
Pipe solitary anguish" and then commented
on the whole passage: "does not this Fit and
is it not Fitting most Exquisitely too but to
what not to Mind but to the Vile Body only

and to its Laws of Good and Evil and its En-
mities against Mind."
things to come Wordsworth's own note cites
Shakespeare's Sonnet CVII: ". . . the prophetic
soul / Of the wide world dreaming on things to
come."

Tintern Abbey

Here, under Coleridge's direct influence, Wordsworth arrives at his myth of memory. Coming again into the presence of a remembered place, he attains a more complete understanding of his poetic self than he enjoyed before. What he persuades himself he has learned is a principle of reciprocity between himself and nature, a mutual generosity, an exchange of his disinterested love for nature's disinterested beauty. In the poet's recognition of this sharing, there comes into being a state of aesthetic contemplation, in which his will ceases to attempt to relate knowledge of the natural world to discursive knowledge of any kind. Nature is a reality to him, one that he will not murder by dissecting.

Yet this great poem is not a celebration, though it would like to be. It is almost a lament. Wordsworth wants the poem to be about renovation, about carrying the past alive into the present, and so being able to live on into the future with a full sense of continuity. "Tintern Abbey" is all the more powerful for breaking away from Wordsworth's intention. The poem's subject, despite the poet, is memory. Is the story he tells himself about memory a visionary lie? Though he is eager to renew his covenant with nature, has he adequate cause to trust that nature will renew her past movements toward him?

The poem does not trust its own answers to these questions. What Emerson, following Coleridge, called the law of compensation, now comes into operation. "Nothing is got for nothing," Emerson grimly observed. Wordsworth now *knows* consciously his love for nature, as he begins to know his bond to other men, but this knowing is darkened by shadows of mortality. An urgency enters the second half of the poem, as the poet begins to press for evidences of continuity with the ardors of his earlier self. Simply, he seeks what in religion is called salvation, but his quest is displaced into a wholly naturalistic context. He knows only nature and his own mind; he remembers when nature gave him a more direct joy than he now has; and farther back there was a time when he knew himself only in union with nature. Desperately, he affirms that nature will not betray him, but the deep reverberations of this seminal poem hint distinctly at how troubled he is.

Lines
Composed a Few Miles Above Tintern Abbey
On Revisiting the Banks of the Wye During a Tour. July 13, 1798°

Five years have passed; five summers, with the length
Of five long winters! and again I hear
These waters, rolling from their mountain-springs
With a soft inland murmur.°—Once again
Do I behold these steep and lofty cliffs,
That on a wild secluded scene impress

Lines . . . July 13, 1798 Wordsworth noted: "I have not ventured to call this Poem an Ode; but it was written with a hope that in the transitions, and the impassioned music of the versification, would be found the principal requisites of that species of composition." The tradition of the Sublime ode hovers in the background throughout, and the thematic connections to the later "Intimations of Immortality" ode should become clearer with each rereading.
soft inland murmur See "Though inland far we be" in the "Intimations" ode, l.162.

Thoughts of more deep seclusion; and connect
The landscape with the quiet of the sky.
The day is come when I again repose
10 Here, under this dark sycamore, and view
These plots of cottage-ground, these orchard-tufts,
Which at this season, with their unripe fruits,
Are clad in one green hue, and lose themselves
'Mid groves and copses. Once again I see
These hedge-rows, hardly hedge-rows, little lines
Of sportive wood run wild: these pastoral farms,
Green to the very door; and wreaths of smoke
Sent up, in silence, from among the trees!
With some uncertain notice, as might seem
20 Of vagrant dwellers in the houseless woods,
Or of some Hermit's cave, where by his fire
The Hermit sits alone.

               These beauteous forms,
Through a long absence, have not been to me
As is a landscape to a blind man's eye:
But oft, in lonely rooms, and 'mid the din
Of towns and cities, I have owed to them
In hours of weariness, sensations sweet,
Felt in the blood, and felt along the heart;
And passing even into my purer mind,°
30 With tranquil restoration:°—feelings too
Of unremembered pleasure: such, perhaps,
As have no slight or trivial influence
On that best portion of a good man's life,
His little, nameless, unremembered, acts
Of kindness and of love. Nor less, I trust,
To them I may have owed another gift,
Of aspect more sublime; that blessed mood
In which the burthen of the mystery,
In which the heavy and the weary weight
40 Of all this unintelligible world,
Is lightened:—that serene and blessed mood,
In which the affections gently lead us on,—
Until, the breath of this corporeal frame
And even the motion of our human blood
Almost suspended, we are laid asleep
In body, and become a living soul:
While with an eye made quiet by the power
Of harmony, and the deep power of joy,
We see into the life of things.°

purer mind not that the mind is purer than the
heart or blood; he means a purer part or, like-
lier, state of the mind
tranquil restoration Involved here is the "emotion recollected in tranquillity" of the 1800

Preface to *Lyrical Ballads*, but restoration has
a very strong meaning, almost "renovation."
that serene . . . things (ll. 41–49) Not a
mystical reverie, but an aesthetic state of contemplation is described.

If this
50 Be but a vain belief, yet, oh! how oft—
In darkness and amid the many shapes
Of joyless daylight; when the fretful stir
Unprofitable, and the fever of the world,
Have hung upon the beatings of my heart—
How oft, in spirit, have I turned to thee,
O sylvan Wye! thou wanderer through the woods,
How often has my spirit turned to thee!

And now, with gleams of half-extinguished thought,
With many recognitions dim and faint,
60 And somewhat of a sad perplexity,°
The picture of the mind revives again:
While here I stand, not only with the sense
Of present pleasure, but with pleasing thoughts
That in this moment there is life and food
For future years. And so I dare to hope,
Though changed, no doubt, from what I was when first
I came among these hills; when like a roe
I bounded o'er the mountains, by the sides
Of the deep rivers, and the lonely streams,
70 Wherever nature led: more like a man
Flying from something that he dreads° than one
Who sought the thing he loved. For nature then
(The coarser pleasures of my boyish days,°
And their glad animal movements all gone by)
To me was all in all.°—I cannot paint
What then I was. The sounding cataract
Haunted me like a passion: the tall rock,
The mountain, and the deep and gloomy wood,
Their colours and their forms, were then to me
80 An appetite; a feeling and a love,
That had no need of a remoter charm,
By thought supplied, nor any interest
Unborrowed from the eye.—That time is past,
And all its aching joys are now no more,
And all its dizzy raptures.° Not for this
Faint I, nor mourn nor murmur; other gifts
Have followed; for such loss, I would believe,
Abundant recompense.° For I have learned

sad perplexity There is evidently a felt sense of loss in the contrast between memory and the scene before him; the dark undersong of the poem has begun.
Flying . . . dreads Flying from time; what he dreads is mortality, the poem's hidden subject.
my boyish days his first stage, so much at one with Nature that he was not aware of her
all in all The second stage, when he was aware of Nature and loved her without anxiety, five years before; the third stage is the "now" of the poem, when he is conscious of the possibility of estrangement both from Nature and from his own former self.
dizzy raptures like "aching joys." This is an ambiguous phrase; "dizzy" and "aching" seek to qualify negatively, yet primarily they testify to the intensity and authenticity of the now past raptures and joys.
other gifts . . . recompense first central verse statement of Wordsworth's great idea of the compensatory imagination, which converts experiential loss into poetic and (Wordsworth desperately insisted) human gain

To look on nature, not as in the hour
90 Of thoughtless youth; but hearing oftentimes
The still, sad music of humanity,
Nor harsh nor grating, though of ample power
To chasten and subdue. And I have felt
A presence that disturbs me with the joy
Of elevated thoughts; a sense sublime
Of something far more deeply interfused,
Whose dwelling is the light of setting suns,
And the round ocean and the living air,
And the blue sky, and in the mind of man:
100 A motion and a spirit, that impels
All thinking things, all objects of all thought,
And rolls through all things. Therefore am I still
A lover of the meadows and the woods,
And mountains; and of all that we behold
From this green earth; of all the mighty world
Of eye, and ear,—both what they half create,°
And what perceive; well pleased to recognize
In nature and the language of the sense
The anchor of my purest thoughts, the nurse,°
110 The guide, the guardian of my heart, and soul
Of all my moral being.   Nor perchance,
If I were not thus taught, should I the more
Suffer my genial spirits° to decay:
For thou art with me here upon the banks
Of this fair river; thou my dearest Friend,
My dear, dear Friend;° and in thy voice I catch
The language of my former heart, and read
My former pleasures in the shooting lights
Of thy wild eyes. Oh! yet a little while
120 May I behold in thee what I was once,
My dear, dear Sister! and this prayer I make,°
Knowing that Nature never did betray
The heart that loved her; 'tis her privilege,
Through all the years of this our life, to lead
From joy to joy: for she can so inform
The mind that is within us, so impress

half create crucial and controversial phrase, deliberately echoed in Yeats's "Adam's Curse,"
and itself a conscious echo from Edward Young's
Night Thoughts VI.427, where the human senses
"half create the wondrous world they see." It
may be interpreted as follows: Man half creates
as well as perceives Nature because his senses
are not wholly passive but selective, to a high
degree; Man's choice among what his senses
present to him is a kind of creation, one that
is guided by memory, and that strives to attain
continuity by linking together earlier and later
presences of Nature.
nurse as in the "Intimations" ode, l. 81

genial spirits The source is Milton's Samson
Agonistes, ll. 594–98; the fearful descendant is
Coleridge's "Dejection: An Ode," l. 39.
Friend his sister Dorothy. It is a shock to learn
in l. 114 that she is present in the scene at all;
it is another shock to remember that she was
only a year-and-a-half younger than the poet,
though he reads in her "the language of my
former heart."
this prayer I make Does he ever make it in
this poem? Some critics interpret the prayer as
beginning in l. 134, but that seems a blessing,
not a prayer.

With quietness and beauty, and so feed
With lofty thoughts, that neither evil tongues,
Rash judgments, nor the sneers of selfish men,
130   Nor greetings where no kindness is, nor all
The dreary intercourse of daily life,
Shall e'er prevail against us, or disturb
Our cheerful faith, that all which we behold
Is full of blessings. Therefore let the moon
Shine on thee in thy solitary walk;°
And let the misty mountain-winds be free
To blow against thee: and, in after years,
When these wild ecstasies shall be matured
Into a sober pleasure;° when thy mind
140   Shall be a mansion for all lovely forms,
Thy memory be as a dwelling-place
For all sweet sounds and harmonies; oh! then,
If solitude, or fear, or pain, or grief,
Should be thy portion, with what healing thoughts
Of tender joy wilt thou remember me,
And these my exhortations! Nor, perchance—
If I should be where I no more can hear
Thy voice, nor catch from thy wild eyes these gleams
Of past existence—wilt thou then forget
150   That on the banks of this delightful stream
We stood together; and that I, so long
A worshipper of Nature, hither came
Unwearied in that service: rather say
With warmer love—oh! with far deeper zeal
Of holier love.° Nor wilt thou then forget,
That after many wanderings, many years
Of absence, these steep woods and lofty cliffs,
And this green pastoral landscape, were to me
More dear, both for themselves and for thy sake!
1798   1798

Nutting°

—————————It seems a day
(I speak of one from many singled out)
One of those heavenly days that cannot die;

---

solitary walk The passage is clearly indebted to Coleridge's "Frost at Midnight," written less than a half-year before.
sober pleasure It is difficult to prefer a sober pleasure to a wild ecstasy, but this is Wordsworth's desperate wisdom, for which see again the "Intimations" ode, ll. 196–98.
holier love The displacement of the vocabulary of religious devotion into a naturalistic context here has been noted by many critics, and made Wordsworth very nervous in later years; so in 1814 he denied that he was ever "a worshipper of Nature," and deprecated "a passionate expression, uttered incautiously in the poem upon the Wye. . . ."
Nutting rejected from *The Prelude*, but akin to the crucial episodes of Bk. I

When, in the eagerness of boyish hope,
I left our cottage-threshold, sallying forth
With a huge wallet o'er my shoulders slung,
A nutting-crook in hand; and turned my steps
Toward some far-distant wood, a Figure quaint,
Tricked out in proud disguise of cast-off weeds
10   Which for that service had been husbanded,
By exhortation of my frugal Dame—
Motley accoutrement, of power to smile
At thorns, and brakes, and brambles,—and, in truth,
More ragged than need was! O'er path-less rocks,
Through beds of matted fern, and tangled thickets,
Forcing my way, I came to one dear nook
Unvisited, where not a broken bough
Drooped with its withered leaves, ungracious sign
Of devastation; but the hazels rose
20   Tall and erect, with tempting clusters hung,
A virgin scene!—A little while I stood,
Breathing with such suppression of the heart
As joy delights in; and, with wise restraint
Voluptuous, fearless of a rival, eyed
The banquet;—or beneath the trees I sate
Among the flowers, and with the flowers I played;
A temper known to those who, after long
And weary expectation, have been blest
With sudden happiness beyond all hope.
30   Perhaps it was a bower beneath whose leaves
The violets of five seasons re-appear
And fade, unseen by any human eye;
Where fairy water-breaks do murmur on
Forever; and I saw the sparkling foam,
And—with my cheek on one of those green stones
That, fleeced with moss, under the shady trees,
Lay round me, scattered like a flock of sheep—
I heard the murmur and the murmuring sound,
In that sweet mood when pleasure loves to pay
40   Tribute to ease; and, of its joy secure,
The heart luxuriates with indifferent things,
Wasting its kindliness on stocks and stones,
And on the vacant air. Then up I rose,
And dragged to earth both branch and bough, with crash
And merciless ravage: and the shady nook
Of hazels, and the green and mossy bower,
Deformed and sullied, patiently gave up
Their quiet being: and, unless I now
Confound my present feelings with the past,
50   Ere from the mutilated bower I turned
Exulting, rich beyond the wealth of kings,

I felt a sense of pain when I beheld
The silent trees, and saw the intruding sky.—
Then, dearest Maiden, move along these shades
In gentleness of heart; with gentle hand
Touch—for there is a spirit in the woods.
1798   1800

The Lucy Poems

These five poems are traditionally grouped, and do seem to create an extraordinary unity, though Wordsworth himself never printed them as a sequence. Coleridge, commenting on "A Slumber Did My Spirit Seal," surmised that the poem recorded a gloomy moment in which Wordsworth experienced a passing fear that Dorothy might die. The most persuasive modern speculation is that of H. M. Margoliouth, who identified "Lucy" as Margaret (Peggy) Hutchinson, younger sister of the Mary whom Wordsworth married, and of the Sara whom Coleridge wished to marry but could not. Margaret, born in 1772, died in 1796. Margoliouth noted that "I travelled among unknown men" is a subtle declaration of love for Mary, "beloved not only for herself but as part of England, not only for herself but as inheriting also Wordsworth's unfulfilled love for her dead sister." This must all remain surmise, as no definitive evidence exists.

Strange Fits of Passion

Strange fits of passion have I known:
And I will dare to tell,
But in the Lover's ear alone,
What once to me befell.

When she I loved looked every day
Fresh as a rose in June,
I to her cottage bent my way,
Beneath an evening-moon.

Upon the moon I fixed my eye,
10   All over the wide lea;
With quickening pace my horse drew nigh
Those paths so dear to me.

And now we reached the orchard-plot;
And, as we climbed the hill,
The sinking moon to Lucy's cot
Came near, and nearer still.

In one of those sweet dreams I slept,
Kind Nature's gentlest boon!
And all the while my eyes I kept
20   On the descending moon.

My horse moved on; hoof after hoof
He raised, and never stopped:
When down behind the cottage roof,
At once, the bright moon dropped.

What fond and wayward thoughts will slide
Into a Lover's head!
'O mercy!' to myself I cried,
'If Lucy should be dead!'
1799   1800

She Dwelt Among the Untrodden Ways

She dwelt among the untrodden ways
    Beside the springs of Dove,°
A Maid whom there were none to praise
    And very few to love:

A violet by a mossy stone
    Half hidden from the eye!
—Fair as a star, when only one
    Is shining in the sky.

She lived unknown, and few could know
    When Lucy ceased to be;
But she is in her grave, and, oh,
    The difference to me!°
1799   1800

Three Years She Grew in Sun and Shower

Three years she grew in sun and shower,°
Then Nature said, 'A lovelier flower
On earth was never sown;
This Child I to myself will take;
She shall be mine, and I will make
A Lady of my own.

'Myself will to my darling be
Both law and impulse: and with me
The Girl, in rock and plain,
In earth and heaven, in glade and bower,
Shall feel an overseeing power
To kindle or restrain.

Dove any of several English streams
The . . . me! a line in which Keats found
"perfect pathos"
Three . . . shower almost certainly means she
lived for three years after the "I" of the poem
fell in love with her, not that she was a three-
year-old child when she died (see the next-to-
the-last stanza).

'She shall be sportive as the fawn
That wild with glee across the lawn
Or up the mountain springs;
And hers shall be the breathing balm,
And hers the silence and the calm
Of mute insensate things.

'The floating clouds their state shall lend
20   To her; for her the willow bend;
Nor shall she fail to see
Even in the motions of the Storm
Grace that shall mould the Maiden's form
By silent sympathy.

'The stars of midnight shall be dear
To her; and she shall lean her ear
In many a secret place
Where rivulets dance their wayward round,
And beauty born of murmuring sound
30   Shall pass into her face.

'And vital feelings of delight
Shall rear her form to stately height,
Her virgin bosom swell;
Such thoughts to Lucy I will give
While she and I together live
Here in this happy dell.'

Thus Nature spake—The work was done—
How soon my Lucy's race was run!
She died, and left to me
40   This heath, this calm, and quiet scene;
The memory of what has been,
And never more will be.
1799   1800

A Slumber Did My Spirit Seal

A slumber did my spirit seal;
    I had no human fears:
She seemed a thing that could not feel
    The touch of earthly years.

No motion has she now, no force;
    She neither hears nor sees;
Rolled round in earth's diurnal° course,
    With rocks, and stones, and trees.
1799   1800

diurnal daily

I Travelled Among Unknown Men

I travelled among unknown men,
   In lands beyond the sea;
Nor, England! did I know till then
   What love I bore to thee.

'Tis past, that melancholy dream!
   Nor will I quit thy shore
A second time; for still I seem
   To love thee more and more.

Among thy mountains did I feel
   The joy of my desire;
And she I cherished turned her wheel
   Beside an English fire.

Thy mornings showed, thy nights concealed,
   The bowers where Lucy played;
And thine too is the last green field
   That Lucy's eyes surveyed.

   1801   1807

Lucy Gray;

Or, Solitude

Oft I had heard of Lucy Gray:
And, when I crossed the wild,
I chanced to see at break of day
The solitary child.

No mate, no comrade Lucy knew;
She dwelt on a wide moor,
—The sweetest thing that ever grew
Beside a human door!

You yet may spy the fawn at play,
The hare upon the green;
But the sweet face of Lucy Gray
Will never more be seen.

'Tonight will be a stormy night—
You to the town must go;
And take a lantern, Child, to light
Your mother through the snow.'

'That, Father! will I gladly do:
'Tis scarcely afternoon—

The minster-clock° has just struck two,
20   And yonder is the moon!'

At this the Father raised his hook,
And snapped a faggot-band;
He plied his work;—and Lucy took
The lantern in her hand.

Not blither is the mountain roe:
With many a wanton stroke
Her feet disperse the powdery snow,
That rises up like smoke.

The storm came on before its time:
30   She wandered up and down;
And many a hill did Lucy climb:
But never reached the town.

The wretched parents all that night
Went shouting far and wide;
But there was neither sound nor sight
To serve them for a guide.

At day-break on a hill they stood
That overlooked the moor;
And thence they saw the bridge of wood,
40   A furlong from their door.

They wept—and, turning homeward, cried,
'In heaven we all shall meet';
—When in the snow the mother spied
The print of Lucy's feet.

Then downwards from the steep hill's edge
They tracked the footmarks small;
And through the broken hawthorn hedge,
And by the long stone-wall;

And then an open field they crossed:
50   The marks were still the same;
They tracked them on, nor ever lost;
And to the bridge they came.

They followed from the snowy bank
Those footmarks, one by one,
Into the middle of the plank;
And further there were none!

—Yet some maintain that to this day
She is a living child;
That you may see sweet Lucy Gray
60   Upon the lonesome wild.

minster-clock church clock

O'er rough and smooth she trips along,
And never looks behind;
And sings a solitary song
That whistles in the wind.
1799   1800

Michael

This is one of Wordsworth's great visions of the dignity of Natural Man, defeated (if at all) neither by circumstance nor by himself, but by the corrupting influence of urban society upon his son. The whole poem, Wordsworth's most beautiful version of pastoral, turns on the idea of covenant, between Michael and Nature, and between Michael and his son. Michael remains true to both covenants, but Nature is more constant than Luke, and the poem ends therefore in profound (though noble) pathos.

Michael

A Pastoral Poem

If from the public way you turn your steps
Up the tumultuous brook of Green-head Ghyll,°
You will suppose that with an upright path
Your feet must struggle; in such bold ascent
The pastoral mountains front you, face to face.
But, courage! for around that boisterous brook
The mountains have all opened out themselves,
And made a hidden valley of their own.
No habitation can be seen; but they
10   Who journey thither find themselves alone
With a few sheep, with rocks and stones, and kites
That overhead are sailing in the sky.
It is in truth an utter solitude;
Nor should I have made mention of this Dell
But for one object which you might pass by,
Might see and notice not. Beside the brook
Appears a straggling heap of unhewn stones!
And to that simple object appertains
A story—unenriched with strange events,
20   Yet not unfit, I deem, for the fireside, ,
Or for the summer shade. It was the first
Of those domestic tales that spake to me
Of Shepherds, dwellers in the valleys, men
Whom I already loved;—not verily

Ghyll   a narrow valley usually wooded and
containing a stream. Greenhead is near Wordsworth's house at Grasmere.

For their own sakes, but for the fields and hills
Where was their occupation and abode.
And hence this Tale, while I was yet a Boy
Careless of books, yet having felt the power
Of Nature, by the gentle agency
Of natural objects, led me on to feel   30
For passions that were not my own, and think
(At random and imperfectly indeed)
On man, the heart of man, and human life.
Therefore, although it be a history
Homely and rude, I will relate the same
For the delight of a few natural hearts;
And, with yet fonder feeling, for the sake
Of youthful Poets, who among these hills
Will be my second self when I am gone.°

Upon the forest-side in Grasmere Vale   40
There dwelt a Shepherd, Michael was his name;
An old man, stout of heart, and strong of limb.
His bodily frame had been from youth to age
Of an unusual strength: his mind was keen,
Intense, and frugal, apt for all affairs,
And in his shepherd's calling he was prompt
And watchful more than ordinary men.
Hence had he learned the meaning of all winds,
Of blasts of every tone; and oftentimes,
When others heeded not, He heard the South   50
Make subterraneous music, like the noise
Of bagpipers on distant Highland hills.
The Shepherd, at such warning, of his flock
Bethought him, and he to himself would say,
'The winds are now devising work for me!'
And, truly, at all times, the storm, that drives
The traveller to a shelter, summoned him
Up to the mountains: he had been alone
Amid the heart of many thousand mists,
That came to him, and left him, on the heights.   60
So lived he till his eightieth year was past.
And grossly that man errs, who should suppose
That the green valleys, and the streams and rocks,
Were things indifferent to the Shepherd's thoughts.
Fields, where with cheerful spirits he had breathed
The common air; hills, which with vigorous step
He had so often climbed; which had impressed
So many incidents upon his mind
Of hardship, skill or courage, joy or fear;

And . . . gone a beautiful prophecy, but sad
because unfulfilled; Wordsworth was reluctant
to recognize the poetic gifts of his best disciples: Shelley, Keats, Clare.

70 Which, like a book, preserved the memory
Of the dumb animals, whom he had saved,
Had fed or sheltered, linking to such acts
The certainty of honourable gain;
Those fields, those hills—what could they less? had laid
Strong hold on his affections, were to him
A pleasurable feeling of blind love,
The pleasure which there is in life itself.

His days had not been passed in singleness.
His Helpmate was a comely matron, old—
80 Though younger than himself full twenty years.
She was a woman of a stirring life,
Whose heart was in her house: two wheels she had
Of antique form; this large, for spinning wool;
That small, for flax; and if one wheel had rest,
It was because the other was at work.
The Pair had but one inmate in their house,
An only Child, who had been born to them
When Michael, telling o'er his years, began
To deem that he was old,—in shepherd's phrase,
90 With one foot in the grave. This only Son,
With two brave sheep-dogs tried in many a storm,
The one of an inestimable worth,
Made all their household. I may truly say,
That they were as a proverb in the vale
For endless industry. When day was gone,
And from their occupations out of doors
The Son and Father were come home, even then,
Their labour did not cease; unless when all
Turned to the cleanly supper-board, and there,
100 Each with a mess of pottage and skimmed milk,
Sat round the basket piled with oaten cakes,
And their plain home-made cheese. Yet when the meal
Was ended, Luke (for so the Son was named)
And his old Father both betook themselves
To such convenient work as might employ
Their hands by the fire-side; perhaps to card
Wool for the Housewife's spindle, or repair
Some injury done to sickle, flail, or scythe,
Or other implement of house or field.

110 Down from the ceiling, by the chimney's edge,
That in our ancient uncouth country style
With huge and black projection overbrowed
Large space beneath, as duly as the light
Of day grew dim the Housewife hung a lamp;
An aged utensil, which had performed
Service beyond all others of its kind.

Early at evening did it burn—and late,
Surviving comrade of uncounted hours,
Which, going by from year to year, had found,
120   And left the couple neither gay perhaps
Nor cheerful, yet with objects and with hopes,
Living a life of eager industry.
And now, when Luke had reached his eighteenth year,
There by the light of this old lamp they sate,
Father and Son, while far into the night
The Housewife plied her own peculiar work,
Making the cottage through the silent hours
Murmur as with the sound of summer flies.
This light was famous in its neighbourhood,
130   And was a public symbol of the life
That thrifty Pair had lived.   For, as it chanced,
Their cottage on a plot of rising ground
Stood single, with large prospect, north and south,
High into Easedale, up to Dunmail-Raise,
And westward to the village near the lake;
And from this constant light, so regular,
And so far seen, the House itself, by all
Who dwelt within the limits of the vale,
Both old and young, was named THE EVENING STAR.

140   Thus living on through such a length of years,
The Shepherd, if he loved himself, must needs
Have loved his Helpmate; but to Michael's heart
This son of his old age was yet more dear—
Less from instinctive tenderness, the same
Fond spirit that blindly works in the blood of all—
Than that a child, more than all other gifts
That earth can offer to declining man,
Brings hope with it, and forward-looking thoughts,
And stirrings of inquietude, when they
150   By tendency of nature needs must fail.
Exceeding was the love he bare to him,
His heart and his heart's joy! For often-times
Old Michael, while he was a babe in arms,
Had done him female service, not alone
For pastime and delight, as is the use
Of fathers, but with patient mind enforced
To acts of tenderness; and he had rocked
His cradle, as with a woman's gentle hand.

        And in a later time, ere yet the Boy
160   Had put on boy's attire, did Michael love,
Albeit of a stern unbending mind,
To have the Young-one in his sight, when he
Wrought in the field, or on his shepherd's stool

Sate with a fettered sheep before him stretched
Under the large old oak, that near his door
Stood single, and, from matchless depth of shade,
Chosen for the Shearer's covert from the sun,
Thence in our rustic dialect was called
The CLIPPING° TREE, a name which yet it bears.
170   There, while they two were sitting in the shade,
With others round them, earnest all and blithe,
Would Michael exercise his heart with looks
Of fond correction and reproof bestowed
Upon the Child, if he disturbed the sheep
By catching at their legs, or with his shouts
Scared them, while they lay still beneath the shears.

And when by Heaven's good grace the boy grew up
A healthy Lad, and carried in his cheek
Two steady roses that were five years old;
180   Then Michael from a winter coppice cut
With his own hand a sapling, which he hooped
With iron, making it throughout in all
Due requisites a perfect shepherd's staff,
And gave it to the Boy; wherewith equipt
He as a watchman oftentimes was placed
At gate or gap, to stem or turn the flock;
And, to his office prematurely called,
There stood the urchin, as you will divine,
Something between a hindrance and a help;
190   And for this cause not always, I believe,
Receiving from his Father hire of praise;
Though nought was left undone which staff, or voice,
Or looks, or threatening gestures, could perform.

But soon as Luke, full ten years old, could stand
Against the mountain blasts; and to the heights,
Not fearing toil, nor length of weary ways,
He with his Father daily went, and they
Were as companions, why should I relate
That objects which the Shepherd loved before
200   Were dearer now? that from the Boy there came
Feelings and emanations—things which were
Light to the sun and music to the wind;
And that the old Man's heart seemed born again?

Thus in his Father's sight the Boy grew up:
And now, when he had reached his eighteenth year,
He was his comfort and his daily hope.

Clipping the word used in the North of England for shearing

While in this sort the simple household lived
From day to day, to Michael's ear there came
Distressful tidings. Long before the time
210   Of which I speak, the Shepherd had been bound
In surety for his brother's son, a man
Of an industrious life, and ample means;
But unforeseen misfortunes suddenly
Had pressed upon him; and old Michael now
Was summoned to discharge the forfeiture,
A grievous penalty, but little less
Than half his substance. This unlooked-for claim,
At the first hearing, for a moment took
More hope out of his life than he supposed
220   That any old man ever could have lost.
As soon as he had armed himself with strength
To look his trouble in the face, it seemed
The Shepherd's sole resource to sell at once
A portion of his patrimonial fields.
Such was his first resolve; he thought again,
And his heart failed him. 'Isabel,' said he,
Two evenings after he had heard the news,
'I have been toiling more than seventy years,
And in the open sunshine of God's love
230   Have we all lived; yet if these fields of ours
Should pass into a stranger's hand, I think
That I could not lie quiet in my grave.
Our lot is a hard lot; the sun himself
Has scarcely been more diligent than I;
And I have lived to be a fool at last
To my own family. An evil man
That was, and made an evil choice, if he
Were false to us; and, if he were not false,
There are ten thousand to whom loss like this
240   Had been no sorrow. I forgive him;—but
'Twere better to be dumb than to talk thus.

'When I began, my purpose was to speak
Of remedies and of a cheerful hope.
Our Luke shall leave us, Isabel; the land
Shall not go from us, and it shall be free;
He shall possess it, free as is the wind
That passes over it. We have, thou knowest,
Another kinsman—he will be our friend
In this distress. He is a prosperous man,
250   Thriving in trade—and Luke to him shall go,
And with his kinsman's help and his own thrift
He quickly will repair this loss, and then
He may return to us. If here he stay,

What can be done? Where every one is poor,
What can be gained?'
           At this the old Man paused,
And Isabel sat silent, for her mind
Was busy, looking back into past times.
There's Richard Bateman, thought she to herself,
He was a parish-boy—at the church-door
260   They made a gathering for him, shillings, pence,
And halfpennies, wherewith the neighbours bought
A basket, which they filled with pedlar's wares;
And, with this basket on his arm, the lad
Went up to London, found a master there,
Who, out of many, chose the trusty boy
To go and overlook his merchandise
Beyond the seas; where he grew wondrous rich,
And left estates and monies to the poor,
And, at his birth-place, built a chapel floored
270   With marble, which he sent from foreign lands.
These thoughts, and many others of like sort,
Passed quickly through the mind of Isabel,
And her face brightened. The old Man was glad,
And thus resumed:—'Well, Isabel! this scheme
These two days has been meat and drink to me.
Far more than we have lost is left us yet.
—We have enough—I wish indeed that I
Were younger;—but this hope is a good hope.
Make ready Luke's best garments, of the best
280   Buy for him more, and let us send him forth
Tomorrow, or the next day, or tonight:
—If he *could* go, the Boy should go tonight.'

    Here Michael ceased, and to the fields went forth
With a light heart. The Housewife for five days
Was restless morn and night, and all day long
Wrought on with her best fingers to prepare
Things needful for the journey of her son.
But Isabel was glad when Sunday came
To stop her in her work: for, when she lay
290   Heard him, how he was troubled in his sleep:
By Michael's side, she through the last two nights
And when they rose at morning she could see
That all his hopes were gone. That day at noon
She said to Luke, while they two by themselves
Were sitting at the door, 'Thou must not go:
We have no other Child but thee to lose,
None to remember—do not go away,
For if thou leave thy Father he will die.'
The Youth made answer with a jocund voice;

300   And Isabel, when she had told her fears,
      Recovered heart. That evening her best fare
      Did she bring forth, and all together sat
      Like happy people round a Christmas fire.

      With daylight Isabel resumed her work;
      And all the ensuing week the house appeared
      As cheerful as a grove in Spring: at length
      The expected letter from their kinsman came,
      With kind assurances that he would do
      His utmost for the welfare of the Boy;
310   To which, requests were added, that forthwith
      He might be sent to him. Ten times or more
      The letter was read over; Isabel
      Went forth to show it to the neighbours round;
      Nor was there at that time on English land
      A prouder heart than Luke's. When Isabel
      Had to her house returned, the old Man said,
      'He shall depart to-morrow.' To this word
      The Housewife answered, talking much of things
      Which, if at such short notice he should go,
320   Would surely be forgotten. But at length
      She gave consent, and Michael was at ease.

      Near the tumultuous brook of Green-head Ghyll,
      In that deep valley, Michael had designed
      To build a Sheep-fold; and, before he heard
      The tidings of his melancholy loss,
      For this same purpose he had gathered up
      A heap of stones, which by the streamlet's edge
      Lay thrown together, ready for the work.
      With Luke that evening thitherward he walked:
330   And soon as they had reached the place he stopped,
      And thus the old Man spake to him:—'My son,
      To-morrow thou wilt leave me: with full heart
      I look upon thee, for thou art the same
      That wert a promise to me ere thy birth,
      And all thy life hast been my daily joy.
      I will relate to thee some little part
      Of our two histories; 'twill do thee good
      When thou art from me, even if I should touch
      On things thou canst not know of.——After thou
340   First cam'st into the world—as oft befalls
      To new-born infants—thou didst sleep away
      Two days, and blessings from thy Father's tongue
      Then fell upon thee. Day by day passed on,
      And still I loved thee with increasing love.
      Never to living ear came sweeter sounds
      Than when I heard thee by our own fire-side

First uttering, without words, a natural tune;
While thou, a feeding babe, didst in thy joy
Sing at thy Mother's breast. Month followed month,
350 And in the open fields my life was passed
And on the mountains; else I think that thou
Hadst been brought up upon thy Father's knees.
But we were playmates, Luke: among these hills,
As well thou knowest, in us the old and young
Have played together, nor with me didst thou
Lack any pleasure which a boy can know.'
Luke had a manly heart; but at these words
He sobbed aloud. The old Man grasped his hand,
And said, 'Nay, do not take it so—I see
360 That these are things of which I need not speak.
—Even to the utmost I have been to thee
A kind and a good Father: and herein
I but repay a gift which I myself
Received at others' hands; for, though now old
Beyond the common life of man, I still
Remember them who loved me in my youth.
Both of them sleep together: here they lived,
As all their Forefathers had done; and when
At length their time was come, they were not loth
370 To give their bodies to the family mould.
I wished that thou should'st live the life they lived,
But 'tis a long time to look back, my Son,
And see so little gain from threescore years.
These fields were burthened when they came to me;
Till I was forty years of age, not more
Than half of my inheritance was mine.
I toiled and toiled; God blessed me in my work,
And till these three weeks past the land was free.
—It looks as if it never could endure
380 Another Master. Heaven forgive me, Luke,
If I judge ill for thee, but it seems good
That thou shouldst go.'
                              At this the old Man paused;
Then, pointing to the stones near which they stood,
Thus, after a short silence, he resumed:
'This was a work for us; and now, my Son,
It is a work for me. But, lay one stone—
Here, lay it for me, Luke, with thine own hands.
Nay, Boy, be of good hope;—we both may live
To see a better day. At eighty-four
390 I still am strong and hale;—do thou thy part;
I will do mine.—I will begin again
With many tasks that were resigned to thee:
Up to the heights, and in among the storms,

Will I without thee go again, and do
All works which I was wont to do alone,
Before I knew thy face.—Heaven bless thee, Boy!
Thy heart these two weeks has been beating fast
With many hopes; it should be so—yes—yes—
I knew that thou couldst never have a wish
400 To leave me, Luke: thou hast been bound to me
Only by links of love: when thou art gone,
What will be left to us!—But I forget
My purposes. Lay now the corner-stone,
As I requested; and hereafter, Luke,
When thou art gone away, should evil men
Be thy companions, think of me, my Son,
And of this moment; hither turn thy thoughts,
And God will strengthen thee: amid all fear
And all temptation, Luke, I pray that thou
410 May'st bear in mind the life thy Fathers lived,
Who, being innocent, did for that cause
Bestir them in good deeds. Now, fare thee well—
When thou return'st, thou in this place wilt see
A work which is not here: a covenant
'Twill be between us; but, whatever fate
Befall thee, I shall love thee to the last,
And bear thy memory with me to the grave.'

      The Shepherd ended here; and Luke stooped down,
And, as his Father had requested, laid
420 The first stone of the Sheep-fold. At the sight
The old Man's grief broke from him; to his heart
He pressed his Son, he kissed him and wept;
And to the house together they returned.
—Hushed was that House in peace, or seeming peace,
Ere the night fell:—with morrow's dawn the Boy
Began his journey, and when he had reached
The public way, he put on a bold face;
And all the neighbours, as he passed their doors,
Came forth with wishes and with farewell prayers,
430 That followed him till he was out of sight.

      A good report did from their Kinsman come,
Of Luke and his well-doing: and the Boy
Wrote loving letters, full of wondrous news,
Which, as the Housewife phrased it, were throughout
'The prettiest letters that were ever seen.'
Both parents read them with rejoicing hearts.
So, many months passed on: and once again
The Shepherd went about his daily work
With confident and cheerful thoughts; and now
440 Sometimes when he could find a leisure hour

He to that valley took his way, and there
Wrought at the Sheep-fold. Meantime Luke began
To slacken in his duty; and, at length,
He in the dissolute city gave himself
To evil courses: ignominy and shame
Fell on him, so that he was driven at last
To seek a hiding-place beyond the seas.

    There is a comfort in the strength of love;
'Twill make a thing endurable, which else
450 Would overset the brain, or break the heart:
I have conversed with more than one who well
Remember the old Man, and what he was
Years after he had heard this heavy news.
His bodily frame had been from youth to age
Of an unusual strength. Among the rocks
He went, and still looked up to sun and cloud,
And listened to the wind; and, as before,
Performed all kinds of labour for his sheep,
And for the land, his small inheritance.
460 And to that hollow dell from time to time
Did he repair, to build the Fold of which
His flock had need. 'Tis not forgotten yet
The pity which was then in every heart
For the old Man—and 'tis believed by all
That many and many a day he thither went,
And never lifted up a single stone.°

    There, by the Sheep-fold, sometimes was he seen
Sitting alone, or with his faithful Dog,
Then old, beside him, lying at his feet.
470 The length of full seven years, from time to time,
He at the building of this Sheep-fold wrought,
And left the work unfinished when he died.
Three years, or little more, did Isabel
Survive her Husband: at her death the estate
Was sold, and went into a stranger's hand.
The Cottage which was named THE EVENING STAR
Is gone—the ploughshare has been through the ground
On which it stood; great changes have been wrought
In all the neighbourhood:—yet the oak is left
480 That grew beside their door; and the remains
Of the unfinished Sheep-fold may be seen
Beside the boisterous brook of Green-head Ghyll.
1800   1800

And . . . stone Matthew Arnold observed that this line epitomizes Wordsworth's peculiar strength: "Nothing subtle in it, no heightening, no study of poetic style, strictly so called, at all; yet it is expression of the highest and most expressive kind."

My Heart Leaps Up°

My heart leaps up when I behold
   A rainbow in the sky:
So was it when my life began;
So is it now I am a man;
So be it when I shall grow old,
   Or let me die!
The Child is father of the Man;
And I could wish my days to be
Bound each to each by natural piety.°
1802   1807

Resolution and Independence

More even than "Tintern Abbey" and the "Intimations of Immortality" ode, this is the archetype that sets the pattern for the modern crisis-lyric, the poem through and in which a poet saves himself for poetry, and by implication for life. In a secularized epiphany or "privileged moment," as Walter Pater was to call it (Wordsworth's own phrase for it, in *The Prelude,* is "spots of time"), the poet receives the equivalent of a "peculiar grace," a "something given" that redeems the time, that allows renovation to begin. Coleridge in Chapter XXII of his *Biographia Literaria* says: "Indeed this fine poem is *especially* characteristic of the author. There is scarce a defect or excellence in his writings of which it would not present a specimen." Something of the defects can be studied in the mad reflecting-glasses of the poem's two great parodies, Lewis Carroll's "The White Knight's Ballad" and Edward Lear's "Incidents in the Life of My Uncle Arly."

Wordsworth based the poem on an actual meeting with an old leech-gatherer, and wrote a strong commentary on his poetic intentions in a letter written to Sara Hutchinson on June 14, 1802 (while the poem was still being composed). She had disliked the latter part of the draft she had read. Wordsworth defended his poem with considerable passion:

> I describe myself as having been exalted to the highest pitch of delight by the joyousness and beauty of Nature and then as depressed, even in the midst of these beautiful objects, to the lowest dejection and despair. A young Poet in the midst of the happiness of Nature is described as overwhelmed by the thought of the miserable reverses which have befallen the happiest of all men, viz Poets—I think of this till I am so deeply impressed by it, that I consider the manner in which I was rescued from my dejection and despair almost as an interposition of Providence. . . . It is in the character of the old man to tell his story in a manner which an *impatient* reader must necessarily feel as tedious. But Good God! Such a figure, in such a place, a pious self-respecting, miserably infirm old man telling such a tale!

My Heart Leaps Up This is the seed of the "Intimations" ode; after 1815, ll. 7–9 were used as an epigraph to that poem.
natural piety Coleridge approved, and said of this poem that it showed men "that continuity in their self-consciousness, which Nature has made the law of their animal Life." But Blake protested bitterly: "There is no such Thing as Natural Piety Because The Natural Man is at Enmity with God."

Chatterton's "Excellent Ballade of Charitie" gave Wordsworth the poem's metrical form and something of its setting. Hovering in the background is the example of Spenser's *Prothalamion,* with its restoration of the poet's spirits from an initial despondency of self.

Resolution and Independence

I

There was a roaring in the wind all night;
The rain came heavily and fell in floods;
But now the sun is rising calm and bright;
The birds are singing in the distant woods;
Over his own sweet voice the Stock-dove broods;°
The Jay makes answer as the Magpie chatters;
And all the air is filled with pleasant noise of waters.

II

All things that love the sun are out of doors;
The sky rejoices in the morning's birth;
10   The grass is bright with rain-drops;—on the moors
The hare is running races in her mirth;
And with her feet she from the plashy earth
Raises a mist; that, glittering in the sun,
Runs with her all the way, wherever she doth run.

III

I was a Traveller then upon the moor;
I saw the hare that raced about with joy;
I heard the woods and distant waters roar;
Or heard them not, as happy as a boy:
The pleasant season did my heart employ:
20   My old remembrances went from me wholly;
And all the ways of men, so vain and melancholy.

IV

But, as it sometimes chanceth, from the might
Of joy in minds that can no further go,
As high as we have mounted in delight
In our dejection do we sink as low;
To me that morning did it happen so;
And fears and fancies thick upon me came;
Dim sadness—and blind thoughts, I knew not, nor could name.

Over . . . broods In his Preface of 1815 Wordsworth commented upon this line: "The stock-dove is said to *coo,* a sound well imitating the note of the bird; but, by the intervention of the metaphor *broods,* the affections are called in by the imagination to assist in marking the manner in which the bird reiterates and prolongs her soft note, as if herself delighting to listen to it. . . ."

V

I heard the sky-lark warbling in the sky;
30   And I bethought me of the playful hare:
Even such a happy Child of earth am I;
Even as these blissful creatures do I fare;
Far from the world I walk, and from all care;
But there may come another day to me—
Solitude, pain of heart, distress, and poverty.

VI

My whole life I have lived in pleasant thought,
As if life's business were a summer mood;
As if all needful things would come unsought
To genial faith, still rich in genial good;
40   But how can He° expect that others should
Build for him, sow for him, and at his call
Love him, who for himself will take no heed at all?

VII

I thought of Chatterton,° the marvellous Boy,
The sleepless Soul that perished in his pride;
Of Him° who walked in glory and in joy
Following his plough, along the mountain-side:
By our own spirits are we deified:
We Poets in our youth begin in gladness;
But thereof come in the end despondency and madness.°

VIII

50   Now, whether it were by peculiar grace,
A leading from above, a something given,
Yet it befell that, in this lonely place,
When I with these untoward thoughts had striven,
Beside a pool bare to the eye of heaven
I saw a Man before me unawares:
The oldest man he seemed that ever wore grey hairs.

IX

As a huge stone is sometimes seen to lie
Couched on the bald top of an eminence;
Wonder to all who do the same espy,
60   By what means it could thither come, and whence;
So that it seems a thing endued with sense:
Like a sea-beast crawled forth, that on a shelf
Of rock or sand reposeth, there to sun itself;

He Coleridge, not just anyone
Chatterton the poet Thomas Chatterton (1752–70), who killed himself at 17. Swinburne particularly admired these two lines about Chatterton.

Him Burns died at 37, desperate and self-ruined.
But . . . madness that is, from the joy itself comes the final madness

X

Such seemed this Man, not all alive nor dead,
Nor all asleep—in his extreme old age:
His body was bent double, feet and head
Coming together in life's pilgrimage;
As if some dire constraint of pain, or rage
Of sickness felt by him in times long past,
70   A more than human weight upon his frame had cast.

XI

Himself he propped, limbs, body, and pale face,
Upon a long grey staff of shaven wood:
And, still as I drew near with gentle pace,
Upon the margin of that moorish flood
Motionless as a cloud the old Man stood,
That heareth not the loud winds when they call;
And moveth all together, if it move at all.

XII

At length, himself unsettling, he the pond
Stirred with his staff, and fixedly did look
80   Upon the muddy water, which he conned,
As if he had been reading in a book:
And now a stranger's privilege I took;
And, drawing to his side, to him did say,
'This morning gives us promise of a glorious day.'

XIII

A gentle answer did the old Man make,
In courteous speech which forth he slowly drew:
And him with further words I thus bespake,
'What occupation do you there pursue?
This is a lonesome place for one like you.'
90   Ere he replied, a flash of mild surprise
Broke from the sable orbs of his yet-vivid eyes.

XIV

His words came feebly, from a feeble chest,
But each in solemn order followed each,
With something of a lofty utterance drest—
Choice word and measured phrase, above the reach
Of ordinary men; a stately speech;
Such as grave Livers do in Scotland use,
Religious men, who give to God and man their dues.

XV

He told, that to these waters he had come
100   To gather leeches,° being old and poor:

leeches still used in early 19th-century medicine,
to let blood to relieve minor illnesses

Employment hazardous and wearisome!
And he had many hardships to endure:
From pond to pond he roamed, from moor to moor;
Housing, with God's good help, by choice or chance;
And in this way he gained an honest maintenance.

XVI

The old Man still stood talking by my side;
But now his voice to me was like a stream
Scarce heard; nor word from word could I divide;
And the whole body of the Man did seem
110   Like one whom I had met with in a dream;
Or like a man from some far region sent,
To give me human strength, by apt admonishment.

XVII

My former thoughts returned: the fear that kills;
And hope that is unwilling to be fed;
Cold, pain, and labour, and all fleshly ills;
And mighty Poets in their misery dead.
—Perplexed, and longing to be comforted,
My question eagerly did I renew,
'How is it that you live, and what is it you do?'

XVIII

120   He with a smile did then his words repeat;
And said that, gathering leeches, far and wide
He travelled; stirring thus about his feet
The waters of the pools where they abide.
'Once I could meet with them on every side;
But they have dwindled long by slow decay;
Yet still I persevere, and find them where I may.'

XIX

While he was talking thus, the lonely place,
The old Man's shape, and speech—all troubled me:
In my mind's eye I seemed to see him pace
130   About the weary moors continually,
Wandering about alone and silently.
While I these thoughts within myself pursued,
He, having made a pause, the same discourse renewed.

XX

And soon with this he other matter blended,
Cheerfully uttered, with demeanour kind,
But stately in the main; and when he ended,
I could have laughed myself to scorn to find
In that decrepit Man so firm a mind.

'God,' said I, 'be my help and stay secure;
140   I'll think of the Leech-gatherer on the lonely moor!'
1802   1807

Composed upon Westminster Bridge, September 3, 1802

Earth has not anything to show more fair:
Dull would he be of soul who could pass by
A sight so touching in its majesty:
This City now doth, like a garment, wear
The beauty of the morning; silent, bare,
Ships, towers, domes, theatres, and temples lie
Open unto the fields, and to the sky;
All bright and glittering in the smokeless air.
Never did sun more beautifully steep
10   In his first splendour, valley, rock, or hill;
Ne'er saw I, never felt, a calm so deep!
The river glideth at his own sweet will:
Dear God! the very houses seem asleep;
And all that mighty heart is lying still!
1802   1807

It Is a Beauteous Evening

It is a beauteous evening, calm and free,
The holy time is quiet as a Nun
Breathless with adoration; the broad sun
Is sinking down in its tranquillity;
The gentleness of heaven broods o'er the Sea:
Listen! the mighty Being° is awake,
And doth with his eternal motion make
A sound like thunder—everlastingly.
Dear Child!° dear Girl! that walkest with me here,
10   If thou appear untouched by solemn thought,
Thy nature is not therefore less divine:
Thou liest in Abraham's bosom° all the year;
And worshippest at the Temple's inner shrine,°
God being with thee when we know it not.
1802   1807

Being the sea, not God
Child almost certainly Caroline, the poet's
daughter by Annette Vallon
Abraham's bosom See Luke 16:22.

inner shrine the Holy of Holies, inner recess
of the Jerusalem Temple, entered by the High
Priest only once a year, on the Day of Atonement

I Wandered Lonely as a Cloud°

I wandered lonely as a cloud
That floats on high o'er vales and hills,
When all at once I saw a crowd,
A host, of golden daffodils;
Beside the lake, beneath the trees,
Fluttering and dancing in the breeze.

Continuous as the stars that shine
And twinkle on the milky way,
They stretched in never-ending line
10   Along the margin of a bay:
Ten thousand saw I at a glance,
Tossing their heads in sprightly dance.

The waves beside them danced; but they
Outdid the sparkling waves in glee;
A poet could not but be gay,
In such a jocund company;
I gazed—and gazed—but little thought
What wealth the show to me had brought:

For oft, when on my couch I lie
20   In vacant or in pensive mood,
They flash upon that inward eye
Which is the bliss of solitude;
And then my heart with pleasure fills,
And dances with the daffodils.

            1807

The World Is Too Much with Us

The world is too much with us; late and soon,
Getting and spending, we lay waste our powers:
Little we see in Nature that is ours;
We have given our hearts away, a sordid boon!
This Sea that bares her bosom to the moon;
The winds that will be howling at all hours,
And are up-gathered now like sleeping flowers;
For this, for everything, we are out of tune;
It moves us not.—Great God! I'd rather be
10   A Pagan suckled in a creed outworn;
So might I, standing on this pleasant lea,°

I Wandered Lonely as A Cloud based on a passage in Dorothy Wordsworth's *Journals,* April 15, 1802: "I never saw daffodils so beautiful. They grew among the mossy stones about and about them, some rested their heads upon these stones as on a pillow for weariness and the rest tossed and reeled and danced and seemed as if they verily laughed with the wind that blew upon them over the lake, they looked so gay, ever glancing, ever changing."
pleasant lea See Spenser's "Colin Clouts Come Home Againe," l. 283: "Yet seemed to be a goodly pleasant lea."

Have glimpses that would make me less forlorn;
Have sight of Proteus rising from the sea;°
Or hear old Triton blow his wreathèd horn.°
1802–4   1807

Ode: Intimations of Immortality from Recollections of Early Childhood

It has been maintained, with justice, that after Milton's *Lycidas* this is the most important shorter poem in the language; certainly it has been one of the most influential upon poets coming after Wordsworth. The Great Ode's effect can be traced in Coleridge, Shelley, Keats, Byron, Clare, Tennyson, Browning, Arnold, Hopkins, Swinburne, and Yeats, among many others, and in American poetry throughout the entire succession that moves between Emerson and Wallace Stevens.

Lionel Trilling succinctly observed that the Ode is not about growing old, but about growing up, with its mingling of painful loss and hard-won gain. Whether, and in what sense, the Ode is also a poem about mortality (rather than about immortality at all) is in perpetual dispute. Wordsworth himself said that "this poem rests entirely upon two recollections of childhood: one that of a splendour in the objects of sense which is passed away; and the other an indisposition to bend to the law of death, as applying to our own particular case." The poet's more general comment on the poem is of great value:

> Two years at least passed between the writing of the first four stanzas and the remaining part. To the attentive and competent reader the whole sufficiently explains itself, but there is no harm in adverting here to particular feelings or experiences of my own mind on which the structure of the poem partly rests. Nothing was more difficult for me in childhood than to admit the notion of death as a state applicable to my own being . . . it was not so much from the source of animal vivacity that *my* difficulty came as from a sense of the indomitableness of the spirit within me. I used to brood over the stories of Enoch and Elijah, and almost to persuade myself that, whatever might become of others, I should be translated in something of the same way to heaven. With a feeling congenial to this, I was often unable to think of external things as having external existence, and I communed with all that I saw as something not apart from, but inherent in, my own immaterial nature. Many times while going to school have I grasped at a wall or a tree to recall myself from this abyss of idealism to the reality. At that time I was afraid of such processes. In later periods of life I have deplored, as we have all reason to do, a subjugation of an opposite character, and have rejoiced over the remembrances, as is expressed in the lines, "obstinate questionings," etc. To that dreamlike vividness and splendour which invest objects of sight in childhood, everyone, I believe, if he would look back, could bear testimony. . . .

Though Wordsworth goes on to deny that the Ode argues for the pre-existence of the soul, his denial is ambivalent, since he asserts that there is nothing in the Christian

from the sea See *Paradise Lost* III.604: "In various shapes old *Proteus* from the Sea." Homer said that Proteus could assume any shape he wished.
horn See Spenser's "Colin Clouts . . . ," ll. 244–45: "Of them the shepherd which hath charge in chief, / Is *Triton* blowing loud his wreathed horne." Triton, a kind of male mermaid, was generally visualized as playing on a conch shelltrumpet. In identifying the Sea with mythological poetry by Spenser and Milton, Wordsworth opposed their tradition to what he felt was a falling away from Nature, and prepared the way for Keats, whose sonnet "On the Sea" owes much to this sonnet.

revelation to contradict it. Despite scholarly tradition, which has found "sources" for the Ode in Plato's *Phaedrus* and his *Phaedo*, it is well to remember that Wordsworth actually denied any Platonic influence.

Structurally, the Ode is in three parts, with stanzas I through IV stating the problem of Wordsworth's sense of loss, and stanzas V through VIII and IX through XI giving contrary reactions to that sense. Trilling's comment has justly attained a kind of classical status:

> That there should be ambivalence in Wordsworth's response to this diminution is quite natural, and the two answers, that of stanzas V–VIII and that of stanzas IX–XI, comprise both the resistance to and the acceptance of growth. Inevitably we resist change and turn back with passionate nostalgia to the stage we are leaving. Still, we fulfill ourselves by choosing what is painful and difficult and necessary, and we develop by moving toward death. In short, organic development is a hard paradox which Wordsworth is stating in the discrepant answers of the second part of the Ode.

Ode

Intimations of Immortality from Recollections of Early Childhood°

> The Child is father of the Man;
> And I could wish my days to be
> Bound each to each by natural piety.°
> PAULÒ MAJORA CANAMUS°

I

There was a time when meadow, grove, and stream,
The earth, and every common° sight,
　　To me did seem
　　Apparelled in celestial light,
The glory and the freshness of a dream.°
It is not now as it hath been of yore;—
　　Turn wheresoe'er I may,
　　By night or day,
The things which I have seen I now can see no more.

II

10   The Rainbow comes and goes,
　　And lovely is the Rose,

Ode . . . Childhood "Intimations" in the title means something very like "signs" or "tokens," and the title therefore suggests that the poem is a searching for evidences, almost a quest for election. The precursor poem, in a deep sense, is the *Lycidas* of Milton, and this ode was intended also primarily to be a dedication to the poet's higher powers, a prologue to the great epic he hoped still to write.
The Child . . . piety the last three lines of "My Heart Leaps Up," reminding us that "bound each to each" means a covenant of continuity with the poet's earlier self

Paulò . . . canamus "Let us sing of somewhat more exalted things," an invocation of the Muses of Sicily (that is, of Pastoral) at the opening of Virgil's *Fourth Eclogue*; Wordsworth is remembering the deliberate echoing of this phrase in l. 17 of *Lycidas:* "Begin, and somewhat loudly sweep the string."
common for Wordsworth, an honorific adjective
The glory . . . dream See the "dreamlike vividness and splendour" in the passage quoted in the Headnote; there is no irony intended here, as dreams to Wordsworth suggest images livelier than those of wakefulness.

The Moon doth with delight
Look round her when the heavens are bare;
   Waters on a starry night
   Are beautiful and fair;
The sunshine is a glorious birth;°
But yet I know, where'er I go,
That there hath past away a glory from the earth.

   III
Now, while the birds thus sing a joyous song,
   And while the young lambs bound
      As to the tabor's sound,°
To me alone there came a thought of grief:
A timely utterance gave that thought relief,°
   And I again am strong:
The cataracts blow their trumpets from the steep;
No more shall grief of mine the season wrong;
I hear the Echoes through the mountains throng,
The Winds come to me from the fields of sleep,°
      And all the earth is gay;
         Land and sea
   Give themselves up to jollity,
      And with the heart of May
   Doth every Beast keep holiday;—
      Thou Child of Joy,
Shout round me, let me hear thy shouts, thou happy Shepherd-boy!

   IV
Ye blessèd Creatures, I have heard the call
   Ye to each other make; I see
The heavens laugh with you in your jubilee;
   My heart is at your festival,
   My head hath its coronal,°
The fulness of your bliss, I feel—I feel it all.
   Oh evil day! if I were sullen°
      While Earth herself is adorning,
         This sweet May-morning,
      And the Children are culling
         On every side,

glorious birth The present tense of stanza II tes-
tifies to the poet's continued vividness of ordinary perception; the loss is real, but is of something extraordinary.
tabor's sound beating of pastoral drum, to
provide rhythm for pipe or flute
A timely . . . relief The "timely utterance"
is presumably a poem; possibly "My Heart
Leaps Up," possibly "Resolution and Independence" (Trilling's suggestion).
The Winds . . . sleep A much-disputed line;
it may mean simply that the poet wakes each
morning with a fresh sense of inspiration.
coronal pastoral garland; see the poignant response of Coleridge in the verse letter to Sara
Hutchinson from which "Dejection: An Ode"
was quarried: "I too will crown me with a
Coronal—" (l. 136)
Oh . . . sullen a Dantesque touch; as in
"Resolution and Independence," Wordsworth
fears the hellish condition he thinks he observes in Coleridge, that of being sullen in the
sweet air

In a thousand valleys far and wide,
    Fresh flowers; while the sun shines warm,
And the Babe leaps up on his Mother's arm:—
50   I hear, I hear, with joy I hear!
    —But there's a Tree, of many, one,°
A single Field which I have looked upon,
Both of them speak of something that is gone:
        The Pansy at my feet
        Doth the same tale repeat:
Whither is fled the visionary gleam?
Where is it now,° the glory and the dream?

       v

Our birth is but a sleep and a forgetting:
The Soul that rises with us, our life's Star,°
60   Hath had elsewhere its setting,
        And cometh from afar:
        Not in entire forgetfulness,
        And not in utter nakedness,
But trailing clouds of glory do we come
        From God, who is our home:
Heaven lies about us in our infancy!
Shades of the prison-house begin to close
        Upon the growing Boy,
        But He
70 Beholds the light, and whence it flows,
        He sees it in his joy;
The Youth, who daily farther from the east
        Must travel, still is Nature's Priest,
        And by the vision splendid
        Is on his way attended;
At length the Man perceives it die away,
And fade into the light of common day.

       vi

Earth fills her lap with pleasures of her own;
Yearnings she hath in her own natural kind,
80 And, even with something of a Mother's mind,
        And no unworthy aim,
        The homely° Nurse doth all she can
To make her Foster-child, her Inmate Man,
        Forget the glories he hath known,
And that imperial palace whence he came.

But . . . one not an archetypal or Platonic tree, but simply a particular tree whose individual appearance Wordsworth had noticed, and now remembers. Blake (according to Crabb Robinson) was deeply moved by ll. 51–57.
Where is it now not necessarily the same question as "whither is fled" in the line just before
our life's Star not an astrological image, but "the Sun" is not an adequate interpretation
homely archaic sense, familiar or homelike

VII

Behold the Child° among his new-born blisses,
A six years' Darling of a pigmy size!
See, where 'mid work of his own hand he lies,
Fretted° by sallies of his mother's kisses,
90 With light upon him from his father's eyes!
See, at his feet, some little plan or chart,
Some fragment from his dream of human life,
Shaped by himself with newly-learned art;
     A wedding or a festival,
     A mourning or a funeral;
      And this hath now his heart,
      And unto this he frames his song:
       Then will he fit his tongue
To dialogues of business, love, or strife;
00   But it will not be long
      Ere this be thrown aside,
      And with new joy and pride
The little Actor cons another part;
Filling from time to time his 'humorous stage'°
With all the Persons, down to palsied Age,
That Life brings with her in her equipage;
     As if his whole vocation
     Were endless imitation.

VIII

Thou, whose exterior semblance doth belie
10   Thy Soul's immensity;
Thou best Philosopher, who yet dost keep
Thy heritage, thou Eye among the blind,
That, deaf and silent, read'st the eternal deep,
Haunted for ever by the eternal mind,—
     Mighty Prophet! Seer blest!
     On whom those truths do rest,
Which we are toiling all our lives to find,
In darkness lost, the darkness of the grave;
Thou, over whom thy Immortality
20 Broods like the Day, a Master o'er a Slave,
A Presence which is not to be put by;°
Thou little Child, yet glorious in the might
Of heaven-born freedom on thy being's height,
Why with such earnest pains dost thou provoke
The years to bring the inevitable yoke,

Child Hartley Coleridge, who always found a second father in Wordsworth
Fretted vexed, bothered
'humorous stage' from the sonnet dedicating *Musophilus* by Samuel Daniel (1562–1619), one of Wordsworth's acknowledged precursors
A Presence . . . by followed originally by four lines Wordsworth discarded, possibly because Coleridge disliked them so much, but they are a loss from the poem: "To whom the grave / Is but a lonely bed without the sense or sight / Of day or the warm light, / A place of thought where we in waiting lie"

Thus blindly with thy blessedness at strife?
Full soon thy Soul shall have her earthly freight,
And custom lie upon thee with a weight,
Heavy as frost, and deep almost as life!

IX

130   O joy! that in our embers
        Is something that doth live,
        That nature yet remembers
        What was so fugitive!
The thought of our past years in me doth breed
Perpetual benediction: not indeed
For that which is most worthy to be blest;
Delight and liberty, the simple creed
Of Childhood, whether busy or at rest,
With new-fledged hope still fluttering in his breast:—
140   Not for these I raise
        The song of thanks and praise;
        But for those obstinate questionings
        Of sense and outward things,
        Fallings from us, vanishings;°
        Blank misgivings of a Creature
Moving about in worlds not realized,°
High instincts before which our mortal Nature
Did tremble like a guilty Thing surprised:
        But for those first affections,
150   Those shadowy recollections,
        Which, be they what they may,
Are yet the fountain light of all our day,
Are yet a master light of all our seeing;
        Uphold us, cherish, and have power to make
Our noisy years seem moments in the being
Of the eternal Silence: truths that wake,
        To perish never;
Which neither listlessness, nor mad endeavour,
        Nor Man nor Boy,
160 Nor all that is at enmity with joy,
Can utterly abolish or destroy!
        Hence in a season of calm weather
        Though inland far we be,
Our Souls have sight of that immortal sea
        Which brought us hither,
        Can in a moment travel thither,
And see the Children sport upon the shore,
And hear the mighty waters rolling evermore.°

vanishings when external things began to assert an external existence, previously not acknowledged
realized perhaps in the double sense, "made real" and "made conscious of"

And see . . . evermore This vision of the children, and of the immortal sea ("the oceanic sense," as Freud ironically named it), is the prime intimation of immortality in the Ode.

X

Then sing, ye Birds, sing, sing a joyous song!
170   And let the young Lambs bound
          As to the tabor's sound!
We in thought will join your throng,
          Ye that pipe and ye that play,
          Ye that through your hearts today
          Feel the gladness of the May!
What though the radiance which was once so bright
Be now for ever taken from my sight,
          Though nothing can bring back the hour
Of splendour in the grass, of glory in the flower;
180   We will grieve not, rather find
          Strength in what remains behind;
          In the primal sympathy
          Which having been must ever be;
          In the soothing thoughts that spring
          Out of human suffering;
          In the faith that looks through death,
In years that bring the philosophic mind.°

XI

And O, ye Fountains, Meadows, Hills, and Groves,
Forebode not any severing of our loves!
190 Yet in my heart of hearts I feel your might;
I only have relinquished one delight
To live beneath your more habitual sway.
I love the Brooks which down their channels fret,
Even more than when I tripped lightly as they;
The innocent brightness of a new-born Day
          Is lovely yet;
The Clouds that gather round the setting sun
Do take a sober colouring° from an eye
That hath kept watch o'er man's mortality;
200 Another race hath been, and other palms are won.°
Thanks to the human heart by which we live,
Thanks to its tenderness, its joys, and fears,
To me the meanest flower that blows° can give
Thoughts that do often lie too deep for tears.°
1802–4   1807

---

philosophic mind the reflective or mature mind,
not necessarily a metaphysical one
sober colouring the visual equivalent of "the
still, sad music" of "Tintern Abbey," l. 91
other . . . won that is, different rewards are
given for the contests of maturity as opposed
to the contests of childhood and youth
meanest . . . blows a living flower, however
unsightly
too . . . tears thoughts so profound that even
mourning cannot express them; a suggestion
that joy is ultimately deeper than sorrow

She Was a Phantom of Delight

She° was a Phantom of delight
When first she gleamed upon my sight;
A lovely Apparition, sent
To be a moment's ornament;
Her eyes as stars of Twilight fair;
Like Twilight's, too, her dusky hair;
But all things else about her drawn
From May-time and the cheerful Dawn;
A dancing Shape, an Image gay,
To haunt, to startle, and way-lay.

I saw her upon nearer view,
A Spirit, yet a Woman too!
Her household motions light and free,
And steps of virgin-liberty;
A countenance in which did meet
Sweet records, promises as sweet;
A Creature not too bright or good
For human nature's daily food;
For transient sorrows, simple wiles,
Praise, blame, love, kisses, tears, and smiles.

And now I see with eye serene
The very pulse of the machine;
A Being breathing thoughtful breath,
A Traveller between life and death;
The reason firm, the temperate will,
Endurance, foresight, strength, and skill;
A perfect Woman, nobly planned,
To warn, to comfort, and command;
And yet a Spirit still, and bright
With something of angelic light.

1804   1807

Ode to Duty°

Jam non consilio bonus, sed more eò perductus, ut non tantum
rectè facere possim, sed nisi rectè facere non possim.°

Stern Daughter of the Voice of God!°
O Duty! if that name thou love
Who art a light to guide, a rod

To check the erring, and reprove;
Thou, who art victory and law
When empty terrors overawe;
From vain temptations dost set free;
And calmest the weary strife of frail humanity!

There are who ask not if thine eye
Be on them; who, in love and truth,
Where no misgiving is, rely
Upon the genial sense° of youth;
Glad Hearts! without reproach or blot;
Who do thy work, and know it not:
Oh! if through confidence misplaced
They fail, thy saving arms, dread Power! around them cast.

Serene will be our days and bright,
And happy will our nature be,
When love is an unerring light,
And joy its own security.
And they a blissful course may hold
Even now, who, not unwisely bold,
Live in the spirit of this creed;
Yet seek thy firm support, according to their need.

I, loving freedom, and untried;
No sport of every random gust,
Yet being to myself a guide,
Too blindly have reposed my trust:
And oft, when in my heart was heard
Thy timely mandate, I deferred
The task, in smoother walks to stray;
But thee I now would serve more strictly, if I may.

Through no disturbance of my soul,
Or strong compunction° in me wrought,
I supplicate for thy control;
But in the quietness of thought:
Me this unchartered freedom tires;
I feel the weight of chance-desires:
My hopes no more must change their name,
I long for a repose that ever is the same.°

[Yet not the less would I throughout
Still act according to the voice
Of my own wish; and feel past doubt
That my submissiveness was choice:
Not seeking in the school of pride

---

genial sense vital sense, the primal exuberance
of youth
compunction contrition, or moral uneasiness

I long . . . same "I have sought for a joy
without pain, / For a solid without fluctuation,"
said Blake's Urizen.

For 'precepts over dignified,'°
Denial and restraint I prize
No farther than they breed a second Will more wise.°]

Stern Lawgiver! yet thou dost wear
50   The Godhead's most benignant grace;
Nor know we anything so fair
As is the smile upon thy face:
Flowers laugh before thee on their beds
And fragrance in thy footing treads;
Thou dost preserve the stars from wrong;
And the most ancient heavens, through Thee, are fresh and strong.

To humbler functions, awful Power!
I call thee: I myself commend
Unto thy guidance from this hour;
60   Oh, let my weakness have an end!
Give unto me, made lowly wise,°
The spirit of self-sacrifice;
The confidence of reason° give;
And in the light of truth thy Bondman let me live!
1804   1807

The Solitary Reaper°

Behold her, single in the field,
Yon solitary Highland Lass!
Reaping and singing by herself;
Stop here, or gently pass!
Alone she cuts and binds the grain,
And sings a melancholy strain;
O listen! for the Vale profound
Is overflowing with the sound.

No Nightingale did ever chaunt
10   More welcome notes to weary bands
Of travellers in some shady haunt,
Among Arabian sands:

'precepts over dignified' from Milton's plea for divorce, where he defends the dignity of man from "empty and over dignified precepts"
Yet not . . . wise Wordsworth later excised this stanza, but it is too good to lose, with its powerful notion of "a second Will."
lowly wise See *Paradise Lost* VIII.173–74, where Raphael warns Adam: "Heaven is for thee too high / To know what passes there. Be lowly wise; / Think only what concerns thee and thy being."
reason a moral as well as an analytical faculty, as in its Miltonic usage
The Solitary Reaper Wordsworth acknowledged

his debt to his friend Thomas Wilkinson's *Tours to the British Mountains* (not published until 1824), where a sentence reads: "Passed a female who was reaping alone; she sung in Erse as she bended over her sickle; the sweetest human voice I ever heard: her strains were tenderly melancholy, and felt delicious, long after they were heard no more." Notice that Wordsworth's imagination is moved to surmise because he does not know the language in which the Highland girl sings. The best modern analogue, as many critics have noted, is Wallace Stevens's Wordsworthian poem "The Idea of Order at Key West."

A voice so thrilling ne'er was heard
In spring-time from the Cuckoo-bird,
Breaking the silence of the seas
Among the farthest Hebrides.

Will no one tell me what she sings?—
Perhaps the plaintive numbers flow
For old, unhappy, far-off things,
20   And battles long ago:
Or is it some more humble lay,
Familiar matter of today?
Some natural sorrow, loss, or pain,
That has been, and may be again?

Whate'er the theme, the Maiden sang
As if her song could have no ending;
I saw her singing at her work,
And o'er the sickle bending:—
I listened, motionless and still;
30   And, as I mounted up the hill,
The music in my heart I bore,
Long after it was heard no more.
1805   1807

Elegiac Stanzas°

Suggested by A Picture of Peele Castle,° in A Storm, Painted by Sir George Beaumont°

I was thy neighbour once, thou rugged Pile!
Four summer weeks I dwelt in sight of thee:
I saw thee every day; and all the while
Thy Form was sleeping on a glassy sea.

So pure the sky, so quiet was the air!
So like, so very like, was day to day!
Whene'er I looked, thy Image still was there;
It trembled, but it never passed away.

How perfect was the calm! it seemed no sleep;
10   No mood, which season takes away, or brings:
I could have fancied that the mighty Deep
Was even the gentlest of all gentle Things.

Elegiac Stanzas Wordsworth's beloved brother
John was drowned by shipwreck on February
5, 1805. This poem was written more than a
year later, and does not represent a first shocked
reaction of grief, but a deeply considered loss
of faith in both nature and the imagination. This
loss, on the evidence of Wordsworth's later
poetry, was more complex and deeper than the
poet himself could realize.
Peele Castle stands on an island near the coast
of Lancashire.
Beaumont Wordsworth's friend and patron; a
rich amateur artist

Ah! THEN, if mine had been the Painter's hand,
To express what then I saw; and add the gleam,
The light that never was, on sea or land,
The consecration, and the Poet's dream;°

I would have planted thee, thou hoary Pile
Amid a world how different from this!
Beside a sea that could not cease to smile;
20   On tranquil land, beneath a sky of bliss.

Thou shouldst have seemed a treasure-house divine
Of peaceful years; a chronicle of heaven;—
Of all the sunbeams that did ever shine
The very sweetest had to thee been given.

A Picture had it been of lasting ease,
Elysian quiet, without toil or strife;
No motion but the moving tide, a breeze,
Or merely silent Nature's breathing life.

Such, in the fond illusion of my heart,
30   Such Picture would I at that time have made:
And seen the soul of truth in every part,
A steadfast peace that might not be betrayed.

So once it would have been,—'tis so no more;
I have submitted to a new control:°
A power is gone, which nothing can restore;°
A deep distress hath humanised my Soul.°

Not for a moment could I now behold
A smiling sea, and be what I have been:
The feeling of my loss will ne'er be old;
40   This, which I know, I speak with mind serene.°

Then, Beaumont, Friend! who would have been the Friend,
If he had lived, of Him whom I deplore,°
This work of thine I blame not, but commend;
This sea in anger, and that dismal shore.

O 'tis a passionate Work!—yet wise and well,
Well chosen is the spirit that is here;
That Hulk which labours in the deadly swell,
This rueful sky, this pageantry of fear!

And this huge Castle, standing here sublime,
50   I love to see the look with which it braves,

Poet's dream "Dream" has a negative meaning
here, very close to "delusion."
new control not the reciprocal relation with
Nature, but obedience to the moral law
A power . . . restore See the "Intimations"
ode, ll. 177–78.

A deep . . . Soul Before this, joy had humanized Wordsworth's soul.
with mind serene not in the immediate grief of
John's death
deplore mourn

Cased in the unfeeling armour of old time,
The lightning, the fierce wind, and trampling waves.

Farewell, farewell the heart that lives alone,
Housed in a dream, at distance from the Kind!°
Such happiness, wherever it be known,
Is to be pitied; for 'tis surely blind.

But welcome fortitude, and patient cheer,
And frequent sights of what is to be borne!
Such sights, or worse, as are before me here.—
60 Not without hope we suffer and we mourn.
1806   1807

The Prelude

The first version of this internalized romance (see period Headnote) was completed in 1805, but Wordsworth refused to publish the poem, and resented Coleridge's publication of "To William Wordsworth," the poem giving his reactions at having heard Wordsworth read aloud this major work. Wordsworth revised it over several decades, and the 1850 version, published posthumously, is rhetorically superior to the 1805 text, and is the source of the substantial selections that follow. Yet Wordsworth's reasons for declining publication were not stylistic. "The Poem to Coleridge," as he always called it (the title The Prelude was chosen by his widow), is the summation of his earlier self, the central poem of his Great Decade (1797–1807). The poet aged very quickly, and only a double handful of strong poems came out of the second half of his life. Though he would not have accepted such a judgment, something in him was unable to confront his own earlier self. He could not abandon The Prelude, but also he could not live with it as a public presence. Perhaps his sense of survival compelled him to keep the poem to himself, as a talisman against death. With Wordsworth, massive simplicity is usually the accurate formula for understanding; perhaps he just did not want to be reminded, or have others reminded, of how much he had lost.

The Prelude is not a "confessional" poem, as is so much recent verse in America. Its subject is subjectivity, and the poet maps the growth of his consciousness in the faith that he is wholly representative of the best potentialities of mankind. Unlike St. Augustine, whose crises were resolved by the realization he was hardly alone in the universe, but shared it with God as well as with other men, Wordsworth is essentially alone with the universe. If The Prelude is a religious poem, then the religion is not quite Christianity, though it is certainly closer to Christianity than to the natural religion of eighteenth-century England or of Rousseau. The God of The Prelude is neither nature nor Wordsworth's imagination but an unnamed third presence which, at crucial moments, can subsume both. Yet The Prelude is not a quest after that presence, or a quest after nature. It is, like some works of Ruskin and Proust and Beckett after it, a search for lost time, a journey seeking a remembered world. That world belonged to imagination, and Wordsworth finds it again by returning to a perception that was also creation, a way of thinking that was a way of recognition.

Kind mankind

The persistent theme of *The Prelude* is the power of the poet's mind over the universe it inhabits. This power is so great that it could be saved for the discipline of poetry, Wordsworth believed, only because nature worked to subdue and chasten it. Wordsworth feared the strength of his own imagination, and showed himself the terror of such strength in figures like Margaret and the Solitary of *The Excursion,* and in the dream-figure of the Arab in Book V of *The Prelude.* His imagination pressed for autonomy, as against nature, and would have been wholly and dangerously free of nature had Wordsworth yielded to it. He did not, but this did not make him only a nature poet, as *The Prelude* shows throughout. The poem's theme, like that of "Tintern Abbey," is not the humanizing of nature (a more Coleridgean ambition) and not the naturalizing of the human imagination (Arnold's interpretation of Wordsworth). The poet knows he is wholly apart from nature, once he is mature, but he confronts in nature presences from whom he fears (and cannot accept) estrangement. His theme is the tempering of imagination by nature, an educational process that leads to renovation, and to a balanced power of imagining that neither yields to a universe of decay nor seeks (as Blake did) to burn through that universe.

The Prelude

Or, Growth of a Poet's Mind
An Autobiographical Poem

From *Book First*

INTRODUCTION—CHILDHOOD
AND SCHOOL-TIME

O there is blessing in this gentle breeze,
A visitant that while it fans my cheek
Doth seem half-conscious of the joy it brings
From the green fields, and from yon azure sky.°
Whate'er its mission, the soft breeze can come
To none more grateful than to me; escaped
From the vast city, where I long had pined
A discontented sojourner: now free,
Free as a bird to settle where I will.°
10   What dwelling shall receive me? in what vale
Shall be my harbour? underneath what grove
Shall I take up my home? and what clear stream
Shall with its murmur lull me into rest?
The earth is all before me.° With a heart

O there . . . sky (ll. 1–4) Wordsworth said that the poem's opening lines were written extempore as he walked from Bristol to Racedown in 1795; what matters is that the wind rises, and the spirit of the poet rises with it.
Free . . . will Escaping London, where he had lived unhappily for half a year in 1795, the poet celebrates his recovered liberty, to return to nature and compose again (made possible by a legacy).
The earth . . . me a beautiful contrast to poor Adam and Eve in *Paradise Lost* XII.646

Joyous, nor scared at its own liberty,
I look about; and should the chosen guide
Be nothing better than a wandering cloud,
I cannot miss my way.° I breathe again!
Trances of thought and mountings of the mind
20   Come fast upon me: it is shaken off,
That burthen of my own unnatural self,°
The heavy weight of many a weary day
Not mine, and such as were not made for me.
Long months of peace (if such bold word accord
With any promises of human life),
Long months of ease and undisturbed delight
Are mine in prospect; whither shall I turn,
By road or pathway, or through trackless field,
Up hill or down, or shall some floating thing
30   Upon the river point me out my course?

Dear Liberty! Yet what would it avail
But for a gift that consecrates the joy?
For I, methought, while the sweet breath of heaven
Was blowing on my body, felt within
A correspondent breeze, that gently moved
With quickening virtue, but is now become
A tempest, a redundant energy,
Vexing its own creation.° Thanks to both,
And their congenial powers, that, while they join
40   In breaking up a long-continued frost,
Bring with them vernal promises, the hope
Of active days urged on by flying hours,—
Days of sweet leisure, taxed with patient thought
Abstruse, nor wanting punctual service high,
Matins and vespers of harmonious verse!

Thus far, O Friend! did I, not used to make
A present joy° the matter of a song,
Pour forth that day my soul in measured strains
That would not be forgotten, and are here
50   Recorded: to the open fields I told
A prophecy: poetic numbers came
Spontaneously to clothe in priestly robe
A renovated spirit singled out,°
Such hope was mine, for holy services.

and should . . . way another contrast, to the pillar of cloud the Israelites followed across the desert on their way to the Promised Land
it is shaken . . . unnatural self Compare "Tintern Abbey," ll. 37–41, written three years later.
For I . . . creation (ll. 33–38) The breeze rising within him is like an over-prepared event, which cannot come off; the wise passivity he needs is lacking.

A present joy Having defied what he will term later, in the 1800 Preface to *Lyrical Ballads*, as the mood in which successful composition generally begins, he is defeated by "a present joy."
singled out The sense of election is already strong here, the spirit already renovated.

My own voice cheered me, and, far more, the mind's
Internal echo of the imperfect sound;
To both I listened, drawing from them both
A cheerful confidence in things to come.

       . . .

It was a splendid evening, and my soul
Once more made trial of her strength, nor lacked
Aeolian visitations; but the harp
Was soon defrauded, and the banded host
Of harmony dispersed in straggling sounds,
And lastly utter silence! 'Be it so;
100   Why think of any thing but present good?'°
So, like a home-bound labourer I pursued
My way beneath the mellowing sun, that shed
Mild influence;° nor left in me one wish
Again to bend the Sabbath of that time
To a servile yoke. What need of many words?
A pleasant loitering journey, through three days
Continued, brought me to my hermitage.
I spare to tell of what ensued, the life
In common things—the endless store of things,
110   Rare, or at least so seeming, every day
Found all about me in one neighbourhood—
The self-congratulation, and, from morn
To night, unbroken cheerfulness serene.
But speedily an earnest longing rose
To brace myself to some determined aim,
Reading or thinking; either to lay up
New stores, or rescue from decay the old
By timely interference: and therewith
Came hopes still higher, that with outward life
120   I might endue some airy phantasies
That had been floating loose about for years,
And to such beings temperately deal forth
The many feelings that oppressed my heart.
That hope hath been discouraged; welcome light
Dawns from the east, but dawns to disappear
And mock me with a sky that ripens not
Into a steady morning: if my mind,
Remembering the bold promise of the past,
Would gladly grapple with some noble theme,
130   Vain is her wish; where'er she turns she finds
Impediments from day to day renewed.

       . . .

Why . . . good There is no anxiety in this mis-
adventure of redundant inspiration; anxiety will
come, overwhelmingly, with the problem of an
epic theme, and its hidden burden of the anxiety
of influence, Wordsworth's own fear that he may
be only a latecomer, arriving after all the stories
of poetry have been told.
Mild influence See *Paradise Lost* VII.375.

Sometimes it suits me better to invent
A tale from my own heart, more near akin
To my own passions and habitual thoughts;
Some variegated story, in the main
Lofty, but the unsubstantial structure melts
Before the very sun that brightens it,
Mist into air dissolving! Then a wish,
My best and favourite aspiration, mounts
With yearning toward some philosophic song
230 Of Truth that cherishes our daily life;
With meditations passionate from deep
Recesses in man's heart, immortal verse
Thoughtfully fitted to the Orphean lyre;
But from this awful burthen I full soon
Take refuge and beguile myself with trust
That mellower years will bring a riper mind
And clearer insight. Thus my days are passed
In contradiction; with no skill to part
Vague longing, haply bred by want of power,
240 From paramount impulse not to be withstood,
A timorous capacity from prudence,
From circumspection, infinite delay.
Humility and modest awe themselves
Betray me, serving often for a cloak
To a more subtle selfishness; that now
Locks every function up in blank reserve,
Now dupes me, trusting to an anxious eye
That with intrusive restlessness beats off
Simplicity and self-presented truth.
250 Ah! better far than this, to stray about
Voluptuously through fields and rural walks,
And ask no record of the hours, resigned
To vacant musing, unreproved neglect
Of all things, and deliberate holiday.
Far better never to have heard the name
Of zeal and just ambition, than to live
Baffled and plagued by a mind that every hour
Turns recreant to her task; takes heart again,
Then feels immediately some hollow thought
260 Hang like an interdict upon her hopes.
This is my lot; for either still I find
Some imperfection in the chosen theme,
Or see of absolute accomplishment
Much wanting, so much wanting, in myself,
That I recoil and droop, and seek repose
In listlessness from vain perplexity,
Unprofitably travelling toward the grave,

Like a false steward who hath much received
And renders nothing back.°
                Was it for this
270 That one, the fairest of all rivers, loved
To blend his murmurs with my nurse's song,
And, from his alder shades and rocky falls,
And from his fords and shallows, sent a voice
That flowed along my dreams? For this, didst thou,
O Derwent! winding among grassy holms°
Where I was looking on, a babe in arms,
Make ceaseless music that composed my thoughts
To more than infant softness, giving me
Amid the fretful dwellings of mankind
280 A foretaste, a dim earnest, of the calm
That Nature breathes among the hills and groves.°
When he had left the mountains and received
On his smooth breast the shadow of those towers
That yet survive, a shattered monument
Of feudal sway, the bright blue river passed
Along the margin of our terrace walk;
A tempting playmate whom we dearly loved.
Oh, many a time have I, a five years' child,
In a small mill-race severed from his stream,
290 Made one long bathing of a summer's day;
Basked in the sun, and plunged and basked again
Alternate, all a summer's day, or scoured
The sandy fields, leaping through flowery groves
Of yellow ragwort; or when rock and hill,
The woods, and distant Skiddaw's lofty height,
Were bronzed with deepest radiance, stood alone
Beneath the sky, as if I had been born
On Indian plains, and from my mother's hut
Had run abroad in wantonness, to sport
300 A naked savage, in the thunder shower.

    Fair seed-time had my soul, and I grew up
Fostered alike by beauty and by fear:
Much favoured in my birth-place, and no less
In that beloved Vale to which erelong
We were transplanted—there were we let loose
For sports of wider range. Ere I had told
Ten birth-days, when among the mountain slopes
Frost, and the breath of frosty wind, had snapped
The last autumnal crocus, 'twas my joy

Unprofitably . . . back the starting crisis-point
of the poem; almost a death-in-life condition
for a strong poet with Wordsworth's ambitions
holms low land at riverside
Was it . . . groves (ll. 269–281) With more-
than-Proustian skill, the Derwent River is transformed from an agent of admonishment to the
messenger of the poetic theme, the development
of the poet's own imagination.

310 With store of springes° o'er my shoulder hung
To range the open heights where woodcocks run
Along the smooth green turf. Through half the night,
Scudding° away from snare to snare, I plied
That anxious visitation;—moon and stars
Were shining o'er my head. I was alone,
And seemed to be a trouble to the peace
That dwelt among them. Sometimes it befel
In these night wanderings, that a strong desire
O'erpowered my better reason, and the bird
320 Which was the captive of another's toil
Became my prey; and when the deed was done
I heard among the solitary hills
Low breathings coming after me, and sounds
Of undistinguishable motion, steps
Almost as silent as the turf they trod.

Nor less when spring had warmed the cultured Vale,
Roved we as plunderers where the mother-bird
Had in high places built her lodge; though mean
Our object and inglorious, yet the end
330 Was not ignoble. Oh! when I have hung
Above the raven's nest, by knots of grass
And half-inch fissures in the slippery rock
But ill sustained, and almost (so it seemed)
Suspended by the blast that blew amain,
Shouldering the naked crag, oh, at that time
While on the perilous ridge I hung alone,
With what strange utterance did the loud dry wind
Blow through my ear! the sky seemed not a sky
Of earth—and with what motion moved the clouds!

340 Dust as we are, the immortal spirit grows
Like harmony in music; there is a dark
Inscrutable workmanship that reconciles
Discordant elements, makes them cling together
In one society. How strange that all
The terrors, pains, and early miseries,
Regrets, vexations, lassitudes interfused
Within my mind, should e'er have borne a part,
And that a needful part, in making up
The calm existence that is mine when I
350 Am worthy of myself! Praise to the end!
Thanks to the means which Nature deigned to employ;
Whether her fearless visitings, or those
That came with soft alarm, like hurtless light
Opening the peaceful clouds; or she may use

Springes traps or snares   **Scudding** moving hurriedly

Severer interventions, ministry
More palpable, as best might suit her aim.

    One summer evening (led by her) I found
A little boat tied to a willow tree
Within a rocky cave, its usual home.
360 Straight I unloosed her chain, and stepping in
Pushed from the shore. It was an act of stealth
And troubled pleasure, nor without the voice
Of mountain-echoes did my boat move on;
Leaving behind her still, on either side,
Small circles glittering idly in the moon,
Until they melted all into one track
Of sparkling light. But now, like one who rows,
Proud of his skill, to reach a chosen point
With an unswerving line, I fixed my view
370 Upon the summit of a craggy ridge,
The horizon's utmost boundary; far above
Was nothing but the stars and the grey sky.
She was an elfin pinnace; lustily
I dipped my oars into the silent lake,
And, as I rose upon the stroke, my boat
Went heaving through the water like a swan;
When, from behind that craggy steep till then
The horizon's bound, a huge peak, black and huge,
As if with voluntary power instinct
380 Upreared its head. I struck and struck again,
And growing still in stature the grim shape
Towered up between me and the stars, and still,
For so it seemed, with purpose of its own
And measured motion like a living thing,
Strode after me. With trembling oars I turned,
And through the silent water stole my way
Back to the covert of the willow tree;
There in her mooring-place I left my bark,—
And through the meadows homeward went, in grave
390 And serious mood; but after I had seen
That spectacle, for many days, my brain
Worked with a dim and undetermined sense
Of unknown modes of being; o'er my thoughts
There hung a darkness, call it solitude
Or blank desertion. No familiar shapes
Remained, no pleasant images of trees,
Of sea or sky, no colours of green fields;
But huge and mighty forms, that do not live
Like living men, moved slowly through the mind
400 By day, and were a trouble to my dreams.

Wisdom and Spirit of the universe!
Thou Soul that art the eternity of thought,
That givest to forms and images a breath
And everlasting motion, not in vain
By day or star-light thus from my first dawn
Of childhood didst thou intertwine for me
The passions that build up our human soul;
Not with the mean and vulgar works of man,
But with high objects, with enduring things—
410   With life and nature, purifying thus
The elements of feeling and of thought,
And sanctifying, by such discipline,
Both pain and fear, until we recognise
A grandeur in the beatings of the heart.
Nor was this fellowship vouchsafed to me
With stinted kindness. In November days,
When vapours rolling down the valley made
A lonely scene more lonesome, among woods,
At noon and 'mid the calm of summer nights,
420   When, by the margin of the trembling lake,
Beneath the gloomy hills homeward I went
In solitude, such intercourse was mine;
Mine was it in the fields both day and night,
And by the waters, all the summer long.

And in the frosty season, when the sun
Was set, and visible for many a mile
The cottage windows blazed through twilight gloom,
I heeded not their summons: happy time
It was indeed for all of us—for me
430   It was a time of rapture! Clear and loud
The village clock tolled six,—I wheeled about,
Proud and exulting like an untired horse
That cares not for his home. All shod with steel,
We hissed along the polished ice in games
Confederate, imitative of the chase
And woodland pleasures,—the resounding horn,
The pack loud chiming, and the hunted hare.
So through the darkness and the cold we flew,
And not a voice was idle; with the din
440   Smitten, the precipices rang aloud;
The leafless trees and every icy crag
Tinkled like iron; while far distant hills
Into the tumult sent an alien sound
Of melancholy not unnoticed, while the stars
Eastward were sparkling clear, and in the west
The orange sky of evening died away.

Not seldom from the uproar I retired
Into a silent bay, or sportively
Glanced sideway, leaving the tumultuous throng,
450   To cut across the reflex of a star
That fled, and, flying still before me, gleamed
Upon the glassy plain; and oftentimes,
When we had given our bodies to the wind,
And all the shadowy banks on either side
Came sweeping through the darkness, spinning still
The rapid line of motion, then at once
Have I, reclining back upon my heels,
Stopped short; yet still the solitary cliffs
Wheeled by me—even as if the earth had rolled
460   With visible motion her diurnal round!
Behind me did they stretch in solemn train,
Feebler and feebler, and I stood and watched
Till all was tranquil as a dreamless sleep.

Ye Presences of Nature in the sky
And on the earth! Ye Visions of the hills!
And Souls of lonely places! can I think
A vulgar hope was yours when ye employed
Such ministry, when ye through many a year
Haunting me thus among my boyish sports,
470   On caves and trees, upon the woods and hills,
Impressed upon all forms the characters
Of danger or desire; and thus did make
The surface of the universal earth
With triumph and delight, with hope and fear,
Work like a sea? . . .

From *Book Second*

SCHOOL-TIME

Those incidental charms which first attached
My heart to rural objects, day by day
200   Grew weaker, and I hasten on to tell
How Nature, intervenient° till this time
And secondary, now at length was sought
For her own sake. But who shall parcel out
His intellect by geometric rules,
Split like a province into round and square?
Who knows the individual hour in which
His habits were first sown, even as a seed?
Who that shall point as with a wand and say
'This portion of the river of my mind
210   Came from yon fountain?' Thou, my Friend!° art one

intervenient something extraneous   **Friend** Coleridge

More deeply read in thy own thoughts; to thee
Science appears but what in truth she is,
Not as our glory and our absolute boast,
But as a succedaneum,° and a prop
To our infirmity. No officious slave
Art thou of that false secondary power
By which we multiply distinctions, then
Deem that our puny boundaries are things
That we perceive, and not that we have made.
220   To thee, unblinded by these formal arts,
The unity of all hath been revealed,
And thou wilt doubt with me, less aptly skilled
Than many are to range the faculties
In scale and order, class the cabinet
Of their sensations, and in voluble phrase
Run through the history and birth of each
As of a single independent thing.
Hard task, vain hope, to analyse the mind,
If each most obvious and particular thought,
230   Not in a mystical and idle sense,
But in the words of Reason deeply weighed,
Hath no beginning.
          Blest the infant Babe,
(For with my best conjecture I would trace
Our Being's earthly progress,) blest the Babe,
Nursed in his Mother's arms, who sinks to sleep
Rocked on his Mother's breast; who with his soul
Drinks in the feelings of his Mother's eye!
For him, in one dear Presence, there exists
A virtue which irradiates and exalts
240   Objects through widest intercourse of sense.
No outcast he, bewildered and depressed:
Along his infant veins are interfused
The gravitation and the filial bond
Of nature that connect him with the world.
Is there a flower, to which he points with hand
Too weak to gather it, already love
Drawn from love's purest earthly fount for him
Hath beautified that flower; already shades
Of pity cast from inward tenderness
250   Do fall around him upon aught that bears
Unsightly marks of violence or harm.
Emphatically such a Being lives,
Frail creature as he is, helpless as frail,
An inmate of this active universe.
For feeling has to him imparted power

succedaneum replacement

That through the growing faculties of sense
Doth like an agent of the one great Mind
Create, creator and receiver both,
Working but in alliance with the works
260   Which it beholds.—Such, verily, is the first
Poetic spirit of our human life,
By uniform control of after years,
In most, abated or suppressed; in some,
Through every change of growth and of decay,
Pre-eminent till death.
             From early days,
Beginning not long after that first time
In which, a Babe, by intercourse of touch
I held mute dialogues with my Mother's heart,
I have endeavoured to display the means
270   Whereby this infant sensibility,
Great birthright of our being, was in me
Augmented and sustained. Yet is a path
More difficult before me; and I fear
That in its broken windings we shall need
The chamois'° sinews, and the eagle's wing:
For now a trouble came into my mind
From unknown causes. I was left alone
Seeking the visible world, nor knowing why.°
The props of my affections were removed,
280   And yet the building stood, as if sustained
By its own spirit! All that I beheld
Was dear, and hence to finer influxes
The mind lay open to a more exact
And close communion. Many are our joys
In youth, but oh! what happiness to live
When every hour brings palpable access
Of knowledge, when all knowledge is delight,
And sorrow is not there! The seasons came,
And every season wheresoe'er I moved
290   Unfolded transitory qualities,
Which, but for this most watchful power of love,
Had been neglected; left a register
Of permanent relations, else unknown.
Hence life, and change, and beauty, solitude
More active even than 'best society'—
Society made sweet as solitude
By silent inobtrusive sympathies,
And gentle agitations of the mind
From manifold distinctions, difference

chamois' an agile, goat-like antelope   lack reality, including a full sense of other
nor knowing why The crisis of a lifelong   selves) begins to be revealed here.
solipsist (a person for whom external things

300 Perceived in things, where, to the unwatchful eye,
No difference is, and hence, from the same source,
Sublimer joy; for I would walk alone,
Under the quiet stars, and at that time
Have felt whate'er there is of power in sound
To breathe an elevated mood, by form
Or image unprofaned; and I would stand,
If the night blackened with a coming storm,
Beneath some rock, listening to notes that are
The ghostly language of the ancient earth,
310 Or make their dim abode in distant winds.
Thence did I drink the visionary power;
And deem not profitless those fleeting moods
Of shadowy exultation: not for this,
That they are kindred to our purer mind
And intellectual life; but that the soul,
Remembering how she felt, but what she felt
Remembering not, retains an obscure sense
Of possible sublimity, whereto
With growing faculties she doth aspire,
320 With faculties still growing, feeling still
That whatsoever point they gain, they yet
Have something to pursue.°. . .

From *Book Fourth*

SUMMER VACATION

It seemed the very garments that I wore
Preyed on my strength, and stopped the quiet stream
Of self-forgetfulness.
                    Yes, that heartless chase
Of trivial pleasures was a poor exchange
For books and nature at that early age.
300 'Tis true, some casual knowledge might be gained
Of character or life; but at that time,
Of manners put to school I took small note,
And all my deeper passions lay elsewhere.
For better had it been to exalt the mind
By solitary study, to uphold
Intense desire through meditative peace;
And yet, for chastisement of these regrets,
The memory of one particular hour
Doth here rise up against me. 'Mid a throng
310 Of maids and youths, old men, and matrons staid,
A medley of all tempers, I had passed

but that . . . pursue (ll. 315–22) Compare this
"possible sublimity" with Book VI.608 "and
something evermore about to be."

The night in dancing, gaiety, and mirth,
With din of instruments and shuffling feet,
And glancing forms, and tapers glittering,
And unaimed prattle flying up and down;
Spirits upon the stretch, and here and there
Slight shocks of young love-liking interspersed,
Whose transient pleasure mounted to the head,
And tingled through the veins. Ere we retired,
320 The cock had crowed, and now the eastern sky
Was kindling, not unseen, from humble copse
And open field, through which the pathway wound,
And homeward led my steps. Magnificent
The morning rose, in memorable pomp,
Glorious as e'er I had beheld—in front,
The sea lay laughing at a distance; near,
The solid mountains shone, bright as the clouds,
Grain-tinctured, drenched in empyrean light;
And in the meadows and the lower grounds
330 Was all the sweetness of a common dawn—
Dews, vapours, and the melody of birds,
And labourers going forth to till the fields.°

Ah! need I say, dear Friend! that to the brim
My heart was full; I made no vows, but vows
Were then made for me; bond unknown to me
Was given, that I should be, else sinning greatly,
A dedicated Spirit. On I walked
In thankful blessedness, which yet survives.

        · · ·

From *Book Fifth*

BOOKS

When Contemplation, like the night-calm felt
Through earth and sky, spreads widely, and sends deep
Into the soul its tranquillizing power,
Even then I sometimes grieve for thee, O Man,
Earth's paramount Creature! not so much for woes
That thou endurest; heavy though that weight be,
Cloud-like it mounts, or touched with light divine
Doth melt away; but for those palms achieved,
Through length of time, by patient exercise
10 Of study and hard thought; there, there, it is
That sadness finds its fuel. Hitherto,
In progress through this Verse, my mind hath looked
Upon the speaking face of earth and heaven

Magnificent . . . fields This moment of moments (ll. 323–32) is revivalistic in its structure, peculiarly Protestant in its temper,
because of the acute sense of election it conveys.

As her prime teacher, intercourse with man
Established by the sovereign Intellect,
Who through that bodily image hath diffused,
As might appear to the eye of fleeting time,
A deathless spirit. Thou also, man! hast wrought,
For commerce of thy nature with herself,
20   Things that aspire to unconquerable life;
And yet we feel—we cannot choose but feel—
That they must perish. Trembling of the heart
It gives, to think that our immortal being
No more shall need such garments; and yet man,
As long as he shall be the child of earth,
Might almost 'weep to have'° what he may lose,
Nor be himself extinguished, but survive,
Abject, depressed, forlorn, disconsolate.
A thought is with me sometimes, and I say,—
30   Should the whole frame of earth by inward throes
Be wrenched, or fire come down from far to scorch
Her pleasant habitations, and dry up
Old Ocean, in his bed left singed and bare,
Yet would the living Presence still subsist
Victorious, and composure would ensue,
And kindlings like the morning—presage sure
Of day returning and of life revived.
But all the meditations of mankind,
Yea, all the adamantine holds of truth
40   By reason built, or passion, which itself
Is highest reason in a soul sublime;
The consecrated works of Bard and Sage,
Sensuous or intellectual, wrought by men,
Twin labourers and heirs of the same hopes;
Where would they be? Oh! why hath not the Mind
Some element to stamp her image on
In nature somewhat nearer to her own?
Why, gifted with such powers to send abroad
Her spirit, must it lodge in shrines so frail?

50   One day, when from my lips a like complaint
Had fallen in presence of a studious friend,
He with a smile made answer, that in truth
'Twas going far to seek disquietude;
But on the front of his reproof confessed
That he himself had oftentimes given way
To kindred hauntings. Whereupon I told,
That once in the stillness of a summer's noon,
While I was seated in a rocky cave

'weep to have' See Shakespeare, Sonnet LXIV,
l. 14.

By the sea-side, perusing, so it chanced,
60   The famous history of the errant knight
Recorded by Cervantes, these same thoughts
Beset me, and to height unusual rose,
'While listlessly I sate, and, having closed
The book, had turned my eyes toward the wide sea.
On poetry and geometric truth,
And their high privilege of lasting life,
From all internal injury exempt,
I mused, upon these chiefly: and at length,
My senses yielding to the sultry air,
70   Sleep seized me, and I passed into a dream.°
I saw before me stretched a boundless plain
Of sandy wilderness, all black and void,
And as I looked around, distress and fear
Came creeping over me, when at my side,
Close at my side, an uncouth shape appeared
Upon a dromedary,° mounted high.
He seemed an Arab of the Bedouin tribes:
A lance he bore, and underneath one arm
A stone, and in the opposite hand, a shell
80   Of a surpassing brightness. At the sight
Much I rejoiced, not doubting but a guide
Was present, one who with unerring skill
Would through the desert lead me; and while yet
I looked and looked, self-questioned what this freight
Which the new-comer carried through the waste
Could mean, the Arab told me that the stone
(To give it in the language of the dream)
Was 'Euclid's Elements'; and 'This,' said he,
'Is something of more worth'; and at the word
90   Stretched forth the shell, so beautiful in shape,
In colour so resplendent, with command
That I should hold it to my ear. I did so,
And heard that instant in an unknown tongue,
Which yet I understood, articulate sounds,
A loud prophetic blast of harmony;
An Ode, in passion uttered, which foretold
Destruction to the children of the earth
By deluge, now at hand. No sooner ceased
The song, than the Arab with calm look declared
100   That all would come to pass of which the voice
Had given forewarning, and that he himself
Was going then to bury those two books:
The one that held acquaintance with the stars,
And wedded soul to soul in purest bond

Sleep . . . dream not actually Wordsworth's
own dream, but founded on a dream of the
great French philosopher Descartes (1596–1650)
dromedary camel with one hump

Of reason, undisturbed by space or time;
The other that was a god, yea many gods,
Had voices more than all the winds, with power
To exhilarate the spirit, and to soothe,
Through every clime, the heart of human kind.
110   While this was uttering, strange as it may seem,
I wondered not, although I plainly saw
The one to be a stone, the other a shell;
Nor doubted once but that they both were books,
Having a perfect faith in all that passed.
Far stronger, now, grew the desire I felt
To cleave unto this man; but when I prayed
To share his enterprise, he hurried on
Reckless of me: I followed, not unseen,
For oftentimes he cast a backward look,
120   Grasping his twofold treasure.—Lance in rest,°
He rode, I keeping pace with him; and now
He, to my fancy, had become the knight
Whose tale Cervantes tells; yet not the knight,
But was an Arab of the desert too;
Of these was neither, and was both at once.
His countenance, meanwhile, grew more disturbed;
And, looking backwards when he looked, mine eyes
Saw, over half the wilderness diffused,
A bed of glittering light:° I asked the cause:
130   'It is,' said he, 'the waters of the deep
Gathering upon us'; quickening then the pace
Of the unwieldy creature he bestrode,
He left me: I called after him aloud;
He heeded not; but, with his twofold charge
Still in his grasp, before me, full in view,
Went hurrying o'er the illimitable waste,
With the fleet waters of a drowning world
In chase of him; whereat I waked in terror,
And saw the sea before me, and the book,
140   In which I had been reading, at my side.

    Full often, taking from the world of sleep
This Arab phantom, which I thus beheld,
This semi-Quixote, I to him have given
A substance, fancied him a living man,
A gentle dweller in the desert, crazed
By love and feeling, and internal thought
Protracted among endless solitudes;
Have shaped him wandering upon this quest!

Lance in rest Previously the Arab held both shell and lance; now, farther along in his saving quest, he holds both shell and stone.
glittering light Wordsworth's consciousness does not fear engulfment, which appears as a kind of glory, but fears instead the black and void sandy wilderness in which the dream began.

Nor have I pitied him; but rather felt
150   Reverence was due to a being thus employed;
And thought that, in the blind and awful lair
Of such a madness, reason did lie couched.
Enow there are on earth to take in charge
Their wives, their children, and their virgin loves,
Or whatsoever else the heart holds dear;
Enow to stir for these; yea, will I say,
Contemplating in soberness the approach
Of an event so dire, by signs in earth
Or heaven made manifest, that I could share
160   That maniac's fond anxiety, and go
Upon like errand. Oftentimes at least
Me hath such strong entrancement overcome,
When I have held a volume in my hand,
Poor earthly casket of immortal verse,
Shakespeare, or Milton, labourers divine!

.   .   .

There was a Boy:° ye knew him well, ye cliffs
And islands of Winander!—many a time
At evening, when the earliest stars began
To move along the edges of the hills,
Rising or setting, would he stand alone
Beneath the trees or by the glimmering lake,
370   And there, with fingers interwoven, both hands
Pressed closely palm to palm, and to his mouth
Uplifted, he, as through an instrument,
Blew mimic hootings to the silent owls,
That they might answer him; and they would shout
Across the watery vale, and shout again,
Responsive to his call, with quivering peals,
And long halloos and screams, and echoes loud,
Redoubled and redoubled, concourse wild
Of jocund din; and, when a lengthened pause
380   Of silence came and baffled his best skill,
Then sometimes, in that silence while he hung
Listening, a gentle shock of mild surprise
Has carried far into his heart the voice
Of mountain torrents; or the visible scene
Would enter unawares into his mind,
With all its solemn imagery, its rocks,
Its woods, and that uncertain heaven, received
Into the bosom of the steady lake.°

This Boy was taken from his mates, and died
390   In childhood, ere he was full twelve years old.

Boy In the first draft the boy is Wordsworth himself.
Its woods . . . lake Coleridge said of ll. 387–   88: "Had I met these lines running wild in the deserts of Arabia, I should have instantly screamed out 'Wordsworth!' "

Fair is the spot, most beautiful the vale
Where he was born; the grassy churchyard hangs
Upon a slope above the village school,
And through that churchyard when my way has led
On summer evenings, I believe that there
A long half hour together I have stood
Mute, looking at the grave in which he lies!
Even now appears before the mind's clear eye
That self-same village church; I see her sit
400   (The thronèd Lady whom erewhile we hailed)
On her green hill, forgetful of this Boy
Who slumbers at her feet,—forgetful, too,
Of all her silent neighbourhood of graves,
And listening only to the gladsome sounds
That, from the rural school ascending, play
Beneath her and about her. May she long
Behold a race of young ones like to those
With whom I herded!—(easily, indeed,
We might have fed upon a fatter soil
410   Of arts and letters—but be that forgiven)—
A race of real children; not too wise,
Too learned, or too good; but wanton, fresh,
And bandied up and down by love and hate;
Not unresentful where self-justified;
Fierce, moody, patient, venturous, modest, shy;
Mad at their sports like withered leaves in winds;
Though doing wrong and suffering, and full oft
Bending beneath our life's mysterious weight
Of pain, and doubt, and fear, yet yielding not
420   In happiness to the happiest upon earth.
Simplicity in habit, truth in speech,
Be these the daily strengtheners of their minds;
May books and Nature be their early joy!
And knowledge, rightly honoured with that name—
Knowledge not purchased by the loss of power!°

430   . . . that very week,
While I was roving up and down alone,
Seeking I knew not what, I chanced to cross
One of those open fields, which, shaped like ears,
Make green peninsulas on Esthwaite's Lake:
Twilight was coming on, yet through the gloom
Appeared distinctly on the opposite shore
A heap of garments, as if left by one
Who might have there been bathing. Long I watched,
But no one owned them; meanwhile the calm lake

Knowledge . . . power a concern central to
Wordsworth, since the compensatory imagination
verges on a kind of increase in knowledge at
the expense of a drain upon experience.

Wordsworth's terms here influenced De Quincey
and Shelley, and play their part in Yeats, as in
the final question of "Leda and the Swan."

440   Grew dark with all the shadows on its breast,
And, now and then, a fish up-leaping snapped
The breathless stillness. The succeeding day,
Those unclaimed garments telling a plain tale
Drew to the spot an anxious crowd; some looked
In passive expectation from the shore,
While from a boat others hung o'er the deep,
Sounding with grappling irons and long poles.
At last, the dead man, 'mid that beauteous scene
Of trees and hills and water, bolt upright
450   Rose, with his ghastly face, a spectre shape
Of terror; yet no soul-debasing fear,
Young as I was, a child not nine years old,
Possessed me, for my inner eye had seen
Such sights before, among the shining streams
Of faery land, the forest of romance.
Their spirit hallowed the sad spectacle
With decoration of ideal grace;
A dignity, a smoothness, like the works
Of Grecian art, and purest poesy.°

.   .   .

A gracious spirit o'er this earth presides,
And o'er the heart of man: invisibly
It comes, to works of unreproved delight,
And tendency benign, directing those
Who care not, know not, think not what they do.
The tales that charm away the wakeful night
In Araby, romances; legends penned
For solace by dim light of monkish lamps;
Fictions, for ladies of their love, devised
500   By youthful squires; adventures endless, spun
By the dismantled warrior in old age,
Out of the bowels of those very schemes
In which his youth did first extravagate;
These spread like day, and something in the shape
Of these will live till man shall be no more.
Dumb yearnings, hidden appetites, are ours,
And *they must* have their food. Our childhood sits,
Our simple childhood, sits upon a throne
That hath more power than all the elements.
510   I guess not what this tells of Being past,
Nor what it augurs of the life to come;
But so it is, and, in that dubious hour,
That twilight when we first begin to see
This dawning earth, to recognise, expect,
And in the long probation that ensues,

---

yet no . . poesy An extraordinarily difficult argument is implicit here (ll. 451–59), but the kernal is the contention that early immersion in the romance world serves to defend the mind from too early an exposure to experiential horrors.

The time of trial, ere we learn to live
In reconcilement with our stinted powers;
To endure this state of meagre vassalage,
Unwilling to forego, confess, submit,
520 Uneasy and unsettled, yoke-fellows
To custom, mettlesome, and not yet tamed
And humbled down; oh! then we feel, we feel,
We know where we have friends. Ye dreamers, then,
Forgers of daring tales! we bless you then,
Impostors, drivellers, dotards, as the ape
Philosophy will call you: *then* we feel
With what, and how great might ye are in league,
Who make our wish, our power, our thought a deed,
An empire, a possession,—ye whom time
530 And seasons serve; all Faculties to whom
Earth crouches, the elements are potter's clay,
Space like a heaven filled up with northern lights,
Here, nowhere, there, and everywhere at once.°

.   .   .

Here must we pause: this only let me add,
From heart-experience, and in humblest sense
Of modesty, that he, who in his youth
A daily wanderer among woods and fields
With living Nature hath been intimate,
Not only in that raw unpractised time
590 Is stirred to extasy, as others are,
By glittering verse; but further, doth receive,
In measure only dealt out to himself,
Knowledge and increase of enduring joy
From the great Nature that exists in works
Of mighty Poets. Visionary power
Attends the motions of the viewless winds,
Embodied in the mystery of words:
There, darkness makes abode, and all the host
Of shadowy things work endless changes,—there,
600 As in a mansion like their proper home,
Even forms and substances are circumfused
By that transparent veil with light divine,
And, through the turnings intricate of verse,
Present themselves as objects recognised,
In flashes, and with glory not their own.

From *Book Sixth*

CAMBRIDGE AND THE ALPS

When the third summer freed us from restraint,
A youthful friend, he too a mountaineer,

Space . . . once See the opening section of
Wallace Stevens's *The Auroras of Autumn.*

Not slow to share my wishes, took his staff,
And sallying forth, we journeyed side by side,
Bound to the distant Alps. A hardy slight
Did this unprecedented course imply
Of college studies and their set rewards;
Nor had, in truth, the scheme been formed by me
330   Without uneasy forethought of the pain,
The censures, and ill-omening of those
To whom my worldly interests were dear.
But Nature then was sovereign in my mind,
And mighty forms, seizing a youthful fancy,
Had given a charter to irregular hopes.
In any age of uneventful calm
Among the nations, surely would my heart
Have been possessed by similar desire;
But Europe at that time was thrilled with joy,
340   France standing on the top of golden hours,°
And human nature seeming born again.

    . . .

       That very day,
From a bare ridge we also first beheld
Unveiled the summit of Mont Blanc, and grieved
To have a soulless image on the eye
That had usurped upon a living thought
That never more could be. The wondrous Vale
Of Chamouny stretched far below, and soon
530   With its dumb cataracts and streams of ice,
A motionless array of mighty waves,
Five rivers broad and vast, made rich amends,
And reconciled us to realities;
There small birds warble from the leafy trees,
The eagle soars high in the element,
There doth the reaper bind the yellow sheaf,
The maiden spread the haycock in the sun,
While Winter like a well-tamed lion walks,
Descending from the mountain to make sport
540   Among the cottages by beds of flowers.

Whate'er in this wide circuit we beheld,
Or heard, was fitted to our unripe state
Of intellect and heart. With such a book
Before our eyes, we could not choose but read
Lessons of genuine brotherhood, the plain
And universal reason of mankind,
The truths of young and old. Nor, side by side
Pacing, two social pilgrims, or alone

the top of golden hours See Shakespeare, Sonnet
XVI, l. 5: "Now stand you on the top of happy
hours."

Each with his humour, could we fail to abound
550   In dreams and fictions, pensively composed:
Dejection taken up for pleasure's sake,
And gilded sympathies, the willow wreath,
And sober posies of funereal flowers,
Gathered among those solitudes sublime
From formal gardens of the lady Sorrow,
Did sweeten many a meditative hour.

        Yet still in me with those soft luxuries
Mixed something of stern mood,° an under-thirst
Of vigour seldom utterly allayed.
560   And from that source how different a sadness
Would issue, let one incident make known.
When from the Vallais we had turned, and clomb
Along the Simplon's steep and rugged road,
Following a band of muleteers, we reached
A halting-place, where all together took
Their noon-tide meal. Hastily rose our guide,
Leaving us at the board; awhile we lingered,
Then paced the beaten downward way that led
Right to a rough stream's edge, and there broke off;
570   The only track now visible was one
That from the torrent's further brink held forth
Conspicuous invitation to ascend
A lofty mountain. After brief delay
Crossing the unbridged stream, that road we took,
And clomb with eagerness, till anxious fears
Intruded, for we failed to overtake
Our comrades gone before. By fortunate chance,
While every moment added doubt to doubt,
A peasant met us, from whose mouth we learned
580   That to the spot which had perplexed us first
We must descend, and there should find the road,
Which in the stony channel of the stream
Lay a few steps, and then along its banks;
And, that our future course, all plain to sight,
Was downwards, with the current of that stream.
Loth to believe what we so grieved to hear,
For still we had hopes that pointed to the clouds,
We questioned him again, and yet again;
But every word that from the peasant's lips
590   Came in reply, translated by our feelings,
Ended in this,—*that we had crossed the Alps.*°

stern mood Geoffrey Hartman observes: "The
stern mood to which Wordsworth refers can only
be his premonition of spiritual autonomy, of an
independence from sense-experience. . . ."
Loth . . . Alps (ll. 586–91) Hartman: "The

poet recognizes at last that the power he has
looked for in the outside world is really within
and frustrating his search. A shock of recognition
then feeds the very blindness toward the external world which helped to produce that shock."

Imagination—here the Power so called
Through sad incompetence of human speech,
That awful Power rose from the mind's abyss
Like an unfathered vapour that enwraps,
At once, some lonely traveller. I was lost;
Halted without an effort to break through;
But to my conscious soul I now can say—
'I recognise thy glory': in such strength
600   Of usurpation, when the light of sense
Goes out, but with a flash that has revealed
The invisible world, doth greatness make abode,
There harbours; whether we be young or old,
Our destiny, our being's heart and home,
Is with infinitude, and only there;
With hope it is, hope that can never die,
Effort, and expectation, and desire,
And something evermore about to be.
Under such banners militant, the soul
610   Seeks for no trophies, struggles for no spoils
That may attest her prowess, blest in thoughts
That are their own perfection and reward,
Strong in herself and in beatitude
That hides her, like the mighty flood of Nile
Poured from his fount of Abyssinian clouds
To fertilise the whole Egyptian plain.°

The melancholy slackening that ensued
Upon those tidings by the peasant given
Was soon dislodged. Downwards we hurried fast,
620   And, with the half-shaped road which we had missed,
Entered a narrow chasm. The brook and road
Were fellow-travellers in this gloomy strait,
And with them did we journey several hours
At a slow pace. The immeasurable height
Of woods decaying, never to be decayed,
The stationary blasts of waterfalls,
And in the narrow rent at every turn
Winds thwarting winds, bewildered and forlorn,
The torrents shooting from the clear blue sky,
630   The rocks that muttered close upon our ears,
Black drizzling crags that spake by the way-side
As if a voice were in them, the sick sight
And giddy prospect of the raving stream,
The unfettered clouds and region of the Heavens,
Tumult and peace, the darkness and the light—
Were all like workings of one mind, the features

Imagination . . . plain This passage (ll. 592–
616) is a sublime afterthought, nearly fourteen years after the event.

Of the same face, blossoms upon one tree;
Characters of the great Apocalypse,°
The types and symbols of Eternity,
40   Of first, and last, and midst, and without end.°

         .   .   .

From *Book Seventh*

RESIDENCE IN LONDON

         Rise up, thou monstrous ant-hill on the plain
50   Of a too busy world! Before me flow,
Thou endless stream of men and moving things!
Thy every-day appearance, as it strikes—
With wonder heightened, or sublimed by awe—
On strangers, of all ages; the quick dance
Of colours, lights, and forms; the deafening din;
The comers and the goers face to face,
Face after face; the string of dazzling wares,
Shop after shop, with symbols, blazoned names,
And all the tradesman's honours overhead:
60   Here, fronts of houses, like a title-page,
With letters huge inscribed from top to toe,
Stationed above the door, like guardian saints;
There, allegoric shapes, female or male,
Or physiognomies of real men,
Land-warriors, kings, or admirals of the sea,
Boyle,° Shakespeare, Newton, or the attractive head
Of some quack-doctor, famous in his day.

         Meanwhile the roar continues, till at length,
Escaped as from an enemy, we turn
70   Abruptly into some sequestered nook,
Still as a sheltered place when winds blow loud!
At leisure, thence, through tracts of thin resort,
And sights and sounds that come at intervals,
We take our way. A raree-show° is here,
With children gathered round; another street
Presents a company of dancing dogs,
Or dromedary, with an antic pair
Of monkeys on his back; a minstrel band
Of Savoyards; or, single and alone,
80   An English ballad-singer. Private courts,

Apocalypse Revelation, the last book of the New Testament, and also the last act in the Christian drama of history; here natural objects are seen as being at once written words of Revelation and actors in the final drama of redemption.
Of first . . . without end See *Paradise Lost* V.165.

Boyle Robert Boyle, 17th-century physical scientist
raree-show Savoyard pronunciation of rare-show, a show-in-a-box or a peep-show; Savoyards were immigrants from the duchy of Savoy on the border between France and Italy.

Gloomy as coffins, and unsightly lanes
Thrilled by some female vendor's scream, belike
The very shrillest of all London cries,
May then entangle our impatient steps;
Conducted through those labyrinths, unawares,
To privileged regions and inviolate,
Where from their airy lodges studious lawyers
Look out on waters, walks, and gardens green.

.   .   .

    As the black storm upon the mountain top
620 Sets off the sunbeam in the valley, so
That huge fermenting mass of human-kind
Serves as a solemn back-ground, or relief,
To single forms and objects, whence they draw,
For feeling and contemplative regard,
More than inherent liveliness and power.
How oft, amid those overflowing streets,
Have I gone forward with the crowd, and said
Unto myself, 'The face of every one
That passes by me is a mystery!'
630 Thus have I looked, nor ceased to look, oppressed
By thoughts of what and whither, when and how,
Until the shapes before my eyes became
A second-sight procession, such as glides
Over still mountains, or appears in dreams;
And once, far-travelled in such mood, beyond
The reach of common indication, lost
Amid the moving pageant, I was smitten
Abruptly, with the view (a sight not rare)
Of a blind Beggar, who, with upright face,
640 Stood, propped against a wall, upon his chest
Wearing a written paper, to explain
His story, whence he came, and who he was.
Caught by the spectacle my mind turned round
As with the might of waters; an apt type
This label seemed of the utmost we can know,
Both of ourselves and of the universe;
And, on the shape of that unmoving man,
His steadfast face and sightless eyes, I gazed,
As if admonished from another world.°

650 Though reared upon the base of outward things,
Structures like these the excited spirit mainly
Builds for herself; scenes different there are,
Full-formed, that take, with small internal help,
Possession of the faculties,—the peace

And . . . world The blind Beggar belongs to the visionary world of the Leech-gatherer in "Resolution and Independence," for here too "the might of waters" is invoked.

That comes with night; the deep solemnity
Of nature's intermediate hours of rest,
When the great tide of human life stands still;
The business of the day to come, unborn,
Of that gone by, locked up, as in the grave;
660 The blended calmness of the heavens and earth,
Moonlight and stars, and empty streets, and sounds
Unfrequent as in deserts; at late hours
Of winter evenings, when unwholesome rains
Are falling hard, with people yet astir,
The feeble salutation from the voice
Of some unhappy woman, now and then
Heard as we pass, when no one looks about,
Nothing is listened to. But these, I fear,
Are falsely catalogued; things that are, are not,
670 As the mind answers to them, or the heart
Is prompt, or slow, to feel. What say you, then,
To times, when half the city shall break out
Full of one passion, vengeance, rage, or fear?
To executions, to a street on fire,
Mobs, riots, or rejoicings? From these sights
Take one,—that ancient festival, the Fair,
Holden where martyrs suffered in past time,
And named of St. Bartholomew;° there, see
A work completed to our hands, that lays,
680 If any spectacle on earth can do,
The whole creative powers of man asleep!—
For once, the Muse's help will we implore,
And she shall lodge us, wafted on her wings,
Above the press and danger of the crowd,
Upon some showman's platform. What a shock
For eyes and ears! what anarchy and din,
Barbarian and infernal,—a phantasma,°
Monstrous in colour, motion, shape, sight, sound!
Below, the open space, through every nook
690 Of the wide area, twinkles, is alive
With heads; the midway region, and above,
Is thronged with staring pictures and huge scrolls,
Dumb proclamations of the Prodigies;°
With chattering monkeys dangling from their poles,
And children whirling in their roundabouts;°
With those that stretch the neck and strain the eyes,
And crack the voice in rivalship, the crowd
Inviting; with buffoons against buffoons

that ancient . . . St. Bartholomew This fair took place in Smithfield, where Protestants were martyred when the Catholic Queen Mary ruled, from 1553 to 1558.

phantasma illusion
Prodigies wonders; here, freaks
roundabouts merry-go-rounds

Grimacing, writhing, screaming,—him who grinds
700   The hurdy-gurdy, at the fiddle weaves,
Rattles the salt-box, thumps the kettle-drum,
And him who at the trumpet puffs his cheeks,
The silver-collared Negro with his timbrel,
Equestrians, tumblers, women, girls, and boys,
Blue-breeched, pink-vested, with high-towering plumes.
All moveables of wonder, from all parts,
Are here—Albinos, painted Indians, Dwarfs,
The Horse of knowledge, and the learned Pig,
The Stone-eater, the man that swallows fire,
710   Giants, Ventriloquists, the Invisible Girl,
The Bust that speaks and moves its goggling eyes,
The Wax-work, Clock-work, all the marvellous craft
Of modern Merlins, Wild Beasts, Puppet-shows,
All out-o'-the-way, far-fetched, perverted things,
All freaks of nature, all Promethean thoughts
Of man, his dullness, madness, and their feats
All jumbled up together, to compose
A Parliament of Monsters. Tents and Booths
Meanwhile, as if the whole were one vast mill,
720   Are vomiting, receiving on all sides,
Men, Women, three-years Children, Babes in arms.

Oh, blank confusion! true epitome
Of what the mighty City is herself
To thousands upon thousands of her sons,
Living amid the same perpetual whirl
Of trivial objects, melted and reduced
To one identity, by differences
That have no law, no meaning, and no end—
Oppression, under which even highest minds
730   Must labour, whence the strongest are not free.
But though the picture weary out the eye,
By nature an unmanageable sight,
It is not wholly so to him who looks
In steadiness, who hath among least things
An under-sense of greatest; sees the parts
As parts, but with a feeling of the whole.

.   .   .

From *Book Eighth*

RETROSPECT

But lovelier far than this, the paradise
Where I was reared; in Nature's primitive gifts
100   Favoured no less, and more to every sense
Delicious, seeing that the sun and sky,

The elements, and seasons as they change,
Do find a worthy fellow-labourer there—
Man free, man working for himself, with choice
Of time, and place, and object; by his wants,
His comforts, native occupations, cares,
Cheerfully led to individual ends
Or social, and still followed by a train
Unwooed, unthought-of even—simplicity,
10   And beauty, and inevitable grace.

    Yea, when a glimpse of those imperial bowers
Would to a child be transport over-great,
When but a half-hour's roam through such a place
Would leave behind a dance of images,
That shall break in upon his sleep for weeks;
Even then the common haunts of the green earth,
And ordinary interests of man,
Which they embosom, all without regard
As both may seem, are fastening on the heart
20   Insensibly, each with the other's help.
For me, when my affections first were led
From kindred, friends, and playmates, to partake
Love for the human creature's absolute self,
That noticeable kindliness of heart
Sprang out of fountains, there abounding most
Where sovereign Nature dictated the tasks
And occupations which her beauty adorned,
And Shepherds were the men that pleased me first;

    . . . For this he quits his home
At day-spring, and no sooner doth the sun
Begin to strike him with a fire-like heat,
Than he lies down upon some shining rock,
And breakfasts with his dog. When they have stolen,
As is their wont, a pittance from strict time,
240   For rest not needed or exchange of love,
Then from his couch he starts; and now his feet
Crush out a livelier fragrance from the flowers
Of lowly thyme, by Nature's skill enwrought
In the wild turf: the lingering dews of morn
Smoke round him, as from hill to hill he lies,
His staff protending° like a hunter's spear,
Or by its aid leaping from crag to crag,
And o'er the brawling beds of unbridged streams.
Philosophy, methinks, at Fancy's call,
250   Might deign to follow him through what he does
Or sees in his day's march; himself he feels,
In those vast regions where his service lies,

protending stretching out

A freeman, wedded to his life of hope
And hazard, and hard labour interchanged
With that majestic indolence so dear
To native man. A rambling school-boy, thus
I felt his presence in his own domain,
As of a lord and master, or a power,
Or genius, under Nature, under God,
260   Presiding; and severest solitude
Had more commanding looks when he was there.
When up the lonely brooks on rainy days
Angling I went, or trod the trackless hills
By mists bewildered, suddenly mine eyes
Have glanced upon him distant a few steps,
In size a giant, stalking through thick fog,
His sheep like Greenland bears; or, as he stepped
Beyond the boundary line of some hill-shadow,
His form hath flashed upon me, glorified
270   By the deep radiance of the setting sun:
Or him have I descried in distant sky,
A solitary object and sublime,
Above all height! like an aerial cross
Stationed alone upon a spiry rock
Of the Chartreuse,° for worship. Thus was man
Ennobled outwardly before my sight,
And thus my heart was early introduced
To an unconscious love and reverence
Of human nature; hence the human form
280   To me became an index of delight,
Of grace and honour, power and worthiness.
Meanwhile this creature—spiritual almost
As those of books, but more exalted far;
Far more of an imaginative form
Than the gay Corin° of the groves, who lives
For his own fancies, or to dance by the hour,
In coronal, with Phyllis in the midst—
Was, for the purposes of kind, a man
With the most common; husband, father; learned,
290   Could teach, admonish; suffered with the rest
From vice and folly, wretchedness and fear;
Of this I little saw, cared less for it,
But something must have felt.
                              Call ye these appearances—
Which I beheld of shepherds in my youth,
This sanctity of Nature given to man—
A shadow, a delusion, ye who pore

Chartreuse the mountains near Grenoble; the Carthusian monks placed crosses on the tops of them

Corin Corin and Phyllis are traditional names in literary pastoral.

On the dead letter, miss the spirit of things;
Whose truth is not a motion or a shape
Instinct with vital functions, but a block
Or waxen image which yourselves have made,
And ye adore! But blessed be the God
Of Nature and of Man that this was so;
That men before my inexperienced eyes
Did first present themselves thus purified,
Removed, and to a distance that was fit:

. . .

From *Book Tenth*

RESIDENCE IN FRANCE

. . . It pleased me more
To abide in the great City,° where I found
The general air still busy with the stir
Of that first memorable onset made
By a strong levy of humanity
Upon the traffickers in Negro blood;°
Effort which, though defeated, had recalled
To notice old forgotten principles,
And through the nation spread a novel heat
Of virtuous feeling. For myself, I own
That this particular strife had wanted power
To rivet my affections; nor did now
Its unsuccessful issue much excite
My sorrow; for I brought with me the faith
That, if France prospered, good men would not long
Pay fruitless worship to humanity,
And this most rotten branch of human shame,
Object, so seemed it, of superfluous pains,
Would fall together with its parent tree.
What, then, were my emotions, when in arms
Britain put forth her free-born strength in league,
Oh, pity and shame! with those confederate Powers!°
Not in my single self alone I found,
But in the minds of all ingenuous youth,
Change and subversion from that hour. No shock
Given to my moral nature had I known

great City London. Wordsworth went to France late in 1791, and stayed for one year, intensely sympathizing with the moderate Girondist faction among the revolutionaries, and falling in love (and fathering a daughter) with Annette Vallon; on his return to England, he experienced the double guilt of not sharing the Girondists' fate, when most were executed by the radical Jacobins in the Terror, and of having abandoned his mistress and their daughter.

Of that . . . Negro blood William Wilberforce's bill for abolishing the slave trade passed the House of Commons in April 1792, but was killed in the House of Lords; abolition did not come until 1807.
What . . . Powers On February 11, 1793, England declared war against France, thus joining itself to the most tyrannical European nations in their league against the Revolution.

270   Down to that very moment;° neither lapse
       Nor turn of sentiment that might be named
       A revolution, save at this one time;
       All else was progress on the self-same path
       On which, with a diversity of pace,
       I had been travelling: this a stride at once
       Into another region. As a light
       And pliant harebell, swinging in the breeze
       On some grey rock—its birth-place—so had I
       Wantoned, fast rooted on the ancient tower
280   Of my beloved country, wishing not
       A happier fortune than to wither there:
       Now was I from that pleasant station torn
       And tossed about in whirlwind. I rejoiced,
       Yea, afterwards—truth most painful to record!—
       Exulted, in the triumph of my soul,
       When Englishmen by thousands were o'erthrown,
       Left without glory on the field, or driven,
       Brave hearts! to shameful flight.° It was a grief,—
       Grief call it not, 'twas anything but that,—
290   A conflict of sensations without name,
       Of which *he* only, who may love the sight
       Of a village steeple, as I do, can judge,
       When, in the congregation bending all
       To their great Father, prayers were offered up,
       Or praises for our country's victories;
       And, 'mid the simple worshippers, perchance
       I only, like an uninvited guest
       Whom no one owned, sate silent, shall I add,
       Fed on the day of vengeance yet to come.

                       .   .   .

       It was a lamentable time for man,
       Whether a hope had e'er been his or not;
       A woeful time for them whose hopes survived
       The shock; most woeful for those few who still
       Were flattered, and had trust in human kind:
       They had the deepest feeling of the grief.
390   Meanwhile the Invaders fared as they deserved:
       The Herculean Commonwealth had put forth her arms,
       And throttled with an infant godhead's might
       The snakes about her cradle; that was well,
       And as it should be; yet no cure for them
       Whose souls were sick with pain of what would be
       Hereafter brought in charge against mankind.

No shock . . . moment Not even the failure of
the Revolution affected Wordsworth as strongly
as the English counter-revolutionary crusade;
this holds true for Blake and Coleridge also.

shameful flight retreat of the Duke of York's
army after the battle of Hondshoote, in September 1793

Most melancholy at that time, O Friend!
Were my day-thoughts,—my nights were miserable;
Through months, through years, long after the last beat
400 Of those atrocities,° the hour of sleep
To me came rarely charged with natural gifts,
Such ghastly visions had I of despair
And tyranny, and implements of death;
And innocent victims sinking under fear,
And momentary hope, and worn-out prayer,
Each in his separate cell, or penned in crowds
For sacrifice, and struggling with fond mirth
And levity in dungeons, where the dust
Was laid with tears. Then suddenly the scene
410 Changed, and the unbroken dream entangled me
In long orations, which I strove to plead
Before unjust tribunals,—with a voice
Labouring, a brain confounded, and a sense,
Death-like, of treacherous desertion,° felt
In the last place of refuge—my own soul.

. . .

From *Book Eleventh*

FRANCE

O pleasant exercise of hope and joy!°
For mighty were the auxiliars which then stood
Upon our side, us who were strong in love!
Bliss was it in that dawn to be alive,
But to be young was very Heaven! O times,
110 In which the meagre, stale, forbidding ways
Of custom, law, and statute, took at once
The attraction of a country in romance!
When Reason seemed the most to assert her rights
When most intent on making of herself
A prime enchantress—to assist the work,
Which then was going forward in her name!
Not favoured spots alone, but the whole Earth,
The beauty wore of promise—that which sets
(As at some moments might not be unfelt
120 Among the bowers of Paradise itself)
The budding rose above the rose full blown.
What temper at the prospect did not wake

---

those atrocities the Reign ot Terror, autumn
1793 to summer 1794
treacherous desertion His guilt is complex here;
the manifest element is having abandoned the
Girondists, but the latent, stronger anxiety is
for having abandoned Annette and his child.

hope and joy This rhapsody (ll. 105–44) on the
original prospects of the Revolution should be
compared with the concluding passage from
"Home at Grasmere" used as the "Prospectus"
to *The Excursion.*

To happiness unthought of? The inert
Were roused, and lively natures rapt away!
They who had fed their childhood upon dreams,
The play-fellows of fancy, who had made
All powers of swiftness, subtilty, and strength
Their ministers,—who in lordly wise had stirred
Among the grandest objects of the sense,
130   And dealt with whatsoever they found there
As if they had within some lurking right
To wield it;—they, too, who of gentle mood
Had watched all gentle motions, and to these
Had fitted their own thoughts, schemers more mild,
And in the region of their peaceful selves;—
Now was it that *both* found, the meek and lofty
Did both find helpers to their hearts' desire,
And stuff at hand, plastic as they could wish,—
Were called upon to exercise their skill,
140   Not in Utopia,—subterranean fields,—
Or some secreted island, Heaven knows where!
But in the very world, which is the world
Of all of us,—the place where, in the end,
We find our happiness, or not at all!

.   .   .

But now, become oppressors in their turn,°
Frenchmen had changed a war of self-defence
For one of conquest, losing sight of all
Which they had struggled for: now mounted up,
210   Openly in the eye of earth and heaven,
The scale of liberty. I read her doom,
With anger vexed, with disappointment sore,
But not dismayed, nor taking to the shame
Of a false prophet. While resentment rose
Striving to hide, what nought could heal, the wounds
Of mortified presumption, I adhered
More firmly to old tenets, and, to prove
Their temper, strained them more; and thus, in heat
Of contest, did opinions every day
220   Grow into consequence, till round my mind
They clung, as if they were its life, nay more,
The very being of the immortal soul.°

.   .   .

I summoned my best skill, and toiled, intent
280   To anatomize the frame of social life,
Yea, the whole body of society

But . . . turn By early 1795, French armies were thrusting deep into Italy, Spain, and Germany.

immortal soul This passage (ll. 206–22) is the start of Wordsworth's *intellectual* crisis, as contrasted to the *poetic* crisis depicted in Book First.

Searched to its heart.° Share with me, Friend! the wish
That some dramatic tale, endued with shapes
Livelier, and flinging out less guarded words
Than suit the work we fashion, might set forth
What then I learned, or think I learned, of truth,
And the errors into which I fell, betrayed
By present objects, and by reasonings false
From their beginnings, inasmuch as drawn
290   Out of a heart that had been turned aside
From Nature's way by outward accidents,
And which was thus confounded, more and more
Misguided, and misguiding. So I fared,
Dragging all precepts, judgments, maxims, creeds,
Like culprits to the bar; calling the mind,
Suspiciously, to establish in plain day
Her titles and her honours; now believing,
Now disbelieving; endlessly perplexed
With impulse, motive, right and wrong, the ground
300   Of obligation, what the rule and whence
The sanction; till, demanding formal *proof,*
And seeking it in every thing, I lost
All feeling of conviction, and, in fine,
Sick, wearied out with contrarieties,
Yielded up moral questions in despair.°

. . .

From *Book Twelfth*

IMAGINATION AND TASTE, HOW IMPAIRED AND RESTORED

In such strange passion, if I may once more
Review the past, I warred against myself—
A bigot to a new idolatry—
Like a cowled monk who hath forsworn the world,
Zealously laboured to cut off my heart
80   From all the sources of her former strength;
And as, by simple waving of a wand,
The wizard instantaneously dissolves
Palace or grove, even so could I unsoul
As readily by syllogistic words
Those mysteries of being which have made,
And shall continue evermore to make,

I summoned . . . heart He falls into the imaginative error of the rationalist analysts of society and human nature, who do not begin and end with the human heart, as his best poetry does.
till, demanding . . . despair (ll. 301–5) the low point of this crisis, from which his former self, in the shape of Dorothy and his own "spots of time," will save him. Wordsworth is describing the pernicious effects of having become, however briefly, a follower of the intellectual and social theories of William Godwin, the Necessitarian Anarchist philosopher.

Of the whole human race one brotherhood.

What wonder, then, if, to a mind so far
Perverted, even the visible Universe
90   Fell under the dominion of a taste
Less spiritual, with microscopic view
Was scanned, as I had scanned the moral world?

.   .   .

I speak in recollection of a time
When the bodily eye, in every stage of life
The most despotic of our senses, gained
130   Such strength in *me* as often held my mind
In absolute dominion.° Gladly here,
Entering upon abstruser argument,
Could I endeavour to unfold the means
Which Nature studiously employs to thwart
This tyranny, summons all the senses each
To counteract the other, and themselves,
And makes them all, and the objects with which all
Are conversant, subservient in their turn
To the great ends of Liberty and Power.
140   But leave we this: enough that my delights
(Such as they were) were sought insatiably.
Vivid the transport, vivid though not profound;
I roamed from hill to hill, from rock to rock,
Still craving combinations of new forms,
New pleasure, wider empire for the sight,
Proud of her own endowments, and rejoiced
To lay the inner faculties asleep.

.   .   .

In truth, the degradation—howsoe'er
Induced, effect, in whatsoe'er degree,
Of custom that prepares a partial scale
In which the little oft outweighs the great;
Or any other cause that hath been named;
Or lastly, aggravated by the times
And their impassioned sounds, which well might make
200   The milder minstrelsies of rural scenes
Inaudible—was transient; I had known
Too forcibly, too early in my life,
Visitings of imaginative power
For this to last: I shook the habit off
Entirely and forever, and again
In Nature's presence stood, as now I stand,
A sensitive being, a *creative* soul.

I speak . . . dominion (ll. 126–31) He seeks the power of the mind over the universe of sense; in his crisis time, he rightly feared enslavement to the eye, the ultimate fate of visionaries when their energies are fled; see, for instance, Thoreau's later journals.

There are in our existence spots of time,°
That with distinct pre-eminence retain
210   A renovating virtue, whence, depressed
By false opinion and contentious thought,
Or aught of heavier or more deadly weight,
In trivial occupations, and the round
Of ordinary intercourse, our minds
Are nourished and invisibly repaired;
A virtue, by which pleasure is enhanced,
That penetrates, enables us to mount,
When high, more high, and lifts us up when fallen.
This efficacious spirit chiefly lurks
220   Among those passages of life that give
Profoundest knowledge to what point, and how,
The mind is lord and master—outward sense
The obedient servant of her will.° Such moments
Are scattered everywhere, taking their date
From our first childhood. I remember well,
That once, while yet my inexperienced hand
Could scarcely hold a bridle, with proud hopes
I mounted, and we journeyed towards the hills:
An ancient servant of my father's house
230   Was with me, my encourager and guide:
We had not travelled long, ere some mischance
Disjoined me from my comrade; and, through fear
Dismounting, down the rough and stony moor
I led my horse, and, stumbling on, at length
Came to a bottom, where in former times
A murderer had been hung in iron chains.
The gibbet-mast had mouldered down, the bones
And iron case were gone; but on the turf,
Hard by, soon after that fell deed was wrought,
240   Some unknown hand had carved the murderer's name.
The monumental letters were inscribed
In times long past; but still, from year to year,
By superstition of the neighbourhood,
The grass is cleared away, and to this hour
The characters are fresh and visible:
A casual glance had shown them, and I fled,
Faltering and faint, and ignorant of the road:
Then, reascending the bare common, saw
A naked pool that lay beneath the hills,
250   The beacon on the summit, and, more near,
A girl, who bore a pitcher on her head,

---

spots of time The most important conceptual image in *The Prelude*; the "spots of time" are also what might be termed "moments of space," the equivalent of Blake's pulsation of an artery in which the poet's work is done, their function is to enshrine "the spirit of the Past for future restoration" (see ll. 285–86).

her will the creative mind or imagination's will

And seemed with difficult steps to force her way
Against the blowing wind. It was, in truth,
An ordinary sight; but I should need
Colours and words that are unknown to man,
To paint the visionary dreariness
Which, while I looked all round for my lost guide,
Invested moorland waste, and naked pool,
The beacon crowning the lone eminence,
260   The female and her garments vexed and tossed
By the strong wind. When, in the blessed hours
Of early love, the loved one at my side,
I roamed, in daily presence of this scene,
Upon the naked pool and dreary crags,
And on the melancholy beacon fell
A spirit of pleasure and youth's golden gleam;
And think ye not with radiance more sublime
For these remembrances, and for the power
They had left behind? So feeling comes in aid
270   Of feeling, and diversity of strength
Attends us, if but once we have been strong.°
Oh! mystery of man, from what a depth
Proceed thy honours. I am lost, but see
In simple childhood something of the base
On which thy greatness stands; but this I feel,
That from thyself it comes, that thou must give,
Else never canst receive. The days gone by
Return upon me almost from the dawn
Of life: the hiding-places of man's power
280   Open; I would approach them, but they close.
I see by glimpses now; when age comes on,
May scarcely see at all; and I would give,
While yet we may, as far as words can give,
Substance and life to what I feel, enshrining,
Such is my hope, the spirit of the Past
For future restoration.—Yet another
Of these memorials:—

                    One Christmas-time,
On the glad eve of its dear holidays,
Feverish, and tired, and restless, I went forth
290   Into the fields, impatient for the sight
Of those led palfreys that should bear us home;
My brothers and myself. There rose a crag,
That, from the meeting-point of two highways
Ascending, overlooked them both, far stretched;
Thither, uncertain on which road to fix

if . . . strong   the   kernel   of   Wordsworth's
faith; his confidence that he began as a strong
poet, a capable imagination

My expectation, thither I repaired,
Scout-like, and gained the summit; 'twas a day
Tempestuous, dark, and wild, and on the grass
I sate half-sheltered by a naked wall;
300   Upon my right hand couched a single sheep,
Upon my left a blasted hawthorn stood;
With those companions at my side, I watched,
Straining my eyes intensely, as the mist
Gave intermitting prospect of the copse
And plain beneath. Ere we to school returned,—
That dreary time,—ere we had been ten days
Sojourners in my father's house, he died,
And I and my three brothers, orphans then,
Followed his body to the grave. The event,
310   With all the sorrow that it brought, appeared
A chastisement; and when I called to mind
That day so lately past, when from the crag
I looked in such anxiety of hope;
With trite reflections of morality,
Yet in the deepest passion, I bowed low
To God, Who thus corrected my desires;
And, afterwards, the wind and sleety rain,
And all the business of the elements,
The single sheep, and the one blasted tree,
320   And the bleak music from that old stone wall,
The noise of wood and water, and the mist
That on the line of each of those two roads
Advanced in such indisputable shapes;
All these were kindred spectacles and sounds
To which I oft repaired, and thence would drink,
As at a fountain; and on winter nights,
Down to this very time, when storm and rain
Beat on my roof, or, haply, at noon-day,
While in a grove I walk, whose lofty trees,
330   Laden with summer's thickest foliage, rock
In a strong wind, some working of the spirit,
Some inward agitations thence are brought,
Whate'er their office, whether to beguile
Thoughts over busy in the course they took,
Or animate an hour of vacant ease.

From *Book Fourteenth*

CONCLUSION

In one of those excursions (may they ne'er
Fade from remembrance!) through the Northern tracts
Of Cambria° ranging with a youthful friend,
Cambria Wales

I left Bethgelert's° huts at couching-time,
And westward took my way, to see the sun
Rise from the top of Snowdon. To the door
Of a rude cottage at the mountain's base
We came, and roused the shepherd who attends
The adventurous stranger's steps, a trusty guide;
10   Then, cheered by short refreshment, sallied forth.

It was a close, warm, breezeless summer night,
Wan, dull, and glaring, with a dripping fog
Low-hung and thick that covered all the sky;
But, undiscouraged, we began to climb
The mountain-side. The mist soon girt us round,
And, after ordinary travellers' talk
With our conductor, pensively we sank
Each into commerce with his private thoughts:
Thus did we breast the ascent, and by myself
20   Was nothing either seen or heard that checked
Those musings or diverted, save that once
The shepherd's lurcher,° who, among the crags,
Had to his joy unearthed a hedgehog, teased
His coiled-up prey with barkings turbulent.
This small adventure, for even such it seemed
In that wild place and at the dead of night,
Being over and forgotten, on we wound
In silence as before. With forehead bent
Earthward, as if in opposition set
30   Against an enemy, I panted up
With eager pace, and no less eager thoughts.
Thus might we wear a midnight hour away,
Ascending at loose distance each from each,
And I, as chanced, the foremost of the band;
When at my feet the ground appeared to brighten,
And with a step or two seemed brighter still;
Nor was time given to ask or learn the cause,
For instantly a light upon the turf
Fell like a flash, and lo! as I looked up,
40   The Moon hung naked in a firmament
Of azure without cloud, and at my feet
Rested a silent sea of hoary mist.
A hundred hills their dusky backs upheaved
All over this still ocean; and beyond,
Far, far beyond, the solid vapours stretched,
In headlands, tongues, and promontory shapes,
Into the main Atlantic, that appeared
To dwindle, and give up his majesty,

Bethgelert's village near Snowdon, the highest   **lurcher** hunting dog
mountain in Wales

Usurped upon far as the sight could reach.
50 Not so the ethereal vault; encroachment none
Was there, nor loss; only the inferior stars
Had disappeared, or shed a fainter light
In the clear presence of the full-orbed Moon,
Who, from her sovereign elevation, gazed
Upon the billowy ocean, as it lay
All meek and silent, save that through a rift—
Not distant from the shore whereon we stood,
A fixed, abysmal, gloomy, breathing-place—
Mounted the roar of waters, torrents, streams
60 Innumerable, roaring with one voice!
Heard over earth and sea, and, in that hour,
For so it seemed, felt by the starry heavens.

    When into air had partially dissolved
That vision, given to spirits of the night
And three chance human wanderers, in calm thought
Reflected, it appeared to me the type
Of a majestic intellect, its acts
And its possessions, what it has and craves,
What in itself it is, and would become.
70 There I beheld the emblem of a mind
That feeds upon infinity, that broods
Over the dark abyss, intent to hear
Its voices issuing forth to silent light
In one continuous stream; a mind sustained
By recognitions of transcendent power,
In sense conducting to ideal form,
In soul of more than mortal privilege.
One function, above all, of such a mind
Had Nature shadowed there, by putting forth,
80 'Mid circumstances awful and sublime,
That mutual domination which she loves
To exert upon the face of outward things,
So moulded, joined, abstracted, so endowed
With interchangeable supremacy,
That men, least sensitive, see, hear, perceive,
And cannot choose but feel. The power, which all
Acknowledge when thus moved, which Nature thus
To bodily sense exhibits, is the express
Resemblance of that glorious faculty°
90 That higher minds bear with them as their own.
This is the very spirit in which they deal
With the whole compass of the universe:
They from their native selves can send abroad

glorious faculty the higher Reason or poetic
imagination

Kindred mutations; for themselves create
A like existence; and, whene'er it dawns
Created for them, catch it, or are caught
By its inevitable mastery,
Like angels stopped upon the wing by sound
Of harmony from Heaven's remotest spheres.°
100   Them the enduring and the transient both
Serve to exalt; they build up greatest things
From least suggestions; ever on the watch,
Willing to work and to be wrought upon,
They need not extraordinary calls
To rouse them; in a world of life they live,
By sensible impressions not enthralled,
But by their quickening impulse made more prompt
To hold fit converse with the spiritual world,
And with the generations of mankind
110   Spread over time, past, present, and to come,
Age after age, till Time shall be no more.
Such minds are truly from the Deity,
For they are Powers; and hence the highest bliss
That flesh can know is theirs—the consciousness
Of Whom° they are, habitually infused
Through every image and through every thought,
And all affections by communion raised
From earth to heaven, from human to divine;
Hence endless occupation for the Soul,
120   Whether discursive or intuitive;°
Hence cheerfulness for acts of daily life,
Emotions which best foresight need not fear,
Most worthy then of trust when most intense.
Hence, amid ills that vex and wrongs that crush
Our hearts—if here the words of Holy Writ
May with fit reverence be applied—that peace
Which passeth understanding,° that repose
In moral judgments which from this pure source
Must come, or will by man be sought in vain.

                        . . .
430   Oh! yet a few short years of useful life,
And all will be complete, thy° race be run,
Thy monument of glory will be raised;
Then, though (too weak to tread the ways of truth)
This age fall back to old idolatry,

Like angels . . . spheres Frank Kermode noted
Wallace Stevens's debt to this and subsequent
passages in *Notes Toward a Supreme Fiction,*
"It Must Give Pleasure" VIII.
Whom refers to a composite poetic selfhood,
and not to God
And all . . . intuitive (ll. 117–20) See *Paradise*

Lost V.483–90 where Raphael discourses to
Adam on the "gradual scale sublimed" which
distinguishes human from angelic faculties, a
passage crucial also for Coleridge's formulation
of the Secondary Imagination.
that peace . . . understanding Philippians 4:7
thy Coleridge's

Though men return to servitude as fast
As the tide ebbs, to ignominy and shame
By nations sink together, we shall still
Find solace—knowing what we have learnt to know,
Rich in true happiness if allowed to be
440 Faithful alike in forwarding a day
Of firmer trust, joint labourers in the work
(Should Providence such grace to us vouchsafe)
Of their deliverance, surely yet to come.
Prophets of Nature, we to them will speak
A lasting inspiration, sanctified
By reason, blest by faith: what we have loved,
Others will love, and we will teach them how;
Instruct them how the mind of man becomes
A thousand times more beautiful than the earth
450 On which he dwells, above this frame of things
(Which, 'mid all revolution in the hopes
And fears of men, doth still remain unchanged)
In beauty exalted, as it is itself
Of quality and fabric more divine.
1799–1805   1850

Surprised by Joy

Surprised by joy—impatient as the Wind
I turned to share the transport—Oh! with whom
But Thee,° deep buried in the silent tomb,
That spot which no vicissitude can find?
Love, faithful love, recalled thee to my mind—
But how could I forget thee? Through what power,
Even for the least division of an hour,
Have I been so beguiled as to be blind
To my most grievous loss!—That thought's return
10 Was the worst pang that sorrow ever bore,
Save one, one only, when I stood forlorn,
Knowing my heart's best treasure was no more;
That neither present time, nor years unborn
Could to my sight that heavenly face restore.
                                1815

Thee the poet's daughter Catherine, who had
died in June 1812, three years old

Composed upon an Evening of Extraordinary Splendour and Beauty°

I

Had this effulgence disappeared
With flying haste, I might have sent,
Among the speechless clouds, a look
Of blank astonishment;
But 'tis endued with power to stay,
And sanctify one closing day,
That frail Mortality may see—
What is?—ah no, but what *can* be!
Time was when field and watery cove
10   With modulated echoes rang,
While choirs of fervent Angels sang
Their vespers in the grove;
Or, crowning, star-like, each some sovereign height,
Warbled, for heaven above and earth below,
Strains suitable to both.—Such holy rite,
Methinks, if audibly repeated now
From hill or valley, could not move
Sublimer transport, purer love,
Than doth this silent spectacle—the gleam—
20   The shadow—and the peace supreme!

II

No sound is uttered,—but a deep
And solemn harmony pervades
The hollow vale from steep to steep,
And penetrates the glades.
Far-distant images draw nigh,
Called forth by wondrous potency
Of beamy radiance, that imbues
Whate'er it strikes with gem-like hues!
In vision exquisitely clear,
30   Herds range along the mountain side;
And glistening antlers are descried;
And gilded flocks appear.
Thine is the tranquil hour, purpureal Eve!
But long as god-like wish, or hope divine,
Informs my spirit, ne'er can I believe
That this magnificence is wholly thine!
—From worlds not quickened by the sun
A portion of the gift is won;

Composed . . . Beauty Wordsworth's own note to this very poignant poem: "The multiplication of mountain-ridges, described at the commencement of the third stanza of this Ode, as a kind of Jacob's Ladder, leading to Heaven, is produced either by watery vapours, or sunny haze;—in the present instance by the latter cause. Allusions to the Ode, entitled 'Intimations of Immortality,' pervade the last stanza."

An intermingling of Heaven's pomp is spread
40 On grounds which British shepherds tread!

                III
And, if there be whom broken ties
Afflict, or injuries assail,
Yon hazy ridges to their eyes
Present a glorious scale,
Climbing suffused with sunny air,
To stop—no record hath told where!
And tempting Fancy to ascend,
And with immortal Spirits blend!
—Wings at my shoulders seem to play;
50 But, rooted here, I stand and gaze
On those bright steps that heavenward raise
Their practicable way.
Come forth, ye drooping old men, look abroad,
And see to what fair countries ye are bound!
And if some traveller, weary of his road,
Hath slept since noon-tide on the grassy ground,
Ye Genii! to his covert speed;
And wake him with such gentle heed
As may attune his soul to meet the dower
60 Bestowed on this transcendent hour!

                IV
Such hues from their celestial Urn
Were wont to stream before mine eye,
Where'er it wandered in the morn
Of blissful infancy.
This glimpse of glory, why renewed?
Nay, rather speak with gratitude;
For, if a vestige of those gleams
Survived, 'twas only in my dreams.
Dread Power! whom peace and calmness serve
70 No less than Nature's threatening voice,
If aught unworthy be my choice,
From THEE if I would swerve;
Oh, let Thy grace remind me of the light
Full early lost, and fruitlessly deplored;
Which, at this moment, on my waking sight
Appears to shine, by miracle restored:
My soul, though yet confined to earth,
Rejoices in a second birth!
—'Tis past, the visionary splendour fades;
80 And night approaches with her shades.
1817   1820

Mutability

From low to high doth dissolution climb,
And sink from high to low, along a scale
Of awful notes, whose concord shall not fail;
A musical but melancholy chime,
Which they can hear who meddle not with crime,
Nor avarice, nor over-anxious care.
Truth fails not; but her outward forms that bear
The longest date do melt like frosty rime,
That in the morning whitened hill and plain
And is no more; drop like the tower sublime
Of yesterday, which royally did wear
His crown of weeds, but could not even sustain
Some casual shout that broke the silent air,
Or the unimaginable touch of Time.°

1821   1822

Extempore Effusion upon the Death of James Hogg°

When first, descending from the moorlands,
I saw the Stream of Yarrow° glide
Along a bare and open valley,
The Ettrick Shepherd was my guide.

When last along its banks I wandered,
Through groves that had begun to shed
Their golden leaves upon the pathways,
My steps the Border-minstrel° led.

The mighty Minstrel breathes no longer,
'Mid mouldering ruins low he lies;
And death upon the braes° of Yarrow,
Has closed the Shepherd-poet's eyes:

Nor has the rolling year twice measured,
From sign to sign, its stedfast course,
Since every mortal power of Coleridge
Was frozen at its marvellous source;

The rapt One, of the godlike forehead,
The heaven-eyed creature sleeps in earth:°

Or . . . Time Samuel Monk points out that this alludes to Milton's tract, *Of Education,* where he mentions the "unimaginable touches" of music.
James Hogg Scottish poet known as "the Ettrick Shepherd," died November 21, 1835
Yarrow river in southern Scotland

Border-minstrel Sir Walter Scott had died in 1832.
braes hillsides
The rapt . . . earth Coleridge had died in 1834; the two men had been reconciled, but Wordsworth waited a year before elegizing his closest friend, as he so movingly does here.

20 And Lamb, the frolic and the gentle,
   Has vanished from his lonely hearth.°

   Like clouds that rake the mountain-summits,
   Or waves that own no curbing hand,
   How fast has brother followed brother,
   From sunshine to the sunless land!

   Yet I, whose lids from infant slumber
   Were earlier raised, remain to hear
   A timid voice, that asks in whispers,
   'Who next will drop and disappear?'

   Our haughty life is crowned with darkness,
30 Like London with its own black wreath,
   On which with thee, O Crabbe!° forth-looking.
   I gazed from Hampstead's breezy heath.

   As if but yesterday departed,
   Thou too art gone before; but why,
   O'er ripe fruit, seasonably gathered,
   Should frail survivors heave a sigh?

   Mourn rather for that holy Spirit,
   Sweet as the spring, as ocean deep;
   For Her° who, ere her summer faded,
40 Has sunk into a breathless sleep.

   No more of old romantic sorrows,
   For slaughtered Youth or love-lorn Maid!
   With sharper grief is Yarrow smitten,
   And Ettrick mourns with her their Poet dead.
   1835   1835

SAMUEL TAYLOR COLERIDGE
1772–1834

Coleridge was the youngest of fourteen children of a country clergyman, a precocious and lonely child, a kind of changeling in his own family. Early a dreamer and (as he said) a "character," he suffered the loss of his father (who had loved him best) when he was only nine. At Christ's Hospital in London, soon after his father's death, he found an excellent school that gave him the intellectual nurture he needed, as well as a lifelong friend in the future essayist, Charles Lamb. Early a poet, he fell deeply in love with Mary Evans, a schoolfellow's sister, but nothing came of it.

At Jesus College, Cambridge, Coleridge started well, but temperamentally he was not suited to academic discipline, and failed of distinction. Fleeing Cambridge, and

And Lamb . . . hearth Charles Lamb also had died in 1834.
Crabbe George Crabbe had died in 1832.
Her Felicia Hemans, a rather unfortunate poetess, who died at the age of forty-two in 1835; she was very popular for many decades afterward, in America and in England, but is now remembered only for the splendidly bad lyric "Casabianca," with its memorable first line: "The boy stood on the burning deck."

much in debt, he enlisted in the cavalry under the immortal name of Silas Tomkyn Comberbacke, but kept falling off his horse. Though he proved useful to his fellow dragoons at writing love letters, he was good for little else but stable-cleaning, and the cavalry allowed his brothers to buy him out. He returned to Cambridge, but his characteristic guilt impeded academic labor, and when he abandoned Cambridge in 1794 he had no degree.

A penniless young poet, radical in politics, original in religion, he fell in with the then equally radical bard Robert Southey, remembered today as the Conservative Laureate constantly savaged in Byron's satirical verse. Like our contemporary communards, the two poetical youths projected what they named a Pantisocracy. With the right young ladies, and other choice spirits, they would found a communistic agrarian-literary settlement on the banks of the Susquehanna in exotic Pennsylvania. At Southey's urging, Coleridge made a Pantisocratic engagement to the not very brilliant Miss Sara Fricker, whose sister Southey was to marry. Pantisocracy died at birth, and Coleridge in time woke up to find himself unsuitably married, the largest misfortune of his life.

He turned to Wordsworth, whom he had met early in 1795. His poetry influenced Wordsworth's, and helped Wordsworth attain his characteristic mode. It is not too much to say that Coleridge's poetry disappeared into Wordsworth's. We remember *Lyrical Ballads* (1798) as Wordsworth's book; yet about a third of it (in length) was Coleridge's, and "Tintern Abbey," the crown of the volume except for *The Ancient Mariner*, is immensely indebted to Coleridge's "Frost at Midnight." Nor is there much evidence of Wordsworth's admiring or encouraging his friend's poetry; toward *The Ancient Mariner* he was always very grudging, and he was discomfited (but inevitably so) by both "Dejection: An Ode" and "To William Wordsworth." Selfless where Wordsworth's poetry was concerned, Coleridge had to suffer his closest friend's neglect of his own poetic ambitions.

This is not an easy matter to be fair about, since literature necessarily is as much a matter of personality as it is of character. Coleridge, like Keats (and to certain readers, Shelley) is lovable. Byron is at least always fascinating, and Blake in his lonely magnificence is a hero of the imagination. But Wordsworth's personality, like Milton's or Dante's, does not stimulate affection for the poet in the common reader. Coleridge has, as Walter Pater observed, a "peculiar charm"; he seems to lend himself to myths of failure, which is astonishing when the totality of his work is contemplated.

Yet it is his life, and his self-abandonment of his poetic ambitions, that continue to convince us that we ought to find in him parables of the failure of genius. His best poetry was all written in the year and a half in which he saw Wordsworth daily (1797–98); yet even his best poetry, with the single exception of *The Ancient Mariner*, is fragmentary. The pattern of his life is fragmentary also. When he received an annuity from the Wedgwood family, he left Wordsworth and Dorothy to study language and philosophy in Germany (1798–99). Soon after returning, his miserable middle years began, though he was only twenty-seven. He moved near the Wordsworths again, and fell in love, permanently and unhappily, with Sara Hutchinson, whose sister Mary was to become Wordsworth's wife in 1802. His own marriage was hopeless, and his health rapidly deteriorated, perhaps for psychological reasons. To help endure the pain he began to drink laudanum, liquid opium, and thus contracted an addiction he never entirely cast off. In 1804, seeking better health, he went to work in Malta, but returned two years later in the worst condition of his life. Separating from his wife, he moved to London, and began another career as lecturer, general man-of-letters, and periodical editor, while his miseries augmented. The inevitable quarrel with Wordsworth in 1810 was ostensibly reconciled in 1812, but real friendship was not re-established until 1828.

From 1816 on, Coleridge lived in the household of a physician, James Gillman, so as to be able to keep working, and thus avoid total breakdown. Prematurely aged, his poetry over, Coleridge entered into a major last phase as critic and philosopher, upon which his historical importance depends; but this, like his earlier prose achievements, is beyond the scope of an introduction to his poetry. It remains to ask, what was his achievement as a poet, and extraordinary as that was, why did his poetry effectively cease after about 1807? Wordsworth went on with poetry after 1807, but mostly very badly. The few poems Coleridge wrote, from the age of thirty-five on, are powerful but occasional. Did not the poetic will fail in him, since his imaginative powers remained always fresh?

Coleridge's large poetic ambitions included the writing of a philosophic epic on the origin of evil, and a sequence of hymns to the sun, moon, and elements. These high plans died, slowly but definitively, and were replaced by the dream of a philosophic *opus maximum*, a huge work of synthesis that would reconcile German Idealist philosophy with the orthodox truths of Christianity. Though only fragments of this work were ever written, much was done in its place—speculations on theology, political theory, and criticism that had a profound influence on conservative British thought in the Victorian period, and in quite another way on the American Transcendentalism led by Emerson and Theodore Parker.

Coleridge's actual achievement as poet divides into two remarkably diverse groups, remarkable because they are almost simultaneous. The daemonic group, necessarily more famous, is the triad of The Ancient Mariner, Christabel and "Kubla Khan." The conversational group includes the conversation-poems proper, of which "The Eolian Harp" and "Frost at Midnight" are the most important, as well as the irregular ode, "Dejection," and "To William Wordsworth." The late fragments "Limbo" and "Ne Plus Ultra" mark a kind of return to the daemonic mode. To have written only nine poems that really matter, for a poet of Coleridge's gifts, is a sorrow, but the uniqueness of the two groups partly compensates for the slenderness of the canon.

The daemonic poems break through the orthodox censor set up by Coleridge's moral fears of his own imaginative impulses. Unifying the group is a magical quest-pattern which intends as its goal a reconciliation between the poet's self-consciousness and a higher order of being, associated with divine forgiveness, but this reconciliation fortunately lies beyond the border of all these poems. The Mariner attains a state of purgation, but cannot get beyond that process. Christabel is violated by Geraldine, but this too is a purgation, rather than damnation, as her utter innocence is her only flaw. Coleridge himself, in the most piercing moment in his poetry, is tempted to assume the state of an Apollo-rebirth, the youth with flashing eyes and floating hair in "Kubla Khan," but he withdraws from his vision of a poet's paradise, judging it to be only another purgatory.

The conversational group, though so immensely different in mode, speaks more directly of an allied theme: the desire to go home, not to the past, but to what Hart Crane beautifully called "an improved infancy." Each of these poems, like the daemonic group, verges upon a kind of vicarious and purgatorial atonement, in which Coleridge must fail or suffer so that someone he loves may succeed or experience joy. There is a subdued implication that somehow the poet will yet be accepted into a true home this side of the grave, if he can perfect an atonement.

Where Wordsworth, in his primordial power, masters the subjective world, and aids his readers in the difficult art of feeling, Coleridge deliberately courts defeat by subjectivity, and is content to be confessional. But, though he cannot help us to feel, as Wordsworth does, he gives us to understand how deeply felt his own sense of reality is. Though in a way his poetry is a testament of defeat, a yielding to the anxiety of influence, and to the fear of self-glorification, it is one of the most enduringly poignant of such testaments that literature affords us.

Sonnet°

To the River Otter

Dear native Brook!° wild Streamlet of the West!
  How many various-fated years have past,
  What happy and what mournful hours, since last
I skimmed the smooth thin stone along thy breast,
Numbering its light leaps! yet so deep imprest
Sink the sweet scenes of childhood, that mine eyes
  I never shut amid the sunny ray,
But straight with all their tints thy waters rise,
  Thy crossing plank, thy marge with willows grey,
And bedded sand that veined with various dyes
Gleamed through thy bright transparence! On my way,
  Visions of Childhood! oft have ye beguiled
Lone manhood's cares, yet waking fondest sighs:
  Ah! that once more I were a careless Child!
1793?   1796

The Eolian Harp°

COMPOSED AT CLEVEDON, SOMERSETSHIRE°

My pensive Sara! thy soft cheek reclined
Thus on mine arm, most soothing sweet it is
To sit beside our Cot, our Cot o'ergrown
With white-flowered Jasmin, and the broad-leaved Myrtle,
(Meet emblems they of Innocence and Love!)
And watch the clouds, that late were rich with light,

Sonnet See Bowles's "To the River Itchin" for Coleridge's model.
native Brook The Otter ran near Coleridge's birthplace, Ottery St. Mary.
The Eolian Harp from Aeolus, Greek god of the winds; this was an instrument of strings stretched across a sound box; attached to an open window, it produced a quasi-music when the wind swept over it. For the poets of Sensibility and the Romantics the Harp provided an emblem for inspiration, its natural strength and also its limitations.
Clevedon, Somersetshire place of Coleridge's honeymoon with Sara Fricker. This, grimly and prophetically, was a honeymoon poem.

Slow saddening round, and mark the star of eve
Serenely brilliant (such should Wisdom be)
Shine opposite! How exquisite the scents
10   Snatched from yon bean-field! and the world so hushed!
The stilly murmur of the distant Sea
Tells us of silence.
                    And that simplest Lute,
Placed length-ways in the clasping casement, hark!
How by the desultory breeze caressed,
Like some coy maid half yielding to her lover,
It pours such sweet upbraiding, as must needs
Tempt to repeat the wrong! And now, its strings
Boldlier swept, the long sequacious° notes
Over delicious surges sink and rise,
20   Such a soft floating witchery of sound
As twilight Elfins make, when they at eve
Voyage on gentle gales from Fairy-Land,
Where Melodies round honey-dropping flowers,
Footless and wild, like birds of Paradise,
Nor pause, nor perch, hovering on untamed wing!
O! the one Life within us and abroad,
Which meets all motion and becomes its soul,
A light in sound, a sound-like power in light,
Rhythm in all thought, and joyance everywhere—
30   Methinks, it should have been impossible
Not to love all things in a world so filled;
Where the breeze warbles, and the mute still air
Is Music slumbering on her instrument.°

    And thus, my Love! as on the midway slope
Of yonder hill I stretch my limbs at noon,
Whilst through my half-closed eye-lids I behold
The sunbeams dance, like diamonds, on the main,
And tranquil muse upon tranquillity;
Full many a thought uncalled and undetained,
40   And many idle flitting phantasies,
Traverse my indolent and passive brain,
As wild and various as the random gales
That swell and flutter on this subject Lute!
    And what if all of animated nature
Be but organic Harps diversely framed,
That tremble into thought, as o'er them sweeps
Plastic and vast, one intellectual breeze,
At once the Soul of each, and God of all?°

sequacious successive
O . . . instrument Ll. 26–33 are an afterthought, as is the title, both being added in
1817.
At . . . all Influenced by the Idealist philosopher Bishop George Berkeley (1685–1753),
but more daring in speculation; in one manuscript Coleridge added: "Thus God would be
the universal Soul,/Mechanized matter as the
organic harps/And each one's Tubes be that,
which each calls I."

But thy more serious eye a mild reproof
50 Darts, O belovèd Woman! nor such thoughts
Dim and unhallowed dost thou not reject,
And biddest me walk humbly with my God.
Meek Daughter in the family of Christ!
Well hast thou said and holily dispraised
These shapings of the unregenerate mind;
Bubbles that glitter as they rise and break
On vain Philosophy's aye-babbling spring.
For never guiltless may I speak of him,
The Incomprehensible! save when with awe
60 I praise him, and with Faith that inly *feels*;
Who with his saving mercies healed me,
A sinful and most miserable man,
Wildered and dark, and gave me to possess
Peace, and this Cot, and thee, heart-honored Maid!
1795   1796

The Rime of the Ancient Mariner°

In Seven Parts

Facile credo, plures esse Naturas invisibiles quam visibiles in rerum univer-
sitate. Sed horum omnium familiam quis nobis enarrabit? et gradus et cogna-
tiones et discrimina et singulorum munera? Quid agunt? quae loca habitant?
Harum rerum notitiam semper ambivit ingenium humanum, nunquam attigit.
Juvat, interea, non diffiteor, quandoque in animo, tanquam in tabula, majoris
et melioris mundi imaginem contemplari: ne mens assuefacta hodiernae vitae
minutiis se contrahat nimis, et tota subsidat in pusillas cogitationes. Sed veritati
interea invigilandum est, modusque servandus, ut certa ab incertis, diem a
nocte, distinguamus.—T. BURNET,° *Archaeol. Phil.* p. 68.

ARGUMENT

How a Ship having passed the Line was driven by storms to the cold Country
towards the South Pole; and how from thence she made her course to the

The Rime of the Ancient Mariner First published in *Lyrical Ballads;* this is the revised
version, to which the marginal glosses were
added in 1816; Coleridge's most helpful comment on the poem was recorded in 1830, in
reply to the celebrated Bluestocking, Mrs. Bar-
bauld, who had objected that the poem lacked
a moral: "I told her that in my own judgment
the poem had too much; and that the only, or
chief fault, if I might say so, was the obtrusion
of the moral sentiment so openly on the reader
as a principle or cause of action in a work of
pure imagination. It ought to have had no more
moral than the *Arabian Nights'* tale of the merchant's sitting down to eat dates by the side of
a well and throwing the shells aside, and lo! a
genie starts up and says he *must* kill the afore-
said merchant *because* one of the date shells
had, it seems, put out the eye of the genie's son."
T. Burnet Thomas Burnet (1635?–1715), Eng-

lish churchman, best known for his mythologizing cosmogony, *The Sacred Theory of the Earth.*
The motto can be rendered: "I easily believe
that there are more invisible than visible beings
in the universe. But who will tell us the families of all these? And the ranks, affinities, differences, and functions of each? What do they do?
Where do they live? The human mind has always circled after knowledge of these things,
but has never attained it. But I do not deny
that it is good sometimes to contemplate in
thought, as in a picture, the image of a greater
and better world; otherwise the mind, habituated to the petty matters of daily life, may con-
tract itself too much, and subside entirely into
trivial thoughts. But meanwhile we must be vigi-
lant for truth, and keep proportion, that we may
distinguish certain from uncertain, day from
night."

tropical Latitude of the Great Pacific Ocean; and of the strange things that befell; and in what manner the Ancyent Marinere came back to his own Country.°

PART I

An ancient
Mariner meet-
eth three Gal-
lants bidden
to a wedding-
feast, and de-
taineth one.

It is an ancient Mariner,
And he stoppeth one of three.
'By thy long grey beard and glittering eye,°
Now wherefore stopp'st thou me?

'The Bridegroom's doors are opened wide,
And I am next of kin;
The guests are met, the feast is set:
May'st hear the merry din.'

10

He holds him with his skinny hand,
'There was a ship,' quoth he.
'Hold off! unhand me, grey-beard loon!'
Eftsoons° his hand dropped he.

The Wedding-
Guest is spell-
bound by the
eye of the old
seafaring man,
and con-
strained to
hear his tale.

He holds him with his glittering eye—
The Wedding-Guest stood still,
And listens like a three years' child:
The Mariner hath his will.

The Wedding-Guest sat on a stone:
He cannot choose but hear;
And thus spake on that ancient man,
The bright-eyed Mariner.

20

'The ship was cheered, the harbour cleared,
Merrily did we drop
Below the kirk, below the hill,

The Mariner
tells how the
ship sailed
southward
with a good
wind and fair
weather, till it
reached the
line.

Below the lighthouse top.

'The Sun came up upon the left,
Out of the sea came he!
And he shone bright, and on the right
Went down into the sea.

'Higher and higher every day,
Till over the mast at noon—'
The Wedding-Guest here beat his breast,
For he heard the loud bassoon.

30

How . . . Country This is the Argument in
Lyrical Ballads, 1798; in the 1800 edition Coleridge inserted: "how the Ancient Mariner cru-
elly and in contempt of the laws of hospitality
killed a sea-bird and how he was followed by
many and strange Judgments."

glittering eye The Mariner is a mesmerist or
hypnotist, like the vampire Geraldine in *Christabel.*
Eftsoons immediately

The Wedding-Guest heareth the bridal music; but the Mariner continueth his tale.

The bride hath paced into the hall,
Red as a rose is she;
Nodding their heads before her goes
The merry minstrelsy.

The Wedding-Guest he beat his breast,
Yet he cannot choose but hear;
And thus spake on that ancient man,
40 The bright-eyed Mariner.

The ship driven by a storm toward the south pole.

'And now the STORM-BLAST came, and he
Was tyrannous and strong:
He struck with his o'ertaking wings,
And chased us south along.

'With sloping masts and dipping prow,
As who pursued with yell and blow
Still treads the shadow of his foe,
And forward bends his head,
The ship drove fast, loud roared the blast,
50 And southward aye we fled.

'And now there came both mist and snow,
And it grew wondrous cold:
And ice, mast-high, came floating by,
As green as emerald.

The land of ice, and of fearful sounds where no living thing was to be seen.

'And through the drifts the snowy clifts
Did send a dismal sheen:
Nor shapes of men nor beasts we ken—
The ice was all between.

'The ice was here, the ice was there,
60 The ice was all around:
It cracked and growled, and roared and howled,
Like noises in a swound!°

Till a great sea-bird, called the Albatross, came through the snow-fog, and was received with great joy and hospitality.

'At length did cross an Albatross,
Thorough the fog it came;
As if it had been a Christian soul,
We hailed it in God's name.

'It ate the food it ne'er had eat,
And round and round it flew.
The ice did split with a thunder-fit;
70 The helmsman steered us through!

And lo! the Albatross proveth a bird of good omen, and followeth

'And a good south wind sprung up behind;
The Albatross did follow,
And every day, for food or play,
Came to the mariner's hollo!

swound swoon

the ship as it returned northward through fog and floating ice.

'In mist or cloud, on mast or shroud,°
It perched for vespers nine;
Whiles all the night, through fog-smoke white,
Glimmered the white Moon-shine.'

The ancient Mariner inhospitably killeth the pious bird of good omen.

80

'God save thee, ancient Mariner!
From the fiends, that plague thee thus!—
Why lookest thou so?'—With my cross-bow
I shot the ALBATROSS.

PART II

The Sun now rose upon the right:°
Out of the sea came he,
Still hid in mist, and on the left
Went down into the sea.

And the good south wind still blew behind,
But no sweet bird did follow,
Nor any day for food or play
Came to the mariners' hollo!

90

His shipmates cry out against the ancient Mariner, for killing the bird of good luck.

And I had done a hellish thing,
And it would work 'em woe:
For all averred, I had killed the bird
That made the breeze to blow.
Ah wretch! said they, the bird to slay,
That made the breeze to blow!

But when the fog cleared off, they justify the same, and thus make themselves accomplices in the crime.

100

Nor dim nor red, like God's own head,
The glorious Sun uprist:
Then all averred, I had killed the bird
That brought the fog and mist.
'Twas right, said they, such birds to slay,
That bring the fog and mist.

The fair breeze continues; the ship enters the Pacific Ocean, and sails northward, even till it reaches the Line.

The fair breeze blew, the white foam flew,
The furrow followed free;
We were the first that ever burst
Into that silent sea.

110

The ship hath been suddenly becalmed.

Down dropped the breeze, the sails dropped down,
'Twas sad as sad could be;
And we did speak only to break
The silence of the sea!

All in a hot and copper sky,
The bloody Sun, at noon,
Right up above the mast did stand,
No bigger than the Moon.

shroud a set of ropes which supports the mast   **The Sun . . . right** The ship had rounded **Cape Horn** and now headed north.

Day after day, day after day,
We stuck, nor breath nor motion;
As idle as a painted ship
Upon a painted ocean.

And the Alba-
120 tross begins to
be avenged.

Water, water, every where,
And all the boards did shrink;
Water, water, every where,
Nor any drop to drink.

The very deep did rot: O Christ!
That ever this should be!
Yea, slimy things did crawl with legs
Upon the slimy sea.

About, about, in reel and rout
The death-fires° danced at night;
The water, like a witch's oils,
130 Burnt green, and blue and white.

A Spirit had
followed them;
one of the in-
visible inhabi-
tants of this
planet, neither

And some in dreams assurèd were
Of the Spirit° that plagued us so;
Nine fathom deep he had followed us
From the land of mist and snow.

departed souls nor angels; concerning whom the learned Jew, Josephus, and the Platonic
Constantinopolitan, Michael Psellus, may be consulted. They are very numerous, and there
is no climate or element without one or more.

And every tongue, through utter drought,
Was withered at the root;
We could not speak, no more than if
We had been choked with soot.

The shipmates,
140 in their sore
distress, would
fain throw the
whole guilt on
the ancient

Ah! well a-day! what evil looks
Had I from old and young!
Instead of the cross, the Albatross
About my neck was hung.

Mariner: in sign whereof they hang the dead sea-bird round his neck.

PART III

There passed a weary time. Each throat
Was parched, and glazed each eye.
A weary time! a weary time!
How glazed each weary eye,
The ancient
Mariner be-
holdeth a sign
in the element
afar off.

When looking westward, I beheld
A something in the sky.

At first it seemed a little speck,
150 And then it seemed a mist;

death-fires electrical effect like lights, called St.
Elmo's fire; by sailors' superstition, they are
death-omens

Spirit a daemon, intermediary between men
and gods

It moved and moved, and took at last
A certain shape, I wist.°

A speck, a mist, a shape, I wist!
And still it neared and neared:
As if it dodged a water-sprite,
It plunged and tacked and veered.

At its nearer
approach, it
seemeth him
to be a ship;
and at a dear
ransom he
freeth his
speech from
the bonds of
thirst.

A flash of joy;

With throats unslaked, with black lips baked
We could nor laugh nor wail;
Through utter drought all dumb we stood!
I bit my arm, I sucked the blood,
And cried, A sail! a sail!

With throats unslaked, with black lips baked
Agape they heard me call:
Gramercy!° they for joy did grin,
And all at once their breath drew in,
As they were drinking all.

And horror
follows. For
can it be a
ship that
comes onward
without wind
or tide?

See! see! (I cried) she tacks no more!
Hither to work us weal;°
Without a breeze, without a tide,
She steadies with upright keel!

The western wave was all a-flame.
The day was well nigh done!
Almost upon the western wave
Rested the broad bright Sun;
When that strange shape drove suddenly
Betwixt us and the Sun.

It seemeth
him but the
skeleton of
a ship.

And straight the Sun was flecked with bars,
(Heaven's Mother send us grace!)
As if through a dungeon-grate he peered
With broad and burning face.

And its ribs
are seen as
bars on the
face of the
setting Sun.

Alas! (thought I, and my heart beat loud)
How fast she nears and nears!
Are those *her* sails that glance in the Sun,
Like restless gossameres?

The Spectre-
Woman and
her Death-
mate, and no
other on
board the
skeleton ship.

Are those *her* ribs through which the Sun
Did peer, as through a grate?
And is that Woman all her crew?
Is that a DEATH? and are there two?
Is DEATH that woman's mate?

Like vessel,
like crew!

Her lips were red, *her* looks were free,
Her locks were yellow as gold:

wist knew   **weal** good
Gramercy "great thanks" (French, *grand-merci*)

Death and
Life-in-Death
have diced for
the ship's
crew, and she
(the latter)
winneth the
ancient
Mariner.

Her skin was as white as leprosy,
The Night-mare LIFE-IN-DEATH was she,
Who thicks man's blood with cold.

The naked hulk alongside came,
And the twain were casting dice;
'The game is done! I've won! I've won!'
Quoth she, and whistles thrice.

200   No twilight
within the
courts of the
Sun.

The Sun's rim dips; the stars rush out:
At one stride comes the dark;
With far-heard whisper, o'er the sea,
Off shot the spectre-bark.

At the rising
of the Moon,

We listened and looked sideways up!
Fear at my heart, as at a cup,
My life-blood seemed to sip!
The stars were dim, and thick the night,
The steersman's face by his lamp gleamed white;
From the sails the dew did drip—

210

Till clomb above the eastern bar
The hornèd Moon, with one bright star
Within the nether tip.

One after
another,

One after one, by the star-dogged Moon,°
Too quick for groan or sigh,
Each turned his face with a ghastly pang,
And cursed me with his eye.

His shipmates
drop down
dead.

Four times fifty living men,
(And I heard nor sigh nor groan)
With heavy thump, a lifeless lump,
They dropped down one by one.

220   But Life-in-
Death begins
her work on
the ancient
Mariner.

The souls did from their bodies fly,—
They fled to bliss or woe!
And every soul, it passed me by,
Like the whizz of my cross-bow!

PART IV

The Wedding-
Guest feareth
that a Spirit
is talking to
him;

'I fear thee, ancient Mariner!
I fear thy skinny hand!
And thou art long, and lank, and brown,
As is the ribbed sea-sand.

'I fear thee and thy glittering eye,
And thy skinny hand, so brown.'—

230   But the
ancient Ma-
riner assureth

Fear not, fear not, thou Wedding-Guest!
This body dropped not down.

star-dogged Moon "It is a common superstition   happen whenever a star dogs the Moon" (Cole-
among sailors that something evil is about to   ridge).

him of his
bodily life, and
proceedeth to
relate his hor-
rible penance.

Alone, alone, all, all alone,
Alone on a wide wide sea!
And never a saint took pity on
My soul in agony.

He despiseth
the creatures
of the calm,

The many men, so beautiful!
And they all dead did lie:
And a thousand thousand slimy things
Lived on; and so did I.

240

And envieth
that *they*
should live,
and so many
lie dead.

I looked upon the rotting sea,
And drew my eyes away;
I looked upon the rotting deck,
And there the dead men lay.

I looked to heaven, and tried to pray;
But or ever a prayer had gusht,
A wicked whisper came, and made
My heart as dry as dust.

250

I closed my lids, and kept them close,
And the balls like pulses beat;
For the sky and the sea, and the sea and the sky
Lay like a load on my weary eye,
And the dead were at my feet.

But the curse
liveth for him
in the eye of
the dead men.

The cold sweat melted from their limbs,
Nor rot nor reek did they:
The look with which they looked on me
Had never passed away.

An orphan's curse would drag to hell
A spirit from on high;
But oh! more horrible than that
Is the curse in a dead man's eye!
Seven days, seven nights, I saw that curse,
And yet I could not die.

260

In his lone-
liness and
fixedness he
yearneth to-
wards the
journeying
Moon, and the
stars that still
sojourn, yet
still move
onward; and
every where
the blue sky
belongs to

The moving Moon went up the sky,
And no where did abide:
Softly she was going up,
And a star or two beside—

Her beams bemocked the sultry main,
Like April hoar-frost spread;
But where the ship's huge shadow lay,
The charmèd water burnt alway
A still and awful red.

270

them, and is their appointed rest, and their native country and their own natural homes,
which they enter unannounced, as lords that are certainly expected and yet there is a
silent joy at their arrival.

By the light
of the Moon he
beholdeth
God's crea-
tures of the
great calm.

Beyond the shadow of the ship,
I watched the water-snakes:
They moved in tracks of shining white,
And when they reared, the elfish light
Fell off in hoary flakes.

Within the shadow of the ship
I watched their rich attire:
Blue, glossy green, and velvet black,
They coiled and swam; and every track
Was a flash of golden fire.

280

Their beauty
and their
happiness.

O happy living things! no tongue
Their beauty might declare:
A spring of love gushed from my heart,
And I blessed them unaware:
Sure my kind saint took pity on me,
And I blessed them unaware.

He blesseth
them in his
heart.

The spell
begins to
break.

The self-same moment I could pray;
And from my neck so free
The Albatross fell off, and sank
Like lead into the sea.

290

PART V

Oh sleep! it is a gentle thing,
Beloved from pole to pole!
To Mary Queen the praise be given!
She sent the gentle sleep from Heaven,
That slid into my soul.

By grace of
the holy
Mother, the
ancient
Mariner is
refreshed with
rain.

The silly° buckets on the deck,
That had so long remained,
I dreamt that they were filled with dew;
And when I awoke, it rained.

300

My lips were wet, my throat was cold,
My garments all were dank;
Sure I had drunken in my dreams,
And still my body drank.

I moved, and could not feel my limbs:
I was so light—almost
I thought that I had died in sleep,
And was a blessèd ghost.

He heareth
sounds and
seeth strange
sights and
commotions in
the sky and
the element.

And soon I heard a roaring wind:
It did not come anear;
But with its sound it shook the sails,
That were so thin and sere.

310

silly in the archaic sense of "simple" or
"homely," perhaps also "blessed"

The upper air burst into life!
And a hundred fire-flags sheen,°
To and fro they were hurried about!
And to and fro, and in and out,
The wan stars danced between.

And the coming wind did roar more loud,
And the sails did sigh like sedge;°
And the rain poured down from one black cloud;
The Moon was at its edge.

The thick black cloud was cleft, and still
The Moon was at its side:
Like waters shot from some high crag,
The lightning fell with never a jag,
A river steep and wide.

The loud wind never reached the ship,
Yet now the ship moved on!
Beneath the lightning and the Moon
The dead men gave a groan.

They groaned, they stirred, they all uprose,
Nor spake, nor moved their eyes;
It had been strange, even in a dream,
To have seen those dead men rise.

The helmsman steered, the ship moved on;
Yet never a breeze up-blew;
The mariners all 'gan work the ropes,
Where they were wont to do;
They raised their limbs like lifeless tools—
We were a ghastly crew.

The body of my brother's son
Stood by me, knee to knee:
The body and I pulled at one rope,
But he said nought to me.

'I fear thee, ancient Mariner!'
Be calm, thou Wedding-Guest!
'Twas not those souls that fled in pain,
Which to their corses came again,
But a troop of spirits blest:

For when it dawned—they dropped their arms,
And clustered round the mast;
Sweet sounds rose slowly through their mouths,
And from their bodies passed.

The bodies of the ship's crew are inspired and the ship moves on;

But not by the souls of the men, nor by daemons of earth or middle air, but by a blessed troop of angelic spirits, sent down by the invocation

320
330
340
350

And . . . sheen lights waving as if they were flags   **sedge** coarse, grassy plant bordering lakes and streams

of the guar-
dian saint.

Around, around, flew each sweet sound,
Then darted to the Sun;
Slowly the sounds came back again,
Now mixed, now one by one.

360

Sometimes a-dropping from the sky
I heard the sky-lark sing;
Sometimes all little birds that are,
How they seemed to fill the sea and air
With their sweet jargoning!°

And now 'twas like all instruments,
Now like a lonely flute;
And now it is an angel's song,
That makes the heavens be mute.

It ceased; yet still the sails made on
A pleasant noise till noon,
A noise like of a hidden brook

370

In the leafy month of June,
That to the sleeping woods all night
Singeth a quiet tune.

Till noon we quietly sailed on,
Yet never a breeze did breathe:
Slowly and smoothly went the ship,
Moved onward from beneath.

The lonesome
Spirit from
the south-pole
carries on the

380

ship as far as
the Line, in
obedience to
the angelic
troop, but still
requireth
vengeance.

Under the keel nine fathom deep,
From the land of mist and snow,
The spirit slid: and it was he
That made the ship to go.
The sails at noon left off their tune,
And the ship stood still also.

The Sun, right up above the mast,
Had fixed her to the ocean:
But in a minute she 'gan stir,
With a short uneasy motion—
Backwards and forwards half her length
With a short uneasy motion.

390

Then like a pawing horse let go,
She made a sudden bound:
It flung the blood into my head,
And I fell down in a swound.

The Polar
Spirit's fellow-
daemons, the
invisible in-

How long in that same fit I lay,
I have not to declare;
But ere my living life returned,

jargoning archaic sense, "warbling"

I heard and in my soul discerned
Two voices in the air.

'Is it he?' quoth one, 'Is this the man?
By him who died on cross,
With his cruel bow he laid full low
The harmless Albatross.

'The spirit who bideth by himself
In the land of mist and snow,
He loved the bird that loved the man
Who shot him with his bow.'

The other was a softer voice,
As soft as honey-dew:
Quoth he, 'The man hath penance done,
And penance more will do.'

PART VI

FIRST VOICE

'But tell me, tell me! speak again,
Thy soft response renewing—
What makes that ship drive on so fast?
What is the ocean doing?'

SECOND VOICE

'Still as a slave before his lord,
The ocean hath no blast;
His great bright eye most silently
Up to the Moon is cast—

'If he may know which way to go;
For she guides him smooth or grim.
See, brother, see! how graciously
She looketh down on him.'

FIRST VOICE

'But why drives on that ship so fast,
Without or wave or wind?'

SECOND VOICE

'The air is cut away before,
And closes from behind.

'Fly, brother, fly! more high, more high!
Or we shall be belated:
For slow and slow that ship will go,
When the Mariner's trance is abated.'

habitants of the element, take part in his wrong; and two of them relate, one to the other, that penance long and heavy for the ancient Mariner hath been accorded to the Polar Spirit, who returneth southward.

00

410

420

The Mariner hath been cast into a trance; for the angelic power causeth the vessel to drive northward faster than human life could endure.

430 The super-
     natural motion
     is retarded;
     the Mariner
     awakes, and
     his penance
     begins anew.

I woke, and we were sailing on
As in a gentle weather:
'Twas night, calm night, the moon was high;
The dead men stood together.

All stood together on the deck,
For a charnel-dungeon° fitter:
All fixed on me their stony eyes,
That in the Moon did glitter.

The pang, the curse, with which they died,
Had never passed away:
440 I could not draw my eyes from theirs,
Nor turn them up to pray.

The curse is
finally ex-
piated.

And now this spell was snapped: once more
I viewed the ocean green,
And looked far forth, yet little saw
Of what had else been seen—

Like one, that on a lonesome road
Doth walk in fear and dread,
And having once turned round walks on,
And turns no more his head;
450 Because he knows, a frightful fiend
Doth close behind him tread.

But soon there breathed a wind on me,
Nor sound nor motion made:
Its path was not upon the sea,
In ripple or in shade.

It raised my hair, it fanned my cheek
Like a meadow-gale° of spring—
It mingled strangely with my fears,
Yet it felt like a welcoming.

460 Swiftly, swiftly flew the ship,
Yet she sailed softly too:
Sweetly, sweetly blew the breeze—
On me alone it blew.

And the
ancient
Mariner be-
holdeth his
native
country.

Oh! dream of joy! is this indeed
The light-house top I see?
Is this the hill? is this the kirk?
Is this mine own countree?

We drifted o'er the harbour-bar,
And I with sobs did pray—
470 O let me be awake, my God!
Or let me sleep alway.

charnel-dungeon where dead bodies are piled   meadow-gale breeze

The harbour-bay was clear as glass,
So smoothly it was strewn!
And on the bay the moonlight lay,
And the shadow of the Moon.

The rock shone bright, the kirk no less,
That stands above the rock:
The moonlight steeped in silentness
The steady weathercock.

480

*The angelic
spirits leave
the dead
bodies,*

*And appear in
their own
forms of light.*

And the bay was white with silent light,
Till rising from the same,
Full many shapes, that shadows were,
In crimson colours came.

A little distance from the prow
Those crimson shadows were:
I turned my eyes upon the deck—
Oh, Christ! what saw I there!

Each corse lay flat, lifeless and flat,
And, by the holy rood!°
490   A man all light, a seraph-man,
On every corse there stood.

This seraph-band, each waved his hand:
It was a heavenly sight!
They stood as signals to the land,
Each one a lovely light;

This seraph-band, each waved his hand,
No voice did they impart—
No voice; but oh! the silence sank
Like music on my heart.

500   But soon I heard the dash of oars,
I heard the Pilot's cheer;
My head was turned perforce away
And I saw a boat appear.

The Pilot and the Pilot's boy,
I heard them coming fast:
Dear Lord in Heaven! it was a joy
The dead men could not blast.

I saw a third—I heard his voice:
It is the Hermit good!
510   He singeth loud his godly hymns
That he makes in the wood.
He'll shrieve my soul, he'll wash away
The Albatross's blood.

rood cross

PART VII

The Hermit of
the Wood,

This Hermit good lives in that wood
Which slopes down to the sea.
How loudly his sweet voice he rears!
He loves to talk with marineres
That come from a far countree.

520

He kneels at morn, and noon, and eve—
He hath a cushion plump:
It is the moss that wholly hides
The rotted old oak-stump.

The skiff-boat neared: I heard them talk,
'Why, this is strange, I trow!
Where are those lights so many and fair,
That signal made but now?'

Approacheth
the ship with
wonder.

'Strange, by my faith!' the Hermit said—
'And they answered not our cheer!
The planks looked warped! and see those sails,
530
How thin they are and sere!
I never saw aught like to them,
Unless perchance it were

'Brown skeletons of leaves that lag
My forest-brook along;
'When the ivy-tod° is heavy with snow,
And the owlet whoops to the wolf below,
That eats the she-wolf's young.'

'Dear Lord! it hath a fiendish look—
(The Pilot made reply)
540
I am a-feared'—'Push on, push on!'
Said the Hermit cheerily.

The boat came closer to the ship,
But I nor spake nor stirred;
The boat came close beneath the ship,
And straight a sound was heard.

The ship
suddenly
sinketh.

Under the water it rumbled on,
Still louder and more dread:
It reached the ship, it split the bay;
The ship went down like lead.

550   The ancient
Mariner is
saved in the
Pilot's boat.

Stunned by that loud and dreadful sound,
Which sky and ocean smote,
Like one that hath been seven days drowned
My body lay afloat;

ivy-tod ivy bush

But swift as dreams, myself I found
Within the Pilot's boat.

Upon the whirl, where sank the ship,
The boat spun round and round;
And all was still, save that the hill
Was telling of the sound.

560

I moved my lips—the Pilot shrieked
And fell down in a fit;
The holy Hermit raised his eyes,
And prayed where he did sit.

I took the oars: the Pilot's boy,
Who now doth crazy go,
Laughed loud and long, and all the while
His eyes went to and fro.
'Ha! ha!' quoth he, 'full plain I see,
The Devil knows how to row.'

570

And now, all in my own countree,
I stood on the firm land!
The Hermit stepped forth from the boat,
And scarcely he could stand.

The ancient Mariner earnestly entreateth the Hermit to shrieve him; and the penance of life falls on him.

'O shrieve° me, shrieve me, holy man!'
The Hermit crossed his brow.
'Say quick,' quoth he, 'I bid thee say—
What manner of man art thou?'

580

Forthwith this frame of mine was wrenched
With a woeful agony,
Which forced me to begin my tale;
And then it left me free.

And ever and anon throughout his future life an agony constraineth him to travel from land to land;

Since then, at an uncertain hour,
That agony returns:
And till my ghastly tale is told,
This heart within me burns.

I pass, like night, from land to land;°
I have strange power of speech;
That moment that his face I see,
I know the man that must hear me:
To him my tale I teach.

590

What loud uproar bursts from that door!
The wedding-guests are there:
But in the garden-bower the bride
And bride-maids singing are:

shrieve me hear my confession and give me   I pass . . . land like the Wandering Jew, or
absolution   Cain

And hark the little vesper bell,
Which biddeth me to prayer!

O Wedding-Guest! this soul hath been
Alone on a wide wide sea:
So lonely 'twas, that God himself
600   Scarce seemèd there to be.

O sweeter than the marriage-feast,
'Tis sweeter far to me,
To walk together to the kirk
With a goodly company!—

To walk together to the kirk,
And all together pray,
While each to his great Father bends,
Old men, and babes, and loving friends
And youths and maidens gay!

610   *And to teach,
by his own
example, love
and reverence
to all things
that God made
and loveth.*

Farewell, farewell! but this I tell
To thee, thou Wedding-Guest!
He prayeth well, who loveth well
Both man and bird and beast.

He prayeth best, who loveth best
All things both great and small;
For the dear God who loveth us,
He made and loveth all.

The Mariner, whose eye is bright,
Whose beard with age is hoar,
620   Is gone: and now the Wedding-Guest
Turned from the bridegroom's door.

He went like one that hath been stunned,
And is of sense forlorn:
A sadder and a wiser man,
He rose the morrow morn.
1797–98   1798

Kubla Khan:

Or, a Vision in a Dream. A Fragment.

The following fragment is here published at the request of a poet [1] of great and deserved celebrity, and, as far as the Author's own opinions are concerned, rather as a *psychological* curiosity, than on the ground of any supposed *poetic* merits.

1. Lord Byron.

In the summer of the year 1797, the Author, then in ill health, had retired
to a lonely farm-house between Porlock and Linton, on the Exmoor confines of
Somerset and Devonshire. In consequence of a slight indisposition, an anodyne
had been prescribed, from the effects of which he fell asleep in his chair at the
moment that he was reading the following sentence, or words of the same
substance, in 'Purchas's Pilgrimage': 'Here the Khan Kubla commanded a
palace to be built, and a stately garden thereunto. And thus ten miles of fertile
ground were inclosed with a wall.'[2] The Author continued for about three
hours in a profound sleep,[3] at least of the external senses, during which time
he has the most vivid confidence, that he could not have composed less than
from two to three hundred lines; if that indeed can be called composition in
which all the images rose up before him as *things*, with a parallel production
of the correspondent expressions, without any sensation or consciousness of
effort. On awaking he appeared to himself to have a distinct recollection of
the whole, and taking his pen, ink, and paper, instantly and eagerly wrote down
the lines that are here preserved. At this moment he was unfortunately called
out by a person on business from Porlock, and detained by him above an hour,
and on his return to his room, found, to his no small surprise and mortification,
that though he still retained some vague and dim recollection of the general
purport of the vision, yet, with the exception of some eight or ten scattered
lines and images, all the rest had passed away like the images on the surface
of a stream into which a stone has been cast, but, alas! without the after restoration of the latter!

> Then all the charm
> Is broken—all that phantom-world so fair
> Vanishes, and a thousand circlets spread,
> And each mis-shape[s] the other. Stay awhile,
> Poor youth! who scarcely dar'st lift up thine eyes—
> The stream will soon renew its smoothness, soon
> The visions will return! And lo, he stays,
> And soon the fragments dim of lovely forms
> Come trembling back, unite, and now once more
> The pool becomes a mirror.
> [From *The Picture; or, the Lover's Resolution*, ll. 91–100.]

Yet from the still surviving recollections in his mind, the Author has frequently purposed to finish for himself what had been originally, as it were,

2. The correct quotation from Samuel Purchas, *Purchas His Pilgrimage* (1613), is: "In
Xamdu did Cublai Can build a stately Palace, encompassing sixteene miles of plaine
ground with a wall, wherein are fertile Meddowes, pleasant springs, delightfull Streams,
and all sorts of beasts of chase and game, and in the middest thereof a sumptuous
house of pleasure, which may be removed from place to place." J. L. Lowes demonstrated
that other borrowings from Purchas are important, particularly from the account of
Alvadine, the Old Man of the Mountain, who employed his earthly paradise or garden
of delights to train the assassins whom he sent against his enemies.
3. In a manuscript note Coleridge confessed that his supposed sleep was actually an
opium-induced reverie.

given to him. Σαμερον αδιον ασω [4] [Αὔριον ἅδιον ἅσω[5] *1834*]: but the to-morrow is yet to come.

In Xanadu did Kubla Khan
A stately pleasure-dome decree:
Where Alph,° the sacred river, ran
Through caverns measureless to man
　　Down to a sunless sea.
So twice five miles of fertile ground
　With walls and towers were girdled round:
And there were gardens bright with sinuous rills,
　Where blossomed many an incense-bearing tree;
10　And here were forests ancient as the hills,
Enfolding sunny spots of greenery.

But oh! that deep romantic chasm which slanted
Down the green hill athwart a cedarn cover!
A savage place! as holy and enchanted
As e'er beneath a waning moon was haunted
By woman wailing for her demon-lover!
And from this chasm, with ceaseless turmoil seething,
As if this earth in fast thick pants were breathing,
A mighty fountain momently was forced:
20　Amid whose swift half-intermitted burst
Huge fragments vaulted like rebounding hail,
Or chaffy grain beneath the thresher's flail:
And 'mid these dancing rocks at once and ever
It flung up momently the sacred river.
Five miles meandering with a mazy motion
Through wood and dale the sacred river ran,
Then reached the caverns measureless to man,
And sank in tumult to a lifeless ocean:
And 'mid this tumult Kubla heard from far
30　Ancestral voices prophesying war!
　　The shadow of the dome of pleasure
　　Floated midway on the waves;
　　Where was heard the mingled measure°
　　From the fountain and the caves.
It was a miracle of rare device,
A sunny pleasure-dome with caves of ice!

　A damsel with a dulcimer
　In a vision once I saw:

4. From Theocritus, *Idylls* I.145, "I'll sing to you a sweeter song another day."
5. "I'll sing to you a sweeter song tomorrow."

Alph Scholars agree that Coleridge compounded the first letter of the Greek alphabet, "Alpha," with mythological speculations that the Garden of Eden, where language began, was in Abys-sinia, and with memories of the classical river Alpheus, which ran underground.
mingled measure See William Collins's ode "The Passions," l. 64.

It was an Abyssinian maid,
40   And on her dulcimer she played,
Singing of Mount Abora.°
Could I revive within me
Her symphony and song,
To such a deep delight 'twould win me,
That with music loud and long,
I would build that dome in air,
That sunny dome! those caves of ice!
And all who heard should see them there,
And all should cry, Beware! Beware!
50   His flashing eyes, his floating hair!
Weave a circle round him thrice,
And close your eyes with holy dread,
For he on honey-dew hath fed,
And drunk the milk of Paradise.°
1798   1816

Christabel [1]

Preface

The first part of the following poem was written in the year 1797, at Stowey, in the county of Somerset. The second part, after my return from Germany, in the year 1800, at Keswick, Cumberland. It is probable that if the poem had been finished at either of the former periods, or if even the first and second part had been published in the year 1800, the impression of its originality would have been much greater than I dare at present expect. But for this I have only my own indolence to blame. The dates are mentioned for the exclusive purpose of precluding charges of plagiarism or servile imitation from myself. For there is amongst us a set of critics, who seem to hold, that every possible thought and image is traditional; who have no notion that there are such things as fountains in the world, small as well as great; and who would therefore charitably derive every rill they behold flowing, from a perforation made in some other man's tank. I am confident, however, that as far as the present poem is concerned, the celebrated poets [2] whose writings I might be suspected of having imitated,

---

Mount Abora See *Paradise Lost* IV.280–82: "where *Abassin* Kings their issue Guard, / Mount *Amara*, though this by some supposed / True Paradise under the Ethiop Line."

milk of Paradise See Plato's *Ion* 534 a-b, where a poet's inspiration is compared to the Dionysiac women who receive honey and milk from the rivers of a Muses' paradise.

1. This is perhaps best read as a sequence of fragments, or four poems linked together, only partly by subject, and partly by the theme best described by W. J. Bate as "the open admission of evil by innocence." Coleridge said that the poem was "founded on the notion, that the virtuous of this world save the wicked," and he remarked also that, in composing *Christabel*, he was haunted by lines from Richard Crashaw's "A Hymn to the Name and Honour of the Admirable Saint Teresa": "Since 'tis not to be had at home / She'll travel to a martyrdome. / No home for her confesses she, / But where she may a martyr be." But in the fragments as they stand, there are no indications that Geraldine will be redeemed by the sacrifice (apparently sexual) of Christabel.
2. Sir Walter Scott and Lord Byron.

either in particular passages, or in the tone and the spirit of the whole, would
be among the first to vindicate me from the charge, and who, on any striking
coincidence, would permit me to address them in this doggerel version of two
monkish Latin hexameters.

> 'Tis mine and it is likewise yours;
> But an if this will not do;
> Let it be mine, good friend! for I
> Am the poorer of the two.

I have only to add that the metre of Christabel is not, properly speaking,
irregular, though it may seem so from its being founded on a new principle:
namely, that of counting in each line the accents, not the syllables. Though the
latter may vary from seven to twelve, yet in each line the accents will be found
to be only four. Nevertheless, this occasional variation in number of syllables
is not introduced wantonly, or for the mere ends of convenience, but in correspondence with some transition in the nature of the imagery or passion.

PART I

'Tis the middle of night by the castle clock,
And the owls have awakened the crowing cock;
Tu—whit!——Tu—whoo!
And hark, again! the crowing cock,
How drowsily it crew.
Sir Leoline, the Baron rich,
Hath a toothless mastiff bitch;
From her kennel beneath the rock
She maketh answer to the clock,
10   Four for the quarters, and twelve for the hour;
Ever and aye, by shine and shower,
Sixteen short howls, not over loud;
Some say, she sees my lady's shroud.

Is the night chilly and dark?
The night is chilly, but not dark.
The thin grey cloud is spread on high,
It covers but not hides the sky.
The moon is behind, and at the full;
And yet she looks both small and dull.
20   The night is chill, the cloud is grey:
'Tis a month before the month of May,
And the Spring comes slowly up this way.

The lovely lady, Christabel,
Whom her father loves so well,
What makes her in the wood so late,
A furlong from the castle gate?
She had dreams all yesternight
Of her own betrothèd knight;

And she in the midnight wood will pray
30   For the weal° of her lover that's far away.

She stole along, she nothing spoke,
The sighs she heaved were soft and low,
And naught was green upon the oak
But moss and rarest mistletoe:
She kneels beneath the huge oak tree,
And in silence prayeth she.

The lady sprang up suddenly,
The lovely lady, Christabel!
It moaned as near, as near can be,
40   But what it is she cannot tell.—
On the other side it seems to be,
Of the huge, broad-breasted, old oak tree.

The night is chill; the forest bare;
Is it the wind that moaneth bleak?
There is not wind enough in the air
To move away the ringlet curl
From the lovely lady's cheek—
There is not wind enough to twirl
The one red leaf, the last of its clan,
50   That dances as often as dance it can,
Hanging so light, and hanging so high,
On the topmost twig that looks up at the sky.

Hush, beating heart of Christabel!
Jesu, Maria, shield her well!
She folded her arms beneath her cloak,
And stole to the other side of the oak.
        What sees she there?

There she sees a damsel bright,
Dressed in a silken robe of white,
60   That shadowy in the moonlight shone:
The neck that made that white robe wan,
Her stately neck, and arms were bare;
Her blue-veined feet unsandaled were,
And wildly glittered here and there
The gems entangled in her hair.
I guess, 'twas frightful there to see
A lady so richly clad as she—
Beautiful exceedingly!

Mary mother, save me now!
70   (Said Christabel,) And who art thou?

weal welfare

The lady strange made answer meet,
And her voice was faint and sweet:—
Have pity on my sore distress,
I scarce can speak for weariness:
Stretch forth thy hand, and have no fear!
Said Christabel, How camest thou here?
And the lady, whose voice was faint and sweet,
Did thus pursue her answer meet:—

My sire is of noble line,
80   And my name is Geraldine:
Five warriors seized me yestermorn,
Me, even me, a maid forlorn:
They choked my cries with force and fright,
And tied me on a palfrey white.
The palfrey was as fleet as wind,
And they rode furiously behind.

They spurred amain,° their steeds were white:
And once we crossed the shade of night.
As sure as Heaven shall rescue me,
90   I have no thought what men they be;
Nor do I know how long it is
(For I have lain entranced I wis)°
Since one, the tallest of the five,
Took me from the palfrey's back,
A weary woman, scarce alive.
Some muttered words his comrades spoke:
He placed me underneath this oak;
He swore they would return with haste;
Whither they went I cannot tell—
100   I thought I heard, some minutes past,
Sounds as of a castle bell.
Stretch forth thy hand (thus ended she).
And help a wretched maid to flee.

Then Christabel stretched forth her hand,
And comforted fair Geraldine:
O well, bright dame! may you command
The service of Sir Leoline;
And gladly our stout chivalry
Will he send forth and friends withal
110   To guide and guard you safe and free
Home to your noble father's hall.

She rose: and forth with steps they passed
That strove to be, and were not, fast.
Her gracious stars the lady blest,

amain vehemently, exceedingly   wis think

And thus spake on sweet Christabel:
All our household are at rest,
The hall as silent as the cell;
Sir Leoline is weak in health,
And may not well awakened be,
120   But we will move as if in stealth,
And I beseech your courtesy,
This night, to share your couch with me.

They crossed the moat, and Christabel
Took the key that fitted well;
A little door she opened straight,
All in the middle of the gate;
The gate that was ironed within and without,
Where an army in battle array had marched out.
The lady sank, belike through pain,
130   And Christabel with might and main
Lifted her up,° a weary weight,
Over the threshold of the gate:
Then the lady rose again,
And moved, as she were not in pain.

So free from danger, free from fear,
They crossed the court: right glad they were.
And Christabel devoutly cried
To the lady by her side,
Praise we the Virgin all divine
140   Who hath rescued thee from thy distress!
Alas, alas! said Geraldine,
I cannot speak for weariness.
So free from danger, free from fear,
They crossed the court: right glad they were.

Outside her kennel, the mastiff old
Lay fast asleep, in moonshine cold.
The mastiff old did not awake,
Yet she an angry moan did make!
And what can ail the mastiff bitch?
150   Never till now she uttered yell
Beneath the eye of Christabel.
Perhaps it is the owlet's scritch:°
For what can ail the mastiff bitch?

They passed the hall, that echoes still,
Pass as lightly as you will!
The brands were flat, the brands were dying,
Amid their own white ashes lying;
But when the lady passed, there came

Lifted her up Evil beings cannot enter without   **scritch** screech
the aid of the innocent.

A tongue of light, a fit of flame;
160   And Christabel saw the lady's eye,
And nothing else saw she thereby,
Save the boss of the shield of Sir Leoline tall,
Which hung in a murky old niche in the wall.
O softly tread, said Christabel,
My father seldom sleepeth well.

Sweet Christabel her feet doth bare,
And jealous of the listening air
They steal their way from stair to stair,
Now in glimmer, and now in gloom,
170   And now they pass the Baron's room,
As still as death, with stifled breath!
And now have reached her chamber door;
And now doth Geraldine press down
The rushes° of the chamber floor.

The moon shines dim in the open air,
And not a moonbeam enters here.
But they without its light can see
The chamber carved so curiously,
Carved with figures strange and sweet,
180   All made out of the carver's brain,
For a lady's chamber meet:
The lamp with twofold silver chain
Is fastened to an angel's feet.

The silver lamp burns dead and dim;
But Christabel the lamp will trim.
She trimmed the lamp, and made it bright,
And left it swinging to and fro,
While Geraldine, in wretched plight,
Sank down upon the floor below.

190   O weary lady, Geraldine,
I pray you, drink this cordial wine!
It is a wine of virtuous powers;
My mother made it of wild flowers.

And will your mother pity me,
Who am a maiden most forlorn?
Christabel answered—Woe is me!
She died the hour that I was born.
I have heard the grey-haired friar tell
How on her death-bed she did say,
200   That she should hear the castle-bell
Strike twelve upon my wedding-day.

rushes spread as floor covering, a general medieval custom

O mother dear! that thou wert here!
I would, said Geraldine, she were!

But soon with altered voice, said she—
'Off, wandering mother! Peak° and pine!
I have power to bid thee flee.'
Alas! what ails poor Geraldine?
Why stares she with unsettled eye?
Can she the bodiless dead espy?
210   And why with hollow voice cries she,
'Off, woman, off! this hour is mine—
Though thou her guardian spirit be,
Off, woman, off! 'tis given to me.'

Then Christabel knelt by the lady's side,
And raised to heaven her eyes so blue—
Alas! said she, this ghastly ride—
Dear lady! it hath wildered you!
The lady wiped her moist cold brow,
And faintly said, ''tis over now!'

220   Again the wild-flower wine she drank:
Her fair large eyes 'gan glitter bright,
And from the floor whereon she sank,
The lofty lady stood upright:
She was most beautiful to see,
Like a lady of a far countree.

And thus the lofty lady spake—
'All they who live in the upper sky,
Do love you, holy Christabel!
And you love them, and for their sake
230   And for the good which me befel,
Even I in my degree will try,
Fair maiden, to requite you well.
But now unrobe yourself; for I
Must pray, ere yet in bed I lie.'

Quoth Christabel, So let it be!
And as the lady bade, did she.
Her gentle limbs did she undress,
And lay down in her loveliness.

But through her brain of weal and woe
240   So many thoughts moved to and fro,
That vain it were her lids to close;
So half-way from the bed she rose,
And on her elbow did recline
To look at the lady Geraldine.

Peak grow thin; see *Macbeth* I.iii.23, where the
witches incant: "dwindle, peak and pine"

Beneath the lamp the lady bowed,
And slowly rolled her eyes around;
Then drawing in her breath aloud,
Like one that shuddered, she unbound
The cincture from beneath her breast:
250   Her silken robe, and inner vest,
Dropped to her feet, and full in view,
Behold! her bosom and half her side——
A sight to dream of, not to tell!
O shield her! shield sweet Christabel!

Yet Geraldine nor speaks nor stirs;
Ah! what a stricken look was hers!
Deep from within she seems half-way
To lift some weight with sick assay,°
And eyes the maid and seeks delay;
260   Then suddenly, as one defied,
Collects herself in scorn and pride,
And lay down by the Maiden's side!—
And in her arms the maid she took,
        Ah wel-a-day!
And with low voice and doleful look
These words did say:
'In the touch of this bosom there worketh a spell,
Which is lord of thy utterance, Christabel!
Thou knowest tonight, and wilt know tomorrow,
270   This mark of my shame, this seal of my sorrow;
        But vainly thou warrest,
            For this is alone in
            Thy power to declare,
                That in the dim forest
            Thou heardest a low moaning.
And foundest a bright lady, surpassingly fair;
And didst bring her home with thee in love and in charity,
To shield her and shelter her from the damp air.'

THE CONCLUSION TO PART I

It was a lovely sight to see
280   The lady Christabel, when she
Was praying at the old oak tree.
        Amid the jaggèd shadows
        Of mossy leafless boughs,
        Kneeling in the moonlight,
        To make her gentle vows;
Her slender palms together prest,
Heaving sometimes on her breast;
Her face resigned to bliss or bale—

assay attempt

Her face, oh call it fair not pale,
290 And both blue eyes more bright than clear,
Each about to have a tear.

With open eyes (ah woe is me!)
Asleep, and dreaming fearfully,
Fearfully dreaming, yet, I wis,
Dreaming that alone, which is—
O sorrow and shame! Can this be she,
The lady, who knelt at the old oak tree?
And lo! the worker of these harms,
That holds the maiden in her arms,
300 Seems to slumber still and mild,
As a mother with her child.

A star hath set, a star hath risen,
O Geraldine! since arms of thine
Have been the lovely lady's prison.
O Geraldine! one hour was thine—
Thou'st had thy will! By tairn° and rill,
The night-birds all that hour were still.
But now they are jubilant anew,
From cliff and tower, tu—whoo! tu—whoo!
310 Tu—whoo! tu—woo! from wood and fell!°

And see! the lady Christabel
Gathers herself from out her trance;
Her limbs relax, her countenance
Grows sad and soft; the smooth thin lids
Close o'er her eyes; and tears she sheds—
Large tears that leave the lashes bright!
And oft the while she seems to smile
As infants at a sudden light!

Yea, she doth smile, and she doth weep,
320 Like a youthful hermitess,°
Beauteous in a wilderness,
Who, praying always, prays in sleep.
And, if she move unquietly,
Perchance, 'tis but the blood so free
Comes back and tingles in her feet.
No doubt, she hath a vision sweet.
What if her guardian spirit 'twere,
What if she knew her mother near?
But this she knows, in joys and woes,
330 That saints will aid if men will call:
For the blue sky bends over all!
1797   1798

---

tairn mountain pool
fell moor, hill

hermitess perhaps a remembrance of Crashaw's
St. Teresa (see note 1)

PART II

Each matin bell, the Baron saith,
Knells us back to a world of death.
These words Sir Leoline first said,
When he rose and found his lady dead:
These words Sir Leoline will say
Many a morn to his dying day!

And hence the custom and law began
That still at dawn the sacristan,
340   Who duly pulls the heavy bell,
Five and forty beads must tell
Between each stroke—a warning knell,
Which not a soul can choose but hear
From Bratha Head to Wyndermere.°

Saith Bracy the bard, So let it knell!
And let the drowsy sacristan
Still count as slowly as he can!
There is no lack of such, I ween,°
As well fill up the space between.
350   In Langdale Pike° and Witch's Lair,
And Dungeon-ghyll° so foully rent,
With ropes of rock and bells of air
Three sinful sextons' ghosts are pent,
Who all give back, one after t'other,
The death-note to their living brother;
And oft too, by the knell offended,
Just as their one! two! three! is ended,
The devil mocks the doleful tale
With a merry peal from Borodale.

360   The air is still! through mist and cloud
That merry peal comes ringing loud;
And Geraldine shakes off her dread,
And rises lightly from the bed;
Puts on her silken vestments white,
And tricks her hair in lovely plight,°
And nothing doubting of her spell
Awakens the lady Christabel.
'Sleep you, sweet lady Christabel?
I trust that you have rested well.'

370   And Christabel awoke and spied
The same who lay down by her side—
O rather say, the same whom she

Wyndermere The place names in Part II are all
in the Lake Country.
ween believe

Pike peak
ghyll bed of a stream
plight fashion

Raised up beneath the old oak tree!
Nay, fairer yet! and yet more fair!
For she belike hath drunken deep
Of all the blessedness of sleep!
And while she spake, her looks, her air
Such gentle thankfulness declare,
That (so it seemed) her girded vests
380   Grew tight beneath her heaving breasts.
'Sure I have sinned!' said Christabel,
'Now heaven be praised if all be well!'
And in low faltering tones, yet sweet,
Did she the lofty lady greet
With such perplexity of mind
As dreams too lively leave behind.

So quickly she rose, and quickly arrayed
Her maiden limbs, and having prayed
That He, who on the cross did groan,
390   Might wash away her sins unknown,
She forthwith led fair Geraldine
To meet her sire, Sir Leoline.

The lovely maid and the lady tall
Are pacing both into the hall,
And pacing on through page and groom,
Enter the Baron's presence-room.

The Baron rose, and while he prest
His gentle daughter to his breast,
With cheerful wonder in his eyes
400   The lady Geraldine espies,
And gave such welcome to the same,
As might beseem so bright a dame!

But when he heard the lady's tale,
And when she told her father's name,
Why waxed Sir Leoline so pale,
Murmuring o'er the name again,
Lord Roland de Vaux of Tryermaine?

Alas! they had been friends in youth;
But whispering tongues can poison truth;
410   And constancy lives in realms above;
And life is thorny; and youth is vain;
And to be wroth with one we love
Doth work like madness in the brain.
And thus it chanced, as I divine,
With Roland and Sir Leoline.
Each spake words of high disdain
And insult to his heart's best brother:

They parted—ne'er to meet again!
But never either found another
To free the hollow heart from paining—
They stood aloof, the scars remaining,
Like cliffs which had been rent asunder;
A dreary sea now flows between;—
But neither heat, nor frost, nor thunder,
Shall wholly do away, I ween,
The marks of that which once hath been.

Sir Leoline, a moment's space,
Stood gazing on the damsel's face:
And the youthful Lord of Tryermaine
Came back upon his heart again.

O then the Baron forgot his age,
His noble heart swelled high with rage;
He swore by the wounds in Jesu's side
He would proclaim it far and wide,
With trump and solemn heraldry,
That they, who thus had wronged the dame,
Were base as spotted infamy!
'And if they dare deny the same,
My herald shall appoint a week,
And let the recreant traitors seek
My tourney court—that there and then
I may dislodge their reptile souls
From the bodies and forms of men!'
He spake: his eye in lightning rolls!
For the lady was ruthlessly seized; and he kenned°
In the beautiful lady the child of his friend!

And now the tears were on his face,
And fondly in his arms he took
Fair Geraldine, who met the embrace,
Prolonging it with joyous look.
Which when she viewed, a vision fell
Upon the soul of Christabel,
The vision of fear, the touch and pain!
She shrunk and shuddered, and saw again—
(Ah, woe is me! Was it for thee,
Thou gentle maid! such sights to see?)

Again she saw that bosom old,
Again she felt that bosom cold,
And drew in her breath with a hissing sound:
Whereat the Knight turned wildly round,
And nothing saw, but his own sweet maid
With eyes upraised, as one that prayed.

kenned recognized

The touch, the sight, had passed away,
And in its stead that vision blest,
Which comforted her after-rest
While in the lady's arms she lay,
Had put a rapture in her breast,
And on her lips and o'er her eyes
Spread smiles like light!
                          With new surprise,
470   'What ails then my belovèd child?'
The Baron said—His daughter mild
Made answer, 'All will yet be well!'
I ween, she had no power to tell
Aught else: so mighty was the spell.

Yet he, who saw this Geraldine,
Had deemed her sure a thing divine:
Such sorrow with such grace she blended,
As if she feared she had offended
Sweet Christabel, that gentle maid!
480   And with such lowly tones she prayed
She might be sent without delay
Home to her father's mansion.
                                'Nay!
Nay, by my soul!' said Leoline.
'Ho! Bracy the bard, the charge be thine!
Go thou, with music sweet and loud,
And take two steeds with trappings proud,
And take the youth whom thou lovest best
To bear thy harp, and learn thy song,
And clothe you both in solemn vest,
490   And over the mountains haste along,
Lest wandering folk, that are abroad,
Detain you on the valley road.

'And when he has crossed the Irthing flood,
My merry bard! he hastes, he hastes
Up Knorren Moor, through Halegarth Wood,
And reaches soon that castle good
Which stands and threatens Scotland's wastes.

'Bard Bracy! bard Bracy! your horses are fleet,
Ye must ride up the hall, your music so sweet,
500   More loud than your horses' echoing feet!
And loud and loud to Lord Roland call,
Thy daughter is safe in Langdale hall!
Thy beautiful daughter is safe and free—
Sir Leoline greets thee thus through me!
He bids thee come without delay
With all thy numerous array

And take thy lovely daughter home:
And he will meet thee on the way
With all his numerous array
510   White with their panting palfreys' foam:
And, by mine honour! I will say,
That I repent me of the day
When I spake words of fierce disdain
To Roland de Vaux of Tryermaine!—
—For since that evil hour hath flown,
Many a summer's sun hath shone;
Yet ne'er found I a friend again
Like Roland de Vaux of Tryermaine.'

The lady fell, and clasped his knees,
520   Her face upraised, her eyes o'erflowing;
And Bracy replied, with faltering voice,
His gracious Hail on all bestowing!—
'Thy words, thou sire of Christabel,
Are sweeter than my harp can tell;
Yet might I gain a boon of thee,
This day my journey should not be,
So strange a dream hath come to me,
That I have vowed with music loud
To clear yon wood from thing unblest,
530   Warned by a vision in my rest!
For in my sleep I saw that dove,
That gentle bird, whom thou dost love,
And callest by thy own daughter's name—
Sir Leoline! I saw the same
Fluttering, and uttering fearful moan,
Among the green herbs in the forest alone.
Which when I saw and when I heard,
I wondered what might ail the bird;
For nothing near it could I see,
540   Save the grass and green herbs underneath the old tree.

'And in my dream methought I went
To search out what might there be found;
And what the sweet bird's trouble meant,
That thus lay fluttering on the ground.
I went and peered, and could descry
No cause for her distressful cry;
But yet for her dear lady's sake
I stooped, methought, the dove to take,
When lo! I saw a bright green snake
550   Coiled around its wings and neck.
Green as the herbs on which it couched,
Close by the dove's its head it crouched;
And with the dove it heaves and stirs,

Swelling its neck as she swelled hers!
I woke; it was the midnight hour,
The clock was echoing in the tower;
But though my slumber was gone by,
This dream it would not pass away—
It seems to live upon my eye!
560   And thence I vowed this self-same day
With music strong and saintly song
To wander through the forest bare,
Lest aught unholy loiter there.'

Thus Bracy said: the Baron, the while,
Half-listening heard him with a smile;
Then turned to Lady Geraldine,
His eyes made up of wonder and love;
And said in courtly accents fine,
'Sweet maid, Lord Roland's beauteous dove,
570   With arms more strong than harp or song,
Thy sire and I will crush the snake!'
He kissed her forehead as he spake,
And Geraldine in maiden wise
Casting down her large bright eyes,
With blushing cheek and courtesy fine
She turned her from Sir Leoline;
Softly gathering up her train,
That o'er her right arm fell again;
And folded her arms across her chest,
580   And couched her head upon her breast,
And looked askance at Christabel——
Jesu, Maria, shield her well!

A snake's small eye blinks dull and shy;
And the lady's eyes they shrunk in her head,
Each shrunk up to a serpent's eye,
And with somewhat of malice, and more of dread,
At Christabel she looked askance!—
One moment—and the sight was fled!
But Christabel in dizzy trance
590   Stumbling on the unsteady ground
Shuddered aloud, with a hissing sound;
And Geraldine again turned round,
And like a thing, that sought relief,
Full of wonder and full of grief,
She rolled her large bright eyes divine
Wildly on Sir Leoline.

The maid, alas! her thoughts are gone
She nothing sees—no sight but one!
The maid, devoid of guile and sin,

600   I know not how, in fearful wise,
      So deeply had she drunken in
      That look, those shrunken serpent eyes,
      That all her features were resigned
      To this sole image in her mind:
      And passively did imitate
      That look of dull and treacherous hate!
      And thus she stood, in dizzy trance,
      Still picturing that look askance
      With forced unconscious sympathy
610   Full before her father's view——
      As far as such a look could be
      In eyes so innocent and blue!

      And when the trance was o'er, the maid
      Paused awhile, and inly prayed:
      Then falling at the Baron's feet,
      'By my mother's soul do I entreat
      That thou this woman send away!'
      She said: and more she could not say:
      For what she knew she could not tell,
620   O'er-mastered by the mighty spell.

      Why is thy cheek so wan and wild,
      Sir Leoline? Thy only child
      Lies at thy feet, thy joy, thy pride,
      So fair, so innocent, so mild;
      The same, for whom thy lady died!
      O by the pangs of her dear mother
      Think thou no evil of thy child!
      For her, and thee, and for no other,
      She prayed the moment ere she died:
630   Prayed that the babe for whom she died,
      Might prove her dear lord's joy and pride!
          That prayer her deadly pangs beguiled,
              Sir Leoline!
          And wouldst thou wrong thy only child,
              Her child and thine?

      Within the Baron's heart and brain
      If thoughts, like these, had any share,
      They only swelled his rage and pain,
      And did but work confusion there.
640   His heart was cleft with pain and rage,
      His cheeks they quivered, his eyes were wild,
      Dishonoured thus in his old age;
      Dishonoured by his only child,
      And all his hospitality
      To the wronged daughter of his friend

By more than woman's jealousy
Brought thus to a disgraceful end—
He rolled his eye with stern regard
Upon the gentle minstrel bard,
650   And said in tones abrupt, austere—
'Why, Bracy! dost thou loiter here?
I bade thee hence!' The bard obeyed;
And turning from his own sweet maid,
The agèd knight, Sir Leoline,
Led forth the lady Geraldine!
1797–1800   1816

THE CONCLUSION TO PART II

A little child,° a limber elf,
Singing, dancing to itself,
A fairy thing with red round cheeks,
That always finds, and never seeks,
660   Makes such a vision to the sight
As fills a father's eyes with light;
And pleasures flow in so thick and fast
Upon his heart, that he at last
Must needs express his love's excess
With words of unmeant bitterness.
Perhaps 'tis pretty to force together
Thoughts so all unlike each other;
To mutter and mock a broken charm,
To dally with wrong that does no harm.
670   Perhaps 'tis tender too and pretty
At each wild word to feel within
A sweet recoil of love and pity.
And what, if in a world of sin
(O sorrow and shame should this be true!)
Such giddiness of heart and brain
Comes seldom save from rage and pain,
So talks as it's most used to do.
1801   1816

Frost at Midnight°

The Frost performs its secret ministry,
Unhelped by any wind. The owlet's cry
Came loud—and hark, again! loud as before.
The inmates of my cottage, all at rest,

child Hartley Coleridge
Frost at Midnight This poem, the perfection of Coleridge's conversation group, is greatly indebted to Cowper's *The Task* IV.286–310, "The Winter Evening"; in turn, it strongly influenced Wordsworth's "Tintern Abbey," as a comparison of the conclusions of the two poems will show.

Have left me to that solitude, which suits
Abstruser musings: save that at my side
My cradled infant slumbers peacefully.
'Tis calm indeed! so calm, that it disturbs
And vexes meditation with its strange
10   And extreme silentness. Sea, hill, and wood,
This populous village! Sea, and hill, and wood,
With all the numberless goings-on of life,
Inaudible as dreams! the thin blue flame
Lies on my low-burnt fire, and quivers not;
Only that film,° which fluttered on the grate,
Still flutters there, the sole unquiet thing.
Methinks, its motion in this hush of nature
Gives it dim sympathies with me who live,
Making it a companionable form,
20   Whose puny flaps and freaks the idling Spirit
By its own moods interprets, everywhere
Echo or mirror seeking of itself,
And makes a toy of Thought.

                     But O! how oft,
How oft, at school,° with most believing mind,
Presageful, have I gazed upon the bars,
To watch that fluttering *stranger*! and as oft
With unclosed lids, already had I dreamt
Of my sweet birth-place, and the old church-tower,
Whose bells, the poor man's only music, rang
30   From morn to evening, all the hot Fair-day,
So sweetly, that they stirred and haunted me
With a wild pleasure, falling on mine ear
Most like articulate sounds of things to come!
So gazed I, till the soothing things, I dreamt,
Lulled me to sleep, and sleep prolonged my dreams!
And so I brooded all the following morn,
Awed by the stern preceptor's face, mine eye
Fixed with mock study on my swimming book:
Save if the door half opened, and I snatched
40   A hasty glance, and still my heart leaped up,
For still I hoped to see the *stranger's* face,
Townsman, or aunt, or sister more beloved,
My play-mate° when we both were clothed alike!

    Dear Babe, that sleepest cradled by my side,
Whose gentle breathings, heard in this deep calm,
Fill up the interspersèd vacancies

---

film soot on the grate; Coleridge noted: "In all parts of the Kingdom these films are called *strangers* and supposed to portend the arrival of some absent friend"

school Christ's Hospital, London
play-mate Coleridge's sister Ann

And momentary pauses of the thought!
My babe so beautiful! it thrills my heart
With tender gladness, thus to look at thee,
50   And think that thou shalt learn far other lore,
And in far other scenes! For I was reared
In the great city, pent 'mid cloisters° dim,
And saw nought lovely but the sky and stars.
But *thou*, my babe! shalt wander like a breeze
By lakes and sandy shores, beneath the crags
Of ancient mountain, and beneath the clouds,
Which image in their bulk both lakes and shores
And mountain crags: so shalt thou see and hear
The lovely shapes and sounds intelligible
60   Of that eternal language,° which thy God
Utters, who from eternity doth teach
Himself in all, and all things in himself.
Great universal Teacher! he shall mould
Thy spirit, and by giving make it ask.

  Therefore all seasons shall be sweet to thee,
Whether the summer clothe the general earth
With greenness, or the redbreast sit and sing
Betwixt the tufts of snow on the bare branch
Of mossy apple-tree, while the nigh thatch
70   Smokes in the sun-thaw; whether the eave-drops fall
Heard only in the trances of the blast,
Or if the secret ministry of frost
Shall hang them up in silent icicles,
Quietly shining to the quiet Moon.
1798   1798

Dejection: An Ode

This began as a long verse-letter to Sara Hutchinson, whom Coleridge hopelessly loved, and who was soon to become Wordsworth's sister-in-law. The occasion for the letter was Wordsworth's reading aloud to Coleridge of the first four stanzas of the "Intimations of Immortality" ode. When the verse-letter was worked into an ode, many of the direct references to Wordsworth's stanzas were removed, together with all overt references to Sara Hutchinson and Coleridge's unhappy marriage. The person addressed became "William" rather than "Sara" while still in manuscript, then "Edmund" in the first publication of the poem on the very day of Wordsworth's marriage, and finally "Lady" when first included in a book.

  The central argument Coleridge conducts with Wordsworth is most crucial in stanza IV, where the origin of joy is located only in the human viewer and not in the external scene.

cloisters of Christ's Hospital   **eternal language** of natural appearances

Dejection: An Ode

Late, late yestreen I saw the new Moon,
With the old Moon in her arms;
And I fear, I fear, my Master dear!
We shall have a deadly storm.
BALLAD OF SIR PATRICK SPENCE

I

Well! If the Bard was weather-wise, who made
   The grand old ballad of Sir Patrick Spence,
   This night, so tranquil now, will not go hence
Unroused by winds, that ply a busier trade
Than those which mould yon cloud in lazy flakes,
Or the dull sobbing draft, that moans and rakes
Upon the strings of this Aeolian lute,
     Which better far were mute.
   For lo! the New-moon winter-bright!
10   And overspread with phantom light,
    (With swimming phantom light o'erspread
    But rimmed and circled by a silver thread)
I see the old Moon in her lap, foretelling
   The coming-on of rain and squally blast.
And oh! that even now the gust were swelling,
   And the slant night-shower driving loud and fast!
Those sounds which oft have raised me, whilst they awed,
    And sent my soul abroad,
Might now perhaps their wonted impulse give,
20 Might startle this dull pain, and make it move and live!

II

A grief without a pang, void, dark, and drear,
   A stifled, drowsy, unimpassioned grief,
   Which finds no natural outlet, no relief,
     In word, or sigh, or tear—
O Lady! in this wan and heartless mood,
To other thoughts by yonder throstle wooed,
   All this long eve, so balmy and serene,
Have I been gazing on the western sky,
   And its peculiar tint of yellow green:
30 And still I gaze—and with how blank an eye!
And those thin clouds above, in flakes and bars,
That give away their motion to the stars;
Those stars, that glide behind them or between,
Now sparkling, now bedimmed, but always seen:
Yon crescent Moon, as fixed as if it grew
In its own cloudless, starless lake of blue;
I see them all so excellently fair,
I see, not feel, how beautiful they are!

III

My genial spirits° fail;
40   And what can these avail
To lift the smothering weight from off my breast?
        It were a vain endeavour,
        Though I should gaze forever
On that green light that lingers in the west:
I may not hope from outward forms to win
The passion and the life, whose fountains are within.

IV

O Lady! we receive but what we give,
And in our life alone does Nature live:
Ours is her wedding garment, ours her shroud!
50   And would we aught behold, of higher worth,
Than that inanimate cold world allowed
To the poor loveless ever-anxious crowd,
        Ah! from the soul itself must issue forth
A light, a glory, a fair luminous cloud
        Enveloping the Earth—
And from the soul itself must there be sent
        A sweet and potent voice, of its own birth,
Of all sweet sounds the life and element!

V

O pure of heart! thou needest not ask of me
60   What this strong music in the soul may be!
What, and wherein it doth exist,
This light, this glory, this fair luminous mist,
This beautiful and beauty-making power.
        Joy, virtuous Lady! Joy that ne'er was given,
Save to the pure, and in their purest hour,
Life, and Life's effluence, cloud at once and shower,
Joy, Lady! is the spirit and the power,
Which, wedding Nature to us, gives in dower
        A new Earth and new Heaven,
70   Undreamt of by the sensual and the proud—
Joy is the sweet voice, Joy the luminous cloud—
        We in ourselves rejoice!
And thence flows all that charms or ear or sight,
        All melodies the echoes of that voice,
All colours a suffusion from that light.

VI

There was a time when, though my path was rough,
        This joy within me dallied with distress,

---

genial spirits See Milton's *Samson Agonistes*, ll.
594–98, and Wordsworth's "Tintern Abbey,"
l. 113.

And all misfortunes were but as the stuff
Whence Fancy made me dreams of happiness:
80 For hope grew round me, like the twining vine,
And fruits, and foliage, not my own, seemed mine.
But now afflictions bow me down to earth:
Nor care I that they rob me of my mirth;
      But oh! each visitation
Suspends what nature gave me at my birth,
      My shaping spirit of Imagination.
For not to think of what I needs must feel,
      But to be still and patient, all I can;
And haply by abstruse research to steal
90   From my own nature all the natural man—
This was my sole resource, my only plan:
Till that which suits a part infects the whole,
And now is almost grown the habit of my soul.

      VII
Hence, viper thoughts, that coil around my mind,
      Reality's dark dream!
I turn from you, and listen to the wind,
      Which long has raved unnoticed. What a scream
Of agony by torture lengthened out
That lute sent forth! Thou Wind, that rav'st without,
100   Bare crag, or mountain tairn,° or blasted tree,
Or pine-grove whither woodman never clomb,
Or lonely house, long held the witches' home,
      Methinks were fitter instruments for thee,
Mad Lutanist! who in this month of showers,
Of dark-brown gardens, and of peeping flowers,
Makest Devils' yule, with worse than wintry song,
The blossoms, buds, and timorous leaves among.
      Thou Actor, perfect in all tragic sounds!
Thou mighty Poet, e'en to frenzy bold!
110   What tellest thou now about?
      'Tis of the rushing of an host in rout,
With groans, of trampled men, with smarting wounds—
At once they groan with pain, and shudder with the cold!
But hush! there is a pause of deepest silence!
      And all that noise, as of a rushing crowd,
With groans, and tremulous shudderings—all is over—
      It tells another tale, with sounds less deep and loud!
      A tale of less affright,
      And tempered with delight,
120 As Otway's self had framed the tender lay,°—

tairn pool
As Otway's . . . lay Thomas Otway (1652–
85), Restoration dramatist, is merely an absurd
cover here; the original manuscript read "William's self" and the reference is clearly to
Wordsworth's "Lucy Gray."

'Tis of a little child
Upon a lonesome wild,
Not far from home, but she hath lost her way:
And now moans low in bitter grief and fear,
And now screams loud, and hopes to make her mother hear.

VIII

'Tis midnight, but small thoughts have I of sleep:
Full seldom may my friend such vigils keep!
Visit her, gentle Sleep! with wings of healing,
    And may this storm be but a mountain-birth,°
30 May all the stars hang bright above her dwelling,
    Silent as though they watched the sleeping Earth!
        With light heart may she rise,
        Gay fancy, cheerful eyes,
    Joy lift her spirit, joy attune her voice;
To her may all things live, from pole to pole,
Their life the eddying of her living soul!
    O simple spirit, guided from above,
Dear Lady! friend devoutest of my choice,
Thus mayest thou ever, evermore rejoice.
1802   1802

Phantom°

All look and likeness caught from earth
All accident of kin and birth,
Had passed away. There was no trace
Of aught on that illumined face,
Upraised beneath the rifted stone
But of one spirit all her own;—
She, she herself, and only she,
Shone through her body visibly.
1805   1834

To William Wordsworth

COMPOSED ON THE NIGHT AFTER HIS RECITATION
OF A POEM ON THE GROWTH OF AN INDIVIDUAL MIND°
Friend of the wise! and Teacher of the Good!°

mountain-birth The probable reference is to the famous tag in Horace's *Ars Poetica*, l. 139, where the mountain labors and brings forth a mouse. **Phantom** evidently a description of Sara Hutchinson as she appeared to Coleridge in a dream **Composed . . . Mind** Wordsworth read *The Prelude* aloud to Coleridge (it took some two weeks) when Coleridge returned from Malta, a somewhat broken man, in 1806. Wordsworth asked Coleridge not to publish this poem; Coleridge printed it anyway, at first under the bland title, *To a Gentleman*. After the quarrel between the two friends in 1810, the poem underwent significant revision, but much of it was equivocal from the first, though its tribute to *The Prelude* is still unsurpassed. **Friend . . . Good** In 1807 this first line read, "O Friend! O Teacher! God's great gift to me."

Into my heart have I received that Lay
More than historic, that prophetic Lay
Wherein (high theme by thee first sung aright)
Of the foundations and the building up
Of a Human Spirit thou hast dared to tell
What may be told, to the understanding mind
Revealable; and what within the mind
By vital breathings secret as the soul
Of vernal growth, oft quickens in the heart
Thoughts all too deep for words!°—

                          Theme hard as high!
Of smiles spontaneous, and mysterious fears°
(The first-born they of Reason° and twin-birth),
Of tides obedient to external force,
And currents self-determined, as might seem,
  Or by some inner Power; of moments awful,
Now in thy inner life, and now abroad,
When power streamed from thee, and thy soul received
The light reflected, as a light bestowed—
Of fancies fair, and milder hours of youth,
Hyblean° murmurs of poetic thought
Industrious in its joy, in vales and glens
Native or outland, lakes and famous hills!
Or on the lonely high-road, when the stars
Were rising; or by secret mountain streams,
The guides and the companions of thy way!

Of more than Fancy, of the Social Sense
Distending wide, and man beloved as man,
Where France in all her towns lay vibrating
Like some becalmèd bark beneath the burst
Of Heaven's immediate thunder, when no cloud
Is visible, or shadow on the main.
For thou wert there, thine own brows garlanded,
Amid the tremor of a realm aglow,
Amid a mighty nation jubilant,
When from the general heart of human kind
Hope sprang forth like a full-born Deity!
——Of that dear Hope afflicted and struck down,
So summoned homeward, thenceforth calm and sure
From the dread watch-tower of man's absolute self,
With light unwaning on her eyes, to look
Far on—herself a glory to behold,
The Angel of the vision! Then (last strain)

10
20
30
40

Thoughts . . . words See the last line of the
Intimations of Immortality ode.
mysterious fears See *The Prelude* I and II.
Reason in the transcendental sense, a higher
faculty than the mere Understanding, which
deals only with the realm of experience
Hyblean Ancient Hybla, in Sicily, was renowned
for its honey.

Of Duty, chosen Laws controlling choice,
Action and joy!—An Orphic° song indeed,
A song divine of high and passionate thoughts
To their own music chaunted!

                O great Bard!
Ere yet that last strain dying awed the air,
With stedfast eye I viewed thee in the choir
50   Of ever-enduring men. The truly great
Have all one age, and from one visible space
Shed influence! They, both in power and act,
Are permanent, and Time is not with them,
Save as it worketh for them, they in it.
Nor less a sacred roll, than those of old,
And to be placed, as they, with gradual fame
Among the archives of mankind, thy work
Makes audible a linkèd lay of Truth,
Of Truth profound a sweet continuous lay,
60   Not learnt, but native, her own natural notes!
Ah! as I listened with a heart forlorn,
The pulses of my being beat anew:
And even as Life returns upon the drowned,
Life's joy rekindling roused a throng of pains—
Keen pangs of Love, awakening as a babe
Turbulent, with an outcry in the heart;
And fears self-willed, that shunned the eye of Hope;
And Hope that scarce would know itself from Fear;
Sense of past Youth, and Manhood come in vain,
70   And Genius given, and Knowledge won in vain;
And all which I had culled in wood-walks wild,
And all which patient toil had reared, and all,
Commune with thee had opened out—but flowers
Strewed on my corse, and borne upon my bier
In the same coffin, for the self-same grave!

    That way no more! and ill beseems it me,
Who came a welcomer in herald's guise,
Singing of Glory, and Futurity,
To wander back on such unhealthful road,
80   Plucking the poisons of self-harm! And ill
Such intertwine beseems triumphal wreaths
Strewed before thy advancing!

                Nor do thou,
Sage Bard! impair the memory of that hour,
Of thy communion with my nobler mind°
By pity or grief, already felt too long!

Orphic pertaining to the legendary bard, Or-   **nobler mind** i.e. nobler in 1798 than in 1807
pheus; hence a synonym for "oracular"

Nor let my words import more blame than needs.
The tumult rose and ceased: for Peace is nigh
Where Wisdom's voice has found a listening heart.
Amid the howl of more than wintry storms,
90   The Halcyon° hears the voice of vernal hours
Already on the wing.

          Eve following eve,
Dear tranquil time, when the sweet sense of Home
Is sweetest! moments for their own sake hailed
And more desired, more precious, for thy song,
In silence listening, like a devout child,
My soul lay passive, by thy various strain
Driven as in surges now beneath the stars,
With momentary stars of my own birth,
Fair constellated foam, still darting off
100 Into the darkness; now a tranquil sea,
Outspread and bright, yet swelling to the moon.

And when—O Friend! my comforter and guide!
Strong in thyself, and powerful to give strength!—
Thy long sustainèd Song finally closed,
And thy deep voice had ceased—yet thou thyself
Wert still before my eyes, and round us both
That happy vision of belovèd faces—
Scarce conscious, and yet conscious of its close
I sate, my being blended in one thought
110 (Thought was it? or aspiration? or resolve?)
Absorbed, yet hanging still upon the sound—
And when I rose, I found myself in prayer.
1807   1817

On Donne's Poetry°

With Donne, whose muse on dromedary° trots,
Wreathe iron pokers into true-love knots;
Rhyme's sturdy cripple, fancy's maze and clue,
Wit's forge and fire-blast, meaning's press and screw.
1818?   1836

Halcyon mythological bird credited with so
calming the ocean as to nest upon it; from the
story of Halcyone, who drowned herself after
finding her husband Ceyx drowned; the gods
changed them into magical birds
On Donne's Poetry Coleridge remarked that "to
read Dryden, Pope, etc., you need only count
syllables; but to read Donne you must measure
Time, and discover the Time of each word by
the sense of the Passion."
dromedary fleet, one-humped camel

Limbo°

The sole true Something—This! In Limbo's Den
It frightens Ghosts, as here Ghosts frighten men.
Thence cross'd unseized—and shall some fated hour
Be pulverised by Demogorgon's° power,
And given as poison to annihilate souls—
Even now it shrinks them—they shrink in as Moles
(Nature's mute monks, live mandrakes° of the ground)
Creep back from Light—then listen for its sound;—
See but to dread, and dread they know not why—
10   The natural alien of their negative eye.

'Tis a strange place, this Limbo!—not a Place,
Yet name it so;—where Time and weary Space
Fettered from flight, with night-mare sense of fleeing,
Strive for their last crepuscular° half-being;—
Lank Space, and scytheless Time with branny hands
Barren and soundless as the measuring sands,
Not marked by flit of Shades,—unmeaning they
As moonlight on the dial of the day!
But that is lovely—looks like Human Time,
20   An Old Man with a steady look sublime,
That stops his earthly task to watch the skies;
But he is blind—a Statue hath such eyes;—
Yet having moonward turned his face by chance,
Gazes the orb with moon-like countenance,
With scant white hairs, with foretop bald and high,
He gazes still,—his eyeless face all eye;—
As 'twere an organ full of silent sight,
His whole face seemeth to rejoice in light!
Lip touching lip, all moveless, bust and limb—
30   He seems to gaze at that which seems to gaze on him!
    No such sweet sights doth Limbo den immure,
Walled round, and made a spirit-jail secure,
By the mere horror of blank Naught-at-all,
Whose circumambience doth these ghosts enthral.
A lurid thought is growthless, dull Privation,
Yet that is but a Purgatory curse;
Hell knows a fear far worse,
A fear—a future state;—'tis positive Negation!
1817   1893

Limbo From one of Coleridge's notebooks, where it is followed by the fragment "Ne Plus Ultra"; George Ridenour demonstrates both fragments' debts to Coleridge's earlier "Ode to the Departing Year," and to the theosophical writings of Jacob Boehme. David Perkins usefully cites Aphorism XIX from Coleridge's *Aids to Reflection:* "There is another death, not the mere negation of life, but its positive opposite." Coleridge's Limbo is evidently not the traditional one (on Hell's borders, for the virtuous unbap-tized) but a state on the ambiguous line between what is and what is not, a kind of half-phantasmagoria or waking nightmare.
Demogorgon's god of the abyss; see the note to l.207 of Shelley's *Prometheus Unbound*
mandrakes poisonous plants, whose forked roots were thought to resemble humans; legend held that mandrakes shrieked when picked
crepuscular relating to twilight, hence indistinct or dim

Ne Plus Ultra°

Sole Positive of Night!
Antipathist° of Light!
Fate's only essence! primal scorpion rod°—
The one permitted opposite of God!—
Condensèd blackness and abysmal storm
Compacted to one sceptre
Arms the Grasp enorm—
The Intercepter—
The Substance that still casts the shadow Death!—
10   The Dragon foul and fell—
The unrevealable,
And hidden one, whose breath
Gives wind and fuel to the fires of Hell!
Ah! sole despair
Of both the eternities° in Heaven!
Sole interdict of all-bedewing prayer,
The all-compassionate!
Save to the Lampads Seven°
Revealed to none of all the Angelic State,
20   Save to the Lampads Seven,
That watch the throne of Heaven!
1826?   1834

To Nature°

It may indeed be phantasy, when I
Essay to draw from all created things
Deep, heartfelt, inward joy that closely clings;
And trace in leaves and flowers that round me lie
Lessons of love and earnest piety.
So let it be; and if the wide world rings
In mock of this belief, it brings
Nor fear, nor grief, nor vain perplexity.
So will I build my altar in the fields,
10   And the blue sky my fretted dome shall be,
And the sweet fragrance that the wild flower yields
Shall be the incense I will yield to Thee,
Thee only God! and thou shalt not despise
Even me, the priest of this poor sacrifice.
1820?   1836

Ne Plus Ultra literally, "nothing more beyond," here meaning something like "nothing worse than this condition"
Antipathist natural enemy
scorpion rod the contrary to Aaron's rod, Exodus 7:10–12

both the eternities the two are Divine Love and Divine Knowledge
Lampads Seven seven lamps of fire burning before the Divine Throne in Revelation 4:5
To Nature This late sonnet is a touching return to the earlier vision Coleridge had tried to share with Wordsworth.

Epitaph°

Stop, Christian passer-by!—Stop, child of God,
And read with gentle breast. Beneath this sod
A poet lies, or that which once seemed he.
O, lift one thought in prayer for S. T. C.;
That he who many a year with toil of breath
Found death in life, may here find life in death!
Mercy for praise—to be forgiven for° fame
He asked, and hoped, through Christ. Do thou the same!
1833   1834

GEORGE GORDON, LORD BYRON
1788–1824

Byron's life and personality are at least as fascinating as his poetry. No author before or since has enjoyed and suffered such notoriety, or had a literary and social influence so much out of proportion with his actual imaginative achievement, considerable as that was. Somehow Byron was at once a man of incredible personal beauty, and yet congenitally half-lame and incessantly struggling against a tendency to grow fat. The most brilliant conversationalist of his time, except for the incomparable Coleridge, he glorified solitude and at last attained it. Celebrated as the highest of High Romantics (the only one to attain a European reputation, in part because he does not lose too much by translation, but primarily because of his life), he despised Romanticism, and insisted that English poetry all but died with the death of Pope. A virtual synonym for the greatest of lovers, he was passive toward women, sodomistic, sado-masochistic, fundamentally homosexual, and early disgusted with all sexual experience anyway. Outcast for his incest with his half-sister, he nevertheless seems to have gotten beyond narcissistic self-regard only in relation to her, yet she was in no way remarkable. A radical by the English standards of his day, and an active revolutionary in Italy, he was wholly skeptical as to the benefits of either reform or revolution. Acclaimed to this day as the martyr-hero of the Greek Revolution against the Turks, he despised the modern Greeks even as he financed, trained, and led them in rebellion. Apparently emancipated in religion, he was shocked by his closest friend Shelley's polemic against Christianity, could not rid himself of a Calvinistic temper, and inclined secretly toward Catholicism. A superb athlete and champion swimmer, he had to compel his reluctant, sluggish body to keep up with his restless spirit. To sum up: he was the most antithetical of men, and one of the most self-divided of poets.

   Byron's father, widely known as a rakehell, died when the poet was three, leaving him with a neurotic, unstable mother and a governess who both seduced and chastised him. He attended Harrow, and Trinity College, Cambridge, where he had homosexual experience. When his early lyrics, *Hours of Idleness* (1807), were attacked in *The Edinburgh Review*, Byron retaliated in his first satire, *English Bards and Scotch Reviewers* (1809). Returning from a grand tour of Iberia and Greece (1809–11), he published his verse diary, *Childe Harold's Pilgrimage*, Cantos I and II, in 1812, and his

---

Epitaph not actually written for his own me-   **for** instead of
morial stone, but intended for the final page of
an edition of his poems

true career began: "I awoke one morning and found myself famous." Enormous success in Regency society followed, including love affairs with Lady Oxford and with Caroline Lamb, who terrorized him to the extent that he sought refuge in marriage with Annabella Milbanke, a virtuous lady much given to mathematical interests, and a very improbable choice on his part. A number of verse tales (*Lara* is the best of them) enjoyed the same popularity as *Childe Harold,* and meanwhile Byron devoted himself also to the left wing of the Whig party. In eloquent speeches to the House of Lords, he urged Catholic Emancipation and defended the "framebreakers," workers who had destroyed machines that had displaced them.

Though a daughter was born to Lady Byron, the marriage soon became insupportable, evidently because of Byron's periodic rages, continued incest with his half-sister, and sodomistic demands on his highly conventional wife. They separated, amid much public scandal, and Byron, after encountering many social snubs, abandoned England for good in April 1816. He went to Geneva, and began his close friendship with Shelley, which lasted unbroken—though with strains—until Shelley drowned in 1822. Under Shelley's influence (and, paradoxically, of Wordsworth's through Shelley) he wrote Canto III of *Childe Harold,* and entered on a new phase of his poetry. Moving to Italy in autumn 1817, he enjoyed an orgiastic season in Venice, involving many scores of women. During this time, he completed the second Romantic phase of his work, writing Canto IV of *Childe Harold* and finishing *Manfred,* which he had begun in Shelley's company. More important, he discovered his true mode in the poem *Beppo,* a light satire in ottava rima that soon led him to begin his masterpiece, *Don Juan.*

From 1819 until he left for Greece in 1823, Byron settled down in a domestic relationship with the Countess Teresa Guiccioli, joining her family in revolutionary plots against the Austrians, and following them to Pisa, where he was again in daily association with Shelley. To this time belong much the largest part of *Don Juan,* the brilliant satire *The Vision of Judgment,* and an effective, apocalyptic drama, *Cain* (a work difficult to represent by excerpts).

Weary of his life, Byron went to Greece to seek a soldier's death at thirty-six, and found it. He found also, though, a last, bitter, frustrated homosexual passion for his Greek page boy Loukas, and his final verses and letters betray profound self-disgust but an unwearied intelligence and quick humor. His death at Missolonghi in April 1824 saved him from middle age, and made his legend imperishable.

If we can put aside the phenomenon of Byronism, which flowered extravagantly all over Europe after so Romantic a death, we are left with two parts of Byron's accomplishment—*Don Juan* and everything else. Of the latter, there is clearly lasting value in a handful of lyrics, in aspects of *Childe Harold* III and IV and of *Manfred,* and major achievement in *Cain* and in *The Vision of Judgment.* But, taken together, this is little compared with *Don Juan,* which only Shelley of Byron's contemporaries judged accurately and adequately, as being something wholly new and yet completely relevant to the Romantic Age.

From English Bards and Scotch Reviewers°

Behold! in various throngs the scribbling crew,
For notice eager, pass in long review:
Each spurs his jaded Pegasus apace,
And rhyme and blank maintain an equal race;
Sonnets on sonnets crowd, and ode on ode;
And Tales of Terror° jostle on the road;
Immeasurable measures move along;
150 For simpering folly loves a varied song,
To strange mysterious dulness still the friend,
Admires the strain she cannot comprehend.
Thus Lays of Minstrels°—may they be the last!—
On half-strung harps whine mournful to the blast.
While mountain spirits prate to river sprites,
That dames may listen to the sound at nights;
And goblin brats, of Gilpin Horner's brood,°
Decoy young border-nobles through the wood,
And skip at every step, Lord knows how high,
160 And frighten foolish babes, the Lord knows why;
While high-born ladies in their magic cell,
Forbidding knights to read who cannot spell,
Dispatch a courier to a wizard's grave,
And fight with honest men to shield a knave.

Next view in state, proud prancing on his roan,
The golden-crested haughty Marmion,°
Now forging scrolls, now foremost in the fight,
Not quite a felon, yet but half a knight,
The gibbet or the field prepared to grace;
170 A mighty mixture of the great and base.
And think'st thou, Scott! by vain conceit perchance,
On public taste to foist thy stale romance,
Though Murray with his Miller° may combine
To yield thy muse just half-a-crown per line?
No! when the sons of song descend to trade,
Their bays are sear, their former laurels fade.
Let such forego the poet's sacred name,
Who rack their brains for lucre, not for fame:
Still for stern Mammon may they toil in vain!
180 And sadly gaze on gold they cannot gain!

English Bards and Scotch Reviewers Byron was at work on this poem, as *English Bards*, when his volume of lyrics, *Hours of Idleness*, was savaged (not unjustly) by Lord Brougham in *The Edinburgh Review* of January 1808. The poem consequently was enlarged to include *Scotch Reviewers*, but the portions given here are all devoted to the older generation of Romantics— Scott, Southey, Wordsworth, and Coleridge. Byron later repudiated the poem and had its fifth edition burned, but could not suppress it.

Tales of Terror refers to the vogue of the Gothic novel, but particularly to works of Sir Walter Scott and Matthew Gregory Lewis (1775–1818), notorious author of *The Monk*
Lays of Minstrels Scott's metrical romance *The Lay of the Last Minstrel* (1805)
Horner's brood Scott's poem uses the border legend of Gilpin Horner.
Marmion Scott's long poem of 1808
Murray . . . Miller London publisher

Such be their meed, such still the just reward
Of prostituted muse and hireling bard!
For this we spurn Apollo's venal son,
And bid a long 'good night to Marmion.'°

These are the themes that claim our plaudits now;
These are the bards to whom the muse must bow;
While Milton, Dryden, Pope, alike forgot,
Resign their hallowed bays to Walter Scott.

The time has been, when yet the muse was young,
190   When Homer swept the lyre, and Maro° sung,
An epic scarce ten centuries could claim,
While awe-struck nations hailed the magic name:
The work of each immortal bard appears
The single wonder of a thousand years.
Empires have mouldered from the face of earth,
Tongues have expired with those who gave them birth,
Without the glory such a strain can give,
As even in ruin bids the language live.
Not so with us, though minor bards, content,
200   On one great work a life of labour spent:
With eagle pinion soaring to the skies,
Behold the ballad-monger Southey° rise!
To him let Camoëns,° Milton, Tasso° yield,
Whose annual strains, like armies, take the field.
First in the ranks see Joan of Arc° advance,
The scourge of England and the boast of France!
Though burnt by wicked Bedford° for a witch,
Behold her statue placed in glory's niche;
Her fetters burst, and just released from prison,
210   A virgin phoenix from her ashes risen.
Next see tremendous Thalaba° come on,
Arabia's monstrous, wild, and wondrous son;
Domdaniel's dread destroyer,° who o'erthrew
More mad magicians than the world e'er knew.
Immortal hero! all thy foes o'ercome,
For ever reign—the rival of Tom Thumb!°
Since startled metre fled before thy face,
Well wert thou doomed the last of all thy race!

'good . . . Marmion' spoken on Marmion's death (*Marmion* VI.869)
Maro Virgil
ballad-monger Southey the first of many attacks upon Southey, to culminate in *Don Juan* and *The Vision of Judgment*
Camoëns Luis de Camoëns (1524–80), Portugal's great poet, wrote the epic *Lusiads*
Tasso Torquato Tasso (1544–95), Italian epic poet, wrote *Jerusalem Delivered*
Joan of Arc Southey's revolutionary poem on her was published in 1796.

Bedford Duke of Bedford, English commander, who burned Joan at the stake
Thalaba Southey's mythological epic *Thalaba the Destroyer* (1801)
destroyer Thalaba destroys a horde of evil magicians who live in Domdaniel, an undersea palace.
Tom Thumb *The Tragedy of Tragedies; or, the Life and Death of Tom Thumb the Great* (1730), a farce by Henry Fielding

Well might triumphant genii bear thee hence,
220   Illustrious conqueror of common sense!
Now, last and greatest, Madoc° spreads his sails,
Cacique° in Mexico, and prince in Wales;
Tells us strange tales, as other travellers do,
More old than Mandeville's,° and not so true.
Oh! Southey! Southey! cease thy varied song!
A bard may chant too often and too long:
As thou art strong in verse, in mercy, spare!
A fourth, alas! were more than we could bear.
But if, in spite of all the world can say,
230   Thou still wilt verseward plod thy weary way;
If still in Berkley ballads most uncivil,
Thou wilt devote old women to the devil,°
The babe unborn thy dread intent may rue:
'God help thee,' Southey, and thy readers too.

Next comes the dull disciple of thy school,
That mild apostate from poetic rule,
The simple Wordsworth, framer of a lay
As soft as evening in his favourite May,
Who warns his friend 'to shake off toil and trouble,
240   And quit his books, for fear of growing double';°
Who, both by precept and example, shows
That prose is verse, and verse is merely prose;°
Convincing all, by demonstration plain,
Poetic souls delight in prose insane;
And Christmas stories tortured into rhyme
Contain the essence of the true sublime.
Thus, when he tells the tale of Betty Foy,
The idiot mother of 'an idiot boy';
A moon struck, silly lad, who lost his way,
250   And, like his bard, confounded night with day;
So close on each pathetic part he dwells,
And each adventure so sublimely tells,
That all who view the 'idiot in his glory'
Conceive the bard the hero of the story.°

Shall gentle Coleridge pass unnoticed here,
To turgid ode and tumid stanza dear?
Though themes of innocence amuse him best,
Yet still obscurity's a welcome guest.
If Inspiration should her aid refuse

Madoc epic by Southey (1805)
Cacique native chief
Mandeville's Sir John Mandeville (died 1372), credited with a famous travel book
devil Southey's ballad, "The Old Woman of Berkeley," a rather good poem about a witch

to shake . . . double from Wordsworth's "The Tables Turned" (1798)
That . . . prose See the Preface to the Second Edition of Lyrical Ballads (1800).
That . . . story See Wordsworth's "The Idiot Boy," included in Lyrical Ballads.

260   To him who takes a pixy for a muse,°
       Yet none in lofty numbers can surpass
       The bard who soars to elegize an ass.°
       So well the subject suits his noble mind,
       He brays, the laureate of the long-eared kind.
       1807–08   1809

From Lara°

XVII

       In him inexplicably mixed appeared
290   Much to be loved and hated, sought and feared;
       Opinion varying o'er his hidden lot,
       In praise or railing ne'er his name forgot:
       His silence formed a theme for others' prate—
       They guessed—they gazed—they fain would know his fate.
       What had he been? what was he, thus unknown,
       Who walked their world, his lineage only known?
       A hater of his kind? yet some would say,
       With them he could seem gay amidst the gay;
       But owned that smile, if oft observed and near,
300   Waned in its mirth, and withered to a sneer;
       That smile might reach his lip but passed not by,
       None e'er could trace its laughter to his eye:
       Yet there was softness too in his regard,
       At times, a heart as not by nature hard,
       But once perceived, his spirit seemed to chide
       Such weakness as unworthy of its pride,
       And steeled itself, as scorning to redeem
       One doubt from others' half withheld esteem;
       In self-inflicted penance of a breast
310   Which tenderness might once have wrung from rest;
       In vigilance of grief that would compel
       The soul to hate for having loved too well.

XVIII

       There was in him a vital scorn of all:
       As if the worst had fallen which could befall,
       He stood a stranger in this breathing world,
       An erring spirit from another hurled;
       A thing of dark imaginings, that shaped
       By choice the perils he by chance escaped;
       But 'scaped in vain, for in their memory yet

To . . . muse See Coleridge's "Song of the
Pixies" (1796).
The bard . . . ass See Coleridge's unfortunate
poem "To a Young Ass" (1794).
Lara Though this Gothic romance is not of high
poetic interest, the portrait of Lara in these
sections is a remarkable epitome of the High
Romantic hero and a splendid idealized self-
portrait of Byron. The flavor of Milton's Satan
can be tasted throughout.

320 His mind would half exult and half regret.
With more capacity for love than earth
Bestows on most of mortal mould and birth,
His early dreams of good outstripped the truth,
And troubled manhood followed baffled youth;
With thought of years in phantom chase misspent,
And wasted powers for better purpose lent;
And fiery passions that had poured their wrath
In hurried desolation o'er his path,
And left the better feelings all at strife
330 In wild reflection o'er his stormy life;
But haughty still and loth himself to blame,
He called on Nature's self to share the shame,
And charged all faults upon the fleshly form
She gave to clog the soul, and feast the worm;
Till he at last confounded good and ill,
And half mistook for fate the acts of will.
Too high for common selfishness, he could
At times resign his own for others' good,
But not in pity, not because he ought,
340 But in some strange perversity of thought,
That swayed him onward with a secret pride
To do what few or none would do beside;
And this same impulse would, in tempting time,
Mislead his spirit equally to crime;
So much he soared beyond, or sunk beneath,
The men with whom he felt condemned to breathe,
And longed by good or ill to separate
Himself from all who shared his mortal state.
His mind abhorring this had fixed her throne
350 Far from the world, in regions of her own:
Thus coldly passing all that passed below,
His blood in temperate seeming now would flow:
Ah! happier if it ne'er with guilt had glowed,
But ever in that icy smoothness flowed!
'Tis true, with other men their path he walked,
And like the rest in seeming did and talked,
Nor outraged Reason's rules by flaw nor start,
His madness was not of the head, but heart;
And rarely wandered in his speech, or drew
360 His thoughts so forth as to offend the view.

XIX
With all that chilling mystery of mien,
And seeming gladness to remain unseen,
He had (if 'twere not Nature's boon) an art
Of fixing memory on another's heart:
It was not love perchance, nor hate, nor aught

That words can image to express the thought;
But they who saw him did not see in vain,
And once beheld, would ask of him again:
And those to whom he spake remembered well,
370   And on the words, however light, would dwell:
None knew, nor how, nor why, but he entwined
Himself perforce around the hearer's mind;
There he was stamped, in liking, or in hate,
If greeted once; however brief the date
That friendship, pity, or aversion knew,
Still there within the inmost thought he grew.
You could not penetrate his soul, but found,
Despite your wonder, to your own he wound;
His presence haunted still; and from the breast
380   He forced an all unwilling interest:
Vain was the struggle in that mental net,
His spirit seemed to dare you to forget!
1814   1814

Stanzas for Music°

There be none of Beauty's daughters
    With a magic like thee;
And like music on the waters
    Is thy sweet voice to me:
When, as if its sound were causing
The charmed ocean's pausing,
The waves lie still and gleaming,
And the lulled winds seem dreaming.

And the midnight moon is weaving
10   Her bright chain o'er the deep;
Whose breast is gently heaving,
    As an infant's asleep:
So the spirit bows before thee,
To listen and adore thee;
With a full but soft emotion,
Like the swell of Summer's ocean.
1816   1816

Stanzas for Music This rather Shelleyan lyric
traditionally was believed to refer to Claire
Clairmont, but almost certainly refers to John
Edleston, a choirboy who moved the noble lord
rather more than any of "Beauty's daughters."

Childe Harold's Pilgrimage, A Romaunt°

From *Canto the Third*

I

Is thy face like thy mother's, my fair child!
ADA! sole daughter of my house and heart?
When last I saw thy young blue eyes they smiled,
And then we parted,—not as now we part,
But with a hope.°—
               Awaking with a start,
The waters heave around me; and on high
The winds lift up their voices: I depart,
Whither I know not; but the hour's gone by,
When Albion's lessening shores could grieve or glad mine eye.

II

10 Once more upon the waters! yet once more!°
And the waves bound beneath me as a steed
That knows his rider. Welcome to their roar!
Swift be their guidance, wheresoe'er it lead!
Though the strained mast should quiver as a reed,
And the rent canvass fluttering strew the gale,
Still must I on; for I am as a weed,
Flung from the rock on Ocean's foam, to sail
Where'er the surge may sweep, the tempest's breath prevail.

III

In my youth's summer I did sing of One,°
20 The wandering outlaw of his own dark mind;
Again I seize the theme, then but begun,
And bear it with me, as the rushing wind
Bears the cloud onwards: in that Tale I find
The furrows of long thought, and dried-up tears,
Which, ebbing, leave a sterile track behind,
O'er which all heavily the journeying years
Plod the last sands of life,—where not a flower appears.

IV

Since my young days of passion—joy, or pain—
Perchance my heart and harp have lost a string,
30 And both may jar: it may be that in vain
I would essay as I have sung to sing.
Yet, though a dreary strain, to this I cling,

Romaunt romance
When . . . hope Byron had last seen his daughter, Augusta Ada, when she was just a month old, in January 1816, when Lady Byron left him. He now acknowledges that he will never see the child again (and he did not).
Once . . . more! Byron echoes Henry V's speech to his soldiers in Shakespeare's *Henry V* III.i.19.
One Childe Harold, or Byron at twenty-one

So that it wean me from the weary dream
Of selfish grief or gladness—so it fling
Forgetfulness around me—it shall seem
To me, though to none else, a not ungrateful theme.

V

He, who grown aged in this world of woe,
In deeds, not years, piercing the depths of life,
So that no wonder waits him; nor below
40 Can love, or sorrow, fame, ambition, strife,
Cut to his heart again with the keen knife
Of silent, sharp endurance: he can tell
Why thought seeks refuge in lone caves, yet rife
With airy images, and shapes which dwell
Still unimpaired, though old, in the soul's haunted cell.

VI

'Tis to create, and in creating live
A being more intense, that we endow
With form our fancy, gaining as we give
The life we image, even as I do now.
50 What am I? Nothing: but not so art thou,
Soul of my thought! with whom I traverse earth,
Invisible but gazing, as I glow
Mixed with thy spirit, blended with thy birth,
And feeling still with thee in my crushed feelings' dearth.

VII

Yet must I think less wildly:—I *have* thought
Too long and darkly, till my brain became,
In its own eddy boiling and o'erwrought,
A whirling gulf of phantasy and flame:
And thus, untaught in youth my heart to tame,
60 My springs of life were poisoned. 'Tis too late!
Yet am I changed; though still enough the same
In strength to bear what time can not abate,
And feed on bitter fruits without accusing Fate.

VIII

Something too much of this:°—but now 'tis past,
And the spell closes with its silent seal.°
Long absent HAROLD re-appears at last;
He of the breast which fain no more would feel,
Wrung with the wounds which kill not but ne'er heal;
Yet Time, who changes all, had altered him
70 In soul and aspect as in age: years steal

Something . . . this See *Hamlet* III.ii.69.   **silent seal** seal enforcing silence

Fire from the mind as vigour from the limb,
And life's enchanted cup but sparkles near the brim.

IX

His had been quaffed too quickly, and he found
The dregs were wormwood; but he filled again,
And from a purer fount, on holier ground,°
And deemed its spring perpetual; but in vain!
Still round him clung invisibly a chain
Which galled for ever, fettering though unseen,
And heavy though it clanked not; worn with pain,
80   Which pined although it spoke not, and grew keen,
Entering with every step he took through many a scene.

X

Secure in guarded coldness, he had mixed
Again in fancied safety with his kind,
And deemed his spirit now so firmly fixed
And sheathed with an invulnerable mind,
That, if no joy, no sorrow lurked behind;
And he, as one, might 'midst the many stand
Unheeded, searching through the crowd to find
Fit speculation—such as in strange land
90   He found in wonder-works of God and Nature's hand.

XI

But who can view the ripened rose, nor seek
To wear it? who can curiously behold
The smoothness and the sheen of beauty's cheek,
Nor feel the heart can never all grow old?
Who can contemplate Fame through clouds unfold
The star which rises o'er her steep, nor climb?
Harold, once more within the vortex, rolled
On with the giddy circle, chasing Time,
Yet with a nobler aim than in his youth's fond° prime.

XII

100   But soon he knew himself the most unfit
Of men to herd with Man, with whom he held
Little in common; untaught to submit
His thoughts to others, though his soul was quelled
In youth by his own thoughts; still uncompelled,
He would not yield dominion of his mind
To spirits against whom his own rebelled;
Proud though in desolation; which could find
A life within itself, to breathe without mankind.

holier ground Greece, where Byron was to die   **fond** foolish
his heroic death

XIII

Where rose the mountains, there to him were friends;
Where rolled the ocean, thereon was his home;
Where a blue sky, and glowing clime, extends,
He had the passion and the power to roam;
The desert, forest, cavern, breaker's foam,
Were unto him companionship; they spake
A mutual language, clearer than the tome
Of his land's tongue, which he would oft forsake
For Nature's pages glassed° by sunbeams on the lake.

XIV

Like the Chaldean,° he could watch the stars,
Till he had peopled them with beings bright
As their own beams; and earth, and earth-born jars,
And human frailties, were forgotten quite:
Could he have kept his spirit to that flight
He had been happy; but this clay will sink
Its spark immortal, envying it the light
To which it mounts, as if to break the link
That keeps us from yon heaven which woos us to its brink.

XV

But in Man's dwellings he became a thing
Restless and worn, and stern and wearisome,
Drooped as a wild-born falcon with clipt wing,
To whom the boundless air alone were home:
Then came his fit° again, which to o'ercome,
As eagerly the barred-up bird will beat
His breast and beak against his wiry dome
Till the blood tinge his plumage, so the heat
Of his impeded soul would through his bosom eat.

XVI

Self-exiled Harold wanders forth again,
With nought of hope left, but with less of gloom;
The very knowledge that he lived in vain,
That all was over on this side the tomb,
Had made Despair a smilingness assume,
Which, though 'twere wild,—as on the plundered wreck
When mariners would madly meet their doom
With draughts intemperate on the sinking deck,—
Did yet inspire a cheer which he forbore to check.

glassed either made like glass or made reflected
Chaldean Babylonian; Babylon was famous for

its astrologers; see Yeats's "Two Songs from a
Play."
Then . . . fit See *Macbeth* III.iv.21.

XVII

Stop!°—for thy tread is on an Empire's dust!
An Earthquake's spoil is sepulchred below!
Is the spot marked with no colossal bust,
Nor column trophied for triumphal show?
None; but the moral's truth tells simpler so,
As the ground was before, thus let it be;—
How that red rain hath made the harvest grow!
And is this all the world has gained by thee,
Thou first and last of fields, king-making° Victory?

150

XVIII

And Harold stands upon this place of skulls,
The grave of France, the deadly Waterloo!
How in an hour the power which gave annuls
Its gifts, transferring fame as fleeting too!
In 'pride of place'° here last the eagle flew,
Then tore with bloody talon the rent plain,
Pierced by the shaft of banded nations through;
Ambition's life and labours all were vain;
He wears the shattered links of the world's broken chain.°

160

XIX

Fit retribution! Gaul° may champ the bit
And foam in fetters;—but is Earth more free?
Did nations combat to make *One* submit;
Or league to teach all kings true sovereignty?
What! shall reviving Thraldom again be
The patched-up idol of enlightened days?°
Shall we, who struck the Lion° down, shall we
Pay the Wolf° homage? proffering lowly gaze
And servile knees to thrones? No; *prove*° before ye praise!

170

XX

If not, o'er one fallen despot boast no more!
In vain fair cheeks were furrowed with hot tears
For Europe's flowers long rooted up before
The trampler of her vineyards; in vain years
Of death, depopulation, bondage, fears,
Have all been borne, and broken by the accord
Of roused-up millions: all that most endears

Stop because we are on the field of Waterloo, only a year after the battle
king-making making Louis XVIII the King of France again
'pride of place' highest point of flight, the eagle being Napoleon, but also see *Macbeth* II.iv.12
He . . . chain at St. Helena, where he was kept until he died

Gaul Roman name for France
enlightened days a reference to the 18th century, before the Revolution
Lion Napoleon
Wolf possibly Metternich, or Wellington
prove have it proved to you

Glory, is when the myrtle wreathes a sword
180 Such as Harmodius° drew on Athens' tyrant lord.

XXI

There was a sound of revelry by night,°
And Belgium's Capital had gathered then
Her Beauty and her Chivalry, and bright
The lamps shone o'er fair women and brave men;
A thousand hearts beat happily; and when
Music arose with its voluptuous swell,
Soft eyes looked love to eyes which spake again,
And all went merry as a marriage-bell;—
But hush! hark! a deep sound strikes like a rising knell!

XXII

190 Did ye not hear it?—No; 'twas but the wind,
Or the car rattling o'er the stony street;
On with the dance! let joy be unconfined;
No sleep till morn, when Youth and Pleasure meet
To chase the glowing Hours with flying feet—
But hark!—that heavy sound breaks in once more,
As if the clouds its echo would repeat;
And nearer, clearer, deadlier than before!
Arm! Arm! it is—it is—the cannon's opening roar!

XXIII

Within a windowed niche of that high hall
200 Sate Brunswick's fated chieftain;° he did hear
That sound the first amidst the festival,
And caught its tone with Death's prophetic ear;
And when they smiled because he deemed it near,
His heart more truly knew that peal too well
Which stretched his father on a bloody bier,
And roused the vengeance blood alone could quell:
He rushed into the field, and, foremost fighting, fell.

XXIV

Ah! then and there was hurrying to and fro,
And gathering tears, and tremblings of distress,
210 And cheeks all pale, which but an hour ago
Blushed at the praise of their own loveliness;
And there were sudden partings, such as press
The life from out young hearts, and choking sighs
Which ne'er might be repeated; who could guess

Harmodius who killed the tyrant Hipparchus, with a dagger hidden in a myrtle branch **There . . . night** at the ball given in Brussels by the Duchess of Richmond on the eve of the battle

chieftain Duke of Brunswick, killed the day after the ball; his father had died in battle in 1806

If ever more should meet those mutual eyes,
Since upon night so sweet such awful morn could rise!

XXV

And there was mounting in hot haste: the steed,
The mustering squadron, and the clattering car,
When pouring forward with impetuous speed,
220   And swiftly forming in the ranks of war;
And the deep thunder peal on peal afar;
And near, the beat of the alarming drum
Roused up the soldier ere the morning star;
While thronged the citizens with terror dumb,
Or whispering, with white lips—'The foe! They come! they come!'

XXVI

And wild and high the 'Cameron's gathering'° rose!
The war-note of Lochiel,° which Albyn's° hills
Have heard, and heard, too, have her Saxon° foes:—
How in the noon of night that pibroch° thrills,
230   Savage and shrill! But with the breath which fills
Their mountain-pipe, so fill the mountaineers
With the fierce native daring which instils
The stirring memory of a thousand years,
And Evan's, Donald's° fame rings in each clansman's ears!

XXVII

And Ardennes° waves above them her green leaves,
Dewy with nature's tear-drops, as they pass,
Grieving, if aught inanimate e'er grieves,
Over the unreturning brave,—alas!
Ere evening to be trodden like the grass
240   Which now beneath them, but above shall grow
In its next verdure, when this fiery mass
Of living valour, rolling on the foe
And burning with high hope, shall moulder cold and low.

XXVIII

Last noon beheld them full of lusty life,
Last eve in Beauty's circle proudly gay,
The midnight brought the signal-sound of strife,
The morn the marshalling in arms,—the day
Battle's magnificently-stern array!

'Cameron's gathering' war song of the Highland clan, the Cameronians
Lochiel title of Cameronian chief
Albyn's Gaelic for Scotland
Saxon English
pibroch battle-call of the bagpipes
Evan's, Donald's Sir Evan Cameron, who fought against Cromwell, and later for James II; Donald Cameron, his descendant, fought for the Young Pretender, and was wounded at Culloden, the last stand of the Highlanders as an independent fighting force
Ardennes forest area not actually the site of this battle; Byron wanted it for its Shakespearean associations (see *As You Like It*)

The thunder-clouds close o'er it, which when rent
250   The earth is covered thick with other clay,
Which her own clay shall cover, heaped and pent,
Rider and horse,—friend, foe,—in one red burial blent!

        .   .   .

XLI

If, like a tower upon a headlong rock,
Thou° hadst been made to stand or fall alone,
Such scorn of man had helped to brave the shock;
But men's thoughts were the steps which paved thy throne,
Their admiration thy best weapon shone;
The part of Philip's son° was thine, not then
(Unless aside thy purple had been thrown)
Like stern Diogenes° to mock at men;
For sceptred cynics earth were far too wide a den.

XLII

370   But quiet to quick bosoms is a hell,
And *there* hath been thy bane; there is a fire
And motion of the soul which will not dwell
In its own narrow being, but aspire
Beyond the fitting medium of desire;
And, but once kindled, quenchless evermore,
Preys upon high adventure, nor can tire
Of aught but rest; a fever at the core,
Fatal to him who bears, to all who ever bore.

XLIII

This makes the madmen who have made men mad
380   By their contagion; Conquerors and Kings,
Founders of sects and systems, to whom add
Sophists, Bards, Statesmen, all unquiet things
Which stir too strongly the soul's secret springs,
And are themselves the fools to those they fool;
Envied, yet how unenviable! what stings
Are theirs! One breast laid open were a school
Which would unteach mankind the lust to shine or rule.

XLIV

Their breath is agitation, and their life
A storm whereon they ride, to sink at last;
390   And yet so nursed and bigoted to strife,
That should their days, surviving perils past,
Melt to calm twilight, they feel overcast
With sorrow and supineness, and so die;

Thou Napoleon
Philip's son Alexander the Great

Diogenes Greek Cynic philosopher of Alexander's time

Even as a flame unfed which runs to waste
With its own flickering, or a sword laid by,
Which eats into itself and rusts ingloriously.

XLV

He who ascends to mountain-tops, shall find
The loftiest peaks most wrapt in clouds and snow;
He who surpasses or subdues mankind,
400   Must look down on the hate of those below.
Though high *above* the sun of glory glow,
And far *beneath* the earth and ocean spread,
Round him are icy rocks, and loudly blow
Contending tempests on his naked head,
And thus reward the toils which to those summits led.

. . .

LXXII

680   I live not in myself, but I become
Portion of that around me; and to me
High mountains are a feeling,° but the hum
Of human cities torture: I can see
Nothing to loathe in nature, save to be
A link reluctant in a fleshly chain,
Classed among creatures, when the soul can flee,
And with the sky, the peak, the heaving plain
Of ocean, or the stars, mingle, and not in vain.

LXXIII

And thus I am absorbed, and this is life:
690   I look upon the peopled desert past,
As on a place of agony and strife,
Where, for some sin, to sorrow I was cast,
To act and suffer, but remount at last
With a fresh pinion; which I feel to spring,
Though young, yet waxing vigorous, as the blast
Which it would cope with, on delighted wing,
Spurning the clay-cold bonds which round our being cling.

LXXIV

And when, at length, the mind shall be all free
From what it hates in this degraded form,
700   Reft of its carnal life, save what shall be
Existent happier in the fly and worm,—
When elements to elements conform,
And dust is as it should be, shall I not

I live . . . feeling The Wordsworthian influence, through Shelley, is palpable here; Wordsworth was not pleased.

Feel all I see, less dazzling, but more warm?
The bodiless thought? the Spirit of each spot?
Of which, even now, I share at times the immortal lot?

LXXV

Are not the mountains, waves, and skies, a part
Of me and of my soul, as I of them?
Is not the love of these deep in my heart
710   With a pure passion? should I not contemn
All objects, if compared with these? and stem
A tide of suffering, rather than forego
Such feelings for the hard and worldly phlegm
Of those whose eyes are only turned below,
Gazing upon the ground, with thoughts which dare not glow?

1816   1816

. . .

From *Canto the Fourth*

CXXI

Oh Love! no habitant of earth thou art—
An unseen seraph, we believe in thee,
A faith whose martyrs are the broken heart,
But never yet hath seen, nor e'er shall see
The naked eye, thy form, as it should be;
The mind hath made thee, as it peopled heaven,
Even with its own desiring phantasy,
And to a thought such shape and image given,
As haunts the unquenched soul—parched—wearied—wrung—and riven.

CXXII

1090   Of its own beauty is the mind diseased,
And fevers into false creation:—where,
Where are the forms the sculptor's soul hath seized?—
In him alone. Can Nature show so fair?
Where are the charms and virtues which we dare
Conceive in boyhood and pursue as men,
The unreached Paradise of our despair,
Which o'er-informs the pencil and the pen,
And overpowers the page where it would bloom again?

CXXIII

Who loves, raves—'tis youth's frenzy; but the cure
1100   Is bitterer still; as charm by charm unwinds
Which robed our idols, and we see too sure
Nor worth nor beauty dwells from out the mind's
Ideal shape of such; yet still it binds

The fatal spell, and still it draws us on,
Reaping the whirlwind from the oft-sown winds;°
The stubborn heart, its alchemy begun,
Seems ever near the prize,—wealthiest when most undone.

CXXIV
We wither from our youth, we gasp away—
Sick—sick; unfound the boon—unslaked the thirst,
110   Though to the last, in verge of our decay,
Some phantom lures, such as we sought at first—
But all too late,—so are we doubly curst.
Love, fame, ambition, avarice—'tis the same,
Each idle—and all ill—and none the worst—
For all are meteors with a different name,
And Death the sable smoke where vanishes the flame.

CXXV
Few—none—find what they love or could have loved,
Though accident, blind contact, and the strong
Necessity of loving, have removed
120   Antipathies—but to recur, ere long,
Envenomed with irrevocable wrong;
And Circumstance, that unspiritual god
And miscreator, makes and helps along
Our coming evils with a crutch-like rod,
Whose touch turns Hope to dust,—the dust we all have trod.

CXXVI
Our life is a false nature—'tis not in
The harmony of things,—this hard decree,
This uneradicable taint of sin,
This boundless upas, this all-blasting tree°
130   Whose root is earth, whose leaves and branches be
The skies which rain their plagues on men like dew—
Disease, death, bondage—all the woes we see—
And worse, the woes we see not—which throb through
The immedicable soul, with heart-aches ever new.

.   .   .

CXXXVII
But I have lived, and have not lived in vain:
My mind may lose its force, my blood its fire,
And my frame perish even in conquering pain;
But there is that within me which shall tire
Torture and Time, and breathe when I expire;
230   Something unearthly which they deem not of,

Reaping . . . winds See Hosea 8:7.
This boundless . . . tree The upas-tree, capable of devastating all vegetation near it, was a
pure product of Romantic visionary botany.

Like the remembered tone of a mute lyre,
Shall on their softened spirits sink, and move
In hearts all rocky now the late remorse of love.

CXXXVIII

The seal is set.—Now welcome, thou dread power!
Nameless, yet thus omnipotent, which here°
Walkest in the shadow of the midnight hour
With a deep awe, yet all distinct from fear;
Thy haunts are ever where the dead walls rear
Their ivy mantles, and the solemn scene
1240   Derives from thee a sense so deep and clear
That we become a part of what has been,
And grow unto the spot, all-seeing but unseen.

· · ·

CLXIII

And if it be Prometheus stole from Heaven
1460   The fire which we endure, it was repaid
By him to whom the energy was given
Which this poetic marble hath arrayed
With an eternal glory—which, if made
By human hands, is not of human thought;
And Time himself hath hallowed it, nor laid
One ringlet in the dust—nor hath it caught
A tinge of years, but breathes the flame with which 'twas wrought.

CLXIV

But where is he, the Pilgrim of my song,
The being who upheld it through the past?
1470   Methinks he cometh late and tarries long.
He is no more—these breathings are his last;
His wanderings done, his visions ebbing fast,
And he himself as nothing:—if he was
Aught but a phantasy, and could be classed
With forms which live and suffer—let that pass—
His shadow fades away into Destruction's mass,

· · ·

CLXXVII

Oh! that the Desert were my dwelling-place,
With one fair Spirit° for my minister,
That I might all forget the human race,
And, hating no one, love but only her!
Ye Elements!—in whose ennobling stir
1590   I feel myself exalted—Can ye not

here Rome   **Spirit** his sister Augusta

Accord me such a being? Do I err
In deeming such inhabit many a spot?
Though with them to converse can rarely be our lot.

CLXXVIII

There is a pleasure in the pathless woods,
There is a rapture on the lonely shore,
There is society where none intrudes,
By the deep Sea, and music in its roar:
I love not Man the less, but Nature more,
From these our interviews, in which I steal
600   From all I may be, or have been before,
To mingle with the Universe, and feel
What I can ne'er express, yet can not all conceal.

CLXXIX

Roll on, thou deep and dark blue Ocean—roll!
Ten thousand fleets sweep over thee in vain;
Man marks the earth with ruin—his control
Stops with the shore;—upon the watery plain
The wrecks are all thy deed, nor doth remain
A shadow of man's ravage, save his own,
When, for a moment, like a drop of rain,
610   He sinks into thy depths with bubbling groan,
Without a grave, unknelled, uncoffined, and unknown.

CLXXX

His steps are not upon thy paths,—thy fields
Are not a spoil for him,—thou dost arise
And shake him from thee; the vile strength he wields
For earth's destruction thou dost all despise,
Spurning him from thy bosom to the skies,
And sendest him, shivering in thy playful spray
And howling, to his Gods, where haply lies
His petty hope in some near port or bay,
620   And dashest him again to earth:—there let him lay.°

CLXXXI

The armaments which thunderstrike the walls
Of rock-built cities, bidding nations quake
And monarchs tremble in their capitals,
The oak leviathans,° whose huge ribs make
Their clay creator the vain title take
Of lord of thee, and arbiter of war,—
These are thy toys, and, as the snowy flake,

lay lie. This notorious solecism, quite deliberate on Byron's part, was meant to remind his readers that, after all, he was a nobleman who could be aristocratically slapdash.
oak leviathans warships

They melt into thy yeast of waves, which mar
Alike the Armada's pride or spoils of Trafalgàr.°

CLXXXII

1630   Thy shores are empires, changed in all save thee—
Assyria, Greece, Rome, Carthage, what are they?
Thy waters washed them power while they were free,
And many a tyrant since; their shores obey
The stranger, slave, or savage; their decay
Has dried up realms to deserts:—not so thou,
Unchangeable save to thy wild-waves' play;
Time writes no wrinkle on thine azure brow—
Such as creation's dawn beheld, thou rollest now.

CLXXXIII

Thou glorious mirror, where the Almighty's form
1640   Glasses° itself in tempests; in all time,
Calm or convulsed—in breeze, or gale, or storm,
Icing the pole, or in the torrid clime
Dark-heaving;—boundless, endless, and sublime—
The image of Eternity—the throne
Of the Invisible; even from out thy slime
The monsters of the deep are made; each zone
Obeys thee; thou goest forth, dread, fathomless, alone.

CLXXXIV

And I have loved thee, Ocean! and my joy
Of youthful sports was on thy breast to be
1650   Borne, like thy bubbles, onward: from a boy
I wantoned with thy breakers—they to me
Were a delight; and if the freshening sea
Made them a terror—'twas a pleasing fear,
For I was as it were a child of thee,
And trusted to thy billows far and near,
And laid my hand upon thy mane—as I do here.

CLXXXV

My task is done—my song hath ceased—my theme
Has died into an echo; it is fit
The spell should break of this protracted dream.
1660   The torch shall be extinguished which hath lit
My midnight lamp—and what is writ, is writ,—
Would it were worthier! but I am not now
That which I have been—and my visions flit

Trafalgàr Half or more of the Spanish Armada was lost to bad weather, in 1588; many of the French ships at the battle of Trafalgar, in 1805, were similarly lost.
Glasses reflects

Less palpably before me—and the glow
Which in my spirit dwelt is fluttering, faint, and low.

CLXXXVI

Farewell! a word that must be, and hath been—
A sound which makes us linger;—yet—farewell!
Ye! who have traced the Pilgrim to the scene
Which is his last, if in your memories dwell
A thought which once was his, if on ye swell
A single recollection, not in vain
He wore his sandal-shoon and scallop-shell;°
Farewell! with *him* alone may rest the pain,
If such there were—with *you*, the moral of his strain!
1817   1818

Prometheus°

Titan! to whose immortal eyes
    The sufferings of mortality,
    Seen in their sad reality,
Were not as things that gods despise;
What was thy pity's recompense?
A silent suffering, and intense;
The rock, the vulture, and the chain,
All that the proud can feel of pain,
The agony they do not show,
The suffocating sense of woe,
    Which speaks but in its loneliness,
And then is jealous lest the sky
Should have a listener, nor will sigh
    Until its voice is echoless.

Titan! to thee the strife was given
    Between the suffering and the will,
    Which torture where they cannot kill;
And the inexorable Heaven,
And the deaf tyranny of Fate,
The ruling principle of Hate,
Which for its pleasure doth create
The things it may annihilate,
Refused thee even the boon to die:
The wretched gift eternity
Was thine—and thou hast borne it well.
All that the Thunderer wrung from thee

670

10

20

---

sandal-shoon and scallop-shell pilgrim's emblems, the sandals for land-journeying, and the
scallop shell (usually worn on the hat) for sea-
voyaging

Prometheus written in Shelley's company, and
partly under his influence, but with a kind of
Calvinistic tempering very far from Shelley's
spirit

Was but the menace which flung back
On him the torments of thy rack;
The fate thou didst so well foresee,
30　But would not to appease him tell;
And in thy Silence was his Sentence,
And in his Soul a vain repentance,
And evil dread so ill dissembled,
That in his hand the lightnings trembled.

Thy Godlike crime was to be kind,
　To render with thy precepts less
　The sum of human wretchedness,
And strengthen Man with his own mind;
But baffled as thou wert from high,
40　Still in thy patient energy,
In the endurance, and repulse
　Of thine impenetrable Spirit,
Which Earth and Heaven could not convulse,
　A mighty lesson we inherit:
Thou art a symbol and a sign
　To Mortals of their fate and force;
Like thee, Man is in part divine,
　A troubled stream from a pure source;
And Man in portions can foresee
50　His own funereal destiny;
His wretchedness, and his resistance,
And his sad unallied existence:
To which his Spirit may oppose
Itself—and equal to all woes,
　And a firm will, and a deep sense,
Which even in torture can descry
　Its own concentered recompense,
Triumphant where it dares defy,
And making Death a Victory.°
1816　　　　　　　　　　1816

Darkness°

I had a dream, which was not all a dream.
The bright sun was extinguished, and the stars
Did wander darkling in the eternal space,
Rayless, and pathless, and the icy earth
Swung blind and blackening in the moonless air;
Morn came and went—and came, and brought no day,

And making . . . Victory See I Corinthians 15:55, and also the stanzas chanted by Demogorgon that end Shelley's *Prometheus Unbound*. **Darkness** This is Byron's version of a prevalent Romantic nightmare, "The Last Man" theme, upon which Thomas Campbell and Thomas Hood wrote poems and Mary Shelley a novel. "Darkness" profoundly influenced Poe, and should be compared with his "The City in the Sea."

And men forgot their passions in the dread
Of this their desolation; and all hearts
Were chilled into a selfish prayer for light:
10   And they did live by watchfires—and the thrones,
The palaces of crowned kings—the huts,
The habitations of all things which dwell,
Were burnt for beacons; cities were consumed,
And men were gathered round their blazing homes
To look once more into each other's face;
Happy were those who dwelt within the eye
Of the volcanos, and their mountain-torch:
A fearful hope was all the world contained;
Forests were set on fire—but hour by hour
20   They fell and faded—and the crackling trunks
Extinguished with a crash—and all was black.
The brows of men by the despairing light
Wore an unearthly aspect, as by fits
The flashes fell upon them; some lay down
And hid their eyes and wept; and some did rest
Their chins upon their clenched hands, and smiled;
And others hurried to and fro, and fed
Their funeral piles with fuel, and looked up
With mad disquietude on the dull sky,
30   The pall of a past world; and then again
With curses cast them down upon the dust,
And gnashed their teeth and howled: the wild birds shrieked
And, terrified, did flutter on the ground,
And flap their useless wings; the wildest brutes
Came tame and tremulous; and vipers crawled
And twined themselves among the multitude,
Hissing, but stingless—they were slain for food.
And War, which for a moment was no more,
Did glut himself again:—a meal was bought
40   With blood, and each sate sullenly apart
Gorging himself in gloom: no love was left;
All earth was but one thought—and that was death
Immediate and inglorious; and the pang
Of famine fed upon all entrails—men
Died, and their bones were tombless as their flesh;
The meagre by the meagre were devoured,
Even dogs assailed their masters, all save one,
And he was faithful to a corse, and kept
The birds and beasts and famished men at bay,
50   Till hunger clung° them, or the dropping dead
Lured their lank jaws; himself sought out no food,
But with a piteous and perpetual moan,
And a quick desolate cry, licking the hand

clung in its original sense of "stuck fast to"

Which answered not with a caress—he died.
The crowd was famished by degrees; but two
Of an enormous city did survive,
And they were enemies: they met beside
The dying embers of an altar-place
Where had been heaped a mass of holy things
60   For an unholy usage; they raked up,
And shivering scraped with their cold skeleton hands
The feeble ashes, and their feeble breath
Blew for a little life, and made a flame
Which was a mockery; then they lifted up
Their eyes as it grew lighter, and beheld
Each other's aspects—saw, and shrieked and died—
Even of their mutual hideousness they died,
Unknowing who he was upon whose brow
Famine had written Fiend. The world was void,
70   The populous and the powerful was a lump,
Seasonless, herbless, treeless, manless, lifeless,
A lump of death—a chaos of hard clay.
The rivers, lakes, and ocean all stood still,
And nothing stirred within their silent depths;
Ships sailorless lay rotting on the sea,
And their masts fell down piecemeal: as they dropped
They slept on the abyss without a surge—
The waves were dead; the tides were in their grave,
The moon, their mistress, had expired before;
80   The winds were withered in the stagnant air,
And the clouds perished; Darkness had no need
Of aid from them—She was the Universe.
1816   1816

From Manfred°

A Dramatic Poem

ACT III, SCENE IV

Interior of the Tower
[MANFRED *alone*]
The stars are forth, the moon above the tops
Of the snow-shining mountains.—Beautiful!
I linger yet with Nature, for the night

Manfred This is the closing scene of Byron's Promethean "dramatic poem," best characterized by Goethe as possessing "the gloomy heat of an unbounded and exuberant despair." Manfred, a Faustian magus, has emulated Byron himself, by the crime of deliberate, knowing incest with his sister, Astarte, who evidently killed herself in remorse. Weary of the human condition, but rejecting immortality and seeking only oblivion, Manfred invokes the preternatural powers, presided over by Arimanes, a kind of Gnostic Satan, or god of nature. He is granted a vision of Astarte, who tells him "tomorrow ends thy earthly ills." On the morrow, an abbot unsuccessfully attempts to reconcile Manfred with the church, but he courteously declines. This last scene, which repudiates the Faust story, as Manfred yields only to himself, then follows.

Hath been to me a more familiar face
Than that of man; and in her starry shade
Of dim and solitary loveliness,
I learned the language of another world.
I do remember me, that in my youth,
When I was wandering,—upon such a night
10 I stood within the Coliseum's wall,
Midst the chief relics of almighty Rome.
The trees which grew along the broken arches
Waved dark in the blue midnight, and the stars
Shone through the rents of ruin; from afar
The watch-dog bayed beyond the Tiber; and
More near from out the Caesars' palace came
The owl's long cry, and, interruptedly,
Of distant sentinels the fitful song
Begun and died upon the gentle wind.
20 Some cypresses beyond the time-worn breach
Appeared to skirt the horizon, yet they stood
Within a bowshot. Where the Caesars dwelt,
And dwell the tuneless birds of night, amidst
A grove which springs through levelled battlements
And twines its roots with the imperial hearths,
Ivy usurps the laurel's place of growth;—
But the gladiators' bloody Circus stands,
A noble wreck in ruinous perfection!
While Caesar's chambers, and the Augustan halls,
30 Grovel on earth in indistinct decay.—
And thou didst shine, thou rolling moon, upon
All this, and cast a wide and tender light,
Which softened down the hoar austerity
Of rugged desolation, and filled up,
As 'twere anew, the gaps of centuries;
Leaving that beautiful which still was so,
And making that which was not, till the place
Became religion, and the heart ran o'er
With silent worship of the great of old,—
40 The dead, but sceptred sovereigns, who still rule
Our spirits from their urns.—
                              'Twas such a night!
'Tis strange that I recall it at this time;
But I have found our thoughts take wildest flight
Even at the moment when they should array
Themselves in pensive order.
        [*Enter the* ABBOT]
    ABBOT   My good lord!
I crave a second grace for this approach;
But yet let not my humble zeal offend
By its abruptness—all it hath of ill
Recoils on me; its good in the effect

50 May light upon your head—could I say *heart*—
Could I touch *that,* with words or prayers, I should
Recall a noble spirit which hath wandered
But is not yet all lost.
    MANFRED   Thou knowest me not;
My days are numbered, and my deeds recorded:
Retire, or 'twill be dangerous—Away!
    ABBOT   Thou dost not mean to menace me?
    MANFRED   Not I;
I simply tell thee peril is at hand,
And would preserve thee.
    ABBOT   What dost thou mean?
    MANFRED   Look there!
What dost thou see?
    ABBOT   Nothing.
    MANFRED   Look there, I say,
60 And steadfastly;—now tell me what thou seest.
    ABBOT   That which should shake me—but I fear it not:
I see a dusk and awful figure rise,
Like an infernal god, from out the earth;
His face wrapt in a mantle, and his form
Robed as with angry clouds: he stands between
Thyself and me—but I do fear him not.
    MANFRED   Thou hast no cause; he shall not harm thee, but
His sight may shock thine old limbs into palsy.
I say to thee—Retire!
    ABBOT   And I reply—
70 Never—till I have battled with this fiend:—
What doth he here?
    MANFRED   Why—ay—what doth he here?—
I did not send for him,—he is unbidden.
    ABBOT   Alas! lost mortal! what with guests like these
Hast thou to do? I tremble for thy sake:
Why doth he gaze on thee, and thou on him?
Ah! he unveils his aspect: on his brow
The thunder-scars are graven;° from his eye
Glares forth the immortality of hell—
Avaunt!—
    MANFRED   Pronounce—what is thy mission?
    SPIRIT   Come!
    ABBOT   What art thou, unknown being? answer!—
80   speak!
    SPIRIT   The genius of this mortal.—Come! 'tis time.
    MANFRED   I am prepared for all things, but deny
The power which summons me. Who sent thee here?
    SPIRIT   Thou'lt know anon—Come! Come!

on his brow . . . graven See *Paradise Lost*
I.600 ff.

MANFRED   I have commanded
Things of an essence greater far than thine,
And striven with thy masters. Get thee hence!
    SPIRIT   Mortal! thine hour is come—Away! I say.
    MANFRED   I knew, and know my hour is come, but not
To render up my soul to such as thee:
90   Away! I'll die as I have lived—alone.
    SPIRIT   Then I must summon up my brethren.—Rise!
        [*Other Spirits rise up*]
    ABBOT   Avaunt! ye evil ones!—Avaunt! I say,—
Ye have no power where piety hath power,
And I do charge ye in the name—
    SPIRIT   Old man!
We know ourselves, our mission, and thine order;
Waste not thy holy words on idle uses,
It were in vain: this man is forfeited.
Once more I summon him—Away! away!
    MANFRED   I do defy ye,—though I feel my soul
100 Is ebbing from me, yet I do defy ye;
Nor will I hence, while I have earthly breath
To breathe my scorn upon ye—earthly strength
To wrestle, though with spirits; what ye take
Shall be ta'en limb by limb.
    SPIRIT   Reluctant mortal!
Is this the Magian who would so pervade
The world invisible, and make himself
Almost our equal?—Can it be that thou
Art thus in love with life? the very life
Which made thee wretched!
    MANFRED   Thou false fiend, thou liest!
110 My life is in its last hour,—*that* I know,
Nor would redeem a moment of that hour.
I do not combat against death, but thee
And thy surrounding angels; my past power
Was purchased by no compact with thy crew,
But by superior science—penance—daring—
And length of watching—strength of mind—and skill
In knowledge of our fathers—when the earth
Saw men and spirits walking side by side
And gave ye no supremacy: I stand
120 Upon my strength—I do defy—deny—
Spurn back, and scorn ye!—
    SPIRIT   But thy many crimes
Have made thee—
    MANFRED   What are they to such as thee?
Must crimes be punished but by other crimes,
And greater criminals?—Back to thy hell!
Thou hast no power upon me, *that* I feel;

Thou never shalt possess me, *that* I know:
What I have done is done; I bear within
A torture which could nothing gain from thine:
The mind which is immortal makes itself
130   Requital for its good or evil thoughts,
Is its own origin of ill and end,
And its own place and time°—its innate sense,
When stripp'd of this mortality, derives
No colour from the fleeting things without,
But is absorbed in sufferance or in joy,
Born from the knowledge of its own desert.
Thou didst not tempt me, and thou couldst not tempt me;
I have not been thy dupe nor am thy prey—
But was my own destroyer, and will be
140   My own hereafter.—Back, ye baffled fiends!
The hand of death is on me—but not yours!
    [*The Demons disappear*]
    ABBOT   Alas! how pale thou art—thy lips are white—
And thy breast heaves—and in thy gasping throat
The accents rattle. Give thy prayers to Heaven—
Pray—albeit but in thought,—but die not thus.
    MANFRED   'Tis over—my dull eyes can fix thee not;
But all things swim around me, and the earth
Heaves as it were beneath me. Fare thee well—
Give me thy hand.
    ABBOT   Cold—cold—even to the heart—
150   But yet one prayer—Alas! how fares it with thee?
    MANFRED   Old man! 'tis not so difficult to die.°
    [MANFRED *expires*]
    ABBOT   He's gone—his soul hath ta'en its earthless flight—
Whither? I dread to think—but he is gone.
1816–17   1817

'So We'll Go No More A-Roving'°

So we'll go no more a-roving
    So late into the night,
Though the heart be still as loving,
    And the moon be still as bright.

The mind . . . time See *Paradise Lost* I.254 ff.
Old . . . die After his publisher, Murray, omitted this line in the first edition, Byron wrote to him angrily: "You have destroyed the whole effect and moral of the poem."

'So We'll . . . A-Roving' part of a letter to Thomas Moore. Its motto might be, from the same letter: "At present I am on the invalid regimen myself."

For the sword outwears its sheath,°
And the soul wears out the breast,
And the heart must pause to breathe,
And Love itself have rest.

10   Though the night was made for loving,
And the day returns too soon,
Yet we'll go no more a-roving
By the light of the moon.
1817   1830

For . . . sheath the will to make love is stronger than potency, or as Byron also remarks in the letter: "Though I did not dissipate much upon the whole, yet I find 'the sword wearing out the scabbard,' though I have but just turned the corner of twenty-nine."

Don Juan

"This crammed, various creation renders the Romantic view of a world too large in all directions and too complex in its workings to be captured and arranged in any neat system of thought or formal pattern." This description by Alvin Kernan best characterizes the open universe of Byron's great satire, his only work that reflects both the immensity and paradoxes of his own character and personality.

In reading a series of excerpts from *Don Juan*, we need not feel that we are betraying the poem, which is frankly digressive, unfinished and unfinishable (it would have gone on as long as Byron did), and unified only by the identity of the narrator with the poet himself. Byron is not Don Juan, and indeed Don Juan is scarcely a person, but rather a traditional hero of the picaresque mode, who remains unaltered by experience (no matter how violent) and remarkably passive in most of his love affairs. He is eminently seducible, this being his principal point of resemblance to his creator.

The best comments on the poem, in its own day, after Shelley's (he considered it the great poem of the age, superior to the work of Wordsworth and Goethe), were by Hazlitt, and of course by Byron himself. Hazlitt accurately saw Byron's poetry as the record of "a mind preying upon itself." Despite the poem's infectious vitalism, it masks throughout a thoroughgoing transvaluation of values and perhaps, finally, a hopelessness as to the human condition which is precisely prophetic of much more recent literature. Yet the poem's grand defense is Byron's own: "Confess, confess— you dog," he says to us as readers even as he exclaimed in a letter, "it may be bawdy but is it not good English? It may be profligate but is it not *life*, is it not *the thing?*"

The style, first used by him in the slight but charming *Beppo*, comes from the comic poets of the Italian Renaissance, Pulci and Boiardo in particular. Byron had been preceded in this adaptation by a contemporary, John Hookham Frere, but far out- does Frere. In a deeper sense, the poem stems from English tradition, rather than Italian. Its true precursors are Butler, Swift, and Sterne.

Don Juan°

Difficile est propriè communia dicere.
HORACE.°

Dost thou think, because thou art virtuous, there shall be no more cakes
and ale? Yes, by Saint Anne, and ginger shall be hot i' the mouth, too!
Shakespeare, Twelfth Night, or What You Will

Fragment
On the back of the Poet's MS. of Canto I

I would to heaven that I were so much clay,
    As I am blood, bone, marrow, passion, feeling—
Because at least the past were passed away—
    And for the future—(but I write this reeling,
Having got drunk exceedingly today,
    So that I seem to stand upon the ceiling)
I say—the future is a serious matter—
And so—for God's sake—hock and soda-water!°

Dedication°

I

Bob Southey! You're a poet—Poet-laureate,
    And representative of all the race,
Although 'tis true that you turned out a Tory at
    Last,—yours has lately been a common case,—
And now, my Epic Renegade! what are ye at?
    With all the Lakers,° in and out of place?
A nest of tuneful persons, to my eye
Like 'four and twenty Blackbirds in a pye;°

II

'Which pye being opened they began to sing'
    (This old song and new simile holds good),
'A dainty dish to set before the King,'
    Or Regent,° who admires such kind of food;—
And Coleridge, too, has lately taken wing,
    But like a hawk encumbered with his hood,—
Explaining metaphysics to the nation—
I wish he would explain his Explanation.°

10

Don Juan to be pronounced in the English, not the Spanish, manner
Horace Byron's own translation: " 'Tis no slight task to write on common things"
hock and soda-water Hock is Rhine wine; the mixture was a hangover remedy.
Dedication Southey evidently was telling the story that Byron and Shelley, Mary Godwin and Claire Clairmont, were involved in a "League of Incest" in their time together at Geneva;

Don Juan begins the *sparagmos* or tearing apart of the egregious Southey, which is completed in *The Vision of Judgment.*
Lakers the "school" of Wordsworth, Southey, and Coleridge, all resident in the Lake District
pye Henry James Pye (1745–1813), absurd Poet Laureate before Southey
Regent Prince Regent, and later George IV
I wish . . . Explanation a reference to the *Biographia Literaria* (1817)

III

You, Bob! are rather insolent, you know,
    At being disappointed in your wish
To supersede all warblers here below,
20   And be the only Blackbird in the dish;
And then you overstrain yourself, or so,
    And tumble downward like the flying fish
Gasping on deck, because you soar too high, Bob,
And fall, for lack of moisture quite a-dry, Bob!°

IV

And Wordsworth, in a rather long *Excursion*
    (I think the quarto holds five hundred pages),
Has given a sample from the vasty version
    Of his new system to perplex the sages;
'Tis poetry—at least by his assertion,
30   And may appear so when the dog-star rages—
And he who understands it would be able
To add a story to the Tower of Babel.

V

You—Gentlemen! by dint of long seclusion
    From better company, have kept your own
At Keswick, and, through still continued fusion
    Of one another's minds, at last have grown
To deem as a most logical conclusion,
    That Poesy has wreaths for you alone:
There is a narrowness in such a notion,
40 Which makes me wish you'd change your lakes for ocean.

VI

I would not imitate the petty thought,
    Nor coin my self-love to so base a vice,
For all the glory your conversion brought,
    Since gold alone should not have been its price.
You have your salary; was't for that you wrought?
    And Wordsworth has his place in the Excise.°
You're shabby fellows—true—but poets still,
And duly seated on the immortal hill.

VII

Your bays may hide the baldness of your brows—
50   Perhaps some virtuous blushes;—let them go—

---

quite a-dry, Bob! The double meaning is that
Southey is both a fish, out of the water, gasping
on deck, and sexually unable to come.
And . . . Excise Byron's cruel note: "Wordsworth's place may be in the Customs—it is, I
think, in that or the Excise—besides another at
Lord Lonsdale's table, where this poetical charlatan and political parasite licks up the crumbs
with a hardened alacrity; the converted Jacobin
having long subsided into the clownish syco-
phant of the worse prejudices of the aristocracy."

To you I envy neither fruit nor boughs—
   And for the fame you would engross below,
The field is universal, and allows
   Scope to all such as feel the inherent glow:
Scott, Rogers, Campbell, Moore, and Crabbe, will try
'Gainst you the question with posterity.

VIII

For me, who, wandering with pedestrian Muses,
   Contend not with you on the wingèd steed,
I wish your fate may yield ye, when she chooses,
60   The fame you envy, and the skill you need;
And recollect a poet nothing loses
   In giving to his brethren their full meed
Of merit, and complaint of present days
Is not the certain path to future praise.

IX

He that reserves his laurels for posterity
   (Who does not often claim the bright reversion)
Has generally no great crop to spare it, he
   Being only injured by his own assertion;
And although here and there some glorious rarity
70   Arise like Titan from the sea's immersion,
The major part of such appellants go
To—God knows where—for no one alse can know.

X

If, fallen in evil days on evil tongues,°
   Milton appealed to the Avenger, Time,
If Time, the Avenger, execrates his wrongs,
   And makes the word 'Miltonic' mean 'sublime,'
He deigned not to belie his soul in songs,
   Nor turn his very talent to a crime;
He did not loathe the Sire to laud the Son,°
80   But closed the tyrant-hater he begun.

XI

Think'st thou, could he—the blind Old Man—arise,
   Like Samuel° from the grave, to freeze once more
The blood of monarchs with his prophecies,
   Or be alive again—again all hoar
With time and trials, and those helpless eyes,
   And heartless daughters—worn—and pale—and poor;

If . . . tongues *Paradise Lost* VII.25–26
He . . . the Son Having despised Charles I,
Milton was courageous enough to go on de-
spising Charles II, in defiance of the Restora-
tion.
Samuel I Samuel 27:13–14

Would *he* adore a sultan? *he* obey
The intellectual eunuch Castlereagh?°

XII

Cold-blooded, smooth-faced, placid miscreant!
90   Dabbling its sleek young hands in Erin's gore,°
And thus for wider carnage taught to pant,
    Transferred to gorge upon a sister shore,
The vulgarest tool that Tyranny could want,
    With just enough of talent, and no more,
To lengthen fetters by another fixed,
And offer poison long already mixed.

XIII

An orator of such set trash of phrase
    Ineffably—legitimately vile,
That even its grossest flatterers dare not praise,
100   Nor foes—all nations—condescend to smile,—
Not even a sprightly blunder's spark can blaze
    From that Ixion° grindstone's ceaseless toil,
That turns and turns to give the world a notion
Of endless torments and perpetual motion.

XIV

A bungler even in its disgusting trade,
    And botching, patching, leaving still behind
Something of which its masters are afraid,
    States to be curbed, and thoughts to be confined,
Conspiracy or Congress to be made—
110   Cobbling at manacles for all mankind—
A tinkering slave-maker, who mends old chains,
With God and man's abhorrence for its gains.

XV

If we may judge of matter by the mind,
    Emasculated to the marrow *It*
Hath but two objects, how to serve, and bind,
    Deeming the chain it wears even men may fit,
Eutropius° of its many masters,—blind
    To worth as freedom, wisdom as to wit,
Fearless—because *no* feeling dwells in ice,
120   Its very courage stagnates to a vice.

Castlereagh Viscount Castlereagh (1769–1822), Foreign Secretary in the right-wing government from 1812 to 1822, hated ferociously by Byron, Shelley, Hunt, and their friends
Erin's gore Castlereagh had repressed an Irish rebellion.

Ixion Ungrateful to Zeus, he was bound to an ever-turning wheel.
Eutropius a eunuch who gained power in the Byzantine empire; see Gibbon's *History of the Decline and Fall of the Roman Empire*, chap. 32.

XVI

Where shall I turn me not to *view* its bonds,
  For I will never *feel* them;—Italy!
Thy late reviving Roman soul desponds
  Beneath the lie this State-thing breathed o'er thee°—
Thy clanking chain, and Erin's yet green wounds,
  Have voices—tongues to cry aloud for me.
Europe has slaves, allies, kings, armies still,
And Southey lives to sing them very ill.

XVII

Meantime, Sir Laureate, I proceed to dedicate,
130 In honest simple verse, this song to you.
And, if in flattering strains I do not predicate,
  'Tis that I still retain my 'buff and blue';°
My politics as yet are all to educate:
  Apostasy's so fashionable, too,
To keep *one* creed's a task grown quite Herculean:
Is it not so, my Tory, Ultra-Julian?°
    VENICE, SEPTEMBER 16, 1818

From *Canto the First*

I

I want a hero: an uncommon want,
  When every year and month sends forth a new one,
Till, after cloying the gazettes with cant,
  The age discovers he is not the true one;
Of such as these I should not care to vaunt,
  I'll therefore take our ancient friend Don Juan—
We all have seen him, in the pantomime,°
Sent to the devil somewhat ere his time.

            .   .   .

V

Brave men were living before Agamemnon
  And since, exceeding valorous and sage,
A good deal like him too, though quite the same none;
  But then they shone not on the poet's page,
And so have been forgotten:—I condemn none,
  But can't find any in the present age
Fit for my poem (that is, for my new one);
40 So, as I said, I'll take my friend Don Juan.

Thy late . . . thee Castlereagh was widely hated in Italy for selling out the city of Genoa, after first upholding it.
'buff and blue' Whig party colors, worn by followers of Charles James Fox, Byron among them

Ultra-Julian an apostate, like the Roman Emperor Julian
We . . . pantomime The story of Don Juan had been a popular English pantomime for some time, showing the great lover as a dupe and a failure.

VI

Most epic poets plunge 'in medias res'°
   (Horace makes this the heroic turnpike road),
And then your hero tells, whene'er you please,
   What went before—by way of episode,
While seated after dinner at his ease,
   Beside his mistress in some soft abode,
Palace, or garden, paradise, or cavern,
Which serves the happy couple for a tavern.

VII

That is the usual method, but not mine—
50   My way is to begin with the beginning;
The regularity of my design
   Forbids all wandering as the worst of sinning,
And therefore I shall open with a line
   (Although it cost me half an hour in spinning)
Narrating somewhat of Don Juan's father,
And also of his mother, if you'd rather.

     . . .

X

His mother was a learnèd lady, famed
   For every branch of every science known—
In every Christian language ever named,
   With virtues equalled by her wit alone:
She made the cleverest people quite ashamed,
   And even the good with inward envy groan,
Finding themselves so very much exceeded
80   In their own way by all the things that she did.

     . . .

XVIII

Perfect she was, but as perfection is
   Insipid in this naughty world of ours,
Where our first parents never learned to kiss
140   Till they were exiled from their earlier bowers,
Where all was peace, and innocence, and bliss
   (I wonder how they got through the twelve hours),
Don José, like a lineal son of Eve,
Went plucking various fruit without her leave.

XIX

He was a mortal of the careless kind,
   With no great love for learning, or the learned,
Who chose to go where'er he had a mind,

'in medias res' "into the midst of things,"
from Horace's *Ars Poetica*, 1.148

And never dreamed his lady was concerned;
The world, as usual, wickedly inclined
150   To see a kingdom or a house o'erturned
Whispered he had a mistress, some said *two*,
But for domestic quarrels *one* will do.

· · ·

LIV

Young Juan now was sixteen years of age,
    Tall, handsome, slender, but well knit: he seemed
Active, though not so sprightly, as a page;
    And everybody but his mother deemed
Him almost man; but she flew in a rage
430   And bit her lips (for else she might have screamed)
If any said so, for to be precocious
Was in her eyes a thing the most atrocious.

LV

Amongst her numerous acquaintance, all
    Selected for discretion and devotion,
There was the Donna Julia, whom to call
    Pretty were but to give a feeble notion
Of many charms in her as natural
    As sweetness to the flower, or salt to ocean,
Her zone to Venus, or his bow to Cupid,
440   (But this last simile is trite and stupid).

LVI

The darkness of her Oriental eye
    Accorded with her Moorish origin;
(Her blood was not all Spanish, by the by;
    In Spain, you know, this is a sort of sin).
When proud Granada fell, and, forced to fly,
    Boabdil° wept, of Donna Julia's kin
Some went to Africa, some stayed in Spain,
Her great great grandmamma chose to remain.

· · ·

LIX

However this might be, the race went on
    Improving still through every generation,
Until it centred in an only son,
    Who left an only daughter: my narration
May have suggested that this single one
470   Could be but Julia (whom on this occasion

Boabdil last Moorish king of Granada, reported to have wept when his capital fell to
the Spanish in 1491

I shall have much to speak about), and she
Was married, charming, chaste, and twenty-three.

LX

Her eye (I'm very fond of handsome eyes)
   Was large and dark, suppressing half its fire
Until she spoke, then through its soft disguise
   Flashed an expression more of pride than ire
And love than either; and there would arise
   A something in them which was not desire,
But would have been, perhaps, but for the soul
480 Which struggled through and chastened down the whole.

LXI

Her glossy hair was clustered o'er a brow
   Bright with intelligence, and fair, and smooth;
Her eyebrow's shape was like the aerial bow,
   Her cheek all purple with the beam of youth,
Mounting, at times, to a transparent glow,
   As if her veins ran lightning; she, in sooth,
Possessed an air and grace by no means common:
Her stature tall—I hate a dumpy woman.

LXII

Wedded she was some years, and to a man
490   Of fifty, and such husbands are in plenty;
And yet, I think, instead of such a ONE
   'Twere better to have TWO of five-and-twenty,
Especially in countries near the sun:
   And now I think on't, 'mi vien in mente,'°
Ladies even of the most uneasy virtue
Prefer a spouse whose age is short of thirty.

LXIII

'Tis a sad thing, I cannot choose but say,
   And all the fault of that indecent sun,
Who cannot leave alone our helpless clay,
500   But will keep baking, broiling, burning on,
That howsoever people fast and pray,
   The flesh is frail, and so the soul undone:
What men call gallantry, and gods adultery,
Is much more common where the climate's sultry.

LXIV

Happy the nations of the moral North!
   Where all is virtue, and the winter season

'mi vien in mente' "it comes to my mind"

Sends sin, without a rag on, shivering forth
   ('Twas snow that brought St. Anthony to reason);°
Where juries cast up what a wife is worth,
510   By laying whate'er sum, in mulct, they please on
The lover, who must pay a handsome price,
Because it is a marketable vice.

LXV

Alfonso was the name of Julia's lord,
   A man well looking for his years, and who
Was neither much beloved nor yet abhorred:
   They lived together as most people do,
Suffering each other's foibles by accord,
   And not exactly either *one* or *two;*
Yet he was jealous, though he did not show it,
520 For jealousy dislikes the world to know it.

LXVI

Julia was—yet I never could see why—
   With Donna Inez quite a favourite friend;
Between their tastes there was small sympathy,
   For not a line had Julia ever penned:
Some people whisper (but, no doubt, they lie,
   For malice still imputes some private end)
That Inez had, ere Don Alfonso's marriage,
Forgot with him her very prudent carriage;

LXVII

And that still keeping up the old connexion,
530   Which time had lately rendered much more chaste,
She took his lady also in affection,
   And certainly this course was much the best:
She flattered Julia with her sage protection,
   And complimented Don Alfonso's taste;
And if she could not (who can?) silence scandal,
At least she left it a more slender handle.

LXVIII

I can't tell whether Julia saw the affair
   With other people's eyes, or if her own
Discoveries made, but none could be aware
540   Of this, at least no symptom e'er was shown;
Perhaps she did not know, or did not care,
   Indifferent from the first, or callous grown:
I'm really puzzled what to think or say,
She kept her counsel in so close a way.

'Twas . . . reason In a note Byron called this a "recipe for hot blood in cold weather" and correctly supposed it was St. Francis "who had the wife of snow."

LXIX

Juan she saw, and, as a pretty child,
    Caressed him often—such a thing might be
Quite innocently done, and harmless styled,
    When she had twenty years, and thirteen he;
But I am not so sure I should have smiled
550   When he was sixteen, Julia twenty-three;
These few short years make wondrous alterations,
Particularly amongst sun-burnt nations.

LXX

Whate'er the cause might be, they had become
    Changed; for the dame grew distant, the youth shy,
Their looks cast down, their greetings almost dumb,
    And much embarrassment in either eye;
There surely will be little doubt with some
    That Donna Julia knew the reason why,
But as for Juan, he had no more notion
560   Than he who never saw the sea of ocean.

LXXI

Yet Julia's very coldness still was kind,
    And tremulously gentle her small hand
Withdrew itself from his, but left behind
    A little pressure, thrilling, and so bland
And slight, so very slight, that to the mind
    'Twas but a doubt; but ne'er magician's wand
Wrought change with all Armida's fairy art°
Like what this light touch left on Juan's heart.

LXXII

And if she met him, though she smiled no more,
570   She looked a sadness sweeter than her smile,
As if her heart had deeper thoughts in store
    She must not own, but cherished more the while
For that compression in its burning core;
    Even innocence itself has many a wile,
And will not dare to trust itself with truth,
And love is taught hypocrisy from youth.

LXXIII

But passion most dissembles, yet betrays
    Even by its darkness; as the blackest sky
Foretells the heaviest tempest, it displays
580   Its workings through the vainly guarded eye,

Armida's . . . art Armida, a witch in Tasso's
Jerusalem Delivered, enchanted Rinaldo, thus
impeding his crusader's career.

And in whatever aspect it arrays
    Itself, 'tis still the same hypocrisy;
Coldness or anger, even disdain or hate,
Are masks it often wears, and still too late.

LXXIV

Then there were sighs, the deeper for suppression,
    And stolen glances, sweeter for the theft,
And burning blushes, though for no transgression,
    Tremblings when met, and restlessness when left;
All these are little preludes to possession,
590   Of which young passion cannot be bereft,
And merely tend to show how greatly love is
Embarrassed at first starting with a novice.

LXXV

Poor Julia's heart was in an awkward state;
    She felt it going, and resolved to make
The noblest efforts for herself and mate,
    For honour's, pride's, religion's, virtue's sake.
Her resolutions were most truly great,
    And almost might have made a Tarquin° quake:
She prayed the Virgin Mary for her grace,
600 As being the best judge of a lady's case.

LXXVI

She vowed she never would see Juan more,
    And next day paid a visit to his mother,
And looked extremely at the opening door,
    Which, by the Virgin's grace, let in another;
Grateful she was, and yet a little sore—
    Again it opens, it can be no other,
'Tis surely Juan now—No! I'm afraid
That night the Virgin was no further prayed.

LXXVII

She now determined that a virtuous woman
610   Should rather face and overcome temptation,
That flight was base and dastardly, and no man
    Should ever give her heart the least sensation;
That is to say, a thought beyond the common
    Preference, that we must feel upon occasion,
For people who are pleasanter than others,
But then they only seem so many brothers.

Tarquin an early Roman royal family, distinguished by its savagery, as in the rape of Lu-
crece by one Tarquin

LXXVIII

And even if by chance—and who can tell?
   The devil's so very sly—she should discover
That all within was not so very well,
620   And, if still free, that such or such a lover
Might please perhaps, a virtuous wife can quell
   Such thoughts, and be the better when they're over;
And if the man should ask, 'tis but denial:
I recommend young ladies to make trial.

LXXIX

And then there are such things as love divine,
   Bright and immaculate, unmixed and pure,
Such as the angels think so very fine,
   And matrons, who would be no less secure,
Platonic, perfect, 'just such love as mine':
630   Thus Julia said—and thought so, to be sure;
And so I'd have her think, were I the man
On whom her reveries celestial ran.

LXXX

Such love is innocent, and may exist
   Between young persons without any danger.
A hand may first, and then a lip be kissed;
   For my part, to such doings I'm a stranger,
But *hear* these freedoms form the utmost list
   Of all o'er which such love may be a ranger:
If people go beyond, 'tis quite a crime,
640   But not my fault—I tell them all in time.

LXXXI

Love, then, but love within its proper limits,
   Was Julia's innocent determination
In young Don Juan's favour, and to him its
   Exertion might be useful on occasion;
And, lighted at too pure a shrine to dim its
   Ethereal lustre, with what sweet persuasion
He might be taught, by love and her together—
I really don't know what, nor Julia either.

LXXXII

Fraught with this fine intention, and well fenced
650   In mail of proof—her purity of soul,
She, for the future of her strength convinced,
   And that her honour was a rock, or mole,
Exceeding sagely from that hour dispensed
   With any kind of troublesome control;

But whether Julia to the task was equal
Is that which must be mention'd in the sequel.

LXXXIII

Her plan she deemed both innocent and feasible,
     And, surely, with a stripling of sixteen
Not scandal's fangs could fix on much that's seizable,
660   Or if they did so, satisfied to mean
Nothing but what was good, her breast was peaceable:
     A quiet conscience makes one so serene!
Christians have burnt each other, quite persuaded
That all the Apostles would have done as they did.

LXXXIV

And if in the mean time her husband died,
     But Heaven forbid that such a thought should cross
Her brain, though in a dream! (and then she sighed)
     Never could she survive that common loss;
But just suppose that moment should betide,
670   I only say suppose it—*inter nos.*
(This should be *entre nous,* for Julia thought
In French, but then the rhyme would go for nought.)

LXXXV

I only say, suppose this supposition:
     Juan being then grown up to man's estate
Would fully suit a widow of condition,
     Even seven years hence it would not be too late;
And in the interim (to pursue this vision)
     The mischief, after all, could not be great,
For he would learn the rudiments of love,
680 I mean the seraph way of those above.

                    .   .   .

XC

Young Juan wandered by the glassy brooks,
     Thinking unutterable things; he threw
Himself at length within the leafy nooks
     Where the wild branch of the cork forest grew;
There poets find materials for their books,
     And every now and then we read them through,
So that their plan and prosody are eligible,
720 Unless, like Wordsworth, they prove unintelligible.

XCI

He, Juan (and not Wordsworth), so pursued
     His self-communion with his own high soul,
Until his mighty heart, in its great mood,
     Had mitigated part, though not the whole

Of its disease; he did the best he could
    With things not very subject to control,
And turned, without perceiving his condition,
    Like Coleridge, into a metaphysician.

XCII

He thought about himself, and the whole earth,
    Of man the wonderful, and of the stars,
And how the deuce they ever could have birth;
    And then he thought of earthquakes, and of wars,
How many miles the moon might have in girth,
    Of air-balloons, and of the many bars
To perfect knowledge of the boundless skies;—
And then he thought of Donna Julia's eyes.

XCIII

In thoughts like these true wisdom may discern
    Longings sublime, and aspirations high,
Which some are born with, but the most part learn
    To plague themselves withal, they know not why:
'Twas strange that one so young should thus concern
    His brain about the action of the sky;
If *you* think 'twas philosophy that this did,
I can't help thinking puberty assisted.

XCIV

He pored upon the leaves, and on the flowers,
    And heard a voice in all the winds; and then
He thought of wood-nymphs and immortal bowers,
    And how the goddesses came down to men:
He missed the pathway, he forgot the hours,
    And when he looked upon his watch again,
He found how much old Time had been a winner—
He also found that he had lost his dinner.

· · ·

CI

But Inez was so anxious, and so clear
    Of sight, that I must think, on this occasion,
She had some other motive much more near
    For leaving Juan to this new temptation;
But what that motive was, I shan't say here;
    Perhaps to finish Juan's education,
Perhaps to open Don Alfonso's eyes,
In case he thought his wife too great a prize.

CII

It was upon a day, a summer's day;—
    Summer's indeed a very dangerous season,

730

740

750

810

And so is spring about the end of May;
    The sun, no doubt, is the prevailing reason;
But whatsoe'er the cause is, one may say,
    And stand convicted of more truth than treason,
That there are months which nature grows more merry in,—
March has its hares, and May must have its heroine.

CIII
'Twas on a summer's day—the sixth of June:—
    I like to be particular in dates,
Not only of the age, and year, but moon;
820   They are a sort of post-house, where the Fates
Change horses, making history change its tune,
    Then spur away o'er empires and o'er states,
Leaving at last not much besides chronology,
Excepting the post-obits° of theology.

CIV
'Twas on the sixth of June, about the hour
    Of half-past six—perhaps still nearer seven—
When Julia sate within as pretty a bower
    As e'er held houri in that heathenish heaven
Described by Mahomet, and Anacreon Moore,°
830   To whom the lyre and laurels have been given,
With all the trophies of triumphant song—
He won them well, and may he wear them long!

CV
She sate, but not alone; I know not well
    How this same interview had taken place,
And even if I knew, I should not tell—
    People should hold their tongues in any case;
No matter how or why the thing befell,
    But there were she and Juan, face to face—
When two such faces are so, 'twould be wise,
840   But very difficult, to shut their eyes.

CVI
How beautiful she looked! her conscious heart
    Glow'd in her cheek, and yet she felt no wrong.
Oh Love! how perfect is thy mystic art,
    Strengthening the weak, and trampling on the strong,
How self-deceitful is the sagest part
    Of mortals whom thy lure hath led along—
The precipice she stood on was immense,
So was her creed in her own innocence.

post-obits sum paid on a person's death
Anacreon Moore Thomas Moore's first publication was a translation of Anacreon (born about
570 B.C.), a witty Greek lyric poet.

CVII

She thought of her own strength, and Juan's youth,
850   And of the folly of all prudish fears,
Victorious virtue, and domestic truth,
     And then of Don Alfonso's fifty years:
I wish these last had not occurred, in sooth,
     Because that number rarely much endears,
And through all climes, the snowy and the sunny,
Sounds ill in love, whate'er it may in money.

CVIII

When people say, 'I've told you *fifty* times.'
     They mean to scold, and very often do;
When poets say, 'I've written *fifty* rhymes,'
860   They make you dread that they'll recite them too;
In gangs of *fifty*, thieves commit their crimes;
     At *fifty* love for love is rare, 'tis true,
But then, no doubt, it equally as true is,
A good deal may be bought for *fifty* Louis.

CIX

Julia had honour, virtue, truth, and love
     For Don Alfonso; and she inly swore,
By all the vows below to powers above,
     She never would disgrace the ring she wore,
Nor leave a wish which wisdom might reprove;
870   And while she pondered this, besides much more,
One hand on Juan's carelessly was thrown,
Quite by mistake—she thought it was her own;

CX

Unconsciously she leaned upon the other,
     Which played within the tangles of her hair;
And to contend with thoughts she could not smother
     She seemed, by the distraction of her air.
'Twas surely very wrong in Juan's mother
     To leave together this imprudent pair,
She who for many years had watched her son so—
880   I'm very certain *mine* would not have done so.

CXI

The hand which still held Juan's, by degrees
     Gently, but palpably confirm'd its grasp,
As if it said, 'Detain me, if you please';
     Yet there's no doubt she only meant to clasp
His fingers with a pure Platonic squeeze;
     She would have shrunk as from a toad, or asp,

Had she imagined such a thing could rouse
A feeling dangerous to a prudent spouse.

CXII

I cannot know what Juan thought of this,
890   But what he did, is much what you would do;
His young lip thanked it with a grateful kiss,
    And then, abashed at its own joy, withdrew
In deep despair, lest he had done amiss,—
    Love is so very timid when 'tis new:
She blushed, and frowned not, but she strove to speak,
And held her tongue, her voice was grown so weak.

CXIII

The sun set, and up rose the yellow moon:
    The devil's in the moon for mischief; they
Who called her CHASTE, methinks, began too soon
900   Their nomenclature; there is not a day,
The longest, not the twenty-first of June,
    Sees half the business in a wicked way
On which three single hours of moonshine smile—
And then she looks so modest all the while.

CXIV

There is a dangerous silence in that hour,
    A stillness, which leaves room for the full soul
To open all itself, without the power
    Of calling wholly back its self-control;
The silver light which, hallowing tree and tower,
910   Sheds beauty and deep softness o'er the whole,
Breathes also to the heart, and o'er it throws
A loving languor, which is not repose.

CXV

And Julia sate with Juan, half embraced
    And half retiring from the glowing arm,
Which trembled like the bosom where 'twas placed;
    Yet still she must have thought there was no harm
Or else 'twere easy to withdraw her waist;
    But then the situation had its charm,
And then—God knows what next—I can't go on;
920   I'm almost sorry that I e'er begun.

CXVI

Oh Plato! Plato! you have paved the way,
    With your confounded fantasies, to more
Immoral conduct by the fancied sway
    Your system feigns o'er the controlless core

Of human hearts, than all the long array
  Of poets and romancers:—You're a bore,
A charlatan, a coxcomb—and have been,
At best, no better than a go-between.

CXVII

And Julia's voice was lost, except in sighs,
930   Until too late for useful conversation;
The tears were gushing from her gentle eyes,
  I wish, indeed, they had not had occasion,
But who, alas! can love, and then be wise?
  Not that remorse did not oppose temptation;
A little still she strove, and much repented,
And whispering 'I will ne'er consent'—consented.

CXVIII

'Tis said that Xerxes offered a reward
  To those who could invent him a new pleasure:
Methinks the requisition's rather hard,
940   And must have cost his majesty a treasure:
For my part, I'm a moderate-minded bard,
  Fond of a little love (which I call leisure);
I care not for new pleasures, as the old
Are quite enough for me, so they but hold.

CXIX

Oh Pleasure! you're indeed a pleasant thing,
  Although one must be damned for you, no doubt:
I make a resolution every spring
  Of reformation, ere the year run out,
But somehow, this my vestal vow takes wing,
950   Yet still, I trust, it may be kept throughout:
I'm very sorry, very much ashamed,
And mean, next winter, to be quite reclaimed.

CXX

Here my chaste Muse a liberty must take—
  Start not! still chaster reader—she'll be nice hence-
Forward, and there is no great cause to quake;
  This liberty is a poetic licence,
Which some irregularity may make
  In the design, and as I have a high sense
Of Aristotle and the Rules, 'tis fit
960   To beg his pardon when I err a bit.

CXXI

This licence is to hope the reader will
  Suppose from June the sixth (the fatal day

Without whose epoch my poetic skill
　　For want of facts would all be thrown away),
But keeping Julia and Don Juan still
　　In sight, that several months have passed; we'll say
'Twas in November, but I'm not so sure
About the day—the era's more obscure.

CXXII

We'll talk of that anon.—'Tis sweet to hear
970　　At midnight on the blue and moonlit deep
The song and oar of Adria's gondolier,°
　　By distance mellowed, o'er the waters sweep;
'Tis sweet to see the evening star appear;
　　'Tis sweet to listen as the night-winds creep
From leaf to leaf; 'tis sweet to view on high
The rainbow, based on ocean, span the sky.

CXXIII

'Tis sweet to hear the watch-dog's honest bark
　　Bay deep-mouthed welcome as we draw near home;
'Tis sweet to know there is an eye will mark
980　　Our coming, and look brighter when we come;
'Tis sweet to be awakened by the lark,
　　Or lulled by falling waters; sweet the hum
Of bees, the voice of girls, the song of birds,
The lisp of children, and their earliest words.

CXXIV

Sweet is the vintage, when the showering grapes
　　In Bacchanal° profusion reel to earth,
Purple and gushing: sweet are our escapes
　　From civic revelry to rural mirth;
Sweet to the miser are his glittering heaps,
990　　Sweet to the father is his first-born's birth;
Sweet is revenge—especially to women,
Pillage to soldiers, prize-money° to seamen.

CXXV

Sweet is a legacy, and passing sweet
　　The unexpected death of some old lady
Or gentleman of seventy years complete,
　　Who've made 'us youth'° wait too—too long already
For an estate, or cash, or country seat,
　　Still breaking, but with stamina so steady

The song . . . gondolier Venetian gondoliers
sang as they rowed.
Bacchanal wanton
prize-money property captured at sea, and hence
legal booty
'us youth' See Falstaff's "They hate us youth,"
I *Henry IV* II.ii.93.

That all the Israelites are fit to mob its
Next owner for their double-damned post-obits.

CXXVI

'Tis sweet to win, no matter how, one's laurels,
   By blood or ink! 'tis sweet to put an end
To strife; 'tis sometimes sweet to have our quarrels,
   Particularly with a tiresome friend:
Sweet is old wine in bottles, ale in barrels;
   Dear is the helpless creature we defend
Against the world; and dear the schoolboy spot
We ne'er forget, though there we are forgot.

CXXVII

But sweeter still than this, than these, than all,
   Is first and passionate love—it stands alone,
Like Adam's recollection of his fall;
   The tree of knowledge has been plucked—all's known—
And life yields nothing further to recall
   Worthy of this ambrosial sin, so shown,
No doubt in fable, as the unforgiven
Fire which Prometheus filched for us from heaven.

CXXVIII

Man's a strange animal, and makes strange use
   Of his own nature, and the various arts,
And likes particularly to produce
   Some new experiment to show his parts;
This is the age of oddities let loose,
   Where different talents find their different marts;
You'd best begin with truth, and when you've lost your
Labour, there's a sure market for imposture.

CXXIX

What opposite discoveries we have seen!
   (Signs of true genius, and of empty pockets.)
One makes new noses, one a guillotine,
   One breaks your bones, one sets them in their sockets;
But vaccination certainly has been
   A kind antithesis to Congreve's rockets,°
With which the Doctor paid off an old pox,
By borrowing a new one from an ox.

CXXX

Bread has been made (indifferent) from potatoes;
   And galvanism has set some corpses grinning,°

Congreve's rockets a new kind of shell employed in the Battle of Leipzig (1813)
And . . . grinning Luigi Galvani had experimented with the supposed medical possibilities of electricity; his nephew, one Aldini, attempted to revive a murderer with electricity in 1803, undoubtedly contributing to the mythology culminating in Mary Shelley's novel *Frankenstein.*

But has not answer'd like the apparatus
    Of the Humane Society's beginning,
By which men are unsuffocated gratis:
    What wondrous new machines have late been spinning!
I said the small pox has gone out of late;
1040   Perhaps it may be followed by the great.°

CXXXI

'Tis said the great came from America;
    Perhaps it may set out on its return,—
The population there so spreads, they say
    'Tis grown high time to thin it in its turn,°
With war, or plague, or famine, any way,
    So that civilisation they may learn;
And which in ravage the more loathsome evil is—
Their real lues,° or our pseudo-syphilis?

CXXXII

This is the patent age of new inventions
1050   For killing bodies, and for saving souls,
All propagated with the best intentions;
    Sir Humphry Davy's lantern,° by which coals
Are safely mined for in the mode he mentions,
    Tombuctoo travels, voyages to the Poles,
Are ways to benefit mankind, as true,
Perhaps, as shooting them at Waterloo.

. . .

CXXXVI

'Twas midnight—Donna Julia was in bed,
    Sleeping, most probably,—when at her door
Arose a clatter might awake the dead,
    If they had never been awoke before,
And that they have been so we all have read,
    And are to be so, at the least, once more;—
The door was fastened, but with voice and fist
First knocks were heard, then 'Madam—Madam—hist!

CXXXVII

'For God's sake, Madam—Madam—here's my master,
1090   With more than half the city at his back—
Was ever heard of such a curst disaster!
    'Tis not my fault—I kept good watch—Alack!
Do pray undo the bolt a little faster—
    They're on the stair just now, and in a crack

the great syphilis, known as the "great pox"
The population . . . turn the doctrine of
Malthus, expounded in 1798

lues syphilis
lantern coal miner's safety lamp

Will all be here; perhaps he yet may fly—
Surely the window's not so *very* high!'

CXXXVIII

By this time Don Alfonso was arrived,
    With torches, friends, and servants in great number;
The major part of them had long been wived,
    And therefore paused not to disturb the slumber
Of any wicked woman, who contrived
    By stealth her husband's temples to encumber:
Examples of this kind are so contagious,
Were *one* not punished, *all* would be outrageous.

CXXXIX

I can't tell how, or why, or what suspicion
    Could enter into Don Alfonso's head;
But for a cavalier of his condition
    It surely was exceedingly ill-bred,
Without a word of previous admonition,
    To hold a levee round his lady's bed,
And summon lackeys, armed with fire and sword,
To prove himself the thing he most abhorred.

CXL

Poor Donna Julia! starting as from sleep
    (Mind—that I do not say—she had not slept),
Began at once to scream, and yawn, and weep;
    Her maid, Antonia, who was an adept,
Contrived to fling the bed-clothes in a heap,
    As if she had just now from out them crept:
I can't tell why she should take all this trouble
To prove her mistress had been sleeping double.

CXLI

But Julia mistress, and Antonia maid,
    Appeared like two poor harmless women, who
Of goblins, but still more of men afraid,
    Had thought one man might be deterred by two,
And therefore side by side were gently laid,
    Until the hours of absence should run through,
And truant husband should return, and say,
'My dear, I was the first who came away.'

CXLII

Now Julia found at length a voice, and cried,
    'In heaven's name, Don Alfonso, what d'ye mean?
Has madness seized you? would that I had died
    Ere such a monster's victim I had been!

What may this midnight violence betide,
    A sudden fit of drunkenness or spleen?
Dare you suspect me, whom the thought would kill?
Search, then, the room!'—Alfonso said, 'I will.'

CXLIII

He searched, they searched, and rummaged everywhere,
    Closet and clothes-press, chest and window-seat,
And found much linen, lace, and several pair
1140   Of stockings, slippers, brushes, combs, complete,
With other articles of ladies fair,
    To keep them beautiful, or leave them neat:
Arras they pricked and curtains with their swords,
And wounded several shutters, and some boards.

CXLIV

Under the bed they searched, and there they found—
    No matter what—it was not that they sought;
They opened windows, gazing if the ground
    Had signs or footmarks, but the earth said nought;
And then they stared each other's faces round:
1150   'Tis odd, not one of all these seekers thought,
And seems to me almost a sort of blunder,
Of looking in the bed as well as under.

CXLV

During this inquisition Julia's tongue
    Was not asleep—'Yes, search and search,' she cried,
'Insult on insult heap, and wrong on wrong!
    It was for this that I became a bride!
For this in silence I have suffered long
    A husband like Alfonso at my side;
But now I'll bear no more, nor here remain,
1160   If there be law or lawyers in all Spain.

CXLVI

'Yes, Don Alfonso! husband now no more,
    If ever you indeed deserved the name,
Is't worthy of your years?—you have three-score—
    Fifty, or sixty, it is all the same—
Is't wise or fitting, causeless to explore
    For facts against a virtuous woman's fame?
Ungrateful, perjured, barbarous Don Alfonso,
How dare you think your lady would go on so?

CXLVII

'Is it for this I have disdained to hold
1170   The common privileges of my sex?

That I have chosen a confessor so old
    And deaf, that any other it would vex,
And never once he has had cause to scold,
    But found my very innocence perplex
So much, he always doubted I was married—
How sorry you will be when I've miscarried!

CXLVIII

'Was it for this that no Cortejo° e'er
    I yet have chosen from out the youth of Seville?
Is it for this I scarce went anywhere,
    Except to bull-fights, mass, play, rout, and revel?
Is it for this, whate'er my suitors were,
    I favoured none—nay, was almost uncivil?
Is it for this that General Count O'Reilly,°
Who took Algiers, declares I used him vilely?

CXLIX

'Did not the Italian Musico Cazzani°
    Sing at my heart six months at least in vain?
Did not his countryman, Count Corniani,°
    Call me the only virtuous wife in Spain?
Were there not also Russians, English, many?
    The Count Strongstroganoff I put in pain,
And Lord Mount Coffeehouse, the Irish peer,
Who killed himself for love (with wine) last year.

CL

'Have I not had two bishops at my feet?
    The Duke of Ichar, and Don Fernan Nunez?
And is it thus a faithful wife you treat?
    I wonder in what quarter now the moon is:
I praise your vast forbearance not to beat
    Me also, since the time so opportune is—
Oh, valiant man! with sword drawn and cocked trigger,
Now, tell me, don't you cut a pretty figure?

CLI

'Was it for this you took your sudden journey,
    Under pretence of business indispensable,
With that sublime of rascals your attorney,
    Whom I see standing there, and looking sensible
Of having played the fool? though both I spurn, he
    Deserves the worst, his conduct's less defensible,

180

190

200

Cortejo Byron's note: "The Spanish 'Cortejo' is much the same as the Italian 'Cavalier Servente'" (as Byron was to Teresa Guiccioli). **O'Reilly** As Byron noted, Count O'Reilly "did not take Algiers—but Algiers very nearly took him"; he withdrew in some disorder after a fiasco in 1775.
Cazzani perhaps playing on *cazzo*, the phallus
Corniani from *cornuto*, a cuckold

Because, no doubt, 'twas for his dirty fee,
And not from any love to you nor me.

CLII

'If he comes here to take a deposition,
1210   By all means let the gentleman proceed;
You've made the apartment in a fit condition:—
    There's pen and ink for you, sir, when you need—
Let everything be noted with precision,
    I would not you for nothing should be fee'd—
But as my maid's undrest, pray turn your spies out.'
'Oh!' sobbed Antonia, 'I could tear their eyes out.'

CLIII

'There is the closet, there the toilet, there
    The antechamber—search them under, over;
There is the sofa, there the great arm-chair,
1220   The chimney—which would really hold a lover.
I wish to sleep, and beg you will take care
    And make no further noise, till you discover
The secret cavern of this lurking treasure—
And when 'tis found, let me, too, have that pleasure.

CLIV

'And now, Hidalgo!° now that you have thrown
    Doubt upon me, confusion over all,
Pray have the courtesy to make it known
    Who is the man you search for? How d'ye call
Him? what his lineage? let him but be shown—
1230   I hope he's young and handsome—is he tall?
Tell me—and be assured, that since you stain
Mine honour thus, it shall not be in vain.

CLV

'At least, perhaps, he has not sixty years,
    At that age he would be too old for slaughter,
Or for so young a husband's jealous fears—
    (Antonia! let me have a glass of water.)
I am ashamed of having shed these tears,
    They are unworthy of my father's daughter;
My mother dreamed not in my natal hour,
1240   That I should fall into a monster's power.

CLVI

'Perhaps 'tis of Antonia you are jealous,
    You saw that she was sleeping by my side

Hidalgo Spanish gentleman

When you broke in upon us with your fellows:
    Look where you please—we've nothing, sir, to hide;
Only another time, I trust, you'll tell us,
    Or for the sake of decency abide
A moment at the door, that we may be
Dressed to receive so much good company.

CLVII

'And now, sir, I have done, and say no more;
250   The little I have said may serve to show
The guileless heart in silence may grieve o'er
    The wrongs to whose exposure it is slow:—
I leave you to your conscience as before,
    'Twill one day ask you *why* you used me so?
God grant you feel not then the bitterest grief!
Antonia! where's my pocket-handkerchief?'

CLVIII

She ceased, and turned upon her pillow; pale
    She lay, her dark eyes flashing through their tears,
Like skies that rain and lighten; as a veil,
260   Waved and o'ershading her wan cheek, appears
Her streaming hair: the black curls strive, but fail,
    To hide the glossy shoulder, which uprears
Its snow through all;—her soft lips lie apart,
And louder than her breathing beats her heart.

CLIX

The Senhor Don Alfonso stood confused;
    Antonia bustled around the ransacked room,
And, turning up her nose, with looks abused
    Her master, and his myrmidons, of whom
Not one, except the attorney, was amused;
270   He, like Achates,° faithful to the tomb,
So there were quarrels, cared not for the cause,
Knowing they must be settled by the laws.

CLX

With prying snub-nose, and small eyes, he stood,
    Following Antonia's motions here and there,
With such suspicion in his attitude;
    For reputations he had little care;
So that a suit or action were made good,
    Small pity had he for the young and fair,
And ne'er believed in negatives, till these
280   Were proved by competent false witnesses.

Achates the best friend of Aeneas

CLXI

But Don Alfonso stood with downcast looks,
    And, truth to say, he made a foolish figure;
When, after searching in five hundred nooks,
    And treating a young wife with so much rigour,
He gained no point, except some self-rebukes,
    Added to those his lady with such vigour
Had poured upon him for the last half-hour,
Quick, thick, and heavy—as a thunder-shower.

CLXII

At first he tried to hammer an excuse,
    To which the sole reply was tears and sobs,
And indications of hysterics, whose
    Prologue is always certain throes, and throbs,
Gasps, and whatever else the owners choose:
    Alfonso saw his wife, and thought of Job's;°
He saw too, in perspective, her relations,
And then he tried to muster all his patience.

CLXIII

He stood in act to speak, or rather stammer,
    But sage Antonia cut him short before
The anvil of his speech received the hammer,
    With 'Pray, sir, leave the room, and say no more,
Or madam dies.'—Alfonso mutter'd, 'D—n her.'
    But nothing else, the time of words was o'er;
He cast a rueful look or two, and did,
He knew not wherefore, that which he was bid.

CLXIV

With him retired his *'posse comitatus,'*°
    The attorney last, who lingered near the door
Reluctantly, still tarrying there as late as
    Antonia let him—not a little sore
At this most strange and unexplained *'hiatus'*
    In Don Alfonso's facts, which just now wore
An awkward look; as he revolved the case,
The door was fastened in his legal face.

CLXV

No sooner was it bolted, than—Oh shame!
    Oh sin! Oh sorrow! and Oh womankind!
How can you do such things and keep your fame,
    Unless this world, and t'other too, be blind?

1290

1300

1310

Job's who said to him in his misery "Dost thou   **'posse comitatus'** company
still retain thine integrity? Curse god, and die"
(Job 2:9)

Nothing so dear as an unfilched good name!
    But to proceed—for there is more behind:
With much heartfelt reluctance be it said,
320   Young Juan slipped, half-smothered, from the bed.

        CLXVI
He had been hid—I don't pretend to say
    How, nor can I indeed describe the where—
Young, slender, and packed easily, he lay,
    No doubt, in little compass, round or square;
But pity him I neither must nor may
    His suffocation by that pretty pair;
'Twere better, sure, to die so, than be shut
With maudlin Clarence in his Malmsey butt.°

        CLXVII
And, secondly, I pity not, because
330   He had no business to commit a sin,
Forbid by heavenly, fined by human laws,
    At least 'twas rather early to begin;
But at sixteen the conscience rarely gnaws
    So much as when we call our old debts in
At sixty years, and draw the accompts of evil,
And find a deuced balance with the devil.

        CLXVIII
Of his position I can give no notion:
    'Tis written in the Hebrew Chronicle,°
How the physicians, leaving pill and potion,
340   Prescribed, by way of blister, a young belle,
When old King David's blood grew dull in motion,
    And that the medicine answered very well;
Perhaps 'twas in a different way applied,
For David lived, but Juan nearly died.

        CLXIX
What's to be done? Alfonso will be back
    The moment he has sent his fools away.
Antonia's skill was put upon the rack,
    But no device could be brought into play—
And how to parry the renewed attack?
350   Besides, it wanted but few hours of day:
Antonia puzzled; Julia did not speak,
But pressed her bloodless lip to Juan's cheek.

With . . . butt See Shakespeare, *Richard III*   **Hebrew Chronicle** See I Kings 1:1–3.
I.iv.276.

CLXX

He turned his lip to hers, and with his hand
　　Called back the tangles of her wandering hair;
Even then their love they could not all command,
　　And half forgot their danger and despair:
Antonia's patience now was at a stand—
　　'Come, come, 'tis no time now for fooling there,'
She whispered, in great wrath—'I must deposit
1360　This pretty gentleman within the closet:

CLXXI

'Pray, keep your nonsense for some luckier night—
　　Who can have put my master in this mood?
What will become on't—I'm in such a fright,
　　The devil's in the urchin, and no good—
Is this a time for giggling? this a plight?
　　Why, don't you know that it may end in blood?
You'll lose your life, and I shall lose my place,
My mistress all, for that half-girlish face.

CLXXII

'Had it but been for a stout cavalier
1370　Of twenty-five or thirty—(come, make haste)
But for a child, what piece of work is here!
　　I really, madam, wonder at your taste—
(Come, sir, get in)—my master must be near:
　　There, for the present, at the least, he's fast,
And if we can but till the morning keep
Our counsel—Juan, mind, you must not sleep).'

CLXXIII

Now, Don Alfonso entering, but alone,
　　Closed the oration of the trusty maid:
She loitered, and he told her to be gone,
1380　An order somewhat sullenly obeyed;
However, present remedy was none,
　　And no great good seemed answer'd if she stayed:
Regarding both with slow and sidelong view,
She snuffed the candle, curtsied, and withdrew.

CLXXIV

Alfonso paused a minute—then begun
　　Some strange excuses for his late proceeding;
He would not justify what he had done,
　　To say the best, it was extreme ill-breeding;
But there were ample reasons for it, none
1390　Of which he specified in this his pleading:

His speech was a fine sample, on the whole,
Of rhetoric, which the learned call 'rigmarole.'

CLXXV

Julia said nought; though all the while there rose
    A ready answer, which at once enables
A matron, who her husband's foible knows,
    By a few timely words to turn the tables,
Which, if it does not silence, still must pose,—
    Even if it should comprise a pack of fables;
'Tis to retort with firmness, and when he
Suspects with *one,* do you reproach with *three.*

CLXXVI

Julia, in fact, had tolerable grounds,—
    Alfonso's loves with Inez were well known;
But whether 'twas that one's own guilt confounds—
    But that can't be, as has been often shown,
A lady with apologies abounds;—
    It might be that her silence sprang alone
From delicacy to Don Juan's ear,
To whom she knew his mother's fame was dear.

CLXXVII

There might be one more motive, which makes two;
    Alfonso ne'er to Juan had alluded,—
Mentioned his jealousy, but never who
    Had been the happy lover, he concluded,
Concealed amongst his premises; 'tis true,
    His mind the more o'er this its mystery brooded;
To speak of Inez now were, one may say,
Like throwing Juan in Alfonso's way.

CLXXVIII

A hint, in tender cases, is enough;
    Silence is best, besides there is a *tact*—
(That modern phrase appears to me sad stuff,
    But it will serve to keep my verse compact)—
Which keeps, when pushed by questions rather rough,
    A lady always distant from the fact:
The charming creatures lie with such a grace,
There's nothing so becoming to the face.

CLXXIX

They blush, and we believe them; at least I
    Have always done so; 'tis of no great use,
In any case, attempting a reply,
    For then their eloquence grows quite profuse;

And when at length they're out of breath, they sigh,
1430   And cast their languid eyes down, and let loose
A tear or two, and then we make it up;
And then—and then—and then—sit down and sup.

CLXXX

Alfonso closed his speech, and begged her pardon,
    Which Julia half withheld, and then half granted,
And laid conditions, he thought very hard on,
    Denying several little things he wanted:
He stood like Adam lingering near his garden,
    With useless penitence perplexed and haunted,
Beseeching she no further would refuse,
1440   When, lo! he stumbled o'er a pair of shoes.

CLXXXI

A pair of shoes!—what then? not much, if they
    Are such as fit with ladies' feet, but these
(No one can tell how much I grieve to say)
    Were masculine; to see them, and to seize,
Was but a moment's act.—Ah! well-a-day!
    My teeth begin to chatter, my veins freeze—
Alfonso first examined well their fashion,
And then flew out into another passion.

CLXXXII

He left the room for his relinquished sword,
1450   And Julia instant to the closet flew.
'Fly, Juan, fly! for heaven's sake—not a word—
    The door is open—you may yet slip through
The passage you so often have explored—
    Here is the garden-key—Fly—fly—Adieu!
Haste—haste! I hear Alfonso's hurrying feet—
Day has not broke—there's no one in the street.'

CLXXXIII

None can say that this was not good advice,
    The only mischief was, it came too late;
Of all experience 'tis the usual price,
1460   A sort of income-tax laid on by fate:
Juan had reached the room-door in a trice,
    And might have done so by the garden-gate,
But met Alfonso in his dressing-gown,
Who threatened death—so Juan knocked him down.

CLXXXIV

Dire was the scuffle, and out went the light;
    Antonia cried out 'Rape!' and Julia 'Fire!'

But not a servant stirred to aid the fight.
    Alfonso, pommelled to his heart's desire,
Swore lustily he'd be revenged this night;
470   And Juan, too, blasphemed an octave higher;
His blood was up: though young, he was a Tartar,
And not at all disposed to prove a martyr.

CLXXXV

Alfonso's sword had dropped ere he could draw it,
    And they continued battling hand to hand,
For Juan very luckily ne'er saw it;
    His temper not being under great command,
If at that moment he had chanced to claw it,
    Alfonso's days had not been in the land
Much longer.—Think of husbands', lovers' lives!
480 And how ye may be doubly widows—wives!

CLXXXVI

Alfonso grappled to detain the foe,
    And Juan throttled him to get away,
And blood ('twas from the nose) began to flow;
    At last, as they more faintly wrestling lay,
Juan contrived to give an awkward blow,
    And then his only garment quite gave way;
He fled, like Joseph, leaving it; but there,
I doubt, all likeness ends between the pair.°

CLXXXVII

Lights came at length, and men, and maids, who found
490   An awkward spectacle their eyes before;
Antonia in hysterics, Julia swooned,
    Alfonso leaning, breathless, by the door;
Some half-torn drapery scattered on the ground,
    Some blood, and several footsteps, but no more:
Juan the gate gained, turned the key about,
And liking not the inside, locked the out.

CLXXXVIII

Here ends this canto.—Need I sing, or say,
    How Juan, naked, favoured by the night,
Who favours what she should not, found his way,
500   And reached his home in an unseemly plight?
The pleasant scandal which arose next day,
    The nine days' wonder which was brought to light,
And how Alfonso sued for a divorce,
Were in the English newspapers, of course.

the pair See Genesis 39:12.

CLXXXIX

If you would like to see the whole proceedings,
    The depositions, and the cause at full,
The names of all the witnesses, the pleadings
    Of counsel to nonsuit, or to annul,
There's more than one edition, and the readings
1510   Are various, but they none of them are dull;
The best is that in short-hand ta'en by Gurney,°
Who to Madrid on purpose made a journey.

CXC

But Donna Inez, to divert the train
    Of one of the most circulating scandals
That had for centuries been known in Spain,
    At least since the retirement of the Vandals,
First vowed (and never had she vowed in vain)
    To Virgin Mary several pounds of candles;
And then, by the advice of some old ladies,
1520   She sent her son to be shipped off from Cadiz.

CXCI

She had resolved that he should travel through
    All European climes, by land or sea,
To mend his former morals, and get new,
    Especially in France and Italy
(At least this is the thing most people do).
    Julia was sent into a convent: she
Grieved, but, perhaps, her feelings may be better
Shown in the following copy of her Letter:°—

CXCII

'They tell me 'tis decided; you depart:
1530   'Tis wise—'tis well, but not the less a pain;
I have no further claim on your young heart,
    Mine is the victim, and would be again;
To love too much has been the only art
    I used;—I write in haste, and if a stain
Be on this sheet, 'tis not what it appears;
My eyeballs burn and throb, but have no tears.

CXCIII

'I loved, I love you, for this love have lost
    State, station, heaven, mankind's, my own esteem,
And yet can not regret what it hath cost,
1540   So dear is still the memory of that dream;
Yet, if I name my guilt, 'tis not to boast,

Gurney W. B. Gurney, shorthand trial reporter   Julia's part, and suggesting that her convent
her Letter a marvelous document, demonstrat-   existence was not particularly repressive
ing enormous advances in sophistication on

None can deem harshlier of me than I deem:
I trace this scrawl because I cannot rest—
I've nothing to reproach or to request.

CXCIV

'Man's love is of man's life a thing apart,
    'Tis woman's whole existence;° man may range
The court, camp, church, the vessel, and the mart;
    Sword, gown, gain, glory, offer in exchange
Pride, fame, ambition, to fill up his heart,
    And few there are whom these cannot estrange;
Men have all these resources, we but one,
To love again, and be again undone.

CXCV

'You will proceed in pleasure, and in pride,
    Beloved and loving many; all is o'er
For me on earth, except some years to hide
    My shame and sorrow deep in my heart's core;
These I could bear, but cannot cast aside
    The passion which still rages as before,—
And so farewell—forgive me, love me—No,
That word is idle now—but let it go.

CXCVI

'My breast has been all weakness, is so yet;
    But still I think I can collect my mind;
My blood still rushes where my spirit's set,
    As roll the waves before the settled wind;
My heart is feminine, nor can forget—
    To all, except one image, madly blind;
So shakes the needle, and so stands the pole,
As vibrates my fond heart to my fixed soul.

CXCVII

'I have no more to say, but linger still,
    And dare not set my seal upon this sheet,
And yet I may as well the task fulfil,
    My misery can scarce be more complete:
I had not lived till now, could sorrow kill;
    Death shuns the wretch who fain the blow would meet,
And I must even survive this last adieu,
And bear with life, to love and pray for you!'

CXCVIII

This note was written upon gilt-edged paper
    With a neat little crow-quill, slight and new;

Man's . . . existence lifted by Byron from
the celebrated Madame de Staël, whom he knew

Her small white hand could hardly reach the taper,
1580   It trembled as magnetic needles do,
And yet she did not let one tear escape her;
    The seal a sun-flower; '*Elle vous suit partout*,'°
The motto, cut upon a white cornelian;
The wax was superfine, its hue vermilion.

CXCIX

This was Don Juan's earliest scrape; but whether
    I shall proceed with his adventures is
Dependent on the public altogether;
    We'll see, however, what they say to this,
Their favour in an author's cap's a feather,
1590   And no great mischief's done by their caprice;
And if their approbation we experience,
Perhaps they'll have some more about a year hence.

CC

My poem's epic, and is meant to be
    Divided in twelve books; each book containing,
With love, and war, a heavy gale at sea,
    A list of ships, and captains, and kings reigning,
New characters; the episodes are three:
    A panoramic view of hell's in training,
After the style of Virgil and of Homer,
1600 So that my name of Epic's no misnomer.

CCI

All these things will be specified in time,
    With strict regard to Aristotle's rules,
The *Vade Mecum*° of the true sublime,
    Which makes so many poets, and some fools:
Prose poets like blank-verse, I'm fond of rhyme,
    Good workmen never quarrel with their tools;
I've got new mythological machinery,
And very handsome supernatural scenery.

CCII

There's only one slight difference between
1610   Me and my epic brethren gone before,
And here the advantage is my own, I ween
    (Not that I have not several merits more,
But this will more peculiarly be seen);
    They so embellish, that 'tis quite a bore
Their labyrinth of fables to thread through,
Whereas this story's actually true.

'**Elle vous suit partout**' "she follows you every-   **Vade Mecum** a guidebook, literally "go with
where"   me"

CCIII

If any person doubt it, I appeal
  To history, tradition, and to facts,
To newspapers, whose truth all know and feel,
  To plays in five, and operas in three acts;
All these confirm my statement a good deal,
  But that which more completely faith exacts
Is, that myself, and several now in Seville,
Saw Juan's last elopement with the devil.

CCIV

If ever I should condescend to prose,
  I'll write poetical commandments, which
Shall supersede beyond all doubt all those
  That went before; in these I shall enrich
My text with many things that no one knows,
  And carry precept to the highest pitch:
I'll call the work 'Longinus o'er a Bottle,
Or, Every Poet his *own* Aristotle.'°

CCV

Thou shalt believe in Milton, Dryden, Pope;
  Thou shalt not set up Wordsworth, Coleridge, Southey;
Because the first is crazed beyond all hope,
  The second drunk,° the third so quaint and mouthy:
With Crabbe it may be difficult to cope,
  And Campbell's Hippocrene is somewhat drouthy:
Thou shalt not steal from Samuel Rogers,° nor
Commit—flirtation with the muse of Moore.

CCVI

Thou shalt not covet Mr. Sotheby's° Muse,
  His Pegasus, nor anything that's his;
Thou shalt not bear false witness like 'the Blues'°—
  (There's one,° at least, is very fond of this);
Thou shalt not write, in short, but what I choose:
  This is true criticism, and you may kiss—
Exactly as you please, or not,—the rod;
But if you don't, I'll lay it on, by G—d!

CCVII

If any person should presume to assert
  This story is not moral, first, I pray,

'Longinus . . . Aristotle' Aristotle was made
the authority for poetic "rules" by Renaissance
and later critics; the more Romantic Longinus
(3rd century A.D.) was interpreted as authority
for yielding to inspiration
The . . . drunk Coleridge was a heavy brandy
drinker

Samuel Rogers (1763–1855) better known as
a conversationalist than as a poet
Sotheby's William Sotheby (1757–1833), poetic
translator
'the Blues' "bluestockings," or literary women
There's one perhaps Lady Byron, or else Caroline Lamb, a cast-off mistress of Byron's

That they will not cry out before they're hurt,
    Then that they'll read it o'er again, and say
(But, doubtless, nobody will be so pert),
    That this is not a moral tale, though gay;
Besides, in Canto Twelfth, I mean to show
The very place where wicked people go.

CCVIII

If, after all, there should be some so blind
    To their own good this warning to despise,
Let by some tortuosity of mind,
    Not to believe my verse and their own eyes,
And cry that they 'the moral cannot find,'
    I tell him, if a clergyman, he lies;
Should captains the remark, or critics, make,
They also lie too—under a mistake.

CCIX

The public approbation I expect,
    And beg they'll take my word about the moral,
Which I with their amusement will connect
    (So children cutting teeth receive a coral);
Meantime they'll doubtless please to recollect
    My epical pretensions to the laurel:
For fear some prudish readers should grow skittish,
I've bribed my grandmother's review—the British.

CCX

I sent it in a letter to the Editor,
    Who thanked me duly by return of post—
I'm for a handsome article his creditor;
    Yet, if my gentle Muse he please to roast,
And break a promise after having made it her,
    Denying the receipt of what it cost,
And smear his page with gall instead of honey,
All I can say is—that he had the money.

CCXI

I think that with this holy new alliance
    I may ensure the public, and defy
All other magazines of art or science,
    Daily, or monthly, or three monthly; I
Have not essayed to multiply their clients,
    Because they tell me 'twere in vain to try,
And that the Edinburgh Review and Quarterly
Treat a dissenting author very martyrly.

CCXII

'*Non ego hoc ferrem calida juventâ*
690   *Consule Planco,*' Horace said,° and so
Say I; by which quotation there is meant a
    Hint that some six or seven good years ago
(Long ere I dreamt of dating from the Brenta)
    I was most ready to return a blow,
And would not brook at all this sort of thing
In my hot youth—when George the Third was King.

CCXIII

But now at thirty years my hair is grey—
    (I wonder what it will be like at forty?
I thought of a peruke° the other day—)
700   My heart is not much greener; and, in short, I
Have squandered my whole summer while 'twas May,
    And feel no more the spirit to retort; I
Have spent my life, both interest and principal,
And deem not, what I deemed, my soul invincible.

CCXIV

No more—no more—Oh! never more on me
    The freshness of the heart can fall like dew,
Which out of all the lovely things we see
    Extracts emotions beautiful and new,
Hived in our bosom like the bag of the bee:
1710   Think'st thou the honey with those objects grew?
Alas! 'twas not in them, but in thy power
To double even the sweetness of a flower.

CCXV

No more—no more—Oh! never more, my heart,
    Canst thou be my sole world, my universe!
Once all in all, but now a thing apart,
    Thou canst not be my blessing or my curse:
The illusion's gone for ever, and thou art
    Insensible, I trust, but none the worse,
And in thy stead I've got a deal of judgment,
1720   Though heaven knows how it ever found a lodgment.°

CCXVI

My days of love are over;° me no more
    The charms of maid, wife, and still less of widow,
Can make the fool of which they made before,—

Horace said *Odes* III.xiv: "I should not have
borne this in the heat of youth when Plancus
was Consul"
peruke wig
lodgment These stanzas (CCXIV, CCXV) are
Byron's version of Wordsworth's "Intimations
of Immortality" ode.
My . . . over paraphrase of Horace, *Odes* IV.
i.29–32

In short, I must not lead the life I did do;
The credulous hope of mutual minds is o'er,
    The copious use of claret is forbid too,
So for a good old-gentlemanly vice,
I think I must take up with avarice.

CCXVII

Ambition was my idol, which was broken
    Before the shrines of Sorrow, and of Pleasure;
And the two last have left me many a token
    O'er which reflection may be made at leisure:
Now, like Friar Bacon's brazen head,° I've spoken,
    'Time is, Time was, Time's past:'—a chymic° treasure
Is glittering youth, which I have spent betimes—
My heart in passion, and my head on rhymes.

CCXVIII

What is the end of fame? 'tis but to fill
    A certain portion of uncertain paper:
Some liken it to climbing up a hill,
    Whose summit, like all hills, is lost in vapour;
For this men write, speak, preach, and heroes kill,
    And bards burn what they call their 'midnight taper,'
To have, when the original is dust,
A name, a wretched picture, and worse bust.

CCXIX

What are the hopes of man? Old Egypt's King
    Cheops erected the first pyramid
And largest, thinking it was just the thing
    To keep his memory whole, and mummy hid:
But somebody or other rummaging,
    Burglariously broke his coffin's lid:
Let not a monument give you or me hopes,
Since not a pinch of dust remains of Cheops.

CCXX

But, I being fond of true philosophy,
    Say very often to myself, 'Alas!
All things that have been born were born to die,
    And flesh (which Death mows down to hay) is grass;
You've passed your youth not so unpleasantly,
    And if you had it o'er again—'twould pass—
So thank your stars that matters are no worse,
And read your Bible, sir, and mind your purse.'

Now . . . head See Robert Greene's *Friar Bacon*   chymic alchemical
and Friar Bungay IV.i.

CCXXI

But for the present, gentle reader! and
    Still gentler purchaser! the bard—that's I—
Must, with permission, shake you by the hand,
    And so your humble servant, and good-bye!
We meet again, if we should understand
    Each other; and if not, I shall not try
Your patience further than by this short sample—
'Twere well if others followed my example.

CCXXII

'Go, little book, from this my solitude!
    I cast thee on the waters—go thy ways!
And if, as I believe, thy vein be good,
    The world will find thee after many days.'°
When Southey's read, and Wordsworth understood,
    I can't help putting in my claim to praise—
The four first rhymes are Southey's, every line:
For God's sake, reader! take them not for mine!
1818   1819

From *Canto the Third*

I

Hail, Muse! *et caetera*.—We left Juan sleeping,
    Pillowed upon a fair and happy breast,
And watched by eyes that never yet knew weeping,
    And loved by a young heart, too deeply blessed
To feel the poison through her spirit creeping,
    Or know who rested there, a foe to rest,
Had soiled the current of her sinless years,
And turned her pure heart's purest blood to tears!

II

Oh, Love! what is it in this world of ours
    Which makes it fatal to be loved? Ah why
With cypress branches hast thou wreathed thy bowers,
    And made thy best interpreter a sigh?
As those who dote on odours pluck the flowers,
    And place them on their breast—but place to die—
Thus the frail beings we would fondly cherish
Are laid within our bosoms but to perish.

III

In her first passion woman loves her lover,
    In all the others all she loves is love,

'Go . . . days' from the last stanza of Southey's
Epilogue to the Lay of the Laureate

Which grows a habit she can ne'er get over,
20   And fits her loosely—like an easy glove,
As you may find, whene'er you like to prove her:
    One man alone at first her heart can move;
She then prefers him in the plural number,
Not finding that the additions much encumber.

            IV
I know not if the fault be men's or theirs;
    But one thing's pretty sure; a woman planted
(Unless at once she plunge for life in prayers)
    After a decent time must be gallanted;
Although, no doubt, her first of love affairs
30   Is that to which her heart is wholly granted;
Yet there are some, they say, who have had *none*,
But those who have ne'er end with only *one*.

            V
'Tis melancholy, and a fearful sign
    Of human frailty, folly, also crime,
That love and marriage rarely can combine,
    Although they both are born in the same clime;
Marriage from love, like vinegar from wine—
    A sad, sour, sober beverage—by time
Is sharpened from its high celestial flavour,
40 Down to a very homely household savour.

            VI
There's something of antipathy, as 'twere,
    Between their present and their future state;
A kind of flattery that's hardly fair
    Is used until the truth arrives too late—
Yet what can people do, except despair?
    The same things change their names at such a rate;
For instance—passion in a lover's glorious,
But in a husband is pronounced uxorious.

            VII
Men grow ashamed of being so very fond;
50   They sometimes also get a little tired
(But that, of course, is rare), and then despond:
    The same things cannot always be admired,
Yet 'tis 'so nominated in the bond,'
    That both are tied till one shall have expired.
Sad thought! to lose the spouse that was adorning
Our days, and put one's servants into mourning.

VIII

There's doubtless something in domestic doings
  Which forms, in fact, true love's antithesis;
Romances paint at full length people's wooings,
60 But only give a bust of marriages;
For no one cares for matrimonial cooings,
  There's nothing wrong in a connubial kiss:
Think you, if Laura had been Petrarch's wife,
He would have written sonnets all his life?

IX

All tragedies are finished by a death,
  All comedies are ended by a marriage;
The future states of both are left to faith,
  For authors fear description might disparage
The worlds to come of both, or fall beneath,
70 And then both worlds would punish their miscarriage;
So leaving each their priest and prayer-book ready,
They say no more of Death or of the Lady.°

X

The only two that in my recollection
  Have sung of heaven and hell, or marriage, are
Dante and Milton, and of both the affection
  Was hapless in their nuptials, for some bar
Of fault or temper ruined the connexion
  (Such things, in fact, it don't ask much to mar);
But Dante's Beatrice and Milton's Eve
80 Were not drawn from their spouses, you conceive.

XI

Some persons say that Dante meant theology
  By Beatrice, and not a mistress—I,
Although my opinion may require apology,
  Deem this a commentator's phantasy,
Unless indeed it was from his own knowledge he
  Decided thus, and showed good reason why;
I think that Dante's more abstruse ecstatics
Meant to personify the mathematics.

. . .

XCI

Milton's the prince of poets—so we say;
  A little heavy, but no less divine:
An independent being in his day—
820 Learned, pious, temperate in love and wine;

They . . . Lady refers to popular ballad
"Death and the Lady"

But his life falling into Johnson's way,
   We're told this great high priest of all the Nine
Was whipped at college—a harsh sire—odd spouse,
For the first Mrs. Milton left his house.

     XCII
All these are, *certes*, entertaining facts,
   Like Shakespeare's stealing deer, Lord Bacon's bribes;
Like Titus' youth, and Caesar's earliest acts;°
   Like Burns (whom Doctor Currie well describes);°
Like Cromwell's pranks;—but although truth exacts
830   These amiable descriptions from the scribes,
As most essential to their hero's story,
They do not much contribute to his glory.

     XCIII
All are not moralists, like Southey, when
   He prated to the world of 'Pantisocracy';
Or Wordsworth unexcised, unhired, who then
   Seasoned his pedlar poems with democracy;
Or Coleridge, long before his flighty pen
   Let to the Morning Post its aristocracy;°
When he and Southey, following the same path,
840   Espoused two partners (milliners of Bath).°

     XCIV
Such names at present cut a convict figure,
   The very Botany Bay° in moral geography;
Their loyal treason, renegado rigour,
   Are good manure for their more bare biography.
Wordsworth's last quarto, by the way, is bigger
   Than any since the birthday of typography;
A drowsy frowzy poem, called the 'Excursion,'
Writ in a manner which is my aversion.

     XCV
He there builds up a formidable dike
850   Between his own and others' intellect;
But Wordsworth's poem, and his followers, like
   Joanna Southcote's Shiloh,° and her sect,
Are things which in this century don't strike
   The public mind,—so few are the elect;

Like . . . acts Suetonious said the Emperor
Titus, in his youth, was a forger, and Caesar a
torturer.
Like . . . describes A life of Burns published
in 1800 by James Currie detailed much scandal
about the poet.
Or Coleridge . . . aristocracy In 1800 Coleridge began to write for the *Morning Post*.
When . . . Bath In autumn 1795, Coleridge
and Southey married the Fricker sisters, of Bath.
Botany Bay penal colony in Australia
Joanna . . . Shiloh The prophetess Joanna Southcott (1750–1814) insisted she would bear the
second Messiah, Shiloh.

And the new births of both their stale virginities
Have proved but dropsies, taken for divinities.

XCVI

But let me to my story: I must own,
    If I have any fault, it is digression—
Leaving my people to proceed alone,
860   While I soliloquize beyond expression;
But these are my addresses from the throne,
    Which put off business to the ensuing session:
Forgetting each omission is a loss to
The world, not quite so great as Ariosto.°

XCVII

I know that what our neighbours call 'longueurs,'°
    (We've not so good a word, but have the thing,
In that complete perfection which insures
    An epic from Bob Southey every Spring—)
Form not the true temptation which allures
870   The reader; but 'twould not be hard to bring
Some fine examples of the epopée,°
To prove its grand ingredient is ennui.

XCVIII

We learn from Horace, 'Homer sometimes sleeps';
    We feel without him, Wordsworth sometimes wakes,—
To show with what complacency he creeps,
    With his dear 'Waggoners,' around his lakes.°
He wishes for 'a boat' to sail the deeps—
    Of ocean?—No, of air; and then he makes
Another outcry for 'a little boat,'
880   And drivels seas to set it well afloat.°

XCIX

If he must fain sweep o'er the ethereal plain,
    And Pegasus runs restive in his 'Waggon,'
Could he not beg the loan of Charles's Wain?
    Or pray Medea for a single dragon?°
Or if, too classic for his vulgar brain,
    He feared his neck to venture such a nag on,
And he must needs mount nearer to the moon,
Could not the blockhead ask for a balloon?

Ariosto Ludovico Ariosto (1474–1533) wrote *Orlando Furioso*, greatest of the Italian epic romances.
'longueurs' tediousness
epopée épopée, epic poetry

lakes See Wordsworth's *The Waggoner* (1819).
And . . . afloat See the opening passage of Wordsworth's *Peter Bell*.
Or . . . dragon In the *Medea* of Euripides, she escapes in a chariot pulled by dragons.

C

'Pedlars,' and 'Boats,' and 'Waggons!' Oh! ye shades
890   Of Pope and Dryden, are we come to this?
That trash of such sort not alone evades
    Contempt, but from the bathos' vast abyss
Floats scumlike uppermost, and these Jack Cades°
    Of sense and song above your graves may hiss—
The 'little boatman' and his 'Peter Bell'
Can sneer at him who drew 'Achitophel!'

        . . .

1819   1821

From *Canto the Fourth*

I

Nothing so difficult as a beginning
    In poesy, unless perhaps the end;
For oftentimes when Pegasus seems winning
    The race, he sprains a wing, and down we tend,
Like Lucifer when hurled from heaven for sinning;
    Our sin the same, and hard as his to mend,
Being pride, which leads the mind to soar too far,
Till our own weakness shows us what we are.

II

But time, which brings all beings to their level,
10   And sharp Adversity, will teach at last
Man,—and, as we would hope,—perhaps the devil,
    That neither of their intellects are vast:
While youth's hot wishes in our red veins revel,
    We know not this—the blood flows on too fast:
But as the torrent widens towards the ocean,
We ponder deeply on each past emotion.

III

As boy, I thought myself a clever fellow,
    And wished that others held the same opinion;
They took it up when my days grew more mellow,
20   And other minds acknowledged my dominion:
Now my sere fancy 'falls into the yellow
    Leaf,'° and Imagination droops her pinion,
And the sad truth which hovers o'er my desk
Turns what was once romantic to burlesque.

IV

And if I laugh at any mortal thing,
    'Tis that I may not weep; and if I weep,

Jack Cades Cade, a Pretender to the throne, led
a rebellion in 1450.

'falls . . . Leaf' See *Macbeth* V.iii.22–23, one
of Byron's favorite passages.

'Tis that our nature cannot always bring
    Itself to apathy, for we must steep
Our hearts first in the depths of Lethe's spring,
30   Ere what we least wish to behold will sleep:
Thetis baptized her mortal son in Styx;
    A mortal mother would on Lethe fix.

       V

Some have accused me of a strange design
    Against the creed and morals of the land,
And trace it in this poem every line:
    I don't pretend that I quite understand
My own meaning when I would be *very* fine;
    But the fact is that I have nothing planned,
Unless it were to be a moment merry,
40   A novel word in my vocabulary.

      VI

To the kind reader of our sober clime
    This way of writing will appear exotic;
Pulci° was sire of the half-serious rhyme,
    Who sang when chivalry was more Quixotic,
And revelled in the fancies of the time,
    True knights, chaste dames, huge giants, kings despotic;
But all these, save the last, being obsolete,
I chose a modern subject as more meet.

       . . .

1819–20   1821

From *Canto the Fifth*

    XXX

I wonder if his appetite was good?
    Or, if it were, if also his digestion?
Methinks at meals some odd thoughts might intrude,
    And conscience ask a curious sort of question,
About the right divine how far we should
    Sell flesh and blood. When dinner has oppressed one,
I think it is perhaps the gloomiest hour
240 Which turns up out of the sad twenty-four.

    XXXI

Voltaire says 'No;' he tells you that Candide
    Found life most tolerable after meals;
He's wrong—unless man were a pig, indeed,
    Repletion rather adds to what he feels,

Pulci Luigi Pulci (1432–84), Florentine poet whose *Morgante Maggiore* begins the mode that leads to *Don Juan;* Byron translated the first canto of Pulci's poem

Unless he's drunk, and then no doubt he's freed
    From his own brain's oppression while it reels.
Of food I think with Philip's son, or rather
Ammon's (ill pleased with one world and one father°);

XXXII

I think with Alexander, that the act
    Of eating, with another act or two,
250 Makes us feel our mortality in fact
    Redoubled; when a roast and a ragout,
And fish, and soup, by some side dishes backed,
    Can give us either pain or pleasure; who
Would pique himself on intellects, whose use
Depends so much upon the gastric juice?

XXXIII

The other evening ('twas on Friday last)—
    This is a fact, and no poetic fable—
Just as my great coat was about me cast,
260   My hat and gloves still lying on the table,
I heard a shot—'twas eight o'clock scarce past—
    And, running out as fast as I was able,
I found the military commandant
Stretched in the street, and able scarce to pant.

XXXIV

Poor fellow! for some reason, surely bad,
    They had slain him with five slugs; and left him there
To perish on the pavement: so I had
    Him borne into the house and up the stair,
And stripped, and looked to,—But why should I add
270   More circumstances? vain was every care;
The man was gone: in some Italian quarrel
Killed by five bullets from an old gun-barrel.

XXXV

I gazed upon him, for I knew him well;
    And though I have seen many corpses, never
Saw one, whom such an accident befell,
    So calm; though pierced through stomach, heart, and liver,
He seemed to sleep,—for you could scarcely tell
    (As he bled inwardly, no hideous river
Of gore divulged the cause) that he was dead:
280 So as I gazed on him, I thought or said—

Of . . . father Plutarch tells us that the god
Ammon, in a serpent's form, begot Alexander
the Great upon King Philip's wife; Plutarch
also says that Alexander felt his supposed
godhood threatened only by sleep and sexual
intercourse.

XXXVI

'Can this be death? then what is life or death?
    Speak!' but he spoke not: 'wake!' but still he slept:—
'But yesterday, and who had mightier breath?
    A thousand warriors by his word were kept
In awe: he said, as the centurion saith,
    "Go," and he goeth; "come," and forth he stepped.
The trump and bugle till he spake were dumb—
And now nought left him but the muffled drum.'

XXXVII

And they who waited once and worshipped—they
    With their rough faces thronged about the bed
To gaze once more on the commanding clay
    Which for the last, though not the first, time bled:
And such an end! that he who many a day
    Had faced Napoleon's foes until they fled,—
The foremost in the charge or in the sally,
Should now be butchered in a civic alley.

XXXVIII

The scars of his old wounds were near his new,
    Those honourable scars which brought him fame;
And horrid was the contrast to the view——
    But let me quit the theme; as such things claim
Perhaps even more attention than is due
    From me: I gazed (as oft I have gazed the same)
To try if I could wrench aught out of death
Which should confirm, or shake, or make a faith;

XXXIX

But it was all a mystery. Here we are,
    And there we go:—but *where?* five bits of lead,
Or three, or two, or one, send very far!
    And is this blood, then, formed but to be shed?
Can every element our elements mar?
    And air—earth—water—fire live—and we dead?
We, whose minds comprehend all things? No more;
But let us to the story as before.

1820   · · ·   1821

From *Canto the Seventh*

I

O Love! O Glory! what are you who fly
    Around us ever, rarely to alight?
There's not a meteor in the Polar sky

Of such transcendent and more fleeting flight.
Chill, and chained to cold earth, we lift on high
    Our eyes in search of either lovely light;
A thousand and a thousand colours they
Assume, then leave us on our freezing way.

II

And such as they are, such my present tale is,
10   A nondescript and ever-varying rhyme,
A versified Aurora Borealis, '
    Which flashes o'er a waste and icy clime.
When we know what all are, we must bewail us,
    But ne'ertheless I hope it is no crime
To laugh at *all* things—for I wish to know
What, after *all*, are *all* things—but a *show?*

III

They accuse me—*Me*—the present writer of
    The present poem—of—I know not what—
A tendency to under-rate and scoff
20   At human power and virtue, and all that;
And this they say in language rather rough.
    Good God! I wonder what they would be at!
I say no more than hath been said in Dante's
Verse, and by Solomon and by Cervantes;

IV

By Swift, by Machiavel, by Rochefoucault,°
    By Fénelon,° by Luther, and by Plato;
By Tillotson,° and Wesley,° and Rousseau,
    Who knew this life was not worth a potato.
'Tis not their fault, nor mine, if this be so,—
30   For my part, I pretend not to be Cato,°
Nor even Diogenes.°—We live and die,
But which is best, you know no more than I.

V

Socrates said, our only knowledge was
    'To know that nothing could be known;' a pleasant
Science enough, which levels to an ass
    Each man of wisdom, future, past, or present.
Newton (that proverb of the mind), alas!
    Declared, with all his grand discoveries recent,

Rochefoucault François, Duke of La Roche-
foucauld, 17th-century French secular moralist
Fénelon 17th-century French Quietist and religious moralist
Tillotson John Tillotson, 17th-century English
divine and prose stylist

Wesley John Wesley, 18th-century Methodist
leader
Cato Cato the Younger (Roman politician, 1st
century B.C.), known for his moral uprightness
Diogenes ascetic and Cynic philosopher

That he himself felt only 'like a youth
40 Picking up shells by the great ocean—Truth.'

VI

Ecclesiastes said, 'that all is vanity'—
    Most modern preachers say the same, or show it
By their examples of true Christianity:
    In short, all know, or very soon may know it;
And in this scene of all-confessed inanity,
    By saint, by sage, by preacher, and by poet,
Must I restrain me, through the fear of strife,
From holding up the nothingness of life?

VII

Dogs, or men!—for I flatter you in saying
50   That ye are dogs—your betters far—ye may
Read, or read not, what I am now essaying
    To show ye what ye are in every way.
As little as the moon stops for the baying
    Of wolves, will the bright Muse withdraw one ray
From out her skies—then howl your idle wrath!
While she still silvers o'er your gloomy path.

VIII

'Fierce loves and faithless wars'—I am not sure
    If this be the right reading—'tis no matter;°
The fact's about the same, I am secure;
60   I sing them both, and am about to batter
A town which did a famous siege endure,
    And was beleaguer'd both by land and water
By Souvaroff, or Anglicè Suwarrow,°
Who loved blood as an alderman loves marrow.

        .   .   .

1822   1823

From *Canto the Ninth*

LXII

Though somewhat large, exuberant, and truculent,
490   When *wroth*—while *pleased*, she° was as fine a figure
As those who like things rosy, ripe, and succulent,
    Would wish to look on, while they are in vigour.
She could repay each amatory look you lent
    With interest, and in turn was wont with rigour

'**Fierce . . . matter** Byron deliberately reverses
Spenser's "Fierce wars and faithful loves shall
moralize my song," the last line of *The Faerie
Queene's* first stanza.
Suwarrow The Russian general Suvaroff attacked

Ismael, a Danubian Turkish fortress-town, on
November 30, 1790; "Anglicè" means "the
English spelling."
she Catherine the Great, Empress of Russia,
notorious for her intense sexual life

To exact of Cupid's bills the full amount
At sight, nor would permit you to discount.

LXIII

With her the latter, though at times convenient,
    Was not so necessary; for they tell
That she was handsome, and though fierce *looked* lenient,
500   And always used her favourites too well.
If once beyond her boudoir's precincts in ye went,
    Your 'fortune' was in a fair way 'to swell
A man' (as Giles says°); for though she would widow all
Nations, she liked man as an individual.

LXIV

What a strange thing is man! and what a stranger
    Is woman! What a whirlwind is her head,
And what a whirlpool full of depth and danger
    Is all the rest about her! Whether wed,
Or widow, maid, or mother, she can change her
510   Mind like the wind: whatever she has said
Or done, is light to what she'll say or do;—
The oldest thing on record, and yet new!

LXV

Oh Catherine! (for of all interjections,
    To thee both *oh!* and *ah!* belong of right
In love and war) how odd are the connexions
    Of human thoughts, which jostle in their flight!
Just now *yours* were cut out in different sections:
    First Ismail's capture caught your fancy quite;
Next of new knights, the fresh and glorious batch;
520   And *thirdly* he who brought you the despatch!

LXVI

Shakespeare talks of 'the herald Mercury
    New lighted on a heaven-kissing hill:'°
And some such visions crossed her majesty,
    While her young herald knelt before her still.
'Tis very true the hill seemed rather high,
    For a lieutenant to climb up; but skill
Smooth'd even the Simplon's steep,° and by God's blessing,
With youth and health all kisses are 'heaven-kissing.'

Giles says See Philip Massinger's *A New Way To Pay Old Debts* V.i, where Sir Giles Overreach says: "His fortune swells him: 'tis rank, he's married."

Shakespeare . . . hill see *Hamlet* III.iv.58–59
Simplon's steep side of mountain pass in Swiss Alps

LXVII

Her majesty looked down, the youth looked up—
530   And so they fell in love;—she with his face,
His grace, his God-knows-what: for Cupid's cup
    With the first draught intoxicates apace,
A quintessential laudanum or 'black drop,'
    Which makes one drunk at once, without the base
Expedient of full bumpers; for the eye
In love drinks all life's fountains (save tears) dry.

LXVIII

He, on the other hand, if not in love,
    Fell into that no less imperious passion,
Self-love—which, when some sort of thing above
540   Ourselves, a singer, dancer, much in fashion,
Or duchess, princess, empress, 'deigns to prove'
    ('Tis Pope's phrase°) a great longing, though a rash one.
For one especial person out of many,
Makes us believe ourselves as good as any.

LXIX

Besides, he was of that delighted age
    Which makes all female ages equal—when
We don't much care with whom we may engage,
    As bold as Daniel in the lions' den,
So that we can our native sun assuage
550   In the next ocean, which may flow just then,
To make a twilight in, just as Sol's heat is
Quenched in the lap of the salt sea, or Thetis.

LXX

And Catherine (we must say thus much for Catherine),
    Though bold and bloody, was the kind of thing
Whose temporary passion was quite flattering,
    Because each lover looked a sort of king,
Made up upon an amatory pattern,
    A royal husband in all save the *ring*—
Which, being the damnedest part of matrimony,
560   Seemed taking out the sting to leave the honey.

LXXI

And when you add to this, her womanhood
    In its meridian, her blue eyes or gray—
(The last, if they have soul, are quite as good,
    Or better, as the best examples say:
Napoleon's, Mary's (queen of Scotland), should

Pope's phrase See *Eloisa to Abelard*, ll. 87–88.

Lend to that colour a transcendent ray;
And Pallas also sanctions the same hue,
Too wise to look through optics black or blue)—

LXXII
Her sweet smile, and her then majestic figure,
570   Her plumpness, her imperial condescension,
Her preference of a boy to men much bigger
(Fellows whom Messalina's self would pension),
Her prime of life, just now in juicy vigour,
With other *extras*, which we need not mention,—
All these, or any one of these, explain
Enough to make a stripling very vain.

LXXIII
And that's enough, for love is vanity,
Selfish in its beginning as its end,
Except where 'tis a mere insanity,
580   A maddening spirit which would strive to blend
Itself with beauty's frail inanity,
On which the passion's self seems to depend:
And hence some heathenish philosophers
Make love the main-spring of the universe.

LXXIV
Besides Platonic love, besides the love
Of God, the love of sentiment, the loving
Of faithful pairs—I needs must rhyme with dove,
That good old steam-boat which keeps verses moving
'Gainst reason—Reason ne'er was hand-and-glove
590   With rhyme, but always leant less to improving
The sound than sense) besides all these pretences
To love, there are those things which words name senses;

LXXV
Those movements, those improvements in our bodies
Which make all bodies anxious to get out
Of their own sand-pits, to mix with a goddess,
For such all women are at first no doubt.
How beautiful that moment! and how odd is
That fever which precedes the languid rout
Of our sensations! What a curious way
600   The whole thing is of clothing souls in clay!

LXXVI
The noblest kind of love is love Platonical,
To end or to begin with; the next grand
Is that which may be christened love canonical,

Because the clergy take the thing in hand;
The third sort to be noted in our chronicle
    As flourishing in every Christian land,
Is, when chaste matrons to their other ties
Add what may be called *marriage in disguise*.

LXXVII

Well, we won't analyse—our story must
    Tell for itself: the sovereign was smitten,
Juan much flattered by her love, or lust;—
    I cannot stop to alter words once written,
And the two are so mixed with human dust,
    That he who *names one*, both perchance may hit on:
But in such matters Russia's mighty empress
Behaved no better than a common sempstress.

. . .

1822   1823

From *Canto the Eleventh*

LIII

Juan knew several languages—as well
    He might—and brought them up with skill, in time
To save his fame with each accomplished belle,
    Who still regretted that he did not rhyme.
There wanted but this requisite to swell
    His qualities (with them) into sublime:
Lady Fitz-Frisky, and Miss Maevia Mannish,
Both longed extremely to be sung in Spanish.

LIV

However, he did pretty well, and was
    Admitted as an aspirant to all
The coteries, and, as in Banquo's glass,
    At great assemblies or in parties small,
He saw ten thousand living authors pass,
    That being about their average numeral;
Also the eighty 'greatest living poets,'
As every paltry magazine can show *it's*.

LV

In twice five years the 'greatest living poet,'
    Like to the champion in the fisty ring,
Is called on to support his claim, or show it,
    Although 'tis an imaginary thing.
Even I—albeit I'm sure I did not know it,
    Nor sought of foolscap subjects to be king,—
Was reckoned, a considerable time,
The grand Napoleon of the realms of rhyme.

LVI

But Juan was my Moscow,° and Faliero°
My Leipsic,° and my Mont Saint Jean° seems Cain:°
'La Belle Alliance' of dunces down at zero,
  Now that the Lion's fallen, may rise again:
But I will fall at least as fell my hero;
  Nor reign at all, or as a *monarch* reign;
Or to some lonely isle of gaolers go,
With turncoat Southey for my turnkey Lowe.°

LVII

Sir Walter reigned before me; Moore and Campbell
450 Before and after: but now grown more holy,
The Muses upon Sion's hill must ramble
  With poets almost clergymen, or wholly;
And Pegasus has a psalmodic amble
  Beneath the very Reverend Rowley Powley,°
Who shoes the glorious animal with stilts,
A modern Ancient Pistol°—by the hilts!

LVIII

Still he excels that artificial hard
  Labourer in the same vineyard, though the vine
Yields him but vinegar for his reward,—
460 That neutralised dull Dorus of the Nine;
That swarthy Sporus,° neither man nor bard;
  That ox of verse, who *ploughs* for every line:—
Cambyses' roaring Romans beat at least
The howling Hebrews of Cybele's priest.°—

LIX

Then there's my gentle Euphues; who, they say,
  Sets up for being a sort of *moral me;*°
He'll find it rather difficult some day
  To turn out both, or either, it may be.
Some persons think that Coleridge hath the sway;
470 And Wordsworth has supporters, two or three;

But . . . Moscow Paralleling his literary career with Napoleon's military one, Byron dates his decline with the reading public from the publication of Canto I of *Don Juan.*
Faliero *Marino Faliero: An Historical Tragedy,* by Byron
Leipsic "The Battle of the Nations," where Napoleon was defeated in 1813
Mont Saint Jean farmhouse on Waterloo battlefield, symbol of Napoleon's final defeat
Cain Byron's great dramatic poem; much denounced for impiety and incest when it was published in 1821
Lowe Sir Hudson Lowe, captor of Napoleon on St. Helena

Powley the Reverend George Croly, a contemporary poet who had imitated Byron's work
Pistol See I *Henry IV* II.iv.197.
Sporus Pope's satirical name for Lord Hervey in his *Epistle to Dr. Arbuthnot*
That ox . . . priest Henry Hart Milman, Professor of Poetry at Oxford, whom Byron considered a critical enemy, is the "Ox of verse"; Leslie Marchand identifies the roaring Romans as being from Croly's *Cataline* and the howling Hebrews from Milman's *Fall of Jerusalem.*
Then . . . me B. W. Procter, a poet who wrote under the name of "Barry Cornwall"

And that deep-mouthed Boeotian 'Savage Landor'°
Has taken for a swan rogue Southey's gander.

LX

John Keats, who was killed off by one critique,
 Just as he really promised something great,
If not intelligible, without Greek
 Contrived to talk about the Gods of late,
Much as they might have been supposed to speak.°
 Poor fellow! His was an untoward fate;
'Tis strange the mind, that fiery particle,
Should let itself be snuffed out by an article.

LXI

The list grows long of live and dead pretenders
 To that which none will gain—or none will know
The conqueror at least; who, ere Time renders
 His last award, will have the long grass grow
Above his burnt-out brain, and sapless cinders.
 If I might augur, I should rate but low
Their chances;—they're too numerous, like the thirty
Mock tyrants, when Rome's annals waxed but dirty.

LXII

This is the literary *lower* empire,
 Where the praetorian bands take up the matter;—
A 'dreadful trade,' like his who 'gathers samphire,'°
 The insolent soldiery to soothe and flatter,
With the same feelings as you'd coax a vampire.
 Now, were I once at home, and in good satire,
I'd try conclusions with those Janizaries,°
And show them *what* an intellectual war is.

LXIII

I think I know a trick or two, would turn
 Their flanks;—but it is hardly worth my while
With such small gear to give myself concern:
 Indeed I've not the necessary bile;
My natural temper's really aught but stern,
 And even my Muse's worst reproof's a smile;
And then she drops a brief and modern curtsy,
And glides away, assured she never hurts ye.

480

490

500

Landor The Greeks thought the Boeotians to be savage and stupid; Landor was neither, but had a fierce temper; Landor was also on excellent terms with Southey.
John . . . speak in the great fragment *Hype-*rion; this is Byron's first praise for Keats's poetry
A . . . samphire See *King Lear* IV.vi.15.
Janizaries Turkish soldiers, particularly of the Sultan's Guard

LXIV

My Juan, whom I left in deadly peril
   Amongst live poets and blue ladies, passed
With some small profit through that field so sterile,
   Being tired in time, and neither least nor last,
Left it before he had been treated very ill;
510   And henceforth found himself more gaily classed
Amongst the higher spirits of the day,
The sun's true son, no vapour, but a ray.

              .   .   .

1822   ———————————————— 1823

Stanzas to the Po°

River, that rollest by the ancient walls,
   Where dwells the Lady of my love, when she
Walks by thy brink, and there perchance recalls
   A faint and fleeting memory of me;

What if thy deep and ample stream should be
   A mirror of my heart, where she may read
The thousand thoughts I now betray to thee,
   Wild as thy wave, and headlong as thy speed!

What do I say—a mirror of my heart?
10   Are not thy waters sweeping, dark, and strong?
Such as my feelings were and are, thou art;
   And such as thou art were my passions long.

Time may have somewhat tamed them,—not for ever;
   Thou overflowest thy banks, and not for aye
Thy bosom overboils, congenial river!
   Thy floods subside, and mine have sunk away—

But left long wrecks behind: and now again,
   Borne in our old unchanged career, we move:
Thou tendest wildly onwards to the main.
20   And I—to loving *one* I should not love.

The current I behold will sweep beneath
   Her native walls, and murmur at her feet;
Her eyes will look on thee, when she shall breathe
   The twilight air, unharmed by summer's heat.

She will look on thee,—I have looked on thee,
   Full of that thought; and, from that moment, ne'er

Stanzas to the Po This lyric, Byron's most accomplished, echoes the firm diction and grave sweet style of some of Dante's love poems. The poem was written only a few weeks after Byron, aged thirty-one, fell in love with the Countess Teresa Guiccioli, aged nineteen, who had been married only a year or so to the fifty-eight-year-old Count. Briefly separated from Teresa, he wrote the first draft of this poem, in which he struggles not to yield to love.

Thy waters could I dream of, name, or see,
   Without the inseparable sigh for her!

Her bright eyes will be imaged in thy stream,—
30   Yes! they will meet the wave I gaze on now:
Mine cannot witness, even in a dream,
   That happy wave repass me in its flow!

The wave that bears my tears returns no more:
   Will she return by whom that wave shall sweep?—
Both tread thy banks, both wander on thy shore,
   I by thy source, she by the dark-blue deep.

But that which keepeth us apart is not
   Distance, nor depth of wave, nor space of earth,
But the distraction of a various lot,
40   As various as the climates of our birth.

A stranger loves the Lady of the land,
   Born far beyond the mountains, but his blood
Is all meridian,° as if never fanned
   By the black wind that chills the polar flood.

My blood is all meridian; were it not,
   I had not left my clime, nor should I be,
In spite of tortures, ne'er to be forgot,
   A slave again of love,—at least of thee.

'Tis vain to struggle—let me perish young—
50   Live as I lived, and love as I have loved;
To dust if I return, from dust I sprung,
   And then, at least, my heart can ne'er be moved.°
  1819   1824

The Vision of Judgment

This is a satire on Robert Southey, a talented and highly productive man of letters, but generally a bad poet; Byron is quite kind to the deceased monarch George III, who needed kindness, as he had been a miserable failure, and died blind and crazy. Southey, like his friends of genius, Wordsworth and Coleridge, was a political

---

meridian the point at which the sun attains its highest altitude

My blood . . . moved Less than two months later, Byron ceased to hesitate and moved to join Teresa, and then redrafted the last two stanzas:

   My heart is all meridian, were it not
     I had not suffered now, nor should
     I be
   Despite old tortures ne'er to be forgot
     The slave again—Oh! Love! at least
     of thee!

'Tis vain to struggle, I have
   struggled long
To love again no more as once I
   loved,
Oh! Time! why leave this worst of
   earliest Passions strong?
To tear a heart which pants to be
   unmoved?

Revealing as this is, Byron was wise to keep to the first version.

turncoat, but also had accepted appointment as Poet Laureate upon the death of the bad poet Pye in 1813. This was enough for Byron to despise him, but Byron heard in 1817 that Southey was active in spreading scandalous rumors about him. The 1818 Dedication to the First Canto of *Don Juan* began the destruction of Southey; this brilliant poem completed it, and has given poor Southey the only immortality he has.

Southey's *A Vision of Judgment*, as befits an official lament for George III, opens with a preface in which the Laureate attacks "the Satanic School" of rebels and immoralists: Byron, Shelley, and their friends. The Laureate then goes into a trance, and "sees" the King gloriously accepted into Heaven.

The Vision of Judgment

I

Saint Peter sat by the celestial gate:
   His keys were rusty, and the lock was dull,
So little trouble had been given of late;
   Not that the place by any means was full,
But since the Gallic era 'eighty-eight'°
   The devils had ta'en a longer, stronger pull,
And 'a pull altogether,' as they say
At sea—which drew most souls another way.

II

The angels all were singing out of tune,
10   And hoarse with having little else to do,
Excepting to wind up the sun and moon,
   Or curb a runaway young star or two,
Or wild colt of a comet, which too soon
   Broke out of bounds o'er the ethereal blue,
Splitting some planet with its playful tail,
As boats are sometimes by a wanton whale.

III

The guardian seraphs had retired on high,
   Finding their charges past all care below;
Terrestrial business filled nought in the sky
20   Save the recording angel's black bureau;
Who found, indeed, the facts to multiply
   With such rapidity of vice and woe,
That he had stripped off both his wings in quills,
And yet was in arrear of human ills.

IV

His business so augmented of late years,
   That he was forced, against his will no doubt,

'eighty-eight' Byron takes 1788 as the start of
the French Revolution.

(Just like those cherubs, earthly ministers,)
  For some resource to turn himself about,
And claim the help of his celestial peers,
30   To aid him ere he should be quite worn out
By the increased demand for his remarks;
  Six angels and twelve saints were named his clerks.

v

This was a handsome board—at least for heaven;
  And yet they had even then enough to do,
So many conquerors' cars were daily driven,
  So many kingdoms fitted up anew;
Each day too slew its thousands six or seven,
  Till at the crowning carnage, Waterloo,
They threw their pens down in divine disgust—
40 The page was so besmeared with blood and dust.

vi

This by the way; 'tis not mine to record
  What angels shrink from: even the very devil
On this occasion his own work abhorred,
  So surfeited with the infernal revel:
Though he himself had sharpened every sword,
  It almost quenched his innate thirst of evil.
(Here Satan's sole good work deserves insertion—
'Tis, that he has both generals in reversion.°)

vii

Let's skip a few short years of hollow peace,
50   Which peopled earth no better, hell as wont,
And heaven none—they form the tyrant's lease,
  With nothing but new names subscribed upon't;
'Twill one day finish: meantime they increase,
  'With seven heads and ten horns,' and all in front,
Like Saint John's foretold beast; but ours are born
Less formidable in the head than horn.

viii

In the first year of freedom's second dawn°
  Died George the Third; although no tyrant, one
Who shielded tyrants, till each sense withdrawn
60   Left him nor mental nor external sun:
A better farmer ne'er brushed dew from lawn,
  A worse king never left a realm undone!
He died—but left his subjects still behind,
One half as mad—and t'other no less blind.

Here . . . reversion Napoleon and Wellington   the first revolutionary upsurge since the Congress
are marked out for Satan.   of Vienna (1814–15).
second dawn 1820, when George III died, saw

IX

He died! his death made no great stir on earth;
  His burial made some pomp; there was profusion
Of velvet, gilding, brass, and no great dearth
  Of aught but tears—save those shed by collusion.
For these things may be bought at their true worth;
70 Of elegy there was the due infusion—
Bought also; and the torches, cloaks, and banners,
Heralds, and relics of old Gothic manners,

X

Formed a sepulchral melodrame. Of all
  The fools who flocked to swell or see the show,
Who cared about the corpse? The funeral
  Made the attraction, and the black the woe.
There throbbed not there a thought which pierced the pall;
  And when the gorgeous coffin was laid low,
It seemed the mockery of hell to fold
80 The rottenness of eighty years in gold.

XI

So mix his body with the dust! It might
  Return to what it *must* far sooner, were
The natural compound left alone to fight
  Its way back into earth, and fire, and air;
But the unnatural balsams merely blight
  What nature made him at his birth, as bare
As the mere million's base unmummied clay—
Yet all his spices but prolong decay.

XII

He's dead—and upper earth with him has done;
90 He's buried; save the undertaker's bill,
Or lapidary° scrawl, the world is gone
  For him, unless he left a German will;°
But where's the proctor who will ask his son?
  In whom his qualities are reigning still,
Except that household virtue, most uncommon,
Of constancy to a bad, ugly woman.

XIII

'God save the king!' It is a large economy
  In God to save the like; but if he will
Be saving, all the better; for not one am I
100 Of those who think damnation better still:
I hardly know too if not quite alone am I

lapidary a polisher of precious stones   III, hid away the will of his father, George I.
a German will George II, grandfather of George

In this small hope of bettering future ill
By circumscribing, with some slight restriction,
The eternity of hell's hot jurisdiction.

XIV

I know this is unpopular; I know
    'Tis blasphemous; I know one may be damned
For hoping no one else may e'er be so;
    I know my catechism; I know we're crammed
With the best doctrines till we quite o'erflow;
    I know that all save England's church have shammed,
And that the other twice two hundred churches
And synagogues have made a *damned* bad purchase.

XV

God help us all! God help me too! I am,
    God knows, as helpless as the devil can wish,
And not a whit more difficult to damn,
    Than is to bring to land a late-hooked fish,
Or to the butcher to purvey the lamb;
    Not that I'm fit for such a noble dish,
As one day will be that immortal fry
Of almost everybody born to die.

XVI

Saint Peter sat by the celestial gate,
    And nodded o'er his keys; when, lo! there came
A wondrous noise he had not heard of late—
    A rushing sound of wind, and stream, and flame;
In short, a roar of things extremely great,
    Which would have made aught save a saint exclaim;
But he, with first a start and then a wink,
Said, 'There's another star gone out, I think!'

XVII

But ere he could return to his repose,
    A cherub flapped his right wing o'er his eyes—
At which St. Peter yawned, and rubbed his nose:
    'Saint porter,' said the angel, 'prithee rise!'
Waving a goodly wing, which glowed, as glows
    An earthly peacock's tail, with heavenly dyes:
To which the saint replied, 'Well, what's the matter?
Is Lucifer come back with all this clatter?'

XVIII

'No,' quoth the cherub; 'George the Third is dead.'
    'And who *is* George the Third?' replied the apostle:
'*What George? what Third?*' 'The king of England,' said

140 The angel. 'Well! he won't find kings to jostle
Him on his way; but does he wear his head;
  Because the last we saw here had a tustle,°
And ne'er would have got into heaven's good graces,
Had he not flung his head in all our faces.°

    XIX
'He was, if I remember, king of France;
  That head of his, which could not keep a crown
On earth, yet ventured in my face to advance
  A claim to those of martyrs—like my own:
If I had had my sword, as I had once
150 When I cut ears off, I had cut him down;
But having but my *keys*, and not my brand,
I only knocked his head from out his hand.

    XX
'And then he set up such a headless howl,
  That all the saints came out and took him in;
And there he sits by St. Paul, cheek by jowl;
  That fellow Paul—the parvenù! The skin
Of St. Bartholomew, which makes his cowl
  In heaven, and upon earth redeemed his sin°
So as to make a martyr, never sped
160 Better than did this weak and wooden head.

    XXI
'But had it come up here upon its shoulders,
  There would have been a different tale to tell:
The fellow-feeling in the saint's beholders
  Seems to have acted on them like a spell;
And so this very foolish head heaven solders
  Back on its trunk: it may be very well,
And seems the custom here to overthrow
Whatever has been wisely done below.'

    XXII
The angel answered, 'Peter! do not pout:
170 The king who comes has head and all entire,
And never knew much what it was about—
  He did as doth the puppet—by its wire,
And will be judged like all the rest, no doubt:
  My business and your own is not to inquire
Into such matters, but to mind our cue—
Which is to act as we are bid to do.'

tustle tussle
Had . . . faces Louis XVI of France, guillotined
in 1793

The skin . . . sin St. Bartholomew was first
skinned alive, and then crucified.

XXIII

While thus they spake, the angelic caravan,
    Arriving like a rush of mighty wind,
Cleaving the fields of space, as doth the swan
    Some silver stream (say Ganges, Nile, or Inde,
Or Thames, or Tweed), and 'midst them an old man
    With an old soul, and both extremely blind,
Halted before the gate, and in his shroud
Seated their fellow-traveller on a cloud.

XXIV

But bringing up the rear of this bright host
    A Spirit of a different aspect waved
His wings, like thunder-clouds above some coast
    Whose barren beach with frequent wrecks is paved;
His brow was like the deep when tempest-tossed;
    Fierce and unfathomable thoughts engraved
Eternal wrath on his immortal face,
And *where* he gazed a gloom pervaded space.

XXV

As he drew near, he gazed upon the gate
    Ne'er to be entered more by him or Sin,
With such a glance of supernatural hate,
    As made Saint Peter wish himself within;
He patterned with his keys at a great rate,
    And sweated through his apostolic skin:
Of course his perspiration was but ichor,°
Or some such other spiritual liquor.

XXVI

The very cherubs huddled all together,
    Like birds when soars the falcon; and they felt
A tingling to the tip of every feather,
    And formed a circle like Orion's belt
Around their poor old charge; who scarce knew whither
    His guards had led him, though they gently dealt
With royal manes (for by many stories,
And true, we learn the angels all are Tories).

XXVII

As things were in this posture, the gate flew
    Asunder, and the flashing of its hinges
Flung over space an universal hue
    Of many-coloured flame, until its tinges
Reached even our speck of earth, and made a new

---

ichor The gods had ichor, an ethereal liquid,
rather than blood in their veins.

180

190

200

210

Aurora borealis spread its fringes
O'er the North Pole; the same seen, when ice-bound,
By Captain Parry's crew, in 'Melville's Sound.'°

XXVIII

And from the gate thrown open issued beaming
    A beautiful and mighty Thing of Light,
Radiant with glory, like a banner streaming
220   Victorious from some world-o'erthrowing fight:
My poor comparisons must needs be teeming
    With earthly likenesses, for here the night
Of clay obscures our best conceptions, saving
Johanna Southcote,° or Bob Southey raving.

XXIX

'Twas the archangel Michael: all men know
    The make of angels and archangels, since
There's scarce a scribbler has not one to show,
    From the fiends' leader to the angels' prince.
There also are some altar-pieces, though
230   I really can't say that they much evince
One's inner notions of immortal spirits;
But let the connoisseurs explain *their* merits.

XXX

Michael flew forth in glory and in good;
    A goodly work of him from whom all glory
And good arise; the portal past—he stood;
    Before him the young cherubs and saints hoary—
(I say *young*, begging to be understood
    By looks, not years; and should be very sorry
To state, they were not older than St. Peter,
240   But merely that they seemed a little sweeter).

XXXI

The cherubs and the saints bowed down before
    That arch-angelic hierarch, the first
Of essences angelical, who wore
    The aspect of a god; but this ne'er nursed
Pride in his heavenly bosom, in whose core
    No thought, save for his Master's service, durst
Intrude, however glorified and high;
He knew him but the viceroy of the sky.

'Melville's Sound' described by Sir William
Edward Parry in his account of his voyages in
quest of the Northwest Passage (1819–20)
Johanna Southcote Joanna Southcott (1750–
1814), authoress of the *Book of Wonders*, a
prophetess who expected to bear the Messiah,
but died of a brain malady instead

XXXII

He and the sombre silent Spirit met—
    They knew each other both for good and ill;
Such was their power, that neither could forget
    His former friend and future foe; but still
There was a high, immortal, proud regret
    In either's eye, as if 'twere less their will
Than destiny to make the eternal years
Their date of war, and their 'champ clos'° the spheres.

XXXIII

But here they were in neutral space: we know
    From Job,° that Satan hath the power to pay
A heavenly visit thrice a year or so;
    And that the 'sons of God,' like those of clay,
Must keep him company; and we might show
    From the same book, in how polite a way
The dialogue is held between the Powers
Of Good and Evil—but 'twould take up hours.

XXXIV

And this is not a theologic tract,
    To prove with Hebrew and with Arabic
If Job be allegory or a fact,
    But a true narrative; and thus I pick
From out the whole but such and such an act
    As sets aside the slightest thought of trick.
'Tis every tittle true, beyond suspicion,
And accurate as any other vision.

XXXV

The spirits were in neutral space, before
    The gate of heaven; like eastern thresholds is
The place where Death's grand cause is argued o'er,°
    And souls dispatched to that world or to this;
And therefore Michael and the other wore
    A civil aspect: though they did not kiss,
Yet still between his Darkness and his Brightness
There passed a mutual glance of great politeness.

XXXVI

The Archangel bowed, not like a modern beau,
    But with a graceful oriental bend,
Pressing one radiant arm just where below
    The heart in good men is supposed to tend.

'champ clos' tournament field, therefore closed off
Job Job 1:2

The spirits . . . o'er Oriental cities frequently debated policy and dealt out justice in their gateways.

He turned as to an equal, not too low,
 But kindly; Satan met his ancient friend
With more hauteur, as might an old Castilian
Poor noble meet a mushroom rich civilian.

XXXVII

He merely bent his diabolic brow
290   An instant; and then raising it, he stood
In act to assert his right or wrong, and show
 Cause why King George by no means could or should
Make out a case to be exempt from woe
 Eternal, more than other kings, endued
With better sense and hearts, whom history mentions,
Who long have 'paved hell with their good intentions.'

XXXVIII

Michael began: 'What wouldst thou with this man,
 Now dead, and brought before the Lord? What ill
Hath he wrought since his mortal race began,
300   That thou canst claim him? Speak! and do thy will,
If it be just: if in this earthly span
 He hath been greatly failing to fulfil
His duties as a king and mortal, say,
And he is thine; if not, let him have way.'

XXXIX

'Michael!' replied the Prince of Air, 'even here,
 Before the Gate of him thou servest, must
I claim my subject: and will make appear
 That as he was my worshipper in dust,
So shall he be in spirit, although dear
310   To thee and thine, because nor wine nor lust
Were of his weaknesses; yet on the throne
He reigned o'er millions to serve me alone.

XL

Look to *our* earth, or rather *mine;* it was,
 Once, more thy master's: but I triumph not
In this poor planet's conquest; nor, alas!
 Need he thou servest envy me my lot:
With all the myriads of bright worlds which pass
 In worship round him, he may have forgot
Yon weak creation of such paltry things:
320   I think few worth damnation save their kings,—

XLI

'And these but as a kind of quit-rent,° to
 Assert my right as lord: and even had

quit-rent feudal arrangement in which small
fixed sum was paid to overlord in lieu of
services due

I such an inclination, 'twere (as you
   Well know) superfluous; they are grown so bad,
That hell has nothing better left to do
   Than leave them to themselves: so much more mad
And evil by their own internal curse,
Heaven cannot make them better, nor I worse.

      XLII
'Look to the earth, I said, and say again:
330   When this old, blind, mad, helpless, weak, poor worm
Began in youth's first bloom and flush to reign,
   The world and he both wore a different form,
And much of earth and all the watery plain
   Of ocean called him king: through many a storm
His isles had floated on the abyss of time;
For the rough virtues chose them for their clime.

      XLIII
'He came to his sceptre young; he leaves it old:
   Look to the state in which he found his realm,
And left it; and his annals too behold,
340   How to a minion first he gave the helm;°
How grew upon his heart a thirst for gold,
   The beggar's vice, which can but overwhelm
The meanest hearts; and for the rest, but glance
Thine eye along America and France.

      XLIV
' 'Tis true, he was a tool from first to last
   (I have the workmen safe); but as a tool
So let him be consumed. From out the past
   Of ages, since mankind have known the rule
Of monarchs—from the bloody rolls amassed
350   Of sin and slaughter—from the Caesar's school,
Take the worst pupil; and produce a reign
More drenched with gore, more cumbered with the slain.

      XLV
'He ever warred with freedom and the free:
   Nations as men, home subjects, foreign foes,
So that they uttered the word "Liberty!"
   Found George the Third their first opponent. Whose
History was ever stained as his will be
   With national and individual woes?
I grant his household abstinence; I grant
360   His neutral virtues, which most monarchs want;

How . . . helm The minion was the Earl of
Bute, Prime Minister (1762–63).

XLVI

'I know he was a constant consort; own
   He was a decent sire, and middling lord.
All this is much, and most upon a throne;
   As temperance, if at Apicius' board,°
Is more than at an anchorite's supper shown.
   I grant him all the kindest can accord;
And this was well for him, but not for those
Millions who found him what oppression chose.

XLVII

'The New World shook him off; the Old yet groans
370   Beneath what he and his prepared, if not
Completed: he leaves heirs on many thrones
   To all his vices, without what begot
Compassion for him—his tame virtues; drones
   Who sleep, or despots who have now forgot
A lesson which shall be re-taught them, wake
Upon the thrones of earth; but let them quake!

XLVIII

'Five millions of the primitive, who hold
   The faith which makes ye great on earth, implored
A *part* of that vast *all* they held of old,—
380   Freedom to worship—not alone your Lord,
Michael, but you, and you, Saint Peter! Cold
   Must be your souls, if you have not abhorred
The foe to Catholic participation
In all the license of a Christian nation.°

XLIX

'True! he allowed them to pray God; but as
   A consequence of prayer, refused the law
Which would have placed them upon the same base
   With those who did not hold the saints in awe.'
But here Saint Peter started from his place,
390   And cried, 'You may the prisoner withdraw:
Ere heaven shall ope her portals to this Guelph,°
While I am guard, may I be damned myself!

L

'Sooner will I with Cerberus° exchange
   My office (and *his* is no sinecure)
Than see this royal Bedlam bigot range

Apicius' board Apicius was a famous epicure in Augustan Rome.
The foe . . . nation George III had opposed the enfranchisement of the Catholic Irish.

Guelph family name of House of Hanover, the line of George III
Cerberus three-headed dog who guarded the gates of Hades

The azure fields of heaven, of that be sure!'
'Saint!' replied Satan, 'you do well to avenge
   The wrongs he made your satellites endure;
And if to this exchange you should be given,
400   I'll try to coax *our* Cerberus up to heaven.

      LI
Here Michael interposed: 'Good saint! and devil!
   Pray, not so fast; you both outrun discretion.
Saint Peter! you were wont to be more civil!
   Satan! excuse this warmth of his expression,
And condescension to the vulgar's level:
   Even saints sometimes forget themselves in session.
Have you got more to say?'—'No.'—'If you please,
I'll trouble you to call your witnesses.'

      LII
Then Satan turned and waved his swarthy hand,
410   Which stirred with its electric qualities
Clouds farther off than we can understand,
   Although we find him sometimes in our skies;
Infernal thunder shook both sea and land
   In all the planets, and hell's batteries
Let off the artillery, which Milton mentions°
As one of Satan's most sublime inventions.

      LIII
This was a signal unto such damned souls
   As have the privilege of their damnation
Extended far beyond the mere controls
420   Of worlds past, present, or to come; no station
Is theirs particularly in the rolls
   Of hell assigned; but where their inclination
Or business carries them in search of game,
They may range freely—being damned the same.

      LIV
They're proud of this—as very well they may,
   It being a sort of knighthood, or gilt key°
Stuck in their loins; or like to an 'entré'
   Up the back stairs, or such free-masonry.
I borrow my comparisons from clay,
430   Being clay myself. Let not those spirits be
Offended with such base low likenesses;
We know their posts are nobler far than these.

Milton mentions *Paradise Lost* VI.484–85   gilt key insignia of court officials

LV

When the great signal ran from heaven to hell—
  About ten million times the distance reckoned
From our sun to its earth, as we can tell
  How much time it takes up, even to a second,
For every ray that travels to dispel
  The fogs of London, through which, dimly beaconed,
The weathercocks are gilt some thrice a year,
440 If that the *summer* is not too severe:°—

LVI

I say that I can tell—'twas half a minute:
  I know the solar beams take up more time
Ere, packed up for their journey, they begin it;
  But then their telegraph° is less sublime,
And if they ran a race, they would not win it
  'Gainst Satan's couriers bound for their own clime.
The sun takes up some years for every ray
To reach its goal—the devil not half a day.

LVII

Upon the verge of space, about the size
450 Of half-a-crown, a little speck appeared
(I've seen a something like it in the skies
  In the Aegean, ere a squall); it neared,
And, growing bigger, took another guise;
  Like an aerial ship it tacked, and steered,
Or *was* steered (I am doubtful of the grammar
Of the last phrase, which makes the stanza stammer:—

LVIII

But take your choice); and then it grew a cloud;
  And so it was—a cloud of witnesses.
But such a cloud! No land e'er saw a crowd
460 Of locusts numerous as the heavens saw these;
They shadowed with their myriads space; their loud
  And varied cries were like those of wild geese
(If nations may be likened to a goose),
And realised the phrase of 'hell broke loose.'°

LIX

Here crashed a sturdy oath of stout John Bull,
  Who damned away his eyes as heretofore:
There Paddy brogued 'By Jasus!'—'What's your wull?'
  The temperate Scot exclaimed: the French ghost swore

If . . . severe Byron steals the joke from
Horace Walpole: "The summer has set in with
its usual severity"

telegraph presumably the London-Portsmouth
semaphore
'hell broke loose' *Paradise Lost* IV.918

In certain terms I shan't translate in full,
470   As the first coachman will; and 'midst the war,
The voice of Jonathan° was heard to express,
'*Our* president is going to war, I guess.'

LX

Besides there were the Spaniard, Dutch, and Dane;
    In short, an universal shoal of shades,
From Otaheite's isle° to Salisbury Plain,
    Of all climes and professions, years and trades,
Ready to swear against the good king's reign,
    Bitter as clubs in cards are against spades;
All summoned by this grand 'subpoena,' to
480   Try if kings mayn't be damned like me or you.

LXI

When Michael saw this host, he first grew pale,
    As angels can; next, like Italian twilight,
He turned all colours—as a peacock's tail,
    Or sunset streaming through a Gothic skylight
In some old abbey, or a trout not stale,
    Or distant lightning on the horizon *by* night,
Or a fresh rainbow, or a grand review
Of thirty regiments in red, green, and blue.

LXII

Then he addressed himself to Satan: 'Why—
490   My good old friend, for such I deem you, though
Our different parties make us fight so shy,
    I ne'er mistake you for a *personal* foe;
Our difference is *political,* and I
    Trust that, whatever may occur below,
You know my great respect for you: and this
Makes me regret whate'er you do amiss—

LXIII

'Why, my dear Lucifer, would you abuse
    My call for witnesses? I did not mean
That you should half of earth and hell produce;
500   'Tis even superfluous, since two honest, clean,
True testimonies are enough: we lose
    Our time, nay, our eternity, between
The accusation and defence: if we
Hear both, 'twill stretch our immortality.'

Jonathan that is, the United States, from   **Otaheite's isle** Tahiti
Jonathan Trumbull, American politician (1710–
85)

LXIV

Satan replied, 'To me the matter is
    Indifferent, in a personal point of view:
I can have fifty better souls than this
    With far less trouble than we have gone through
Already; and I merely argued his
510   Late majesty of Britain's case with you
Upon a point of form: you may dispose
Of him; I've kings enough below, God knows!'

LXV

Thus spoke the Demon (late called 'multifaced'
    By multo-scribbling Southey). 'Then we'll call
One or two persons of the myriads placed
    Around our congress, and dispense with all
The rest,' quoth Michael: 'Who may be so graced
    As to speak first? there's choice enough—who shall
It be?' Then Satan answered, 'There are many;
520   But you may choose Jack Wilkes° as well as any.'

LXVI

A merry, cock-eyed, curious-looking sprite
    Upon the instant started from the throng,
Dressed in a fashion now forgotten quite;
    For all the fashions of the flesh stick long
By people in the next world; where unite
    All the costumes since Adam's, right or wrong,
From Eve's fig-leaf down to the petticoat,
Almost as scanty, of days less remote.

LXVII

The spirit looked around upon the crowds
530   Assembled, and exclaimed, 'My friends of all
The spheres, we shall catch cold amongst these clouds;
    So let's to business: why this general call?
If those are freeholders I see in shrouds,
    And 'tis for an election that they bawl,
Behold a candidate with unturned coat!
Saint Peter, may I count upon your vote?'

LXVIII

'Sir,' replied Michael, 'you mistake; these things
    Are of a former life, and what we do
Above is more august; to judge of kings
540   Is the tribunal met: so now you know.'

Jack Wilkes noted Radical politician and libertine, a leader of the opposition to George III,
who jailed and exiled him, but vainly, as
Wilkes returned to the House of Commons,
vindicated by the populace

'Then I presume those gentlemen with wings,'
  Said Wilkes, 'are cherubs; and that soul below
Looks much like George the Third, but to my mind
  A good deal older—Bless me! is he blind?'

LXIX

'He is what you behold him, and his doom
  Depends upon his deeds,' the Angel said.
'If you have aught to arraign in him, the tomb
  Gives license to the humblest beggar's head
To lift itself against the loftiest.'—'Some,'
550   Said Wilkes, 'don't wait to see them laid in lead,
For such a liberty—and I, for one,
Have told them what I thought beneath the sun.'

LXX

'*Above* the sun repeat, then, what thou hast
  To urge against him,' said the Archangel. 'Why,'
Replied the spirit, 'since old scores are past,
  Must I turn evidence? In faith, not I.
Besides, I beat him hollow at the last,°
  With all his Lords and Commons: in the sky
I don't like ripping up old stories, since
560   His conduct was but natural in a prince.

LXXI

'Foolish, no doubt, and wicked, to oppress
  A poor unlucky devil without a shilling;
But then I blame the man himself much less
  Than Bute and Grafton,° and shall be unwilling
To see him punished here for their excess,
  Since they were both damned long ago, and still in
Their place below: for me, I have forgiven,
And vote his "habeas corpus" into heaven.'

LXXII

'Wilkes,' said the Devil, 'I understand all this;
570   You turned to half a courtier ere you died,
And seem to think it would not be amiss
  To grow a whole one on the other side
Of Charon's ferry; you forget that *his*
  Reign is concluded; whatsoe'er betide,
He won't be sovereign more: you've lost your labour
For at the best he will but be your neighbour.

Besides . . . last In 1782 the resolutions expelling Wilkes in 1764 were stricken from the Commons journals.

Grafton the Duke of Grafton, like the Earl of Bute a minister of George III

LXXIII

'However, I knew what to think of it,
    When I beheld you in your jesting way
Flitting and whispering round about the spit
580   Where Belial, upon duty for the day,
With Fox's lard° was basting William Pitt,
    His pupil; I knew what to think, I say:
That fellow even in hell breeds farther ills;
I'll have him *gagged*—'twas one of his own bills.

LXXIV

'Call Junius!'° From the crowd a shadow stalked,
    And at the name there was a general squeeze,
So that the very ghosts no longer walked
    In comfort, at their own aerial ease,
But were all rammed, and jammed (but to be balked,
590   As we shall see), and jostled hands and knees,
Like wind compressed and pent within a bladder,
Or like a human colic, which is sadder.

LXXV

The shadow came°—a tall, thin, grey-haired figure,
    That looked as it had been a shade on earth;
Quick in its motions, with an air of vigour,
    But nought to mark its breeding or its birth:
Now it waxed little, then again grew bigger,
    With now an air of gloom, or savage mirth;
But as you gazed upon its features, they
600   Changed every instant—to *what*, none could say.

LXXVI

The more intently the ghosts gazed, the less
    Could they distinguish whose the features were;
The Devil himself seemed puzzled even to guess;
    They varied like a dream—now here, now there;
And several people swore from out the press,
    They knew him perfectly; and one could swear
He was his father: upon which another
Was sure he was his mother's cousin's brother:

LXXVII

Another, that he was a duke, or knight,
610   An orator, a lawyer, or a priest,
A nabob, a man-midwife; but the wight

Fox's lard Charles James Fox, the Whig
leader, was rather fat.
Junius pseudonym of eloquent author who
satirized George III and the Tories; his title

page had the motto *Stat Nominis Umbra* ("A
Shadow Stands for the Name")
The shadow came The reference is to the motto
of Junius.

Mysterious changed his countenance at least
As oft as they their minds: though in full sight
He stood, the puzzle only was increased;
    The man was a phantasmagoria in
Himself—he was so volatile and thin.

LXXVIII

The moment that you had pronounced him *one,*
Presto! his face changed, and he was another;
And when that change was hardly well put on,
620   It varied, till I don't think his own mother
(If that he had a mother) would her son
Have known, he shifted so from one to t'other;
    Till guessing from a pleasure grew a task,
At this epistolary 'Iron Mask.'°

LXXIX

For sometimes he like Cerberus would seem—
'Three gentlemen at once' (as sagely says
Good Mrs. Malaprop°); then you might deem
    That he was not even *one;* now many rays
Were flashing round him; and now a thick stream
630   Hid him from sight—like fogs on London days:
    Now Burke,° now Tooke,° he grew to people's fancies,
And certes often like Sir Philip Francis.°

LXXX

I've an hypothesis—'tis quite my own;
    I never let it out till now, for fear
Of doing people harm about the throne,
    And injuring some minister or peer,
On whom the stigma might perhaps be blown;
    It is—my gentle public, lend thine ear!
'Tis, that what Junius we are wont to call
640   Was *really, truly,* nobody at all.

LXXXI

I don't see wherefore letters should not be
    Written without hands, since we daily view
Them written without heads; and books, we see,
    Are filled as well without the latter too:
And really till we fix on somebody

'Iron Mask' The "Man in the Iron Mask" was imprisoned in the Bastille by Louis XIV; Byron's point is that Junius too remains unknown.
Mrs. Malaprop delightful misuser of words in R. B. Sheridan's comedy, *The Rivals* (1775), hence the term "malapropism." The most splendid of her remarks: "as headstrong as an allegory on the banks of the Nile."
Burke Edmund Burke (1729–97), great Whig orator and author
Tooke John Horne Tooke (1736–1812), another opponent of the American War
Sir Philip Francis (1740–1818) probably was Junius.

For certain sure to claim them as his due,
Their author, like the Niger's mouth,° will bother
The world to say if *there* be mouth or author.

LXXXII

'And who and what art thou?' the Archangel said.
650 'For *that* you may consult my title-page,'
Replied this mighty shadow of a shade:
 'If I have kept my secret half an age,
I scarce shall tell it now.'—'Canst thou upbraid,'
 Continued Michael, 'George Rex, or allege
Aught further?' Junius answered, 'You had better
First ask him for *his* answer to my letter:

LXXXIII

'My charges upon record will outlast
 The brass of both his epitaph and tomb.'
'Repent'st thou not,' said Michael, 'of some past
660 Exaggeration? something which may doom
Thyself if false, as him if true? Thou wast
 Too bitter—is it not so?—in thy gloom
Of passion?'—'Passion!' cried the phantom dim,
'I loved my country, and I hated him.

LXXXIV

'What I have written, I have written:° let
 The rest be on his head or mine!' So spoke
Old 'Nominis Umbra;' and while speaking yet,
 Away he melted in celestial smoke.
Then Satan said to Michael, 'Don't forget
670 To call George Washington, and John Horne Tooke,
And Franklin;'—but at this time there was heard
A cry for room, though not a phantom stirred.

LXXXV

At length with jostling, elbowing, and the aid
 Of cherubim appointed to that post,
The devil Asmodeus° to the circle made
 His way, and looked as if his journey cost
Some trouble. When his burden down he laid,
 'What's this?' cried Michael; 'why, 'tis not a ghost?'
'I know it,' quoth the incubus; 'but he
680 Shall be one, if you leave the affair to me.

LXXXVI

'Confound the renegado! I have sprained
 My left wing, he's so heavy; one would think

Niger's mouth allusion to recent explorations in
Africa

What . . . written John 19:22
Asmodeus name for the devil

Some of his works about his neck were chained.
   But to the point; while hovering o'er the brink
Of Skiddaw° (where as usual it still rained),
     I saw a taper, far below me, wink,
And stooping, caught this fellow at a libel—
No less on history than the Holy Bible.

       LXXXVII
'The former is the devil's scripture, and
690   The latter yours, good Michael: so the affair
Belongs to all of us, you understand.
     I snatched him up just as you see him there,
And brought him off for sentence out of hand:
     I've scarcely been ten minutes in the air—
At least a quarter it can hardly be:
I dare say that his wife is still at tea.'

       LXXXVIII
Here Satan said, 'I know this man of old,
     And have expected him for some time here;
A sillier fellow you will scarce behold,
700   Or more conceited in his petty sphere:
But surely it was not worth while to fold
     Such trash below your wing, Asmodeus dear:
We had the poor wretch safe (without being bored
With carriage) coming of his own accord.

       LXXXIX
'But since he's here, let's see what he has done.'
     'Done!' cried Asmodeus, 'he anticipates
The very business you are now upon,
     And scribbles as if head clerk to the Fates.
Who knows to what his ribaldry may run,
710   When such an ass as this, like Balaam's,° prates?'
'Let's hear,' quoth Michael, 'what he has to say:
You know we're bound to that in every way.'

       XC
Now the bard, glad to get an audience, which
     By no means often was his case below,
Began to cough, and hawk, and hem, and pitch
     His voice into that awful note of woe
To all unhappy hearers within reach
     Of poets when the tide of rhyme's in flow;
But stuck fast with his first hexameter,
720   Not one of all whose gouty feet would stir.

Skiddaw mountain in the Lake District; Southey   **Balaam's** Numbers 22:28
resided near it

XCI

But ere the spavined dactyls could be spurred
　　Into recitative, in great dismay
Both cherubim and seraphim were heard
　　To murmur loudly through their long array;
And Michael rose ere he could get a word
　　Of all his foundered verses under way,
And cried, 'For God's sake stop, my friend! 'twere best—
Non Di, non homines°—you know the rest.'

XCII

A general bustle spread throughout the throng,
730　　Which seemed to hold all verse in detestation;
The angels had of course enough of song
　　When upon service; and the generation
Of ghosts had heard too much in life, not long
　　Before, to profit by a new occasion:
The monarch, mute till then, exclaimed, 'What! what!
Pye° come again? No more—no more of that!'

XCIII

The tumult grew; an universal cough
　　Convulsed the skies, as during a debate,
When Castlereagh has been up long enough
740　　(Before he was first minister of state,
I mean—the *slaves hear now*); some cried 'Off, off!'
　　As at a farce; till, grown quite desperate,
The bard Saint Peter prayed to interpose
(Himself an author) only for his prose.

XCIV

The varlet was not an ill-favoured knave;
　　A good deal like a vulture in the face,
With a hook nose and a hawk's eye, which gave
　　A smart and sharper-looking sort of grace
To his whole aspect, which, though rather grave,
750　　Was by no means so ugly as his case;
But that, indeed, was hopeless as can be,
Quite a poetic felony *'de se.'*°

XCV

Then Michael blew his trump, and stilled the noise
　　With one still greater, as is yet the mode
On earth besides; except some grumbling voice,
　　Which now and then will make a slight inroad

Non . . . homines Horace's *Ars Poetica*, ll.
372–73, "Neither gods nor men can stand
mediocre poets."

Pye Henry James Pye, wretched Laureate
before Southey
felony 'de se' suicide

Upon decorous silence, few will twice
   Lift up their lungs when fairly overcrowed;
And now the bard could plead his own bad cause,
760 With all the attitudes of self-applause.

XCVI

He said—(I only give the heads)—he said,
   He meant no harm in scribbling; 'twas his way
Upon all topics; 'twas, besides, his bread,
   Of which he buttered both sides; 'twould delay
Too long the assembly (he was pleased to dread),
   And take up rather more time than a day,
To name his works—he would but cite a few—
'Wat Tyler'—'Rhymes on Blenheim'—'Waterloo.'

XCVII

He had written praises of a regicide;°
770   He had written praises of all kings whatever;
He had written for republics far and wide,
   And then against them bitterer than ever:
For pantisocracy he once had cried
   Aloud, a scheme less moral than 'twas clever;
Then grew a hearty anti-jacobin—
Had turned his coat—and would have turned his skin.

XCVIII

He had sung against all battles, and again
   In their high praise and glory; he had called
Reviewing 'the ungentle craft,'° and then
780   Become as base a critic as e'er crawled—
Fed, paid, and pampered by the very men
   By whom his muse and morals had been mauled:
He had written much blank verse, and blanker prose,
And more of both than anybody knows.

XCIX

He had written Wesley's life:—here turning round
   To Satan, 'Sir, I'm ready to write yours,
In two octavo volumes, nicely bound,
   With notes and preface, all that most allures
The pious purchaser; and there's no ground
790   For fear, for I can choose my own reviewers:
So let me have the proper documents,
That I may add you to my other saints.'

He . . . regicide Southey wrote a poem praising Henry Marten, one of the judges who commanded the execution of Charles I.

'the ungentle craft' memorable characterization of reviewers by Southey, in his edition of the poet Kirke White

C

Satan bowed, and was silent. 'Well, if you,
    With amiable modesty, decline
My offer, what says Michael? There are few
    Whose memoirs could be rendered more divine.
Mine is a pen of all work; not so new
    As it was once, but I would make you shine
Like your own trumpet. By the way, my own
800   Has more of brass in it, and is as well blown.

CI

'But talking about trumpets, here's my Vision!
    Now you shall judge, all people; yes, you shall
Judge with my judgment, and by my decision
    Be guided who shall enter heaven or fall.
I settle all these things by intuition,
    Times present, past, to come, heaven, hell, and all.
Like King Alfonso.° When I thus see double,
I save the Deity some worlds of trouble.'

CII

He ceased, and drew forth an MS.; and no
810   Persuasion on the part of devils, saints,
Or angels, now could stop the torrent; so
    He read the first three lines of the contents;
But at the fourth, the whole spiritual show
    Had vinished, with variety of scents,
Ambrosial and sulphureous, as they sprang,
Like lightning, off from his 'melodious twang.'°

CIII

Those grand heroics acted as a spell:
    The angels stopped their ears and plied their pinions;
The devils ran howling, deafened, down to hell;
820   The ghosts fled, gibbering, for their own dominions—
(For 'tis not yet decided where they dwell,
    And I leave every man to his opinions);
Michael took refuge in his trump—but, lo!
His teeth were set on edge, he could not blow!

CIV

Saint Peter, who has hitherto been known
    For an impetuous saint, upraised his keys,
And at the fifth line knocked the poet down;
    Who fell like Phaeton,° but more at ease,

Alfonso Byron's note: "King Alfonso, speaking
of the Ptolomean System, said that 'had he been
consulted at the creation of the world, he would
have spared the Maker some absurdities'."
'melodious twang' Byron's note cites John
Aubrey's *Miscellanies* (1696) as speaking of
a ghost that vanished with "a curious perfume,
and most melodious twang."
Phaeton Apollo's son, who fell to destruction
when he usurped the chariot of the sun

Into his lake, for there he did not drown;
830   A different web being by the Destinies
Woven for the Laureate's final wreath, whene'er
Reform shall happen either here or there.

CV

He first sank to the bottom—like his works,
    But soon rose to the surface—like himself;
For all corrupted things are buoyed like corks,
    By their own rottenness, light as an elf,
Or wisp that flits o'er a morass: he lurks,
    It may be, still, like dull books on a shelf,
In his own den, to scrawl some 'Life' or 'Vision,'
840   As Welborn° says—'the devil turn'd precisian.'°

CVI

As for the rest, to come to the conclusion
    Of this true dream, the telescope is gone
Which kept my optics free from all delusion,
    And showed me what I in my turn have shown;
All I saw farther, in the last confusion,
    Was, that King George slipped into heaven for one;
And when the tumult dwindled to a calm,
I left him practising the hundredth psalm.°
1821   1822

On This Day I Complete My Thirty-sixth Year°

'Tis time this heart should be unmoved,°
    Since others it hath ceased to move:
Yet, though I cannot be beloved,
        Still let me love!

My days are in the yellow leaf;°
    The flowers and fruits of love are gone;
The worm, the canker, and the grief
        Are mine alone!

The fire that on my bosom preys
10   Is lone as some volcanic isle;
No torch is kindled at its blaze—
        A funeral pile.

Welborn character in Philip Massinger's drama *A New Way To Pay Old Debts* (1633)
precisian Puritan
hundredth psalm See Psalm 100:4: "Enter into his gates with thanksgiving . . .".
Thirty-sixth Year written at Missolonghi in Greece, where he was to die three months later, a martyr of the Greek Revolution against the Turks
unmoved See the last line of "Stanzas to the Po."
yellow leaf See Shakespeare's Sonnet LXXIII and *Macbeth* V.III.21 ff.

The hope, the fear, the jealous care,
   The exalted portion of the pain
And power of love, I cannot share,
      But wear the chain.

But 'tis not *thus*—and 'tis not *here*—
   Such thoughts should shake my soul, nor *now*,
Where glory decks the hero's bier,
20   Or binds his brow.

The sword, the banner, and the field,
   Glory and Greece, around me see!
The Spartan, borne upon his shield,°
      Was not more free.

Awake! (not Greece—she *is* awake!)
   Awake, my spirit! Think through *whom*°
Thy life-blood tracks its parent lake,
      And then strike home!

Tread those reviving passions down,
30   Unworthy manhood!—unto thee
Indifferent should the smile or frown
      Of beauty be.°

If thou regret'st thy youth, *why live?*
   The land of honourable death
Is here:—up to the field, and give
      Away thy breath!

Seek out—less often sought than found—
   A soldier's grave, for thee the best;
Then look around, and choose thy ground,
40   And take thy rest.
      1824   1824

PERCY BYSSHE SHELLEY
1792–1822

Shelley, the most intense and original lyrical poet in the language, was born on August 4, 1792, to a very wealthy family of country gentry in Sussex. His extremely radical religious and political vision came to him very early and led him to rebel against the system at Eton. He was expelled from University College, Oxford, in March 1811, after less than half a year in residence, during which he co-authored and published *The Necessity of Atheism*. Going to London, he met Leigh Hunt, mixed in

---

The . . . **shield** Wounded or dead Spartans were honored by being so carried off the battle-field.
whom Byron was descended (through his mother) from the ancient kings of Scotland.

Tread . . . **be** Byron was in love again, during the closing months of his life, with his page boy Loukas, but evidently this love was not reciprocated.

radical circles, and eloped with Harriet Westbrook, he having just turned nineteen, she being sixteen. With the astonishing rapidity that always characterized his life and his poetry ("I always go on until I am stopped and I never am stopped"), he proceeded to announce himself to the Necessitarian philosopher-reformer William Godwin as a true disciple, journeyed to Ireland to agitate against the English government, poured out pamphlets, was shadowed by royal agents, privately printed the revolutionary poem Queen Mab, fathered a daughter upon Harriet and then abandoned her, again pregnant, to elope with Mary Godwin, the brilliant seventeen-year-old daughter of Godwin and the late woman's liberation pioneer Mary Wollstonecraft.

In the autumn of 1815, fearing imminent death from tuberculosis (which he did not have), he wrote his first considerable poem, Alastor, in a Wordsworthian style but subtly directed against Wordsworth. In May 1816, Shelley left England, and went to Geneva, where his friendship with Byron commenced, and where his genius found its true direction in the composing of the "Hymn to Intellectual Beauty" and "Mont Blanc." Soon after he had returned to England, in the autumn, Harriet drowned herself, freeing him to legalize his union with Mary Godwin. In 1817, the Lord Chancellor Eldon refused Shelley custody of his two children by Harriet, ostensibly on moral grounds. In March 1818, Shelley went into exile to Italy, never to return.

During his four Italian years, in his later twenties (he drowned a month before his thirtieth birthday), Shelley wrote his succession of major poems: Julian and Maddalo, Prometheus Unbound, The Cenci, The Sensitive Plant, The Witch of Atlas, Epipsychidion, Adonais, Hellas, the unfinished death-poem, The Triumph of Life, scores of magnificent lyrics, and the major prose essay, his Defence of Poetry. These years were also crowded with intense friendships, love affairs, revolutionary politics, and continual study and meditation. Personally all but selfless, almost preternaturally benevolent, Shelley was also habitually gentle, urbane, and by all accounts the most lovable of human beings. Byron, a bitter judge of character, said of him after his death that everyone else he knew seemed a beast compared to Shelley. Nevertheless, Shelley was constantly reviled in England as an immoralist and an atheist, an opponent of everything supposedly decent in established society. One prominent English obituary trumpeted: "Shelley the Atheist is dead. Now he knows whether there is a Hell or not."

Shelley's posthumous poetic reputation is the most volatile and hardest-fought-over of the last hundred and fifty years. Eminent modern critics have agreed with one another that he is all but totally worthless, an opinion held in his own time by Charles Lamb, and developed later by Carlyle and Arnold. T. S. Eliot, F. R. Leavis, Allen Tate, and W. H. Auden are typical of the majority view in modern criticism that prevailed until recently. Their Shelley is a confused emotionalist, a bad craftsman, a mock lyrist, a perpetual adolescent.

All this is not even good nonsense. Shelley is a crucial, sometimes the dominant, influence upon Beddoes, Browning, Swinburne, Yeats, Shaw, and Hardy. His emotions are very powerful, but his urbane control more powerful still. He is a superb craftsman, a lyrical poet without rival, and one of the most advanced and mature skeptical intellects ever to write a poem. He is as close to being both an English Pindar and an English Lucretius as anyone has been, and in his greater works challenges both those classical precursors. His poetry clearly does not have universal appeal among literary people; it never had and never will, probably because it is idiosyncratic enough to be menacing. Also, beyond question, the sheer violence of dissent in Shelley's political, religious, and sexual views is going to continue to alienate certain readers. But to the common readers of poetry, where we still have them, Shelley's position seems fixed. He stands as the modern lyrical poet proper, the passionately erotic idealist who attempts to find ultimate values in this world more perpetually than most of us can bear to try, and who goes on questing even though he fails to find what he seeks.

The central form of Shelley's poetry is remorseless quest, for a world where Eros is triumphant always, where desire shall not fail, and a confrontation of life by life is always taking place. Shelley, much scholarly opinion aside, was no Platonist, though he loved Plato's writings. Rather, he was a visionary skeptic, who found he could not reconcile heart and head, and could not bear to deceive either. A passionately religious temperament, Shelley evolved what might be termed a Protestant Orphism as his personal faith, a strenuous prophecy of human renovation in which fallen men would rise to "Man, one harmonious soul of many a soul, / Whose nature is its own divine control, / Where all things flow to all, as rivers to the sea. . . ." As the poet matured, he saw more clearly that this hope could not be realized by reform or revolution (though he always remained on the Left) but must come, if at all, through an overcoming of each natural selfhood by imagination. Though this approximates Blake's faith, the two poets never met, and evidently never read one another (though both personally knew Godwin, and others). Shelley differs from Blake in not systemizing his emergent myth of salvation, for his intellectual skepticism (the true ground of his being) compelled him to doubt profoundly his own idealizations.

There is, despite his own yearnings, an unmistakable pattern of deepening despair in the cycle of Shelley's poetry. From the dead end of *Alastor,* Shelley rose to the highly qualified hope of *Prometheus Unbound,* and then came full circle again to the natural defeat of imaginative quest in *Adonais* and in the unfinished but totally hopeless *The Triumph of Life,* which is not a *Purgatorio* but an *Inferno* (though most Shelley scholars would dispute this). Shelley's heart, when he died, had begun to touch the limits of desire, as his final love lyrics show. A tough but subtle temperament, he had worn himself out, and was ready to depart.

Alastor

The title of Shelley's first major poem was suggested by Thomas Love Peacock after he had read the completed work, and means (according to Peacock) "an evil genius"; "a relentless daemon" or a kind of Nemesis might be closer to Shelley's poem, where the Spirit of Solitude is an implicit being in pursuit of the Poet, but a being that is the solipsistic part of him (his Spectre, Blake would have said). Shelley's Poet is haunted by his own acute self-consciousness, even as he pursues his narcist dream vision of a beloved woman. Shelley's Preface does not blame his Poet, nor does the poem, for the Poet represents the most dangerous but also the most attractive part of Shelley's own mind, the questing element we rightly identify with him. *Alastor* stems directly from Wordsworth's account of the Solitary in *The Excursion,* and had an immense effect upon subsequent nineteenth-century poetry. Keats's *Endymion,* Browning's *Pauline* and *Paracelsus,* Yeats's *The Wanderings of Oisin* and *The Shadowy Waters* (among others) take up Shelley's version of internalized quest romance, which is parodied in our century by Wallace Stevens's *The Comedian as the*

Letter C. The excerpts that follow are meant to indicate the poem's central sequence, the Poet's idealistic but remorselessly self-destructive drive, against all natural limitation or even human obligation, to attain an impossibly complete union with his vision.

From Alastor

or The Spirit of Solitude

Preface

The poem entitled *Alastor* may be considered as allegorical of one of the most interesting situations of the human mind. It represents a youth of uncorrupted feelings and adventurous genius led forth by an imagination inflamed and purified through familiarity with all that is excellent and majestic, to the contemplation of the universe. He drinks deep of the fountains of knowledge, and is still insatiate. The magnificence and beauty of the external world sinks profoundly into the frame of his conceptions, and affords to their modifications a variety not to be exhausted. So long as it is possible for his desires to point towards objects thus infinite and unmeasured, he is joyous, and tranquil, and self-possessed. But the period arrives when these objects cease to suffice. His mind is at length suddenly awakened and thirsts for intercourse with an intelligence similar to itself. He images to himself the Being whom he loves. Conversant with speculations of the sublimest and most perfect natures, the vision in which he embodies his own imaginations unites all of wonderful, or wise, or beautiful, which the poet, the philosopher, or the lover could depicture. The intellectual faculties, the imagination, the functions of sense, have their respective requisitions on the sympathy of corresponding powers in other human beings. The Poet is represented as uniting these requisitions, and attaching them to a single image. He seeks in vain for a prototype of his conception. Blasted by his disappointment, he descends to an untimely grave.

The picture is not barren of instruction to actual men. The Poet's self-centred seclusion was avenged by the furies of an irresistible passion pursuing him to speedy ruin. But that Power° which strikes the luminaries of the world with sudden darkness and extinction, by awakening them to too exquisite a perception of its influences, dooms to a slow and poisonous decay those meaner spirits that dare to abjure its dominion. Their destiny is more abject and inglorious as their delinquency is more contemptible and pernicious. They who, deluded by no generous error, instigated by no sacred thirst of doubtful knowledge, duped by no illustrious superstition, loving nothing on this earth, and cherishing no hopes beyond, yet keep aloof from sympathies with their kind, rejoicing neither in human joy nor mourning with human grief; these, and such as they, have their apportioned curse. They languish, because none feel with them their common nature. They are morally dead. They are neither friends, nor lovers, nor fathers, nor citizens of the world, nor benefactors of their country. Among those who attempt to exist without human sympathy, the pure and tender-

that **Power** the imagination

hearted perish through the intensity and passion of their search after its communities, when the vacancy of their spirit suddenly makes itself felt. All else, selfish, blind, and torpid, are those unforeseeing multitudes who constitute, together with their own, the lasting misery and loneliness of the world. Those who love not their fellow-beings live unfruitful lives, and prepare for their old age a miserable grave.

> The good die first,
> And those whose hearts are dry as summer dust,
> Burn to the socket!°

DECEMBER 14, 1815

> Nondum amabam, et amare amabam, quaerebam quid
> amarem, amans amare.°—*Confess. St. August.*

Earth, ocean, air, belovèd brotherhood!°
If our great Mother° has imbued my soul
With aught of natural piety° to feel
Your love, and recompense the boon with mine;
If dewy morn, and odorous noon, and even,
With sunset and its gorgeous ministers,
And solemn midnight's tingling silentness;
If autumn's hollow sighs in the sere wood,
And winter robing with pure snow and crowns
10 Of starry ice the grey grass and bare boughs;
If spring's voluptuous pantings when she breathes
Her first sweet kisses, have been dear to me;
If no bright bird, insect, or gentle beast
I consciously have injured, but still loved
And cherished these my kindred; then forgive
This boast, belovèd brethren, and withdraw
No portion of your wonted favour now!

Mother of this unfathomable world!
Favour my solemn song, for I have loved
20 Thee ever, and thee only; I have watched
Thy shadow, and the darkness of thy steps,
And my heart ever gazes on the depth
Of thy deep mysteries. I have made my bed
In charnels and on coffins, where black death
Keeps record of the trophies won from thee,
Hoping to still these obstinate questionings°
Of thee and thine, by forcing some lone ghost
Thy messenger, to render up the tale
Of what we are. In lone and silent hours,

The good . . . socket Wordsworth's *The Excursion* I.500–502, slightly modified
Nondum . . . amare "Not yet I loved, and I loved to love; I sought what I should love, loving to love"
Earth . . . brotherhood Shelley speaks as the Promethean element of fire, addressing his brother-elements as a Muse-principle
Mother Wordsworthian Nature
natural piety from Wordsworth's lyric, "My Heart Leaps Up," l. 9
obstinate questionings See Wordsworth, "Intimations of Immortality" ode, l. 145

30   When night makes a weird sound of its own stillness,
Like an inspired and desperate alchemist
Staking his very life on some dark hope,
Have I mixed awful talk and asking looks
With my most innocent love, until strange tears
 Uniting with those breathless kisses, made
Such magic as compels the charmèd night
To render up thy charge: . . . and, though ne'er yet
Thou hast unveiled thy inmost sanctuary,
Enough from incommunicable dream,
40   And twilight phantasms, and deep noon-day thought,
Has shone within me, that serenely now
And moveless, as a long-forgotten lyre°
Suspended in the solitary dome
Of some mysterious and deserted fane,
I wait thy breath, Great Parent, that my strain
May modulate with murmurs of the air,
And motions of the forests and the sea,
And voice of living beings, and woven hymns
Of night and day, and the deep heart of man.

            . . .

When early youth had passed, he left
His cold fireside and alienated home
To seek strange truths in undiscovered lands.
Many a wide waste and tangled wilderness
Has lured his fearless steps; and he has bought
80   With his sweet voice and eyes, from savage men,
His rest and food. Nature's most secret steps
He like her shadow has pursued, where'er
The red volcano overcanopies
Its fields of snow and pinnacles of ice
With burning smoke, or where bitumen lakes
On black bare pointed islets ever beat
With sluggish surge, or where the secret caves°
Rugged and dark, winding among the springs
Of fire and poison, inaccessible
90   To avarice or pride, their starry domes
Of diamond and of gold expand above
Numberless and immeasurable halls,
Frequent° with crystal column, and clear shrines
Of pearl, and thrones radiant with chrysolite.
Nor had that scene of ampler majesty
Than gems or gold, the varying roof of heaven
And the green earth lost in his heart its claims
To love and wonder; he would linger long

---

lyre the Romantic wind-lyre or Aeolian harp   **Frequent** crowded
secret caves the first of several echoes of Coleridge's *Kubla Khan*

In lonesome vales, making the wild his home,
100   Until the doves and squirrels would partake
From his innocuous hand his bloodless food,°
Lured by the gentle meaning of his looks,
And the wild antelope, that starts whene'er
The dry leaf rustles in the brake,° suspend
Her timid steps to gaze upon a form
More graceful than her own.

          . . .

140   The Poet wandering on, through Arabie
And Persia, and the wild Carmanian waste,°
And o'er the aerial mountains which pour down
Indus and Oxus from their icy caves,
In joy and exultation held his way;
Till in the vale of Cashmire, far within
Its loneliest dell, where odorous plants entwine
Beneath the hollow rocks a natural bower,
Beside a sparkling rivulet he stretched
His languid limbs. A vision on his sleep
150   There came, a dream of hopes that never yet
Had flushed his cheek. He dreamed a veilèd maid
Sate near him, talking in low solemn tones.
Her voice was like the voice of his own soul
Heard in the calm of thought; its music long,
Like woven sounds of streams and breezes, held
His inmost sense suspended in its web
Of many-coloured woof and shifting hues.
Knowledge and truth and virtue were her theme,
And lofty hopes of divine liberty,
160   Thoughts the most dear to him, and poesy,
Herself a poet. Soon the solemn mood
Of her pure mind kindled through all her frame
A permeating fire: wild numbers then
She raised, with voice stifled in tremulous sobs
Subdued by its own pathos: her fair hands
Were bare alone, sweeping from some strange harp
Strange symphony, and in their branching veins
The eloquent blood told an ineffable tale.
The beating of her heart was heard to fill
170   The pauses of her music, and her breath
Tumultuously accorded with those fits
Of intermitted song. Sudden she rose,
As if her heart impatiently endured
Its bursting burthen: at the sound he turned,
And saw by the warm light of their own life
Her glowing limbs beneath the sinuous veil

bloodless food Shelley was a notorious vegetar-
ian

brake thicket
Carmanian waste desert in Persia

Of woven wind, her outspread arms now bare,
Her dark locks floating in the breath of night,
Her beamy bending eyes, her parted lips
180 Outstretched, and pale, and quivering eagerly.
His strong heart sunk and sickened with excess
Of love. He reared his shuddering limbs and quelled
His gasping breath, and spread his arms to meet
Her panting bosom: . . . she drew back a while,
Then, yielding to the irresistible joy,
With frantic gesture and short breathless cry
Folded his frame in her dissolving arms.
Now blackness veiled his dizzy eyes, and night
Involved and swallowed up the vision; sleep,
190 Like a dark flood suspended in its course,
Rolled back its impulse on his vacant brain.

        . . .

    At length upon the lone Chorasmian° shore
He paused, a wide and melancholy waste
Of putrid marshes. A strong impulse urged
His steps to the sea-shore. A swan was there,°
Beside a sluggish stream among the reeds.
It rose as he approached, and with strong wings
Scaling the upward sky, bent its bright course
High over the immeasurable main.
280 His eyes pursued its flight.—'Thou hast a home,
Beautiful bird; thou voyagest to thine home,
Where thy sweet mate will twine her downy neck
With thine, and welcome thy return with eyes
Bright in the lustre of their own fond joy.
And what am I that I should linger here,
With voice far sweeter than thy dying notes,
Spirit more vast than thine, frame more attuned
To beauty, wasting these surpassing powers
In the deaf air, to the blind earth, and heaven
290 That echoes not my thoughts?' A gloomy smile
Of desperate hope wrinkled his quivering lips.
For sleep, he knew, kept most relentlessly
Its precious charge, and silent death exposed,
Faithless perhaps as sleep, a shadowy lure,
With doubtful smile mocking its own strange charms.

    Startled by his own thoughts he looked around.
There was no fair fiend near him, not a sight
Or sound of awe but in his own deep mind.
A little shallop floating near the shore
300 Caught the impatient wandering of his gaze.

Chorasmian Aral Sea   **A swan was there** This passage (ll. 275–90)
                                        echoes throughout Yeats's poetry.

It had been long abandoned, for its sides
Gaped wide with many a rift, and its frail joints
Swayed with the undulations of the tide.
A restless impulse urged him to embark
And meet lone Death on the drear ocean's waste;
For well he knew that mighty Shadow loves
The slimy caverns of the populous deep.

The day was fair and sunny, sea and sky
Drank its inspiring radiance, and the wind
310   Swept strongly from the shore, blackening the waves.
Following his eager soul, the wanderer
Leaped in the boat, he spread his cloak aloft
On the bare mast, and took his lonely seat,
And felt the boat speed o'er the tranquil sea
Like a torn cloud before the hurricane.

.   .   .

When on the threshold of the green recess
The wanderer's footsteps fell, he knew that death
Was on him. Yet a little, ere it fled,
Did he resign his high and holy soul
To images of the majestic past,
630   That paused within his passive being now,
Like winds that bear sweet music, when they breathe
Through some dim latticed chamber. He did place
His pale lean hand upon the rugged trunk
Of the old pine. Upon an ivied stone
Reclined his languid head, his limbs did rest,
Diffused and motionless, on the smooth brink
Of that obscurest chasm;—and thus he lay,
Surrendering to their final impulses
The hovering powers of life. Hope and despair,
640   The torturers, slept; no mortal pain or fear
Marred his repose, the influxes of sense,
And his own being unalloyed by pain,
Yet feebler and more feeble, calmly fed
The stream of thought, till he lay breathing there
At peace, and faintly smiling:—his last sight
Was the great moon, which o'er the western line
Of the wide world her mighty horn suspended,
With whose dun beams inwoven darkness seemed
To mingle. Now upon the jaggèd hills
650   It rests, and still as the divided frame
Of the vast meteor sunk, the Poet's blood,
That ever beat in mystic sympathy
With nature's ebb and flow, grew feebler still:
And when two lessening points of light alone
Gleamed through the darkness, the alternate gasp
Of his faint respiration scarce did stir

The stagnate night:—till the minutest ray
Was quenched, the pulse yet lingered in his heart.
It paused—it fluttered. But when heaven remained
60 Utterly black, the murky shades involved
An image, silent, cold, and motionless,
As their own voiceless earth and vacant air.
Even as a vapour fed with golden beams
That ministered on sunlight, ere the west
Eclipses it, was now that wondrous frame—
No sense, no motion, no divinity—
A fragile lute, on whose harmonious strings
The breath of heaven did wander—a bright stream
Once fed with many-voicèd waves—a dream
70 Of youth, which night and time have quenched for ever,
Still, dark, and dry, and unremembered now.
    O, for Medea's wondrous alchemy,°
Which wheresoe'er it fell made the earth gleam
With bright flowers, and the wintry boughs exhale
From vernal blooms fresh fragrance! O, that God,
Profuse of poisons, would concede the chalice
Which but one living man° has drained, who now,
Vessel of deathless wrath, a slave that feels
No proud exemption in the blighting curse
80 He bears, over the world wanders for ever,
Lone as incarnate death! O, that the dream
Of dark magician in his visioned cave,°
Raking the cinders of a crucible
For life and power, even when his feeble hand
Shakes in its last decay, were the true law
Of this so lovely world! But thou art fled
Like some frail exhalation; which the dawn
Robes in its golden beams,—ah! thou hast fled!
The brave, the gentle, and the beautiful,
90 The child of grace and genius. Heartless things
Are done and said in the world, and many worms
And beasts and men live on, and mighty Earth
From sea and mountain, city and wilderness,
In vesper low or joyous orison,
Lifts still its solemn voice:—but thou art fled—
Thou canst no longer know or love the shapes
Of this phantasmal scene, who have to thee
Been purest ministers, who are, alas!
Now thou art not. Upon those pallid lips
700 So sweet even in their silence, on those eyes
That image sleep in death, upon that form
Yet safe from the worm's outrage, let no tear

Medea's . . . alchemy i.e. she could restore the
dead to life
one living man Ahasuerus, the Wandering Jew,
a late-medieval legend of an eternally condemned outcast, and one of Shelley's heroes
visioned cave cave of visions

Be shed—not even in thought. Nor, when those hues
Are gone, and those divinest lineaments,
Worn by the senseless wind, shall live alone
In the frail pauses of this simple strain,
Let not high verse, mourning the memory
Of that which is no more, or painting's woe
Or sculpture, speak in feeble imagery
710   Their own cold powers. Art and eloquence,
And all the shows o' the world are frail and vain
To weep a loss that turns their lights to shade.
It is a woe too 'deep for tears,'° when all
Is reft at once, when some surpassing Spirit,
Whose light adorned the world around it, leaves
Those who remain behind, not sobs or groans,
The passionate tumult of a clinging hope;
But pale despair and cold tranquillity,
Nature's vast frame, the web of human things,
720   Birth and the grave, that are not as they were.
1815   1816

Hymn to Intellectual° Beauty

I

The awful shadow of some unseen Power
  Floats though unseen among us,—visiting
  This various world with as inconstant wing
As summer winds that creep from flower to flower,—
Like moonbeams that behind some piny mountain shower,
    It visits with inconstant glance
    Each human heart and countenance;
Like hues and harmonies of evening,—
    Like clouds in starlight widely spread,—
10   Like memory of music fled,—
    Like aught that for its grace may be
Dear, and yet dearer for its mystery.

II

Spirit of BEAUTY, that dost consecrate
  With thine own hues all thou dost shine upon
  Of human thought or form,—where art thou gone?
Why dost thou pass away and leave our state,
This dim vast vale of tears, vacant and desolate?
    Ask why the sunlight not for ever
    Weaves rainbows o'er yon mountain-river,
20   Why aught should fail and fade that once is shown,

'deep for tears' "Intimations" ode, l. 203   Intellectual in its 18-century meaning of "be-
                                                   yond the senses"

Why fear and dream and death and birth
Cast on the daylight of this earth
Such gloom,—why man has such a scope
For love and hate, despondency and hope?

III

No voice° from some sublimer world hath ever
 To sage or poet these responses given—
Therefore the names of Demon, Ghost, and Heaven,
Remain the records of their vain endeavour,
Frail spells—whose uttered charm might not avail to sever,
30 From all we hear and all we see,
  Doubt, chance, and mutability.
Thy light alone—like mist o'er mountains driven,
 Or music by the night-wind sent
 Through strings of some still instrument,°
 Or moonlight on a midnight stream,
Gives grace and truth to life's unquiet dream.

IV

Love, Hope, and Self-esteem,° like clouds depart
 And come, for some uncertain moments lent.
 Man were immortal, and omnipotent,
40 Didst thou, unknown and awful as thou art,
Keep with thy glorious train firm state within his heart.
  Thou messenger of sympathies,
  That wax and wane in lovers' eyes—
Thou—that to human thought art nourishment,
 Like darkness to a dying flame!
 Depart not as thy shadow came,
 Depart not—lest the grave should be,
Like life and fear, a dark reality.

V

While yet a boy I sought for ghosts, and sped
50 Through many a listening chamber, cave and ruin,
 And starlight wood, with fearful steps pursuing
Hopes of high talk with the departed dead.
I called on poisonous names° with which our youth is fed;
  I was not heard—I saw them not—
  When musing deeply on the lot
Of life, at that sweet time when winds are wooing
 All vital things that wake to bring
 News of birds and blossoming,—
 Sudden, thy shadow fell on me;
60 I shrieked, and clasped my hands in ecstasy!°

No voice Shelley's "atheism"
instrument Aeolian harp
Love . . . Self-esteem Shelley's version of the
three prime Pauline virtues, with Self-esteem
replacing Faith

poisonous names God and Christ
I shrieked . . . ecstasy This line deliberately
adopts the Sibylline stance.

VI

I vowed that I would dedicate my powers
    To thee and thine—have I not kept the vow?
    With beating heart and streaming eyes, even now
I call the phantoms of a thousand hours
Each from his voiceless grave: they have in visioned bowers
        Of studious zeal or love's delight
        Outwatched with me the envious night—
They know that never joy illumed my brow
        Unlinked with hope that thou wouldst free
70   This world from its dark slavery,
        That thou—O awful LOVELINESS,
Wouldst give whate'er these words cannot express.

VII

The day becomes more solemn and serene
    When noon is past—there is a harmony
    In autumn, and a lustre in its sky,
Which through the summer is not heard or seen,
As if it could not be, as if it had not been!°
        Thus let thy power, which like the truth
        Of nature on my passive youth
80 Descended, to my onward life supply
        Its calm—to one who worships thee,
        And every form containing thee,
Whom, SPIRIT fair, thy spells did bind
To fear° himself, and love all human kind.
1816   1817

Mont Blanc°

Lines Written in the Vale of Chamouni

I

The everlasting universe of things°
Flows through the mind,° and rolls its rapid waves,
Now dark—now glittering—now reflecting gloom—

As if . . . been Shelley's version of the "sober colouring" of Wordsworth's "Intimations" ode, l. 198
fear hold in reverence
Mont Blanc in the Swiss Alps, the highest mountain in Europe. This poem is the sister-hymn to Shelley's invocation of the Intellectual Beauty, but where that saluted a transient, though benign, force, this addresses a Power at once constant, indifferent, and removed; the best analogues to Shelley's complex myth-makings here are to be found, not in platonism or in any philosophy contemporary with Shelley, but in various forms of the Gnostic religion, or heretical Christianity, or in Blake. An illuminating modern analogue is provided by Wallace Stevens's *The Auroras of Autumn,* where the initially terrifying Northern Lights intimate to the poet his own dangerous imaginative freedom from a naturalistically manifested hidden Power that has no regard for him.
universe of things at once the Arve river and all natural phenomena, in their relation to the adverting mind
mind at once the Ravine of Arve and a universal mind, such as is represented by Prometheus in Shelley's lyrical drama

Now lending splendour, where from secret springs
The source of human thought its tribute brings
Of waters,—with a sound but half its own,
Such as a feeble brook° will oft assume
In the wild woods, among the mountains lone,
Where waterfalls around it leap for ever,
10 Where woods and winds contend, and a vast river
Over its rocks ceaselessly bursts and raves.

II

Thus thou, Ravine of Arve—dark, deep Ravine—
Thou many-coloured, many-voicèd vale,
Over whose pines, and crags, and caverns sail
Fast cloud-shadows and sunbeams: awful scene,
Where Power in likeness of the Arve comes down
From the ice-gulfs that gird his secret throne,°
Bursting through these dark mountains like the flame
Of lightning through the tempest;—thou dost lie,
20 Thy giant brood of pines around thee clinging,
Children of elder time, in whose devotion
The chainless winds still come and ever came
To drink their odours, and their mighty swinging
To hear—an old and solemn harmony;
Thine earthly rainbows stretched across the sweep
Of the aethereal waterfall, whose veil
Robes some unsculptured image; the strange sleep
Which when the voices of the desert fail
Wraps all in its own deep eternity;—
30 Thy caverns echoing to the Arve's commotion,
A loud, lone sound no other sound can tame;
Thou art pervaded with that ceaseless motion,
Thou art the path of that unresting sound—
Dizzy Ravine! and when I gaze on thee
I seem as in a trance sublime and strange
To muse on my own separate fantasy,
My own, my human mind, which passively
Now renders and receives fast influencings,
Holding an unremitting interchange
40 With the clear universe of things around;
One legion of wild thoughts, whose wandering wings
Now float above thy darkness, and now rest
Where that or thou art no unbidden guest,
In the still cave of the witch Poesy,
Seeking among the shadows that pass by
Ghosts of all things that are, some shade of thee,

---

feeble brook like the individual human mind
(see l. 37)

Where Power . . . throne anticipation of Demogorgon, in *Prometheus Unbound*

Some phantom, some faint image; till the breast
From which they fled recalls them, thou art there!°

III

Some say that gleams of a remoter world
50   Visit the soul in sleep,—that death is slumber,
And that its shapes the busy thoughts outnumber
Of those who wake and live.—I look on high;
Has some unknown omnipotence unfurled
The veil of life and death? or do I lie
In dream, and does the mightier world of sleep
Spread far around and inaccessibly
Its circles? For the very spirit fails,
Driven like a homeless cloud from steep to steep
That vanishes among the viewless gales!
60   Far, far above, piercing the infinite sky,
Mont Blanc appears,—still, snowy, and serene—
Its subject mountains their unearthly forms
Pile around it, ice and rock; broad vales between
Of frozen floods, unfathomable deeps,
Blue as the overhanging heaven, that spread
And wind among the accumulated steeps;
A desert peopled by the storms alone,
Save when the eagle brings some hunter's bone,
And the wolf tracks her there—how hideously
70   Its shapes are heaped around! rude, bare, and high,
Ghastly, and scarred, and riven.—Is this the scene
Where the old Earthquake-daemon taught her young
Ruin? Were these their toys? or did a sea
Of fire envelop once this silent snow?
None can reply—all seems eternal now.
The wilderness has a mysterious tongue
Which teaches awful doubt, or faith so mild,
So solemn, so serene, that man may be,
But for such faith, with nature reconciled;°
80   Thou hast a voice, great Mountain, to repeal
Large codes of fraud and woe;° not understood
By all, but which the wise, and great, and good
Interpret, or make felt, or deeply feel.°

IV

The fields, the lakes, the forests, and the streams,
Ocean, and all the living things that dwell

thou art there when the poet ceases to search for an image of the Power, he finds it in the scene that he confronts
that man . . . reconciled Wordsworthian "faith so mild" is an idealism that prevents us from being reconciled with nature's indifference, unlike the Shelleyan "awful doubt"
Large . . . woe The codes of fraud are Christianity's; the codes of woe are made by the governments of counter-revolutionary Europe.
the wise . . . feel Godwin represents the "wise" who can "interpret"; Wordsworth the "great" who can make the mountain's voice "felt"; Coleridge the "good" who can "deeply feel"; Shelley, as skeptical visionary, stands apart from all three.

Within the daedal° earth; lightning, and rain,
Earthquake, and fiery flood, and hurricane,
The torpor of the year when feeble dreams
Visit the hidden buds, or dreamless sleep
90   Holds every future leaf and flower;—the bound
With which from that detested trance they leap;
The works and ways of man, their death and birth,
And that of him and all that his may be;
All things that move and breathe with toil and sound
Are born and die; revolve, subside, and swell.
Power dwells apart in its tranquillity,
Remote, serene, and inaccessible:
And *this*, the naked countenance of earth,
On which I gaze, even these primaeval mountains
100   Teach the adverting mind. The glaciers creep
Like snakes that watch their prey, from their far fountains,
Slow rolling on; there, many a precipice,
Frost and the Sun in scorn of mortal power
Have piled: dome, pyramid, and pinnacle,
A city of death, distinct with many a tower
And wall impregnable of beaming ice.
Yet not a city, but a flood of ruin
Is there, that from the boundaries of the sky
Rolls its perpetual stream; vast pines are strewing
110   Its destined path, or in the mangled soil
Branchless and shattered stand; the rocks, drawn down
From yon remotest waste, have overthrown
The limits of the dead and living world,
Never to be reclaimed. The dwelling-place
Of insects, beasts, and birds, becomes its spoil
Their food and their retreat for ever gone,
So much of life and joy is lost. The race
Of man flies far in dread; his work and dwelling
Vanish, like smoke before the tempest's stream,
120   And their place is not known. Below, vast caves
Shine in the rushing torrents' restless gleam,
Which from those secret chasms in tumult welling
Meet in the vale, and one majestic River,
The breath and blood of distant lands, for ever
Rolls its loud waters to the ocean-waves,
Breathes its swift vapours to the circling air.°

v

Mont Blanc yet gleams on high:—the power is there,
The still and solemn power of many sights,
And many sounds, and much of life and death.

daedal from Daedalus, great artificer of labyrinths; Shelley uses the word to mean "won-
derfully made"

Below . . . air This passage (ll. 120–26)
closely echoes Coleridge's *Kubla Khan*.

130 In the calm darkness of the moonless nights,
In the lone glare of day, the snows descend
Upon that Mountain; none beholds them there,
Nor when the flakes burn in the sinking sun,
Or the star-beams dart through them:—Winds contend
Silently there, and heap the snow with breath
Rapid and strong, but silently! Its home
The voiceless lightning in these solitudes
Keeps innocently, and like vapour broods
Over the snow. The secret Strength of things
140 Which governs thought, and to the infinite dome
Of Heaven is as a law, inhabits thee!
And what were thou, and earth, and stars, and sea,
If to the human mind's imaginings
Silence and solitude were vacancy?°
1816   1817

Ozymandias°

I met a traveller from an antique land
Who said: Two vast and trunkless legs of stone
Stand in the desert . . . Near them, on the sand,
Half sunk, a shattered visage lies, whose frown,
And wrinkled lip, and sneer of cold command,
Tell that its sculptor well those passions read
Which yet survive, stamped on these lifeless things,
The hand that mocked° them, and the heart that fed:
And on the pedestal these words appear:
10 'My name is Ozymandias, king of kings:
Look on my works, ye Mighty, and despair!'
Nothing beside remains. Round the decay
Of that colossal wreck, boundless and bare
The lone and level sands stretch far away.
1817   1818

And what . . . vacancy What would the Power, or any phenomenon mean in human terms, if our imagination could not create out of silence and solitude? Shelley ends the poem by celebrating the "violence from within," the imagination, in its response to the "violence from without," the "Dizzy Ravine."
Ozymandias another name for Rameses II of Egypt (13th century B.C.), whose colossal tomb at Thebes was in the shape of a male Sphinx. Yeats's "The Second Coming" and Stevens's Notes Toward a Supreme Fiction both make use of this sonnet.
mocked Shelley uses this to mean "artistically imitated" as well as "disdained."

From Julian and Maddalo°

A Conversation

I rode one evening with Count Maddalo
Upon the bank of land° which breaks the flow
Of Adria° towards Venice: a bare strand
Of hillocks, heaped from ever-shifting sand,
Matted with thistles and amphibious weeds,
Such as from earth's embrace the salt ooze breeds,
Is this; an uninhabited sea-side,
Which the lone fisher, when his nets are dried,
Abandons; and no other object breaks
10 The waste, but one dwarf tree and some few stakes
Broken and unrepaired, and the tide makes
A narrow space of level sand thereon,
Where 'twas our wont to ride while day went down.
This ride was my delight. I love all waste
And solitary places; where we taste
The pleasure of believing what we see
Is boundless, as we wish our souls to be:
And such was this wide ocean, and this shore
More barren than its billows; and yet more
20 Than all, with a remembered friend I love
To ride as then I rode;—for the winds drove
The living spray along the sunny air
Into our faces; the blue heavens were bare,
Stripped to their depths by the awakening north;
And, from the waves, sound like delight broke forth
Harmonising with solitude, and sent
Into our hearts aereal merriment.
So, as we rode, we talked; and the swift thought,
Winging itself with laughter, lingered not,
30 But flew from brain to brain,—such glee was ours,
Charged with light memories of remembered hours,
None slow enough for sadness: till we came
Homeward, which always makes the spirit tame.
This day had been cheerful but cold, and now
The sun was sinking, and the wind also.
Our talk grew somewhat serious, as may be
Talk interrupted with such raillery
As mocks itself, because it cannot scorn
The thoughts it would extinguish:—'twas forlorn,
40 Yet pleasing, such as once, so poets tell,
The devils held within the dales of Hell

Julian and Maddalo Julian is Shelley, Maddalo is Lord Byron; the poem undoubetdly records actual conversations between them; the poem's landscape and other details deeply influenced Browning, for which see "Two in the Campagna," "Love Among the Ruins," and *Childe Roland to the Dark Tower Came,* in particular.
bank of land the Lido
Adria Adriatic sea

Concerning God, freewill and destiny:°
Of all that earth has been or yet may be,
All that vain men imagine or believe,
Or hope can paint or suffering may achieve,
We descanted, and I (for ever still
Is it not wise to make the best of ill?)
Argued against despondency, but pride
Made my companion take the darker side.
50   The sense that he was greater than his kind
Had struck, methinks, his eagle spirit blind
By gazing on its own exceeding light.
Meanwhile the sun paused ere it should alight,
Over the horizon of the mountains;—Oh,
How beautiful is sunset, when the glow
Of Heaven descends upon a land like thee,
Thou Paradise of exiles, Italy!
Thy mountains, seas, and vineyards, and the towers
Of cities they encircle!—it was ours
60   To stand on thee, beholding it: and then,
Just where we had dismounted, the Count's men
Were waiting for us with the gondola.—
As those who pause on some delightful way
Though bent on pleasant pilgrimage, we stood
Looking upon the evening, and the flood
Which lay between the city and the shore,
Paved with the image of the sky . . . the hoar
And aery Alps towards the North appeared
Through mist, an heaven-sustaining bulwark reared
70   Between the East and West; and half the sky
Was roofed with clouds of rich emblazonry
Dark purple at the zenith, which still grew
Down the steep West into a wondrous hue
Brighter than burning gold, even to the rent
Where the swift sun yet paused in his descent
Among the many-folded hills: they were
Those famous Euganean hills, which bear,
As seen from Lido through the harbour piles,
The likeness of a clump of peakèd isles—
80   And then—as if the Earth and Sea had been
Dissolved into one lake of fire, were seen
Those mountains towering as from waves of flame
Around the vaporous sun, from which there came
The inmost purple spirit of light, and made
Their very peaks transparent. 'Ere it fade,'
Said my companion, 'I will show you soon
A better station'—so, o'er the lagune°

'twas forlorn . . . destiny See *Paradise Lost*   lagune lagoon
II.555–69.

We glided; and from that funereal bark
I leaned, and saw the city, and could mark
90   How from their many isles, in evening's gleam,
Its temples and its palaces did seem
Like fabrics of enchantment piled to Heaven.
I was about to speak, when—'We are even
Now at the point I meant,' said Maddalo,
And bade the gondolieri cease to row.
'Look, Julian, on the west, and listen well
If you hear not a deep and heavy bell.'
I looked, and saw between us and the sun
A building on an island; such a one
100   As age to age might add, for uses vile,
A windowless, deformed and dreary pile;
And on the top an open tower, where hung
A bell, which in the radiance swayed and swung;
We could just hear its hoarse and iron tongue:
The broad sun sunk behind it, and it tolled
In strong and black relief.—'What we behold
Shall be the madhouse and its belfry tower,'
Said Maddalo, 'and ever at this hour
Those who may cross the water, hear that bell
110   Which calls the maniacs, each one from his cell,
To vespers.'—'As much skill as need to pray
In thanks or hope for their dark lot have they
To their stern maker,' I replied. 'O ho!
You talk as in years past,' said Maddalo.
' 'Tis strange men change not. You were ever still
Among Christ's flock a perilous infidel,
A wolf for the meek lambs—if you can't swim
Beware of Providence.'° I looked on him,
But the gay smile had faded in his eye.
120   'And such,'—he cried, 'is our mortality,
And this must be the emblem and the sign
Of what should be eternal and divine!—
And like that black and dreary bell, the soul,
Hung in a heaven-illumined tower, must toll
Our thoughts and our desires to meet below
Round the rent heart and pray—as madmen do
For what? they know not,—till the night of death
As sunset that strange vision, severeth
Our memory from itself, and us from all
130   We sought and yet were baffled.' I recall
The sense of what he said, although I mar
The force of his expressions. The broad star

if you . . . Providence Byron was a swimmer of European reputation; Shelley declined to
learn.

Of day meanwhile had sunk behind the hill,
And the black bell became invisible,
And the red tower looked gray, and all between
The churches, ships and palaces were seen
Huddled in gloom;—into the purple sea
The orange hues of heaven sunk silently.
We hardly spoke, and soon the gondola
140   Conveyed me to my lodging by the way.
     The following morn was rainy, cold and dim:
Ere Maddalo arose, I called on him,
And whilst I waited with his child° I played;
A lovelier toy sweet Nature never made,
A serious, subtle, wild, yet gentle being,
Graceful without design and unforeseeing,
With eye—Oh speak not of her eyes!—which seem
Twin mirrors of Italian Heaven, yet gleam
With such deep meaning, as we never see
150   But in the human countenance: with me
She was a special favourite: I had nursed
Her fine and feeble limbs when she came first
To this bleak world; and she yet seemed to know
On second sight her ancient playfellow,
Less changed than she was by six months or so;
For after her first shyness was worn out
We sate there, rolling billiard balls about,
When the Count entered. Salutations past—
'The word you spoke last night might well have cast
160   A darkness on my spirit—if man be
The passive thing you say, I should not see
Much harm in the religions and old saws
(Though I may never own such leaden laws)
Which break a teachless nature to the yoke:
Mine is another faith'—thus much I spoke
And noting he replied not, added: 'See
This lovely child, blithe, innocent and free;
She spends a happy time with little care,
While we to such sick thoughts subjected are
170   As came on you last night—it is our will
That thus enchains us to permitted ill—
We might be otherwise—we might be all
We dream of happy, high, majestical.
Where is the love, beauty, and truth we seek
But in our mind? and if we were not weak
Should we be less in deed than in desire?'
'Ay, if we were not weak—and we aspire

his child Allegra, the natural daughter of Byron
and Claire Clairmont, Mary Shelley's foster-
sister

How vainly to be strong!' said Maddalo:
'You talk Utopia.' 'It remains to know,'
180   I then rejoined, 'and those who try may find
How strong the chains are which our spirit bind;
Brittle perchance as straw . . . We are assured
Much may be conquered, much may be endured,
Of what degrades and crushes us. We know
That we have power over ourselves to do
And suffer—what, we know not till we try;
But something nobler than to live and die—
So taught those kings of old philosophy
Who reigned, before Religion made men blind;
190   And those who suffer with their suffering kind
Yet feel their faith, religion.' . . .

   . . . then we lingered not,
520   Although our argument was quite forgot,
But calling the attendants, went to dine
At Maddalo's; yet neither cheer nor wine
Could give us spirits, for we talked of him°
And nothing else, till daylight made stars dim;
And we agreed his was some dreadful ill
Wrought on him boldly, yet unspeakable,
By a dear friend; some deadly change in love
Of one vowed deeply which he dreamed not of;
For whose sake he, it seemed, had fixed a blot
530   Of falsehood on his mind which flourished not
But in the light of all-beholding truth;
And having stamped this canker on his youth
She had abandoned him—and how much more
Might be his woe, we guessed not—he had store
Of friends and fortune once, as we could guess
From his nice habits and his gentleness;
These were now lost . . . it were a grief indeed
If he had changed one unsustaining reed
For all that such a man might else adorn.
540   The colours of his mind seemed yet unworn;
For the wild language of his grief was high,
Such as in measure were called poetry;
And I remember one remark which then
Maddalo made. He said: 'Most wretched men
Are cradled into poetry by wrong,
They learn in suffering what they teach in song.'
   If I had been an unconnected man
I, from this moment, should have formed some plan

him a nameless mad poet (probably Tasso)
whose confinement is the subject of the middle
part of the poem

Never to leave sweet Venice,—for to me
550   It was delight to ride by the lone sea;
And then, the town is silent—one may write
Or read in gondolas by day or night,
Having the little brazen lamp alight,
Unseen, uninterrupted; books are there,
Pictures, and casts from all those statues fair
Which were twin-born with poetry, and all
We seek in towns, with little to recall
Regrets for the green country. I might sit
In Maddalo's great palace, and his wit
560   And subtle talk would cheer the winter night
And make me know myself, and the firelight
Would flash upon our faces, till the day
Might dawn and make me wonder at my stay:
But I had friends in London too: the chief
Attraction here, was that I sought relief
From the deep tenderness that maniac wrought
Within me—'twas perhaps an idle thought—
But I imagined that if day by day
I watched him, and but seldom went away,
570   And studied all the beatings of his heart
With zeal, as men study some stubborn art
For their own good, and could by patience find
An entrance to the caverns of his mind,
I might reclaim him from his dark estate:
In friendships I had been most fortunate—
Yet never saw I one whom I would call
More willingly my friend; and this was all
Accomplished not; such dreams of baseless good
Oft come and go in crowds or solitude
580   And leave no trace—but what I now designed
Made for long years impression on my mind.
The following morning, urged by my affairs,
I left bright Venice . . .
1818   1824

Prometheus Unbound

The Greek Orphic tradition maintained that the Titans, whom Zeus and the Olympian gods overthrew, were our ancestors. Hesiod said that the name, Titans, meant "punished overreachers." Of these overreachers, Prometheus (whose name means "foresighted," "prophetic") is the most celebrated. Aeschylus, the Athenian tragic dramatist, wrote a trilogy on Prometheus, of which only the first play, *Prometheus Bound*, survives. In it, Zeus (Shelley's Jupiter) is a tyrant who tortures Prometheus, but the Titan has faults also, being prideful and unrestrained. The surviving fragments of Aeschylus' second play, *Prometheus Unbound*, indicate that Zeus is reforming himself, as he has partly restored the Titan, and has given up his threats to destroy mankind. He still seeks to induce Prometheus to reveal a fatal secret, known only to the Titan, which will destroy Olympian rule, the secret being that any child Zeus begets upon Thetis, a mortal woman, will rise eventually to destroy his father.

Shelley rejects the outcome of Aeschylus' lost second play, which reconciles Zeus and Prometheus, and which permits Zeus to be warned in time. Shelley's Romantic Prometheus never yields to Jupiter, but he ceases to hate Jupiter, and in doing so begins a process that destroys the High God, whom Shelley regards as being beyond redemption. This process is imaginatively difficult, but is undoubtedly the supreme poetic invention in Shelley's work. To understand it, a reader needs to clarify for himself the curious shape of Shelley's myth in the poem.

As in Blake's *The Four Zoas,* the postulate is that a unitary Man fell, and separated out into torturing and tortured components, and into male and female forms as well. Jupiter is not an ultimate evil, even though he would like to be; he is too limited, because he has been invented by his victim, Prometheus, and cannot survive long once Prometheus abandons hatred of his own invention. As for Prometheus himself, he is limited also, for though he contains the human imagination and sexual energy, he can only begin the process of freeing imagination and sexuality. To complete it he requires Asia, who is again a limited being. Despite much scholarly interpretation to the contrary, she does not contain a universal Love or what Shelley termed the Intellectual Beauty, though in her apotheosis (at the end of Act II) she momentarily becomes one with these high powers. Mostly she remains subject to nature and can best be thought of as that provisional strength in humanity (much celebrated by Wordsworth) that holds the natural world, even in its dreadfully fallen condition, open to the love and beauty that hover perpetually (according to Shelley) just beyond the range of our senses.

Demogorgon is the lyrical drama's prime difficulty. Unlike the Demogorgon of Spenser, Milton, and Coleridge (see his fragment, "Limbo"), Shelley's daemon is not the pagan god of the abyss, but rather the god of skepticism, of our appalled but honest question: "What can we know?" He is a dialectical entity, who governs the turning-over of historical cycles, resembling in this the Marxist dialectic of history (Engels and Marx greatly admired Shelley's poem). He is also a parody of the descent of the Holy Spirit in some Christian accounts of fallen history. His limitation is what most characterizes him, for he represents the imagelessness of ultimates, like the dread, morally unallied Power behind the ravine in Shelley's *Mont Blanc.*

Though it is very much a poem of Shelley's own revolutionary age, *Prometheus Unbound* transcends the limiting context of any particular time, or rather becomes sharply relevant in any new time-of-troubles. Shelley, always a revolutionary temperament, is not teaching quietism or acceptance. But he shows, in agonizing, deeply inward ways, how difficult the path of regeneration is, and how much both the head and the heart need to purge in themselves if and when regeneration is ever to begin.

Prometheus Unbound

A Lyrical Drama in Four Acts

Audisne haec amphiarae, sub terram abdite? [1]

Preface

The Greek tragic writers, in selecting as their subject any portion of their national history or mythology, employed in their treatment of it a certain arbitrary discretion. They by no means conceived themselves bound to adhere to the common interpretation or to imitate in story as in title their rivals and predecessors. Such a system would have amounted to a resignation of those claims to preference over their competitors which incited the composition. The Agamemnonian story was exhibited on the Athenian theatre with as many variations as dramas.

I have presumed to employ a similar licence. The *Prometheus Unbound* of Aeschylus supposed the reconciliation of Jupiter with his victim as the price of the disclosure of the danger threatened to his empire by the consummation of his marriage with Thetis. Thetis, according to this view of the subject, was given in marriage to Peleus, and Prometheus, by the permission of Jupiter, delivered from his captivity by Hercules. Had I framed my story on this model, I should have done no more than have attempted to restore the lost drama of Aeschylus; an ambition which, if my preference to this mode of treating the subject had incited me to cherish, the recollection of the high comparison such an attempt would challenge might well abate. But, in truth, I was averse from a catastrophe so feeble as that of reconciling the Champion with the Oppressor of mankind. The moral interest of the fable, which is so powerfully sustained by the sufferings and endurance of Prometheus, would be annihilated if we could conceive of him as unsaying his high language and quailing before his successful and perfidious adversary. The only imaginary being resembling in any degree Prometheus, is Satan; and Prometheus is, in my judgement, a more poetical character than Satan, because, in addition to courage, and majesty, and firm and patient opposition to omnipotent force, he is susceptible of being described as exempt from the taints of ambition, envy, revenge, and a desire for personal aggrandisement, which, in the Hero of *Paradise Lost*, interfere with the interest. The character of Satan engenders in the mind a pernicious casuistry which leads us to weigh his faults with his wrongs, and to excuse the former because the latter exceed all measure. In the minds of those who consider that magnificent fiction with a religious feeling it engenders something worse. But Prometheus is, as it were, the type of the highest perfection of moral and intellectual nature, impelled by the purest and the truest motives to the best and noblest ends.

---

1. "Do you hear this, Amphiaraus, in your home beneath the earth?" This verse, by an unknown translator of a lost play by Aeschylus, is quoted in Cicero's *Tusculan Disputations*, as a reproach to a wavering stoic. Amphiaraus, a renowned Seer, was one of the Seven against Thebes, who later became an oracular god in a cave beneath the earth. Shelley's epigraph (perhaps over-subtle) seems directed against Wordsworth and Coleridge, once rebels but now oracular in their piety. They are asked to hear this play, which voices the stoic defiance of Prometheus (and of Shelley).

This Poem was chiefly written upon the mountainous ruins of the Baths of Caracalla,[2] among the flowery glades, and thickets of odoriferous blossoming trees, which are extended in ever winding labyrinths upon its immense platforms and dizzy arches suspended in the air. The bright blue sky of Rome, and the effect of the vigorous awakening spring in that divinest climate, and the new life with which it drenches the spirits even to intoxication, were the inspiration of this drama.

The imagery which I have employed will be found, in many instances, to have been drawn from the operations of the human mind, or from those external actions by which they are expressed. This is unusual in modern poetry, although Dante and Shakespeare are full of instances of the same kind: Dante indeed more than any other poet, and with greater success. But the Greek poets, as writers to whom no resource of awakening the sympathy of their contemporaries was unknown, were in the habitual use of this power; and it is the study of their works (since a higher merit would probably be denied me) to which I am willing that my readers should impute this singularity.

One word is due in candour to the degree in which the study of contemporary writings may have tinged my composition, for such has been a topic of censure with regard to poems far more popular, and indeed more deservedly popular, than mine. It is impossible that any one who inhabits the same age with such writers as those who stand in the foremost ranks of our own, can conscientiously assure himself that his language and tone of thought may not have been modified by the study of the productions of those extraordinary intellects. It is true, that, not the spirit of their genius, but the forms in which it has manifested itself, are due less to the peculiarities of their own minds than to the peculiarity of the moral and intellectual condition of the minds among which they have been produced. Thus a number of writers possess the form, whilst they want the spirit of those whom, it is alleged, they imitate; because the former is the endowment of the age in which they live, and the latter must be the uncommunicated lightning of their own mind.

The peculiar style of intense and comprehensive imagery which distinguishes the modern literature of England, has not been, as a general power, the product of the imitation of any particular writer. The mass of capabilities remains at every period materially the same; the circumstances which awaken it to action perpetually change. If England were divided into forty republics, each equal in population and extent to Athens, there is no reason to suppose but that, under institutions not more perfect than those of Athens, each would produce philosophers and poets equal to those who (if we except Shakespeare) have never been surpassed. We owe the great writers of the golden age of our literature to that fervid awakening of the public mind which shook to dust the oldest and most oppressive form of the Christian religion. We owe Milton to the progress and development of the same spirit: the sacred Milton was, let it ever be remembered, a republican, and a bold inquirer into morals and religion. The great writers of our own age are, we have reason to suppose, the companions and forerunners of some unimagined change in our social condition or the opinions which cement it. The cloud of mind is discharging its

2. Ancient sprawling baths of Rome named for the Emperor Caracalla (188-217 A.D.).

collected lightning, and the equilibrium between institutions and opinions is now restoring, or is about to be restored.

As to imitation, poetry is a mimetic art. It creates, but it creates by combination and representation. Poetical abstractions are beautiful and new, not because the portions of which they are composed had no previous existence in the mind of man or in nature, but because the whole produced by their combination has some intelligible and beautiful analogy with those sources of emotion and thought, and with the contemporary condition of them: one great poet is a masterpiece of nature which another not only ought to study but must study. He might as wisely and as easily determine that his mind should no longer be the mirror of all that is lovely in the visible universe, as exclude from his contemplation the beautiful which exists in the writings of a great contemporary. The pretence of doing it would be a presumption in any but the greatest; the effect, even in him, would be strained, unnatural, and ineffectual. A poet is the combined product of such internal powers as modify the nature of others; and of such external influences as excite and sustain these powers; he is not one, but both. Every man's mind is, in this respect, modified by all the objects of nature and art; by every word and every suggestion which he ever admitted to act upon his consciousness; it is the mirror upon which all forms are reflected, and in which they compose one form. Poets, not otherwise than philosophers, painters, sculptors, and musicians, are, in one sense, the creators, and, in another, the creations, of their age. From this subjection the loftiest do not escape. There is a similarity between Homer and Hesiod, between Aeschylus and Euripides, between Virgil and Horace, between Dante and Petrarch, between Shakespeare and Fletcher, between Dryden and Pope; each has a generic resemblance under which their specific distinctions are arranged. If this similarity be the result of imitation, I am willing to confess that I have imitated.

Let this opportunity be conceded to me of acknowledging that I have, what a Scotch philosopher characteristically terms, 'a passion for reforming the world': what passion incited him to write and publish his book, he omits to explain. For my part I had rather be damned with Plato and Lord Bacon, than go to Heaven with Paley and Malthus.[3] But it is a mistake to suppose that I dedicate my poetical compositions solely to the direct enforcement of reform, or that I consider them in any degree as containing a reasoned system on the theory of human life. Didactic poetry is my abhorrence; nothing can be equally well expressed in prose that is not tedious and supererogatory in verse. My purpose has hitherto been simply to familiarise the highly refined imagination of the more select classes of poetical readers with beautiful idealisms of moral excellence; aware that until the mind can love, and admire, and trust, and hope, and endure, reasoned principles of moral conduct are seeds cast upon the highway of life which the unconscious passenger tramples into dust, although they would bear the harvest of his happiness. Should I live to accomplish what I purpose, that is, produce a systematical history of what

3. William Paley (1743–1805), popular theologian, maintained the case for natural religion, and argued the moral usefulness of Hell. Thomas Robert Malthus (1776–1834), popular economist, demonstrated war, famine, and pestilence to be necessary due to the excess of population growth over food production. Shelley, as a revolutionary reformer, despised both as apologists for things-as-they-are.

appear to me to be the genuine elements of human society, let not the advocates of injustice and superstition flatter themselves that I should take Aeschylus rather than Plato as my model.

The having spoken of myself with unaffected freedom will need little apology with the candid; and let the uncandid consider that they injure me less than their own hearts and minds by misrepresentation. Whatever talents a person may possess to amuse and instruct others, be they ever so inconsiderable, he is yet bound to exert them: if his attempt be ineffectual, let the punishment of an unaccomplished purpose have been sufficient; let none trouble themselves to heap the dust of oblivion upon his efforts; the pile they raise will betray his grave which might otherwise have been unknown.

DRAMATIS PERSONAE

PROMETHEUS	APOLLO	HERCULES
DEMOGORGON	MERCURY	THE PHANTASM OF JUPITER
JUPITER	ASIA ⎫	THE SPIRIT OF THE EARTH
THE EARTH	PANTHEA ⎬ *Oceanides.*	THE SPIRIT OF THE MOON
OCEAN	IONE ⎭	SPIRITS OF THE HOURS
SPIRITS ECHOES FAUNS FURIES		

From ACT I

SCENE *A Ravine of Icy Rocks in the Indian Caucasus.* PROMETHEUS *is discovered bound to the Precipice.* PANTHEA *and* IONE *are seated at his feet. Time, night. During the Scene, morning slowly breaks.*

PROMETHEUS   Monarch of Gods and Daemons, and all Spirits
But One,° who throng those bright and rolling worlds
Which Thou and I alone of living things
Behold with sleepless eyes! regard this Earth
Made multitudinous with thy slaves, whom thou
Requitest for knee-worship, prayer, and praise,
And toil, and hecatombs° of broken hearts,
With fear and self-contempt and barren hope.°
Whilst me, who am thy foe, eyeless in hate,
10   Hast thou made reign and triumph, to thy scorn,°
O'er mine own misery and thy vain revenge.
Three thousand years of sleep-unsheltered hours,
And moments aye divided by keen pangs
Till they seemed years, torture and solitude,
Scorn and despair,—these are mine empire:—
More glorious far than that which thou surveyest
From thine unenvied throne, O Mighty God!
Almighty, had I deigned to share the shame
Of thine ill tyranny, and hung not here
20   Nailed to this wall of eagle-baffling mountain,

One probably Demogorgon
hecatombs gigantic sacrifices
With fear . . . hope the negations of the

Shelleyan virtues: love, self-esteem, hope
Whilst me . . . scorn making you (Jupiter) an
object of scorn

Black, wintry, dead, unmeasured; without herb,
Insect, or beast, or shape or sound of life.
Ah me! alas, pain, pain ever, forever!

No change, no pause, no hope! Yet I endure.
I ask the Earth, have not the mountains felt?
I ask yon Heaven, the all-beholding Sun,
Has it not seen? The sea, in storm or calm,
Heaven's ever-changing Shadow, spread below,
Have its deaf waves not heard my agony?
30 Ah me! alas, pain, pain ever, forever!

The crawling glaciers pierce me with the spears
Of their moon-freezing crystals, the bright chains
Eat with their burning cold into my bones.
Heaven's wingèd hound, polluting from thy lips
His beak in poison not his own, tears up
My heart;° and shapeless sights come wandering by,
The ghastly people of the realm of dream,
Mocking me: and the Earthquake-fiends are charged
To wrench the rivets from my quivering wounds
40 When the rocks split and close again behind:
While from their loud abysses howling throng
The genii of the storm, urging the rage
Of whirlwind, and afflict me with keen hail.
And yet to me welcome is day and night,
Whether one breaks the hoar frost of the morn,
Or starry, dim, and slow, the other climbs
The leaden-coloured east; for then they lead
The wingless, crawling hours, one among whom
—As some dark Priest hales the reluctant victim
50 Shall drag thee, cruel King, to kiss the blood
From these pale feet, which then might trample thee
If they disdained not such a prostrate slave.
Disdain! Ah no! I pity thee.° What ruin
Will hunt thee undefended through wide Heaven!
How will thy soul, cloven to its depth with terror,
Gape like a hell within! I speak in grief,
Not exultation, for I hate no more,
As then ere misery made me wise. The curse
Once breathed on thee I would recall. Ye Mountains,
60 Whose many-voicèd Echoes, through the mist
Of cataracts, flung the thunder of that spell!
Ye icy Springs, stagnant with wrinkling frost,
Which vibrated to hear me, and then crept
Shuddering through India! Thou serenest Air,

Heaven's . . . heart The vulture perpetually
kissed Jupiter, and then proceeded to its daily
torture of Prometheus.

I pity thee the turning over of the Promethean
cycle

Through which the Sun walks burning without beams!
And ye swift Whirlwinds, who on poisèd wings
Hung mute and moveless o'er yon hushed abyss,
As thunder, louder than your own, made rock
The orbèd world! If then my words had power,
70   Though I am changed so that aught evil wish
Is dead within; although no memory be
Of what is hate, let them not lose it now!
What was that curse? for ye all heard me speak.

. . .

PROMETHEUS   Venerable mother!°
All else who live and suffer take from thee
Some comfort; flowers, and fruits, and happy sounds,
And love, though fleeting; these may not be mine.
190 But mine own words, I pray, deny me not.
THE EARTH They shall be told. Ere Babylon was dust,
The Magus Zoroaster, my dead child,
Met his own image walking in the garden.°
That apparition, sole of men, he saw.
For know there are two worlds of life and death:
One that which thou beholdest; but the other
Is underneath the grave, where do inhabit
The shadows of all forms that think and live
Till death unite them and they part no more;°
200 Dreams and the light imaginings of men,
And all that faith creates or love desires,
Terrible, strange, sublime and beauteous shapes.
There thou art, and dost hang, a writhing shade,
'Mid whirlwind-peopled mountains; all the gods
Are there, and all the powers of nameless worlds,
Vast, sceptred phantoms; heroes, men, and beasts;
And Demogorgon,° a tremendous gloom;
And he, the supreme Tyrant, on his throne
Of burning gold. Son, one of these shall utter
210 The curse which all remember. Call at will

Venerable mother After the scatterd components of a fallen world have refused to repeat
his forgotten curse, the Titan appeals to the
Earth, his mother.
Zoroaster . . . garden Zoroaster, a 6th-century
B.C. Persian, founded a dualistic religion, as the
prophet of Ormazd, spirit of good, against Ahriman (or Ahuramazda), spirit of evil. The story
of his meeting his double is Shelley's invention,
and repeats the ancient superstition that to meet
one's double is to be close to one's death. There
is a legend that Shelley met his double a few
days before he drowned, and fainted when the
double asked him: "How long do you mean to
be content?"
Till . . . more an anticipation of the modern

German poet R.M. Rilke's myth that we become
complete by marrying our own deaths
Demogorgon The most difficult interpretative
problem in the poem; late medieval and early
Renaissance mythologists made Demogorgon the
father of all the Gentile gods, and the original
ruler of the Abyss or Chaos, a role he fills in
Spenser, Milton, and in Coleridge's "Limbo."
In Shelley's poem he is more a dialectic or
process of how things happen than he is a personage; he is morally unallied, and thus the god
of skepticism, preceptor of our appalling freedom to imagine well or badly. As such, he resembles both the historical dialectic of the
Marxists, and the descent of the Holy Spirit in
Christian readings of history. He may be a deliberate parody of the Holy Spirit.

Thine own ghost, or the ghost of Jupiter,
Hades or Typhon,° or what mightier Gods
From all-prolific Evil, since thy ruin
Have sprung, and trampled on my prostrate sons.
Ask, and they must reply: so the revenge
Of the Supreme may sweep through vacant shades,
As rainy wind through the abandoned gate
Of a fallen palace.

. . .

PHANTASM OF JUPITER
    Fiend, I defy thee! with a calm, fixed mind,°
      All that thou canst inflict I bid thee do;
    Foul Tyrant both of Gods and Human-kind,
      One only being shalt thou not subdue.
    Rain then thy plagues upon me here,
    Ghastly disease, and frenzying fear;
    And let alternate frost and fire
    Eat into me, and be thine ire
270   Lightning, and cutting hail, and legioned forms
    Of furies, driving by upon the wounding storms,

    Ay, do thy worst. Thou art omnipotent.
      O'er all things but thyself I gave thee power,
    And my own will. Be thy swift mischiefs sent
      To blast mankind, from yon ethereal tower.
    Let thy malignant spirit move
    In darkness over those I love:
    On me and mine I imprecate
    The utmost torture of thy hate;
280   And thus devote to sleepless agony,
    This undeclining head while thou must reign on high.

    But thou, who art the God and Lord: O, thou,
      Who fillest with thy soul this world of woe,
    To whom all things of Earth and Heaven do bow
      In fear and worship: all-prevailing foe!
    I curse thee! let a sufferer's curse
    Clasp thee, his torturer, like remorse;
    Till thine Infinity shall be
    A robe of envenomed agony;°
290   And thine Omnipotence a crown of pain,
    To cling like burning gold round thy dissolving brain.

Hades or Typhon Hades here is Pluto, lord of Hades; Typhon is a monster with many heads, responsible for earthquakes.
mind The mind is that of Prometheus, but the speaker is the Phantasm or shadow-form, the double of Jupiter, uttering a curse of which he will be the victim, and which Prometheus now seeks vainly to recall.
thine . . . agony the Infinity of Jupiter will torture him even as the shirt of the centaur Nessus tormented Heracles, a suffering that caused Heracles to mount his death-pyre

Heap on thy soul, by virtue of this Curse,
   Ill deeds, then be thou damned, beholding good;°
Both infinite as is the universe,
   And thou, and thy self-torturing solitude.
An awful image of calm power
Though now thou sittest, let the hour
Come, when thou must appear to be
That which thou art internally;
300   And after many a false and fruitless crime
Scorn track thy lagging fall through boundless space and time.

PROMETHEUS   Were these my words, O Parent?
THE EARTH   They were thine.
PROMETHEUS   It doth repent me: words are quick and vain;
Grief for awhile is blind, and so was mine.
I wish no living thing to suffer pain.

      .   .   .

FURY   Behold an emblem: those who do endure
Deep wrongs for man, and scorn, and chains, but heap
Thousandfold torment on themselves and him.°
PROMETHEUS   Remit the anguish of that lighted stare;
Close those wan lips; let that thorn-wounded brow
Stream not with blood; it mingles with thy tears!
600   Fix, fix those tortured orbs in peace and death,
So thy sick throes shake not that crucifix,
So those pale fingers play not with thy gore.
O, horrible! Thy name I will not speak,
It hath become a curse.° I see, I see
The wise, the mild, the lofty, and the just,
Whom thy slaves hate for being like to thee,
Some hunted by foul lies from their heart's home,
An early-chosen, late-lamented home;
As hooded ounces° cling to the driven hind;
610   Some linked to corpses in unwholesome cells:
Some—Hear I not the multitude laugh loud?—
Impaled in lingering fire: and mighty realms
Float by my feet, like sea-uprooted isles,
Whose sons are kneaded down in common blood
By the red light of their own burning homes.
FURY   Blood thou canst see, and fire; and canst hear groans;
Worse things, unheard, unseen, remain behind.
PROMETHEUS   Worse?
FURY   In each human heart terror survives

Heap . . . good Prometheus cursed Jupiter as Milton's God cursed Satan, a peculiarly Shelleyan irony; see *Paradise Lost* I.209–20.
Behold . . . him The Furies, sent by Jupiter to torment Prometheus, have given him a vision of the moral failure of the French Revolution; the last and subtlest Fury now demonstrates that the sacrifice of Christ only brought about a new tyranny, historical and institutional Christianity, which has martyred man afresh.
It . . . curse In the sense that societal Christianity has driven out Shelley, Byron, and others for supposed moral offenses, and deprived Shelley of his children by his first marriage.
ounces trained leopards kept hooded until released to hunt down the hind, or deer

The ravin° it has gorged: the loftiest fear
620   All that they would disdain to think were true:
Hypocrisy and custom make their minds
The fanes of many a worship, now outworn.
They dare not devise good for man's estate,
And yet they know not that they do not dare.
The good want power, but to weep barren tears.
The powerful goodness want: worse need for them.
The wise want love; and those who love want wisdom;
And all best things are thus confused to ill.°
Many are strong and rich, and would be just,
630   But live among their suffering fellow-men
As if none felt: they know not what they do.°
    PROMETHEUS   Thy words are like a cloud of wingèd snakes;
And yet I pity those they torture not.
    FURY   Thou pitiest them? I speak no more!
[*Vanishes*]

·   ·   ·

    ACT II
From SCENE IV°   *The Cave of* DEMOGORGON. ASIA *and* PANTHEA.
    PANTHEA   What veilèd form sits on that ebon throne?
    ASIA   The veil has fallen.
    PANTHEA   I see a mighty darkness
Filling the seat of power, and rays of gloom
Dart round, as light from the meridian sun.
—Ungazed upon and shapeless; neither limb,
Nor form, nor outline; yet we feel it is
A living Spirit.
    DEMOGORGON   Ask what thou wouldst know.
    ASIA   What canst thou tell?
    DEMOGORGON   All things thou dar'st demand.
    ASIA   Who made the living world?
    DEMOGORGON   God.°
    ASIA   Who made all
10   That it contains? thought, passion, reason, will,
Imagination?
    DEMOGORGON   God: Almighty God.°
    ASIA   Who made that sense which, when the winds of Spring
In rarest visitation, or the voice

ravin carrion
The wise . . . ill Compare Yeats's "The Second
Coming," which echoes this passage; the wise
who lack love include Godwin and Shelley's own
revolutionary intelligentsia, while those who love
but lack wisdom include Wordsworth and Coleridge.
they know . . . do See Luke 23:34.
Scene IV Asia, the wife of Prometheus, long
separated from him by Jupiter, has descended to
the oracular cave of Demogorgon, to find out

how and when the overthrow of Jupiter, and her
subsequent reunion with Prometheus, will take
place. In her difficult dialogue with Demogorgon, he is not so much evasive as relatively unknowing; she learns only what she already knows
and is, but this is enough, since the time of
renovation is now.
God not Jupiter, but a figure closer to Prometheus himself
Almighty God the ultimate Power, as in "Mont
Blanc"

Of one beloved heard in youth alone,
Fills the faint eyes with falling tears which dim
The radiant looks of unbewailing flowers,
And leaves this peopled earth a solitude
When it returns no more?°

DEMOGORGON   Merciful God.°

20 ASIA   And who made terror, madness, crime, remorse,
Which from the links of the great chain of things,
To every thought within the mind of man
Sway and drag heavily, and each one reels
Under the load towards the pit of death;
Abandoned hope, and love that turns to hate;
And self-contempt,° bitterer to drink than blood;
Pain, whose unheeded and familiar speech
Is howling, and keen shrieks, day after day;
And Hell, or the sharp fear of Hell?

DEMOGORGON   He reigns.°

ASIA   Utter his name: a world pining in pain
30 Asks but his name: curses shall drag him down.

DEMOGORGON   He reigns.

ASIA   I feel, I know it: who?

DEMOGORGON   He reigns.

ASIA   Who reigns? There was the Heaven and Earth at first,°
And Light and Love; then Saturn, from whose throne
Time fell, an envious shadow: such the state
Of the earth's primal spirits beneath his sway,
As the calm joy of flowers and living leaves
Before the wind or sun has withered them
And semivital worms; but he refused
The birthright of their being, knowledge, power,
40 The skill which wields the elements, the thought
Which pierces this dim universe like light,
Self-empire, and the majesty of love;
For thirst of which they fainted. Then Prometheus
Gave wisdom, which is strength, to Jupiter,
And with this law alone, 'Let man be free,'
Clothed him with the dominion of wide Heaven.°
To know nor faith, nor love, nor law; to be
Omnipotent but friendless is to reign;
And Jove now reigned; for on the race of man
50 First famine, and then toil, and then disease,

Who made . . . more Asia's experience recalls
the "Hymn to Intellectual Beauty."
Merciful God the Intellectual Beauty
self-contempt the greatest of vices in Shelley's
moral universe
He reigns Jupiter
at first Asia's complex cosmogony describes (ll.
32–38), as Blake's does, an original Saturnian
or happy and unfallen universe, rather than an

initial chaos, as in the Hebraic account.
Then Prometheus . . . Heaven Saturn, king of
the Titans, refused to give us the equivocal gift
of consciousness, which Prometheus (as in the
poetry of Empedocles, a pre-Socratic philosopher) insisted was necessary for us to be wholly
human; Jupiter, the agent of Prometheus, betrayed him and us, imposing the tyranny of
Heaven.

Strife, wounds, and ghastly death unseen before,
Fell; and the unseasonable seasons drove
With alternating shafts of frost and fire,
Their shelterless, pale tribes to mountain caves:
And in their desert hearts fierce wants he sent,
And mad disquietudes, and shadows idle
Of unreal good, which levied mutual war,
So ruining the lair wherein they raged.
Prometheus saw, and waked the legioned hopes
60   Which sleep within folded Elysian flowers,
Nepenthe, Moly, Amaranth,° fadeless blooms,
That they might hide with thin and rainbow wings
The shape of Death; and Love he sent to bind
The disunited tendrils of that vine
Which bears the wine of life, the human heart;
And he tamed fire which, like some beast of prey,
Most terrible, but lovely, played beneath
The frown of man; and tortured to his will
Iron and gold, the slaves and signs of power,
70   And gems and poisons, and all subtlest forms
Hidden beneath the mountains and the waves.
He gave man speech, and speech created thought,
Which is the measure of the universe;
And Science struck the thrones of earth and heaven,
Which shook, but fell not; and the harmonious mind
Poured itself forth in all-prophetic song;
And music lifted up the listening spirit
Until it walked, exempt from mortal care.
Godlike, o'er the clear billows of sweet sound;
80   And human hands first mimicked and then mocked,
With moulded limbs more lovely than its own,
The human form, till marble grew divine;
And mothers, gazing, drank the love men see
Reflected in their race, behold, and perish.
He told the hidden power of herbs and springs,
And Disease drank and slept. Death grew like sleep.
He taught the implicated orbits woven
Of the wide-wandering stars; and how the sun
Changes his lair, and by what secret spell
90   The pale moon is transformed, when her broad eye
Gazes not on the interlunar sea:
He taught to rule, as life directs the limbs,
The tempest-wingèd chariots of the Ocean,
And the Celt knew the Indian. Cities then
Were built, and through their snow-like columns flowed
The warm winds, and the azure aether shone,

Nepenthe was a drug giving forgetfulness,
Moly a herb to protect against enchantment,
and Amaranth an undying, unfading flower.

1. The Royal Pavilion at Brighton, reconstructed in 1818 by John Nash (1752–1835), a monumental plaything of the Regency period, reflecting a vogue for orientalizing décor on a sizable scale. *The Granger Collection.*

2. The British Museum, London, from a wood engraving of 1844. It was designed by Sir Robert Smirke (1781–1867), and built 1823–47, to house the collections of classical antiquities which had been augmented by such treasures as the Elgin marbles from the Parthenon in Athens. *The Granger Collection.*

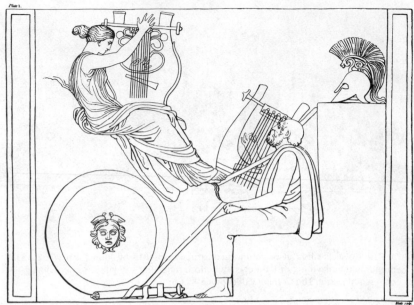

3. The illustrations for Homer, Hesiod, and Dante by the sculptor John Flaxman (1775–1826) were notably influential both in England and abroad. *Homer Invoking the Muse* was engraved by Blake himself (1793). *New York Public Library.*

ENGLISH NEOCLASSICAL STYLE

4. *The Furies,* from Dante's *Inferno* IX.46–48: "This is Megaera, on the left; she who weeps on the right is Alecto; Tisiphone is in the middle." This series was engraved by Thomas Pirolli. *New York Public Library.*

5. *The Nightmare*, 1781, by the Swiss-born Henry Fuseli (1741–1825), visionary artist and friend of Blake who anticipated the concerns of Surrealist painting with his interest in dream and derangement. *Frankfurter Goethemuseum.*

6. *Titania, Bottom, and Fairies*, 1793–94, by Fuseli shows a concern not with the pageantry or the dramatic moment in Shakespeare usually rendered by late Victorian narrative painters, but with moments of terror and transformation, like this epitome of *A Midsummer Night's Dream*. Kunsthaus, Zürich.

7. William Blake's Head of Spenser, from a series done in 1800–1801 for the library of William Hayley in Felpham, Sussex. Spenser is shown in a laurel garland, with Queen Elizabeth, as Cynthia, resting in a crescent moon ("Eliza" is inscribed on the medal Spenser wears); on the right, regarding her meditatively, an old man with two stars above him and a shepherd's staff. Nymphs fly about the wreath. The imagery may refer to the April Eclogue of Spenser's *The Shepheardes Calendar*. *City Art Gallery*, Manchester.

8. William Blake in 1807, detail from the portrait by Thomas Phillips (1770–1845). *National Portrait Gallery*, London.

9. Blake, "The Little Black Boy," from *Songs of Innocence and Experience*. The Library of Congress, Rosenwald Collection, Washington, D.C.

10. Blake, "The Tyger," from *Songs of Innocence and Experience.* The Library of Congress, Rosenwald Collection.

11. Blake, *The Ancient of Days;* the painting for the frontispiece to *Europe: a Prophecy,* 1794, shows Urizen bent over the fallen world, marking out its limits with compasses in a complex parody, perhaps, of Proverbs 8:27: "When he set a compass upon the face of the depth." *The Whitworth Art Gallery,* Manchester.

12. Blake, *Newton*, 1795, a color print, showing an absorption in contraction and bounding, parallel to Urizen's, but here set at the bottom of a sea of time and space. *The Tate Gallery*, London.

13. Blake, frontispiece to *Visions of the Daughters of Albion*, showing *left to right*, Bromion, Oothoon, and Theotormon. The scene does not literally occur in the poem but is, rather, Theotormon's vision of what is happening. (See *Visions of the Daughters of Albion*). *The Tate Gallery.*

14. Blake, *Nebuchadnezzar*, 1795, a color print showing the fallen Babylonian king who, "driven from men . . . did eat grass as oxen, and his body was wet with the dew of heaven, till his hairs were grown like eagles' feathers, and his nails like birds' claws" (Daniel 4:33). *The Tate Gallery.*

15. Plate 24 of *The Marriage of Heaven and Hell*, upon which the print above was based. *The Pierpont Morgan Library*, New York.

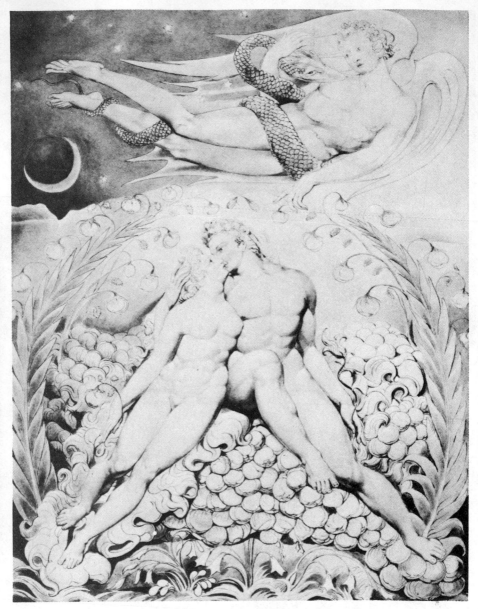

16. *Satan with Adam and Eve*, 1808, Blake's watercolor illustrating *Paradise Lost*, IX. *Museum of Fine Arts*, Boston.

17. *Pandemonium*, 1824, John Martin's (1789–1854) mezzotint illustration of Book II of *Paradise Lost* showing the Romantic reading of Milton at its most theatrical. *The Metropolitan Museum of Art*, New York, *Harris Brisbane Dick Fund, 1949.*

18. *Manfred on the Jungfrau,* 1837, by John Martin. Byron and the Ossianic poems of Macpherson joined Milton and Shakespeare in providing subjects and images for Romantic painting in England. Here, the tormented hero of Byron's drama is about to fling himself ʿrom the Alpine peak:

> . . . Farewell, ye opening heavens!
> Look not upon me thus reproachfully—
> You were not meant for me—Earth! take these atoms!

He is restrained by a chamois hunter behind him. *Birmingham* (**England**) *Museum and Art Gallery.*

19. *The Valley Thick with Corn*, 1825, brush and pen in sepia. The visionary paintings of Samuel Palmer (1805–81), friend and follower of Blake, were done mostly in Shoreham, Kent, during the painter's youth, and depict a condition of life not unlike Blake's Beulah, rich and moonlit. Unlike Blake's vision of Beulah, however, this is not equivocal: what Blake saw as a necessary but dangerous state of repose from intellectual warfare, Palmer saw as a final good. *Ashmolean Museum*, Oxford.

20. *The Valley with a Bright Cloud*, 1825, brush and pen in sepia. *Ashmolean Museum.*

21. Samuel Palmer, *A Hilly Scene*, c. 1826, water color and tempera. *The Tate Gallery.*

22. Samuel Palmer, *Early Morning*, 1825, brush and pen in sepia. *Ashmolean Museum.*

23. Samuel Palmer, *Shepherds under a Full Moon*, c. 1830, brush and pen in sepia. *Ashmolean Museum.*

24. *The Bellman*, Samuel Palmer's mezzotint done in 1879 (near the end of his life), for Milton's "Il Penseroso":

> Where glowing embers through the room
> Teach light to counterfeit a gloom,
> Far from all resort of mirth
> Save the cricket on the hearth,
> Or the Bellman's drowsy charm,
> To bless the doors from nightly harm.

Museum of Fine Arts, Boston.

25. Samuel Palmer, *The Lonely Tower,* also from "Il Penseroso":

> Or let my Lamp at midnight hour,
> Be seen in some high lonely tower,
> Where I may oft out-watch the Bear . . .

William Butler Yeats in "The Phases of the Moon" celebrated this print and

> . . . the candelight
> From the far tower where Milton's Platonist
> Sat late, or Shelley's visionary prince:
> The lonely light that Samuel Palmer engraved,
> An image of mysterious wisdom won by toil . . .

British Museum.

26. Samuel Palmer, *Coming from Evening Church*, 1830, oil and tempera on canvas.
The Tate Gallery.

27. Samuel Palmer, *The Magic Apple Tree,* 1830, watercolor.
Fitzwilliam Museum, Cambridge.

28. Wordsworth in 1805, a drawing by Henry Edridge (1769–1821). *The Granger Collection.*

29. Coleridge in 1814, a portrait by the American Romantic painter Washington Allston (1779–1843). *The Granger Collection.*

30. *Chirk Aqueduct,* 1804, by John Sell Cotman (1782–1842). This watercolor of a newly constructed aqueduct in Yorkshire represents the finest work of one of the greatest English water-colorists. Cotman's bold, almost abstract planes look forward to modern art; in general, his work displays the triumph of a peculiarly English landscape idiom. *Victoria and Albert Museum,* London.

THE VISION OF LANDSCAPE

31. *Stonehenge,* here shown in a storm, by J. M. W. Turner (1775–1851); drawn between 1820 and 1830. *British Museum.*

32. *Stonehenge*, by John Constable, another of the pre-eminent English painters (1776–1837). Along with Turner, Constable dominates the sphere of landscape in early nineteenth-century painting. His scene, penetrated by rainbows, is fully as agitated as Turner's, but in a different mode. *Victoria and Albert Museum.*

33. Mount Snowdon in Wales, c. 1800, painted by John Varley (1778–1842). Compare with Wordsworth's description in *The Prelude*, Bk. XIV. *Walker Art Gallery*, Liverpool.

34. *The Ploughman,* by Edward Calvert (1789–1883), Palmer's friend and associate at Shoreham. The Romantic pastoral vision is of a secondary paradise, with the serpent transfixed, and musical graces dancing on a low rise. *Victoria and Albert Museum.*

35. *The Primitive City*, 1822, Edward Calvert's watercolor, shows imaginative affinities with both Blake and Palmer in its way of generating a mythology of its own. *British Museum.*

36. Shelley in 1819, a portrait by Amelia Curran. *National Portrait Gallery*.

37. Keats in 1821, painted in Rome by Joseph Severn (1783–1879). *National Portrait Gallery*.

38. Lord Byron in 1814, in Albanian costume, painted by Thomas Phillips (1770–1845). *National Portrait Gallery.*

39. J. M. W. Turner (1775–1851), *Slavers Throwing Overboard the Dead and Dying —
Typhon Coming On,* 1840. In his Romantic vision Turner sees beyond this manifest
attack on the slave trade (becoming extinct at the time of the painting; the incident
suggesting it had probably occurred in 1783). He extends his censure to the whole world
of trade, of "getting and spending," and in his own verses accompanying the painting
he makes it clear that the typhoon is no mere natural cataclysm:

> Aloft all hands, strike the top-masts and belay;
> You angry setting sun and fierce-edged clouds
> Declare the Typhon's coming.
> Before it sweeps your decks, throw overboard
> The dead and dying—ne'er heed their chains.
> Hope, Hope, fallacious Hope!
> Where is thy market now?

Museum of Fine Arts, Boston.

40. *Rain, Steam and Speed* (The Great Western Railway), by J. M. W. Turner. Exhibited in 1844, this great canvas represents a complex response to the industrial revolution's ability to produce new natural phenomena. That response lies beyond Wordsworth's resolve, in his sonnet of 1835 called "Steamboats, Viaducts, and Railways," that technology

> . . . howsoe'er it mar
> The loveliness of Nature

never

> prove a bar
> To the Mind's gaining that prophetic sense
> Of future change, that point of vision. . . .

For Turner's total vision of a world made of light, the railway does not "mar," but participates. *National Gallery*, London.

And the blue sea and shadowy hills were seen.
Such, the alleviations of his state,
Prometheus gave to man, for which he hangs
100 Withering in destined pain: but who rains down
Evil, the immedicable plague, which, while
Man looks on his creation like a God
And sees that it is glorious, drives him on,
The wreck of his own will, the scorn of earth,
The outcast, the abandoned, the alone?
Not Jove: while yet his frown shook Heaven, ay, when
His adversary from adamantine chains
Cursed him, he trembled like a slave. Declare
Who is his master? Is he too a slave?
110   DEMOGORGON   All spirits are enslaved which serve things evil:
Thou knowest if Jupiter be such or no.
   ASIA   Whom calledst thou God?
   DEMOGORGON   I spoke but as ye speak,
For Jove is the supreme of living things.
   ASIA   Who is the master of the slave?
   DEMOGORGON   If the abysm
Could vomit forth its secrets. . . . But a voice
Is wanting, the deep truth is imageless;°
For what would it avail to bid thee gaze
On the revolving world? What to bid speak
Fate, Time, Occasion, Chance, and Change? To these
120 All things are subject but eternal Love.°
   ASIA   So much I asked before, and my heart gave
The response thou hast given; and of such truths
Each to itself must be the oracle.°
One more demand; and do thou answer me
As mine own soul would answer, did it know
That which I ask. Prometheus shall arise
Henceforth the sun of this rejoicing world:
When shall the destined hour arrive?
   DEMOGORGON   Behold!°

                . . .

From SCENE V   *The Car pauses within a Cloud on the top of a snowy Mountain.*
   VOICE IN THE AIR, *singing*°
   Life of Life! thy lips enkindle
      With their love the breath between them;

deep . . . imageless Demogorgon expresses the central truth of skepticism, that ultimates cannot be known or portrayed.
Love This transcendent love is identical with the Intellectual Beauty, but it is not manifested or represented in the poem, not even by Asia, except in her momentary transfiguration at the end of Act II.
So much . . . oracle She has learned, as F. A. Pottle phrased it, "to give up her demand for an ultimate Personal Evil, to combine an unshak-able faith that the universe is sound at the core with a realization that, as regards man, Time is radically and incurably evil."
Behold! The chariot of the Hours descends, to take Asia back up to the soon-to-be-transformed world.
singing The Voice in the Air, confronting a transfigured Asia, in her moment-of-moments in which she becomes a kind of heavenly Venus, attempts to image the imageless, and fails, but brilliantly and unforgettably.

50   And thy smiles before they dwindle
            Make the cold air fire; then screen them
        In those looks, where whoso gazes
        Faints, entangled in their mazes.

        Child of Light! thy limbs are burning
            Through the vest which seems to hide them;
        As the radiant lines of morning
            Through the clouds ere they divide them;
        And this atmosphere divinest
        Shrouds thee wheresoe'er thou shinest.

60   Fair are others; none beholds thee,
            But thy voice sounds low and tender
        Like the fairest, for it folds thee
            From the sight, that liquid splendour,
        And all feel, yet see thee never,
        As I feel now, lost forever!

        Lamp of Earth! where'er thou movest
            Its dim shapes are clad with brightness,
        And the souls of whom thou lovest
            Walk upon the winds with lightness,
70   Till they fail, as I am failing,
        Dizzy, lost, yet unbewailing!

            ASIA
        My soul is an enchanted boat,
        Which, like a sleeping swan, doth float
        Upon the silver waves of thy sweet singing;
            And thine doth like an angel sit
            Beside a helm conducting it,
        Whilst all the winds with melody are ringing.
            It seems to float ever, forever,
            Upon that many-winding river,
80   Between mountains, woods, abysses,
            A paradise of wildernesses!
        Till, like one in slumber bound,
        Borne to the ocean, I float down, around,
        Into a sea profound, of ever-spreading sound:

            Meanwhile thy spirit lifts its pinions
            In music's most serene dominions;
        Catching the winds that fan that happy heaven.
            And we sail on, away, afar,
            Without a course, without a star,
90   But, by the instinct of sweet music driven;
            Till through Elysian garden islets
            By thee, most beautiful of pilots,
            Where never mortal pinnace glided,
            The boat of my desire is guided:

Realms where the air we breathe is love,
Which in the winds and on the waves doth move,
Harmonizing this earth with what we feel above.

We have passed Age's icy caves,
And Manhood's dark and tossing waves,
100 And Youth's smooth ocean, smiling to betray:
Beyond the glassy gulfs we flee
Of shadow-peopled Infancy,
Through Death and Birth, to a diviner day;
A paradise of vaulted bowers,
Lit by downward-gazing flowers,
And watery paths that wind between
Wildernesses calm and green,
Peopled by shapes too bright to see,°
And rest, having beheld; somewhat like thee;
110 Which walk upon the sea, and chant melodiously!
END OF THE SECOND ACT

ACT III

SCENE I *Heaven.* JUPITER *on his Throne;* THETIS *and the other Deities
assembled.*

JUPITER Ye congregated powers of heaven, who share
The glory and the strength of him ye serve,
Rejoice! henceforth I am omnipotent.
All else had been subdued to me; alone
The soul of man, like unextinguished fire,
Yet burns towards heaven with fierce reproach, and doubt,
And lamentation, and reluctant prayer,
Hurling up insurrection, which might make
Our antique empire insecure, though built
10 On eldest faith, and hell's coeval,° fear;
And though my curses through the pendulous air,
Like snow on herbless peaks, fall flake by flake,
And cling to it; though under my wrath's night
It climbs the crags of life, step after step,
Which wound it, as ice wounds unsandalled feet,
It yet remains supreme o'er misery,
Aspiring, unrepressed, yet soon to fall:
Even now have I begotten a strange wonder,
That fatal child,° the terror of the earth,
20 Who waits but till the destined hour arrive,
Bearing from Demogorgon's vacant throne°

A paradise . . . see (ll. 104–8) She describes,
in her apotheosis, a return to a divine infancy,
like "the Shining Ones" described by John Bunyan or Blake's children of Beulah or Wordsworth's children on the shore in his "Intimations" Ode.
coeval of equal age

fatal child Jupiter's unintentional irony, as Jupiter's son by Thetis will be fatal for him, precisely
because the son is unbegotten
vacant throne another irony; the throne is vacant only because Demogorgon is in the act of
rising up from it

The dreadful might of ever-living limbs
Which clothed that awful spirit unbeheld,
To redescend, and trample out the spark.
Pour forth heaven's wine, Idaean Ganymede,°
And let it fill the Daedal cups like fire,
And from the flower-inwoven soil divine
Ye all-triumphant harmonies arise,
As dew from earth under the twilight stars:
30   Drink! be the nectar circling through your veins
The soul of joy, ye ever-living Gods,
Till exultation burst in one wide voice
Like music from Elysian winds.
                               And thou
Ascend beside me, veilèd in the light
Of the desire which makes thee one with me,
Thetis, bright image of eternity!
When thou didst cry, 'Insufferable might!
God! Spare me! I sustain not the quick flames,
The penetrating presence; all my being,
40   Like him whom the Numidian seps° did thaw
Into a dew with poison, is dissolved,°
Sinking through its foundations:' even then
Two mighty spirits, mingling, made a third
Mightier than either, which, unbodied now,
Between us floats, felt, although unbeheld,
Waiting the incarnation, which ascends,
(Hear ye the thunder of the fiery wheels
Griding° the winds?) from Demogorgon's throne.
Victory! victory! Feel'st thou not, O world,
50   The earthquake of his chariot thundering up
Olympus?
[*The Car of the* HOUR *arrives.* DEMOGORGON *descends,
and moves towards the Throne of* JUPITER.]
                     Awful shape, what art thou? Speak!
   DEMOGORGON   Eternity. Demand no direr name.°
Descend, and follow me down the abyss.
I am thy child, as thou wert Saturn's child;°
Mightier than thee: and we must dwell together
Henceforth in darkness. Lift thy lightnings not.
The tyranny of heaven none may retain,
Or reassume, or hold, succeeding thee:
Yet if thou wilt, as 'tis the destiny
60   Of trodden worms to writhe till they are dead,
Put forth thy might.

Ganymede boy abducted from Mt. Ida to be
Jupiter's cupbearer
seps serpent whose bite caused decomposition
dissolved she could not sustain him, and so
did not conceive

Griding cutting with a strident sound
Eternity . . . name whatever one wishes to call
one's own dialectic or process of doom
child usurper only

JUPITER   Detested prodigy!
Even thus beneath the deep Titanian prisons
I trample thee! thou lingerest?
                              Mercy! mercy!
No pity, no release, no respite! Oh,
That thou wouldst make mine enemy my judge,
Even where he hangs, seared by my long revenge,
On Caucasus! he would not doom me thus.
Gentle, and just, and dreadless, is he not
The monarch of the world? What then art thou?
No refuge! No appeal!
70   Sink with me then,
We two will sink on the wide waves of ruin,
      Even as a vulture and a snake outspent°
Drop, twisted in inextricable fight,
Into a shoreless sea. Let hell unlock
Its mounded oceans of tempestuous fire,
And whelm on them into the bottomless void
This desolated world, and thee, and me,
The conqueror and the conquered, and the wreck
Of that for which they combated.
                              Ai! Ai!°
80   The elements obey me not. I sink
Dizzily down, ever, forever, down.
And, like a cloud, mine enemy above
Darknes my fall with victory! Ai, Ai!

SCENE II   *The Mouth of a great River in the Island Atlantis.* OCEAN *is discovered
reclining near the Shore;* APOLLO *stands beside him.*
      OCEAN   He fell, thou sayest, beneath his conqueror's frown?
      APOLLO   Ay, when the strife was ended which made dim
The orb I rule, and shook the solid stars,
The terrors of his eye illumined heaven
With sanguine light, through the thick ragged skirts
Of the victorious darkness, as he fell:
Like the last glare of day's red agony,
Which, from a rent among the fiery clouds,
Burns far along the tempest-wrinkled deep.
10   OCEAN   He sunk to the abyss? To the dark void?
      APOLLO   Ay, when the strife was ended which made dim
On Caucasus, his thunder-baffled wings
Entangled in the whirlwind, and his eyes
Which gazed on the undazzling sun, now blinded
By the white lightning, while the ponderous hail
Beats on his struggling form, which sinks at length

Even . . . outspent The image of a serpent
wrestling to the death with a vulture or eagle
haunted Shelley, and is crucial in his early
Spenserian epic, *The Revolt of Islam;* for a
modern instance, indebted to Shelley, see the
end of "The Dance" in Hart Crane's *The Bridge.*
Ai! "woe!" in Greek

Prone, and the aereal ice clings over it.

OCEAN   Henceforth the fields of heaven-reflecting sea
Which are my realm, will heave, unstained with blood,
20   Beneath the uplifting winds, like plains of corn
Swayed by the summer air; my streams will flow
Round many-peopled continents, and round
Fortunate isles; and from their glassy thrones
Blue Proteus° and his humid nymphs shall mark
The shadow of fair ships, as mortals see
The floating bark of the light-laden moon
With that white star, its sightless pilot's crest,
Borne down the rapid sunset's ebbing sea;
Tracking their path no more by blood and groans,
30   And desolation, and the mingled voice
Of slavery and command; but by the light
Of wave-reflected flowers, and floating odours,
And music soft, and mild, free, gentle voices,
And sweetest music, such as spirits love.

APOLLO   And I shall gaze not on the deeds which make
My mind obscure with sorrow, as eclipse
Darkens the sphere I guide; but list, I hear
The small, clear, silver lute of the young Spirit
That sits in the morning star.

OCEAN   Thou must away;
40   Thy steeds will pause at even, till when farewell:
The loud deep calls me home even now to feed it
With azure calm out of the emerald urns
Which stand for ever full beside my throne.
Behold the Nereids° under the green sea,
Their wavering limbs borne on the wind-like stream,
Their white arms lifted o'er their streaming hair
With garlands pied and starry sea-flower crowns,
Hastening to grace their mighty sister's joy.
[*A sound of waves is heard*]
It is the unpastured sea hungering for calm.
Peace, monster; I come now. Farewell.
50   APOLLO   Farewell.

From SCENE III   *Caucasus.*

SPIRIT OF THE EARTH   Mother, I am grown wiser, though a child
Cannot be wise like thee, within this day;
And happier too; happier and wiser both.
Thou knowest that toads, and snakes, and loathly worms,
And venomous and malicious beasts, and boughs
That bore ill berries in the woods, were ever

Proteus an older sea god, a shape-shifter and   Nereids fifty sea nymphs, daughters of Nereus,
prophet; if caught and held while he exhausts   good-natured Old Man of the Sea
his changes, he will reveal the future

An hindrance to my walks o'er the green world:
40   And that, among the haunts of humankind,
Hard-featured men, or with proud, angry looks,
Or cold, staid gait, or false and hollow smiles,
Or the dull sneer of self-loved ignorance,
Or other such foul masks, with which ill thoughts
Hide that fair being whom we spirits call man;
And women too, ugliest of all things evil,
(Though fair, even in a world where thou art fair,
When good and kind, free and sincere like thee),
When false or frowning made me sick at heart
50   To pass them, though they slept, and I unseen.
Well, my path lately lay through a great city
Into the woody hills surrounding it:
A sentinel was sleeping at the gate:
When there was heard a sound, so loud, it shook
The towers amid the moonlight, yet more sweet
Than any voice but thine, sweetest of all;
A long, long sound, as it would never end:
And all the inhabitants leaped suddenly
Out of their rest, and gathered in the streets,
60   Looking in wonder up to Heaven, while yet
The music pealed along. I hid myself
Within a fountain in the public square,
Where I lay like the reflex of the moon
Seen in a wave under green leaves; and soon
Those ugly human shapes and visages
Of which I spoke as having wrought me pain,
Passed floating through the air, and fading still
Into the winds that scattered them; and those
From whom they passed seemed mild and lovely forms
70   After some foul disguise had fallen, and all
Were somewhat changed, and after brief surprise
And greetings of delighted wonder, all
Went to their sleep again:° and when the dawn
Came, wouldst thou think that toads, and snakes, and efts,
Could e'er be beautiful? yet so they were,
And that with little change of shape or hue:
All things had put their evil nature off:
I cannot tell my joy, when o'er a lake
Upon a drooping bough with nightshade twined,
80   I saw two azure halcyons clinging downward
And thinning one bright bunch of amber berries,°
With quick long beaks, and in the deep there lay
Those lovely forms imaged as in a sky;

all went . . . again surely the gentlest and   I saw . . . berries deadly nightshade is now
most urbane Apocalypse in literature   harmless

So, with my thoughts full of these happy changes,
We meet again, the happiest change of all.

.   .   .

[*The* SPIRIT OF THE HOUR *enters*]
PROMETHEUS   We feel what thou hast heard and seen: yet speak.
SPIRIT OF THE HOUR   Soon as the sound had ceased whose thunder filled
The abysses of the sky and the wide earth,
100   There was a change: the impalpable thin air
And the all-circling sunlight were transformed,
As if the sense of love dissolved in them
Had folded itself round the spherèd world.
My vision then grew clear, and I could see
Into the mysteries of the universe:
Dizzy as with delight I floated down,
Winnowing the lightsome air with languid plumes,
My coursers sought their birthplace in the sun,
Where they henceforth will live exempt from toil,
110   Pasturing flowers of vegetable fire;
And where my moonlike car will stand within
A temple, gazed upon by Phidian forms°
Of thee, and Asia, and the Earth, and me,
And you fair nymphs looking the love we feel,—
In memory of the tidings it has borne,—
Beneath a dome fretted with graven flowers,
Poised on twelve columns of resplendent stone,
And open to the bright and liquid sky.
Yoked to it by an amphisbaenic snake°
120   The likeness of those wingèd steeds will mock°
The flight from which they find repose. Alas,
Whither has wandered now my partial tongue
When all remains untold which ye would hear?
As I have said, I floated to the earth:
It was, as it is still, the pain of bliss
To move, to breathe, to be; I wandering went
Among the haunts and dwellings of mankind,
And first was disappointed not to see
Such mighty change as I had felt within
130   Expressed in outward things; but soon I looked,
And behold, thrones were kingless, and men walked
One with the other even as spirits do,
None fawned, none trampled; hate, disdain, or fear,
Self-love or self-contempt, on human brows
No more inscribed, as o'er the gate of hell,
'All hope abandon ye who enter here;'°

Phidian forms Phidias was the greatest of Greek
sculptors (5th century B.C.).
amphisbaenic snake with a head at each end,
and so capable of moving either way

mock "imitate" and perhaps "disdain"
All . . . here See Dante's *Inferno* III, where
this is the inscription over the gate of Hell.

None frowned, none trembled, none with eager fear
Gazed on another's eye of cold command,
Until the subject of a tyrant's will
140 Became, worse fate, the abject of his own,
Which spurred him, like an outspent horse, to death.
None wrought his lips in truth-entangling lines
Which smiled the lie his tongue disdained to speak;
None, with firm sneer, trod out in his own heart
The sparks of love and hope till there remained
Those bitter ashes, a soul self-consumed,
And the wretch crept a vampire among men,
Infecting all with his own hideous ill;
None talked that common, false, cold, hollow talk
150 Which makes the heart deny the *yes* it breathes,
Yet question that unmeant hypocrisy
With such a self-mistrust as has no name.
And women, too, frank, beautiful, and kind
As the free heaven which rains fresh light and dew
On the wide earth, past; gentle radiant forms,
From custom's evil taint exempt and pure;
Speaking the wisdom once they could not think,
Looking emotions once they feared to feel,
And changed to all which once they dared not be,
160 Yet being now, made earth like heaven; nor pride,
Nor jealousy, nor envy, nor ill shame,
The bitterest of those drops of treasured gall,
Spoilt the sweet taste of the nepenthe, love.

Thrones, altars, judgement-seats, and prisons; wherein,
And beside which, by wretched men were borne
Sceptres, tiaras, swords, and chains, and tomes
Of reasoned wrong, glozed on° by ignorance,
Were like those monstrous and barbaric shapes,
The ghosts of a no-more-remembered fame,
170 Which, from their unworn obelisks, look forth
In triumph o'er the palaces and tombs
Of those who were their conquerors: mouldering round,
These imaged to the pride of kings and priests
A dark yet mighty faith, a power as wide
As is the world it wasted, and are now
But an astonishment; even so the tools
And emblems of its last captivity,
Amid the dwellings of the peopled earth,
Stand, not o'erthrown, but unregarded now.
180 And those foul shapes, abhorred by god and man,—
Which, under many a name and many a form
Strange, savage, ghastly, dark and execrable,

glozed on commented on

Were Jupiter, the tyrant of the world;
And which the nations, panic-stricken, served
With blood, and hearts broken by long hope, and love
Dragged to his altars soiled and garlandless,
And slain amid men's unreclaiming tears,
Flattering the thing they feared, which fear was hate,—
Frown, mouldering fast, o'er their abandoned shrines:
190   The painted veil, by those who were, called life,
Which mimicked, as with colours idly spread,
All men believed or hoped, is torn aside;
The loathsome mask has fallen, the man remains
Sceptreless, free, uncircumscribed, but man
Equal, unclassed, tribeless, and nationless,
Exempt from awe, worship, degree, the king
Over himself; just, gentle, wise: but man
Passionless?——no, yet free from guilt or pain,
Which were, for his will made or suffered them,
200   Nor yet exempt, though ruling them like slaves,
From chance, and death, and mutability,
The clogs of that which else might oversoar
The loftiest star of unascended heaven,
Pinnacled dim in the intense inane.°

    END OF THE THIRD ACT

        From ACT IV°
SCENE   *A Part of the Forest near the Cave of* PROMETHEUS.
    PANTHEA   But see where through two openings in the forest
Which hanging branches overcanopy,
And where two runnels of a rivulet,
Between the close moss violet-inwoven,
Have made their path of melody, like sisters
Who part with sighs that they may meet in smiles,
200   Turning their dear disunion to an isle
Of lovely grief, a wood of sweet sad thoughts;
Two visions of strange radiance float upon
The ocean-like enchantment of strong sound,
Which flows intenser, keener, deeper yet
Under the ground and through the windless air.
        IONE   I see a chariot like that thinnest boat,°
In which the Mother of the Months° is borne
By ebbing light into her western cave,
When she upsprings from interlunar dreams;

---

inane formless void of infinite space, a Lucre-
tian concept
Act IV A great afterthought, composed just
after the "Ode to the West Wind," opens with
songs and dances of Spirits and Hours celebrating the New Day; the "two visions of strange
radiance," now described by Panthea and Ione,

Asia's sisters, are the symbolic center of the Act.
boat the old moon in the new moon's arms,
bearing an apocalyptic infant who heralds a
storm of change
Mother . . . Months Diana, the moon, bears
the months.

210   O'er which is curved an orblike canopy
       Of gentle darkness, and the hills and woods,
       Distinctly seen through that dusk aery veil,
       Regard° like shapes in an enchanter's glass;
       Its wheels are solid clouds, azure and gold,
       Such as the genii of the thunderstorm
       Pile on the floor of the illumined sea
       When the sun rushes under it; they roll
       And move and grow as with an inward wind;
       Within it sits a wingèd infant, white°
220   Its countenance, like the whiteness of bright snow,
       Its plumes are as feathers of sunny frost,
       Its limbs gleam white, through the wind-flowing folds
       Of its white robe, woof of ethereal pearl.
       Its hair is white, the brightness of white light
       Scattered in strings; yet its two eyes are heavens
       Of liquid darkness, which the Deity
       Within seems pouring, as a storm is poured
       From jaggèd clouds, out of their arrowy lashes,
       Tempering the cold and radiant air around,
230   With fire that is not brightness; in its hand
       It sways a quivering moonbeam, from whose point
       A guiding power directs the chariot's prow
       Over its wheelèd clouds, which as they roll
       Over the grass, and flowers, and waves, wake sounds,
       Sweet as a singing rain of silver dew.
           PANTHEA   And from the other opening in the wood
       Rushes, with loud and whirlwind harmony,
       A sphere, which is as many thousand spheres,
       Solid as crystal, yet through all its mass
240   Flow, as through empty space, music and light:
       Ten thousand orbs involving and involved,
       Purple and azure, white, and green, and golden,
       Sphere within sphere; and every space between
       Peopled with unimaginable shapes,
       Such as ghosts dream dwell in the lampless deep,
       Yet each inter-transpicuous,° and they whirl
       Over each other with a thousand motions,
       Upon a thousand sightless axles spinning,
       And with the force of self-destroying swiftness,
250   Intensely, slowly, solemnly roll on,
       Kindling with mingled sounds, and many tones,
       Intelligible words and music wild.
       With mighty whirl the multitudinous orb
       Grinds the bright brook into an azure mist

Regard appear
Within . . . white based on the Enthroned

Man in Ezekiel 1:27, and the Son of Man in
Revelation 1:14
inter-transpicuous inter-transparent

Of elemental subtlety, like light;
And the wild odour of the forest flowers,
The music of the living grass and air,
The emerald light of leaf-entangled beams
Round its intense yet self-conflicting speed,
260   Seem kneaded into one aëreal mass
Which drowns the sense. Within the orb itself,
Pillowed upon its alabaster arms,
Like to a child o'erwearied with sweet toil,
On its own folded wings, and wavy hair,
The Spirit of the Earth is laid asleep,
And you can see its little lips are moving,
Amid the changing light of their own smiles,
Like one who talks of what he loves in dream.°
     IONE   'Tis only mocking the orb's harmony.°
270   PANTHEA   And from a star upon its forehead, shoot,
Like swords of azure fire, or golden spears
With tyrant-quelling myrtle° overtwined,
Embleming heaven and earth united now,
Vast beams like spokes of some invisible wheel
Which whirl as the orb whirls, swifter than thought,
Filling the abyss with sun-like lightenings,
And perpendicular now, and now transverse,
Pierce the dark soil, and as they pierce and pass,
Make bare the secrets of the earth's deep heart;
280   Infinite mines of adamant and gold,
Valueless° stones, and unimagined gems,
And caverns on crystalline columns poised
With vegetable silver overspread;
Wells of unfathomed fire, and water springs
Whence the great sea, even as a child is fed,
Whose vapours clothe earth's monarch mountain-tops
With kingly, ermine snow. The beams flash on
And make appear the melancholy ruins
Of cancelled cycles; anchors, beaks of ships;
290   Planks turned to marble; quivers, helms, and spears,
And gorgon-headed targes,° and the wheels
Of scythèd chariots,° and the emblazonry
Of trophies, standards, and armorial beasts,°
Round which death laughed, sepulchred emblems
Of dead destruction, ruin within ruin!
The wrecks beside of many a city vast,

loves in dream (ll. 236–68) See Ezekiel's vision of "the wheels and their work," Ezekiel
1:16–18, and *Paradise Lost* V.618–25; Shelley
describes an earth whirling itself on toward finality.
'Tis . . . harmony an example of Shelley's ur-
banity in apocalyptic writing: the sleeping infant Spirit mocks the inhuman harmony of its
own vehicle
myrtle emblem of love
Valueless beyond value, priceless
targes shields
scythèd chariots war chariots with bladed
wheels
armorial beasts heraldic emblems

Whose population which the earth grew over
Was mortal, but not human; see, they lie,
Their monstrous works, and uncouth skeletons,
00   Their statues, homes and fanes; prodigious shapes
Huddled in gray annihilation, split,
Jammed in the hard, black deep; and over these,
The anatomies of unknown wingèd things,
And fishes which were isles of living scale,
And serpents, bony chains, twisted around
The iron crags, or within heaps of dust
To which the tortuous strength of their last pangs
Had crushed the iron crags; and over these
The jaggèd alligator, and the might
310   Of earth-convulsing behemoth,° which once
Were monarch beasts, and on the slimy shores,
And weed-overgrown continents of earth,
Increased and multiplied like summer worms
On an abandoned corpse, till the blue globe°
Wrapped deluge round it like a cloak, and they
Yelled, gasped, and were abolished; or some God
Whose throne was in a comet, passed, and cried,
'Be not!' And like my words they were no more.

. . .

DEMOGORGON
Man, who wert once a despot and a slave;
550   A dupe and a deceiver; a decay;
A traveller from the cradle to the grave
Through the dim night of this immortal day:°
ALL
Speak: thy strong words may never pass away.
DEMOGORGON
This is the day, which down the void abysm
At the Earth-born's spell° yawns for Heaven's despotism,
And Conquest is dragged captive through the deep:
Love, from its awful throne of patient power
In the wise heart, from the last giddy hour
Of dread endurance, from the slippery, steep,
560   And narrow verge of crag-like agony, springs
And folds over the world its healing wings.°

Gentleness, Virtue, Wisdom, and Endurance,
These are the seals of that most firm assurance

---

behemoth The alligator is Shelley's version of
Job's Leviathan, who appears with Behemoth
(perhaps a mythologized hippopotamus) in Job
40:15–24.
blue globe covered by water
Man . . . day Demogorgon has summoned up
the scattered Spirits of the Universe for a final
accounting; this quatrain should be compared to

Blake's "To the Accuser Who Is the God of This
World" from *The Gates of Paradise*.
spell Prometheus, child of Earth, has made
this magic.
And folds . . . wings Love here takes the role
of the Christian Holy Spirit as Paraclete or
comforter.

Which bars the pit over Destruction's strength;
And if, with infirm hand, Eternity,
Mother of many acts and hours, should free
    The serpent that would clasp her with his length;
These are the spells by which to reassume
An empire o'er the disentangled doom.°

570   To suffer woes which Hope thinks infinite;
To forgive wrongs darker than death or night;
    To defy Power, which seems omnipotent;
To love, and bear; to hope till Hope creates
From its own wreck the thing it contemplates;°
    Neither to change, nor falter, nor repent;
This, like thy glory, Titan, is to be
Good, great and joyous, beautiful and free;
This is alone Life, Joy, Empire, and Victory.
1818–19   1820

England in 1819

An old, mad, blind, despised, and dying king,°—
Princes, the dregs of their dull race,° who flow
Through public scorn,—mud from a muddy spring,—
Rulers who neither see, nor feel, nor know,
But leech-like to their fainting country cling,
Till they drop, blind in blood, without a blow,—
A people starved and stabbed in the untilled field,°—
An army, which liberticide and prey
Makes as a two-edged sword to all who wield,—
10   Golden and sanguine laws which tempt and slay;
Religion Christless, Godless—a book sealed;
A Senate,—Time's worst statute unrepealed,°—
Are graves, from which a glorious Phantom may
Burst, to illumine our tempestuous day.
1819   1839

doom the serpent, Eternity, which may undo
the Renewal
to hope . . . contemplates M.H. Abrams, in
his *Natural Supernaturalism,* usefully relates
Demogorgon's final lyric to Wordsworth's "Prospectus" to *The Excursion,* which speaks "Of
blessèd consolations in distress" and like Shelley
emphasizes humanistic Hope as a cardinal virtue.
An old . . . king George III, who died the next
year; he had been blind and mentally ill for
some time. See Byron's *Vision of Judgment.*

Princes . . . race The Prince Regent was neither
virtuous nor popular.
stabbed . . . field the "Peterloo Massacre" at
Manchester, August 16, 1819, where a peaceful
assembly was dispersed by mounted troops, who
killed or injured a number of the unarmed protesters. As the assault took place on St. Peter's
Field, the public sardonically called it "Peterloo," so as to discredit Wellington's more glorious victory at Waterloo.
Time's . . . unrepealed the law barring Dissenters and Roman Catholics from holding office

Ode to the West Wind

Shelley's supreme lyric was composed simultaneously with Act III of *Prometheus Unbound*, and is close in spirit to the Psalms and the prophetic poetry of the Old Testament. On one level, it is a prophecy of political revolution against the Europe established by the Congress of Vienna in 1815. On another, it attempts to find in natural cycle a harbinger of a human finality beyond cyclic change. Most profoundly, the poem is Jobean, concerned with purgatorial trial and a highly personal yet universal despair, the sense of having failed one's own creative powers. It should be noted that the fourth and fifth sections propose exactly contrary answers to the dilemma implicitly developed in the first three.

The poem's form is a unique amalgam of Dante's *terza rima* and the English or Shakespearean sonnet.

Ode to the West Wind

This poem was conceived and chiefly written in a wood that skirts the Arno, near Florence, and on a day when that tempestuous wind, whose temperature is at once mild and animating, was collecting the vapours which pour down the autumnal rains. They began, as I foresaw, at sunset with a violent tempest of hail and rain, attended by that magnificent thunder and lightning peculiar to the Cisalpine regions.

The phenomenon alluded to at the conclusion of the third stanza is well known to naturalists. The vegetation at the bottom of the sea, of rivers, and of lakes, sympathizes with that of the land in the change of seasons, and is consequently influenced by the winds which announce it.—

I

O wild West Wind,° thou breath of Autumn's being,
Thou, from whose unseen presence the leaves dead
Are driven, like ghosts from an enchanter fleeing,

Yellow, and black, and pale, and hectic red,
Pestilence-stricken multitudes: O thou,
Who chariotest to their dark wintry bed

The wingèd seeds, where they lie cold and low,
Each like a corpse within its grave, until
Thine azure sister of the Spring shall blow

10 Her clarion o'er the dreaming earth, and fill
(Driving sweet buds like flocks to feed in air)
With living hues and odours plain and hill:

Wild Spirit, which art moving everywhere;
Destroyer and preserver; hear, oh, hear!

West Wind Westerly winds rule in the Cisalpine most of the year; Shelley is observing the action of the wind marking the end of summer; another westerly wind ("thine azure sister of the Spring") will mark the end of winter for the western coast of Italy.

II

Thou on whose stream, mid the steep sky's commotion,
Loose clouds like earth's decaying leaves are shed,
Shook from the tangled boughs of Heaven and Ocean,°

Angels of rain and lightning: there are spread
On the blue surface of thine aery surge,
20   Like the bright hair uplifted from the head

Of some fierce Maenad,° even from the dim verge
Of the horizon to the zenith's height,
The locks of the approaching storm. Thou dirge

Of the dying year, to which this closing night
Will be the dome of a vast sepulchre,
Vaulted with all thy congregated might

Of vapours, from whose solid atmosphere
Black rain, and fire, and hail will burst: oh, hear!

III

Thou who didst waken from his summer dreams
30   The blue Mediterranean, where he lay,
Lulled by the coil of his crystàlline streams,

Beside a pumice° isle in Baiae's° bay,
And saw in sleep old palaces and towers
Quivering within the wave's intenser day,

All overgrown with azure moss and flowers
So sweet, the sense faints picturing them! Thou
For whose path the Atlantic's level powers

Cleave themselves into chasms, while far below
The sea-blooms and the oozy woods which wear
40   The sapless foliage of the ocean, know

Thy voice, and suddenly grow grey with fear,
And tremble and despoil themselves: oh, hear!

IV

If I were a dead leaf thou mightest bear;
If I were a swift cloud to fly with thee;
A wave to pant beneath thy power, and share

The impulse of thy strength, only less free
Than thou, O uncontrollable! If even
I were as in my boyhood, and could be

Loose . . . Ocean High up is a canopy of solid, relatively stationary clouds; below are smaller, 'loose' clouds driven swiftly along by the wind. Shelley calls the upper stationary cloud-formations the boughs of Heaven and Ocean because it consists of condensed water-

vapor drawn up from the ocean by the heat of the sun."—F.A. Pottle
Maenad the "frenzied woman"; Maenads were followers of Dionysus, who tore Orpheus apart
pumice porous, volcanic stone
Baiae's resort near Naples; frequented by Roman emperors

The comrade of thy wanderings over Heaven,
50 As then, when to outstrip thy skiey speed
Scarce seemed a vision; I would ne'er have striven

As thus with thee in prayer in my sore need.
Oh, lift me as a wave, a leaf, a cloud!
I fall upon the thorns of life!° I bleed!

A heavy weight of hours has chained and bowed
One too like thee: tameless, and swift, and proud.

V

Make me thy lyre,° even as the forest is:
What if my leaves are falling like its own!
The tumult of thy mighty harmonies

60 Will take from both a deep, autumnal tone,
Sweet though in sadness. Be thou, Spirit fierce,
My spirit! Be thou me, impetuous one!

Drive my dead thoughts over the universe
Like withered leaves to quicken a new birth!
And, by the incantation of this verse,

Scatter, as from an unextinguished hearth
Ashes and sparks, my words among mankind!
Be through my lips to unawakened earth

The trumpet of a prophecy! O, Wind,
70 If Winter comes, can Spring be far behind?
        1819   1820

To a Skylark°

Hail to thee, blithe Spirit!
  Bird thou never wert,
  That from Heaven, or near it,
    Pourest thy full heart
In profuse strains of unpremeditated art.

Higher still and higher
  From the earth thou springest
  Like a cloud of fire;
    The blue deep thou wingest,
10 And singing still dost soar, and soaring ever singest.

thorns of life a grimly ironic echo of Keats's *Sleep and Poetry*, l. 245, which Shelley evidently judged to be an attack upon him rather than Byron; there are Jobean overtones
lyre the aeolian harp
To a Skylark This famous lyric, written about a year after the "Ode to the West Wind," is a plangent farewell to the theme of the poet's pro-

phetic relation to a Power hidden behind Nature. It is important to keep in mind that the skylark is already out of sight when this poem begins; the bird flies too high for visibility, and can just barely be heard. Throughout the lyric, Shelley emphasizes his estrangement from the joy he intuits, and so ecstatically conveys.

In the golden lightning
  Of the sunken sun,
O'er which clouds are brightening,
  Thou dost float and run;
Like an unbodied joy whose race is just begun.

The pale purple even
  Melts around thy flight;
Like a star of Heaven,
  In the broad daylight
20 Thou art unseen, but yet I hear thy shrill delight,

Keen as are the arrows
  Of that silver sphere,°
Whose intense lamp narrows
  In the white dawn clear
Until we hardly see—we feel that it is there.

All the earth and air
  With thy voice is loud,
As, when night is bare,
  From one lonely cloud
30 The moon rains out her beams, and Heaven is overflowed.

What thou art we know not;
  What is most like thee?
From rainbow clouds there flow not
  Drops so bright to see
As from thy presence showers a rain of melody.

Like a Poet hidden
  In the light of thought,
Singing hymns unbidden,
  Till the world is wrought
40 To sympathy with hopes and fears it heeded not:

Like a high-born maiden
  In a palace-tower,
Soothing her love-laden
  Soul in secret hour
With music sweet as love, which overflows her bower:

Like a glow-worm golden
  In a dell of dew,
Scattering unbeholden
  Its aereal hue
50 Among the flowers and grass, which screen it from the view!

Like a rose embowered
  In its own green leaves,

silver sphere the Morning Star

By warm winds deflowered,
　Till the scent it gives
Makes faint with too much sweet those heavy-wingèd thieves:

Sound of vernal showers
　On the twinkling grass,
Rain-awakened flowers,
　All that ever was
60 Joyous, and clear, and fresh, thy music doth surpass:

Teach us, Sprite or Bird,
　What sweet thoughts are thine:
I have never heard
　Praise of love or wine
That panted forth a flood of rapture so divine.

Chorus Hymeneal,°
　Or triumphal chant,
Matched with thine would be all
　But an empty vaunt,
70 A thing wherein we feel there is some hidden want.

What objects are the fountains
　Of thy happy strain?
What fields, or waves, or mountains?
　What shapes of sky or plain?
What love of thine own kind? what ignorance of pain?

With thy clear keen joyance
　Languor cannot be:
Shadow of annoyance
　Never came near thee:
80 Thou lovest—but ne'er knew love's sad satiety.

Waking or asleep,
　Thou of death must deem
Things more true and deep
　Than we mortals dream,
Or how could thy notes flow in such a crystal stream?

We look before and after,
　And pine for what is not:
Our sincerest laughter
　With some pain is fraught;
90 Our sweetest songs are those that tell of saddest thought.

Yet if we could scorn
　Hate, and pride, and fear;
If we were things born
　Not to shed a tear,
I know not how thy joy we ever should come near.

Hymeneal pertaining to marriage

Better than all measures
  Of delightful sound,
Better than all treasures
  That in books are found,
100 Thy skill to poet were, thou scorner of the ground!

Teach me half the gladness
  That thy brain must know,
Such harmonious madness
  From my lips would flow
The world should listen then—as I am listening now.
1820   1820

From The Sensitive Plant°

CONCLUSION

Whether the Sensitive Plant, or that
Which within its boughs like a Spirit sat,
Ere its outward form had known decay,
Now felt this change, I cannot say.

Whether that Lady's gentle mind,
No longer with the form combined
120 Which scattered love, as stars do light,
Found sadness, where it left delight,

I dare not guess; but in this life
Of error, ignorance, and strife,
Where nothing is, but all things seem,
And we the shadows of the dream,

It is a modest creed, and yet
Pleasant if one considers it,
To own that death itself must be,
Like all the rest, a mockery.

130 That garden sweet, that lady fair,
And all sweet shapes and odours there,
In truth have never passed away:
'Tis we, 'tis ours, are changed; not they.

For love, and beauty, and delight,
There is no death nor change: their might
Exceeds our organs, which endure
No light, being themselves obscure.
1820   1820

The Sensitive Plant These urbane, skeptical, yet still idealistic quatrains are a coda to a poem ostensibly about a mimosa or sensitive plant (the leaves react to darkness, or to touch, by closing together, with an upward movement). The plant, the pastoral Lady who attends it, and the gar- den in which both live are shown in their vision- ary prime, interpenetrated by a mutual love, and then all three are destroyed by winter. The Conclusion questions the reality of this destruc- tion.

Hymn of Apollo

I

The sleepless Hours who watch me as I lie,
   Curtained with star-inwoven tapestries
From the broad moonlight of the sky,
   Fanning the busy dreams from my dim eyes,—
Waken me when their Mother, the grey Dawn,
Tells them that dreams and that the moon is gone.

II

Then I arise, and climbing Heaven's blue dome,
   I walk over the mountains and the waves,
Leaving my robe upon the ocean foam;
10   My footsteps pave the clouds with fire; the caves
Are filled with my bright presence, and the air
Leaves the green Earth to my embraces bare.

III

The sunbeams are my shafts, with which I kill
   Deceit, that loves the night and fears the day;
All men who do or even imagine ill
   Fly me, and from the glory of my ray
Good minds and open actions take new might,
Until diminished by the reign of Night.

IV

I feed the clouds, the rainbows and the flowers
20   With their aethereal colours; the moon's globe
And the pure stars in their eternal bowers
   Are cinctured° with my power as with a robe;
Whatever lamps on Earth or Heaven may shine
Are portions of one power, which is mine.

V

I stand at noon upon the peak of Heaven,
   Then with unwilling steps I wander down
Into the clouds of the Atlantic even;
   For grief that I depart they weep and frown:
What look is more delightful than the smile
30   With which I soothe them from the western isle?

VI

I am the eye with which the Universe
   Beholds itself and knows itself divine;°
All harmony of instrument or verse,

cinctured encompassed, girded

I am . . . divine the highest praise given poetry, even by Shelley

453

All prophecy, all medicine is mine,
All light of art or nature;—to my song
Victory and praise in its own right belong.
1820   1824

The Two Spirits: An Allegory°

FIRST SPIRIT

O thou, who plumed with strong desire
    Wouldst float above the earth, beware!
A Shadow° tracks thy flight of fire—
        Night is coming!
    Bright are the regions of the air,
And among the winds and beams
    It were delight to wander there—
        Night is coming!

SECOND SPIRIT

The deathless stars are bright above;
10   If I would cross the shade of night,°
Within my heart is the lamp of love,°
        And that is day!
And the moon will smile with gentle light
On my golden plumes where'er they move;
    The meteors will linger round my flight,
        And make night day.

FIRST SPIRIT

But if the whirlwinds of darkness waken
    Hail, and lightning, and stormy rain;
See, the bounds of the air are shaken—
        Night is coming!
20   The red swift clouds of the hurricane
Yon declining sun have overtaken,
    The clash of the hail sweeps over the plain—
        Night is coming!

SECOND SPIRIT

I see the light, and I hear the sound;
    I'll sail on the flood of the tempest dark,
With the calm within and the light around
        Which makes night day:
And thou, when the gloom is deep and stark,

The Two Spirits: An Allegory The Second Spirit
represents infinite desire, the First is a Spirit of
repression, of finite limits; more specifically, the
Second Spirit is first love, and the First Spirit
everything that attempts to defeat it.

Shadow the ruin haunting love, or frustration
of desire
shade of night the shadow thrown into the
heavens by our earth
lamp of love the sphere of Venus, the Evening
Star, where earth's shadow ends

30 Look from thy dull earth, slumber-bound,
        My moon-like flight thou then mayst mark
            On high, far away.

Some say there is a precipice
    Where one vast pine is frozen to ruin
O'er piles of snow and chasms of ice
        Mid Alpine mountains;
    And that the languid storm pursuing
That wingèd shape, forever flies
    Round those hoar branches, aye renewing
40   Its aery fountains.°

Some say when nights are dry and clear,
    And the death-dews sleep on the morass,
Sweet whispers are heard by the traveller,
        Which make night day:
And a silver shape like his early love doth pass
Upborne by her wild and glittering hair,
    And when he awakes on the fragrant grass,
        He finds night day.°
    1820   1824

Epipsychidion

This is Shelley's most original and most rhapsodic poem. The theme, as in Blake's *Visions of the Daughters of Albion,* is the necessity of free love, but Shelley characteristically at last sees love defeated not by societal and individual repressions, but by the separateness that irreparably shadows the human condition. Taking its occasion from Shelley's love affair with Emilia Viviani, which ended badly, the poem emulates Dante by seeking to make Emilia a kind of Beatrice, a guide to a higher, more visionary existence. The title, which means "a work about the soul out of my soul," expresses an intention to universalize this experience of passion.

The first of these selections, three pungent sermons against the restrictiveness of marriage, is followed by a passage near the poem's conclusion, where desire touches its limits, and gloriously fails.

From Epipsychidion

        [Three Sermons on Free Love]
        Thy° wisdom speaks in me, and bids me dare
Beacon the rocks on which high hearts are wrecked.
I never was attached to that great sect,
150 Whose doctrine is, that each one should select

Some . . . fountains This stanza (ll. 33–40) is the First Spirit's vision of the Second Spirit's ruinous fate, a cyclic and frozen pursuit.

Some . . . day (ll. 41–48) The "traveller" sees the shape of early desire in the Second Spirit. Thy Emilia's

Out of the crowd a mistress or a friend,
And all the rest, though fair and wise, commend
To cold oblivion, though it is in the code
Of modern morals, and the beaten road
Which those poor slaves with weary footsteps tread,
Who travel to their home among the dead
By the broad highway of the world, and so
With one chained friend, perhaps a jealous foe,
The dreariest and the longest journey° go.

160   True Love in this differs from gold and clay,
That to divide is not to take away.
Love is like understanding, that grows bright,
Gazing on many truths; 'tis like thy light,
Imagination! which from earth and sky,
And from the depths of human fantasy,
As from a thousand prisms and mirrors, fills
The Universe with glorious beams, and kills
Error, the worm, with many a sun-like arrow
Of its reverberated lightning. Narrow
170   The heart that loves, the brain that contemplates,
The life that wears, the spirit that creates
One object, and one form, and builds thereby
A sepulchre° for its eternity.

Mind from its object differs most in this:
Evil from good; misery from happiness;
The baser from the nobler; the impure
And frail, from what is clear and must endure.
If you divide suffering and dross, you may
Diminish till it is consumed away;
180   If you divide pleasure and love and thought,
Each part exceeds the whole; and we know not
How much, while any yet remains unshared,
Of pleasure may be gained, of sorrow spared:
This truth is that deep well, whence sages draw
The unenvied light of hope; the eternal law
By which those live, to whom this world of life
Is as a garden ravaged,° and whose strife
Tills for the promise of a later birth
The wilderness of this Elysian earth.

. . .

[The Annihilation of Love]
Let us become the overhanging day,
The living soul of this Elysian isle,
540   Conscious, inseparable, one. Meanwhile
We two will rise, and sit, and walk together,

longest journey marriage; used by E. M. Forster   **sepulchre** marriage
as a title for his novel (1907)   **ravaged** by marriage

Under the roof of blue Ionian weather,
And wander in the meadows, or ascend
The mossy mountains, where the blue heavens bend
With lightest winds, to touch their paramour;
Or linger, where the pebble-paven shore,
Under the quick, faint kisses of the sea
Trembles and sparkles as with ecstasy,—
Possessing and possessed by all that is
550　Within that calm circumference of bliss,
And by each other, till to love and live
Be one:—or, at the noontide hour, arrive
Where some old cavern hoar seems yet to keep
The moonlight of the expired night asleep,
Through which the awakened day can never peep;
A veil for our seclusion, close as night's,
Where secure sleep may kill thine innocent lights;
Sleep, the fresh dew of languid love, the rain
Whose drops quench kisses till they burn again.
560　And we will talk, until thought's melody
Become too sweet for utterance, and it die
In words, to live again in looks, which dart
With thrilling tone into the voiceless heart,
Harmonizing silence without a sound.
Our breath shall intermix, our bosoms bound,
And our veins beat together; and our lips
With other eloquence than words, eclipse
The soul that burns between them, and the wells
Which boil under our being's inmost cells,
570　The fountains of our deepest life, shall be
Confused in Passion's golden purity,
As mountain-springs under the morning sun.
We shall become the same, we shall be one
Spirit within two frames, oh! wherefore two?
One passion in twin-hearts, which grows and grew,
Till like two meteors of expanding flame,
Those spheres instinct with it become the same,
Touch, mingle, are transfigured; ever still
Burning, yet ever inconsumable:
580　In one another's substance finding food,
Like flames too pure and light and unimbued
To nourish their bright lives with baser prey,
Which point to Heaven and cannot pass away:
One hope within two wills, one will beneath
Two overshadowing minds, one life, one death,
One Heaven, one Hell, one immortality,
And one annihilation . . .
1821　　　　　　1839

Adonais

Adonais is one of the major pastoral elegies, and like the others it both laments a dead poet and speculates darkly on its author's own possible fate. Shelley's poem is unique, partly for the extraneous reason that he mourns a poet of his own stature, John Keats, but largely because of its scope and ambition, which break down the limits of elegy. The last seventeen stanzas of *Adonais* are closer to their descendants, Yeats's "Sailing to Byzantium" and "Byzantium," than to their ancestors: the second-century (B.C.) Hellenic poems, Bion's "Lament of Venus for Adonis" and Moschus' "Lament for Bion," and the great English Renaissance elegies, Spenser's *Astrophel* for Sir Philip Sidney and Milton's *Lycidas* for Edward King. Bion mourns the death of Adonis, god of the vegetative year and lover of Venus. Moschus laments the untimely death of the mourner for Adonis, and the Renaissance elegists follow, though with astonishing departures in Milton's poem. But Shelley, in the last third of his poem, is not mourning at all. He struggles to attain a luminous self-recognition that will prepare him for his own death, which he accurately senses is coming shortly (only a year away), and he strives to secure also some vision of the state of being of poetry itself, in its border relations both to life and to death.

Adonais°

An Elegy on the Death of John Keats, Author of
Endymion, Hyperion, Etc.

Ἀστὴρ πρὶν μὲν ἔλαμπες ἐνὶ ζωοῖσιν Ἑῷος·
νῦν δὲ θανὼν λάμπεις Ἕσπερος ἐν φθιμένοις. —PLATO°

I

I weep for Adonais—he is dead!
O, weep for Adonais! though our tears
Thaw not the frost which binds so dear a head!
And thou, sad Hour, selected from all years
To mourn our loss, rouse thy obscure compeers,
And teach them thine own sorrow, say: 'With me
Died Adonais; till the Future dares
Forget the Past, his fate and fame shall be
An echo and a light unto eternity!'

II

10 Where wert thou, mighty Mother,° when he lay,
When thy Son lay, pierced by the shaft which flies
In darkness?° where was lorn Urania

Adonais W. M. Rossetti first suggested that the title had some reference to the Hebrew "Adonai," a name for God meaning "Lord," and substituted by Jewish tradition for the sacred name, Jehovah, but this seems unlikely. The best suggestion is still that "Adonais" is a variant on "Adonias," the annual lament for Adonis by his female votaries.
Plato Shelley himself translated this motto (which is probably not by Plato):

Thou wert the morning star among the living,
    Ere thy fair light had fled:—
Now, having died, thou art as Hesperus, giving
    New splendour to the dead.
Mother Venus Urania, Muse of sublime poetry, of astronomy, and of spiritual love
the shaft . . . darkness The reference is to anonymous criticism.

When Adonais died? With veilèd eyes,
'Mid listening Echoes, in her Paradise
She sate, while one, with soft enamoured breath,
Rekindled all the fading melodies,
With which, like flowers that mock the corse beneath,
He had adorned and hid the coming bulk of Death.

III

Oh, weep for Adonais—he is dead!
Wake, melancholy Mother, wake and weep!
Yet wherefore? Quench within their burning bed
Thy fiery tears, and let thy loud heart keep
Like his, a mute and uncomplaining sleep;
For he is gone, where all things wise and fair
Descend;—oh, dream not that the amorous Deep
Will yet restore him to the vital air;
Death feeds on his mute voice, and laughs at our despair.

IV

Most musical of mourners, weep again!
Lament anew, Urania!—He died,°
Who was the Sire of an immortal strain,
Blind, old, and lonely, when his country's pride,
The priest, the slave, and the liberticide,
Trampled and mocked with many a loathèd rite
Of lust and blood; he went, unterrified,
Into the gulf of death; but his clear Sprite
Yet reigns o'er earth; the third among the sons of light.°

V

Most musical of mourners, weep anew!
Not all to that bright station dared to climb;
And happier they their happiness who knew,
Whose tapers yet burn through that night of time
In which suns perished; others more sublime,
Struck by the envious wrath of man or god,
Have sunk, extinct in their refulgent prime;
And some yet live, treading the thorny road,
Which leads, through toil and hate, to Fame's serene abode.°

VI

But now, thy youngest, dearest one, has perished—
The nursling of thy widowhood, who grew,
Like a pale flower by some sad maiden cherished,

He died Milton, Keats's precursor, and father
of what Shelley took to be the true tradition of
English poetry
sons of light Homer, Dante, Milton: the three
greatest Western writers of epic

And some . . . abode Destined for this abode,
Shelley believed, were Wordsworth, Byron, and
Coleridge.

And fed with true-love tears, instead of dew;
50   Most musical of mourners, weep anew!
Thy extreme hope, the loveliest and the last,
The bloom, whose petals nipped before they blew
Died on the promise of the fruit, is waste;
The broken lily lies—the storm is overpast.

VII

To that high Capital,° where kingly Death
Keeps his pale court in beauty and decay,
He came; and bought, with price of purest breath,
A grave among the eternal.—Come away!
Haste, while the vault of blue Italian day
60   Is yet his fitting charnel-roof! while still
He lies, as if in dewy sleep he lay;
Awake him not! surely he takes his fill
Of deep and liquid rest, forgetful of all ill.

VIII

He will awake no more, oh, never more!—
Within the twilight chamber spreads apace
The shadow of white Death, and at the door
Invisible Corruption waits to trace
His extreme way to her dim dwelling-place;
The eternal Hunger sits, but pity and awe
70   Soothe her pale rage, nor dares she to deface
So fair a prey, till darkness, and the law
Of change, shall o'er his sleep the mortal curtain draw.

IX

Oh, weep for Adonais!—The quick Dreams,
The passion-wingèd Ministers of thought,
Who were his flocks, whom near the living streams
Of his young spirit he fed, and whom he taught
The love which was its music, wander not,—
Wander no more, from kindling brain to brain,
But droop there, whence they sprung; and mourn their lot
80   Round the cold heart, where, after their sweet pain,
They ne'er will gather strength, or find a home again.

X

And one with trembling hands clasps his cold head,
And fans him with her moonlight wings, and cries;
'Our love, our hope, our sorrow, is not dead;
See, on the silken fringe of his faint eyes,
Like dew upon a sleeping flower, there lies

Capital Rome

A tear some Dream has loosened from his brain.'
Lost Angel of a ruined Paradise!
She knew not 'twas her own; as with no stain
90   She faded, like a cloud which had outwept its rain.

XI

One from a lucid urn of starry dew
Washed his light limbs as if embalming them;
Another clipped her profuse locks, and threw
The wreath upon him, like an anadem,°
Which frozen tears instead of pearls begem;
Another in her wilful grief would break
Her bow and wingèd reeds, as if to stem
A greater loss with one which was more weak;
And dull the barbèd fire against his frozen cheek.

XII

100   Another Splendour on his mouth alit,
That mouth, whence it was wont to draw the breath
Which gave it strength to pierce the guarded wit,°
And pass into the panting heart beneath
With lightning and with music: the damp death
Quenched its caress upon his icy lips;
And, as a dying meteor stains a wreath
Of moonlight vapour, which the cold night clips,°
It flushed through his pale limbs, and passed to its eclipse.

XIII

And others came . . . Desires and Adorations,
110   Wingèd Persuasions and veiled Destinies,
Splendours, and Glooms, and glimmering Incarnations
Of hopes and fears, and twilight Phantasies;
And Sorrow, with her family of Sighs,
And Pleasure, blind with tears, led by the gleam
Of her own dying smile instead of eyes,
Came in slow pomp;—the moving pomp might seem
Like pageantry of mist on an autumnal stream.

XIV

All he had loved, and moulded into thought,
From shape, and hue, and odour, and sweet sound,
120   Lamented Adonais. Morning sought
Her eastern watch-tower, and her hair unbound,
Wet with the tears which should adorn the ground,
Dimmed the aereal eyes that kindle day;
Afar the melancholy thunder moaned,

anadem garland   **clips** embraces
guarded wit defensive minds of potential readers

Pale Ocean in unquiet slumber lay,
And the wild Winds flew round, sobbing in their dismay.

XV

Lost Echo° sits amid the voiceless mountains,
And feeds her grief with his remembered lay,
And will no more reply to winds or fountains,
130   Or amorous birds perched on the young green spray,
Or herdsman's horn, or bell at closing day;
Since she can mimic not his lips, more dear
Than those for whose disdain she pined away
Into a shadow of all sounds:—a drear
Murmur, between their songs, is all the woodmen hear.

XVI

Grief made the young Spring wild, and she threw down
Her kindling buds, as if she Autumn were,
Or they dead leaves; since her delight is flown,
For whom should she have waked the sullen year?
140   To Phoebus was not Hyacinth° so dear
Nor to himself Narcissus,° as to both
Thou, Adonais: wan they stand and sere
Amid the faint companions of their youth,
With dew all turned to tears; odour, to sighing ruth.

XVII

Thy spirit's sister, the lorn nightingale°
Mourns not her mate with such melodious pain;
Not so the eagle, who like thee could scale
Heaven, and could nourish in the sun's domain
Her mighty youth with morning,° doth complain,
150   Soaring and screaming round her empty nest,
As Albion wails for thee: the curse of Cain
Light on his head who pierced thy innocent breast,
And s⌐ared the angel soul that was its earthly guest!

XVIII

Ah, woe is me! Winter is come and gone,
But grief returns with the revolving year;°
The airs and streams renew their joyous tone;
The ants, the bees, the swallows reappear;
Fresh leaves and flowers deck the dead Seasons' bier;

Echo Echo was a nymph in love with Narcissus, who was in love with himself; consequently, as Shelley says, "she pined away."
Hyacinth a youth beloved by Phoebus Apollo, but accidentally slain by that god, who changed the youth's blood into the flower hyacinth, whose markings were interpreted by the Greeks as "ai ai" ("woe! woe!")

Narcissus as much the flower he became as the self-enamored youth he was
nightingale a reference to Keats's great ode
Not so . . . morning By legend, old eagles regain youth by flying high enough, and thus melting down.
But . . . year Compare l. 472.

The amorous birds now pair in every brake,°
160 And build their mossy homes in field and brere;°
And the green lizard, and the golden snake,
Like unimprisoned flames, out of their trance awake.

XIX

Through wood and stream and field and hill and Ocean
A quickening life from the Earth's heart has burst
As it has ever done, with change and motion,
From the great morning of the world when first
God dawned on Chaos; in its stream immersed,
The lamps of Heaven flash with a softer light;
All baser things pant with life's sacred thirst;
170 Diffuse themselves; and spend in love's delight,
The beauty and the joy of their renewèd might.

XX

The leprous corpse, touched by this spirit tender,
Exhales itself in flowers of gentle breath;
Like incarnations of the stars, when splendour
Is changed to fragrance, they illumine death
And mock the merry worm that wakes beneath;
Nought we know, dies. Shall that alone which knows
Be as a sword consumed before the sheath
By sightless lightning?—the intense atom glows
180 A moment, then is quenched in a most cold repose.

XXI

Alas! that all we loved of him should be,
But for our grief, as if it had not been,
And grief itself be mortal! Woe is me!
Whence are we, and why are we? of what scene
The actors or spectators? Great and mean
Meet massed in death, who lends what life must borrow.
As long as skies are blue, and fields are green,
Evening must usher night, night urge the morrow,
Month follow month with woe, and year wake year to sorrow.

XXII

190 *He* will awake no more, oh, never more!
'Wake thou,' cried Misery, 'childless Mother, rise
Out of thy sleep, and slake, in thy heart's core,
A wound more fierce than his, with tears and sighs.'
And all the Dreams that watched Urania's eyes,
And all the Echoes whom their sister's song
Had held in holy silence, cried: 'Arise!'

brake thicket   brere briar

Swift as a Thought by the snake Memory stung,
From her ambrosial rest the fading Splendour sprung.

XXIII

She rose like an autumnal Night, that springs
200   Out of the East, and follows wild and drear
The golden Day, which, on eternal wings,
Even as a ghost abandoning a bier,
Had left the Earth a corpse. Sorrow and fear
So struck, so roused, so rapt Urania;
So saddened round her like an atmosphere
Of stormy mist; so swept her on her way
Even to the mournful place where Adonais lay.

XXIV

Out of her secret Paradise she sped,
Through camps and cities rough with stone, and steel,
210   And human hearts, which to her aery tread
Yielding not, wounded the invisible
Palms of her tender feet where'er they fell:
And barbèd tongues, and thoughts more sharp than they,
Rent the soft Form they never could repel,
Whose sacred blood, like the young tears of May,
Paved with eternal flowers that undeserving way.

XXV

In the death-chamber for a moment Death,
Shamed by the presence of that living Might,
Blushed to annihilation, and the breath
220   Revisited those lips, and Life's pale light
Flashed through those limbs, so late her dear delight.
'Leave me not wild and dread and comfortless,
As silent lightning leaves the starless night!
Leave me not!' cried Urania: her distress
Roused Death: Death rose and smiled, and met her vain caress.

XXVI

'Stay yet awhile! speak to me once again;
Kiss me, so long but as a kiss may live;
And in my heartless breast and burning brain
That word, that kiss, shall all thoughts else survive,
230   With food of saddest memory kept alive,
Now thou art dead, as if it were a part
Of thee, my Adonais! I would give
All that I am to be as thou now art!
But I am chained to Time, and cannot thence depart!

XXVII

'O gentle child, beautiful as thou wert,
Why didst thou leave the trodden paths of men
Too soon, and with weak hands though mighty heart
Dare the unpastured dragon in his den?
Defenceless as thou wert, oh, where was then
240   Wisdom the mirrored shield,° or scorn the spear?
Or hadst thou waited the full cycle, when
Thy spirit should have filled its crescent sphere,°
The monsters of life's waste had fled from thee like deer.

XXVIII

'The herded wolves, bold only to pursue;
The obscene ravens, clamorous o'er the dead;
The vultures° to the conqueror's banner true
Who feed where Desolation first has fed,
And whose wings rain contagion;—how they fled,
When, like Apollo, from his golden bow
250   The Pythian° of the age one arrow sped
And smiled!—The spoilers tempt no second blow,
They fawn on the proud feet that spurn them lying low.

XXIX

'The sun comes forth, and many reptiles spawn;
He sets, and each ephemeral insect then
Is gathered into death without a dawn,
And the immortal stars awake again;
So is it in the world of living men:
A godlike mind soars forth, in its delight
Making earth bare and veiling heaven, and when
260   It sinks, the swarms that dimmed or shared its light
Leave to its kindred lamps the spirit's awful night.'

XXX

Thus ceased she: and the mountain shepherds came,
Their garlands sere, their magic mantles rent;
The Pilgrim of Eternity,° whose fame
Over his living head like Heaven is bent,
An early but enduring monument,
Came, veiling all the lightnings of his song
In sorrow; from her wilds Ierne sent

mirrored shield Perseus, given a mirror-shield by Athena, and a sword by Hermes, cut off Medusa's head, by looking at her reflection in the shield; otherwise, she would have turned him into stone.
crescent sphere i.e. full maturity
vultures critics; so also, wolves and ravens

Pythian Apollo Pythius or the Python-slayer; here, Lord Byron, for his *English Bards and Scotch Reviewers*
Pilgrim of Eternity Byron, foremost of the "mountain shepherds" or contemporary poets; the Pilgrim because of *Childe Harold's Pilgrimage*

The sweetest lyrist° of her saddest wrong,
270   And Love taught Grief to fall like music from his tongue.

XXXI

Midst others of less note, came one frail Form,°
A phantom among men; companionless
As the last cloud of an expiring storm
Whose thunder is its knell; he, as I guess,
Had gazed on Nature's naked loveliness,
Actaeon-like, and now he fled astray
With feeble steps o'er the world's wilderness,
And his own thoughts, along that rugged way,
Pursued, like raging hounds, their father and their prey.°

XXXII

280   A pardlike Spirit beautiful and swift°—
A Love in desolation masked;—a Power
Girt round with weakness;—it can scarce uplift
The weight of the superincumbent hour;
It is a dying lamp, a falling shower,
A breaking billow;—even whilst we speak
Is it not broken? On the withering flower
The killing sun smiles brightly: on a cheek
The life can burn in blood, even while the heart may break.

XXXIII

His head was bound with pansies overblown,
290   And faded violets, white, and pied, and blue;
And a light spear topped with a cypress cone,°
Round whose rude shaft dark ivy-tresses grew
Yet dripping with the forest's noonday dew,
Vibrated, as the ever-beating heart
Shook the weak hand that grasped it; of that crew
He came the last, neglected and apart;
A herd-abandoned deer struck by the hunter's dart.

XXXIV

All stood aloof, and at his partial moan
Smiled through their tears; well knew that gentle band
300   Who in another's fate now wept his own,
As in the accents of an unknown land

---

sweetest lyrist Byron's friend Thomas Moore, poet of the *Irish Melodies* (Ierne = Ireland). In fact, both Moore and Byron despised Keats's poetry.
Form not so much Shelley, as his antithetical self, the Poet of *Alastor*
Actaeon-like . . . prey Actaeon had the misfortune to peep at Diana when she was bathing; she punished him by turning the unfortunate hunter into a stag, and he was torn to pieces by his own dogs.
A pardlike . . . swift The leopard image suggests Dionysus.
cypress cone Shelley bears the thyrsus or Dionysiac wand, as well as the mourning cypress, the pansies of acute self-consciousness, and other emblems of a poet bound for self-destruction.

He sung new sorrow; sad Urania scanned
The Stranger's mien, and murmured: 'Who art thou?'
He answered not, but with a sudden hand
Made bare his branded and ensanguined brow,
Which was like Cain's° or Christ's—oh! that it should be so!

XXXV

What softer voice is hushed over the dead?
Athwart what brow is that dark mantle thrown?
What form leans sadly o'er the white death-bed,
310   In mockery° of monumental stone,
The heavy heart heaving without a moan?
If it be He, who, gentlest of the wise,°
Taught, soothed, loved, honoured the departed one,
Let me not vex, with inharmonious sighs,
The silence of that heart's accepted sacrifice.

XXXVI

Our Adonais has drunk poison—oh!
What deaf and viperous murderer could crown
Life's early cup with such a draught of woe?
The nameless worm° would now itself disown:
320   It felt, yet could escape, the magic tone
Whose prelude held all envy, hate, and wrong,
But what was howling in one breast alone,
Silent with expectation of the song,
Whose master's hand is cold, whose silver lyre unstrung.

XXXVII

Live thou, whose infamy is not thy fame!
Live! fear no heavier chastisement from me,
Thou noteless blot on a remembered name!
But be thyself, and know thyself to be!
And ever at thy season be thou free
330   To spill the venom when thy fangs o'erflow;
Remorse and Self-contempt shall cling to thee;
Hot Shame shall burn upon thy secret brow,
And like a beaten hound tremble thou shalt—as now.

XXXVIII

Nor let us weep that our delight is fled
Far from these carrion kites that scream below;
He wakes or sleeps with the enduring dead;
Thou canst not soar where he is sitting now.—
Dust to the dust! but the pure spirit shall flow

Cain's perhaps guilt for not having protected his "brother," Keats   **mockery** imitation   **gentlest . . . wise** Leigh Hunt   **nameless worm** anonymous reviewer

Back to the burning fountain whence it came,
340   A portion of the Eternal, which must glow
Through time and change, unquenchably the same,
Whilst thy cold embers choke the sordid hearth of shame.

XXXIX

Peace, peace! he is not dead, he doth not sleep—
He hath awakened from the dream of life—
'Tis we, who lost in stormy visions, keep
With phantoms an unprofitable strife,
And in mad trance, strike with our spirit's knife
Invulnerable nothings.°—*We* decay
Like corpses in a charnel; fear and grief
350   Convulse us and consume us day by day,
And cold hopes swarm like worms within our living clay.

XL

He has outsoared the shadow of our night;°
Envy and calumny and hate and pain,
And that unrest which men miscall delight,
Can touch him not and torture not again;
From the contagion of the world's slow stain
He is secure, and now can never mourn
A heart grown cold, a head grown gray in vain;
Nor, when the spirit's self has ceased to burn,
360   With sparkless ashes load an unlamented urn.°

XLI

He lives, he wakes—'tis Death is dead, not he;
Mourn not for Adonais.—Thou young Dawn,
Turn all thy dew to splendour, for from thee
The spirit thou lamentest is not gone;
Ye caverns and ye forests, cease to moan!
Cease, ye faint flowers and fountains, and thou Air,
Which like a mourning veil thy scarf hadst thrown
O'er the abandoned Earth, now leave it bare
Even to the joyous stars which smile on its despair!

XLII

370   He is made one with Nature: there is heard
His voice in all her music, from the moan
Of thunder, to the song of night's sweet bird;°
He is a presence to be felt and known
In darkness and in light, from herb and stone,

And in . . . nothings the situation of *Macbeth* II.i.33–34
shadow . . . night shadow cast upward by earth into the heavens

an unlamented urn the fate of Wordsworth and Coleridge
sweet bird another reference to Keats's ode

Spreading itself where'er that Power may move
Which has withdrawn his being to its own;
Which wields the world with never-wearied love,
Sustains it from beneath, and kindles it above.

XLIII

He is a portion of the loveliness
380   Which once he made more lovely: he doth bear
His part, while the one Spirit's plastic stress°
Sweeps through the dull dense world, compelling there,
All new successions to the forms they wear;
Torturing the unwilling dross° that checks its flight
To its own likeness, as each mass may bear;
And bursting in its beauty and its might
From trees and beasts and men into the Heaven's light.

XLIV

The splendours of the firmament of time
May be eclipsed, but are extinguished not;
390   Like stars° to their appointed height they climb,
And death is a low mist which cannot blot
The brightness it may veil. When lofty thought
Lifts a young heart above its mortal lair,
And love and life contend in it, for what
Shall be its earthly doom, the dead live there
And move like winds of light on dark and stormy air.

XLV

The inheritors of unfulfilled renown
Rose from their thrones, built beyond mortal thought,
Far in the Unapparent. Chatterton°
400   Rose pale,—his solemn agony had not
Yet faded from him; Sidney,° as he fought
And as he fell and as he lived and loved
Sublimely mild, a Spirit without spot,
Arose; and Lucan,° by his death approved:
Oblivion as they rose shrank like a thing reproved.

XLVI

And many more, whose names on Earth are dark,
But whose transmitted effluence cannot die

plastic stress shaping pressure; see Coleridge's "The Eolian Harp," ll. 46–48
unwilling dross the natural recalcitrance of all substance to become spirit
Like stars Shelley uses the same image for true poets in The Triumph of Life.
Chatterton Thomas Chatterton (1752–70); the agony is from his suicide at seventeen; Shelley knew that Chatterton was peculiarly important to Keats.

Sidney Sir Philip Sidney (1554–86) died in battle at thirty-two.
Lucan Marcus Annaeus Lucanus (39–65 A.D.), Roman poet remembered for his Pharsalia, on the Civil Wars, killed himself at twenty-six, when his participation in a plot against Nero was revealed; Shelley is saying that his death was the one good thing about him.

So long as fire outlives the parent spark,
Rose, robed in dazzling immortality.
'Thou art become as one of us,' they cry,
'It was for thee yon kingless sphere has long
Swung blind in unascended majesty,
Silent alone amid an Heaven of Song.
Assume thy wingèd throne, thou Vesper° of our throng!'

XLVII

Who mourns for Adonais? Oh, come forth,
Fond° wretch! and know thyself and him aright.
Clasp with thy panting soul the pendulous° Earth;
As from a centre, dart thy spirit's light
Beyond all worlds, until its spacious might
Satiate the void circumference: then shrink
Even to a point within our day and night;
And keep thy heart light lest it make thee sink
When hope has kindled hope, and lured thee to the brink.

XLVIII

Or go to Rome, which is the sepulchre,
Oh, not of him, but of our joy: 'tis nought
That ages, empires, and religions there
Lie buried in the ravage they have wrought;
For such as he can lend,—they borrow not
Glory from those who made the world their prey;
And he is gathered to the kings of thought
Who waged contention with their time's decay,
And of the past are all that cannot pass away.

XLIX

Go thou to Rome,—at once the Paradise,
The grave, the city, and the wilderness;
And where its wrecks like shattered mountains rise,
And flowering weeds, and fragrant copses dress
The bones of Desolation's nakedness
Pass, till the spirit of the spot shall lead
Thy footsteps to a slope of green access
Where, like an infant's smile, over the dead
A light of laughing flowers along the grass is spread;

L

And gray walls moulder round, on which dull Time
Feeds, like slow fire upon a hoary brand;
And one keen pyramid with wedge sublime,°

Vesper Hesperus, the Evening Star
Fond foolish
pendulous hanging
And one . . . sublime the pyramid-tomb of
the Roman tribune Gaius Cestus, near the Protestant cemetery where Keats was buried (and where Shelley was to be buried)

Pavilioning the dust of him who planned
This refuge for his memory, doth stand
Like flame transformed to marble; and beneath,
A field is spread, on which a newer band
Have pitched in Heaven's smile their camp of death,
450 Welcoming him we lose with scarce extinguished breath.

LI

Here pause: these graves are all too young as yet
To have outgrown the sorrow which consigned
Its charge to each; and if the seal is set,
Here, on one fountain of a mourning mind,°
Break it not thou! too surely shalt thou find
Thine own well full, if thou returnest home,
Of tears and gall. From the world's bitter wind
Seek shelter in the shadow of the tomb.
What Adonais is, why fear we to become?

LII

460 The One remains, the many change and pass;
Heaven's light forever shines, Earth's shadows fly;
Life, like a dome of many-coloured glass,
Stains the white radiance of Eternity,
Until Death tramples it to fragments.—Die,
If thou wouldst be with that which thou dost seek!
Follow where all is fled!—Rome's azure sky,
Flowers, ruins, statues, music, words, are weak
The glory they transfuse with fitting truth to speak.°

LIII

Why linger, why turn back, why shrink, my Heart?
470 Thy hopes are gone before: from all things here
They have departed; thou shouldst now depart!
A light is passed from the revolving year,
And man, and woman; and what still is dear
Attracts to crush, repels to make thee wither.
The soft sky smiles,—the low wind whispers near:
'Tis Adonais calls! oh, hasten thither,
No more let Life divide what Death can join together.

LIV

That Light whose smile kindles the Universe,
That Beauty in which all things work and move,

---

mourning mind Shelley's three-year-old son William was buried in the same cemetery a year and one-half before Keats.
The One . . . speak Though the language here (ll. 460–68) derives from Platonic tradition, this famous stanza blends Platonic Idealism with Shelley's own visionary skepticism. Here the One or Eternal radiance, and phenomenal life or the many-colored glass, are opposing realities (where in a purer Platonism only the Eternal would be real). Life is a staining, and in some sense, therefore, a loss, but "stains" here means coloring, and the colors are identical with "azure sky, / Flowers, ruins, statues, music, words," which fall short of Eternal glory yet are valuable and lovely in themselves.

480   That Benediction which the eclipsing Curse
Of birth can quench not, that sustaining Love
Which through the web of being blindly wove
By man and beast and earth and air and sea,
Burns bright or dim, as each° are mirrors of
The fire for which all thirst; now beams on me,
Consuming the last clouds of cold mortality.

LV

The breath whose might I have invoked in song°
Descends on me; my spirit's bark is driven,
Far from the shore, far from the trembling throng
490   Whose sails were never to the tempest given;
The massy earth and spherèd skies are riven!
I am borne darkly, fearfully, afar;
Whilst, burning through the inmost veil of Heaven,
The soul of Adonais, like a star,
Beacons from the abode where the Eternal are.°
1821   1821

To Night

I

Swiftly walk o'er the western wave,
        Spirit of Night!
Out of the misty eastern cave,°
Where, all the long and lone daylight,
Thou wovest dreams of joy and fear,
Which make thee terrible and dear,—
        Swift be thy flight!

II

Wrap thy form in a mantle grey,
        Star-inwrought!
10   Blind with thine hair the eyes of Day;
Kiss her until she be wearied out,
Then wander o'er city, and sea, and land,
Touching all with thine opiate wand—
        Come, long-sought!

III

When I arose and saw the dawn,
        I sighed for thee;
When light rode high, and the dew was gone,

as each to the degree that each
song in the "Ode to the West Wind"
The soul . . . are Contrast the close of *Lycidas*,
where the dead poet becomes "the Genius of
the shore."

Out . . . cave As the day closes, the first core
of darkness is in the east, and in its relation to
the light of the whole sky, it seems the dark
mouth of a cave.

And noon lay heavy on flower and tree,
And the weary Day turned to his° rest,
20 Lingering like an unloved guest,
       I sighed for thee.

       IV
Thy brother Death came, and cried,
       Wouldst thou me?
Thy sweet child Sleep, the filmy-eyed,
Murmured like a noontide bee,
Shall I nestle near thy side?
Wouldst thou me?—And I replied,
       No, not thee!

       V
Death will come when thou art dead,
30   Soon, too soon—
Sleep will come when thou art fled;
Of neither would I ask the boon
I ask of thee, belovèd Night—
Swift be thine approaching flight,
       Come soon, soon!
    1821   1824

From Hellas°

     CHORUS
060 The world's great age begins anew,
    The golden years return,
The earth doth like a snake renew
    Her winter weeds° outworn:
Heaven smiles, and faiths and empires gleam,
Like wrecks of a dissolving dream.

A brighter Hellas rears its mountains
    From waves serener far;
A new Peneus rolls his fountains
    Against the morning star.
070 Where fairer Tempes° bloom, there sleep
Young Cyclads° on a sunnier deep.

Day . . . his This "Day" is the Sun only, hence male, and not the mythic female "Day" of stanza II.
Hellas A lyrical drama celebrating the Greek rebellion against the Turks in 1821, roughly founded on *The Persians* of Aeschylus. In his own note to this the final Chorus, Shelley indicates a skeptical reserve as to his own prophecy: "It will remind the reader . . . of Isaiah and Virgil, whose ardent spirits overleaping the actual reign of evil which we endure and be- wail, already saw the possible and perhaps approaching state of society in which the *'lion shall lie down with the lamb.'* . . ." Compare Yeats's "Two Songs from a Play" (the play is *The Resurrection*).
weeds garments
Tempes the vale of Tempe in Thessaly, near Mt. Pelion, where the river Peneus flows; the daughter of Peneus, Daphne, was transformed into the laurel, sacred to Apollo
Cyclads islands in the Aegean

A loftier Argo° cleaves the main,
　　Fraught with a later prize;
Another Orpheus sings again,
　　And loves, and weeps, and dies.
A new Ulysses leaves once more
Calypso for his native shore.

Oh, write no more the tale of Troy,
　　If earth Death's scroll must be!
1080　Nor mix with Laian° rage the joy
　　Which dawns upon the free:
Although a subtler Sphinx renew
Riddles of death Thebes never knew.°

Another Athens shall arise,
　　And to remoter time
Bequeath, like sunset to the skies,
　　The splendour of its prime;
And leave, if nought so bright may live,
All earth can take or Heaven can give.

1090　Saturn and Love their long repose
　　Shall burst, more bright and good
Than all who fell, than One° who rose,
　　Than many unsubdued:
Not gold, not blood, their altar dowers,
But votive tears and symbol flowers.

Oh, cease! must hate and death return?
　　Cease! must men kill and die?
Cease! drain not to its dregs the urn
　　Of bitter prophecy.
1100　The world is weary of the past,
Oh, might it die or rest at last!
1821　　　　　　　　　　1822

With a Guitar, To Jane°

Ariel to Miranda:°—Take
This slave of Music, for the sake
Of him who is the slave of thee,

Argo Jason's ship in his quest of the Golden
Fleece
Laian Laius was the father of Oedipus.
Although . . . knew The Sphinx of Thebes,
overcome by Oedipus, asked riddles of life, particularly of human origins; "a subtler Sphinx"
will concern itself with the mystery of human
death.
One Identified by Shelley's own note as Christ;
"all who fell," he said, were the Gods of Greece,
Asia, and Egypt, while the "many unsubdued"
were the surviving religions of China, India,
"and the native tribes of America."
Jane Jane Williams, with whom Shelley was
in love during the closing months of his life; he
drowned with her husband, Edward Williams,
in circumstances still mysterious. This poem
accompanied the present of a guitar.
Ariel to Miranda characters in Shakespeare's
The Tempest, as are Ferdinand and Prospero

And teach it all the harmony
In which thou canst, and only thou,
Make the delighted spirit glow,
Till joy denies itself again,
And, too intense, is turned to pain;
For by permission and command
10 Of thine own Prince Ferdinand,°
Poor Ariel sends this silent token
Of more than ever can be spoken;
Your guardian spirit, Ariel, who,
From life to life, must still pursue
Your happiness;—for thus alone
Can Ariel ever find his own.
From Prospero's enchanted cell,
As the mighty verses tell,
To the throne of Naples, he
20 Lit you o'er the trackless sea,
Flitting on, your prow before,
Like a living meteor.
When you die, the silent Moon,
In her interlunar swoon,°
Is not sadder in her cell
Than deserted Ariel.
When you live again on earth,
Like an unseen star of birth,
Ariel guides you o'er the sea
30 Of life from your nativity.
Many changes have been run
Since Ferdinand and you begun
Your course of love, and Ariel still
Has tracked your steps, and served your will;
Now, in humbler, happier lot,
This is all remembered not;
And now, alas! the poor sprite is
Imprisoned, for some fault of his,
In a body like a grave;—
40 From you he only dares to crave,
For his service and his sorrow,
A smile today, a song tomorrow.
The artist who this idol wrought,
To echo all harmonious thought,
Felled a tree, while on the steep
The woods were in their winter sleep,
Rocked in that repose divine
On the wind-swept Apennine;
And dreaming, some of Autumn past,

Ferdinand i.e. Edward Williams   **swoon** time between the old and the new moon

50   And some of Spring approaching fast,
      And some of April buds and showers,
      And some of songs in July bowers,
      And all of love; and so this tree,—
      O that such our death may be!—
      Died in sleep, and felt no pain,
      To live in happier form again:
      From which, beneath Heaven's fairest star,
      The artist wrought this loved Guitar,
      And taught it justly to reply,
60   To all who question skilfully,
      In language gentle as thine own;
      Whispering in enamoured tone
      Sweet oracles of woods and dells,
      And summer winds in sylvan cells;
      For it had learned all harmonies
      Of the plains and of the skies,
      Of the forests and the mountains,
      And the many-voicèd fountains;
      The clearest echoes of the hills,
70   The softest notes of falling rills,
      The melodies of birds and bees,
      The murmuring of summer seas,
      And pattering rain, and breathing dew,
      And airs of evening; and it knew
      That seldom-heard mysterious sound,
      Which, driven on its diurnal round,
      As it floats through boundless day,
      Our world enkindles on its way.—
      All this it knows, but will not tell
80   To those who cannot question well
      The Spirit that inhabits it;
      It talks according to the wit
      Of its companions; and no more
      Is heard than has been felt before,
      By those who tempt it to betray
      These secrets of an elder day:
      But, sweetly as its answers will
      Flatter hands of perfect skill,
      It keeps its highest, holiest tone
90   For our belovèd Jane alone.
      1822   1832

Lines Written in the Bay of Lerici°

She left me at the silent time
When the moon had ceased to climb
The azure path of Heaven's steep,
And like an albatross asleep,
Balanced on her wings of light,
Hovered in the purple night,
Ere she sought her ocean nest
In the chambers of the West.
She left me, and I stayed alone
10   Thinking over every tone
Which, though silent to the ear,
The enchanted heart could hear,
Like notes which die when born, but still
Haunt the echoes of the hill;
And feeling ever—oh, too much!—
The soft vibration of her touch,
As if her gentle hand, even now,
Lightly trembled on my brow;
And thus, although she absent were,
20   Memory gave me all of her
That even Fancy dares to claim:—
Her presence had made weak and tame
All passions, and I lived alone
In the time which is our own;
The past and future were forgot,
As they had been, and would be, not.
But soon, the guardian angel gone,
The daemon° reassumed his throne
In my faint heart. I dare not speak
30   My thoughts, but thus disturbed and weak
I sat and saw the vessels glide
Over the ocean bright and wide,
Like spirit-wingèd chariots sent
O'er some serenest element
For ministrations strange and far;
As if to some Elysian star
Sailed for drink to medicine
Such sweet and bitter pain as mine.
And the wind that winged their flight
40   From the land came fresh and light,
And the scent of wingèd flowers,
And the coolness of the hours
Of dew, and sweet warmth left by day,
Were scattered o'er the twinkling bay.

Lines . . . Lerici another lyric to Jane Williams; Shelley left it untitled

daemon presumably the spirit that dominated
the poet in *Alastor*

And the fisher with his lamp
And spear about the low rocks damp
Crept, and struck the fish which came
To worship the delusive flame.
Too happy they, whose pleasure sought
50   Extinguishes all sense and thought
Of the regret that pleasure leaves,
Destroying life° alone, not peace!
1822   1862

The Triumph of Life

Shelley's last poem, left unfinished when he drowned, manifests a new severity of impulse and extraordinary purgation of style, and yet it is the most despairing poem he wrote, even darker in its implications than *Adonais*. Many readers want to believe that the poem would have ended in some affirmation, had it been completed, but there is little in the poem to encourage such speculation. The poem's best critics, from Hazlitt to Yeats, have seen its sadness, and the extent to which it constitutes a palinode or recantation of Shelley's more positive visions, such as *Prometheus Unbound*. What Yeats called the *antithetical* quest, undertaken against the natural man and his human affections, which Shelley had begun to pursue in *Alastor*, here attains its shattering climax. The best (and most restrained) statement of a more hopeful reading of the poem can be found in M. H. Abrams's *Natural Supernaturalism*.

Shelley's poem takes its tone from Dante's *Purgatorio*, but the action and context of *The Triumph of Life* share more with the *Inferno*. Rousseau, prophet of nature, serving as a surrogate for Wordsworth, enters the poem as Virgil, the guide to Shelley's Dante. But Shelley here is no Pilgrim of the Absolute. What he sees in this magnificent fragment is horror, the defeat of all human integrity by life, our life, which is only a lively death. This vision is not nihilistic, for all its hopelessness, not because anything in the text suggests that Shelley will clamber out of the abyss, but because he will not join the dance, will not be seduced by Nature as his precursor Rousseau was. And yet he stands in the hell of life's triumph, and sees around him all men who have lived save for a sacred few of Athens and Jerusalem, whom he declines to name.

Amid this frightening splendor, two elements stand forth: the chastening of Shelley's idiom and mythic inventiveness, and the provocative distinction between three realms of light—poetry (the stars), nature (the sun), life (the chariot's glare). As nature outshines imagination, so the chariot's horrible splendor outshines Nature. In the fragment's closing passages, Shelley writes his last and most convincing critique of Wordsworthianism. Nature, whether she desires otherwise or not, always does betray the heart that loves her. The "shape all light," Wordsworthian Nature, offers her cup of communion, Rousseau drinks, and his imagination becomes as sand. Shelley, perhaps hours from his death, is at the height of his powers, but gazes out at a universe of death that offers only a parody of his own vitalism.

The text printed here was prepared and edited by Donald H. Reiman and published in 1965 in *Shelley's "The Triumph of Life": A Critical Study.*

life in the same sense as "life" is used in *The Triumph of Life*

The Triumph of Life°

Swift as a spirit hastening to his task
   Of glory & of good, the Sun sprang forth
Rejoicing in his splendour, & the mask

   Of darkness fell from the awakened Earth.°
The smokeless altars of the mountain snows
   Flamed above crimson clouds, & at the birth

Of light, the Ocean's orison arose
   To which the birds tempered their matin lay.°
All flowers in field or forest which unclose

10   Their trembling eyelids to the kiss of day,
Swinging their censers in the element,
   With orient incense lit by the new ray

Burned slow & inconsumably, & sent
   Their odorous sighs up to the smiling air,
And in succession due, did Continent,

   Isle, Ocean, & all things that in them wear
The form & character of mortal mould
   Rise as the Sun their father rose, to bear

Their portion of the toil which he of old
20   Took as his own & then imposed on them;°
But I, whom thoughts which must remain untold

   Had kept as wakeful as the stars that gem
The cone of night,° now they were laid asleep,
   Stretched my faint limbs beneath the hoary stem

Which an old chestnut flung athwart the steep
   Of a green Apennine: before me fled
The night; behind me rose the day; the Deep

   Was at my feet, & Heaven above my head
When a strange trance over my fancy grew
30   Which was not slumber, for the shade it spread

Was so transparent that the scene came through
   As clear as when a veil of light is drawn
O'er evening hills they glimmer; and I knew

The Triumph of Life As in Petrarch's *Triumphs*, the title means a triumphal procession, but "Life" ironically means "Death-in-Life," or everything in life that can triumph over imaginative integrity.
the Sun . . . Earth The Sun is swift *as* a beneficent spirit, but its task here is morally ambiguous; the emotional temper of this opening resembles the lyric "To Night."

matin lay The religious vocabulary suggests a Wordsworthian displacement of sacramentalism into nature worship, but this is a scene from which Shelley consciously stands apart.
imposed on them As Yeats noted, the Sun here is something of a despot.
cone of night earth's shadow, which is a cone-like shape

That I had felt the freshness of that dawn,
Bathed in the same cold dew my brow & hair
And sate as thus upon that slope of lawn

Under the self same bough, & heard as there
The birds, the fountains & the Ocean hold
Sweet talk in music through the enamoured air.°

40   And then a Vision on my brain was rolled.

——————————

As in that trance of wondrous thought I lay
This was the tenour of my waking dream.
Methought I sate beside a public way

Thick strewn with summer dust, & a great stream
Of people there was hurrying to & fro
Numerous as gnats upon the evening gleam,

All hastening onward, yet none seemed to know
Whither he went, or whence he came, or why
He made one of the multitude, yet so

50   Was born amid the crowd as through the sky
One of the million leaves of summer's bier.°—
Old age & youth, manhood & infancy,

Mixed in one mighty torrent did appear,
Some flying from the thing they feared & some
Seeking the object of another's fear,

And others as with steps towards the tomb
Pored on the trodden worms that crawled beneath,
And others mournfully within the gloom

Of their own shadow walked, and called it death . . .
60   And some fled from it as it were a ghost,
Half fainting in the affliction of vain breath.

But more with motions which each other crost
Pursued or shunned the shadows the clouds threw
Or birds within the noonday ether lost,

Upon that path where flowers never grew;
And weary with vain toil & faint for thirst
Heard not the fountains whose melodious dew

Out of their mossy cells forever burst
Nor felt the breeze which from the forest told
70   Of grassy paths, & wood lawns interspersed

---

enamoured air The vision is recurrent, and enchanted.

summer's bier See the opening of "Ode to the
West Wind."

With overarching elms & caverns cold,
  And violet banks where sweet dreams brood, but they
Pursued their serious folly as of old . . . .

And as I gazed methought that in the way
  The throng grew wilder, as the woods of June
  When the South wind shakes the extinguished day.—

And a cold glare, intenser than the noon
  But icy cold, obscured with   light
The Sun as he the stars. Like the young moon

80 When on the sunlit limits of the night
Her white shell trembles amid crimson air
  And whilst the sleeping tempest gathers might

Doth, as a herald of its coming, bear
  The ghost of her dead Mother, whose dim form
Bends in dark ether from her infant's chair,°

So came a chariot on the silent storm
  Of its own rushing splendour, and a Shape°
So sate within as one whom years deform

Beneath a dusky hood & double cape
90 Crouching within the shadow of a tomb,
And o'er what seemed the head, a cloud like crape,

Was bent a dun & faint aetherial gloom
  Tempering the light; upon the chariot's beam
A Janus-visaged Shadow° did assume

The guidance of that wonder-wingèd team.
  The Shapes which drew it in thick lightnings
Were lost:° I heard alone on the air's soft stream

The music of their ever moving wings.
  All the four faces° of that charioteer
100 Had their eyes banded°. . . little profit brings

Speed in the van & blindness in the rear,
  Nor then avail the beams that quench the Sun
Or that his banded eyes could pierce the sphere

Of all that is, has been, or will be done.—
  So ill was the car guided, but it past
With solemn speed majestically on . . .

infant's chair the old moon in the new moon's
arms; see the epigraph to Coleridge's "Dejection" and the chariot-vision in *Prometheus Unbound* IV.206–35
Shape Life the Conqueror
Shadow a parody of the cherubim or guiding
angels of the divine chariot in Ezekiel, Revelation, Dante, and Milton; "Janus-visaged" because looking before and after (though here
seeing nothing), like the Roman god Janus
lost because though a parody of the divine
chariot, it is self-propelled as that was
four faces again in parody of Ezekiel's four
"living creatures" (Blake's Zoas), each with his
four faces
banded probably means blindfolded, whereas
Ezekiel and Dante emphasize a plethora of open
eyes.

The crowd gave way, & I arose aghast,
    Or seemed to rise, so mighty was the trance,
And saw like clouds upon the thunder blast

110   The million with fierce song and maniac dance
Raging around; such seemed the jubilee
    As when to greet some conqueror's advance

Imperial Rome poured forth her living sea
    From senatehouse & prison & theatre
When Freedom left those who upon the free

    Had bound a yoke which soon they stooped to bear.°
Nor wanted here the true similitude
    Of a triumphal pageant, for where'er

The chariot rolled a captive multitude
120   Was driven; all those who had grown old in power
Or misery,—all who have their age subdued,

    By action or by suffering, and whose hour
Was drained to its last sand in weal or woe,
    So that the trunk survived both fruit & flower;

All those whose fame or infamy must grow
    Till the great winter lay the form & name
Of their own earth with them forever low,

    All but the sacred few who could not tame
Their spirits to the Conqueror, but as soon
130   As they had touched the world with living flame

Fled back like eagles to their native noon,°
    Or those who put aside the diadem
Of earthly thrones or gems, till the last one

    Were there;—for they of Athens & Jerusalem
Were neither mid the mighty captives seen
    Nor mid the ribald crowd that followed them°

Or fled before . . Now swift, fierce & obscene
    The wild dance maddens in the van, & those
Who lead it, fleet as shadows on the green,

140   Outspeed the chariot & without repose
Mix with each other in tempestuous measure
    To savage music . . . . Wilder as it grows,

Had . . . bear Like the "mind-forged manacles" of Blake's "London," this yoke relies upon
the oppressed and their failure of will.
Fled . . . noon as Keats did in *Adonais*
for they . . . them Since Shelley does not name

Socrates and Jesus, we should grant him his deliberate ambiguity; there are some in the traditions of Athens and Jerusalem who did not yield
to Life, but we are not certain who they were.

They, tortured by the agonizing pleasure,
  Convulsed & on the rapid whirlwinds spun
Of that fierce spirit, whose unholy leisure

  Was soothed by mischief since the world begun,
Throw back their heads & loose their streaming hair,
  And in their dance round her who dims the Sun

Maidens & youths fling their wild arms in air
150   As their feet twinkle; they recede, and now
Bending within each other's atmosphere

  Kindle invisibly; and as they glow
Like moths by light attracted & repelled,
  Oft to new bright destruction come & go.°

Till like two clouds into one vale impelled
  That shake the mountains when their lightnings mingle
And die in rain,—the fiery band which held

  Their natures, snaps . . . ere the shock cease to tingle
One falls and then another in the path
160   Senseless, nor is the desolation single,

Yet ere I can say *where* the chariot hath
  Past over them; nor other trace I find
But as of foam° after the Ocean's wrath

  Is spent upon the desert shore.—Behind,
Old men, and women foully disarrayed
  Shake their grey hair in the insulting wind,

Limp in the dance & strain with limbs decayed
  To reach the car of light which leaves them still
Farther behind & deeper in the shade.

170   But not the less with impotence of will
They wheel, though ghastly shadows interpose
  Round them & round each other, and fulfill

Their work and to the dust whence they arose
  Sink & corruption veils them as they lie
And frost in these performs what fire in those.°

  Struck to the heart by this sad pageantry,
Half to myself I said, 'And what is this?
  Whose shape is that within the car? & why'—

Maidens . . . go Shelley's final vision of sexual love; the contrast with *Epipsychidion* is instructive.
foam the foam of Aphrodite

And frost . . . those Contrast the "frost" of the opening of *Adonais* and the "burning through" fire of its close.

I would have added—'is all here amiss?'
180   But a voice answered . . 'Life' . . . I turned & knew
(O Heaven have mercy on such wretchedness!)

That what I thought was an old root which grew
To strange distortion out of the hill side
      Was indeed one of that deluded crew,

And that the grass which methought hung so wide
      And white, was but his thin discoloured hair,
And that the holes it vainly sought to hide

Were or had been eyes.°—'If thou canst forbear
To join the dance, which I had well forborne.'
190   Said the grim Feature,° of my thought aware,

'I will now tell that which to this deep scorn
      Led me & my companions, and relate
The progress of the pageant since the morn;

'If thirst of knowledge doth not thus abate,
Follow it even to the night, but I
      Am weary'. . . . Then like one who with the weight

Of his own words is staggered, wearily
      He paused, and ere he could resume, I cried,
'First who art thou?'. . . 'Before thy memory

200   'I feared, loved, hated, suffered, did, & died,
And if the spark with which Heaven lit my spirit
      Earth had with purer nutriment supplied

'Corruption would not now thus much inherit
      Of what was once Rousseau—nor this disguise
Stained that within which still disdains to wear it.°—

'If I have been extinguished, yet there rise
A thousand beacons from the spark I bore.'°—
      'And who are those chained to the car?' 'The Wise,

'The great, the unforgotten: they who wore
210   Mitres & helms & crowns, or wreathes of light,°
Signs of thought's empire over thought; their lore

'Taught them not this—to know themselves; their might
Could not repress the mutiny within,°
      And for the morn of truth they feigned, deep night

the holes . . . eyes Rousseau, a great poet (in Shelley's judgment) and thus one of "heaven's living eyes," is fearfully ashamed of his loss, which parallels the blindfolding of the charioteer.
grim Feature See *Paradise Lost* X.279; "Feature" used in the sense of form or shape.
Corruption . . . it The disdain is like that of Farinata (*Inferno* X.36) and the other heroic damned in Dante.
spark I bore as one of the founders of Romanticism
wreathes of light The saints too are chained to the chariot.
mutiny within the unregenerate selfhood

'Caught them ere evening.' 'Who is he with chin
    Upon his breast and hands crost on his chain?'
'The Child of a fierce hour; he sought to win

'The world, and lost all it did contain
Of greatness, in its hope destroyed; & more
220   Of fame & peace than Virtue's self can gain

'Without the opportunity which bore
    Him on its eagle's pinion to the peak
From which a thousand climbers have before

'Fall'n as Napoleon fell.'—I felt my cheek
Alter to see the great form pass away
    Whose grasp had left the giant world so weak

That every pigmy kicked it as it lay—
    And much I grieved to think how power & will
In opposition rule our mortal day—

230   And why God made irreconcilable
Good & the means of good,° and for despair
    I half disdained mine eye's desire to fill

With the spent vision of the times that were
    And scarce have ceased to be . . . 'Dost thou behold,'
Said then my guide, 'those spoilers spoiled, Voltaire,

'Frederic, & Kant, Catherine, & Leopold,°
Chained hoary anarchs, demagogue & sage
    Whose name the fresh world thinks already old—

'For in the battle Life & they did wage
240   She remained conqueror—I was overcome
By my own heart alone, which neither age

'Nor tears nor infamy nor now the tomb
Could temper to its object.'°—'Let them pass'—
    I cried—'the world & its mysterious doom

'Is not so much more glorious than it was
    That I desire to worship those who drew
New figures on its false & fragile glass

    'As the old faded.'—'Figures ever new
Rise on the bubble, paint them how you may;
250   We have but thrown, as those before us threw,

God . . . good Shelley's central and most sorrowful insight
Frederic . . . Leopold the "enlightened despots," Frederick the Great of Prussia, Catherine the Great of Russia, and Leopold II of Austria, together with Voltaire, the Enlightenment man of letters, who inspired them to "reforms," and Immanuel Kant, culminating philosopher of the Enlightenment. These make an odd company, but in the view of the emotional naturalist Rousseau they all neglected the heart and its impulses.
For in . . . object (ll. 239–43) The Enlightened fell victim to life; Rousseau fell victim too, but to his heart's infinite desires, which could not temper themselves to any attainable objects.

'Our shadows on it as it past away.
　　But mark, how chained to the triumphal chair
　　The mighty phantoms of an elder day—

　　'All that is mortal of great Plato there
　　Expiates the joy & woe his master knew not,°
　　　That star that ruled his doom was far too fair—

'And Life, where long that flower of Heaven grew not,
　　Conquered the heart by love which gold or pain
Or age or sloth or slavery could subdue not—

260　　　And near　　　walk the　　　twain,
　　The tutor & his pupil,° whom Dominion
　　　Followed as tame as vulture in a chain.—

'The world was darkened beneath either pinion
　　Of him whom from the flock of conquerors
Fame singled as her thunderbearing minion;

　　'The other long outlived both woes & wars,
Throned in new thoughts of men, and still had kept
　　The jealous keys of truth's eternal doors

'If Bacon's spirit°　　　had not leapt
270　　Like lightning out of darkness; he compelled
　　The Proteus shape of Nature's as it slept

　　'To wake & to unbar the caves that held
The treasure of the secrets of its reign—
　　See the great bards of old who inly quelled

'The passions which they sung, as by their strain
　　May well be known: their living melody
Tempers its own contagion to the vein

　　'Of those who are infected with it°—I
Have suffered what I wrote, or viler pain!—

280　　'And so my words were seeds of misery—
Even as the deeds of others.'—'Not as theirs,'
　　I said—he pointed to a company

In which I recognized amid the heirs
　　Of Caesar's crime from him to Constantine,°
The Anarchs old whose force & murderous snares

---

master knew not Socrates was invulnerable to
Eros, but Plato (by legend) experienced passionate homosexual love for a youth named
Aster, whose name means "star" but in English
also a flower (l. 257); see the elegiac epigram
on Aster, attributed to Plato, used by Shelley as
the epigraph to Adonais.
tutor & his pupil Aristotle and Alexander the
Great

Bacon's spirit Francis Bacon (1561–1626),
whose empiricism helped overturn the Aristotel-
ian intellectual authority
infected with it Rousseau, who as a Romantic
suffers what he writes, stands apart from classical writers and their readers.
Constantine 4th-century Roman emperor who
established Christianity as the state religion

Had founded many a sceptre bearing line
And spread the plague of blood & gold abroad,
 And Gregory & John° and men divine

Who rose like shadows between Man & god
290 Till that eclipse, still hanging under Heaven,
Was worshipped by the world o'er which they strode

 For the true Sun it quenched.°—'Their power was given
But to destroy,' replied the leader—'I
 Am one of those who have created, even

'If it be but a world of agony.'—
 'Whence camest thou & whither goest thou?
How did thy course begin,' I said, '& why?

 'Mine eyes are sick of this perpetual flow
Of people, & my heart of one sad thought.—
300 Speak.' 'Whence I came, partly I seem to know,

'And how & by what paths I have been brought
 To this dread pass, methinks even thou mayst guess;
Why this should be my mind can compass not;

 'Whither the conqueror hurries me still less.
But follow thou, & from spectator turn
 Actor or victim in this wretchedness,

'And what thou wouldst be taught I then may learn
 From thee.—Now listen . . . In the April prime°
When all the forest tops began to burn

310 'With kindling green, touched by the azure clime
Of the young year, I found myself asleep
 Under a mountain which from unknown time

'Had yawned into a cavern high & deep,
 And from it came a gentle rivulet
Whose water like clear air in its calm sweep

 'Bent the soft grass & kept for ever wet
The stems of the sweet flowers, and filled the grove
 With sound which all who hear must needs forget

'All pleasure & all pain, all hate & love,
320 Which they had known before that hour of rest:
A sleeping mother then would dream not of

 'The only child who died upon her breast
At eventide, a king would mourn no more
 The crown of which his brow was dispossest

Gregory & John Pope Gregory the Great (c. 540–604) traditionally is credited with establishing the Papacy as a secular entity; John, a name frequently assumed by popes

it quenched the "eclipse" of historical, institutionalized Christianity destroys the true God **April prime** spring of the year, and second birth of Rousseau into adolescence and poetry

'When the sun lingered o'er the Ocean floor
   To gild his rival's new prosperity.—
Thou wouldst forget thus vainly to deplore

   'Ills, which if ills, can find no cure from thee,
The thought of which no other sleep will quell
330   Nor other music blot from memory—

'So sweet & deep is the oblivious spell.—
   Whether my life had been before that sleep
The Heaven which I imagine, or a Hell

'Like this harsh world in which I wake to weep,
I know not. I arose & for a space
   The scene of woods & waters seemed to keep,

'Though it was now broad day, a gentle trace
   Of light diviner than the common Sun
Sheds on the common Earth,° but all the place

340   'Was filled with many sounds woven into one
Oblivious melody, confusing sense°
   Amid the gliding waves & shadows dun;

'And as I looked the bright omnipresence
   Of morning through the orient cavern flowed,
And the Sun's image radiantly intense

'Burned on the waters of the well that glowed
Like gold, and threaded all the forest maze
   With winding paths of emerald fire—there stood

'Amid the sun, as he amid the blaze
350   Of his own glory, on the vibrating
Floor of the fountain, paved with flashing rays,

   'A shape all light,° which with one hand did fling
Dew on the earth, as if she were the Dawn
   Whose invisible rain forever seemed to sing

'A silver music on the mossy lawn,
   And still before her on the dusky grass
Iris her many coloured scarf had drawn.°—

   'In her right hand she bore a crystal glass
Mantling with bright Nepenthe;°—the fierce splendour
360   Fell from her as she moved under the mass

common Earth The use of "common" is Wordsworthian, and the remainder of the fragment
deliberately parodies the "Intimations of Immortality" ode.
confusing sense the synesthesia that typifies
Wordsworthian-Coleridgean Imagination
A shape all light Wordsworthian Nature, mask-
ing as the "celestial light" or "glory" of the
"Intimations" ode. Whatever her intentions
(Shelley leaves them ambiguous), her pragmatic
effect upon Rousseau is malevolent.
Iris . . . drawn the rainbow, emblem of the
Wordsworthian covenant with Nature, as in the
epigraph to the "Intimations" ode
Nepenthe drug of forgetfulness; here, what is
forgotten is the Divine Vision or childood in-
tensity of imagination

'Of the deep cavern, & with palms so tender
   Their tread broke not the mirror of its billow,
Glided along the river, and did bend her

'Head under the dark boughs, till like a willow
Her fair hair swept the bosom of the stream
   That whispered with delight to be their pillow.—

'As one enamoured is upborne in dream
   O'er lily-paven lakes mid silver mist
To wondrous music, so this shape might seem

370   'Partly to tread the waves with feet which kist
The dancing foam, partly to glide along
   The airs that roughened the moist amethyst,

'Or the slant morning beams that fell among
   The trees, or the soft shadows of the trees;
And her feet ever to the ceaseless song

'Of leaves & winds & waves & birds & bees
And falling drops moved in a measure new
   Yet sweet, as on the summer evening breeze

'Up from the lake a shape of golden dew
380   Between two rocks, athwart the rising moon,
Moves up the east, where eagle never flew.—

'And still her feet, no less than the sweet tune
To which they moved, seemed as they moved, to blot
   The thoughts of him who gazed on them, & soon

'All that was seemed as if it had been not,
   As if the gazer's mind was strewn beneath
Her feet like embers, & she, thought by thought,

'Trampled its fires into the dust of death,°
   As Day upon the threshold of the east
390   Treads out the lamps of night, until the breath

'Of darkness reillumines even the least
   Of heaven's living eyes°—like day she came,
Making the night a dream; and ere she ceased

'To move, as one between desire and shame
Suspended, I said—"If, as it doth seem,
   Thou comest from the realm without a name,

' "Into this valley of perpetual dream,
   Shew whence I came, and where I am, and why—
Pass not away upon the passing stream."

dust of death the end of Rousseau's greater
vision, as he yields to the Muse of Nature

living eyes the stars, who are the poets, as in
Adonais XLIV

400   ' "Arise and quench thy thirst,"° was her reply.
And as a shut lily, stricken by the wand
    Of dewy morning's vital alchemy,

'I rose; and, bending at her sweet command,
    Touched with faint lips the cup she raised,
And suddenly my brain became as sand

    'Where the first wave had more than half erased
The track of deer on desert Labrador,
    Whilst the fierce wolf from which they fled amazed

'Leaves his stamp visibly upon the shore
410   Until the second bursts—so on my sight
Burst a new Vision never seen before.—

    'And the fair shape waned in the coming light
As veil by veil the silent splendour drops
    From Lucifer,° amid the chrysolite

'Of sunrise ere it strike the mountain tops—
    And as the presence of that fairest planet
Although unseen is felt by one who hopes

    'That his day's path may end as he began it
In that star's smile, whose light is like the scent
420   Of a jonquil when evening breezes fan it,

'Or the soft note in which his dear lament
    The Brescian shepherd breathes,° or the caress
That turned his weary slumber to content.—

    'So knew I in that light's severe excess
The presence of that shape which on the stream
    Moved, as I moved along the wilderness,

'More dimly than a day appearing dream,
    The ghost of a forgotten form of sleep,
A light from Heaven whose half extinguished beam

430   'Through the sick day in which we wake to weep
Glimmers, forever sought, forever lost.—
    So did that shape its obscure tenour keep

'Beside my path, as silent as a ghost,
    But the new Vision, and its cold bright car,
With savage music, stunning music, crost

    'The forest, and as if from some dread war
Triumphantly returning, the loud million
    Fiercely extolled the fortune of her star.—

"Arise . . . thirst" Her reply is ambiguous, as he did not understand.
Lucifer the Morning Star, "light-bearer"

Or the . . . breathes national song of Brescia (northern Italy) which begins, "I am weary of pasturing the sheep"

'A moving arch of victory the vermilion
440   And green & azure plumes of Iris had
Built high over her wind-winged pavilion,

'And underneath aetherial glory clad
The wilderness, and far before her flew
The tempest of the splendour which forbade

'Shadow to fall from leaf or stone;—the crew
Seemed in that light like atomies° that dance
Within a sunbeam.—Some upon the new

'Embroidery of flowers that did enhance
The grassy vesture of the desert, played,
450   Forgetful of the chariot's swift advance;

'Others stood gazing till within the shade
Of the great mountain its light left them dim.—
Others outspeeded it, and others made

'Circles around it like the clouds that swim
Round the high moon in a bright sea of air,
And more did follow, with exulting hymn,

'The chariot & the captives fettered there,
But all like bubbles on an eddying flood
Fell into the same track at last & were

460   'Borne onward.—I among the multitude
Was swept; me sweetest flowers delayed not long,
Me not the shadow nor the solitude,

'Me not the falling stream's Lethean song,
Me, not the phantom of that early form
Which moved upon its motion,—but among

'The thickest billows of the living storm
I plunged, and bared my bosom to the clime
Of that cold light, whose airs too soon deform.—

'Before the chariot had begun to climb
470   The opposing steep of that mysterious dell,
Behold a wonder worthy of the rhyme

'Of him whom from the lowest depths of Hell
Through every Paradise & through all glory
Love led serene, & who returned to tell

'In words of hate & awe the wondrous story
How all things are transfigured, except Love;°
For deaf as is a sea which wrath makes hoary

atomies bits of dust   Of him . . . Love (ll. 472–76) Dante, pro-
                                         tected by Beatrice's love

'The world can hear not the sweet notes that move
    The sphere whose light is melody to lovers°—
480   A wonder worthy of his rhyme—the grove

'Grew dense with shadows to its inmost covers,
    The earth was grey with phantoms, & the air
Was peopled with dim forms, as when there hovers

'A flock of vampire-bats before the glare
Of the tropic sun, bringing ere evening
    Strange night upon some Indian isle,—thus were

'Phantoms diffused around, & some did fling
    Shadows of shadows, yet unlike themselves,
Behind them, some like eaglets on the wing

490   'Were lost in the white blaze, others like elves
Danced in a thousand unimagined shapes
    Upon the sunny streams & grassy shelves;

'And others sate chattering like restless apes
    On vulgar paws and voluble like fire.
Some made a cradle of the ermined capes

'Of kingly mantles, some upon the tiar°
Of pontiffs sate like vultures, others played
    Within the crown which girt with empire

'A baby's or an idiot's brow, & made
500   Their nests in it; the old anatomies°
Sate hatching their bare brood under the shade

'Of demon wings, and laughed from their dead eyes
To reassume the delegated power
    Arrayed in which these worms did monarchize

'Who make this earth their charnel.°—Others more
    Humble, like falcons sate upon the fist
Of common men, and round their heads did soar,

'Or like small gnats & flies, as thick as mist
On evening marshes, thronged about the brow
510   Of lawyer, statesman, priest & theorist,

'And others like discoloured flakes of snow
    On fairest bosoms & the sunniest hair
Fell, and were melted by the youthful glow

'Which they extinguished; for like tears, they were
A veil to those from whose faint lids they rained
    In drops of sorrow.—I became aware

The sphere . . . lovers the sphere of Venus   anatomies skeletons
tiar tiara, crown of the Papacy   charnel cemetery

'Of whence those forms proceeded which thus stained
    The track in which we moved; after brief space
From every form the beauty slowly waned,

520   'From every firmest limb & fairest face
The strength & freshness fell like dust, & left
    The action & the shape without the grace

'Of life; the marble brow of youth was cleft
    With care, and in the eyes where once hope shone
Desire like a lioness bereft

    'Of its last cub, glared ere it died; each one
Of that great crowd sent forth incessantly
    These shadows, numerous as the dead leaves blown

'In Autumn evening from a poplar tree—
530   Each, like himself & like each other were,
At first, but soon distorted, seemed to be

    'Obscure clouds moulded by the casual air;
And of this stuff the car's creative ray°
    Wrought all the busy phantoms that were there

'As the sun shapes the clouds—thus, on the way
    Mask after mask fell from the countenance
And form of all, and long before the day

    'Was old, the joy which waked like Heaven's glance
The sleepers in the oblivious valley, died,
540   And some grew weary of the ghastly dance

'And fell, as I have fallen by the way side,
    Those soonest from whose forms most shadows past
And least of strength & beauty did abide.'—

    'Then, what is Life?' I said . . . the cripple cast
His eye upon the car which now had rolled
    Onward, as if that look must be the last,

And answered . . . . 'Happy those for whom the fold
    Of
1822   1824

JOHN KEATS
1795–1821

Keats was born October 31, 1795, in London, the first of four children in the family of a prosperous coachman. His father died in a riding accident when the future poet was eight, his mother of tuberculosis when he was fourteen. He grew up, despite

creative ray The terrible bitterness of "creative"
in this context should be noted.

the tubercular inheritance, to be pugnacious and handsome, but stunted in size at five feet. Apprenticed to a surgeon by his dishonest guardian, he went on in 1815 to Guy's Hospital, London, as a medical student. His earliest poetry was mawkish, but "Sleep and Poetry" in 1816 demonstrated a genuine voice rising in him, and consolidated his poetic ambitions.

Haunted, like all his major contemporaries, by the shadow of Milton's splendor, Keats was also both burdened and aided by his perceptive reading of Wordsworth. His long poem *Endymion* rightly seemed a failure even to him, and he probably did not suffer as keenly from its negative reviews as tradition has held. Intellectually, the principal influence upon him was Hazlitt, but, from early 1818 on, his matchless letters show a rugged independence of mind, and a speculative development well in advance of his own poetry. One of the puzzles of Keats's rapid development was that the poet in him did not catch up with the man until the autumn of 1818. In the year between the ages of twenty-three and twenty-four, certainly one of the most fecund ever experienced by any poet, Keats wrote almost all of his major poetry.

Yet this brilliant year was full of sorrows. A summer walking tour, largely in Scotland, ended suddenly in August 1818 with the first signs of the tuberculosis that was to kill him. Autumn 1818, when the glorious year of poetry started, was largely spent nursing his brother Tom, who was dying, with agonizing slowness, of the family disease. In December, Tom died, and soon after Keats fell genuinely in love with Fanny Brawne—a relationship that was never to be fulfilled, as Keats gradually began to realize but naturally could not accept. He worked at his first *Hyperion* fragment, but could not advance in it. In January 1819, surely in tribute to Fanny Brawne, he wrote *The Eve of St. Agnes,* his least tragic major poem. The great self-recognition of his imaginative life began in April, with the composition of "Ode to Psyche" and "La Belle Dame sans Merci." In May, the great odes "On a Grecian Urn," "On Melancholy," and "To a Nightingale" were written. *Lamia,* probably his only poem to be over-rated consistently in our century, began to be drafted in June and July. Culmination came in August–September, with the superb fragment, *The Fall of Hyperion,* and the perfect ode "To Autumn." But with the transition to middle and fuller autumn, an ultimate despair followed all these gifts of the spirit, and effectively ended Keats's poetry.

By February 1820, Keats came to understand that he might have only a year or so to live, and consequently had no hope of marriage to Fanny Brawne. After a terrible half-year, he sailed to Italy in September, on the outside chance of improving his health, but he lingered only until February 23, 1821, when he died in Rome, aged twenty-five years and four months.

Of all nineteenth-century poets who wrote in English, Keats has demonstrated the most universal power to move readers in our own time. His effect upon later nineteenth-century poets was extraordinary, from Thomas Hood through Tennyson, Arnold (an unwilling and even unrecognized case of influence), Hopkins, Rossetti, and Morris, but a vast audience did not come to him until the twentieth century. The modern common reader and literary critic have agreed on Keats, for somewhat different reasons, and his influence is still vital in several major twentieth-century poets, particularly in Wallace Stevens. It seems justified to observe that Keats has the most secure and uncontested reputation of any poet since the Renaissance, an astonishing eminence for a unique but flawed artist who did not live long enough to perfect more than a handful of works.

Even the poet's letters, which were viciously deprecated as "unmanly" during the

Victorian period, enjoy a prestige today second to none in the language. Keats-idolatry is a benign malady, compared with many other literary disorders, and this editor has no desire to deplore it. But why does Keats appear a more timeless phenomenon than his great contemporaries now seem to be? What accounts for the generous over-praise that consistently links him with Shakespeare in modern criticism? Clearly he is the most sympathetic of modern poets, though he does not compare to Blake in conceptual power or to Wordsworth in originality. To define this power of sympathy is to identify what intrinsically belongs to Keats, what could not have come to us without him.

The prime element is Keats's thoroughgoing naturalistic humanism, in him a tough-minded and healthy doctrine very difficult to parallel in any writer since. Here he stemmed from Wordsworth, particularly the poet of *Home at Grasmere* (*The Recluse* fragment), who, by words which speak of nothing more than what we already are, would rouse us from the sleep of death to show us we are at home in a nature fitted to our minds. But Wordsworth's naturalism, his sense that the earth was enough, remained uneasy. Even in "Tintern Abbey" it wavers at the borders of a theophany, as though the visible world threatened to go out with the light of sense, and only infinity remained as an emblem of the deepest truth. From at least the "Ode to Psyche" on, Keats proclaims a more strenuously naturalistic confidence: "I see, and sing, by my own eyes inspired."

Allied to this heroic priesthood of the visible is Keats's extraordinary detachment, a capacity for disinterestedness so rare in a poet of all men as to be especially refreshing. He himself, in the crucial letter of December 21–27, 1817, to his brothers, developed this gift into the difficult but radiant quality "which Shakespeare possessed so enormously—I mean *Negative Capability*, that is when man is capable of being in uncertainties, Mysteries, doubts, without any irritable reaching after fact and reason—." No better description could be made of the poet-quester of *The Fall of Hyperion*, or of the voice that chants the great odes.

Beyond the uncompromising sense that we are completely physical in a physical world, and the allied realization that we are compelled to imagine more than we can know or understand, there is a third quality in Keats more clearly present than in any other poet since Shakespeare. This is the gift of tragic acceptance, which persuades us again that Keats was the least solipsistic of poets, the one most able to grasp the individuality and reality of selves totally distinct from his own, and of an outward world that would survive his perception of it. In his final poems he succeeds miraculously in communicating to us what it would be like if we shared this most uncommon and most gracious of human gifts.

On First Looking into Chapman's Homer°

Much have I travelled in the realms of gold,
  And many goodly states and kingdoms seen;
  Round many western islands have I been

On First . . . Homer Keats had been reading George Chapman's translation (published between 1598 and 1616) with his friend Charles Cowden Clarke; as he had no Greek, this was Keats's true introduction to the greatest Western poet.

Which bards in fealty to Apollo hold.
Oft of one wide expanse had I been told
   That deep-browed Homer ruled as his demesne;
   Yet did I never breathe its pure serene°
Till I heard Chapman speak out loud and bold:
Then felt I like some watcher of the skies
10   When a new planet swims into his ken;
Or like stout Cortez° when with eagle eyes
   He stared at the Pacific—and all his men
Looked at each other with a wild surmise—
   Silent, upon a peak in Darien.
1816   1816

On the Grasshopper and Cricket°

The poetry of earth is never dead:
   When all the birds are faint with the hot sun,
   And hide in cooling trees, a voice will run
From hedge to hedge about the new-mown mead;
That is the Grasshopper's—he takes the lead
   In summer luxury,—he has never done
   With his delights; for when tired out with fun
He rests at ease beneath some pleasant weed.
The poetry of earth is ceasing never:
10   On a lone winter evening, when the frost
      Has wrought a silence, from the stove there shrills
The Cricket's song, in warmth increasing ever,
   And seems to one in drowsiness half lost,
      The Grasshopper's among some grassy hills.
1816   1817

From Sleep and Poetry°

O for ten years, that I may overwhelm
Myself in poesy; so I may do the deed
That my own soul has to itself decreed.
Then will I pass the countries that I see
100   In long perspective, and continually

pure serene clear air; presumably remembered from Coleridge's poem, "Hymn Before Sunrise, in the Vale of Chamouni," l. 72
Cortez a celebrated mistake; it should be Balboa, who discovered the Pacific in 1513
On the Grasshopper and Cricket written in a sonnet competition with Leigh Hunt, who had suggested the subject
Sleep and Poetry Though not a mature work (Keats was barely twenty-one), this is thematically a crucial poem in Keats's development, showing both his indebtedness to Wordsworth and his passionate intention to swerve away from that great original, while abiding in a naturalistic humanism still recognizably Wordsworthian; sleep, in the title and throughout, is taken as a mode of half-wakeful consciousness, almost equivalent to the poetic state proper.

Taste their pure fountains. First the realm I'll pass
Of Flora, and old Pan:° sleep in the grass,
Feed upon apples red, and strawberries,
And choose each pleasure that my fancy sees;
Catch the white-handed nymphs in shady places,
To woo sweet kisses from averted faces,—
Play with their fingers, touch their shoulders white
Into a pretty shrinking with a bite
As hard as lips can make it: till agreed,
110 A lovely tale of human life we'll read.
And one will teach a tame dove how it best
May fan the cool air gently o'er my rest;
Another, bending o'er her nimble tread,
Will set a green robe floating round her head,
And still will dance with ever varied ease,
Smiling upon the flowers and the trees:
Another will entice me on, and on
Through almond blossoms and rich cinnamon;
Till in the bosom of a leafy world
120 We rest in silence, like two gems upcurled
In the recesses of a pearly shell.
And can I ever bid these joys farewell?
Yes, I must pass them for a nobler life,
Where I may find the agonies, the strife
Of human hearts:° for lo! I see afar,
O'er sailing the blue cragginess, a car
And steeds with streamy manes—the charioteer
Looks out upon the winds with glorious fear:°
And now the numerous tramplings quiver lightly
130 Along a huge cloud's ridge; and now with sprightly
Wheel downward come they into fresher skies,
Tipped round with silver from the sun's bright eyes.
Still downward with capacious whirl they glide;
And now I see them on the green-hill's side
In breezy rest among the nodding stalks.
The charioteer with wondrous gesture talks
To the trees and mountains; and there soon appear
Shapes of delight, of mystery, and fear,
Passing along before a dusky space
140 Made by some mighty oaks: as they would chase
Some ever-fleeting music on they sweep.
Lo! how they murmur, laugh, and smile, and weep:

Flora . . . Pan Flora was the Roman goddess of flowers; Pan, the Greek god of flocks, shepherds.
hearts The passage, up to this point, is heavily influenced by Wordsworth's *Tintern Abbey*, with its three stages of poetic development: "boyish days," aesthetic response to nature, and sympathy with other mortals.

I see . . . fear This vision of the chariot of imagination, akin to visions in Gray and Shelley, has a distinct tonal coloring of Collins, as Douglas Bush notes; Keats's charioteer, like Collins's, is not so much daemonic himself as a fearful invoker of the daemonic world.

Some with upholden hand and mouth severe;
Some with their faces muffled to the ear
Between their arms; some, clear in youthful bloom,
Go glad and smilingly athwart the gloom;
Some looking back, and some with upward gaze;
Yes, thousands in a thousand different ways
Flit onward—now a lovely wreath of girls
150 Dancing their sleek hair into tangled curls;
And now broad wings. Most awfully intent
The driver of those steeds is forward bent,
And seems to listen: O that I might know
All that he writes with such a hurrying glow.

The visions all are fled—the car is fled
Into the light of heaven, and in their stead
A sense of real things comes doubly strong,
And, like a muddy stream, would bear along
My soul to nothingness: but I will strive
160 Against all doubtings, and will keep alive
The thought of that same chariot, and the strange
Journey it went.

          Is there so small a range
In the present strength of manhood, that the high
Imagination cannot freely fly
As she was wont of old? Prepare her steeds,
Paw up against the light, and do strange deeds
Upon the clouds? Has she not shown us all?
From the clear space of ether, to the small
Breath of new buds unfolding? From the meaning
170 Of Jove's large eye-brow, to the tender greening
Of April meadows? Here her altar shone,
Even in this isle; and who could paragon
The fervid choir that lifted up a noise
Of harmony, to where it aye will poise
Its mighty self of convoluting sound,
Huge as a planet, and like that roll round,
Eternally around a dizzy void?
Ay, in those days the Muses were nigh cloyed
With honours; nor had any other care
180 Than to sing out and sooth their wavy hair.

Could all this be forgotten? Yes, a schism
Nurtured by foppery and barbarism,
Made great Apollo blush for this his land.
Men were thought wise who could not understand
His glories: with a puling infant's force
They swayed about upon a rocking horse,

And thought it Pegasus.° Ah dismal souled!
The winds of heaven blew, the ocean rolled
Its gathering waves—ye felt it not. The blue
190 Bared its eternal bosom, and the dew
Of summer nights collected still to make
The morning precious: beauty was awake!
Why were ye not awake? But ye were dead
To things ye knew not of,—were closely wed
To musty laws lined out with wretched rule
And compass vile: so that ye taught a school
Of dolts to smooth, inlay, and clip, and fit,
Till, like the certain wands of Jacob's wit,°
Their verses tallied. Easy was the task:
200 A thousand handicraftsmen wore the mask
Of Poesy. Ill-fated, impious race!
That blasphemed the bright Lyrist° to his face,
And did not know it,—no, they went about,
Holding a poor, decrepid standard out
Marked with most flimsy mottos, and in large
The name of one Boileau!°

                          O ye whose charge
It is to hover round our pleasant hills!
Whose congregated majesty so fills
My boundly reverence, that I cannot trace
210 Your hallowed names, in this unholy place,
So near those common folk; did not their shames
Affright you? Did our old lamenting Thames
Delight you? Did ye never cluster round
Delicious Avon, with a mournful sound,
And weep? Or did ye wholly bid adieu
To regions where no more the laurel grew?
Or did ye stay to give a welcoming
To some lone spirits who could proudly sing
Their youth away, and die?° 'Twas even so:
220 But let me think away those times of woe:
Now 'tis a fairer season; ye have breathed
Rich benedictions o'er us; ye have wreathed
Fresh garlands: for sweet music has been heard
In many places;°—some has been upstirred

They swayed . . . Pegasus This attack on the Popean couplet is derived from William Hazlitt, who said that Pope and Dr. Johnson would have converted Milton's "vaulting Pegasus into a rocking-horse," Pegasus being the steed of the Muses.
Jacob's wit See Genesis 30:31–43; but here, as generally, Keats's biblical allusions come from other poets; see *The Merchant of Venice* I.iii.85.
Lyrist Apollo

Boileau Nicolas Boileau-Despréaux (1636–1711), French poet and critic, who was probably only a name to Keats, and who was regarded by Leigh Hunt and others as the true founder of "the French school" of English poetry, that is, the neoclassical school of Pope
To some . . . die Thomas Chatterton, the 18th-century poet
places an attempt to particularize the "Romantic Revival" of English poetry

From out its crystal dwelling in a lake,°
By a swan's ebon bill; from a thick brake,
Nested and quiet in a valley mild,
Bubbles a pipe;° fine sounds are floating wild
About the earth: happy are ye and glad.

230   These things are doubtless: yet in truth we've had
Strange thunders from the potency of song;
Mingled indeed with what is sweet and strong,
From majesty: but in clear truth the themes
Are ugly clubs, the Poets Polyphemes
Disturbing the grand sea.° A drainless shower
Of light is poesy; 'tis the supreme of power;
'Tis might half slumbering on its own right arm.°
The very archings of her eye-lids charm
A thousand willing agents to obey,
240   And still she governs with the mildest sway:
But strength alone though of the Muses born
Is like a fallen angel: trees uptorn,
Darkness, and worms, and shrouds, and sepulchres
Delight it; for it feeds upon the burrs,
And thorns of life;° forgetting the great end
Of poesy, that it should be a friend
To sooth the cares, and lift the thoughts of man.°

1816   · · ·   1817

On the Sea°

It keeps eternal whisperings around
    Desolate shores, and with its mighty swell
    Gluts twice ten thousand Caverns, till the spell
Of Hecate° leaves them their old shadowy sound.
Often 'tis in such gentle temper found,
    That scarcely will the very smallest shell
    Be moved for days from where it sometime fell,
When last the winds of Heaven were unbound.

some . . . lake Wordsworth
from . . . pipe Leigh Hunt; Keats was to
change his mind as to Hunt's poetical eminence.
Poets . . . sea The sea is poetry; the poets,
even Wordsworth and certainly Byron, are
thematically tendentious and have a design
upon us, which they subdue their poems to expressing; such poets are like Homer's blind
Cyclops, Polyphemus, who threw rocks into the
sea at Odysseus, vainly; Wordsworth and Byron
will miss us because they are club-wielders,
thematically obsessed.
'Tis . . . arm Keats's definition of true poetry
as always keeping some of its strength in reserve

thorns of life The "fallen angel" suggests Byron,
but Shelley divined some reference to himself,
and appropriated this phrase with extraordinary
effect in his "Ode to the West Wind," l. 54.
To sooth . . . man This climax of the passage
is Wordsworthian again, in its conception of the
purpose of poetry.
On the Sea See King Lear IV.vi.4: "Hark! do
you hear the sea," which Keats said was his
starting point for this sonnet; it seems inescap-
able that the Sea, to Keats, represented primarily the universe of poetry.
Hecate goddess of the netherworld and of witch-
craft, and associated by Keats with the moon
goddess governing the tides

Oh ye! who have your eyeballs vexed and tired,
10   Feast them upon the wideness of the Sea;
        Oh ye! whose ears are dinned with uproar rude,
        Or fed too much with cloying melody—
        Sit ye near some old Cavern's Mouth and brood,
    Until ye start, as if the sea-nymphs quired!
    1817   1848

In Drear-Nighted December

I
In drear-nighted December,
    Too happy, happy tree,
Thy branches ne'er remember
    Their green felicity:
    The north cannot undo them
    With a sleety whistle through them;
    Nor frozen thawings glue them
        From budding at the prime.

II
In drear-nighted December,
10   Too happy, happy brook,
Thy bubblings ne'er remember
    Apollo's summer look;
    But with a sweet forgetting,
    They stay their crystal fretting,
    Never, never petting°
        About the frozen time.

III
Ah! would 'twere so with many
    A gentle girl and boy!
But were there ever any
20   Writhed not of passèd joy?
    The feel of not to feel it,
    When there is none to heal it,
    Nor numbèd sense to steel it,
        Was never said in rhyme.
        1817   1829

petting complaining

From Epistle to John Hamilton Reynolds°

O that our dreamings all, of sleep or wake,
Would all their colours from the sunset take:
From something of material sublime,
70   Rather than shadow our own soul's day-time
In the dark void of night. For in the world
We jostle,—but my flag is not unfurled
On the admiral-staff,—and to philosophise
I dare not yet! Oh, never will the prize,
High reason, and the lore of good and ill,
Be my award! Things cannot to the will
Be settled, but they tease us out of thought;°
Or is it that imagination brought
Beyond its proper bound, yet still confined,
80   Lost in a sort of Purgatory blind,
Cannot refer to any standard law
Of either earth or heaven? It is a flaw
In happiness, to see beyond our bourn,—
It forces us in summer skies to mourn,
It spoils the singing of the nightingale.

Dear Reynolds! I have a mysterious tale,
And cannot speak it: the first page I read
Upon a lampit° rock of green sea-weed
Among the breakers; 'twas a quiet eve,
90   The rocks were silent, the wide sea did weave
An untumultuous fringe of silver foam
Along the flat brown sand; I was at home
And should have been most happy,—but I saw
Too far into the sea, where every maw°
The greater on the less feeds evermore.—
But I saw too distinct into the core
Of an eternal fierce destruction,
And so from happiness I far was gone.
Still am I sick of it, and though, today,
100   I've gathered young spring-leaves, and flowers gay
Of periwinkle and wild strawberry,
Still do I that most fierce destruction see,—
The shark at savage prey,—the hawk at pounce,—
The gentle robin, like a pard or ounce,°
Ravening a worm,—Away, ye horrid moods!
Moods of one's mind! You know I hate them well.

Epistle to John Hamilton Reynolds These lines are from a verse-and-prose letter, March 25, 1818, that Keats wrote to his friend, Reynolds (1796–1852), a poet now best remembered for a verse-satire on Wordsworth's poem *Peter Bell,* which work Shelley also satirized.

tease . . . thought used again in "On a Grecian Urn," l. 44
lampit limpit, mollusk
maw stomach
pard or ounce lynx or leopard

502

You know I'd sooner be a clapping bell
To some Kamschatkan° missionary church,
Than with these horrid moods be left i' the lurch.—
110 Do you get health—and Tom the same—I'll dance,
And from detested moods in new romance°
Take refuge—Of bad lines a centaine dose
Is sure enough—and so 'here follows prose.'°—
1818   1848

When I Have Fears

When I have fears that I may cease to be
    Before my pen has gleaned my teeming brain,
Before high-piled books, in charactery,°
    Hold like rich garners the full ripened grain;
When I behold, upon the night's starred face,
    Huge cloudy symbols of a high romance,
And think that I may never live to trace
    Their shadows, with the magic hand of chance;
And when I feel, fair creature of an hour,
10   That I shall never look upon thee more,
Never have relish in the faery power
    Of unreflecting love;—then on the shore
Of the wide world I stand alone, and think
Till love and fame to nothingness do sink.
1818   1848

Fragment of an Ode to Maia

Mother of Hermes! and still youthful Maia!°
        May I sing to thee
As thou wast hymned on the shores of Baiae?°
        Or may I woo thee
In earlier Sicilian?° or thy smiles
Seek as they once were sought, in Grecian isles,
By bards who died content on pleasant sward,°
    Leaving great verse unto a little clan?
O, give me their old vigour, and unheard
10   Save of the quiet primrose, and the span
        Of heaven and few ears,

Kamschatkan Kamchatka, in Siberia
new romance presumably refers to a contemplated poem
'here . . . prose' See *Twelfth Night* II.v.154.
charactery writing
Maia mother, by Zeus, of Hermes, god of lucky

finds, shepherds, thieves, and travelers
Baiae Roman colony near Naples
Sicilian in the pastoral mode of the poet Theocritus (d. 260? B.C.)
sward grassy turf

Rounded by thee, my song should die away
        Content as theirs,
Rich in the simple worship of a day.
1818   1848

Hyperion

Rejecting the sentimentality of much of his earlier work, including *Endymion,* Keats wrote *Hyperion* in what he called "a more naked and grecian Manner." Though he had abandoned the fragment by April 1819, and it is undeniably an inconsistent work, few more powerful attempts at the Sublime exist. The view taken of the conflict between Olympians and Titans is an original one, and contrasts strongly with those of Shelley and Byron (see Headnote to *Prometheus Unbound*). In an atmosphere at once strong and cool, *Hyperion* surveys the fallen condition of the Titans without either a Miltonic didactic emphasis or a Shelleyan personalizing self-dramatization. Here is the first triumph of Keats's earlier idea of poetry as a disinterested mode.

The situation in which the poem begins is that difficult moment in myth when the old gods are departing and the new are not yet securely themselves. In particular, Hyperion, Titan of the sun, uneasily abides in heaven, and the young Apollo, down on earth, is "dying into life," becoming the god of poetry. Though an overt march-of-mind moral, of history as necessary progress, is given to Oceanus, displaced god of the sea, there is small reason to believe that he speaks for Keats himself. The poem hesitates at the verge of becoming an allegory of the history of imagination, and this hesitation is one of its strengths.

We can surmise that Keats gave up this first *Hyperion* for two reasons, first that the fragment is so complete in itself that any continuation would have meant redundancy, and second that he either could not or more likely would not maintain the beautiful but strained Miltonic high style of the first two books. The brief fragment of Book III shows a return to the subjective, romance style of *Endymion,* which was to be transformed into the harsh, purgatorial style of *The Fall of Hyperion.* Something vital and open in Keats had begun to discover his own personalizing involvement in this magnificent but abortive epic, and he was too honest to go on. But he had made already the most successful single emulation of Miltonic style and procedure in the Romantic tradition. Even the use throughout of sonorous Titanic names is a return of the Miltonic glory of a Sublime cataloguing.

Hyperion

A Fragment

Book I

Deep in the shady sadness of a vale
Far sunken from the healthy breath of morn,
Far from the fiery noon, and eve's one star,

Sat grey-haired Saturn, quiet as a stone,
Still as the silence round about his lair;
Forest on forest hung about his head
Like cloud on cloud. No stir of air was there,
Not so much life as on a summer's day
Robs not one light seed from the feathered grass,
10   But where the dead leaf fell, there did it rest.
A stream went voiceless by, still deadened more
By reason of his fallen divinity
Spreading a shade: the Naiad° mid her reeds
Pressed her cold finger closer to her lips.

Along the margin-sand large foot-marks went,
No further than to where his feet had stayed,°
And slept there since. Upon the sodden ground
His old right hand lay nerveless, listless, dead,
Unsceptred; and his realmless eyes were closed;
20   While his bowed head seemed listening to the Earth,
His ancient mother, for some comfort yet.

It seemed no force could wake him from his place;
But there came one,° who with a kindred hand
Touched his wide shoulders, after bending low
With reverence, though to one who knew it not.
She was a Goddess of the infant world;
By her in stature the tall Amazon
Had stood a pigmy's height: she would have ta'en
Achilles by the hair and bent his neck;
30   Or with a finger stayed Ixion's wheel.°
Her face was large as that of Memphian sphinx,°
Pedestaled haply in a palace court,
When sages looked to Egypt for their lore.
But oh! how unlike marble was that face:
How beautiful, if sorrow had not made
Sorrow more beautiful than Beauty's self.
There was a listening fear in her regard,
As if calamity had but begun;
As if the vanward clouds of evil days
40   Had spent their malice, and the sullen rear
Was with its stored thunder labouring up.
One hand she pressed upon that aching spot
Where beats the human heart, as if just there,
Though an immortal, she felt cruel pain:
The other upon Saturn's bended neck
She laid, and to the level of his ear

Naiad water nymph
stayed Douglas Bush's emendation for "strayed"
one Thea, Hyperion's wife and sister
Ixion's wheel Ixion's punishment in Hades
was to be bound to a perpetually revolving
wheel because he had dared to love Hera, the
wife of Zeus.
sphinx the Egyptian sphinx at Memphis, not
the Theban one of the Oedipus story

Leaning with parted lips, some words she spake
In solemn tenour and deep organ tone:
Some mourning words, which in our feeble tongue
Would come in these like accents; O how frail
50   To that large utterance of the early Gods!
'Saturn, look up!—though wherefore, poor old King?°
I have no comfort for thee, no not one:
I cannot say, "O wherefore sleepest thou?"
For heaven is parted from thee, and the earth
Knows thee not, thus afflicted, for a God;
And ocean too, with all its solemn noise,
Has from thy sceptre passed; and all the air
Is emptied of thine hoary majesty.
60   Thy thunder, conscious of the new command,
Rumbles reluctant o'er our fallen house;
And thy sharp lightning in unpractised hands
Scorches and burns our once serene domain.
O aching time! O moments big as years!
All as ye pass swell out the monstrous truth,
And press it so upon our weary griefs
That unbelief has not a space to breathe.
Saturn, sleep on:—O thoughtless, why did I
Thus violate thy slumbrous solitude?
70   Why should I ope thy melancholy eyes?
Saturn, sleep on! while at thy feet I weep.'

As when, upon a trancèd summer-night,
Those green-robed senators of mighty woods,
Tall oaks, branch-charmèd by the earnest stars,
Dream, and so dream all night without a stir,
Save from one gradual solitary gust
Which comes upon the silence, and dies off,
As if the ebbing air had but one wave;
So came these words and went; the while in tears
80   She touched her fair large forehead to the ground,
Just where her falling hair might be outspread
A soft and silken mat for Saturn's feet.
One moon, with alteration slow, had shed
Her silver seasons four upon the night,
And still these two were posturèd motionless,
Like natural sculpture in cathedral cavern;
The frozen God still couchant on the earth,
And the sad Goddess weeping at his feet:
Until at length old Saturn lifted up
90   His faded eyes, and saw his kingdom gone,

poor old King The association between Saturn
and Shakespeare's King Lear seems deliberate
throughout.

And all the gloom and sorrow of the place,
And that fair kneeling Goddess; and then spake,
As with a palsied tongue, and while his beard
Shook horrid° with such aspen-malady:
'O tender spouse of gold Hyperion,
Thea, I feel thee ere I see thy face;
Look up, and let me see our doom in it;
Look up, and tell me if this feeble shape
Is Saturn's; tell me, if thou hear'st the voice
00   Of Saturn; tell me, if this wrinkling brow,
Naked and bare of its great diadem,
Peers like the front of Saturn. Who had power
To make me desolate? whence came the strength?
How was it nurtured to such bursting forth,
While Fate seemed strangled in my nervous° grasp?
But it is so; and I am smothered up,
And buried from all godlike exercise
Of influence benign on planets pale,
Of admonitions to the winds and seas,
10   Of peaceful sway above man's harvesting,
And all those acts which Deity supreme
Doth ease its heart of love in.—I am gone
Away from my own bosom: I have left
My strong identity, my real self,
Somewhere between the throne, and where I sit
Here on this spot of earth. Search, Thea, search!
Open thine eyes eterne, and sphere them round
Upon all space: space starred, and lorn of light;
Space regioned with life-air; and barren void;
Spaces of fire, and all the yawn of hell.—
120   Search, Thea, search! and tell me, if thou seest
A certain shape or shadow, making way
With wings or chariot fierce to repossess
A heaven he lost erewhile: it must—it must
Be of ripe progress—Saturn must be King.
Yes, there must be a golden victory;
There must be Gods thrown down, and trumpets blown
Of triumph calm, and hymns of festival
Upon the gold clouds metropolitan,
Voices of soft proclaim, and silver stir
130   Of strings in hollow shells; and there shall be
Beautiful things made new, for the surprise
Of the sky-children; I will give command:
Thea! Thea! Thea! where is Saturn?'

This passion lifted him upon his feet,
And made his hands to struggle in the air,

horrid bristling   **nervous** powerful

His Druid locks° to shake and ooze with sweat,
His eyes to fever out, his voice to cease.
He stood, and heard not Thea's sobbing deep;
140 A little time, and then again he snatched
Utterance thus.—'But cannot I create?
Cannot I form? Cannot I fashion forth
Another world, another universe,
To overbear and crumble this to naught?
Where is another chaos? Where?'—That word
Found way unto Olympus, and made quake
The rebel three.°—Thea was startled up,
And in her bearing was a sort of hope,
As thus she quick-voiced spake, yet full of awe.
150 'This cheers our fallen house: come to our friends,
O Saturn! come away, and give them heart;
I know the covert, for thence came I hither.'
Thus brief; then with beseeching eyes she went
With backward footing through the shade a space:
He followed, and she turned to lead the way
Through agèd boughs, that yielded like the mist
Which eagles cleave upmounting from their nest.

Meanwhile in other realms big tears were shed,
More sorrow like to this, and such like woe,
160 Too huge for mortal tongue or pen of scribe:
The Titans fierce, self-hid, or prison-bound,
Groaned for the old allegiance once more,
And listened in sharp pain for Saturn's voice.
But one of the whole mammoth-brood still kept
His sovereignty, and rule, and majesty;—
Blazing Hyperion on his orbèd fire
Still sat, still snuffed the incense, teeming up
From man to the sun's God; yet unsecure:
For as among us mortals omens drear
170 Fright and perplex, so also shuddered he—
Not at dog's howl, or gloom-bird's hated screech,
Or the familiar visiting of one
Upon the first toll of his passing-bell,
Or prophesyings of the midnight lamp;
But horrors, portioned to a giant nerve,
Oft made Hyperion ache. His palace bright
Bastioned with pyramids of glowing gold,
And touched with shade of bronzèd obelisks,
Glared a blood-red through all its thousand courts,
180 Arches, and domes, and fiery galleries;

Druid locks Later 18th-century antiquarians attempted to identify the Celtic Druids or pagan priests with the Titans.

rebel three Jupiter, Neptune, Pluto; Saturn's sons by Rhea and rulers respectively of sky, sea, and underworld

And all its curtains of Aurorian° clouds
Flushed angerly: while sometimes eagle's wings,
Unseen before by Gods or wondering men,
Darkened the place; and neighing steeds were heard,
Not heard before by Gods or wondering men.
Also, when he would taste the spicy wreaths
Of incense, breathed aloft from sacred hills,
Instead of sweets, his ample palate took
Savour of poisonous brass and metal sick:
190 And so, when harboured in the sleepy west,
After the full completion of fair day,—
For rest divine upon exalted couch
And slumber in the arms of melody,
He paced away the pleasant hours of ease
With stride colossal, on from hall to hall;
While far within each aisle and deep recess,
His wingèd minions in close clusters stood,
Amazed and full of fear; like anxious men
Who on wide plains gather in panting troops,
200 When earthquakes jar their battlements and towers.
Even now, while Saturn, roused from icy trance,
Went step for step with Thea through the woods,
Hyperion, leaving twilight in the rear,
Came slope upon the threshold of the west;
Then, as was wont, his palace-door flew ope
In smoothest silence, save what solemn tubes,
Blown by the serious Zephyrs, gave of sweet
And wandering sounds, slow-breathèd melodies;
And like a rose in vermeil° tint and shape,
210 In fragrance soft, and coolness to the eye,
That inlet to severe magnificence
Stood full blown, for the God to enter in.

He entered, but he entered full of wrath;
His flaming robes streamed out beyond his heels,
And gave a roar, as if of earthly fire,
That scared away the meek ethereal Hours°
And made their dove-wings tremble. On he flared,
From stately nave to nave, from vault to vault,
Through bowers of fragrant and enwreathèd light,
220 And diamond-pavèd lustrous long arcades,
Until he reached the great main cupola;
There standing fierce beneath, he stamped his foot,
And from the basement deep to the high towers
Jarred his own golden region; and before
The quavering thunder thereupon had ceased,

Aurorian from Aurora, the dawn goddess
vermeil vermilion

Hours female divinities who presided over the
changes of the seasons

His voice leapt out, despite of godlike curb,
To this result: 'O dreams of day and night!
O monstrous forms! O effigies of pain!
O spectres busy in a cold, cold gloom!
230   O lank-eared Phantoms of black-weeded pools!
Why do I know ye? why have I seen ye? why
Is my eternal essence thus distraught
To see and to behold these horrors new?
Saturn is fallen, am I too to fall?
Am I to leave this haven of my rest,
This cradle of my glory, this soft clime,
This calm luxuriance of blissful light,
These crystalline pavilions, and pure fanes,
Of all my lucent empire? It is left
240   Deserted, void, nor any haunt of mine.
The blaze, the splendour, and the symmetry,
I cannot see—but darkness, death and darkness.
Even here, into my centre of repose,
The shady visions come to domineer,
Insult, and blind, and stifle up my pomp.—
Fall!—No, by Tellus° and her briny robes!
Over the fiery frontier of my realms
I will advance a terrible right arm
Shall scare that infant thunderer, rebel Jove,
250   And bid old Saturn take his throne again.'—
He spake, and ceased, the while a heavier threat
Held struggle with his throat but came not forth;
For as in theatres of crowded men
Hubbub increases more they call out 'Hush!'
So at Hyperion's words the Phantoms pale
Bestirred themselves, thrice horrible and cold;
And from the mirrored level where he stood
A mist arose, as from a scummy marsh.
At this, through all his bulk an agony
260   Crept gradual, from the feet unto the crown,
Like a lithe serpent vast and muscular
Making slow way, with head and neck convulsed
From over-strainèd might. Released, he fled
To the eastern gates, and full six dewy hours
Before the dawn in season due should blush,
He breathed fierce breath against the sleepy portals,
Cleared them of heavy vapours, burst them wide
Suddenly on the ocean's chilly streams.
The planet orb of fire, whereon he rode
270   Each day from east to west the heavens through,
Spun round in sable curtaining of clouds;

Tellus Earth

Not therefore veilèd quite, blindfold, and hid,
But ever and anon the glancing spheres,
Circles, and arcs, and broad-belting colure,°
Glowed through, and wrought upon the muffling dark
Sweet-shapèd lightnings from the nadir deep
Up to the zenith,—hieroglyphics old
Which sages and keen-eyed astrologers
Then living on the earth, with labouring thought
280   Won from the gaze of many centuries:
Now lost, save what we find on remnants huge
Of stone, or marble swart;° their import gone,
Their wisdom long since fled.—Two wings this orb
Possessed for glory, two fair argent° wings,
Ever exalted at the God's approach:
And now, from forth the gloom their plumes immense
Rose, one by one, till all outspreaded were;
While still the dazzling globe maintained eclipse,
Awaiting for Hyperion's command.
290   Fain would he have commanded, fain took throne
And bid the day begin, if but for change.
He might not:—No, though a primeval God:
The sacred seasons might not be disturbed.
Therefore the operations of the dawn
Stayed in their birth, even as here 'tis told.
Those silver wings expanded sisterly,
Eager to sail their orb; the porches wide
Opened upon the dusk demesnes of night;
And the bright Titan, frenzied with new woes,
300   Unused to bend, by hard compulsion bent
His spirit to the sorrow of the time;
And all along a dismal rack of clouds,
Upon the boundaries of day and night,
He stretched himself in grief and radiance faint.
There as he lay, the Heaven with its stars
Looked down on him with pity, and the voice
Of Coelus, from the universal space,
Thus whispered low and solemn in his ear.
'O brightest of my children dear, earth-born
310   And sky-engendered, Son of Mysteries
All unrevealèd even to the powers
Which met at thy creating; at whose joys
And palpitations sweet, and pleasures soft,
I, Coelus, wonder, how they came and whence;
And at the fruits thereof what shapes they be,
Distinct, and visible; symbols divine,

colure a great circle on the celestial sphere   swart dark, dusky
passing through the poles and the equinoxes or   argent silver
solstices

Manifestations of that beauteous life
Diffused unseen throughout eternal space:
Of these new-formed art thou, oh brightest child!
320 Of these, thy brethren and the Goddesses!
There is sad feud among ye, and rebellion
Of son against his sire. I saw him fall,
I saw my first-born° tumbled from his throne!
To me his arms were spread, to me his voice
Found way from forth the thunders round his head!
Pale wox I, and in vapours hid my face.
Art thou, too, near such doom? Vague fear there is:
For I have seen my sons most unlike Gods.
Divine ye were created, and divine
330 In sad demeanour, solemn, undisturbed,
Unruffled, like high Gods, ye lived and ruled:
Now I behold in you fear, hope, and wrath;
Actions of rage and passion; even as
I see them, on the mortal world beneath,
In men who die.—This is the grief, O Son!
Sad sign of ruin, sudden dismay, and fall!
Yet do thou strive; as thou art capable,
As thou canst move about, an evident God;
And canst oppose to each malignant hour
340 Ethereal presence:—I am but a voice;
My life is but the life of winds and tides,
No more than winds and tides can I avail:—
But thou canst.—Be thou therefore in the van
Of circumstance; yea, seize the arrow's barb
Before the tense string murmur.—To the earth!
For there thou wilt find Saturn, and his woes.
Meantime I will keep watch on thy bright sun,
And of thy seasons be a careful nurse.'—
Ere half this region-whisper had come down,
350 Hyperion arose, and on the stars
Lifted his curvèd lids, and kept them wide
Until it ceased; and still he kept them wide:
And still they were the same bright, patient stars.
Then with a slow incline of his broad breast,
Like to a diver in the pearly seas,
Forward he stooped over the airy shore,
And plunged all noiseless into the deep night.

Book II

Just at the self-same beat of Time's wide wings
Hyperion slid into the rustled air,
And Saturn gained with Thea that sad place

first-born Saturn

Where Cybele° and the bruisèd Titans mourned.
It was a den where no insulting light
Could glimmer on their tears; where their own groans
They felt, but heard not, for the solid roar
Of thunderous waterfalls and torrents hoarse,
Pouring a constant bulk, uncertain where.
10   Crag jutting forth to crag, and rocks that seemed
Ever as if just rising from a sleep,
Forehead to forehead held their monstrous horns;
And thus in thousand hugest phantasies
Made a fit roofing to this nest of woe.
Instead of thrones, hard flint they sat upon,
Couches of rugged stone, and slaty ridge
Stubborned with iron. All were not assembled:
Some chained in torture, and some wandering.
Coeus, and Gyges, and Briareus,
20   Typhon, and Dolor, and Porphyrion,°
With many more, the brawniest in assault,
Were pent in regions of laborious breath;
Dungeoned in opaque element, to keep
Their clenchèd teeth still clenched, and all their limbs
Locked up like veins of metal, cramped and screwed;
Without a motion, save of their big hearts
Heaving in pain, and horribly convulsed
With sanguine feverous boiling gurge° of pulse.
Mnemosyne° was straying in the world;
30   Far from her moon had Phoebe° wanderèd;
And many else were free to roam abroad,
But for the main, here found they covert drear.
Scarce images of life, one here, one there,
Lay vast and edgeways; like a dismal cirque°
Of Druid stones, upon a forlorn moor,
When the chill rain begins at shut of eve,
In dull November, and their chancel vault,
The Heaven itself, is blinded throughout night.
Each one kept shroud, nor to his neighbour gave
40   Or word, or look, or action of despair.
Creus was one; his ponderous iron mace
Lay by him, and a shattered rib of rock
Told of his rage, ere he thus sank and pined.
Iapetus another; in his grasp,
A serpent's plashy° neck; its barbèd tongue

Cybele in mythology, wife of Saturn and so
mother of all the other gods
Coeus . . . Porphyrion Coeus is a Titan; Gyges
and Briareus giants with a hundred hands;
Typhon, a monster with a hundred heads;
Dolor (Latin for sorrow), a Titan created by
Keats; Porphyrion, a giant of obscure origins.

gurge whirlpool
Mnemosyne Mother of the Muses, daughter of
Coelus, her name means "Memory."
Phoebe goddess of the moon
cirque circle, ring
plashy splashed with colors

Squeezed from the gorge, and all its uncurled length
Dead; and because the creature could not spit
Its poison in the eyes of conquering Jove.
Next Cottus: prone he lay, chin uppermost,
50 As though in pain; for still upon the flint
He ground severe his skull, with open mouth
And eyes at horrid working. Nearest him
Asia,° born of most enormous Caf,
Who cost her mother Tellus keener pangs,
Though feminine, than any of her sons:
More thought than woe was in her dusky face,
For she was prophesying of her glory;
And in her wide imagination stood
Palm-shaded temples, and high rival fanes,
60 By Oxus or in Ganges' sacred isles.
Even as Hope upon her anchor leans,
So leant she, not so fair, upon a tusk
Shed from the broadest of her elephants.
Above her, on a crag's uneasy shelf,
Upon his elbow raised, all prostrate else,
Shadowed Enceladus; once tame and mild
As grazing ox unworried in the meads;
Now tiger-passioned, lion-thoughted, wroth,
He meditated, plotted, and even now
70 Was hurling mountains in that second war,
Not long delayed, that scared the younger Gods
To hide themselves in forms of beast and bird.
Not far hence Atlas; and beside him prone
Phorcus, the sire of Gorgons.° Neighboured close
Oceanus, and Tethys, in whose lap
Sobbed Clymene° among her tangled hair.
In midst of all lay Themis,° at the feet
Of Ops° the queen all clouded round from sight;
No shape distinguishable, more than when
80 Thick night confounds the pine-tops with the clouds:
And many else whose names may not be told.
For when the Muse's wings are air-ward spread,
Who shall delay her flight? And she must chaunt°
Of Saturn, and his guide, who now had climbed
With damp and slippery footing from a depth
More horrid still. Above a sombre cliff
Their heads appeared, and up their stature grew

Asia in mythology, daughter of the Titans
Oceanus and Tethys
Phorcus . . . Gorgons Phorcus is a sea god; the
Gorgons are his three daughters—Medusa being
the most famous—noted for their snaky locks
and their ability to turn people to stone with
a glance.
Clymene in mythology, daughter of Oceanus and

wife of Iapetus, but Keats seems to mean the
mother of Phaethon, as in Ovid's *Metamor-*
phoses II
Themis Her name means "Law"; daughter of
Coelus.
Ops another name for Cybele
chaunt chant

Till on the level height their steps found ease:
Then Thea spread abroad her trembling arms
90   Upon the precincts of this nest of pain,
And sidelong fixed her eye on Saturn's face:
There saw she direst strife; the supreme God
At war with all the frailty of grief,
Of rage, of fear, anxiety, revenge,
Remorse, spleen, hope, but most of all despair.
Against these plagues he strove in vain; for Fate
Had poured a mortal oil upon his head,°
A disanointing poison: so that Thea,
Affrighted, kept her still, and let him pass
100 First onwards in, among the fallen tribe.

As with us mortal men, the laden heart
Is persecuted more, and fevered more,
When it is nighing to the mournful house
Where other hearts are sick of the same bruise;
So Saturn, as he walked into the midst,
Felt faint, and would have sunk among the rest,
But that he met Enceladus's eye,
Whose mightiness, and awe of him, at once
Came like an inspiration; and he shouted,
110 'Titans, behold your God!' at which some groaned;
Some started on their feet; some also shouted;
Some wept, some wailed, all bowed with reverence;
And Ops, uplifting her black folded veil,
Showed her pale cheeks, and all her forehead wan,
Her eye-brows thin and jet, and hollow eyes.
There is a roaring in the bleak-grown pines
When Winter lifts his voice; there is a noise
Among immortals when a God gives sign,
With hushing finger, how he means to load
120 His tongue with the full weight of utterless thought,
With thunder, and with music, and with pomp:
Such noise is like the roar of bleak-grown pines:
Which, when it ceases in this mountained world,
No other sound succeeds; but ceasing here,
Among these fallen, Saturn's voice therefrom
Grew up like organ, that begins anew
Its strain, when other harmonies, stopped short,
Leave the dinned air vibrating silverly.
Thus grew it up—'Not in my own sad breast,
130 Which is its own great judge and searcher out,
Can I find reason why ye should be thus:
Not in the legends of the first of days,

for Fate . . . head thus making **him human,**
and so weaker

Studied from that old spirit-leavèd book
Which starry Uranus with finger bright
Saved from the shores of darkness, when the waves
Low-ebbed still hid it up in shallow gloom;—
And the which book ye know I ever kept
For my firm-based footstool:—Ah, infirm!
Not there, nor in sign, symbol, or portent
140   Of element, earth, water, air, and fire,—
At war, at peace, or inter-quarreling
One against one, or two, or three, or all
Each several one against the other three,
As fire with air loud warring when rain-floods
Drown both, and press them both against earth's face,
Where, finding sulphur, a quadruple wrath
Unhinges the poor world;—not in that strife,
Wherefrom I take strange lore, and read it deep,
Can I find reason why ye should be thus:
150   No, nowhere can unriddle, though I search,
And pore on Nature's universal scroll
Even to swooning, why ye, Divinities,
The first-born of all shaped and palpable Gods,
Should cower beneath what, in comparison,
Is untremendous might. Yet ye are here,
O'erwhelmed, and spurned, and battered, ye are here!
O Titans, shall I say, "Arise!"—Ye groan:
Shall I say "Crouch!"—Ye groan. What can I then?
O Heaven wide! O unseen parent dear!
160   What can I? Tell me, all ye brethren Gods,
How we can war, how engine our great wrath!
O speak your counsel now, for Saturn's ear
Is all a-hungered. Thou, Oceanus,
Ponderest high and deep; and in thy face
I see, astonied,° that severe content
Which comes of thought and musing: give us help!'

So ended Saturn; and the God of the Sea,
Sophist° and sage, from no Athenian grove,°
But cogitation in his watery shades,
170   Arose, with locks not oozy, and began,
In murmurs, which his first-endeavouring tongue
Caught infant-like from the far-foamèd sands.
'O ye, whom wrath consumes! who, passion-stung,
Writhe at defeat, and nurse your agonies!
Shut up your senses, stifle up your ears,
My voice is not a bellows unto ire.

---

astonied astonished
Sophist probably in a positive sense, as being wise, yet its negative aspect of rhetorician and casuist may suggest that Keats had some reservations as to the following speech
Athenian grove Plato's Academy

Yet listen, ye who will, whilst I bring proof
How ye, perforce, must be content to stoop:
And in the proof much comfort will I give,
180   If ye will take that comfort in its truth.
We fall by course of Nature's law, not force
Of thunder, or of Jove. Great Saturn, thou
Hast sifted well the atom-universe;
But for this reason, that thou art the King,
And only blind from sheer supremacy,
One avenue was shaded from thine eyes,
Through which I wandered to eternal truth.
And first, as thou wast not the first of powers,
So art thou not the last; it cannot be:
190   Thou art not the beginning nor the end.
From chaos and parental darkness came
Light, the first fruits of that intestine broil,
That sullen ferment, which for wondrous ends
Was ripening in itself. The ripe hour came,
And with it light, and light, engendering
Upon its own producer, forthwith touched
The whole enormous matter into life.
Upon that very hour, our parentage,
The Heavens, and the Earth, were manifest:
200   Then thou first born, and we the giant race,
Found ourselves ruling new and beauteous realms.
Now comes the pain of truth, to whom 'tis pain;
O folly! for to bear all naked truths,
And to envisage circumstance, all calm,
That is the top of sovereignty. Mark well!
As Heaven and Earth are fairer, fairer far
Than Chaos and blank Darkness, though once chiefs;
And as we show beyond that Heaven and Earth
In form and shape compact and beautiful,
210   In will, in action free, companionship,
And thousand other signs of purer life;
So on our heels a fresh perfection treads,
A power more strong in beauty, born of us
And fated to excel us, as we pass
In glory that old Darkness: nor are we
Thereby more conquered, than by us the rule
Of shapeless Chaos. Say, doth the dull soil
Quarrel with the proud forests it hath fed,
And feedeth still, more comely than itself?
220   Can it deny the chiefdom of green groves?
Or shall the tree be envious of the dove
Because it cooeth, and hath snowy wings
To wander wherewithal and find its joys?
We are such forest-trees, and our fair boughs

Have bred forth, not pale solitary doves,
But eagles golden-feathered, who do tower
Above us in their beauty, and must reign
In right thereof; for 'tis the eternal law
That first in beauty should be first in might:
230   Yea, by that law, another race may drive
Our conquerors to mourn as we do now.
Have ye beheld the young God of the Seas,°
My dispossessor? Have ye seen his face?
Have ye beheld his chariot, foamed along
By noble wingèd creatures he hath made?
I saw him on the calmèd waters scud,°
With such a glow of beauty in his eyes,
That it enforced me to bid sad farewell
To all my empire: farewell sad I took,
240   And hither came, to see how dolorous fate
Had wrought upon ye; and how I might best
Give consolation in this woe extreme.
Receive the truth, and let it be your balm.'

Whether through pozed° conviction, or disdain,
They guarded silence, when Oceanus
Left murmuring, what deepest thought can tell?
But so it was, none answered for a space,
Save one whom none regarded, Clymene;
And yet she answered not, only complained,
250   With hectic lips, and eyes up-looking mild,
Thus wording timidly among the fierce:
'O Father, I am here the simplest voice,
And all my knowledge is that joy is gone,
And this thing woe crept in among our hearts,
There to remain forever, as I fear:
I would not bode of evil, if I thought
So weak a creature could turn off the help
Which by just right should come of mighty Gods;
Yet let me tell my sorrow, let me tell
260   Of what I heard, and how it made me weep,
And know that we had parted from all hope.
I stood upon a shore, a pleasant shore,
Where a sweet clime was breathèd from a land
Of fragrance, quietness, and trees, and flowers.
Full of calm joy it was, as I of grief;
Too full of joy and soft delicious warmth;
So that I felt a movement in my heart
To chide, and to reproach that solitude
With songs of misery, music of our woes;

God of the Seas Neptune   **pozed** puzzled
scud move rapidly

270 And sat me down, and took a mouthèd shell
And murmured into it, and made melody—
O melody no more! for while I sang,
And with poor skill let pass into the breeze
The dull shell's echo, from a bowery strand
Just opposite, an island of the sea,
There came enchantment with the shifting wind,
That did both drown and keep alive my ears.
I threw my shell away upon the sand,
And a wave filled it, as my sense was filled
280 With that new blissful golden melody.
A living death was in each gush of sounds,
Each family of rapturous hurried notes,
That fell, one after one, yet all at once,
Like pearl beads dropping sudden from their string:
And then another, then another strain,
Each like a dove leaving its olive perch,
With music winged instead of silent plumes,
To hover round my head, and make me sick
Of joy and grief at once. Grief overcame,
290 And I was stopping up my frantic ears,
When, past all hindrance of my trembling hands,
A voice came sweeter, sweeter than all tune,
And still it cried, "Apollo! young Apollo!
The morning-bright Apollo! young Apollo!"
I fled, it followed me, and cried "Apollo!"
O Father, and O Brethren, had ye felt
Those pains of mine; O Saturn, hadst thou felt,
Ye would not call this too indulgèd tongue
Presumptuous, in thus venturing to be heard.'

300 So far her voice flowed on, like timorous brook
That, lingering along a pebbled coast,
Doth fear to meet the sea: but sea it met,
And shuddered; for the overwhelming voice
Of huge Enceladus swallowed it in wrath:
The ponderous syllables, like sullen waves
In the half-glutted hollows of reef-rocks,
Came booming thus, while still upon his arm
He leaned; not rising, from supreme contempt.
'Or shall we listen to the over-wise,
310 Or to the over-foolish, Giant-Gods?
Not thunderbolt on thunderbolt, till all
That rebel Jove's whole armoury were spent,
Not world on world upon these shoulders piled,
Could agonize me more than baby-words
In midst of this dethronement horrible.
Speak! roar! shout! yell! ye sleepy Titans all.

Do ye forget the blows, the buffets vile?
Are ye not smitten by a youngling arm?
Dost thou forget, sham Monarch of the Waves,
320   Thy scalding in the seas? What, have I roused
Your spleens with so few simple words as these?
O joy! for now I see ye are not lost:
O joy! for now I see a thousand eyes
Wide-glaring for revenge!'—As this he said,
He lifted up his stature vast, and stood,
Still without intermission speaking thus:
'Now ye are flames, I'll tell you how to burn,
And purge the ether of our enemies;
How to feed fierce the crooked stings of fire,
330   And singe away the swollen clouds of Jove,
Stifling that puny essence in its tent.
O let him feel the evil he hath done;
For though I scorn Oceanus's lore,
Much pain have I for more than loss of realms:
The days of peace and slumberous calm are fled;
Those days, all innocent of scathing war,
When all the fair Existences of heaven
Came open-eyed to guess what we would speak:—
That was before our brows were taught to frown,
340   Before our lips knew else but solemn sounds;
That was before we knew the wingèd thing,
Victory, might be lost, or might be won.
And be ye mindful that Hyperion,
Our brightest brother, still is undisgraced—
Hyperion, lo! his radiance is here!'

All eyes were on Enceladus's face,
And they beheld, while still Hyperion's name
Flew from his lips up to the vaulted rocks,
A pallid gleam across his features stern:
350   Not savage, for he saw full many a God
Wroth as himself. He looked upon them all,
And in each face he saw a gleam of light,
But splendider in Saturn's, whose hoar locks
Shone like the bubbling foam about a keel
When the prow sweeps into a midnight cove.
In pale and silver silence they remained,
Till suddenly a splendour, like the morn,
Pervaded all the beetling gloomy steeps,
All the sad spaces of oblivion,
360   And every gulf, and every chasm old,
And every height, and every sullen depth,
Voiceless, or hoarse with loud tormented streams:
And all the everlasting cataracts,

And all the headlong torrents far and near,
Mantled before in darkness and huge shade,
Now saw the light and made it terrible.
It was Hyperion:—a granite peak
His bright feet touched, and there he stayed to view
The misery his brilliance had betrayed
370 To the most hateful seeing of itself.
Golden his hair of short Numidian curl,
Regal his shape majestic, a vast shade
In midst of his own brightness, like the bulk
Of Memnon's image at the set of sun
To one who travels from the dusking East:
Sighs, too, as mournful as that Memnon's harp°
He uttered, while his hands contemplative
He pressed together, and in silence stood.
Despondence seized again the fallen Gods
380 At sight of the dejected King of Day,
And many hid their faces from the light:
But fierce Enceladus sent forth his eyes
Among the brotherhood; and, at their glare,
Uprose Iapetus, and Creus too,
And Phorcus, sea-born, and together strode
To where he towered on his eminence.
There those four shouted forth old Saturn's name;
Hyperion from the peak loud answered, 'Saturn!'
Saturn sat near the Mother of the Gods,°
390 In whose face was no joy, though all the Gods
Gave from their hollow throats the name of 'Saturn!'

      Book III
Thus in alternate uproar and sad peace,
Amazèd were those Titans utterly.
O leave them, Muse! O leave them to their woes;
For thou art weak to sing such tumults dire:
A solitary sorrow best befits
Thy lips, and antheming a lonely grief.
Leave them, O Muse! for thou anon wilt find
Many a fallen old Divinity
Wandering in vain about bewildered shores.
10   Meantime touch piously the Delphic harp,
And not a wind of heaven but will breathe
In aid soft warble from the Dorian flute;°
For lo! 'tis for the Father of all verse.°
Flush every thing that hath a vermeil hue,

Memnon's harp Memnon, son of Aurora and
Tithonus, was a mythical king of Ethiopia slain
by Achilles; his statue, in the Egyptian city of
Thebes, made mourning sounds when touched
by the rising and setting sun.

Mother of the Gods Cybele
Dorian flute See *Paradise Lost* I.550–51, for
Keats's thematic reference.
Father . . . verse Apollo

Let the rose glow intense and warm the air,
And let the clouds of even and of morn
Float in voluptuous fleeces o'er the hills;
Let the red wine within the goblet boil,
Cold as a bubbling well; let faint-lipped shells,
20   On sands, or in great deeps, vermilion turn
Through all their labyrinths; and let the maid
Blush keenly, as with some warm kiss surprised.
Chief isle of the embowered Cyclades,
Rejoice, O Delos,° with thine olives green,
And poplars, and lawn-shading palms, and beech,
In which the Zephyr breathes the loudest song,
And hazels thick, dark-stemmed beneath the shade:
Apollo is once more the golden theme!
Where was he, when the Giant of the Sun
30   Stood bright, amid the sorrow of his peers?
Together had he left his mother° fair
And his twin-sister° sleeping in their bower,
And in the morning twilight wandered forth
Beside the osiers of a rivulet,
Full ankle-deep in lilies of the vale.
The nightingale had ceased, and a few stars
Were lingering in the heavens, while the thrush
Began calm-throated. Throughout all the isle
There was no covert, no retired cave
40   Unhaunted by the murmurous noise of waves,
Though scarcely heard in many a green recess.
He listened, and he wept, and his bright tears
Went trickling down the golden bow he held.
Thus with half-shut suffusèd eyes he stood,
While from beneath some cumbrous boughs hard by
With solemn step an awful Goddess° came,
And there was purport in her looks for him,
Which he with eager guess began to read
Perplexed, the while melodiously he said:
50   'How cam'st thou over the unfooted sea?
Oh hath that antique mien and robèd form
Moved in these vales invisible till now?
Sure I have heard those vestments sweeping o'er
The fallen leaves, when I have sat alone
In cool mid-forest. Surely I have traced
The rustle of those ample skirts about
These grassy solitudes, and seen the flowers
Lift up their heads, as still the whisper passed.
Goddess! I have beheld those eyes before,

Delos small, sacred island, the birthplace of   **mother** Leto
Apollo; it is one of a group of islands in the   **twin-sister** Diana
Aegean known as the Cyclades   **Goddess** Mnemosyne

60 And their eternal calm, and all that face,
Or I have dreamed.'—'Yes,' said the supreme shape,
Thou hast dreamed of me; and awaking up
Didst find a lyre all golden by thy side,
Whose strings touched by thy fingers, all the vast
Unwearied ear of the whole universe
Listened in pain and pleasure at the birth
Of such new tuneful wonder. Is't not strange
That thou shouldst weep, so gifted? Tell me, youth,
What sorrow thou canst feel; for I am sad

70 When thou dost shed a tear: explain thy griefs
To one who in this lonely isle hath been
The watcher of thy sleep and hours of life,
From the young day when first thy infant hand
Plucked witless the weak flowers, till thine arm
Could bend that bow heroic to all times.
Show thy heart's secret to an ancient Power
Who hath forsaken old and sacred thrones
For prophecies of thee, and for the sake
Of loveliness new born.'—Apollo then,

80 With sudden scrutiny and gloomless eyes,
Thus answered, while his white melodious throat
Throbbed with the syllables.—'Mnemosyne!
Thy name is on my tongue, I know not how;
Why should I tell thee what thou so well seest?
Why should I strive to show what from thy lips
Would come no mystery? For me, dark, dark,
And painful vile oblivion seals my eyes:
I strive to search wherefore I am so sad,
Until a melancholy numbs my limbs;

90 And then upon the grass I sit, and moan,
Like one who once had wings.—O why should I
Feel cursed and thwarted, when the liegeless air
Yields to my step aspirant? Why should I
Spurn the green turf as hateful to my feet?
Goddess benign, point forth some unknown thing:
Are there not other regions than this isle?
What are the stars? There is the sun, the sun!
And the most patient brilliance of the moon!
And stars by thousands! Point me out the way

100 To any one particular beauteous star,
And I will flit into it with my lyre
And make its silvery splendour pant with bliss.
I have heard the cloudy thunder: Where is power?
Whose hand, whose essence, what divinity
Makes this alarum in the elements,
While I here idle listen on the shores
In fearless yet in aching ignorance?

O tell me, lonely Goddess, by thy harp,
That waileth every morn and eventide,
110   Tell me why thus I rave, about these groves!
Mute thou remainest—mute! Yet I can read
A wondrous lesson in thy silent face:
Knowledge enormous makes a God of me.
Names, deeds, grey legends, dire events, rebellions,
Majesties, sovereign voices, agonies,
Creations and destroyings, all at once
Pour into the wide hollows of my brain,
And deify me, as if some blithe wine
Or bright elixir peerless I had drunk,
120   And so become immortal.'—Thus the God,
While his enkindled eyes, with level glance
Beneath his white soft temples, stedfast kept
Trembling with light upon Mnemosyne.
Soon wild commotions shook him, and made flush
All the immortal fairness of his limbs;
Most like the struggle at the gate of death;
Or liker still to one who should take leave
Of pale immortal death, and with a pang
As hot as death's is chill, with fierce convulse
130   Die into life:° so young Apollo anguished:
His very hair, his golden tresses famed
Kept undulation round his eager neck.
During the pain Mnemosyne upheld
Her arms as one who prophesied.—At length
Apollo shrieked;—and lo! from all his limbs
Celestial   *   *   *   *   *   *   *
*   *   *   *   *   *   *   *   *

THE END
1818–19   1820

The Eve of St. Agnes°

I

St. Agnes' Eve—Ah, bitter chill it was!
The owl, for all his feathers, was a-cold;
The hare limped trembling through the frozen grass,
And silent was the flock in woolly fold:

Die into life hardly in the Christian or Pauline sense, which is a paradoxical one; probably it means "to become a poet"
The Eve of St. Agnes By superstition, a girl may have a vision of her future husband on St. Agnes's Eve (January 20), if she performs the proper magical rituals. Using the Spenserian stanza, Keats writes a Spenserian version of *Romeo and Juliet,* but with a romantic and happy ending; though St. Agnes is the patroness of virgins, Keats seems happily skeptical in this poem as to her influence.

Numb were the Beadsman's° fingers, while he told
His rosary, and while his frosted breath,
Like pious incense from a censer old,
Seemed taking flight for heaven, without a death,
Past the sweet Virgin's picture, while his prayer he saith.

II

His prayer he saith, this patient, holy man;
Then takes his lamp, and riseth from his knees,
And back returneth, meagre, barefoot, wan,
Along the chapel aisle by slow degrees:
The sculptured dead, on each side, seem to freeze,
Imprisoned in black, purgatorial rails:
Knights, ladies, praying in dumb orat'ries,°
He passeth by; and his weak spirit fails
To think how they may ache in icy hoods and mails.

III

Northward he turneth through a little door,
And scarce three steps, ere Music's golden tongue
Flattered to tears this aged man and poor;
But no—already had his deathbell rung:
The joys of all his life were said and sung:
His was harsh penance on St. Agnes' Eve:
Another way he went, and soon among
Rough ashes sat he for his soul's reprieve,
And all night kept awake, for sinners' sake to grieve.

IV

That ancient Beadsman heard the prelude soft;
And so it chanced, for many a door was wide,
From hurry to and fro. Soon, up aloft,
The silver, snarling trumpets 'gan to chide:
The level chambers, ready with their pride,
Were glowing to receive a thousand guests:
The carvèd angels, ever eager-eyed,
Stared, where upon their heads the cornice rests,
With hair blown back, and wings put cross-wise on their breasts.

V

At length burst in the argent° revelry,
With plume, tiara, and all rich array,
Numerous as shadows haunting faerily
The brain, new stuffed, in youth, with triumphs gay

10
20
30
40

Beadsman's A beadsman was a pauper paid to pray for one, the reference being to the beads of his rosary.

orat'ries oratories, chapels
argent silver

Of old romance. These let us wish away,
And turn, sole-thoughted, to one Lady there,
Whose heart had brooded, all that wintry day,
On love, and winged St. Agnes' saintly care,
As she had heard old dames full many times declare.

VI

They told her how, upon St. Agnes' Eve,
Young virgins might have visions of delight,
And soft adorings from their loves receive
Upon the honeyed middle of the night,
50   If ceremonies due they did aright;
As, supperless to bed they must retire,
And couch supine their beauties, lilly white;
Nor look behind, nor sideways, but require
Of Heaven with upward eyes for all that they desire.

VII

Full of this whim was thoughtful Madeline:
The music, yearning like a God in pain,
She scarcely heard: her maiden eyes divine,
Fixed on the floor, saw many a sweeping train°
Pass by—she heeded not at all: in vain
60   Came many a tiptoe, amorous cavalier,
And back retired; not cooled by high disdain,
But she saw not: her heart was otherwhere:
She sighed for Agnes' dreams, the sweetest of the year.

VIII

She danced along with vague, regardless eyes,
Anxious her lips, her breathing quick and short:
The hallowed hour was near at hand: she sighs
Amid the timbrels,° and the thronged resort
Of whisperers in anger, or in sport;
'Mid looks of love, defiance, hate, and scorn,
70   Hoodwinked° with faery fancy; all amort,°
Save to St. Agnes and her lambs unshorn,°
And all the bliss to be before tomorrow morn.

IX

So, purposing each moment to retire,
She lingered still. Meantime, across the moors,
Had come young Porphyro, with heart on fire
For Madeline. Beside the portal doors,

train skirts sweeping the floor
timbrels snare drums
hoodwinked blinded
amort as if dead

unshorn On St. Agnes's Day, two lambs were offered at the altar during Mass, their wool later being spun and woven by nuns.

Buttressed from moonlight, stands he, and implores
All saints to give him sight of Madeline,
But for one moment in the tedious hours,
80   That he might gaze and worship all unseen;
Perchance speak, kneel, touch, kiss—in sooth such things have been.

X

He ventures in: let no buzzed whisper tell:
All eyes be muffled, or a hundred swords
Will storm his heart, Love's feverous citadel:
For him, those chambers held barbarian hordes,
Hyena foemen, and hot-blooded lords,
Whose very dogs would execrations howl
Against his lineage: not one breast affords
Him any mercy, in that mansion foul,
90   Save one old beldame,° weak in body and in soul.

XI

Ah, happy chance! the aged creature came,
Shuffling along with ivory-headed wand,
To where he stood, hid from the torch's flame,
Behind a broad hall-pillar, far beyond
The sound of merriment and chorus bland:
He startled her; but soon she knew his face,
And grasped his fingers in her palsied hand,
Saying, 'Mercy, Porphyro! hie thee from this place:
They are all here tonight, the whole blood-thirsty race!

XII

100   'Get hence! get hence! there's dwarfish Hildebrand;
He had a fever late, and in the fit
He cursed thee and thine, both house and land:
Then there's that old Lord Maurice, not a whit
More tame for his grey hairs—Alas me! flit!
Flit like a ghost away.'—'Ah, Gossip dear,
We're safe enough; here in this arm-chair sit,
And tell me how'—'Good Saints! not here, not here;
Follow me, child, or else these stones will be thy bier.'

XIII

He followed through a lowly archèd way,
110   Brushing the cobwebs with his lofty plume,
And as she muttered 'Well-a—well-a-day!'
He found him in a little moonlight room,
Pale, latticed, chill, and silent as a tomb.
'Now tell me where is Madeline,' said he,

beldame old woman, hag

'O tell me, Angela, by the holy loom
Which none but secret sisterhood may see,
When they St. Agnes' wool are weaving piously.'

XIV

'St. Agnes! Ah! it is St. Agnes' Eve—
Yet men will murder upon holy days:
120   Thou must hold water in a witch's sieve,°
And be liege-lord of all the Elves and Fays,
To venture so: it fills me with amaze
To see thee, Porphyro!—St. Agnes' Eve!
God's help! my lady fair the conjuror plays
This very night: good angels her deceive!
But let me laugh awhile, I've mickle° time to grieve.'

XV

Feebly she laugheth in the languid moon,
While Porphyro upon her face doth look,
Like puzzled urchin on an aged crone
130   Who keepeth closed a wondrous riddle-book,
As spectacled she sits in chimney nook.
But soon his eyes grew brilliant, when she told
His lady's purpose; and he scarce could brook
Tears, at the thought of those enchantments cold,
And Madeline asleep in lap of legends old.

XVI

Sudden a thought came like a full-blown rose,
Flushing his brow, and in his pained heart
Made purple riot: then doth he propose
A stratagem, that makes the beldame start:
140   'A cruel man and impious thou art:
Sweet lady, let her pray, and sleep, and dream
Alone with her good angels, far apart
From wicked men like thee. Go, go!—I deem
Thou canst not surely be the same that thou didst seem.'

XVII

'I will not harm her, by all saints I swear,'
Quoth Porphyro: 'O may I ne'er find grace
When my weak voice shall whisper its last prayer,
If one of her soft ringlets I displace,
Or look with ruffian passion in her face:
150   Good Angela, believe me by these tears;
Or I will, even in a moment's space,
Awake, with horrid shout, my foemen's ears,
And beard them, though they be more fanged than wolves and bears.'

sieve bewitched so as to hold water   **mickle** much

XVIII

'Ah! why wilt thou affright a feeble soul?
A poor, weak, palsy-stricken, churchyard thing,
Whose passing-bell may ere the midnight toll;
Whose prayers for thee, each morn and evening,
Were never missed.'—Thus plaining, doth she bring
A gentler speech from burning Porphyro;
160   So woful, and of such deep sorrowing,
That Angela gives promise she will do
Whatever he shall wish, betide her weal or woe.

XIX

Which was, to lead him, in close secrecy,
Even to Madeline's chamber, and there hide
Him in a closet, of such privacy
That he might see her beauty unespied,
And win perhaps that night a peerless bride,
While legioned faeries paced the coverlet,
And pale enchantment held her sleepy-eyed.
170   Never on such a night have lovers met,
Since Merlin paid his Demon all the monstrous debt.°

XX

'It shall be as thou wishest,' said the Dame:
'All cates° and dainties shall be stored there
Quickly on this feast-night: by the tambour frame°
Her own lute thou wilt see: no time to spare,
For I am slow and feeble, and scarce dare
On such a catering trust my dizzy head.
Wait here, my child, with patience; kneel in prayer
The while: Ah! thou must needs the lady wed,
180   Or may I never leave my grave among the dead.'—

XXI

So saying, she hobbled off with busy fear.
The lover's endless minutes slowly passed;
The dame returned, and whispered in his ear
To follow her; with aged eyes aghast
From fright of dim espial. Safe at last,
Through many a dusky gallery, they gain
The maiden's chamber, silken, hushed, and chaste;
Where Porphyro took covert, pleased amain.°
His poor guide hurried back with agues in her brain.

Since . . . debt The Demon presumably was
the temptress Vivien, who trapped Merlin after
coaxing his spells from him.
cates delicacies

tambour frame drum-shaped frame for embroidery
amain exceedingly

XXII

190 Her faltering hand upon the balustrade,
Old Angela was feeling for the stair,
When Madeline, St. Agnes' charmèd maid,
Rose, like a missioned spirit, unaware:
With silver taper's light, and pious care,
She turned, and down the aged gossip led
To a safe level matting. Now prepare,
Young Porphyro, for gazing on that bed;
She comes, she comes again, like ring-dove frayed° and fled.

XXIII

Out went the taper as she hurried in;
200 Its little smoke, in pallid moonshine, died:
She closed the door, she panted, all akin
To spirits of the air, and visions wide:
No uttered syllable, or, woe betide!
But to her heart, her heart was voluble,
Paining with eloquence her balmy side;
As though a tongueless nightingale should swell
Her throat in vain, and die, heart-stifled, in her dell.

XXIV

A casement high and triple-arched there was,
All garlanded with carven imag'ries
210 Of fruits, and flowers, and bunches of knot-grass,
And diamonded with panes of quaint device,
Innumerable of stains and splendid dyes,
As are the tiger-moth's deep-damasked wings;
And in the midst, 'mong thousand heraldries,
And twilight saints, and dim emblazonings,
A shielded scutcheon blushed with blood of queens and kings.

XXV

Full on this casement shone the wintry moon,
And threw warm gules° on Madeline's fair breast,
As down she knelt for heaven's grace and boon;
220 Rose-bloom fell on her hands, together pressed,
And on her silver cross soft amethyst,
And on her hair a glory, like a saint:
She seemed a splendid angel, newly dressed,
Save wings, for heaven:—Porphyro grew faint:
She knelt, so pure a thing, so free from mortal taint.

XXVI

Anon his heart revives: her vespers done,
Of all its wreathèd pearls her hair she frees;

frayed frightened   gules the heraldic name for red

Unclasps her warmèd jewels one by one;
Loosens her fragrant bodice; by degrees
230   Her rich attire creeps rustling to her knees:
Half-hidden, like a mermaid in sea-weed,
Pensive awhile she dreams awake, and sees,
In fancy, fair St. Agnes in her bed,
But dares not look behind, or all the charm is fled.

      XXVII
Soon, trembling in her soft and chilly nest,
In sort of wakeful swoon, perplexed she lay,
Until the poppied warmth of sleep oppressed
Her soothèd limbs, and soul fatigued away;
Flown, like a thought, until the morrow-day;
240   Blissfully havened both from joy and pain;
Clasped like a missal where swart Paynims pray;°
Blinded alike from sunshine and from rain,
As though a rose should shut, and be a bud again.

      XXVIII
Stol'n to this paradise, and so entranced,
Porphyro gazed upon her empty dress,
And listened to her breathing, if it chanced
To wake into a slumberous tenderness;
Which when he heard, that minute did he bless,
And breathed himself: then from the closet crept,
250   Noiseless as fear° in a wide wilderness,
And over the hushed carpet, silent, stepped,
And 'tween the curtains peeped, where, lo!—how fast she slept.

      XXIX
Then by the bed-side, where the faded moon
Made a dim, silver twilight, soft he set
A table, and, half anguished, threw thereon
A cloth of woven crimson, gold, and jet:—
O for some drowsy Morphean° amulet!
The boisterous, midnight, festive clarion,
The kettle-drum, and far-heard clarinet,
260   Affray his ears, though but in dying tone:—
The hall door shuts again, and all the noise is gone.

      XXX
And still she slept an azure-lidded sleep,
In blanchèd linen, smooth, and lavendered,
While he from forth the closet brought a heap
Of candied apple, quince, and plum, and gourd;

Clasped . . . pray kept shut as a Christian
prayer book would be where pagans pray

fear frightened person
Morphean pertaining to the god of sleep

With jellies soother° than the creamy curd,
And lucent syrups, tinct° with cinnamon;
Manna and dates, in argosy transferred
From Fez;° and spiced dainties, every one,
270   From silken Samarcand° to cedared Lebanon.

XXXI

These delicates he heaped with glowing hand
On golden dishes and in baskets bright
Of wreathed silver: sumptuous they stand
In the retired quiet of the night,
Filling the chilly room with perfume light.—
'And now, my love, my seraph fair, awake!
Thou art my heaven, and I thine eremite:°
Open thine eyes, for meek St. Agnes' sake,
Or I shall drowse beside thee, so my soul doth ache.'

XXXII

280   Thus whispering, his warm, unnervèd arm
Sank in her pillow. Shaded was her dream
By the dusk curtains:—'twas a midnight charm
Impossible to melt as icèd stream:
The lustrous salvers in the moonlight gleam;
Broad golden fringe upon the carpet lies:
It seemed he never, never could redeem
From such a stedfast spell his lady's eyes;
So mused awhile, entoiled in woofèd° phantasies.

XXXIII

Awakening up, he took her hollow lute,—
290   Tumultuous,—and, in chords that tenderest be,
He played an ancient ditty, long since mute,
In Provence called, 'La belle dame sans merci:'°
Close to her ear touching the melody;—
Wherewith disturbed, she uttered a soft moan:
He ceased—she panted quick—and suddenly
Her blue affrayèd eyes wide open shone:
Upon his knees he sank, pale as smooth-sculptured stone.

XXXIV

Her eyes were open, but she still beheld,
Now wide awake, the vision of her sleep:
300   There was a painful change, that nigh expelled
The blisses of her dream so pure and deep

soother smoother
tinct tinctured
Fez commercial city in northern Morocco
Samarcand today a city in southern Russia, and
still noted for its silks

eremite hermit, usually has religious connotations
woofèd woven
'La belle . . . merci' poem by Alain Chartier,
medieval French poet, as well as a poem by
Keats (see below)

At which fair Madeline began to weep,
And moan forth witless words with many a sigh;
While still her gaze on Porphyro would keep;
Who knelt, with joinèd hands and piteous eye,
Fearing to move or speak, she looked so dreamingly.

XXXV

'Ah, Porphyro!' said she, 'but even now
Thy voice was at sweet tremble in mine ear,
Made tuneable with every sweetest vow;
310 And those sad eyes were spiritual and clear:
How changed thou art! how pallid, chill, and drear!
Give me that voice again, my Porphyro,
Those looks immortal, those complainings dear!
Oh leave me not in this eternal woe,
For if thou diest, my Love, I know not where to go.'

XXXVI

Beyond a mortal man impassioned far
At these voluptuous accents, he arose,
Ethereal, flushed, and like a throbbing star
Seen mid the sapphire heaven's deep repose;
320 Into her dream he melted, as the rose
Blendeth its odour with the violet,—
Solution sweet: meantime the frost-wind blows
Like Love's alarum pattering the sharp sleet
Against the window-panes; St. Agnes' moon hath set.

XXXVII

'Tis dark: quick pattereth the flaw-blown° sleet:
'This is no dream, my bride, my Madeline!'
'Tis dark: the icèd gusts still rave and beat:
'No dream, alas! alas! and woe is mine!
Porphyro will leave me here to fade and pine.—
330 Cruel! what traitor could thee hither bring?
I curse not, for my heart is lost in thine,
Though thou forsakest a deceivèd thing;—
A dove forlorn and lost with sick unprunèd wing.'

XXXVIII

'My Madeline! sweet dreamer! lovely bride!
Say, may I be for aye thy vassal blest?
Thy beauty's shield, heart-shaped and vermeil° dyed?
Ah, silver shrine, here will I take my rest
After so many hours of toil and quest,
A famished pilgrim,—saved by miracle.

---

flaw-blown gust-blown   **vermeil** vermilion

340   Though I have found, I will not rob thy nest
       Saving of thy sweet self; if thou thinkest well
     To trust, fair Madeline, to no rude infidel.

          XXXIX
       'Hark! 'tis an elfin-storm from faery land,
       Of haggard° seeming, but a boon indeed:
       Arise—arise! the morning is at hand;—
       The bloated wassaillers will never heed:—
       Let us away, my love, with happy speed;
       There are no ears to hear, or eyes to see,—
       Drowned all in Rhenish° and the sleepy mead:°
350   Awake! arise! my love, and fearless be,
     For o'er the southern moors I have a home for thee.'

          XL
       She hurried at his words, beset with fears,
       For there were sleeping dragons all around,
       At glaring watch, perhaps, with ready spears—
       Down the wide stairs a darkling way they found.—
       In all the house was heard no human sound.
       A chain-drooped lamp was flickering by each door;
       The arras,° rich with horseman, hawk, and hound,
       Fluttered in the besieging wind's uproar;
360   And the long carpets rose along the gusty floor.

          XLI
       They glide, like phantoms, into the wide hall;
       Like phantoms, to the iron porch, they glide;
       Where lay the Porter, in uneasy sprawl,
       With a huge empty flagon by his side:
       The wakeful bloodhound rose, and shook his hide,
       But his sagacious eye an inmate owns:
       By one, and one, the bolts full easy slide:—
       The chains lie silent on the footworn stones;—
     The key turns, and the door upon its hinges groans.

          XLII
370   And they are gone: aye, ages long ago
       These lovers fled away into the storm.
       That night the Baron dreamt of many a woe,
       And all his warrior-guests, with shade and form
       Of witch, and demon, and large coffin-worm,
       Were long be-nightmared. Angela the old
       Died palsy-twitched, with meagre face deform;

haggard wild   **mead** fermented liquor, made of malt and honey
Rhenish Rhine wine   **arras** tapestry

The Beadsman, after thousand aves° told,
For aye unsought for slept among his ashes cold.
1819   1820

La Belle Dame Sans Merci°

A Ballad

O, what can ail thee, knight-at-arms,
    Alone and palely loitering?
The sedge has withered from the lake,
    And no birds sing.

O, what can ail thee, knight-at-arms,
    So haggard and so woe-begone?
The squirrel's granary is full,
    And the harvest's done.

I see a lily on thy brow,
10   With anguish moist and fever dew;
And on thy cheeks a fading rose
    Fast withereth too.

I met a lady in the meads,
    Full beautiful—a faery's child,
Her hair was long, her foot was light,
    And her eyes were wild.°

I made a garland for her head,
    And bracelets too, and fragrant zone;°
She looked at me as she did love,
20   And made sweet moan.

I set her on my pacing steed,
    And nothing else saw all day long;
For sidelong would she bend, and sing
    A faery's song.

She found me roots of relish sweet,
    And honey wild, and manna dew,°
And sure in language strange she said—
    'I love thee true.'

She took me to her elfin grot,
30   And there she wept and sighed full sore,

aves Hail Marys (*Ave Maria*)
La Belle Dame Sans Merci The title, which means "The Beautiful Lady Without Pity," is taken from a medieval poem by Alain Chartier, but the lady of this poem is not so much without pity as unable to make herself understood by the infatuated knight, since they speak different languages; the poem is complex and perhaps deliberately confused, since the lady combines aspects of two absolutely opposing Spenserian ladies, the whore Duessa and the Faerie Queene herself.
And . . . wild See Wordsworth's lyric "Her Eyes Are Wild."
zone girdle
And honey . . . dew See Coleridge's *Kubla Khan*, l. 53.

And there I shut her wild wild eyes
  With kisses four.

And there she lullèd me asleep
  And there I dreamed—Ah! woe betide!
The latest dream I ever dreamed
  On the cold hill side.

I saw pale kings and princes too,
  Pale warriors, death-pale were they all;
40 They cried—'La Belle Dame sans Merci
  Hath thee in thrall!'

I saw their starved lips in the gloam,
  With horrid warning gapèd wide,
And I awoke and found me here,
  On the cold hill's side.

And this is why I sojourn here
  Alone and palely loitering,
Though the sedge has withered from the lake,
  And no birds sing.
1819   1820

On the Sonnet°

If by dull rhymes our English must be chained,
And, like Andromeda,° the Sonnet sweet
Fettered, in spite of painèd loveliness,
Let us find out, if we must be constrained,
Sandals more interwoven and complete
To fit the naked foot of Poesy:
Let us inspect the Lyre, and weigh the stress
Of every chord, and see what may be gained
By ear industrious, and attention meet;
10 Misers of sound and syllable, no less
Than Midas° of his coinage, let us be
Jealous of dead leaves in the bay wreath crown;
So, if we may not let the Muse be free,
She will be bound with garlands of her own.
1819   1848

On the Sonnet The experimental rhyme scheme (*abca bdca bcde de*) attempts to avoid what Keats called "the pouncing rhymes" of the Petrarchan sonnet and the closing couplet of the Shakespearean kind, which Keats found "too elegiac."
Andromeda Andromeda was being sacrificed to a sea monster, to appease Poseidon, the sea god, when Perseus arrived, liberated her from her rock, killed the dragon, turned another suitor to stone, and married the lady; Keats presents himself as Perseus to the English sonnet's Andromeda.
Midas King Midas of Phrygia greedily requested of Dionysus (who owed him a favor) the power to turn everything he touched to gold; after involuntarily transforming his food, his drink, and even his loving daughter to gold, Midas was repentant, and successfully begged to lose his redundant power.

Ode to Psyche°

O Goddess! hear these tuneless numbers, wrung
   By sweet enforcement and remembrance dear,
And pardon that thy secrets should be sung
   Even into thine own soft-conchèd° ear:
Surely I dreamt today, or did I see
   The wingèd Psyche with awakened eyes?°
I wandered in a forest thoughtlessly,
   And, on the sudden, fainting with surprise,
Saw two fair creatures, couchèd side by side°
10   In deepest grass, beneath the whispering roof
     Of leaves and trembled blossoms, where there ran
       A brooklet, scarce espied:

'Mid hushed, cool-rooted flowers, fragrant-eyed,
   Blue, silver-white, and budded Tyrian,°
They lay calm-breathing on the bedded grass;
   Their arms embracèd, and their pinions too;
   Their lips touched not, but had not bade adieu,
As if disjoinèd by soft-handed slumber,
   And ready still past kisses to outnumber
20   At tender eye-dawn of aurorean love:
     The wingèd boy I knew;
   But who wast thou, O happy, happy dove?
       His Psyche true!

O latest born and loveliest vision far
   Of all Olympus' faded hierarchy!
Fairer than Phoebe's° sapphire-regioned star,
   Or Vesper,° amorous glow-worm of the sky;
Fairer than these, though temple thou hast none,
     Nor altar heaped with flowers;
30 Nor virgin-choir to make delicious moan
     Upon the midnight hours;
No voice, no lute, no pipe, no incense sweet
   From chain-swung censer teeming;

Ode to Psyche This first of the great odes
(written during the month April 20–May 20,
1819) is addressed to a goddess largely of
Keat's own creation. W. J. Bate interprets her
as the "inner life," which one could amend to
the "inner life-in-love," or the internalized
quest turned outward again by the impulse of
sharing. The Hellenistic Psyche (for her story
see *The Golden Ass* by Apuleius, Latin author
of the 2nd century A.D.) was a mortal with
whom Cupid or Eros fell in love. Fearing the
wrath of his mother Venus, he visited Psyche
only in darkness, until the naturally curious girl
exposed him by the sudden lighting of a torch
(see the poem's last stanza). After separation
and suffering, Cupid and Psyche were reunited
among the gods, with Psyche made immortal.
Keats begins his poem by bringing the reunited
lovers down to earth, and proceeds to declare
himself Psyche's priest. In this declaration, he
writes a manifesto for his imagination, and
begins his major poetry. See his journal-letter
of February–May 1819, to George and Georgiana Keats.
soft-conchèd shaped like a soft shell
awakened eyes See Spenser's *Amoretti* LXXVII:
"Was it a dreame, or did I see it playne . . . ?"
side by side See *Paradise Lost* IV.741, 790.
Tyrian famous purple-blue dye of ancient Tyre;
see Browning's poem on Keats, "Popularity"
Phoebe's the moon, Diana
Vesper the Evening Star, Hesperus

No shrine, no grove, no oracle, no heat
   Of pale-mouthed prophet dreaming.

O brightest! though too late for antique vows,
   Too, too late for the fond° believing lyre,
When holy were the haunted forest boughs,
   Holy the air, the water, and the fire;
40 Yet even in these days so far retired
   From happy pieties, thy lucent fans,°
Fluttering among the faint Olympians,
I see, and sing, by my own eyes inspired.
So let me be thy choir, and make a moan
      Upon the midnight hours;
Thy voice, thy lute, thy pipe, thy incense sweet
   From swingèd censer teeming;
Thy shrine, thy grove, thy oracle, thy heat
   Of pale-mouthed prophet dreaming.

50 Yes, I will be thy priest, and build a fane°
   In some untrodden region of my mind,°
Where branchèd thoughts, new grown with pleasant pain,
   Instead of pines shall murmur in the wind:
Far, far around shall those dark-clustered trees
   Fledge the wild-ridgèd mountains steep by steep;
And there by zephyrs, streams, and birds, and bees,
   The moss-lain Dryads° shall be lulled to sleep;
And in the midst of this wide quietness
A rosy sanctuary will I dress
60 With the wreathed trellis of a working brain,
   With buds, and bells, and stars without a name,
With all the gardener Fancy e'er could feign,
   Who breeding flowers, will never breed the same:
And there shall be for thee all soft delight
   That shadowy thought can win,
A bright torch, and a casement ope° at night,
   To let the warm Love in!
   1819   1820

Ode to a Nightingale

I

My heart aches, and a drowsy numbness pains
   My sense, as though of hemlock° I had drunk,

---

fond probably has both the older meaning of "foolish" and the modern one of "affectionate"
fans wings
fane temple
and build . . . mind See Spenser's *Amoretti* XXII: "Her temple fayre is built within my mind . . .".

moss-lain Dryads wood nymphs reclining on banks of moss
casement ope See "To a Nightingale," l. 69.
hemlock poisonous herb, and not the American tree of that name

Or emptied some dull opiate to the drains
   One minute past, and Lethe-wards° had sunk:
'Tis not through envy of thy happy lot,
   But being too happy in thine happiness,—
      That thou, light-wingèd Dryad° of the trees,
        In some melodious plot
   Of beechen green, and shadows numberless,
10   Singest of summer in full-throated ease.

      II

O, for a draught of vintage! that hath been
   Cooled a long age in the deep-delved earth,
Tasting of Flora° and the country green,
   Dance, and Provençal° song, and sunburnt mirth!
O for a beaker full of the warm South,
   Full of the true, the blushful Hippocrene,°
      With beaded bubbles winking at the brim,
        And purple-stainèd mouth;
   That I might drink, and leave the world unseen,
20   And with thee fade away into the forest dim:

      III

Fade far away, dissolve, and quite forget
   What thou among the leaves hast never known,
The weariness, the fever, and the fret
   Here, where men sit and hear each other groan;
Where palsy shakes a few, sad, last grey hairs,
   Where youth grows pale, and spectre-thin, and dies;°
      Where but to think is to be full of sorrow
        And leaden-eyed despairs,
   Where Beauty cannot keep her lustrous eyes,
30   Or new Love pine at them beyond tomorrow.

      IV

Away! away! for I will fly to thee,
   Not charioted by Bacchus and his pards,°
But on the viewless° wings of Poesy,
   Though the dull brain perplexes and retards:
Already with thee! tender is the night,
   And haply the Queen-Moon is on her throne,
      Clustered around by all her starry Fays;°
        But here there is no light,

Lethe-wards down to the river of forgetfulness in the underworld
Dryad wood nymph
Flora Roman goddess of fertility
Provençal province in southern France associated with the troubadours and the origins of Romantic poetry

Hippocrene fountain of the Muses on Mt. Helicon
Where youth . . . dies Keats's brother Tom died of tuberculosis in December 1818.
pards leopards drawing the chariot of Bacchus, god of intoxication
viewless flying too high to have any view
Fays fairies

Save what from heaven is with the breezes blown
40   Through verdurous glooms and winding mossy ways.

V

I cannot see what flowers are at my feet,
    Nor what soft incense hangs upon the boughs,
But, in embalmèd° darkness, guess each sweet
    Wherewith the seasonable month endows
The grass, the thicket, and the fruit-tree wild;
    White hawthorn, and the pastoral eglantine;
        Fast fading violets covered up in leaves;
            And mid-May's eldest child,
    The coming musk-rose, full of dewy wine,
50   The murmurous haunt of flies on summer eves.

VI

Darkling° I listen; and, for many a time
I have been half in love with easeful Death,
Called him soft names in many a musèd rhyme,
    To take into the air my quiet breath;
Now more than ever seems it rich to die,
    To cease upon the midnight with no pain,
        While thou art pouring forth thy soul abroad
            In such an ecstasy!
    Still wouldst thou sing, and I have ears in vain—
60   To thy high requiem become a sod.

VII

Thou wast not born for death, immortal Bird!
    No hungry generations tread thee down;
The voice I hear this passing night was heard
    In ancient days by emperor and clown:
Perhaps the self-same song that found a path
    Through the sad heart of Ruth,° when, sick for home,
        She stood in tears amid the alien corn;
            The same that oft-times hath
    Charmed magic casements, opening on the foam
70   Of perilous seas, in faery lands forlorn.

VIII

Forlorn! the very word is like a bell
    To toll me back from thee to my sole self!
Adieu! the fancy cannot cheat so well
    As she is famed to do, deceiving elf.

---

embalmèd perfumed
Darkling in the darkness; see *Paradise Lost*
III.39, where the blind Milton compares him-
self to the nightingale that "sings darkling"

Ruth See Ruth 2 in the Bible, but Keats's vision has more in common with Wordsworth's
"The Solitary Reaper."

Adieu! adieu! thy plaintive anthem fades
  Past the near meadows, over the still stream,
    Up the hill-side; and now 'tis buried deep
      In the next valley-glades:
    Was it a vision, or a waking dream?°
80   Fled is that music:—Do I wake or sleep?
    1819   1819

Ode on a Grecian Urn

I

Thou still unravished bride of quietness,
  Thou foster-child of silence and slow time,
Sylvan historian, who canst thus express
  A flowery tale more sweetly than our rhyme:
What leaf-fringed legend haunts about thy shape
  Of deities or mortals, or of both,
    In Tempe° or the dales of Arcady?°
What men or gods are these? What maidens loth?
What mad pursuit? What struggle to escape?
10   What pipes and timbrels? What wild ecstasy?

II

Heard melodies are sweet, but those unheard
  Are sweeter; therefore, ye soft pipes, play on;
Not to the sensual° ear, but, more endeared,
  Pipe to the spirit ditties of no tone:
Fair youth, beneath the trees, thou canst not leave
  Thy song, nor ever can those trees be bare;
    Bold Lover, never, never canst thou kiss,
Though winning near the goal—yet, do not grieve;
  She cannot fade, though thou hast not thy bliss,
20   Forever wilt thou love, and she be fair!

III

Ah, happy, happy boughs! that cannot shed
  Your leaves, nor ever bid the Spring adieu;
And, happy melodist, unwearièd,
  Forever piping songs forever new;
More happy love! more happy, happy love!
  Forever warm and still to be enjoyed,
    Forever panting, and forever young;

waking dream Douglas Bush usefully cites Hazlitt's lecture "On Chaucer and Spenser" (which Keats heard delivered): "Spenser was the poet of our waking dreams . . . lulling the senses into a deep oblivion of the jarring noises of the world, from which we have no wish to be ever recalled"
Tempe valley in Thessaly
Arcady a region of ancient Greece, but primarily a vision of the pastoral ideal
sensual sensuous

All breathing human passion far above,
   That leaves a heart high-sorrowful and cloyed,
30   A burning forehead, and a parching tongue.

IV

Who are these coming to the sacrifice?
   To what green altar, O mysterious priest,
Lead'st thou that heifer lowing at the skies,
   And all her silken flanks with garlands dressed?
What little town by river or sea shore,
   Or mountain-built with peaceful citadel,
     Is emptied of this folk, this pious morn?
And, little town, thy streets for evermore
   Will silent be; and not a soul to tell
40   Why thou art desolate, can e'er return.°

V

O Attic° shape! Fair attitude! with brede°
   Of marble men and maidens overwrought,
With forest branches and the trodden weed;
   Thou, silent form, dost tease us out of thought°
As doth eternity: Cold Pastoral!
   When old age shall this generation waste,
     Thou shalt remain, in midst of other woe
Than ours, a friend to man, to whom thou say'st,
   'Beauty is truth, truth beauty,—that is all
50   Ye know on earth, and all ye need to know.'°
    1819   1820

Ode on Melancholy°

I

No, no, go not to Lethe,° neither twist
   Wolf's-bane,° tight-rooted, for its poisonous wine;
Nor suffer thy pale forehead to be kissed
   By nightshade, ruby grape of Proserpine;°

And . . . return The "little town" is not on the urn, but exists only in the implications of art.
Attic pertaining to Attica, i.e. Athens
brede embroidery
tease . . . thought as in the "Epistle to John Hamilton Reynolds" l. 77
Beauty . . . know There has been much critical controversy as to where Keats intended the quotation to end; I follow Douglas Bush in assigning the last two lines to the urn, and not just the first five words of l. 49.
Ode on Melancholy The ode originally opened with the following stanza, which Keats later canceled:

Though you should build a bark of dead men's bones,
   And rear a phantom gibbet for a mast,
Stitch creeds together for a sail, with groans
   To fill it out, blood-stainèd and aghast;
Although your rudder be a dragon's tail
   Long severed, yet still hard with agony,
   Your cordage large uprootings from the skull
Of bald Medusa, certes you would fail
   To find the Melancholy—whether she
    Dreameth in any isle of Lethe dull.
Lethe See "To a Nightingale," l. 4.
Wolf's-bane poisonous plant, as is nightshade
Proserpine queen of the underworld; wife of Pluto

Make not your rosary of yew-berries,°
   Nor let the beetle,° nor the death-moth° be
      Your mournful Psyche,° nor the downy owl
    A partner in your sorrow's mysteries;
      For shade to shade will come too drowsily,
10   And drown the wakeful anguish of the soul.

        II
But when the melancholy fit shall fall
   Sudden from heaven like a weeping cloud,
    That fosters the droop-headed flowers all,
      And hides the green hill in an April shroud;
    Then glut thy sorrow on a morning rose,
      Or on the rainbow of the salt sand-wave,
      Or on the wealth of globèd peonies;
Or if thy mistress some rich anger shows,
   Emprison her soft hand, and let her rave,
20   And feed deep, deep upon her peerless eyes.

        III
She° dwells with Beauty—Beauty that must die;
   And Joy, whose hand is ever at his lips
Bidding adieu; and aching Pleasure nigh,
   Turning to poison while the bee-mouth sips:
Ay, in the very temple of Delight
   Veiled Melancholy has her sovereign shrine,°
      Though seen of none save him whose strenuous tongue
Can burst Joy's grape against his palate fine;
   His soul shall taste the sadness of her might,
30   And be among her cloudy trophies hung.°
     1819   1820

The Fall of Hyperion

This purgatorial fragment is parallel to Shelley's *The Triumph of Life,* in that each poem derives its structure and procedure from Dante (by way of the Cary translation, in Keats's case), each has elements of palinode or recantation, and shows also a new severity of style and firmer discipline of mythopoetic invention. Keats too is writing his vision of judgment, but his vision, though tragic, is not as dark or as deliberately universalizing as Shelley's. Where Shelley passively renders Rousseau's terrifying story, Keats actively confronts his Muse, Moneta, and compels her not only to accept him as a true poet but to modify her harsh and narrow categorizations of

---

yew-berries associated with mourning
beetle coffin emblem, as Egyptian scarab
death-moth moth with skull-like markings
Psyche the soul, symbolized by the butterfly
She refers both to "thy mistress" and the goddess Melancholy.

shrine See the shrine of Moneta in *The Fall of Hyperion.*
And . . . hung See Shakespeare's Sonnet XXXI: "Hung with the trophies of my lovers gone."

poets and of humanist men of action. He does this not by asserting his own identity, but by finding a truer form in the merged, higher identify of a more humanistic poethood than the world has known.

Incomplete as it is (probably Keats did not go on because he was no longer healthy enough, in spirit or in body), *The Fall of Hyperion* shows the start of a different kind of tragic theme and procedure, one that is founded upon a realization that every credence attending literary and spiritual tradition is now dead. Moneta presides over a ruined shrine of all the dead faiths, and the lesson Keats searches out in her countenance is that tragedy is not enough, though he still desires to be a tragic poet. The burden of history, of the fused but broken splendor of past poetic achievements, is heroically taken on by Keats as a necessary prelude to a new level of achievement he believes he can attain. He did not live to do so, but this fragment persuades us that he was the chosen man to make the attempt.

The Fall of Hyperion

A Dream

Canto I

Fanatics have their dreams, wherewith they weave
A paradise for a sect; the savage too
From forth the loftiest fashion of his sleep
Guesses at Heaven; pity these have not
Traced upon vellum or wild Indian leaf
The shadows of melodious utterance.
But bare of laurel they live, dream, and die;
For Poesy alone can tell her dreams,
With the fine spell of words alone can save
10   Imagination from the sable charm
And dumb enchantment. Who alive can say,
'Thou art no Poet—mayst not tell thy dreams?'
Since every man whose soul is not a clod
Hath visions, and would speak, if he had loved,
And been well nurtured in his mother tongue.
Whether the dream now purposed to rehearse
Be poet's or fanatic's will be known
When this warm scribe my hand is in the grave.

20   Methought I stood where trees of every clime,
Palm, myrtle, oak, and sycamore, and beech,
With plantain, and spice-blossoms, made a screen;
In neighbourhood of fountains (by the noise
Soft-showering in my ears), and (by the touch
Of scent) not far from roses. Turning round
I saw an arbour with a drooping roof
Of trellis vines, and bells, and larger blooms,°

I saw . . . blooms See "Ode to Psyche," ll.
60–63.

Like floral censers, swinging light in air;
Before its wreathèd doorway, on a mound
Of moss, was spread a feast of summer fruits,
30 Which, nearer seen, seemed refuse of a meal
By angel tasted or our Mother Eve;°
For empty shells were scattered on the grass,
And grape-stalks but half bare, and remnants more,
Sweet-smelling, whose pure kinds I could not know.
Still was more plenty than the fabled horn°
Thrice emptied could pour forth, at banqueting
For Proserpine returned to her own fields,
Where the white heifers low. And appetite
More yearning than on Earth I ever felt
40 Growing within, I ate deliciously;
And, after not long, thirsted, for thereby
Stood a cool vessel of transparent juice
Sipped by the wandered bee, the which I took,
And, pledging all the mortals of the world,
And all the dead whose names are in our lips,°
Drank. That full draught is parent of my theme.
No Asian poppy nor elixir fine
Of the soon-fading jealous Caliphat;°
No poison gendered in close monkish cell,
50 To thin the scarlet conclave° of old men,
Could so have rapt unwilling life away.
Among the fragrant husks and berries crushed,
Upon the grass I struggled hard against
The domineering potion; but in vain:
The cloudy swoon came on, and down I sank,
Like a Silenus° on an antique vase.
How long I slumbered 'tis a chance to guess.
When sense of life returned, I started up
As if with wings; but the fair trees were gone,
60 The mossy mound and arbour were no more:
I looked around upon the carvèd sides
Of an old sanctuary with roof august,
Builded so high, it seemed that filmèd clouds
Might spread beneath, as o'er the stars of heaven;
So old the place was, I remembered none
The like upon the Earth: what I had seen
Of grey cathedrals, buttressed walls, rent towers,
The superannuations of sunk realms,
Or Nature's rocks toiled hard in waves and winds,
70 Seemed but the faulture of decrepit things
To that eternal domèd Monument.—

Eve See *Paradise Lost* V.321–49.
horn cornucopia or horn of plenty, from a goat
whose milk fed the infant Jupiter
And all . . . lips dead poets, still spoken of
Caliphat council of Caliphs, successors to Mo-
hammed's power, notorious for poisoning one
another
scarlet conclave the College of Cardinals
Silenus drunken satyr who instructed Bacchus

Upon the marble at my feet there lay
Store of strange vessels and large draperies,
Which needs had been of dyed asbestos wove,
Or in that place the moth could not corrupt,°
So white the linen, so, in some, distinct
Ran imageries from a sombre loom.
All in a mingled heap confused there lay
Robes, golden tongs, censer and chafing-dish,
80   Girdles, and chains, and holy jewelries.

Turning from these with awe, once more I raised
My eyes to fathom the space every way;
The embossed roof, the silent massy range
Of columns north and south, ending in mist
Of nothing, then to eastward, where black gates
Were shut against the sunrise evermore.—
Then to the west° I looked, and saw far off
An image, huge of feature as a cloud,
At level of whose feet an altar slept,
90   To be approached on either side by steps,
And marble balustrade, and patient travail
To count with toil the innumerable degrees.
Towards the altar sober-paced I went,
Repressing haste, as too unholy there;
And, coming nearer, saw beside the shrine
One ministering;° and there arose a flame.—
When in mid-May the sickening East wind°
Shifts sudden to the south, the small warm rain
Melts out the frozen incense from all flowers,
100   And fills the air with so much pleasant health
That even the dying man forgets his shroud;—
Even so that lofty sacrificial fire,
Sending forth Maian° incense, spread around
Forgetfulness of everything but bliss,
And clouded all the altar with soft smoke;
From whose white fragrant curtains thus I heard
Language pronounced: 'If thou canst not ascend
These steps,° die on that marble where thou art.
Thy flesh, near cousin to the common dust,
110   Will parch for lack of nutriment—thy bones
Will wither in few years, and vanish so

moth . . . corrupt See Matthew 6:19.
west the direction of conclusions, of personal death
One ministering Moneta, at once Keats's Virgil and his Beatrice; an admonisher (so her name) who replaces the Mnemosyne of the first Hyperion
East wind See Purgatorio XXV.145 ff.: "And, as the May breeze, the herald / of the dawn, blows and is fragrant, / steeped in the odour of grass and flowers, / so I felt a fanning on the middle of my brow / and the moving of a wing / which brought the fragrance of ambrosia"; this is followed by a blessing upon those "who hunger always in right measure."
Maian one of the Pleiades or Daughters of Atlas, and mother of Hermes. For Keats, "Maian" is almost a synonym for "naturalistic."
steps as in Dante's Purgatorio IV, IX, XII–XIII

That not the quickest eye could find a grain
Of what thou now art on that pavement cold.
The sands of thy short life are spent this hour,
And no hand in the universe can turn
Thy hourglass, if these gummed leaves be burnt
Ere thou canst mount up these immortal steps.'
I heard, I looked: two senses both at once,
So fine, so subtle, felt the tyranny
120   Of that fierce threat and the hard task proposed.
Prodigious seemed the toil; the leaves were yet
Burning—when suddenly a palsied chill
Struck from the pavèd level up my limbs,
And was ascending quick to put cold grasp
Upon those streams that pulse beside the throat:
I shrieked, and the sharp anguish of my shriek
Stung my own ears—I strove hard to escape
The numbness; strove to gain the lowest step.
Slow, heavy, deadly was my pace: the cold°
130   Grew stifling, suffocating, at the heart;
And when I clasped my hands I felt them not.
One minute before death, my iced foot touched
The lowest stair; and as it touched, life seemed
To pour in at the toes: I mounted up,
As once fair angels on a ladder° flew
From the green turf to Heaven—'Holy Power,'
Cried I, approaching near the hornèd shrine,
'What am I that should so be saved from death?
What am I that another death come not
140   To choke my utterance sacrilegious, here?'
Then said the veiled shadow—'Thou hast felt
What 'tis to die and live again° before
Thy fated hour, that thou hadst power to do so
Is thy own safety; thou hast dated on
Thy doom.'—'High Prophetess,' said I, 'purge off,
Benign, if so it please thee, my mind's film.'—
'None can usurp this height,' returned that shade,
'But those to whom the miseries of the world
Are misery, and will not let them rest.
150   All else who find a haven in the world,
Where they may thoughtless sleep away their days,
If by a chance into this fane they come,
Rot on the pavement where thou rottedst half.'—
'Are there not thousands in the world,' said I,
Encouraged by the sooth voice of the shade,

---

cold See *Purgatorio* XXX.97–100.
ladder Jacob's vision; Keats's allusion is probably to *Paradise Lost* III.510–15 rather than to
Genesis 28:12

live again as in *Hyperion* III.130, where Apollo
"dies into life"

'Who love their fellows even to the death,
Who feel the giant agony of the world,
And more, like slaves to poor humanity,
Labour for mortal good? I sure should see
160   Other men here; but I am here alone.'
'Those whom thou spak'st of are no visionaries,'
Rejoined that voice—'They are no dreamers weak,
They seek no wonder but the human face;
No music but a happy-noted voice—
They come not here, they have no thought to come—
And thou art here, for thou art less than they—
What benefit canst thou do, or all thy tribe,
To the great world? Thou art a dreaming thing,
A fever of thyself—think of the Earth;
170   What bliss even in hope is there for thee?
What haven? every creature hath its home;
Every sole man hath days of joy and pain,
Whether his labours be sublime or low—
The pain alone; the joy alone; distinct:
Only the dreamer venoms all his days,
Bearing more woe than all his sins deserve.
Therefore, that happiness be somewhat shared,
Such things as thou art are admitted oft
Into like gardens thou didst pass erewhile,
180   And suffered in these temples: for that cause
Thou standest safe beneath this statue's knees.'
'That I am favoured for unworthiness,
By such propitious parley medicined
In sickness not ignoble, I rejoice,
Aye, and could weep for love of such award.'
So answered I, continuing, 'If it please,
Majestic shadow, tell me: sure not all
Those melodies sung into the World's ear
Are useless: sure a poet is a sage;°
190   A humanist, physician to all men.
That I am none I feel, as vultures feel
They are no birds when eagles are abroad.
What am I then: Thou spakest of my tribe:
What tribe?' The tall shade veiled in drooping white
Then spake, so much more earnest, that the breath
Moved the thin linen folds that drooping hung
About a golden censer from the hand
Pendent—'Art thou not of the dreamer tribe?
The poet and the dreamer are distinct,
200   Diverse, sheer opposite, antipodes.
The one pours out a balm upon the World,

sage as Dante invoked Virgil, *Inferno* I.85

The other vexes it.' Then shouted I
Spite of myself, and with a Pythia's spleen,°
'Apollo! faded! O far flown Apollo!
Where is thy misty pestilence to creep
Into the dwellings, through the door crannies
Of all mock lyrists, large self worshippers
And careless Hectorers in proud bad verse.°
Though I breathe death with them it will be life
210   To see them sprawl before me into graves.
Majestic shadow, tell me where I am,
Whose altar this; for whom this incense curls;
What image this whose face I cannot see,
For the broad marble knees; and who thou art,
Of accent feminine so courteous?'

    Then the tall shade, in drooping linens veiled,
Spoke out, so much more earnest, that her breath
Stirred the thin folds of gauze that drooping hung
About a golden censer from her hand
220   Pendent; and by her voice I knew she shed
Long-treasured tears. 'This temple, sad and lone,
Is all spared from the thunder of a war
Foughten long since by giant hierarchy
Against rebellion: this old image here,
Whose carvèd features wrinkled as he fell,
Is Saturn's; I Moneta, left supreme
Sole Priestess of this desolation,'—
I had no words to answer, for my tongue,
Useless, could find about its roofèd home
230   No syllable of a fit majesty
To make rejoinder to Moneta's mourn.
There was a silence, while the altar's blaze
Was fainting for sweet food: I looked thereon,
And on the pavèd floor, where nigh were piled
Faggots of cinnamon, and many heaps
Of other crispèd spice-wood—then again
I looked upon the altar, and its horns
Whitened with ashes, and its languorous flame,
And then upon the offerings again;
240   And so by turns—till sad Moneta cried,
'The sacrifice is done, but not the less
Will I be kind to thee for thy good will.
My power, which to me is still a curse,
Shall be to thee a wonder; for the scenes
Still swooning vivid through my globèd brain,

with . . . spleen with anger like that of the
priestess of Apollo's temple at Delphi
Of all . . . bad verse This appears to be an
attack upon Keats's greatest contemporaries;
"mock lyrists": Shelley; "large self worshippers": Wordsworth; "careless Hectorers": Byron.

With an electral changing misery,
Thou shalt with those dull mortal eyes behold,
Free from all pain, if wonder pain thee not.'
As near as an immortal's spherèd words
250 Could to a mother's soften, were these last:
And yet I had a terror of her robes,
And chiefly of the veils, that from her brow
Hung pale, and curtained her in mysteries,
That made my heart too small to hold its blood.
This saw that Goddess, and with sacred hand
Parted the veils. Then saw I a wan face,°
Not pined by human sorrows, but bright-blanched
By an immortal sickness which kills not;
It works a constant change, which happy death
260 Can put no end to; deathwards progressing
To no death was that visage; it had passed
The lily and the snow; and beyond these
I must not think now, though I saw that face—
But for her eyes I should have fled away.
They held me back, with a benignant light,
Soft mitigated by divinest lids
Half-closed, and visionless entire they seemed
Of all external things;—they saw me not,
But in blank splendour, beamed like the mild moon,
270 Who comforts those she sees not, who knows not
What eyes are upward cast. As I had found
A grain of gold upon a mountain side,
And twinged with avarice strained out my eyes
To search its sullen entrails rich with ore,
So at the view of sad Moneta's brow,
I ached to see what things the hollow brain
Behind enwombèd: what high tragedy
In the dark secret chambers of her skull
Was acting, that could give so dread a stress
280 To her cold lips, and fill with such a light
Her planetary eyes; and touch her voice
With such a sorrow—'Shade of Memory!'—
Cried I, with act adorant at her feet,
'By all the gloom hung round thy fallen house,
By this last temple, by the golden age,
By great Apollo, thy dear Foster Child,
And by thyself, forlorn divinity,
The pale Omega° of a withered race,
Let me behold, according as thou saidst,
290 What in thy brain so ferments to and fro!'

wan face For a possible source, see *Purgatorio*
XXXI.117 ff.
Omega final letter of Greek alphabet, and so
the ultimate, revealed form, as in Revelation
1:8, 11, and *Paradiso* XXVI.19

No sooner had this conjuration passed
My devout lips, than side by side we stood
(Like a stunt bramble by a solemn pine)
Deep in the shady sadness of a vale,°
Far sunken from the healthy breath of morn,
Far from the fiery noon and eve's one star.
Onward I looked beneath the gloomy boughs,
And saw, what first I thought an image huge,
Like to the image pedestaled so high
300   In Saturn's temple. Then Moneta's voice
Came brief upon mine ear—'So Saturn sat
When he had lost his Realms—' whereon there grew
A power within me of enormous ken
To see as a god sees, and take the depth
Of things as nimbly as the outward eye
Can size and shape pervade. The lofty theme
At those few words hung vast before my mind,
With half-unraveled web. I sat myself
Upon an eagle's watch, that I might see,
310   And seeing ne'er forget. No stir of life
Was in this shrouded vale, not so much air
As in the zoning° of a summer's day
Robs not one light seed from the feathered grass,
But where the dead leaf fell there did it rest:
A stream went voiceless by, still deadened more
By reason of the fallen divinity
Spreading more shade; the Naiad 'mid her reeds
Pressed her cold finger closer to her lips.

       Along the margin-sand large footmarks went
320   No farther than to where old Saturn's feet
Had rested, and there slept, how long a sleep!
Degraded, cold, upon the sodden ground
His old right hand lay nerveless, listless, dead,
Unsceptred; and his realmless eyes were closed,
While his bowed head seemed listening to the Earth,
His ancient mother, for some comfort yet.

       It seemed no force could wake him from his place;
But there came one who, with a kindred hand
Touched his wide shoulders after bending low
330   With reverence, though to one who knew it not.
Then came the grieved voice of Mnemosyne,°
And grieved I hearkened. 'That divinity
Whom thou saw'st step from yon forlornest wood,

Deep . . . vale Keats now returns to the first
Hyperion (this is the very first line), revising
it as he goes on.
zoning moving from zone to zone

Mnemosyne perhaps a mistake for "Moneta,"
or perhaps Keats intended the names to be
alternate, once the story-telling had commenced;
see II.50

And with slow pace approach our fallen King,
Is Thea, softest-natured of our Brood.'
I marked the Goddess in fair statuary
Surpassing wan Moneta by the head,
And in her sorrow nearer woman's tears.
There was a listening fear in her regard,
340   As if calamity had but begun;
As if the vanward clouds of evil days
Had spent their malice, and the sullen rear
Was with its storèd thunder labouring up.
One hand she pressed upon that aching spot
Where beats the human heart, as if just there,
Though an immortal, she felt cruel pain;
The other upon Saturn's bended neck
She laid, and to the level of his hollow ear
Leaning with parted lips, some words she spake
350   In solemn tenor and deep organ tune;
Some mourning words, which in our feeble tongue
Would come in this-like accenting; how frail
To that large utterance of the early Gods!

    'Saturn! look up—and for what, poor lost King?
I have no comfort for thee; no not one;
I cannot cry, wherefore thus sleepest thou?
For Heaven is parted from thee, and the Earth
Knows thee not, so afflicted, for a God;
And Ocean too, with all its solemn noise,
360   Has from thy sceptre passed, and all the air
Is emptied of thine hoary majesty:
Thy thunder, captious at the new command,
Rumbles reluctant o'er our fallen house;
And thy sharp lightning, in unpracticed hands,
Scorches and burns our once serene domain.
With such remorseless speed still come new woes,
That unbelief has not a space to breathe.
Saturn! sleep on:—Me thoughtless, why should I
Thus violate thy slumbrous solitude?
370   Why should I ope thy melancholy eyes?
Saturn, sleep on, while at thy feet I weep.'

    As when upon a trancèd summer-night
Forests, branch-charmèd by the earnest stars,
Dream, and so dream all night without a noise,
Save from one gradual solitary gust,
Swelling upon the silence; dying off;
As if the ebbing air had but one wave;
So came these words, and went; the while in tears
She pressed her fair large forehead to the earth,
380   Just where her fallen hair might spread in curls,

A soft and silken mat for Saturn's feet.
Long, long those two were postured motionless,
Like sculpture builded-up upon the grave
Of their own power. A long awful time
I looked upon them: still they were the same;
The frozen God still bending to the earth,
And the sad Goddess weeping at his feet,
Moneta silent. Without stay or prop,
But my own weak mortality, I bore
390   The load of this eternal quietude,
The unchanging gloom, and the three fixèd shapes
Ponderous upon my senses, a whole moon.
For by my burning brain I measured sure
Her silver seasons shedded on the night,
And ever day by day methought I grew
More gaunt and ghostly.—Oftentimes I prayed
Intense, that Death would take me from the Vale
And all its burthens—gasping with despair
Of change, hour after hour I cursed myself;
400   Until old Saturn raised his faded eyes,
And looked around and saw his kingdom gone,
And all the gloom and sorrow of the place,
And that fair kneeling Goddess at his feet.
As the moist scent of flowers, and grass, and leaves,
Fills forest dells with a pervading air,
Known to the woodland nostril, so the words
Of Saturn filled the mossy glooms around,
Even to the hollows of time-eaten oaks,
And to the windings of the foxes' hole,
410   With sad low tones, while thus he spake, and sent
Strange musings to the solitary Pan.
'Moan, brethren, moan; for we are swallowed up
And buried from all Godlike exercise
Of influence benign on planets pale,
And peaceful sway above man's harvesting,
And all those acts which Deity supreme
Doth ease its heart of love in. Moan and wail,
Moan, brethren, moan; for lo, the rebel spheres
Spin round, the stars their ancient courses keep,
420   Clouds still with shadowy moisture haunt the earth,
Still suck their fill of light from sun and moon;
Still buds the tree, and still the sea-shores murmur;
There is no death in all the Universe,
No smell of death—there shall be death—Moan, moan,
Moan, Cybele, moan; for thy pernicious Babes
Have changed a god into a shaking Palsy.
Moan, brethren, moan, for I have no strength left,
Weak as the reed—weak—feeble as my voice—

O, O, the pain, the pain of feebleness.
430 Moan, moan, for still I thaw—or give me help;
Throw down those imps, and give me victory.
Let me hear other groans, and trumpets blown
Of triumph calm, and hymns of festival,
From the gold peaks of Heaven's high-pilèd clouds;
Voices of soft proclaim, and silver stir
Of strings in hollow shells; and let there be
Beautiful things made new for the surprise
Of the sky-children.' So he feebly ceased,
With such a poor and sickly sounding pause,
440 Methought I heard some old man of the earth
Bewailing earthly loss; nor could my eyes
And ears act with that pleasant unison of sense
Which marries sweet sound with the grace of form,
And dolorous accent from a tragic harp
With large-limbed visions.—More I scrutinized:
Still fixed he sat beneath the sable trees,
Whose arms spread straggling in wild serpent forms,
With leaves all hushed; his awful presence there
(Now all was silent) gave a deadly lie
450 To what I erewhile heard—only his lips
Trembled amid the white curls of his beard.
They told the truth, though, round, the snowy locks
Hung nobly, as upon the face of heaven
A mid-day fleece of clouds. Thea arose,
And stretched her white arm through the hollow dark,
Pointing some whither: whereat he too rose
Like a vast giant, seen by men at sea
To grow pale from the waves at dull midnight.
They melted from my sight into the woods;
460 Ere I could turn, Moneta cried, 'These twain
Are speeding to the families of grief,
Where roofed in by black rocks they waste, in pain
And darkness, for no hope.'°—And she spake on,
As ye may read who can unwearied pass
Onward from the Antechamber of this dream,
Where even at the open doors awhile
I must delay, and glean my memory
Of her high phrase:—perhaps no further dare.

Canto II
'Mortal, that thou may'st understand aright,
I humanize my sayings to thine ear,
Making comparisons of earthly things;
Or thou might'st better listen to the wind,

no hope See *Inferno* IV.

Whose language is to thee a barren noise,
Though it blows legend-laden through the trees.—
In melancholy realms big tears are shed,
More sorrow like to this, and such like woe,
Too huge for mortal tongue, or pen of scribe.
10 The Titans fierce, self hid or prison bound,
Groan for the old allegiance once more,
Listening in their doom for Saturn's voice.
But one of our whole eagle-brood still keeps
His sovereignty, and rule, and majesty;
Blazing Hyperion on his orbèd fire
Still sits, still snuffs the incense teeming up
From Man to the Sun's God: yet unsecure.
For as upon the earth dire prodigies
Fright and perplex, so also shudders he:
20 Nor at dog's howl or gloom-bird's Even screech,
Or the familiar visitings of one
Upon the first toll of his passing bell:
But horrors, portioned to a giant nerve,
Make great Hyperion ache. His palace bright,
Bastioned with pyramids of glowing gold,
And touched with shade of bronzèd obelisks,
Glares a blood-red through all the thousand courts,
Arches, and domes, and fiery galleries:
And all its curtains of Aurorian clouds
30 Flush angerly; when he would taste the wreaths
Of incense breathed aloft from sacred hills,
Instead of sweets, his ample palate takes
Savour of poisonous brass and metals sick.
Wherefore when harboured in the sleepy West,
After the full completion of fair day,
For rest divine upon exalted couch
And slumber in the arms of melody,
He paces through the pleasant hours of ease
With strides colossal, on from hall to hall;
40 While far within each aisle and deep recess
His wingèd minions in close clusters stand
Amazed, and full of fear; like anxious men,
Who on a wide plain gather in sad troops,
When earthquakes jar their battlements and towers.
Even now, while Saturn, roused from icy trance,
Goes, step for step, with Thea from yon woods,
Hyperion, leaving twilight in the rear,
Is sloping to the threshold of the West.—
Thither we tend.'—Now in clear light I stood,
50 Relieved from the dusk vale. Mnemosyne
Was sitting on a square-edged polished stone,
That in its lucid depth reflected pure

Her priestess-garments.—My quick eyes ran on
From stately nave to nave, from vault to vault,
Through bowers of fragrant and enwreathèd light
And diamond-pavèd lustrous long arcades.
Anon rushed by the bright Hyperion;
His flaming robes streamed out beyond his heels,
And gave a roar, as if of earthly fire,
60   That scared away the meek ethereal hours,
And made their dove-wings tremble. On he flared.
1819   1856

To Autumn°

I

Season of mists and mellow fruitfulness,
    Close bosom-friend of the maturing sun;
Conspiring with him how to load and bless
    With fruit the vines that round the thatch-eves run;
To bend with apples the mossed cottage-trees,°
    And fill all fruit with ripeness to the core;
        To swell the gourd, and plump the hazel shells
With a sweet kernel; to set budding more,
    And still more, later flowers for the bees,
10   Until they think warm days will never cease,
        For Summer has o'er-brimmed their clammy cells.

II

Who hath not seen thee oft amid thy store?
    Sometimes whoever seeks abroad may find
Thee sitting careless on a granary floor,
    Thy hair soft-lifted by the winnowing wind;
Or on a half-reaped furrow sound asleep,
    Drowsed with the fume of poppies, while thy hook
        Spares the next swath and all its twinèd flowers:
And sometimes like a gleaner thou dost keep
20   Steady thy laden head across a brook;
        Or by a cider-press, with patient look,
        Thou watchest the last oozings hours by hours.

To Autumn Two days after writing this ode, Keats commented upon it in a letter to Reynolds: "How beautiful the season is now—How fine the air. A temperate sharpness about it. Really, without joking, chaste weather—Dian skies—I never lik'd stubble fields so much as now—Aye better than the chilly green of the spring. Somehow a stubble plain looks warm—in the same way that some pictures look warm—this struck me so much in my Sunday's walk that I composed upon it."

To bend . . . cottage-trees The line recalls Chatterton, and Keats in his September 21 letter to Reynolds says: "I always somehow associate Chatterton with autumn." See Chatterton's *Aella*, ll. 184–85: "When the fair apple, red as even sky, / Do bend the tree unto the fruitful ground." In associating Chatterton with autumn, Keats compelled himself to remember an admired young poet who died before he had gathered in the harvest of his poetry.

III

Where are the songs of Spring? Aye, where are they?
  Think not of them, thou hast thy music too,—
While barred clouds bloom the soft-dying day,
  And touch the stubble-plains with rosy hue;
Then in a wailful choir the small gnats mourn
  Among the river sallows,° borne aloft
    Or sinking as the light wind lives or dies;
30 And full-grown lambs loud bleat from hilly bourn;
  Hedge-crickets sing; and now with treble soft
  The red-breast whistles from a garden-croft;
    And gathering swallows twitter in the skies.
    1819   1820

To——————°

What can I do to drive away
Remembrance from my eyes? For they have seen,
Aye, an hour ago, my brilliant Queen!
Touch has a memory. O say, love, say,
What can I do to kill it and be free
In my old liberty?°
When every fair one that I saw was fair,
Enough to catch me in but half a snare,
Not keep me there:
10 When, howe'er poor or particoloured things,
My muse had wings,
And ever ready was to take her course
Whither I bent her force,
Unintellectual, yet divine to me;—
Divine, I say!—What sea-bird o'er the sea
Is a philosopher the while he goes
Winging along where the great water throes?°

  How shall I do
  To get anew
20 Those moulted feathers, and so mount once more
  Above, above
  The reach of fluttering Love,
And make him cower lowly while I soar?

Shall I gulp wine? No, that is vulgarism,
A heresy and schism,
  Foisted into the canon law of love;—
No,—wine is only sweet to happy men;

sallows willows
To—— almost certainly to Fanny Brawne
What can . . . liberty a desperate attempt by

the frustrated lover to free himself from love
throes i.e. is in throes

More dismal cares
Seize on me unawares,—
30   Where shall I learn to get my peace again?
To banish thoughts of that most hateful land,°
Dungeoner of my friends, that wicked strand
Where they were wrecked and live a weckèd life;
That monstrous region, whose dull rivers pour,
Ever from their sordid urns unto the shore,
Unowned of any weedy-hairèd gods;
Whose winds, all zephyrless, hold scourging rods,
Iced in the great lakes, to afflict mankind;
Whose rank-grown forests, frosted, black, and blind,
40   Would fright a Dryad;° whose harsh herbaged meads
Make lean and lank the starved ox while he feeds;
There flowers have no scent, birds no sweet song,
And great unerring Nature once seems wrong.

O, for some sunny spell
To dissipate the shadows of this hell!
Say they are gone,—with the new dawning light
Steps forth my lady bright!
O, let me once more rest
My soul upon that dazzling breast!
50   Let once again these aching arms be placed,
The tender gaolers of thy waist!
And let me feel that warm breath here and there
To spread a rapture in my very hair,—
O, the sweetness of the pain!
Give me those lips again!
Enough! Enough! it is enough for me
To dream of thee!
1819   1848

Bright Star°

[Written on a Blank Page in Shakespeare's Poems,
facing 'A Lover's Complaint']

Bright star, would I were stedfast as thou art—
    Not in lone splendour hung aloft the night
And watching, with eternal lids° apart,
    Like nature's patient, sleepless Eremite,°

hateful land the United States, where Keats's
brother and sister-in-law were in acute financial distress
Dryad wood nymph
Bright Star Keats copied out this revised version of an earlier sonnet while journeying to
Italy with Severn, possibly on October 1, 1820.
lids In his letter to his brother Tom (June 25–

27, 1818), Keats said that natural scenes in the
Lake Country "refine one's sensual vision into
a sort of north star which can never cease to
be open lidded and stedfast over the wonders
of the great Power."
Eremite hermit (with usually a religious con-
notation)

The moving waters at their priestlike task
   Of pure ablution° round earth's human shores,
Or gazing on the new soft-fallen mask
   Of snow upon the mountains and the moors—
No—yet still stedfast, still unchangeable,
10   Pillowed upon my fair love's ripening breast,
To feel forever its soft fall and swell,
   Awake forever in a sweet unrest,
Still, still to hear her tender-taken breath,
And so live ever—or else swoon to death.
1819–20   1838

This Living Hand°

This living hand, now warm and capable
Of earnest grasping, would, if it were cold
And in the icy silence of the tomb,
So haunt thy days and chill thy dreaming nights
That thou wouldst wish thine own heart dry of blood
So in my veins red life might stream again,
And thou be conscience-calmed—see here it is—
I hold it towards you.
1819–20   1898

OTHER ROMANTIC POETS

The eleven poets gathered together here were all contemporaries of the six major Romantic poets. One of them, John Clare, is all but a major poet in his own right. At least two others, Landor and Beddoes, wrote perfect poems within the limitations of their chosen modes. The others are both valuable in themselves and important reflectors of the greater poets of the period.

William Lisle Bowles (1762–1850), a clergyman of the Church of England, matters because of his little volume of 1789, *Fourteen Sonnets,* which influenced much of Coleridge's early poetry, and which is discussed in Chapter 1 of Coleridge's *Biographia Literaria.*

Sir Walter Scott (1771–1832) was formerly accounted a major poet, but time has demonstrated that his permanent work was done in the novel (*Ivanhoe, The Heart of Midlothian,* etc.). Born in Edinburgh, he practiced law, and began his literary career as a translator and ballad collector. From 1805 to 1812, when Byron's competing success helped turn him toward prose fiction, Scott wrote a sequence of metrical tales, of which the best are *The Lay of the Last Minstrel, Marmion,* and *The Lady of the Lake.* But his best poems are lyrics like the three given here: ballad-like,

ablution the act of washing clean; associated with religious rites (hence "priestlike")
This Living Hand probably the last lines of poetry that Keats wrote, perhaps as late as January 1820. Though there is a tradition that they were addressed to Fanny Brawne, they would fit more readily into a Romantic drama of the Jacobean mode, like those by Beddoes and Darley.

archaic, restrained, but with undertones of the deeper emotions to be found in Wordsworth and Coleridge.

Walter Savage Landor (1775–1864) is too large a poetic figure to be justly represented here, though the nine poems chosen do show his elegiac powers. A vehement and overwhelming personality whose career spans much of the history of nineteenth-century poetry, he associated both with the major Romantic and the major Victorian writers. His life was a series of lawsuits, controversies, quarrels with parents, wife, children, friends, and strangers, but his art, in the prose *Imaginary Conversations* and in the deliberately classical, epigrammatic poems, is rightly described as "marmoreal." He died in Italy, at ninety, still turbulent in personality, still restrained and disciplined in style.

Thomas Love Peacock (1785–1866), Shelley's close friend and George Meredith's father-in-law, did his best work as comic novelist (*Nightmare Abbey, Headlong Hall, Crotchet Castle*) and in the shrewd essay "The Four Ages of Poetry" that inspired Shelley's rhapsodic "A Defence of Poetry." Self-educated and wealthy, he delayed steady work until he entered the East India Company, with which he remained for the rest of his life. His best verse, like the delightful novels, is on the border between intellectual satire and fantastic comedy.

With **John Clare** (1793–1864) we come to a poet whose range is narrow, but so intense and pure are his best poems that in them he matches the major Romantics. Though in his madness Clare identified himself with Byron, he is a Wordsworthian poet, and a genuine visionary of nature. More than Burns, he was a peasant poet, whose father was a Northamptonshire farm laborer. In 1820 he published *Poems Descriptive of Rural Life and Scenery,* followed by *The Village Minstrel* in 1821, both of which were popular for a brief while. But his success passed, and the strains of supporting his wife and children aggravated schizoid tendencies always present in him. From 1836 until 1841, when he ran off, Clare was confined in a private asylum, a victim of an acute manic-depressive cycle. From 1841 until 1864, when he died, poor Clare lived in the Northampton General Lunatic Asylum, where he continued to write copiously.

The eleven poems and fragments given here are representative of what is best in Clare, from the overt exploration of Wordsworthian-Coleridgean ideas in "Pastoral Poesy" to the astonishing visionary group of Blake-like lyrics. What is unique to Clare is difficult to describe, but unmistakable. Though he lacks Wordsworth's power and Blake's insight, he can write in the modes of both with a freedom from self-consciousness that makes him one of the most direct and decently human poets in the language. And his indeliberate pathos, which might be expected to be an aesthetic liability, is redeemed by his immediacy, and moves us because in its integrity it seems not to need us. A poem like "A Vision" stands beyond the contraries of human existence, and persuades us that Clare himself, for all his life's horror and defeat, knew a final triumph in the spirit.

The remaining poets, like Clare, are in the generation of Keats and Shelley, and led mostly desperate lives, like the greater poets they imitated. **George Darley** (1795–1846), an Anglo-Irishman born and educated in Dublin, came to London to earn his living as a literary hack, writing art and literary reviews for the periodicals, and mathematical textbooks, as well as tragedies in the Jacobean style, like those of Beddoes, Procter, and Wade. Darley's genius was for lyrical poetry, particularly exemplified in the astonishing *Nepenthe,* which takes *Alastor* and *Endymion* as its models.

But Darley was defeated by his own nature; a struggle with his own inversions made him a compulsive stutterer, and augmented a melancholia that carried him to the borders of madness. His relation to the Muse is beautifully summed up by him in what can serve as the epitaph for his entire generation of poets: "He who the Syren's hair would win / Is mostly strangled in the tide."

Hartley Coleridge (1796–1849), first-born son of his illustrious father, spent his life in the shadows of his father and of Wordsworth and Southey, who were almost his foster-fathers. Poor Hartley could fulfill the prophecies of "Frost at Midnight" only ironically, yet the sweetness of his temperament made him a beloved figure in the Lake Country. He drank his way out of his Oxford fellowship, and was a near-alcoholic all his life, but he left behind a few good sonnets as a small extension of the family tradition.

Thomas Hood's life (1799–1845) war still sadder, as Hood had a larger talent to dissipate. Born in London, the son of a Scottish bookseller, Hood became a popular man of lettters, writing in most available forms. Tuberculosis and poverty deadened his poetic ambitions, and turned him from his earlier, Keatsian poetry to the comic verse for which he is now mostly recalled.

With **Thomas Lovell Beddoes** (1803–1849), we return to doomed genius, as with Clare, but Beddoes is a very different poet, closely influenced by Shelley's more despairing work. Though less famous than Poe, he is a much better poet than his American analogue, for Beddoes achieved mastery in his revival of Gothic morbidities. Born near Bristol, he was the son of a famous eccentric literary physician. At Pembroke College, Oxford, he began to write his peculiar versions of Jacobean tragedy, and lamented the death of Shelley in a radiant outburst of 1822. He proceeded to Germany, where he studied anatomy, in which he became rather grimly learned. Most of his life was spent in Germany and Switzerland, and was occupied by revolutionary activity, the practice of medicine, and many unhappy homosexual love affairs. In 1829, he made his first attempt at suicide; his last and successful attempt came at Basel, when he was forty-six.

For the last twenty years of his life, Beddoes worked at the composition of his masterpiece, *Death's Jest-Book; or The Fool's Tragedy,* a monumental visionary drama that breaks the confines of its quasi-Jacobean form. Interspersed throughout the play are haunting songs, unlike those even of Shelley, whom Beddoes loved and constantly imitated. The deliberate contrast between the unearthly delicacy of tone, and the grotesque vision of death everywhere insinuating itself into life, is the basis of Beddoes's narrow but eminently satisfying lyrical art.

Samuel Palmer (1805–1881), represented in this volume by several of his pictures as well as one visionary lyric, was in his very early work one of Blake's disciples and one of England's best painters. In after years, he aged into a relatively mediocre Victorian landscapist, but the paintings done at Shoreham in his youth are more vivid and successful visual realizations of the lower paradise Blake called Beulah than Blake could manage himself.

Thomas Wade (1805–1875), the last of these poets, is now almost forgotten. Another Jacobean revivalist, and Shelleyan enthusiast, he outlived his brief reputation, but a few of his meditations on sublime scenes recapture something of the Shelleyan intensity of *Alastor* and "Julian and Maddalo."

WILLIAM LISLE BOWLES

To the River Itchin, Near Winton°

Itchin, when I behold thy banks again,
    Thy crumbling margin, and thy silver breast,
    On which the self-same tints still seem to rest,
Why feels my heart the shivering sense of pain?
Is it—that many a summer's day has past
    Since, in life's morn, I caroled on thy side?
    Is it—that oft, since then, my heart has sighed,
As Youth, and Hope's delusive gleams, flew fast?
    Is it—that those, who circled on thy shore,
10   Companions of my youth, now meet no more?
Whate'er the cause, upon thy banks I bend
    Sorrowing, yet feel such solace at my heart,
As at the meeting of some long-lost friend,
    From whom, in happier hours, we wept to part.

1789

SIR WALTER SCOTT

The Dreary Change°

The sun upon the Weirdlaw Hill,
    In Ettrick's vale, is sinking sweet;
The westland wind is hush and still,
    The lake lies sleeping at my feet.
Yet not the landscape to mine eye
    Bears those bright hues that once it bore;
Though evening, with her richest dye,
    Flames o'er the hills of Ettrick's shore.

With listless look along the plain,
10   I see Tweed's silver current glide,
And coldly mark the holy fane
    Of Melrose rise in ruined pride.
The quiet lake, the balmy air,
    The hill, the stream, the tower, the tree,—
Are they still such as once they were?
    Or is the dreary change in me?

Alas, the warped and broken board,
    How can it bear the painter's dye!
The harp of strained and tuneless chord,
20   How to the minstrel's skill reply!

To the River Itchin, Near Winton This and similar sonnets by Bowles provided the model for Coleridge's early "Sonnet: To the River Otter."

The Dreary Change This is Scott's modest equivalent of Wordsworth's "Intimations" ode.

To aching eyes each landscape lowers,
   To feverish pulse each gale blows chill;
And Araby's or Eden's bowers
   Were barren as this moorland hill.

1817

'Proud Maisie'°

Proud Maisie is in the wood,
   Walking so early;
Sweet Robin sits on the bush,
   Singing so rarely.

'Tell me, thou bonny bird,
   When shall I marry me?'
'When six braw° gentlemen
   Kirkward shall carry ye.'

'Who makes the bridal bed,
10   Birdie, say truly?'
'The grey-headed sexton
   That delves the grave duly.

'The glow-worm o'er grave and stone
   Shall light thee steady.
The owl from the steeple sing,
   "Welcome, proud lady".'

1818

The Song of the Reim-kennar°

Stern eagle of the far north-west,
Thou that bearest in thy grasp the thunderbolt,
Thou whose rushing pinions stir ocean to madness,
Thou the destroyer of herds, thou the scatterer of navies,
Amidst the scream of thy rage,
Amidst the rushing of thy onward wings,
Though thy scream be loud as the cry of a perishing nation,
Though the rushing of thy wings be like the roar of ten thousand waves,
Yet hear, in thine ire and thy haste,
10 Hear thou the voice of the Reim-kennar.

Thou hast met the pine-trees of Drontheim,
Their dark-green heads lie prostrate beside their up-rooted stems;

Proud Maisie sung by Madge Wildfire on her
deathbed in the novel *The Heart of Midlothian;*
it is in the tradition of the mad song
braw fine
Reim-kennar Scott's own pseudo-archaism,
formed from Germanic *reim* (rhyme) and *kenner*
(knower), to mean one of the Norns or Fates
skilled in magic rhymes or runic verse; the song
is from the novel *The Pirate*

Thou hast met the rider of the ocean,
The tall, the strong bark of the fearless rover,
And she has struck to thee the topsail
That she had not veiled to a royal armada;
Thou hast met the tower that bears its crest among the clouds,
The battled massive tower of the Jarl° of former days,
And the cope-stone of the turret
20 Is lying upon its hospitable hearth;
But thou too shalt stoop, proud compeller of clouds,
When thou hearest the voice of the Reim-kennar.

There are verses that can stop the stag in the forest,
Ay, and when the dark-coloured dog is opening on his track;
There are verses can make the wild hawk pause on the wing,
Like the falcon that wears the hood and the jesses,°
And who knows the shrill whistle of the fowler;
Thou who canst mock at the scream of the drowning mariner,
And the crash of the ravaged forest,
30 And the groan of the overwhelmed crowds,
When the church hath fallen in the moment of prayer,
There are sounds which thou also must list,
When they are chaunted by the voice of the Reim-kennar.

Enough of woe hast thou wrought on the ocean,
The widows wring their hands on the beach;
Enough of woe hast thou wrought on the land,
The husbandman folds his arms in despair;
Cease thou the waving of thy pinions,
Let the ocean repose in her dark strength;
40 Cease thou the flashing of thine eye,
Let the thunderbolt sleep in the armoury of Odin;°
Be thou still at my bidding, viewless racer of the north-western heaven,
Sleep thou at the voice of Norna° the Reim-kennar.

Eagle of the far north-western waters,
Thou hast heard the voice of the Reim-kennar,
Thou hast closed thy wide sails at her bidding,
And folded them in peace by thy side.
My blessing be on thy retiring path;
When thou stoopest from thy place on high,
50 Soft be thy slumbers in the caverns of the unknown ocean,
Rest till destiny shall again awaken thee;
Eagle of the north-west, thou hast heard the voice of the Reim-kennar.
1821?   1822

Jarl an earl   Odin Scandinavian god of war
jesses short straps fastened about each leg of a   Norna Latinized name of Norn, one of the
falcon   three Fates

WALTER SAVAGE LANDOR

'Lately Our Poets'

Lately our poets loitered in green lanes,
Content to catch the ballads of the plains;°
I fancied I had strength enough to climb
A loftier station at no distant time,
And might securely from intrusion doze
Upon the flowers through which Ilissus° flows.
In those pale olive grounds all voices cease,
And from afar dust fills the paths of Greece.
My slumber broken and my doublet torn,
I find the laurel also bears a thorn.
                              1863

[Rose Aylmer, 1779–1800]°

Ah what avails the sceptred race,°
    Ah what the form divine!
What every virtue, every grace!
    Rose Aylmer, all were thine.
Rose Aylmer, whom these wakeful eyes
    May weep, but never see,
A night of memories and of sighs
    I consecrate to thee.
                              1806

Dirce

Stand close around, ye Stygian set,°
    With Dirce in one boat conveyed!
Or Charon,° seeing, may forget
    That he is old and she a shade
                              1831

On His Seventy-fifth Birthday

I strove with none, for none was worth my strife:
    Nature I loved, and next to Nature, Art:
I warmed both hands before the fire of Life;
    It sinks; and I am ready to depart.
                              1853

the plains a reference to the Lake School of
Wordsworth, Coleridge, and Landor's close
friend Southey
Ilissus river near Athens, mentioned in Plato's
Phaedrus
[Rose Aylmer, 1779–1800] an epitaph for a
young woman, befriended by Landor

sceptred race She was the daughter of a nobleman.
Stygian set the dead being carried across the
river Styx to Hades
Charon ferryman of the dead

Death Stands Above Me

Death stands above me, whispering low
    I know not what into my ear:
Of his strange language all I know
    Is, there is not a world of fear.

             1853

Poem

I cannot tell, not I, why she
Awhile so gracious, now should be
So grave: I cannot tell you why
The violet hangs its head awry.
It shall be culled,° it shall be worn,
In spite of every sign of scorn,
Dark look, and overhanging thorn.

             1846

Autumnal Song

Very true, the linnets sing
Sweetest in the leaves of spring:
You have found in all these leaves
That which changes and deceives,
And, to pine by sun or star,
Left them, false ones as they are.
But there be who walk beside
Autumn's, till they all have died,
And who lend a patient ear
10 To low notes from branches sere.°

             1846

Memory

The Mother of the Muses, we are taught,
Is Memory: she has left me; they remain,
And shake my shoulder, urging me to sing
About the summer days, my loves of old.

culled gathered, picked   **sere** withered, dry

Alas! alas! is all I can reply.
Memory has left with me that name alone,
Harmonious name, which other bards may sing,
But her bright image in my darkest hour
Comes back, in vain comes back, called or uncalled.
10   Forgotten are the names of visitors
Ready to press my hand but yesterday;
Forgotten are the names of earlier friends
Whose genial converse and glad countenance
Are fresh as ever to mine ear and eye;
To these, when I have written and besought
Remembrance of me, the word *Dear* alone
Hangs on the upper verge, and waits in vain.
A blessing wert thou, O oblivion,
If thy stream carried only weeds away,
20   But vernal° and autumnal flowers alike
It hurries down to wither on the strand.

                                    1863

To Wordsworth

Those who have laid the harp aside
    And turned to idler things,
From very restlessness have tried
    The loose and dusty strings,
And, catching back some favourite strain,
Run with it o'er the chords again.

But Memory is not a Muse,
    O Wordsworth! though 'tis said
They all descend from her, and use
10   To haunt her fountain-head:
That other men should work for me
In the rich mines of Poesie,

Pleases me better than the toil
    Of smoothing under hardened hand
With attic emery and oil,
    The shining point for Wisdom's wand,
Like those thou temperest 'mid the rills
Descending from thy native hills.

Without his governance, in vain
20   Manhood is strong, and youth is bold.
If oftentimes the o'erpiled strain

vernal spring

Clogs in the furnace, and grows cold
Beneath his pinions deep and frore,
And swells and melts and flows no more,

That is because the heat beneath
   Pants in its cavern poorly fed.
Life springs not from the couch of Death,
   Nor Muse nor Grace can raise the dead;
Unturned then let the mass remain,
30   Intractable to sun or rain.

A marsh where only flat leaves lie,
And showing but the broken sky,
Too surely is the sweetest lay
That wins the ear and wastes the day,
Where youthful Fancy pouts alone
And lets not Wisdom touch her zone.
He who would build his fame up high,
The rule and plummet must apply,
Nor say, 'I'll do what I have planned,'
40   Before he try if loam or sand
Be still remaining in the place
Delved for each polished pillar's base.
With skilful eye and fit device
Thou raisest every edifice,
Whether in sheltered vale it stand,
Or overlook the Dardan strand,°
Amid the cypresses that mourn
Laodameia's love forlorn.°

We both have run o'er half the space,
50   Listed for mortal's earthly race;
We both have crossed life's fervid line,
And other stars before us shine:
May they be bright and prosperous
As those that have been stars for us!
Our course by Milton's light was sped,
And Shakespeare shining overhead:
Chatting on deck was Dryden too,
The Bacon of the rhyming crew;°
None ever crossed our mystic sea
60   More richly stored with thought than he;
Though never tender nor sublime,
He wrestles with and conquers Time.
To learn my lore on Chaucer's knee,

Dardan strand Trojan shore
Laodameia's . . . forlorn Wordsworth wrote a strong classic poem, "Laodamia" (1814), which ends with the image of trees growing out of the tomb of Laodamia's husband, an emblem of her frustrated love for him; Landor discusses the poem in his "Southey and Porson," one of the *Imaginary Conversations*.
Bacon . . . crew a tribute to Dryden; to be the Sir Francis Bacon among poets is to excel in pithy expressions of prudence and wisdom

I left much prouder company;
Thee gentle Spenser fondly led,
But me he mostly sent to bed.
I wish them every joy above
That highly blessed spirits prove,
Save one: and that too shall be theirs,
70 But after many rolling years,
When 'mid their light thy light appears.
1833   1834

THOMAS LOVE PEACOCK

Song by Mr. Cypress°

There is a fever of the spirit,
  The brand of Cain's unresting doom,
Which in the lone dark souls that bear it
  Glows like the lamp in Tullia's tomb.°
Unlike the lamp, its subtle fire
  Burns, blasts, consumes its cell, the heart.
Till, one by one, hope, joy, desire,
  Like dreams of shadowy smoke depart.

When hope, love, life itself, are only
10   Dust—spectral memories—dead and cold—
The unfed fire burns bright and lonely,
  Like that undying lamp of old:
And by that drear illumination,
  Till time its clay-built home has rent,
Thought broods on feeling's desolation—
  The soul is its own monument.
                                        1818

The War-Song of Dinas Vawr°

The mountain sheep are sweeter,
But the valley sheep are fatter;
We therefore deemed it meeter

Song by Mr. Cypress (from the novel, *Nightmare Abbey*) a parody of Lord Byron. The fashionably melancholy young Mr. Cypress is about to go into exile, explaining that he has quarreled with his wife, and so is free of any further obligations to his country; he sings this lyric, so good a parody of *Childe Harold's Pilgrimage* that little in Byron's poem is worthy of it.
Tullia's tomb Cicero's daughter, who died still a young woman. Cicero, in remorse, attempted to make a shrine of her tomb; in the early 16th century a Roman tomb was discovered on the Appian Way with the embalmed, perfectly preserved body of a young woman, and a lamp; and it was taken, rather dubiously, to be Tullia's tomb.
The War-Song of Dinas Vawr (from the novel, *The Misfortunes of Elphin*) a minor Welsh king in King Arthur's time. As Peacock observed: this is "the quintessence of all war-songs that ever were written, and the sum and substance of all appetencies, tendencies, and consequences of military."

To carry off the latter,
We made an expedition;
We met a host, and quelled it;
We forced a strong position,
And killed the men who held it.

On Dyfed's° richest valley,
10   Where herds of kine were browsing,
We made a mighty sally,
To furnish our carousing.
Fierce warriors rushed to meet us;
We met them, and o'erthrew them:
They struggled hard to beat us;
But we conquered them, and slew them.

As we drove our prize at leisure.
The king marched forth to catch us;
His rage surpassed all measure,
20   But his people could not match us.
He fled to his hall-pillars;
And, ere our force we led off,
Some sacked his house and cellars,
While others cut his head off.

We there, in strife bewildr'ing,
Spilt blood enough to swim in:
We orphaned many children,
And widowed many women.
The eagles and the ravens
30   We glutted with our foemen;
The heroes and the cravens,
The spearmen and the bowmen.

We brought away from battle,
And much their land bemoaned them,
Two thousand head of cattle.
And the head of him who owned them:
Ednyfed, king of Dyfed,
His head was borne before us;
His wine and beasts supplied our feasts,
40   And his overthrow, our chorus.

1829

Dyfed's archaic name for region in Wales

JOHN CLARE

Pastoral Poesy

True poesy is not in words,
    But images that thoughts express,
By which the simplest hearts are stirred
    To elevated happiness.

Mere books would be but useless things
    Where none had taste or mind to read,
Like unknown lands where beauty springs
    And none are there to heed.

But poesy is a language meet,
10   And fields are every one's employ;
The wild flower 'neath the shepherd's feet
    Looks up and gives him joy;

A language that is ever green,
    That feelings unto all impart,
As hawthorn blossoms, soon as seen,
    Give May to every heart.

An image to the mind is brought,
    Where happiness enjoys
An easy thoughtlessness of thought
20   And meets excess of joys.

And such is poesy; its power
    May varied lights employ,
Yet to all minds it gives the dower
    Of self-creating joy.°

And whether it be hill or moor,
    I feel where'er I go
A silence that discourses more
    That any tongue can do.

Unruffled quietness hath made
30   A peace in every place,
And woods are resting in their shade
    Of social loneliness.

The storm, from which the shepherd turns
    To pull his beaver° down,
While he upon the heath sojourns,
    Which autumn pleaches° brown.

---

self-creating joy The poem echoes the dispute between Wordsworth's "Intimations of Immortality" ode and Coleridge's "Dejection: An Ode"; in phrases like this, Clare appears to take Coleridge's side.
beaver hat made of beaver's fur
pleaches bleaches

Is music, ay, and more indeed
    To those of musing mind
Who through the yellow woods proceed
40   And listen to the wind.

The poet in his fitful glee
    And fancy's many moods
Meets it as some strange melody,
    A poem of the woods,

And now a harp that flings around
    The music of the wind;
The poet often hears the sound
    When beauty fills the mind.

So would I my own mind employ,
50   And my own heart impress,
That poesy's self's a dwelling joy
    Of humble quietness.
      1824–32   1935

From Signs of Winter

The cat runs races with her tail. The dog
Leaps o'er the orchard hedge and knarls° the grass.
The swine run round and grunt and play with straw,
Snatching out hasty mouthfuls from the stack.
Sudden upon the elm-tree tops the crows
Unceremonious visit pays and croaks,
Then swops away. From mossy barn the owl
Bobs hasty out—wheels round and, scared as soon,
As hastily retires. The ducks grow wild
10 And from the muddy pond fly up and wheel
A circle round the village and soon tired
Plunge in the pond again. The maids in haste
Snatch from the orchard hedge the mizled° clothes
And laughing hurry in to keep them dry.

             · · ·

1832–35   1920

From Badger

When midnight comes a host of dogs and men
Go out and track the badger to his den,
And put a sack within the hole, and lie
Till the old grunting badger passes by.

knarls nibbles   **mizled** wet with drizzle

He comes and hears—they let the strongest loose.
The old fox hears the noise and drops the goose.
The poacher shoots and hurries from the cry,
And the old hare half wounded buzzes by.
They get a forkèd stick to bear him down
10   And clapt the dogs and bare him to the town,
And bait him all the day with many dogs,
And laugh and shout and fright the scampering hogs.
He runs along and bites at all he meets:
They shout and hollo down the noisy streets.

He turns about to face the loud uproar
And drives the rebels to their very door.
The frequent stone is hurled where 'er they go;
When badgers fight, and every one's a foe.
The dogs are clapt and urged to join the fray;
20   The badger turns and drives them all away.
Though scarcely half as big, dimute° and small,
He fights with dogs for hours and beats them all.
The heavy mastiff, savage in the fray,
Lies down and licks his feet and turns away.
The bulldog knows his match and waxes cold,
The badger grins and never leaves his hold.
He drives the crowd and follows at their heels
And bites them through—the drunkard swears and reels.

The frighted women take the boys away,
30   The blackguard laughs and hurries on the fray.
He tries to reach the woods, an awkward race,
But sticks and cudgels quickly stop the chase.
He turns agen and drives the noisy crowd
And beats the many dogs in noises loud.
He drives away and beats them every one,
And then they loose them all and set them on.
He falls as dead and kicked by boys and men,
Then starts and grins and drives the crowd agen;
Till kicked and torn and beaten out he lies
40   And leaves his hold and cackles, groans, and dies.

· · ·

1835–37   1920

To Wordsworth

Wordsworth I love, his books are like the fields,
    Not filled with flowers, but works of human kind;
The pleasant weed a fragrant pleasure yields,

dimute diminished

The briar and broomwood shaken by the wind,
The thorn and bramble o'er the water shoot
  A finer flower than gardens e'er gave birth,
The aged huntsman grubbing up the root—
  I love them all as tenants of the earth:
Where genius is, there often die the seeds;
  What critics throw away I love the more;
I love to stoop and look among the weeds,
  To find a flower I never knew before;
Wordsworth, go on—a greater poet be;
Merit will live, though parties disagree!
1840–41   1949

[Poem]

I feel I am, I only know I am,
  And plod upon the earth as dull and void:
Earth's prison chilled my body with its dram
  Of dullness, and my soaring thoughts destroyed.
I fled to solitudes from passion's dream,
  But strife pursued—I only know I am.
I was a being created in the race
  Of men, disdaining bounds of place and time,
A spirit that could travel o'er the space
  Of earth and heaven, like a thought sublime—
Tracing creation, like my Maker free,—
  A soul unshackled—like eternity:
Spurning earth's vain and soul debasing thrall—
But now I only know I am,—that's all.
after 1842   1935

Song [Secret Love]

I hid my love when young while I
Couldn't bear the buzzing of a fly;
I hid my love to my despite
Till I could not bear to look at light:
I dare not gaze upon her face
But left her memory in each place;
Where'er I saw a wild flower lie
I kissed and bade my love good-bye.

I met her in the greenest dells,
Where dewdrops pearl the wood bluebells;
The lost breeze kissed her bright blue eye,
The bee kissed and went singing by,

A sunbeam found a passage there,
A gold chain round her neck so fair;
As secret as the wild bee's song
She lay there all the summer long.

I hid my love in field and town
Till e'en the breeze would knock me down;
The bees seemed singing ballads o'er,
20   The fly's buss° turned a lion's roar;
And even silence found a tongue,
To haunt me all the summer long;
The riddle nature could not prove
Was nothing else but secret love.
after 1842   1920

Hesperus°

Hesperus! the day is gone,
Soft falls the silent dew,
A tear is now on many a flower
And heaven lives in you.

Hesperus! the evening mild
Falls round us soft and sweet.
'Tis like the breathings of a child
When day and evening meet.

Hesperus! the closing flower
10   Sleeps on the dewy ground,
While dews fall in a silent shower
And heaven breathes around.

Hesperus! thy twinkling ray
Beams in the blue of heaven,
And tells the traveller on his way
That Earth shall be forgiven!
after 1842   1949

Written in Prison°

I envy e'en the fly its gleams of joy
In the green woods; from being but a boy
Among the vulgar and the lowly bred,
I envied e'en the hare her grassy bed.
Inured to strife and hardship from a child,

buss a kiss, and also a variant of "buzz"   **Prison** when Clare was confined in an asylum
Hesperus the Evening Star

I traced with lonely step the desert wild,
Sighed o'er bird pleasures, but no nest destroyed,
With pleasure felt the singing they enjoyed,
Saw nature smile on all and shed no tears,
10   A slave through ages, though a child in years—
The mockery and scorn of those more old,
An Aesop° in the world's extended fold.
The fly I envy settling in the sun
On the green leaf, and wish my goal was won.
after 1842   1935

The Maid o' the West

In the mountains o' the west
Lives the girl I love the best
With her red rose cheeks and her coal black hair,
Her face is like the rose and her rose breast the lily fair.
In the mountains of the west lives the girl I love the best,
O there's nothing half so sweet as Love, and fair.

In the lands not made of clay
Where the sun ne'er sets away,
But shineth through the midnight bright and fair,
10   I love the lassie best wi' the bright auburn hair,
And she liveth in the land that knoweth no decay,
And the maid I love the best is for ever bright and fair.

The birds sing on the clouds in that eternal land,
Jewels and siller° are they a', and gouden° is the sand.
The sun is one vast world of fire that burneth a' to-day,
And night wi' hells of darkness for ever keeps away.
And dearly I love the queen o' that bright land,
The lily flowers o' woman that meeteth no decay.

Her eyes are springs of light
20   And the blue veins in the white
Of her bosom, may love there
For ever bright and ever fair.
How beautiful she seems to mortal sight,
The white robed maiden with the auburn hair.

And lips of amaranth° and eyes of light
And cheeks the rose of heaven as bright,
Angel of heaven—Maiden o' the West—
She is the maiden that I love the best.

Aesop 6th-century B.C. teller of moralized fables   **amaranth** imaginary purple flower that never
siller silver   fades
gouden golden

Her very eyes are suns o' living light,
30   And dear I love the lady o' the west.
after 1842   1949

The Peasant Poet

He loved the brook's soft sound,
   The swallow swimming by,
He loved the daisy-covered ground,
   The cloud-bedappled sky.
To him the dismal storm appeared
   The very voice of God;
And when the evening rock was reared
   Stood Moses with his rod.
And everything his eyes surveyed,
10   The insects i' the brake,
Were creatures God Almighty made,
   He loved them for his sake—
A silent man in life's affairs,
   A thinker from a boy,
A peasant in his daily cares,
   A poet in his joy.
after 1842 1920

Poets Love Nature

Poets love nature, and themselves are love,
The scorn of fools, and mock of idle pride.
The vile in nature worthless deeds approve,
They court the vile and spurn all good beside.
Poets love nature; like the calm of heaven,
Her gifts like heaven's love spread far and wide:
In all her works there are no signs of leaven,
Sorrow abashes from her simple pride.
Her flowers, like pleasures, have their season's birth,
10   And bloom through regions here below;
They are her very scriptures upon earth,
And teach us simple mirth where'er we go.
Even in prison they can solace me,
For where they bloom God is, and I am free.
after 1842   1873

I Am°

I am: yet what I am none cares or knows;
   My friends forsake me like a memory lost;
I am the self-consumer of my woes—
   They rise and vanish in oblivion's host,
Like shadows in love, frenzied, stifled throes:—
And yet I am, and live—like vapours tost

Into the nothingness of scorn and noise,
   Into the living sea of waking dreams,
Where there is neither sense of life or joys,
10   But the vast shipwreck of my life's esteems;
Even the dearest, that I love the best
Are strange—nay, rather stranger than the rest.

I long for scenes, where man hath never trod,
   A place where woman never smiled or wept
There to abide with my Creator God,
   And sleep as I in childhood sweetly slept,
Untroubling and untroubled where I lie,
The grass below, above, the vaulted sky.
1844?   1865

An Invite to Eternity

Wilt thou go with me, sweet maid
Say, maiden, wilt thou go with me
Through the valley depths of shade,
Of night and dark obscurity,
Where the path hath lost its way,
Where the sun forgets the day,
Where there's nor life nor light to see,
Sweet maiden, wilt thou go with me?

Where stones will turn to flooding streams,
10 Where plains will rise like ocean waves,
Where life will fade like visioned dreams
And mountains darken into caves,
Say, maiden, wilt thou go with me
Through this sad non-identity,
Where parents live and are forgot,
And sisters live and know us not?

Say, maiden, wilt thou go with me
In this strange death of life to be,

I Am perhaps an ironical reflection of Jehovah's "I am That I am," Exodus 3:14; perhaps even a reaction to Coleridge's definition of the Primary Imagination in *Biographia Literaria* XIII

To live in death and be the same
20   Without this life, or home, or name,
At once to be and not to be—
That was and is not—yet to see
Things pass like shadows and the sky
Above, below, around us lie?

The land of shadows wilt thou trace,
And look, nor know each other's face;
The present mixed with reasons gone,
And past and present all as one?
Say, maiden, can thy life be led
30   To join the living with the dead?
Then trace thy footsteps on with me;
We're wed to one eternity.
1844?   1920

A Vision

I lost the love of heaven above,
    I spurned the lust of earth below,
I felt the sweets of fancied love,
    And hell itself my only foe.

I lost earth's joys, but felt the glow
    Of heaven's flame abound in me,
Till loveliness and I did grow
    The bard of immortality.

I loved but woman fell away,
10   I hid me from her faded flame,
I snatched the sun's eternal ray
    And wrote till earth was but a name.

In every language upon earth,
    On every shore, o'er every sea,
I gave my name immortal birth
    And kept my spirit with the free.
    1844   1924

Clock-a-Clay°

In the cowslip peeps I lie
Hidden from the buzzing fly,
While green grass beneath me lies
Pearled wi' dew like fishes' eyes.

Clock-a-Clay the ladybird

Here I lie, a clock-a-clay,
Waiting for the time o' day.

While grassy forests quake surprise,
And the wild wind sobs and sighs,
My gold home rocks as like to fall
10   On its pillar green and tall;
When the parting rain drives by
Clock-a-clay keeps warm and dry.

Day by day and night by night
All the week I hide from sight.
In the cowslip peeps I lie,
In rain and dew still warm and dry.
Day and night, and night and day,
Red, black-spotted clock-a-clay.

My home it shakes in wind and shows
20   Pale green pillar topped wi' flowers,
Bending at the wild wind's breath
Till I touch the grass beneath.
Here I live, lone clock-a-clay,
Watching for the time of day.
1848?   1873

Fragment: Language Has Not the Power

Language has not the power to speak what love indites:
The Soul lies buried in the ink that writes.
                    1950

Bird's Nests

'Tis spring, warm glows the south,
Chaffinch carries the moss in his mouth
To filbert hedges all day long,
And charms the poet with his beautiful song;
The wind blows bleak o'er the sedgy fen,
But warm the sun shines by the little wood,
Where the old cow at her leisure chews her cud.
1863   1935

GEORGE DARLEY

It Is Not Beauty I Demand°

It is not Beauty I demand,
    A crystal brow, the moon's despair,
Nor the snow's daughter, a white hand,
    Nor mermaid's yellow pride of hair.

Tell me not of your starry eyes,
    Your lips that seem on roses fed,
Your breasts where Cupid trembling lies,
    Nor sleeps for kissing of his bed.

A bloomy pair of vermeil cheeks,
10   Like Hebe's° in her ruddiest hours,
A breath that softer music speaks
    Than summer winds a-wooing flowers.

These are but gauds; nay, what are lips?
    Coral beneath the ocean-stream,
Whose brink when your adventurer sips
    Full oft he perisheth on them.

And what are cheeks but ensigns oft
    That wave hot youth to fields of blood?
Did Helen's breast though ne'er so soft,
20   Do Greece or Ilium any good?

Eyes can with baleful ardour burn,
    Poison can breath that erst perfumed,
There's many a white hand holds an urn
    With lovers' hearts to dust consumed.

For crystal brows—there's naught within,
    They are but empty cells for pride;
He who the Syren's hair would win
    Is mostly strangled in the tide.°

Give me, instead of beauty's bust,°
30   A tender heart, a loyal mind,
Which with temptation I could trust,
    Yet never linked with error find.

One in whose gentle bosom I
    Could pour my secret heart of woes,

It Is Not Beauty I Demand This stately lyric has something of a 17th-century flavor, though its High Romantic vision of love should have warned the anthologist Francis Turner Palgrave, who included it in *The Golden Treasury* (where it is still so to be found) as a 17th-century lyric, sandwiched in between poems of Milton and Carew under the Palgrave-invented title "The Loveliness of Love."
Hebe's daughter of Zeus and Hera, and herself goddess of youth; she married Heracles
For crystal . . . tide a stanza, glorious in itself, that should have warned Palgrave
beauty's bust possibly a bust of Pallas Athena or of Venus

Like the care-burthened honey-fly
　　That hides his murmurs in the rose.

My earthly comforter! whose love
　　So indefeasible° might be,
That when my spirit won above
40　　Hers could not stay for sympathy.

　　　　　　　　　　　　　1828

The Phoenix°

I

O blest unfabled Incense Tree,
That burns in glorious Araby,
With red scent chalicing° the air,
Till earth-life grow Elysian there!

Half buried to her flaming breast
In this bright tree, she makes her nest,
Hundred-sunned Phoenix! when she must
Crumble at length to hoary dust!

Her gorgeous death-bed! her rich pyre
10　Burnt up with aromatic fire!
Her urn, sight high from spoiler men!
Her birthplace when self-born again!

The mountainless green wilds among,
Here ends she her unechoing song!
With amber tears and odorous sighs
Mourned by the desert where she dies!

II

Laid like the young fawn mossily
In sun-green vales of Araby,
I woke hard by the Phoenix tree
20　That with shadeless boughs flamed over me;
And upward called by a dumb cry
With moonbroad orbs of wonder, I
Beheld the immortal Bird on high
Glassing the great sun in her eye.
Stedfast she gazed upon his fire,
Still her destroyer and her sire!
As if to his her soul of flame
Had flown already, whence it came;

indefeasible not to be forfeited, never to be voided
The Phoenix (from the long poem *Nepenthe*) a legendary bird of great size and beauty, which after hundreds of years would burn up; from its ashes another Phoenix would arise, or perhaps the same one. The association with the sun is traditional and not Darley's invention.
chalicing as in the Eucharist, where the chalice is the Communion cup

Like those that sit and glare so still,
30   Intense with their death struggle, till
We touch, and curdle at their chill!—
But breathing yet while she doth burn,
    The deathless Daughter of the sun!
Slowly to crimson embers turn
    The beauties of the brightsome one.
O'er the broad nest her silver wings
Shook down their wasteful glitterings;
Her brinded° neck high-arched in air
Like a small rainbow faded there;
40   But brighter glowed her plumy crown
Mouldering to golden ashes down;
With fume of sweet woods, to the skies,
Pure as a Saint's adoring sighs,
Warm as a prayer in Paradise,
Her life-breath rose in sacrifice!
The while with shrill triumphant tone
Sounding aloud, aloft, alone
Ceaseless her joyful deathwail she
Sang to departing Araby!
50   Deep melancholy wonder drew
Tears from my heartspring at that view;
Like cresset° shedding its last flare
Upon some wistful mariner,
The Bird, fast blending with the sky,
Turned on me her dead-gazing eye
Once—and as surge to shallow spray
Sank down to vapoury dust away!

      III
O, fast her amber blood doth flow
    From the heart-wounded Incense Tree,
60   Fast as earth's deep-embosomed woe
    In silent rivulets to the sea!

Beauty may weep her fair first-born,
    Perchance in as resplendent tears,
Such golden dewdrops bow the corn
    When the stern sickleman appears.

But oh! such perfume to a bower
    Never allured sweet-seeking bee,
As to sip fast that nectarous shower
    A thirstier minstrel drew in me!
        1835

brinded streaked or spotted, with tawny color   cresset iron basket with burning light in it

HARTLEY COLERIDGE
Dedicatory Sonnet to S. T. Coleridge

Father, and Bard revered! to whom I owe,
Whate'er it be, my little art of numbers,
Thou, in thy night-watch o'er my cradled slumbers,
Didst meditate the verse that lives to show
(And long shall live, when we alike are low),
Thy prayer how ardent, and thy hope how strong,
That I should learn of Nature's self the song,
The lore which none but Nature's pupils know.

The prayer was heard: I 'wandered like a breeze,'°
10 By mountain brooks and solitary meres,
And gathered there the shapes and phantasies
Which, mixed with passions of my sadder years,
Composed this book. If good therein there be,
That good, my sire, I dedicate to thee.
1832   1833

THOMAS HOOD
Ode°

Autumn

I

I saw old Autumn in the misty morn
Stand shadowless like Silence, listening
To silence, for no lonely bird would sing
Into his hollow ear from woods forlorn,
Nor lowly hedge nor solitary thorn;
Shaking his languid locks all dewy bright
With tangled gossamer that fell by night,
     Pearling his coronet of golden corn.

II

Where are the songs of Summer?°—With the sun,
10 Oping the dusky eyelids of the south,
Till shade and silence waken up as one,
And Morning sings with a warm odorous mouth.
Where are the merry birds?—Away, away,
On panting wings through the inclement skies,
     Lest owls should prey

'wandered . . . breeze' See the beautiful prayer in "Frost at Midnight," ll. 54–64.
Ode a deliberate and beautiful elaboration upon, and tribute to, Keats's great ode "To Autumn," with echoes also of the "Ode to Psyche" and "Ode on Melancholy"
songs of Summer See "Where are the songs of Spring?" in "To Autumn," l. 23.

Undazzled at noonday,
And tear with horny beak their lustrous eyes.

III

Where are the blooms of Summer?—In the west,
Blushing their last to the last sunny hours,
20   When the mild Eve by sudden Night is prest
Like tearful Proserpine,° snatched from her flowers
    To a most gloomy breast.
Where is the pride of Summer,—the green prime,—
The many, many leaves all twinkling?—Three
    On the mossed elm; three on the naked lime
Trembling,—and one upon the old oak tree!
    Where is the Dryads' immortality?°
Gone into mournful cypress and dark yew,
Or wearing the long gloomy Winter through
30   In the smooth holly's green eternity.

IV

The squirrel gloats on his accomplished hoard,
The ants have brimmed their garners with ripe grain,
    And honey bees have stored
The sweets of Summer in their luscious cells;
The swallows all have winged across the main;
But here the Autumn melancholy dwells,
And sighs her tearful spells,
Amongst the sunless shadows of the plain.
    Alone, alone,
40   Upon a mossy stone,
She sits and reckons up the dead and gone
With the last leaves for a love-rosary,
Whilst all the withered world looks drearily,
Like a dim picture of the drownèd past
In the hushed mind's mysterious far away,
Doubtful what ghostly thing will steal the last
Into the distance, grey upon the grey.

V

O go and sit with her, and be o'ershaded
Under the languid downfall of her hair:
50   She wears a coronal of flowers faded
Upon her forehead, and a face of care;
There is enough of withered everywhere
To make her bower,—and enough of gloom;
There is enough of sadness to invite,
If only for the rose that died,—whose doom

Proserpine involuntary queen of Hades, ab- Dryads' immortality See "Ode to Psyche," l. 57.
ducted by Pluto

Is Beauty's,°—she that with the living bloom
Of conscious cheeks most beautifies the light;
There is enough of sorrowing, and quite
Enough of bitter fruits the earth doth bear,—
60   Enough of chilly droppings for her bowl;
Enough of fear and shadowy despair,
To frame her cloudy prison° for the soul!
1822

THOMAS LOVELL BEDDOES
Lines°
Written in a Blank Leaf of the Prometheus Unbound

Write it in gold—a Spirit of the sun,
An Intellect ablaze with heavenly thoughts,
A Soul with all the dews of pathos shining,
Odorous with love, and sweet to silent woe
With the dark glories of concentrate song,
Was sphered in mortal earth. Angelic sounds
Alive with panting thoughts sunned the dim world.
The bright creations of an human heart
Wrought magic in the bosoms of mankind.
10   A flooding summer burst on Poetry;
Of which the crowning sun, the night of beauty,
The dancing showers, the birds whose anthems wild
Note after note unbind the enchanted leaves
Of breaking buds, eve, and the flow of dawn,
Were centred and condensed in his one name
As in a providence—and that was SHELLEY.
1822   1851

Song°

Old Adam, the carrion crow,
  The old crow of Cairo;
He sat in the shower, and let it flow
Under his tail and over his crest;
    And through every feather
    Leaked the wet weather;
And the bough swung under his nest;
For his beak it was heavy with marrow.
  Is that the wind dying? O no;

If . . . Beauty's See "Ode on Melancholy,"
l. 21.
cloudy prison See "Ode on Melancholy," l. 30
Lines Beddoes wrote this in his copy of Pro-

metheus Unbound when news reached him that
Shelley had drowned.
Song sung by Isbrand, the revenger disguised
as a court jester in the play Death's Jest-Book

10   It's only two devils, that blow
        Through a murderer's bones, to and fro,
            In the ghosts' moonshine.

        Ho! Eve, my grey carrion wife,
            When we have supped on king's marrow,
        Where shall we drink and make merry our life?
        Our nest it is queen Cleopatra's skull,
                'Tis cloven and cracked,
                And battered and hacked,
        But with tears of blue eyes it is full:
20   Let us drink then, my raven of Cairo.
            Is that the wind dying? O no;
            It's only two devils, that blow
            Through a murderer's bones, to and fro,
                In the ghosts' moonshine.
                1825?   1850

The New Cecilia°

Whoever has heard of St. Gingo°
    Must know that the gipsy
    He married was tipsy
    Every day of her life with old Stingo.°

And after the death of St. Gingo
    The wonders he did do
    The incredulous widow
    Denied with unladylike lingo:

'For St. Gingo a fig's and a feather-end!°
10   He no more can work wonder
    Than a clyster-pipe° thunder
    Or I sing a psalm with my nether-end.'

As she said it, her breakfast beginning on
    A tankard of home-brewed inviting ale,
    Lo! the part she was sitting and sinning on
    Struck the old hundredth° up like a nightingale.

Loud as psophia° in an American forest or
    The mystic Memnonian marble in
    A desert at daybreak,° that chorister
20   Breathed forth his Aeolian warbling.

Cecilia St. Cecilia was patroness of music.
St. Gingo a saint canonized by Beddoes
Stingo particularly strong ale
feather-end She affirms that the good saint
lacked an adequate member; a "fig" here is a
small, contemptible thing or, as she nastily adds,
a "feather-end."

clyster-pipe an enema
old hundredth Psalm 100, "Make a joyful noise
unto the lord . . . "
psophia a wise bird
The mystic . . . daybreak the statue of Memnon at Thebes, Egypt, which sang in the dawn-
light

That creature seraphic and spherical,
Her firmament,° kept up its clerical
  Thanksgivings, until she did aged die
Cooing and praising and chirping alert in
Her petticoat, swung like a curtain
  Let down o'er the tail of a Tragedy.

Therefore, Ladies, repent and be sedulous°
 In praising your lords, lest, ah! well a day!
Such judgement befall the incredulous
30 And your latter ends melt into melody.
  1829–49   1935

Song of the Stygian Naiades°

   What do you think the mermaids of the Styx were singing as
   I watched them bathing the other day—

I

Proserpine° may pull her flowers,
 Wet with dew or wet with tears,
 Red with anger, pale with fears;
Is it any fault of ours,
If Pluto be an amorous king
 And come home nightly, laden
Underneath his broad bat-wing
 With a gentle earthly maiden?
Is it so, Wind, is it so?
10 All that I and you do know
Is that we saw fly and fix
    'Mongst the flowers and reeds of Styx,
      Yesterday,
Where the Furies made their hay
For a bed of tiger cubs,
A great fly of Beelzebub's,°
The bee of hearts, which mortals name
Cupid, Love, and Fie for shame.

II

Proserpine may weep in rage,
20 But ere I and you have done
 Kissing, bathing in the sun,
What I have in yonder cage,
 She shall guess and ask in vain,
 Bird or serpent, wild or tame;

But if Pluto does't again,
It shall sing out loud his shame.
　What hast caught then? What hast caught?
Nothing but a poet's thought,
　Which so light did fall and fix
30　'Mongst the flowers and reeds of Styx,
　　　　Yesterday,
Where the Furies made their hay
For a bed of tiger cubs,
A great fly of Beelzebub's,
The bee of hearts, which mortals name
Cupid, Love, and Fie for shame.
1835?　　　　　　　1851

SAMUEL PALMER

Shoreham: Twilight Time°

And now the trembling light
Glimmers behind the little hills and corn,
Lingering as loth to part; yet part thou must
And though than open day far pleasing more
(Ere yet the fields and pearlèd cups of flowers
　　　Twinkle in the parting light;)
Thee night shall hide, sweet visionary gleam
That softly lookest through the rising dew;
　　　Till all like silver bright,
10　　　The faithful witness, pure and white,
　　　Shall look o'er yonder grassy hill,
　　　At this village, safe and still.
　　　All is safe and all is still,
　　　Save what noise the watch-dog makes
　　　Or the shrill cock the silence breaks.
　　　Now and then—
　　　And now and then—
　　　Hark! Once again,
　　　The wether's° bell
20　　　To us doth tell
Some little stirring in the fold.
Methinks the lingering dying ray
Of twilight time, doth seem more fair,
And lights the soul up more than day
When wide-spread sultry sunshines are:
Yet all is right and all most fair,
For thou, dear God, has formèd all;
Thou deckest every little flower,

Shoreham: Twilight Time Palmer wrote a few poems and some Virgilian translations; this pastoral lyric is a remarkable description of the world of many of his best paintings, the world his master Blake called Beulah or Innocence. wether's gelded male sheep's

Thou girdest every planet ball,
30 And mark'st when sparrows fall.
1825   1960

THOMAS WADE
The Winter Shore

A mighty change it is, and ominous
Of mightier, sleeping in Eternity.
The bare cliffs seem half-sinking in the sand,
Heaved high by winter seas; and their white crowns,
Struck by the whirlwinds, shed their hair-like snow
Upon the desolate air. Sullen and black,
Their huge backs rearing far along the waves,
The rocks lie barrenly, which there have lain,
Revealed, or hidden, from immemorial time;
10 And o'er them hangs a sea-weed drapery,
Like some old Triton's° hair, beneath which lurk
Myriads of crowned shell-fish, things whose life,
Like a celled hermit's, seemeth profitless.
Vast slimy masses hardened into stone
Rise smoothly from the surface of the Deep,
Each with a hundred thousand fairy cells
Perforate, like a honeycomb, and, cup-like,
Filled with the sea's salt crystal—the soft beds
Once of so many pebbles, thence divorced
20 By the continual waters, as they grew
Slowly to rock. The bleak shore is o'erspread
With sea-weeds green and sere, curled and dishevelled
As they were mermaids' tresses, wildly torn
For some sea-sorrow. The small mountain-stream,
Swollen to a river, laves the quivering beach,
And flows in many channels to the sea
Between high shingly banks, that shake for ever.
The solitary sea-bird, like a spirit,
Balanced in air upon his crescent wings,
30 Hangs floating in the winds, as he were lord
Of the drear vastness round him, and alone
Natured for such dominion. Spring and Summer
And stored Autumn, of their liveries
Here is no vestige; Winter, tempest-robed,
In gloomy grandeur o'er the hills and seas
Reigneth omnipotent.
1835

Triton's minor sea god; see Wordsworth's sonnet
"The World Is Too Much with Us"

Romantic Prose

That prose and poetry are of their natures antithetical to each other is an old and stubborn idea. The extremity of their presumed difference is suggested by part of the definition of prose given by the *Oxford English Dictionary*: "Plain, simple, matter of fact (and hence) dull or commonplace, expression, quality, spirit, etc. (The opposite of Poetry.)" It was one of the achievements of the Romantic Movement that it demonstrated that prose need not be restricted to mere practical purposes, that, so far from being necessarily plain, simple, and matter of fact, let alone dull or commonplace, it might be (to quote the *OED*'s definition of one meaning of poetry) "the expression or embodiment of beautiful or elevated thought, imagination, or feeling in language adapted to stir the imagination and emotions." Wordsworth's Preface to *Lyrical Ballads* (see below), which said that between the language of prose and of poetry there was no essential dissimilarity and that prose can be just as poetical as poetry itself, may be thought of as the trumpet which brought down the wall separating the two modes of expression.

Walter Pater, in his essay *Style*, says of what he calls "imaginative prose" that it is the "special art of the modern world." The three great practitioners of the new art, Hazlitt, Lamb, and De Quincey, would have wished to qualify Pater's temporal characterization. They saw themselves as being in a line of descent from a great, though in their time discredited, tradition, and they claimed one or another degree of kinship with the prose masters of the seventeenth century. The lucid rhetoric of the eighteenth century had a greater effect upon the shape of their sentences than is commonly said, but they took their conscious inspiration from the textured and adumbrative style of the writers of an earlier time, from the grave sonorities of John Milton, Jeremy Taylor, and Sir Thomas Browne, or from the lighter manner of Izaak Walton and Charles Cotton. Yet of course Pater was right in suggesting that they had brought a new art into being. Of the great trio, De Quincey was the most overtly intentional and theoretical in his conception of prose. He took seriously an idea to which poets had often given a merely conventional utterance, that music is the most affecting and most nearly autonomous of the arts, and envisaged an "impassioned prose" which would rival music in the subtlety of its evocations and the hypnotic power of its cadences. Hazlitt and Lamb were neither so explicit nor so elaborate in their intentions, but their artistry in the medium of prose was scarcely less conscious. They loved it for itself, as poets love verse, and they cherished it as the means by which, to paraphrase Pater, they might express not mere fact but their imaginative sense of fact—fact as they themselves experienced it. They were committed to the personal authority of their vision perhaps even more intensely than were the Romantic poets.

If, as Pater says, "imaginative prose" is indeed to be regarded as "the special art of the modern world," its present status lends support to the idea advanced by some critics and cultural historians that the modern world has come to an end and that we are now in what is coming to be called the "post-modern" era. Imaginative prose was indeed a pre-eminent genre of the nineteenth century, both in its Romantic and in its Victorian phases. The great Victorian practitioners of the art, Carlyle, Ruskin, Newman, Dickens, Arnold (sometimes), and Pater himself, are not in all ways continuous with the Romantic prose writers, but each of them, equally with his predecessors, was concerned to shape a prose that would express not mere fact but his sense of it, what Pater calls "his peculiar intuition of the world." Eventually, however, such prose came to seem less appropriate to serious intellectual and artistic purposes than it had formerly been. After a certain point it becomes impossible to discover in the utterances of any notable literary or intellectual figures a concern with a prose which will be an object of interest in itself because it so well expresses the writer's peculiar intuition of the world in language adapted to stir the imagination and the emotions. This is not to say that we are not responsive to peculiar intuitions of the world or that we resist having our imagination and emotions stirred, but only that, for reasons which are numerous and complex, our culture has decided not to trust or take pleasure in such use of language as avows the writer's conscious purpose of communicating his peculiar intuition and his delight in doing so.

We have, in short, a different relation to the written word than that which prevailed among the Romantics. Not merely the work of the three conscious prose artists, Lamb, Hazlitt and De Quincey, but all the examples of Romantic prose included in this volume, whatever their genre, suggest that their words had been put on paper with a peculiar eagerness and urgency, as if the act of writing, like the act of love, was the happy gratuitous expression of vital existence. Even Wordsworth, who disliked the physical art of writing and avoided prose composition because it had to be carried on with pen in hand, when he got down to it displayed in the undertaking a gusto—to use that word of Hazlitt's so much liked by Keats—which no critic of our day can match. For Keats in his letters or for Dorothy Wordsworth in her journals to describe an experience, he with his brilliance, she with her modest immediacy, is as natural as having the experience, is, indeed, part of having it. For all these writers the written word has what Wordsworth said nature itself had, "a breathing life."

WILLIAM WORDSWORTH
1770–1850

Preface to Lyrical Ballads (1802)

When Wordsworth and Coleridge published *Lyrical Ballads* in 1798, they prefaced it with a brief "Advertisement" written by Wordsworth. This peremptory document puts the reader on notice that the poems he is about to encounter will probably not suit his taste and instructs him how to revise his settled standards of judgment with a view to finding pleasure in the poems, as it is right that he should. He is to understand that the majority of the poems were written as "experiments," the purpose of which is to "ascertain how far the language of conversation in the lower and middle classes of society is adapted to the purpose of poetic pleasure." This being the case, he might wonder whether what he is reading is rightly to be called poetry, for the chances are that he takes the defining characteristic of poetry to be "the gaudiness and inane phraseology of many modern writers." He is advised that he can rescue himself from this ignorant opinion only by recognizing that poetry is a difficult subject and requires much severe thought.

In 1800, when a second edition of *Lyrical Ballads* was called for, Wordsworth developed the position taken in the "Advertisement" to make the famous Preface. He revised and expanded it in 1802, the most notable of his additions being the eloquent passage which describes the nature and function of the poet.

The Preface is less peremptory than the "Advertisement" only because it consents to give reasons for its imperatives. Even so, its voice rings with a confident and uncompromising militancy which is unique in the history of criticism, as if a rebel general were announcing the terms on which he will accept the leadership of the state whose corrupt government he is about to overthrow. Toward the government itself, the poets and critics who have misled the people's taste, it takes the tone of Cromwell to the Rump Parliament: "It is not fit that you should sit here any longer! . . . you shall now give place to better men." To the misguided people its language is courteous though stern, for truth is truth and not to be paltered with, and the Preface is firm in its intention that, under the new poetic dispensation, the public shall be given, in Cromwell's phrase, "not what they want but what is good for them."

That poetry is good for people is not a new idea, but never before has so much potentiality of beneficence been claimed for it, and with so much moral fervor. One of the elements of the Preface which make it, of all great documents of literary criticism, the most dramatically urgent is its explicit sense of cultural crisis. Like Rousseau before him, Wordsworth is conscious of something new that has come into society which tends to deteriorate the mind, to "blunt its discriminatory powers," "to unfit it for all voluntary exertion," and thus to "reduce it to a state of almost savage torpor." In specifying the "multitude of causes unknown to former times" which lead to this state of affairs—among them the crowding of men in cities and the ennui of urban work which produces a craving for excitement all too readily gratified by sensational news and entertainment—Wordsworth is responding to the early stages of that mass society and mass culture which we recognize as among the defining characteristics of modern life. It is as a countervailing force against the malign effects of this development—they are manifestly political as well as individual and personal—that Wordsworth defines the nature and function of poetry. In his own way he is describing the condition of human existence which nowadays preoccupies our thought under the name of "alienation." The informing idea of Wordsworth's theory of poetry, as of his practice, is that poetry has the power to prevent and reverse modern man's alienation, his estrangement from himself, from his fellow men, and from the universe. To the enforcement of this idea and to the explication of the particular means by which the poet realizes it, the Preface is devoted.

In a letter of 1802, Coleridge says of the Preface that it is "half a child of my own Brain," arising out of conversations between him and Wordsworth which were so frequent "that we could scarcely either of us perhaps positively say, which first started any particular thought." Yet Coleridge goes on to assert that he is "far from going all lengths with Wordsworth," that, indeed, he rather suspects "that somewhere or other there is a radical difference in our theoretical opinions respecting Poetry." What these differences were Coleridge was to make plain fourteen years later in Chapters XVII through XXII of *Biographia Literaria* (see below).

Preface to Lyrical Ballads (1802)

The first volume of these poems has already been submitted to general perusal. It was published, as an experiment, which, I hoped,[1] might be of some use to ascertain, how far, by fitting to metrical arrangement a selection of the real language of men in a state of vivid sensation, that sort of pleasure and that quantity of pleasure may be imparted, which a poet may rationally endeavour to impart.

I had formed no very inaccurate estimate of the probable effect of those poems: I flattered myself that they who should be pleased with them would read them with more than common pleasure: and, on the other hand, I was well aware, that by those who should dislike them they would be read with more than common dislike. The result has differed from my expectation in this only, that I have pleased a greater number, than I ventured to hope I should please.

For the sake of variety, and from a consciousness of my own weakness, I was induced to request the assistance of a friend, who furnished me with the poems of the *Ancient Mariner*, the 'Foster-Mother's Tale,' the *Nightingale*, and the poem entitled *Love*. I should not, however, have requested this assistance, had I not believed that the poems of my friend would in a great measure have the same tendency as my own, and that, though there would be found a difference, there would be found no discordance in the colours of our style; as our opinions on the subject of poetry do almost entirely coincide.

Several of my friends are anxious for the success of these poems from a belief, that, if the views with which they were composed were indeed realized, a class of poetry would be produced, well adapted to interest mankind permanently, and not unimportant in the multiplicity, and in the quality of its moral relations: and on this account they have advised me to prefix a systematic defence of the theory, upon which the poems were written. But I was unwilling to undertake the task, because I knew that on this occasion the reader would look coldly upon my arguments, since I might be suspected of having been principally influenced by the selfish and foolish hope of *reasoning* him into an approbation of these particular poems: and I was still more unwilling to undertake the task, because, adequately to display my opinions, and fully to enforce my arguments, would require a space wholly disproportionate to the nature of a preface. For to treat the subject with the clearness and coherence, of which I believe it susceptible, it would be necessary to give a full account

1. Wordsworth speaks as if *Lyrical Ballads* was his alone, a not unjustifiable view since all the poems that were added to the second edition of the volume were his.

of the present state of the public taste in this country, and to determine how far this taste is healthy or depraved; which, again, could not be determined, without pointing out, in what manner language and the human mind act and react on each other, and without retracing the revolutions, not of literature alone, but likewise of society itself. I have therefore altogether declined to enter regularly upon this defence; yet I am sensible, that there would be some impropriety in abruptly obtruding upon the public, without a few words of introduction, poems so materially different from those, upon which general approbation is at present bestowed.

It is supposed, that by the act of writing in verse an author makes a formal engagement that he will gratify certain known habits of association; that he not only thus apprizes the reader that certain classes of ideas and expressions will be found in his book, but that others will be carefully excluded. This exponent or symbol held forth by metrical language must in different eras of literature have excited very different expectations: for example, in the age of Catullus, Terence, and Lucretius and that of Statius or Claudian; [2] and in our own country, in the age of Shakespeare and Beaumont and Fletcher, and that of Donne and Cowley, or Dryden, or Pope. I will not take upon me to determine the exact import of the promise which by the act of writing in verse an author, in the present day, makes to his reader; but I am certain, it will appear to many persons that I have not fulfilled the terms of an engagement thus voluntarily contracted. They who have been accustomed to the gaudiness and inane phraseology of many modern writers, if they persist in reading this book to its conclusion, will, no doubt, frequently have to struggle with feelings of strangeness and awkwardness: they will look round for poetry, and will be induced to inquire by what species of courtesy these attempts can be permitted to assume that title. I hope therefore the reader will not censure me, if I attempt to state what I have proposed to myself to perform; and also (as far as the limits of a preface will permit), to explain some of the chief reasons which have determined me in the choice of my purpose: that at least he may be spared any unpleasant feeling of disappointment, and that I myself may be protected from the most dishonourable accusation which can be brought against an author, namely, that of an indolence which prevents him from endeavouring to ascertain what is his duty, or, when his duty is ascertained, prevents him from performing it.[3]

The principal object, then, which I proposed to myself in these poems was to choose incidents and situations from common life and to relate or describe them, throughout, as far as was possible, in a selection of language really used by men; and, at the same time, to throw over them a certain colouring of imagination, whereby ordinary things should be presented to the mind in an unusual way; and, further, and above all, to make these incidents and situations

2. Wordsworth seems to be saying that the earlier Roman and the earlier English poets used verse less self-consciously than did the poets who came at a later time. An adverse judgment on the later poets is probably, though not necessarily, implied.

3. Wordsworth writes here under the influence of the view, prevalent through the Renaissance and especially strong in the 18th century, that the poet owes it as a "duty" to his audience to satisfy its expectations. Actually, of course, he and Coleridge did much to vitiate the force of this obligation.

interesting by tracing in them, truly though not ostentatiously, the primary laws of our nature: [4] chiefly, as far as regards the manner in which we associate ideas in a state of excitement. Low and rustic life was generally chosen, because in that condition, the essential passions of the heart find a better soil in which they can attain their maturity, are less under restraint, and speak a plainer and more emphatic language; because in that condition of life our elementary feelings co-exist in a state of greater simplicity, and, consequently, may be more accurately contemplated, and more forcibly communicated; because the manners of rural life germinate from those elementary feelings; and, from the necessary character of rural occupations, are more easily comprehended; and are more durable; and lastly, because in that condition the passions of men are incorporated with the beautiful and permanent forms of nature. The language, too, of these men is adopted (purified indeed from what appear to be its real defects, from all lasting and rational causes of dislike or disgust) because such men hourly communicate with the best objects from which the best part of language is originally derived; and because, from their rank in society and the sameness and narrow circle of their intercourse, being less under the influence of social vanity they convey their feelings and notions in simple and unelaborated expressions. Accordingly, such a language, arising out of repeated experience and regular feelings, is a more permanent, and a far more philosophical language, than that which is frequently substituted for it by poets, who think that they are conferring honour upon themselves and their art, in proportion as they separate themselves from the sympathies of men, and indulge in arbitrary and capricious habits of expression, in order to furnish food for fickle tastes, and fickle appetites, of their own creation.[5]

I cannot, however, be insensible of the present outcry against the triviality and meanness both of thought and language, which some of my contemporaries have occasionally introduced into their metrical compositions; and I acknowledge, that this defect, where it exists, is more dishonourable to the writer's own character than false refinement or arbitrary innovation, though I should contend at the same time that it is far less pernicious in the sum of its consequences. From such verses the poems in these volumes will be found distinguished at least by one mark of difference, that each of them has a worthy *purpose*. Not that I mean to say, that I always began to write with a distinct purpose formally conceived; but I believe that my habits of meditation have so formed my feelings, as that my descriptions of such objects as strongly excite those feelings, will be found to carry along with them a *purpose*. If in this opinion I am mistaken, I can have little right to the name of a poet. For all good poetry is the spontaneous overflow of powerful feelings: [6] but

4. Compare Coleridge's account of the undertaking in *Biographia Literaria* XIV and XVII. Note that Wordsworth does not refer to the intention, realized in *The Ancient Mariner*, to write poems that set forth supernatural incidents.

5. "It is worthwhile here to observe, that the affecting parts of Chaucer are almost always expressed in language pure and universally intelligible even to this day" (Wordsworth). See Coleridge's disagreement with Wordsworth on the virtues of the language of low and rustic life, *Biographia Literaria* XVII.

6. It is often erroneously supposed that this famous statement constitutes a *definition* of poetry. Not only does Wordsworth immediately qualify the statement, but from the first he does not mean it to say what poetry *is* but only to suggest what the process of making poetry is.

though this be true, poems to which any value can be attached, were never produced on any variety of subjects but by a man, who being possessed of more than usual organic sensibility, had also thought long and deeply. For our continued influxes of feeling are modified and directed by our thoughts, which are indeed the representatives of all our past feelings; and, as by contemplating the relation of these general representatives to each other we discover what is really important to men, so, by the repetition and continuance of this act, our feelings will be connected with important subjects, till at length, if we be originally possessed of much sensibility, such habits of mind will be produced, that, by obeying blindly and mechanically the impulses of those habits, we shall describe objects, and utter sentiments, of such a nature and in such connection with each other, that the understanding of the being to whom we address ourselves, if he be in a healthful state of association, must necessarily be in some degree enlightened, and his affections ameliorated.

I have said that each of these poems has a purpose. I have also informed my reader what this purpose will be found principally to be: namely to illustrate the manner in which our feelings and ideas are associated in a state of excitement. But, speaking in language somewhat more appropriate, it is to follow the fluxes and refluxes of the mind when agitated by the great and simple affections of our nature. This object I have endeavoured in these short essays to attain by various means; by tracing the maternal passion through many of its more subtle windings, as in the poems of the *Idiot Boy* and the *Mad Mother*; by accompanying the last struggles of a human being, at the approach of death, cleaving in solitude to life and society, as in the poem of the 'Forsaken Indian'; by showing, as in the stanzas entitled 'We Are Seven,' the perplexity and obscurity which in childhood attend our notion of death, or rather our utter inability to admit that notion; or by displaying the strength of fraternal, or to speak more philosophically, of moral attachment when early associated with the great and beautiful objects of nature, as in *The Brothers*; or, as in the incident of 'Simon Lee,' by placing my reader in the way of receiving from ordinary moral sensations another and more salutary impression than we are accustomed to receive from them. It has also been part of my general purpose to attempt to sketch characters under the influence of less impassioned feelings, as in the 'Two April Mornings,' 'The Fountain,' *The Old Man Travelling*, *The Two Thieves*, etc. characters of which the elements are simple, belonging rather to nature than to manners, such as exist now, and will probably always exist, and which from their constitution may be distinctly and profitably contemplated. I will not abuse the indulgence of my reader by dwelling longer upon this subject; but it is proper that I should mention one other circumstance which distinguishes these poems from the popular poetry of the day; it is this, that the feeling therein developed gives importance to the action and situation, and not the action and situation to the feeling. My meaning will be rendered perfectly intelligible by referring my reader to the poems entitled 'Poor Susan' and the 'Childless Father,' particularly to the last stanza of the latter poem.

I will not suffer a sense of false modesty to prevent me from asserting, that I point my reader's attention to this mark of distinction, far less for the sake of these particular poems than from the general importance of the subject. The subject is indeed important! For the human mind is capable of being excited without the application of gross and violent stimulants; and he must have a very faint perception of its beauty and dignity who does not know this, and who does not further know, that one being is elevated above another, in proportion as he possesses this capability. It has therefore appeared to me, that to endeavour to produce or enlarge this capability is one of the best services in which, at any period, a writer can be engaged; but this service, excellent at all times, is especially so at the present day. For a multitude of causes, unknown to former times, are now acting with a combined force to blunt the discriminating powers of the mind, and unfitting it for all voluntary exertion to reduce it to a state of almost savage torpor. The most effective of these causes are the great national events which are daily taking place, and the increasing accumulation of men in cities, where the uniformity of their occupations produces a craving for extraordinary incident, which the rapid communication of intelligence hourly gratifies.[7] To this tendency of life and manners the literature and theatrical exhibitions of the country have conformed themselves. The invaluable works of our elder writers, I had almost said the works of Shakespeare and Milton, are driven into neglect by frantic novels, sickly and stupid German tragedies, and deluges of idle and extravagant stories in verse.[8]—When I think upon this degrading thirst after outrageous stimulation, I am almost ashamed to have spoken of the feeble effort with which I have endeavoured to counteract it; and, reflecting upon the magnitude of the general evil, I should be oppressed with no dishonourable melancholy, had I not a deep impression of certain inherent and indestructible qualities of the human mind, and likewise of certain powers in the great and permanent objects that act upon it which are equally inherent and indestructible; and did I not further add to this impression a belief, that the time is approaching when the evil will be systematically opposed, by men of greater powers, and with far more distinguished success.

Having dwelt thus long on the subjects and aim of these poems, I shall request the reader's permission to apprize him of a few circumstances relating to their *style,* in order, among other reasons, that I may not be censured for not having performed what I never attempted. The reader will find that personifications of abstract ideas rarely occur in these volumes; and, I hope, are utterly rejected as an ordinary device to elevate the style, and raise it above prose.[9] I have proposed to myself to imitate, and, as far as is possible,

7. Although Wordsworth writes out of his own observation of the drastic changes that were taking place in the culture of his time, he probably was confirmed in his anxiety by his reading of Rousseau, one of whose characteristic themes was the loss of personal autonomy that results from urban life and from the proliferation of literature and of organized public opinion. "[T]he rapid communication of intelligence" (i.e. of news) refers to the striking increase in the number of daily newspapers in England in the last quarter of the 18th century.

8. A reference to the "Gothic" novels of terror, of which Horace Walpole's The Castle of Otranto (1764) was the prototype; among the best known examples of the genre are Ann Radcliffe's The Mysteries of Udolpho (1794) and Matthew Gregory Lewis's The Monk (1795). Jane Austen parodied such novels in Northanger Abbey. The most notorious of the German sentimental melodramatists was August von Kotzebue (1761–1819); one of his plays, Lovers' Vows, figures in Jane Austen's Mansfield Park.

9. Personification is a figure of speech which attributes human form and feeling to inanimate objects or abstract ideas, e.g. "Secure from flames, from Envy's fiercer rages" (Pope). It was common in the 18th century. For a developed example, see Wordsworth's own "Ode to Duty."

to adopt the very language of men; and assuredly such personifications do not make any natural or regular part of that language. They are, indeed, a figure of speech occasionally prompted by passion, and I have made use of them as such; but I have endeavoured utterly to reject them as a mechanical device of style, or as a family language which writers in metre seem to lay claim to by prescription. I have wished to keep my reader in the company of flesh and blood, persuaded that by so doing I shall interest him. I am, however, well aware that others who pursue a different track may interest him likewise; I do not interfere with their claim, I only wish to prefer a different claim of my own. There will also be found in these volumes little of what is usually called poetic diction; [10] I have taken as much pains to avoid it as others ordinarily take to produce it; this I have done for the reason already alleged, to bring my language near to the language of men, and further, because the pleasure which I have proposed to myself to impart is of a kind very different from that which is supposed by many persons to be the proper object of poetry. I do not know how without being culpably particular I can give my reader a more exact notion of the style in which I wished these poems to be written than by informing him that I have at all times endeavoured to look steadily at my subject, consequently, I hope that there is in these poems little falsehood of description, and that my ideas are expressed in language fitted to their respective importance. Something I must have gained by this practice, as it is friendly to one property of all good poetry, namely, good sense; [11] but it has necessarily cut me off from a large portion of phrases and figures of speech which from father to son have long been regarded as the common inheritance of poets. I have also thought it expedient to restrict myself still further, having abstained from the use of many expressions, in themselves proper and beautiful, but which have been foolishly repeated by bad poets, till such feelings of disgust are connected with them as it is scarcely possible by any art of association to overpower.

If in a poem there should be found a series of lines, or even a single line, in which the language, though naturally arranged and according to the strict laws of metre, does not differ from that of prose, there is a numerous class of critics, who, when they stumble upon these prosaisms as they call them, imagine that they have made a notable discovery, and exult over the poet as over a man ignorant of his own profession. Now these men would establish a canon of criticism which the reader will conclude he must utterly reject, if he wishes to be pleased with these volumes. And it would be a most easy task to prove to him, that not only the language of a large portion of every good poem, even of the most elevated character, must necessarily, except with reference to the metre, in no respect differ from that of good prose, but likewise that some of the most interesting parts of the best poems will be found to be strictly the language of prose, when prose is well written. The truth of this assertion might be demonstrated by innumerable passages from almost all the poetical

10. "Diction" is a neutral word which means simply the choice of words. "Poetic diction" refers to words or phrases which have established themselves as appropriate to poetry, perhaps especially because they are not used in prose or speech.

11. Cf. Coleridge in *Biographia Literaria* IV: "Finally, GOOD SENSE is the BODY of poetic genius."

writings, even of Milton himself. I have not space for much quotation; but, to illustrate the subject in a general manner, I will here adduce a short composition of Gray, who was at the head of those who by their reasonings have attempted to widen the space of separation betwixt prose and metrical composition, and was more than any other man curiously elaborate in the structure of his own poetic diction.[12]

> In vain to me the smiling mornings shine,
> And reddening Phoebus lifts his golden fire:
> The birds in vain their amorous descant join,
> Or cheerful fields resume their green attire:
> These ears alas! for other notes repine;
> *A different object do these eyes require;*
> *My lonely anguish melts no heart but mine;*
> *And in my breast the imperfect joys expire;*
> Yet Morning smiles the busy race to cheer,
> And new-born pleasure brings to happier men;
> The fields to all their wonted tribute bear;
> To warm their little loves the birds complain.
> *I fruitless mourn to him that cannot hear*
> *And weep the more because I weep in vain.*

It will easily be perceived that the only part of this sonnet which is of any value is the lines printed in italics: it is equally obvious, that, except in the rhyme, and in the use of the single word 'fruitless' for fruitlessly, which is so far a defect, the language of these lines does in no respect differ from that of prose.

By the foregoing quotation I have shown that the language of prose may yet be well adapted to poetry; and I have previously asserted that a large portion of the language of every good poem can in no respect differ from that of good prose. I will go further. I do not doubt that it may be safely affirmed, that there neither is, nor can be, any essential difference between the language of prose and metrical composition. We are fond of tracing the resemblance between poetry and painting, and, accordingly, we call them sisters: but where shall we find bonds of connection sufficiently strict to typify the affinity betwixt metrical and prose composition? They both speak by and to the same organs; the bodies in which both of them are clothed may be said to be of the same substance, their affections are kindred and almost identical, not necessarily differing even in degree; poetry [13] sheds no tears 'such as Angels weep,' [14] but

12. The poem of Thomas Gray's is the "Sonnet on the Death of Richard West." The italics are Wordsworth's. It was in a letter to West, later published, that Gray said that "the language of the age is never the language of poetry."
13. "I here use the word 'poetry' (though against my own judgment) as opposed to the word prose, and synonymous with metrical composition. But much confusion has been introduced into criticism by this contradistinction of poetry and prose, instead of the more philosophical one of poetry and matter of fact, or science. The only strict antithesis to prose is metre; nor is this, in truth, a *strict* antithesis, because lines and passages of metre so naturally occur in writing prose, that it would be scarcely possible to avoid them, even were it desirable." (Wordsworth)
14. *Paradise Lost* I.620.

natural and human tears; she can boast of no celestial ichor [15] that distinguishes her vital juices from those of prose; the same human blood circulates through the veins of them both.

If it be affirmed that rhyme and metrical arrangement of themselves constitute a distinction which overturns what I have been saying on the strict affinity of metrical language with that of prose, and paves the way for other artificial distinctions which the mind voluntarily admits, I answer that the language of such poetry as I am recommending is, as far as is possible, a selection of the language really spoken by men; that this selection, wherever it is made with true taste and feeling, will of itself form a distinction far greater than would at first be imagined, and will entirely separate the composition from the vulgarity and meanness of ordinary life; and, if metre be superadded thereto, I believe that a dissimilitude will be produced altogether sufficient for the gratification of a rational mind. What other distinction would we have? Whence is it to come? And where is it to exist? Not, surely, where the poet speaks through the mouths of his characters: it cannot be necessary here, either for elevation of style, or any of its supposed ornaments: for, if the poet's subject be judiciously chosen, it will naturally, and upon fit occasion, lead him to passions the language of which, if selected truly and judiciously, must necessarily be dignified and variegated, and alive with metaphors and figures. I forbear to speak of an incongruity which would shock the intelligent reader, should the poet interweave any foreign splendour of his own with that which the passion naturally suggests: it is sufficient to say that such addition is unnecessary. And, surely, it is more probable that those passages, which with propriety abound with metaphors and figures, will have their due effect, if, upon other occasions where the passions are of a milder character, the style also be subdued and temperate.

But, as the pleasure which I hope to give by the poems I now present to the reader must depend entirely on just notions upon this subject, and, as it is in itself of the highest importance to our taste and moral feelings, I cannot content myself with these detached remarks. And if, in what I am about to say, it shall appear to some that my labour is unnecessary, and that I am like a man fighting a battle without enemies, I would remind such persons, that, whatever may be the language outwardly holden by men, a practical faith in the opinions which I am wishing to establish is almost unknown. If my conclusions are admitted, and carried as far as they must be carried if admitted at all, our judgments concerning the works of the greatest poets both ancient and modern will be far different from what they are at present, both when we praise, and when we censure: and our moral feelings influencing, and influenced by these judgments will, I believe, be corrected and purified.[16]

Taking up the subject, then, upon general grounds, I ask what is meant by the word poet? What is a poet? To whom does he address himself? And what language is to be expected from him? He is a man speaking to men: a man, it is true, endued with more lively sensibility, more enthusiasm and tenderness, who has a greater knowledge of human nature, and a more comprehensive soul,

15. The ethereal fluid that was said to run, instead of blood, in the veins of the Greek gods.
16. Wordsworth expresses here his consciousness of the revolutionary effect his poetic theory would have upon the taste of future readers.

than are supposed to be common among mankind; a man pleased with his own passions and volitions, and who rejoices more than other men in the spirit of life that is in him; delighting to contemplate similar volitions and passions as manifested in the goings-on of the universe, and habitually impelled to create them where he does not find them. To these qualities he has added a disposition to be affected more than other men by absent things as if they were present; an ability of conjuring up in himself passions, which are indeed far from being the same as those produced by real events, yet (especially in those parts of the general sympathy which are pleasing and delightful) do more nearly resemble the passions produced by real events, than any thing which, from the motions of their own minds merely, other men are accustomed to feel in themselves; whence, and from practice, he has acquired a greater readiness and power in expressing what he thinks and feels, and especially those thoughts and feelings which, by his own choice, or from the structure of his own mind, arise in him without immediate external excitement.

But, whatever portion of this faculty we may suppose even the greatest poet to possess, there cannot be a doubt but that the language which it will suggest to him, must, in liveliness and truth, fall far short of that which is uttered by men in real life, under the actual pressure of those passions, certain shadows of which the poet thus produces, or feels to be produced, in himself. However exalted a notion we would wish to cherish of the character of a poet, it is obvious, that, while he describes and imitates passions, his situation is altogether slavish and mechanical,[17] compared with the freedom and power of real and substantial action and suffering. So that it will be the wish of the poet to bring his feelings near to those of the persons whose feelings he describes, nay, for short spaces of time perhaps, to let himself slip into an entire delusion, and even confound and identify his own feelings with theirs; modifying only the language which is thus suggested to him, by a consideration that he describes for a particular purpose, that of giving pleasure. Here, then, he will apply the principle on which I have so much insisted, namely, that of selection; on this he will depend for removing what would otherwise be painful or disgusting in the passion; he will feel that there is no necessity to trick out or to elevate nature: and, the more industriously he applies this principle, the deeper will be his faith that no words, which his fancy or imagination can suggest, will be to be compared with those which are the emanations of reality and truth.

But it may be said by those who do not object to the general spirit of these remarks, that, as it is impossible for the poet to produce upon all occasions language as exquisitely fitted for the passion as that which the real passion itself suggests, it is proper that he should consider himself as in the situation of a translator, who deems himself justified when he substitutes excellences of another kind for those which are unattainable by him; and endeavours occasionally to surpass his original, in order to make some amends for the general inferiority to which he feels that he must submit. But this would be to encourage idleness and unmanly despair. Further, it is the language of men who

17. Wordsworth is using "mechanical" in the old derogatory sense in which it denoted manual labor and subservience. In a later version of the Preface, Wordsworth altered the phrase to read "in some degree mechanical."

speak of what they do not understand; who talk of poetry as of a matter of amusement and idle pleasure; who will converse with us as gravely about a *taste* for poetry, as they express it, as if it were a thing as indifferent as a taste for rope-dancing, or frontiniac [18] or sherry. Aristotle, I have been told, hath said, that poetry is the most philosophic of all writing: [19] it is so: its object is truth, not individual and local, but general, and operative; not standing upon external testimony, but carried alive into the heart by passion; truth which is its own testimony, which gives strength and divinity to the tribunal to which it appeals, and receives them from the same tribunal. Poetry is the image of man and nature. The obstacles which stand in the way of the fidelity of the biographer and historian, and of their consequent utility, are incalculably greater than those which are to be encountered by the poet who has an adequate notion of the dignity of his art. The poet writes under one restriction only, namely, that of the necessity of giving immediate pleasure to a human being possessed of that information which may be expected from him, not as a lawyer, a physician, a mariner, an astronomer or a natural philosopher, but as a man. Except this one restriction, there is no object standing between the poet and the image of things; between this, and the biographer and historian there are a thousand.

Nor let this necessity of producing immediate pleasure be considered as a degradation of the poet's art.[20] It is far otherwise. It is an acknowledgment of the beauty of the universe, an acknowledgment the more sincere because it is not formal, but indirect; it is a task light and easy to him who looks at the world in the spirit of love: further, it is a homage paid to the native and naked dignity of man, to the grand elementary principle of pleasure, by which he knows, and feels, and lives, and moves. We have no sympathy but what is propagated by pleasure: I would not be misunderstood; but wherever we sympathize with pain it will be found that the sympathy is produced and carried on by subtle combinations with pleasure. We have no knowledge, that is, no general principles drawn from the contemplation of particular facts, but what has been built up by pleasure, and exists in us by pleasure alone. The man of science, the chemist and mathematician, whatever difficulties and disgusts they may have had to struggle with, know and feel this. However painful may be the objects with which the anatomist's knowledge is connected, he feels that his knowledge is pleasure; and where he has no pleasure he has no knowledge. What then does the poet? He considers man and the objects that surround him as acting and reacting upon each other, so as to produce an infinite complexity of pain and pleasure; he considers man in his own nature and in his ordinary life as contemplating this with a certain quantity of immediate knowledge, with certain convictions, intuitions, and deductions which by habit become of the nature of intuitions; he considers him as looking

18. One of the rich sweet wines produced in France, Italy, and Spain from muscat grapes; more commonly called Frontignan.
19. Actually Aristotle, in his *Poetics*, said only that poetry is more philosophical than history. It is a striking comment on the literary culture of the time that Wordsworth had not read this important work of criticism but cites it from hearsay.
20. Wordsworth has in mind what the *Oxford English Dictionary* calls the "unfavourable sense" of the word "pleasure"—"sensuous enjoyment as . . . an end in itself. . . . The indulgence of the appetites."

upon this complex scene of ideas and sensations, and finding every where objects that immediately excite in him sympathies which, from the necessities of his nature, are accompanied by an overbalance of enjoyment.

To this knowledge which all men carry about with them, and to these sympathies in which without any other discipline than that of our daily life we are fitted to take delight, the poet principally directs his attention. He considers man and nature as essentially adapted to each other,[21] and the mind of man as naturally the mirror of the fairest and most interesting qualities of nature. And thus the poet, prompted by this feeling of pleasure which accompanies him through the whole course of his studies, converses with general nature with affections akin to those, which, through labour and length of time, the man of science has raised up in himself, by conversing with those particular parts of nature which are the objects of his studies. The knowledge both of the poet and the man of science is pleasure; but the knowledge of the one cleaves to us as a necessary part of our existence, our natural and unalienable inheritance; the other is a personal and individual acquisition, slow to come to us, and by no habitual and direct sympathy connecting us with our fellow-beings. The man of science seeks truth as a remote and unknown benefactor; he cherishes and loves it in his solitude: the poet, singing a song in which all human beings join with him, rejoices in the presence of truth as our visible friend and hourly companion. Poetry is the breath and finer spirit of all knowledge; it is the impassioned expression which is in the countenance of all science. Emphatically may it be said of the poet, as Shakespeare hath said of man, 'that he looks before and after.' [22] He is the rock of defence of human nature; an upholder and preserver, carrying every where with him relationship and love. In spite of difference of soil and climate, of language and manners, of laws and customs, in spite of things silently gone out of mind and things violently destroyed, the poet binds together by passion and knowledge the vast empire of human society, as it is spread over the whole earth, and over all time. The objects of the poet's thoughts are every where; though the eyes and senses of man are, it is true, his favourite guides, yet he will follow wheresoever he can find an atmosphere of sensation in which to move his wings. Poetry is the first and last of all knowledge—it is as immortal as the heart of man. If the labours of men of science should ever create any material revolution, direct or indirect, in our condition, and in the impressions which we habitually receive, the poet will sleep then no more than at present, but

21. In the Preface to *The Excursion* (1814) Wordsworth quotes a passage from his unfinished poem *The Recluse*, in which he gives eloquent expression to the idea that nature and the mind of man are adapted—"fitted"—to each other.

> . . . my voice proclaims
> How exquisitely the individual Mind
> (And the progressive powers perhaps no less
> Of the whole Species) to the external world
> Is fitted: and how exquisitely, too
>
> . . .
>
> The external world is fitted to the mind;
> And the creation (by no lower name
> Can it be called) which they with blended might
> Accomplish . . .

22. *Hamlet* IV.iv.37.

he will be ready to follow the steps of the man of science, not only in those general indirect effects, but he will be at his side, carrying sensation into the midst of the objects of the science itself. The remotest discoveries of the chemist, the botanist, or mineralogist, will be as proper objects of the poet's art as any upon which it can be employed, if the time should ever come when these things shall be familiar to us, and the relations under which they are contemplated by the followers of these respective sciences shall be manifestly and palpably material to us as enjoying and suffering beings. If the time should ever come when what is now called science, thus familiarized to men, shall be ready to put on, as it were, a form of flesh and blood, the poet will lend his divine spirit to aid the transfiguration, and will welcome the being thus produced, as a dear and genuine inmate of the household of man.[23]—It is not, then, to be supposed that any one, who holds that sublime notion of poetry which I have attempted to convey, will break in upon the sanctity and truth of his pictures by transitory and accidental ornaments, and endeavour to excite admiration of himself by arts, the necessity of which must manifestly depend upon the assumed meanness of his subject.

What I have thus far said applies to poetry in general; but especially to those parts of composition where the poet speaks through the mouths of his characters; and upon this point it appears to have such weight that I will conclude, there are few persons, of good sense, who would not allow that the dramatic parts of composition are defective, in proportion as they deviate from the real language of nature, and are coloured by a diction of the poet's own, either peculiar to him as an individual poet, or belonging simply to poets in general, to a body of men who, from the circumstance of their compositions being in metre, it is expected will employ a particular language.

It is not, then, in the dramatic parts of composition that we look for this distinction of language; but still it may be proper and necessary where the poet speaks to us in his own person and character. To this I answer by referring my reader to the description which I have before given of a poet. Among the qualities which I have enumerated as principally conducing to form a poet, is implied nothing differing in kind from other men, but only in degree. The sum of what I have there said is, that the poet is chiefly distinguished from other men by a greater promptness to think and feel without immediate external excitement, and a greater power in expressing such thoughts and feelings as are produced in him in that manner. But these passions and thoughts and feelings are the general passions and thoughts and feelings of men. And with what are they connected? Undoubtedly with our moral sentiments and animal sensations, and with the causes which excite these; with the operations of the elements and the appearances of the visible universe; with storm and sunshine, with the revolutions of the seasons, with cold and heat, with loss of friends and kindred, with injuries and resentments, gratitude and hope, with fear and sorrow. These, and the like, are the sensations and objects which the poet describes, as they are the sensations of other men, and the objects which interest them. The poet thinks and feels in the spirit of the passions of men.

23. Alas, this has not come to pass. Science, so far from being "familiarized to men," has developed to the point where it is beyond the comprehension of most men, including poets.

How, then, can his language differ in any material degree from that of all other men who feel vividly and see clearly? It might be *proved* that it is impossible. But supposing that this were not the case, the poet might then be allowed to use a peculiar language, when expressing his feelings for his own gratification, or that of men like himself. But poets do not write for poets alone, but for men. Unless therefore we are advocates for that admiration which depends upon ignorance, and that pleasure which arises from hearing what we do not understand, the poet must descend from this supposed height, and, in order to excite rational sympathy, he must express himself as other men express themselves. To this it may be added, that while he is only selecting from the real language of men, or, which amounts to the same thing, composing accurately in the spirit of such selection, he is treading upon safe ground, and we know what we are to expect from him. Our feelings are the same with respect to metre; for, as it may be proper to remind the reader, the distinction of metre is regular and uniform, and not like that which is produced by what is usually called poetic diction, arbitrary, and subject to infinite caprices upon which no calculation whatever can be made. In the one case, the reader is utterly at the mercy of the poet respecting what imagery or diction he may choose to connect with the passion, whereas, in the other, the metre obeys certain laws, to which the poet and reader both willingly submit because they are certain, and because no interference is made by them with the passion but such as the concurring testimony of ages has shown to heighten and improve the pleasure which co-exists with it.

It will now be proper to answer an obvious question, namely, why, professing these opinions, have I written in verse? To this, in addition to such answer as is included in what I have already said, I reply in the first place, because, however I may have restricted myself, there is still left open to me what confessedly constitutes the most valuable object of all writing whether in prose or verse, the great and universal passions of men, the most general and interesting of their occupations, and the entire world of nature, from which I am at liberty to supply myself with endless combinations of forms and imagery. Now, supposing for a moment that whatever is interesting in these objects may be as vividly described in prose, why am I to be condemned, if to such description I have endeavoured to superadd the charm which, by the consent of all nations, is acknowledged to exist in metrical language? To this, by such as are unconvinced by what I have already said, it may be answered, that a very small part of the pleasure given by poetry depends upon the metre, and that it is injudicious to write in metre, unless it be accompanied with the other artificial distinctions of style with which metre is usually accompanied, and that by such deviation more will be lost from the shock which will be thereby given to the reader's associations, than will be counterbalanced by any pleasure which he can derive from the general power of numbers. In answer to those who still contend for the necessity of accompanying metre with certain appropriate colours of style in order to the accomplishment of its appropriate end, and who also, in my opinion, greatly underrate the power of metre in itself, it might perhaps, as far as relates to these poems, have been almost sufficient to observe, that poems are extant, written upon more humble subjects, and in a more naked and simple style than I have aimed at, which poems have continued to give pleasure from generation to generation. Now, if nakedness and simplicity be a defect, the fact here mentioned affords a strong presumption that poems somewhat less naked and simple are capable of affording pleasure at the present day; and, what I wished *chiefly* to attempt, at present, was to justify myself for having written under the impression of this belief.

But I might point out various causes why, when the style is manly, and the subject of some importance, words metrically arranged will long continue to impart such a pleasure to mankind as he who is sensible of the extent of that pleasure will be desirous to impart. The end of poetry is to produce excitement in co-existence with an overbalance of pleasure. Now, by the supposition, excitement is an unusual and irregular state of the mind; ideas and feelings do not in that state succeed each other in accustomed order. But, if the words by which this excitement is produced are in themselves powerful, or the images and feelings have an undue proportion of pain connected with them, there is some danger that the excitement may be carried beyond its proper bounds. Now the co-presence of something regular, something to which the mind has been accustomed in various moods and in a less excited state, cannot but have great efficacy in tempering and restraining the passion by an intertexture of ordinary feeling, and of feeling not strictly and necessarily connected with the passion. This is unquestionably true, and hence, though the opinion will at first appear paradoxical, from the tendency of metre to divest language in a certain degree of its reality, and thus to throw a sort of half consciousness of unsubstantial existence over the whole composition, there can be little doubt but that more pathetic situations and sentiments, that is, those which have a greater proportion of pain connected with them, may be endured in metrical composition, especially in rhyme, than in prose. The metre of the old ballads is very artless; yet they contain many passages which would illustrate this opinion, and, I hope, if the following poems be attentively perused, similar instances will be found in them. This opinion may be further illustrated by appealing to the reader's own experience of the reluctance with which he comes to the re-perusal of the distressful parts of *Clarissa Harlowe,* or the *Gamester.*[24] While Shakespeare's writings, in the most pathetic scenes, never act upon us as pathetic beyond the bounds of pleasure—an effect which, in a much greater degree than might at first be imagined, is to be ascribed to small, but continual and regular impulses of pleasurable surprise from the metrical arrangement.—On the other hand (what it must be allowed will much more frequently happen) if the poet's words should be incommensurate with the passion, and inadequate to raise the reader to a height of desirable excitement, then, (unless the poet's choice of his metre has been grossly injudicious) in the feelings of pleasure which the reader has been accustomed to connect with metre in general, and in the feeling, whether cheerful or melancholy, which he has been accustomed to connect with that particular movement of metre, there will be found something which will greatly contribute to impart passion to the words, and to effect the complex end which the poet proposes to himself.

If I had undertaken a systematic defence of the theory upon which these

24. Samuel Richardson's novel *Clarissa* (1747–48) and Edward Moore's play (1753).

poems are written, it would have been my duty to develop the various causes upon which the pleasure received from metrical language depends. Among the chief of these causes is to be reckoned a principle which must be well known to those who have made any of the arts the object of accurate reflection; I mean the pleasure which the mind derives from the perception of similitude in dissimilitude. This principle is the great spring of the activity of our minds, and their chief feeder. From this principle the direction of the sexual appetite, and all the passions connected with it take their origin: it is the life of our ordinary conversation; and upon the accuracy with which similitude in dissimilitude, and dissimilitude in similitude are perceived, depend our taste and our moral feelings. It would not have been a useless employment to have applied this principle to the consideration of metre, and to have shown that metre is hence enabled to afford much pleasure, and to have pointed out in what manner that pleasure is produced. But my limits will not permit me to enter upon this subject, and I must content myself with a general summary.

I have said that poetry is the spontaneous overflow of powerful feelings: it takes its origin from emotion recollected in tranquillity: [25] the emotion is contemplated till by a species of reaction the tranquillity gradually disappears, and an emotion, kindred to that which was before the subject of contemplation, is gradually produced, and does itself actually exist in the mind. In this mood successful composition generally begins, and in a mood similar to this it is carried on; but the emotion, of whatever kind and in whatever degree, from various causes is qualified by various pleasures, so that in describing any passions whatsoever, which are voluntarily described, the mind will upon the whole be in a state of enjoyment. Now, if nature be thus cautious in preserving in a state of enjoyment a being thus employed, the poet ought to profit by the lesson thus held forth to him, and ought especially to take care, that whatever passions he communicates to his reader, those passions, if his reader's mind be sound and vigorous, should always be accompanied with an overbalance of pleasure. Now the music of harmonious metrical language, the sense of difficulty overcome, and the blind association of pleasure which has been previously received from works of rhyme or metre of the same or similar construction, an indistinct perception perpetually renewed of language closely resembling that of real life, and yet, in the circumstance of metre, differing from it so widely, all these imperceptibly make up a complex feeling of delight, which is of the most important use in tempering the painful feeling which will always be found intermingled with powerful descriptions of the deeper passions. This effect is always produced in pathetic and impassioned poetry; while, in lighter compositions, the ease and gracefulness with which the poet manages his numbers are themselves confessedly a principal source of the gratification of the reader. I might perhaps include all which it is *necessary* to say upon this subject by affirming, what few persons will deny, that, of two descriptions, either of passions, manners, or characters, each of them equally well executed, the one in prose and the other in verse, the verse will be read a hundred times where the prose is read once. We see that Pope by the power of verse alone, has contrived to render the plainest common sense interesting, and even fre-

25. This statement is often remembered and quoted as if it said that poetry *is* "emotion recollected in tranquillity." See note 6.

quently to invest it with the appearance of passion. In consequence of these convictions I related in metre the tale of *Goody Blake and Harry Gill*, which is one of the rudest of this collection. I wished to draw attention to the truth that the power of the human imagination is sufficient to produce such changes even in our physical nature as might almost appear miraculous. The truth is an important one; the fact (for it is a *fact*) is a valuable illustration of it. And I have the satisfaction of knowing that it has been communicated to many hundreds of people who would never have heard of it, had it not been narrated as a ballad, and in a more impressive metre than is usual in ballads.

Having thus explained a few of the reasons why I have written in verse, and why I have chosen subjects from common life, and endeavoured to bring my language near to the real language of men, if I have been too minute in pleading my own cause, I have at the same time been treating a subject of general interest; and it is for this reason that I request the reader's permission to add a few words with reference solely to these particular poems, and to some defects which will probably be found in them. I am sensible that my associations must have sometimes been particular instead of general, and that, consequently, giving to things a false importance, sometimes from diseased impulses I may have written upon unworthy subjects; but I am less apprehensive on this account, than that my language may frequently have suffered from those arbitrary connexions of feelings and ideas with particular words and phrases, from which no man can altogether protect himself. Hence I have no doubt, that, in some instances, feelings even of the ludicrous may be given to my readers by expressions which appeared to me tender and pathetic. Such faulty expressions, were I convinced they were faulty at present, and that they must necessarily continue to be so, I would willingly take all reasonable pains to correct. But it is dangerous to make these alterations on the simple authority of a few individuals, or even of certain classes of men; for where the understanding of an author is not convinced, or his feelings altered, this cannot be done without great injury to himself: for his own feelings are his stay and support, and, if he sets them aside in one instance, he may be induced to repeat this act till his mind loses all confidence in itself, and becomes utterly debilitated. To this it may be added, that the reader ought never to forget that he is himself exposed to the same errors as the poet, and perhaps in a much greater degree: for there can be no presumption in saying, that it is not probable he will be so well acquainted with the various stages of meaning through which words have passed, or with the fickleness or stability of the relations of particular ideas to each other; and above all, since he is so much less interested in the subject, he may decide lightly and carelessly.

Long as I have detained my reader, I hope he will permit me to caution him against a mode of false criticism which has been applied to poetry in which the language closely resembles that of life and nature. Such verses have been triumphed over in parodies of which Dr. Johnson's stanza is a fair specimen.

> I put my hat upon my head,
> And walked into the Strand,
> And there I met another man
> Whose hat was in his hand.

Immediately under these lines I will place one of the most justly admired stanzas of the 'Babes in the Wood.'

> These pretty Babes with hand in hand
> Went wandering up and down;
> But never more they saw the Man
> Approaching from the Town.

In both these stanzas the words, and the order of the words, in no respect differ from the most unimpassioned conversation. There are words in both, for example, 'the Strand,' and 'the Town,' connected with none but the most familiar ideas; yet the one stanza we admit as admirable, and the other as a fair example of the superlatively contemptible. Whence arises this difference? Not from the metre, not from the language, not from the order of the words; but the *matter* expressed in Dr. Johnson's stanza is contemptible. The proper method of treating trivial and simple verses to which Dr. Johnson's stanza would be a fair parallelism is not to say, this is a bad kind of poetry, or this is not poetry; but this wants sense; it is neither interesting in itself, nor can *lead* to any thing interesting; the images neither originate in that sane state of feeling which arises out of thought, nor can excite thought or feeling in the reader. This is the only sensible manner of dealing with such verses: Why trouble yourself about the species till you have previously decided upon the genus? Why take pains to prove that an ape is not a Newton when it is self-evident that he is not a man?

I have one request to make of my reader, which is, that in judging these poems he would decide by his own feelings genuinely, and not by reflection upon what will probably be the judgment of others. How common is it to hear a person say, 'I myself do not object to this style of composition or this or that expression, but to such an such classes of people it will appear mean or ludicrous.' This mode of criticism, so destructive of all sound unadulterated judgment, is almost universal: I have therefore to request, that the reader would abide independently by his own feelings, and that if he finds himself affected he would not suffer such conjectures to interfere with his pleasure.

If an author by any single composition has impressed us with respect for his talents, it is useful to consider this as affording a presumption, that, on other occasions where we have been displeased, he nevertheless may not have written ill or absurdly; and, further, to give him so much credit for this one composition as may induce us to review what has displeased us with more care than we should otherwise have bestowed upon it. This is not only an act of justice, but in our decisions upon poetry especially, may conduce in a high degree to the improvement of our own taste: for an *accurate* taste in poetry, and in all the other arts, as Sir Joshua Reynolds has observed,[26] is an *acquired* talent, which can only be produced by thought and a long continued intercourse with the best models of composition. This is mentioned, not with so ridiculous a purpose as to prevent the most inexperienced reader from judging for him-

---

26. The great portrait painter of the 18th century, friend of Johnson, Burke, and Goldsmith. As the first president of the Royal Academy of Arts, he delivered between 1769 and 1790 annual *Discourses* on the principles of art. Wordsworth paraphrases a remark in Discourse XII.

self (I have already said that I wish him to judge for himself), but merely to temper the rashness of decision, and to suggest, that, if poetry be a subject on which much time has not been bestowed, the judgment may be erroneous; and that in many cases it necessarily will be so.

I know that nothing would have so effectually contributed to further the end which I have in view as to have shown of what kind the pleasure is, and how that pleasure is produced, which is confessedly produced by metrical composition essentially different from that which I have here endeavoured to recommend: for the reader will say that he has been pleased by such composition; and what can I do more for him? The power of any art is limited; and he will suspect, that, if I propose to furnish him with new friends, it is only upon condition of his abandoning his old friends. Besides, as I have said, the reader is himself conscious of the pleasure which he has received from such composition, composition to which he has peculiarly attached the endearing name of poetry; and all men feel an habitual gratitude, and something of an honourable bigotry for the objects which have long continued to please them: we not only wish to be pleased, but to be pleased in that particular way in which we have been accustomed to be pleased. There is a host of arguments in these feelings; and I should be the less able to combat them successfully, as I am willing to allow, that, in order entirely to enjoy the poetry which I am recommending, it would be necessary to give up much of what is ordinarily enjoyed. But, would my limits have permitted me to point out how this pleasure is produced, I might have removed many obstacles, and assisted my reader in perceiving that the powers of language are not so limited as he may suppose; and that it is possible that poetry may give other enjoyments, of a purer, more lasting, and more exquisite nature. This part of my subject I have not altogether neglected; but it has been less my present aim to prove, that the interest excited by some other kinds of poetry is less vivid, and less worthy of the nobler powers of the mind, than to offer reasons for presuming, that, if the object which I have proposed to myself were adequately attained, a species of poetry would be produced, which is genuine poetry; in its nature well adapted to interest mankind permanently, and likewise important in the multiplicity and quality of its moral relations.

From what has been said, and from a perusal of the poems, the reader will be able clearly to perceive the object which I have proposed to myself: he will determine how far I have attained this object; and, what is a much more important question, whether it be worth attaining; and upon the decision of these two questions will rest my claim to the approbation of the public.

1800, 1802   1802

DOROTHY WORDSWORTH
1771–1855

The article on Dorothy Wordsworth in an authoritative encyclopedia identifies her as "English writer and diarist." A writer in the most common meaning of the word she was not. She put many words on paper, enough to fill two sizable volumes, but nothing she wrote was intended for publication and she said that she would "detest" setting up as an author. For her *Recollections of a Tour Made in Scotland* (1803) she did indeed have in mind a small audience, "a few friends," but the Grasmere journal, which is the most memorable of all the records of her existence that she made, was intended to be read only by herself and her brother William.

Part of the interest of the journal is of course historical. No other document gives us so intimate a sense of the tone and temper of the first generation of English Romantic poets—not even in their own letters do Wordsworth and Coleridge stand so present before us as they do through Dorothy Wordsworth's loving references to them. And the clues to Wordsworth's creative processes which the journal affords are of decisive significance. But quite apart from its evidential importance, the journal has an inherent value, surely its greatest, as the expression of a rare spirit.

Dorothy, the third of the five Wordsworth children and the only girl, was born in 1771, a year and a half after the birth of William. She was seven years old when their mother died and for the next seventeen years she lived with one or another family of relatives, sometimes happily, sometimes not. William had always had a special place in her affections, as she in his, and for many years they entertained the hope of living together. This was made possible when Wordsworth received the famous bequest from his friend Raisley Calvert; in 1795 the brother and sister set up house together at Racedown in Dorsetshire. *The Prelude* makes plain the thera-peutic effect which the reunion with Dorothy had upon Wordsworth's development, how when he was alienated from humanity by his despair over the course taken by the French Revolution, and from nature, and from his vocation as a poet, "the beloved woman" maintained for him "a saving intercourse" with his "true self."

In 1794 Wordsworth had made the acquaintance of Coleridge, who was to be the other salutary influence on his development as a poet, and in 1797 he and Dorothy moved from Racedown to Alfoxden in order to be near this most valued of all their friends. The association was of exceptional closeness; they were, in the phrase at-tributed to Coleridge, "three persons, but one soul." Dorothy's influence upon Coleridge's intellectual and imaginative life at this time was only less profound than upon her brother's. It was at Alfoxden that Dorothy first undertook to keep a journal, starting in January and ending in May of 1798, and she continued the practice through the first weeks of the visit which she, William, and Coleridge made to Germany in the autumn and part of the winter of 1798–99. In December 1799 Wordsworth and Dorothy realized their long-cherished plan of returning to live in their native Lake District. They established themselves in the little house known as Dove Cottage in the town of Grasmere, in full view of the lovely lake of the same name.

Of the journal that Dorothy kept at Grasmere between May 14, 1800, and January 16, 1803, it seems possible to say that in the whole range of literature no equal number of pages is so crammed and crowded with life. The life of nature is a ceaseless and urgent presence—every budding, flowering, falling, every change of aspect wrought by the process of the seasons or the hours is a vital event to which precise and delighted notice must be given. Yet intense as is Dorothy's response to what her brother called "Nature's breathing life," her consciousness of human life is even more salient and more memorable. The gentry of the neighborhood who make up the Wordsworths' social circle are pretty much taken for granted and are but faintly delineated, but persons lower in the social scale—the working people of the town and most especially the wandering population of the roads—are perceived with an often startling realization of their perdurable solidity and uniqueness. Times were bad and many persons were being displaced from their occupations and homes. Their suffering and their fortitude make one of Wordsworth's great recurrent themes, and one has the sense that before they might be seen in the transcendent momentousness in which they appear in his poems, they had first to be encountered in their immediate actuality by Dorothy.

No least part of the life with which the journal is charged is Dorothy's own passionate existence. It moves, if not toward what can properly be called tragedy, then at least toward great suffering. Of some part of what was to befall her she was inevitably conscious, that she must share her brother's love with another woman. Her feeling for Mary Hutchinson, whom Wordsworth married in 1802, was truly sisterly. But her feeling for her brother was more than that, at any rate more than sisterly feeling is commonly conceived to be, and when we have become aware of this from the tenor of her references to William in the Journal, we cannot read her account of her brother's wedding day without concluding that for her it was a kind of death, the end not of life but of joy. It says much for the strength and largeness of her spirit that it was by no means the end of her tenderness and devotion. For more than thirty years she lived in her brother's household, sharing its joys and sorrows, a cherished and honored figure. But in 1835, presumably as the result of arteriosclerosis, she suffered a drastic physical and mental deterioration which confined her to bed or to a wheelchair and cut her off from human intercourse. It was thus that she, once the most sentient of beings, survived for two decades, outliving her brother by five years.

So that the full flavor of the original may be preserved, the text of our selections from the Grasmere Journals has been taken, without change, from the edition of the Journals prepared by Mary Moorman, published by Oxford University Press in 1971. Miss Moorman worked from the manuscripts of the Grasmere Journals preserved at the Wordsworth Library in Grasmere, and has kept, in virtually every particular, to the punctuation, orthography, and dating of the original.

From The Grasmere Journals
1800–1802

1800

May 14 1800 [*Wednesday*] Wm and John set off into Yorkshire [1] after dinner at ½ past 2 o'clock, cold pork in their pockets. I left them at the turning of the Low-wood bay under the trees. My heart was so full that I could hardly speak to W. when I gave him a farewell kiss. I sate a long time upon a stone at the margin of the lake, and after a flood of tears my heart was easier. The lake looked to me I knew not why dull and melancholy, and the weltering on the shores seemed a heavy sound. I walked as long as I could amongst the stones of the shore. The wood rich in flowers. A beautiful yellow, palish yellow flower, that looked thick round and double, and smelt very sweet—I

1. To visit Mary Hutchinson, who was to become William's wife in 1802. John is John Wordsworth (1771–1805), William and Dorothy's younger brother.

supposed it was a ranunculus—Crowfoot, the grassy-leaved Rabbit-toothed white flower, strawberries, geranium—scentless violet, anemones two kinds, orchises, primroses. The heck-berry very beautiful, the crab coming out as a low shrub. Met a blind man, driving a very large beautiful Bull and a cow —he walked with two sticks. Came home by Clappersgate. The valley very green, many sweet views up to Rydale head when I could juggle away the fine houses, but they disturbed me even more than when I have been happier. One beautiful view of the Bridge, without Sir Michael's.[2] Sate down very often, though it was cold. I resolved to write a journal of the time till W. and J. return, and I set about keeping my resolve because I will not quarrel with myself, and because I shall give Wm Pleasure by it when he comes home again. At Rydale a woman of the village, stout and well dressed, begged a halfpenny—she had never she said done it before, but these hard times— — Arrived at home with a bad head-ach, set some slips of privett. The evening cold, had a fire—my face now flame-coloured. It is nine o'clock. I shall soon go to bed. A young woman begged at the door—she had come from Manchester on Sunday morn with two shillings and a slip of paper which she supposed a Bank note—it was a cheat. She had buried her husband and three children within a year and a half—all in one grave—burying very dear —paupers all put in one place—20 shillings paid for as much ground as will bury a man—a stone to be put over it or the right will be lost—11/6 each time the ground is opened. Oh! that I had a letter from William!

May 15 Thursday A coldish dull morning—hoed the first row of peas, weeded etc. etc., sat hard to mending till evening. The rain which had threatened all day came on just when I was going to walk.

Friday morning [*16th*] Warm and mild, after a fine night of rain. Transplanted raddishes after breakfast, walked to Mr Gell's[3] with the Books, gathered mosses and plants. The woods extremely beautiful with all autumnal variety and softness. I carried a basket for mosses, and gathered some wild plants. Oh! that we had a book of botany. All flowers now are gay and deliciously sweet. The primrose still pre-eminent among the later flowers of the spring. Foxgloves very tall, with their heads budding. I went forward round the lake at the foot of Loughrigg fell.[4] I was much amused with the business of a pair of stone chats. Their restless voices as they skimmed along the water following each other their shadows under them, and their returning back to the stones on the shore, chirping with the same unwearied voice. Could not cross the water so I went round by the stepping-stones. The morning clear but cloudy, that is the hills were not overhung by mists. After dinner Aggy[5] weeded onions and carrots. I helped for a little—wrote to Mary Hutchinson— washed my head—worked. After tea went to Ambleside[6]—a pleasant cool

2. Rydal Hall, the house of Sir Michael de Fleming.
3. William Gell (1777–1836), an archeologist and topographer; he was knighted in 1803.
4. "Fell" is a North of England word for a hill or a mountain.
5. Agnes Fisher lived with her husband John in a cottage near by. John's sister Mary —called Molly—did housework for the Wordsworths.
6. A walk of about 3 miles.

but not cold evening. Rydale was very beautiful with spear-shaped streaks of polished steel. No letters!—only one newspaper. I returned by Clappersgate Grasmere ⁷ was very solemn in the last glimpse of twilight it calls home the heart to quietness. I had been very melancholy in my walk back. I had many of my saddest thoughts and I could not keep the tears within me. But when I came to Grasmere I felt that it did me good. I finished my letter to M. H. Ate hasty pudding,⁸ and went to bed. As I was going out in the morning I met a half crazy old man. He shewed me a pincushion and begged a pin, afterwards a halfpenny. He began in a kind of indistinct voice in this manner: 'Matthew Jobson's lost a cow. Tom Nichol has two good horses strayed. Jim Jones's cow's brokken her horn, etc. etc.' He went into Aggy's and persuaded her to give him some whey ⁹ and let him boil some porridge. She declares he ate two quarts.

Saturday [17th] Incessant rain from morning till night. T. Ashburner ¹⁰ brought us coals. Worked hard and read Mid-summer Night's Dream, Ballads —sauntered a little in the garden. The Skobby sate quietly in its nest rocked by the winds and beaten by the rain.

Sunday 19th Went to church, slight showers, a cold air. The mountains from this window look much greener and I think the valley is more green than ever. The corn begins to shew itself. The ashes are still bare. Went part of the way home with Miss Simpson.¹¹ A little girl from Coniston came to beg. She had lain out all night—her step-mother had turned her out of doors. Her father could not stay at home 'She flights so.' Walked to Ambleside in the evening round the lake. The prospect exceedingly beautiful from Loughrigg fell. It was so green, that no eye could be weary of reposing upon it. The most beautiful situation for a house in the field next to Mr Benson's. It threatened rain all the evening but was mild and pleasant. I was overtaken by 2 Cumberland people on the other side of Rydale who complimented me upon my walking. They were going to sell cloth, and odd things which they make themselves in Hawkshead and the neighbourhood. The post was not arrived so I walked thro' the town, past Mrs Taylor's, and met him.¹² Letters from Coleridge and Cottle.¹³ John Fisher overtook me on the other side of Rydale. He talked much about the alteration in the times, and observed that in a short time there would be only two ranks of people, the very rich and the very poor, for those who have small estates says he are forced to sell, and all the land goes into one hand. Did not reach home till 10 o'clock.

Monday [19th] Sauntered a good deal in the garden, bound carpets, mended old clothes. Read Timon of Athens. Dried linen. Molly weeded the turnips, John stuck the peas. We had not much sunshine or wind but no rain till about 7 o'clock when we had a slight shower just after I had set out

7. The name of both the lake and the town; here the lake.
8. A porridge of flour and oatmeal boiled with seasonings in watered milk.
9. The watery part of milk not separated from the curds in making cheese.
10. Thomas Ashburner was a neighbor who supplied the Wordsworths with coal from Keswick.
11. Daughter of a clergyman of the district.
12. That is, the post—the postman.
13. Joseph Cottle of Bristol published *Lyrical Ballads* in 1798.

upon my walk. I did not return but walked up into the Black Quarter.[14] I sauntered a long time among the rocks above the church. The most delightful situation possible for a cottage commanding two distinct views of the vale and of the lake, is among those rocks. I strolled on, gathered mosses, etc. The quietness and still seclusion of the valley affected me even to producing the deepest melancholy. I forced myself from it. The wind rose before I went to bed. No rain—. . .

Tuesday Morning [20th] A fine mild rain. After Breakfast the sky cleared and before the clouds passed from the hills I went to Ambleside. It was a sweet morning. Everything green and overflowing with life, and the streams making a perpetual song with the thrushes and all little birds, not forgetting the Stone chats. The post was not come in. I walked as far as Windermere.[15] and met him there. No letters! no papers. Came home by Clappersgate. I was sadly tired, ate a hasty dinner and had a bad head-ach. Went to bed and slept at least 2 hours. Rain came on in the Evening—Molly washing.

Wednesday [21st] Went often to spread the linen which was bleaching— a rainy day and very wet night.

Thursday [22nd] A very fine day with showers—dried the linen and starched. Drank tea at Mr Simpson's. Brought down Batchelor's Buttons (Rock Ranunculus) and other plants—went part of the way back. A showery, mild evening—all the peas up.

Friday 23rd Ironing till tea time. So heavy a rain that I could not go for letters—put by the linen, mended stockings etc.

Saturday May 24th Walked in the morning to Ambleside. I found a letter from Wm and from Mary Hutchinson and Douglass.[16] Returned on the other side of the lakes—wrote to William after dinner, nailed up the beds, worked in the garden, sate in the evening under the trees. I went to bed soon with a bad head-ache. A fine day.

Sunday [25th] A very fine warm day, had no fire. Read Macbeth in the morning, sate under the trees after dinner. Miss Simpson came just as I was going out and she sate with me. I wrote to my Brother Christopher, and sent John Fisher to Ambleside after tea. Miss Simpson and I walked to the foot of the lake—her Brother met us. I went with them nearly home and on my return found a letter from Coleridge and from Charles Lloyd,[17] and three papers.

Monday May 26 A very fine morning, worked in the garden till after 10 when old Mr Simpson came and talked to me till after 12. Molly weeding. Wrote letters to J. H.,[18] Coleridge, C. Ll., and W. I walked towards Rydale and turned aside at my favorite field. The air and the lake were still—one cottage light in the vale, and so much of day left that I could distinguish objects, the woods; trees and houses. Two or three different kinds of Birds

---

14. The name given by the Wordsworths to the locality of Easedale.
15. The head of the lake.
16. Charles Douglas of Jamaica, a barrister, a Cambridge friend of Wordsworth's.
17. For a time the friend of Coleridge and Lamb. At this period he lived in the district, near Clappersgate.
18. Joanna Hutchinson, youngest sister of Mary Hutchinson.

sang at intervals on the opposite shore. I sate till I could hardly drag myself away I grew so sad. 'When pleasant thoughts,' etc. . . .[19]

Tuesday 27th I walked to Ambleside with letters—met the post before I reached Mr Partridge's, one paper, only a letter for Coleridge—I expected a letter from Wm. It was a sweet morning, the ashes in the valley nearly in full leaf but still to be distinguished, quite bare on the higher grounds. I was warm in returning, and becoming cold with sitting in the house—I had a bad headach—went to bed after dinner, and lay till after 5—not well after tea. I worked in the garden, but did not walk further. A delightful evening before the Sun set but afterwards it grew colder. Mended stockings etc.

Wednesday [*28th*] In the morning walked up to the rocks above Jenny Dockeray's sate a long time upon the grass the prospect divinely beautiful. If I had three hundred pounds and could afford to have a bad interest for my money I would buy that estate, and we would build a cottage there to end our days in. I went into her garden and got white and yellow lilies, periwinkle, etc., which I planted. Sate under the trees with my work. No fire in the morning. Worked till between 7 and 8, and then watered the garden, and was about to go up to Mr Simpson's, when Miss S. and her visitors passed the door. I went home with them, a beautiful evening the crescent moon hanging above Helm crag.

Thursday [*29th*] In the morning worked in the garden a little, read King John. Miss Simpson, and Miss Falcon and Mr S. came very early. Went to Mr Gell's boat before tea. We fished upon the lake and amongst us caught 13 Bass. Miss Simpson brought gooseberries *and cream*. Left the water at near nine o'clock, very cold. Went part of the way home with the party.

Friday [*30th*] In the morning went to Ambleside, forgetting that the post does not come till the evening. How was I grieved when I was so informed. I walked back resolving to go again in the evening. It rained very mildly and sweetly in the morning as I came home, but came on a wet afternoon and evening—but chilly. I caught Mr Olliff's Lad as he was going for letters, he brought me one from Wm and 2 papers. I planted London pride upon the well and many things on the Borders. John sodded the well. As I came past Rydale in the morning I saw a Heron swimming with only its neck out of water—it beat and struggled amongst the water when it flew away and was long in getting loose.

Saturday [*31st*] A sweet mild rainy morning. Grundy the carpet man called. I paid him 1-10/-. Went to the Blind man's for plants. I got such a load that I was obliged to leave my Basket in the Road and send Molly for it. Planted till after dinner when I was putting up vallances. . . .

Sunday June 1st Rain in the night—a sweet mild morning. Read Ballads; went to church. Singers from Wytheburn. Went part of the way home with Miss Simpson. Walked upon the hill above the house till dinner time—went again to church—a Christening and singing which kept us very late. The pew-side came down with me. Walked with Miss Simpson nearly home. After tea went to Ambleside, round the lakes—a very fine warm evening. I

---

19. "In that sweet mood when pleasant thoughts / Bring sad thoughts to the mind." Wordsworth, "Lines Written in Early Spring."

lay upon the steep of Loughrigg my heart dissolved in what I saw when I was not startled but re-called from my reverie by a noise as of a child paddling without shoes. I looked up and saw a lamb close to me. It approached nearer and nearer as if to examine me and stood a long time. I did not move. At last it ran past me and went bleating along the pathway seeming to be seeking its mother. I saw a hare in the high road. The post was not come in; waited in the Road till John's apprentice came with a letter from Coleridge and 3 papers. The moon shone upon the water—reached home at 10 o'clock—went to bed immediately. Molly brought Daisies etc. which we planted.

Monday [*2nd*] A cold dry windy morning. I worked in the garden and planted flowers, etc. Sate under the trees after dinner till tea time. John Fisher stuck the peas, Molly weeded and washed. I went to Ambleside after tea, crossed the stepping-stones at the foot of Grasmere and pursued my way on the other side of Rydale and by Clappersgate. I sate a long time to watch the hurrying waves and to hear the regularly irregular sound of the dashing waters. The waves round about the little [Island] seemed like a dance of spirits that rose out of the water, round its small circumference of shore. Inquired about lodgings for Coleridge, and was accompanied by Mrs Nicholson as far as Rydale. This was very kind, but God be thanked I want not society by a moonlight lake—It was near 11 when I reached home. I wrote to Coleridge and went late to bed.

Tuesday [*3rd*]   Sent off my letter by the Butcher—a boisterous drying day. I worked in the garden before dinner. Read R[ichar]d Second—was not well after dinner and lay down. Mrs Simpson's grandson brought me some gooseberries. . . . After tea the wind fell. I walked towards Mr Simpson's. Gave the newspapers to the Girl, reached home at 10. No letter, no William—a letter from R[ichar]d [20] to John.

Wednesday [*4th*]   A very fine day. I sate out of doors most of the day, wrote to Mr Jackson.[21] Ambleside fair. I walked to the lake-side in the morning, took up plants and sate upon a stone reading Ballads. In the Evening I was watering plants when Mr and Miss Simpson called. I accompanied them home, and we went to the waterfall at the head of the valley. It was very interesting in the Twilight. I brought home lemon thyme and several other plants, and planted them by moonlight. I lingered out of doors in the hope of hearing my Brothers tread.

Thursday [*5th*]   I sate out of doors great part of the day and worked in the garden—had a letter from Mr Jackson, and wrote an answer to Coleridge. The little birds busy making love and pecking the blossoms and bits of moss off the trees, they flutter about and about and thrid the trees as I lie under them. Molly went out to tea, I would not go far from home, expecting my Brothers. I rambled on the hill above the house gathered wild thyme and took up roots of wild Columbine. . . .

. . .

Saturday [*7th*]   A very warm cloudy morning, threatening to rain. I walked up to Mr Simpson's to gather gooseberries—it was a very fine afternoon. Little

20. The eldest of Dorothy's three brothers.
21. About letting his house, Greta Hall, to the Coleridges.

Tommy [22] came down with me, ate gooseberry pudding and drank tea with me. We went up the hill to gather sods and plants and went down to the lake side and took up orchises etc. I watered the garden and weeded. I did not leave home in the expectation of Wm and John, and sitting at work till after 11 o'clock I heard a foot go to the front of the house, turn round, and open the gate. It was William——After our first joy was over, we got some tea. We did not go to bed till 4 o'clock in the morning so he had an opportunity of seeing our improvements. The birds were singing, and all looked fresh, though not day. There was a greyness on earth and sky. We did not rise till near 10 in the morning [Sunday]. . . .

. . .

Tuesday [*10th*]   On Tuesday, May 27th, a very tall woman,[23] tall much beyond the measure of tall women, called at the door. She had on a very long brown cloak, and a very white cap without Bonnet—her face was excessively brown, but it had plainly once been fair. She led a little bare-footed child about 2 years old by the hand and said her husband who was a tinker was gone before with the other children. I gave her a piece of Bread. Afterwards on my road to Ambleside, beside the Bridge at Rydale, I saw her husband sitting by the roadside, his two asses feeding beside him and the two young children at play upon the grass. The man did not beg. I passed on and about ¼ of a mile further I saw two boys before me, one about 10 the other about 8 years old at play chasing a butterfly. They were wild figures, not very ragged, but without shoes and stockings; the hat of the elder was wreathed round with yellow flowers, the younger whose hat was only a rimless crown, had stuck it round with laurel leaves. They continued at play till I drew very near and then they addressed me with the Beggars' cant and the whining voice of sorrow. I said I served your mother this morning. (The Boys were so like the woman who had called at the door that I could not be mistaken.) O! says the elder you could not serve my mother for she's dead and my father's on at the next town—he's a potter. I persisted in my assertion and that I would give them nothing. Says the elder Come, let's away, and away they flew like lightning. They had however sauntered so long in their road that they did not reach Ambleside before me, and I saw them go up to Matthew Harrison's house with their wallet upon the elder's shoulder, and creeping with a Beggar's complaining foot. On my return through Ambleside I met in the street the mother driving her asses; in the two Panniers of one of which were the two little children whom she was chiding and threatening with a wand which she used to drive on her asses, while the little things hung in wantonness over the Pannier's edge. The woman had told me in the morning that she was of Scotland, which her accent fully proved, but that she had lived (I think at Wigton), that they could not keep a house and so they travelled.

. . .

Monday [*16th*]   Wm and I went to Brathay by Little Langdale and Collath and Skelleth. It was a warm mild morning with threatening of rain. The vale

22. Probably a grandson of Mr. Simpson's.
23. This woman and the incident with her sons became the subject of Wordsworth's poem "Beggars."

of Little Langdale looked bare and unlovely. Collath was wild and interesting, from the Peat carts and peat gatherers—the valley all perfumed with the Gale and wild thyme. The woods about the waterfall veined with rich yellow Broom. A succession of delicious views from Skelleth to Brathay. We met near Skelleth a pretty little Boy with a wallet over his shoulder—he came from Hawkshead and was going to 'late' a lock [24] of meal. He spoke gently and without complaint. When I asked him if he got enough to eat he looked surprized and said 'Nay'. He was 7 years old but seemed not more than 5. . . .

. . .

Thursday [*19th*]   A very hot morning. W. and I walked up to Mr Simpson's. W. and old Mr S. went to fish in Wytheburn water. I dined with John, and lay under the trees. The afternoon changed from clear to cloudy and to clear again. John and I walked up to the waterfall and to Mr Simpson's, and with Miss Simpson met the fishers. W. caught a pike weighing 4¾ lbs. There was a gloom almost terrible over Grasmere water and vale. A few drops fell but not much rain. No Coleridge whom we fully expected.

Friday [*20th*]   I worked in the garden in the morning. Wm prepared Pea sticks. Threatening for rain but yet it comes not. On Wednesday evening a poor man called, a hatter—he had been long ill, but was now recovered and his wife was lying in of her 4th child. The parish would not help him because he had implements of trade etc. etc. We gave him 6d.

Saturday [*21st*]   In the morning W. and I went to Ambleside to get his tooth drawn, and put in. A fine clear morning but cold. W.'s tooth drawn with very little pain—he slept till 3 o'clock. Young Mr S. drank tea and supped with us then fished in Rydale water and they caught 2 small fishes —W. no bite—John 3. Miss Simpson and 3 children called—I walked with them to Rydale. The evening cold and clear and frosty, but the wind was falling as I returned. I staid at home about an hour and then walked up the hill to Rydale lake. Grasmere looked so beautiful that my heart was almost melted away. It was quite calm only spotted with sparkles of light. The church visible. On our return all distant objects had faded away—all but the hills. The reflection of the light bright sky above Black quarter was very solemn. Mr S. did not go till 12 o'clock.

Sunday [*22nd*]   In the morning W. and I walked towards Rydale and up into the wood but finding it not very pleasant we returned—sauntered in the garden—a showery day. In the evening I planted a honeysuckle round the yew tree. In the evening we walked for letters. No letters: no news of Coleridge. Jimmy Benson came home drunk beside us.

. . .

Wednesday [*25th*] [25]   A very rainy day. I made a shoe. Wm and John went to fish in Langdale. In the evening I went above the house, and gathered flowers which I planted, fox-gloves, etc. On Sunday [29 June] Mr and Mrs Coleridge and Hartley came. The day was very warm. We sailed to the foot of Loughrigg. They staid with us three weeks and till the Thursday following, i.e. till the 23 [24th] of July. On the Friday preceding their departure

24. Dialect for "beg a measure."
25. The month is July, the journal having been interrupted by the three-week visit of the Coleridges, briefly summarized in this entry.

we drank tea at the island. The weather very delightful, and on the Sunday we made a great fire, and drank tea in Bainriggs with the Simpsons. I accompanied Mrs C. to Wytheburne, and returned with W.—to tea at Mr Simpson's—it was excessively hot, but the day after Friday July 24th [25th] still hotter. All the morning I was engaged in unpacking our Somersetshire goods [26] and in making pies. The house was a hot oven but yet we could not bake the pies. I was so weary I could not walk, so I went and sate with Wm in the orchard. We had a delightful half hour in the warm still evening.

Saturday 25th   Still hotter. I sate with W. in the orchard all the morning and made my shoes. In the afternoon from excessive heat I was ill in the headach and toothach and went to bed—I was refreshed with washing myself after I got up, but it was too hot to walk till near dark, and then I sate upon the wall finishing my shoes.

. . .

Monday morning [28th]   Received a letter from Coleridge enclosing one from Mr Davy [27] about the Lyrical Ballads. Intensely hot. I made pies in the morning. Wm went into the wood and altered his poems. In the Evening it was so very warm that I was too much tired to walk.

Tuesday [29th]   Still very hot. We gathered peas for dinner. We walked up in the Evening to find out Hewetson's cottage but it was too dark. I was sick and weary.

. . .

Thursday [31st]   All the morning I was busy copying poems. Gathered peas, and in the afternoon Coleridge came, very hot, he brought the 2nd volume of the Anthology.[28] The men went to bathe, and we afterwards sailed down to Loughrigg. Read poems on the water, and let the boat take its own course. We walked a long time upon Loughrigg and returned in the grey twilight. The moon just setting as we reached home.

Friday 1st August   In the morning I copied The Brothers.[29] Coleridge and Wm went down to the lake. They returned and we all went together to Mary Point [30] where we sate in the breeze and the shade, and read Wm's poems. Altered The Whirlblast [31] etc. Mr Simpson came to tea and Mr B. Simpson afterwards. We drank tea in the orchard.

Saturday Morning 2nd   Wm and Coleridge went to Keswick. John went with them to Wytheburn and staid all day fishing and brought home 2 small pikes at night. I accompanied them to Lewthwaite's cottage and on my return papered Wm's room. I afterwards lay down till tea time and after tea worked at my shifts in the orchard. A grey evening. About 8 o'clock it gathered for rain and I had the scatterings of a shower, but afterwards the lake became of a glassy calmness and all was still. I sate till I could see no longer and then continued my work in the house.

Sunday Morning 3rd   I made pies and stuffed the pike—baked a loaf. Head-

26. Presumably household possessions that had been in storage.
27. Who was to become famous as Sir Humphrey Davy the chemist (1778–1829). He was a friend of Joseph Cottle.
28. The Annual Anthology, edited by Southey.
29. Wordsworth's poem.
30. Named by the Wordsworths for Mary Hutchinson.
31. Wordsworth's poem, written in 1798.

ach after dinner—I lay down. A letter from Wm rouzed me, desiring us to go
to Keswick. After writing to Wm we walked as far as Mr Simpson's and ate
black cherries. A Heavenly warm evening with scattered clouds upon the hills.
There was a vernal greenness upon the grass from the rains of the morning
and afternoon. Peas for dinner.

. . .

Wednesday 3rd September   Coleridge Wm and John went from home to
go upon Helvellyn [32] with Mr Simpson. They set out after breakfast. I accompanied them up near the Blacksmith's. A fine coolish morning. I ironed
till ½ past three—now very hot. I then went to a funeral at John Dawson's.
About 10 men and 4 women. Bread cheese and ale. They talked sensibly and
chearfully about common things. The dead person 56 years of age buried by
the parish. The coffin was neatly lettered and painted black and covered with
a decent cloth. They set the corpse down at the door and while we stood
within the threshold the men with their hats off sang with decent and solemn
countenances a verse of a funeral psalm. The corpse was then borne down
the hill and they sang till they had got past the Town-end. I was affected to
tears while we stood in the house, the coffin lying before me. There were
no near kindred, no children. When we got out of the dark house the sun
was shining and the prospect looked so divinely beautiful as I never saw it.
It seemed more sacred than I had ever seen it, and yet more allied to human
life. The green fields, neighbours of the churchyard, were as green as possible
and with the brightness of the sunshine looked quite gay. I thought she was
going to a quiet spot and I could not help weeping very much. When we came
to the bridge they began to sing again and stopped during 4 lines before
they entered the churchyard. The priest met us—he did not look as a man
ought to do on such an occasion—I had seen him half-drunk the day before
in a pot-house. Before we came with the corpse one of the company observed
he wondered what sort of cue 'our Parson would be in.' N.B. it was the day
after the Fair. I had not finished ironing till 7 o'clock. The wind was now high
and I did not walk—writing my journal now at 8 o'clock. Wm and John came
home at 10 o'clock.

. . .

Saturday Morning 13th September   William writing his preface [33] did not
walk. Jones [34] and Mr Palmer came to tea. We walked with them to Borricks—a
lovely evening but the air frosty—worked when I returned home. Wm walked
out. John came home from Mr Marshall. Sent back word to Mrs Clarkson.
Sunday Morning 14th   Made bread. A sore thumb from a cut. A lovely day
—read Boswell in the house in the morning and after dinner under the bright
yellow leaves of the orchard. The pear trees a bright yellow, the apple trees
green still. A sweet lovely afternoon.

. . .

Friday 3rd October   Very rainy all the morning. Little Sally learning to
mark. Wm walked to Ambleside after dinner. I went with him part of the

32. One of the highest mountains in the Lake District (3118 feet).
33. To the 1800 edition of *Lyrical Ballads*.
34. The Reverend Robert Jones, with whom Wordsworth made his Continental tour in
1790.

way—he talked much about the object of his Essay for the 2nd volume of LB. I returned expecting the Simpsons—they did not come. I should have met Wm but my teeth ached and it was showery and late—he returned after 10. Amos Cottle's [35] death in the Morning Post. . . .

N.B. When Wm and I returned from accompanying Jones we met an old man almost double,[36] he had on a coat thrown over his shoulders above his waistcoat and coat. Under this he carried a bundle and had an apron on and a night cap. His face was interesting. He had dark eyes and a long nose. John who afterwards met him at Wythburn took him for a Jew. He was of Scotch parents but had been born in the army. He had had a wife 'and a good woman and it pleased God to bless us with ten children.' All these were dead but one of whom he had not heard for many years, a sailor. His trade was to gather leeches, but now leeches are scarce and he had not strength for it. He lived by begging and was making his way to Carlisle where he should buy a few godly books to sell. He said leeches were very scarce partly owing to this dry season, but many years they have been scarce—he supposed it owing to their being much sought after, that they did not breed fast, and were of slow growth. Leeches were formerly 2/6 [per] 100; they are now 30/. He had been hurt in driving a cart, his leg broke his body driven over his skull fractured. He felt no pain till he recovered from his first insensibility. 'It was then later in the evening, when the light was just going away.'

Saturday October 4th [1800]   A very rainy, or rather showery and gusty morning for often the sun shines. Thomas Ashburner could not go to Keswick. Read a part of Lamb's play.[37] The language is often very beautiful, but too imitative in particular phrases, words etc. The characters except Margaret's unintelligible, and except Margaret's do not shew themselves in action. Coleridge came in while we were at dinner very wet.—We talked till 12 o'clock. He had sate up all the night before writing Essays for the newspaper.—His youngest child had been very ill in convulsion fits. Exceedingly delighted with the 2nd part of Christabel.

Sunday Morning 5th October   Coleridge read a 2nd time Christabel [38]— we had increasing pleasure. A delicious morning. Wm and I were employed all the morning in writing an addition to the preface. Wm went to bed very ill after working after dinner. Coleridge and I walked to Ambleside after dark with the letter. Returned to tea at 9 o'clock. Wm still in bed and very ill. . . .

Monday [6th]   A rainy day. Coleridge intending to go but did not get off. We walked after dinner to Rydale. After tea read The Pedlar.[39] Determined not to print Christabel with the LB.

Tuesday [7th]   Coleridge went off at 11 o'clock.—I went as far as Mr

---

35. Brother of Joseph Cottle.
36. The original of the leech-gatherer in Wordsworth's great poem *Resolution and Independence*.
37. *John Woodvil*, at this time called *Pride's Cure*. It was rejected for production, and when Lamb published it (at his own expense) it was harshly received by the critics.
38. His never to be finished poem.
39. A long poem begun in 1785; part of it was incorporated in *The Excursion* and part used in the second and third books of *The Prelude*.

Simpson's. . . . I was very ill in the evening at the Simpsons—went to bed —supped there. Returned with Miss S. and Mrs. J.[40]—heavy showers. Found Wm at home. I was still weak and unwell—went to bed immediately.

. . .

Wednesday Morning [*22nd*]   We walked to Mr Gell's a very fine morning. Wm composed without much success at the Sheepfold.[41] Coleridge came in to dinner. He had done nothing. We were very merry. C. and I went to look at the prospect from his seat. In the evening Stoddart came in when we were at tea, and after tea Mr and Miss Simpson with large potatoes and plumbs. Wm read after supper, Ruth etc.—Coleridge Christabel.

1801

Tuesday [*November*]*10th*   Poor C. left us [42] and we came home together. We left Keswick at 2 o'clock and did not arrive at G. till 9 o'clock. Drank tea at John Stanley's very comfortably. I burnt myself with Coleridge's Aquafortis.[43] Mary's feet sore. C. had a sweet day for his ride. Every sight and every sound reminded me of him dear dear fellow—of his many walks to us by day and by night—of all dear things. I was melancholy and could not talk, but at last I eased my heart by weeping—nervous blubbering says William. It is not so. O how many, many reasons have I to be anxious for him.

Wednesday 11th   Baked bread and giblet pie—put books in order— mended stockings. Put aside dearest C.'s letters, and now at about 7 o'clock we are all sitting by a nice fire—W. with his book and a candle and Mary [44] writing to Sara.

. . .

Friday 27th   Snow upon the ground thinly scattered. It snowed after we got up and then the sun shone and it was very warm though frosty—now the sun shines sweetly. A woman came who was travelling with her husband —he had been wounded and was going with her to live at Whitehaven. She had been at Ambleside the night before, offered 4d at the Cock for a bed— they sent her to one Harrison's where she and her husband had slept upon the hearth and bought a pennyworth of chips for a fire. Her husband was gone before very lame—'Aye' says she 'I was once an officer's wife I, as you see me now. My first husband married me at Appleby. I had 18£ a year for teaching a school and because I had no fortune his father turned him out of doors. I have been in the West Indies. I lost the use of this Finger just before he died he came to me and said he must bid farewell to his dear children and me. I had a muslin gown on like yours—I seized hold of his coat as he went from me and slipped the joint of my finger. He was shot directly. I came to London and married this man. He was clerk to Judge Chambray, *that man,* that man that's going on the Road now. If he, Judge

---

40. Presumably a married sister of Miss Simpson's.
41. The poem that was to become *Michael*. Wordsworth would seem to have begun it on October 11; the entries for several of the intervening days record his difficulty with its composition.
42. To spend the winter in London.
43. Nitric acid, used for etching.
44. Mary Hutchinson was visiting the Wordsworths. Sara was her sister, the object of Coleridge's affections.

Chambray,[45] had been at Kendal he would [have] given us a guinea or two and made nought of it, for he is very generous.' . . .

. . .

Tuesday 22nd [December]   Still thaw. I washed my head. Wm and I went to Rydale for letters. The road was covered with dirty snow, rough and rather slippery. We had a melancholy letter from C., for he had been very ill, though he was better when he wrote. We walked home almost without speaking. Wm composed a few lines of the Pedlar. We talked about Lamb's Tragedy as we went down the White Moss. We stopped a long time in going to watch a little bird with a salmon coloured breast—a white cross or T upon its wings, and a brownish back with faint stripes. It was pecking the scattered Dung upon the road. It began to peck at the distance of 4 yards from us and advanced nearer and nearer till it came within the length of Wm's stick without any apparent fear of us. As we came up the White Moss we met an old man, who I saw was a beggar by his two bags hanging over his shoulder, but from a half laziness, half indifference and a wanting to *try* him if he would speak I let him pass. He said nothing, and my heart smote me. I turned back and said You are begging? 'Ay,' says he. I gave him a halfpenny. William, judging from his appearance joined in I suppose you were a sailor? 'Ay,' he replied, 'I have been 57 years at sea, 12 of them on board a man-of-war under Sir Hugh Palmer.' Why have you not a pension? 'I have no pension, but I could have got into Greenwich hospital [46] but all my officers are dead.' He was 75 years of age, had a freshish colour in his cheeks, grey hair, a decent hat with a binding round the edge, the hat worn brown and glossy, his shoes were small thin shoes low in the quarters, pretty good. They had belonged to a gentleman. His coat was blue, frock shaped coming over his thighs, it had been joined up at the seams behind with paler blue to let it out, and there were three Bell-shaped patches of darker blue behind where the Buttons had been. His breeches were either of fustian or grey cloth, with strings hanging down, whole and tight; he had a checked shirt on, and a small coloured handkerchief tyed round his neck. His bags were hung over each shoulder and lay on each side of him, below his breast. One was brownish and of coarse stuff, the other was white with meal on the outside, and his blue waistcoat was whitened with meal. In the coarse bag I guessed he put his scraps of meat etc. He walked with a slender stick decently stout, but his legs bowed outwards. We overtook old Fleming [47] at Rydale, leading his little Dutchman-like grandchild along the slippery road. The same pace seemed to be natural to them both, the old man and the little child, and they went hand in hand, the grandfather cautious, yet looking proud of his charge. He had two patches of new cloth at the shoulder blades of his faded claret coloured coat, like eyes at each shoulder, not worn elsewhere. I found Mary at home in her riding-habit all her clothes being put up. We were very sad about Coleridge. Wm walked further. When he came home he cleared a path to the necessary—called me out to see it but before we got there a whole housetop full of snow had fallen from the

---

45. Sir Alan Chambré; he was known for his benevolence.
46. For distressed sailors.
47. He kept an inn at Rydal.

roof upon the path and it echoed in the ground beneath like a dull beating upon it. . . .

1802

Friday 29th January   William was very unwell. Worn out with his bad night's rest—he went to bed—I read to him to endeavour to make him sleep. Then I came into the other room, and read the 1st Book of Paradise Lost. After dinner we walked to Ambleside. Found Lloyds at Luff's—we stayed and drank tea by ourselves. A heart-rending letter from Coleridge—we were sad as we could be. Wm wrote to him. We talked about Wm's going to London. It was a mild afternoon—there was an unusual softness in the prospects as we went, a rich yellow upon the fields, and a soft grave purple on the waters. When we returned, many stars were out, the clouds were moveless, in the sky soft purple, the Lake of Rydale calm, Jupiter behind, Jupiter at least *we* call him, but William says we always call the largest star Jupiter. When we came home we both wrote to C. I was stupefied.

Saturday January 30th   A cold dark morning. William chopped wood—I brought it in in a basket. A cold wind. Wm slept better but he thinks he looks ill—he is shaving now. . . .

. . .

Tuesday [9th February]   William had slept better. He fell to work, and made himself unwell. We did not walk. A funeral came by of a poor woman who had drowned herself, some say because she was hardly treated by her husband, others that he was a very decent respectable man and *she* but an indifferent wife. However this was she had only been married to him last Whitsuntide and had had very indifferent health ever since. She had got up in the night and drowned herself in the pond. She had requested to be buried beside her mother and so she was brought in a hearse. She was followed by several decent-looking men on horseback, her Sister, Thomas Fleming's wife, in a Chaise, and some others with her, and a cart full of women. Molly says folks thinks o' their mothers. Poor Body *she* has been little thought of by any body else. We did a little of Lessing. I attempted a fable, but my head ached my bones were sore with the cold of the day before and I was downright stupid. We went to bed but not till William had tired himself.

. . .

Friday 12th   A very fine bright, clear, hard frost. William working again. I recopied the Pedlar, but poor William all the time at work. Molly tells me 'What! little Sally's gone to visit at Mr Simpson's. They says she's very smart she's got on a new bed-gown that her Cousin gave her. It's a very bonny one they tell me, but I've not seen it. Sally and me's in Luck.' In the afternoon a poor woman came, *she said* to beg some rags for her husband's leg which had been wounded by a slate from the Roof in the great wind—but she has been used to go a-begging, for she has often come here. Her father lived to the age of 105. She is a woman of strong bones with a complexion that has been beautiful, and remained very fresh last year, but now she looks broken, and her little Boy, a pretty little fellow, and whom I have loved for the sake of Basil,[48] looks thin and pale. I observed this to her. Aye says she we have

---

48. The son of Wordsworth's friend Basil Montague. He lived with the Wordsworths from 1795 to 1798 and is the child who figures in "Anecdote for Fathers."

all been ill. Our house was unroofed in the storm nearly and *so* we lived in it for more than a week. The Child wears a ragged drab coat and a fur cap, poor little fellow, I think he seems scarcely at all grown since the first time I saw him. William was with me—we met him in a lane going to Skelwith Bridge. He looked very pretty. He was walking lazily in the deep narrow lane, overshadowed with the hedge-rows, his meal poke hung over his shoulder. He said he was going 'a laiting.'⁴⁹ [49] He now wears the same coat he had on at that time. Poor creatures! When the woman was gone, I could not help thinking that we are not half thankful enough that we are placed in that condition of life in which we are. We do not so often bless god for this as we wish for this 50 £ that 100 £ etc. etc. We have not, however to reproach ourselves with ever breathing a murmur. This woman's was but a *common* case.—The snow still lies upon the ground. Just at the closing in of the Day I heard a cart pass the door, and at the same time the dismal sound of a crying Infant. I went to the window and had light enough to see that a man was driving a cart which seemed not to be very full, and that a woman with an infant in her arms was following close behind and a dog close to her. It was a wild and melancholy sight.—William rubbed his Table after candles were lighted, and we sate a long time with the windows unclosed. I almost finished writing The Pedlar, but poor William wore himself and me out with labour. We had an affecting conversation. Went to bed at 12 o'clock.

.   .   .

Thursday [*4th March*]   Before we had quite finished Breakfast Calvert's man brought the horses for Wm.⁵⁰ [50] We had a deal to do to shave—pens to make —poems to put in order for writing, to settle the dress pack up etc. The man came before the pens were made and he was obliged to leave me with only two. Since he has left me (at ½ past 11) it is now 2 I have been putting the Drawers into order, laid by his clothes which we had thrown here and there and everywhere, filed two months' newspapers and got my dinner 2 boiled eggs and 2 apple tarts. I have set Molly on to clear the garden a little, and I myself have helped. I transplanted some snowdrops—The Bees are busy— Wm has a nice bright day. It was hard frost in the night. The Robins are singing sweetly. Now for my walk. I *will* be busy, I *will* look well and be well when he comes back to me. O the Darling! Here is one of his bitten apples! I can hardly find in my heart to throw it into the fire. I must wash myself, then off—I walked round the two Lakes crossed the stepping stones at Rydale Foot. State down where we always sit. I was full of thoughts about my darling. Blessings on him. I came home at the foot of our own hill under Loughrigg. They are making sad ravages in the woods. Benson's Wood is going and the wood above the River. The wind has blown down a [?small] fir tree on the Rock that terminates John's path—I suppose the wind of Wednesday night. I read German after my return till tea time. After tea I worked and read the LB, enchanted with the Idiot Boy. Wrote to Wm then went to Bed. It snowed when I went to Bed.

Friday [*5th*]   First walked in the garden and orchard. A frosty sunny morning. After dinner I gathered mosses in Easedale. I saw before me sitting

49. Begging.
50. To ride to Keswick on a visit to Coleridge.

in the open field upon his Sack of Rags the old Ragman that I know. His coat is of scarlet in a thousand patches. His Breeches knees were untied—the breeches have been given him by some one. He has a round hat pretty good, small crowned but large rimmed. When I came to him he said Is there a brigg yonder that'll carry me ow'r t'watter? He seemed half stupid. When I came home Molly had shook the carpet and cleaned every thing upstairs. When I see her so happy in her work and exulting in her own importance I often think of that affecting expression which she made use of to me one evening lately. Talking of her good luck in being in this house, 'Aye Mistress them 'at's Low laid would have been a proud creature could they but have [seen] where I is now fra what they thought mud [51] be my Doom.'—I was tired when I reached home. I sent Molly Ashburner to Rydale. No letters! I was sadly mortified. I expected one fully from Coleridge. Wrote to William. Read the L B, got into sad thoughts, tried at German but could not go on —Read LB.—Blessings on that Brother of mine! Beautiful new moon over Silver How.

. . .

Sunday Morning [*14th*]   William had slept badly—he got up at 9 o'clock, but before he rose he had finished the Beggar Boys—and while we were at Breakfast that is (for I had breakfasted) he, with his Basin of Broth before him untouched and a little plate of Bread and butter he wrote the Poem to a Butterfly! He ate not a morsel, nor put on his stockings but sate with his shirt neck unbuttoned, and his waistcoat open while he did it. The thought first came upon him as we were talking about the pleasure we both always feel at the sight of a Butterfly. I told him that I used to chase them a little but that I was afraid of brushing the dust off their wings, and did not catch them— He told me how they used to kill all the white ones when he went to school because they were frenchmen. Mr Simpson came in just as he was finishing the Poem. After he was gone I wrote it down and the other poems and I read them all over to him. We then called at Mr Olliff's. Mr O. walked with us to within sight of Rydale—the sun shone very pleasantly, yet it was extremely cold. We dined and then Wm went to bed. I lay upon the fur gown before the fire but I could not sleep—I lay there a long time—it is now half past 5 I am going to write letters. . . .—William rose without having slept we sate comfortably by the fire till he began to try to alter the butterfly, and tired himself—he went to bed tired.

Monday Morning [*15th*]   We sate reading the poems and I read a little German. Mr Luff came in at one o'clock. He had a long talk with William —he went to Mr Olliff's after dinner and returned to us to tea. During his absence a sailor who was travelling from Liverpool to Whitehaven called he was faint and pale when he knocked at the door, a young Man very well dressed. We sate by the kitchen fire talking with him for 2 hours—he told us [? most] interesting stories of his life. His name was Isaac Chapel—he had been at sea since he was 15 years old. He was by trade a sail-maker. His last voyage was to the Coast of Guinea. He had been on board a slave ship the Captain's name Maxwell where one man had been killed a Boy put to

51. "Might."

lodge with the pigs and was half eaten, one Boy set to watch in the hot sun till he dropped down dead. He had been cast away in North America and had travelled 30 days among the Indians where he had been well treated— He had twice swum from a King's ship in the night and escaped, he said he would rather be in hell than be pressed. He was now going to wait in England to appear against Captain Maxwell. 'O he's a Rascal, Sir, he ought to be put in the papers!' The poor man had not been in bed since Friday Night. He left Liverpool at 2 o'clock on Saturday morning. He had called at a farm house to beg victuals and had been refused. The woman said she would give him nothing. 'Won't you? Then I can't help it.' He was excessively like my Brother John.[52] . . .

Wednesday [*17th*] William went up into the orchard and finished the Poem. Mrs Luff and Mrs Olliff called I went with Mrs O. to the top of the White Moss—Mr O. met us and I went to their house he offered me manure for the garden. I went and sate with W. and walked backwards and forwards in the orchard till dinner time—he read me his poem. I broiled Beefsteaks. After dinner we made a pillow of my shoulder, I read to him and my Beloved slept. . . .

Friday [*19th*] A very rainy morning. I went up into the lane to collect a few green mosses to make the chimney gay against my darling's return. Poor C! I did not wish for, or expect him it rained so. Mr Luff came in before my dinner. We had a long talk. He left me before 4 o'clock, and about ½ an hour after Coleridge came in. His eyes were a little swollen with the wind. I was much affected with the sight of him—he seemed half stupefied.[53] William came in soon after. Coleridge went to bed late, and Wm and I sate up till 4 o'clock. A letter from Sara sent by Mary. They disputed about Ben Jonson. My spirits were agitated very much.

Sunday [*21st*] A showery day. Coleridge and William lay long in bed. We sent up to G. Mackareth's for the horse to go to Keswick but we could not have it. Went with C. to Borwick's where he left us. William was very unwell this evening. We had a sweet and tender conversation. I wrote to Mary and Sara.

Monday [*22nd*] A rainy day. William very poorly. Mr Luff came in after dinner and brought us 2 letters from Sara H. and one from poor Annette. I read Sara's letters while he was here. I finished my letters to M. and S. and wrote to my Br Richard. We talked a good deal about C. and other interesting things. We resolved to see Annette,[54] and that Wm should go to Mary. We wrote to Coleridge not to expect us till Thursday or Friday.

52. Also a sailor; in 1805 he perished in the wreck of the ship he commanded.
53. Possibly from the effects of opium. This and the troubled state of Coleridge's relations with his wife might account for Dorothy's agitated spirits.
54. Although Wordsworth's love affair with Annette Vallon, by whom he had a daughter, was not "discovered" until early in the 20th century, it was never a secret in the Wordsworth family, nor, as is apparent, was it hidden from Mary Hutchinson. Wordsworth, in company with Dorothy, went to Calais in August of 1802 to see Annette and the child.

Tuesday [*23rd*]   A mild morning. William worked at the Cuckow poem.[55] I sewed beside him. After dinner he slept I read German, and at the closing in of day went to sit in the orchard. He came to me, walked backwards and forwards. We talked about C. Wm repeated the poem to me. I left him there and in 20 minutes he came in, rather tired with attempting to write. He is now reading Ben Jonson and I am going to read German it is about 10 o'clock, a quiet night. The fire flutters and the watch ticks I hear nothing else save the Breathing of my Beloved and he now and then pushes his book forward and turns over a leaf. . . . No letter from C. . . .

. . .

Friday [*26th*]   A beautiful morning. William wrote to Annette then worked at the Cuckow. I was ill and in bad spirits—after dinner I sate 2 hours in the orchard. William and I walked together after tea first to the top of White Moss, then to Mr Olliff's. I left Wm and while he was absent wrote out poems. I grew alarmed and went to seek him—I met him at Mr Olliff's. He had been trying without success to alter a passage in Silver How poem [56]—he had written a conclusion just before he went out. While I was getting into bed he wrote the Rainbow.[57]

Saturday [*27th*]   A divine morning. At Breakfast Wm wrote part of an ode.[58] Mr Olliff sent the dung and Wm went to work in the garden. We sate all day in the orchard.

. . .

Thursday 29th [*April*]   A beautiful morning. The sun shone and all was pleasant. We sent off our parcel to Coleridge by the waggon. Mr Simpson heard the Cuckow today. Before we went out after I had written down the Tinker (which William finished this morning) Luff called. He was very lame, limped into the kitchen—he came on a little Pony. We then went to John's Grove, sate a while at first. Afterwards William lay, and I lay in the trench under the fence—he with his eyes shut and listening to the waterfalls and the Birds. There was no one waterfall above another—it was a sound of waters in the air—the voice of the air. William heard me breathing and rustling now and then but we both lay still, and unseen by one another. He thought that it would be as sweet thus to lie so in the grave, to hear the *peaceful* sounds of the earth and just to know that our dear friends were near. The Lake was still. There was a Boat out. Silver How reflected with delicate purple and yellowish hues as I have seen Spar. Lambs on the island and running races together by the half dozen in the round field near us. The copses green*ish*, hawthorn green. . . .

. . .

Saturday May 1st   Rose not till ½ past 8. A heavenly morning. As soon as Breakfast was over we went into the garden and sowed the scarlet beans about the house. It was a clear sky a heavenly morning. I sowed the flowers William helped me. We then went and sate in the orchard till dinner time. It was very hot. William wrote the Celandine.[59] We planned a shed for the sun was

55. "To the Cuckoo."
56. Perhaps *The Firgrove.*
57. "My Heart Leaps Up."
58. "Intimations" Ode, of which "My Heart Leaps Up" became the epigraph.
59. "To the Small Celandine."

too much for us. After dinner we went again to our old resting place in the Hollins under the Rock. We first lay under a holly where we saw nothing but the holly tree and a budding elm mossed with [?] and the sky above our heads. But that holly tree had a beauty about it more than its own, knowing as we did where we were. When the sun had got low enough we went to the Rock shade. Oh the overwhelming beauty of the vale below—greener than green. Two Ravens flew high high in the sky and the sun shone upon their bellys and their wings long after there was none of his light to be seen but a little space on the top of Loughrigg Fell. We went down to tea at 8 o'clock—had lost the poem and returned after tea. The Landscape was fading, sheep and lambs quiet among the Rocks. . . . The sky was perfectly cloudless. N.B. Is it often so? 3 solitary stars in the middle of the blue vault one or two on the points of the high hills. Wm wrote the Celandine 2nd part tonight. Heard the cuckow today this first of May.[60]

Sunday 2nd May   Again a heavenly morning. Letter from Coleridge.

. . .

Sunday Morning May 9th 1802   The air considerably colder today but the sun shone all day. William worked at the Leech gatherer almost incessantly from morning till tea-time. I copied the Leech-gatherer and other poems for Coleridge. I was oppressed and sick at heart for he wearied himself to death. After tea he wrote 2 stanzas in the manner of Thomson's Castle of Indolence,[61] and was tired out. Bad news of Coleridge.

. . .

Monday 31st   I was much better. We sate out all the day. Mary Jameson dined. I wrote out the poem on 'Our Departure'[62] which he seemed to have finished. In the evening Miss Simpson brought us a letter from M. H. and a complimentary and critical letter to W. from John Wilson of Glasgow [63] Post Paid. I went a little way with Miss S. My tooth broke today. They will soon be gone.[64] Let that pass I shall be beloved—I want no more.

. . .

Wednesday 2nd June 1802   In the morning we observed that the scarlet Beans were drooping in the leaves in great numbers owing, we guess, to an insect. We sate a while in the orchard—then we went to the old carpenter's about the hurdles. Yesterday an old man called, a grey-headed man, above 70 years of age. He said he had been a soldier, that his wife and children had died in Jamaica. He had a Beggar's wallet over his shoulders, a coat of shreds and patches altogether of a drab colour—he was tall and though his body was bent he had the look of one used to have been upright. I talked a while to him, and then gave him a piece of cold Bacon and a penny. Said he 'You're a fine woman!' I could not help smiling. I suppose he meant 'You're a kind woman.' Afterwards a woman called travelling to Glasgow. After dinner

---

60. The editor of the text, Mary Moorman, notes that "this sentence is written in large letters across the page."
61. *The Castle of Indolence,* an allegorical poem in the manner of Spenser, by James Thomson (1700–1748), was published in 1748.
62. "A Farewell."
63. He later wrote under the name of Christopher North and was one of the founders of *Blackwood's Magazine.*
64. She means her teeth.

William was very unwell. We went into Frank's field, crawled up the little glen and planned a seat then went to Mr Olliff's Hollins and sate there—found a beautiful shell-like purple fungus in Frank's field. After tea we walked to Butterlip How and backwards and forwards there. All the young oak tree leaves are dry as powder. A cold south wind portending Rain. After we came in we sate in deep silence at the window—I on a chair and William with his hand on my shoulder. We were deep in Silence and Love, a blessed hour. We drew to the fire before bed-time and ate some Broth for our suppers. . . .

Thursday 17th William had slept well. I took castor oil and lay in bed till 12 o'clock. William injured himself with working a little.—When I got up we sate in the orchard, a sweet mild day. Miss Hudson called. I went with her to the top of the hill. When I came home I found William at work, attempting to alter a stanza in the poem on our going for Mary [65] which I convinced him did not need altering. We sate in the house after dinner. In the evening walked on our favourite path. A short letter from Coleridge. William added a little to the Ode he is writing.[66]

Thursday 7th [July] A rainy morning. I paid Thomas Ashburner, and Frank Baty. When I was coming home, a post chaise passed with a little girl behind in a patched ragged red cloak. The child and cloak—Alice Fell's own self.[67] We sate in tranquillity together by the fire in the morning. In the afternoon after we had talked a little, Wm fell asleep, I read the Winter's Tale. Then I went to bed but did not sleep. The Swallows stole in and out of their nest, and sate there *whiles* quite still, *whiles* they sung low for 2 minutes or more at a time just like a muffled Robin. William was looking at the Pedlar when I got up. He arranged it, and after tea I wrote it out—280 lines. In the meantime the evening being fine he carried his coat to the Tailor's and went to George Mackareth's to engage the horse. He came in to me at about ½ past nine pressing me to go out; he had got letters which we were to read out of doors—I was rather unwilling, fearing I could not see to read the letters, but I saw well enough. One was from M. H., a very tender affecting letter, another from Sara to C., from C. to us, and from my B[rothe]r R[ichar]d. The moon was behind. William hurried me out in hopes that I should see her. We walked first to the top of the hill to see Rydale. It was dark and dull but our own vale was very solemn. The shape of Helm Crag was quite distinct, though black. We walked backwards and forwards on the White Moss path there was a sky-like white brightness on the lake. The Wyke Cottage Light at the foot of Silver How. Glowworms out, but not so numerous as last night. O beautiful place! Dear Mary William. The horse is come Friday morning, so I must give over. William is eating his Broth. I must prepare to go. The Swallows I must leave them the well the garden the Roses, all. Dear creatures!!

65. "A Farewell."
66. "Intimations" ode.
67. "Alice Fell; or, Poverty" relates that the poet, traveling by post-chaise, continually hears a cry that he cannot account for; at one of the post stops he discovers that a little girl, poor and orphaned, has been riding behind the chaise and weeping because her ragged cloak was caught in the wheel.

they sang last night after I was in bed—seemed to be singing to one another, just before they settled to rest for the night. Well, I must go. Farewell.— — —

1896, 1904

SAMUEL TAYLOR COLERIDGE
1772–1834

"Through a natural development," André Gide has said, "all great poets eventually become critics." The statement is of course too categorical to be literally true, but that it approaches truth is attested by even a partial roster of the poets whose critical writing is of the highest interest: Dante, Goethe, Schiller, Wordsworth, Shelley, Arnold, Baudelaire, Valéry, Eliot. Of all poets who became critics, none became so wholly and passionately a critic as Coleridge. From his early youth he was deeply engaged by the theory of literature; in his difficult middle years, when his poetic genius had deserted him, he was preoccupied, we might almost say obsessed, with the effort to comprehend and explicate literature in its innermost being, in its essential and ideal nature. To this arduous undertaking he brought a combination of intellectual powers which is perhaps unique in the history of criticism—the boldness and profundity of his philosophic speculation, the precision of his particular observations, and the acuity of his psychological insight have won for him, at least in the English-speaking world, an immense prestige.

Coleridge is not a critic who offers himself to easy comprehension. His concepts are sometimes inherently difficult and they are made the more so by being often formulated in the intellectual idiom of the German philosophers whose seminal thought on aesthetic questions had a decisive influence upon his own. The difficulty is compounded by the circumstance that Coleridge's criticism never achieved a systematic form. Much of it exists as disjointed fragments, unfinished manuscripts, reports which others made of his lectures, notes for and outlines of work to be undertaken. Even *Biographia Literaria* (1817), his best-known work in criticism and the one that comes nearest to being fully composed, is not so much completed as brought to a stop. Yet no one who seriously gives himself to the inchoate canon of Coleridge's criticism is likely to doubt its essential coherence.

It is commonly and correctly said that the idea which informs Coleridge's critical speculation is his conception of the function of literature, or, to use his own word, poetry. This is indeed momentous—nothing less than that of mediating between man and Nature, of confirming and sustaining a mode of perceiving the world which discovers in it, or (what for Coleridge is the same thing) bestows upon it, those attributes which make it responsive and hospitable to man.

This central idea of Coleridge's criticism is given an especially memorable expression in his last great utterance as a poet, *Dejection: An Ode*. The subject of the poem is the painful state into which the poet has fallen in consequence of his being no longer able to exercise what he calls his "shaping spirit of Imagination." It was through the active power of imagination that animation and beauty had been bestowed upon—actually infused into—"that inanimate cold world" which ordinary vision perceives. And the animated world, as if in return for this gift of life made to it by the creative imagination, had confirmed and sustained the imagination in its joyous activity. But now this happy reciprocation of creativity is disastrously at an end. The misfortunes with which the poet has been long afflicted have, he says, incapacitated his imagination, and because he cannot bring it into play to animate the world, the world cannot animate him—"We receive but what we give, / And in our life alone does Nature live." In Coleridge's view the imagination is the presiding faculty or "soul" of literature and as such defines its function. The chief intention of his critical enterprise is to discover the laws by which the imagination operates in carrying on its life-bestowing activity.

That the imagination operates by its own laws is a fundamental assumption of Coleridge's criticism and is the reason for his intense antagonism to the prescriptive criticism of the preceding age. French and English critical theory since the late seventeenth century gave large credence to the idea of "rules"—that is, formulated standards of judgment which were designed to guide the writer toward achieving literary works equal in quality to the admired works of the past. It is true that the tradition of the "rules," which goes back ultimately to Horace's *Ars Poetica,* was from the first quite willing to take account of "genius," to which it gave license to break the rules on due occasion; Pope and Johnson are explicit in their liberality on this score. But the obvious implication of even a permissive formulation of rules is that the work of art is a thing that is *made,* and for a certain purpose, that of satisfying the expectations of the audience. This was a conception of art which Coleridge passionately rejected, as did all the Romanticists—a work of art was not to be thought of as an object consciously contrived, like a mechanical device, with the end in view of gratifying the settled taste of the public, but as an autonomous and living entity, coming into being and growing and developing as a tree does, by the laws of its own nature. If it gives pleasure, as a tree may indeed give pleasure and of the highest kind, this is not its defining purpose, which is, rather, simply to come into being, to fulfill, as it were, the demands of its own nature. Its author does, to be sure, in some sense bring it into being, but in doing so his conscious intention and intellect play but a secondary part. This conception of the process of literary creation as being "organic" rather than "mechanical" was pre-eminently exemplified for Coleridge, as for the Romanticists generally, by Shakespeare. The formulation of the idea of organicism which Coleridge made in the notebook entry given below is its classic expression in English. It will be seen that the idea is salient in Shelley's *Defence of Poetry.*

Biographia Literaria

From *Chapter I*
The discipline of his taste at school—Bowles's sonnets—Comparison between the poets before and since Mr. Pope.

At school I enjoyed the inestimable advantage of a very sensible, though at the same time a very severe master. He [1] early moulded my taste to the preference of Demosthenes to Cicero, of Homer and Theocritus to Virgil, and

---

1. "The Rev. James Bowyer, many years Head Master of the Grammar School, Christ's Hospital" (Coleridge). See below Lamb's account of Bowyer in *Christ's Hospital Five and Thirty Years Ago.*

again of Virgil to Ovid.[2] He habituated me to compare Lucretius (in such extracts as I then read), Terence, and above all the chaster poems of Catullus, not only with the Roman poets of the, so called, silver and brazen ages; but with even those of the Augustan era: and on grounds of plain sense and universal logic to see and assert the superiority of the former in the truth and nativeness, both of their thoughts and diction. At the same time that we were studying the Greek Tragic Poets, he made us read Shakespeare and Milton as lessons: and they were the lessons too, which required most time and trouble to *bring up*, so as to escape his censure. I learnt from him, that Poetry, even that of the loftiest and, seemingly, that of the wildest odes, had a logic of its own, as severe as that of science; and more difficult, because more subtle, more complex, and dependent on more, and more fugitive causes. In the truly great poets, he would say, there is a reason assignable, not only for every word, but for the position of every word; and I will remember that, availing himself of the synonyms to the Homer of Didymus,[3] he made us attempt to show, with regard to each, *why* it would not have answered the same purpose; and *wherein* consisted the peculiar fitness of the word in the original text.

In our own English compositions (at least for the last three years of our school education) he showed no mercy to phrase, metaphor, or image, unsupported by a sound sense, or where the same sense might have been conveyed with equal force and dignity in plainer words. Lute, harp, and lyre, muse, muses, and inspirations, Pegasus, Parnassus, and Hippocrene[4] were all an abomination to him. In fancy I can almost hear him now, exclaiming 'Harp? Harp? Lyre? Pen and ink, boy, you mean! Muse, boy, Muse? Your Nurse's daughter, you mean! Pierian spring? Oh aye! the cloister-pump, I suppose!' Nay, certain introductions, similes, and examples, were placed by name on a list of interdiction. Among the similes, there was, I remember, that of the manchineel fruit,[5] as suiting equally well with too many subjects; in which however it yielded the palm at once to the example of Alexander and Clytus,[6] which was equally good and apt, whatever might be the theme. Was it ambition? Alexander and Clytus!—Flattery? Alexander and Clytus!—Anger? Drunkenness? Pride? Friendship? Ingratitude? Late repentance? Still, still Alexander and Clytus! At length, the praises of agriculture having been exemplified in the sagacious observation, that, had Alexander been holding the plough, he would not have run his friend Clytus through with a spear, this tried and serviceable old friend was banished by public edict in *secula*

2. The particular reasons for the preferences which Coleridge mentions in this and the next sentence need not be gone into—what he is saying in sum is that Bowyer taught him to regard the ancient classics as living literature.

3. Didymus (*c.* 65 B.C.–10 A.D.) was an Alexandrian literary scholar, author of a commentary on Homer. He was nicknamed *Chalkenteros*, Brazen-guts, because of his relentless industry.

4. Pegasus was the winged horse of the Muses. Parnassus was a mountain in Greece, one of whose two summits was the home of Apollo and the Muses. Hippocrene was the fountain of the Muses on another of their homes, Mount Helicon.

5. The manchineel is a tropical American tree, having poisonous sap and poisonous fruit.

6. Clytus—more usually, Cleitus—was a friend of Alexander's and the brother of his foster mother, and had once in battle saved Alexander's life. Alexander killed him in a moment of drunken rage and was overcome with remorse.

seculorum.[7] I have sometimes ventured to think, that a list of this kind, or an *index expurgatorius* [8] of certain well known and ever returning phrases, both introductory, and transitional, including a large assortment of modest egoisms, and flattering illeisms,[9] &c., &c., might be hung up in our law-courts, and both houses of parliament, with great advantage to the public, as an important saving of national time, an incalculable relief to his Majesty's ministers, but above all, as ensuring the thanks of country attorneys, and their clients, who have private bills to carry through the House.

Be this as it may, there was one custom of our master's, which I cannot pass over in silence, because I think it imitable and worthy of imitation. He would often permit our exercises, under some pretext of want of time, to accumulate, till each lad had four or five to be looked over. Then placing the whole number *abreast* on his desk, he would ask the writer, why this or that sentence might not have found as appropriate a place under this or that other thesis: and if no satisfying answer could be returned, and two faults of the same kind were found in one exercise, the irrevocable verdict followed, the exercise was torn up, and another on the same subject to be produced, in addition to the tasks of the day. The reader will, I trust, excuse this tribute of recollection to a man, whose severities, even now, not seldom furnish the dreams, by which the blind fancy would fain interpret to the mind the painful sensations of distempered sleep; but neither lessen nor dim the deep sense of my moral and intellectual obligations. He sent us to the University excellent Latin and Greek scholars, and tolerable Hebraists. Yet our classical knowledge was the least of the good gifts, which we derived from his zealous and conscientious tutorage. He is now gone to his final reward, full of years, and full of honours, even of those honours, which were dearest to his heart, as gratefully bestowed by that school, and still binding him to the interests of that school, in which he had been himself educated, and to which during his whole life he was a dedicated thing.

From causes, which this is not the place to investigate, no models of past times, however perfect, can have the same vivid effect on the youthful mind, as the productions of contemporary genius. . . . The great works of past ages seem to a young man things of another race, in respect to which his faculties must remain passive and submiss, even as to the stars and mountains. But the writings of a contemporary, perhaps not many years older than himself, surrounded by the same circumstances, and disciplined by the same manners, possess a *reality* for him, and inspire an actual friendship as of a man for a man. His very admiration is the wind which fans and feeds his hope. The poems themselves assume the properties of flesh and blood. To recite, to extol, to contend for them is but the payment of a debt due to one, who exists to receive it.

. . .

I had just entered on my seventeenth year, when the sonnets of Mr. Bowles,[10] twenty in number, and just then published in a quarto pamphlet, were first

7. In perpetuity—for "centuries of centuries."
8. The phrase commonly refers to a list of books that Roman Catholics were once not permitted to read until certain parts were expunged.
9. The excessive use of *he* (Latin: *ille*), especially when meaning oneself.
10. William Lisle Bowles (1762–1850) published *Fourteen Sonnets* in 1789. To Cole-

made known and presented to me, by a schoolfellow who had quitted us for the University, and who, during the whole time that he was in our first form (or in our school language a Grecian [11]) had been my patron and protector. I refer to Dr. Middleton, the truly learned, and every way excellent Bishop of Calcutta. . . .

It was a double pleasure to me, and still remains a tender recollection, that I should have received from a friend so revered the first knowledge of a poet, by whose works, year after year, I was so enthusiastically delighted and inspired. My earliest acquaintances will not have forgotten the undisciplined eagerness and impetuous zeal, with which I laboured to make proselytes, not only of my companions, but of all with whom I conversed, of whatever rank, and in whatever place. As my school finances did not permit me to purchase copies, I made, within less than a year and a half, more than forty transcriptions, as the best presents I could offer to those, who had in any way won my regard. And with almost equal delight did I receive the three or four following publications of the same author.

Though I have seen and known enough of mankind to be well aware, that I shall perhaps stand alone in my creed, and that it will be well, if I subject myself to no worse charge than that of singularity; I am not therefore deterred from avowing, that I regard, and ever have regarded the obligations of intellect among the most sacred of the claims of gratitude. A valuable thought, or a particular train of thoughts, gives me additional pleasure, when I can safely refer and attribute it to the conversation or correspondence of another. My obligations to Mr. Bowles were indeed important, and for radical good. At a very premature age, even before my fifteenth year, I had bewildered myself in metaphysics, and in theological controversy. Nothing else pleased me. History, and particular facts, lost all interest in my mind. Poetry (though for a schoolboy of that age, I was above par in English versification, and had already produced two or three compositions which, I may venture to say, without reference to my age, were somewhat above mediocrity, and which had gained me more credit than the sound, good sense of my old master was at all pleased with), poetry itself, yea, novels and romances, became insipid to me. In my friendless wanderings on our leave-days (for I was an orphan, and had scarcely any connexions in London), highly was I delighted, if any passenger, especially if he were dressed in black,[12] would enter into conversation with me. For I soon found the means of directing it to my favourite subjects

---

ridge they came as a revelation by reason of the simplicity of their diction, their air of sincerity, and their responsiveness to nature. In 1806 Bowles produced an edition of Pope in the preface of which he expressed an adverse view of Pope's style. This involved him in a heated and extended controversy with Pope's admirers, of whom Byron was one of the most ardent.

11. The name given to the gifted older pupils of the school who were being prepared for the university. The numbering of "forms" or classes at Christ's Hospital would seem to have been different from that in use in other English schools; usually the youngest class is the first form.

12. That is, a clergyman. He would be the more willing to enter into conversation with the young Coleridge because, from the uniform of long blue coat and bright yellow stockings, he would identify the youth as a member of the school of Christ's Hospital whose pupils, Charles Lamb tells us, were affectionately regarded by Londoners. The uniform is still sometimes worn by pupils of the school.

Of providence, fore-knowledge, will, and fate,
Fixed fate, free will, fore-knowledge absolute,
And found no end in wandering mazes lost.[13]

This preposterous pursuit was, beyond doubt, injurious both to my natural powers, and to the progress of my education. It would perhaps have been destructive, had it been continued; but from this I was auspiciously withdrawn, partly indeed by an accidental introduction to an amiable family,[14] chiefly however, by the genial influence of a style of poetry, so tender and yet so manly, so natural and real, and yet so dignified and harmonious, as the sonnets etc. of Mr. Bowles! Well were it for me, perhaps, had I never relapsed into the same mental disease; if I had continued to pluck the flower and reap the harvest from the cultivated surface, instead of delving in the unwholesome quicksilver mines of metaphysic depths. But if in after time I have sought a refuge from bodily pain and mismanaged sensibility in abstruse researches, which exercised the strength and subtlety of the understanding without awakening the feelings of the heart; still there was a long and blessed interval, during which my natural faculties were allowed to expand, and my original tendencies to develop themselves: my fancy, and the love of nature, and the sense of beauty in forms and sounds.

The second advantage, which I owe to my early perusal, and admiration of these poems (to which let me add, though known to me at a somewhat later period, the *Lewesdon Hill* of Mr. Crowe [15]), bears more immediately on my present subject. Among those with whom I conversed, there were, of course, very many who had formed their taste, and their notions of poetry, from the writings of Mr. Pope and his followers: or to speak more generally, in that school of French poetry, condensed and invigorated by English understanding, which had predominated from the last century. I was not blind to the merits of this school, yet as from inexperience of the world, and consequent want of sympathy with the general subjects of these poems, they gave me little pleasure, I doubtless undervalued the *kind*, and with the presumption of youth withheld from its masters the legitimate name of poets. I saw that the excellence of this kind consisted in just and acute observations on men and manners in an artificial state of society, as its matter and substance: and in the logic of wit, conveyed in smooth and strong epigrammatic couplets, as its *form*. Even when the subject was addressed to the fancy, or the intellect, as in the *Rape of the Lock*, or the *Essay on Man;* nay, when it was a consecutive narration, as in that astonishing product of matchless talent and ingenuity, Pope's translation of the *Iliad;* still a *point* was looked for at the end of each second line, and the whole was as it were a sorites,[16] or, if I may exchange a logical for a grammatical metaphor, a *conjunction disjunctive*, of epigrams.[17] Meantime

13. *Paradise Lost* II.559–61.
14. The widowed mother and three sisters of a school friend, Tom Evans. Coleridge fell in love with the eldest sister, Mary.
15. William Crowe (1745–1829), a clergyman and scholar, published *Lewesdon Hill* in 1788. It is a long descriptive poem in blank verse and in its day much admired.
16. A series of linked syllogisms.
17. A "conjunction disjunctive" is a grammatical element that both joins part of a sentence and suggests an opposition between them—e.g. *either-or, neither-nor, but-although*.

the matter and diction seemed to me characterized not so much by poetic thoughts, as by thoughts *translated* into the language of poetry. On this last point, I had occasion to render my own thoughts gradually more and more plain to myself, by frequent amicable disputes concerning Darwin's *Botanic Garden*,[18] which, for some years, was greatly extolled, not only by the reading public in general, but even by those, whose genius and natural robustness of understanding enabled them afterwards to act foremost in dissipating these 'painted mists' that occasionally rise from the marshes at the foot of Parnassus. During my first Cambridge vacation, I assisted a friend in a contribution for a literary society in Devonshire: and in this I remember to have compared Darwin's work to the Russian palace of ice, glittering, cold and transitory. In the same essay too, I assigned sundry reasons, chiefly drawn from a comparison of passages in the Latin poets with the original Greek, from which they were borrowed, for the preference of Collins' odes to those of Gray; and of the simile in Shakespeare:

> How like a younker or a prodigal,
> The scarfed bark puts from her native bay,
> Hugged and embraced by the strumpet wind!
> How like the prodigal doth she return,
> With over-weathered ribs and ragged sails,
> Lean, rent, and beggared by the strumpet wind! [19]

to the imitation in *The Bard:*

> Fair laughs the morn, and soft the zephyr blows,
> While proudly riding o'er the azure realm
> In gallant trim the gilded vessel goes,
> YOUTH at the prow and PLEASURE at the helm;
> Regardless of the sweeping whirlwind's sway,
> That hushed in grim repose, expects its evening prey.[20]

(In which, by the bye, the words 'realm' and 'sway' are rhymes dearly purchased.) I preferred the original on the ground, that in the imitation it depended wholly on the compositor's putting, or not putting, a *small capital*, both in this, and in many other passages of the same poet, whether the words should be personifications, or mere abstractions. I mention this, because, in referring various lines in Gray to their original in Shakespeare and Milton, and in the clear perception how completely all the propriety was lost in the transfer, I was, at that early period, led to a conjecture, which, many years afterwards was recalled to me from the same thought having been started in conversation, but far more ably, and developed more fully, by Mr. Wordsworth; namely, that this style of poetry, which I have characterized above, as translations of prose thoughts into poetic language, had been kept up by, if it did not wholly arise

---

18. Erasmus Darwin (1731–1802) was the grandfather of Charles Darwin. *The Botanic Garden* (1789, 1791) is a didactic poem in rhymed couplets on plants and flowers. Some of Erasmus Darwin's scientific views are absurd, some brilliant, and the same can be said of his verse.
19. *The Merchant of Venice* II.vi.14–19.
20. Thomas Gray, *The Bard*, ll. 71–74.

from, the custom of writing Latin verses, and the great importance attached to these exercises, in our public schools. Whatever might have been the case in the fifteenth century, when the use of the Latin tongue was so general among learned men, that Erasmus is said to have forgotten his native language; yet in the present day it is not to be supposed, that a youth can *think* in Latin, or that he can have any other reliance on the force or fitness of his phrases, but the authority of the writer from whence he has adopted them. Consequently he must first prepare his thoughts, and then pick out, from Virgil, Horace, Ovid, or perhaps more compendiously from his *Gradus*,[21] halves and quarters of lines, in which to embody them.

I never object to a certain degree of disputatiousness in a young man from the age of seventeen to that of four or five and twenty, provided I find him always arguing on one side of the question. The controversies, occasioned by my unfeigned zeal for the honour of a favourite contemporary, then known to me only by his works, were of great advantage in the formation and establishment of my taste and critical opinions. In my defence of the lines running into each other, instead of closing at each couplet, and of natural language, neither bookish, nor vulgar, neither redolent of the lamp, nor of the kennel, such as *I will remember thee*; instead of the same thought tricked up in the rag-fair finery of

> ————Thy image on her wing
> Before my Fancy's eye shall Memory bring,

I had continually to adduce the metre and diction of the Greek poets from Homer to Theocritus inclusive; and still more of our elder English poets from Chaucer to Milton. Nor was this all. But as it was my constant reply to authorities brought against me from later poets of great name, that no authority could avail in opposition to Truth, Nature, Logic, and the Laws of Universal Grammar; actuated too by my former passion for metaphysical investigations; I laboured at a solid foundation, on which permanently to ground my opinions, in the component faculties of the human mind itself, and their comparative dignity and importance. According to the faculty or source, from which the pleasure given by any poem or passage was derived, I estimated the merit of such poem or passage. As the result of all my reading and meditation, I abstracted two critical aphorisms, deeming them to comprise the conditions and criteria of poetic style; first, that not the poem which we have *read*, but that to which we *return*, with the greatest pleasure, possesses the genuine power, and claims the name of *essential poetry*. Second, that whatever lines can be translated into other words of the same language, without diminution of their significance, either in sense, or association, or in any worthy feeling, are so far vicious in their diction. Be it however observed, that I excluded from the list of worthy feelings, the pleasure derived from mere novelty in the reader, and the desire of exciting wonderment at his powers in the author. Oftentimes since then, in pursuing French tragedies, I have fancied two marks

---

21. Short for *Gradus ad Parnassum* (Step to Parnassus). This was a dictionary of Latin poetical phrases once used in English schools to aid pupils in the composition of Latin verse.

of admiration at the end of each line, as hieroglyphics of the author's own admiration at his own cleverness. Our genuine admiration of a great poet is a continuous *undercurrent* of feeling; it is everywhere present, but seldom anywhere as a separate excitement. I was wont boldly to affirm, that it would be scarcely more difficult to push a stone out from the pyramids with the bare hand, than to alter a word, or the position of a word, in Milton or Shakespeare (in their most important works at least) without making the author say something else, or something worse, than he does say. One great distinction, I appeared to myself to see plainly, between, even the characteristic faults of our elder poets, and the false beauty of the moderns. In the former, from Donne to Cowley, we find the most fantastic out-of-the-way thoughts, but in the most pure and genuine mother English; in the latter, the most obvious thoughts, in language the most fantastic and arbitrary. Our faulty elder poets sacrificed the passion and passionate flow of poetry, to the subtleties of intellect, and to the starts of wit; the moderns to the glare and glitter of a perpetual, yet broken and heterogeneous imagery, or rather to an amphibious something, made up, half of image, and half of abstract meaning.[22] The one sacrificed the heart to the head; the other both heart and head to point and drapery . . .

From *Chapter IV*
Mr. Wordsworth's earlier poems—On fancy and imagination—The investigation of the distinction important to the fine arts.

During the last year of my residence at Cambridge, I became acquainted with Mr. Wordsworth's first publication entitled *Descriptive Sketches;* [1] and seldom, if ever, was the emergence of an original poetic genius above the literary horizon more evidently announced. In the form, style, and manner of the whole poem, and in the structure of the particular lines and periods, there is an harshness and acerbity connected and combined with words and images all aglow, which might recall those products of the vegetable world, where gorgeous blossoms rise out of the hard and thorny rind and shell, within which the rich fruit was elaborating. The language was not only peculiar and strong, but at times knotty and contorted, as by its own impatient strength; while the novelty and struggling crowd of images, acting in conjunction with the difficulties of the style, demanded always a greater closeness of attention, than poetry (at all events, than descriptive poetry) has a right to claim. It not seldom therefore justified the complaint of obscurity. In the following extract I have sometimes fancied, that I saw an emblem of the poem itself, and of the author's genius as it was then displayed.

'Tis storm; and hid in mist from hour to hour,
All day the floods a deepening murmur pour;
The sky is veiled, and every cheerful sight:
Dark is the region as with coming night;

22. "I remember a ludicrous instance in the poem of a young tradesman: No more will I endure love's pleasing pain, / Or round my *heart's leg* tie his galling chain." (Coleridge)

1. Published in 1793. The poem sets forth Wordsworth's impressions and emotions on his walking trip through the Alps in the summer of 1790. The same tour is described in a much more impressive way in *The Prelude VI.*

And yet what frequent bursts of overpowering light!
Triumphant on the bosom of the storm,
Glances the fire-clad eagle's wheeling form;
Eastward, in long perspective glittering, shine
The wood-crowned cliffs that o'er the lake recline;
Wide o'er the Alps a hundred streams unfold,
At once to pillars turned that flame with gold;
Behind his sail the peasant strives to shun
The West, that burns like one dilated sun,
Where in a mighty crucible expire
The mountains, glowing hot, like coals of fire.[2]

The poetic Psyche, in its process to full development, undergoes as many changes as its Greek namesake, the butterfly.[3] And it is remarkable how soon genius clears and purifies itself from the faults and errors of its earliest products; faults which, in its earliest compositions, are the more obtrusive and confluent, because as heterogeneous elements, which had only a temporary use, they constitute the very *ferment*, by which themselves are carried off. Or we may compare them to some diseases, which must work on the humours, and be thrown out on the surface, in order to secure the patient from their future recurrence. I was in my twenty-fourth year, when I had the happiness of knowing Mr. Wordsworth personally, and while memory lasts, I shall hardly forget the sudden effect produced on my mind, by his recitation of a manuscript poem, which still remains unpublished, but of which the stanza, and tone of style, were the same as those of the 'Female Vagrant,' as originally printed in the first volume of the *Lyrical Ballads*.[4] There was here no mark of strained thought, or forced diction, no crowd or turbulence of imagery; and, as the poet hath himself well described in his lines 'On Re-visiting the Wye,' manly reflection, and human associations had given both variety, and an additional interest to natural objects, which in the passion and appetite of the first love they had seemed to him neither to need or permit.[5] The occasional obscurities, which had risen from an imperfect control over the resources of his native language, had almost wholly disappeared, together with that worse defect of arbitrary and illogical phrases, at once hackneyed, and fantastic, which hold so distinguished a place in the *technique* of ordinary poetry, and will,

2. *Descriptive Sketches*, ll. 332–47. Coleridge quotes the passage as it appeared in a revised version in 1815.
3. "The fact, that in Greek Psyche is the common name for the soul, and the butterfly, is thus alluded to in the following stanzas from an unpublished poem of the author:

The butterfly the ancient Grecians made
The soul's fair emblem, and its only name—
But of the soul, escaped the slavish trade
Of mortal life! For in this earthly frame
Ours is the reptile's lot, much toil, much blame,
Manifold motions making little speed,
And to deform and kill the things, whereon we feed." (Coleridge)
4. The manuscript poem was *Guilt and Sorrow*, which Wordsworth composed between 1791 and 1794. He revised part of the poem and, under the title "The Female Vagrant," included it in *Lyrical Ballads*.
5. Coleridge refers to *Tintern Abbey*, ll. 72–102.

more or less, alloy the earlier poems of the truest genius, unless the attention has been specifically directed to their worthlessness and incongruity. I did not perceive anything particular in the mere style of the poem alluded to during its recitation, except indeed such difference as was not separable from the thought and manner; and the Spenserian stanza, which always, more or less, recalls to the reader's mind Spenser's own style, would doubtless have authorized, in my then opinion, a more frequent descent to the phrases of ordinary life, than could without an ill effect have been hazarded in the heroic couplet. It was not however the freedom from false taste, whether as to common defects, or to those more properly his own, which made so unusual an impression on my feelings immediately, and subsequently on my judgement. It was the union of deep feeling with profound thought; the fine balance of truth in observing, with the imaginative faculty in modifying the objects observed; and above all the original gift of spreading the tone, the *atmosphere*, and with it the depth and height of the ideal world around forms, incidents, and situations, of which, for the common view, custom had bedimmed all the lustre, had dried up the sparkle and the dew drops. 'To find no contradiction in the union of old and new; to contemplate the Ancient of Days and all his works with feelings as fresh, as if all had then sprang forth at the first creative fiat; characterizes the mind that feels the riddle of the world, and may help to unravel it. To carry on the feelings of childhood into the powers of manhood; to combine the child's sense of wonder and novelty with the appearances, which every day for perhaps forty years had rendered familiar;

> With sun and moon and stars throughout the year,
> And man and woman; [6]

this is the character and privilege of genius, and one of the marks which distinguish genius from talents. And therefore is it the prime merit of genius and its most unequivocal mode of manifestation, so to represent familiar objects as to awaken in the minds of others a kindred feeling concerning them and that freshness of sensation which is the constant accompaniment of mental, no less than of bodily, convalescence. Who has not a thousand times seen snow fall on water? Who has not watched it with a new feeling, from the time that he has read Burns' comparison of sensual pleasure

> To snow that falls upon a river
> A moment white—then gone forever! [7]

In poems, equally as in philosophic disquisitions, genius produces the strongest impressions of novelty, while it rescues the most admitted truths from the impotence caused by the very circumstance of their universal admission. 'Truths of all others the most awful and mysterious, yet being at the same time of universal interest, are too often considered as *so* true, that they lose all the life and efficiency of truth, and lie bed-ridden in the dormitory of the soul,

6. Milton, "Sonnet, To Mr. Cyriak Skinner upon His Blindness," somewhat altered.
7. *Tam O'Shanter*, ll. 61–62: "Or like the snow falls in the river— / A moment white, then melts forever."

side by side with the most despised and exploded errors.'—*The Friend,* p. 76, No. 5.[8]

This excellence, which in all Mr. Wordsworth's writings is more or less predominant, and which constitutes the character of his mind, I no sooner felt, than I sought to understand. Repeated meditations led me first to suspect (and a more intimate analysis of the human faculties, their appropriate marks, functions, and effects matured my conjecture into full conviction) that fancy and imagination were two distinct and widely different faculties, instead of being, according to the general belief, either two names with one meaning, or, at furthest, the lower and higher degree of one and the same power. It is not, I own, easy to conceive a more opposite translation of the Greek *phantasia* than the Latin *imaginatio;* but it is equally true that in all societies there exists an instinct of growth, a certain collective, unconscious good sense working progressively to desynonymize those words originally of the same meaning, which the conflux of dialects had supplied to the more homogeneous languages, as the Greek and German: and which the same cause, joined with accidents of translation from original works of different countries, occasion in mixed languages like our own. The first and most important point to be proved is, that two conceptions perfectly distinct are confused under one and the same word, and (this done) to appropriate that word exclusively to one meaning, and the synonym (should there be one) to the other. But if (as will be often the case in the arts and sciences) no synonym exists, we must either invent or borrow a word. In the present instance the appropriation has already begun, and been legitimated in the derivative adjective: Milton had a highly *imaginative,* Cowley a very *fanciful* mind. If therefore I should succeed in establishing the actual existences of two faculties generally different, the nomenclature would be at once determined. To the faculty by which I had characterized Milton, we should confine the term *imagination;* while the other would be contra-distinguished as *fancy.* Now were it once fully ascertained, that this division is no less grounded in nature, than that of delirium from mania, or Otway's

> Lutes, lobsters, seas of milk, and ships of amber,[9]

from Shakespeare's

> What! have his daughters brought him to this pass?[10]

or from the preceding apostrophe to the elements; the theory of the fine arts, and of poetry in particular, could not, I thought, but derive some additional and important light. It would in its immediate effects furnish a torch of guidance to the philosophical critic; and ultimately to the poet himself. In energetic minds, truth soon changes by domestication into power; and from directing in the discrimination and appraisal of the product, becomes influencive

8. *The Friend: A Literary, Moral, and Political Weekly Paper* (of minute circulation) was written and published by Coleridge in 1809–10.

9. Thomas Otway, *Venice Preserved* (1682), V.ii.151. Coleridge is being unkind in the way he quotes the line—absurd as it is, it does not read "Lutes, lobsters . . ." but "Lutes, laurels. . . ."

10. *King Lear* III.iv.65.

in the production. To admire on principle, is the only way to imitate without loss of originality . . .

Chapter XIV
Occasion of the Lyrical Ballads, and the objects originally proposed—Preface to the second edition—The ensuing controversy, its causes and acrimony— Philosophic definitions of a poem and poetry with scholia.[1]

During the first year that Mr. Wordsworth and I were neighbours,[2] our conversations turned frequently on the two cardinal points of poetry, the power of exciting the sympathy of the reader by a faithful adherence to the truth of nature, and the power of giving the interest of novelty by the modifying colours of imagination. The sudden charm, which accidents of light and shade, which moonlight or sunset diffused over a known and familiar landscape, appeared to represent the practicability of combining both. These are the poetry of nature. The thought suggested itself (to which of us I do not recollect) that a series of poems might be composed of two sorts. In the one, the incidents and agents were to be, in part at least, supernatural; and the excellence aimed at was to consist in the interesting of the affections by the dramatic truth of such emotions, as would naturally accompany such situations, supposing them real. And real in *this* sense they have been to every human being who, from whatever source of delusion, has at any time believed himself under supernatural agency. For the second class, subjects were to be chosen from ordinary life; the characters and incidents were to be such, as will be found in every village and its vicinity, where there is a meditative and feeling mind to seek after them, or to notice them, when they present themselves.

In this idea originated the plan of the *Lyrical Ballads;* in which it was agreed, that my endeavours should be directed to persons and characters supernatural, or at least romantic; yet so as to transfer from our inward nature a human interest and a semblance of truth sufficient to procure for these shadows of imagination that willing suspension of disbelief for the moment, which constitutes poetic faith. Mr. Wordsworth, on the other hand, was to propose to himself as his object, to give the charm of novelty to things of every day, and to excite a feeling analogous to the supernatural, by awakening the mind's attention from the lethargy of custom, and directing it to the loveliness and the wonders of the world before us; an inexhaustible treasure, but for which, in consequence of the film of familiarity and selfish solicitude we have eyes, yet see not, ears that hear not, and hearts that neither feel nor understand.[3]

With this view I wrote *The Ancient Mariner*, and was preparing among other poems, 'The Dark Ladie,' and the *Christabel*, in which I should have more nearly realized my ideal, than I had done in my first attempt. But Mr. Wordsworth's industry had proved so much more successful, and the number of his poems so much greater, that my compositions, instead of forming a balance, appeared rather an interpolation of heterogeneous matter. Mr. Wordsworth added two or three poems written in his own character, in the impassioned,

1. Plural of *scholium* (Latin), an explanatory note or commentary.
2. In 1797 at Nether Stowey and Alfoxden. See Hazlitt's *My First Acquaintance with Poets.*
3. *Isaiah* 6: 9–10.

lofty, and sustained diction, which is characteristic of his genius.[4] In this form the *Lyrical Ballads* were published; and were presented by him, as an *experiment*,[5] whether subjects, which from their nature rejected the usual ornaments and extra-colloquial style of poems in general, might not be so managed in the language of ordinary life as to produce the pleasureable interest, which it is the peculiar business of poetry to impart. To the second edition he added a preface of considerable length; in which, notwithstanding some passages of apparently a contrary import, he was understood to contend for the extension of this style to poetry of all kinds, and to reject as vicious and indefensible all phrases and forms of style that were not included in what he (unfortunately, I think, adopting an equivocal expression) called the language of *real* life. From this preface, prefixed to poems in which it was impossible to deny the presence of original genius, however mistaken its direction might be deemed, arose the whole long-continued controversy.[6] For from the conjunction of perceived power with supposed heresy I explain the inveteracy and in some instances, I grieve to say, the acrimonious passions, with which the controversy has been conducted by the assailants.

Had Mr. Wordsworth's poems been the silly, the childish things, which they were for a long time described as being; had they been really distinguished from the compositions of other poets merely by meanness of language and inanity of thought; had they indeed contained nothing more than what is found in the parodies and pretended imitations of them; they must have sunk at once, a dead weight, into the slough of oblivion, and have dragged the preface along with them. But year after year increased the number of Mr. Wordsworth's admirers. They were found too not in the lower classes of the reading public, but chiefly among young men of strong sensibility and meditative minds; and their admiration (inflamed perhaps in some degree by opposition) was distinguished by its intensity, I might almost say, by its *religious* fervour. These facts, and the intellectual energy of the author, which was more or less consciously felt, where it was outwardly and even boisterously denied, meeting with sentiments of aversion to his opinions, and of alarm at their consequences, produced an eddy of criticism, which would of itself have borne up the poems by the violence, with which it whirled them round and round. With many parts of this preface, in the sense attributed to them, and which the words undoubtedly seem to authorize, I never concurred; but on the contrary objected to them as erroneous in principle, and as contradictory (in appearance at least) both to other parts of the same preface, and to the author's own practice in the greater number of the poems themselves. Mr. Wordsworth in his recent collection[7] has, I find, degraded this prefatory disquisition to the end of his second volume, to

4. Coleridge means those of Wordsworth's poems, of which *Tintern Abbey* is the pre-eminent example, which were not among the "experiments" referred to in the next sentence.
5. Wordsworth uses the word in the brief "Advertisement" to the first edition of *Lyrical Ballads* as well as in his Preface to the second edition (1800). The concept of conscious "experiment" in art became of great consequence in the later 19th century, although without reference to Wordsworth.
6. The often acrimonious debate over Wordsworth's theory of the language appropriate to poetry.
7. *Poems,* two volumes, 1815.

be read or not at the reader's choice. But he has not, as far as I can discover, announced any change in his poetic creed. At all events, considering it as the source of a controversy, in which I have been honoured more than I deserve by the frequent conjunction of my name with his, I think it expedient to declare once for all, in what points I coincide with his opinions, and in what points I altogether differ. But in order to render myself intelligible I must previously, in as few words as possible, explain my ideas, first, of a POEM; and secondly, of POETRY itself, in *kind*, and in *essence*.

The office of philosophical *disquisition* consists in just *distinction;* while it is the privilege of the philosopher to preserve himself constantly aware, that distinction is not division. In order to obtain adequate notions of any truth, we must intellectually separate its distinguishable parts; and this is the technical *process* of philosophy. But having so done, we must then restore them in our conceptions to the unity, in which they actually co-exist; and this is the *result* of philosophy. A poem contains the same elements as a prose composition; the difference therefore must consist in a different combination of them, in consequence of a different object being proposed. According to the difference of the object will be the difference of the combination. It is possible, that the object may be merely to facilitate the recollection of any given facts or observations by artificial arrangement; and the composition will be a poem, merely because it is distinguished from prose by metre, or by rhyme, or by both conjointly. In this, the lowest sense, a man might attribute the name of a poem to the well-known enumeration of the days in the several months;

> Thirty days hath September,
> April, June, and November, etc.

and others of the same class and purpose. And as a particular pleasure is found in anticipating the recurrence of sounds and quantities, all compositions that have this charm super-added, whatever be their contents, *may* be entitled poems.

So much for the superficial *form.* A difference of object and contents supplies an additional ground of distinction. The immediate purpose may be the communication of truths; either of truth absolute and demonstrable, as in works of science; or of facts experienced and recorded, as in history. Pleasure, and that of the highest and most permanent kind, may *result* from the *attainment* of the end; but it is not itself the immediate end. In other works the communication of pleasure may be the immediate purpose; and though truth, either moral or intellectual, ought to be the *ultimate* end, yet this will distinguish the character of the author, not the class to which the work belongs. Blest indeed is that state of society, in which the immediate purpose would be baffled by the perversion of the proper ultimate end; in which no charm of diction or imagery could exempt the Bathyllus even of an Anacreon, or the Alexis of Virgil, from disgust and aversion! [8]

But the communication of pleasure may be the immediate object of a work

8. The adverse feelings to which Coleridge refers are those which might be occasioned by the representation of homosexuality. The beauty of the youth Bathyllus is celebrated by Anacreon (6th century B.C.); in Virgil's Second Eclogue the shepherd Corydon loves the young Alexis.

not metrically composed; and that object may have been in a high degree attained, as in novels and romances. Would then the mere superaddition of metre, with or without rhyme, entitle *these* to the name of poems? The answer is, that nothing can permanently please, which does not contain in itself the reason why it is so, and not otherwise. If metre be super-added, all other parts must be made consonant with it. They must be such, as to justify the perpetual and distinct attention to each part, which an exact correspondent recurrence of accent and sound are calculated to excite. The final definition then, so deduced, may be thus worded. A poem is that species of composition, which is opposed to works of science, by proposing for its *immediate* object pleasure, not truth; and from all other species (having *this* object in common with it) it is discriminated by proposing to itself such delight from the *whole*, as is compatible with a distinct gratification from each component *part*.

Controversy is not seldom excited in consequence of the disputants attaching each a different meaning to the same word; and in few instances has this been more striking, than in disputes concerning the present subject. If a man chooses to call every composition a poem, which is rhyme, or measure, or both, I must leave his opinion uncontroverted. The distinction is at least competent to characterize the writer's intention. If it were subjoined, that the whole is likewise entertaining or affecting, as a tale, or as a series of interesting reflections, I of course admit this as another fit ingredient of a poem, and an additional merit. But if the definition sought for be that of a *legitimate* poem, I answer, it must be one, the parts of which mutually support and explain each other; all in their proportion harmonizing with, and supporting the purpose and known influences of metrical arrangement. The philosophic critics of all ages coincide with the ultimate judgement of all countries, in equally denying the praises of a just poem, on the one hand, to a series of striking lines or distichs,[9] each of which, absorbing the whole attention of the reader to itself, disjoins it from its context, and makes it a separate whole, instead of an harmonizing part; and on the other hand, to an unsustained composition, from which the reader collects rapidly the general result, unattracted by the component parts. The reader should be carried forward, not merely or chiefly by the mechanical impulse of curiosity, or by a restless desire to arrive at the final solution; but by the pleasureable activity of mind excited by the attractions of the journey itself. Like the motion of a serpent, which the Egyptians made the emblem of intellectual power; or like the path of sound through the air; at every step he pauses and half recedes, and from the retrogressive movement collects the force which again carries him onward. 'Praecipitandus est, liber *spiritus*,' says Petronius Arbiter most happily.[10] The epithet, *liber*, here balances the preceding verb; and it is not easy to conceive more meaning condensed in fewer words.

But if this should be admitted as a satisfactory character of a poem, we have still to seek for a definition of poetry. The writings of Plato, and Bishop

9. A distich is a group of two lines of verse. The word is used in reference to Greek verse. The English rhymed distich is called a couplet.
10. "The free spirit must be impelled forward." Petronius (d. 66 A.D.), whom Tacitus called *Arbiter Elegantiae* (judge of elegance), was a member of Nero's court and the reputed author of *Satyricon*, a brilliant satirical novel of Roman life.

Taylor, and the *Theoria Sacra* of Burnet,[11] furnish undeniable proofs that poetry of the highest kind may exist without metre, and even without the contradistinguishing objects of a poem. The first chapter of Isaiah (indeed a very large portion of the whole book) is poetry in the most emphatic sense; yet it would be not less irrational than strange to assert, that pleasure, and not truth, was the immediate object of the prophet. In short, whatever *specific* import we attach to the word, poetry, there will be found involved in it, as a necessary consequence, that a poem of any length neither can be, or ought to be, all poetry. Yet if an harmonious whole is to be produced, the remaining parts must be preserved *in keeping* with the poetry; and this can be no otherwise effected than by such a studied selection and artificial arrangement, as will partake of *one*, though not a *peculiar* property of poetry. And this again can be no other than the property of exciting a more continuous and equal attention than the language of prose aims at, whether colloquial or written.

My own conclusions on the nature of poetry, in the strictest use of the word, have been in part anticipated in the preceding disquisition on the fancy and imagination. What is poetry? is so nearly the same question with, what is a poet? that the answer to the one is involved in the solution of the other. For it is a distinction resulting from the poetic genius itself, which sustains and modifies the images, thoughts, and emotions of the poet's own mind.

The poet, described in *ideal* perfection, brings the whole soul of man into activity, with the subordination of its faculties to each other, according to their relative worth and dignity. He diffuses a tone and spirit of unity, that blends, and (as it were) *fuses*, each into each, by that synthetic and magical power, to which we have exclusively appropriated the name of imagination. This power, first put in action by the will and understanding, and retained under their irremissive, though gentle and unnoticed, controul (*laxis effertur habenis* [12]) reveals itself in the balance or reconciliation of opposite or discordant qualities: of sameness, with difference; of the general, with the concrete; the idea, with the image; the individual, with the representative; the sense of novelty and freshness, with old and familiar objects; a more than usual state of emotion, with more than usual order; judgement ever awake and steady self-possession, with enthusiasm and feeling profound or vehement; and while it blends and harmonizes the natural and the artificial, still subordinates art to nature; the manner to the matter; and our admiration of the poet to our sympathy with the poetry. 'Doubtless,' as Sir John Davies observes of the soul (and his words may with slight alteration be applied, and even more appropriately, to the poetic IMAGINATION),

> Doubtless this could not be, but that she turns
> Bodies to spirit by sublimation strange,

---

11. Jeremy Taylor (1613–67), the author of *Holy Living* and *Holy Dying*. The chief work of Thomas Burnet (1635–1715) is *Telluris Theoria Sacra*, first composed in Latin and then rendered into English as *The Sacred Theory of the Earth*. The scientific views expressed in the book are fanciful, but Coleridge admired Burnet's prose, as he did the prose of Taylor, for its richness and stately eloquence, qualities that often characterized the work of 17th-century authors but not those of the 18th century, at least until Burke.
12. "Driven with a loose rein."

As fire converts to fire the things it burns,
    As we our food into our nature change.

From their gross matter she abstracts their forms,
    And draws a kind of quintessence from things;
Which to her proper nature she transforms,
    To bear them light on her celestial wings.

Thus does she, when from individual states
    She doth abstract the universal kinds;
Which then re-clothed in divers names and fates
    Steal access through our senses to our minds.[13]

Finally, GOOD SENSE is the BODY of poetic genius, FANCY its DRAPERY, MOTION its LIFE, and IMAGINATION the SOUL that is everywhere, and in each; and forms all into one graceful and intelligent whole.

From *Chapter XVII*
Examination of the tenets peculiar to Mr. Wordsworth—Rustic life (above all, low and rustic life) especially unfavourable to the formation of a human diction —The best parts of language the product of philosophers, not of clowns or shepherds—Poetry essentially ideal and generic—The language of Milton as much the language of real life, yea, incomparably more so than that of the cottager.

As far then as Mr. Wordsworth in his preface contended, and most ably contended, for a reformation in our poetic diction, as far as he has evinced the truth of passion, and the *dramatic* propriety of those figures and metaphors in the original poets, which, stripped of their justifying reasons, and converted into mere artifices of connection or oranament, constitute the characteristic falsity in the poetic style of the moderns; and as far as he has, with equal acuteness and clearness, pointed out the process by which this change was effected, and the resemblances between that state into which the reader's mind is thrown by the pleasureable confusion of thought from an unaccustomed train of words and images; and that state which is induced by the natural language of impassioned feeling; he undertook a useful task, and deserves all praise, both for the attempt and for the execution. The provocations to this remonstrance in behalf of truth and nature were still of perpetual recurrence before and after the publication of this preface. I cannot likewise but add, that the comparison of such poems of merit, as have been given to the public within the last ten or twelve years, with the majority of those produced previously to the appearance of that preface, leave no doubt on my mind, that Mr. Wordsworth is fully justified in believing his efforts to have been by no means ineffectual. Not only in the verses of those who have professed their admiration of his genius, but even of those who have distinguished themselves by hostility to his theory, and depreciation of his writings, are the impressions of his principles plainly visible. It is possible, that with these principles others may have been blended, which are not equally evident; and some which are un-

---

13. Coleridge quotes, with some significant alterations, from *Nosce Teipsum* (Know Thyself), a long poem by Sir John Davies (1569–1626) on the nature of the soul, with emphasis on its immortality.

steady and subvertible from the narrowness or imperfection of their basis. But it is more than possible, that these errors of defect or exaggeration, by kindling and feeding the controversy, may have conduced not only to the wider propagation of the accompanying truths, but that, by their frequent presentation to the mind in an excited state, they may have won for them a more permanent and practical result. A man will borrow a part from his opponent the more easily, if he feels himself justified in continuing to reject a part. While there remain important points in which he can still feel himself in the right, in which he still finds firm footing for continued resistance, he will gradually adopt those opinions, which were the least remote from his own convictions, as not less congruous with his own theory than with that which he reprobates. In like manner with a kind of instinctive prudence, he will abandon by little and little his weakest posts, till at length he seems to forget that they had ever belonged to him, or affects to consider them at most as accidental and 'petty annexments,' the removal of which leaves the citadel unhurt and unendangered.

My own differences from certain supposed parts of Mr. Wordsworth's theory ground themselves on the assumption, that his words had been rightly interpreted, as purporting that the proper diction for poetry in general consists altogether in a language taken, with due exceptions, from the mouths of men in real life, a language which actually constitutes the natural conversation of men under the influence of natural feelings.[1] My objection is, first, that in *any* sense this rule is applicable only to *certain* classes of poetry; secondly, that even to these classes it is not applicable, except in such a sense, as hath never by any one (as far as I know or have read) been denied or doubted; and lastly, that as far as, and in that degree in which it is *practicable*, yet as a *rule* it is useless, if not injurious, and therefore either need not, or ought not to be practised. The poet informs his reader, that he had generally chosen *low and rustic* life; but not *as* low and rustic, or in order to repeat that pleasure of doubtful moral effect, which persons of elevated rank and of superior refinement oftentimes derive from a happy *imitation* of the rude unpolished manners and discourse of their inferiors. For the pleasure so derived may be traced to three exciting causes. The first is the naturalness, in *fact*, of the things represented. The second is the apparent naturalness of the *representation*, as raised and qualified by an imperceptible infusion of the author's own knowledge and talent, which infusion does, indeed, constitute it an *imitation* as distinguished from a mere *copy*. The third cause may be found in the reader's conscious feeling of his superiority awakened by the contrast presented to him; even as for the same purpose the kings and great barons of yore retained sometimes *actual* clowns and fools, but more frequently shrewd and witty fellows in that *character*. These, however, were not Mr. Wordsworth's objects. *He* chose low and rustic life, 'because in that condition the essential passions of the heart find a better soil, in which they can attain their maturity, are less under restraint, and speak a plainer and more emphatic language; because in that condition of life our elementary feelings coexist in a state of greater simplicity, and consequently may be more accurately contemplated, and more forcibly

1. See Preface to *Lyrical Ballads*.

communicated; because the manners of rural life germinate from those elementary feelings; and from the necessary character of rural occupations are more easily comprehended, and are more durable; and lastly, because in that condition the passions of men are incorporated with the beautiful and permanent forms of nature.' [2]

Now it is clear to me, that in the most interesting of the poems, in which the author is more or less dramatic, as *The Brothers, Michael, Ruth, The Mad Mother*, etc., the persons introduced are by no means taken *from low or rustic life* in the common acceptation of those words; and it is not less clear, that the sentiments and language, as far as they can be conceived to have been really transferred from the minds and conversation of such persons, are attributable to causes and circumstances not necessarily connected with 'their occupations and abode.' The thoughts, feelings, language, and manners of the shepherd-farmers in the vales of Cumberland and Westmoreland, as far as they are actually adopted in those poems, may be accounted for from causes, which will and do produce the same results in *every* state of life, whether in town or country. As the two principal I rank that INDEPENDENCE, which raises a man above servitude, or daily toil for the profit of others, yet not above the necessity of industry and a frugal simplicity of domestic life; and the accompanying unambitious, but solid and religious, EDUCATION, which has rendered few books familiar, but the Bible, and the liturgy or hymn book. To this latter cause, indeed, which is so far *accidental*, that it is the blessing of particular countries and a particular age, not the product of particular places or employments, the poet owes the show of probability, that his personages might really feel, think, and talk with any tolerable resemblance to his representation. . . .

It is, moreover, to be considered that to the formation of healthy feelings, and a reflecting mind, *negations* involve impediments not less formidable than sophistication and vicious intermixture. I am convinced, that for the human soul to prosper in rustic life a certain vantage-ground is prerequisite. It is not every man that is likely to be improved by a country life or by country labours. Education, or original sensibility, or both, must pre-exist, if the changes, forms, and incidents of nature are to prove a sufficient stimulant. And where these are not sufficient, the mind contracts and hardens by want of stimulants: and the man becomes selfish, sensual, gross, and hard-hearted. Let the management of the Poor Laws in Liverpool, Manchester, or Bristol be compared with the ordinary dispensation of the poor rates in agricultural villages, where the *farmers* are the overseers and guardians of the poor. If my own experience have not been particularly unfortunate, as well as that of the many respectable country clergymen with whom I have conversed on the subject, the result would engender more than scepticism concerning the desireable influences of low and rustic life in and for itself. Whatever may be concluded on the other side, from the stronger local attachments and enterprising spirit of the Swiss, and other mountaineers, applies to a particular mode of pastoral life, under forms of property that permit and beget manners truly republican, not to rustic life in general, or to the absence of artificial cultivation. On the contrary the mountaineers, whose manners have been so often eulogized, are in general

2. In the Preface.

better educated and greater readers than men of equal rank elsewhere. But where this is not the case, as among the peasantry of North Wales, the ancient mountains, with all their terrors and all their glories, are pictures to the blind, and music to the deaf.

I should not have entered so much into detail upon this passage, but here seems to be the point, to which all the lines of difference converge as to their source and centre. (I mean, as far as, and in whatever respect, my poetic creed *does* differ from the doctrines promulged in this preface.) I adopt with full faith the principle of Aristotle, that poetry as poetry is essentially *ideal*, that it avoids and excludes all *accident;* that its apparent individualities of rank, character, or occupation must be *representative* of a class; and that the *persons* of poetry must be clothed with *generic* attributes, with the *common* attributes of the class: not with such as one gifted individual might *possibly* possess, but such as from his situation it is most probable beforehand that he *would* possess.[3]

· · ·

Here let me be permitted to remind the reader, that the positions, which I controvert, are contained in the sentences—'a selection of the REAL *language of men';*—'*the language of these men*' (i.e. men in low and rustic life) '*I propose to myself to imitate, and, as far as is possible, to adopt the very language of men.*' '*Between the language of prose and that of metrical composition, there neither is, nor can be any essential difference.*' It is against these exclusively that my opposition is directed.

I object, in the very first instance, to an equivocation in the use of the word 'real.' Every man's language varies, according to the extent of his knowledge, the activity of his faculties, and the depth or quickness of his feelings. Every man's language has, first, its *individualities;* secondly, the common properties of the *class* to which he belongs; and thirdly, words and phrases of *universal* use. The language of Hooker, Bacon, Bishop Taylor, and Burke[4] differs from the common language of the learned class only by the superior number and novelty of the thoughts and relations which they had to convey. The language of Algernon Sidney[5] differs not at all from that, which every well-educated gentleman would wish to write, and (with due allowances for the undeliberateness, and less connected train, of thinking natural and proper to conversation) such as he would wish to talk. Neither one nor the other differ half so much from the general language of cultivated society, as the language of Mr. Wordsworth's homeliest composition differs from that of a common peasant. For 'real' therefore, we must substitute *ordinary*, or *lingua communis*.[6] And this, we have proved, is no more to be found in the phraseology of low and rustic life than

---

3. "Say not that I am recommending abstractions; for these class-characteristics which constitute the instructiveness of a character, are so modified and particularized in each person of the Shakespearean drama, that life itself does not excite more distinctly that sense of individuality which belongs to real existence. . . ." (Coleridge)

4. The works of the four men whose use of language Coleridge cites as admirable span two centuries—the first part of Richard Hooker's great *Laws of Ecclesiastical Polity* was published in 1593, Edmund Burke's *Reflections on the French Revolution* in 1790.

5. Algernon Sidney (1622?–83) was the grand-nephew of Sir Philip Sidney. His dramatic political life was controlled by his strong republican principles, which he expressed in his posthumous *Discourses Concerning Government* (1698).

6. "The common tongue."

in that of any other class. Omit the peculiarities of each, and the result of course must be common to all. And assuredly the omissions and changes to be made in the language of rustics, before it could be transferred to any species of poem, except the drama or other professed imitation, are at least as numerous and weighty, as would be required in adapting to the same purpose the ordinary language of tradesmen and manufacturers. Not to mention, that the language so highly extolled by Mr. Wordsworth varies in every county, nay in every village, according to the accidental character of the clergyman, the existence or non-existence of schools; or even, perhaps, as the exciseman, publican, or barber, happen to be, or not to be, zealous politicians, and readers of the weekly newspaper *pro bono publico*.[7] Anterior to cultivation, the *lingua communis* of every country, as Dante has well observed,[8] exists everywhere in parts, and nowhere as a whole.

Neither is the case rendered at all more tenable by the addition of the words, *in a state of excitement*. For the nature of a man's words, where he is strongly affected by joy, grief, or anger, must necessarily depend on the number and quality of the general truths, conceptions and images, and of the words expressing them, with which his mind had been previously stored. For the property of passion is not to *create*; but to set in increased activity. At least, whatever new connections of thoughts or images, or (which is equally, if not more than equally, the appropriate effect of strong excitement) whatever generalizations of truth or experience, the heat of passion may produce; yet the terms of their conveyance must have pre-existed in his former conversations, and are only collected and crowded together by the unusual stimulation. It is indeed very possible to adopt in a poem the unmeaning repetitions, habitual phrases, and other blank counters, which an unfurnished or confused understanding interposes at short intervals, in order to keep hold of his subject, which is still slipping from him, and to give him time for recollection; or in mere aid of vacancy, as in the scanty companies of a country stage the same player pops backwards and forwards, in order to prevent the appearance of empty spaces, in the procession of *Macbeth*, or *Henry VIII*. But what assistance to the poet, or ornament to the poem, these can supply, I am at a loss to conjecture. Nothing assuredly can differ either in origin or in mode more widely from the *apparent* tautologies of intense and turbulent feeling, in which the passion is greater and of longer endurance than to be exhausted or satisfied by a single representation of the image or incident exciting it. Such repetitions I admit to be a beauty of the highest kind; as illustrated by Mr. Wordsworth himself from the song of Deborah. '*At her feet he bowed, he fell, he lay down; at her feet he bowed, he fell; where he bowed, there he fell down dead.*'[9]

1817

7. "For the public good."
8. In his essay *De Vulgari Eloquentia* ("On the Speech of the People") Dante puts the case for the use in poetry of colloquial Italian purged of the peculiarities of regional dialects.
9. *Judges* 5:27. Wordsworth cites this passage in a note to *The Thorn* in which he defends the repetitions that mark the poem as being appropriate to a state of heightened feeling.

Organic Form

[In the course of the nineteenth century the idea of the organic nature of the creative process (see Headnote) established itself as an orthodox doctrine of aesthetic thought. Walter Pater, in his comprehensive essay on Coleridge (1866, 1880), comments on it in a cogent way. He gives it his general assent but goes on to remark the paradox that, in insisting on the organic model of artistic creation as against the older classical view that the work of art is *made* by the artist, Coleridge represents the artist as "almost a mechanical agent." Here is the whole of Pater's objection:

> Instead of the most luminous and self-possessed phase of consciousness, the associative act in art or poetry is made to look like some blindly organic process of assimilation. The work of art is likened to a living organism. That expresses truly the sense of self-delighting, independent life which the finished work of art gives us: it hardly figures that process by which such work was produced. Here there is no blind ferment of lifeless elements toward the realization of a type. By exquisite analysis the artist attains clearness of idea; then, through many stages of refining, clearness of expression. He moves slowly over his work, calculating the tenderest tone, and restraining the subtlest curve, never letting hand or fancy move at large, gradually enforcing flaccid spaces to the higher degree of expressiveness. The philosophic critic, at least, will value, even in works of imagination, seemingly the most intuitive, the power of the understanding in them, their logical process of construction, the spectacle of a supreme intellectual dexterity which they afford.

The passage which follows is a notebook entry for one of Coleridge's public lectures on Shakespeare, which he never prepared for publication. The text is that of T. M. Raysor, published in *Coleridge's Shakespearean Criticism*.]

The subject of the present lecture is no less than a question submitted to your understandings, emancipated from national prejudice: Are the plays of Shakespeare works of rude uncultivated genius, in which the splendour of the parts compensates, if aught can compensate, for the barbarous shapelessness and irregularity of the whole? To which not only the French critics, but even his own English admirers, say [yes].[1] Or is the form equally admirable with the matter, the judgement of the great poet not less deserving of our wonder than his genius? Or to repeat the question in other words, is Shakespeare a great dramatic poet on account only of these beauties and excellencies which he possesses in common with the ancients, but with diminished claims to our love and honour to the full extent of his difference from them? Or are these very differences additional proofs of poetic wisdom, at once results and symbols of living power as contrasted with lifeless mechanism, of free and rival originality as contra-distinguished from servile imitation, or more accurately, [from] a blind copying of effects instead of a true imitation of the essential principles? Imagine not I am about to oppose genius to rules. No! the comparative value of these rules is the very cause to be tried. The spirit of poetry, like all other living powers, must of necessity circumscribe itself by rules, were it only to unite power with beauty. It must embody in order to reveal itself; but a living body is of necessity an organized one,—and what is organization, but the

---

1. Coleridge rightly singles out Voltaire as the extreme example of the French critics holding this view; but it is hard to think of an English critic who went so far as to impute to Shakespeare a "barbarous shapelessness."

connection of parts to a whole, so that each part is at once end and means! This is no discovery of criticism; it is a necessity of the human mind—and all nations have felt and obeyed it, in the invention of metre and measured sounds as the vehicle and involucrum [2] of poetry, itself a fellow-growth from the same life, even as the bark is to the tree.

No work of true genius dare want its appropriate form; neither indeed is there any danger of this. As it must not, so neither can it, be lawless! For it is even this that constitutes it genius—the power of acting creatively under laws of its own origination. How then comes it that not only single Zoili,[3] but whole nations have combined in unhesitating condemnation of our great dramatist, as a sort of African nature, fertile in beautiful monsters, as a wild heath where islands of fertility look greener from the surrounding waste, where the loveliest plants now shine out among unsightly weeds and now are choked by their parasitic growth, so intertwined that we cannot disentangle the weed without snapping the flower. In this statement I have had no reference to the vulgar abuse of Voltaire, save as far as his charges are coincident with the decisions of his commentators and (so they tell you) his almost idolatrous admirers. The true ground of the mistake, as has been well remarked by a continental critic,[4] lies in the confounding mechanical regularity with organic form. The form is mechanic when on any given material we impress a predetermined form, not necessarily arising out of the properties of the material, as when to a mass of wet clay we give whatever shape we wish it to retain when hardened. The organic form, on the other hand, is innate; it shapes as it develops itself from within, and the fullness of its development is one and the same with the perfection of its outward form. Such is the life, such the form. Nature, the prime genial [5] artist, inexhaustible in diverse powers, is equally inexhaustible in forms. Each exterior is the physiognomy of the being within, its true image reflected and thrown out from the concave mirror. And even such is the appropriate excellence of her chosen poet, of our own Shakespeare, himself a nature humanized, a genial understanding directing self-consciously a power and an implicit wisdom deeper than consciousness.

1930

CHARLES LAMB
1775–1834

London was to Charles Lamb what the Lake Country was to his friend William Wordsworth—the beloved place, the scene uniquely appropriate to his spirit. He was not being wholly serious when he said that he had "an almost insurmountable aversion from solitude and rural scenes," but the joking hyperbole expresses the militancy of his

---

2. Case or envelope, especially around a flower.
3. Zoilus—Zoili is the plural which generalizes him into a type—was a critic of the 4th century B.C. notorious for the bitterness of his attacks on Plato and Homer.
4. This is August Wilhelm von Schlegel, the German critic, from whom Coleridge derived many of his ideas about literature, including the one that he here sets forth.
5. This word was used by the Romanticists—in Germany as well as England—in the sense that connects it with "genius" and suggests generation.

feeling for the town at a time when it was becoming received opinion that sensibility could flourish only in the country.

He was born in the very heart of the metropolis, in the district which was once the ancient walled town and is still called "the City," and in, we might say, its heart's core, the Inner Temple, one of the four curious institutions known as the Inns of Court. Although these are voluntary societies, not chartered by the state, they have in charge the whole of the legal profession of England. They came into being in the fourteenth century and are descended from organizations which combined the functions of trade guilds and law schools. Their buildings, some of which are of great antiquity, are extensive; they include churches, libraries, and dining halls, and they accommodate not only professional offices but also residences.

Lamb's having been born and reared in the Inner Temple suggests the paradox of his social position. His father in his youth had gone into domestic service and although he subsequently rose a little in the social scale by becoming a scrivener, that is, a professional legal copyist, he served his employer, a successful lawyer named Samuel Salt, not only in the capacity of confidential clerk but also as a trusted servant. Lamb's maternal grandmother had been housekeeper to a country family, and his mother was Salt's housekeeper. In a society charged with class feeling one might expect the menial callings of his family to have been a source of distress to a highly conscious young man, but this seems not to have been the case. Lamb writes of his father with affectionate respect as a man of proud and independent spirit and some intellectual attainment; he cherished the memory of his grandmother, and of his mother he said that she was a "perfect gentlewoman."

At the age of seven Lamb was enrolled in the famous school of Christ's Hospital, not far from the Temple. He remained a pupil there until he was fifteen, and his account of his experience is to be read in his great autobiographical essay, *Christ's Hospital Five and Thirty Years Ago* (see below). The friendship with Coleridge that he formed at the school was a strong and lasting one, although it had its vicissitudes. It was through Coleridge that he met Wordsworth, and it says much about Lamb that between him and the craggy and difficult person that Wordsworth became in his later years there was the warmest affection.

After leaving school, Lamb was briefly employed in South Sea House and in 1792 he was appointed to a clerkship in India House, the office of the great private but quasi-official body which, until 1858, had charge of the government of India. He remained a member of the staff for thirty years. In his twenty-second year the event occurred which determined the course of his life. There was in his mother's family a strain of insanity which on one occasion showed itself in Lamb himself. It manifested itself in a terrible way in his sister Mary, who was eleven years his senior: in a fit of rage she mortally stabbed their mother. Lamb was witness to the catastrophe. The authorities did not contemplate criminal prosecution but it seemed likely that Mary would be remanded to a public insane asylum. However, through the intervention of influential friends she was released in the custody of her young brother. There was an older and relatively prosperous brother, but he had cut himself off from the family, and Charles was quite alone in his responsibility, which included the care of his senile father. He placed Mary in a private and decent home where he could visit her and from which he removed her some three years later when her rationality was restored. Henceforward the brother and sister were inseparable, except for the periods (which were frequent) when Mary's reason again gave way; the terrible violence would begin to rise and Mary had to be put under the constraint which she herself would ask for. Lamb's devotion through all his life—he predeceased Mary by thirteen years—was entire. Although his domestic affections were strong, his situation made marriage impossible. No resentment over the sacrifice he was making seems ever to have figured in his feelings for Mary, with whom he lived in a reciprocation of tenderness and admiration. When she was in health she was a person of considerable charm and she was liked and highly regarded by Lamb's many distinguished friends. Although unschooled, she read widely and wrote with simple grace.

It was not until he was in his forties that Lamb began to do the work upon which his fame rests. He had had literary ambitions since early youth, and over the following years he was to make several forays toward fame which were either inconclusive or disastrous. In 1796 he published four sonnets in Coleridge's first volume of poems; to these he added when a second edition of the work appeared in the following year. In 1798 he published a slight volume with his friend Charles Lloyd, which included his well-known and still affecting poem *Old Familiar Faces*. He attempted to write for the theater, but his tragedy *John Woodvil* was rejected for production and damned when it was published (1802), and his comedy *Mr. H.* failed dismally when it was staged—Lamb himself joined in hissing it. In 1807 he and Mary wrote a children's book, *Tales from Shakespeare*, which was to be for many years one of the staples of juvenile literature. The publication of *Specimens of English Dramatic Poets Contemporary with Shakespeare* (1808) brought him a certain small reputation as a critic. In 1820, through the good offices of Hazlitt, he was introduced to the editor of the new *London Magazine*, who invited him to contribute occasional essays. The first of these was a reminiscence of his brief time in South Sea House, in the course of which he made mention of an obscure old clerk called Elia; on a whim he signed the essay with that name. Thereafter it was as Elia—he wanted it pronounced "Ellia"—that Lamb wrote. Of the circumstantial details by which he gave substance to this *persona* of the aging harmless bachelor, some were drawn from his own life, some were invented, some compounded of actuality and invention. Within the next two years he contributed twenty-five essays to the *London Magazine;* in 1823 they were gathered together in a volume, *Essays of Elia*, which, although it did not sell well, established itself in the canon of English prose. A decade later *Last Essays of Elia* appeared; with the exception of one piece, "The Superannuated Man," it is inferior to its predecessor.

The power of the *Elia* essays is of a curious kind and baffles explanation. If one undertakes to name their manifest characteristics, one comes up with a list which, although it might account for the admiration given to the essays in an earlier day, can only suggest that they are bound to alienate contemporary taste. They are sentimental: they cherish emotion for its own sake, and have a special predilection for such emotions as are associated with transience, with the pathos of what once was with us and is now forever gone. They are whimsical: they seize upon trivial subjects and with conscious caprice attribute to them large significance. They are quaint: they are given to proposing the peculiar charm which is presumed to lie in the customs and manners of a distant time and they often affect language that long ago fell into disuse. But then, suddenly, they are none of these things; or if they continue to be, it does not matter. The preciousness and self-consciousness come to seem merely adventitious, and what we are aware of as esssential is a strong, clear intelligence, commanding in its centrality, its courage, its refusal of deception, and its vital irony. So formidable a judge as A. C. Bradley said of Lamb that he was the greatest critic of his age; the estimate is an extravagant one, the more because what might be called the canon of Lamb's actual criticism must be gathered mostly from statements made by the way and would make but a slim volume; yet it may serve to suggest something of the effect that the unexpected authority of Lamb's intelligence might have upon a percipient and responsive reader.

Christ's Hospital Five and Thirty Years Ago

[Christ's Hospital was founded in 1552 by Edward VI, its purpose being to "take out of the streets all the fatherless children and other poor men's children" and to give them shelter, food, and schooling. Later the intention of beneficence was changed, and the children admitted were those of respectable parents in reduced financial circumstances rather than those of the very poor. By the eighteenth century the school was the chief enterprise of the foundation. It was commonly called the Blue Coat School from its uniform, which was completed by knee-breeches and yellow stockings. Until 1902, when it was moved to new buildings in the country, the school was housed in the old Grey Friars (Franciscan) monastery on Newgate Street.

In this reminiscence of his schooldays, Lamb plays a curious game of identities. At the beginning of the essay he speaks of himself in the third person, and the "I" recalls circumstances and feelings which are actually those of Lamb's schoolfellow Coleridge. But as the essay proceeds, the "I" becomes Lamb himself.]

In Mr. Lamb's *Works*,[1] published a year or two since, I find a magnificent eulogy on my old school, such as it was, or now appears to him to have been, between the years 1782 and 1789. It happens, very oddly, that my own standing at Christ's was nearly corresponding with his; and, with all gratitude to him for his enthusiasm for the cloisters, I think he has contrived to bring together whatever can be said in praise of them, dropping all the other side of the argument most ingeniously.

I remember L. at school; and can well recollect that he had some peculiar advantages, which I and others of his school-fellows had not. His friends lived in town, and were near at hand; and he had the privilege of going to see them, almost as often as he wished, through some invidious distinction, which was denied to us. The present worthy sub-treasurer to the Inner Temple[2] can explain how that happened. He had his tea and hot rolls in a morning, while we were battening upon our quarter of a penny loaf—our *crug*[3]—moistened with attenuated small beer, in wooden piggins, smacking of the pitched

---

1. A collection of Lamb's miscellaneous prose and verse published in 1818. The essay to which he refers was published in the *Gentleman's Magazine* in 1813.

2. This was Randal Norris, a friend of Lamb's father; he took a paternal interest in Charles, who held him in great affection.—The Inner Temple is one of the four societies, called Inns of Court, which license the practice of law in England. The name applies also to the group of buildings, containing offices and residences, in which the society is housed.

3. The word for bread in Christ's Hospital slang.

leathern jack it was poured from.[4] Our Monday's milk porritch,[5] blue and tasteless, and the pease soup of Saturday, coarse and choking, were enriched for him with a slice of 'extraordinary bread and butter,' from the hot-loaf of the Temple. The Wednesday's mess of millet, somewhat less repugnant—(we had three banyan [6] to four meat days in the week)—was endeared to his palate with a lump of double-refined,[7] and a smack of ginger (to make it go down the more glibly) or the fragrant cinnamon. In lieu of our *half-pickled* Sundays, or *quite fresh* boiled beef on Thursdays (strong as *caro equina* [8]), with detestable marigolds floating in the pail to poison the broth—our scanty mutton crags [9] on Fridays—and rather more savoury, but grudging, portions of the same flesh, rotten-roasted or rare, on the Tuesdays (the only dish which excited our appetites, and disappointed our stomachs, in almost equal proportion)—he had his hot plate of roast veal, or the more tempting griskin [10] (exotics unknown to our palates), cooked in the paternal kitchen (a great thing), and brought him daily by his maid or aunt! I remember the good old relative (in whom love forbade pride) squatting down upon some odd stone in a by-nook of the cloisters, disclosing the viands (of higher regale than those cates which the ravens ministered to the Tishbite [11]); and the contending passions of L. at the unfolding. There was love for the bringer; shame for the thing brought, and the manner of its bringing; sympathy for those who were too many to share in it; and, at top of all, hunger (eldest, strongest of the passions!) predominant, breaking down the stony fences of shame, and awkwardness, and a troubling over-consciousness.

I was a poor friendless boy. My parents, and those who should care for me, were far away. Those few acquaintances of theirs, which they could reckon upon being kind to me in the great city, after a little forced notice, which they had the grace to take of me on my first arrival in town, soon grew tired of my holiday visits. They seemed to them to recur too often, though I thought them few enough; and, one after another, they all failed me, and I felt myself alone among six hundred playmates.

O the cruelty of separating a poor lad from his early homestead! The yearnings which I used to have towards it in those unfledged years! How, in my dreams, would my native town (far in the west) come back, with its church, and trees, and faces! How I would wake weeping, and in the anguish of my heart exclaim upon sweet Calne in Wiltshire! [12]

To this late hour of my life, I trace impressions left by the recollection of

---

4. Small beer is weak beer; a piggin is a small wooden pail with an upright handle, a sort of dipper; leather receptacles for liquids were once common.
5. Porridge; oatmeal.
6. A banian is a member of a Hindu caste which abstains from meat; English sailors used the word to signify a mess at which no meat was served.
7. Sugar.
8. Horse meat.
9. Necks.
10. A pork loin.
11. Cates are dainties. The Tishbite is the prophet Elijah, to whom, at the command of God, ravens brought food when he was in hiding: I Kings 17: 4–6.
12. Under this name Lamb conceals the actual place of Coleridge's home, Ottery St. Mary, in Devonshire.

those friendless holidays. The long warm days of summer never return but they bring with them a gloom from the haunting memory of those *whole-day-leaves*, when, by some strange arrangement, we were turned out, for the livelong day, upon our own hands, whether we had friends to go to, or none. I remember those bathing-excursions to the New-River,[13] which L. recalls with such relish, better, I think, than he can—for he was a home-seeking lad, and did not much care for such water-pastimes:—How merrily we would sally forth into the fields; and strip under the first warmth of the sun; and wanton like young dace [14] in the streams; getting us appetites for noon, which those of us that were pennyless (our scanty morning crust long since exhausted) had not the means of allaying—while the cattle, and the birds, and the fishes, were at feed about us, and we had nothing to satisfy our cravings—the very beauty of the day, and the exercise of the pastime, and the sense of liberty, setting a keener edge upon them!—How faint and languid, finally, we would return, towards nightfall, to our desired morsel, half-rejoicing, half-reluctant, that the hours of our uneasy liberty had expired!

It was worse in the days of winter, to go prowling about the streets objectless—shivering at cold windows of print-shops, to extract a little amusement; or haply, as a last resort, in the hope of a little novelty, to pay a fifty-times repeated visit (where our individual faces should be as well known to the warden as those of his own charges) to the Lions in the Tower—to whose levée,[15] by courtesy immemorial, we had a prescriptive title to admission.

L.'s governor (so we called the patron who presented us to the foundation) [16] lived in a manner under his paternal roof. Any complaint which he had to make was sure of being attended to. This was understood at Christ's, and was an effectual screen to him against the severity of masters, or worse tyranny of the monitors. The oppressions of these young brutes are heart-sickening to call to recollection. I have been called out of my bed, and *waked for the purpose*, in the coldest winter nights—and this not once, but night after night—in my shirt, to receive the discipline of a leathern thong, with eleven other sufferers, because it pleased my callow overseer, when there has been any talking heard after we were gone to bed, to make the six last beds in the dormitory, where the youngest children of us slept, answerable for an offence they neither dared to commit, nor had the power to hinder.—The same execrable tyranny drove the younger part of us from the fires, when our feet were perishing with snow; and, under the cruelest penalties, forbad the indulgence of a drink of water, when we lay in sleepless summer nights, fevered with the season, and the day's sports.

13. A stream brought into London (1609–13) to augment the city's water supply.
14. A minnow-like fish.
15. The Tower of London is a group of buildings, the earliest dating back to William the Conqueror, which has served as fortress, royal residence, and prison for eminent persons accused of crimes against the state. The crown jewels are still kept here but the menagerie is no longer maintained. A levée is the ceremonial reception held by a monarch (here the King of Beasts) upon arising from bed.
16. The substantial citizen who arranged the admission of a boy to Christ's Hospital. In Lamb's case, this was Samuel Salt, his father's employer, a well-known lawyer and member of Parliament. Lamb has described him at length in *Old Benchers of the Inner Temple*.

There was one H——, who, I learned, in after days, was seen expiating some maturer offence in the hulks.[17] (Do I flatter myself in fancying that this might be the planter of that name, who suffered—at Nevis, I think, or St. Kitts,[18]—some few years since? My friend Tobin was the benevolent instrument of bringing him to the gallows.) This petty Nero actually branded a boy, who had offended him, with a red hot iron; and nearly starved forty of us, with exacting contributions, to the one half of our bread, to pamper a young ass, which, incredible as it may seem, with the connivance of the nurse's daughter (a young flame of his) he had contrived to smuggle in, and keep upon the leads of the *ward*, as they called our dormitories. This game went on for better than a week, till the foolish beast, not able to fare well but he must cry roast meat—happier than Caligula's minion,[19] could he have kept his own counsel—but, foolisher, alas! than any of his species in the fables—waxing fat, and kicking, in the fulness of bread, one unlucky minute would needs proclaim his good fortune to the world below; and, laying out his simple throat, blew such a ram's horn blast, as (toppling down the walls of his own Jericho)[20] set concealment any longer at defiance. The client was dismissed, with certain attentions, to Smithfield;[21] but I never understood that the patron underwent any censure on the occasion. This was in the stewardship of L.'s admired Perry.[22]

Under the same *facile* administration, can L. have forgotten the cool impunity with which the nurses used to carry away openly, in open platters, for their own tables, one out of two of every hot joint, which the careful matron had been seeing scrupulously weighed out for our dinners? These things were daily practised in that magnificent apartment, which L. (grown connoisseur since, we presume) praises so highly for the grand paintings 'by Verrio,[23] and others,' with which it is 'hung round and adorned.' But the sight of sleek well-fed blue-coat boys in pictures was, at that time, I believe, little consolatory to him, or us, the living ones, who saw the better part of our provisions carried away before our faces by harpies; and ourselves reduced (with the Trojan in the hall of Dido)

To feed our mind with idle portraiture.[24]

L. has recorded the repugnance of the school to *gags*, or the fat of fresh beef boiled; and sets it down to some superstition. But these unctuous morsels are never grateful to young palates (children are universally fat-haters) and

17. Stationary, demasted ships used as prisons.
18. Islands in the West Indies.
19. The mad Roman emperor Caligula assigned a retinue of slaves to his favorite horse and appointed it consul.
20. The story of how Joshua brought down the walls of Jericho by marching around it with seven priests blowing trumpets is told in Joshua 6: 2–20.
21. A horse and cattle market.
22. In his first essay on the school Lamb writes affectionately of its steward, or superintendent, John Perry.
23. Antonio Verrio was an Italian painter of the 17th century who lived in England and decorated royal residences. Verrio's large picture shows the mathematics students of the school being received by James II.
24. In Bk. I of the *Aeneid*, when Aeneas and his companions reach Dido's city, they see on the wall of the temple to Juno paintings which depict the fall of Troy.

in strong, coarse, boiled meats, *unsalted,* are detestable. A *gag-eater* in our time was equivalent to a *goul,* and held in equal detestation. —— suffered under the imputation.

>   —— 'Twas said
> He ate strange flesh.[25]

He was observed, after dinner, carefully to gather up the remnants left at his table (not many, nor very choice fragments, you may credit me)—and, in an especial manner, these disreputable morsels, which he would convey away, and secretly stow in the settle that stood at his bed-side. None saw when he ate them. It was rumoured that he privately devoured them in the night. He was watched, but no traces of such midnight practices were discoverable. Some reported, that, on leave-days, he had been seen to carry out of the bounds a large blue check handkerchief, full of something. This then must be the accursed thing. Conjecture next was at work to imagine how he could dispose of it. Some said he sold it to the beggars. This belief generally prevailed. He went about moping. None spake to him. No one would play with him. He was excommunicated; put out of the pale of the school. He was too powerful a boy to be beaten, but he underwent every mode of that negative punishment, which is more grievous than many stripes. Still he persevered. At length he was observed by two of his school-fellows, who were determined to get at the secret, and had traced him one leave-day for that purpose, to enter a large worn-out building, such as there exist specimens of in Chancery-lane, which are let out to various scales of pauperism with open door, and a common staircase. After him they silently slunk in, and followed by stealth up four flights, and saw him tap at a poor wicket, which was opened by an aged woman, meanly clad. Suspicion was now ripened into certainty. The informers had secured their victim. They had him in their toils. Accusation was formally preferred, and retribution most signal was looked for. Mr. Hathaway, the then steward (for this happened a little after my time), with that patient sagacity which tempered all his conduct, determined to investigate the matter, before he proceeded to sentence. The result was, that the supposed mendicants, the receivers or purchasers of the mysterious scraps, turned out to be the parents of ——, an honest couple come to decay,—whom this seasonable supply had, in all probability, saved from mendicancy; and that this young stork, at the expense of his own good name, had all this while been only feeding the old birds!—The governors on this occasion, much to their honour, voted a present relief to the family of ——, and presented him with a silver medal. The lesson which the steward read upon RASH JUDGMENT, on the occasion of publicly delivering the medal to ——, I believe, would not be lost upon his auditory.—I had left school then, but I well remember ——. He was a tall, shambling youth, with a cast in his eye, not at all calculated to conciliate hostile prejudices. I have since seen him carrying a baker's basket. I think I heard he did not do quite so well by himself, as he had done by the old folks.

I was a hypochondriac lad; and the sight of a boy in fetters, upon the day of my first putting on the blue clothes, was not exactly fitted to assuage the natural terrors of initiation. I was of tender years, barely turned of seven;

25. Derived from *Antony and Cleopatra* I.iv.67.

and had only read of such things in books, or seen them but in dreams. I was told he had *run away*. This was the punishment for the first offence.—As a novice I was soon after taken to see the dungeons. These were little, square, Bedlam [25] cells, where a boy could just lie at his length upon straw and a blanket—a mattress, I think, was afterwards substituted—with a peep of light, let in askance, from a prison-orifice at top, barely enough to read by. Here the poor boy was locked in by himself all day, without sight of any but the porter who brought him his bread and water—who *might not speak to him;* —or of the beadle, who came twice a week to call him out to receive his periodical chastisement, which was almost welcome, because it separated him for a brief interval from solitude:—and here he was shut up by himself *of nights,* out of the reach of any sound, to suffer whatever horrors the weak nerves, and superstition incident to his time of life, might subject him to.[26] This was the penalty for the second offence.—Wouldst thou like, reader, to see what became of him in the next degree?

The culprit, who had been a third time an offender, and whose expulsion was at this time deemed irreversible, was brought forth, as at some solemn *auto da fe,*[27] arrayed in uncouth and most appalling attire—all trace of his late 'watchet weeds' [28] carefully affaced, he was exposed in a jacket, resembling those which London lamplighters formerly delighted in, with a cap of the same. The effect of this divestiture was such as the ingenious devisers of it could have anticipated. With his pale and frighted features, it was as if some of those disfigurements in Dante had seized upon him. In this disguisement he was brought into the hall (*L.'s favourite state-room*), where awaited him the whole number of his school-fellows, whose joint lessons and sports he was thenceforth to share no more; the awful presence of the steward, to be seen for the last time; of the executioner beadle, clad in his state robe for the occasion; and of two faces more, of direr import, because never but in these extremities visible. These were governors; two of whom, by choice, or charter, were always accustomed to officiate at these *Ultima Supplicia;* [29] not to mitigate (so at least we understood it), but to enforce the uttermost stripe. Old Bamber Gascoigne, and Peter Aubert, I remember, were colleagues on one occasion, when the beadle turning rather pale, a glass of brandy was ordered to prepare him for the mysteries. The scourging was, after the old Roman fashion, long and stately. The lictor [30] accompanied the criminal quite round the hall. We were generally too faint with attending to the previous disgusting circumstances, to make accurate report with our eyes of the degree of corporal suffering inflicted. Report, of course, gave out the back knotty and livid. After

25. Bedlam, corrupted pronunciation of "Bethlehem," i.e. the Hospital of St. Mary of Bethlehem, in London, in which insane persons were confined.
26. "One or two instances of lunacy, or attempted suicide, accordingly, at length convinced the governors of the impolicy of this part of the sentence, and the midnight torture of the spirits was dispensed with. . . ." (Lamb)
27. "Act of faith" (Spanish): the public execution of sentences upon persons condemned by the Inquisition.
28. Clothes of a blue color—the reference is to his school coat.
29. "Extreme punishments."
30. A Roman functionary who walked before a magistrate, carrying a bundle of rods, bound around an axe.

scourging, he was made over, in his *San Benito*,[31] to his friends, if he had any (but commonly such poor runagates were friendless), or to his parish officer, who, to enhance the effect of the scene, had his station allotted to him on the outside of the hall gate.

These solemn pageantries were not played off so often as to spoil the general mirth of the community. We had plenty of exercise and recreation *after* school hours; and, for myself, I must confess, that I was never happier, than *in* them. The Upper and the Lower Grammar Schools were held in the same room; and an imaginary line only divided their bounds. Their character was as different as that of the inhabitants on the two sides of the Pyrennes. The Rev. James Boyer was the Upper Master; [32] but the Rev. Matthew Field presided over that portion of the apartment, of which I had the good fortune to be a member. We lived a life as careless as birds. We talked and did just what we pleased, and nobody molested us. We carried an accidence,[33] or a grammar, for form; but, for any trouble it gave us, we might take two years in getting through the verbs deponent,[34] and another two in forgetting all that we had learned about them. There was now and then the formality of saying a lesson, but if you had not learned it, a brush across the shoulders (just enough to disturb a fly) was the sole remonstrance. Field never used the rod; and in truth he wielded the cane with no great good will—holding it 'like a dancer.' It looked in his hands rather like an emblem than an instrument of authority; and an emblem, too, he was ashamed of. He was a good easy man, that did not care to ruffle his own peace, nor perhaps set any great consideration upon the value of juvenile time. He came among us, now and then, but often stayed away whole days from us; and when he came, it made no difference to us—he had his private room to retire to, the short time he stayed, to be out of the sound of our noise. Our mirth and uproar went on. We had classics of our own, without being beholden to 'insolent Greece or haughty Rome,' [35] that passed current among us—*Peter Wilkins*—*The Adventures of the Hon. Capt. Robert Boyle*—*The Fortunate Blue Coat Boy* [36]—and the like. Or we cultivated a turn for mechanic or scientific operations; making little sun-dials of paper; or weaving those ingenious parentheses, called *cat-cradles;* or making dry peas to dance upon the end of a tin pipe; or studying the art military over that laudable game 'French and English,' and a hundred other such devices to pass away the time—mixing the useful with the agreeable—as would have made the souls of Rousseau and John Locke chuckle to have seen us.[37]

Matthew Field belonged to that class of modest divines who affect to mix in equal proportion the *gentleman,* the *scholar,* and the *Christian;* but, I know not how, the first ingredient is generally found to be the predominating dose

31. The garment of yellow sackcloth worn by the condemned person at an *auto da fé.*
32. See Coleridge's account of him (as James Bowyer) in chapter I of *Biographia Literaria* (above).
33. Lists of the declensions of nouns and the conjugation of verbs in Latin or Greek.
34. A verb in Latin or Greek having an active meaning but a passive form.
35. Ben Jonson, "To the Memory of My Beloved Master, William Shakespeare," l. 39.
36. Widely read adventure stories of the day. *Peter Wilkins* is still of considerable interest as an early work of science fiction.
37. In their writings on the education of young children the two philosophers proposed the usefulness of "doing" as a way of learning.

in the composition. He was engaged in gay parties, or with his courtly bow at some episcopal levée, when he should have been attending upon us. He had for many years the classical charge of a hundred children, during the four or five first years of their education; and his very highest form seldom proceeded further than two or three of the introductory fables of Phaedrus.[38] How things were suffered to go on thus, I cannot guess. Boyer, who was the proper person to have remedied these abuses, always affected, perhaps felt, a delicacy in interfering in a province not strictly his own. I have not been without my suspicions, that he was not altogether displeased at the contrast we presented to his end of the school. We were a sort of Helots to his young Spartans.[39] He would sometimes, with ironic deference, send to borrow a rod of the Under Master, and then, with sardonic grin, observe to one of his upper boys, 'how neat and fresh the twigs looked.' While his pale students were battering their brains over Xenophon and Plato, with a silence as deep as that enjoined by the Samite,[40] we were enjoying ourselves at our ease in our little Goshen.[41] We saw a little into the secrets of his discipline, and the prospect did but the more reconcile us to our lot. His thunders rolled innocuous for us; his storms came near, but never touched us; contrary to Gideon's miracle, while all around were drenched, our fleece was dry.[42] His boys turned out the better scholars; we, I suspect, have the advantage in temper. His pupils cannot speak of him without something of terror allaying their gratitude; the remembrance of Field comes back with all the soothing images of indolence, and summer slumbers, and work like play, and innocent idleness, and Elysian exemptions, and life itself a 'playing holiday.'

Thought sufficiently removed from the jurisdiction of Boyer, we were near enough (as I have said) to understand a little of his system. We occasionally heard sounds of the *Ululantes,* and caught glances of Tartarus.[43] B. was a rabid pedant. His English style was cramped to barbarism. His Easter anthems (for his duty obliged him to those periodical flights) were grating as scrannel pipes.[44]—He would laugh, ay, and heartily, but then it must be at Flaccus's quibble about *Rex*—or at the *tristis severitas in vultu,* or *inspicere in patinas,* of Terence—thin jests, which at their first broaching could hardly have had *vis* enough to move a Roman muscle.[45]—He had two wigs, both pedantic, but

---

38. A Roman author of the reign of Augustus best known for his beast fables, many of which are based on those of Aesop.

39. Helots were the serfs or slaves in Sparta. In order to disgust their sons with drunkenness, the Spartans would exhibit a besotted member of this despised class.

40. The Greek philosopher Pythagoras of Samos, who enjoined his students to silence until they had listened to his lectures for five years.

41. The region of ancient Egypt where the Israelites were allowed to live from the time of Joseph until the Exodus.

42. Actually, in Judges 6:36–40, Gideon asks God for *two* miraculous signs, that his sleeping-fleece be wet when the ground is dry and that it be dry when the ground is wet.

43. Tartarus is the region of Hades where the wicked are punished. The *Ulalantes* are those whose cries of pain Aeneas hears on his visit to the underworld in Bk. VI of the *Aeneid.*

44. That is, harsh pipes; see *Lycidas,* l. 124.

45. In the first of his *Satires,* Horace—Quintus Horatius Flaccus—makes play with *Rex* as meaning *king* and as a man's name. In Terence's comedy *Andrea,* a character says of a patent rogue that there is to be seen "a sad severity in his countenance"; in the same

of differing omen. The one serene, smiling, fresh powdered, betokening a mild day. The other, an old discoloured, unkempt, angry caxon,[46] denoting frequent and bloody execution. Woe to the school, when he made his morning appearance in his *passy*, or *passionate wig*. No comet expounded surer.[47]—J. B. had a heavy hand. I have known him double his knotty fist at a poor trembling child (the maternal milk hardly dry upon its lips) with a 'Sirrah, do you presume to set your wits at me?'—Nothing was more common than to see him make a headlong entry into the schoolroom, from his inner recess, or library, and, with turbulent eye, singling out a lad, roar out, 'Od's my life, Sirrah,' (his favourite adjuration) 'I have a great mind to whip you,'—then, with as sudden a retracting impulse, fling back into his lair—and, after a cooling lapse of some minutes (during which all but the culprit had totally forgotten the context) drive headlong out again, piecing out his imperfect sense, as if it had been some Devil's Litany, with the expletory yell—'*and I* WILL, *too.*'—In his gentler moods, when the *rabidus furor* [48] was assuaged, he had resort to an ingenious method, peculiar, for what I have heard, to himself, of whipping the boy, and reading the Debates,[49] at the same time; a paragraph, and a lash between; which in those times, when parliamentary oratory was most at a height and flourishing in these realms, was not calculated to impress the patient with a veneration for the diffuser graces of rhetoric.

Once, and but once, the uplifted rod was known to fall ineffectual from his hand—when droll squinting W—— having been caught putting the inside of the master's desk to a use for which the architect had clearly not designed it, to justify himself, with great simplicity averred, that *he did not know that the thing had been forewarned.* This exquisite irrecognition of any law antecedent to the *oral* or *declaratory*, struck so irresistibly upon the fancy of all who heard it (the pedagogue himself not excepted) that remission was unavoidable.

L. has given credit to B.'s great merits as an instructor. Coleridge, in his literary life,[50] has pronounced a more intelligible and ample encomium on them. The author of the *Country Spectator* [51] doubts not to compare him with the ablest teachers of antiquity. Perhaps we cannot dismiss him better than with the pious ejaculation of C.—when he heard that his old master was on his death-bed—'Poor J.B.!—may all his faults be forgiven; and may he be wafted to bliss by little cherub boys, all head and wings, with no *bottoms* to reproach his sublunary infirmities.'

Under him were many good and sound scholars bred.—First Grecian [52] of

author's *Adelphi*, in mockery of a father who has adjured his son to look into men's lives as into a mirror, the comic slave solemnly tells the kitchen force to look into the pans. *Vis* is "force."
46. A kind of wig, especially a shabby one.
47. A comet was once thought to portend disaster.
48. "Mad fury."
49. Reports of the proceedings of Parliament.
50. *Biographia Literaria*.
51. A weekly periodical (1792–93) edited and largely written by Lamb's schoolmate, Thomas Fanshaw Middleton.
52. "Grecians" was the name given to the small group of Christ's Hospital pupils who, by reason of their scholarly abilities, were prepared for the university; they usually went to Cambridge.

my time was Lancelot Pepys Stevens, kindest of boys and men, since Co-grammar-master (and inseparable companion) with Dr. T——e. What an edifying spectacle did this brace of friends present to those who remembered the anti-socialities of their predecessors!—You never met the one by chance in the street without a wonder, which was quickly dissipated by the almost immediate sub-appearance of the other. Generally arm in arm, these kindly coadjutors lightened for each other the toilsome duties of their profession, and when, in advanced age, one found it convenient to retire, the other was not long in discovering that it suited him to lay down the fasces [53] also. Oh, it is pleasant, as it is rare, to find the same arm linked in yours at forty, which at thirteen helped it to turn over the *Cicero De Amicitia*,[54] or some tale of Antique Friendship, which the young heart even then was burning to anticipate!—Co-Grecian with S. was Th——, who has since executed with ability various diplomatic functions at the Northern courts. Th—— was a tall, dark, saturnine youth, sparing of speech, with raven locks.—Thomas Fanshaw Middleton followed him (now Bishop of Calcutta) a scholar and a gentleman in his teens. He has the reputation of an excellent critic; and is author (besides the *Country Spectator*) of a treatise on the Greek Article, against Sharpe.—M. is said to bear his mitre high in India, where the *regni novitas* [55] (I dare say) sufficiently justifies the bearing. A humility quite as primitive as that of Jewel or Hooker [56] might not be exactly fitted to impress the minds of those Anglo-Asiatic diocesans with a reverence for home institutions, and the church which those fathers watered. The manners of M. at school, though firm, were mild, and unassuming.—Next to M. (if not senior to him) was Richards, author of the *Aboriginal Britons*, the most spirited of the Oxford Prize Poems; a pale, studious Grecian.—Then followed poor S——, ill-fated M——! of these the Muse is silent.[57]

> Finding some of Edward's race
> Unhappy, pass their annals by.[58]

Come back into memory, like as thou wert in the day-spring of thy fancies, with hope like a fiery column before thee—the dark pillar not yet turned—Samuel Taylor Coleridge—Logician, Metaphysician, Bard!—How have I seen the casual passer through the Cloisters stand still, entranced with admiration (while he weighed the disproportion between the *speech* and the *garb* of the young Mirandola),[59] to hear thee unfold, in thy deep and sweet intonations, the mysteries of Jamblichus, or Plotinus [60] (for even in those years thou

53. The bundle of rods bound around an axe carried by the lictor (see note 30) before a Roman magistrate as a sign of his authority.
54. Cicero's discourse "On Friendship."
55. "Newness of the reign."
56. Famous ecclesiastics of the 16th century, when the authority of the Roman Church was repudiated in England and the Anglican Church was constituted.
57. Identified by Lamb as Scott, who died in a hospital for the insane, and Maunde, who was expelled from school.
58. Lamb alters Matthew Prior's *Carmen Seculare* (1700) viii.4–5. "Edward's race" because Christ's Hospital had been founded by Edward VI.
59. Pico della Mirandola (1463–94), the brilliant and engaging Italian humanist.
60. Jamblichus—usually Iamblichus—a mystic and neoplatonic philosopher of the 4th century; Plotinus, who flourished a century earlier, is the chief exponent of neoplatonism.

waxedst not pale at such philosophic draughts), or reciting Homer in his Greek, or Pindar——while the walls of the old Grey Friars re-echoed to the accents of the *inspired charity-boy!*—Many were the 'wit-combats,' (to dally awhile with the words of old Fuller,[61]) between him and C. V. Le G——, 'which two I behold like a Spanish great gallion, and an English man of war; Master Coleridge, like the former, was built far higher in learning, solid, but slow in his performance. C. V. L., with the English man of war, lesser in bulk, but lighter in sailing, could turn with all tides, tack about, and take advantage of all winds, by the quickness of his wit and invention.'

Nor shalt thou, their compeer, be quickly forgotten, Allen, with the cordial smile, and still more cordial laugh, with which thou wert wont to make the old Cloisters shake, in thy cognition of some poignant jest of theirs; or the anticipation of some more material, and, peradventure, practical one, of thine own. Extinct are those smiles, with that beautiful countenance, with which (for thou wert the *Nireus formosus*[62] of the school), in the days of thy maturer waggery, thou didst disarm the wrath of infuriated town-damsel, who, incensed by provoking pinch, turning tigress-like round, suddenly converted by thy angel-look, exchanged the half-formed terrible '*bl*——,' for a gentler greeting—'*bless thy handsome face!*'

Next follow two, who ought to be now alive, and the friends of Elia—the junior Le G—— [63] and F——; [64] who impelled, the former by a roving temper, the latter by too quick a sense of neglect—ill capable of enduring the slights poor Sizars [65] are sometimes subject to in our seats of learning—exchanged their Alma Mater for the camp; perishing, one by climate, and one on the plains of Salamanca:—Le G——, sanguine, volatile, sweet-natured; F—— dogged, faithful, anticipative of insult, warm-hearted, with something of the old Roman height about him.

Fine, frank-hearted Fr——,[66] the present master of Hertford, with Marma-duke T——,[67] mildest of Missionaries—and both my good friends still—close the catalogue of Grecians in my time.

1820

The Two Races of Men

The human species, according to the best theory I can form of it, is composed of two distinct races, *the men who borrow*, and *the men who lend*. To these two original diversities may be reduced all those impertinent classifications of Gothic and Celtic tribes, white men, black men, red men. All the dwellers upon earth,

---

61. Thomas Fuller, from whose *Worthies of England* (1662) Lamb takes the description of the "wit-combats" between Shakespeare and Ben Jonson, adapting it to Coleridge and Charles Valentine Le Grice.
62. "Beautiful Nireus." He was one of the Greek warriors who besieged Troy.
63. Samuel Le Grice, a military man who died in the West Indies.
64. Joseph Favell.
65. At Cambridge, a student who receives financial help. He was formerly required to perform certain menial services.
66. Frederick William Franklin.
67. Marmaduke Thompson.

'Parthians, and Medes, and Elamites,'[1] flock hither, and do naturally fall in with one or other of these primary distinctions. The infinite superiority of the former, which I choose to designate as the *great race*, is discernible in their figure, port, and a certain instinctive sovereignty. The latter are born degraded. 'He shall serve his brethren.'[2] There is something in the air of one of this cast, lean and suspicious; contrasting with the open, trusting, generous manners of the other.

Observe who have been the greatest borrowers of all ages—Alcibiades—Falstaff—Sir Richard Steele—our late incomparable Brinsley[3]—what a family likeness in all four!

What a careless, even deportment hath your borrower! what rosy gills! what a beautiful reliance on Providence doth he manifest,—taking no more thought than lilies! What contempt for money,—accounting it (yours and mine especially) no better than dross. What a liberal confounding of those pedantic distinctions of *meum* and *tuum!*[4] or rather, what a noble simplification of language (beyond Tooke),[5] resolving these supposed opposites into one clear, intelligible pronoun adjective!—What near approaches doth he make to the primitive *community*,[6]—to the extent of one half of the principle at least!—

He is the true taxer who 'calleth all the world up to be taxed;'[7] and the distance is as vast between him and *one of us*, as subsisted betwixt the Augustan Majesty and the poorest obolary Jew[8] that paid it tribute-pittance at Jerusalem! —His exactions, too, have such a cheerful, voluntary air! So far removed from your sour parochial or state-gatherers,—those ink-horn varlets, who carry their want of welcome in their faces! He cometh to you with a smile, and troubleth you with no receipt; confining himself to no set season. Every day is his Candlemas, or his Feast of Holy Michael.[9] He applieth the *lene tormentum*[10] of a pleasant look to your purse,—which to that gentle warmth expands her silken leaves, as naturally as the cloak of the traveller, for which sun and wind contended! He is the true Propontic[11] which never ebbeth! The sea which taketh handsomely at each man's hand. In vain the victim, whom he delighteth to honour, struggles with destiny; he is in the net. Lend therefore cheerfully,

1. Acts 2:9.
2. Genesis 9:25.
3. Alcibiades, the brilliant, ambitious, dissolute, and traitorous Athenian, friend of Socrates; Falstaff, the most famous of Shakespeare's comic characters (I and II *Henry IV*, *The Merry Wives of Windsor*); Richard Steele, the essayist and dramatist (1672–1729) was notoriously improvident; Brinsley is Richard Brinsley Sheridan (1751–1816), author of *The Rivals* and *The School for Scandal* who was also notorious for his improvidence.
4. "Mine" and "thine."
5. John Horne Tooke (1736–1812), in addition to being an active political radical, was a well-known philologist who emphasized the importance of studying Gothic and Anglo-Saxon.
6. The Apostles "had all things in common; And sold their possessions and goods, and parted them to all men as every man had need, . . ." Acts 2:44–45.
7. The decree of the Emperor, in Luke 2:1.
8. A Jew who had at least an *obolus*, a small coin.
9. Candlemas and Michaelmas are, respectively, Scottish and English "quarter-days," that is, days on which rents, etc., were to be paid.
10. "The gentle spur." Horace, *Odes* III.21, 13.
11. The sea of Marmora. Doubtless Lamb had in mind Othello's reference to it (III. iii. 453–56).

O man ordained to lend—that thou lose not in the end, with thy worldly penny, the reversion promised.[12] Combine not preposterously in thine own person the penalties of Lazarus and of Dives! [13]—but, when thou seest the proper authority coming, meet it smilingly, as it were half-way. Come, a handsome sacrifice! See how light *he* makes of it! Strain not courtesies with a noble enemy.

Reflections like the foregoing were forced upon my mind by the death of my old friend, Ralph Bigod, Esq.,[14] who departed this life on Wednesday evening; dying, as he had lived, without much trouble. He boasted himself a descendant from mighty ancestors of that name, who heretofore held ducal dignities in this realm. In his actions and sentiments he belied not the stock to which he pretended. Early in life he found himself invested with ample revenues; which, with that noble disinterestedness which I have noticed as inherent in men of the *great race*, he took almost immediate measures entirely to dissipate and bring to nothing: for there is something revolting in the idea of a king holding a private purse; and the thoughts of Bigod were all regal. Thus furnished, by the very act of disfurnishment; getting rid of the cumbersome luggage of riches, more apt (as one sings)

> To slacken virtue, and abate her edge,
> Than prompt her to do aught may merit praise,[15]

he set forth, like some Alexander, upon his great enterprise, 'borrowing and to borrow!' [16]

In his periegesis, or triumphant progress throughout this island, it has been calculated that he laid a tythe part of the inhabitants under contribution. I reject this estimate as greatly exaggerated:—but having had the honour of accompanying my friend, divers times, in his perambulations about this vast city, I own I was greatly struck at first with the prodigious number of faces we met, who claimed a sort of respectful acquaintance with us. He was one day so obliging as to explain the phenomenon. It seems, these were his tributaries; feeders of his exchequer; gentlemen, his good friends (as he was pleased to express himself), to whom he had occasionally been beholden for a loan. Their multitudes did no way disconcert him. He rather took a pride in numbering them; and, with Comus, seemed pleased to be 'stocked with so fair a herd.' [17]

With such sources, it was a wonder how he contrived to keep his treasury always empty. He did it by force of an aphorism, which he had often in his mouth, that 'money kept longer than three days stinks.' So he made use of it while it was fresh. A good part he drank away (for he was an excellent tosspot), some he gave away, the rest he threw away, literally tossing and hurling it violently from him—as boys do burrs, or as if it had been infectious,—into

12. Proverbs 9:17: "He that hath pity upon the poor lendeth to the Lord; and that which he hath given will he pay him again."
13. Not the Lazarus whom Jesus raised from the dead but the one who begged daily at the gate of the rich man Dives (Luke 16:19).
14. Under this name, Lamb speaks of a friend, John Fenwick.
15. *Paradise Regained* II.455–56.
16. Revelation 6:2.
17. *Comus*, ll. 151–53.

ponds, or ditches, or deep holes,—inscrutable cavities of the earth;—or he would bury it (where he would never seek it again) by a river's side under some bank, which (he would facetiously observe) paid no interest—but out away from him it must go peremptorily, as Hagar's offspring [18] into the wilderness, while it was sweet. He never missed it. The streams were perennial which fed his fisc.[19] When new supplies became necessary, the first person that had the felicity to fall in with him, friend or stranger, was sure to contribute to the deficiency. For Bigod had an *undeniable* way with him. He had a cheerful, open exterior, a quick jovial eye, a bald forehead, just touched with grey (*cana fides*).[20] He anticipated no excuse, and found none. And, waiving for a while my theory as to the *great race,* I would put it to the most untheorising reader, who may at times have disposable coin in his pocket, whether it is not more repugnant to the kindliness of his nature to refuse such a one as I am describing, than to say *no* to a poor petitionary rogue (your bastard borrower), who, by his mumping visnomy,[21] tells you, that he expects nothing better; and, therefore, whose preconceived notions and expectations you do in reality so much less shock in the refusal.

When I think of this man; his fiery glow of heart; his swell of feeling; how magnificent, how *ideal* he was; how great at the midnight hour; and when I compare with him the companions with whom I have associated since, I grudge the saving of a few idle ducats, and think that I am fallen into the society of *lenders,* and *little men.*

To one like Elia, whose treasures are rather cased in leather covers than closed in iron coffers, there is a class of alienators more formidable than that which I have touched upon; I mean your *borrowers of books*—those mutilators of collections, spoilers of the symmetry of shelves, and creators of odd volumes. There is Comberbatch,[22] matchless in his depredations!

That foul gap in the bottom shelf facing you, like a great eye-tooth knocked out—(you are now with me in my little back study in Bloomsbury,[23] reader!) ——with the huge Switzer-like [24] tomes on each side (like the Guildhall giants,[25] in their reformed posture, guardant of nothing) once held the tallest of my folios, *Opera Bonaventurae,* choice and massy divinity, to which its two supporters (school divinity also, but of a lesser calibre,—Bellarmine, and Holy Thomas),[26] showed but as dwarfs,—itself an Ascapart! [27]—*that* Comberbatch

18. Genesis 21. Hagar's son by Abraham was Ishmael. Both were cast out into the wilderness by Abraham.
19. The treasury of a kingdom or a state.
20. Virgil, *Aeneid* I. 292. The phrase means "ancient honor"—by extension, "gray hair."
21. "To mump" is to mumble like a beggar; "visnomy" is an obsolete form of "physiognomy" for which Lamb had a fondness.
22. When Coleridge as a young man enlisted in the Dragoons, he did so, as his old friends knew, under the name of Silas Tomkyn Comberbacke.
23. A district of London. Lamb did not actually live in it.
24. That is, like the Swiss Guards of the French kings and the pope; they were chosen for their stature.
25. Statues in the London Guildhall, which had been moved from their original places.
26. St. Bonaventure, "The Seraphic Doctor," a 13th-century theologian; Bellarmine, St. Robert Bellarmine, 16th-century theologian; Holy Thomas is St. Thomas Aquinas (13th century), one of the most famous theologians of the time.
27. A giant slain by Bevis of Southampton in Michael Drayton's *Polyolbion* (1613–22).

abstracted upon the faith of a theory he holds, which is more easy, I confess, for me to suffer by than to refute, namely, that 'the title to property in a book (my Bonaventure, for instance), is in exact ratio to the claimant's powers of understanding and appreciating the same.' Should he go on acting upon this theory, which of our shelves is safe?

The slight vacuum in the left-hand case—two shelves from the ceiling— scarcely distinguishable but by the quick eye of a loser—was whilom the commodious resting-place of Browne on *Urn Burial*.[28] C. will hardly allege that he knows more about that treatise than I do, who introduced it to him, and was indeed the first (of the moderns) to discover its beauties—but so have I known a foolish lover to praise his mistress in the presence of a rival more qualified to carry her off than himself.—Just below, Dodsley's dramas [29] want their fourth volume, where Vittoria Corombona is! [30] The remainder nine are as distasteful as Priam's refuse sons, when the Fates *borrowed* Hector.[31] Here stood the *Anatomy of Melancholy*,[32] in sober state.—There loitered the *Complete Angler;* [33] quiet as in life, by some stream side.—In yonder nook, John Buncle,[34] a widower-volume, with 'eyes closed,' mourns his ravished mate.

One justice I must do my friend, that if he sometimes, like the sea, sweeps away a treasure, at another time, sea-like, he throws up as rich an equivalent to match it. I have a small under-collection of this nature (my friend's gatherings in his various calls), picked up, he has forgotten at what odd places, and deposited with as little memory as mine. I take in these orphans, the twice-deserted. These proselytes of the gate are welcome as the true Hebrews. There they stand in conjunction; natives, and naturalised. The latter seem as little disposed to inquire out their true lineage as I am.—I charge no warehouse-room for these deodands,[35] nor shall ever put myself to the ungentlemanly trouble of advertising a sale of them to pay expenses.

To lose a volume to C. carries some sense and meaning in it. You are sure that he will make one hearty meal on your viands, if he can give no account of the platter after it. But what moved thee, wayward, spiteful K.,[36] to be so importunate to carry off with thee, in spite of tears and adjurations to thee to forbear, the Letters of that princely woman, the thrice noble Margaret New-

28. Sir Thomas Browne's *Urn Burial*, or *Hydriotaphia*, was published in 1658. Lamb's pride in his "discovery" of this book is justified. His praise of the prose writers of the 17th century was influential in establishing them in modern taste.

29. Robert Dodsley published his *Select Collection of Old Plays* in 1744. The book did much to revive the interest in Elizabethan drama, which was furthered by Lamb's *Specimens of English Dramatic Poets.*

30. That is, Webster's *The White Devil,* of which Vittoria Corombona is the chief female character.

31. Of Priam's fifty sons, the slain Hector was the most cherished.

32. By Robert Burton, published 1621.

33. By Izaak Walton, published 1653, 1655.

34. *The Life of John Buncle, Esq.,* by Thomas Amory. It was published in two volumes, 1756–66. The phrase "widower-volume" is apt because the hero of the novel was a widower seven times.

35. A deodand—"that which is to be given to God." By English law, a thing which having been the immediate cause of a person's death, is forfeited to the Crown to be used for pious purposes. Lamb uses the word inaccurately.

36. James Kenney (1780–1849), a dramatist and a good friend of Lamb's.

castle? [37]—knowing at the time, and knowing that I knew also, thou most assuredly wouldst never turn over one leaf of the illustrious folio:—what but the mere spirit of contradiction, and childish love of getting the better of thy friend?—Then, worst cut of all! to transport it with thee to the Gallican lands [38]

> Unworthy land to harbour such a sweetness,
> A virtue in which all ennobling thoughts dwelt,
> Pure thoughts, kind thoughts, high thoughts, her sex's wonder! [39]

—hadst thou not thy play-books, and books of jests and fancies, about thee, to keep thee merry, even as thou keepest all companies with thy quips and mirthful tales?—Child of the Green-room, it was unkindly done of thee. Thy wife, too, that part-French, better-part Englishwoman!—that *she* could fix upon no other treatise to bear away, in kindly token of remembering us, than the works of Fulke Greville, Lord Brook [40]—of which no Frenchman, nor woman of France, Italy, or England, was ever by nature constituted to comprehend a tittle! *Was there not Zimmerman on Solitude?* [41]

Reader, if haply thou art blessed with a moderate collection, be shy of showing it; or if thy heart overfloweth to lend them, lend thy books; but let it be to such a one as S. T. C.—he will return them (generally anticipating the time appointed) with usuary; enriched with annotations, tripling their value. I have had experience. Many are these precious MSS of his—(in *matter* oftentimes, and almost in *quantity* not unfrequently, vying with the originals) —in no very clerkly hand—legible in my Daniel; [42] in old Burton; in Sir Thomas Browne; and those abstruser cogitations of the Greville, now, alas! wandering in Pagan lands.—I counsel thee, shut not thy heart, nor thy library, against S. T. C. [43]

1820

New Year's Eve

[Death was a more immediate element of human life in the early nineteenth century than it was later to be. Its actual occurrence was more likely to be witnessed; its mystery and terror were more present to consciousness. And in the degree that this was so, what religion had to offer in the way of light and comfort was still cherished by many. It is therefore not surprising that Lamb's essay, with its frank avowal of the dread of death and its refusal of the hope of, or desire for, an afterlife, should have

37. Margaret, Duchess of Newcastle (1624?–74), wrote in many genres—the essay, drama, poetry, biography (of her husband), autobiography, and *Sociable Letters*, the book whose loss Lamb laments.
38. France—at this time Kenney lived at Versailles.
39. It is thought that these lines are by Lamb.
40. Sir Fulke Greville, 1st Baron Brooke (1554–1628), was the friend and biographer of Sir Philip Sidney.
41. Johann Georg von Zimmerman (1728–95), a Swiss doctor and writer. His sentimental *On Solitude* (1755; 1785), now forgotten, was translated from German into almost every European language.
42. Samuel Daniel (1562–1619), the poet.
43. Coleridge often referred to himself by his initials.

proved distressing to the sensibilities of some of his contemporary readers, a few of whom, including his friend, the poet Robert Southey, took him to task for his deficiency of religious feeling.]

Every man hath two birthdays: two days at least, in every year, which set him upon revolving the lapse of time, as it affects his mortal duration. The one is that which in an especial manner he termeth *his*. In the gradual desuetude of old observances, this custom of solemnising our proper birthday hath nearly passed away, or is left to children, who reflect nothing at all about the matter, nor understand anything in it beyond cake and orange. But the birth of a New Year is of an interest too wide to be pretermitted by king or cobbler. No one ever regarded the First of January with indifference. It is that from which all date their time, and count upon what is left. It is the nativity of our common Adam.

Of all sound of all bells—(bells, the music nighest bordering upon heaven) —most solemn and touching is the peal which rings out the Old Year. I never hear it without a gathering-up of my mind to a concentration of all the images that have been diffused over the past twelvemonth; all I have done or suffered, performed or neglected, in that regretted time. I begin to know its worth, as when a person dies. It takes a personal colour; nor was it a poetical flight in a contemporary, when he exclaimed—

I saw the skirts of the departing Year.[1]

It is no more than what in sober sadness every one of us seems to be conscious of, in that awful leave-taking. I am sure I felt it, and all felt it with me, last night; though some of my companions affected rather to manifest an exhilaration at the birth of the coming year, than any very tender regrets for the decease of its predecessor. But I am none of those who—

Welcome the coming, speed the parting guest.[2]

I am naturally, beforehand, shy of novelties; new books, new faces, new years,—from some mental twist which makes it difficult in me to face the prospective. I have almost ceased to hope; and am sanguine only in the prospects of other (former) years. I plunge into foregone vision and conclusions. I encounter pell-mell with past disappointments. I am armour-proof against old discouragements. I forgive, or overcome in fancy, old adversaries. I play over again *for love*, as the gamesters phrase it, games for which I once paid so dear. I would scarce now have any of those untoward accidents and events of my life reversed. I would no more alter them than the incidents of some well-contrived novel. Methinks, it is better that I should have pined away seven of my goldenest years, when I was thrall to the fair hair, and fairer eyes, of Alice W——n,[3] than that so passionate a love adventure should be lost. It was better that our family should have missed that legacy, which old

1. From Coleridge's *Ode to the Departing Year* in the version of 1796. In a later version "skirts" becomes "train."
2. Pope's translation of the *Odyssey* XV.84; the line appears also in Pope's Horatian *Satires* II. ii. 160.
3. Winterton, the fictitious name Lamb used to indicate the object of a youthful adoration, Ann Simmons.

Dorrell cheated us of,[4] than that I should have at this moment two thousand pounds *in banco*,[5] and be without the idea of that specious old rogue.

In a degree beneath manhood, it is my infirmity to look back upon those early days. Do I advance a paradox when I say, that, skipping over the intervention of forty years, a man may have leave to love *himself*, without the imputation of self-love?

If I know aught of myself, no one whose mind is introspective—and mine is painfully so—can have a less respect for his present identity than I have for the man Elia. I know him to be light, and vain, and humoursome; a notorious ***;[6] addicted to ***; averse from counsel, neither taking it, nor offering it;—*** besides; a stammering[7] buffoon; what you will; lay it on, and spare not; I subscribe to it all, and much more, than thou canst be willing to lay at his door:—but for the child Elia—that 'other me,' there, in the background—I must take leave to cherish the remembrance of that young master—with as little reference, I protest, to this stupid changeling of five-and-forty, as if it had been a child of some other house, and not of my parents. I can cry over its patient smallpox at five, and rougher medicaments. I can lay its poor fevered head upon the sick pillow at Christ's,[8] and wake with it in surprise at the gentle posture of maternal tenderness hanging over it, that unknown had watched its sleep. I know how it shrank from any the least colour of falsehood.—God help thee, Elia, how art thou changed!—Thou art sophisticated.[9]—I know how honest, how courageous (for a weakling) it was —how religious, how imaginative, how hopeful! From what have I not fallen, if the child I remember was indeed myself,—and not some dissembling guardian, presenting a false identity, to give the rule to my unpractised steps, and regulate the tone of my moral being!

That I am fond of indulging, beyond a hope of sympathy, in such retrospection, may be the symptom of some sickly idiosyncrasy. Or is it owing to another cause: simply, that being without wife or family, I have not learned to project myself enough out of myself; and having no offspring of my own to dally with, I turn back upon memory, and adopt my own early idea, as my heir and favourite? If these speculations seem fantastical to thee, reader —(a busy man, perchance), if I tread out of the way of thy sympathy, and am singularly conceited only, I retire, impenetrable to ridicule, under the phantom cloud of Elia.

The elders, with whom I was brought up, were of a character not likely to let slip the sacred observance of any old institution; and the ringing out of the Old Year was kept by them with circumstances of peculiar ceremony.—In those days the sound of those midnight chimes, though it seemed to raise

---

4. William Dorrell was one of the witnesses to the will of Lamb's father, and Lamb believed that he had engaged in some sharp practice which deprived the Lamb children of their inheritance.
5. "In the bank."
6. Lamb leaves the reader to supply the pejorative words.
7. Lamb's stammer, at its worst in boyhood but continuing all his life, kept him from training for a career as clergyman.
8. Christ's Hospital, Lamb's school.
9. In the old sense of adulterated or weakened, rather than in the sense of being less naïve.

hilarity in all around me, never failed to bring a train of pensive imagery into my fancy. Yet I then scarce conceived what it meant, or thought of it as a reckoning that concerned me. Not childhood alone, but the young man till thirty, never feels practically that he is mortal.[10] He knows it indeed, and, if need were, he could preach a homily on the fragility of life; but he brings it not home to himself, any more than in a hot June we can appropriate to our imagination the freezing days of December. But now, shall I confess a truth? —I feel these audits but too powerfully. I begin to count the probabilities of my duration, and to grudge at the expenditure of moments and shortest periods, like misers' farthings. In proportion as the years both lessen and shorten, I set more count upon their periods, and would fain lay my ineffectual finger upon the spoke of the great wheel. I am not content to pass away 'like a weaver's shuttle.'[11] Those metaphors solace me not, nor sweeten the unpalatable draught of mortality. I care not to be carried with the tide, that smoothly bears human life to eternity; and reluct at the inevitable course of destiny. I am in love with this green earth; the face of town and country; the unspeakable rural solitudes, and the sweet security of streets. I would set up my tabernacle here. I am content to stand still at the age to which I am arrived; I, and my friends: to be no younger, no richer, no handsomer. I do not want to be weaned by age; or drop, like mellow fruit, as they say, into the grave.—Any alteration, on this earth of mine, in diet or in lodging, puzzles and discomposes me. My household-gods plant a terrible fixed foot, and are not rooted up without blood. They do not willingly seek Lavinian shores.[12] A new state of being staggers me.

Sun, and sky, and breeze, and solitary walks, and summer holidays, and the greenness of fields, and the delicious juices of meats and fishes, and society, and the cheerful glass, and candlelight, and fireside conversations, and innocent vanities, and jests, and *irony itself*—do these things go out with life?

Can a ghost laugh, or shake his gaunt sides, when you are pleasant with him?

And you, my midnight darlings, my Folios; must I part with the intense delight of having you (huge armfuls) in my embraces? Must knowledge come to me, if it come at all, by some awkward experiment of intuition, and no longer by this familiar process of reading?

Shall I enjoy friendships there, wanting the smiling indications which point me to them here,—the recognizable face—the 'sweet assurance of a look'?[13]

In winter this intolerable disinclination to dying—to give it its mildest name —does more especially haunt and beset me. In a genial August noon, beneath a sweltering sky, death is almost problematic.[14] At those times do such poor snakes as myself enjoy an immortality. Then we expand and burgeon. Then

10. See Hazlitt's essay *On the Feeling of Immortality in Youth.*
11. Job 7:6: "My days are swifter than a weaver's shuttle."
12. In the *Aeneid,* Aeneas transports his household gods (*penates*) from Troy to Italy, where he founds the town of Lavinium, naming it for his Italian wife Lavinia. Lavinian shores are thus the shores of Italy, attained by the wandering Aeneas on orders from the gods. Lamb is saying he is not inclined so to wander.
13. Adapted from the elegy on Sir Philip Sidney by Matthew Roydon.
14. De Quincey records the opposite feeling—see the passage in *The Confessions of an English Opium Eater* dated June 1819.

we are as strong again, as valiant again, as wise again, and a great deal taller. The blast that nips and shrinks me, puts me in thoughts of death. All things allied to the insubstantial, wait upon that master feeling; cold, numbness, dreams, perplexity; moonlight itself, with its shadowy and spectral appearances, —that cold ghost of the sun, or Phoebus' sickly sister, like that innutritious one denounced in the Canticles: [15]—I am none of her minions—I hold with the Persian.[16]

Whatsoever thwarts, or puts me out of my way, brings death unto my mind. All partial evils, like humours, run into that capital plague-sore.—I have heard some profess an indifference to life. Such hail the end of their existence as a port of refuge; and speak of the grave as of some soft arms, in which they may slumber as on a pillow. Some have wooed death——but out upon thee, I say, thou foul, ugly phantom! I detest, abhor, execrate, and (with Friar John) give thee to six score thousand devils, as in no instance to be excused or tolerated, but shunned as an universal viper; to be branded, proscribed, and spoken evil of! In no way can I be brought to digest thee, thou thin, melancholy *Privation*, or more frightful and confounding *Positive!* [17]

Those antidotes, prescribed against the fear of thee, are altogether frigid and insulting, like thyself. For what satisfaction hath a man, that he shall 'lie down with kings and emperors in death,' [18] who in his lifetime never greatly coveted the society of such bed-fellows?—or, forsooth, that 'so shall the fairest face appear'? [19]—why, to comfort me, must Alice W——n be a goblin? More than all, I conceive disgust at those impertinent and misbecoming familiarities, inscribed upon your ordinary tombstones. Every dead man must take upon himself to be lecturing me with his odious truism, that 'Such as he now is I must shortly be.' Not so shortly, friend, perhaps, as thou imaginest. In the meantime I am alive. I move about. I am worth twenty of thee. Know thy betters! Thy New Years' days are past. I survive, a jolly candidate for 1821. Another cup of wine—and while that turncoat bell, that just now mournfully chanted the obsequies of 1820 departed, with changed notes lustily rings in a successor, let us attune to its peal the song made on a like occasion, by hearty, cheerful Mr. Cotton.[20]

THE NEW YEAR

Hark, the cock crows, and yon bright star
Tells us, the day himself's not far;
And see where, breaking from the night,
He gilds the western hills with light.

15. That is, the Song of Songs, also called the Song of Solomon. Presumably the "innutritious one" derives from 8:8: "We have a little sister, and she hath no breasts," but there is no ground for supposing, as Lamb brilliantly does suppose, that this refers to the moon!
16. The ancient Persians worshiped the sun.
17. Lamb is playing with the not uncommon idea that death may not be the absence of life but another, and terrible, form of existence.
18. Job 3:13–14 has "kings and counselors."
19. David Mallet, *William and Margaret* l. 9. In this 18th-century ballad, young Margaret dies and appears in ghostly form to her faithless lover William.
20. Charles Cotton (1630–87). He is remembered chiefly as the author of the dialogue between Piscator and Victor in the second part of Izaak Walton's *Compleat Angler*.

With him old Janus doth appear,
Peeping into the future year,
With such a look as seems to say
The prospect is not good that way.
Thus do we rise ill sights to see,
And 'gainst ourselves to prophesy;
When the prophetic fear of things
A more tormenting mischief brings,
More full of soul-tormenting gall
Than direst mischiefs can befall.
But stay! but stay! methinks my sight,
Better informed by clearer light,
Discerns sereneness in that brow
That all contracted seemed but now.
His reversed face may show distaste,
And frown upon the ills are past;
But that which this way looks is clear,
And smiles upon the New-born Year.
He looks too from a place so high,
The year lies open to his eye;
And all the moments open are
To the exact discoverer.
Yet more and more he smiles upon
The happy revolution.
Why should we then suspect or fear
The influences of a year,
So smiles upon us the first morn,
And speaks us good so soon as born?
Plague on't! the last was ill enough,
This cannot but make better proof;
Or, at the worst, as we brushed through
The last, why so we may this too;
And then the next in reason should
Be superexcellently good:
For the worst ills (we daily see)
Have no more perpetuity
Than the best fortunes that do fall;
Which also bring us wherewithal
Longer their being to support,
Than those do of the other sort:
And who has one good year in three,
And yet repines at destiny,
Appears ungrateful in the case,
And merits not the good he has.
Then let us welcome the New Guest
With lusty brimmers of the best:
Mirth always should Good Fortune meet,
And renders e'en Disaster sweet:

And though the Princess turn her back,
Let us but line ourselves with sack,
We better shall by far hold out,
Till the next year she face about.

How say you, reader—do not these verses smack of the rough magnanimity of the old English vein? Do they not fortify like a cordial; enlarging the heart, and productive of sweet blood, and generous spirits, in the concoction? Where be those puling fears of death, just now expressed or affected?—Passed like a cloud—absorbed in the purging sunlight of clear poetry—clean washed away by a wave of genuine Helicon,[21] your only spa [22] for these hypochondries. And now another cup of the generous! and a merry New Year, and many of them to you all, my masters!

1821

On the Artificial Comedy of the Last Century

[The critical position taken by Lamb in this brilliant essay was attacked—although with sincere protestations of admiration for its author—by Macaulay, who said that its argument was "ingenious" but "altogether sophisticated." "In the name of art, as well as in the name of virtue," he said, "we protest against the principle that the world of pure comedy is one in which no moral enters." And an eminent American critic, the late Joseph Wood Krutch, in his *Comedy and Conscience in the Restoration*, said that Lamb, in the view he took of Restoration comedy, had been "blinded by its brilliance . . . and [saw] only the wit." Both writers mean to suggest that the comedy of the Restoration represented manners and morals as they really were and should therefore be understood as offering an occasion for moral judgment. But this is to miss Lamb's intention, which has nothing to do with the congruence, or lack of it, between what is actually the moral situation of the society and the representation of it on the stage, but reaches far beyond that to propose one of the possible functions of art. Friedrich von Schiller is the last man in the world to be accused of light-mindedness and he took what is essentially Lamb's position. In his far-ranging work *Letters on the Aesthetic Education of Mankind* (1795) he says that the "mere play," which is what the experience of art can be and ultimately should be, suggests to man the possibility of his freedom, giving him a taste of what it feels like to overcome the "earnestness of duty and destiny"; it makes the paradigm of man's true being; it teaches him what he must hope to be. "Man," Schiller says, "only plays when he is in the fullest sense of the word a human being, and he is only a human being when he plays." Lamb, in his own unsystematic way, is saying the same thing.]

The artificial comedy, or comedy of manners, is quite extinct on our stage. Congreve and Farquhar [1] show their heads once in seven years only, to be

21. A mountain sacred to the Muses; just below its summit is the spring Hippocrene, whose waters inspire poets.
22. A resort in which a mineral spring of presumed health-giving properties is situated.

1. William Congreve (1670–1729) was the most brilliant practitioner of the Restoration comedy of manners. His masterpiece is *The Way of the World* (1700). The most admired of the comedies of George Farquhar (1678–1707) is *The Beaux' Stratagem* (1707).

exploded and put down instantly. The times cannot bear them. Is it for a few wild speeches, an occasional license of dialogue? I think not altogether. The business of their dramatic characters will not stand the moral test. We screw everything up to that. Idle gallantry [2] in a fiction, a dream, the passing pageant of an evening, startles us in the same way as the alarming indications of profligacy in a son or ward in real life should startle a parent or guardian. We have no such middle emotions as dramatic interests left. We see a stage libertine playing his loose pranks of two hours' duration, and of no after consequence, with the severe eyes which inspect real vices with their bearings upon two worlds. We are spectators to a plot or intrigue (not reducible in life to the point of strict morality), and take it all for truth. We substitute a real for a dramatic person, and judge him accordingly. We try him in our courts, from which there is no appeal to the *dramatis personae*, his peers. We have been spoiled with—not sentimental comedy—but a tyrant far more pernicious to our pleasures which has succeeded to it, the exclusive and all-devouring drama of common life; where the moral point is everything; where, instead of the fictitious half-believed personages of the stage (the phantoms of old comedy), we recognize ourselves, our brothers, aunts, kinsfolk, allies, patrons, enemies,—the same as in life,—with an interest in what is going on so hearty and substantial, that we cannot afford our moral judgment, in its deepest and most vital results, to compromise or slumber for a moment. What is *there* transacting, by no modification is made to affect us in any other manner than the same events or characters would do in our relationships of life. We carry our fireside concerns to the theatre with us. We do not go thither like our ancestors, to escape from the pressure of reality, so much as to confirm our experience of it; to make assurance double, and take a bond of fate. We must live our toilsome lives twice over, as it was the mournful privilege of Ulysses to descend twice to the shades.[3] All that neutral ground of character, which stood between vice and virtue; or which in fact was indifferent to neither, where neither properly was called in question; that happy breathing-place from the burthen of a perpetual moral questioning—the sanctuary and quiet Alsatia of hunted casuistry [4]—is broken up and disfranchised, as injurious to the interests of society. The privileges of the place are taken away by law. We dare not dally with images, or names, of wrong. We bark like foolish dogs at shadows. We dread infection from the scenic representation of disorder, and fear a painted pustule. In our anxiety that our morality should not take cold, we wrap it up in a great blanket surtout [5] of precaution against the breeze and sunshine.

I confess for myself that (with no great delinquencies to answer for) I am glad for a season to take an airing beyond the diocese of the strict conscience,

2. In the sense not of courage but of sexual adventure.
3. Once, as the *Odyssey* relates, while still a living man, to consult the shade of the prophet Tiresias; a second time when at his death he himself becomes a shade.
4. Lamb uses the word "casuistry" not in its now usual sense of specious reasoning, but in its older sense, in which it denotes the ecclesiastical science of dealing with cases of conscience, of resolving questions of right and wrong. Alsatia was the name given to White-friars, a district of London, which was long a sanctuary for insolvent debtors and criminals.
5. An overcoat.

—not to live always in the precincts of the law courts,—but now and then, for a dream-while or so, to imagine a world with no meddling restrictions—to get into recesses, whither the hunter cannot follow me—

> —Secret shades
> Of woody Ida's inmost grove,
> While yet there was no fear of Jove.[6]

I come back to my cage and my restraint the fresher and more healthy for it. I wear my shackles more contentedly for having respired the breath of an imaginary freedom. I do not know how it is with others, but I feel the better always for the perusal of one of Congreve's—nay, why should I not add even of Wycherley's [7]—comedies. I am the gayer at least for it; and I could never connect those sports of a witty fancy in any shape with any result to be drawn from them to imitation in real life. They are a world of themselves almost as much as fairy land. Take one of their characters, male or female (with few exceptions they are alike), and place it in a modern play, and my virtuous indignation shall rise against the profligate wretch as warmly as the Catos of the pit [8] could desire; because in a modern play I am to judge of the right and the wrong. The standard of *police* is the measure of *political justice*. The atmosphere will blight it; it cannot live here. It has got into a moral world, where it has no business, from which it must needs fall headlong; as dizzy, and incapable of making a stand, as a Swedenborgian bad spirit [9] that has wandered unawares into the sphere of one of his Good Men, or Angels. But in its own world do we feel the creature is so very bad?—The Fainalls and the Mirabels, the Dorimants and the Lady Touchwoods,[10] in their own sphere, do not offend my moral sense; in fact, they do not appeal to it at all. They seem engaged in their proper element. They break through no laws or conscientious restraints. They know of none. They have got out of Christendom into the land— what shall I call it?—of cuckoldry—the Utopia of gallantry, where pleasure is duty, and the manners perfect freedom. It is altogether a speculative scene of things, which has no reference whatever to the world that is. No good person can be justly offended as a spectator, because no good person suffers on the stage. Judged morally, every character in these plays—the few exceptions only are *mistakes*—is alike essentially vain and worthless. The great art of Congreve

6. Milton, "Il Penseroso," ll. 28–30.

7. William Wycherley (1640–1716) is one of the most notable of the Restoration comic dramatists. His best-known plays are *The Country Wife* (1672) and *The Plain Dealer* (1674). Lamb says "even Wycherley" because his comedies, unlike those of Congreve and Farquhar, are savage and cynical in their satire and often coarse in their language.

8. What Americans call the orchestra of a theater the English call the pit. In the 18th century, people of superior social position did not sit there. Marcius Porcius Cato (234–149 B.C.) known as Cato the Elder and Cato the Censor, was the exponent of a stern, "old-Roman" moral rectitude and the implacable enemy of new ways of thought and conduct. His name has become synonymous with harsh judgment.

9. In the theological system of the Swedish scientist, philosopher, and mystic Emmanuel Swedenborg (1688–1772), evil spirits strive to prevent the approximation of God and man, which is the goal of creation.

10. Fainall and Mirabel are characters in Congreve's *The Way of the World;* Dorimant is a character in Sir George Etherege's *The Man of Mode;* Lady Touchwood is a character in Congreve's *The Double Dealer.*

is especially shown in this, that he has entirely excluded from his scenes—some little generosities in the part of Angelica [11] perhaps excepted—not only anything like a faultless character, but any pretensions to goodness or good feelings whatsoever. Whether he did this designedly, or instinctively, the effect is as happy as the design (if design) was bold. I used to wonder at the strange power which his *Way of the World* in particular possesses of interesting you all along in the pursuits of characters, for whom you absolutely care nothing—for you neither hate nor love his personages—and I think it is owing to this very indifference for any, that you endure the whole. He has spread a privation of moral light, I will call it, rather than by the ugly name of palpable darkness, over his creations; and his shadows flit before you without distinction or preference. Had he introduced a good character, a single gush of moral feeling, a revulsion of the judgment to actual life and actual duties, the impertinent Goshen [12] would have only lighted to the discovery of deformities, which now are none, because we think them none.

Translated into real life, the characters of his, and his friend Wycherley's dramas, are profligates and strumpets,—the business of their brief existence, the undivided pursuit of lawless gallantry. No other spring of action, or possible motive of conduct, is recognized; principles which, universally acted upon, must reduce this frame of things to a chaos. But we do them wrong in so translating them. No such effects are produced, in *their* world. When we are among them, we are amongst a chaotic people. We are not to judge them by our usages. No reverend institutions are insulted by their proceedings—for they have none among them. No peace of families is violated—for no family ties exist among them. No purity of the marriage bed is stained—for none is supposed to have a being. No deep affections are disquieted, no holy wedlock bands are snapped asunder—for affection's depth and wedded faith are not of the growth of that soil. There is neither right nor wrong,—gratitude or its opposite,—claim or duty,—paternity or sonship. Of what consequence is it to Virtue, or how is she at all concerned about it, whether Sir Simon or Dapperwit steal away Miss Martha; or who is the father of Lord Froth's or Sir Paul Pliant's children? [13]

The whole is a passing pageant, where we should sit as unconcerned at the issues, for life or death, as at the battle of the frogs and mice.[14] But, like Don Quixote, we take part against the puppets, and quite as impertinently.[15] We dare not contemplate an Atlantis,[16] a scheme, out of which our coxcombical moral sense is for a little transitory ease excluded. We have not the courage

11. The heroine of Congreve's *Love for Love.*
12. Genesis 47:1–4, the part of Egypt which the Pharaoh assigned to the family of Joseph and where the Israelites were allowed to live until they left Egypt; in Exodus 8:22 it is related that the flies sent to plague the Egyptians did not come into Goshen. Hence, a place of refuge; see "Alsatia" in note 4.
13. Sir Simon, Dapperwit, and Martha are characters in Wycherley's *Love in a Wood;* Lord Froth and Sir Paul Pliant are characters in Congreve's *The Double Dealer.*
14. *The Battle of the Frogs and the Mice* is an ancient parody of epic poetry; at one time it was attributed to Homer himself.
15. *Don Quixote* II.xxv. At a puppet play Don Quixote takes literally the plight of the hero and heroine, intervenes in their behalf, and destroys the puppets unfriendly to them.
16. In two of his dialogues, *Timaeus* and *Critias,* Plato speaks of this mythical island, of great extent, which long ago vanished in the sea.

to imagine a state of things for which there is neither reward nor punishment. We cling to the painful necessities of shame and blame. We would indict our very dreams.

Amidst the mortifying circumstances attendant upon growing old, it is something to have seen *The School for Scandal*[17] in its glory. This comedy grew out of Congreve and Wycherley, but gathered some allays of the sentimental comedy which followed theirs. It is impossible that it should be now *acted*, though it continues, at long intervals, to be announced in the bills. Its hero, when Palmer played it at least, was Joseph Surface.[18] When I remember the gay boldness, the graceful solemn plausibility, the measured step, the insinuating voice—to express it in a word—the downright *acted* villany of the part, so different from the pressure of conscious actual wickedness,—the hypocritical assumption of hypocrisy,—which made Jack so deservedly a favourite in that character, I must needs conclude the present generation of playgoers more virtuous than myself, or more dense. I freely confess that he divided the palm with me with his better brother; that, in fact, I liked him quite as well. Not but there are passages,—like that, for instance, where Joseph is made to refuse a pittance to a poor relation,—incongruities which Sheridan was forced upon by the attempt to join the artificial with the sentimental comedy, either of which must destroy the other—but over these obstructions Jack's manner floated him so lightly, that a refusal from him no more shocked you, than the easy compliance of Charles gave you in reality any pleasure; you got over the paltry question as quickly as you could, to get back into the regions of pure comedy, where no cold moral reigns. The highly artificial manner of Palmer in this character counteracted every disagreeable impression which you might have received from the contrast, supposing them real, between the two brothers. You did not believe in Joseph with the same faith with which you believed in Charles. The latter was a pleasant reality, the former a no less pleasant poetical foil to it. The comedy, I have said, is incongruous; a mixture of Congreve with sentimental incompatibilities; the gaiety upon the whole is buoyant; but it required the consummate art of Palmer to reconcile the discordant elements.

A player with Jack's talents, if we had one now, would not dare to do the part in the same manner. He would instinctively avoid every turn which might tend to unrealize,[19] and so to make the character fascinating. He must take his cue from his spectators, who would expect a bad man and a good man as rigidly opposed to each other as the death-beds of those geniuses are contrasted in the prints, which I am sorry to say have disappeared from the windows of my old friend Carrington Bowles,[20] of St. Paul's churchyard

17. By Richard Brinsley Sheridan (1751–1816). First performed in 1777, it has remained one of the most popular comedies in the language.
18. Joseph Surface, of course, is actually the "villain" of the play. John Palmer (1742?– 1798) was one of the most gifted and popular comic actors of his time. He played Joseph Surface in the first performance of *The School for Scandal* and was ever after identified with the role. He was himself a quite unprincipled man and his hypocrisy is suggested by his nickname, Jack Plausible.
19. Lamb is saying that the modern actor, unlike Palmer, would play Joseph Surface in a style that would lead us to take his wickedness seriously.
20. Carrington Bowles was a publisher of engravings. These were often of a moralizing character, depicting the consequences of improvidence and wrongdoing as contrasted with those of probity and industry. Lamb greatly admired Hogarth, the pre-eminent practitioner of this artistic genre.

memory—(an exhibition as venerable as the adjacent cathedral, and almost coeval) of the bad and good man at the hour of death; where the ghastly apprehensions of the former,—and truly the grim phantom with his reality of a toasting-fork is not to be despised,—so finely contrast with the meek complacent kissing of the rod,—taking it in like honey and butter,—with which the latter submits to the scythe of the gentle bleeder,[21] Time, who wields his lancet with the apprehensive finger of a popular young ladies' surgeon. What flesh, like loving grass, would not covet to meet half-way the stroke of such a delicate mower?—John Palmer was twice an actor in this exquisite part. He was playing to you all the while that he was playing upon Sir Peter and his lady.[22] You had the first intimation of a sentiment before it was on his lips. His altered voice was meant to you, and you were to suppose that his fictitious co-flutterers on the stage perceived nothing at all of it. What was it to you if that half reality, the husband, was overreached by the puppetry—or the thin thing (Lady Teazle's reputation) was persuaded it was dying of a plethory? The fortunes of Othello and Desdemona were not concerned in it. Poor Jack has passed from the stage of good time, that he did not live to this our age of seriousness. The pleasant old Teazle King,[23] too, is gone in good time. His manner would scarce have passed current in our day. We must love or hate— acquit or condemn—censure or pity—exert our detestable coxcombry of moral judgment upon everything. Joseph Surface, to go down now, must be a downright revolting villain—no compromise—his first appearance must shock and give horror—his specious plausibilities, which the pleasurable faculties of our fathers welcomed with such hearty greetings, knowing that no harm (dramatic harm even) could come, or was meant to come, of them, must inspire a cold and killing aversion. Charles (the real canting person of the scene—for the hypocrisy of Joseph has its ulterior legitimate ends, but his brother's professions of a good heart centre in downright self-satisfaction) must be *loved*, and Joseph *hated*. To balance one disagreeable reality with another, Sir Peter Teazle must be no longer the comic idea of a fretful old bachelor bridegroom, whose teasings (while King acted it) were evidently as much played off at you, as they were meant to concern anybody on the stage,—he must be a real person, capable in law of sustaining an injury—a person towards whom duties are to be acknowledged—the genuine crim. con. [24] antagonist of the villainous seducer Joseph. To realize him more, his sufferings under his unfortunate match must have the downright pungency of life—must (or should) make you not mirthful but uncomfortable, just as the same predicament would move you in a neighbour or old friend.

The delicious scenes which give the play its name and zest, must affect you in the same serious manner as if you heard the reputation of a dear female friend attacked in your real presence. Crabtree and Sir Benjamin [25]—those

---

21. One who bleeds another person for medical reasons, once a standard procedure in the treatment of certain illnesses.
22. Sir Peter and Lady Teazle in *The School for Scandal*.
23. Thomas King (1730–1805), one of the most admired actors of his day, played innumerable comic roles and was the first Sir Peter Teazle.
24. A common abbreviation of "criminal conversation," i.e. adultery.
25. Characters in *The School for Scandal*, as is Mrs. Candour. Parsons, Dodd, and Miss Pope were accomplished actors of Lamb's day.

poor snakes that live but in the sunshine of your mirth—must be ripened by this hot-bed process of realization into asps or amphisbaenas; [26] and Mrs. Candour—O! frightful!—become a hooded serpent. O! who that remembers Parsons and Dodd—the wasp and butterfly of *The School for Scandal*—in those two characters; and charming natural Miss Pope, the perfect gentlewoman as distinguished from the fine lady of comedy, in this latter part—would forego the true scenic delight—the escape from life—the oblivion of consequences—the holiday barring out [27] of the pedant Reflection—those Saturnalia [28] of two or three brief hours, well won from the world—to sit instead at one of our modern plays—to have his coward conscience (that forsooth must not be left for a moment) stimulated with perpetual appeals—dulled rather, and blunted, as a faculty without repose must be—and his moral vanity pampered with images of notional justice, notional beneficence, lives saved without the spectator's risk, and fortunes given away that cost the author nothing? . . .[29]

1823

Sanity of True Genius

[The idea that the poet is "mad" was given its most famous expression by Plato, in two of whose dialogues, *Phaedrus* and *Ion*, Socrates takes the line that what poets say cannot be construed as making ordinary sense and that their utterances are to be understood as the expression of a "noble madness." The intention of this view is chiefly ironic, a way of proposing the idea that poetry is not under the dominion of the rational intellect; Plato certainly did not mean to say anything more to the discredit of poetry than that it is not philosophy. The idea that the poet does not speak in the voice of reason, or, indeed, in his own voice, but is "possessed" or "inspired," associates him with the prophet or the shaman through whom a god or a spirit communicates, often in language not comprehensible to human intellect. The madness of the poet became part of popular lore—see Shakespeare's "The lunatic, the lover, and the poet" and "The poet's eye in a fine frenzy rolling" (*A Midsummer Night's Dream* V.i.7, 12)—and as such was generally thought to be benign, if it was taken seriously at all. It could, however, be used to belittle the value of poetry in an age which, as Lamb felt, was increasingly concerned with fact and practicality. The question of how far the processes of creative fancies are "abnormal" became salient in the nineteenth century and continues into the twentieth. We may suppose that Lamb felt that he might claim a special authority in dealing with the question—not only did he live intimately with the often realized threat to his sister's reason, but he himself had brief episodes of insanity.]

26. A mythological serpent having a head at each end of its body.
27. The act of schoolboys closing a schoolroom to the master. This was once a common prank in English schools.
28. The Roman festival, held at about the time of our Christmas; at that festival moral restraints were relaxed and decorum forgotten.
29. The rest of the essay discusses the abilities of the actor John Kemble, a member of the astonishing family of actors of whom his sister Mrs. Siddons was the greatest.

So far from the position holding true, that great wit (or genius, in our modern way of speaking), has a necessary alliance with insanity,[1] the greatest wits, on the contrary, will ever be found to be the sanest writers. It is impossible for the mind to conceive of a mad Shakspeare. The greatness of wit, by which the poetic talent is here chiefly to be understood, manifests itself in the admirable balance of all the faculties. Madness is the disproportionate straining or excess of any one of them. 'So strong a wit,' says Cowley, speaking of a poetical friend,

> ———did Nature to him frame,
> As all things but his judgment overcame,
> His judgment like the heavenly moon did show,
> Tempering that mighty sea below. [2]

The ground of the mistake is, that men, finding in the raptures of the higher poetry a condition of exaltation, to which they have no parallel in their own experience, besides the spurious resemblance of it in dreams and fevers, impute a state of dreaminess and fever to the poet. But the true poet dreams being awake. He is not possessed by his subject, but has dominion over it. In the groves of Eden he walks familiar as in his native paths. He ascends the empyrean heaven, and is not intoxicated. He treads the burning marl [3] without dismay; he wins his flight without self-loss through realms of chaos 'and old night.' [4] Or if, abandoning himself to that severer chaos of a 'human mind untuned,' [5] he is content awhile to be mad with Lear, or to hate mankind (a sort of madness) with Timon,[6] neither is that madness, nor this misanthropy, so unchecked, but that,—never letting the reins of reason wholly go, while most he seems to do so,—he has his better genius still whispering at his ear, with the good servant Kent suggesting saner counsels,[7] or with the honest steward Flavius [8] recommending kindlier resolutions. Where he seems most to recede from humanity, he will be found the truest to it. From beyond the scope of Nature if he summon possible existences, he subjugates them to the law of her consistency. He is beautifully loyal to that sovereign directress, even when he appears most to betray and desert her. His ideal tribes submit to policy; his very monsters are tamed to his hand, even as that wild sea-brood, shepherded by Proteus.[9] He tames, and he clothes them with attributes of flesh and blood, till they wonder at themselves, like Indian Islanders forced to submit to European vesture. Caliban, the Witches,[10] are as true to the laws

1. Lamb refers to Dryden's famous couplet (in *Absalom and Achitophel* I.164–65) "Great wits are sure to madness near allied, / And thin partitions do their bounds divide."
2. Abraham Cowley (1618–67), *On the Death of Mr. William Harvey*, stanza 13.
3. *Paradise Lost* I.296.
4. *Ibid.* I.543.
5. Probably a reminiscence of *King Lear* IV.vii.16–17: "The untuned and jarring senses, wind up / Of this child-changèd father."
6. Shakespeare, *Timon of Athens.*
7. In *King Lear* Kent braves the anger of the king by urging him not to misunderstand Cordelia; Lear banishes him, but Kent returns in disguise to serve his master.
8. In *Timon of Athens*, the faithful steward of Timon.
9. In Bk. IV of the *Odyssey*, Proteus, an aged prophet who has the power of assuming any form he wishes, is in charge of a herd of seals or sea cows.
10. Caliban, the misshapen monster, Prospero's recalcitrant slave, in *The Tempest*. The witches in *Macbeth* prophesy the tragic hero's destiny.

of their own nature (ours with a difference), as Othello, Hamlet, and Macbeth. Herein the great and the little wits are differenced; that if the latter wander ever so little from nature or actual existence, they lose themselves, and their readers. Their phantoms are lawless; their visions nightmares. They do not create, which implies shaping and consistency. Their imaginations are not active —for to be active is to call something into act and form—but passive, as men in sick dreams. For the supernatural, or something super-added to what we know of nature, they give you the plainly non-natural. And if this were all, and that these mental hallucinations were discoverable only in the treatment of subjects out of nature, or transcending it, the judgment might with some plea be pardoned if it ran riot, and a little wantonized: but even in the describing of real and every day life, that which is before their eyes, one of these lesser wits shall more deviate from nature—show more of that inconsequence, which has a natural alliance with frenzy,—than a great genius in his 'maddest fits,' as Wither [11] somewhere calls them. We appeal to any one that is acquainted with the common run of Lane's novels,[12]—as they existed some twenty or thirty years back,—those scanty intellectual viands of the whole female reading public, till a happier genius arose, and expelled for ever the innutritious phantoms,—whether he has not found his brain more 'betossed,' his memory more puzzled, his sense of when and where more confounded, among the improbable events, the incoherent incidents, the inconsistent characters, or no-characters, of some third-rate love intrigue—where the persons shall be a Lord Glendamour and a Miss Rivers, and the scene only alternate between Bath and Bond-street—a more bewildering dreaminess induced upon him, than he has felt wandering over all the fairy grounds of Spenser. In the productions we refer to, nothing but names and places is familiar; the persons are neither of this world nor of any other conceivable one; an endless string of activities without purpose, of purposes destitute of motive:—we meet phantoms in our known walks; *fantasques* [13] only christened. In the poet we have names which announce fiction; and we have absolutely no place at all, for the things and persons of *The Fairy Queen* prate not of their 'whereabout.' But in their inner nature, and the law of their speech and actions, we are at home and upon acquainted ground. The one turns life into a dream; the other to the wildest dreams gives the sobrieties of every day occurrences. By what subtle art of tracing the mental processes it is effected, we are not philosophers enough to explain, but in that wonderful episode of the cave of Mammon,[14] in which the Money God appears first in the lowest form of a miser, is then a worker of metals, and becomes the god of all the treasures of the world; and has a daughter, Ambition, before whom all the world kneels for favours—

11. George Wither (1588–1667), in addition to being a poet, was a most voluminous Puritan pamphleteer.

12. Lamb is referring to the Minerva Press, which at the turn of the century was notorious for the trashy sentimental novels it issued.

13. "Odd, strange" (French).

14. In Spenser's *The Faerie Queene* II.vii Sir Guyon comes to the cave of Mammon, who, as the Money God (see Matthew 6:24 and Luke 16:9–13) is identified with the figures of Greek mythology, Plutus, god of wealth, and Pluto, ruler of the underworld. Mammon tries to tempt the knight with offers of riches and with marriage to his daughter, Ambition, but wholly without success.

with the Hesperian fruit,[15] the waters of Tantalus,[16] with Pilate washing his hands vainly, but not impertinently, in the same stream [17]—that we should be at one moment in the cave of an old hoarder of treasures, at the next at the forge of the Cyclops,[18] in a palace and yet in hell, all at once, with the shifting mutations of the most rambling dream, and our judgment yet all the time awake, and neither able nor willing to detect the fallacy,—is a proof of that hidden sanity which still guides the poet in his widest seeming-aberrations.

It is not enough to say that the whole episode is a copy of the mind's conceptions in sleep; it is, in some sort—but what a copy! Let the most romantic of us, that has been entertained all night with the spectacle of some wild and magnificent vision, recombine it in the morning, and try it by his waking judgment. That which appeared so shifting, and yet so coherent, while that faculty was passive, when it comes under cool examination, shall appear so reasonless and so unlinked, that we are ashamed to have been so deluded; and to have taken, though but in sleep, a monster for a god. But the transitions in this episode are every whit as violent as in the most extravagant dream, and yet the waking judgment ratifies them.

1833

WILLIAM HAZLITT
1778–1830

Of the three great prose writers of the Romantic period, it is Hazlitt who makes the most immediate appeal to modern taste. Lamb's conscious sentimentality and quaint archaism are likely to delay our perception of his essential cogency and force. And it may require a conscious effort for the modern reader to come to terms with the gorgeous elaborations yielded by De Quincey's theory of an "impassioned prose" which would rival music in its potentiality for depth and grandeur. But Hazlitt's prose is likely to reach us at once—it is all speed, energy, and masculine decisiveness. It is not, certainly, prose as it is now written for expository purposes; it is more arbitrary, more stamped with personality, and, at moments, more eloquent than modern practice encourages. Yet in its characteristic downright middle style, in what might be called its *working* mode, it can serve as at least a partial model for the modern writer, as the prose of Lamb and De Quincey cannot possibly do. Its superb urgency is as much a function of intellect as of artistry. Hazlitt's earliest commitment had been to systematic philosophy, and although he did not achieve much in this line, his years of preoccupation with it may be thought to account in some part for the inspiriting

15. The Hesperides—"daughters of evening"—were nymphs who guarded a tree on which grew golden apples.
16. In Hades, Tantalus was set in a pool of water which, whenever he sought to allay the thirst with which he was afflicted, receded from him.
17. Pontius Pilate, the Roman governor of Judaea, who wished to release Jesus but yielded to the importunity of the crowd (John 19:1–16); calling for a basin of water, he symbolically washed his hands of the blood of Jesus (Matthew 27:24). Lamb remarks on the appropriateness of the same water figuring in the punishment of Pilate and of Tantalus.
18. The Cyclops were one-eyed giants. In the *Odyssey* they are shepherds but in Hesiod's *Theogony* they are smiths who forge thunderbolts for Zeus.

purposiveness of his style, its eagerness to reach conclusions, whether about literature or about life.

William Hazlitt was born in 1778, the son of a Unitarian minister of strong libertarian principles. When he was five, his father made a missionary voyage to America, taking his family with him. Of the four years' sojourn in the new nation, first in Philadelphia, then in the environs of Boston, surprisingly little seems to have stayed in Hazlitt's memory, for it is referred to scarcely at all in his mature writing. His later and apparently happy boyhood was spent in the little town of Wem in Shropshire, where his father had a small congregation. In 1793 he was sent to the Unitarian New College at Hackney, a district of London, to prepare for the ministry. He remained there for some three years, a recalcitrant pupil who neglected his prescribed studies to pursue his philosophical interests and who moved ever closer to his eventual repudiation of Christianity. His meeting, in 1798, with Coleridge, who was a great name in Unitarian circles, was decisive in his career, confirming him in his dedication to a life of art and thought (see below, *My First Acquaintance with Poets*) and leading to his entry into the society of the rising poets of his day.

With these friends of his youth Hazlitt was not to continue in happy relations. He was by no means a person of easy and conformable temperament—quite the contrary, indeed, he was touchy and suspicious, and at least in his youth and early middle age his behavior was often heedless and calculated to give offense. But what chiefly accounts for the bitter antagonism which grew up between him and Coleridge and Wordsworth is the unremitting passion of his political opinions. All through his life he maintained a passionate commitment to the radical views which he had first received from his father, while his friends, disenchanted by the developments of the French Revolution, abandoned their youthful hopes, in Hazlitt's eyes an unforgivable apostasy. Yet his bitterness was matched by his critical magnanimity, and in his writings, while deploring their politics, he expressed his strong though discriminating admiration for the genius of Coleridge and Wordsworth. It is pleasant to recall that his friendship with Charles Lamb, who was present at his deathbed, was able to transcend all difficulties and that Keats, who said of Hazlitt's "depth of Taste" that it was one of the few things to rejoice at in the age, found his company nothing but congenial.

Hazlitt's first professional venture was not in literature but in painting. His older brother John was a portraitist of some ability and establishment, and Hazlitt put himself under his instruction. One of William's portraits, of Charles Lamb in the dress of a Venetian senator, is well known and quite striking, but he was doubtless right in the conclusion he came to in 1805 that his abilities were not of an order to justify his hopes of artistic excellence. From this time forward he devoted himself to writing, though not for some years to come did he turn to the work by which he is remembered, which began in 1813 when he became the parliamentary reporter and subsequently the dramatic critic of the *Morning Chronicle*. Of the very large canon of his work a chief part was written for periodical publication, usually in haste under the pressure of deadliness, and it is a cause for wonder how much of it is of high value.

Of Hazlitt's characteristics as a critic perhaps the first to be remarked is his comprehensiveness—in his essays and lectures he covers the whole range of English literature from the age of Elizabeth to his own day. Cognate with this is the catholicity of his taste; his judgments are strict but seldom doctrinaire and partisan, a virtue the more to be praised because it was exercised at a time of warring critical creeds. What he chiefly sought in literature, as in painting, was the quality of "gusto," which he defined and celebrated in one of his most attractive critical essays (see below), and he found it in Pope as well as in Shakespeare. Keats was right to speak of the *depth* rather than of the *breadth* of Hazlitt's taste—his phrase suggests the activity by which Hazlitt sees beneath the merely adventitious attributes of the work of art to discern in its design and in its parts the energies which animate it. This is not to say, however, that Hazlitt is to be called a "profound" critic, as Coleridge commonly is; his particular concern is not to explicate the essential nature of art or its processes but, rather, to point out and validate its achievements.

In the genre of the personal or familiar essay Hazlitt is surely the pre-eminent master in English. This is a literary form which apparently is no longer viable—it ceased to be so, indeed, with the death of its great Romantic practitioners, and although from time to time there have been attempts to revive it, they have met with but faint success. The secret which Montaigne discovered for the world, of speaking colloquially and modestly but unabashedly as "I," seems to have been lost. Hazlitt is not Montaigne's equal—although the comparison is by no means an improper one—but like his greater predecessor (whom he much admired), he commands the curious knack of putting "I" boldly forward, indulging the First Person Singular in all its impulses of self-reference and autobiography, and exactly through the activity of egoism conjuring up considerations in which the ego is forgotten and only the actualities of the moral life are of moment.

My First Acquaintance with Poets

My father was a Dissenting [1] Minister at W—m [2] in Shropshire; and in the year 1798 (the figures that composed that date are to me like the 'dreaded name of Demogorgon') [3] Mr. Coleridge came to Shrewsbury, to succeed Mr. Rowe in the spiritual charge of a Unitarian Congregation there. He did not come till late on the Saturday afternoon before he was to preach; and Mr. Rowe, who himself went down to the coach in a state of anxiety and expectation, to look for the arrival of his successor, could find no one at all answering the description but a round-faced man in a short black coat (like a shooting jacket) which hardly seemed to have been made for him, but who seemed to be talking at a great rate to his fellow-passengers. Mr. Rowe had scarce returned to give an account of his disappointment, when the round-faced man in black entered, and dissipated all doubts on the subject, by beginning to

1. "Dissenters" were those who belonged to any of the English Protestant sects—Presbyterians, Independents, Methodists, Unitarians, etc. They dissented from the doctrines of the established Church of England and did not recognize its temporal authority.
2. Wem. It is difficult to know what degree of anonymity Hazlitt thought he had gained for the little town by the omission of one letter—or why he wanted it!
3. *Paradise Lost* II.964–65. Demogorgon was a terrible deity, the very utterance of whose name was believed to have disastrous effects. See note to Shelley's *Prometheus Unbound*, l. 207. Hazlitt, by the reference to him, means to suggest that the great event of 1798, his meeting with Coleridge and Wordsworth, had the dire consequence of committing him to the literary life.

talk. He did not cease while he stayed; nor has he since, that I know of. He held the good town of Shrewsbury in delightful suspense for three weeks that he remained there, 'fluttering the *proud Salopians* like an eagle in a dove-cote'; [4] and the Welsh mountains that skirt the horizon with their tempestuous confusion, agree to have heard no such mystic sounds since the days of

High-born Hoel's harp or soft Llewellyn's lay! [5]

As we passed along between W—m and Shrewsbury, and I eyed their blue tops seen through the wintry branches, or the red rustling leaves of the sturdy oak-trees by the roadside, a sound was in my ears as of a Siren's song; I was stunned, startled with it, as from deep sleep; but I had no notion then that I should ever be able to express my admiration to others in motley imagery or quaint allusion, till the light of his genius shone into my soul, like the sun's rays glittering in the puddles of the road. I was at that time dumb, inarticulate, helpless, like a worm by the wayside, crushed, bleeding, lifeless; but now, bursting from the deadly bands that 'bound them,

With Styx nine times round them,' [6]

my ideas float on winged words, and as they expand their plumes, catch the golden light of other years. My soul has indeed remained in its original bondage, dark, obscure, with longings infinite and unsatisfied; my heart, shut up in the prison-house of this rude clay, has never found, nor will it ever find, a heart to speak to; but that my understanding also did not remain dumb and brutish, or at length found a language to express itself, I owe to Coleridge. But this is not to my purpose.

My father lived ten miles from Shrewsbury, and was in the habit of exchanging visits with Mr. Rowe, and with Mr. Jenkins of Whitchurch (nine miles farther on) according to the custom of Dissenting Ministers in each other's neighbourhood. A line of communication is thus established, by which the flame of civil and religious liberty is kept alive, and nourishes its smouldering fire unquenchable, like the fires in the *Agamemnon* of Aeschylus, placed at different stations, that waited for ten long years to announce with their blazing pyramids the destruction of Troy. Coleridge had agreed to come over to see my father, according to the courtesy of the country, as Mr. Rowe's probable successor; but in the meantime I had gone to hear him preach the Sunday after his arrival. A poet and a philosopher getting up into a Unitarian pulpit to preach the Gospel, was a romance in these degenerate days, a sort of revival of the primitive spirit of Christianity, which was not to be resisted.

It was in January, 1798, that I rose one morning before daylight, to walk ten miles in the mud, and went to hear this celebrated person preach. Never, the longest day I have to live, shall I have such another walk as this cold, raw,

---

4. Hazlitt is playing with a passage in *Coriolanus* (V.vi.114–15) in which a military exploit of the hero is described—for the war-like Volscians he substitutes Salopians, i.e. inhabitants of Salop, an old name for the county of Shropshire; he counts on this to seem mildly comical to his contemporary readers because "salop" or "saloop" was the name of a hot drink made of milk, sugar, and sassafras that was formerly sold in the London streets in the night and early morning.
5. Gray, *The Bard*, l. 28.
6. Pope, *Ode on St. Cecelia's Day*, ll. 90–91.

comfortless one, in the winter of the year 1798. *Il y a des impressions que ni le tems ni les circonstances peuvent effacer. Dusse-je vivre des siècles entiers, le doux tems de ma jeunesse ne peut renaître pour moi, ni s'effacer jamais dans ma mémoire.*[7] When I got there, the organ was playing the hundredth psalm, and, when it was done, Mr. Coleridge rose and gave out his text, 'And he went up into the mountain to pray, HIMSELF, ALONE.'[8] As he gave out his text, his voice 'rose like a steam of rich distilled perfumes,'[9] and when he came to the two last words, which he pronounced loud, deep, and distinct, it seemed to me, who was then young, as if the sounds had echoed from the bottom of the human heart, and as if that prayer might have floated in solemn silence through the universe. The idea of St. John came into mind, 'of one crying in the wilderness, who had his loins girt about, and whose food was locusts and wild honey.'[10] The preacher then launched into his subject, like an eagle dallying with the wind. The sermon was upon peace and war; upon church and state—not their alliance, but their separation[11]—on the spirit of the world and the spirit of Christianity, not as the same, but as opposed to one another. He talked of those who had 'inscribed the cross of Christ on banners dripping with human gore.' He made a poetical and pastoral excursion,—and to show the fatal effects of war, drew a striking contrast between the simple shepherd boy, driving his team afield, or sitting under the hawthorn, piping to his flock, 'as though he should never be old,'[12] and the same poor country-lad, crimped,[13] kidnapped, brought into town, made drunk at an alehouse, turned into a wretched drummer-boy, with his hair sticking on end with powder and po-matum, a long cue at his back, and tricked out in the loathsome finery of the profession of blood.

Such were the notes our once-loved poet sung.[14]

And for myself, I could not have been more delighted if I had heard the music of the spheres. Poetry and Philosophy had met together. Truth and Genius had embraced, under the eye and with the sanction of Religion. This was even beyond my hopes. I returned home well satisfied. The sun that was still labouring pale and wan through the sky, obscured by thick mists, seemed an emblem of the *good cause;* and the cold dank drops of dew that hung half melted on the beard of the thistle, had something genial and refreshing in them; for there was a spirit of hope and youth in all nature, that turned every thing into good. The face of nature had not then the brand of *Jus Divinum*[15] on it:

7. "There are impressions which neither time nor circumstance is able to efface. Were I to live whole centuries, the sweet time of my youth never could be reborn for me, but neither could it ever be erased from my memory." An approximate quotation from Rousseau's enormously popular novel *La Nouvelle Héloïse* (1761), Part VI, Letter 7.
8. Matthew 14:23 and John 6:15.
9. Milton, *Comus*, l. 556.
10. Matthew 3:3–4 and Mark 1:3.
11. Coleridge was later to change his opinion on this score.
12. Sir Philip Sidney, *Arcadia* I.2.
13. Tricked or coerced into military (or naval) service.
14. Pope, "Epistle to Robert, Earl of Oxford," l. 1.
15. "The divine right," i.e. of kings, the doctrine that a king receives his right to rule from God.

Like to that sanguine flower inscribed with woe.[16]

On the Tuesday following, the half-inspired speaker came. I was called down into the room where he was, and went half-hoping, half-afraid. He received me very graciously, and I listened for a long time without uttering a word. I did not suffer in his opinion by my silence. 'For those two hours,' he afterwards was pleased to say, 'he was conversing with W. H.'s forehead!' His appearance was different from what I had anticipated from seeing him before. At a distance, and in the dim light of the chapel, there was to me a strange wildness in his aspect, a dusky obscurity, and I thought him pitted with the smallpox. His complexion was at that time clear, and even bright—

As are the children of yon azure sheen.[17]

His forehead was broad and high, light as if built of ivory, with large projecting eyebrows, and his eyes rolling beneath them like a sea with darkened lustre. 'A certain tender bloom his face o'erspread,'[18] a purple tinge as we see it in the pale thoughtful complexions of the Spanish portrait painters, Murillo and Velasquez. His mouth was gross, voluptuous, open, eloquent; his chin good-humoured and round; but his nose, the rudder of the face, the index of the will, was small, feeble, nothing—like what he has done.[19] It might seem that the genius of his face as from a height surveyed and projected him (with sufficient capacity and huge aspiration) into the world unknown of thought and imagination, with nothing to support or guide his veering purpose, as if Columbus had launched his adventurous course for the New World in a scallop,[20] without oars or compass. So at least I comment on it after the event. Coleridge in his person was rather above the common size, inclining to the corpulent, or like Lord Hamlet, 'somewhat fat and pursy.'[21] His hair (now, alas! grey) was then black and glossy as the raven's, and fell in smooth masses over his forehead. This long pendulous hair is peculiar to enthusiasts, to those whose minds tend heavenward; and is traditionally inseparable (though of a different colour) from the pictures of Christ. It ought to belong, as a character, to all who preach *Christ crucified*, and Coleridge was at that time one of those! It was curious to observe the contrast between him and my father, who was a veteran in the cause, and then declining into the vale of years. He had been a poor Irish lad, carefully brought up by his parents, and sent to the

16. *Lycidas*, l. 106. The flower is the hyacinth (not, however, the modern flower of that name), which was thought to be marked with the letters *ai*, the Greek cry of woe. Hazlitt is saying that as a young man he thought of nature only as beneficent, not as tyrannical and cruel. See *On the Feeling of Immortality in Youth*.
17. Thomson, *The Castle of Indolence* II.xxxiii.
18. *Ibid.* I.lvii.3: "A certain tender gloom o'erspread his face." It is likely that "bloom" is a misprint for "gloom."
19. The idea that Coleridge accomplished "nothing" was once commonly held. It arose partly from the circumstance that Coleridge projected more works than he completed. But even the list of works published in his lifetime is formidable and the edition of his complete works, including his unfinished manuscripts, will run to many volumes.
20. This would seem to be a miswriting or misprinting of "shallop," a small open sailing boat.
21. Hazlitt's memory has conflated two lines of *Hamlet*—III.iv.153, "For in the fatness of these pursy times," and V.ii.298, "He's fat and scant of breath."

University of Glasgow (where he studied under Adam Smith [22]) to prepare him for his future destination. It was his mother's proudest wish to see her son a Dissenting Minister. So if we look back to past generations (as far as eye can reach) we see the same hopes, fears, wishes, followed by the same disappointments, throbbing in the human heart; and so we may see them (if we look forward) rising up for ever, and disappearing, like vapourish bubbles, in the human breast! After being tossed about from congregation to congregation in the heats of the Unitarian controversy,[23] and squabbles about the American war, he had been relegated to an obscure village, where he was to spend the last thirty years of his life, far from the only converse that he loved, the talk about disputed texts of Scripture and the cause of civil and religious liberty. Here he passed his days, repining but resigned, in the study of the Bible, and the perusal of the Commentators,—huge folios, not easily got through, one of which would outlast a winter! Why did he pore on these from morn to night (with the exception of a walk in the fields or a turn in the garden to gather broccoli-plants or kidney-beans of his own rearing, with no small degree of pride and pleasure)?—Here were 'no figures nor no fantasies,' [24] —neither poetry nor philosophy—nothing to dazzle, nothing to excite modern curiosity; but to his lacklustre eyes there appeared, within the pages of the ponderous, unwieldy, neglected tomes, the sacred name of JEHOVAH in Hebrew capitals: pressed down by the weight of the style, worn to the last fading thinness of the understanding, there were glimpses, glimmering notions of the patriarchal wanderings, with palm trees hovering in the horizon, and processions of camels at the distance of three thousand years; there was Moses with the Burning Bush, the number of the Twelve Tribes, types,[25] shadows, glosses on the law and the prophets; there were discussions (dull enough) on the age of Methuselah, a mighty speculation! there were outlines, rude guesses at the shape of Noah's Ark and of the riches of Solomon's Temple; questions as to the date of the creation, predictions of the end of all things; the great lapses of time, the strange mutations of the globe were unfolded with the voluminous leaf, as it turned over; and though the soul might slumber with an hieroglyphic veil of inscrutable mysteries drawn over it, yet it was in a slumber ill exchanged for all the sharpened realities of sense, wit, fancy, or reason. My father's life was comparatively a dream; but it was a dream of infinity and eternity, of death, the resurrection, and a judgment to come!

No two individuals were ever more unlike than were the host and his guest.

---

22. Although he is now remembered chiefly for *The Wealth of Nations* (1776), his pioneering work in economic theory, Adam Smith (1723–90) was also renowned as a moral philosopher.

23. Unitarianism is a system of Christian thought which derives its name from its belief in the single personality of God the Father, as against the doctrine that God has a threefold being, Father, Son, and Holy Spirit. It holds Jesus Christ in highest regard as the greatest of spiritual teachers but does not worship Him as divine. Until 1813 Unitarians in England were under threat of the laws against those who denied the Trinity; their struggle for their civil liberties made them sympathetic with radical causes, including that of American independence.

24. Shakespeare, *Julius Caesar* II.i.231.

25. In theology, "types" are the foreshadowings of the Christian dispensation in the events and persons of the Old Testament.

A poet was to my father a sort of nondescript: yet whatever added grace to the Unitarian cause was to him welcome. He could hardly have been more surprised or pleased, if our visitor had worn wings. Indeed, his thoughts had wings; and as the silken sounds rustled round our little wainscoted parlour, my father threw back his spectacles over his forehead, his white hairs mixing with its sanguine hue; and a smile of delight beamed across his rugged cordial face, to think that Truth had found a new ally in Fancy! [26] Besides, Coleridge seemed to take considerable notice of me, and that of itself was enough. He talked very familiarly, but agreeably, and glanced over a variety of subjects. At dinner-time he grew more animated, and dilated in a very edifying manner on Mary Wollstonecraft and Mackintosh.[27] The last, he said, he considered (on my father's speaking of his *Vindiciae Gallicae* as a capital performance) as a clever scholastic man—a master of the topics,—or as the ready warehouseman of letters, who knew exactly where to lay his hand on what he wanted, though the goods were not his own. He thought him no match for Burke, either in style or matter. Burke was a metaphysician, Mackintosh a mere logician. Burke was an orator (almost a poet) who reasoned in figures, because he had an eye for nature: Mackintosh, on the other hand, was a rhetorician, who had only an eye to commonplaces. On this I ventured to say that I had always entertained a great opinion of Burke, and that (as far as I could find) the speaking of him with contempt might be made the test of a vulgar democratical mind.[28] This was the first observation I ever made to Coleridge, and he said it was a very just and striking one. I remember the leg of Welsh mutton and the turnips on the table that day had the finest flavour imaginable. Coleridge added that Mackintosh and Tom Wedgwood [29] (of whom, however, he spoke highly) had expressed a very indifferent opinion of his friend Mr. Wordsworth, on which he remarked to them—'He strides on so far before you, that he dwindles in the distance!' Godwin [30] had once boasted to him of having carried on an argument with Mackintosh for three hours with dubious success; Coleridge told him—'If there had been a man of genius in the room, he would have settled the question in five minutes.' He asked me if I had ever seen Mary Wollstonecraft, and I said, I had once for a few moments,

26. "My father was one of those who mistook his talent after all. He used to be very much dissatisfied that I preferred his Letters to his Sermons. The last were forced and dry; the first came naturally from him. For ease, half-plays on words, and a supine, monkish, indolent pleasantry, I have never seen them equalled." (Hazlitt)

27. Mary Wollstonecraft (1759–97) is best known for her *Vindication of the Rights of Women* (1792). She married William Godwin in 1797 and died giving birth to their daughter Mary, who became the second wife of Shelley. Sir James Mackintosh (1765–1832), Scottish writer, lawyer, and civil servant, in 1791 published *Vindiciae Gallicae* (Defense of France) in answer to Edmund Burke's *Reflections on the French Revolution* (1790).

28. In England the words "democracy," "democratic," etc., were likely to be used with a pejorative intention in the early part of the 19th century.

29. The son of Josiah Wedgwood, the founder of the famous English firm of potters. He is sometimes called the first photographer. He was greatly admired by all who knew him, and is remembered for his benefaction to Coleridge.

30. William Godwin (1756–1836) had great influence over two generations of Romantic poets with his *Enquiry Concerning Political Justice* (1793), one of the classics of anarchist theory. He is also remembered for his novels, especially *The Adventures of Caleb Williams* (1794).

and that she seemed to me to turn off Godwin's objections to something she advanced with quite a playful, easy air. He replied, that 'this was only one instance of the ascendancy which people of imagination exercised over those of mere intellect.' He did not rate Godwin very high [31] (this was caprice or prejudice, real or affected) but he had a great idea of Mrs. Wollstonecraft's powers of conversation, none at all of her talent for bookmaking. We talked a little about Holcroft.[32] He had been asked if he was not much struck *with* him, and he said, he thought himself in more danger of being struck *by* him. I complained that he would not let me get on at all, for he required a definition of every the commonest word, exclaiming, 'What do you mean by a *sensation*, Sir? What do you mean by an *idea?*' This, Coleridge said, was barricadoing the road to truth:—it was setting up a turnpike-gate at every step we took. I forget a great number of things, many more than I remember; but the day passed off pleasantly, and the next morning Mr. Coleridge was to return to Shrewsbury. When I came down to breakfast, I found that he had just received a letter from his friend T. Wedgwood, making him an offer of 150 £ a year if he chose to waive his present pursuit, and devote himself entirely to the study of poetry and philosophy. Coleridge seemed to make up his mind to close with this proposal in the act of tying on one of his shoes. It threw an additional damp on his departure. It took the wayward enthusiast quite from us to cast him into Deva's [33] winding vales, or by the shores of old romance. Instead of living at ten miles distance, of being the pastor of a Dissenting congregation at Shrewsbury, he was henceforth to inhabit the Hill of Parnassus, to be a shepherd on the Delectable Mountains.[34] Alas! I knew not the way thither, and felt very little gratitude for Mr. Wedgwood's bounty. I was presently relieved from this dilemma; for Mr. Coleridge, asking for a pen and ink, and going to a table to write something on a bit of card, advanced towards me with undulating step, and giving me the precious document, said that that was his address, *Mr. Coleridge, Nether-Stowey, Somersetshire;* and that he should be glad to see me there in a few weeks' time, and, if I chose, would come half-way to meet me. I was not less surprised than the shepherd boy (this simile is to be found in *Cassandra*[35]) when he sees a thunderbolt fall close at his feet. I stammered out my acknowledgments and acceptance of this

31. "He complained in particular of the presumption of attempting to establish the future immortality of man 'without' (as he said) 'knowing what Death was or what Life was'— and the tone in which he pronounced these two words seemed to convey a complete image of both." (Hazlitt)

32. Thomas Holcroft (1745–1809), the self-educated son of poor parents, became a journalist, dramatist, and novelist and the admired friend of Godwin, Lamb, and Hazlitt, the last of whom edited his interesting *Memoirs*. He was a strong partisan of the French Revolution and in 1794 his radical activities led to his being indicted for high treason; he was, however, discharged without a trial.

33. The Latin name for the river Dee. Hazlitt has in mind l. 54 of *Lycidas*, in which Deva is spoken of as a "wizard stream"—it was reputed to have prophetic powers, like the "old Bards, the famous Druids," spoken of two lines before. The whole passage deals with the profession of poetry.

34. Mount Parnassus in Greek mythology was sacred to Apollo and the Muses. In *Pilgrim's Progress* the Delectable Mountains are reached by Christian and Hopeful after they escape from Doubting Castle and the Giant Despair.

35. An interminable—ten-volume!—romance by Gauthier de Costes de la Calprenède much admired in the 17th century.

offer (I thought Mr. Wedgwood's annuity a trifle to it) as well as I could; and this mighty business being settled, the poet-preacher took leave, and I accompanied him six miles on the road. It was a fine morning in the middle of winter, and he talked the whole way. The scholar in Chaucer is described as going—

   Sounding on his way.[36]

So Coleridge went on his. In digressing, in dilating, in passing from subject to subject, he appeared to me to float in air, to slide on ice. He told me in confidence (going along) that he should have preached two sermons before he accepted the situation at Shrewsbury, one on Infant Baptism, the other on the Lord's Supper, showing that he could not administer either, which would have effectually disqualified him for the object in view. I observed that he continually crossed me on the way by shifting from one side of the foot-path to the other. This struck me as an odd movement; but I did not at that time connect it with any instability of purpose or involuntary change of principle, as I have done since. He seemed unable to keep on in a straight line. He spoke slightly of Hume [37] (whose "Essay on Miracles" he said was stolen from an objection started in one of South's sermons—*Credat Judaeus Apella!* [38]). I was not very much pleased at this account of Hume, for I had just been reading, with infinite relish, that completest of all metaphysical *choke-pears,* his *Treatise on Human Nature,* to which the *Essays,* in point of scholastic subtlety and close reasoning, are mere elegant trifling, light summer-reading. Coleridge even denied the excellence of Hume's general style, which I think betrayed a want of taste or candour. He however made me amends by the manner in which he spoke of Berkeley.[39] He dwelt particularly on his *Essay on Vision* as a masterpiece of analytical reasoning. So it undoubtedly is. He was exceedingly angry with Dr. Johnson for striking the stone with his foot, in allusion to this author's Theory of Matter and Spirit, and saying, 'Thus I confute him, Sir.' [40] Coleridge drew a parallel (I don't know how he brought about the connection) between Bishop Berkeley and Tom Paine.[41] He said the one was an instance

36. Hazlitt both misremembers and misunderstands l. 307 of the General Prologue of *The Canterbury Tales,* which reads, "Sounynge in moral vertu was his speche"; "sounynge in" means tending toward, consonant with.
37. David Hume (1711–76), the Scottish philosopher. His skepticism, which had great influence on subsequent philosophical thought, was anathema to Coleridge.
38. The Latin phrase ("let the Jew Apella believe it"—i.e. I do not) is from Horace, *Satires* I.100. Dr. Robert South (1634–1716) was a noted English ecclesiastic.
39. George Berkeley (1685–1753), Bishop of Cloyne in Ireland, was one of the most influential philosophers of his time. Coleridge found his "idealistic" position very congenial.
40. The incident is one of the famous episodes in Boswell's *Life of Johnson.* "After we came out of the church, we stood talking for some time together of Bishop Berkeley's ingenious sophistry to prove the non-existence of matter, and that everything in the universe is merely ideal. I observed, that though we are satisfied that the doctrine is not true, it is impossible to refute it. I shall never forget the alacrity with which Johnson answered, striking his foot with mighty force against a large stone, till he rebounded from it, 'I refute it *thus*' " (1763). Dr. Johnson's "refutation" made plain his failure to understand what Berkeley was saying.
41. Thomas Paine (1737–1809), the political radical who supported and participated in both the American and the French revolutions. He is the author of *Common Sense* (1776) and *The Rights of Man* (1791–92).

of a subtle, the other of an acute mind, than which no two things could be more distinct. The one was a shop-boy's quality, the other the characteristic of a philosopher. He considered Bishop Butler [42] as a true philosopher, a profound and conscientious thinker, a genuine reader of nature and of his own mind. He did not speak of his *Analogy*, but of his *Sermons at the Rolls' Chapel*, of which I had never heard. Coleridge somehow always contrived to prefer the *unknown* to the *known*. In this instance he was right. The *Analogy* is a tissue of sophistry, of wire-drawn, theological special-pleading; the *Sermons* (with the Preface to them) are in a fine vein of deep, matured reflection, a candid appeal to our observation of human nature, without pedantry and without bias. I told Coleridge I had written a few remarks, and was sometimes foolish enough to believe that I had made a discovery on the same subject (the *Natural Disinterestedness of the Human Mind* [43])—and I tried to explain my view of it to Coleridge, who listened with great willingness, but I did not succeed in making myself understood. I sat down to the task shortly afterwards for the twentieth time, got new pens and paper, determined to make clear work of it, wrote a few meagre sentences in the skeleton-style of a mathematical demonstration, stopped half-way down the second page; and, after trying in vain to pump up any words, images, motions, apprehensions, facts, or observations, from that gulf of abstraction in which I had plunged myself for four or five years preceding, gave up the attempt as labour in vain, and shed tears of helpless despondency on the blank unfinished paper. I can write fast enough now. Am I better than I was then? Oh no! One truth discovered, one pang of regret at not being able to express it, is better than all the fluency and flippancy in the world. Would that I could go back to what I then was! Why can we not revive past times as we can revisit old places? If I had the quaint Muse of Sir Philip Sidney to assist me, I would write a *Sonnet to the Road between W—m and Shrewsbury*, and immortalize every step of it by some fond enigmatical conceit. I would swear that the very milestones had ears, and that Harmer-hill stooped with all its pines, to listen to a poet, as he passed! I remember but one other topic of discourse in this walk. He mentioned Paley,[44] praised the naturalness and clearness of his style, but condemned his sentiments, thought him a mere time-serving casuist, and said that 'the fact of his work on Moral and Political Philosophy being made a text-book in our Universities was a disgrace to the national character.' We parted at the six-mile stone; and I returned homeward pensive but much pleased. I had met with unexpected notice from a person, whom I believed to have been prejudiced against me. 'Kind and affable to me had been his condescension, and should

42. Joseph Butler (1692–1752), the moral philosopher and divine whose famous work, *The Analogy of Religion, Natural and Revealed, to the Course and Constitution of Nature,* once had great authority as a defense of the probability of revealed religion.

43. "Disinterestedness" means the state of being free of bias and self-interest. Hazlitt published the work to which he refers under the title *An Essay on the Principles of Human Action* (1805).

44. William Paley (1743–1805), theologian and philosopher, whose *View of the Evidences of Christianity,* a rationalistic defense of religion, was celebrated in its day. It was at Cambridge that his *Principles of Moral Political Philosophy* became a textbook upon its publication in 1785.

be honoured ever with suitable regard.'[45] He was the first poet I had known, and he certainly answered to that inspired name. I had heard a great deal of his powers of conversation, and was not disappointed. In fact, I never met with any thing at all like them, either before or since. I could easily credit the accounts which were circulated of his holding forth to a large party of ladies and gentlemen, an evening or two before, on the Berkeleian Theory, when he made the whole material universe look like a transparency of fine words; and another story (which I believe he has somewhere told himself) of his being asked to a party at Birmingham, of his smoking tobacco and going to sleep after dinner on a sofa, where the company found him to their no small surprise, which was increased to wonder when he started up of a sudden, and rubbing his eyes, looked about him, and launched into a three-hours' description of the third heaven, of which he had had a dream, very different from Mr. Southey's *Vision of Judgment,* and also from that other *Vision of Judgment,* [46] which Mr. Murray, the Secretary of the Bridge-street Junto,[47] has taken into his especial keeping!

On my way back, I had a sound in my ears, it was the voice of Fancy: I had a light before me, it was the face of Poetry. The one still lingers there, the other has not quitted my side! Coleridge in truth met me half-way on the ground of philosophy, or I should not have been won over to his imaginative creed. I had an uneasy, pleasurable sensation all the time, till I was to visit him. During those months the chill breath of winter gave me a welcoming; the vernal air was balm and inspiration to me. The golden sunsets, the silver star of evening, lighted me on my way to new hopes and prospects. *I was to visit Coleridge in the spring.* This circumstance was never absent from my thoughts, and mingled with all my feelings. I wrote to him at the time proposed, and received an answer postponing my intended visit for a week or two, but very cordially urging me to complete my promise then. This delay did not damp, but rather increased my ardour. In the meantime, I went to Llangollen Vale,[48] by way of initiating myself in the mysteries of natural scenery; and I must say I was enchanted with it. I had been reading Coleridge's description of England in his fine *Ode on the Departing Year,* and I applied it, *con amore,*[49] to the objects before me. That valley was to me (in a manner) the

45. At the end of Bk. VIII of *Paradise Lost* Adam says to the angel Raphael, "Gentle to me and affable hath been / Thy condescension and shall be honoured ever / With suitable regard."
46. Robert Southey's A *Vision of Judgment* (1821) describes in a sanctimonious way the reception in heaven of the unhappy George III. In the preface to the poem Southey refers to the "lewdness and impiety" of Byron, who responded with his own *The Vision of Judgment* (1822), a parody of Southey's and a satire on the late king and his government.
47. Byron's *The Vision of Judgment* appeared in the first issue of the *Liberal,* a periodical edited by Leigh Hunt and published by his brother John. It made a great scandal and the prosecution of John Hunt was initiated by Charles Murray of Bridge Street, an officer of the Constitutional Association, on the ground that he had published "a gross, impious, and slanderous" libel on George III "calculated to destroy the comfort and happiness of his present majesty."
48. In Wales, some forty miles from Wem.
49. "With love," warmly.

cradle of a new existence: in the river that winds through it, my spirit was baptised in the waters of Helicon! [50]

I returned home, and soon after set out on my journey with unworn heart and untried feet. My way lay through Worcester and Gloucester, and by Upton, where I thought of Tom Jones and the adventure of the muff.[51] I remember getting completely wet through one day, and stopping at an inn (I think it was at Tewkesbury) where I sat up all night to read *Paul and Virginia*.[52] Sweet were the showers in early youth that drenched my body, and sweet the drops of pity that fell upon the books I read! I recollect a remark of Coleridge's upon this very book, that nothing could shew the gross indelicacy of French manners and the entire corruption of their imagination more strongly than the behaviour of the heroine in the last fatal scene, who turns away from a person on board the sinking vessel, that offers to save her life, because he has thrown off his clothes to assist him in swimming. Was this a time to think of such a circumstance? I once hinted to Wordsworth, as we were sailing in his boat on Grasmere lake, that I thought he had borrowed the idea of his *Poems on the Naming of Places* from the local inscriptions of the same kind in *Paul and Virginia*. He did not own the obligation, and stated some distinction without a difference, in defence of his claim to originality. Any the slightest variation would be sufficient for this purpose in his mind; for whatever *he* added or omitted would inevitably be worth all that any one else had done, and contain the marrow of the sentiment. I was still two days before the time fixed for my arrival, for I had taken care to set out early enough. I stopped these two days at Bridgewater, and when I was tired of sauntering on the banks of its muddy river, returned to the inn, and read *Camilla*.[53] So have I loitered my life away, reading books, looking at pictures, going to plays, hearing, thinking, writing on what pleased me best. I have wanted only one thing to make me happy; but wanting that, have wanted everything!

I arrived, and was well received. The country about Nether Stowey is beautiful, green and hilly, and near the seashore. I saw it but the other day, after an interval of twenty years, from a hill near Taunton. How was the map of my life spread out before me, as the map of the country lay at my feet! In the afternoon, Coleridge took me over to All-Foxden,[54] a romantic old family-mansion of the St. Aubins, where Wordsworth lived. It was then in the possession of a friend of the poet's who gave him the free use of it.[55] Somehow that period (the time just after the French Revolution) was not a time when *nothing was given for nothing*. The mind opened, and a softness might be perceived coming over the heart of individuals, beneath 'the scales that fence' our self-interest. Wordsworth himself was from home, but his sister kept house,

---

50. A mountain which the ancient Greeks thought of as one of the homes of the Muses, the other being Parnassus.
51. Henry Fielding, *The History of Tom Jones, A Foundling* (1749), X.v–vi.
52. An enormously popular novel of young love in an Edenic setting (1787) by Bernadin de Saint-Pierre.
53. *Camilla; or, A Picture of Youth* (1796) is a novel by Fanny Burney.
54. Hazlitt's spelling of Alfoxden.
55. Actually Wordsworth paid a rental of £23 for the year of his occupancy.

and set before us a frugal repast; and we had free access to her brother's poems, the *Lyrical Ballads*, which were still in manuscript, or in the form of *Sybilline Leaves*.[56] I dipped into a few of these with great satisfaction, and with the faith of a novice. I slept that night in an old room with blue hangings, and covered with the round-faced family-portraits of the age of George I and II, and from the wooded declivity of the adjoining part that overlooked my window, at the dawn of day, could

———hear the loud stag speak.[57]

In the outset of life (and particularly at this time I felt it so) our imagination has a body to it. We are in a state between sleeping and waking, and have indistinct but glorious glimpses of strange shapes, and there is always something to come better than what we see. As in our dreams the fulness of the blood gives warmth and reality to the coinage of the brain, so in youth our ideas are clothed, and fed, and pampered with our good spirits; we breathe thick with thoughtless happiness, the weight of future years presses on the strong pulses of the heart, and we repose with undisturbed faith in truth and good. As we advance, we exhaust our fund of enjoyment and of hope. We are no longer wrapped in *lamb's-wool*, lulled in Elysium. As we taste the pleasures of life, their spirit evaporates, the sense palls; and nothing is left but the phantoms, the lifeless shadows of what *has been*!

That morning, as soon as breakfast was over, we strolled out into the park, and seating ourselves on the trunk of an old ash-tree that stretched along the ground, Coleridge read aloud with a sonorous and musical voice, the ballad of *Betty Foy*.[58] I was not critically or sceptically inclined. I saw touches of truth and nature, and took the rest for granted. But in the *Thorn*, the *Mad Mother*, and the *Complaint of a Poor Indian Woman*, I felt that deeper power and pathos which have been since acknowledged,

In spite of pride, in erring reason's spite,[59]

as the characteristics of this author; and the sense of a new style and a new spirit in poetry came over me. It had to me something of the effect that arises from the turning up of the fresh soil, or of the first welcome breath of Spring,

While yet the trembling year is unconfirmed.[60]

Coleridge and myself walked back to Stowey that evening, and his voice sounded high

Of Providence, foreknowledge, will, and fate,
Fixed fate, free-will, foreknowledge absolute,[61]

56. Although the two poets worked closely together on their early poems and although *Lyrical Ballads* was a joint enterprise, it is difficult to know what Hazlitt means by Wordsworth's poems being "in the form of *Sybilline Leaves*," which was the title of Coleridge's volume of 1817. A sibyl—the more usual spelling—was a prophetess thought by the Greeks and Romans to be inspired by Apollo.
57. Ben Jonson, "To Sir Robert Wroth," l. 22.
58. Wordsworth's *The Idiot Boy*. It was included in *Lyrical Ballads*, as were the other poems mentioned in the paragraph.
59. Pope, *An Essay on Man* I.293.
60. Thomson, *The Seasons*, Spring, l. 18.
61. *Paradise Lost* II.559–60.

as we passed through echoing grove, by fairy stream or waterfall, gleaming in the summer moonlight! He lamented that Wordsworth was not prone enough to believe in the traditional superstitions of the place, and that there was a something corporeal, a *matter-of-fact-ness*, a clinging to the palpable, or often to the petty, in his poetry, in consequence. His genius was not a spirit that descended to him through the air; it sprung out of the ground like a flower, or unfolded itself from a green spray, on which the goldfinch sang. He said, however (if I remember right), that this objection must be confined to his descriptive pieces, that his philosophic poetry had a grand and comprehensive spirit in it, so that his soul seemed to inhabit the universe like a palace, and to discover truth by intuition, rather than by deduction. The next day Wordsworth arrived from Bristol at Coleridge's cottage. I think I see him now. He answered in some degree to his friend's description of him, but was more gaunt and Don Quixote-like. He was quaintly dressed (according to the *costume* of that unconstrained period) in a brown fustian [62] jacket and striped pantaloons. There was something of a roll, a lounge in his gait, not unlike his own Peter Bell.[63] There was a severe, worn pressure of thought about his temples, a fire in his eye (as if he saw something in objects more than the outward appearance), an intense high narrow forehead, a Roman nose, cheeks furrowed by strong purpose and feeling, and a convulsive inclination to laughter about the mouth, a good deal at variance with the solemn, stately expression of the rest of his face. Chantrey's [64] bust wants the marking traits; but he was teazed into making it regular and heavy: Haydon's [65] head of him, introduced into the *Entrance of Christ into Jerusalem,* is the most like his drooping weight of thought and expression. He sat down and talked very naturally and freely, with a mixture of clear gushing accents in his voice, a deep guttural intonation, and a strong tincture of the northern *burr,* like the crust on wine. He instantly began to make havoc of the half of a Cheshire cheese on the table, and said triumphantly that 'his marriage with experience had not been so unproductive as Mr. Southey's in teaching him a knowledge of the good things of this life.' He had been to see the *Castle Spectre* by Monk Lewis, while at Bristol, and described it very well.[66] He said 'it fitted the taste of the audience like a glove.' This *ad captandum* [67] merit was however by no means a recommendation of it, according to the severe principles of the new school, which reject rather than court popular effect. Wordsworth, looking out of the low, latticed window, said, 'How beautifully the sun sets on that yellow bank!' I thought within myself, 'With what eyes these poets see nature!' and ever after, when I saw the sunset stream upon the objects facing it, conceived I had made a discovery, or thanked Mr. Wordsworth for having made one for me! We went over to All-Foxden again the day following, and Wordsworth read us the story of Peter Bell in the open air; and the comment made upon it by his face and voice was very differ-

62. A coarse sturdy cloth made of cotton and flax.
63. Of the poem of that name.
64. Sir Francis Chantrey (1781–1841), a portrait sculptor well known in his day.
65. Benjamin Robert Haydon (1786–1846) exhibited this huge painting in 1820. It contained portraits not only of Wordsworth but also of Keats and Hazlitt.
66. Matthew Gregory Lewis (1775–1818) derived his nickname of Monk from his famous novel of "Gothic" terror, *The Monk* (1795).
67. Designed to capture the fancy of the audience.

ent from that of some later critics! Whatever might be thought of the poem, 'his face was as a book where men might read strange matters,'[68] and he announced the fate of his hero in prophetic tones. There is a *chaunt* in the recitation both of Coleridge and Wordsworth, which acts as a spell upon the hearer, and disarms the judgment. Perhaps they have deceived themselves by making habitual use of this ambiguous accompaniment. Coleridge's manner is more full, animated, and varied; Wordsworth's more equable, sustained, and internal. The one might be termed more *dramatic*, the other more *lyrical*. Coleridge has told me that he himself liked to compose in walking over uneven ground, or breaking through the straggling branches of a copse-wood; whereas Wordsworth always wrote (if he could) walking up and down a straight gravel-walk, or in some spot where the continuity of his verse met with no collateral interruption. Returning that same evening, I got into a metaphysical argument with Wordsworth, while Coleridge was explaining the different notes of the nightingale to his sister, in which we neither of us succeeded in making ourselves perfectly clear and intelligible. Thus I passed three weeks at Nether Stowey and in the neighbourhood, generally devoting the afternoons to a delightful chat in an arbour made of bark by the poet's friend Tom Poole,[69] sitting under two fine elm-trees, and listening to the bees humming round us, while we quaffed our *flip*.[70] It was agreed, among other things, that we should make a jaunt down the Bristol-Channel, as far as Linton. We set off together on foot, Coleridge, John Chester, and I. This Chester was a native of Nether Stowey, one of those who were attracted to Coleridge's discourse as flies are to honey, or bees in swarming-time to the sound of a brass pan. He 'followed in the chase, like a dog who hunts, not like one that made up the cry.'[71] He had on a brown cloth coat, boots, and corduroy breeches, was low in stature, bowlegged, had a drag in his walk like a drover, which he assisted by a hazel switch, and kept on a sort of trot by the side of Coleridge, like a running footman by a state coach, that he might not lose a syllable or sound that fell from Coleridge's lips. He told me his private opinion, that Coleridge was a wonderful man. He scarcely opened his lips, much less offered an opinion the whole way: yet of the three, had I to choose during that journey, I would be John Chester. He afterwards followed Coleridge into Germany, where the Kantean philosophers were puzzled how to bring him under any of their categories. When he sat down at table with his idol, John's felicity was complete; Sir Walter Scott's, or Mr. Blackwood's, when they sat down at the same table with the King, was not more so.[72] We passed Dunster on our right, a small town between the brow of a hill and the sea. I remember eyeing it wistfully as it lay below us: contrasted with the woody scene around, it looked as clear, as pure, as *embrowned* and ideal as any landscape I have

68. *Macbeth* I.v.63–64.
69. Thomas Poole (1765–1837), for many years Coleridge's friend and benefactor. The son of a rough tanner who refused him proper schooling, he acquired an education by his own efforts and won the regard and affection of many distinguished persons.
70. A mixed drink, variously made, usually containing beaten eggs.
71. Based on *Othello* II.iii.369–70.
72. William Blackwood, publisher of *Blackwood's Magazine,* and Sir Walter Scott were staunch Tories. Hazlitt probably refers to their attendance at the banquet given to George IV in Edinburgh in 1822.

seen since, of Gaspar Poussin's or Domenichino's.[73] We had a long day's march
—(our feet kept time to the echoes of Coleridge's tongue)—through Minehead
and by the Blue Anchor, and on to Linton, which we did not reach till near
midnight, and where we had some difficulty in making a lodgment. We however
knocked the people of the house up at last, and we were repaid for our apprehensions and fatigue by some excellent rashers of fried bacon and eggs. The
view in coming along had been splendid. We walked for miles and miles on dark
brown heaths overlooking the Channel, with the Welsh hills beyond, and at
times descended into little sheltered valleys close by the seaside, with a smug-
gler's face scowling by us, and then had to ascend conical hills with a path winding up through a coppice to a barren top, like a monk's shaven crown, from one
of which I pointed out to Coleridge's notice the bare masts of a vessel on the
very edge of the horizon and within the red-orbed disk of the setting sun, like
his own spectre-ship in the *Ancient Mariner*. At Linton the character of the
seacoast becomes more marked and rugged. There is a place called the *Valley
of Rocks* (I suspect this was only the poetical name for it) bedded among
precipices overhanging the sea, with rocky caverns beneath, into which the
waves dash, and where the sea-gull for ever wheels its screaming flight. On
the tops of these are huge stones thrown transverse, as if an earthquake had
tossed them there, and behind these is a fretwork of perpendicular rocks,
something like the *Giant's Causeway*.[74] A thunder-storm came on while we
were at the inn, and Coleridge was running out bare-headed to enjoy the
commotion of the elements in the *Valley of Rocks*, but as if in spite, the clouds
only muttered a few angry sounds, and let fall a few refreshing drops. Coleridge told me that he and Wordsworth were to have made this place the
scene of a prose-tale, which was to have been in the manner of, but far
superior to, the *Death of Abel*, but they relinquished the design.[75] In the
morning of the second day, we breakfasted luxuriously in an old-fashioned
parlour, on tea, toast, eggs, and honey, in the very sight of the beehives from
which it had been taken, and a garden full of thyme and wild flowers that
had produced it. On this occasion Coleridge spoke of Virgil's Georgics, but
not well. I do not think he had much feeling for the classical or elegant. It was
in this room that we found a little worn-out copy of the *Seasons*,[76] lying in
a window-seat, on which Coleridge exclaimed, 'That is true fame!' He said
Thomson was a great poet, rather than a good one; his style was as meretri-
cious as his thoughts were natural. He spoke of Cowper as the best modern
poet. He said the *Lyrical Ballads* were an experiment about to be tried by
him and Wordsworth, to see how far the public taste would endure poetry
written in a more natural and simple style than had hitherto been attempted;
totally discarding the artifices of poetical diction, and making use only of

73. Gaspar Poussin (1613–75), whose real name was Gaspar Dughet, was the brother-in-
law and pupil of the more famous Nicolas Poussin; his landscapes were popular in the
18th century. Il Domenichino is Domenico Zampieri (1581–1641), a well-known Italian
painter.
74. A celebrated formation of basaltic columns extending into the sea on the north coast
of Ireland.
75. The *Death of Abel* (1758), by the Swiss poet and painter Salomon Gessner, was
once very popular. The abandoned tale was *The Wanderings of Cain*.
76. By James Thomson (1726–30).

such words as had probably been common in the most ordinary language since the days of Henry II.[77] Some comparison was introduced between Shakespeare and Milton. He said 'he hardly knew which to prefer. Shakespeare appeared to him a mere stripling in the art; he was as tall and as strong, with infinitely more activity than Milton, but he never appeared to have come to man's estate; or if he had, he would not have been a man, but a monster.' He spoke with contempt of Gray, and with intolerance of Pope. He did not like the versification of the latter. He observed that 'the ears of these couplet-writers might be charged with having short memories, that could not retain the harmony of whole passages.' He thought little of Junius [78] as a writer; he had a dislike of Dr. Johnson; and a much higher opinion of Burke as an orator and politician, than of Fox or Pitt.[79] He however thought him very inferior in richness of style and imagery to some of our elder prose-writers, particularly Jeremy Taylor.[80] He liked Richardson, but not Fielding; [81] nor could I get him to enter into the merits of *Caleb Williams*.[82] In short, he was profound and discriminating with respect to those authors whom he liked, and where he gave his judgment fair play; capricious, perverse, and prejudiced in his antipathies and distastes. We loitered on the 'ribbed sea-sands,' [83] in such talk as this, a whole morning, and I recollect met with a curious seaweed, of which John Chester told us the country name! A fisherman gave Coleridge an account of a boy that had been drowned the day before, and that they had tried to save him at the risk of their own lives. He said 'he did not know how it was that they ventured, but, Sir, we have a *nature* towards one another.' This expression, Coleridge remarked to me, was a fine illustration of that theory of disinterestedness which I (in common with Butler) had adopted. I broached to him an argument of mine to prove that *likeness* was not mere association of ideas. I said that the mark in the sand put one in mind of a man's foot, not because it was part of a former impression of a man's foot (for it was quite new) but because it was like the shape of a man's foot. He assented to the justness of this distinction (which I have explained at length elsewhere, for the benefit of the curious) and John Chester listened; not from any interest

77. See Wordsworth's Preface to *Lyrical Ballads*.
78. The anonymous author of a famous series of political pamphlets (1769–72) which attacked the government of George III. His identity has never been established.
79. Charles James Fox (1749–1806), one of the most brilliant and fascinating figures in English political history, defended many liberal and radical causes, including American independence and the French Revolution. He was devoted to gambling only more than to literature; he admired Wordsworth, with whom he corresponded. William Pitt (1759–1806), called "the Younger Pitt" to distinguish him from his equally famous father, became prime minister in 1783 and held office until 1801. In many respects his policies were liberal.
80. In large part because of the beauty of his prose, Taylor is one of the best-remembered of the divines of the 17th century. His most admired works are *Holy Living* (1650) and *Holy Dying* (1651).
81. Samuel Richardson (1689–1761) and Henry Fielding (1707–54) are the two pre-eminent English novelists of the 18th century. The latter began his career by parodying the former. In the 18th and early 19th century their relative merits were commonly debated. Coleridge, for once, is in agreement with Dr. Johnson, who also preferred Richardson to Fielding.
82. A novel by William Godwin, 1794.
83. *The Rime of the Ancient Mariner*, l. 237.

in the subject, but because he was astonished that I should be able to suggest anything to Coleridge that he did not already know. We returned on the third morning, and Coleridge remarked the silent cottage-smoke curling up the valleys where, a few evenings before, we had seen the lights gleaming through the dark.

In a day or two after we arrived at Stowey, we set out, I on my return home, and he for Germany. It was a Sunday morning, and he was to preach that day for Dr. Toulmin of Taunton. I asked him if he had prepared anything for the occasion? He said he had not even thought of the text, but should as soon as we parted. I did not go to hear him,—this was a fault,—but we met in the evening at Bridgewater. The next day we had a long day's walk to Bristol, and sat down, I recollect, by a well-side on the road, to cool ourselves and satisfy our thirst, when Coleridge repeated to me some descriptive lines from his tragedy of *Remorse;* which I must say became his mouth and that occasion better than they, some years after, did Mr. Elliston's and the Drury-lane boards,[84]—

> Oh memory! shield me from the world's poor strife,
> And give those scenes thine everlasting life.

I saw no more of him for a year or two, during which period he had been wandering in the Hartz Forest in Germany; and his return was cometary, meteorous, unlike his setting out. It was not till some time after that I knew his friends Lamb and Southey. The last always appears to me (as I first saw him) with a commonplace book [85] under his arm, and the first with a *bon-mot* in his mouth. It was at Godwin's that I met him with Holcroft and Coleridge, where they were disputing fiercely which was the best—*Man as he was, or man as he is to be*. 'Give me,' says Lamb, 'man as he is *not* to be.' This saying was the beginning of a friendship between us, which I believe still continues. —Enough of this for the present.

> But there is matter for another rhyme,
> And I to this may add a second tale.[86]

1823

On the Feeling of Immortality in Youth

Life is a pure flame, and we live by an invisible sun within us.
SIR THOMAS BROWNE [1]

No young man believes he shall ever die. It was a saying of my brother's,[2] and a fine one. There is a feeling of Eternity in youth, which makes us amends for every thing. To be young is to be as one of the Immortal Gods. One half

---

84. Robert William Elliston (1774–1831) was one of the best-known actors of the day, much admired by Charles Lamb. *Remorse* was produced at the Drury Lane Theatre in 1813.

84. A notebook in which one enters passages from one's reading for later reference.

86. Wordsworth, *Hart-Leap Well*, ll. 95–96.

1. Sir Thomas Browne, *Hydriotaphia* or *Urn Burial* V.

2. John Hazlitt, a year older than William, had studied under Sir Joshua Reynolds and had some success as a portrait painter.

of time indeed is flown—the other half remains in store for us with all its countless treasures; for there is no line drawn, and we see no limit to our hopes and wishes. We make the coming age our own.——

> The vast, the unbounded prospect lies before us.[3]

Death, old age, are words without a meaning, that pass by us like the idle air which we regard not. Others may have undergone, or may still be liable to them—we 'bear a charmed life,'[4] which laughs to scorn all such sickly fancies. As in setting out on a delightful journey, we strain our eager gaze forward——

> Bidding the lovely scenes at distance hail,[5]

—and see no end to the landscape, new objects presenting themselves as we advance; so, in the commencement of life, we set no bounds to our inclinations, nor to the unrestricted opportunities of gratifying them. We have as yet found no obstacle, no disposition to flag; and it seems that we can go on so forever. We look round in a new world, full of life, and motion, and ceaseless progress; and feel in ourselves all the vigour and spirit to keep pace with it, and do not foresee from any present symptoms how we shall be left behind in the natural course of things, decline into old age, and drop into the grave. It is the simplicity, and as it were *abstractedness* of our feelings in youth, that (so to speak) identifies us with nature, and (our experience being slight and our passions strong) deludes us into a belief of being immortal like it. Our short-lived connexion with existence, we fondly flatter ourselves, is an indissoluble and lasting union—a honeymoon that knows neither coldness, jar, nor separation. As infants smile and sleep, we are rocked in the cradle of our wayward fancies, and lulled into security by the roar of the universe around us—we quaff the cup of life with eager haste without draining it, instead of which it only overflows the more—objects press around us, filling the mind with their magnitude and with the throng of desires that wait upon them, so that we have no room for the thoughts of death. From that plenitude of our being, we cannot change all at once to dust and ashes, we cannot imagine 'this sensible, warm motion, to become a kneaded clod'[6]—we are too much dazzled by the brightness of the waking dream around us to look into the darkness of the tomb. We no more see our end than our beginning: the one is lost in oblivion and vacancy, as the other is hid from us by the crowd and hurry of approaching events. Or the grim shadow is seen lingering in the horizon, which we are doomed never to overtake, or whose last, faint, glimmering outline touches upon Heaven and translates us to the skies! Nor would the hold that life has taken of us permit us to detach our thoughts from present objects and pursuits, even if we would. What is there more opposed to health, than sickness; to strength and beauty, than decay and dissolution; to the active search of knowledge than mere oblivion? Or is there none of the usual advantage to bar the

3. Addison, *Cato* V.i.13. Hazlitt misquotes; the line is "The wide, the unbounded prospect lies before us."
4. *Macbeth* V.viii.12.
5. Collins, "The Passions," l. 32.
6. *Measure for Measure* III.i.119–20.

approach of Death, and mock his idle threats; Hope supplies their place, and draws a veil over the abrupt termination of all our cherished schemes. While the spirit of youth remains unimpaired, ere the 'wine of life is drank up,' [7] we are like people intoxicated or in a fever, who are hurried away by the violence of their own sensations: it is only as present objects begin to pall upon the sense, as we have been disappointed in our favourite pursuits, cut off from our closest ties, that passion loosens its hold upon the breast, that we by degrees become weaned from the world, and allow ourselves to contemplate, 'as in a glass, darkly,' [8] the possibility of parting with it for good. The example of others, the voice of experience, has no effect upon us whatever. Casualties we must avoid: the slow and deliberate advances of age we can play at *hide-and-seek* with. We think ourselves too lusty and too nimble for that blear-eyed decrepit old gentleman to catch us. Like the foolish fat scullion, in Sterne, when she hears that Master Bobby is dead, our only reflection is—'So am not I!' [9] The idea of death, instead of staggering our confidence, rather seems to strengthen and enhance our possession and our enjoyment of life. Others may fall around us like leaves, or be mowed down like flowers by the scythe of Time: these are but tropes and figures [10] to the unreflecting ears and overweening presumption of youth. It is not till we see the flowers of Love, Hope, and Joy, withering around us, and our own pleasures cut up by the roots, that we bring the moral home to ourselves, that we abate something of the wanton extravagance of our pretensions, or that the emptiness and dreariness of the prospect before us reconciles us to the stillness of the grave!

> Life! thou strange thing, that hast a power to feel
> Thou art, and to perceive that others are. [11]

Well might the poet begin his indignant invective against an art, whose professed object is its destruction, with this animated apostrophe to life. Life is indeed a strange gift, and its privileges are most miraculous. Nor is it singular that when the splendid boon is first granted us, our gratitude, our admiration, and our delight should prevent us from reflecting our own nothingness, or from thinking it will ever be recalled. Our first and strongest impressions are taken from the mighty scene that is opened to us, and we very innocently transfer its durability as well as magnificence to ourselves. So newly found, we cannot make up our minds to parting with it yet and at least put off that consideration to an indefinite term. Like a clown [12] at a fair, we are full of amazement and rapture, and have no thoughts of going home, or that it will soon be night. We know our existence only from external objects, and we measure it by them.

7. Hazlitt doubtless has in mind *Macbeth* II.iii.94: "The wine of life is drawn."
8. I *Corinthians* 13:12. "For now we see through a glass, darkly." Hazlitt's tampering with the King James text makes its sense more apparent, for the "glass" is a mirror, which, in modern idiom, we see "in" rather than "through."
9. *Tristram Shandy* V.vii.
10. A "trope" is the use of a word in a sense different from that which it usually has, a "figure" of speech.
11. "Fawcett's *Art of War*, a poem, 1794" (Hazlitt). Joseph Fawcett (1758?–1804) was a dissenting minister of liberal political views who achieved considerable fame as a preacher in London. He was a friend of Hazlitt's.
12. In the old meaning of the word—a rustic and naïve person.

We can never be satisfied with gazing; and nature will still want us to look on and applaud. Otherwise, the sumptuous entertainment, 'the feast of reason and the flow of soul,' [13] to which we were invited, seems little better than a mockery and a cruel insult. We do not go from a play till the scene is ended, and the lights are ready to be extinguished. But the fair face of things still shines on; shall we be called away, before the curtain falls, or ere we have scarce had a glimpse of what is going on? Like children, our stepmother Nature holds us up to see the raree-show [14] of the universe; and then, as if life were a burthen to support, lets us instantly down again. Yet in that short interval, what 'brave sublunary things' [15] does not the spectacle unfold; like a bubble, at one minute reflecting the universe, and the next, shook to air!—To see the golden sun and the azure sky, the outstretched ocean, to walk upon the green earth, and to be lord of a thousand creatures, to look down giddy precipices or over distant flowery vales, to see the world spread out under one's finger in a map, to bring the stars near, to view the smallest insects in a microscope, to read history, and witness the revolutions of empires and the succession of generations, to hear of the glory of Sidon and Tyre, of Babylon and Susa, as of a faded pageant, and to say all these were, and are now nothing, to think that we exist in such a point of time, and in such a corner of space, to be at once spectators and a part of the moving scene, to watch the return of the seasons, of spring and autumn, to hear—

> The stockdove plain amid the forest deep,
> That drowsy rustles to the sighing gale [16]

—to traverse desert wildernesses, to listen to the midnight choir, to visit lighted halls, or plunge into the dungeon's gloom, or sit in crowded theatres and see life itself mocked, to feel heat and cold, pleasure and pain, right and wrong, truth and falsehood, to study the works of art and refine the sense of beauty to agony, to worship fame and to dream of immortality, to have read Shakespeare and belong to the same species as Sir Isaac Newton; [17] to be and to do all this, and then in a moment to be nothing, to have it all snatched from one like a juggler's ball or a phantasmagoria; there is something revolting and incredible to sense in the transition, and no wonder that, aided by youth and warm blood, and the flush of enthusiasm, the mind contrives for a long time to reject it with disdain and loathing as a monstrous and improbable fiction, like a monkey on a house-top, that is loath, amidst its fine discoveries and specious antics, to be tumbled headlong into the street, and crushed to atoms, the sport and laughter of the multitude!

13. Pope, *Imitations of Horace,* Satire I, l. 128.
14. A street show.
15. Michael Drayton, "To My Most Dearly-loved Friend, Henry Reynolds, Esquire, of Poets and Poesy," l. 106. Drayton's actual phrase is "brave *translunary* things."
16. Thomson, *The Castle of Indolence* I.33–34.
17. At this point Hazlitt appends a long footnote about a contemptuous comment on Newton which Lady Mary Wortley Montagu (1689–1762) makes in one of her letters, which are famous for their vivacity and wit. He deals severely with this, is led to remark on similar arrogant judgments of Lady Mary's, and goes on to denounce the contempt with which, he says, the aristocracy regards writers of genius who are of lowly social origin.

The change, from the commencement to the close of life, appears like a fable, after it has taken place; how should we treat it otherwise than as a chimera before it has come to pass? There are some things that happened so long ago, places or persons we have formerly seen, of which such dim traces remain, we hardly know whether it was sleeping or waking they occurred; they are like dreams within the dream of life, a mist, a film before the eye of memory, which, as we try to recall them more distinctly, elude our notice altogether. It is but natural that the lone interval that we thus look back upon, should have appeared long and endless in prospect. There are others so distinct and fresh, they seem but of yesterday—their very vividness might be deemed a pledge of their permanence. Then, however far back our impressions may go, we find others still older (for our years are multiplied in youth); descriptions of scenes that we had read, and people before our time, Priam [18] and the Trojan war; and even then, Nestor [19] was old and dwelt delighted on his youth, and spoke of the race of heroes that were no more;—what wonder that, seeing this long line of being pictured in our minds, and reviving as it were in us, we should give ourselves involuntary credit for an indeterminate period of existence? In the Cathedral at Peterborough there is a monument to Mary, Queen of Scots, at which I used to gaze when a boy, while the events of the period, all that had happened since, passed in review before me. If all this mass of feeling and imagination could be crowded into a moment's compass, what might not the whole of life be supposed to contain? We are heirs of the past; we count upon the future as our natural reversion. Besides, there are some of our early impressions so exquisitely tempered, it appears that they must always last—nothing can add to or take away from their sweetness and purity—the first breath of spring, the hyacinth dipped in the dew, the mild lustre of the evening-star, the rainbow after a storm—while we have the full enjoyment of these, we must be young; and what can ever alter us in this respect? Truth, friendship, love, books, are also proof against the canker of time; and while we live, but for them, we can never grow old. We take out a new lease of existence from the objects on which we set our affections, and become abstracted, impassive, immortal in them. We cannot conceive how certain sentiments should ever decay or grow cold in our breasts; and, consequently, to maintain them in their first youthful glow and vigour, the flame of life must continue to burn as bright as ever, or rather, they are the fuel that feed the sacred lamp, that kindle 'the purple light of love,' [20] and spread a golden cloud around our heads! Again, we not only flourish and survive in our affections (in which we will not listen to the possibility of a change, any more than we foresee the wrinkles on the brow of a mistress), but we have a farther guarantee against the thoughts of death in our favourite studies and pursuits, and in their continual advance. Art we know is long; life, we feel, should be so too. We see no end of the difficulties we have to encounter: perfection is slow of attainment, and we must have time to accomplish it in. Rubens [21]

18. Priam was the aged king of Troy when that city was sacked by the Greeks.
19. Nestor was the oldest of the Greek generals who besieged Troy and was esteemed the wisest.
20. Gray, *The Progress of Poesy*, l. 41.
21. Peter Paul Rubens (1577–1640), the great Flemish painter.

complained that when he had just learnt his art, he was snatched away from it: we trust we shall be more fortunate! A wrinkle in an old head takes whole days to finish it properly: but to catch 'the Raphael grace, the Guido air,'[22] no limit should be put to our endeavours. What a prospect for the future! What a task we have entered upon! and shall we be arrested in the middle of it? We do not reckon our time thus employed lost, or our pains thrown away, or our progress slow—we do not droop or grow tired, but 'gain new vigour at our endless task';[23]—and shall Time grudge us the opportunity to finish what we have auspiciously begun, and have formed a sort of compact with nature to achieve? The fame of the great names we look up to is also imperishable; and shall not we, who contemplate it with such intense yearnings, imbibe a portion of ethereal fire, the *divinae particula aurae*,[24] which nothing can extinguish? I remember to have looked at a print of Rembrandt for hours together, without being conscious of the flight of time, trying to resolve it into its component parts, to connect its strong and sharp gradations, to learn the secret of its reflected lights, and found neither satiety nor pause in the prosecution of my studies. The print over which I was poring would last long enough; why should the idea in my mind, which was finer, more impalpable, perish before it? At this, I redoubled the ardour of my pursuit, and by the very subtlety and refinement of my inquiries, seemed to bespeak for them an exemption from corruption and the rude grasp of Death.[25]

Objects, on our first acquaintance with them, have that singleness and integrity of impression that it seems as if nothing could destroy or obliterate them, so firmly are they stamped and rivetted on the brain. We repose on them with a sort of voluptuous indolence, in full faith and boundless confidence. We are absorbed in the present moment, or return to the same point—idling away a great deal of time in youth, thinking we have enough and to spare. There is often a local feeling in the air, which is as fixed as if it were of marble; we loiter in dim cloisters, losing ourselves in thought and in their glimmering arches; a winding road before us seems as long as the journey of life, and as full of events. Time and experience dissipate this illusion; and by reducing them to detail, circumscribe the limits of our expectations. It is only as the pageant of life passes by and the masques turn their backs upon us, that we see through the deception, or believe that the train will have an end. In many cases, the slow progress and monotonous texture of our lives, before we mingle with the world and are embroiled in its affairs, has a tendency to aid the same feeling. We have a difficulty, when left to ourselves, and without the resource of books or some more lively pursuit, to 'beguile the slow and creeping hours of time,'[26] and argue that if it moves on always at this tedious snail's-pace, it can never come to an end. We are willing to skip over certain portions of it that separate us from favourite objects, that irritate ourselves at the unnecessary delay. The young are prodigal of life from

22. Pope, *Epistle to Mr. Jervas*, 1. 36. Raphael (1483–1520) is the famous Italian painter; Guido is Guido Reni (1575–1642), also an Italian painter.
23. Cowper, *Charity*, l. 104.
24. "Parts of the divine breath."
25. "Is it not this that frequently keeps artists alive so long, *viz.*, the constant occupation of their minds with vivid images, with little of the *wear-and-tear* of the body?" (Hazlitt)
26. *As You Like It* II.vii.112.

a superabundance of it; the old are tenacious on the same score, because they have little left, and cannot enjoy even what remains of it.

For my part, I set out in life with the French Revolution, and that event had considerable influence on my early feelings, as on those of others.[27] Youth was then doubly such. It was the dawn on a new era, a new impulse had been given to men's minds, and the sun of Liberty rose upon the sun of Life in the same day, and both were proud to run their race together. Little did I dream, while my first hopes and wishes went hand in hand with those of the human race, that long before my eyes should close, that dawn would be overcast, and set once more in the night of despotism—'total eclipse!'[28] Happy that I did not. I felt for years, and during the best part of my existence, *heart-whole* in that cause, and triumphed in the triumphs over the enemies of man! At that time, while the fairest aspirations of the human mind seemed about to be realized, ere the image of man was defaced and his breast mangled in scorn, philosophy took a higher, poetry could afford a deeper range. At that time, to read *The Robbers*[29] was indeed delicious, and to hear

> From the dungeon of the tower time-rent,
> That fearful voice, a famished father's cry,[30]

could be borne only amidst the fulness of hope, the crash of the fall of the strongholds of power, and the exulting sounds of the march of human freedom. What feelings the death-scene in *Don Carlos*[31] sent into the soul! In that headlong career of lofty enthusiasm, and the joyous opening of the prospects of the world and our own, the thought of death crossing it, smote doubly cold upon the mind; there was a stifling sense of oppression and confinement, an impatience of our present knowledge, a desire to grasp the whole of our existence in one strong embrace, to sound the mystery of life and death, and in order to put an end to the agony of doubt and dread, to burst through our prison-house, and confront the King of Terrors in his grisly palace!—— As I was writing out this passage, my miniature-picture when a child lay on the mantle-piece, and I took it out of the case to look at it. I could perceive few traces of myself in it; but there was the same placid brow, the dimpled mouth, the same timid, inquisitive glance as ever. But its careless smile did not seem to reproach me with having become a recreant to the sentiments that were then sown in my mind, or with having written a sentence that could call up a blush in this image of ingenuous youth!

27. In 1789, when the French Revolution began, Hazlitt was a boy of eleven. For what the French Revolution might mean to young people of the day, see Wordsworth, *The Prelude* VI.342–408 and IX, X, and XI. Wordsworth, like Hazlitt, speaks of the Revolution as a "dawn": "Bliss was it in that dawn to be alive, / But to be young was very Heaven!" (IX.108–9; see the lines that follow for an account of the promise of the renovation of all of life that the Revolution seemed to hold out).
28. Milton, *Samson Agonistes* I.79. The phrase occurs in the famous passage of Samson's lament over his blindness which begins, "O dark, dark, dark, amid the blaze of noon, / Irrecoverably dark, total eclipse / Without all hope of day!"
29. *The Robbers* (1782), a play by Friedrich Schiller (1759–1805), the import of which is socially radical although not revolutionary.
30. Coleridge, "Sonnet to Schiller," ll. 3–4.
31. *Don Carlos* (1787), a play by Schiller of libertarian tendency. It is the basis of Verdi's opera *Don Carlo* (1867).

'That time is past with all its giddy raptures.'[32] Since the future was barred to my progress, I have turned for consolation to the past, gathering up the fragments of my early recollections, and putting them into a form that might live. It is thus, that when we find our personal and substantial identity vanishing from us, we strive to gain a reflected and substituted one in our thoughts: we do not like to perish wholly, and wish to bequeath our names at least to posterity. As long as we can keep alive our cherished thoughts and nearest interests in the minds of others, we do not appear to have retired altogether from the stage, we still occupy a place in the estimation of mankind, [and] exercise a powerful influence over them, and it is only our bodies that are trampled into dust or dispersed to air. Our darling speculations still find favour and encouragement, and we make as good a figure in the eyes of our descendants, nay, perhaps, a better than we did in our lifetime. This is one point gained; the demands of our self-love are so far satisfied. Besides, if by the proofs of intellectual superiority we survive ourselves in this world, by exemplary virtue or unblemished faith, we are taught to ensure an interest in another and a higher state of being, and to anticipate at the same time the applauses of men and angels.

> Even from the tomb the voice of nature cries;
> Even in our ashes live their wonted fires.[33]

As we advance in life, we acquire a keener sense of the value of time. Nothing else, indeed, seems of any consequence; and we become misers in this respect. We try to arrest its few last tottering steps, and to make it linger on the brink of the grave. We can never leave off wondering how that which has ever been should cease to be, and would still live on, that we may wonder at our own shadow, and when 'all the life of life is flown,'[34] dwell on the retrospect of the past. This is accompanied by a mechanical tenaciousness of whatever we possess, by a distrust and a sense of fallacious hollowness in all we see. Instead of the full, pulpy feeling of youth, every thing is flat and insipid. The world is a painted witch, that puts us off with false shows and tempting appearances. The ease, the jocund gaiety, the unsuspecting security of youth are fled: nor can we, without flying in the face of common sense,

> From the last dregs of life, hope to receive
> What its first sprightly runnings could not give.[35]

If we can slip out of the world without notice or mischance, can tamper with bodily infirmity, and frame our minds to the becoming composure of *still-life*,[36] before we sink into total insensibility, it is as much as we ought to expect. We do not in the regular course of nature die all at once: we have mouldered away gradually long before; faculty after faculty, attachment after attachment,

---

32. Wordsworth, *Tintern Abbey*, ll. 83–85: "That time is past, / And all its aching joys are now no more, / And all its dizzy raptures."
33. Gray, *Elegy in a Country Churchyard*, ll. 91–92.
34. Burns, "Lament for James, Earl of Glencairn," vi.
35. Dryden, *Aurengzebe* IV.i.41–42.
36. In painting, the representation of inanimate objects. Hazlitt no doubt had in mind the rather grim French phrase for this—*nature morte*.

we are torn from ourselves piecemeal while living; year after year takes something from us; and death only consigns the last remnant of what we were to
the grave. The revulsion is not so great, and a quiet *euthanasia* [37] is a wind-
ing-up of the plot, that is not out of reason or nature.

That we should thus in a manner outlive ourselves, and dwindle imperceptibly into nothing, is not surprising, when even in our prime the strongest impressions leave so little traces of themselves behind, and the last object is
driven out by the succeeding one. How little effect is produced on us at any
time by the books we have read, the scenes we have witnessed, the sufferings
we have gone through! Think only of the variety of feelings we experience
in reading an interesting romance, or being present at a fine play—what
beauty, what sublimity, what soothing, what heart-rending emotions! You
would suppose these would last for ever, or at least subdue the mind to a
correspondent tone and harmony—while we turn over the page, while the
scene is passing before us, it seems as if nothing could ever after shake our
resolution that 'treason domestic, foreign levy, nothing could touch us farther!' [38]
The first splash of mud we get, on entering the street, the first pettifogging shop-
keeper that cheats us out of twopence, and the whole vanishes clean out of
our remembrance, and we become the idle prey of the most petty and annoy-
ing circumstances. The mind soars by an effort to the grand and lofty: it is at
home in the grovelling, the disagreeable, and the little. This happens in the
height and heyday of our existence, when novelty gives a stronger impulse
to the blood and takes a faster hold of the brain (I have known the impression
on coming out of a gallery of pictures then last half a day)—as we grow old,
we become more feeble and querulous, every object 'reverbs its own hollowness,' [39] and both worlds are not enough to satisfy the peevish importunity
and extravagant presumption of our desires! There are a few superior, happy
beings, who are born with a temper exempt from every trifling annoyance. This
spirit sits serene and smiling as in its native skies, and a divine harmony
(whether heard or not) plays around them. This is to be at peace. Without
this, it is in vain to fly into deserts, or to build a hermitage on the top of
rocks, if regret and ill-humour follow us there: and with this, it is needless
to make the experiment. The only true retirement is that of the heart; the
only true leisure is the repose of the passions. To such persons it makes little
difference whether they are young or old; and they die as they have lived, with
graceful resignation.

1827   1836 / 1850

On Gusto

Gusto in art is power or passion defining any object.—It is not so difficult to
explain this term in what relates to expression (of which it may be said to be
the highest degree) as in what relates to things without expression, to the

37. An easy and painless death. Hazlitt does not use the word as it is commonly used
today, to mean such a death induced for merciful reasons.
38. *Macbeth* III.ii.24–26.
39. *King Lear* I.i.154.

natural appearances of objects, as mere colour or form. In one sense, however, there is hardly any object entirely devoid of expression, without some character of power belonging to it, some precise association with pleasure or pain: and it is in giving this truth of character from the truth of feeling, whether in the highest or the lowest degree, but always in the highest degree of which the subject is capable, that gusto consists.

There is a gusto in the colouring of Titian.[1] Not only do his heads seem to think—his bodies seem to feel. This is what the Italians mean by the *morbidezza* [2] of his flesh-colour. It seems sensitive and alive all over; not merely to have the look and texture of flesh, but the feeling in itself. For example, the limbs of his female figures have a luxurious softness and delicacy, which appears conscious of the pleasure of the beholder. As the objects themselves in nature would produce an impression on the sense, distinct from every other object, and having something divine in it, which the heart owns and the imagination consecrates, the objects in the picture preserve the same impression, absolute, unimpaired, stamped with all the truth of passion, the pride of the eye, and the charm of beauty. Rubens [3] makes his flesh-colour like flowers; Albano's [4] is like ivory; Titian's is like flesh, and like nothing else. It is as different from that of other painters, as the skin is from a piece of white or red drapery thrown over it. The blood circulates here and there, the blue veins just appear, the rest is distinguished throughout only by that sort of tingling sensation to the eye, which the body feels within itself. This is gusto.—Vandyke's [5] flesh-colour, though it has great truth and purity, wants gusto. It has not the internal character, the living principle in it. It is a smooth surface, not a warm, moving mass. It is painted without passion, with indifference. The hand only has been concerned. The impression slides off from the eye, and does not, like the tones of Titian's pencil, leave a sting behind it in the mind of the spectator. The eye does not acquire a taste or appetite for what it sees. In a word, gusto in painting is where the impression made on one sense excites by affinity those of another.

Michael Angelo's [6] forms are full of gusto. They everywhere obtrude the sense of power upon the eye. His limbs convey an idea of muscular strength, of moral grandeur, and even of intellectual dignity: they are firm, commanding, broad, and massy, capable of executing with ease the determined purposes of the will. His faces have no other expression than his figures, conscious power and capacity. They appear only to think what they shall do, and to know that they can do it. This is what is meant by saying that his style is hard and masculine. It is the reverse of Correggio's,[7] which is effeminate. That is, the

1. The name by which the great Venetian painter Tiziano Vecellio (1490?–1576) is commonly known among English-speaking people.
2. Softness, delicacy.
3. Peter Paul Rubens (1577–1640), great Flemish painter; his pictures are notable for their exuberance.
4. Francesco Albani (1578–1660), a painter of the school of Bologna.
5. Sir Anthony Van Dyck (1599–1641), Flemish portraitist, pupil of Rubens. He settled in England in 1632.
6. Michelangelo Buonarroti (1475–1564), Italian painter, sculptor, and architect, generally regarded as the greatest figure of the Italian Renaissance.
7. Antonio Allegri da Correggio (c. 1494–1534), one of the eminent Italian painters of his day.

gusto of Michael Angelo consists in expressing energy of will without proportionable sensibility, Correggio's in expressing exquisite sensibility without energy of will. In Correggio's faces as well as figures we see neither bones nor muscles, but then what a soul is there, full of sweetness and of grace—pure, playful, soft, angelical! There is sentiment enough in a hand painted by Correggio to set up a school of history painters. Whenever we look at the hands of Correggio's women or of Raphael's,[8] we always wish to touch them.

Again, Titian's landscapes have a prodigious gusto, both in the colouring and forms. We shall never forget one that we saw many years ago in the Orleans Gallery[9] of Acteon hunting.[10] It had a brown, mellow, autumnal look. The sky was of the colour of stone. The winds seemed to sing through the rustling branches of the trees, and already you might hear the twanging of bows resound through the tangled mazes of the wood. Mr. West,[11] we understand, has this landscape. He will know if this description of it is just. The landscape background of the St. Peter Martyr[12] is another well-known instance of the power of this great painter to give a romantic interest and an appropriate character to the objects of his pencil, where every circumstance adds to the effect of the scene,—the bold trunks of the tall forest trees, the trailing ground plants, with that cold convent spire rising in the distance, amidst the blue sapphire mountains and the golden sky.

Rubens has a great deal of gusto in his Fauns and Satyrs, and in all that expresses motion, but in nothing else. Rembrandt[13] has it in everything; everything in his pictures has a tangible character. If he puts a diamond in the ear of a Burgomaster's wife, it is of the first water; and his furs and stuffs are proof against a Russian winter. Raphael's gusto was only in expression; he had no idea of the character of anything but the human form. The dryness and poverty of his style in other respects is a phenomenon in the art. His trees are like sprigs of grass stuck in a book of botanical specimens. Was it that Raphael never had time to go beyond the walls of Rome? That he was always in the streets, at church, or in the bath? He was not one of the Society of Arcadians.[14]

Claude's[15] landscapes, perfect as they are, want gusto. This is not easy to explain. They are perfect abstractions of the visible images of things; they speak the visible language of nature truly. They resemble a mirror or microscope. To

8. Raffaello Santi (1483–1520) stands with Leonardo da Vinci and Michelangelo as one of the pre-eminent figures of Italian Renaissance art.
9. An exhibition of paintings of the old Italian masters, most of them from the collection of the Duke of Orleans, which was held in London in 1798–99.
10. The painting is generally called *Diana and Actaeon*.
11. Benjamin West (1738–1820), English historical painter born in America; in 1792 he succeeded Sir Joshua Reynolds as president of the Royal Academy.
12. Hazlitt saw this painting by Titian at the Louvre in 1802. It was destroyed by fire in 1867 after it had been restored to Venice.
13. Rembrandt van Rijn (1606–69), the greatest of the Dutch painters.
14. "Raphael not only could not paint a landscape; he could not paint people in a landscape. He could not have painted the heads or the figures, or even the dresses of the St. Peter Martyr. His figures have always an *in-door* look, that is, a set, determined, voluntary, dramatic character, arising from their own passions, or a watchfulness of those of others, and want that wild uncertainty of expression, which is connected with the accidents of nature and the changes of the elements. He has nothing *romantic* about him." (Hazlitt)
15. Claude Gellée, called Claude Lorrain (1600–1682), French landscape painter.

the eye only they are more perfect than any other landscapes that ever were or will be painted; they give more of nature, as cognizable by one sense alone; but they lay an equal stress on all visible impressions; they do not interpret one sense by another; they do not distinguish the character of different objects as we are taught, and can only be taught, to distinguish them by their effect on the different senses. That is, his eye wanted imagination: it did not strongly sympathize with his other faculties. He saw the atmosphere, but he did not feel it. He painted the trunk of a tree or a rock in the foreground as smooth— with as complete an abstraction of the gross, tangible impression, as any other part of the picture; his trees are perfectly beautiful, but quite immovable; they have a look of enchantment. In short, his landscapes are unequalled imitations of nature, released from its subjection to the elements,—as if all objects were become a delightful fairy vision, and the eye had rarefied and refined away the other senses.

The gusto in the Greek statues is of a very singular kind. The sense of perfect form nearly occupies the whole mind, and hardly suffers it to dwell on any other feeling. It seems enough for them *to be*, without acting or suffering. Their forms are ideal, spiritual. Their beauty is power. By their beauty they are raised above the frailties of pain or passion; by their beauty they are deified.

The infinite quantity of dramatic invention in Shakespeare takes from his gusto. The power he delights to show is not intense, but discursive. He never insists on any thing as much as he might, except a quibble. Milton has great gusto. He repeats his blow twice; grapples with and exhausts his subject. His imagination has a double relish of its objects, an inveterate attachment to the things he describes, and to the words describing them.—

> Or where Chineses drive
> With sails and wind their *cany* waggons *light*.[16]

>   · · ·
> Wild above rule or art, *enormous* bliss.[17]

There is a gusto in Pope's compliments, in Dryden's satires, and Prior's tales; and among prose-writers, Boccaccio and Rabelais had the most of it. We will only mention one other work which appears to us to be full of gusto, and that is the *Beggar's Opera*.[18] If it is not, we are altogether mistaken in our notions on this delicate subject.

1816

THOMAS DE QUINCEY
1785–1859

Thomas De Quincey was born in Manchester, the son of a prosperous merchant of some literary cultivation and of a mother whom he was to describe as intellectually distinguished. De Quincey's father died when Thomas was seven, leaving the large

16. *Paradise Lost* III.438–39.
17. *Ibid.* V.297.
18. By John Gay (1685–1732). It was produced in 1728 and was an extraordinary success.

family in easy financial circumstances. Despite the poor quality of the schools he attended, the boy early acquired an exceptional command of the classical languages—his skill in writing Latin verse was prodigious and by the age of fifteen he could not only write Greek but also speak it fluently. His precocity was intellectual as well as scholastic; he formed friendships with several adults of notable intelligence and learning, read enormously, and resolved upon a life of literary and philosophical pursuits. In 1801 he was sent by his guardians to the Manchester Grammar School, where the quality of instruction was good but the care of the pupils so negligent and the daily routine so oppressively dull that young De Quincey fell into a low state of spirits and health. Unable to prevail upon his guardians to remove him from the school, he ran away in July of 1802, a month before his seventeenth birthday. He went first to Wales, where he delighted in the mountain scenery and, through a chance acquaintance, was introduced to German literature, and then traveled to London.

The London experience was a momentous one and De Quincey has immortalized it in the first part of his *Confessions of an English Opium-Eater*. His small stock of money was soon exhausted and his hopes of raising a loan against his financial expectations when he should come of age were frustrated. A disreputable lawyer in the employ of the money-lenders with whom he negotiated gave him permission to sleep in an untenanted, unfurnished, and unheated house, an accommodation he shared with a miserable child, a ten-year-old girl of unknown parentage. All the clothes he had were on his back and he went hungry for days. It was at this time of self-elected and quite extreme privation that De Quincey made the acquaintance of the young woman who was to play a significant part in his emotional life. Ann, his senior by a year or two, was a prostitute for whom he conceived a tender and presumably unerotic affection, which she reciprocated—as he recalled with undying gratitude, when he once fainted on the street from hunger, she spent her last sixpence for a glass of wine to revive him. This precious relationship ended abruptly. Having been given a sum of money by a friend of his family whom he met by chance, De Quincey took coach for Eton to visit a friend, a young lord, who he hoped would stand as security for a loan; when he returned to London after a few days, Ann was not at the appointed meeting place and was nowhere to be found. De Quincey never saw her again, except in the dreams which soon became the most significant part of his life.

Just how his reconciliation with his guardians came about De Quincey does not make clear, but we next see him at Worcester College, Oxford. The university made but little impression on him and he left without taking a degree. He kept to himself and gave much of his time to studying Hebrew and enlarging his knowledge of German literature. During his Oxford residence, while on a visit to London, he made the step which decided the course of his life and the bent of his genius. To allay a severe toothache and neuralgia, on the advice of a friend he took his first opium.

In the early nineteenth century, opium was far from being a forbidden drug. Laudanum, which is opium dissolved in alcohol, was the standard pain-reliever of the day, to be bought without prescription at any chemist's shop; it was taken as casually as we now take aspirin and it was commonly given to children. Pellets of opium might also be freely bought; in bad times the drug in this form was in common use by the poor to allay the pangs of hunger. The number of eminent and respectable people who habitually used it, with or without extreme deleterious effects, was considerable. Yet it cannot be said that its use was regarded wholly with indifference, as the case of Coleridge makes plain; his extreme addiction dismayed his friends and filled him with intense guilt. De Quincey, who was more nearly in control of his addiction than Coleridge, was consciously ambivalent in his attitude toward the drug. He candidly describes the "pains of opium" and he knows its dangers, but he took opium not only as he was coerced by his addiction but also with some degree of free will. He was aware that his use of the drug diminished certain of his mental processes and curtailed his power of sustained work, but he believed that it was the source of his best artistic effects. The dreams or dream-like states which it produced were his most cherished forms of experience, and he prized even those that terrified him.

In 1807 De Quincey made the acquaintance of Coleridge, whom he had long admired, and subsequently that of Wordsworth; and in 1809 he settled at Dove Cottage in Grasmere, which the Wordsworths had given up two years before. He lived twelve years in the Lake District, married a local farmer's daughter who had been his mistress and borne him a child, and became confirmed in his addiction. His relationship with the Wordsworths was for a time very close, but deteriorated into acrimony on both sides. In 1821 he left the Lake Country and settled in London. His inherited income had been much curtailed by unfortunate investment and he now undertook to support himself and his growing family by periodical writing. His beginning was auspicious—in the first year of his residence in London he published *Confessions of an English Opium-Eater* in the *London Magazine* to great acclaim, which was augmented when the work was brought out as a volume in 1822. Although never exactly a popular author, his work from then on was always in demand. In 1828 he removed from London to Edinburgh, where he lived the rest of his life. His mode of existence was disordered and vagrant and by preference solitary, yet he was an affectionate husband and father, and his personal charm and enchanting conversation made his company much sought after.

Virtually the whole of the large canon of De Quincey's work consists of his contributions to monthly or quarterly journals. Only a small proportion of it is of enduring value. Financial necessity forced him turn his hand to a great variety of subjects, for his erudition was vast and curious, and although brilliant passages occur in most of his all too discursive articles on history, metaphysics, political economy, and literature, in the main these writings are the hackwork of genius. Yet De Quincey never surrendered his ideal of himself as the subtle psychologist and the conscious artist and he fully realized it in a part of his work which, though small in proportion to the whole, is yet in itself quite considerable in extent. His best powers are evoked by the occasions in which he recollects his own experience of persons, of books, most especially of dreams. To the explication of what he called the "germinal principles of the dream" he devoted the best efforts of his often profound intelligence. It was these principles which directed his conception of an "impassioned prose" which, deriving its rhetoric from Milton, Sir Thomas Browne, and Jeremy Taylor, should have the complexity, the power, and the autonomy of music itself. This was not De Quincey's only prose mode (in the best of his narrative or expository writing he could be relatively literal and explicit), but it is the one by which he set highest store, as do his admirers. It is the mode of the unfinished *Suspiria de Profundis* (Sighs from the Depths)—of which "Levana and Our Ladies of Sorrows" (see below) is a part—and De Quincey was probably right in saying that this was his masterpiece.

Confessions of an English Opium-Eater

In 1856 De Quincey undertook to revise the *Confessions of an English Opium-Eater* for a collected edition of his work that was being prepared. In the process he quadrupled the length of the original text. Although doubtless he added some things of value, most admirers of his work prefer the first version, finding it more direct and immediate and closer to the actuality of the experiences described, and it is from this version that the following selection is taken.

The substance of the first of the *Confessions'* three sections has been suggested in the Headnote on De Quincey; it is called "Preliminary Confessions" and opium does not figure in it; perhaps its chief purpose is to acquaint the reader with Ann, the dear lost friend (see below, the dream of June 1819). The second section, "The Pleasures of Opium," describes the sensations of heightened perception and significance which for De Quincey were the drug's chief charm. The selected passage is from "The Pains of Opium," which concludes the book.

From Confessions of an English Opium-Eater

The Pains of Opium

. . . I now pass to what is the main subject of these latter confessions, to the history and journal of what took place in my dreams; for these were the immediate and proximate cause of my acutest suffering.

The first notice I had of any important change going on in this part of my physical economy, was from the re-awakening of a state of eye generally incident to childhood, or exalted states of irritability. I know not whether my reader is aware that many children, perhaps most, have a power of painting, as it were, upon the darkness, all sorts of phantoms; in some, that power is simply a mechanic affection of the eye; others have a voluntary, or a semi-voluntary power to dismiss or to summon them; or, as a child once said to me when I questioned him on this matter, 'I can tell them to go, and they go; but sometimes they come when I don't tell them to come.' Whereupon I told him that he had almost as unlimited command over apparitions as a Roman centurion [1] over his soldiers.—In the middle of 1817, I think it was, that this faculty became positively distressing to me: at night, when I lay awake in bed, vast processions passed along in mournful pomp; friezes of never-ending stories, that to my feelings were as sad and solemn as if they were stories drawn from times before Oedipus or Priam—before Tyre—before Memphis. [2] And, at the same time, a corresponding change took place in my dreams; a theatre seemed suddenly opened and lighted up within my brain, which presented nightly spectacles of more than earthly splendour. And the four following facts may be mentioned, as noticeable at this time:

1. That, as the creative state of the eye increased, a sympathy seemed to arise between the waking and the dreaming states of the brain in one point— that whatsoever I happened to call up and to trace by a voluntary act upon the

1. An officer of the Roman army commanding a century, i.e. a group of 100 men.
2. Oedipus was king of Thebes, Priam king of Troy; Tyre was the great city of Phoenicia; Memphis became the capital of Egypt after the fall of Thebes.

darkness was very apt to transfer itself to my dreams; so that I feared to exercise this faculty; for, as Midas [3] turned all things to gold, that yet baffled his hopes and defrauded his human desires, so whatsoever things capable of being visually represented I did but think of in the darkness, immediately shaped themselves into phantoms of the eye; and, by a process apparently no less inevitable, when thus once traced in faint and visionary colours, like writings in sympathetic ink,[4] they were drawn out by the fierce chemistry of my dreams, into insufferable splendour that fretted my heart.

2. For this, and all other changes in my dreams, were accompanied by deep-seated anxiety and gloomy melancholy, such as are wholly incommunicable by words. I seemed every night to descend, not metaphorically, but literally to descend, into chasms and sunless abysses, depths below depths, from which it seemed hopeless that I could ever reascend. Nor did I, by waking, feel that I *had* reascended. This I do not dwell upon; because the state of gloom which attended these gorgeous spectacles, amounting at least to utter darkness, as of some suicidal despondency, cannot be approached by words.

3. The sense of space, and in the end, the sense of time, were both powerfully affected. Buildings, landscapes, etc. were exhibited in proportions so vast as the bodily eye is not fitted to receive. Space swelled, and was amplified to an extent of unutterable infinity. This, however, did not disturb me so much as the vast expansion of time; I sometimes seemed to have lived for 70 or 100 years in one night; nay, sometimes had feelings representative of a millennium passed in that time, or, however, of a duration far beyond the limits of any human experience.

4. The minutest incidents of childhood, or forgotten scenes of later years, were often revived: I could not be said to recollect them; for if I had been told of them when waking, I should not have been able to acknowledge them as parts of my past experience. But placed as they were before me, in dreams like intuitions, and clothed in all their evanescent circumstances and accompanying feelings, I *recognized* them instantaneously. I was once told by a near relative of mine, that having in her childhood fallen into a river, and being on the very verge of death but for the critical assistance which reached her, she saw in a moment her whole life, in its minutest incidents, arrayed before her simultaneously as in a mirror; and she had a faculty developed as suddenly for comprehending the whole and every part. This, from some opium experiences of mine, I can believe; I have, indeed, seen the same thing asserted twice in modern books, and accompanied by a remark which I am convinced is true; viz. that the dread book of account,[5] which the Scriptures speak of, is, in fact, the mind itself of each individual. Of this at least feel assured, that there is no such thing as *forgetting* possible to the mind; a thousand accidents may, and will interpose a veil between our present consciousness and the secret inscriptions on the mind; accidents of the same sort will also rend away this veil; but alike, whether veiled or unveiled, the inscription remains for ever; just as the stars seem to withdraw before the common light of day, whereas, in fact, we all know

3. When Dionysus offered to gratify any wish that Midas might make, this legendary king asked that everything he touched be turned to gold; to his dismay, he found that this applied to food, as well as everything else.
4. Ink that is invisible until treated by a chemical or by heat.
5. Revelation 20:12.

that it is the light which is drawn over them as a veil—and that they are waiting to be revealed when the obscuring daylight shall have withdrawn.

Having noticed these four facts as memorably distinguishing my dreams from those of health, I shall now cite a case illustrative of the first fact; and shall then cite any others that I remember, either in their chronological order, or any other that may give them more effect as pictures to the reader.

I had been in youth, and even since, for occasional amusement, a great reader of Livy,[6] whom, I confess, that I prefer, both for style and matter, to any other of the Roman historians; and I had often felt as most solemn and appalling sounds, and most emphatically representative of the majesty of the Roman people, the two words so often occurring in Livy—*Consul Romanus;* [7] especially when the consul is introduced in his military character. I mean to say, that the words king —sultan—regent, &c. or any other titles of those who embody in their own persons the collective majesty of a great people, had less power over my reverential feelings. I had also, though no great reader of history, made myself minutely and critically familiar with one period of English history, viz. the period of the Parliamentary War, having been attracted by the moral grandeur of some who figured in that day, and by the many interesting memoirs which survive those unquiet times. Both these parts of my lighter reading, having furnished me often with matter of reflection, now furnished me with matter for my dreams. Often I used to see, after painting upon the blank darkness a sort of rehearsal whilst waking, a crowd of ladies, and perhaps a festival, and dances. And I heard it said, or I said to myself, 'These are English ladies from the unhappy times of Charles I. These are the wives and the daughters of those who met in peace, and sat at the same tables, and were allied by marriage or by blood; and yet, after a certain day in August, 1642,[8] never smiled upon each other again, nor met but in the field of battle; and at Marston Moor, at Newbury, or at Naseby,[9] cut asunder all ties of love by the cruel sabre, and washed away in blood the memory of ancient friendship.' —The ladies danced, and looked as lovely as the court of George IV.[10] Yet I knew, even in my dream, that they had been in the grave for nearly two centuries.—This pageant would suddenly dissolve: and, at a clapping of hands, would be heard the heart-quaking sound of *Consul Romanus:* and immediately came 'sweeping by,' [11] in gorgeous paludaments,[12] Paulus or Marius,[13] girt round by a company of centurions, with the crimson tunic hoisted on a spear,[14] and followed by the *alalagmos* [15] of the Roman legions.

6. Titus Livius (59 B.C.–17 A.D.) wrote an enormous history of Rome; of its 142 books, only 35 have survived.
7. "Roman consul." Under the Republic the consul was the supreme civil and military magistrate of Rome.
8. On August 22 the royal standard was raised at Nottingham and the Civil War began, ending in the deposition and beheading of Charles I.
9. Battles in the Civil War in which the Royalist forces met defeat.
10. The monarch at the time De Quincey was writing.
11. Milton, "Il Penseroso," l. 98: "In scepter'd pall come sweeping by."
12. *Paludamentum:* a military cloak worn by a general.
13. Lucius Paulus (b. 230 B.C.), conqueror of Macedonia, and Gaius Marius (b. 157 B.C.), victor over the invading Germans. Their triumphs were celebrated with great pomp.
14. Token of victory.
15. A loud noise (Greek)—that of the Roman war cry.

Many years ago, when I was looking over Piranesi's [16] *Antiquities of Rome,* Mr. Coleridge, who was standing by, described to me a set of plates by that artist, called his *Dreams,* and which record the scenery of his own visions during the delirium of a fever: some of them (I describe only from memory of Mr. Coleridge's account) representing vast Gothic halls: on the floor of which stood all sorts of engines and machinery, wheels, cables, pulleys, levers, catapults, etc. etc. expressive of enormous power put forth, and resistance overcome. Creeping along the sides of the walls, you perceived a staircase; and upon it, groping his way upwards, was Piranesi himself: follow the stairs a little further, and you perceive it come to a sudden abrupt termination, without any balustrade, and allowing no step onwards to him who had reached the extremity, except into the depths below. Whatever is to become of poor Piranesi, you suppose, at least, that his labours must in some way terminate here. But raise your eyes, and behold a second flight of stairs still higher: on which again Piranesi is perceived, but this time standing on the very brink of the abyss. Again elevate your eye, and a still more aerial flight of stairs is beheld: and again is poor Piranesi busy on his aspiring labours: and so on, until the unfinished stairs and Piranesi both are lost in the upper gloom of the hall.—With the same power of endless growth and self-reproduction did my architecture proceed in dreams. In the early stage of my malady, the splendours of my dreams were indeed chiefly architectural: and I beheld such pomp of cities and palaces as was never yet beheld by the waking eye, unless in the clouds. From a great modern poet [17] I cite part of a passage which describes, as an appearance actually beheld in the clouds, what in many of its circumstances I saw frequently in sleep:

> The appearance, instantaneously disclosed,
> Was of a mighty city—boldly say
> A wilderness of building, sinking far
> And self-withdrawn into a wondrous depth,
> Far sinking into splendour—without end!
> Fabric it seemed of diamond, and of gold,
> With alabaster domes, and silver spires,
> And blazing terrace upon terrace, high
> Uplifted; here, serene pavilions bright
> In avenues disposed; there towers begirt
> With battlements that on their restless fronts
> Bore stars—illumination of all gems!
> By earthly nature had the effect been wrought
> Upon the dark materials of the storm
> Now pacified: on them, and on the coves,
> And mountain-steeps and summits, whereunto

16. Giovanni Battista Piranesi (1720–78) was an engraver who produced innumerable representations of the ancient monuments of Rome. None of the books he published bears the title *Dreams,* but in 1750 he brought out two volumes of prints which depicted not actual buildings but fanciful structures, disturbingly dream-like in their quality and not the less so because of the precision of their detail. One of the volumes, *Carceri,* was devoted to the representation of fantasies of vast prisons.

17. Wordsworth. The passage is from *The Excursion* II.834–51.

The vapours had receded,—taking there
Their station under a cerulean sky, etc. etc.

The sublime circumstance—'battlements that on their *restless* fronts bore stars,'—might have been copied from my architectural dreams, for it often occurred.—We hear it reported of Dryden, and of Fuseli [18] in modern times, that they thought proper to eat raw meat for the sake of obtaining splendid dreams: how much better for such a purpose to have eaten opium, which yet I do not remember that any poet is recorded to have done, except the dramatist Shadwell: [19] and in ancient days, Homer is, I think, rightly reputed to have known the virtues of opium.[20]

To my architecture succeeded dreams of lakes and silvery expanses of water: —these haunted me so much that I feared, though possibly it will appear ludicrous to a medical man, that some dropsical [21] state or tendency of the brain might thus be making itself, to use a metaphysical word, *objective;* and the sentient organ *project* itself as its own object.—For two months I suffered greatly in my head—a part of my bodily structure which had hitherto been so clear from all touch or taint of weakness, physically, I mean, that I used to say of it, as the last Lord Orford [22] said of his stomach, that it seemed likely to survive the rest of my person.—Till now I had never felt a headache even, or any the slightest pain, except rheumatic pains caused by my own folly. However, I got over this attack, though it must have been verging on something very dangerous.

The waters now changed their character,—from translucent lakes, shining like mirrors, they now became seas and oceans. And now came a tremendous change, which, unfolding itself slowly like a scroll, through many months, promised an abiding torment; and, in fact, it never left me until the winding up of my case. Hitherto the human face had mixed often in my dreams, but not despotically, nor with any special power of tormenting. But now that which I have called the tyranny of the human face began to unfold itself. Perhaps some part of my London life might be answerable for this. Be that as it may, now it was that upon the rocking waters of the ocean the human face began to appear: the sea appeared paved with innumerable faces, upturned to the heavens: faces, imploring, wrathful, despairing, surged upwards by thousands, by myriads, by generations, by centuries:—my agitation was infinite,—my mind tossed—and surged with the ocean.

May, 1818. The Malay [23] has been a fearful enemy for months. I have been every night, through his means, transported into Asiatic scenes. I know not

18. Henry Fuseli (1741–1825), a Swiss-born English painter. Many of his pictures are the representation of dreams or dream-like scenes.
19. Thomas Shadwell (1642?–92), dramatist and poet, satirized by Dryden in *The Medal* and *Mac Flecknoe.*
20. In the *Odyssey* IV.220–21 Homer speaks feelingly of a drug—the lotos—that quiets pain and anger and brings forgetfulness of every sorrow.
21. Dropsy is a pathological accumulation of fluid in the tissues and cavities of the body.
22. This was Horace Walpole (1717–97), author of *The Castle of Otranto* (1764).
23. Earlier in his narrative, De Quincey relates that "one day a Malay knocked at my door." He was at that time living in the Lake Country. The man was wholly pacific but his aspect—"small, fierce, restless eyes, thin lips, slavish postures"—was disturbing. He

whether others share in my feelings on this point; but I have often thought that if I were compelled to forego England, and to live in China, and among Chinese manners and modes of life and scenery, I should go mad. The causes of my horror lie deep; and some of them must be common to others. Southern Asia, in general, is the seat of awful images and associations. As the cradle of the human race, it would alone have a dim and reverential feeling connected with it. But there are other reasons. No man can pretend that the wild, barbarous, and capricious superstitions of Africa, or of savage tribes elsewhere, affect him in the way that he is affected by the ancient, monumental, cruel, and elaborate religions of Indostan, etc. The mere antiquity of Asiatic things, of their institutions, histories, modes of faith, etc. is so impressive, that to me the vast age of the race and name overpowers the sense of youth in the individual. A young Chinese seems to me an antediluvian man renewed. Even Englishmen, though not bred in any knowledge of such institutions, cannot but shudder at the mystic sublimity of *castes* [24] that have flowed apart, and refused to mix, through such immemorial tracts of time; nor can any man fail to be awed by the names of the Ganges or the Euphrates. It contributes much to these feelings that southern Asia is, and has been for thousands of years, the part of the earth most swarming with human life; the great *officina gentium*.[25] Man is a weed in those regions. The vast empires also, into which the enormous population of Asia has always been cast, give a further sublimity to the feelings associated with all Oriental names or images. In China, over and above what it has in common with the rest of southern Asia, I am terrified by the modes of life, by the manners, and the barrier of utter abhorrence, and want of sympathy, placed between us by feelings deeper than I can analyse. I could sooner live with lunatics, or brute animals. All this, and much more than I can say, or have time to say, the reader must enter into before he can comprehend the unimaginable horror which these dreams of Oriental imagery, and mythological tortures, impressed upon me. Under the connecting feeling of tropical heat and vertical sun-lights, I brought together all creatures, birds, beasts, reptiles, all trees and plants, usages and appearances, that are found in all tropical regions, and assembled them together in China or Indostan. From kindred feelings, I soon brought Egypt and all her gods under the same law. I was stared at, hooted at, grinned at, chattered at, by monkeys, by paroquets, by cockatoos. I ran into pagodas: and was fixed for centuries at the summit, or in secret rooms; I was the idol; I was the priest; I was worshipped; I was sacrificed. I fled from the wrath of Brama [26] through all the forests of Asia: Vishnu hated me: Seeva laid wait for me. I came

---

spoke no English and communication with him was not possible. De Quincey gave him a large piece of opium; the man bolted down the whole of it, went on his way, and was never heard from again. But, as De Quincey says, he "festered afterwards upon my dreams, and brought other Malays with him, worse than himself, that ran 'a-muck' at me and led me into a world of troubles."

24. Hindu society is divided into four hereditary classes, sharply divided from each other by restrictions on professions and marriage. The system, although less rigorous than formerly, still prevails.

25. "Workshop of the nations."

26. In the religion of the Brahmins, Brahma is the creative power, Vishnu the preserving power, Siva the destructive power.

suddenly upon Isis and Osiris: [27] I had done a deed, they said, which the ibis and the crocodile trembled at. I was buried for a thousand years in stone coffins, with mummies and sphinxes, in narrow chambers at the heart of eternal pyramids. I was kissed, with cancerous kisses, by crocodiles; and laid, confounded with all unutterable slimy things, amongst reeds and Nilotic mud.

I thus give the reader some slight abstraction of my Oriental dreams, which always filled me with such amazement at the monstrous scenery, that horror seemed absorbed, for a while, in sheer astonishment. Sooner or later, came a reflux of feeling that swallowed up the astonishment, and left me, not so much in terror, as in hatred and abomination of what I saw. Over every form, and threat, and punishment, and dim sightless incarceration, brooded a sense of eternity and infinity that drove me into an oppression as of madness. Into these dreams only, it was, with one or two slight exceptions, that any circumstances of physical horror entered. All before had been moral and spiritual terrors. But here the main agents were ugly birds, or snakes, or crocodiles; especially the last. The cursed crocodile became to me the object of more horror than almost all the rest. I was compelled to live with him; and (as was always the case almost in my dreams) for centuries. I escaped sometimes, and found myself in Chinese houses, with cane tables, etc. All the feet of the tables, sofas, etc. soon became instinct with life: the abominable head of the crocodile, and his leering eyes, looked out at me, multiplied into a thousand repetitions: and I stood loathing and fascinated. And so often did this hideous reptile haunt my dreams, that many times the very same dream was broken up in the very same way: I heard gentle voices speaking to me (I hear everything when I am sleeping); and instantly I awoke: it was broad noon; and my children were standing, hand in hand, at my bedside; come to show me their coloured shoes, or new frocks, or to let me see them dressed for going out. I protest that so awful was the transition from the damned crocodile, and the other unutterable monsters and abortions of my dreams, to the sight of innocent *human* natures and of infancy, that, in the mighty and sudden revulsion of mind, I wept, and could not forbear it, as I kissed their faces.

June, 1819. I have had occasion to remark, at various periods of my life, that the deaths of those whom we love, and indeed the contemplation of death generally, is (*caeteris paribus*) [28] more affecting in summer than in any other season of the year. And the reasons are these three, I think: first, that the visible heavens in summer appear far higher, more distant, and (if such a solecism [29] may be excused) more infinite; the clouds, by which chiefly the eye expounds the distance of the blue pavilion stretched over our heads, are in summer more voluminous, massed, and accumulated in far grander and more towering piles: secondly, the light and the appearances of the declining and the setting sun are much more fitted to be types and characters of the Infinite: and, thirdly, which is the main reason, the exuberant and riotous

27. Isis is the Egyptian goddess of fertility, sister and wife of Osiris, the god who, by annually dying and returning to life, personifies the self-renewing power of nature.
28. "Other things being equal."
29. The solecism, or impropriety of language, is the phrase "more infinite," since "infinite" cannot be qualified with respect to degree.

prodigality of life naturally forces the mind more powerfully upon the antagonist thought of death, and the wintry sterility of the grave. For it may be observed, generally, that wherever two thoughts stand related to each other by a law of antagonism, and exist, as it were, by mutual repulsion, they are apt to suggest each other. On these accounts it is that I find it impossible to banish the thought of death when I am walking alone in the endless days of summer; and any particular death, if not more affecting, at least haunts my mind more obstinately and besiegingly in that season. Perhaps this cause, and a slight incident which I omit, might have been the immediate occasions of the following dream; to which, however, a predisposition must always have existed in my mind; but having been once roused, it never left me, and split into a thousand fantastic varieties, which often suddenly reunited, and composed again the original dream.

I thought that it was a Sunday morning in May, that it was Easter Sunday, and as yet very early in the morning. I was standing, as it seemed to me, at the door of my own cottage. Right before me lay the very scene which could really be commanded from that situation, but exalted, as was usual, and solemnized by the power of dreams. There were the same mountains, and the same lovely valley at their feet; but the mountains were raised to more than Alpine height, and there was interspace far larger between them of meadows and forest lawns; the hedges were rich with white roses; and no living creature was to be seen, excepting that in the green churchyard there were cattle tranquilly reposing upon the verdant graves, and particularly round about the grave of a child whom I had tenderly loved, just as I had really beheld them, a little before sunrise in the same summer, when that child died.[30] I gazed upon the well-known scene, and I said aloud (as I thought) to myself, 'It yet wants much of sunrise; and it is Easter Sunday; and that is the day on which they celebrate the first-fruits of resurrection. I will walk abroad; old griefs shall be forgotten today; for the air is cool and still, and the hills are high, and stretch away to heaven; and the forest-glades are as quiet as the churchyard; and, with the dew I can wash the fever from my forehead, and then I shall be unhappy no longer.' And I turned, as if to open my garden gate; and immediately I saw upon the left a scene far different; but which yet the power of dreams had reconciled into harmony with the other. The scene was an Oriental one; and there also it was Easter Sunday, and very early in the morning. And at a vast distance were visible, as a stain upon the horizon, the domes and cupolas of a great city—an image or faint abstraction, caught perhaps in childhood from some picture of Jerusalem. And not a bow-shot from me, upon a stone, and shaded by Judean palms, there sat a woman; and I looked; and it was—Ann! She fixed her eyes upon me earnestly; and I said to her at length: 'So then I have found you at last.' I waited: but she answered me not a word. Her face was the same as when I saw it last, and yet again how different! Seventeen years ago, when the lamp-light fell upon her face, as for the last time I kissed her lips (lips, Ann, that to me were not polluted), her eyes were streaming with tears: the tears were now wiped away; she seemed more beautiful than she was at that time, but in all other

30. The child was little Kate Wordsworth. De Quincey described his feelings about her death in one of his essays.

points the same, and not older. Her looks were tranquil, but with unusual solemnity of expression; and I now gazed upon her with some awe, but suddenly her countenance grew dim, and, turning to the mountains, I perceived vapours rolling between us; in a moment, all had vanished; thick darkness came on; and, in the twinkling of an eye, I was far away from mountains, and by lamplight in Oxford-street, walking again with Ann—just as we walked seventeen years before, when we were both children.

As a final specimen, I cite one of a different character, from 1820.

The dream commenced with a music which now I often heard in dreams—a music of preparation and of awakening suspense; a music like the opening of the Coronation Anthem,[31] and which, like *that*, gave the feeling of a vast march—of infinite cavalcades filing off—and the tread of innumerable armies. The morning was come of a mighty day—a day of crisis and of final hope for human nature, then suffering some mysterious eclipse, and labouring in some dread extremity. Somewhere, I knew not where—somehow, I knew not how —by some beings, I knew not whom—a battle, a strife, an agony, was conducting,—was evolving like a great drama, or piece of music; with which my sympathy was the more insupportable from my confusion as to its place, its cause, its nature, and its possible issue. I, as is usual in dreams (where, of necessity, we make ourselves central to every movement), had the power, and yet had not the power, to decide it. I had the power, if I could raise myself, to will it; and yet again had not the power, for the weight of twenty Atlantics was upon me, or the oppression of inexpiable guilt. 'Deeper than ever plummet sounded,' [32] I lay inactive. Then, like a chorus, the passion deepened. Some greater interest was at stake; some mightier cause than ever yet the sword had pleaded, or trumpet had proclaimed. Then came sudden alarms: hurryings to and fro: trepidations of innumerable fugitives, I knew not whether from the good cause or the bad: darkness and lights: tempest and human faces: and at last, with the sense that all was lost, female forms, and the features that were worth all the world to me, and but a moment allowed,—and clasped hands, and heart-breaking partings, and then—everlasting farewells! and with a sigh, such as the caves of hell sighed when the incestuous mother uttered the abhorred name of death, the sound was reverberated—everlasting farewells! and again, and yet again reverberated—everlasting farewells!

And I awoke in struggles, and cried aloud—'I will sleep no more!' [33]

But I am now called upon to wind up a narrative which has already extended to an unreasonable length. Within more spacious limits, the materials which I have used might have been better unfolded; and much which I have not used might have been added with effect. Perhaps, however, enough has been given. It now remains that I should say something of the way in which this conflict of horrors was finally brought to its crisis. The reader is already aware (form a passage near the beginning of the introduction to the first part) that the opium-eater has, in some way or other, 'unwound, almost to its final links,

31. Written by G. F. Handel (1685–1759) for the coronation of George II in 1727.
32. *The Tempest* III.iii.101.
33. *Macbeth* II.ii.35–43.

the accursed chain which bound him.' By what means? To have narrated this, according to the original intention, would have far exceeded the space which can now be allowed. It is fortunate, as such a cogent reason exists for abridging it, that I should, on a maturer view of the case, have been exceedingly unwilling to injure, by any such unaffecting details, the impression of the history itself, as an appeal to the prudence and the conscience of the yet unconfirmed opium-eater—or even, though a very inferior consideration, to injure its effect as a composition. The interest of the judicious reader will not attach itself chiefly to the subject of the fascinating spells, but to the fascinating power. Not the opium-eater, but the opium, is the true hero of the tale; and the legitimate centre on which the interest revolves. The object was to display the marvellous agency of opium, whether for pleasure or for pain: if that is done, the action of the piece has closed.

However, as some people, in spite of all laws to the contrary, will persist in asking what became of the opium-eater, and in what state he now is, I answer for him thus: The reader is aware that opium had long ceased to found its empire on spells of pleasure; it was solely by the tortures connected with the attempt to abjure it, that it kept its hold. Yet, as other tortures, no less it may be thought, attended the non-abjuration of such a tyrant, a choice only of evils was left; and *that* might as well have been adopted, which, however terrific in itself, held out a prospect of final restoration to happiness. This appears true; but good logic gave the author no strength to act upon it. However, a crisis arrived for the author's life, and a crisis for other objects still dearer to him—and which will always be far dearer to him than his life, even now that it is again a happy one.—I saw that I must die if I continued the opium: I determined, therefore, if that should be required, to die in throwing it off. How much I was at that time taking I cannot say; for the opium which I used had been purchased for me by a friend who afterwards refused to let me pay him; so that I could not ascertain even what quantity I had used within the year. I apprehend, however, that I took it very irregularly: and that I varied from about fifty or sixty grains, to 150 a day. My first task was to reduce it to forty, to thirty, and, as fast as I could, to twelve grains.

I triumphed: but think not, reader, that therefore my sufferings were ended; nor think of me as of one sitting in a *dejected* state. Think of me as of one, even when four months had passed, still agitated, writhing, throbbing, palpitating, shattered; and much, perhaps, in the situation of him who has been racked, as I collect the torments of that state from the affecting account of them left by the most innocent sufferer of the times of James I.[34] Meantime, I derived no benefit from any medicine, except one prescribed to me by an Edinburgh surgeon of great eminence, viz. ammoniated tincture of valerian. Medical account, therefore, of my emancipation I have not much to give: and even that little, as managed by a man so ignorant of medicine as myself, would probably tend only to mislead. At all events, it would be misplaced in this situation. The moral of the narrative is addressed to the opium-eater; and therefore, of necessity, limited in its application. If he is taught to fear and tremble, enough

34. "William Lithgow [1582–1645?]: His book (Travels, &c.) is ill and pedantically written; but the account of his own sufferings on the rack at Malaga is overpoweringly affecting." (De Quincey)

has been effected. But he may say, that the issue of my case is at least a proof that opium, after a seventeen years' use, and an eight years' abuse of its powers, may still be renounced: and that *he* may chance to bring to the task greater energy than I did, or that with a stronger constitution than mine he may obtain the same results with less. This may be true: I would not presume to measure the efforts of other men by my own: I heartily wish him more energy: I wish him the same success. Nevertheless, I had motives external to myself which he may unfortunately want: and these supplied me with conscientious supports which mere personal interests might fail to supply to a mind debilitated by opium.

Lord Bacon conjectures that it may be as painful to be born as to die: I think it probable: and, during the whole period of diminishing the opium, I had the torments of a man passing out of one mode of existence into another. The issue was not death, but a sort of physical regeneration: and I may add, that ever since, at intervals, I have had a restoration of more than youthful spirits, though under the pressure of difficulties, which, in a less happy state of mind, I should have called misfortunes.

One memorial of my former condition still remains: my dreams are not yet perfectly calm: the dread swell and agitation of the storm have not wholly subsided: the legions that encamped in them are drawing off, but not all departed: my sleep is still tumultuous, and, like the gates of Paradise to our first parents when looking back from afar, it is still, in the tremendous line of Milton—

With dreadful faces thronged and fiery arms.[35]

1821   1821

On the Knocking at the Gate in "Macbeth"

[When Macbeth has stabbed King Duncan and his two attendants, and Lady Macbeth carries back to the chamber the grooms' bloody daggers which her husband has inadvertently brought out with him, a knocking at the castle gate is heard. It is repeated three more times before the guilty couple leaves the stage. The knocking continues, growing louder; a drunken porter eventually makes his appearance on the empty stage and in his own good time, after some grimly comic soliloquizing, opens the gate to Macduff and Lennox. The scene has a unique force which De Quincey was the first to remark. It is interesting to note that he makes no reference to the porter's soliloquy and his subsequent dialogue with Macduff, now generally thought very striking but which Coleridge found disgusting and believed could not have been written by Shakespeare. The last paragraph of the famous essay is an extreme example of the Romantic view of Shakespeare as transcending the limits of mere art, as being identical with nature itself.]

From my boyish days I had always felt a great perplexity on one point in *Macbeth*. It was this: the knocking at the gate which succeeds to the murder of Duncan produced to my feelings an effect for which I never could account.

35. *Paradise Lost* XII.644.

The effect was that it reflected back upon the murderer a peculiar awfulness and a depth of solemnity; yet, however obstinately I endeavoured with my understanding to comprehend this, for many years I never could see *why* it should produce such an effect.

Here I pause for one moment, to exhort the reader never to pay any attention to his understanding [1] when it stands in opposition to any other faculty of his mind. The mere understanding, however useful and indispensable, is the meanest faculty in the human mind, and the most to be distrusted; and yet the great majority of people trust to nothing else—which may do for ordinary life, but not for philosophical purposes. Of this out of ten thousand instances that I might produce I will cite one. Ask of any person whatsoever who is not previously prepared for the demand by a knowledge of the perspective to draw in the rudest way the commonest appearance which depends upon the laws of that science—as, for instance, to represent the effect of two walls standing at right angles to each other, or the appearance of the houses on each side of a street as seen by a person looking down the street from one extremity. Now, in all cases, unless the person has happened to observe in pictures how it is that artists produce these effects, he will be utterly unable to make the smallest approximation to it. Yet why? For he has actually seen the effect every day of his life. The reason is that he allows his understanding to overrule his eyes. His understanding, which includes no intuitive knowledge of the laws of vision, can furnish him with no reason why a line which is known and can be proved to be a horizontal line should not *appear* a horizontal line: a line that made any angle with the perpendicular less than a right angle would seem to him to indicate that his houses were all tumbling down together. Accordingly, he makes the line of his houses a horizontal line, and fails, of course, to produce the effect demanded. Here, then, is one instance out of many in which not only the understanding is allowed to overrule the eyes, but where the understanding is positively allowed to obliterate the eyes, as it were; for not only does the man believe the evidence of his understanding in opposition to that of his eyes, but (what is monstrous) the idiot is not aware that his eyes ever gave such evidence. He does not know that he has seen (and therefore *quoad* [2] his consciousness has *not* seen) that which he *has* seen every day of his life.

But to return from this digression. My understanding could furnish no reason why the knocking at the gate in *Macbeth* should produce any effect, direct or reflected. In fact, my understanding said positively that it could *not* produce any effect. But I knew better; I felt that it did; and I waited and clung to the problem until further knowledge should enable me to solve it. At length, in 1812, Mr. Williams made his *début* on the stage of Ratcliffe Highway, and

---

1. De Quincey means to use this word in the special sense which was initiated by the German philosopher Immanuel Kant (1724–1804), who distinguished between understanding (*Verstand*) and reason (*Vernunft*). He conceived *reason* to be the highest faculty of the mind; it is the power by which the mind synthesizes into unity the concepts provided by the understanding or intellect. It is thus the *creative* faculty; "the mere understanding," as De Quincey calls it, is but mechanical and subordinate. Actually, De Quincey, although he has Kant's distinction in mind, is using the word in a much more limited sense than Kant intended.
2. "So far."

executed those unparalleled murders which have procured for him such a brilliant and undying reputation.[3] On which murders, by the way, I must observe that in one respect they have had an ill effect, by making the connoisseur in murder very fastidious in his taste, and dissatisfied by anything that has been since done in that line. All other murders look pale by the deep crimson of his; and, as an amateur [4] once said to me in a querulous tone, 'There has been absolutely nothing *doing* since his time, or nothing that's worth speaking of.' But this is wrong; for it is unreasonable to expect all men to be great artists, and born with the genius of Mr. Williams. Now, it will be remembered that in the first of these murders (that of the Marrs) the same incident (of a knocking at the door soon after the work of extermination was complete) did actually occur which the genius of Shakespeare has invented; and all good judges, and the most eminent dilettanti,[5] acknowledged the felicity of Shakespeare's suggestion as soon as it was actually realized. Here, then, was a fresh proof that I was right in relying on my own feeling, in opposition to my understanding; and I again set myself to study the problem. At length I solved it to my own satisfaction; and my solution is this: murder, in ordinary cases, where the sympathy is wholly directed to the case of the murdered person, is an incident of coarse and vulgar horror; and for this reason—that it flings the interest exclusively upon the natural but ignoble instinct by which we cleave to life: an instinct which, as being indispensable to the primal law of self-preservation, is the same in kind (though different in degree) amongst all living creatures. This instinct, therefore, because it annihilates all distinctions, and degrades the greatest of men to the level of 'the poor beetle that we tread on,' [6] exhibits human nature in its most abject and humiliating attitude. Such an attitude would little suit the purposes of the poet. What then must he do? He must throw the interest on the murderer. Our sympathy must be with *him* (of course I mean a sympathy of comprehension, a sympathy by which we enter into his feelings, and are made to understand them—not a sympathy of pity or approbation).[7] In the murdered person, all strife of thought, ill flux and reflux of passion and of purpose, are crushed by one overwhelming

3. In the winter of 1811–12, in Ratcliffe Highway, a depressed nautical neighborhood, John Williams, a sailor, murdered the members of two households—that of the Marrs (four persons) and that of the Williamsons (three persons). He was apprehended and committed suicide in prison. The tone of whimsically ironic admiration in which De Quincey speaks of his terrible exploit is developed in the essays *On Murder Considered as One of the Fine Arts*, to which is appended a Postcript giving a detailed account of Williams's crimes.
4. In its early sense: a lover of a fine art.
5. Not in the modern sense of those who practice an art without commitment, but lovers of art, connoisseurs.
6. *Measure for Measure* III.i.79.
7. "It seems almost ludicrous to guard and explain my use of a word in a situation where it would naturally explain itself. But it has become necessary to do so, in consequence of the unscholar-like use of the word sympathy, at present so general, by which, instead of taking it in its proper sense, as the act of reproducing in our minds the feelings of another. whether for hatred, indignation, love, pity, or approbation, it is made a mere synonym of the word *pity;* and hence, instead of saying 'sympathy *with* another,' many writers adopt the monstrous barbarism of 'sympathy *for* another.'" (De Quincey)

panic; the fear of instant death smites him 'with its petrific mace.' [8] But in the murderer, such a murderer as a poet will condescend to, there must be raging some great storm of passion—jealousy, ambition, vengeance, hatred—which will create a hell within him; and into this hell we are to look.

In *Macbeth*, for the sake of gratifying his own enormous and teeming faculty of creation, Shakespeare has introduced two murderers: and, as usual in his hands, they are remarkably discriminated: but—though in Macbeth the strife of mind is greater than in his wife, the tiger spirit not so awake, and his feelings caught chiefly by contagion from her—yet, as both were finally involved in the guilt of murder, the murderous mind of necessity is finally to be presumed in both. This was to be expressed; and, on its own account, as well as to make it a more proportionable antagonist to the unoffending nature of their victim, 'the gracious Duncan,' [9] and adequately to expound 'the deep damnation of his taking off,' [10] this was to be expressed with peculiar energy. We were to be made to feel that the human nature—*i.e.* the divine nature of love and mercy, spread through the hearts of all creatures, and seldom utterly withdrawn from man—was gone, vanished, extinct, and that the fiendish nature had taken its place. And, as this effect is marvellously accomplished in the *dialogues* and *soliloquies* themselves, so it is finally consummated by the expedient under consideration; and it is to this that I now solicit the reader's attention. If the reader has ever witnessed a wife, daughter, or sister in a fainting fit, he may chance to have observed that the most affecting moment in such a spectacle is *that* in which a sigh and a stirring announce the recommencement of suspended life. Or, if the reader has ever been present in a vast metropolis on the day when some great national idol was carried in funeral pomp to his grave, and, chancing to walk near the course through which it passed, has felt powerfully, in the silence and desertion of the streets, and in the stagnation of ordinary business, the deep interest which at that moment was possessing the heart of man—if all at once he should hear the death-like stillness broken up by the sound of wheels rattling away from the scene, and making known that the transitory vision was dissolved, he will be aware that at no moment was his sense of the complete suspension and pause in ordinary human concerns so full and affecting as at that moment when the suspension ceases, and the goings-on of human life are suddenly resumed. All action in any direction is best expounded, measured, and made apprehensible, by reaction. Now, apply this to the case in *Macbeth*. Here, as I have said, the retiring of the human heart and the entrance of the fiendish heart was to be expressed and made sensible. Another world has stepped in; and the murderers are taken out of the region of human things, human purposes, human desires. They are transfigured: Lady Macbeth is 'unsexed'; [11] Macbeth has forgot that he was born of woman; both are conformed to the image of devils; and the world of devils is suddenly revealed. But how shall this be conveyed and made palpable?

8. *Paradise Lost* X.294. Petrific: having the power to turn to stone.
9. *Macbeth* III.i.65.
10. *Macbeth* I.vii.20.
11. *Macbeth* I.v.41. Lady Macbeth asks the spirits "that tend on mortal thoughts" to "unsex" her, that is, take away all her womanly feelings so that she can carry out the assassination of King Duncan.

In order that a new world may step in, this world must for a time disappear. The murderers and the murder must be insulated—cut off by an immeasurable gulf from the ordinary tide and succession of human affairs—locked up and sequestered in some deep recess; we must be made sensible that the world of ordinary life is suddenly arrested, laid asleep, tranced, racked into a dread armistice; time must be annihilated, relation to things without abolished; and all must pass self-withdrawn into a deep syncope [12] and suspension of earthly passion. Hence it is that, when the deed is done, when the work of darkness is perfect, then the world of darkness passes away like a pageantry in the clouds: the knocking at the gate is heard, and it makes known audibly that the reaction has commenced; the human has made its reflux upon the fiendish; the pulses of life are beginning to beat again; and the re-establishment of the goings-on of the world in which we live first makes us profoundly sensible of the awful parenthesis that had suspended them.

O mighty poet! Thy works are not as those of other men, simply and merely great works of art, but are also like the phenomena of nature, like the sun and the sea, the stars and the flowers, like frost and snow, rain and dew, hail-storm and thunder, which are to be studied with entire submission of our own faculties, and in the perfect faith that in them there can be no too much or too little, nothing useless or inert, but that, the farther we press in our discoveries, the more we shall see proofs of design and self-supporting arrangement where the careless eye had seen nothing but accident!

1823   1823

Levana and Our Ladies of Sorrow

Oftentimes at Oxford I saw Levana in my dreams. I knew her by her Roman symbols. Who is Levana? Reader, that do not pretend to have leisure for very much scholarship, you will not be angry with me for telling you. Levana was the Roman goddess that performed for the newborn infant the earliest office of ennobling kindness—typical, by its mode, of that grandeur which belongs to man everywhere, and of that benignity in powers invisible which even in Pagan worlds sometimes descends to sustain it. At the very moment of birth, just as the infant tasted for the first time the atmosphere of our troubled planet, it was laid on the ground. *That* might bear different interpretations.[1] But immediately, lest so grand a creature should grovel there for more than one instant, either the paternal hand, as proxy for the goddess Levana, or some near kinsman, as proxy for the father, raised it upright, bade it look erect as the king of all this world, and presented its forehead to the stars, saying, perhaps, in his heart, 'Behold what is greater than yourselves!' This symbolic act represented the function of Levana. And that mysterious lady, who never revealed her face (except to me in dreams), but always acted by delegation, had her name from the Latin verb (as still it is the Italian verb) *levare*, to raise aloft.

12. The word is used here in the now rare sense of a pause, a cessation.

1. De Quincey probably has in mind the mythological story of the giant Antaeus, who was made stronger by contact with his mother, the Earth.

This is the explanation of Levana. And hence it has arisen that some people have understood by Levana the tutelary power that controls the education of the nursery. She, that would not suffer at his birth even a prefigurative or mimic degradation for her awful [2] ward, far less could be supposed to suffer the real degradation attaching to the non-development of his powers. She therefore watches over human education. Now, the word *edŭco*, with the penultimate short, was derived (by a process often exemplified in the crystallization of languages) from the word *edūco*, with the penultimate long. Whatsoever *educes*, or develops, *educates*. By the education of Levana, therefore, is meant, not the poor machinery that moves by spelling-books and grammars, but by that mighty system of central forces hidden in the deep bosom of human life, which by passion, by strife, by temptation, by the energies of resistance, works forever upon children, resting not day or night, any more than the mighty wheel of day and night themselves, whose moments, like restless spokes, are glimmering forever as they revolve.

If, then, *these* are the ministries by which Levana works, how profoundly must she reverence the agencies of grief! But you, reader, think that children generally are not liable to grief such as mine. There are two senses in the word *generally*—the sense of Euclid, where it means *universally* (or in the whole extent of the *genus*), and a foolish sense of this word, where it means *usually*. Now, I am far from saying that children universally are capable of grief like mine. But there are more than you ever heard of who die of grief in this island of ours. I will tell you a common case. The rules of Eton require that a boy on the *foundation* [3] should be there twelve years: he is superannuated at eighteen; consequently he must come at six. Children torn away from mothers and sisters at that age not unfrequently die. I speak of what I know. The complaint is not entered by the registrar as grief; but *that* it is. Grief of that sort, and at that age, has killed more than ever have been counted amongst its martyrs.

Therefore it is that Levana often communes with the powers that shake man's heart; therefore it is that she dotes upon grief. 'These ladies,' said I softly to myself, on seeing the ministers [4] with whom Levana was conversing, 'these are the Sorrows; and they are three in number: as the *Graces* [5] are three, who dress man's life with beauty; the *Parcae* [6] are three, who weave the dark arras [7] of man's life in their mysterious loom always with colours sad in part, sometimes angry with tragic crimson and black; the *Furies* [8] are three, who visit with retributions called from the other side of the grave offences that walk upon this; and once even the *Muses* were but three,[9] who fit the harp, the trumpet, or the lute, to the great burdens of man's impassioned creations.

2. "Awful" not because of his great power but because of his painful destiny.
3. A boy who receives his schooling free of cost.
4. "Minister" in the sense of a person who serves as an agent for another.
5. Greek goddesses personifying charm and beauty.
6. The Latin name for the Fates. They were represented as weaving the fabric of a man's life.
7. Tapestry.
8. Spirits of the underworld who wreaked vengeance upon those who transgressed against the laws, especially those pertaining to the family.
9. Greek female deities of the arts, traditionally nine in number.

These are the Sorrows; all three of whom I know.' That last words I say now; but in Oxford I said, 'one of whom I know, and the others too surely I *shall* know.' For already, in my fervent youth, I saw (dimly relieved upon the dark background of my dreams) the imperfect lineaments of the awful Sisters.

These Sisters—by what name shall we call them? If I say simply 'The Sorrows,' there will be a chance of mistaking the term; it might be understood of individual sorrow—separate cases of sorrow—whereas I want a term expressing the mighty abstractions that incarnate themselves in all individual sufferings of man's heart, and I wish to have these abstractions presented as impersonations, that is, as clothed with human attributes of life, and with functions pointing to flesh. Let us call them, therefore, *Our Ladies of Sorrow.*

I know them thoroughly, and have walked in all their kingdoms. Three sisters they are, of one mysterious household; and their paths are wide apart; but of their dominion there is no end. Them I saw often conversing with Levana, and sometimes about myself. Do they talk, then? O no! Mighty phantoms like these disdain the infirmities of language. They may utter voices through the organs of man when they dwell in human hearts, but amongst themselves is no voice nor sound; eternal silence reigns in *their* kingdoms. They spoke not as they talked with Levana, they whispered not; they sang not; though oftentimes methought they *might* have sung: for I upon earth had heard their mysteries oftentimes deciphered by harp and timbrel, by dulcimer and organ. Like God, whose servants they are, they utter their pleasure not by sounds that perish, or by words that go astray, but by signs in heaven, by changes on earth, by pulses in secret rivers, heraldries painted on darkness, and hieroglyphics written on the tablets of the brain. *They* wheeled in mazes; *I* spelled the steps. *They* telegraphed [10] from afar; *I* read the signals. *They* conspired together; and on the mirrors of darkness *my* eye traced the plots. *Theirs* were the symbols; *mine* are the words.

What is it the Sisters are? What is it that they do? Let me describe their form and their presence, if form it were that still fluctuated in its outline, or presence it were that forever advanced to the front or forever receded amongst shades.

The eldest of the three is named *Mater Lachrymarum,* Our Lady of Tears. She it is that night and day raves and moans, calling for vanished faces. She stood in Rama, where a voice was heard of lamentation—Rachel weeping for her children, and refusing to be comforted.[11] She it was that stood in Bethlehem on the night when Herod's sword swept its nurseries of Innocents, and the little feet were stiffened forever which, heard at times as they trotted along floors overhead, woke pulses of love in household hearts that were not unmarked in heaven. Her eyes are sweet and subtle, wild and sleepy, by turns; oftentimes rising to the clouds, oftentimes challenging the heavens. She wears a diadem

10. Although the word was used for signaling by semaphore, De Quincey probably had in mind the electric telegraph, which was invented in 1844, the year before this essay was written.

11. In Matthew 2, in the account of the massacre of the Innocents, the verse in Jeremiah 31:15 about Rachel weeping for her children is quoted. Rama was Rachel's burying place. Herod ("the Great"), King of Judaea, ordered the slaughter of all male children less than two years old in order that the infant Jesus should be destroyed.

round her head. And I knew by childish memories that she could go abroad upon the winds, when she heard the sobbing of litanies, or the thundering of organs, and when she beheld the mustering of summer clouds. This Sister, the elder, it is that carries keys more than papal [12] at her girdle, which open every cottage and every palace. She, to my knowledge, sat all last summer by the bedside of the blind beggar, him that so often and so gladly I talked with, whose pious daughter, eight years old, with the sunny countenance, resisted the temptations of play and village mirth, to travel all day long on dusty roads with her afflicted father. For this did God send her a great reward. In the spring time of the year, and whilst yet her own spring was budding, He recalled her to himself. But her blind father mourns for ever over *her:* still he dreams at midnight that the little guiding hand is locked within his own; and still he wakens to a darkness that is *now* within a second and a deeper darkness. This *Mater Lachrymarum* also has been sitting all this winter of 1844–5 within the bedchamber of the Czar,[13] bringing before his eyes a daughter (not less pious) that vanished to God not less suddenly, and left behind her a darkness not less profound. By the power of the keys it is that Our Lady of Tears glides, a ghostly intruder, into the chambers of sleepless men, sleepless women, sleepless children, from Ganges to the Nile, from Nile to Mississippi. And her, because she is the first-born of her house, and has the widest empire, let us honour with the title of 'Madonna.' [14]

The second Sister is called *Mater Suspiriorum,* Our Lady of Sighs. She never scales the clouds, nor walks abroad upon the winds. She wears no diadem. And her eyes, if they were ever seen, would be neither sweet nor subtle; no man could read their story; they would be found filled with perishing dreams, and with wrecks of forgotten delirium. But she raises not her eyes; her head, on which sits a dilapidated turban, droops forever, forever fastens on the dust. She weeps not. She groans not. But she sighs inaudibly at intervals. Her sister, Madonna, is oftentimes stormy and frantic, raging in the highest against heaven, and demanding back her darlings. But Our Lady of Sighs never clamours, never defies, dreams not of rebellious aspirations. She is humble to abjectness. Hers is the meekness that belongs to the hopeless. Murmur she may, but it is in her sleep. Whisper she may, but it is to herself in the twilight. Mutter she does at times, but it is in solitary places that are desolate as she is desolate, in ruined cities, and when the sun has gone down to his rest. This Sister is the visitor of the Pariah,[15] of the Jew,[16] of the bondsman to the oar in the Mediterranean galleys; [17] of the English criminal in Norfolk Island,[18] blotted out from the books of remembrance in sweet far-off England; of the baffled penitent reverting his eyes forever upon a solitary grave, which to him seems the altar overthrown of some past and bloody sacrifice, on which altar

---

12. In Matthew 16:19 Jesus says to Peter that he will give him the keys to the kingdom of heaven; the authority of the pope, which descends from Peter, is symbolized by keys.
13. The tyrannical Nicholas I (1796–1855), whose daughter Alexandra died when she was nineteen.
14. "My lady"—a term of respect formerly used in Italy in addressing a married woman.
15. A member of a low caste in India. Although they are not outside the caste system and are not even of the lowest caste, the word in English has come to mean an outcast.
16. In England Jews did not enjoy full civil rights until 1858.
17. Ships propelled by oars as well as sails; criminals were condemned to service in them.
18. An island in the South Pacific belonging to Australia, once a penal colony.

no oblations [19] can now be availing, whether towards pardon that he might implore, or towards reparation that he might attempt. Every slave that at noonday looks up to the tropical sun with timid reproach, as he points with one hand to the earth, our general mother, but for *him* a stepmother, as he points with the other hand to the Bible, our general teacher, but against *him* sealed and sequestered; every woman sitting in darkness, without love to shelter her head, or hope to illumine her solitude, because the heaven-born instincts kindling in her nature germs of holy affections, which God implanted in her womanly bosom, having been stifled by social necessities, now burn sullenly to waste, like sepulchral lamps amongst the ancients; every nun defrauded of her unreturning Maytime by wicked kinsman, whom God will judge; every captive in every dungeon; all that are betrayed, and all that are rejected; outcasts by traditionary law, and children of *hereditary* disgrace: all these walk with Our Lady of Sighs. She also carries a key; but she needs it little. For her kingdom is chiefly amongst the tents of Shem,[20] and the houseless vagrant of every clime. Yet in the very highest ranks of man she finds chapels of her own; and even in glorious England there are some that, to the world, carry their heads as proudly as the reindeer, who yet secretly have received her mark upon their foreheads.

But the third Sister, who is also the youngest——! Hush! whisper whilst we talk of *her!* Her kingdom is not large, or else no flesh should live; but within that kingdom all power is hers. Her head, turreted like that of Cybele,[21] rises almost beyond the reach of sight. She droops not; and her eyes, rising so high, *might* be hidden by distance. But, being what they are, they cannot be hidden: through the treble veil of crape which she wears the fierce light of a blazing misery, that rests not for matins or for vespers, for noon of day or noon of night, for ebbing or for flowing tide, may be read from the very ground. She is the defier of God. She also is the mother of lunacies, and the suggestress of suicides. Deep lie the roots of her power; but narrow is the nation that she rules. For she can approach only those in whom a profound nature has been upheaved by central convulsions; in whom the heart trembles and the brain rocks under conspiracies of tempest from without and tempest from within. Madonna moves with uncertain steps, fast or slow, but still with tragic grace. Our Lady of Sighs creeps timidly and stealthily. But this youngest Sister moves with incalculable motions, bounding, and with tiger's leaps. She carries no key; for, though coming rarely amongst men, she storms all doors at which she is permitted to enter at all. And *her* name is *Mater Tenebrarum* —Our Lady of Darkness.

These were the *Semnai Theai* or Sublime Goddesses, these were the *Eumenides* or Gracious Ladies [22] (so called by antiquity in shuddering propitiation), of my Oxford dreams. Madonna spoke. She spoke by her mysterious hand. Touching my head, she beckoned to Our Lady of Sighs; and *what* she spoke, translated out of the signs which (except in dreams) no man reads, was this:

19. The act of offering something to a deity.

20. The oldest of the sons of Noah. God regarded him with favor. To "dwell in the tents of Shem" (Genesis 9:27) is a phrase of uncertain implication but it is often taken to mean, as here, to live unhappily among strangers.

21. A goddess of contradictory attributes, at once beneficent and terrible; the crown in which she is often represented is in the shape of a city's walls.

22. The Furies, fierce and terrifying in their appearance, were called by this name to propitiate them.

'Lo! here is he whom in childhood I dedicated to my altars. This is he that once I made my darling. Him I led astray, him I beguiled; and from heaven I stole away his young heart to mine. Through me did he become idolatrous; and through me it was, by languishing desires, that he worshipped the worm, and prayed to the wormy grave. Holy was the grave to him; lovely was its darkness; saintly its corruption. Him, this young idolater, I have seasoned for thee, dear gentle Sister of Sighs! Do thou take him now to *thy* heart, and season him for our dreadful sister. And thou,' turning to the *Mater Tenebrarum,* she said, 'wicked sister, that temptest and hatest, do thou take him from *her*. See that thy sceptre lie heavy on his head. Suffer not woman and her tenderness to sit near him in his darkness. Banish the frailties of hope; wither the relenting of love; scorch the fountains of tears; curse him as only *thou* canst curse. So shall he be accomplished in the furnace; so shall he see the things that ought *not* to be seen, sights that are abominable, and secrets that are unutterable. So shall he read elder truths, sad truths, grand truths, fearful truths. So shall he rise again *before* he dies. And so shall our commission be accomplished which from God we had—to plague his heart until we had unfolded the capacities of his spirit.' [23]

1845   1845

The Literature of Knowledge and the Literature of Power [1]

What is it that we mean by *literature?* Popularly, and amongst the thoughtless, it is held to include everything that is printed in a book. Little logic is required to disturb *that* definition. The most thoughtless person is easily made aware that in the idea of *literature* one essential element is some relation to a general and common interest of man—so that what applies only to a local, or professional, or merely personal interest, even though presenting itself in the shape of a book, will not belong to literature. So far the definition is easily narrowed; and it is as easily expanded. For not only is much that takes a station in books not literature; but inversely, much that really *is* literature never reaches a station in books. The weekly sermons of Christendom, that vast pulpit literature which acts so extensively upon the popular mind—to warn, to uphold, to renew, to comfort, to alarm—does not attain the sanctuary of libraries in the ten-thousandth part of its extent. The drama again—as, for instance, the finest of Shakespeare's plays in England, and all leading Athenian plays in the noontide of the Attic stage—operated as a literature on the public mind, and were (according to the strictest letter of that term) *published* through the audiences that witnessed [2] their representation some time before they were published as

---

23. See Keats's letter of February 14–May 3, 1819 on the world as a "Vale of Soul-making."

1. Originally part of a long essay on Pope, this discourse has achieved an independent existence.

2. "Charles I, for example, when Prince of Wales, and many others in his father's court, gained their known familiarity with Shakespeare not through the original quartos so slenderly diffused, nor through the first folio of 1625, but through the court representation of his chief dramas at Whitehall." (De Quincey)

things to be read; and they were published in this scenical mode of publication with much more effect than they could have had as books during ages of costly copying or of costly printing.

Books, therefore, do not suggest an idea coextensive and interchangeable with the idea of literature; since much literature, scenic, forensic, or didactic (as from lecturers and public orators), may never come into books, and much that *does* come into books may connect itself with no literary interest. But a far more important correction, applicable to the common vague idea of literature, is to be sought not so much in a better definition of literature as in a sharper distinction of the two functions which it fulfils. In that great social organ which, collectively, we call literature, there may be distinguished two separate offices that may blend and often *do* so, but capable, severally, of a severe insulation, and naturally fitted for reciprocal repulsion. There is, first, the Literature of *Knowledge;* and, secondly, the Literature of *Power.* The function of the first is —to *teach;* the function of the second is—to *move:* the first is a rudder; the second, an oar or a sail. The first speaks to the *mere* discursive understanding; the second speaks ultimately, it may happen, to the higher understanding or reason, but always *through* affections of pleasure and sympathy. Remotely, it may travel towards an object seated in what Lord Bacon calls *dry* light; [3] but, proximately, it does and must operate—else it ceases to be a Literature of *Power* —on and through that *humid* light which clothes itself in the mists and glittering *iris* [4] of human passions, desires, and genial emotions. Men have so little reflected on the higher functions of literature as to find it a paradox if one should describe it as a mean or subordinate purpose of books to give information. But this is a paradox only in the sense which makes it honourable to be paradoxical. Whenever we talk in ordinary language of seeking information or gaining knowledge, we understand the words as connected with something of absolute novelty. But it is the grandeur of all truth which *can* occupy a very high place in human interests that it is never absolutely novel to the meanest of minds: it exists eternally by way of germ or latent principle in the lowest as in the highest, needing to be developed, but never to be planted. To be capable of transplantation is the immediate criterion of a truth that ranges on a lower scale. Besides which, there is a rarer thing than truth—namely, *power,* or deep sympathy with truth. What is the effect, for instance, upon society, of children? By the pity, by the tenderness, and by the peculiar modes of admiration, which connect themselves with the helplessness, with the innocence, and with the simplicity of children, not only are the primal affections strengthened and continually renewed, but the qualities which are dearest in the sight of heaven—the frailty, for instance, which appeals to forbearance, the innocence which symbolizes the heavenly, and the simplicity which is most alien from the worldly—are kept up in perpetual remembrance, and their ideals are continually refreshed. A purpose of the same nature is answered by the higher literature, viz. the Literature of Power. What do you learn from *Paradise Lost?* Nothing at all. What do you learn from a cookery-book? Something new, something that you did not know before, in every paragraph. But

3. In *Novum Organum, Aphorisms concerning the Interpretation of Nature and the Kingdom of Man,* Aphorism 49.
4. Rainbow.

would you therefore put the wretched cookery-book on a higher level of estimation than the divine poem? What you owe to Milton is not any knowledge, of which a million separate items are still but a million of advancing steps on the same earthly level; what you owe is *power*—that is, exercise and expansion to your own latent capacity of sympathy with the infinite, where every pulse and each separate influx is a step upwards, a step ascending as upon a Jacob's ladder [5] from earth to mysterious altitudes above the earth. *All* the steps of knowledge, from first to last, carry you further on the same plane, but could never raise you one foot above your ancient level of earth: whereas the very *first* step in power is a flight—is an ascending movement into another element where earth is forgotten.

Were it not that human sensibilities are ventilated and continually called out into exercise by the great phenomena of infancy, or of real life as it moves through chance and change, or of literature as it re-combines these elements in the mimicries of poetry, romance, etc., it is certain that, like any animal power or muscular energy falling into disuse, all such sensibilities would gradually droop and dwindle. It is in relation to these great *moral* capacities of man that the Literature of Power, as contradistinguished from that of knowledge, lives and has its field of action. It is concerned with what is highest in man; for the Scriptures themselves never condescended to deal by suggestion or co-operation with the mere discursive understanding: when speaking of man in his intellectual capacity, the Scriptures speak not of the understanding, but of '*the understanding heart*' [6]—making the heart, *i.e.* the great *intuitive* (or non-discursive) organ, to be the interchangeable formula for man in his highest state of capacity for the infinite. Tragedy, romance, fairy tale, or epopee,[7] all alike restore to man's mind the ideals of justice, of hope, of truth, of mercy, of retribution, which else (left to the support of daily life in its realities) would languish for want of sufficient illustration. What is meant, for instance, by *poetic justice?*—It does not mean a justice that differs by its object from the ordinary justice of human jurisprudence; for then it must be confessedly a very bad kind of justice; but it means a justice that differs from common forensic justice by the degree in which it *attains* its object, a justice that is more omnipotent over its own ends, as dealing—not with the refractory elements of earthly life, but with the elements of its own creation, and with materials flexible to its own purest preconceptions. It is certain that, were it not for the Literature of Power, these ideals would often remain amongst us as mere arid notional forms; whereas, by the creative forces of man put forth in literature, they gain a vernal life of restoration, and germinate into vital activities. The commonest novel, by moving in alliance with human fears and hopes, with human instincts of wrong and right, sustains and quickens those affections. Calling them into action, it rescues them from torpor. And hence the pre-eminency over all authors that merely *teach* of the meanest that *moves*, or that teaches, if at all, indirectly *by* moving. The very highest work that has ever existed in the Literature of Knowledge is but a *provisional* work: a book upon trial and sufferance, and *quamdiu bene se gesserit*.[8] Let its teaching be

5. In Genesis 28:12 Jacob dreams of a ladder to heaven with angels going up and down it.
6. In I Kings 3:12 God says to Solomon, "I have given thee . . . an understanding heart."
7. Epic poetry.
8. "So long as it conducts itself well."

even partially revised, let it be but expanded—nay, even let its teaching be but placed in a better order—and instantly it is superseded. Whereas the feeblest works in the Literature of Power, surviving at all, survive as finished and unalterable amongst men. For instance, the *Principia* of Sir Issac Newton was a book *militant* on earth from the first. In all stages of its progress it would have to fight for its existence: first, as regards absolute truth; secondly, when that combat was over, as regards its form or mode of presenting the truth. And as soon as a Laplace,[9] or anybody else, builds higher upon the foundations laid by this book, effectually he throws it out of the sunshine into decay and darkness; by weapons won from this book he superannuates and destroys this book, so that soon the name of Newton remains as a mere *nominis umbra*,[10] but his book, as a living power, has transmigrated into other forms. Now, on the contrary, the *Iliad,* the *Prometheus* of Aeschylus, the *Othello* or *King Lear,* the *Hamlet* or *Macbeth,* and the *Paradise Lost,* are not militant, but triumphant for ever as long as the languages exist in which they speak or can be taught to speak. They never *can* transmigrate into new incarnations. To reproduce *these* in new forms, or variations, even if in some things they should be improved, would be to plagiarize. A good steam-engine is properly superseded by a better. But one lovely pastoral valley is not superseded by another, nor a statue of Praxiteles [11] by a statue of Michael Angelo.[12] These things are separated not by imparity, but by disparity. They are not thought of as unequal under the same standard, but as different in *kind*, and, if otherwise equal, as equal under a different standard. Human works of immortal beauty and works of nature in one respect stand on the same footing: they never absolutely repeat each other, never approach so near as not to differ; and they differ not as better and worse, or simply by more and less: they differ by undecipherable and incommunicable differences, that cannot be caught by mimicries, that cannot be reflected in the mirror of copies, that cannot become ponderable in the scales of vulgar comparison.

All works in this class, as opposed to those in the Literature of Knowledge, first, work by far deeper agencies, and, secondly, are more permanent; in the strictest sense they are κτήματα ἐς ἀεί:[13] and what evil they do, or what good they do, is commensurate with the national language, sometimes long after the nation has departed. At this hour, five hundred years since their creation, the tales of Chaucer, never equalled on this earth for their tenderness, and for life of picturesqueness, are read familiarly by many in the charming language of their natal day, and by others in the modernizations of Dryden, of Pope, and of Wordsworth. . . .

All the Literature of Knowledge builds only ground-nests, that are swept away by floods, or confounded by the plough; but the Literature of Power builds nests in aerial altitudes of temples sacred from violation, or of forests inaccessible to fraud. *This* is a great prerogative of the *power* literature; and it is a greater which lies in the mode of its influence. The *knowledge* literature, like the

9. The great French mathematician and astronomer (1749–1827). Among his many notable achievements is the hypothesis of the nebular origin of the solar system.
10. "Shadow of a name." It is of course not true that this is what Newton's name has become.
11. Greek sculptor of the 4th century B.C.
12. Italian sculptor, painter, architect, and poet (1475–1574).
13. "Eternal possessions."

fashion of this world, passeth away. An encyclopaedia is its abstract; and, in this respect, it may be taken for its speaking symbol—that before one generation has passed an encyclopaedia is superannuated; for it speaks through the dead memory and unimpassioned understanding, which have not the repose of higher faculties, but are continually enlarging and varying their phylacteries.[14] But all literature properly so called—literature κατ' ἐξοχην[15]—for the very same reason that it is so much more durable than the Literature of Knowledge, is (and by the very same proportion it is) more intense and electrically searching in its impressions. The directions in which the tragedy of this planet has trained our human feelings to play, and the combinations into which the poetry of this planet has thrown our human passions of love and hatred, of admiration and contempt, exercise a power for bad or good over human life that cannot be contemplated, when stretching through many generations, without a sentiment allied to awe. And of this let every one be assured—that he owes to the impassioned books which he has read many a thousand more of emotions than he can consciously trace back to them. Dim by their origination, these emotions yet arise in him, and mould him through life, like forgotten incidents of his childhood.

1848   1848

PERCY BYSSHE SHELLEY
1792–1822

A Defence of Poetry

One of the salient characteristics of Romantic thought is the largeness of the claims it made for the power and beneficence of art and, most especially, of poetry. As religion lost its authority with the educated classes, poetry came increasingly to be seen as the basis and guarantor of the spiritual and moral life. This tendency is exemplified by Wordsworth's Preface to the second edition of *Lyrical Ballads* (see above), which assigns to poetry a function more decisive and far-reaching than had ever before been conceived. Yet bold as are the assertions of the power of poetry which the Preface makes, they fall short of those advanced by Shelley in the impassioned eloquence of *A Defence of Poetry*.

The occasion of Shelley's essay was the publication in 1821 of Thomas Love Peacock's *The Four Ages of Poetry*. Peacock was one of Shelley's warmest and most devoted friends despite—or because of—the dissimilarity of the two men in almost every point of temperament. Although manifestly attracted by the ideas and emotions of the Romanticists, Peacock loved the way of the conventional world and set high store by the worldly virtues of amenity, moderation, and good sense. His ambivalence in this regard is perhaps best exemplified by the good nature which informs the caricature he drew of Shelley in *Nightmare Abbey*, one of the five delightful satirical novels he wrote between 1816 and 1861. The same division of mind is to be seen in

---

14. Phylacteries are small leather boxes containing strips of parchment on which are written passages in Hebrew from the books of Deuteronomy and Exodus; orthodox Jewish men strap one to the forehead, the other to the left arm, during morning prayers.
15. "Pre-eminently."

The Four Ages of Poetry. The avowed intention of the essay is to demonstrate that poetry, of its nature, must inevitably decline with the progress of civilization and that in an age of rationality, such as the nineteenth century, it can only be an anachronism which is both barbaric and absurd. Peacock was dealing with a question which was seriously entertained by many people at the time, as it still is—since poetry takes its rise in the modes of thought which are characteristic of relatively primitive societies, must not the development of more rational and practical modes of thought make poetry an unnatural and inappropriate form of expression? That the answer to the question might be affirmative was suggested by the theory and practice of contemporary poets themselves, by Wordsworth, for example, who in his Preface and in many of his poems seeks to reinstitute primitive modes of thought and the language consonant with them. Yet although Peacock is exploiting an entirely serious idea, he does not do so with entire seriousness. By one device or another, by the jocosity of his tone or by the extravagance of his formulations, he signals that his argument is not to be taken literally, that his assault upon poetry is made chiefly as a spoof. He does indeed mean to mock what he takes to be the extravagant claims for poetry made by the Romanticists, but when he frames his denunciation of their absurdity and vanity, his intention is not to give comfort to the Philistine enemies of poetry but, rather, to tease the poets themselves, taking license to do so from his sense of familial connection with them.

And Shelley must surely have understood something of the humorous character of the essay, for he gave no sign of being shocked or grieved by Peacock's profane handling of the thing that in all the world he himself held most sacred. At the same time, however, he took with quite ultimate seriousness such part of Peacock's argument as might be thought substantive and replied to it in a polemic which undertook to say that poetry, so far from being deteriorated and made powerless by the advance of civilization, is actually the decisive and even the sole agent of civilization.

Deeply moving as the essay unquestionably is, it cannot be of material help to us when we try to think about poetry with some degree of particularity. This is so because, as Shelley uses the word, "poetry" does not denote, as it commonly does, the *corpus* of all known poems, or of all known poems that are to be admired, or of these together with all poems yet to be written and admired. For Shelley, "poetry" is a concept or an entity which has its existence apart from and anterior to any actual poem; it may be, although it need not be, embodied in an actual poem, and it may also be embodied in any human creation whatsoever which is beneficent. Shelley is explicit in saying that a poet is anyone who contributes to civilization—poets are not only those who make actual poems, and not only the practitioners of the arts of music, architecture, painting, and sculpture, but also "the institutors of laws, and the founders of civil society and the inventors of the arts of life, and the teachers." Poetry is not a mode of expression but that which is to be expressed—it is possible for Shelley to speak of drama as being admirable "so long as it continues to express poetry." And that which is to be expressed, in whatever human activity, is the harmonious and eternal order of life, the Beauty and Truth which, in Platonic fashion, are conceived to be pre-existent to their expression.

Shelley does recognize that poetry may be spoken of not only in what he calls a "universal sense" but also in what he calls a "restricted sense." Yet when he uses the word in this latter sense and speaks of actual poems, his interest is likely to be confined to those, such as Homer's, Dante's, Milton's, and Shakespeare's, which he understands to be pointing toward that supernal reality which is poetry in the "universal sense." Of actual poems which have a reference less transcendent he takes no account.

One statement that Shelley makes in A Defence of Poetry deserves particular consideration, that in which he speaks in quite specific terms of the part that is played in the moral life by the faculty of imagination, which he represents as a form of love. "The great secret of morals," he says, "is love; or a going out of our own nature, and an identification of ourselves with the beautiful which exists in thought, action, or person, not our own. A man to be greatly good, must imagine intensely and comprehensively; he must put himself in the place of another and of many others; the pains and pleasures of his species must become his own. The great instrument of moral good is the imagination; and poetry [in the "restricted sense"] administers to the effect by acting on the cause." This formulates beautifully and precisely the rationale of the nineteenth-century faith in the moral influence of art, which still has power over us in the face of all the dubieties that have grown up around it.

From A Defence of Poetry

According to one mode of regarding those two classes of mental action, which are called reason and imagination, the former may be considered as mind contemplating the relations borne by one thought to another, however produced; and the latter, as mind acting upon those thoughts so as to colour them with its own light, and composing from them, as from elements, other thoughts, each containing within itself the principle of its own integrity. The one [1] is the τὸ ποιεῖν,[2] or the principle of synthesis, and has for its objects those forms which are common to universal nature and existence itself; the other is the τὸ λογιζειν,[3] or principle of analysis, and its action regards the relations of things, simply as relations; considering thoughts, not in their integral unity, but as the algebraical representations which conduct to certain general results. Reason is the enumeration of quantities already known; imagination is the perception of the value of those quantities, both separately and as a whole. Reason respects the differences, and imagination the similitudes of things. Reason is to imagination as the instrument to the agent, as the body to the spirit, as the shadow to the substance.

Poetry, in a general sense, may be defined to be 'the expression of the imagination': and poetry is connate [4] with the origin of man. . . .

In the youth of the world, men dance and sing and imitate natural objects, observing [5] in these actions, as in all others, a certain rhythm or order. And, although all men observe a similar, they observe not the same order, in the motions of the dance, in the melody of the song, in the combinations of lan-

1. Shelley inverts the order in which, in the preceding sentence, he has mentioned and described the two classes of mental action. "The one" is imagination, "the other" is reason.
2. "Making."
3. "Reasoning."
4. Born at the same time.
5. Not in the sense of "perceive" but in the sense of "adhere to" or "comply with," e.g. "observe the law."

guage, in the series of their imitations of natural objects. For there is a certain order or rhythm belonging to each of these classes of mimetic representation, from which the hearer and the spectator receive an intenser and purer pleasure than from any other: the sense of an approximation to this order has been called taste [6] by modern writers. Every man in the infancy of art, observes an order which approximates more or less closely to that from which his highest delight results: but the diversity is not sufficiently marked, as that its gradations should be sensible, except in those instances where the predominance of this faculty of approximation to the beautiful (for so we may be permitted to name the relation betwen this highest pleasure and its cause) is very great. Those in whom it [7] exists in excess are poets, in the most universal sense of the word; and the pleasure resulting from the manner in which they express the influence of society or nature upon their own minds, communicates itself to others, and gathers a sort of re-duplication from that community. Their language is vitally metaphorical; [8] that is, it marks the before unapprehended relations of things and perpetuates their apprehension, until the words which represent them, become, through time, signs for portions or classes of thoughts instead of pictures of integral thoughts; and then if no new poets should arise to create afresh the associations which have been thus disorganized, language will be dead to all the nobler purposes of human intercourse. These similitudes or relations are finely said by Lord Bacon to be 'the same footsteps of nature impressed' upon the various subjects of the world' [9]—and he considers the faculty which perceives them as the storehouse of axioms common to all knowledge. In the infancy of society every author is necessarily a poet, because language itself is poetry; and to be a poet is to apprehend the true and the beautiful, in a word, the good which exists in the relation, subsisting, first between existence and perception, and secondly between perception and expression. Every original language near to its source is in itself the chaos of a cyclic poem: [10] the copiousness of lexicography [11] and the distinctions of grammar are the works of a later age, and are merely the catalogue and the form of the creations of poetry.

But poets, or those who imagine and express this indestructible order, are not only the authors of language and of music, of the dance and architecture,

6. Although it no longer figures much in aesthetic theory, the concept of "taste," the faculty by which the virtues of a work of art are intuitively perceived and accurately judged, was of great moment in the critical thought of the 18th century and continued to have force through the 19th. Shelley speaks of it here as the faculty which responds to instances of archetypal beauty.

7. That is, "this faculty of approximation to the beautiful."

8. Shelley touches here upon the formation of abstract words from concrete ones and the tendency to forget their concrete origin. For example, "spirit" and "inspiration" derive from the Latin word *spiritus,* meaning breath, the breath of a god; the poet who asks for inspiration—see Shelley's "Ode to the West Wind"—asks that the breath of the god enter into him and give him its powers.

9. *"De Augment. Scient.* Cap. 1, lib. iii" (Shelley). The reference is to *De Augmentis Scientiarum* (Concerning the Enlargement of the Sciences) which has an expanded version of *The Advancement of Learning.*

10. A group of poems dealing with the same hero or event, e.g. the Arthurian cycle, the Trojan cycle.

11. Dictionary-making.

and statuary, and painting; they are the institutors of laws, and the founders of civil society, and the inventors of the arts of life, and the teachers, who draw into a certain propinquity with the beautiful and the true, that partial apprehension of the agencies of the invisible world which is called religion.[12] Hence all original religions are allegorical, or susceptible of allegory, and, like Janus,[13] have a double face of false and true. Poets, according to the circumstances of the age and nation in which they appeared, were called, in the earlier epochs of the world, legislators, or prophets: [14] a poet essentially comprises and unites both these characters. For he not only beholds intensely the present as it is, and discovers those laws according to which present things ought to be ordered, but he beholds the future in the present, and his thoughts are the germs of the flower and the fruit of latest time. Not that I assert poets to be prophets in the gross sense of the word, or that they can foretell the form as surely as they foreknow the spirit of events: such is the pretence of superstition, which would make poetry an attribute of prophecy, rather than prophecy an attribute of poetry. A poet participates in the eternal, the infinite, and the one; as far as relates to his conceptions, time and place and number are not. The grammatical forms which express the moods of time, and the difference of persons, and the distinction of place, are convertible with respect to the highest poetry without injuring it as poetry; and the choruses of Aeschylus, and the book of Job, and Dante's Paradise, would afford, more than any other writings, examples of this fact, if the limits of this essay did not forbid citation. The creations of sculpture, painting, and music, are illustrations still more decisive.

. . .

A poem is the image of life expressed in its eternal truth. There is this difference between a story [15] and a poem, that a story is a catalogue of detached facts, which have no other bond of connexion than time, place, circumstance, cause and effect; the other is the creation of actions according to the unchangeable forms of human nature, as existing in the mind of the creator, which is itself the image of all other minds. The one is partial, and applies only to a definite period of time, and a certain combination of events which can never again recur; the other is universal, and contains within itself the germ of a relation to whatever motives or actions have place in the possible varieties of human nature. Time, which destroys the beauty and the use of the story of particular facts, stripped of the poetry which should invest them, augments that of poetry, and for ever develops new and wonderful applications of the eternal truth which it contains. Hence epitomes [16] have been called the moths of just history; they eat out the poetry of it. The story of

12. Although Shelley had a strong animus against established religion, his belief in an invisible world and in the power of its agencies was intensely held.
13. A Roman god of gates and doorways, represented as having two faces looking in opposite directions. January is named for him.
14. Shelley is referring to the double meaning of the Latin word *vates,* both "prophet" and "poet."
15. As his definition of it makes plain, Shelley is using the word "story" in a curiously limited sense.
16. Abstracts or synopses.

particular facts is as a mirror which obscures and distorts that which should be beautiful: poetry is a mirror which makes beautiful that which is distorted.

The parts of a composition may be poetical, without the composition as a whole being a poem. A single sentence may be considered as a whole, though it be found in a series of unassimilated portions; a single word even may be a spark of inextinguishable thought. And thus all the great historians, Herodotus, Plutarch, Livy, were poets; and although the plan of these writers, espectially that of Livy, restrained them from developing this faculty in its highest degree, they make copious and ample amends for their subjection, by filling all the interstices of their subject with living images.

Having determined what is poetry, and who are poets, let us proceed to estimate its effects upon society.

Poetry is ever accompanied with pleasure: all spirits on which it falls open themselves to receive the wisdom which is mingled with its delight. In the infancy of the world, neither poets themselves nor their auditors are fully aware of the excellence of poetry: for it acts in a divine and unapprehended manner, beyond and above consciousness; and it is reserved for future generations to contemplate and measure the mighty cause and effect in all the strength and splendour of their union. Even in modern times, no living poet ever arrived at the fullness of his fame; the jury which sits in judgment upon a poet, belonging as he does to all time, must be composed of his peers: it must be empanelled by Time from the selectest of the wise of many generations. A Poet is a nightingale, who sits in darkness and sings to cheer its own solitude with sweet sounds; his auditors are as men entranced by the melody of an unseen musician, who feel that they are moved and softened, yet know not whence or why. The poems of Homer and his contemporaries were the delight of infant Greece; they were the elements of that social system which is the column upon which all succeeding civilization has reposed. Homer embodied the ideal perfection of his age in human character; nor can we doubt that those who read his verses were awakened to an ambition of becoming like to Achilles, Hector, and Ulysses: the truth and beauty of friendship, patriotism, and persevering devotion to an object,[17] were unveiled to the depths in these immortal creations: the sentiments of the auditors must have been refined and enlarged by a sympathy with such great and lovely impersonations, until from admiring they imitated, and from imitation they identified themselves with the objects of their admiration. Nor let it be objected, that these characters are remote from moral perfection, and that they can by no means be considered as edifying patterns for general imitation. Every epoch, under names more or less specious, has deified its peculiar errors; revenge is the naked idol of the worship of a semi-barbarous age; and self-deceit is the veiled image of unknown evil, before which luxury and satiety lie prostrate. But a poet considers the vices of his contemporaries as the temporary dress in which his creations must be arrayed, and which cover without concealing the eternal proportions of their beauty. An epic or dramatic personage is understood to wear them around his soul, as he may the ancient armour or the modern uniform around his body; whilst it is

17. Achilles' friendship with Patroclus, Hector's unremitting concern for Troy, Ulysses' intention to return to his home and family.

easy to conceive a dress more graceful than either. The beauty of the internal nature cannot be so far concealed by its accidental vesture, but that the spirit of its form shall communicate itself to the very disguise, and indicate the shape it hides from the manner in which it is worn. A majestic form and graceful motions will express themselves through the most barbarous and tasteless costume. Few poets of the highest class have chosen to exhibit the beauty of their conceptions in its naked truth and splendour; and it is doubtful whether the alloy of costume, habit, etc., be not necessary to temper this planetary music for mortal ears.

The whole objection, however, of the immorality of poetry [18] rests upon a misconception of the manner in which poetry acts to produce the moral improvement of man. Ethical science [19] arranges the elements which poetry has created, and propounds schemes and proposes examples of civil and domestic life: nor is it for want of admirable doctrines that men hate, and despise, and censure, and deceive, and subjugate one another. But poetry acts in another and diviner manner. It awakens and enlarges the mind itself by rendering it the receptacle of a thousand unapprehended combinations of thought. Poetry lifts the veil from the hidden beauty of the world, and makes familiar objects be as if they were not familiar; it reproduces [20] all that it represents, and the impersonations clothed in its Elysian [21] lights stand thenceforward in the minds of those who have once contemplated them, as memorials of that gentle and exalted content [22] which extends itself over all thoughts and actions with which it coexists. The great secret of morals is love; or a going out of our own nature, and an identification of ourselves with the beautiful which exists in thought, action, or person, not our own. A man, to be greatly good, must imagine intensely and comprehensively; he must put himself in the place of another and of many others; the pains and pleasures of his species must become his own.[23] The great instrument of moral good is the imagination; and poetry administers to the effect by acting upon the cause. Poetry enlarges the circumference of the imagination by replenishing it with thoughts of ever new delight, which have the power of attracting and assimilating to their own nature all other thoughts, and which form new intervals and interstices whose void for ever craves fresh food. Poetry strengthens that faculty which is the organ of the moral nature of man, in the same manner as exercise strengthens a limb. A poet therefore would do ill to embody his own conceptions of right and wrong, which are usually those of his place and time, in his poetical creations, which participate in neither. By this assumption of the inferior office of interpreting the effect, in which perhaps after all he might acquit himself but

18. The reference is to Plato's *Republic* which proposes that poets be debarred from the perfect state because of the "immorality" that their representations of human conduct are said to foster.

19. That is, moral philosophy. The word "science" did not yet have its present limited meaning.

20. In the sense of "to bring again into material existence," to create or form anew.

21. Elysium is the abode of the blessed after death.

22. With the accent on the second syllable: although we still use the word as an adjective ("Are you content?"), as a noun it has become obsolete, replaced by "contentment."

23. See, in De Quincey's essay *On the Knocking at the Gate in "Macbeth,"* his footnote (note 7) on the word "sympathy."

imperfectly, he would resign the glory in a participation in the cause. There was little danger that Homer, or any of the eternal poets, should have so far misunderstood themselves as to have abdicated this throne of their widest dominion. Those in whom the poetical faculty, though great, is less intense, as Euripides, Lucan, Tasso, Spenser, have frequently affected a moral aim,[24] and the effect of their poetry is diminished in exact proportion to the degree in which they compel us to advert to this purpose.

[A passage is omitted in which Shelley speaks of the rise of the drama in Athens and of drama in general.]

. . . The author of the *Four Ages of Poetry* has prudently omitted to dispute on the effect of the drama upon life and manners. For, if I know the Knight by the device [25] of his shield, I have only to inscribe Philoctetes or Agamemnon or Othello [26] upon mine to put to flight the giant sophisms which have enchanted him, as the mirror of intolerable light though on the arm of one of the weakest of the Paladines [27] could blind and scatter whole armies of necromancers and pagans. The connexion of scenic exhibitions with the improvement or corruption of the manners of men, has been universally recognized: in other words, the presence or absence of poetry in its most perfect and universal form, has been found to be connected with good and evil in conduct and habit. The corruption which has been imputed to the drama as an effect,[28] begins, when the poetry employed in its constitution ends: I appeal to the history of manners [29] whether the gradations of the growth of the one and the decline of the other have not corresponded with an exactness equal to any other example of moral cause and effect.

The drama at Athens, or wheresoever else it may have approached to its perfection, coexisted with the moral and intellectual greatness of the age. The tragedies of the Athenian poets are as mirrors in which the spectator beholds himself, under a thin disguise of circumstance, stripped of all but that ideal perfection and energy which every one feels to be the internal type of all that he loves, admires, and would become. The imagination is enlarged by a sympathy with pains and passions so mighty, that they distend in their conception the capacity of that by which they are conceived; the good affections are strengthened by pity, indignation, terror and sorrow; [30] and an exalted

24. Shelley's point is that an explicit and didactic morality diminishes the possible moral influence of a work by limiting the activity of the reader's imagination. See Keats's letter on "Negative Capability."

25. A symbol or motto on the shield of a knight to identify him.

26. Respectively, the heroes of Sophocles' *Philoctetes,* of Aeschylus' *Agamemnon,* and of Shakespeare's *Othello.*

27. In the cycle of the Charlemagne legends, the twelve peers who accompanied the king; by extension, a heroic champion, a paragon of chivalry.

28. Shelley doubtless has chiefly in mind the attitude of the Puritans to the theater, of which a late expression was Jeremy Collier's *Short View of the Immorality and Profaneness of the English Stage* (1698), but he may also be thinking of the *Letter to M. d'Alembert on the Theatre* (1758), the work in which Rousseau, whom Shelley greatly admired, imputed to the theater a bad influence on morality.

29. In the sense not of etiquette but of the prevailing mode of conduct of a society.

30. Aristotle said in his *Poetics* that tragedy arouses in the spectator the emotions of pity and terror.

calm [31] is prolonged from the satiety of this high exercise of them into the tumult of familiar life: even crime is disarmed of half its horror and all its contagion by being represented as the fatal consequence of the unfathomable agencies of nature; error is thus divested of its wilfulness; men can no longer cherish it as the creation of their choice. In a drama of the highest order there is little food for censure or hatred; it teaches rather self-knowledge and self-respect. Neither the eye nor the mind can see itself, unless reflected upon that which it resembles. The drama, so long as it continues to express poetry,[32] is as a prismatic and many-sided mirror, which collects the brightest rays of human nature and divides and reproduces them from the simplicity of these elementary forms, and touches them with majesty and beauty, and multiplies all that it reflects, and endows it with the power of propagating its like wherever it may fall.

But in periods of the decay of social life, the drama sympathizes with that decay. Tragedy becomes a cold imitation of the form of the great masterpieces of antiquity, divested of all harmonious accompaniment of the kindred arts; and often the very form misunderstood, or a weak attempt to teach certain doctrines, which the writer considers as moral truths; and which are usually no more than specious flatteries of some gross vice or weakness, with which the author, in common with his auditors, are infected. Hence what has been called the classical and domestic drama. Addison's *Cato* is a specimen of the one; [33] and would it were not superfluous to cite examples of the other! [34] To such purposes poetry cannot be made subservient. Poetry is a sword of lightning, ever unsheathed, which consumes the scabbard that would contain it. And thus we observe that all dramatic writings of this nature are unimaginative in a singular degree; they affect sentiment and passion, which, divested of imagination, are other names for caprice and appetite. The period in our own history of the grossest degradation of the drama is the reign of Charles II, when all forms in which poetry had been accustomed to be expressed became hymns to the triumph of kingly power over liberty and virtue. Milton stood alone illuminating an age unworthy of him. At such periods the calculating principle pervades all the forms of dramatic exhibition, and poetry ceases to be expressed upon them. Comedy loses its ideal universality: wit succeeds to humour; we laugh from self complacency and triumph, instead of pleasure; malignity, sarcasm and contempt, succeed to sympathetic merriment; we hardly laugh, but we smile.[35] Obscenity, which is ever blasphemy against the divine beauty in life, becomes, from the very veil which it assumes, more active if less disgusting: it is a monster for which the corruption of society for ever brings forth new food, which it devours in secret.

31. By this phrase Shelley refers to Aristotle's idea of *catharsis*, the condition of mind that tragedy ideally induces by arousing pity and terror, which, after being experienced, leave the spectator in a state of equilibrium.
32. Here Shelley speaks of poetry not as an activity but as achieved knowledge.
33. Produced in 1713, *Cato* was a great popular success but has become the type of the "correct" and dull classical tragedy.
34. The kind of drama that developed early in the 18th century in reaction to Restoration comedy; written from a middle-class point of view, it set store by a simple prudential morality.
35. For a more favorable view of Restoration comedy, see Lamb's essay *On the Artificial Comedy of the Last Century.*

The drama being that form under which a greater number of modes of expression of poetry are susceptible of being combined than any other, the connexion of poetry and social good is more observable in the drama than in whatever other form. And it is indisputable that the highest perfection of human society has ever corresponded with the highest dramatic excellence; and that the corruption or the extinction of the drama in a nation where it has once flourished, is a mark of a corruption of manners, and an extinction of the energies which sustain the soul of social life. But, as Machiavelli says of political institutions, that life may be preserved and renewed, if men should arise capable of bringing back the drama to its principles.[36] And this is true with respect to poetry in its most extended sense; all language institution and form, require not only to be produced but to be sustained: the office and character of a poet participates in the divine nature as regards providence, no less than as regards creation.

[A passage is omitted in which Shelley takes a general survey of the course of literature up to Dante.]

The poetry of Dante may be considered as the bridge thrown over the stream of time, which unites the modern and ancient world. The distorted notions of invisible things which Dante and his rival Milton have idealized, are merely the mask and the mantle in which these great poets walk through eternity enveloped and disguised. It is a difficult question to determine how far they were conscious of the distinction which must have subsisted in their minds between their own creeds and that of the people. Dante at least appears to wish to mark the full extent of it by placing Riphaeus,[37] whom Virgil calls *justissimus unus*, in Paradise, and observing a most heretical caprice in his distribution of rewards and punishments. And Milton's poem contains within itself a philosophical refutation of that system, of which, by a strange and natural antithesis, it has been a chief popular support. Nothing can exceed the energy and magnificence of the character of Satan as expressed in *Paradise Lost*.[38] It is a mistake to suppose that he could ever have been intended for the popular personification of evil. Implacable hate, patient cunning and a sleepless refinement of device to inflict the extremest anguish on an enemy, these things are evil; and, although venial in a slave, are not to be forgiven in a tyrant; although redeemed by much that ennobles his defeat in one subdued, are marked by all that dishonours his conquest in the victor. Milton's Devil as a moral being is as far superior to his God, as one who perseveres in some

36. All the great Romantic writers were intensely interested in the theater, and hoped for the development of a drama comparable to that of the Elizabethan Age. All the poets among them wrote for the stage, usually without either popular or literary success— although Shelley's own tragedy, *The Cenci*, is in many respects a remarkable work.
37. Riphaeus is the warrior Virgil calls most just among the Trojans, *Aeneid* II. 426.
38. See Blake's "Note" in *The Marriage of Heaven and Hell*: "The reason Milton wrote in fetters when he wrote of Angels and God, and at liberty when of devils and Hell, is because he was a true poet, and of the devil's party without knowing it." Satan as the archetype of the heroic rebel was of great interest in the Romantic period. In the Preface to *Prometheus Unbound*, Shelley neutralizes the view of Satan he expresses in *The Defence of Poetry*. "The character of Satan," he says, "engenders in the mind a pernicious casuistry which leads us to weigh his faults with his wrongs, and to excuse the former because the latter exceed all measure." He offers Prometheus as a preferable—a "more poetical"—example of the heroic rebel.

purpose which he has conceived to be excellent in spite of adversity and torture, is to one who in the cold security of undoubted triumph inflicts the most horrible revenge upon his enemy, not from any mistaken notion of inducing him to repent of a perseverance in enmity, but with the alleged design of exasperating him to deserve new torments.[39] Milton has so far violated the popular creed (if this shall be judged to be a violation) as to have alleged no superiority of moral virtue to his God over his Devil. And this bold neglect of a direct moral purpose is the most decisive proof of the supremacy of Milton's genius. He mingled as it were the elements of human nature as colours upon a single pallet, and arranged them in the composition of his great picture according to the laws of epic truth; that is, according to the laws of that principle by which a series of actions of the external universe and of intelligent and ethical beings is calculated to excite the sympathy of succeeding generations of mankind. The *Divina Commedia* and *Paradise Lost* have conferred upon modern mythology a systematic form; and when change and time shall have added one more superstition to the mass of those which have arisen and decayed upon the earth, commentators will be learnedly employed in elucidating the religion of ancestral Europe, only not utterly forgotten because it will have been stamped with the eternity of genius.

Homer was the first and Dante the second epic poet: that is, the second poet, the series of whose creations bore a defined and intelligible relation to the knowledge and sentiment and religion and political conditions of the age in which he lived, and of the ages which followed it: developing itself in correspondence with their development. For Lucretius had limed the wings of his swift spirit in the dregs of the sensible world; [40] and Virgil, with a modesty which ill became his genius, had affected the fame of an imitator, even whilst he created anew all that he copied; [41] and none among the flock of Mock-birds, though their notes were sweet, Apollonius Rhodius, Quintus Calaber Smyrnetheus, Nonnus, Lucan, Statius, or Claudian,[42] have sought even to fulfil a single condition of epic truth. Milton was the third epic poet. For if the title of epic in its highest sense be refused to the *Aeneid*, still less can it be conceded to the *Orlando Furioso*,[43] the *Gerusalemme Liberata*,[44] the *Lusiad*,[45] or the *Faerie Queene*.

39. In *Paradise Lost*. Perhaps the sexual torments of the rebel angels are implied.
40. Lime is a sticky substance made from holly bark, smeared on trees to catch birds. Lucretius, the Roman philosophical poet (94?–55 B.C.), in his long poem *De Rerum Natura* (On the Nature of Things), undertook to liberate mankind from religious superstition and the fear of death; to this end he reasoned that all things exist by their own mechanical laws and are not in the control of supernatural powers, good or bad. Shelley, while admiring him, would naturally be distressed by his denial of spirit and also by his famous attack on love.
41. Virgil based the *Aeneid* on elements of both the *Iliad* and the *Odyssey*.
42. Greek and Roman poets from the 3rd century B.C. to the 4th century A.D. who wrote long narrative poems.
43. "Orlando Mad," a very popular epic poem by Lodovico Ariosto (1474–1533), first published in 1516 and in an expanded version in 1532.
44. "Jerusalem Delivered," an epic poem by Torquato Tasso (1581), no less popular than *Orlando Furioso*.
45. Usually in the plural *The Lusiads*, or *Lusiadas* (1572), an epic poem by Luis de Camoëns. It relates the great deeds of Lusians—Portuguese—of all ages but chiefly those of the explorer Vasco da Gama.

Dante and Milton were both deeply penetrated with the ancient religion of the civilized world; and its spirit exists in their poetry probably in the same proportion as its forms survived in the unreformed worship of modern Europe. The one preceded and the other followed the Reformation at almost equal intervals. Dante was the first religious reformer, and Luther surpassed him rather in the rudeness and acrimony, than in the boldness of his censures of papal usurpation. Dante was the first awakener of entranced Europe; he created a language, in itself music and persuasion, out of a chaos of inharmonious barbarisms. He was the congregator of those great spirits who presided over the resurrection of learning; the Lucifer of that starry flock which in the thirteenth century shone forth from republican Italy, as from a heaven, into the darkness of the benighted world. His very words are instinct with spirit; each is as a spark, a burning atom of inextinguishable thought; and many yet lie covered in the ashes of their birth, and pregnant with a lightning which has yet found no conductor. All high poetry is infinite; it is as the first acorn, which contained all oaks potentially. Veil after veil may be undrawn, and the inmost naked beauty of the meaning never exposed. A great poem is a fountain forever overflowing with the waters of wisdom and delight; and after one person and one age has exhausted all its divine effluence which their peculiar relations enable them to share, another and yet another succeeds, and new relations are ever developed, the source of an unforeseen and an unconceived delight.

The age immediately succeeding to that of Dante, Petrarch,[46] and Boccaccio,[47] was characterized by a revival of painting, sculpture, music, and architecture. Chaucer caught the sacred inspiration, and the superstructure of English literature is based upon the materials of Italian invention.

But let us not be betrayed from a defence into a critical history of poetry and its influence on society. Be it enough to have pointed out the effects of poets, in the large and true sense of the word, upon their own and all succeeding times, and to revert to the partial instances cited as illustrations of an opinion the reverse of that attempted to be established by the author of *The Four Ages of Poetry*.

But poets have been challenged to resign the civic crown to reasoners and mechanists on another plea. It is admitted that the exercise of the imagination is most delightful, but it is alleged, that that of reason is more useful. Let us examine as the grounds of this distinction, what is here meant by utility. Pleasure or good, in a general sense, is that which the consciousness of a sensitive and intelligent being seeks, and in which, when found, it acquiesces. There are two modes or degrees of pleasure, one durable, universal and permanent; the other transitory and particular. Utility may either express the means of producing the former or the latter. In the former sense, whatever strengthens and purifies the affections, enlarges the imagination, and adds spirit to sense, is useful. But the meaning in which the author of *The Four Ages of Poetry* seems to have employed the word utility is the narrower one

46. Francesco Petrarca (1304–74), Italian poet and scholar, a moving spirit of the Renaissance.
47. Giovanni Boccaccio (1313?–75), a close friend of Petrarch, and, like him, an influential humanist. The author of many works of scholarship and literature, he is now remembered chiefly for the tales of his *Decameron*.

of banishing the importunity of the wants of our animal nature, the surrounding men with security of life, the dispersing the grosser delusions of superstition, and the conciliating such a degree of mutual forbearance among men as
may consist with the motives of personal advantage.[48]

Undoubtedly the promoters of utility, in this limited sense, have their
appointed office in society. They follow the footsteps of poets, and copy the
sketches of their creations into the book of common life. They make space, and
give time. Their exertions are of the highest value, so long as they confine
their administration of the concerns of the inferior powers of our nature within
the limits due to the superior ones. But whilst the sceptic destroys gross superstitions, let him spare to deface, as some of the French writers [49] have defaced,
the eternal truths charactered upon the imaginations of men. Whilst the
mechanist abridges, and the political economist combines, labour, let them
beware that their speculations, for want of correspondence with those first
principles which belong to the imagination, do not tend, as they have in modern
England, to exasperate at once the extremes of luxury and want. They have
exemplified the saying, 'To him that hath, more shall be given; and from him
that hath not, the little that he hath shall be taken away.' [50] The rich have
become richer, and the poor have become poorer; and the vessel of the state
is driven between the Scylla and Charybdis [51] of anarchy and despotism. Such
are the effects which must ever flow from an unmitigated exercise of the calculating faculty.

It is difficult to define pleasure in its highest sense; the definition involving
a number of apparent paradoxes. For, from an inexplicable defect of harmony
in the constitution of human nature, the pain of the inferior is frequently connected with the pleasures of the superior portions of our being. Sorrow, terror,
anguish, despair itself, are often the chosen expressions of an approximation
to the highest good. Our sympathy in tragic fiction depends on this principle;
tragedy delights by affording a shadow of the pleasure which exists in pain.[52]
This is the source also of the melancholy which is inseparable from the sweetest
melody. The pleasure that is in sorrow is sweeter than the pleasure of pleasure
itself. And hence the saying, 'It is better to go to the house of mourning, than
to the house of mirth.' [53] Not that this highest species of pleasure is necessarily
linked with pain. The delight of love and friendship, the ecstasy of the admiration of nature, the joy of the perception and still more of the creation of
poetry is often wholly unalloyed.

The production and assurance of pleasure in this highest sense is true utility.
Those who produce and preserve this pleasure are poets or poetical philosophers.

48. At least in its early development, Utilitarianism defended competition and "free
enterprise." J.S. Mill modified this position.
49. Voltaire most especially. See note 55 below.
50. Matthew 25:29.
51. In Greek mythology, two monsters stationed on either side of the narrow strait
between Italy and Sicily. The phrase means two equal dangers, the avoidance of one
of them leading to the other.
52. Shelley here touches briefly though pointedly upon the question that Keats tries to
solve in his Letter of December 21, 1817—why we find pleasure in tragedy.
53. Ecclesiastes 7:2.

The exertions of Locke, Hume, Gibbon, Voltaire, Rousseau,[54] and their disciples, in favour of oppressed and deluded humanity, are entitled to the gratitude of mankind. Yet it is easy to calculate the degree of moral and intellectual improvement which the world would have exhibited, had they never lived. A little more nonsense would have been talked for a century or two; and perhaps a few more men, women, and children, burnt as heretics. We might not at this moment have been congratulating each other on the abolition of the Inquisition in Spain.[55] But it exceeds all imagination to conceive what would have been the moral condition of the world if neither Dante, Petrarch, Boccaccio, Chaucer, Shakespeare, Calderon, Lord Bacon, nor Milton, had ever existed; if Raphael and Michael Angelo had never been born; if the Hebrew poetry had never been translated; if a revival of the study of Greek literature had never taken place; if no monuments of ancient sculpture had been handed down to us; and if the poetry of the religion of the ancient world had been extinguished together with its belief. The human mind could never, except by the intervention of these excitements, have been awakened to the invention of the grosser sciences, and that application of analytical reasoning to the aberrations of society, which it is now attempted to exalt over the direct expression of the inventive and creative faculty itself.

We have more moral, political and historical wisdom, than we know how to reduce into practice; we have more scientific and economical knowledge than can be accommodated to the just distribution of the produce which it multiplies. The poetry in these systems of thought, is concealed by the accumulation of facts and calculating processes. There is no want of knowledge respecting what is wisest and best in morals, government, and political economy, or at least, what is wiser and better than what men now practise and endure. But we let 'I dare not wait upon I would, like the poor cat in the adage.'[56] We want the creative faculty to imagine that which we know; we want the generous impulse to act that which we imagine; we want the poetry of life: our calculations have outrun conception; we have eaten more than we can digest. The cultivation of those sciences which have enlarged the limits of the empire of man over the external world, has, for want of the poetical faculty, proportionally circumscribed those of the internal world; and man, having enslaved the elements, remains himself a slave. To what but a cultivation of the mechanical arts in a degree disproportioned to the presence of the creative faculty, which is the basis of all knowledge, is to be attributed the abuse of all invention for abridging and combining labour, to the exasperation of the inequality of mankind?[57] From what other cause has it arisen that these inventions which should have lightened, have added a weight to the curse imposed on Adam? Thus poetry, and the principle of self, of which money is the visible incarnation, are the God and Mammon of the world.

54. "I follow the classification by the author of *The Four Ages of Poetry;* but he was essentially a poet. The others, even Voltaire, were mere reasoners." (Shelley)
55. Shelley refers to its temporary abolition by the Liberal Revolution of 1820. The Inquisition was not permanently abolished until 1834.
56. *Macbeth* I.vii.44–45.
57. Shelley refers to the seeming paradox that the "labor-saving" inventions of the Industrial Revolution, so far from lightening the labor of the working classes, had made it heavier.

The functions of the poetical faculty are twofold; by one it creates new materials for knowledge, and power and pleasure; by the other it engenders in the mind a desire to reproduce and arrange them according to a certain rhythm and order which may be called the beautiful and the good. The cultivation of poetry is never more to be desired than at periods when, from an excess of the selfish and calculating principle, the accumulation of the materials of external life exceed the quantity of the power of assimilating them to the internal laws of human nature. The body has then become too unwieldy for that which animates it.

Poetry is indeed something divine. It is at once the centre and circumference of knowledge; it is that which comprehends all science, and that to which all science must be referred. It is at the same time the root and blossom of all other systems of thought; it is that from which all spring, and that which adorns all; and that which, if blighted, denies the fruit and the seed, and withholds from the barren world the nourishment and the succession of the scions of the tree of life. It is the perfect and consummate surface and bloom of things; it is as the odour and the colour of the rose to the texture of the elements which compose it, as the form and the splendour of unfaded beauty to the secrets of anatomy and corruption. What were virtue, love, patriotism, friendship—what were the scenery of this beautiful universe which we inhabit; what were our consolations on this side of the grave, and what were our aspirations beyond it, if poetry did not ascend to bring light and fire from those eternal regions where the owl-winged faculty of calculation dare not ever soar? Poetry is not like reasoning, a power to be exerted according to the determination of the will. A man cannot say, 'I will compose poetry.' The greatest poet even cannot say it: for the mind in creation is as a fading coal, which some invisible influence, like an inconstant wind, awakens to transitory brightness: this power arises from within, like the colour of a flower which fades and changes as it is developed, and the conscious portions of our natures are unprophetic either of its approach or its departure. Could this influence be durable in its original purity and force, it is impossible to predict the greatness of the results; but when composition begins, inspiration is already on the decline, and the most glorious poetry that has ever been communicated to the world is probably a feeble shadow of the original conception of the poet.[58] I appeal to the great poets of the present day, whether it be not an error to assert that the finest passages of poetry are produced by labour and study. The toil and the delay recommended by critics, can be justly interpreted to mean no more than a careful observation of the inspired moments, and an artificial connexion of the spaces between their suggestions by the intertexture of conventional expressions; a necessity only imposed by the limitedness of the poetical faculty itself. For Milton conceived the *Paradise Lost* as a whole before he executed it in portions. We have his own authority also for the Muse having 'dictated' to him the 'unpremeditated song,' and let this be an answer to those who would allege the fifty-six various readings of the first line of the *Orlando Furioso*.[59] Compositions so produced are to poetry what mosaic is to painting.

58. This was perhaps Shelley's own experience, yet many writers find that their best inspirations come in the course of composition.

59. Ariosto was given to much revision and correction of his work.

This instinct and intuition of the poetical faculty is still more observable in the plastic and pictorial arts; a great statue or picture grows under the power of the artist as a child in the mother's womb; and the very mind which directs the hands in formation is incapable of accounting to itself for the origin, the gradations, or the media of the process.[60]

Poetry is the record of the best and happiest moments of the happiest and best minds. We are aware of evanescent visitations of thought and feeling sometimes associated with place or person, sometimes regarding our own mind alone, and always arising unforeseen and departing unbidden, but elevating and delightful beyond all expression: so that even in the desire and the regret they leave, there cannot but be pleasure, participating as it does in the nature of its object. It is as it were the interpenetration of a diviner nature through our own; but its footsteps are like those of a wind over a sea, which the coming calm erases, and whose traces remain only, as on the wrinkled sand which paves it. These and corresponding conditions of being are experienced principally by those of the most delicate sensibility and the most enlarged imagination; and the state of mind produced by them is at war with every base desire. The enthusiasm of virtue, love, patriotism, and friendship, is essentially linked with these emotions; and whilst they last, self appears as what it is, an atom to a universe. Poets are not only subject to these experiences as spirits of the most refined organization, but they can colour all that they combine with the evanescent hues of this ethereal world; a word, or a trait in the representation of a scene or a passion, will touch the enchanted chord, and reanimate, in those who have ever experienced these emotions, the sleeping, the cold, the buried image of the past. Poetry thus makes immortal all that is best and most beautiful in the world; it arrests the vanishing apparitions which haunt the interlunations of life, and veiling them, or in language or in form, sends them forth among mankind, bearing sweet news of kindred joy to those with whom their sisters abide—abide, because there is no portal of expression from the caverns of the spirit which they inhabit into the universe of things. Poetry redeems from decay the visitations of the divinity in Man.

Poetry turns all things to loveliness; it exalts the beauty of that which is most beautiful, and it adds beauty to that which is most deformed; it marries exultation and horror, grief and pleasure, eternity and change; it subdues to union under its light yoke, all irreconcilable things. It transmutes all that it touches, and every form moving within the radiance of its presence is changed by wondrous sympathy to an incarnation of the spirit which it breathes; its secret alchemy turns to potable gold [61] the poisonous waters which flow from death through life; it strips the veil of familiarity from the world, and lays bare the naked and sleeping beauty, which is the spirit of its forms.

60. Shelley's emphasis on the unconscious nature of the creative process is in accord with what Coleridge says about the "organic" nature of art. This view, though doubtless basically right, is stated perhaps too categorically—Pater's comment, which is quoted in the Headnote to Coleridge's statement of organicism (see Organic Form above) applies as well to Shelley's insistence on the unconscious.

61. It was believed that gold, the "noblest" metal, would have sovereign powers if it could be made drinkable.

All things exist as they are perceived; at least in relation to the percipient. 'The mind is its own place, and of itself can make a Heaven of Hell, a Hell of Heaven.' [62] But poetry defeats the curse which binds us to be subjected to the accident of surrounding impressions. And whether it spreads its own figured curtain, or withdraws life's dark veil from before the scene of things, it equally creates for us a being within our being. It makes us the inhabitants of a world to which the familiar world is a chaos. It reproduces the common Universe of which we are portions and percipients, and it purges from our inward sight the film of familiarity which obscures from us the wonder of our being. It compels us to feel that which we perceive, and to imagine that which we know. It creates anew the universe, after it has been annihilated in our minds by the recurrence of impressions blunted by reiteration. It justifies that bold and true word of Tasso: *Non merita nome di creatore, se non Iddio ed il Poeta.*[63]

A poet, as he is the author to others of the highest wisdom, pleasure, virtue and glory, so he ought personally to be the happiest, the best, the wisest, and the most illustrious of men. As to his glory, let Time be challenged to declare whether the fame of any other institutor of human life be comparable to that of a poet. That he is the wisest, the happiest, and the best, inasmuch as he is a poet, is equally incontrovertible: the greatest poets have been men of the most spotless virtue, of the most consummate prudence, and, if we could look into the interior of their lives, the most fortunate of men: and the exceptions, as they regard those who possessed the imaginative faculty in a high yet inferior degree, will be found on consideration to confirm rather than destroy the rule. Let us for a moment stoop to the arbitration of popular breath, and usurping and uniting in our own persons the incompatible characters of accuser, witness, judge and executioner, let us without trial, testimony, or form, determine that certain motives of those who are 'there sitting where we dare not soar,'[64] are reprehensible. Let us assume that Homer was a drunkard, that Virgil was a flatterer, that Horace was a coward, that Tasso was a madman, that Lord Bacon was a peculator, that Raphael was a libertine, that Spenser was a poet laureate.[65] It is inconsistent with this division of our subject to cite living poets, but posterity has done ample justice to the great names now referred to. Their errors have been weighed and found to have been dust in the balance; if their sins were as scarlet, they are now white as snow: [66] they have been washed in the blood of the mediator and the redeemer, Time. Observe in what a ludicrous chaos the imputations of real or fictitious crime have been confused in the contemporary calumnies against poetry and poets;

62. *Paradise Lost* I.254–55.
63. "No one deserves the name of creator save only God and the poet." Shelley's calling this statement "bold" serves to remind us that the word "create" (and its derivatives) was not yet in common use in reference to art—"making" implies a pre-existent material out of which the thing is formed, whereas "creation" implies that the thing is brought into being *ex nihilo*, out of nothing, which was once thought to be what God alone could do.
64. *Paradise Lost* IV.829.
65. All these accusations were made against these persons; some of them are true. In speaking further on of the "contemporary calumnies against . . . poets," Shelley means the scandals from which he and Byron suffered.
66. Isaiah 1:18.

consider how little is, as it appears—or appears, as it is; look to your own motives, and judge not, lest ye be judged.

Poetry, as has been said, in this respect differs from logic, that it is not subject to the control of the active powers of the mind, and that its birth and recurrence has no necessary connexion with consciousness or will. It is presumptuous to determine that these are the necessary conditions of all mental causation, when mental effects are experienced insusceptible of being referred to them. The frequent recurrence of the poetical power, it is obvious to suppose, may produce in the mind an habit of order and harmony correlative with its own nature and with its effects upon other minds. But in the intervals of inspiration, and they may be frequent without being durable, a poet becomes a man, and is abandoned to the sudden reflux of the influences under which others habitually live. But as he is more delicately organized than other men, and sensible to pain and pleasure, both his own and that of others, in a degree unknown to them, he will avoid the one and pursue the other with an ardour proportioned to this difference. And he renders himself obnoxious [67] to calumny, when he neglects to observe the circumstances under which these objects of universal pursuit and flight have disguised themselves in one another's garments.

But there is nothing necessarily evil in this error, and thus cruelty, envy, revenge, avarice, and the passions purely evil, have never formed any portion of the popular imputations on the lives of poets.

I have thought it most favourable to the cause of truth to set down these remarks according to the order in which they were suggested to my mind, by a consideration of the subject itself, instead of following that of the treatise that excited me to make them public.[68] Thus although devoid of the formality of a polemical reply; if the view they contain be just, they will be found to involve a refutation of the doctrines of The Four Ages of Poetry, so far at least as regards the first division of the subject. I can readily conjecture what should have moved the gall of the learned and intelligent author of that paper; I confess myself, like him, unwilling to be stunned by the Theseids [69] of the hoarse Codri of the day. Bavius and Maevius undoubtedly are, as they ever were, insufferable persons. But it belongs to a philosophical critic to distinguish rather than confound.

The first part of these remarks [70] has related to poetry in its elements and principles; and it has been shown, as well as the narrow limits assigned them would permit, that what is called poetry, in a restricted sense, has a common source with all other forms of order and of beauty, according to which the materials of human life are susceptible of being arranged, and which is poetry in an universal sense.

67. The word is used here in a now obsolete sense: exposed to harm or injury.
68. Actually The Defence was not made public in Shelley's lifetime; it was first published in 1840.
69. Epic poems about Theseus. Codrus (plural: Codri) was a poet mocked by Virgil, Horace, and Juvenal, the last of whom ascribes to him a tragedy about Theseus; he may be fictitious. Bavius and Maevius were poetasters contemptuously mentioned by Virgil (Eclogues III); the latter was also the object of Horace's scorn.
70. Shelley meant this Defence to be only the first part of a longer essay, which he meant to continue but did not.

The second part will have for its object an application of these principles to the present state of the cultivation of poetry, and a defence of the attempt to idealize the modern forms of manners and opinions, and compel them into a subordination to the imaginative and creative faculty. For the literature of England, an energetic development of which has ever preceded or accompanied a great and free development of the national will, has arisen as it were from a new birth. In spite of the low-thoughted envy which would undervalue contemporary merit, our own will be a memorable age in intellectual achievements, and we live among such philosophers and poets as surpass beyond comparison any who have appeared since the last national struggle for civil and religious liberty.[71] The most unfailing herald, companion, and follower of the awakening of a great people to work a beneficial change in opinion or institution, is poetry. At such periods there is an accumulation of the power of communicating and receiving intense and impassioned conceptions respecting man and nature. The persons in whom this power resides, may often as far as regards many portions of their nature, have little apparent correspondence with that spirit of good of which they are the ministers. But even whilst they deny and abjure, they are yet compelled to serve, the power which is seated upon the throne of their own soul. It is impossible to read the compositions of the most celebrated writers of the present day without being startled with the electric life which burns within their words. They measure the circumference and sound the depths of human nature with a comprehensive and all-penetrating spirit, and they are themselves perhaps the most sincerely astonished at its manifestations; for it is less their spirit than the spirit of the age.[72] Poets are the hierophants [73] of an unapprehended inspiration; the mirrors of the gigantic shadows which futurity casts upon the present; the words which express what they understand not; the trumpets which sing to battle, and feel not what they inspire; the influence which is moved not, but moves. Poets are the unacknowledged legislators of the world.

1821   1840

JOHN KEATS

1795–1821

Letters

When Matthew Arnold wrote his essay on Keats in 1880 the question to which he chiefly addressed himself was whether Keats was something more than an "enchantingly sensuous" poet, whether there might be found in his work such intellectual and moral elements as would permit him to be thought of as a great poet, or, since he had died so young, as having been potentially a great poet. Arnold answered the question in the affirmative. Yet despite his eloquence and his authority, the prevailing view

---

71. The 17th-century parliamentary movement which resulted in the deposition of Charles I.
72. The idea that a historical period has a unique character and particular intentions, of which individual men are the unconscious agents, was gaining currency at that time.
73. Priests who expound sacred mysteries.

of Keats as a wholly sensuous poet continued in force for quite half a century. It remained possible for Sidney Colvin, one of his biographers and editors, to say of Keats that he had "a mind constitutionally inapt for abstract thinking." Colvin went even farther—"Keats," he said, "had no mind." As late as 1930 it could come as a revelation to so perceptive a reader as George Santayana that Keats really did have a mind. Writing to J. Middleton Murry, the English critic whose *Studies in Keats* did much to change the older view of the poet, Santayana said that Keats had always been a "personal favourite" of his and that what he had been attracted by was exactly the absence of any intellectual or moral depth, "a certain frank sensuality or youthfulness . . . a certain plebeian innocence of great human interests: I called him the *Cockney Genius,* and thought him luscious rather than intellectual." Santayana goes on: "I see now [i.e. after reading Murry's book] how wrong that was and that he was really intuitively contemplative."

No one now is likely to read Keats as Santayana read him before his enlightenment and as he was chiefly read for a century. The intensity of his concern with "great human interests" is now taken for granted, as is its complexity and profundity. In this radical revision of the image of Keats his letters have played a decisive part. All that is now seen in the poetry was of course there to be seen from the beginning. But it is understandable that the enchanting sensuousness and the frank sensuality should have captivated the first attention and interest of readers, and that, being in themselves powerful and significant traits, they should have seemed definitive of the poetry. It was Keats's letters, as they became more available and better known over the years, that made the first characterization of his poetry eventually untenable. Arnold, arguing his view that Keats is a poet of intellectual and moral weight, draws his evidence scarcely at all from the poetry itself; it is the letters that he relies on to make his point. He detested the letters to Fanny Brawne and deplored their having been published, but upon the letters that Keats wrote to his friends and family touching upon art and life he grounded his claims for the poet's profound seriousness.

With the passing years Keats's letters have quite outgrown their earlier validating function. They no longer exist as documents which derive their value from the light they throw on the temperament and intellect of the writer, but in their own right. Indeed, so high do they stand in the admiration and affection of many readers, that critics sometimes feel it necessary to caution against thinking of Keats primarily as the writer of the letters rather than as the writer of the poems. The admonition is proper enough, yet it would seem to have become the case that the poems and the letters exist in happy symbiosis, that they now together make up the canon of Keats. The poems must certainly come first in our thought. But that this needs to be said suggests the difference between our response to the poems and our response to the letters. The poems, even when they are of the highest interest, are seldom perfect, and although, especially when taken together, they quite transcend their imperfections, our response to them is necessarily mediated by complex considerations. The letters are always perfect in their genre, and our response to them is immediate and personal.

Perhaps in our day it requires some effort to think of letters as constituting a genre. Less and less does correspondence play a part in personal relations, the exchange of letters between persons in some intimate connection with each other and concerned to convey the information that intimacy permits, and requires: the casual happenings of the day, gossip, reflections on large matters and small, the news of plans, of troubles, of griefs, of joys. It seems pretty certain that the later twentieth century will have produced a relatively small body of significant collected letters as compared with preceding centuries, beginning with the seventeenth, when letters may be said to have been first thought of as a genre. In the eighteenth century the posthumous collection and publication of the letters of notable persons, especially literary figures, became increasingly common practice. That so many letters were preserved suggests the high store that was set upon them not merely for reasons of sentiment, as personal memorabilia, but because of the intrinsic value they were thought to have.

Not all the criteria of literary excellence bear upon the genre of the letter. Indeed, an especial interest and a chief charm of the form is felt to lie in the opportunity it gives for evading the conventions of public communication. Good letters, it is felt, are those which are free from self-consciousness, which claim their right to be spontaneous and immediate, and even, if the mood dictates and the occasion allows, casual or willful. Yet some of the conventional standards of literary excellence do indeed apply, of which substantiality of subject matter, cogency of observation and reasoning, and sincerity and force of utterance are salient. Judged by these diverse criteria, Keats's letters are pre-eminent in the genre, even unique. No other letters communicate so fully their author's temperament as his do, or display so bold an energy of mind in the confrontation of the problems of art and existence, or move so freely from the trivial to the transcendent and back again, or convey so clearly the actuality of the writer's relation to the person he is writing to, or to himself.

It has become the laudable custom to print Keats's letters in the closest possible approximation to the way he wrote them, that is, without any editorial revision of his spelling and punctuation and with his stricken-out but still legible phrases preserved.

From Letters

To Benjamin Bailey,[1] November 22, 1817

My dear Bailey,

. . . I wish you knew all that I think about Genius and the Heart—and yet I think you are thoroughly acquainted with my innermost breast in that respect or you could not have known me even thus long and still hold me worthy to be your dear friend. In passing however I must say of one thing that has pressed upon me lately and encreased my Humility and capability of submission and that is this truth—Men of Genius are great as certain ethereal Chemicals operating on the Mass of neutral intellect—by [for but] they have not any individuality, any determined Character.[2] I would call the top and head of those who have a proper self Men of Power—

But I am running my head into a Subject which I am certain I could not do justice to under five years s[t]udy and 3 vols octavo—and moreover long to be talking about the Imagination— . . . O I wish I was as certain of the end of

1. A close friend of Keats's, who had recently visited him in Oxford, where Bailey was an undergraduate; it was on this visit that Keats composed the third book of *Endymion*.
2. For the development of this idea, see the letter to Richard Woodhouse, October 27, 1818.

all your troubles as that of your momentary start about the authenticity of the Imagination. I am certain of nothing but of the holiness of the Heart's affections and the truth of Imagination—What the imagination seizes as Beauty must be truth ³—whether it existed before or not—for I have the same Idea of all our Passions as of Love they are all in their sublime, creative of essential Beauty— In a Word, you may know my favorite Speculation by my first Book and the little song I sent in my last ⁴—which is a representation from the fancy of the probable mode of operating in these Matters—The Imagination may be compared to Adam's dream ⁵—he awoke and found it truth. I am the more zealous in this affair, because I have never yet been able to perceive how any thing can be known for truth by consequitive reasoning—and yet it must be—Can it be that even the greatest Philosopher ever arrived at his goal without putting aside numerous objections—However it may be, O for a Life of Sensations rather than of Thoughts! It is 'a Vision in the form of Youth' a Shadow of reality to come—and this consideration has further conv[i]nced me for it has come as auxiliary to another favorite Speculation of mine, that we shall enjoy ourselves here after by having what we called happiness on Earth repeated in a finer tone and so repeated ⁶—And yet such a fate can only befall those who delight in sensation rather than hunger as you do after Truth—Adam's dream will do here and seems to be a conviction that Imagination and its empyreal reflection is the same as human Life and its spiritual repetition. But as I was saying—the simple imaginative Mind may have its rewards in the repeti[ti]on of its own silent Working coming continually on the spirit with a fine suddenness—to compare great things with small—have you never by being surprised with an old Melody —in a delicious place—by a delicious voice, fe[l]t over again your very speculations and surmises at the time it first operated on your soul—do you not remember forming to yourself the singer's face more beautiful that [*for* than] it was possible and yet with the elevation of the Moment you did not think so— even then you were mounted on the Wings of Imagination so high—that the Prototype must be here after—that delicious face you will see—What a time! I am continually running away from the subject—sure this cannot be exactly the case with a complex Mind—one that is imaginative and at the same time careful of its fruits—who would exist partly on sensation partly on thought— to whom it is necessary that years should bring the philosophic Mind ⁷—such an one I consider your's and therefore it is necessary to your eternal Happiness that you not only ~~have~~ drink this old Wine of Heaven which I shall call the redigestion of our most ethereal Musings on Earth; but also increase in knowledge and know all things. I am glad to hear you are in a fair Way for Easter—you will soon get through your unpleasant reading and then!—but the world is full of

3. See the last lines of "Ode on a Grecian Urn."
4. In a letter to Bailey some weeks earlier Keats had included the song "O Sorrow" from *Endymion* IV.
5. *Paradise Lost* VIII.452–90. Adam dreams of Eve and upon awaking finds her present before him.
6. A recurrent idea in Keats's poems is that through certain intense experiences of pleasure man might achieve a kind of divinity, an unconditioned existence which in *Endymion* I.779, he speaks of as "a fellowship with essence." It is this that he suggests by the "finer tone."
7. Wordsworth, the *Intimations of Immortality* Ode, l. 187. Keats loved to repeat this poem.

troubles and I have not much reason to think myself pestered with many—I think Jane or Marianne [8] has a better opinion of me than I deserve—for really and truly I do not think my Brothers illness connected with mine—you know more of the real Cause than they do—nor have I any chance of being rack'd as you have been—you perhaps at one time thought there was such a thing as Worldly Happiness to be arrived at, at certain periods of time marked out—you have of necessity from your disposition been thus led away—I scarcely remember counting upon any Happiness—I look not for it if it be not in the present hour—nothing startles me beyond the Moment. The setting sun will always set me to rights—or if a Sparrow come before my Window I take part in its existince and pick about the Gravel. The first thing that strikes me on hea[r]ing a Misfortune having befalled another is this. 'Well it cannot be helped.—he will have the pleasure of trying the resources of his spirit; [9] and I beg now my dear Bailey that hereafter should you observe any thing cold in me not to but [for put] it to the account of heartlessness but abstraction—for I assure you I sometimes feel not the influence of a Passion or Affection during a whole week—and so long this sometimes continues I begin to suspect myself and the genuiness of my feelings at other times—thinking them a few barren Tragedy-tears—My Brother Tom is much improved—he is going to Devonshire—whither I shall follow him— . . .

Your affectionate friend
John Keats

To George and Tom Keats, December 21, 27 (?), 1817

[In this letter Keats sets forth his doctrine of "Negative Capability," which has captivated the attention of critics and has often been explicated, although by no one so well as by Keats himself. The intellectual attitude he describes and praises is actually not difficult to comprehend, but perhaps it can be realized somewhat more sharply if we bring to mind the response we make to tragedy. When, for example, Macbeth comes to its end, we are not concerned about determining the extent of Macbeth's evil-doing, or the justness of his doom, or the pitfalls of ambition. Although our moral sensibilities have been deeply engaged, we do not make moral judgments at all. On the contrary: we find, perhaps to our surprise, that our hearts in some fashion go out to Macbeth; we separate him from his wickedness. We feel that the events we have witnessed do indeed convey a significance, one that is beyond any practical moral conclusion, but we cannot formulate what it is, and with this "half knowledge" we "remain content"; we find ourselves in "uncertainties, mysteries, doubts" and take pleasure in being there. Keats's formulation of Negative Capability, with its rejection

---

8. Jane and Marianne were sisters of Keats's close friend John Hamilton Reynolds, to whom many of the letters are addressed. Keats's brother Tom was ill of tuberculosis, from which he died on December 1, 1818. The "real cause" of Keats's illness was once thought to be a venereal infection. W. J. Bate, Keats's most authoritative biographer, rejects this. Bailey has been "rack'd" by the pains of an unhappy love affair.
9. Keats develops the implications of this attitude in the famous "Vale of Soul-Making" passage in his letter to George and Georgiana Keats, February 14–May 3, 1819.

of "any irritable reaching after fact and reason," is an instance of the Romantic hostility toward that subordinate faculty of the mind which the German philosopher Immanuel Kant (1724–1804) called *Verstand,* generally translated as "understanding." See the first paragraph of Shelley's *A Defence of Poetry* and the second paragraph of De Quincey's *On the Knocking at the Gate in "Macbeth.")*

My dear Brothers
I must crave your pardon for not having written ere this & & I saw Kean [10] return to the public in Richard III, & finely he did it, & at the request of Reynolds I went to criticise his Luke in Riches [11]—the critique is in todays champion, which I send you with the Examiner in which you will find very proper lamentation on the obsoletion of christmas Gambols & pastimes: but it was mixed up with so much egotism of that drivelling nature that pleasure is entirely lost.[12] . . . I have had two very pleasant evenings with Dilke [13] yesterday & today; & am at this moment just come from him & feel in the humour to go on with this, began in the morning, & from which he came to fetch me. I spent Friday evening with Wells [14] & went the next morning to see *Death on the Pale horse.* It is a wonderful picture, when West's [15] age is considered; But there is nothing to be intense upon; no women one feels mad to kiss; no face swelling into reality. the excellence of every Art is its intensity, capable of making all disagreeables evaporate, from their being in close relationship with Beauty & Truth—Examine King Lear [16] & you will find this examplified throughout; but in this picture we have unpleasantness without any momentous depth of speculation excited, in which to bury its repulsiveness— The picture is larger than Christ rejected—I dined with Haydon [17] the sunday after you left, & had a very pleasant day, I dined too (for I have been out too much lately) with Horace Smith & met his two brothers with Hill & Kingston & one Du Bois,[18] they only served to convince me, how superior humour is to wit in respect to enjoyment—These men say things which make one start,

10. Edmund Kean, the great actor (1787–1833), especially notable for his performances of Shakespeare's tragic heroes.
11. That is, in his performance of Luke Traffic in Sir J. B. Burges's *Riches.*
12. Keats's review appeared in *The Champion* of December 21. The *Examiner* essay on Christmas about which Keats is so severe was by Leigh Hunt (see note 26).
13. Charles Wentworth Dilke (1789–1864) was a close friend of Keats. He achieved reputation as an essayist and editor. The house in Hampstead in which Keats lived with Charles Armitage Brown was part of a two-family structure, of which Dilke owned the other half. The house is now the Keats Museum.
14. Charles Jeremiah Wells (1800–1879), a poet, was a friend of Tom Keats. He played an elaborate hoax on Tom by fabricating letters from a fictitious lady; Keats never forgave him for this.
15. Benjamin West (1738–1820), American by birth, president of the Royal Academy of Art. *Christ Rejected,* mentioned farther on, is another of his paintings.
16. See the sonnet on *King Lear* in the letter following, in which Keats takes a rather more complex view of the effect of "disagreeables."
17. Benjamin Robert Haydon (1786–1846), a painter of note whose pictures were often of inordinate size. Several of Keats's letters are addressed to him. Disappointed in his ambitions, he committed suicide. His *Autobiography* is of considerable interest.
18. Horace, James, and Leonard Smith. The first two were notable wits and are remembered for their volume of parodies, *Rejected Addresses.* Thomas Hill, a book collector; John Kingston, a civil servant; Edward Dubois, an essayist and editor.

without making one feel, they are all alike; their manners are alike; they all know fashionables; they have a mannerism in their very eating & drinking, in their mere handling a Decanter—They talked of Kean & his low company —Would I were with that company instead of yours said I to myself! I know such like acquaintance will never do for me & yet I am going to Reynolds, on wednesday—Brown [19] & Dilke walked with me & back from the Christmas pantomime. I had not a dispute but a disquisition with Dilke, on various subjects; several things dovetailed in my mind, & at once it struck me, what quality went to form a Man of Achievement especially in Literature & which Shakespeare posessed so enormously—I mean *Negative Capability*, that is when man is capable of being in uncertainties, Mysteries, doubts, without any irritable reaching after fact & reason—Coleridge, for instance,[20] would let go by a fine isolated verisimilitude caught from the Penetralium [21] of mystery, from being incapable of remaining content with half knowledge. This pursued through Volumes would perhaps take us no further than this, that with a great poet the sense of Beauty overcomes every other consideration, or rather obliterates all consideration.

Shelley's poem is out & there are words about its being objected too, as much as Queen Mab was.[22] Poor Shelley I think he has his Quota of good qualities, in sooth la!! Write soon to your most sincere friend & affectionate Brother

John

To George and Tom Keats, January 23, 24, 1818

My dear Brothers.

I was thinking what hindered me from writing so long, for I have many things to say to you & know not where to begin. It shall be upon a thing most interesting to you my Poem. Well! I have given the 1st book to Taylor; [23] he seemed more than satisfied with it, & to my surprise proposed publishing it in Quarto if Haydon would make a drawing of some event therein, for a Frontispeice. I called on Haydon, he said he would do anything I liked, but said he would rather paint a finished picture, from it, which he seems eager to do; this in a year or two will be a glorious thing for us; & it will be, for Haydon is struck with the 1st Book. I left Haydon & the next day received a letter from him, proposing to make, as he says, with all his might, a finished chalk sketch of my head, to be engraved in the first style & put at the head of my Poem,

19. Charles Armitage Brown, a close friend of Keats. See note 13.

20. Keats had but little knowledge of the philosophical tendency of Coleridge and erred grievously in choosing it as a bad example. Of Dilke, in whose company the idea of Negative Capability had occurred to him, he later said, "Dilke was a man who cannot feel he has a personal identity unless he has made up his Mind about everything. . . . Dilke will never come at a truth as long as he lives; because he is always trying at it."

21. *Penetralia:* the innermost parts of a building, especially a temple. The word is not used in the singular, as Keats uses it, getting the form wrong; it should be *penetrale.*

22. *Laon and Cythna,* later entitled *The Revolt of Islam.* The publishers were distressed over its theme of incest between brother and sister, and Shelley was forced to revise it. *Queen Mab* (1813), written when Shelley was eighteen, is an attack on virtually every institution of society.

23. The first book of *Endymion.* John Taylor (1781–1864), senior partner of Taylor and Hessey, Keats's second publishers. He was an intelligent and feeling man and his dealings with Keats were honorable and kind.

saying at the same time he had never done the thing for any human being, & that it must have considerable effect as he will put the name to it—I begin today to copy my 2nd Book 'thus far into the bowels of the Land' [24]—You shall hear whether it will be Quarto or non Quarto, picture or non Picture. Leigh Hunt I showed my 1st Book to, he allows it not much merit as a whole; says it is unnatural & made ten objections to it in the mere skimming over.[25] He says the conversation is unnatural & too high-flown for the Brother & Sister. Says it should be simple forgetting do ye mind, that they are both overshadowed by a Supernatural Power, & of force could not speak like Franchesca in the Rimini.[26] He must first prove that Caliban's poetry is unnatural,—This with me completely overturns his objections—the fact is he & Shelley are hurt & perhaps justly, at my not having showed them the affair officiously & from several hints I have had they appear much disposed to dissect & anatomize, any trip or slip I may have made.—But whose afraid Ay! Tom! demme if I am. I went last tuesday, an hour too late, to Hazlitt's Lecture on poetry, got there just as they were coming out . . . —I think a little change has taken place in my intellect lately—I cannot bear to be uninterested or unemployed, I, who for so long a time, have been addicted to passiveness—Nothing is finer for the purposes of great productions, than a very gradual ripening of the intellectual powers—As an instance of this—observe—I sat down yesterday to read King Lear once again the thing appeared to demand the prologue of a Sonnet, I wrote it & began to read—(I know you would like to see it)

'On sitting down to King Lear once Again'
O golden tongued Romance with serene Lute!
Fair plumed syren! Queen! if [of] far away!
Leave melodizing on this wintry day,
Shut up thine olden volume & be mute.
Adieu! for once again the fierce dispute,
Betwixt Hell torment & impassioned Clay
Must I burn through; once more assay
The bitter sweet of this Shakespeareian fruit
Chief Poet! & ye clouds of Albion.
Begettors of our deep eternal theme,
When I am through the old oak forest gone
Let me not wander in a barren dream
But when I am consumed with the Fire
Give me new Phoenix-wings to fly at my desire

So you see I am getting at it, with a sort of determination & strength, though verily I do not feel it at this moment . . .

My dear Brothers Your very affectionate Brother
John

24. *Richard III* V.ii.3.
25. Leigh Hunt (1784–1859), poet, essayist, and publicist, was one of the earliest of Keats's literary friends. It was he who first published Keats's poems, in his paper the *Examiner*. Keats began by admiring Hunt's poetry and fell under the influence of its easy "naturalness"—actually a colloquial looseness of expression—but later became alienated from it and rather impatient with the poet himself.
26. Hunt's *The Story of Rimini* (1816).

To John Hamilton Reynolds,[27] *February 3, 1818*

My dear Reynolds,

I thank you for your dish of Filberts—Would I could get a basket of them by way of desert every day for the sum of two pence [28]—Would we were a sort of ethereal Pigs, & turn'd loose to feed upon spiritual Mast & Acorns—which would be merely being a squirrel & feed upon filberts. for what is a squirrel but an airy pig, or a filbert but a sort of archangelical acorn. . . . It may be said that we ought to read our Contemporaries. that Wordsworth &c should have their due from us. but for the sake of a few fine imaginative or domestic passages, are we to be bullied into a certain Philosophy engendered in the whims of an Egotist [29]—Every man has his speculations, but every man does not brood and peacock over them till he makes a false coinage and deceives himself—Many a man can travel to the very bourne of Heaven, and yet want confidence to put down his halfseeing. Sancho will invent a Journey heavenward as well as any body.[30] We hate poetry that has a palpable design upon us—and if we do not agree, seems to put its hand in its breeches pocket. Poetry should be great & unobtrusive, a thing which enters into one's soul, and does not startle it or amaze it with itself but with its subject.—How beautiful are the retired flowers! how would they lose their beauty were they to throng into the highway crying out, 'admire me I am a violet! dote upon me I am a primrose!' Modern poets differ from the Elizabethans in this. Each of the moderns like an Elector of Hanover governs his petty state, & knows how many straws are swept daily from the Causeways in all his dominions & has a continual itching that all the Housewives should have their coppers well scoured: the antients were Emperors of vast Provinces, they had only heard of the remote ones and scarcely cared to visit them.—I will cut all this—I will have no more of Wordsworth or Hunt in particular—Why should we be of the tribe of Manasseh when we can wander with Esau? [31] why should we kick against the Pricks,[32] when we can walk on Roses? Why should we be owls, when we

27. John Hamilton Reynolds (1794–1852), one of Keats's warmest friends, was at this time a clerk in an insurance office but studied law and practiced as a solicitor. He was devoted to literature and had a gift for comic verse. His tombstone identifies him as "The Friend of Keats."

28. Keats is referring to two sonnets by Reynolds on Robin Hood sent by the twopenny post.

29. Keats held Wordsworth in the highest admiration and submitted to his influence in many ways. Yet no poet moves toward his own style and purposes—his own identity—without some dissatisfaction with the predecessors who have shown him the way. Although Keats further on in this letter speaks of Wordsworth and Leigh Hunt in the same breath and the same tone, he of course discriminated between them. Doubtless in the adverse things he says here about Wordsworth, Keats has much in mind the moralizing tone of *The Excursion* (1814), but his objections go beyond this.

30. In *Don Quixote* II.xli, Sancho Panza, the mad knight's literal-minded squire, having been hoaxed into believing that he has made a sky-journey on a magical wooden horse, gives a full account of the heavenly wonders he has seen.

31. In Genesis 48:17–20, Jacob, blessing his two grandsons by Joseph, says that the tribe descending from Manasseh will be of less account than the tribe of Ephraim. Keats makes Manasseh the type of respectable mediocrity. Esau, the free-ranging hunter, loses his birthright and also the blessing of his father Isaac to his prudent, scheming brother Jacob (Genesis 25:29–34 and 27).

32. Acts 9:5.

can be Eagles? Why be teased with 'nice Eyed wagtails,'[33] when we have in sight 'the Cherub Contemplation'?[34]—Why with Wordsworths 'Matthew with a bough of wilding in his hand'[35] when we can have Jacques 'under an oak[36] &c'—The secret of the Bough of Wilding will run through your head faster than I can write it—Old Matthew spoke to him some years ago on some nothing, & because he happens in an Evening Walk to imagine the figure of the old man—he must stamp it down in black & white, and it is henceforth sacred—I don't mean to deny Wordsworth's grandeur & Hunt's merit, but I mean to say we need not be teazed with grandeur & merit—when we can have them uncontaminated & unobtrusive. Let us have the old Poets, & robin Hood Your letter and its sonnets gave me more pleasure than will the 4th Book of Childe Harold[37] & the whole of any body's life & opinions. In return for your dish of filberts, I have gathered a few Catkins,[38] I hope they'll look pretty.

[Keats here copies two of Hunt's poems, *Robin Hood* and *Lines on the Mermaid Tavern*.]

Yr sincere friend and Coscribbler
John Keats

To John Hamilton Reynolds, February 19, 1818

My dear Reynolds,

I have an idea that a Man might pass a very pleasant life in this manner— let him on any certain day read a certain Page of full Poesy or distilled Prose and let him wander with it, and muse upon it, and reflect from it, and bring home to it, and prophesy upon it, and dream upon it—until it becomes stale— but when will it do so? Never—When Man has arrived at a certain ripeness in intellect any one grand and spiritual passage serves him as a starting post towards all 'the two-and thirty Pallaces'[39] How happy is such a 'voyage of conception,' what delicious diligent Indolence! A doze upon a Sofa does not hinder it, and a nap upon Clover engenders ethereal finger-pointings—the prattle of a child gives it wings, and the converse of middle age a strength to beat them—a strain of musick conducts to 'an odd angle of the Isle'[40] and when the leaves whisper it puts a 'girdle round the earth.'[41] Nor will this sparing touch of noble Books be any irreverance to their Writers—for perhaps the honors paid by Man to Man are trifles in comparison to the Benefit done by great Works to the 'Spirit and pulse of good,'[42] by their mere passive existence. Memory should not be called knowledge—Many have original Minds who do not think it—they are led away by Custom—Now it appears to me that almost

33. From Hunt's *The Nymphs* II.170.
34. Milton, *Il Penseroso*, l.54.
35. "The Two April Mornings" (one of Wordsworth's most moving poems, as Keats in a less irritable moment must surely have known). "Wilding" is the wild apple tree.
36. In *As You Like It* the melancholy Jaques is described sitting "under an oak" philosophizing over the fate of a wounded stag.
37. The last canto of Byron's poem was soon to appear.
38. A scaly spike of blossoms, as of the birch and willow.
39. In Buddhist doctrine.
40. *The Tempest* I.ii.223.
41. *Midsummer Night's Dream* II.i.175.
42. Wordsworth, *The Old Cumberland Beggar*. l. 77.

any Man may like the Spider spin from his own inwards his own airy Citadel
—the points of leaves and twigs on which the Spider begins her work are few
and she fills the Air with a beautiful circuiting: man should be content with
as few points to tip with the fine Webb of his Soul and weave a tapestry
empyrean—full of Symbols for his spiritual eye, of softness for his spiritual
touch, of space for his wandering of distinctness for his Luxury—But the
Minds of Mortals are so different and bent on such diverse Journeys that it
may at first appear impossible for any common taste and fellowship to exist
between two or three under these suppositions—It is however quite the contrary
—Minds would leave each other in contrary directions, traverse each other
in Numberless points, and all [for at] last greet each other at the Journeys
end—A old Man and a child would talk together and the old Man be led on
his Path, and the child left thinking—Man should not dispute or assert but
whisper results to his neighbour, and thus by every germ of Spirit sucking the
Sap from mould ethereal every human might become great, and Humanity
instead of being a wide heath of Furse and Briars with here and there a remote
Oak or Pine, would become a grand democracy of Forest Trees. It has been an
old Comparison for our urging on—the Bee hive—however it seems to me that
we should rather be the flower than the Bee—for it is a false notion that more
is gained by receiving than giving—no the receiver and the giver are equal
in their benefits—The f[l]ower I doubt not receives a fair guerdon from the
Bee—its leaves blush deeper in the next spring—and who shall say between
Man and Woman which is the most delighted? [43] Now it is more noble to sit
like Jove that [for than] to fly like Mercury—let us not therefore go hurrying
about and collecting honey-bee like, buzzing here and there impatiently from a
knowledge of what is to be arrived at: but let us open our leaves like a flower
and be passive and receptive—budding patiently under the eye of Apollo and
taking hints from every noble insect that favors us with a visit—sap will be
given us for Meat and dew for drink—I was led into these thoughts, my dear
Reynolds, by the beauty of the morning operating on a sense of Idleness—I
have not read any Books—the Morning said I was right—I had no Idea but
of the Morning and the Thrush said I was right—seeming to say—

> O thou whose face hath felt the Winter's wind;
>   Whose eye has seen the Snow clouds hung in Mist
> And the black-elm tops 'mong the freezing Stars
> To thee the Spring will be a harvest-time—
> O thou whose only book has been the light
> Of supreme darkness which thou feddest on
> Night after night, when Phœbus was away
> To thee the Spring shall be a tripple morn—
> O fret not after knowledge—I have none
> And yet my song comes native with the warmth

43. That is, in the sexual act. The prophet Tiresias had been both a man and a woman.
When Zeus and Hera asked him to settle a dispute on this point, he said that woman
had the most pleasure. This made Hera so angry that she blinded him; Zeus in recompense
gave him the gift of prophecy.

O fret not after knowledge—I have none
And yet the Evening listens—He who saddens
At thought of Idleness cannot be idle,
And he's awake who thinks himself asleep.

Now I am sensible all this is a mere sophistication, however it may neighbour to any truths, to excuse my own indolence—so I will not deceive myself that Man should be equal with jove—but think himself very well off as a sort of scullion-Mercury or even a humble Bee—It is not [for no] matter whether I am right or wrong either one way or another, if there is sufficient to lift a little time from your Shoulders.

Your affectionate friend
John Keats

To John Taylor, February 27, 1818

My dear Taylor,
Your alteration strikes me as being a great improvement [44]—. . . I am extremely indebted to you for this attention and also for your after admonitions— It is a sorry thing for me that any one should have to overcome Prejudices in reading my Verses—that affects me more than any hypercriticism on any particular Passage. In *Endymion* I have most likely but moved into the Go-cart from the leading strings. In Poetry I have a few Axioms, and you will see how far I am from their Centre. 1st I think Poetry should surprise by a fine excess and not by Singularity—it should strike the Reader as a wording of his own highest thoughts, and appear almost a Remembrance—2nd Its touches of Beauty should never be half way therby making the reader breathless instead of content: the rise, the progress, the setting of imagery should like the Sun come natural natural too him—shine over him and set soberly although in magnificence leaving him in the Luxury of twilight—but it is easier to think what Poetry should be than to write it—and this leads me on to another axiom. That if Poetry comes not as naturally as the Leaves to a tree it had better not come at all. However it may be with me I cannot help looking into new countries with 'O for a Muse of fire to ascend!' [45]—If Endymion serves me as a Pioneer perhaps I ought to be content. I have great reason to be content, for thank God I can read and perhaps understand Shakspeare to his depths, and I have I am sure many friends, who, if I fail, will attribute any change in my Life and Temper to Humbleness rather than to Pride—to a cowering under the Wings of great Poets rather than to a Bitterness that I am not appreciated. I am anxious to get Endymion printed that I may forget it and proceed. . . .

Your sincere and oblig^d friend
John Keats

P.S. You shall have a sho[r]t *Preface* in good time—

44. Taylor, as Keats's publisher, made corrections in the punctuation of *Endymion*.
45. An approximate quotation of the first line of the Prologue of *Henry V*. Despite what the thrush said in the 19 February letter to Reynolds (see above, p. 772), it is plain that Keats *did* fret after knowledge. The letter following expresses the same desire with especial eloquence.

To John Taylor, April 24, 1818

My dear Taylor,

I think I Did very wrong to leave you to all the trouble of Endymion—but I could not help it then—another time I shall be more bent to all sort of troubles and disagreeables—Young Men for some time have an idea that such a thing as happiness is to be had and therefore are extremely impatient under any unpleasant restraining—in time however, of such stuff is the world about them, they know better and instead of striving from Uneasiness greet it as an habitual sensation, a pannier which is to weigh upon them through life.

And in proportion to my disgust at the task is my sense of your kindness & anxiety—the book pleased me much—it is very free from faults; and although there are one or two words I should wish replaced, I see in many places an improvement greatly to the purpose—

. . . I was purposing to travel over the north this Summer—there is but one thing to prevent me—I know nothing I have read nothing and I mean to follow Solomon's directions of 'get Wisdom—get understanding' [46]—I find cavalier days are gone by. I find that I can have no enjoyment in the World but continual drinking of Knowledge—I find there is no worthy pursuit but the idea of doing some good for the world—some do it with their society— some with their wit—some with their benevolence—some with a sort of power of conferring pleasure and good humour on all they meet and in a thousand ways all equally dutiful to the command of Great Nature—there is but one way for me—the road lies th[r]ough application study and thought. I will pursue it and to that end purpose retiring for some years. I have been hovering for some time between an exquisite sense of the luxurious and a love for Philosophy—were I calculated for the former I should be glad—but as I am not I shall turn all my soul to the latter. My Brother Tom is getting better and I hope I shall see both him and Reynolds well before I retire from the World. I shall see you soon and have some talk about what Books I shall take with me—

Your very sincere friend
John Keats

To John Hamilton Reynolds, May 3, 1818

My dear Reynolds.

What I complain of is that I have been in so an uneasy a state of Mind as not to be fit to write to an invalid. I cannot write to any length under a dis-guised feeling. I should have loaded you with an addition of gloom, which I am sure you do not want. I am now thank God in a humour to give you a good groats worth—for Tom, after a Night without a Wink of sleep, and overburdened with fever, has got up after a refreshing day sleep and is better than he has been for a long time; and you I trust have been again round the Common without any effect but refreshment. . . .—Were I to study physic or rather Medicine again,[47]—I feel it would not make the least difference in my Poetry; when the Mind is in its infancy a Bias is in reality a Bias, but when

---

46. Proverbs 4:5.
47. Keats was a Licentiate of the Society of Apothecaries, and as such might treat patients. In a letter of 1819 to George and Georgiana Keats he says that he thinks of going to Edinburgh "to study for a physician," presumably to take the more advanced degree of Doctor of Medicine.

we have acquired more strength, a Bias becomes no Bias. Every department of knowledge we see excellent and calculated towards a great whole. I am so convinced of this, that I am glad at not having given away my medical Books, which I shall again look over to keep alive the little I know thitherwards; and moreover intend through you and Rice to become a sort of Pip-civilian.[48] An extensive knowledge is needful to thinking people—it takes away the heat and fever; and helps, by widening speculation, to ease the Burden of the Mystery: [49] a thing I begin to understand a little, and which weighed upon you in the most gloomy and true sentence in your Letter. The difference of high Sensations with and without knowledge appears to me this—in the latter case we are falling continually ten thousand fathoms deep [50] and being blown up again without wings and with all [the] horror of a bare shoulderd Creature— in the former case, our shoulders are fledge,[51] and we go thro' the same air and space without fear. . . .

You may be anxious to know for fact to what sentence in your Letter I allude. You say 'I fear there is little chance of any thing else in this life.' You seem by that to have been going through with a more painful and acute zest the same labyrinth that I have—I have come to the same conclusion thus far. My Branchings out therefrom have been numerous: one of them is the consideration of Wordsworth's genius and as a help, in the manner of gold being the meridian Line of worldly wealth,—how he differs from Milton.—And here I have nothing but surmises, from an uncertainty whether Miltons apparently less anxiety for Humanity proceeds from his seeing further or no than Wordsworth: And whether Wordsworth has in truth epic passion, and martyrs himself to the human heart, the main region of his song [52]—In regard to his genius alone—we find what he says true as far as we have experienced and we can judge no further but by larger experience—for axioms in philosophy are not axioms until they are proved upon our pulses: We read fine ————things but never feel them to thee full until we have gone the same step as the Author.—I know this is not plain; you will know exactly my meaning when I say, that now I shall relish Hamlet more than I ever have done —Or, better—You are sensible no man can set down Venery [53] as a bestial or joyless thing until he is sick of it and therefore all philosophizing on it would be mere wording. Until we are sick, we understand not;—in fine, as Byron says, 'Knowledge is Sorrow'; [54] and I go on to say that 'Sorrow is Wisdom'—and further for aught we can know for certainty! 'Wisdom is folly'— So you see how I have run away from Wordsworth, and Milton. . . .

48. An amateur lawyer. James Rice, the friend of whom Keats said that he was "the most sensible and ever wise man" he knew, was a lawyer.
49. Wordsworth, *Tintern Abbey*, l. 38. This poem is salient in Keats's mind in this letter, both in his discussion of Wordsworth himself and in his speculations about the nature of human existence; from Wordsworth's account of the stages of his own mental and emotional development, Keats derives the idea of the "Chambers" of human life, discussed later in this letter.
50. *Paradise Lost* II.934; III.267.
51. That is, without wings.
52. A quotation from the fragment of *The Recluse* which Wordsworth had cited in the Preface to *The Excursion*.
53. The pursuit of sexual activity.
54. *Manfred* I.i.10. Actually, "Sorrow is knowledge."

. . .—I will return to Wordsworth—whether or no he has an extended vision or a circumscribed grandeur—whether he is an eagle in his nest, or on the wing—And to be more explicit and to show you how tall I stand by the giant, I will put down a simile of human life as far as I now perceive it; that is, to the point to which I say we both have arrived at—' Well—I compare human life to a large Mansion of Many Apartments, two of which I can only describe, the doors of the rest being as yet shut upon me—The first we step into we call the infant or thoughtless Chamber, in which we remain as long as we do not think—We remain there a long while, and notwithstanding the doors of the second Chamber remain wide open, showing a bright appearance, we care not to hasten to it; but are at length imperceptibly impelled by the awakening of the thinking principle—within us—we no sooner get into the second Chamber, which I shall call the Chamber of Maiden-Thought,[55] than we become intoxicated with the light and the atmosphere, we see nothing but pleasant wonders, and think of delaying there for ever in delight: However among the effects this breathing is father of is that tremendous one of sharpening one's vision into the heart and nature of Man—of convincing ones nerves that the World is full of Misery and Heartbreak, Pain, Sickness and oppression —whereby This Chamber of Maiden Thought becomes gradually darken'd and at the same time on all sides of it many doors are set open—but all dark —all leading to dark passages—We see not the ballance of good and evil. We are in a Mist—*We* are now in that state—We feel the 'burden of the Mystery,' To this point was Wordsworth come, as far as I can conceive when he wrote 'Tintern Abbey' and it seems to me that his Genius is explorative of those dark Passages. Now if we live, and go on thinking, we too shall explore them. he is a Genius and superior [to] us, in so far as he can, more than we, make discoveries, and shed a light in them—Here I must think Wordsworth is deeper than Milton—though I think it has depended more upon the general and gregarious advance of intellect, than individual greatness of Mind—From the Paradise Lost and the other Works of Milton, I hope it is not too presuming, even between ourselves to say, his Philosophy, human and divine, may be tolerably understood by one not much advanced in years, In his time englishmen were just emancipated from a great superstition—and Men had got hold of certain points and resting places in reasoning which were too newly born to be doubted, and too much opposed by the Mass of Europe not to be thought etherial and authentically divine—who could gainsay his ideas on virtue, vice, and Chastity in Comus, just at the time of the dismissal of Cod-pieces [56] and a hundred other disgraces? who would not rest satisfied with his hintings at good and evil in the Paradise Lost, when just free from the inquisition and burrning in Smithfield? [57] The Reformation produced such immediate and great benefits, that Protestantism was considered under the immediate eye of heaven, and its own remaining Dogmas and superstitions, then, as it were, regenerated, constituted those resting places and seeming sure points of Reasoning—from

55. "Maiden" in the sense of first, as in "maiden voyage," "maiden speech," or in the sense of untried, as in "maiden knight." The Chamber of Maiden-Thought corresponds to the stage of existence described by Wordsworth in *Tintern Abbey*, ll. 67–83.

56. A pouch, often elaborately ornamented, at the crotch of the close-fitting breeches worn by men from the 15th to the 17th centuries.

57. The open space outside the walls of the City of London where heretics were burned in the 16th century.

that I have mentioned, Milton, whatever he may have thought in the sequel, appears to have been content with these by his writings—He did not think into the human heart, as Wordsworth has done—Yet Milton as a Philosopher, had sure as great powers as Wordsworth—What is then to be inferr'd? O many things—It proves there is really a grand march of intellect—, It proves that a mighty providence subdues the mightiest Minds to the service of the time being, whether it be in human Knowledge or Religion. After all there is certainly something real in the World . . . Tom has spit a leetle blood this afternoon, and that is rather a damper—but I know—the truth is there is something real in the World Your third Chamber of Life shall be a lucky and a gentle one—stored with the wine of love—and the Bread of Friendship—. . . .

Your affectionate friend
John Keats

To Richard Woodhouse,[58] October 27, 1818

My dear Woodhouse,

Your Letter gave me a great satisfaction; more on account of its friendliness, than any relish of that matter in it which is accounted so acceptable in the 'genus irritabile' [59] The best answer I can give you is in a clerklike manner to make some observations on two principle points, which seem to point like indices into the midst of the whole pro and con, about genius, and views and atchievements and ambition and cœtera. 1st As to the poetical Character itself, (I mean that sort of which, if I am any thing, I am a Member; that sort distinguished from the wordsworthian or egotistical sublime; [60] which is a thing per se and stands alone) it is not itself—it has no self—it is every thing and nothing—It has no character [61]—it enjoys light and shade; it lives in gusto,[62] be it foul or fair, high or low, rich or poor, mean or elevated—It has as much delight in conceiving an Iago as an Imogen.[63] What shocks the virtuous philosop[h]er, delights the camelion Poet. It does no harm from its relish of the dark side of things any more than from its taste for the bright one; because they both end in speculation.[64] A Poet is the most unpoetical of any thing in existence; because he has no Identity [65]—he is continually in for [? informing]

---

58. Woodhouse, seven years older than Keats, was a barrister and the literary adviser to Keats's publishers, Taylor and Hessey. He was educated at Eton and was a good classicist and philologist. To his scholarly habits we owe the preservation of the early versions of Keats's poems.
59. "Irritable tribe"—of poets, so called by Horace, *Epistles* II.ii.102.
60. This striking phrase has established itself as the perfect description of one characteristic mode of Wordsworth's poetry.
61. When Keats says that "the poetical Character . . . has no character," he is playing with two meanings of a word of many meanings—character as the sum of the traits of poets of a class, and character as a strongly defined personal identity. But the reference is clearly to William Collins's allegorical figure in his "Ode on the Poetical Character."
62. See Hazlitt's essay "On Gusto."
63. The devilish villain of Shakespeare's *Othello* and the angelic heroine of his *Cymbeline*.
64. That is, not in action.
65. The paradox is that the poet, who has no identity, makes poems which, if they are truly poems, i.e. good poems, are so because they are themselves and cannot, as the poet can (see what Keats goes on to say), be "annihilated" by other identities. See the following letter, in which Keats makes personal identity, acquired through the experience of pain, the crowning achievement of human life.

—and filling some other Body—The Sun, the Moon, the Sea and Men and Women who are creatures of impulse are poetical and have about them an unchangeable attribute—the poet has none; no identity—he is certainly the most unpoetical of all God's Creatures. If then he has no self, and if I am a Poet, where is the Wonder that I should say I would right write no more? Might I not at that very instant [have] been cogitating on the Characters of saturn and Ops? [66] It is a wretched thing to confess; but is a very fact that not one word I ever utter can be taken for granted as an opinion growing out of my identical nature—how can it, when I have no nature? When I am in a room with People if I ever am free from speculating on creations of my own brain, then not myself goes home to myself: but the identity of every one in the room begins to [for so] to press upon me that, I am in a very little time an [ni]hilated—not only among Men; it would be the same in a Nursery of children: I know not whether I make myself wholly understood: I hope enough so to let you see that no dependence is to be placed on what I said that day.

In the second place I will speak of my views, and of the life I purpose to myself—I am ambitious of doing the world some good: if I should be spared that may be the work of maturer years—in the interval I will assay to reach to as high a summit in Poetry as the nerve bestowed upon me will suffer. The faint conceptions I have of Poems to come brings the blood frequently into my forehead—All I hope is that I may not lose all interest in human affairs —that the solitary indifference I feel for applause even from the finest Spirits, will not blunt any acuteness of vision I may have. I do not think it will—I feel assured I should write from the mere yearning and fondness I have for the Beautiful even if my night's labours should be burnt every morning and no eye ever shine upon them. But even now I am perhaps not speaking from myself; but from some character in whose soul I now live. I am sure however that this next sentence is from myself. I feel your anxiety, good opinion and friendliness in the highest degree, and am

Your's most sincerely
John Keats

To George and Georgiana [67] Keats, October 14–31, 1818

My dear George;

. . . Notwithstand your Happiness and your recommendation I hope I shall never marry. Though the most beautiful Creature were waiting for me at the end of a Journey or a Walk; though the carpet were of Silk, the Curtains of the morning Clouds; the chairs and Sofa stuffed with Cygnet's [68] down; the food

---

66. Characters in *Hyperion*, Keats's unfinished poem which he was working on at this time and which he left unfinished for reasons given in note 89.

67. George Keats married Georgiana Wylie in 1818 and with her emigrated to America, settling in Louisville, Kentucky. After numerous vicissitudes, he prospered for a time and became prominent in the life of the town, but ended in bankruptcy in 1841, the year of his death. Because the mail service between England and America was still disorganized and infrequent, Keats sent his letters to his brother and sister-in-law by private arrangements and he kept on writing a letter until such arrangements could be made; the letter following this one was composed over nearly three months.

68. A cygnet is a young swan.

Manna,[69] the Wine beyond Claret,[70] the Window opening on Winander mere,[71] I should not feel—or rather my Happiness would not be so fine, as [*corrected from* and] my Solitude is sublime. Then instead of what I have described, there is a Sublimity to welcome me home—The roaring of the wind is my wife and the Stars through the windowpane are my Children. The mighty abstract Idea I have of Beauty in all things stifles the more divided and minute domestic happiness—an amiable wife and sweet Children I contemplate as a part of that Bea[u]ty. but I must have a thousand of those beautiful particles to fill up my heart. I feel more and more every day, as my imagination strengthens, that I do not live in this world alone but in a thousand worlds—No sooner am I alone than shapes of epic greatness are stationed around me, and serve my Spirit the office of which is equivalent to a king's body guard—then 'Tragedy, with scepter'd pall, comes sweeping by' [72] According to my state of mind I am with Achilles shouting in the Trenches or with Theocritus in the Vales of Sicily.[73] Or I throw [*corrected from* through] my whole being into Triolus and repeating those lines, 'I wander, like a lost soul upon the stygian Banks staying for waftage,' [74] I melt into the air with a voluptuousness so delicate that I am content to be alone—These things combined with the opinion I have of the generallity of women—who appear to me as children to whom I would rather give a Sugar Plum than my time, form a barrier against Matrimony which I rejoice in. I have written this that you might see I have my share of the highest pleasures and that though I may choose to pass my days alone I shall be no Solitary. You see therre is nothing spleenical [75] in all this. The only thing that can ever affect me personally for more than one short passing day, is any doubt about my powers for poetry—I seldom have any, and I look with hope to the nighing time when I shall have none. I am as happy as a Man can be—that is in myself I should be happy if Tom was well, and I knew you were passing pleasant days—Then I should be most enviable—with the yearning Passion I have for the beautiful, connected and made one with the ambition of my intellect. Th[i]nk of my Pleasure in Solitude, in comparison of my commerce with the world—there I am a child—there they do not know me not even my most intimate acquaintance—I give into their feelings as though I were refraining from irritating [a] little child—Some think me middling, others silly, others foolish—every one thinks he sees my weak side against my will; when in truth it is with my will—I am content to be thought all this because I have in my own breast so great a resource. This is one great reason why they like me so; because they can all show to advantage in a room, and eclipse from a certain tact one who is reckoned to be a good Poet—I hope I am not here playing

69. The food miraculously provided for the Israelites during their flight from Egypt.
70. Keats's favorite wine.
71. Winander, in Wordsworth's Lake District and celebrated by the poet, is too large to be called a "mere," which means a small lake or pond.
72. Milton, *Il Penseroso*, ll. 97–98.
73. Achilles, the fiercest of the Greek captains who besieged Troy, is the central figure of the *Iliad*. Theocritus (*c.* 300–*c.* 260 B.C.) is the founder of the tradition of bucolic or pastoral poetry, which takes for its subjects the lives and loves of rustics, usually herdsmen.
74. Shakespeare, *Troilus and Cressida* III.ii.8–10.
75. The spleen was once considered to be the organ from which melancholy and ill humor arose. The usual adjectival form is "splenetic" or "spleenful."

tricks 'to make the angels weep': I think not: for I have not the least contempt for my species; and though it may sound paradoxical: my greatest elevations of soul leaves me every time more humbled—Enough of this—though in your Love for me you will not think it enough. . . . Tom is rather more easy than he has been: but is still so nervous that I can not speak to him of these Matters [76]—indeed it is the care I have had to keep his Mind aloof from feelings too acute that has made this Letter so short a one—I did not like to write before him a Letter he knew was to reach your hands—I cannot even now ask him for any Message—his heart speaks to you—Be as happy as you can. Think of me and for my sake be cheerful. Believe me my dear Brother and sister

Your anxious and affectionate Brother
John

This day is my Birth day—. . .

To George and Georgiana Keats, February 14–May 3, 1819

My dear Brother & Sister—How is it we have not heard from you from the Settlement yet? The Letters must surely have miscarried—I am in expectation every day. . . .

. . .

A Man's life of any worth is a continual allegory—and very few eyes can see the Mystery of his life—a life like the scriptures, figurative—which such people can no more make out than they can the hebrew Bible. Lord Byron cuts a figure—but he is not figurative—Shakspeare led a life of Allegory; his works are the comments on it. . . .

. . . I have this moment received a note from Haslam [77] in which he expects the death of his Father who has been for some time in a state of insensibility —his mother bears up he says very well—I shall go to twon [for town] tommorrow to see him. This is the world—thus we cannot expect to give way many hours to pleasure—Circumstances are like Clouds continually gathering and bursting—While we are laughing the seed of some trouble is put into the wide arable land of events [78]—while we are laughing it sprouts is [for it] grows and suddenly bears a poison fruit which we must pluck—Even so we have leisure to reason on the misfortunes of our friends; our own touch us too nearly for words. Very few men have ever arrived at a complete disinterestedness of Mind: very few have been influenced by a pure desire of the benefit of

---

76. In a preceding passage which has been omitted Keats refers to the George Keatses' expectation of a child. It is characteristic of his imaginative tact that he does not speak to Tom of a nephew or niece Tom could have no hope of ever seeing. Tom died just a month later.

77. William Haslam (1795–1851), "a most kind and obliging and constant friend," as Keats called him, was in business in London.

78. This striking phrase, and what immediately follows it, may have had their unconscious origin in the famous passage from Milton's *Areopagitica:* "Good and evil we know in the field of this world grow up together and almost inseparably, and the knowledge of good is so involved and interwoven with the knowledge of evil . . . that those confused seeds which were imposed on Psyche as an incessant labor to cull out and sort asunder, were not more intermixed. It was from out the rind of one apple tasted, that the knowledge of good and evil, as two twins cleaving together, leaped forth into the world."

others—in the greater part of the Benefactors of & to Humanity some mere-tricious motive has sullied their greatness—some melodramatic scenery has facinated them—From the manner in which I feel Haslam's misfortune I perceive how far I am from any humble standard of disinterestedness—Yet this feeling ought to be carried to its highest pitch, as there is no fear of its ever injuring society—which it would do I fear pushed to an extremity—For in wild nature the Hawk would loose his Breakfast of Robins and the Robin his of Worms The Lion must starve as well as the swallow—The greater part of Men make their way with the same instinctiveness, the same unwandering eye from their purposes, the same animal eagerness as the Hawk—The Hawk wants a Mate, so docs the Man—look at them both they set about it and pro-cure on[e] in the same manner—They want both a nest and they both set about one in the same manner—they get their food in the same manner—The noble animal Man for his amusement smokes his pipe—the Hawk balances about the Clouds—that is the only difference of their leisures. This it is that makes the Amusement of Life—to a speculative Mind. I go among the Fields and catch a glimpse of a stoat [79] or a fieldmouse peeping out of the withered grass—the creature hath a purpose and its eyes are bright with it—I go amongst the buildings of a city and I see a Man hurrying along—to what? The Creature has a purpose and his eyes are bright with it. But then as Words-worth says, 'We have all one human heart' [80]—there is an ellectric fire in human nature tending to purify—so that among these human creature[s] there is continully some birth of new heroism—The pity is that we must wonder at it: as we should at finding a pearl in rubbish—I have no doubt that thousands of people ncver heard of have had hearts comp[l]etely disinterested: I can remember but two—Socrates and Jesus—their Histories evince it—What I heard a little time ago, Taylor [81] observe with respect to Socrates, may be said of Jesus—That he was so great a man that though he transmitted no writing of his own to posterity, we have his Mind and his sayings and his greatness handed to us by others. It is to be lamented that the history of the latter was written and revised by Men interested in the pious frauds of Religion. Yet through all this I see his splendour. Even here though I myself am pursueing the same instinctive course as the veriest human animal you can think of—I am however young writing at random—straining at particles of light in the midst of a great darkness—without knowing the bearing of any one assertion of any one opinion. Yet may I not in this be free from sin? May there not be superior beings amused with any graceful, though instinctive attitude my mind m[a]y fall into, as I am entertained with the alertness of a Stoat or the anxiety of a Deer? Though a quarrel in the streets is a thing to be hated, the energies displayed in it are fine; the commonest Man shows a grace in his quarrel—By a superior being our reasoning[s] may take the same tone—though erroneous they may be fine—This is the very thing in which consists poetry; and if so it is not so fine a thing as philosophy—For the same reason that an eagle is

---

79. Actually, the ermine in its dark-furred phase. The word is often erroneously used to denote the common weasel.
80. *The Old Cumberland Beggar*, l. 153.
81. John Taylor, Keats's publisher.

not so fine a thing as a truth—Give me this credit—Do you not think I strive
—to know myself? Give me this credit—and you will not think that on my
own accou[n]t I repeat Milton's lines

> How charming is divine Philosophy
> Not harsh and crabbed as dull fools suppose
> But musical as is Apollo's lute [82]—

No—no for myself—feeling grateful as I do to have got into a state of mind
to relish them properly—Nothing ever becomes real till it is experienced—
Even a Proverb is no proverb to you till your Life has illustrated it—I am
ever affraid that your anxiety for me will lead you to fear for the violence of
my temperament continually smothered down: for that reason I did not intend
to have sent you the following sonnet [83]—but look over the two last pages and
ask yourselves whether I have not that in me which will well bear the buffets
of the world. . . .

The common cognomen of this world among the misguided and superstitious
is 'a vale of tears' from which we are to be redeemed by a certain arbitary
interposition of God and taken to Heaven—What a little circumscribe[d]
straightened notion! Call the world if you Please 'The vale of Soul-making'
Then you will find out the use of the world (I am speaking now in the highest
terms [84] for human nature admitting it to be immortal which I will here take
for granted for the purpose of showing a thought which has struck me concerning it) I say 'Soul making' Soul as distinguished from an Intelligence—
There may be intelligences or sparks of the divinity in millions—but they are
not Souls the till they acquire identities, till each one is personally itself.
I[n]telligences are atoms of perception—they know and they see and they are
pure, in short they are God—how then are Souls to be made? How then are
these sparks which are God to have identity given them—so as ever to possess
a bliss peculiar to each ones individual existence? How, but by the medium of
a world like this? This point I sincerely wish to consider because I think it a
grander system of salvation than the chrystain religion—or rather it is a system
of Spirit-creation—This is effected by three grand materials acting the one
upon the other for a series of years—These three Materials are the *Intelligence*
—the *human heart* (as distinguished from intelligence or Mind) and the *World*
or *Elemental space* suited for the proper action of *Mind and Heart* on each
other for the purpose of forming the *Soul* or *Intelligence destined to possess the
sense of Identity*. I can scarcely express what I but dimly perceive—and yet
I think I perceive it—that you may judge the more clearly I will put it in the
most homely form possible—I will call the *world* a School instituted for the
purpose of teaching little children to read—I will call the *human heart* the

---

82. Milton, *Comus*, ll. 475–77.
83. "Why Did I Laugh To-Night?" After copying the sonnet, Keats writes, "I went to
bed, and enjoyed an uninterrupted sleep. Sane I went to bed and sane I arose."
84. Perhaps Keats makes this stipulation because it occurs to him that the idea of the
developmental effect of suffering cannot, in ordinary compassion, be thought to apply to
those who, by reason of the circumstances of their lives and natures, are only passive to
experience. His doctrine, that is, is for persons who are so circumstanced that they can
think of their selves as material out of which something significant can be made.

horn Book [85] used in that School—and I will call the *Child able to read, the Soul* made from that *school* and its *hornbook*. Do you not see how necessary a World of Pains and troubles is to school an Intelligence and make it a soul? A Place where the heart must feel and suffer in a thousand diverse ways! Not merely is the Heart a Hornbook, It is the Minds Bible, it is the Minds experience, it is the teat from which the Mind or intelligence sucks its identity [86]—As various as the Lives of Men are—so various become their souls, and thus does God make individual beings, Souls, Identical Souls of the sparks of his own essence—This appears to me a faint sketch of a system of Salvation which does not affront our reason and humanity—I am convinced that many difficulties which christians labour under would vanish before it—There is one wh[i]ch even now Strikes me—the Salvation of Children—In them the Spark or intelligence returns to God without any identity—it having had no time to learn of, and be altered by, the heart—or seat of the human Passions—It is pretty generally suspected that the chr[i]stian scheme has been coppied from the ancient persian and greek Philosophers. Why may they not have made this simple thing even more simple for common apprehension by introducing Mediators and Personages in the same manner as in the hethen mythology abstractions are personified—Seriously I think it probable that this System of Soul-making—may have been the Parent of all the more palpable and personal Schemes of Redemption, among the Zoroastrians the Christians and the Hindoos. For as one part of the human species must have their carved Jupiter; so another part must have the palpable and named Mediator and saviour, their Christ their Oromanes and their Vishnu [87]—If what I have said should not be plain enough, as I fear it may not be, I will but [*for* put] you in the place where I began in this series of thoughts—I mean, I began by seeing how man was formed by circumstances—and what are circumstances?—but touchstones of his heart—? and what are touch stones?—but proovings of his hearrt?—and what are proovings of his heart but fortifiers or alterers of his nature? and what is his altered nature but his soul?—and what was his soul before it came into the world and had These provings and alterations and perfectionings?— An intelligence—without Identity—and how is this Identity to be made? Through the medium of the Heart? And how is the heart to become this Medium but in a world of Circumstances?—There now I think what with Poetry and Theology you may thank your Stars that my pen is not very long winded. . . .

. . . This is the 3ᵈ of May & every thing is in delightful forwardness; the violets are not withered, before the peeping of the first rose; You must let me know every thing, how parcels go & come, what papers you have, & what Newspapers you want, & other things—God bless you my dear Brother & Sister

Your ever Affectionate Brother

John Keats

85. Children formerly learned to read from a primer consisting of a single page mounted on wood and protected by a sheet of transparent horn.
86. Images drawn from eating and drinking are salient in Keats's thought.
87. Oromanes is a version of Ahriman, in the Zoroastrian religion the principle of evil, which is combatted by Ormazd, the principle of good. In Hinduism, Vishnu, the Preserver, is the Supreme Spirit.

To George and Georgiana Keats, September 21, 1819

My dear George,

. . . In the course of a few months I shall be as good an Italian Scholar as I am a french one—I am reading Ariosto [88] at present: not manageing more than six or eight stanzas at a time. When I have done this language so as to be able to read it tolerably well—I shall set myself to get complete in latin and there my learning must stop. I do not think of venturing upon Greek. I would not go even so far if I were not persuaded of the power the knowlege of any language gives one. the fact is I like to be acquainted with foreign languages. It is besides a nice way of filling up intervals &c Also the reading of Dante in [*for* is] well worth the while. And in latin there is a fund of curious literature of the middle ages—The Works of many great Men Aretine and Sanazarius and Machievel [89]—I shall never become attach'd to a foreign idiom so as to put it into my writings. The Paradise lost though so fine in itself is a curruption of our Language—it should be kept as it is unique—a curiosity. a beautiful and grand Curiosity. The most remarkable Production of the world —A northern dialect accommodating itself to greek and latin inversions and intonations. The purest english I think—or what ought to be the purest—is Chatterton's [90]—The Language had existed long enough to be entirely uncorrupted of Chaucer's gallicisms and still the old words are used—Chatterton's language is entirely northern—I prefer the native music of it to Milton's cut by feet I have but lately stood on my guard against Milton. Life to him would be death to me. Miltonic verse cannot be written but it [*for* in] the vein of art —I wish to devote myself to another sensation.[91]. . .

Your affectionate and anxious brother

John Keats

To Percy Bysshe Shelley, August 16, 1820

[On July 27, 1819, Shelley wrote to Keats from Pisa saying that he had heard of Keats's bad health, cautioning him against the rigors of an English winter, and extending to him a cordial invitation to come to Pisa to live with the Shelleys. He went on to say that he had lately read *Endymion* again "and ever with a new sense of the treasures of poetry it contains, though treasures poured forth with indistinct

88. Ludovico Ariosto (1474–1533), Italian poet, author of the epic poem *Orlando Furioso* (Orlando Mad), 1516, expanded version, 1532.
89. Pietro Aretino (1492–1556), Italian author noted for the audacity of his satire. Jacopo Sannazaro (1458–1530), Italian poet; his *Arcadia* had a direct influence on Sir Philip Sidney's work of the same name. Niccòlo Machiavelli (1469–1527), Italian statesman and political theorist.
90. Thomas Chatterton (1752–70), poetic prodigy, whose pseudo-medieval poems have survived their discovery as fabrications. In despair at his poverty, Chatterton poisoned himself at age 17.
91. Keats made the same comparison between the language of Chatterton and Milton in a letter to Reynolds written the same day. He goes on to say that he has given up *Hyperion*—"There were too many Miltonic inversions in it—Miltonic verse cannot be written but in an artful or rather artist's humour. I wish to give myself to other sensations. English ought to be kept up."

profusion." Then, having spoken of his request to his publisher to send Keats copies of *Prometheus Unbound* and *The Cenci*, he says, "In poetry I have sought to avoid system and mannerism; I wish those who excel me in genius would pursue the same plan." Shelley, Keats's senior by three years, had advantages of social position and education that Keats could not but be conscious of, and, for all his difficulties, he was better established as a poet than Keats, who, in a few references to Shelley in his letters, shows a certain touchiness about him. In his reply to the letter, Keats takes courteous account of the kindness of the invitation and the praise, but seems to see a hint of condescension in Shelley's advice and replies with advice of his own which is not less to the point for having been occasioned by pride.]

My dear Shelley,

I am very much gratified that you, in a foreign country, and with a mind almost over occupied, should write to me in the strain of the Letter beside me. If I do not take advantage of your invitation it will be prevented by a circumstance I have very much at heart to prophesy—There is no doubt that an english winter would put an end to me, and do so in a lingering hateful manner, therefore I must either voyage or journey to Italy as a soldier marches up to a battery. My nerves at present are the worst part of me, yet they feel soothed when I think that come what extreme may, I shall not be destined to remain in one spot long enough to take a hatred of any four particular bed-posts. I am glad you take any pleasure in my poor Poem;—which I would willingly take the trouble to unwrite, if possible, did I care so much as I have done about Reputation. I received a copy of the Cenci, as from yourself from Hunt. There is only one part of it I am judge of; the Poetry, and dramatic effect, which by many spirits now a days is considered the mammon. A modern work it is said must have a purpose,[92] which may be the God—*an artist* must serve Mammon —he must have 'self concentration' selfishness perhaps. You I am sure will forgive me for sincerely remarking that you might curb your magnanimity and be more of an artist, and 'load every rift' of your subject with ore [93] The thought of such discipline must fall like cold chains upon you, who perhaps never sat with your wings furl'd for six Months together. And is not this extraordina[r]y talk for the winter of Endymion? whose mind was like a pack of scattered cards—I am pick'd up and sorted to a pip.[94] My Imagination is a Monastry and I am its Monk—you must explain my metap[cs] [*for* metaphysics] to yourself. I am in expectation of Prometheus every day. Could I have my own wish for its interest effected you would have it still in manuscript—or be but now putting an end to the second act. I remember you advising me not to publish my first-blights, on Hampstead heath—I am returning advice upon your hands. Most of the Poems in the volume I send you have been written above two years, and would never have been publish'd but from a hope of gain; so you see I am inclined enough to take your advice now. I must exp[r]ess once more my deep sense of your kindness, adding my sincere thanks and respects for M[rs] Shelley. In the hope of soon seeing you (I) remain

most sincerely (yours,)

John Keats

92. The statement was made by Wordsworth in his Preface to *Lyrical Ballads*.
93. *The Faerie Queene* II.vii.28, l. 5.
94. The marking on a playing card.

To Charles Brown, November 30, 1820 [95]

Rome. 30 November 1820

My dear Brown,
'Tis the most difficult thing in the world to me to write a letter. My stomach continues so bad, that I feel it worse on opening any book,—yet I am much better than I was in Quarantine. Then I am afraid to encounter the proing and conning of any thing interesting to me in England. I have an habitual feeling of my real life having past, and that I am leading a posthumous existence. God knows how it would have been—but it appears to me—however, I will not speak of that subject. I must have been at Bedhampton nearly at the time you were writing to me from Chichester—how unfortunate—and to pass on the river too! There was my star predominant! I cannot answer any thing in your letter, which followed me from Naples to Rome, because I am afraid to look it over again. I am so weak (in mind) that I cannot bear the sight of any hand writing of a friend I love so much as I do you. Yet I ride the little horse, —and, at my worst, even in Quarantine, summoned up more puns, in a sort of desperation, in one week than in any year of my life. There is one thought enough to kill me—I have been well, healthy, alert &c, walking with her— and now—the knowledge of contrast, feeling for light and shade, all that information (primitive sense) necessary for a poem are great enemies to the recovery of the stomach. There, you rogue, I put you to the torture,—but you must bring your philosophy to bear—as I do mine, really—or how should I be able to live? Dr Clarke is very attentive to me; he says, there is very little the matter with my lungs, but my stomach, he says, is very bad. I am well disappointed in hearing good news from George,—for it runs in my head we shall all die young. I have not written to x x x x x [96] yet, which he must think very neglectful; being anxious to send him a good account of my health, I have delayed it from week to week. If I recover, I will do all in my power to correct the mistakes made during sickness; and if I should not, all my faults will be forgiven. I shall write to x x x to-morrow, or next day. I will write to x x x x x in the middle of next week. Severn is very well, though he leads so dull a life with me. Remember me to all friends, and tell x x x x I should not have left London without taking leave of him, but from being so low in body and mind. Write to George as soon as you receive this, and tell him how I am, as far as you can guess;—and also a note to my sister—who walks about my imagination like a ghost—she is so like Tom. I can scarcely bid you good bye even in a letter. I always made an awkward bow.

God bless you!
John Keats

95. In a hopeless effort to recover his health, Keats sailed for Italy on September 17, 1820, in the care of one of his friends, Joseph Severn, an artist. They arrived in Rome in mid-November. After great suffering, Keats died on February 23, 1821. This is his last known letter.
96. This letter exists only in a copy and the copyist has thus represented the names of four friends to whom Keats refers. They are probably Haslam, Dilke, Woodhouse, and Reynolds.

Glossary

A Commentary on Selected Literary and Historical Terms

Allegory Literally, "other reading"; originally a way of interpreting a narrative or other text in order to extract a more general, or a less literal, meaning from it, e.g. reading Homer's *Odyssey* as the universal voyage of human life—with Odysseus standing for all men—which must be made toward a final goal. In the Middle Ages allegory came to be associated with ways of reading the Bible, particularly the Old Testament in relation to the New. In addition, stories came to be written with the intention of being interpreted symbolically; thus e.g. the *Psychomachia* or "battle for the soul" of Prudentius (b. 348 A.D.) figured the virtues and vices as contending soldiers in a battle (see *Personification*). There is allegorical lyric poetry and allegorical drama as well as allegorical narrative. In works such as Spenser's *The Faerie Queene* and Bunyan's *Pilgrim's Progress* allegory becomes a dominant literary form. See also *Figure,* under *Rhetoric; Type, Typology.*

Alliteration A repeated initial consonant in successive words. In Old English verse, any vowel alliterates with any other, and alliteration is not an unusual or expressive phenomenon but a regularly recurring structural feature of the verse, occurring on the first and third, and often on the first, second, and third, primary-stressed syllables of the four-stressed line. Thus, from "The Seafarer":

> hréran mid hóndum hrímcælde sǽ
> ("to stir with his hand the rime-cold sea")

In later English verse tradition, alliteration becomes expressive in a variety of ways. Spenser uses it decoratively, or to link adjective and noun, verb and object, as in the line: "Much daunted with that dint, her sense was dazed." In the 18th and 19th centuries it becomes even less systematic and more "musical."

Assonance A repeated vowel sound, a part-rhyme, which has great expressive effect when used internally (within lines), e.g. "An old, mad, blind, despised and dying king,—" (Shelley, "Sonnet: England in 1819").

Baroque (1) Originally (and still), an oddly shaped rather than a spherical pearl, and hence something twisted, contorted, involuted. (2) By a complicated analogy, a term designating stylistic periods in art, music, and literature during the 16th and 17th centuries in Europe. The analogies among the arts are frequently strained, and the stylistic periods by no means completely coincide. But the relation between the poetry of Richard Crashaw in English and Latin, and the sculpture and architecture of Gianlorenzo Bernini (1598–1680), is frequently taken to typify the spirit of the baroque. (See Wylie Sypher, *Four Stages of Renaissance Style*, 1955.)

Balade, Ballade   The dominant lyric form in French poetry of the 14th and 15th centuries; a strict form consisting of three stanzas of eight lines each, with an *envoi* (*q.v.*), or four-line conclusion, addressing either a person of importance or a personification. Each stanza, including the *envoi*, ends in a refrain.

Ballad Meter   Or *common meter;* four-lined stanzas, rhyming *abab*, the first and third lines in iambic tetrameter (four beats), and the second and fourth lines in iambic trimeter (three beats). See *Meter*.

Courtly Love   Modern scholarship has coined this name for a set of conventions around which medieval love-poetry was written. It was essentially chivalric and a product of 12th-century France, especially of the troubadours. This poetry involves an idealization of the beloved woman, whose love, like all love, refines and ennobles the lover so that the union of their minds and/or bodies—a union that ought not to be apparent to others—allows them to attain excellence of character.

Dada   A satirical, anti-literary movement in European art and literature, 1916–21, its name having been selected to connote *nothing* (the movement's founders are in dispute over its method of selection). Dadaists engaged in a systematic nullification of reason, religion, and art itself, producing pictures and poems out of the random and the absurd, sculpture out of ordinary objects, and entertainments out of elaborately staged exhibitions that must have been alternately hilarious and tedious. Founded in Zurich by Tristan Tzara, Hans Arp, Hugo Ball, and Richard Huelsenbeck, Dada moved to Paris in 1919, took on a more international character, and was embraced by many young writers who would thereafter become attached to Surrealism (*q.v.*).

Decorum   Propriety of discourse; what is becoming in action, character, and style; the avoidance of impossibilities and incongruities in action, style, and character: "the good grace of everything after his kind" and the "great masterpiece to observe." More formally, a neoclassical doctrine maintaining that literary style—grand, or high, middle, and low—be appropriate to the subject, occasion, and genre. Thus Milton, in *Paradise Lost* (I.13–14), invokes his "adventurous song, / That with no middle flight intends to soar. . . ." See also *Rhetoric*.

Dissenters   In England, members of Protestant churches and sects that do not conform to the doctrines of the established Church of England; from the 16th century on, this would include Baptists, Puritans of various sorts within the Anglican Church, Presbyterians, Congregationalists, and (in the 18th century) Methodists. Another term, more current in the 19th century, is *Nonconformist*.

Elegy   Originally, in Greek and Latin poetry, a poem composed not in the hexameter lines of epic (*q.v.*) and, later, of pastoral, but in the elegiac couplets consisting of one hexameter line followed by a pentameter. Elegiac poetry was amatory, epigrammatic. By the end of the 16th century, English poets were using heroic couplets (*q.v.*), to stand for both hexameters and elegiacs; and an elegiac poem was any serious meditative piece. Perhaps because of the tradition of the pastoral elegy (*q.v.*), the general term "elegy" came to be reserved, in modern terminology, for an elaborate and formal lament, longer than a *dirge* or *threnody,* for a dead person. By extension, "elegiac" has come to mean, in general speech, broodingly sad.

Enjambment The "straddling" of a clause or sentence across two lines of verse, as opposed to closed, or end-stopped, lines. Thus, in the opening lines of Shakespeare's *Twelfth Night:*

> If music be the food of love, play on!
> Give me excess of it, that, surfeiting
> The appetite may sicken and so die . . .

the first line is stopped, the second enjambed. When enjambment becomes strong or violent, it may have an ironic or comic effect.

The Enlightenment A term used very generally, to refer to the late 17th and the 18th century in Europe, a period characterized by a programmatic rationalism—i.e. a belief in the ability of human reason to understand the world and thereby to transform whatever in it needed transforming; an age in which ideas of science and progress accompanied the rise of new philosophies of the relation of man to the state, an age which saw many of its hopes for human betterment fulfilled in the French Revolution.

Envoi, Envoy Short concluding stanza found in certain French poetic forms and their English imitations, e.g. the *ballade* (*q.v.*). It serves as a dedicatory postscript, and a summing up of the poem of which it repeats the refrain.

Epic Or, *heroic poetry;* originally, oral narrative delivered in a style different from that of normal discourse by reason of verse, music, and heightened diction, and concerning the great deeds of a central heroic figure, or group of figures, usually having to do with a crisis in the history of a race or culture. Its setting lies in this earlier "heroic" period, and it will often have been written down only after a long period of oral transmission. The Greek *Iliad* and *Odyssey* and the Old English *Beowulf* are examples of this, in their narration mixing details from both the heroic period described and the actual time of their own composition and narration. What is called *secondary* or *literary* epic is a long, ambitious poem, composed by a single poet on the model of the older, primary forms, and of necessity being more allusive and figurative than its predecessors. Homer's poems lead to Virgil's *Aeneid,* which leads to Milton's *Paradise Lost,* in a chain of literary dependency. Spenser's *Faerie Queene* might be called *romantic epic* of the secondary sort, and Dante's *Divine Comedy* might also be assimilated to post-Virgilian epic tradition.

Epic Simile An extended comparison, in Homeric and subsequently in Virgilian and later epic poetry, between an event in the story (the *fable*) and something in the experience of the epic audience, to the effect of making the fabulous comprehensible in terms of the familiar. From the Renaissance on, additional complications have emerged from the fact that what is the familiar for the classical audience becomes, because of historical change, itself fabled (usually, pastoral) for the modern audience. Epic similes compare the fabled with the familiar usually with respect to one property or element; thus, in the *Odyssey*, when the stalwart forward motion of a ship in high winds is described, the simile goes:

> And as amids a fair field four brave horse
> Before a chariot, stung into their course
> With fervent lashes of the smarting scourge
> That all their fire blows high, and makes them rise
> To utmost speed the measure of their ground:
> So bore the ship aloft her fiery bound
> About whom rushed the billows, black and vast
> In which the sea-roars burst . . .
>   (*Chapman translation*)

Notice the formal order of presentation: "even as . . .": *the familiar event, often described in detail;* "just so . . .": *the fabled one.*

Epicureanism   A system of philosophy founded by the Greek Epicurus (342–270 B.C.), who taught that the five senses are the sole source of ideas and sole criterion of truth, and that the goal of human life is pleasure (i.e. hedonism), though this can be achieved only by practicing moderation. Later the term came to connote bestial self-indulgence, which Epicurus had clearly rejected.

Figurative Language   In a general sense, any shift away from a literal meaning of words, brought about by the use of tropes (*q.v.*) or other rhetorical devices. See *Rhetoric.*

Free Verse, Vers Libre   Generally, any English verse form whose lines are measured neither by the number of 1) stressed syllables (see *Meter* §3, accentual verse), 2) alternations of stressed and unstressed syllables (§4, accentual-syllabic verse), nor syllables alone (§2, syllabic verse). The earliest English free verse —that of Christopher Smart in *Jubilate Agno* (18th century)—imitates the prosody of Hebrew poetry (reflected also in the translation of the English Bible), in maintaining unmeasured units marked by syntactic parallelism. While many free-verse traditions (e.g. that of Walt Whitman) remain close to the impulses of this biblical poetry, yet others, in the 20th century, have developed new *ad hoc* patternings of their own. *Vers libre* usually refers to the experimental, frequently very short unmeasured lines favored by poets of the World War I period, although the term, rather than the form, was adopted from French poetry of the 19th century.

Gothic   Term (originally pejorative, as alluding to the Teutonic barbarians) designating the architectural style of the Middle Ages. The revival of interest in medieval architecture in the later 18th century produced not only pseudo-Gothic castles like Horace Walpole's "Strawberry Hill", and more modest artificial ruins on modern estates, but also a vogue for atmospheric prose romances set in medieval surroundings and involving improbable terrors, and known as Gothic novels. The taste for the Gothic, arising during the Age of Sensibility (*q.v.*), is another reflection of a reaction against earlier 18th-century neoclassicism (*q.v*).

Heroic Couplet In English prosody, a pair of rhyming, iambic pentameter lines, used at first for closure—as at the end of the Shakespearean sonnet (*q.v.*)—or to terminate a scene in blank-verse drama; later adapted to correspond in English poetry to the elegiac couplet of classical verse as well as to the heroic, unrhymed, Greek and Latin hexameter. Octosyllabic couplets, with four stresses (eight syllables) to the line, are a minor, shorter, jumpier form, used satirically unless in implicit allusion to the form of Milton's "Il Penseroso," in which they develop great lyrical power. (See *Meter.*)

Irony Generally, a mode of saying one thing to mean another. *Sarcasm*, in which one means exactly the opposite of what one says, is the easiest and cheapest form; thus, e.g. "Yeah, it's a *nice day–*" when one means that it's a miserable one. But serious literature produces ironies of a much more complex and revealing sort. *Dramatic irony* occurs when a character in a play or story asserts something whose meaning the audience or reader knows will change in time. Thus, in Genesis when Abraham assures his son Isaac (whom he is about to sacrifice) that "God will provide his own lamb," the statement is lighted with dramatic irony when a sacrificial ram is actually provided at the last minute to save Isaac. Or, in the case of Sophocles' *Oedipus,* when almost everything the protagonist says about the predicament of his city is hideously ironic in view of the fact (which he does not know) that he is responsible therefor. The ironies generated by the acknowledged use of non-literal language (see *Rhetoric*) and fictions in drama, song, and narrative are at the core of imaginative literature.

Kenning An Old Norse form designating, strictly, a condensed simile or metaphor of the kind frequently used in Old Germanic poetry; a figurative circumlocution for a thing not actually named—e.g. "swan's path" for sea; "world-candle" or "sky-candle" for sun. More loosely, often used to mean also a metaphorical compound word or phrase such as "ring-necked" or "foamy-necked" for a ship, these being descriptive rather than figurative in character.

Macaronic Verse in which two languages are mingled, usually for burlesque purposes.

Meter Verse may be made to differ from prose and from ordinary speech in a number of ways, and in various languages these ways may be very different. Broadly speaking, lines of verse may be marked out by the following regularities of pattern:

1. *Quantitative Verse,* used in ancient Greek poetry and adopted by the Romans, used a fixed number of what were almost musical measures, called *feet;* they were built up of long and short syllables (like half- and quarter-notes in music), which depended on the vowel and consonants in them. *Stress accent* (the *word* stress which, when accompanied by vowel reduction, distinguishes the English noun "*content*" from the adjective "*content*") did not exist in ancient Greek, and played no part in the rhythm of the poetic line. Thus, the first line of the *Odyssey: Andra moi ennepe mousa, polytropon hos mala polla* ("Sing me, O muse, of that man of many resources who, after great hardship . . .") is composed in *dactyls* of one long syllable followed by two shorts (but, as in musical rhythm, replaceable by two longs, a *spondee*).

With six dactyls to a line, the resulting meter is called *dactylic hexameter* (*hexameter*, for short), the standard form for epic poetry. Other kinds of foot or measure were: the *anapest* ($\cup \cup -$); the *iamb* ($\cup -$); the *trochee* ($- \cup$); and a host of complex patterns used in lyric poetry. Because of substitutions, however, the number of syllables in a classical line was not fixed, only the number of measures.

2. *Syllabic Verse,* used in French, Japanese, and many other languages, and in English poetry of the mid-20th century, measures only the *number* of syllables per line with no regard to considerations of *quantity* or *stress.* Because of the prominence of stress in the English language, two lines of the same purely syllabic length may not necessarily sound at all as though they were in the same meter, e.g.:

> These two incommensurably sounding
> Lines are both written with ten syllables.

3. *Accentual Verse,* used in early Germanic poetry, and thus in Old English poetry, depended upon the number of strong *stress accents* per line. These accents were four in number, with no fixed number of unstressed. Folk poetry and nursery rhymes often preserve this accentual verse, e.g.:

> Sing, sing, what shall I sing?
> The cat's run away with the pudding-bag string

The first line has six syllables, the second, eleven, but they sound more alike (and not merely by reason of their rhyme) than the two syllabic lines quoted above.

4. *Accentual-Syllabic Verse,* the traditional meter of English poetry from Chaucer on, depends upon both numbered *stresses* and numbered *syllables,* a standard form consisting of ten syllables alternately stressed and unstressed, and having five stresses; thus it may be said to consist of five syllable pairs.

For complex historical reasons, accentual-syllabic groups of stressed and unstressed syllables came to be known by the names used for Greek and Latin feet—which can be very confusing. The analogy was made between *long* syllables in the classical languages, and *stressed* syllables in English. Thus, the pair of syllables in the adjective "con*tent*" is called an *iamb,* and in the noun "*con*tent," a *trochee;* the word "*clas*sical" is a *dactyll,* and the phrase "of the *best,*" an *anapest.* When English poetry is being discussed, these terms are always used in their adapted, accentual-syllabic meanings, and hence the ten-syllable line mentioned earlier is called "iambic pentameter" in English. The phrase "high-tide" would be a *spondee* (as would, in general, two monosyllables comprising a proper name, e.g. "John Smith"); whereas compound nouns like "highway" would be *trochaic.* In this adaptation of classical nomenclature, the terms *dimeter, trimeter, tetrameter, pentameter, hexameter* refer not to the number of quantitative feet but to the number of syllable-groups (pairs or triplets, from one to six) composing the line. Iambic pentameter and tetrameter lines are frequently also called *decasyllabic* and *octosyllabic* respectively.

5. *Versification.* In verse, lines may be arranged in patterns called *stichic*

or *strophic*, that is, the same linear form (say, iambic pentameter) repeated without grouping by rhyme or interlarded lines of another form, or varied in just such a way into *stanzas* or *strophes* ("turns"). Unrhymed iambic pentameter, called *blank verse*, is the English stichic form that Milton thought most similar to classic hexameter or *heroic* verse. But in the Augustan period iambic pentameter rhymed pairs, called heroic couplets (*q.v.*), came to stand for this ancient form as well as for the classical elegiac verse (*q.v.*). Taking couplets as the simplest strophic unit, we may proceed to *tercets* (groups of three lines) and to *quatrains* (groups of four), rhymed *abab* or *abcb*, and with equal or unequal line lengths. Other stanzaic forms: *ottava rima*, an eight-line, iambic pentameter stanza, rhyming *abababcc*; *Spenserian stanza*, rhyming *ababbcbcc*, all pentameter save for the last line, an iambic hexameter, or *alexandrine*. There have been adaptations in English (by Shelley, notably, and without rhyme by T. S. Eliot) of the Italian *terza rima* used by Dante in *The Divine Comedy*, interlocking tercets rhyming *aba bcb cdc ded*, etc. More elaborate stanza forms developed in the texts of some Elizabethan songs and in connection with the ode (*q.v.*).

Myth   A primitive story explaining the origins of certain phenomena in the world and in human life, and usually embodying gods or other supernatural forces, heroes (men who are either part human and part divine, or are placed between an ordinary mortal and a divine being), men, and animals. Literature continues to incorporate myths long after the mythology (the system of stories containing them) ceases to be a matter of actual belief. Moreover, discarded beliefs of all sorts tend to become myths when they are remembered but no longer literally clung to, and are used in literature in a similar way. The classical mythology of the Greeks and Romans was apprehended in this literary, or interpreted, way, even in ancient times. The gods and heroes and their deeds came to be read as allegory (*q.v.*). During the Renaissance, *mythography*—the interpretation of myths in order to make them reveal a moral or historical significance (rather than merely remaining entertaining but insignificant stories)—was extremely important, both for literature and for painting and sculpture. In modern criticism, mythical or *archetypal* situations and personages have been interpreted as being central objects of the work of the imagination.

Neoclassicism   (1) In general the term refers to Renaissance and post-Renaissance attempts to model enterprises in the various arts on Roman and Greek originals—or as much as was known of them. Thus, in the late Renaissance, the architectural innovations of Andrea Palladio may be called "neoclassic," as may Ben Jonson's relation, and Alexander Pope's as well, to the Roman poet Horace. The whole Augustan period in English literary history (1660–1740) was a deliberately neoclassical one.

(2) More specifically, neoclassicism refers to that period in the history of all European art spanning the very late 18th and early 19th century, which period may be seen as accompanying the fulfillment, and the termination, of the Enlightenment (*q.v.*). In England such neoclassic artists as Henry Fuseli, John Flaxman, George Romney, and even, in some measure, William Blake, are close to the origins of pictorial and literary Romanticism itself.

Neoplatonism   See *Platonism*.
Nonconformist   See *Dissenters*.

Octosyllabic Couplet   See *Heroic Couplet; Meter*.
Ode   A basic poetic form, originating in Greek antiquity. The *choral ode* was a public event, sung and danced, at a large ceremony, or as part of the tragic and comic drama. Often called *Pindaric ode*, after a great Greek poet, the form consisted of *triads* (groups of three sections each). These were units of song and dance, and had the form *aab*—that is, a *strophe* (or "turn"), an *antistrophe* (or "counter-turn"), and an *epode* (or "stand"), the first two being identical musically and metrically, the third different. In English poetry, the Pindaric ode form, only in its metrical aspects, became in the 17th century a mode for almost essayistic poetic comment, and was often used also as a kind of cantata libretto, in praise of music and poetry (the so-called *musical ode*). By the 18th century the ode became the form for a certain kind of personal, visionary poem, and it is this form that Wordsworth and Coleridge transmitted to Romantic tradition. A second English form, known as *Horatian ode*, was based on the lyric (not choral) poems of Horace, and is written in *aabb* quatrains, with the last two lines shorter than the first two by a pair of syllables or more.

Paradox   In logic, a self-contradictory statement, hence meaningless (or a situation producing one), with an indication that something is wrong with the language in which such a situation can occur, e.g. the famous paradox of Epimenedes the Cretan, who held that all Cretans are liars (and thus could be lying if— and only if—he wasn't), or that of Zeno, of the arrow in flight: since at any instant of time the point of the arrow can always be said to be at one precise point, therefore it is continually at rest at a continuous sequence of such points, and therefore never moves. In literature, however, particularly in the language of lyric poetry, paradox plays another role. From the beginnings of lyric poetry, paradox has been deemed necessary to express feelings and other aspects of human inner states, e.g. Sappho's invention of the Greek word *glykypikron* ("bittersweet") to describe love, or her assertion that she was freezing and burning at the same time. So too the Latin poet Catullus, in his famous couplet

> I'm in hate and I'm in love; why do I? you may ask.
> Well, I don't know, but I feel it, and I'm in agony.

may be declaring thereby that true love poetry must be illogical.

In Elizabethan poetry, paradoxes were frequently baldly laid out in the rhetorical form called *oxymoron* (see *Rhetoric*), as in "the victor-victim," or across a fairly mechanical sentence structure, as in "My feast of joy is but a dish of pain." In the highest poetic art, however, the seeming self-contradiction is removed when one realizes that either, or both, of the conflicting terms is to be taken figuratively, rather than literally. The apparent absurdity, or strangeness, thus gives rhetorical power to the utterance. Elaborate and sophisticated paradoxes, insisting on their own absurdity, typify the poetic idiom of the tradition of John Donne.

Pastoral A literary mode in which the lives of simple country people are celebrated, described, and used allegorically by sophisticated urban poets and writers. The *idylls* of Sicilian poet Theocritus (3rd century B.C.) were imitated and made more symbolic in Virgil's *eclogues;* shepherds in an Arcadian landscape stood for literary and political personages, and the Renaissance adapted these narrative and lyric pieces for moral and aesthetic discussion. Spenser's *Shepheardes Calendar* is an experimental collection of eclogues involving an array of forms and subjects. In subsequent literary tradition, the pastoral imagery of both Old and New Testaments (Psalms, Song of Songs, priest as *pastor* or shepherd of his flock, and so on) joins with the classical mode. Modern critics, William Empson in particular, have seen the continuation of pastoral tradition in other versions of the country-city confrontation, such as child-adult and criminal-businessman. See *Pastoral Elegy.*

Pastoral Elegy A form of lament for the death of a poet, originating in Greek bucolic tradition (Bion's lament for Adonis, a lament for Bion by a fellow poet, Theocritus' first idyll, Virgil's tenth eclogue) and continued in use by Renaissance poets as a public mode for the presentation of private, inner, and even coterie matters affecting poets and their lives, while conventionally treating questions of general human importance. At a death one is moved to ask, "Why this death? Why now?" and funeral elegy must always confront these questions, avoiding easy resignation as an answer. Pastoral elegy handled these questions with formal mythological apparatus, such as the Muses, who should have protected their dead poet, local spirits, and other presences appropriate to the circumstances of the life and death, and perhaps figures of more general mythological power. The end of such poems is the eternalization of the dead poet in a monument of myth, stronger than stone or bronze: Spenser's *Astrophel,* a lament for Sir Philip Sidney, concludes with an Ovidian change—the dead poet's harp, like Orpheus' lyre, becomes the constellation Lyra. Milton's *Lycidas* both exemplifies and transforms the convention. Later examples include Shelley's *Adonais* (for Keats), Arnold's *Thyrsis* (for Clough), and Swinburne's *Ave Atque Vale* (for Baudelaire).

Pathetic Fallacy John Ruskin's term (used in *Modern Painters,* 1856) for the projection of human emotions onto the world in such a way as to personify inanimate things ineptly or falsely.

Personification Treating a thing or, more properly, an abstract quality, as though it were a person. Thus, "Surely *goodness* and *mercy* shall follow me all the days of my life" tends to personify the italicized terms by reason of the metaphoric use of "follow me." On the other hand, a conventional, complete personification, like *Justice* (whom we recognize by her *attributes*—she is blindfolded, she has scales and a sword) might also be called an *allegorical figure* in her own right, and her attributes *symbols* (blindness = impartiality; scales = justly deciding; sword = power to mete out what is deserved). Often the term "personification" applies to momentary, or *ad hoc,* humanizations.

Platonism The legacy of Plato (429–347 B.C.) is virtually the history of philosophy. His *Timaeus* was an important source of later cosmology; his doctrine of ideas is central to Platonic tradition. His doctrine of love (especially in the *Symposium*) had enormous influence in the Renaissance, at which time its applicability was shifted to heterosexual love specifically. The *Republic* and the *Laws* underlie a vast amount of political thought, and the *Republic* contains also a philosophical attack on poetry (fiction) which defenders of the arts have always had to answer. Neoplatonism—a synthesis of Platonism, Pythagoreanism, and Aristotelianism—was dominant in the 3rd century A.D.; and the whole tradition was revived in the 15th and 16th centuries. The medieval Plato was Latinized, largely at second-hand; the revival of Greek learning in the 15th century led to another Neoplatonism: a synthesis of Platonism, the medieval Christian Aristotle, and Christian doctrine. Out of this came the doctrines of love we associate with some Renaissance poetry; a sophisticated version of older systems of allegory and symbol; and notions of the relation of spirit and matter reflected in Marvell and many other poets.

Rhetoric   In classical times, rhetoric was the art of persuading through the use of language. The major treatises on style and structure of discourse—Aristotle's *Rhetoric*, Quintilian's *Institutes of Oratory*, the *Rhetorica ad Herrenium* ascribed for centuries to Cicero—were concerned with the "arts" of language in the older sense of "skills." In the Middle Ages the *trivium* (*q.v.*), or program that led to the degree of Bachelor of Arts, consisted of grammar, logic, and rhetoric, but it was an abstract study, based on the Roman tradition. In the Renaissance, classical rhetorical study became a matter of the first importance, and it led to the study of literary stylistics and the application of principles and concepts of the production and structure of eloquence to the higher eloquence of poetry.

Rhetoricians distinguished three stages in the production of discourse: *inventio* (finding or discovery), *dispositio* (arranging), and *elocutio* (style). Since the classical discipline aimed always at practical oratory (e.g. winning a case in court, or making a point effectively in council), *memoria* (memory) and *pronuntiatio* (delivery) were added. For the Renaissance, however, rhetoric became the art of writing. Under the heading of *elocutio*, style became stratified into three levels, *elevated* or high, *elegant* or middle, and *plain* or low. The proper fitting of these styles to the subject of discourse comprised the subject of decorum (*q.v.*).

Another area of rhetorical theory was concerned with classification of devices of language into *schemes, tropes,* and *figures.* A basic but somewhat confused distinction between figures of speech and figures of thought need not concern us here, but we may roughly distinguish between schemes (or patterns) of words, and tropes as manipulations of meanings, and of making words non-literal.

Common Schemes

anadiplosis   repeating the terminal word in a clause as the start of the next one: "Pleasure might cause her read; reading might cause her know; / Knowledge might pity win, and pity grace obtain" (Sidney, *Astrophel and Stella*).

anaphora   the repetition of a word or phrase at the openings of successive clauses, e.g. "The Lord sitteth above the water floods. The Lord remaineth King forever. The Lord shall give strength unto his people. The Lord shall give his people the blessing of peace."

chiasmus   a pattern of criss-crossing a syntactic structure, whether of noun and adjective, e.g. "Empty his bottle, and his girlfriend gone," or of a reversal of normal syntax with similar effect, e.g. "A fop her passion, and her prize, a sot," reinforced by assonance (*q.v.*). Chiasmus may even extend to assonance, as in Coleridge's line "In Xanadu did Kubla Khan."

Common Tropes

metaphor and simile both involve comparison of one thing to another, the difference being that the *simile* will actually compare, using the words "like" or "as," while the metaphor identifies one with the other, thus producing a non-literal use of a word or attribution. Thus, Robert Burns's "O, my love is like a red, red rose / That's newly sprung in June" is a simile; had Burns written, "My love, thou art a red, red rose . . .", it would have been a metaphor—and indeed, it would not mean that the lady had acquired petals. In modern critical theory, *metaphor* has come to stand for various non-expository kinds of evocative signification. I. A. Richards, the modern critic most interested in a general theory of metaphor in this sense, has contributed the terms *tenor* (as in the case above, the girl) and *vehicle* (the rose) to designate the components. See also *Epic Simile.*

metonymy a trope in which the vehicle is closely and conventionally associated with the tenor, e.g. "crown" and "king," "pen" and "writing," "pencil" and "drawing," "sword" and "warfare."

synecdoche a trope in which the part stands for the whole, e.g. "sail" for "ship."

hyperbole intensifying exaggeration, e.g. the combined synecdoche and hyperbole in which Christopher Marlowe's Faustus asks of Helen of Troy "Is this the face that launched a thousand ships / And burned the topless towers of Ilium?"

oxymoron literally, sharp-dull; a figure of speech involving a witty paradox, e.g. "sweet harm"; "darkness visible" (Milton, *Paradise Lost* I.63).

Satire A literary mode painting a distorted verbal picture of part of the world in order to show its true moral, as opposed merely to its physical, nature. In this sense, Circe, the enchantress in Homer's *Odyssey* who changed Odysseus' men into pigs (because they made pigs of themselves while eating) and would have changed Odysseus into a fox (for he was indeed foxy), was the first satirist. Originally the Latin word *satura* meant a kind of literary grab bag, or medley, and a satire was a fanciful kind of tale in mixed prose and verse; but later a false etymology connected the word with *satyr* and thus with the grotesque. Satire may be in verse or in prose; in the 16th and 17th centuries, the Roman poets Horace and Juvenal were imitated and expanded upon by writers of satiric moral verse, the tone of the verse being wise, smooth, skeptical, and urbane, that of the prose, sharp, harsh, and sometimes nasty. A tradition of English verse satire runs through Donne, Jonson, Dryden, Pope, and Samuel Johnson; of prose satire, Addison, Swift, and Fielding.

Seneca Lucius Annaeus Seneca (4 B.C.–65 A.D.) was an important source of Renaissance stoicism (*q.v.*), a model for the "closet" drama of the period, and an exemplar for the kind of prose that shunned the Ciceronian loquacity of early humanism and cultivated terseness. He was Nero's tutor; in 62 A.D. he retired from public life, and in 65 was compelled to commit suicide for taking part in a political conspiracy. He produced writings on ethics and physics, as well as ten tragedies often imitated in the Renaissance.

Sensibility (1) In the mid-18th century, the term came to be used in a literary context to refer to a susceptibility to fine or tender feelings, particularly involving the feelings and sorrows of others. This became a quality to be cultivated in despite of stoical rejections of unreasonable emotion which the neoclassicism (q.v.) of the earlier Augustan age had prized. The meaning of the word blended easily into "sentimentality"; but the literary period in England characterized by the work of writers such as Sterne, Goldsmith, Gray, Collins, and Cowper is often called the Age of Sensibility.

(2) A meaning more important for modern literature is that of a special kind of total awareness, an ability to make the finest discriminations in its perception of the world, and yet at the same time not lacking in a kind of force by the very virtue of its own receptive power. The varieties of awareness celebrated in French literature from Baudelaire through Marcel Proust have been adapted by modernist English critics, notably T. S. Eliot, for a fuller extension of the meaning of *sensibility*. By the term "dissociation of sensibility," Eliot implied the split between the sensuous and the intellectual faculties which he thought characterized English poetry after the Restoration (1660).

Sententia   A wise, fruitful saying, functioning as a guide to morally correct thought or action.

Sestina   Originally a Provençal lyric form supposedly invented by Arnaut Daniel in the 12th century, and one of the most complex of those structures. It has six stanzas of six lines each, folllowed by an *envoi* (q.v.) or *tornada* of three lines. Instead of rhyming, the end-words of the lines of the first stanza are all repeated in the following stanzas, but in a constant set of permutations. The *envoi* contains all six words, three in the middle of each line. D. G. Rossetti, Swinburne, Pound, Auden, and other modern poets have used the form, and Sir Philip Sidney composed a magnificent double-sestina, "Ye Goat-herd Gods."

Skepticism   A philosophy that denies the possibility of certain knowledge, and, although opposed to Stoicism and Epicureanism (q.v.), advocated *ataraxy*, imperturbability of mind. Skepticism originated with Pyrrhon (c. 360–270 B.C.), and its chief transmitter was Sextus Empiricus (c. 200 B.C.). In the Renaissance, skepticism had importance as questioning the power of the human mind to know truly (for a classic exposition see Donne's *Second Anniversary*, ll. 254–300), and became a powerful influence in morals and religion through the advocacy of Montaigne.

Sonnet   A basic lyric form, consisting of fourteen lines of iambic pentameter rhymed in various patterns. The *Italian* or *Petrarchan* sonnet is divided clearly into *octave* and *sestet,* the first rhyming *abba abba* and the second in a pattern such as *cdc dcd*. The *Shakespearean* sonnet consists of three quatrains followed by a couplet: *abab cdcd efef gg*. In the late 16th century in England, sonnets were written either independently as short epigrammatic forms, or grouped in sonnet sequences, i.e. collections of upwards of a hundred poems, in imitation of Petrarch, purportedly addressed to one central figure or muse—a lady usually with a symbolic name like "Stella" or "Idea." Milton made a new kind of use of the Petrarchan form, and the Romantic poets continued in the Miltonic tradition. Several variations have been devised, including the addition of "tails" or extra lines, or the recasting into sixteen lines, instead of fourteen.

Stoicism, Stoics Philosophy founded by Zeno (335–263 B.C.), and opposing the hedonistic tendencies of Epicureanism (*q.v.*). The Stoics' world-view was pantheistic: God was the energy that formed and maintained the world, and wisdom lay in obedience to this law of nature as revealed by the conscience. Moreover, every man is free because the life according to nature and conscience is available to all; so too is suicide—a natural right. Certain Stoics saw the end of the world as caused by fire. In the Renaissance, Latin Stoicism, especially that of Seneca (*q.v.*), had a revival of influence and was Christianized in various ways.

Stream of Consciousness A literary technique of modern fiction which attempts to imitate or duplicate, in patterns other than those of discourse, the flow of thoughts, impressions, memories, meditations, musings, and other products of an individual character's consciousness. It can result either in the fragmentation of sentence structure, or the overwhelming of it in long strings of eloquence. In James Joyce's *Ulysses,* where it is called "interior monologue," it operates in different styles to represent the thoughts of different characters, but its most celebrated use is in Molly Bloom's forty-two page soliloquy that concludes the book.

Style See *Decorum.*

Sublime "Lofty"; as a literary idea, originally the basic concept of a Greek treatise (by the so-called "Longinus") on style. In the 18th century, however, the *sublime* came to mean a loftiness perceivable in nature, and sometimes in art—a loftiness different from the composed vision of landscape known as the *picturesque,* because of the element of wildness, power, and even terror. The *beautiful,* the picturesque, and the sublime became three modes for the perception of nature.

Surrealism (1) A literary and artistic movement, predominantly French but with vast international influence; initiated after World War I by André Breton and others, and enshrining the irrational as the best mode of perceiving and representing reality. Pathological forms of vision, hallucination, psychotic utterance, automatic writing, free association, and other means of nullifying even the structures of Symbolist poetic tradition were celebrated. Poetic form was abandoned as though it were as inauthentic as bookkeeping or scientific language, and the surrealistic "texts" are neither prose nor verse. The unconscious, the impulsive, and particularly the erotic are the domains of the surrealistic imagination, which occupied many European painters including Pablo Picasso at a phase in his career, and particularly and with greatest success, René Magritte. Among French writers associated with the movement were Paul Eluard, Louis Aragon, Philippe Soupault, Antonin Artaud, René Char, and Raymond Queneau.

(2) In a looser sense, "surrealist" has been commonly (and misleadingly) used to describe representations in modern literature of the visionary, the dreamlike, the fantastic in any of its forms.

Symbolism (1) Broadly, the process by which one phenomenon, in literature, stands for another, or group of others, and usually of a different sort. Clearcut cases of this in medieval and Renaissance literature are *emblems* or *attributes* (see *Personification; Allegory*). Sometimes conventional symbols may be used in more than one way, e.g. a mirror betokening both truth and vanity. See also *Figure,* under *Rhetoric.*

(2) In a specific sense (and often given in its French form, *symbolisme*), an important esthetic concept for modern literature, formulated by French poets and critics of the later 19th century following Baudelaire. In this view, the literary symbol becomes something closer to a kind of commanding, central metaphor, taking precedence over any more discursive linguistic mode for poetic communication. The effects of this concept on literature in English have been immense; and some version of the concept survives in modern notions of the poetic *image*, or *fiction*.

Trope (1) See *Rhetoric*. (2) In the liturgy of the Catholic Church, a phrase, sentence, or verse with its musical setting, introduced to amplify or embellish some part of the text of the mass or the office (i.e. the prayers and Scripture readings recited daily by priests, religious, and even laymen) when chanted in choir. Tropes of this second kind were discontinued in 1570 by the authority of Pope Pius V. Troping new material into older or conventional patterns seems to have been, in a general way, a basic device of medieval literature, and was the genesis of modern drama.

Type, Typology (1) Strictly, in medieval biblical interpretation, the prefiguration of the persons and events of the New Testament by persons and events of the Old, the Old Testament being fulfilled in, but not entirely superseded by, the New. Thus, the Temptation and Fall of Man were held to prefigure the first Temptation of Christ, pride in each case being the root of the temptation, and a warning against gluttony the moral lesson to be drawn from both. The Brazen Serpent raised up by Moses was held to prefigure the crucifixion of Christ; Isaac, as a sacrificial victim ("God will provide his own Lamb," says Abraham to him) is a *type* of Christ. The forty days and nights of the Deluge, the forty years of Israel's wandering in the desert, Moses' forty days in the desert are all typologically related.

(2) In a looser sense, a person or event seen as a model or paradigm. See also *Figure*, under *Rhetoric*.

Villanelle A lyric form originally used in French Renaissance poetry for pastoral subjects, adopted by 19th-century English writers of light verse, and eventually taken up again by poets such as James Joyce, William Empson, and Dylan Thomas for more than trivial effects. The form consists of five (see *Meter* §5) tercets rhyming *aba*, followed by a quatrain rhyming *abaa*. The first and last line of the first tercet are alternately repeated as refrains at the end of each following tercet. Thus, in Edward Arlington Robinson's famous villanelle beginning

> They are all gone away,
>> The house is shut and still,
> There is nothing more to say.

the first and third line are alternated, finally to follow each other in the last tercet. Modern use of the form depends upon subtle variations of the meaning of the refrain lines at each repetition.

Suggestions for Further Reading

The Period in General

Political and Social Backgrounds The most useful single study remains Alfred Cobban's *Edmund Burke and the Revolt Against the Eighteenth Century*, 1929, which emphasizes Burke's influence on the later thought of Wordsworth and Coleridge. G. M. Trevelyan's *English Social History*, 1942, sketches the period with great vividness. Supplemental detail may be sought in R. J. White's *From Waterloo to Peterloo*, 1957, and in Kenneth MacLean's *Agrarian Age*, 1951. Still valuable is Edward Dowden's *The French Revolution and English Literature*, 1897, which can be filled out by Carl Woodring's *Politics in English Romantic Poetry*, 1970. The relevant pages in Raymond Williams's *Culture and Society, 1780–1950*, 1960, provide a vigorous instance of a modern radical view.

Literary History Douglas Bush, *Mythology and the Romantic Tradition in English Poetry*, 1937, remains the classical study of a crucial element in Romantic poetry, though its bias is firmly anti-Romantic. The best literary history is the superbly informed work of Oliver Elton, *A Survey of English Literature*, two vols., 1928. The two relevant volumes in the Oxford History of English Literature are rather inadequate, but much useful information may be derived from Ian Jack, *English Literature, 1815–1832*, 1963, and W. L. Renwick, *English Literature, 1789–1815*, 1963.

Collections of Critical Essays *English Romantic Poets*, ed. M. H. Abrams, 1960, balances a variety of viewpoints on the major poets. *Romanticism Reconsidered*, ed. N. Frye, 1963, sums up leading critical attitudes of the period. *Romanticism and Consciousness*, ed. H. Bloom, 1970, collects essays on the major poets and essays investigating the central Romantic ideas of Nature, literary form, and political revolution. *From Sensibility to Romanticism*, ed. F. W. Hilles and H. Bloom, 1965, gathers essays on the main continuity of English poetry from Pope to Keats.

General Studies Two works by M. H. Abrams, *The Mirror and the Lamp*, 1953, and *Natural Supernaturalism*, 1971, are distinguished and sympathetic studies respectively of Romantic critical theory and Romantic poetry. W. J. Bate, *From Classic to Romantic*, 1946, remains a highly useful account of the development of Romantic attitudes. The most comprehensive volume giving readings of individual Romantic poems is *The Visionary Company* by H. Bloom, rev. ed., 1971. More advanced studies are offered in H. Bloom, *The Ringers in the Tower*, 1971; N. Frye, *A Study of English*

Romanticism, 1968; and G. Hartman, *Beyond Formalism,* 1970. D. G. James, *Scepticism and Poetry,* 1937, is still a useful account of Romantic theories of imagination. F. Kermode, *Romantic Image,* 1957, was a pioneer exploration of the continuity of Romantic and Modern poetry.

Bibliography R. H. Fogle, *Romantic Poets and Prose Writers,* 1967. T. M. Raysor, *The English Romantic Poets,* 1956; C. W. and L. H. Houtchens, *The English Romantic Poets and Essayists,* 1966.

Poetry

WILLIAM BLAKE

Editions *Poetry and Prose,* ed. D. V. Erdman, with commentary by H. Bloom, 1965.

Critical Studies Hazard Adams, *William Blake,* 1963. H. Bloom, *Blake's Apocalypse,* 1963. S. Foster Damon, *William Blake,* 1924, and *A Blake Dictionary,* 1965. D. V. Erdman, *Blake, Prophet against Empire,* 1954. P. F. Fisher, *The Valley of Vision,* 1961. *Blake,* ed. N. Frye, 1966. N. Frye, *Fearful Symmetry,* 1947. *Discussions of Blake,* ed. J. Grant, 1961. J. M. Murry, *William Blake,* 1933. Milton Percival, *Blake's Circle of Destiny,* 1938. *Blake's Visionary Forms Dramatic,* ed. D. V. Erdman and J. Grant, 1970.

Biography The best continues to be Alexander Gilchrist, *Life of William Blake,* 1863, in the edition of Ruthven Todd, 1945.

WILLIAM WORDSWORTH

Editions *Poetical Works,* ed. E. de Selincourt and H. Darbishire, five vols., 1940–49. *The Prelude,* 1805 and 1850 facing texts, ed. E. de Selincourt and H. Darbishire, 1959. Best one-volume edition, ed. T. Hutchinson and E. de Selincourt, 1950.

Critical Studies *Wordsworth,* ed. M. H. Abrams, 1971. L. Abercrombie, *The Art of Wordsworth,* 1952. Matthew Arnold, *Essays in Criticism,* 2nd series, 1888. A. C. Bradley, *Oxford Lectures on Poetry,* 1909. *Wordsworth,* ed. J. Davis, 1963. *Wordsworth,* ed. G. T. Dunklin, 1951. D. Ferry, *The Limits of Mortality,* 1959. G. Hartman, *Wordsworth's Poetry, 1787–1814,* 1965. E. D. Hirsch, *Wordsworth and Schelling,* 1960. J. Jones, *The Egotistical Sublime,* 1953. W. L. Sperry, *Wordsworth's Anti-Climax,* 1935. C. Woodring, *Wordsworth,* 1965.

Biography The best is Mary Moorman's *Wordsworth, A Biography,* two vols., 1957 (corrected 1968) and 1965, respectively.

SAMUEL TAYLOR COLERIDGE

Editions Complete edition at this date in progress, ed. Kathleen Coburn, who is editing the *Notebooks* also (first two vols., 1957–61). *Complete Poetical Works,* ed. E. H. Coleridge, two vols., 1912. *Biographia Literaria,* ed. J. Shawcross, two vols., 1907. *Collected Letters* (through 1819), ed. E. L. Griggs, four vols. 1956–59. *Inquiring Spirit,* ed. K. Coburn, 1951: miscellaneous prose.

Critical Studies W. J. Bate, *Coleridge*, 1967. J. B. Beer, *Coleridge, the Visionary*, 1959. *Coleridge*, ed. K. Coburn, 1967. *New Perspectives on Coleridge and Wordsworth*, ed. G. Hartman, 1972. Humphry House, *Coleridge*, 1953. J. L. Lowes, *The Road to Xanadu*, 1927. I. A. Richards, *Coleridge on Imagination*, 1960.

LORD BYRON

Editions *Works*, 13 vols., ed. E. H. Coleridge and R. E. Prothero, 1898–1904; one-volume ed. of *Poetical Works*, ed. E. H. Coleridge, 1905. *Byron: A Self-Portrait*, ed. P. Quennell, two vols., 1950, gives diaries and selected letters.

Critical Studies M. G. Cooke, *The Blind Man Traces the Circle*, 1969. G. W. Knight, *The Burning Oracle*, 1939. J. J. McGann, *Fiery Dust*, 1968. G. Ridenour, *The Style of "Don Juan,"* 1960. A. Rutherford, *Byron*, 1961. *Byron*, ed. P. West, 1963.

Biography The most comprehensive is L. A. Marchand, *Byron*, three vols., 1957.

PERCY BYSSHE SHELLEY

Editions *Complete Works*, ten vols., ed. R. Ingpen and W. E. Peck, 1926–30. *Complete Poetical Works*, ed. T. Hutchinson, 1904. *Shelley's Prose*, ed. D. L. Clarke, 1954. *Letters*, ed. F. L. Jones, two vols., 1964.

Critical Studies Carlos Baker, *Shelley's Major Poetry*, 1948. H. Bloom, *Shelley's Mythmaking*, 1959. A. M. D. Hughes, *The Nascent Mind of Shelley*, 1947. C. E. Pulos, *The Deep Truth*, 1954. *Shelley*, ed. G. M. Ridenour, 1965. J. Todhunter, *A Study of Shelley*, 1880. E. Wasserman, *Shelley*, 1971. M. Wilson, *Shelley's Later Poetry*, 1959. For *The Triumph of Life* see D. H. Reiman, ed., 1965.

Biography The best are E. Blunden, *Shelley, A Life Story*, 1946 (repr. 1965), and N. I. White, *Shelley*, two vols., 1940.

JOHN KEATS

Editions *Poetical Works*, ed. H. W. Garrod, 1958. *Letters*, ed. H. E. Rollins, two vols., 1958.

Critical Studies W. J. Bate, *Negative Capability*, 1939. *Keats*, ed. W. J. Bate, 1964. J. R. Caldwell, *John Keats' Fancy*, 1945. J. M. Murry, *Keats*, 1955, and *Keats and Shakespeare*, 1926. C. D. Thorpe, *The Mind of Keats*, 1926. M. Dickstein, *Keats and His Poetry*, 1971. E. Wasserman, *The Finer Tone*, 1953.

Biography The best is W. J. Bate, *John Keats*, 1963.

OTHER ROMANTIC POETS

William Lisle Bowles *Poetical Works*, ed. G. Gilfillan, two vols., 1855. S. T. Coleridge, *Biographia Literaria*, Vol. I, chap. 1. A. Symons, *Romantic Movement in English Poetry*, 1909.

Sir Walter Scott   *Poetical Works*, ed. J. L. Robertson, 1904. See Scott chapter in H. J. C. Grierson and J. C. Smith, *A Critical Survey of English Poetry*, 1944.

Walter Savage Landor   *Poetical Works*, ed. S. Wheeler, three vols., 1937. Donald Davie, "The Shorter Poems of Walter Savage Landor," *Essays in Criticism*, ed. F. W. Bateson, Vol. I, 1951. R. Pinsky, *Landor's Poetry*, 1968.

Thomas Love Peacock   *Works*, ed. H. F. B. Brett-Smith and C. E. Jones, ten vols., 1928, and *Poems*, ed. B. Johnson, 1906. O. W. Campbell, *Peacock*, 1953.

John Clare   *Poems*, ed. J. W. Tibble, two vols., 1935; *Poems of John Clare's Madness*, ed. G. Grigson, 1949; *The Later Poems*, ed. E. Robinson and G. Summerfield, 1964. J. M. Murry, *John Clare and Other Studies*, 1950.

George Darley   *Complete Poetical Works*, ed. R. Colles, 1908. C. C. Abbott, *Life and Letters of George Darley*, 1928. J. Heath-Stubbs, *The Darkling Plain*, 1950.

Hartley Coleridge   *Complete Poetical Works*, ed. R. Colles, 1908. E. Blunden, *Votive Tablets*, 1931.

Thomas Hood   *Complete Poetical Works*, ed. W. C. Jerrold, 1911. George Saintsbury, *Collected Essays*, Vol. II, 1923.

Thomas Lovell Beddoes   *Works*, ed. H. W. Donner, 1935. H. W. Donner, *Beddoes: The Making of a Poet*, 1935. N. Frye, *A Study of English Romanticism*, 1968.

Samuel Palmer   G. Grigson, *Samuel Palmer's Valley of Vision*, 1960.

Thomas Wade   H. B. Forman, "Wade: The Poet and His Surroundings," in *Literary Anecdotes of the Nineteenth Century*, ed. W. R. Nicoll and T. J. Wise, Vol. I, 1895.

Prose
THOMAS DE QUINCEY

Editions   *The Collected Writings*, ed. David Masson, 14 vols., 1889–90. *Uncollected Writings*, ed. James Hogg, two vols., 1890. *Posthumous Writings*, ed. A. H. Japp, two vols., 1891–93. *A Diary of Thomas De Quincey for 1803*, ed. H. A. Eaton, 1927. *De Quincey's Literary Criticism*, ed. Helen Darbishire, 1909.

Critical Studies   Albert Goldman, *The Mine and the Mint: Sources for the Writings of De Quincey*, 1965. D. Grant, "Thomas De Quincey," in *Some British Romantics*, ed. J. V. Logan and others, 1966. John E. Jordan, *Thomas De Quincey, Literary Critic*, 1952. J. Hillis Miller, *The Disappearance of God: Five Nineteenth-Century Writers*, 1963. S. Kobayashi, *Rhythm in the Prose of Thomas De Quincey*, 1956. René Wellek, *History of Modern Criticism, 1750–1950*, Vol. II, 1955.

Biography   There is as yet no definitive biography of De Quincey, understandably enough, for the difficulties he puts in the way of a biographer are enormous. The following works are variously useful. M. H. Abrams, *The Milk of Paradise*, 1934, 1970, on De Quincey's use of opium. H. S. Davies, *Thomas De Quincey*, 1964. *De Quincey and His Friends: Personal Recollections, Souvenirs and Anecdotes*, ed. James Hogg, 1895. Horace A. Eaton, *Thomas De Quincey: A Biography*, 1936, the most reliable of the lives. Malcolm Elwin, *Thomas De Quincey*, 1935. Alethea Hayter, *Opium and the Romantic Imagination*, 1968, 1971, on De Quincey's use of opium. John E. Jordan, *De Quincey to Wordsworth: A Biography of a Relationship*, 1962. Edward Sackville-West, *A Flame in Sunlight*, 1936.

WILLIAM HAZLITT

Editions   *The Complete Works*, ed. P. P. Howe, 1930–34. *Selected Essays*, ed. Geoffrey Keynes, 1930. *Hazlitt Painted by Himself and Presented by Catherine Macdonald Maclean*, 1949.

Critical Studies   W. P. Albrecht, *Hazlitt and the Creative Imagination*, 1965. David Cecil, "Hazlitt's Occasional Essays," *The Fine Art of Reading*, 1957. Herschel Baker, *William Hazlitt*, 1962, the most thorough account of Hazlitt's ideas. K. Coburn, "Hazlitt on the Disinterested Imagination," *Some British Romantics*, ed. J. V. Logan and others, 1966. H. W. Garrod, "The Place of Hazlitt in English Criticism," *The Profession of Poetry*, 1929. J. B. Priestley, *Hazlitt*, 1960. Elizabeth Schneider, *The Aesthetics of William Hazlitt*, 1933, 1952. H. M. Sikes, "The Infernal Hazlitt," *Essays Presented to Stanley Pargellis*, ed. H. Bluhm, 1965. René Wellek, *History of Modern Criticism, 1750–1950*, Vol. II, 1955. Stewart C. Wilcox, *Hazlitt in the Workshop*, 1943.

Biography   P. P. Howe, *Life of William Hazlitt*, 1922 (new ed. 1947). Although spoken of as the standard biography, this is both less detailed and less perceptive than Catherine Macdonald Maclean's *Born Under Saturn*, 1944, which is the best biography.

CHARLES LAMB

Editions   *Works of Charles and Mary Lamb*, ed. E. V. Lucas, 1903–05; *Letters*, 1935. *The Letters of Charles Manning to Charles Lamb*, ed. G. A. Anderson, 1925.

Critical Studies   G. L. Barnett, "The Evolution of Elia," Princeton dissertation, 1942. *Lamb's Criticism*, ed. E. M. W. Tillyard, 1923; Tillyard's introductory essay, "Lamb as a Literary Critic," is a useful study. Walter Pater, *Appreciations*, 1889. Mario Praz, *The Hero in Eclipse in Victorian Literature*, 1956. S. M. Rich, *The Elian Miscellany*, 1931. Denys Thompson, "Our Debt to Lamb," *Determinations*, ed. F. R. Leavis, 1934. Geoffrey Tillotson, "The Historical Importance of Certain Essays of Elia," *Some British Romantics*, ed. J. V. Logan and others, 1966. René Wellek, *History of Modern Criticism, 1750–1950*, Vol. II, 1955.

Biography   E. V. Lucas, *Life of Charles Lamb*, 1921; the best biography. Edmund Blunden, *Charles Lamb: His Life Recorded by His Contemporaries*, 1934. W. C. Hazlitt, *The Lambs: Their Lives, Their Friends, and Their Correspondence*, 1897; *Lamb and Hazlitt*, 1900.

Author and Title Index

First-Line Index